Holidays, Festivals, and Celebrations of the World Dictionary

Detailing More than 2,000 Observances from
All 50 States and More than 100 Nations

SECOND EDITION

Holidays, Festivals, and Celebrations of the World Dictionary

Detailing More than 2,000 Observances from All 50 States and More than 100 Nations

SECOND EDITION

A Compendious Reference Guide to Popular, Ethnic, Religious, National, and Ancient Holidays, Festivals, Celebrations, Commemorations, Holy Days, Feasts, and Fasts; Supplemented by Special Sections on Calendar Systems, the Millennium, Admission Days and Facts about the States and Territories, Presidents of the United States, Tourism Information Sources, and Web Sites on Holidays; Special Indexes of Chronological, Ethnic and Geographic, Historical, Religious, Ancient, Folkloric, Calendar, Promotional and Sports Holidays, State and National Legal Holidays, General, and Subject Indexes

Edited by

HELENE HENDERSON

and

SUE ELLEN THOMPSON

Omnigraphics, Inc.

Penobscot Building • Detroit, MI 48226

Editorial Staff, Second Edition

Helene Henderson and Sue Ellen Thompson, *Editors*
Barry Puckett, *Research Associate*
Jacquelyn S. Goodwin, *Assistant Editor*
Frank R. Abate, *Consulting Editor*

Omnigraphics, Inc.

Matthew Barbour, *Production Manager*
Laurie Lanzen Harris, *Vice President, Editorial Director*
Peter E. Ruffner, *Vice President, Administration*
James A. Sellgren, *Vice President, Operations and Finance*
Jane Steele, *Marketing Consultant*

* * *

Frederick G. Ruffner, Jr., *President, Publisher*

Copyright © 1997 Omnigraphics, Inc.
ISBN 0-7808-0074-5

Library of Congress Cataloging-in-Publication Data

Holidays, festivals, and celebrations of the world dictionary : detailing more than 2,000 observances from all 50 states and more than 100 nations / edited by Helene Henderson and Sue Ellen Thompson. —- 2nd ed.
    "A compendium reference guide to popular, ethnic, religious, national, and ancient holidays, festivals, celebrations, commemorations, holy days, feasts, and fasts; supplemented by special sections on calendar systems, the millennium, admission days and facts about the states and territories, Presidents of the United States, tourism information sources, and web sites on holidays; special indexes of chronological, ethnic and geographic, historical, religious, ancient, folkloric, calendar, promotional and sports holidays, state and national legal holidays, general (alphabetical by name and by key-word) and subject indexes."
    "New to this ed. : contact information, source material, and special section on the upcoming millennium."
    Includes bibliographical references and indexes.
    ISBN 0-7808-0074-5 (lib. bdg. : alk. paper)
    1. Holidays — Dictionaries.   2. Festivals — Dictionaries.
I. Henderson, Helene. 1963-   .   II. Thompson, Sue Ellen.
GT3925.T46   1997
394.26 — dc21   97-9160
                                                                          CIP

The information in this publication was compiled from sources cited and from sources considered reliable. While every possible effort has been made to ensure reliability, the publisher will not assume liability for damages caused by inaccuracies in the data, and makes no warranty, express or implied, on the accuracy of the information contained herein.

∞

This book is printed on acid-free paper meeting the ANSI Z39.48 Standard. The infinity symbol that appears above indicates that the paper in this book meets that standard.

Printed in the United States of America.

Table of Contents

Contents by Subject

Foreword

This is the second, greatly enlarged edition of a dictionary devoted to a subject area of perennial interest to everyone.

All countries have their festivals, and many also have secular holidays to mark the achievements of famous individuals or to celebrate historical events. From primitive times onwards, festivals have celebrated the religious mysteries of existence—the enigma of birth, death and rebirth—in the environment and the pattern of human experience. Such festivals filled a deep-seated need in the human psyche, evoking profound emotions associated with the changing pattern of the year: the promise of spring, the joys of summer, the harvest, the decline of the year through fall to the rigors of winter, and the promise of a new spring. The divine origin of this mystery was to be acknowledged, honored and propitiated, so that human prosperity and fertility flourished in the struggle for existence through the progress of the seasons and the passing of time.

Inevitably such festivals required a measurement of time, so that seasonal festivals could be celebrated at appropriate dates in the cycle of the year. But for thousands of years, primitive and pantheistic concepts of the universe inhibited the exact timing of festivals. In the natural division of time, the solar day is the daily revolution of the earth and alternation of light and darkness, the solar year is the circle of seasons in the earth's revolution around the sun. Months are divisions resulting from the lunar phases of the moon. But division of time into hours, days, or a regular month is more arbitrary, and it was not until early Roman times that the calendar as such was formalized for civil convenience; the word "calendar" itself derives from the Latin *Kalendae.* By 46 B.C., the time of Julius Caesar, the Roman civil calendar had become three months out of phase with the true astronomical year. That year was called *ultimus annus confusionis*, 'the last year of the muddled reckoning.' The Julian calendar reform in the first century B.C., which became the standard of Western countries, corrected the discrepancy and regularized a calendar based on the solar cycle. Though far more accurate, the Julian calendar still resulted in a discrepancy, since its "average" year of 365.25 days—requiring the insertion of an extra leap year day once every four years—became progressively out of step with the real solar year of 365.242199 days.

In a papal bull of February 24, 1582, Pope Gregory XIII inaugurated the Gregorian calendar, which required the deletion of ten days from the calendar (to bring it back into phase with the astronomical year) in October 1582, and the occasional adjustment whereby three out of every four round figure "century" years are not leap years (1700,1800, and 1900 were not leap years; 2000 will be). October 4, 1582, was followed by October 15 in the calendar. This rearrangement of the calendar was bewildering to many people, who clamored, "Give us back our ten days!" But the Gregorian calendar was eventually adopted, at least for civil purposes, throughout the West, and remains a worldwide standard to this day. Meanwhile, of course, other ancient calendars such as the Jewish and Islamic have continued to exist side by side with the Gregorian calendar. *Holidays, Festivals, and Celebrations of the World Dictionary* includes a discussion of the history of ancient and modern calendars, and clarifies such complexities.

Different religions have continued to find common ground in the concept of special days to mark the supreme mysteries of life. Three of the great world religions—Judaism, Christianity, and

Islam — have all recognized a holy day of rest from the week of toil for special worship. The Sabbath of Judaism was moved by Christians from Saturday to Sunday, while for Muslims the "day of assembly" in a mosque is Friday.

Many different religions meet in their interpretations of festival times of the year. With the rise of Christianity in Europe, some of the old pagan festivals were retained by the new Church, although given different religious interpretations. Behind the feasting and merrymaking of Christmas, one might still hear dim echoes of ancient winter solstice festivals of light, the Roman Saturnalia, the Druidic rites with mistletoe, Germanic tree-worship, and the strange gods of Saxon mythology.

In addition to religious festivals, the ancient Romans made a distinction between religious and secular events, and the institution of secular holidays has since proliferated in the countries of the world. Even so, holidays still have their roots in the concept of some special significance of certain days, necessitating a break in the daily toil of normal life. The very word "holiday" is derived from "Holy day."

Secular holidays excite special emotions. We love to celebrate the birthdays of family members and friends with greetings and presents. So, too, we feel a special sense of belonging to a social group or nation in the observance of our secular holidays, which unite us in common ties of special interest, ethnicity, or national pride.

The range of religious festivals and secular holidays is now vast in the various countries of the world. In modern times, the proliferation of national and local events has also resulted in scores of special group days, and even whimsical and bizarre observances, ranging from Buzzard Day in Hinckley, Ohio, to the Rat's Wedding Day in China.

In the past, the great festivals and holidays were kept alive by folk memory, or by the many almanacs sold by peddlers, giving the dates of fairs and other events and anniversaries, together with lunar information, tides, eclipses, and even prophecies, spiced with quaint aphorisms and proverbs. In 1732, Benjamin Franklin became author-editor-publisher of the *Poor Richard* series of almanacs that popularized such pithy folk wisdom as "God helps them that help themselves" and "Necessity never made a good bargain." The British counterpart of *Poor Richard* was the *Vox Stellarum* of Dr. Francis Moore, first published in 1700, descendants of which are still published annually under the title *Old Moore's Almanack.*

In nineteenth-century Britain, antiquarians published various volumes of discursive lore, listing the significance of days of the calendar, festivals, and holidays, and their history. The best of these was the delightful work, *The Book of Days: A Miscellany of Popular Antiquities in Connection with the Calendar, Including Anecdote, Biography & History, Curiosities of Literature, and Oddities of Human Life and Character,* by Robert Chambers (2 volumes, 1862–64, reissued by Omnigraphics in 1990).

Such books are fascinating to browse through for their out-of-the-way information and bygone lore of the calendar, but although many of the festivals and holidays discussed are still celebrated, there have been scores of newer holidays in the U.S. and worldwide in the present century.

Publication of the first edition of *Holidays, Festivals, and Celebrations of the World Dictionary* provided a truly comprehensive annotated reference work giving information on national and international festivals and holidays, with descriptive entries covering religious, cultural, ethnic, historical, popular and sports celebrations from all over the world, with special sections on calendar systems, and tables of state and national public holidays. In addition to a General Index of people, places, institutions, and other keywords, easy reference was facilitated by special indexes of Chronological, Religious and Special Subjects (including Ancient/Pagan, Calendar, Folkloric, Historical, Promotional, and Sporting entries).

In this new edition, there are now over 500 new entries covering state, national, and legal holidays as well as source and contact information when available; a listing of admission days for all 50 states; and independence, republic, and national days for countries of the world. There are special sections of biographical information on all U.S. presidents and major landmarks commemorating them; an annotated bibliography of holiday-related books; domestic and international tourism information sources; and web sites on holidays. In addition to a new comprehensive Subject Index and existing special indexes, there are also four other new indexes—General Index, Alphabetical by Name and by Key-Word; Legal Holidays by U.S. State; Legal Holidays by Country; and Ethnic and Geographic.

Detailed information is now listed on more than 2,000 observances from all 50 states and more than 100 nations. There are now eight indexes providing rapid reference to relevant information. The style of the entries is such that they will be equally accessible for scholars, students, and the general public.

This is a key reference work for general use and for schools and public libraries, but it is also a multi-purpose dictionary. Ministers of different denominations will find it valuable for its broad coverage of the festivals of Christianity and also for those of other world religions. Business people planning promotional journeys will find its information of special value when visiting foreign countries and different states in the U.S. Politicians and other dignitaries will find it useful to consult in marking the local and national importance of given days. School children can learn about the meaning of individual holidays and the observances of different religious and ethnic groups, as well as the popular fun festivals of various states and countries.

All kinds of travelers will value the listing of public holidays in the U.S. and other countries, and it will also add special interest to the planning of personal vacations at home and abroad. In addition to the often spectacular religious festivals of the world, there are now scores of lighthearted or tongue-in-cheek popular holiday events, such as the Great American Duck Race in Deming, New Mexico, or the Garlic Festival in Gilroy, California. From state to state and country to country there are humorous, quaint, and diverting events which have become great tourist attractions. Journalists will find this an indispensable desk book for news stories on the significance of days.

This is also a book that can enhance understanding of ethnic groups and different nationalities, through knowledge of the manifold celebrations of life, and the emotions of reverence, joy, and laughter which we share in our individual festivals and holidays.

Leslie Shepard
Dublin, Ireland
January 1997

Introduction

This revised and expanded second edition of *Holidays, Festivals, and Celebrations of the World Dictionary (HFCWD)* contains up-to-date information about more than 2,000 holidays, festivals, celebrations, commemorations, holy days, feasts and fasts, and other observances from all parts of the world, and includes more than 500 new entries. Entries include events for which people come together for a day or periods of up to a few days or (rarely) weeks for special activities, celebrations, commemorations, or rituals. These events have a story to tell, in that each is significant, unusual, or somehow remarkable. Holidays and festivals for more than 100 countries, as well as events specifically observed in every state of the United States, are included.

The entries cover holidays and festivals that are popular, secular, religious, or a combination thereof. The great bulk of entries are events still celebrated or observed, but a few ancient and discontinued events are included because allusions to them still appear in literature or art, or occur in discourse.

Birth or death anniversaries of famous individuals generally are not included, nor are simple anniversaries of historical events. But those few such events that are regularly observed with significant celebrations or special activities, or that have particular cultural significance, such as **Martin Luther King, Jr.'s Birthday** or **Anzac Day**, are included.

Most entries in *HFCWD* have national or wide regional significance, but some local events that are offbeat, colorful, distinctive, or bizarre, such as the **Gilroy Garlic Festival**, have also been included. Entries for well-known days of religious significance, such as **Christmas**, **Rosh Hashanah**, and **Ramadan**, contain information seldom found in other current reference sources.

Organization

Main Entries and Alternate Forms

The book is arranged alphabetically by name of holiday. Main entries appear in **boldface**. As a new feature of this second edition, all main entries are now numbered, and these numbers are used in the indexes. Well-known alternate forms of the main entry appear in parentheses immediately after the main entry, e.g., **Hanukkah (Chanukah)**. Such alternate forms also appear as cross-references in their proper alphabetical position. Less common alternate forms appear in **boldface** within the text of the entry, and cross-references to other entries appear in SMALL CAPITAL letters.

Order of Main Entries

Since people looking for information on a given subject may not know its official title, main entries have been written with the key words first. Thus, words such as *birthday, death of, feast, festa, festival, fête, fiesta, national,* and *international* have normally been transposed to the end of the main entry, e.g.: **Bab, Birth of the; Bastille, Festival de la; Old-Time Fiddlers' Contest, National**, etc.

Spelling and Forms Used for Main Entries

HFCWD deals with events that relate to many cultures, the original names of which involve a number of alphabets and non-Roman writing systems. As much as possible, spellings and forms for main entries were standardized for ease of access. The following were used as guides on spelling standardization:

- For Hindu and Islamic calendars and events: *The Encyclopedia of Religion*, Mircea Eliade, ed., Macmillan, 1987.

- For Jewish calendar and events: *The Jewish Holidays: A Guide and Commentary*, Michael Strassfeld, Harper & Row, 1985, as well as *The Encyclopedia of Religion* by Eliade.

- For Asian and African holidays and events no single standard was used. The form used is that appearing most often in the sources consulted. For many Hindu, Islamic, and Asian terms, diacriticals unfamiliar to the non-specialist were omitted.

- General sources consulted were *Encyclopedia Britannica* (15th edition, 1995), *Columbia Encyclopedia* (fifth edition, 1993), *Merriam-Webster's Biographical Dictionary* (1995), and *Merriam-Webster's Geographical Dictionary* (third edition, 1997).

Dates

On the line below the main entry, the date of celebration or observance is given in italics. For those entries whose date is based on a lunar calendar, we have shown the approximate date in the Gregorian calendar followed by the lunar date. The exception is for events based on the strictly lunar Islamic calendar, where only the Islamic month and day are given. See the section on **Calendar Systems around the World** for a detailed explanation of the Islamic calendar.

Religious Holidays

For the most part, entries for religious holidays are spelled and described in terms of the major religion that observes them. If only some followers of a major religion observe a holiday, or if different branches or sects commemorate something different (or nothing at all) on a given holiday, the entry specifies the practice of the particular group. **St. John the Baptist's Day,** for instance, is recognized by most Christians, and so is described (and indexed) as "Christian," despite the fact that some Christians do not venerate saints. The holy day of **Ashura** is observed quite differently by Sunni and Shi'ite Muslims, and so both practices are described.

Christian Denominations

For Christianity, references to the West or Western church generally include the Roman Catholic Church, the churches of the Anglican Communion, and major Protestant denominations. References to the East or Eastern church include Orthodox Christians, such as Greek and Russian Orthodox, and all those Christians acknowledging the primacy of the Patriarch of Constantinople.

New Entries

More than 500 new entries have been added to this edition. They include independence days, national days, republic days, and liberation days around the world, legal holidays in some of the new countries that were formerly part of the U.S.S.R., and other holidays and festivals of many kinds. Barring time constraints, many more could easily have been added. At the last moment, however, even though the schedule prohibited any more new inclusions, we decided we had to relent and write about just one more event—the Wizard of Oz Festival in Chesterton, Indiana.

New Entry Features

Sources

Abbreviated reference source titles are provided for entries as applicable, followed by the relevant page number(s) where one can find information in that source. For a complete list of all sources used, see the bibliography in Appendix 5.

Contact Information

Names, addresses, phone and fax numbers, and web sites (when applicable) have been added to entries on contemporary public festivals and other events. In some cases, the organization(s) listed are actual sponsors. In others, an embassy or tourist office is given; such agencies are not necessarily responsible for the event, but they are provided as likely sources of information about the event. In a few cases, entries discuss events in several locations, but we have maintained a limit of no more than two contacts per entry. Excluded are such religious or contemplative holidays as **Easter, Hanukkah, Karwachoth,** and **Laylat al Miraj**—for which the obvious contact would be a local church, synagogue, temple, or mosque—as well as holidays that tend to be private or domestic observances, such as **Mother's Day, April Fools' Day,** and **Hina Matsuri**. More general contact information is provided in Appendix 3, *Domestic Tourism Information Sources*; Appendix 4, *International Tourism Information Sources*; and Appendix 6, *Web Sites on Holidays*.

Special Features New to this Edition

As well as more than 500 new entries, we have also added expanded coverage of world calendar systems, a special section on the upcoming Millennium, six appendices, and five indexes. (We have also reduced the type size in hopes of keeping this book out of the "weightlifting" department.)

The Millennium

This special section provides an overview of the end of the second millennium in the year 2000 and includes historical background, utopic and apocalyptic interpretations and predictions, planned celebrations, and a bibliography.

Appendices

1. Admission Days and Facts about the States and Territories

This section lists for each of the fifty states: the date and order of admission to the Union; information about current or past admission day observances, if applicable; state nicknames, mottoes, animals, flowers, and other symbols; reference sources noting the admission day; and offices to contact for further information. This last item includes state tourist or travel offices, state libraries, governors' offices, and secretaries of state. For territories, listed are year of association with the U.S.; nicknames, mottoes, flowers, and other symbols; and offices to contact.

2. United States Presidents

This section lists all U.S. presidents in the order in which they held office, their birth dates and places, spouses, death dates and places, burial sites, political parties, nicknames, career highlights, and notable landmarks commemorating them. It should be noted that some of these landmarks are private residences, and do not permit visitors.

3. **Domestic Tourist Information Sources**

   In alphabetical order by state, this section provides addresses, phone and fax numbers, and web sites (where available) for state tourism and travel bureaus and, for major cities and metropolitan areas within the state, convention and visitors bureaus and chambers of commerce.

4. **International Tourist Information Sources**

   In alphabetical order by country, this section provides addresses, phone and fax numbers for national tourism offices and embassies or consulate offices within the U.S.

5. **Bibliography**

   The annotated bibliography includes sources cited or consulted in *HFCWD*, as well as other sources for further reading. Sources are listed under the following categories: Reference and Other Background Works on Holidays (including Calendars and Time-Reckoning Systems; Festival Organization; Philosophy, Theory and Analysis of Festivity; and Teaching Aids); Holidays of Religious Traditions; Holidays of Ethnic Groups and Geographic Regions; Individual Holidays; and Journals.

6. **Web Sites on Holidays**

   This listing of holiday-related web sites includes descriptions of sites and web site addresses (URL), as well as mailing addresses, phone and fax numbers, and e-mail addresses, when available. Sites chosen represent a broad sampling of holiday, festival, and celebration material available on the World Wide Web, and the sites are thought to be relatively stable as gauged by communication with the sites' sponsors or the well-known status of the sponsoring organization (e.g. B'nai B'rith).

Indexes

Several different Special Indexes provide reference to entries (as appropriate) for each of the following categories. In all indexes in this edition, references to entries are given by entry numbers, not page numbers.

- **Chronological Index**

   Fixed Days and Events—Indexes events that are celebrated on a specific date.

   Movable Days—Indexes events whose date of celebration is not fixed, particularly those that are observed according to non-Gregorian calendars and those that depend on the date of Easter.

- **Religious Groups Index**

   Indexes events with a significant religious element by the religious group observing it. In some cases, the line between culture and religion is not distinct enough to comfortably place an observance in either camp. Therefore, entries that describe events observed by a particular ethnic group that contain sacred components (not affiliated with any major religion) are listed in this index under the ethnic group as well as in the Ethnic and Geographic Index (described below under **Indexes New to this Edition**).

- **Special Subject Indexes**

   Ancient/Pagan—Indexes events rooted in ancient times.

   Calendar—Indexes events that deal specifically with the calendar.

   Folkloric—Indexes events rooted in folklore and tradition.

   Historic—Indexes commemorations of specific events in history.

Promotional — Indexes festivals that promote something, such as a location or activity.

Sporting — Indexes events that are based on or revolve around sports, games, etc.

Some events may be categorized in more than one of the above special subjects. For instance, the **Burning of Judas** in Venezuela is listed under the Religious Groups Index (for its Christian significance), Ancient/Pagan (for its almost certain growth out of similar pagan customs), and Folkloric (for its folkloric aspects).

Indexes New to this Edition

- **Subject Index**

Indexes names of individuals, institutions, and other items of significance appearing within the text of the entries. For example, foods, animals, music, customs, and activities closely associated with an event are indexed — both those that are the subject of an observance and those that play significant roles in observances. We have identified celebratory elements common to various cultures, such as burning (effigies, mock, rituals), courtship (ceremonies and festivals, customs and lore), and planting and weather lore, and these celebrations are indexed accordingly. In addition, some religious groups and geographic locations are listed in this index when entries provide substantial information about a religion's background or a location's history. Such headings in the Subject Index *do not* list every holiday and festival celebrated by those religious groups or in those locations. However, cross references at those headings point to such listings that are provided in, respectively, the Religious Groups Index and the Ethnic and Geographic Index.

- **General Index, Alphabetical by Name and Key-Word**

Indexes names of main entries in *HFCWD*, alternate and foreign names of events, and English translations (when available) of foreign names, by key-word. For instance, the **National Old-Time Fiddlers' Contest** is listed under its main entry name (**Old-Time Fiddlers' Contest, National**), as well as under "Fiddlers'," "Contest," and "National." And the entry **Janmashtami**, for example, is also listed under its alternate rendering, "Krishnastami," as well as by key-word in its English translation, "Krishna's Birthday" and "Birthday of Krishna."

- **Legal Holidays by State Index**

Indexes legal holidays in each of the fifty states and American Samoa, Guam, Puerto Rico, and the U.S. Virgin Islands, in alphabetical order by state or territory.

- **Legal Holidays by Country Index**

Indexes legal holidays in more than 100 countries around the world in alphabetical order by country, including some of the new countries that were formerly part of the U.S.S.R.

- **Ethnic and Geographic Index**

Indexes ethnic groups and peoples observing events, and geographic locales (regions, cities, states, provinces, countries) in which holidays and festivals occur.

Audience

HFCWD is intended for elementary, middle and high schools and public libraries, as well as churches, synagogues, mosques, community affairs groups, and others interested in learning about festive events.

Acknowledgments

Holidays, Festivals, and Celebrations of the World Dictionary would not have been possible without the assistance, inspiration, and diligence of many people. Our thanks go to Donna Rhein, Kathleen Mallory, and Marian J. Darling for the exhaustive research they did to unearth new information for even the most written-about holidays, and to reveal additional details about those less well-known. And thanks to Barbara Carlson for her editorial work on the first edition.

We also wish to recognize the assistance provided by a number of clergymen, especially Rabbi Carl Astor of Congregation Beth-El, the Rev. Ralph W. Merrill, St. James Episcopal Church, and the Rev. Constantine J. Simones, St. Sophia Hellenic Orthodox Church, all in New London, Conn.; and the Rev. Paul E. Lutz, St. Paul Lutheran Church, Old Saybrook, Conn. Their prompt responses to our many questions and their willingness to look up arcane information were indispensable.

For their contributions to the second edition, we are deeply grateful to: Jenifer Swanson for courageously venturing into cyberspace to provide us with holiday web sites; Mary Ann Stavros, for her impeccable eye for page design and presentation; Tanya Gulevich, for lending her firm grounding in the study of cultures to various nooks and crannies of this edition; and Karen Bellenir, for valuable dialogue on calendars, as well as editorial issues of standardization. Barry Puckett came to the rescue many times over with indexing acumen, constant support, and research assistance of every kind. Laurie Harris and Frederick Ruffner have been wonderfully supportive and patient throughout this edition's gestation period.

Finally, we must extend many thanks and best wishes to the countless festival sponsors, embassy and consulate personnel, and tourism professionals who helped put the formidable job of accurate coverage within the realm of possibility.

Even with all the essential contributions of the individuals mentioned above and others, we must add that the responsibility for any errors or omissions in *HFCWD* rests solely with the editors.

Words Relating to Periods of Time

A descriptive listing of words related to periods of time is included below. Many of the words are adjectives in form, but also are commonly used as nouns, e.g., *the bicentennial of the U.S. Constitution*. All terms are defined in two separate lists: first by number referred to, then alphabetically.

Listed by Number

diurnal, per diem, quotidian
  daily; of a day
nocturnal
  nightly, of a night
nichthemeron
  a period of 24 hours
semidiurnal
  twice a day
hebdomadal
  weekly; a period of seven days
semiweekly
  twice a week
biweekly
  1. every two weeks
  2. twice a week
fortnightly
  once every two weeks
triweekly
  1. every three weeks
  2. three times a week
novendial
  a period of nine days
monthly, tricenary
  1. relating to a period of one month
  2. thirty days
bimonthly
  1. every two months
  2. twice a month
semimonthly
  twice a month
bimester
  relating to a period of two months
trimester
  relating to a period of three months

trimonthly
  1. every three months
  2. three times a month
biquarterly
  twice every three months
biannual
  twice a year (not necessarily at equally
  spaced intervals)
triannual
  three times a year
semiannual, semiyearly, semestral
  every half year or six-month period
annual, solennial, quotennial, per annum
  yearly; once a year
biennial, biennium, biyearly, diennial
  relating to a period of two years
triennial, triennium
  relating to a period of three years
quadrennial, quadrennium, quadriennial
  relating to a period of four years
quinquennial, quintennial, quinquennium
  relating to a period of five years
sexennial, sextennial
  relating to a period of six years
septenary, septennial, septennium
  relating to a period of seven years
octennial
  relating to a period of eight years
novennial
  relating to a period of nine years
decennary, decennial, decennium
  relating to a period of 10 years
undecennial
  relating to a period of 11 years

duodecennial
  relating to a period of 12 years
quindecennial
  relating to a period of 15 years
septendecennial
  relating to a period of 17 years
vicennial, vigintennial
  relating to a period of 20 years
tricennial, trigintennial
  relating to a period of 30 years
quinquagenary, semicentennial, semicentenary
  relating to a period of 50 years
centenary, centennial, centennium, centurial
  relating to a period of 100 years
quasquicentennial
  relating to a period of 125 years
sesquicentenary, sesquicentennial
  relating to a period of 150 years
bicentenary, bicentennial, bicentennium
  relating to a period of 200 years
tercentenary, tricentennial, tercentennial
  relating to a period of 300 years
quadricentennial, quatercentennial
  relating to a period of 400 years
quincentenary, quincentennial
  relating to a period of 500 years
sexcentenary
  relating to a period of 600 years
septicentennial
  relating to a period of 700 years
antemillennial, premillennial
  relating to the period before the millennium
millennial, millennium
  relating to a period of 1000 years;
  10 centuries
postmillennial
  relating to the period after the millennium
sesquimillennium
  relating to a period of 1500 years;
  15 centuries
bimillenary, bimillennial, bimillennium
  relating to a period of 2000 years;
  20 centuries
perennial
  occurring year after year
plurennial
  lasting for many years
aeonial
  everlasting

Listed Alphabetically

aeonial
  everlasting
annual
  yearly; once a year
antemillennial
  relating to the period before the millennium
biannual
  twice a year (not necessarily at equally
  spaced intervals)
bicentenary, bicentennial, bicentennium
  relating to a period of 200 years
biennial, biennium
  relating to a period of two years
bimester
  relating to a period of two months
bimillenary, bimillennial, bimillennium
  relating to a period of 2000 years; 20 centuries
bimonthly
  1. every two months
  2. twice a month
biquarterly
  twice every three months
biweekly
  1. every two weeks
  2. twice a week
biyearly
  relating to a period of two years
centenary, centennial, centennium, centurial
  relating to a period of 100 years
decennary, decennial, decennium
  relating to a period of 10 years
diennial
  relating to a period of two years
diurnal
  daily; of a day
duodecennial
  relating to a period of 12 years
fortnightly
  once every two weeks
hebdomadal
  weekly; a period of seven days
millennial, millennium
  relating to a period of 1000 years; 10 centuries
monthly
  1. relating to a period of one month
  2. thirty days
nichthemeron
  a period of 24 hours

nocturnal
nightly, of a night

novendial
a period of nine days

novennial
relating to a period of nine years

octennial
relating to a period of eight years

per annum
yearly; once a year

per diem
daily; of a day

perennial
occurring year after year

plurennial
lasting for many years

postmillennial
relating to the period after the millennium

premillennial
relating to the period before the millennium

quadrennial, quadrennium, quadriennial
relating to a period of four years

quadricentennial
relating to a period of 400 years

quasquicentennial
relating to a period of 125 years

quatercentennial
relating to a period of 400 years

quincentenary, quincentennial
relating to a period of 500 years

quindecennial
relating to a period of 15 years

quinquagenary
relating to a period of 50 years

quinquennial, quinquennium, quintennial
relating to a period of five years

quotennial
yearly; once a year

quotidian
daily; of a day

semestral, semiannual
every half year or six-month period

semicentenary, semicentennial
relating to a period of 50 years

semidiurnal
twice a day

semimonthly
twice a month

semiweekly
twice a week

semiyearly
every half year or six-month period

septenary
relating to a period of seven years

septendecennial
relating to a period of 17 years

septennial, septennium
relating to a period of seven years

septicentennial
relating to a period of 700 years

sesquicentenary, sesquicentennial
relating to a period of 150 years

sesquimillennium
relating to a period of 1500 years; 15 centuries

sexcentenary
relating to a period of 600 years

sexennial, sextennial
relating to a period of six years

solennial
yearly; once a year

tercentenary, tercentennial
relating to a period of 300 years

triannual
three times a year

tricenary
1. relating to a period of one month
2. thirty days

tricennial
relating to a period of 30 years

tricentennial
relating to a period of 300 years

triennial, triennium
relating to a period of three years

trigintennial
relating to a period of 30 years

trimester
relating to a period of three months

trimonthly
1. every three months
2. three times a month

triweekly
1. every three weeks
2. three times a week

undecennial
relating to a period of 11 years

vicennial, vigintennial
relating to a period of 20 years

Calendar Systems around the World: Julian, Gregorian, Jewish, Islamic, Hindu, Buddhist, Chinese, Mayan, and Aztec

A calendar is a means of reckoning time through the application of divisions—days, weeks, months, and years. Some of these divisions, such as months, originate in observations of phenomena in nature. Others, such as weeks, are quite arbitrary. In primitive times, people reckoned by cycles of the moon (months), but when a more convenient, shorter period was needed days were grouped, e.g., intervals between market days probably led to the use of the seven-day week. The originally Jewish seven-day week became a standard throughout Western civilization starting from the third century B.C.

The Day

The day is a fairly natural division, despite the variation in the length of sunlight through the year. The Babylonians introduced divisions of the day into twenty-four hours, but the length of hours varied through the year. Only with the development of accurate clocks, the demand for which was a byproduct of the interest in maritime navigation that came with the Renaissance, was the day given scientific regularity.

The Month

A lunar month, the period of a complete cycle of the phases of the moon, lasts approximately 29.5 days, is easy for all to recognize, short enough to be counted without using large numbers, matches closely with the female menstrual cycle and, given its relation to the tidal cycle, with the duration of cyclic behavior in some marine animals. Its simplicity and minimal ease of observation (if one discounts cloudy skies) led to its great significance, and it was widely used as the basis for calendars in many cultures. The length of each month varied according to the culture, e.g., the Babylonians alternated between twenty-nine- and thirty-day months, the Egyptians fixed them at thirty days, etc.

The Seasons

But the problem inherent in the use of a lunar calendar is that the cycles of the sun, not the moon, determine the seasons, the predictability of which is essential to the success of agriculture. The seasons could be determined by solar observation, either by measuring the cycle of the midday shadow cast by a stick placed vertically in the ground, or by sophisticated astronomical calculations. Either system resulted in a solar year of approximately 365 days, incompatible with the twelve 29.5-day lunar months that resulted in a 354-day year.

Civilizations attempted to reconcile lunar months with the solar year in varied ways. The most influential ancient effort was that of the Egyptian astronomers, working from precise mathematical observations and borrowing from Babylonian astronomy, who drew up the Roman calendar that Julius Caesar introduced.

Julian Calendar

Julius Caesar ordered the change of the reformed Roman lunar calendar to a solar-based one in 46 B.C. The intercalation of ninety days corrected a discrepancy that had been growing between the seasons and the months in which they had traditionally fallen. Prior to this intercalation, the Roman civic year had come to be about three months "ahead" of the seasons, so spring began in June. The year 46 B.C. was assigned 445 days to make the adjustment; it was called *ultimus annus confusionis*, 'the last year of the muddled reckoning.' The new calendar, based on the Egyptian solar calendar, provided for a year of 365 days with an additional day in February every fourth year. The addition of this leap year and day gives the Julian year an average length of 365.25 days—very close to the actual solar cycle. The Julian calendar (O.S., or Old Style) remained in civic use in the West for more than 1,600 years, is still the basis of the "Old Calendarist" Orthodox Christian liturgical calendar, and is used by all Orthodox Christian churches to determine the date of Easter.

Gregorian Calendar

By the late sixteenth century, the difference between the Julian calendar and the seasons had grown to ten days because the Julian year, averaging 365.25 days, was slightly longer than the actual length of a solar year, which, by modern calculation, is known to be 365.242199 days long. Fixed holy days began to occur in the "wrong" season, both for the church and for farmers, who used certain holy days to determine planting and harvesting. Pope Gregory XIII ordered the reform that deleted ten days from the year 1582; in that year, October 15 was the day after October 5. This change, coupled with the elimination of leap days in "century" years unless evenly divisible by 400 (e.g., 1600, 2000), corrected the calendar so that today only occasional "leap seconds" are needed to keep months and seasons synchronized. At first adopted only in Roman Catholic countries, the Gregorian calendar (N.S., or New Style) gradually came to be accepted throughout the West, and today has become the calendar used by most of the world, at least for business and government.

Jewish Calendar

In 358, Hillel II introduced a permanent calendar based on mathematical and astronomical calculations, eliminating the need for eyewitness sightings of the new moon with which the new month begins. Due to doubts as to when the new moon appeared, biblical law stated that those living outside of Israel would observe two days rather than one for each festival, except for Yom Kippur, the Day of Atonement. The Talmud required that this custom continue even after the calendar was formulated. The Jewish era begins with the date of Creation, traditionally set in 3761 B.C.

Only slight modifications were made to Hillel's calendar, and it has remained unchanged since the tenth century. A day is reckoned from sundown to sundown, a week contains seven days, a month is either twenty-nine or thirty days long, and a year has twelve lunar months plus about eleven days, or 353, 354, or 355 days. To reconcile the calendar with the annual solar cycle, a thirteenth month of thirty days is intercalated in the third, sixth, eighth, eleventh, fourteenth, seventeenth, and nineteenth years of a nineteen-year cycle; a leap year may contain from 383 to 385 days. The civil calendar begins with the month of Tishri, the first day of which is Rosh Hashanah, the New Year. The cycle of the religious calendar begins on Nisan 15, Passover (Pesach).

The names of the months of the Jewish calendar were borrowed from the Babylonians. The pre-exilic books of the Bible usually refer to the months according to their numerical order, beginning with Tishri, but there are four months mentioned with different names: Nisan/Abib, Iyyar/Ziv, Tishri/Ethanim, and Heshvan/Bul:

Nisan: mid-March to mid-April

Iyyar: mid-April to mid-May

Sivan: mid-May to mid-June

Tammuz: mid-June to mid-July

Av: mid-July to mid-August

Elul: mid-August to mid-September

Tishri: mid-September to mid-October

Heshvan: mid-October to mid-November

Kislev: mid-November to mid-December

Tevet: mid-December to mid-January

Shevat: mid-January to mid-February

Adar: mid-February to mid-March

The intercalary month of Adar II is inserted before Adar as needed.

Islamic Calendar

The Islamic calendar, called *hijri* or Hegirian, is still strictly lunar-based. Moreover, the *actual* beginning of a month depends on the sighting of the new moon. Traditionally, if the sky is overcast and the new moon is not visible, the previous month runs another thirty days before the new month begins. However, the *practical* beginning of a month is according to astronomical calculations of lunar cycles. The Islamic era begins July 16, 622, the date of the hegira or flight into exile of the Prophet Muhammad from Mecca to Medina.

There are twelve Islamic lunar months, some of twenty-nine, others of thirty days; these yield 354 days in the Islamic year. The fixed holidays set in the Islamic calendar thus move "backward" about ten days each year in relation to the Gregorian calendar. In roughly thirty-six years, Ramadan, the Islamic holy month of fasting, moves back through the entire solar year. The Islamic day runs from sundown to sundown.

Other calendars were developed in Islamic countries for the sake of agriculture, which depends on a solar calendar. The Coptic calendar, a variation of the Julian, was used until recently, but is now limited primarily to use in Egypt and the Sudan, countries with large Coptic populations. The Turkish fiscal calendar, also Julian-based, was used in the Ottoman Empire. Nowadays, the Gregorian calendar is followed nearly everywhere for civic purposes, and the Islamic calendar determines only the days of religious observance. Saudi Arabia is one exception, and, at least officially, uses the Islamic calendar as the calendar of reference.

The names of the Islamic months are an ancient reflection of the seasons of the solar year:

Muharram: the sacred month

Safar: the month which is void

Rabi al-Awwal: the first spring

Rabi ath-Thani: the second spring

Jumada-l-Ula: the first month of dryness

Jumada-th-Thaniyyah: the second month of dryness

Rajab: the revered month

Shaban: the month of division

Ramadan: the month of great heat

Shawwal: the month of hunting

Dhu al-Qadah: the month of rest

Dhu al-Hijjah: the month of pilgrimage

Hindu Calendar

Although each geographical region of India has had its own calendar, all are based on an ancient calendar, the earliest time measurement system in India, found in texts thought to date from as early as 1000 B.C. Of the multitudinous regional Hindu calendars, used only for religious holidays, the majority divide an approximate solar year of 360 days into twelve months. Each day is 1/30th of a month, with the intercalation of a leap month every sixty months. Time measurements based on observations of the constellations are used along with the calendar. Each month is divided into two fortnights: *krsna* (waning or dark half) and *sukla* (waxing or bright half). In southern India, the month begins with the new moon. In other parts of the country, the full moon is considered to be the beginning of the month. Many references to the Hindu calendar (depending on the source) are given as follows: month, fortnight (either S=waxing or K=waning), and number of the day in that fortnight, e.g., Rama Navami: Caitra S. 9.

The names of the Hindu months (with variant spellings) are given below, with the Burmese name for the month in brackets:

Caitra or Chaitra [Tagu]: March-April

Vaisakha [Kasone]: April-May

Jyeshta or Jyaistha [Nayhone]: May-June

Ashadha or Asadha [Waso]: June-July

Sravana [Wagaung]: July-August

Bhadrapada [Tawthalin]: August-September

Asvina [Thadingyut]: September-October

Kartika or Karttika [Tazaungmone]: October-November

Margasirsa or Margashirsha [Nadaw]: November-December

Pausa or Pausha [Pyatho]: December-January

Magha [Tabodwei]: January-February

Phalguna [Tabaung]: February-March

Buddhist Calendar

The Buddhist calendar originated in India and varies among different geographic locations, as does the Hindu calendar, with which it shares many common elements. The method for determining the date of the new year is not uniform among Buddhist sects. Theravada Buddhists (those primarily in Sri Lanka, Laos, Burma/Myanmar, Thailand, and Cambodia), using a Hindu calendar as their basis, calculate the months by the moon and the new year by the sun's position in relation to the twelve segments of the heavens, each named for a sign of the zodiac. The solar new year begins when the sun enters Aries, usually between April 13th and 18th. The lunar months alternate between twenty-nine and thirty days in length. The first lunar month is usually sometime in December, except for the Burmese Buddhist calendar, which begins in April (see **Hindu Calendar** above for Burmese names). Periodically, the seventh month has an intercalary day, and an intercalary month is added every few years. Cambodia, Laos, and Thailand refer to the months by number. Tibetan Buddhists, whose calendar has been heavily influenced by the Chinese calendar, begin their new year at the full moon nearest to the midpoint of Aquarius. Mahayana Buddhists (those primarily in Tibet, Mongolia, China, Korea, and Japan) base their holidays on Buddhist, Chinese, or Gregorian calendars.

Chinese Calendar

The Chinese calendar, widely used in Asian countries, is based on the oldest system of time measurement still in use, with its epoch believed to be 2953 B.C. Part of the reason that the Chinese calendar has survived intact for so long is that, until the middle of the twentieth century, the document was considered sacred. Any changes to the calendar were tightly controlled by imperial authorities, and the penalty for illegally tampering with the time-keeping system was death. Until the rise of Communism in China during the twentieth century, the official calendar was presented to the emperor, governors, and other dignitaries in an annual ceremony. Since 1911, the Gregorian calendar has been in use for civic purposes.

The Chinese New Year takes place on the new moon nearest to the point which is defined in the West as the fifteenth degree of the zodiacal sign of Aquarius. Each of twelve months in the Chinese year is twenty-nine or thirty days long and is divided into two parts, each of which is two weeks long. The Chinese calendar, like all lunisolar systems, requires periodic adjustment to keep the lunar and solar cycles integrated, therefore an intercalary month is added when necessary.

The names of each of the twenty-four two-week periods sometimes correspond to festivals which occur during the period. Beginning with the New Year, which takes place in late January or early February, these periods are known by the following names: Spring Begins (New Year), the Rain Water, the Excited Insects, the Vernal Equinox, the Clear and Bright, the Grain Rains, the Summer Begins, the Grain Fills, the Grain in Ear, the Summer Solstice, the Slight Heat, the Great Heat, the Autumn Begins, the Limit of Heat, the White Dew, the Autumnal Equinox, the Cold Dew, the Hoar Frost Descends, the Winter Begins, the Little Snow, the Heavy Snow, the Winter Solstice, the Little Cold, and the Great Cold.

Mayan and Aztec Calendars

The Mayan and Aztec civilizations both used what is commonly referred to as the Mesoamerican calendar. This ancient calendar may have derived from the Olmec civilization, which thrived between 1300 and 400 B.C. in what is now southeastern Mexico, along the Gulf. The Mesoamerican calendrical system probably originated between 1000–900 B.C. and employed not just one calendar, but a system of two interconnecting calendars: a 260-day calendar and a 365-day calendar. These two calendars ran alongside each other. Every 52 years, a named day from the 260-day calendar would be the same as a named day from the 365-day calendar (there are 18,980 days in 52 years, and 18,980 is the least common multiple of both 365 and 260). This 52-year cycle was observed by both the Mayans and the Aztecs.

Mayan civilization, in what is now southeastern Mexico, Belize, and portions of Guatemala and Honduras, flourished between about 300–900 A.D., a period known as the Classical Mayan era. The Mayans used the 260-day calendar—known as the *tzolkin*—for sacred purposes, and the 365-day solar-based calendar—called the *haab*—for agricultural purposes. The Mayan calendar system employed glyphs, small pictorial inscriptions, to represent such time periods as a day, a month, and a year, as well as to represent specific months of the year and specific days in the months. Each day was named for a god who was thought to be manifest as that day. The days' numbers were written using a combination of dots and bars. The 260-day Mayan calendar was divided into 13 months of 20 named days. The 365-day calendar was divided into 18 months of 20 named days plus a brief month of five days, called *Uayeb*, or 'ominous days'. The 52-year Mayan cycle is known as the Calendar Round. The 260-day system is thought to be the only one of its kind in the world. Scholars are not certain what the significance of 260 is, though some have noted that the average duration of human pregnancy is approximately 260 days long. In addition, the Mayans had a highly developed knowledge of astronomy, and 260 was a number significant in calculating the appearance of Venus—the planet identified with the Mayan god Kukulcan, known as Quetzalcoatl to the Toltec people, who flourished in Mesoamerica (and dominated the Mayans) from the 10th century to the middle of the 12th century.

Mayans also developed the Long Count, an extensive system of time-reckoning which attempted to encompass the time of the world from its creation to its end. The Mayans are thought to have developed the Long Count between 400 B.C. and 100 A.D. From this system, they dated the current creation to have occurred in 3114 B.C. (or 3113 B.C., by some contemporary calculations). This Long Count, according to some scholars, will end in December 2011 (or 2012).

The Aztecs (they called themselves Mexica) were dominant in Mesoamerica after the Toltec empire collapsed, from the early 1300s up until the Spanish began colonization in the early 1600s. Like the Mayans, the Aztecs used the 260-day calendar divided into 13 months of 20 days; they called it *tonalpohualli*, or 'count of day.' Their 365-day calendar also consisted of 18 months of 20 days plus a period of five days, which the Aztecs believed to be unlucky. The Aztecs also named their days after deities, but, unlike the Mayan system, Aztec numerical notation consisted only of dots. Aztecs probably did not use a Long Count. At the end of their 52-year cycle—which they called *xiuhmolpilli*, or 'year bundle'—the Aztecs celebrated the new beginning with a great renewal ceremony (see NEW FIRE CEREMONY).

Today, the 365-day civil calendar predominates throughout the region, though some contemporary Mayans also continue to use the 260-day calendar to observe sacred festivals.

Comparative Table of Calendar Systems

The Gregorian calendar is based on the solar cycle of 365 days per year, while the Jewish, Hindu, and Burmese calendars are based on the lunar cycle of 29½ days per month. The first day of the lunar months depicted here is typically the day of the new moon. The lunar months can overlap with the Gregorian months near which they fall. This is reflected in the chart below. While the Burmese calendar is essentially identical to the Hindu, the names of the months differ and are thus represented below. An asterisk (*) denotes the months in which the various New Years fall.

Gregorian Calendar	Jewish Calendar	Hindu, Jain, Buddhist and Sikh Calendar	Burmese Calendar
January*	Shevat	Magha	Tabodwei
February			
	Adar	Phalguna	Tabaung
March			
	Nisan	Caitra*	Tagu*
April			
	Iyyar	Vaisakha*	Kasone
May			
	Sivan	Jyeshta	Nayhone
June			
	Tammuz	Ashadha	Waso
July			
	Av	Sravana	Wagaung
August			
	Elul	Bhadrapada	Tawthalin
September			
	Tishri*	Asvina	Thadingyut
October			
	Heshvan	Kartika	Tazaungmone
November			
	Kislev	Margasirsa	Nadaw
December			
	Tevet	Pausa	Pyatho

The Millennium

In the Western world, the year 1997 is widely regarded as an exceptional period—the long-awaited Millennium, two thousand years after the birth of Jesus Christ in the Christian chronology indicated by the term "A.D." (Anno Domini—the Year of our Lord). Many religious sects believe that this is a period to be marked by signs and wonders, and the Second Coming of Christ, while a secular public regards the Millennium as an important milestone in the history of the world.

However, the Christian calendar is somewhat misleading, since there is no evidence that Jesus of Nazareth was born in 1 A.D., and the canonical date is approximate—circa 7–8 B.C. (Before Christ), in itself a somewhat paradoxical dating! The actual inception of the Christian era is also somewhat vague. Benedictine legend ascribed it to Dionysius Exiguus, a Scythian monk and abbot of Rome in or about the year 532 A.D., but there are other claimants, perhaps equally legendary. The introduction of dating the Christian era did not come into official use until some time between the tenth and twelfth centuries. It was first indicated in European documents as "anno incarnationis Domini" or "anno ab incarnatione" or "anno a Nativate" or "anno a Passione," eventually as "anno Domini." Early papal documents were often undated, or listed the Kalends, Nones, and Ides of various months, or else the year of the reign of a particular pope. An early use of the incarnation dating in Vatican records was in 938 A.D.

Of course, it must be remembered that the concept of a Messiah or Savior to redeem the world was originally a Jewish belief, taken over by the Christians (together with the Jewish scriptures of the Old Testament) after the crucifixion of Jesus, whom the Christians claimed as the Messiah, foretold in prophecies, although not accepted as such by the Jews. It seems, from vague references in the Talmud, the Jewish book of religious law, that since the claimed Messiah did not reform the hearts of men and restore the kingdom of God on earth, as expected in prophecy as the test of the Messiah, "that man" could not be the Messiah.

The belief in a Golden Age initiated by a Messiah took different forms in Jewish and Christian history. The original Jewish view of the prophet Isaiah was of an anointed king, of the House of David, imbued with the spirit of Yahweh, who would effect the salvation of Israel. At other periods, the concept became that of a divine power which would transform the souls of human beings in fulfilling the covenant with God. Early Jewish converts to Christianity believed in an earthly leader and kingdom, underlining the condemnation of Jesus by the Romans as a heretical political leader. But from time to time, both Jewish and Christian beliefs were modified, encouraged, then discredited in the struggles of the early Christian Church. Millennial hopes became a powerful element in Christian theology. Such beliefs also became known alternatively as "Chiliasm" (from a Greek root), embodying the belief that Christ would reign on earth for a thousand years. The concept of a thousand years derives from Psalms (90:4), which states that one thousand years are as one day before the Lord, and the Mosaic account of creation in six days. The Chiliasts considered the six days as 6,000 years of activity, followed by a sabbath of one thousand years of peace and happiness.

There have been many millennial speculations arising from interpretation of apocalyptic literature, notably the book of Revelations. In the second century, Justin Martyr stated: "I and all Christians whose belief is in every respect correct know that there will be both a resurrection of the flesh and a thousand years in Jerusalem, which will then be rebuilt, adorned and enlarged, as the prophets Ezekiel, Isaiah and others declare." After the Crucifixion, many Christians believed in the Second Coming of a Messiah who would reign in bodily presence upon earth for a thousand years, although this belief was sometimes condemned as "Jewish." Variants of this belief were attacked, modified and reinstated during the period of persecution of Christians and the attempt to develop a uniform theology. After several centuries, millennial beliefs subsided, although partially revived by the end of the tenth century with a general expectation that the end of the world was at hand. By the sixteenth century, the Reformation revived millennial belief with speculation of the downfall of the Roman Catholic Church, but the extravagances of such sects as the Anabaptists discredited millenarianism in the reformed churches.

A new revival of Protestant belief occurred in the eighteenth century through such authorities as Johann Albrecht Bengel, Friedrich Christoph Oetinger, Johan Heinrich Jung-Stilling and others, while the inspired mystic Emanuel Swedenborg believed that the last judgment took place unseen in 1757 and that the Church of New Jerusalem had been formed in both heaven and earth.

By now, millennial beliefs in Christian sects were of two main kinds: first, that the world was already going through an initial period of the reign of evil, in which the saints suffered, and divine judgment was already registered, as a prelude to a thousand years of transformation; second, that there would be a Second Coming of Christ after a thousand years of the Christian era, to be followed by another thousand years of transformation and judgment. Variants of such beliefs were reflected in the many heterodox sects which emerged from the nineteenth century onwards, such as the Catholic Apostolic Church of Edward Irving, and the followers of William Miller, who predicted the Second Coming to take place in 1843, but was obliged to revise the date when that year passed without the divine event. Other Adventist sects have had similar problems of prediction. The followers of Joanna Southcott believed that she would actually give birth to the Messiah, but were disappointed when an apparent pregnancy proved fallacious, and Southcott herself renounced her beliefs as delusive. Well-known millennial sects surviving at the present time include Jehovah's Witnesses and the Mormons (also known as "Latter-Day Saints" indicating the belief that the world is approaching the last days).

In modern times, millennial beliefs have largely disappeared from mainline Christian doctrines, both Catholic and Protestant, but have continued in a popular simplified form through the claims of Catholic visionaries such as those at Fátima, Garabandal, and Medjugorje, where apparitions of the Virgin Mary convey messages of the need for religious revival and observance before the imminent days of signs and wonders. Meanwhile, Jewish messianic belief retains a strong mystic characteristic of the transformation of souls through righteous living in the human covenant with God.

It is interesting to note that Hindu belief in great cycles of creation, decline and rebirth also claims a forthcoming period of world decline and devolution. The *Yugas*, or ages of the world, are measured in years of the gods, each year equal to 360 human years. In the *Krita Yuga*, or Golden Age of 4,800 years, there is a period of righteousness, religious observance, truth and duty; in the *Treta Yuga*, or Silver Age of 3,600 years, righteousness declines to some extent; in the *Dwapara Yuga* of 2,400 years, there is further decline, accompanied by diseases and calamities; in the *Kali Yuga*, or evil age of 1,200 years, there is further decline and calamity until eventual devolution, to be followed by a new cycle of creation and righteousness. The world is said to be passing through *Kali Yuga* at the present time.

There is no doubt that the past few decades have seen a worldwide explosion of crime and decadence, in spite of astonishing scientific and technological innovation, that there are many catastrophic natural disasters and human calamities in a period of political unrest and ruthless wars of conquest, instead of the peace and happiness confidently expected after the horrors of World War II. Even though millennial belief is no longer a dominant aspect of orthodox Christian doctrine, there is widespread popular unease as the world moves into the Millennium.

Various governments plan special events to mark this period, but these will be of a secular character. There are also special technological problems of the millennium with the belated realization that many manufacturers of computers had pre-programmed their dating systems to the twentieth-century calendar by making only the last two digits of the year adjustable. The millennium requires the *first* two digits to be able to read "20" (instead of "19"), thus many computers as well as other electronic devices will wrongly register the year "2000" as "1900" and subsequent years equally inaccurately. As a result, insurance companies may face huge claims as the worldwide cost of apparatus adjustment runs into billions of dollars! An organization named "Taskforce 2000" has been set up by the computer industry to coordinate response to this costly problem. However, in an age of planned consumer product obsolescence, manufacturers of new equipment may relish a sudden increase in sales of newly designed equipment.

Meanwhile, scientific predictions of the condition of the ozone layer and the possibility of giant asteroids hitting the earth and destroying life have something of the character of the ancient prophecies of apocalyptic doom.

Leslie Shepard
Dublin, Ireland
January 1997

The Millennium: An Overview

The end of this millennium, the year 2000, is filled with symbolism and significance. Communications technology and the shrinking of our world combine to make this the most widely shared turn of the millennium and turn of the century ever. To societies that follow the Western Gregorian calendar, the year 2000 marks a convergence of several fascinating strands of history and traditional speculation, from apocalyptic prophesies to utopic visions. While other traditions follow their own calendrical systems — such as the Jewish calendar, when it will be the year 5760; the Islamic, 1420; Chinese, 4698; and Hindu, 2051 — nearly every place in the world follows the Gregorian calendar for business purposes.

The significance of the millennium, which comes from the Christian religious tradition, is based upon the birth of Jesus Christ. *Millennium* is a Latin word meaning a period of one thousand years. The year 2001, not 2000 — as purists are wont to point out — marks the 2000th anniversary of the date traditionally celebrated as the birth of Jesus. That date, however, is in error. Dionysius Exiguus, also known as Dennis the Diminutive, was a Christian monk living during the sixth century A.D., who wrongly calculated the birth year of Christ to be 1 A.D. Most scholars now accept that Jesus was born sometime between 4–7 B.C., which means that we are already in the third millennium. Some make the case for 5 B.C., when a comet, suggested to be the Star of Bethlehem, was visible over Bethlehem. (For a most exacting, and enjoyable, explanation of the debate over the calendrical error, see Gould, 1994).

The word "millennium" also carries a biblical connotation. John of Patmos, author of the New Testament book of Revelation, referred to a 1000-year rule of Christ before the Last Judgment and end of this world (Rev. 20). From this biblical text derive several forms of millennialism, a Judeo-Christian belief that God will bring about the end of the world as we know it, and usher in a new utopic kingdom. These sorts of apocalyptic views are key to understanding the significance many attach to the millennium.

Apocalypticism through History

In Western cultures, many images and ideas about the end of the world come from a literary tradition known as apocalyptic literature. The millennium has nothing to do with apocalypse, but some people draw connections between them. Some claim that because the year 2000 marks the end of the second millennium after Christ's birth, that is when the apocalypse, the end times, will occur. They often put forth a line of reasoning summarized here by theologian William Barclay: "it was held that the age of the world would correspond to the time taken for its creation and that the time of creation was 6,000 years [based on a 4004 B.C. creation date]. 'A thousand years in thy sight are but as yesterday' (Psalm 90:4). 'One day with the Lord is as a thousand years, and a thousand years as one day' (2 Peter 3:8). Each day of creation was said to be 1,000 years. It was, therefore, held that the Messiah would come in the sixth thousand of the years; and the seventh thousand, the equivalent of the Sabbath rest in the creation story, would be the reign of the Messiah" (*The Revelation*, 1976, 2:188). Yet, the Roman Catholic Church has discouraged literal readings of these texts since the time of St. Augustine of Hippo (354–430 A.D.; see Boyer, p. 21; *The Revelation*, 1976). Augustine read Revelation as being about the moral conflicts each person, as well as the Church, undergoes through life. In addition, the Church took seriously what Jesus was reported to have said to his disciples: "But of that day and hour [of the Second Coming] no one knows, neither the angels in heaven, nor the Son, but the Father alone" (Matthew 24:36) and, when asked if he was going to restore the kingdom, Jesus replied, "It is not for you to know the times or seasons that the Father has established by his own authority" (Acts 1:7).

The biblical book of Revelation, also known as the Apocalypse, is one of the most common sources people refer to about the end times (*apocalypse* is a Greek word meaning 'unveiling' or 'revelation'). It belongs to a Jewish and Christian literary genre that was very popular between 200 B.C. and 200 A.D. Revelation was probably written around 90 A.D., placing it squarely within that tradition. The author calls himself John, though most scholars doubt that he was St. John the Evangelist; they do agree that John was a persecuted Christian banished to the island of Patmos, which was a Roman prison of sorts. The book of Revelation also needs to be considered in terms of the author's intent to his audience. John was writing to other Christians scattered throughout the Middle East, who were also either already being persecuted or in danger by Roman authorities. Domitian was the Roman emperor between 81–96 A.D., when John was imprisoned, and, as Barclay has it, "with the exception of Caligula, [Domitian] was the first Emperor to take his divinity seriously and to *demand* Caesar worship" (*The Revelation*, 1976, 1:19). Roman emperors were referred to as "Caesars." People who refused to perform a public act of worship to Caesar (i.e., Domitian) and proclaim that "Caesar is Lord" could be imprisoned or killed.

Apocalyptic literature has some striking characteristics, not the least of which is the extravagant use of a rich collection of symbolic and allegorical language and imagery. These characteristics inform not only John's Revelation in the New Testament (often referred to as "Revelations"), but also the Old Testament books of Daniel, Ezekiel, Zechariah, and Jeremiah, which together comprise the main sources that later ages, including our own, have drawn on. All employ a common stock of literary devices and images, as well as give symbolic meaning to certain numbers, such as six (signifying imperfection), seven (signifying perfection, completeness), and one thousand (meaning any very large number). Generally, Revelation tells a story of God bringing great calamity to earth, punishment to sinners, and Jesus' second coming which brings salvation to the faithful. Some of the most enduring and powerful images of the calamities, or the "Great Tribulation," are: stars falling to earth, the moon turning to blood, the waters of the earth turning to blood, and the dragon (Rev. 6:12-13, 7:14, 8:8, 9:1, 16:3-4, 12, 20). Chapter 13 of Mark's Gospel, sometimes called the "Little Apocalypse," also deals with these themes. Jesus tells his disciples about "signs" to precede his second coming: "wars and reports of wars," "tribulations," "signs and wonders," and "false Messiahs and false prophets" (Mark 13:3-27). One of the most popular images in Revelation is that of the beast, whose number is 666 and who is associated with the Antichrist, an instrument of Satan. He is described as working in conjunction with the false prophet. When they appear on earth, it is a sign that the end will come soon (Rev. 13, 16:13). Next, angels are sent with sickles to harvest the earth (Rev. 14:14-20). Finally, there appears "a new heaven and a new earth," where no one dies, mourns, or suffers (Rev. 21:1-4). We will see later how many of these images recur throughout history in popular imagination.

Early readers of Revelation helped build the tradition of trying to identify "the Beast" by assigning numerical values to letters in names, and seeing whether they add up to 666. The ruthless Roman Emperor Nero (37–68 A.D.), who started the Roman persecution of Christians, was the hands-down favorite for some time, even though he was dead when John wrote Revelation. Similar to the "resurrection" mythology that surrounds Elvis Presley today, many people thought that Nero might return from the dead to rule and terrorize again.

Literary critic Frank Kermode captures some of the classic features of apocalyptic literature:

> There is always reference to some state of affairs contemporary with the author, but the material is presented as belonging to a remoter time. It is represented as occurring in a dream or vision, and the figures of the dream are very artificial and obscure, somewhat in the manner of medieval dream poetry. Readers are always of necessity interpreters; the text is deliberately vague or sometimes bewilderingly precise, and what one gets out of it depends to a large extent on what one puts in, which is why the Beast can be thought to represent not only Nero but also Napoleon or Hitler or a wicked pope. The mysterious numbers allow one to select the date on which the obscure events prophesied will take place, so the work is never out of date; it can be mapped onto almost any set of circumstances, which is why it has had so profound an effect not only on lunatic schismatics but also on serious political thinkers through the centuries. Apocalypse is always a literature of crisis; the unknown past is coming to a catastrophic end, the unknown future is upon us; we are placed, as no one ever was before, at precisely the moment in time when the past may be seen as a pattern and the future, amply predicted in the numerals and images of the text, begins to take exact shapes (Kermode, 1987: 385).

The power of apocalyptic literature also depends upon the Christian view of history as having a beginning and an end. Other traditions view history differently, such as the Mayan and Hindu faiths, which hold that history is cyclical, that ages of the world begin, end, and begin and end again and again.

Theologian Bernard McGinn, writing on apocalyptic sects and movements, adds this:

> Historically, apocalypticism has been the protest literature of out-groups. It thrives in moments when stable cultural systems are undergoing breakdown and provides, by its characteristic separation from the wider culture, a way of getting outside the reigning structure—where reverie and dream can obtain a hearing. That is, it suspends the reality principle and creates space for options, for musing on what if's, might be's, and should be's. As such, apocalypticism can function as either grace or evil force. On the one hand, it is the brewing place of scapegoating pogroms, crusades, revolutions and holy wars; and on the other, it can be a culture's way of declaring that conservatism does not suffice, that no society can prosper without qualitative growth (McGinn, 1996).

Apocalypticism, with its themes of disaster and salvation, has historically offered a way to deal with hopes and fears. As medievalist Robert E. Lerner writes, "Millennial prophecies [in the late Middle Ages] appear to have served the function of instilling hope and fortitude during times of disaster. Millennial prophecies were customarily inspired by meteorological portents or by calamities such as the onslaught of the Mongols, the fall of the Holy Land, the spread of the Black Death, or the outbreak of the Great Schism [breakup of the Roman Catholic Church, 1378–1417]" (Lerner, 1987: 387).

In fact, times of changing rulership, social chaos, and wars—events that affect virtually everyone living in a society—have traditionally been times for those of Judeo-Christian heritage to tap into their store of apocalyptic literature and look for signs, portents, and wonders, particularly in the skies. In pre-Enlightenment Europe, as folklorist Thomas E. Bullard echoes the psalm, "the heavens were telling the will of the gods" (Bullard, 1997). Signs in the skies did a number of things; among others, they "proclaimed the uniqueness and importance of special individuals" (e.g., the Star, or comet, of Bethlehem) and "foretold the future to some degree . . . war, disease, and calamity." Moreover, "sights that appeared to the Romans appeared as well in the Middle Ages and flourished throughout the age of the Reformation." He cautions, however, that one writer oftentimes follows another "in an age-old tradition of imposing a significant message on anomalous aerial phenomena. . . . [In the Christian era,] accurate reporting took second place to advancement of the faith, so the modern reader has good reason to suspect that every account is a distortion mandated by the literary and intellectual fashions of the day. This trend became acute in the sixteenth and seventeenth centuries when propagandists twisted or fabricated prodigy accounts for political purposes."

Throughout recorded history, millenarian sects or movements have sprung up from time to time. Some recent examples include the tragic Heaven's Gate cult, the followers of Elizabeth Clare Prophet, the Jonestown cult, the Branch Davidians, the Solar Temple cult, the Aum Shinrikyo sect, the militia movement, and the survivalist movement (for more information on these, see Barkun, 1974 and Lamy, 1996; for more information on earlier American premillenarian sects, including the Millerites, see Barkun, 1974 and Weber, 1979). But we will take a look at the previous turn of the millennium as well as focus on a few representative moments throughout Judeo-Christian history when, in certain places, large or powerful portions of societies fell under an apocalyptic spell. As we will see, when we approach a calendar year laden with cultural significance, such as 1666 or 2000, apocalyptic literature and tradition become popular. There is also a tendency to look for, and notice, prophesies and potential signs in the sky.

The Eve of the Second Millennium

In the year 999, according to a popular legend dating from the seventeenth century, Europeans were fearful that the world was coming to an end. On the eve of the second millennium, many people supposedly sold their possessions, left their fields neglected, freed slaves and prisoners, forgave debts, and rushed to churches for forgiveness before the tribulation began and Christ returned. It is not necessarily untrue that people repented and were absolved of their sins en masse, that prisoners and slaves were freed, and debts forgiven, since these are precisely the kinds of things that the Roman Catholic pope calls for in a jubilee year—however, the first jubilee year wasn't until 1300 (see **Celebrations and Other Events** below).

Despite the existence of much popular post-medieval literature detailing the mass atonement and fear of Europeans awaiting the end of the world at the stroke of midnight on December 31, 999, there are a number of good reasons why this story may be better read as fiction than as history. Modern historians have found no sound evidence for a widespread panic on the eve of the second millennium. In fact, they have plenty of evidence that 1) the general population did not widely adhere to any calendar (much less the Christian calendar), except of course for the seasons, which guided their agrarian way of life; 2) there was no general consensus on what year it really was due to the variety of competing A.D. dating systems; and 3) people didn't even agree on the month and day of the new year: in Rome, it was December 25; in Florence, March 25 (the Feast of the Annunciation); in France, Easter Sunday; in Spain and Portugal, January 1; and in England, on either March 25, Christmas, or January 1, Feast of the Circumcision.

The case for the terrors of the year 1000 derives from a few sources, including Vatican librarian Caesar Baronius and his 12-volume *History of the Church* (1558–1607), and the nineteenth-century historian Jules Michelet and his Romanticist work in the 1830s, *History of France* (volume 2, 1833; Landes, 1989: 722-23). Michelet's work drew on the chronicles of one Raoul or Radulphus Glaber. Glaber was a Roman Catholic monk who also reported a spectacular sighting of a comet he had in September 1000, which lasted three months and which he interpreted as a sign of some impending unusual occurrence in the world. Glaber wrote, "And indeed a fire soon consumed the church of St. Michael the Archangel built on a promontory in the ocean" (Focillon, 1969: 66). There were also reports of sighting the shape of a dragon in the sky, as well as an earthquake in the year 1000 (Focillon, 1969: 70). Then, as now, the Church did its best to pre-empt fears of the end of the world and spread a message of hope and renewal toward the new millennium, in keeping with its Augustinian doctrine that no human being—only God—knows when the world will end.

Which is not to say that apocalypticism was absent from that period. Actually, there is evidence that the years leading up to 1033—the millennium anniversary of Christ's death—were anxious ones for some Europeans. In 1033, according to Hillel Schwartz, there was a solar eclipse and, in Israel, an earthquake (Schwartz, 1990: 37). Glaber writes of a famine in France in 1033: "Men believed that the orderly processions of the seasons and the laws of nature, which until then had ruled the world, had relapsed into the eternal chaos; and they feared that mankind would end" (quoted in Focillon, 1969: 67). So there was some anxiety, mainly among the clergy. There is as yet no conclusive evidence that it was widespread or popular, though a few historians have recently begun to reopen the question of whether there was an apocalyptic mood about the year 1000.

However, as theologian Bernard McGinn notes, "Medieval people lived with enough daily misery and terror to think often of Antichrist [and, by implication, the end of the world] without needing a rigidly chronological thousand-year theory" (McGinn, 1994a: 99).

The Orthodox Year 7000

As we approach the third millennium, we might ponder the following case. It cannot be said that prophesies never come true when they are supposed to. It's just that they may come true in unexpected ways.

Since the thirteenth century in Russia, a well-known prophecy held that the world would end in the Orthodox calendar year 7000, which was 1492 in the Gregorian calendar. As in other times and places, apocalyptic expectations went hand in hand with social discord. Historian David Goldfrank notes the Muslim defeat of Byzantium in 1453 and Novgorod's loss of independence in the 1470s, and cites "the approaching Orthodox year '7000' (1492), for which there were no available calendars as late as 1487" (Goldfrank, 1984: 127), because they were so convinced the world would end.

Novgorod had been the capital city of an independent republic and the center of economic wealth since 1136. Moscow began invading Novgorod in the 1450s and conquered it in the 1470s. In addition, "as political and economic pressures on Novgorod increased in the fifteenth century the Novgorodian church frequently interpreted negotiations with the West as signs that the end of the church calendar in 1492 would bring an end to history. [Orthodox Christian] Archbishop Gennadius of Novgorod and Pskov took the initiative shortly after his installation in 1485 in imploring a still-reluctant Moscow to prepare for this moment of destiny by cleansing its realm of heretics just as he had in the see of Novgorod. . . . Some of its nervous, apocalyptical quality almost certainly came from the fear that secularization of both intellectual life and church property was imminent in this westerly region, and that the Tsar himself might emulate the new state builders of the West" (Billington, 1966: 87-88).

Of course, the world as Europeans knew it did end after 1492, with Christopher Columbus's finding of the New World. Columbus, by the way, believed that in so doing, he was fulfilling a prophetic role. Influenced by the apocalyptic millennial vision of Joachim of Fiore which depended on the conversion of the Jews, the defeat of Islamic Turkey, and the founding of a New Jerusalem, Columbus seems to have considered himself instrumental in bringing about that millennium. Certainly, his notes record an intense interest in apocalyptic literature and strong shades of messianism: "God made me the messenger of the new heaven and the new earth, of which He spoke in the Apocalypse of St. John, after having spoken of it by the mouth of Isaiah; and He showed me the spot where to find it" (quoted in Sweet, 1986: 379).

This was also a time when the world ended for innumerable Native Americans in Europe's New World. And the world ended for countless Jewish people who were thrown out of Spain in 1492, after about 100 years of being converted to Catholicism under threat of persecution.

Reformation Era

As we look at western Europe in the sixteenth century, we can see that social conditions created fertile soil in which end-of-the-world signs, wonders, and prophesies could flourish. And, in a sense, the unified Christian world did indeed end. Many areas were in crisis. For some years, religious reformers had been calling for cleaning up corruption and abuses of power in the Church, which nonetheless had been a more or less stable center of peoples' lives for centuries. The Reformation movement set off wars, revolts, and power struggles that went on into the next century. The Ottoman Turks were threatening western Europe, and some breakaway Protestant groups, such as the Anabaptists, held millennial ideas. A popular idea in England was that the pope was the Antichrist, whose appearance signalled the end times (Boyer, 1992: 62).

Ever since 1517, when Martin Luther (who died believing that the end was near) posted the 95 theses on the church door at Wittenberg, Germany, people were more motivated to read the Bible, since a fundamental tenet of reform was that each man could attain the truth by himself through reading scripture. The widespread use of the printing press by the early 1500s ensured that written words of all kinds were more available in western Europe than ever before. But, then, as now, some of the most sensationalistic kinds of literature claimed large readerships among the literate.

The idea that the Last Judgment was imminent was reinforced by such publications as *The Doome warning all men to the Judgemente* (1581) by Stephen Bateman, in which is listed every prodigy and sign he had ever read about. In 1532, for example, Bateman reports, "In many countries there were seen dragons flying in the air in flocks covered with crowns, and having pigs' snouts." Other popular publications included *Strange News, or the Historie of Strange Wonders* (1561), John Foxe's *Actes and Monuments of These Latter and Perillous Days* (1563); and "innumerable pamphlets a few pages long proclaiming 'Strange News' to readers" (Bullard, 1997; see also Thomas, 1971: 141). One is reminded of our own supermarket tabloids. At the turn of the century, two of the best-known European artworks with apocalyptic themes were produced: *The Apocalypse* (1498), the famous series of woodcuts by Albrecht Dürer, and *Garden of Earthly Delights* (c. 1500) by Hieronymous Bosch.

In the midst of all this emerged the French physician and astrologer Michel Nostradamus (born Michel de Nostredame, 1503–1566) and his book of prophesies, *Centuries* (1555). A writer of almanacs and poetry that had been popular since 1550, he also helped create our current definition of the word "century" to mean 100 years, rather than just a collection of 100 things. He wrote prophecies, or ambiguous, though evocative, verse, as many would have it. Since its publication, readers have offered interpretations of the quatrains of the *Centuries*. Some thought, for example, he had foreseen the death of Henry II, king of France, in 1559 (Schwartz, 1990: 99). During the second half of the twentieth century, Nostradamus's popularity has again enjoyed a revival of interest. Here is a verse from his *Centuries* that we may expect to hear about as our century comes to a close:

> The year 1999, seven months,
> From the sky will come a great King of terror,
> To resuscitate the great King of Angoulmois;
> Before, after, Mars will reign by good luck.

We don't know what is meant by the King of terror or the King of Angoulmois, but Mars was the ancient Roman god of war. Those who believe the quatrain above refers to the end of the world in July ("seven months"), 1999, should note that Nostradamus wrote that his prophecies went up to the year 3797 (Schwartz: 1990, 97-98). Those engaged in reviving his prophesies under the premise that they are relevant today, might care to consider the many and complex traditional and literary influences informing the *Centuries*. Nostradamus drew on apocalyptic literature of the ancient Judeo-Christian variety as well as its translation into popular almanacs and pamphlets of the time. He may also have been familiar with kabbalah, a medieval system of scriptural interpretation in which each word, number, and letter was considered to have a secret meaning. As an educated man, he may well have been acquainted with *Hypnerotomachia Poliphili* by Francesco Colonna. Published in 1499, this book dealt with Neoplatonism, a mystical philosophy that was derived from Plato's ideas and used highly allegorical language. Nostradamus also translated Egyptian hieroglyphic writing into verse during the 1530s. His friend Julius Caesar Scaliger was known for creating anagrams and other word games in Latin. In addition, Nostradamus was familiar with cryptic symbols used in alchemy. Forerunner of the science of chemistry, alchemy was the ancient practice of attempting to turn ordinary metals into gold or silver. Finally, emblems and animal symbols used in heraldry were commonplace in Europe at this time, and people occasionally used them to stand for famous people (Schwartz, 1990: 98-99).

1666 and Beyond

In England, the mid-1600s were filled with turmoil. The English Civil War raged from 1642 to 1648, and new Protestant millenarian groups like the Ranters, the Quakers, the Fifth Monarchists, and the Muggletonians abounded. Many thought that the tribulation would occur in a year with such numerical significance as 1666, since 666 was the number of the beast in Revelation. (However, competing years for the end in this era were 1656, supposedly the number of years between Creation and the Flood, as well as the last ones of the century [Thomas, 1971: 141-42]). By this time in England, looking for answers in the skies had become rather legitimate through the popularity of astrology, which was considered a science. Astrologers watched the movements of astronomical bodies to assess what was happening on earth and also to predict what might happen (Thomas, 1971: 283-385). Given these social factors, it should not surprise that, as today, people were fascinated with the idea of the events in Revelation somehow coming to pass, reading prophesies and seeing signs in the sky.

According to McGinn, "[In England] in the 1640s and 1650s hundreds of sermons and pamphlets, frequently based on texts from Revelation, fueled the fires of social and political unrest" (McGinn, 1987: 536). Many books drawing on apocalyptic literature appeared at this time, including: *The Whole Prophecies of Scotland, England, France, Ireland and Denmark* (published in Scotland in 1603 and 1615 as *Collection of Ancient Scottish Prophecies*), and *The Prophecy of Thomas Becket* (published in 1666; previously published in 1645 by William Lilly in *A Collection of Ancient and Moderne Prophesies*). These tended to employ images handed down from biblical and apocalyptic books such as Revelation and Daniel (Thomas, 1971: 390-96), as did publications like *Looke Up and See Wonders* (1628); *Prodigies and Apparitions, or England's Warning-Pieces* by John Vicars (1642); *Natura Prodigiorum* by John Gadbury (1660); and perhaps most notably, *Mirabilis Annus, or the Year of Prodigies and Wonders* (1661-62).

Several apocalyptic images found in Revelation and other biblical books — fire coming from the sky, stars falling, the sickle, the blood—were observed in the following sightings reported in England in 1659 and 1660:

In 1659, according to a publication of the same year out of London called *The Five Strange Wonders in the North and West of England*, "several prodigies appeared between Leicester and Nottingham, and among them there was 'the dismal sight in the air, on Sabbath day last was a fortnight, prodigiously representing itself from one of a clock in the forenoon, till about a quarter and a half after three, in the perfect figure and form of a black coffin, with a fiery dart, and a flaming sword flying to and again, backwards and forwards toward the head of the said coffin, which was . . . beheld by many hundreds of people. . . . And very observable it is, that the fiery dart, or arrow, during the time that the coffin lay hovering and flying up and down in the air, seemed as it were to charge each other, and with such clashing, and streaks of fire, as the like is not to be parallel'd in any age; but upon the dissolution of the coffin, abundance of streams of fire proceeded from it'" (Bullard, 1997). According to *Mirabilis Annus*, on October 17, 1660, "at Shenly in Hertfordshire . . . was seen in the air towards the evening . . . the appearance of five naked men exceeding bright and glorious, moving very swiftly." Again in Hertfordshire, a couple of weeks later, "Three persons . . . going before day . . . were on a sudden smitten with a great terrible flash of lightning; after which the air continued very light . . . and [they] concluded that some house at Meisden had been on fire; but they having not ridden much further perceived the fire in a great body to ascend, and the sky opening to receive it; and as it went up, three stars one immediately after another fell down from it perpendicularly. . . . Some part of the body of fire which ascended, remained yet in their view, and after a little space it turned into the direct form of a sickle with a handle . . . and continued . . . till the daylight swallowed it up." On November 5, 1660, near London, "Two men . . . very early in the morning from under it appeared two stars as big as the moon, and . . . they did with great violence contend with each other. One star grew dimmer and the other brighter during the contest of two hours' duration. Streams of fire and blood poured down from the stars."

Shifting eastward, a similar mood and social upheaval was prevalent in Russia. Historian James H. Billington notes that "the two great periods of apocalyptical excitation in Muscovy—at the beginning of the sixteenth century and the middle of the seventeenth—coincide exactly with times of disaster and renewed apocalypticism in the Jewish community and with violent anti-Jewish measures in Muscovy. What began as a crude imitation of Spanish persecution in the purge of 'Judaizers' by believers in the messianic theory of the Third Rome led eventually to a massacre of Jews in 1648 that was unequaled anywhere prior to the twentieth century. By this time, however, the Russians were sufferers as well as persecutors; and one finds both the Muscovite Old Believers and Jewish Sabbataians expecting the end of the world in 1666. . . . More 'messianic expectations [existed through the] late imperial period' [and during the Bolshevik Revolution of 1917]" (Billington, 1966: 72-75).

By 1700, general excitement about new scientific and astronomical advances had greatly cooled the climate against widespread apocalyptic beliefs, at least temporarily. And yet, one of the fathers of modern Western physics, Sir Isaac Newton, was not immune from interest in biblical apocrypha; he penned *Observations upon the Prophecies of Daniel, and the Apocalypse of St. John* (1733). Newton theorized that the Beast would appear and be defeated by 1867, and the millennium of Christ's rule would begin in 2000. And mathematician William Whiston used Halley's recent discoveries about comets to put forth his thesis that not only was the Flood caused by a near-miss, but that another comet could be coming to bring on the Final Judgment (*New Theory of the Earth*, 1696; see also Thomas, 1971: 428-32). Thus we continue to trace our current fears and speculations about wayward astronomical bodies colliding with earth.

Contemporary Mythology of the Year 2000

During the twentieth century, the year 2000 has come to symbolize the Future as well as a sort of deadline. Scholars and observers in virtually every field of inquiry have used the approaching millennium to stand for what lies ahead and to spur us on to take action. In 1994, the World Futurist Society held a conference in Cambridge, Massachusetts, called, predictably enough, "Toward the New Millennium: Living, Learning, and Working." Many writers have offered forecasts for society into the next century. In 1983, literary and social critic Raymond Williams, in his *The Year 2000*, offered an analysis of political, economic and social prospects for the 21st century. The following are more popular examples of the same trend: George Gallup, Jr., with William Proctor's *Forecast 2000* (1984); Arthur C. Clarke's *July 20, 2019: Life in the 21st Century* (1986); former President Richard Nixon's *1999: Victory Without War* (1988); John and Patricia Naisbitt's *Megatrends 2000* (1990); Pat Robertson's *The New Millennium: 10 Trends That Will Impact You and Your Family by the Year 2000* (1990; for another view by Robertson, see below); David Halberstam's *The Next Century* (1991); Jacques Attali's *Millennium: Winners and Losers in the Coming World Order* (1991); and Jeffrey A. Fisher's *Rx 2000: Breakthroughs in Health, Medicine, and Longevity by the Year 2000 and Beyond* (1992). The list goes on.

On the entrepreneurial side of things, we now have (again, a partial list): Hilton's Millennium Hotel, Millennium vitamins, Lever 2000 soap, the Millennium Fund from Fidelity, Mazda Millenia, and no doubt, a thousand others.

Contemporary Anxiety and Utopianism

Popular ideas about the millennium tend to split into two broad camps: utopian visions and dooms-day scenarios. Some people are looking forward to a utopic millennium in active, if marginal, ways. For example, the Unarius (Universal Articulate Interdimensional Understanding of Science) Academy of Science awaits the landing of benevolent Space Brothers on its 67 acres in El Cajon, California, in 2001, at which time Earth will become the 33rd planet in the Interplanetary Confederation (Clark, 1997). On the pessimistic side of the spectrum, we see preparations for doomsday by some members of the survivalist movement that has been growing since the 1980s. Theologian Bernard McGinn cites a Time/CNN poll, performed by Yankelevich Partners, Inc., on April 28-29, 1993, in which 1,000 adult Americans were asked the following question: "Will the second coming of Jesus Christ occur sometime around the year 2000?" Twenty percent said yes, 49 percent said no, and 31 percent responded that they were not sure (McGinn, 1994a: 281 *n*.1). It would seem significant that half the people polled either believed the second coming of Christ would happen around the year 2000 or were not sure. The best-selling nonfiction book of the 1970s was Hal Lindsey's *The Late Great Planet Earth* (1970), which espoused premillenialism with its own system of biblical exegesis, interpreting events in the twentieth century as being signs from Revelation and other apocalyptic books. In 1977, a film company released a documentary based on the book, narrated by none other than Orson Welles (who perpetrated the "War of the Worlds" Mars invasion hoax on a radio show in 1938). Twenty-eight million copies of the book were in print by 1990.

In contemporary culture, one notices the prevalence of the calamity-causing agent, good or bad, that comes from the sky, often either large bodies in space that collide with earth or extraterrestrials making contact. As we have seen, the sky is a place people have searched for millennia for wonders and signs of the times. In addition, the sky is where the gods have lived for many cultures. Sociologist Barry Beyerstein cites the tradition of "all-powerful beings coming from the sky with an ancient history all their own. The idea is that we're making such a mess of things we're going to reach a breaking point, and that breaking point is somehow linked to the numerological significance of the year 2000—which is totally irrelevant, of course, though not in a lot of people's thinking" (Strachen, 1996).

Many recent books, both utopic and dystopic, have been inspired by the millennium. Barry Brummet identifies a popular nonfiction genre he calls secular apocalypticism. This kind of rhetoric follows the form of religious apocrypha, but is secular in nature, even as it relies on human hopes and fears. It uses the all too concrete themes of possible nuclear war, ecological or economic break-down, and population explosion, and is typified by such works as *Apocalypse 2000: Economic Breakdown and the Suicide of Democracy 1989-2000* by Peter Jay (1987); *World War III: Population and the Biosphere at the End of the Millennium* by Michael Tobias (1994); *The Great Depression of 1990* by Ravi Batra (1987); and Roberto Vacca's *The Coming Dark Age* (1973).

The coming year 2000 has also prompted novels by such diverse public figures as evangelist Pat Robertson with *The End of the Age* (1995), in which an asteroid causes doomsday; astronomer Carl Sagan with *Contact* (1985), in which the reality of extraterrestrial beings is discovered just before the millennium (before his death in 1996, he was working on a screenplay about a messiah coming at the millennium); and Pulitzer Prize-winning journalist Jack Anderson, whose novel *Millennium* (1994), involves extraterrestrials coming to pronounce judgment on earth. (But, be aware: this is far from a complete list of novels about the millennium/year 2000; for more, see Dorris and Erdrich, 1988.)

One of the most popular bestsellers of the 1990s has been *The Celestine Prophecy* by James Redfield (1993), whose epigraph comes from the apocalyptic book of Daniel (12:3-4). The jacket blurb notifies the reader that he or she will "suddenly recognize the quantum leap forward humankind is preparing to make as we approach the new millennium." Ken Carey's series of channeled messages from advanced sentient beings, including *The Starseed Transmissions* (1982) and *The Third Millennium: Living in the Posthistoric World* (1995), promises spiritual and social guidance for human evolution.

In addition to books, this fascination has shown up in other media. A Fox-TV show, "Millennium," involves a clandestine group of investigators who track ever more bizarre and horrendous cases of human depravity upon the millennium's approach. Extraterrestrials attack earth in *Independence Day* (Twentieth-Century Fox, 1996), and an asteroid threatens to destroy the world in the made-for-TV movie *Asteroid* (NBC, 1997). On the stage, we've seen, among others, Arthur Kopit's *End of the World: A Play in 3 Acts (with Symposium to Follow)* (New York, 1984; Cambridge, Mass., 1987) and Joan MacLeod's *2000* (Toronto, 1996). And the popular music industry has offered us the likes of Elvis Costello's "Waiting for the End of the World" (1977) and "Hurry Down, Doomsday (The Bugs Are Taking Over) [1991]," "Apocalypse 9/8" by Genesis (1972), and what is certain to be the ubiquitous "1999" (1983) by the artist formerly known as Prince. Finally, there are hundreds of Web sites about the millennium on the Internet.

In the meantime, we can almost surely expect network television and the film industry to serve up more apocalyptic-like disaster movies, infotainment-style documentaries on doomsday predictions, and still more Nostradamus specials, while magazines—from *The New Yorker* to *Weekly World News* —are publishing stories dealing with millennial beliefs and traditions. *Newsweek* has announced that it will periodically publish special millennium issues, along with its new Millennium section in the regular weekly issues.

As editor William Griffin presaged in his *Endtime: The Doomsday Catalog* (1979), "Armageddon has become a growth industry" (Boyer, 1992: 11).

None of which should obscure the fact that the year 2000 is a critical deadline. If computers are not modified to register the accurate year, there really could be dire consequences to the social order. Dubbed the "Millennium Bug," the problem is that most computer programs have been written so that dates are stored using only the last two digits of the year, for example, "98" for 1998. When the programs' internal clocks turn over to "00" in the year 2000, the computer will read "1900," causing mayhem in any calculations that depend on dates, such as loans, insurance, pensions, and Social Security. Recent estimates are that at least 30 percent of the U.S.'s computer systems could crash. IBM assures us that most of its products are now 2000-friendly. And most of the newer Pentium computers are safe. But *Newsweek* reports that 80 percent of businesses and governments, including the U.S. federal government and, of all agencies, NASA, still have not taken the necessary steps to avert this problem. "A 1996 congressional survey of top federal agencies found that only nine of 24 had given [the computer problem] any thought" (*Newsweek*, January 27, 1997: 18). Experts estimate that it will cost the world up to $600 billion to solve the problem by having computer analysts search through existing programs to correct the glitch or replacing all older programs and computers that can't register four-digit years. Computers could still crash if even a few of the date references are missed. Problems are already occurring with programs handling transactions that involve dates in the future, such as mortgages, insurance policies, and driver's licenses. A new industry has developed in response to the Millennium Bug, including insurance companies offering some coverage and computer consultants—some coming out of retirement—making themselves available to deal with the problem.

Celebrations and Other Events

The Third Millennium will begin on January 1, 2001—but that's not likely to stop the vast majority of people from commencing their millennium partying on or around December 31, 1999. To usher in the new millennium, many people are looking to fly on Concorde jets; rent small islands in the Pacific, castles in Scotland, and rooms in the Tower of London; climb Mount Kilimanjaro; tour the Galapagos Islands; and board cruise lines to almost anywhere.

According to the Greenwich Royal Observatory in Greenwich, England—long the official time keeper of the world—the first populated place that will experience the new century and millennium will be in the Chatham Islands of New Zealand, though the island nations of Kiribati and Tonga lay claims to being first as well. Kiribati even moved its part of the International Date Line so that all its islands are on the same side of the line, making it the first nation to experience the new millennium. The first point on the globe, however, at which the new millennium will arrive is at Balleny Island in Antarctica.

The Observatory is located directly along the Prime Meridian, which is the zero longitude mark, and had been point zero for the world's clocks since 1884. Now, Coordinated Universal Time is kept by 150 atomic clocks all over the world. Greenwich's Maritime Museum plans to host an exhibition on "The Story of Time" from November 1999 through the autumn of 2000. In addition, there is talk of building a huge exposition center in Greenwich to hold an exhibit on the time zones of the world.

Many party venues are already booked or have long waiting lists, for example, New York's Rainbow Room, the hotels at Disney World in Florida, and the Seattle Space Needle, which is being rented for a bash by 15 families from Portland, Oregon. Travel company Abercrombie & Kent has sold out its package tours to Egypt, to Kenya and Tanzania, and to India and Nepal. Other venues are not taking reservations until the millennium is closer: the Eiffel Tower restaurant in Paris, France, and Caesars Palace and the MGM Grand in Las Vegas, Nevada. But the Empire State Building will be open to the public.

New York's Times Square is likely to be one of the most densely populated places in the world to meet the new millennium. In 1995, the Times Square Business Improvement District (TSBID) held a contest on what it should do on New Year's Eve, 1999. One entry suggested having 100 yellow taxis with their radios simultaneously playing "It's a Small World." TSBID President Gretchen Dykstra's favorite entry "suggested we turn off all the lights in Times Square and exactly at midnight have Barry Manilow sing 'It's just another New Year's Eve'." That was not the winning entry either. What will happen in Times Square is that 24 TV monitors will cover New Year celebrations in each time zone around the world, in addition to Dick Clark and the dropping of the ball.

Mayflower 2000 is part of England's plan to bring in the new millennium. Based on the ship that brought the Pilgrims to America, this reconstruction will sail from England to the U.S. in 1999. Fleet 2000 will see the launch of several sailing ships on a round-the-globe voyage, hitting Boston, Massachusetts, and 32 other ports around the world. Another cruise, sponsored by Nippon travel agency in Japan, will feature a dramatic crossing of the International Date Line at the stroke of 12 midnight on December 31, 1999. Because they will be sailing eastward from Japan to Hawaii, they will get to celebrate the new millennium more than once. The *Queen Mary* ship, docked in Long Beach, California, is hosting a party, but it will cost $1999.99 to get in.

The Millennium Society is a non-profit organization based in Washington, D.C., whose members will sail to Egypt on the *Queen Elizabeth II* for a World Millennium Charity Ball near the Pyramid of Cheops to be held on December 31, 1999. The Society is also planning to sponsor parties in each of the world's time zones.

A company called The Mitten Group in Chicago, Illinois, bills itself as "The Official Celebration of the Year 2000™" (yes, it has obtained a trademark). The Billennium® is a "series of global media events and products" and plans to promote millennium-related events. The Billennium web site plans to display a "Billennium Countdown Clock" and a "Billennium Time Capsule" (whose contents will be launched via satellite).

Around the world, other millennium plans are in the making:

In Hannover, Germany, EXPO 2000 will be held from June 1 to October 30, 2000, as a world exposition to present ecological and economic problems facing the world. Expo organizers have invited 185 countries and nine international organizations to participate in EXPO 2000 in order to "direct attention to the ongoing process of redefining man's relationship to nature and technology." The Expo will also feature a theme park and a variety of cultural and sporting events.

North Cape, Norway, is the northernmost point of land in Europe, and will host a New Year's Eve concert music celebration. Organizers in Istanbul, Turkey, are billing the location as one from which revelers can experience the millennium arriving in both Europe and Asia. Brazil is planning a beach party in Rio de Janeiro, while Sri Lanka is readying for the same in Colombo. And there will be bonfires in Iceland.

Some more daring partiers have opted for spending the holiday at Volcano House in Hawaii Volcanoes National Park; as its name implies, the hotel is near a volcano—about ten feet away from the edge.

In London, England, the Millennium Wheel Company wants to build a silver-and-white 500-foot Ferris wheel on the banks of the Thames River. In Birmingham, England, a ten-year-long Millennium Festival was kicked off in 1990; the City of Birmingham Symphony presents music from each decade of the twentieth century. An Englishman is constructing a huge airship, called the Millennia, to take a small group of people on a flight around the world during the year 2000. Another British man is organizing people worldwide to light beacons at midnight in each time zone, so that by the end of January 1, 2000, the earth will look like a giant beacon of light from observers, say, in orbit (although there are as yet no reported plans for extraterrestrial millennium trips).

England and France have both erected giant clocks to count down the days to January 1, 2000. England's is located at Greenwich, and the French clock is mounted on the Eiffel Tower.

Finally, cities hosting regularly occurring events, such as the World Cup and the Olympic Games, may be expected to prolong the festivities to include the new millennium.

In commemoration of the birth of Christ, several religious celebrations are planned. The Roman Catholic pope, John Paul II, has designated the year 2000 to be a jubilee year. In that spirit, he is joined by the World Conference of Churches in calling for wealthier nations to cancel debts owed them by poorer nations. In his apostolic letter *Tertio Millenio Adveniente* (November 10, 1994), Pope John Paul II writes, that "preparing for the Year 2000 has become as it were a hermeneutical key of my pontificate." The U.S. Conference of Catholic Bishops even has a subcommittee on the millennium. In Rome, they're building a new subway, dubbed "The Jubilee Line," in preparation for the thousands of tourists expected for pilgrimages, exhibits, and celebrations. On Christmas Eve, 1999, the pope will open the holy door at St. Peter's Basilica, while three specially appointed cardinals will open the holy doors to the three other basilicas. The custom of opening of the "holy door" goes back to the fifteenth century, when in so doing, the pope granted sanctuary to Christians who requested it. How the pope opens the door, which has been walled up, is interesting. He hits the door three times with a silver hammer while singing "Open unto me the gates of justice." On the third hit, the masonry collapses and the pope leads the way into the basilica. The holy doors are then closed after the new year arrives.

In England, the national Millennium Commission is trying to arrange for the simultaneous ringing of church bells throughout the country on January 1, 2000. They expect they will need 10,000 people to do all the bell-ringing.

In the Holy Land, Israel is building Nazareth 2000, a pilgrimage center at the city in Galilee, including a theme park and museum. The city of Jesus' birth, Bethlehem, is controlled by Palestine, and has not found funding for any preparations, though there may yet be plans for the 2,000th birthday anniversary.

When the parties are over, however, we will have to decide what to call the first decade of the new century. Some suggestions are: the noughties, the aughties, the two-thousands, the ohs, the 20-ohs, the double-ohs, the double-zeros, the oh-ohs . . .

* * *

Since the end of the nineteenth century, the year 2000 has been held out as a beacon for where the future begins. As we approach the year designated as the start of the third millennium, we carry all the dreams, fears, and expectations we've collectively been accumulating in anticipation of that future, even as we have been planting its seeds all along. One certainty is that the year 2000 will bring us the challenge of setting our next milepost, sighting the next beacon.

Sources

Appell, David. "The Year 2000." *Internet World* 8,1 (January 1997): 68.

August, Oliver. "Airship to Set Sail for the Millennium." *Times of London* (September 30, 1996).

Barkun, Michael. *Disaster and the Millennium*. New Haven, CT: Yale University Press, 1974.

Bartholomew, Doug. "The Year 2000 Time Bomb: Time's Running Out." *InformationWeek* 565 (February 5, 1996): 30.

Billington, James H. *The Icon and the Axe*. New York: Alfred A. Knopf, 1966.

Boyer, Paul. *When Time Shall Be No More: Prophecy Belief in Modern American Culture*. Cambridge, MA: Harvard University Press, 1992.

Broder, James M., with Laurence Zuckerman. "The Millennium Bug — A Special Report; Computers Are the Future But Remain Unready for It." *New York Times* (April 7, 1997).

Brummett, Barry. *Contemporary Apocalyptic Rhetoric*. (Praeger Series in Political Communication). New York: Praeger Publishers, 1991.

Bullard, Thomas E. "Anomalous Aerial Phenomena before 1800." In Jerome Clark, *The UFO Encyclopedia*, 2nd ed. Detroit, MI: Omnigraphics, Inc., 1997.

Bustos, Alex. "Party Lovers Already Gearing Up for Dec. 31, 1999." *Vancouver* [Canada] *Sun* (December 28, 1996): A1.

Carlson, Peter. "The Vision Thing." *Washington Post* (January 1, 1995): W8.

Clark, Jerome. "Unarius—Science of Life." In his *The UFO Encyclopedia*, 2nd ed. Detroit, MI: Omnigraphics, Inc., 1997.

Cohn, Norman. *The Pursuit of the Millennium*. London, England: Secker & Warburg, 1957.

Collins, Gail, and Dan Collins. *The Millennium Book: Your Essential All-Purpose Guide to the Year 2000*. New York: Doubleday/Dolphin, 1991.

"Countdown to a New Millenium [sic] Under Way." *Newsday* (December 31, 1995): A26.

Davis, Lanny J. "A Look at . . . the Computer Calendar Crisis: Countdown to a Meltdown Before the Year 2000, We Have to Spend Billions to Fix a Very Strange Glitch." *Washington Post* (September 15, 1996): C3.

Dorris, Michael, and Louise Erdrich. "Bangs and Whimpers: Novelists at Armageddon." *New York Times Book Review* (March 13, 1988): 1.

Eaton, Leslie. "Elixers for a Digital Headache; Pain and Profit for Investors as Computers Confront Year 2000." *New York Times* (April 8, 1997).

Editors of *Newsweek*. "Beyond 2000: America in the 21st Century." *Newsweek* (January 27, 1997). Special inaugural/millennium issue.

Ferris, Timothy. "Annals of Space. Is This the End?" *The New Yorker* (January 27, 1997): 44.

Focillon, Henri. *The Year 1000.* New York: Frederick Ungar Publishing Co., 1969.

Full Sail for Fleet 2000." *Boston Globe* (May 31, 1994).

"Germany: World Exhibition to Launch 2000." *South China Morning Post* (October 3, 1996).

Goldfrank, David M. "Judaizers." In Joseph L. Wieczynski, ed. *The Modern Encyclopedia of Russian and Soviet History*, vol. 15: 143-46. Gulf Breeze, FL: Academic International Press, 1980.

———. "Pre-Enlightenment Utopianism in Russian History." *Russian History* 11,2-3 (Summer-Fall 1984): 123-47.

Gould, Stephen Jay. "Dousing Diminutive Dennis's Debate." *Natural History* (April 1994): 4-12.

Grimes, William. "Hot Spots for the Millennium." *New York Times* (December 29, 1996).

Grunwald, Henry. "The Year 2000: Is It the End—Or Just the Beginning?" *Time* (March 30, 1992): 73.

Heard, Alex. "Mommie Dearest: The Millennium Goes Green." *New Republic* 214,18 (April 29, 1996): 19.

John Paul II. *Celebrate 2000! A Three-Year Reader: Reflections on Jesus, the Holy Spirit, and the Father.* Selected and arranged by Paul Thigpen. Ann Arbor, MI: Servant Publications, 1996.

Kermode, Frank. "Introduction to the New Testament." In Robert Alter and Frank Kermode, eds., *The Literary Guide to the Bible*, 375-86. Cambridge, MA: Harvard University Press, 1987.

Kohut, John J., and Roland Sweet, comps. *Countdown to the Millennium: Curious But True News Dispatches Heralding the Last Days of the Planet.* New York: Signet, 1994.

Kristof, Nicholas D. "In Pacific Race to Usher in Millennium, a Date-Line Jog." *New York Times* (March 23, 1997).

Kumar, Krishan, and Stephen Bann. *Utopias and the Millennium.* London, England: Reaktion Books, Ltd., 1993.

Lamy, Philip. *Millennium Rage: Survivalists, White Supremacists, and the Doomsday Prophecy.* New York: Plenum Press, 1996.

Landes, Richard. "The Year 1000." In Joseph R. Strayer, ed. *Dictionary of the Middle Ages*, vol. 12: 722-23. New York: Charles Scribner's Sons, 1989.

Lerner, Robert E. "Christian Millennialism." In Joseph R. Strayer, ed. *Dictionary of the Middle Ages*, vol. 8: 384-88. New York: Charles Scribner's Sons, 1987.

McGinn, Bernard. *Antichrist: Two Thousand Years of the Human Fascination with Evil.* San Francisco, CA: HarperSanFrancisco, 1994a.

———. *Apocalypticism in the Western Tradition.* Aldershot, Hampshire, England: Variorum, 1994b.

———. *Visions of the End: Apocalyptic Traditions in the Middle Ages.* New York: Columbia University Press, 1979.

———. "Revelation." In Robert Alter and Frank Kermode, eds., *The Literary Guide to the Bible*, 523-41. Cambridge, MA: Harvard University Press, 1987.

———. "Apocalyptic Spirituality: Approaching the Third Millennium." *Catholic World* 239,1429 (January-February 1996): 4.

"Millennium Messiah: A Sagan Screenplay." *Toronto Star* (August 9, 1996): D8.

Morrison, Richard. "Rattle of a Not So Simple Man; Simon Rattle." *Times of London* (March 2, 1994).

Morrow, Lance. "A Cosmic Moment." *Time* 140,27 (Fall 1992): 6.

Penenberg, Adam L. "Another Millennia Problem: Computer Files." *New York Times* (April 6, 1997).

Provost, Foster. *"Book of Prophecies." Columbus Dictionary.* Detroit, MI: Omnigraphics, Inc., 1991.

The Revelation of John. Revised edition. Two volumes. Translated with an Introduction and Interpretation by William Barclay. Philadelphia, PA: The Westminster Press, 1976. (The Daily Study Bible Series)

Reynolds, Christopher. "Turning 2000 . . . Where in the World Will You Be?" *Los Angeles Times* (December 29, 1996).

Schwartz, Hillel. *Century's End: A Cultural History of the Fin de Siècle from the 990s through the 1990s.* New York: Doubleday, 1990.

————. "Millenarianism: An Overview." In Mircea Eliade, ed., *The Encyclopedia of Religion.* New York: Macmillan, 1987.

Stableford, Brian, and David Langford. *The Third Millennium; A History of the World: AD 2000-3000.* New York: Alfred A. Knopf, Inc., 1985.

Strachen, Alex. "Paranoia Zone." *Vancouver Sun* (September 30, 1996): C1.

Sweet, Leonard I. "Christopher Columbus and the Millennial Vision of the New World." *Catholic Historical Review* 72,3 (July 1986): 369-82.

Thomas, Keith. *Religion and the Decline of Magic.* New York: Charles Scribner's Sons, 1971.

Wagner, Cynthia. "Toward the New Millennium: Living, Learning, and Working." *Futurist* (November-December 1994): 37.

Walker, Christopher. "Holy Cities Battle for Riches of Millennial Mammon." *Times of London* (December 4, 1996).

Weber, Bruce. "New York Seeks to Be Party Central for the Millennium. Details to Come." *New York Times* (July 22, 1996): B14.

Weber, Timothy P. *Living in the Shadow of the Second Coming: American Premillennialism, 1875-1925.* New York: Oxford University Press, 1979.

Contacts and Web Sites

Greenwich 2000
E-mail: webmaster@greenwich2000.com
WWW: www.greenwich2000.com

The Mitten Group, Inc.
Organizer of the Billennium
1335 W. Altgeld St.
Chicago, IL 60614
Phone: 312-327-2000; fax: 312-327-1999
E-mail: billennium@aol.com
WWW: www.billennium.com

Year 2000 and Millennium Threshold Observances Around the World
The Millennium Institute
1117 N. 19th St., Ste. 900
Arlington, VA 22209-1708
Phone: 703-841-0048; fax: 703-841-0050
E-mail: millennium@igc.apc.org
WWW: www.igc.org/millennium/events/index.html

A

♦ 0001 ♦ **Åarhus Festival Week**
First Saturday in September for nine days

Since 1965 the Danish city of Åarhus has been the site of a nine-day festival whose cultural and sporting events run the gamut from opera to fishing competitions. There are jazz and rock concerts, a cross-country race, public debates, poetry readings, and theatrical productions. The New York City Ballet and the Alvin Ailey American Dance Theatre have performed there, as have the Israel Philharmonic Orchestra, the Orchestre de Paris, and such world-renowned soloists as Isaac Stern, Vladimir Ashkenazy, Boris Christoff, and Claudio Arrau. A group of actors from the Åarhus Theater travels around to hospitals and senior citizens' homes to perform for people who are unable to attend the festival.

The events are held in a variety of indoor and outdoor sites throughout the city, including the Åarhus Theater, an art nouveau structure from the turn of the century, the new Åarhus Concert Hall built in 1981, and the area's many parks, churches, and coffee shops. Åarhus is also the site of Marselisborg Castle, the Danish royal family's summer residence.

CONTACT: SOURCES:
Danish Tourist Board   *Chases-1996*, p. 367
655 Third Ave., 18th Floor   *GdWrldFest-1985*, p. 71
New York, NY 10017   *IntlThFolk-1979*, p. 91
212-949-2333; fax: 212-983-5260   *MusFestEurBrit-1980*, p. 37

♦ 0002 ♦ **Abbey Fair**
Early August

The Abbey Fair in Bethlehem, Connecticut, is a two-day monastic fair sponsored by the Benedictine sisters of the Abbey of Regina Laudis. Since it was first held in 1952, the fair has expanded considerably. It offers a wide variety of unusual events and activities, including performances of Gregorian chant; a sale of food, flowers, and crafts produced by the abbey; blacksmithing demonstrations; and a world-famous Neapolitan crêche in the horse stable formerly owned by an 18th-century Congregational minister. The sisters are responsible for much of the food that is served, and there is a raffle for one of the Abbey's Cheviot lambs and a baby calf. Even the hamburger and hotdog stand uses only Abbey-grown beef. In contrast to the many traditional attractions that are associated with life at the Abbey, there is also a fashion show, a basketball clinic, and sales of used furniture and clothing.

According to the nuns who run the annual fair, its purpose is to celebrate the "true values of life, of friendships that endure, and those happy moments that remain constant in memory."

CONTACT: SOURCES:
Connecticut Tourism Division   *RelHolCal-1993*, p. 55
865 Brook St.
Rocky Hill, CT 06067
800-282-6863 or 860-258-4355
fax: 860-258-4275

♦ 0003 ♦ **Abdu'l-Baha, Ascension of**
November 28

A holy day in the Baha'i religion, commemorating the death of Abbas Effendi, known as Abdu'l-Baha, in 1921 in Haifa, Palestine (now Israel). The eldest son of Mirza Husayn Ali, known as Baha'u'llah, the prophet-founder of the Baha'i faith, he was named the leader of the Baha'i community in his father's will, which also appointed him to interpret Baha'i writings. In turn, Abdu'l-Baha appointed his eldest grandson, Shoghi Effendi (1896–1957) as his successor and Guardian of the Cause. Today the affairs of the worldwide Baha'i community are administered by the Universal House of Justice, a body that meets in Haifa and is elected every five years.

CONTACT: SOURCES:
Baha'is of the U.S.   *AnnivHol-1983*, p. 152
Office of Public Information   *RelHolCal-1993*, p. 58
866 United Nations Plaza, Ste. 120
New York, NY 10017-1822
212-803-2500; fax: 212-803-2573

♦ 0004 ♦ **Aboakyer Festival**
April–May

The Effutu people of Ghana celebrate the **Deer Hunting Festival** by making an offering to the god Panche Otu. Two groups known as the Asafo companies, each consisting of about 150 people ranging in age from young boys to grandfathers, compete in a deer hunt that begins at dawn with the pounding of drums and the ringing of bells. When the first deer is caught, the victorious company brings it back alive and presents it proudly to their chief. Then the deer is taken back to the village, where dancing and drumming continue in an effort to placate Panche Otu so that he will bring them a bountiful year.

SOURCES:
FolkWrldHol-1992, p. 226

♦ 0005 ♦ **Abu Simbel Festival**
February 22 and October 22

This festival celebrates the two days of the year on which the light of the rising sun can reach the 180-foot deep innermost chambers of Abu Simbel, the great temple of Ramses II, in Egypt. The temple was designed so that only on these two days in February and October does the sun shine on the four gods in the sanctuary, Ptah, Amen-Re, Ramses, and Re-Horakhty. This temple, the most colossal in Egypt, was built by Ramses II between 1300 and 1233 B.C., and is famous for its four 65-foot statues of the seated Ramses. It is actually two temples—one for Ramses and one for queen Nefertari and is extraordinary for its grandeur, beauty, and history. It was unknown to the European world until Swiss explorer Johann Burckhardt found it in 1812. The Italian Giovanni Belzoni excavated the entrance and explored the temple in 1816. In 1964, when the new Aswan Dam was to be built, creating a lake that would have drowned the temple, it was cut into 2,000 pieces and reassembled at a site about 180 feet higher. It is not as perfect as it was at the foot of the cliff—but it was saved.

It is thought that there must have been ritual celebrations in ancient times on the days when the sun penetrated the sanctuary. Today, television covers the event, and people gather to see the sunrise and to meditate. The sun now shines on the sanctuary a day earlier than it did before the temple was moved.

CONTACT:
Egyptian Tourist Authority
645 N. Michigan Ave., Ste. 829
Chicago, IL 60611
312-280-4666; fax: 312-280-4788

SOURCES:
Chases-1996, p. 427

♦ 0006 ♦ **Acadian Day**
August

The original Acadians were 17th-century French colonists who settled in the area known as Acadia, which covered what is now Nova Scotia as well as Prince Edward Island, and parts of northern Maine and Quebec. Their French-speaking descendants in the Maritime Provinces continue to honor their heritage by holding many local Acadian Day celebrations, usually during the summer months.

Fifty thousand people attend the **Acadian Festival** in Caraquet, New Brunswick, the largest of these celebrations. The festival takes place for 10 days in August each year and includes Acadian dance performances, cabaret, and concerts as well as sporting contests. The highlight of the festival is "L' Acadie en Fête," a huge celebration involving Acadian musicians, singers, artists, and actors.

CONTACT:
Tourism New Brunswick
P.O. Box 12345
Fredericton, NB
Canada E3B 5C3
800-561-0123

SOURCES:
DictDays-1988, p. 1
GdWrldFest-1985, p. 37

♦ 0007 ♦ **Acadian Festival**
Length varies, usually 3–4 days at the end of June

The Madawaska Territory, which at one time ran along the Canadian border between Maine and New Brunswick, was settled by a small group of farmers who were chased out of Acadia by the English in the late 18th century. As the settlements grew, they were separated into Canadian and American communities, with Edmundston on the Canadian side and Madawaska and St. David on the American side of the St. John River.

In 1978 the local historical society in Madawaska proclaimed June 28 as Acadian Day in the state of Maine, and since that time it has been the site of an Acadian (or French-Canadian) festival lasting anywhere from one day to a week. Regular events include French music and dancing, an Acadian Supper featuring *pot en pot* and *fougère*, a parade with bands and marching units from both Maine and Canada, and an Acadian mass followed by a procession to the white marble cross that marks the site of the original Acadian settlement. The festival usually coincides with a reunion of the original 13 families who settled here.

CONTACT:
Madawaska Chamber of
  Commerce
378 Main St.
Madawaska, ME 04756
207-728-7000

♦ 0008 ♦ **Acadiens, Festivals**
Third weekend in September

A combination of several festivals (food, music, crafts, and more) to celebrate Cajun culture in Lafayette, La., known as the capital of French Louisiana. When they were expelled from Nova Scotia by the British in the 1770s, the French Acadian farmers settled in the area around Lafayette in a region of 22 parishes that came to be known as Acadiana. The word "Cajun" comes from Acadian.

One part of the celebration is the Bayou Food Festival, which offers a range of Cajun cooking from crawfish gumbo to alligator sausage to corn maque-chou. The Louisiana Native Crafts Festival features handmade Cajun crafts and demonstrations by blacksmiths, decoy carvers, alligator skinners, and story tellers. The Festival de Musique Acadienne features centuries-old music sung in French. Modern crafts are also on exhibit, and lectures and workshops on the Acadian language and history are part of the weekend.

CONTACT:
Louisiana Office of Tourism
P.O. Box 94291
Baton Rouge, LA 70804
800-334-8626 or 504-342-8119
fax: 504-342-8390

Adelaide Cup Day
See **Hobart Cup Day**

♦ 0009 ♦ **Adelaide Festival of the Arts**
February–March in even-numbered years

The city of Adelaide, South Australia, was geographically isolated and a cultural wasteland until a group of businessmen got together in 1960 and decided that what their city needed was a festival of the arts. The resulting event, which has been held biennially since that time, put Adelaide on the map and made it one of the world's top performing arts centers. In addition to the events held in the Adelaide Festival Centre, the Festival Theatre, and four other theaters built especially to accommodate the more than 300 festival performances, other programs are held across the city in smaller theaters, town halls, clubs, parks, and in the streets. There is chamber music, classical ballet, symphony concerts, modern jazz, and rock music in addition to experimental plays, poetry readings, mime, and workshops where literary ideas, directions, and styles are discussed.

CONTACT:
Australian Tourist Commission
100 Park Ave., 25th Floor
New York, NY 10017
212-687-6300; fax: 212-661-3340

SOURCES:
GdWrldFest-1985, p. 8
IntlThFolk-1979, pp. 19, 21

♦ 0010 ♦ **Admission Day**
Varies from state to state

Many American states celebrate the anniversary of their admission to the Union by observing a public holiday on or near the actual day. Sometimes the day is referred to by the name of the state—as in Colorado Day, Indiana Day, Nevada Day, or WEST VIRGINIA DAY—and is marked by special celebrations. Other states let the anniversary of their admission pass unnoticed. In Vermont, Admission Day coincides with TOWN MEETING DAY.

For a listing of all states, *see* Appendix A.

Adults Day
See **Seijin-no-Hi**

♦ 0011 ♦ **Advent**
From the Sunday closest to November 30 to December 24 in West; from November 15 to December 24 in East

The Advent season marks the beginning of the Christian year in Western Christianity. Its length varies from 22 to 28 days, beginning on the Sunday nearest St. Andrew's Day and encompassing the next three Sundays, ending on CHRISTMAS EVE.

In the Roman Catholic Church and those of the Anglican Communion the third Sunday is called Gaudete Sunday, from the first word of the introit, "Rejoice." Rose-colored vestments may replace the purple, and flowers may be on the altar. Originally a period of reflection and penitence in preparation for CHRISTMAS—in much the same way that LENT is in preparation for EASTER—Advent has sometimes been referred to as the **Winter Lent**. But over time the restrictions of Advent have become greatly relaxed. Today it is usually associated with the Advent calendars that parents give their children to help them count the days until Christmas.

In Orthodox (Eastern) Christianity, the church year begins on September 1, and Advent begins on November 15. The Advent fast is called the **Little Lent**, because it's shorter than the **Great Lent** preceding Easter.

SOURCES:
AmerBkDays-1978, p. 1059
BkFestHolWrld-1970, p. 127
DaysCustFaith-1957, p. 302
DictWrldRel-1989, pp. 5, 154, 175
FolkWrldHol-1992, p. 573
RelHolCal-1993, p. 55
SaintFestCh-1904, p. xiii

♦ 0012 ♦ **Advent in Germany**
Sunday nearest November 30 through December 24

ADVENT customs in Germany include the lighting of candles and the hanging of special Advent wreaths. In Roman Catholic areas, the candles are lit on each of the four Saturdays during the Advent season; among Protestants, Sunday is the day for lighting candles—one on the first day, two on the second day, three on the third, and so on. Many German households light a "Star of Seven," a seven-branch candelabrum, on CHRISTMAS EVE, and at midnight carry the lit "star" through the dark to the village church for the Christmas Eve service.

Advent wreaths are made of fir and decorated with gold and silver ribbons or scarlet woolen threads. They are often hung from the ceiling or in a doorway, parallel to the floor, so that candles can be placed standing up in the wreath. The lit wreaths may also be displayed on the table, around which family and friends sit while singing carols and preparing handmade gifts.

SOURCES:
BkFestHolWrld-1970, p. 128
FestWestEur-1958, p. 79
FolkWrldHol-1992, p. 573

Afghan Independence Day
See **Jeshn**

♦ 0013 ♦ **African Methodist Quarterly Meeting Day**
Last Saturday in August

The **Big August Quarterly** of the African Union Methodist Protestant Church, which takes place annually in Wilmington, Delaware, celebrates the founding of the A.U.M.P. Church in 1813 as the "Mother Church" for African Americans. The first independent black congregation in Wilmington was started by an influential black religious leader named Peter Spencer, who led a group of 41 followers out of Wilmington's Asbury Methodist Church in 1805 because white members of the congregation refused to let them participate fully in the services. Before the Civil War, slaves in the surrounding areas were given time off to attend this special weekend of revival preaching, gospel singing, and reunions with family and friends.

Modeled on the Quakers' quarterly meetings, it was originally a rousing religious festival that drew tens of thousands of African Americans from Delaware and the surrounding states. Although it no longer draws the crowds it used to, the Big August Quarterly has undergone a resurgence in recent years. It features soul food, musical entertainment, and an opportunity for people to reminisce about the Big August Quarterlies of the past.

CONTACT:
Greater Wilmington Convention
  and Visitors Bureau
1300 N. Market St.
Wilmington, DE 19801
302-652-4088; fax: 302-652-4726

SOURCES:
FolkAmerHol-1991, p. 317
RelHolCal-1993, p. 56

Ages, Festival of the
See **Jidai Matsuri**

♦ 0014 ♦ **Agonalia**
January 9

In Roman mythology, Janus is the god of beginnings and of doorways. The worship of Janus is believed to have been started by Romulus, one of the legendary founders of Rome. Usually depicted with two faces, one looking forward to the future and the other looking back to the past, his image appeared on an early Roman coin with a ship's prow on the reverse side. Roman boys used to toss these coins, calling out "heads or ships" just as youngsters today play "heads or tails." During the festival in honor of Janus known as the Agonalia, the *rex sacrorum* or officiating priest sacrificed a ram. Offerings of barley, incense, wine, and cakes called *Januae* were also common.

Numa Pompilius, the legendary second king of Rome, honored Janus by dedicating the famous *Ianus geminus,* the arcade at the northeast end of the Roman Forum, to him. It was believed that passing through this arcade brought luck to soldiers on their way to war.

SOURCES:
AmerBkDays-1978, p. 1
DictFolkMyth-1984, p. 539

Agricultural Field Days
See **Field Days, National**

♦ 0015 ♦ **Agriculture Fair at Santarém, National**
Second week in June

The most important agricultural fair in Portugal is held during the second week in June each year at Santarém, capital of the rich agricultural province of Ribatejo. Although the focus of the **Ribatejo Fair** is on farming and livestock breeding, there is also a colorful program of bullfighting, folk singing, and dancing, as well as a procession of *campinos,* or bull-herders. Many other European countries exhibit farm animals and machinery at the **Feira Nacional de Agricultura**. Santarém is also the site of an annual gastronomy festival in October, which focuses on traditional cooking from all over the country.

CONTACT:
Portuguese National Tourist
  Office
590 Fifth Ave., 4th Floor
New York, NY 10036
212-354-4403; fax: 212-764-6137

SOURCES:
IntlThFolk-1979, p. 312

♦ 0016 ♦ **Agua, La Fiesta de**
First Sunday in October

A ritual cleansing festival held in San Pedro de Casta, Peru, the **Water Festival** pays homage to Pariapunko, the Incan god of the water. The town mayor goes to the cave where Pariapunko is believed to reside and implores him to flood the community with fresh water. Then La Toma, the gate that holds back the Carhuayumac River, is opened and the water is allowed to course through the irrigation ditches that have just been cleaned and repaired. A procession of horsemen accompanies the water as it makes its way to the gorge of Carhuayumac.

CONTACT:
Embassy of Peru
1700 Massachusetts Ave., N.W.
Washington, D.C. 20036
202-833-9860; fax: 202-659-8124

SOURCES:
FolkWrldHol-1992, p. 505

♦ 0017 ♦ **Agwunsi Festival**
August–September

Agwunsi is the god of healing and divination among the Igbo people of Nigeria. He is also the patron of doctors, because he gives herbs and other medicines their power to cure. On the Agwunsi feast day, patients who have been healed send animals as a token of gratitude to the doctors who cured them.

SOURCES:
FolkWrldHol-1992, p. 471

♦ 0018 ♦ **Airing the Classics**
Sixth day of sixth lunar month

In China the **Double Sixth** is the day when Buddhist monasteries examine the books in their library collections to make sure that they haven't been damaged. It commemorates the time when the boat carrying the Buddhist scriptures from India was upset at a river crossing, and all the books had to be spread out to dry. Also known as **Tiankuang Jie**, or **Heaven's Gift Day**, it is traditional in some regions to set linens and books, as well as bath water, out in the sun. Setting aside a special day for "Airing the Classics" is especially important in tropical climates, where books are more susceptible to mold and insects.

SOURCES:
FolkWrldHol-1992, p. 351

♦ 0019 ♦ **Air Races, National Championship**
September, four days ending on second weekend after Labor Day

A four-day nostalgia trip for air buffs, held since 1964 in Reno, Nev. About 95 to 100 aircraft are generally registered for the races, providing some 150,000 spectators with the sight and sound of piston-engine planes flying around closed-pylon race courses. The planes entered include such World War II planes as the powerful P-51 Mustang and the bent-wing Chance-Vought F2G Corsair; the eerie sound the Corsair made was called "whistling death" by the Japanese of World War II. The race is the only one in the world that covers all four classes: Unlimited (vintage and modified warbirds and homebuilt racers), AT-6 (World War II pilot trainers), Formula One (super-midget planes), and Biplane (double-winged barn stormers). Air shows of military demonstrations, parachuting exhibits, and military fly-bys are also some of the events.

CONTACT:
Reno-Sparks Convention & Visitors Authority
4590 S. Virginia St.
Reno, NV 89502
800-367-7366 or 702-827-7600
fax: 702-827-7686

SOURCES:
GdUSFest-1984, p. 115

♦ 0020 ♦ **Air Show, International**
August

Widely recognized as Canada's national air show, this three-day event is an opportunity for the aviation industry to display the latest developments in civilian aircraft. Since the first show was held in 1962, it has grown to include aerobatic performances by the Canadian Armed Forces, the Royal Air Force, the Snowbirds Jet Team, and the U.S. Air Force's Thunderbirds. Aviation-related equipment is on display, and there is a large banquet featuring well-known personalities in the aviation and aerospace field. The show is held at the airport in Abbotsford, British Columbia, and is regularly attended by upwards of 200,000 people.

CONTACT:
Tourism British Columbia
Parliament Buildings
Victoria, B.C.
Canada V8V 1X4
800-663-6000 or 604-663-6000

SOURCES:
Chases-1996, p. 329
GdWorldFest-1985, p. 31

♦ 0021 ♦ **Ak-Sar-Ben Livestock Exposition and Rodeo**
September–October

Billed as the "World's Largest 4-H Livestock Show," the Ak-Sar-Ben ("Nebraska" spelled backwards) Livestock Exposition and Rodeo in Omaha dates back to 1928, when its purpose was to get the state's young people interested in livestock breeding. It started out as a nationwide breed show, but thoroughbred racing became an important part of the event when, during the 1930s, parimutuel racing became legal—as long as it was administered by nonprofit organizations. A significant percentage of the profits is contributed to agricultural research.

The exposition lasts five days and features a World Championship Rodeo, a Catch-a-Calf contest, and entertainment by well-known country and western stars. But the show's main purpose is to showcase 4-H activities.

CONTACT:
Nebraska Travel and Tourism Division
700 S. 16th St.
Lincoln, NE 68508
800-228-4307 or 402-471-3794
fax: 402-471-3026

SOURCES:
GdUSFest-1984, p. 111

♦ 0022 ♦ **Alabama Blueberry Festival**
Third Saturday in June

A one-day celebration of the blueberry in Brewton which is in the only area of Alabama still shipping blueberries commercially. The celebration, dedicated to Dr. W. T. Brightwell, whose improved varieties of the Rabbiteye blueberry were introduced here in 1961, features tours of the local blueberry farms. Events include live entertainment, children's rides, arts and crafts, a food contest, and food booths selling all kinds of locally prepared blueberry dishes, among them cobbler, waffles, ice cream and cakes. Attendance is about 28,000.

CONTACT:
Alabama Bureau of Tourism and Travel
P.O. Box 4927
Montgomery, AL 36103
800-252-2263 or 334-242-4169
fax: 334-242-4554

♦ 0023 ♦ **Alacitas Fair**
January 24

For hundreds of years the Aymara Indians of Bolivia have held an annual celebration at La Paz in honor of their god of prosperity named Ekeko, a little man with a big belly, an open mouth, outstretched arms, and wearing a backpack. Miniature replicas of Ekeko are sold, as well as miniature items of food, clothing, and other goods that the Aymaras would like to have. They believe that if they fill one of Ekeko's packs with these miniature objects, he will bring them the real things they represent. The children cry "Alacitas!", which means "Buy me!"

CONTACT:
Bolivian Embassy
3014 Massachusetts Ave., N.W.
Washington, D.C. 20008
202-483-4410; fax: 202-328-3712

SOURCES:
AnnivHol-1983, p. 13
BkFestHolWrld-1970, p. 17
BkHolWrld-1986, Jan 24
Chases-1996, p. 74
DictFolkMyth-1984, pp. 33, 342
FolkWrldHol-1992, p. 37

♦ 0024 ♦ **Alamo Day**
March 6

The cry "Remember the Alamo!" has particular significance for the natives of Texas, which was once part of Mexico. In 1836 a garrison of Texans took a stand against the Mexican army at a Franciscan mission in San Antonio named after the grove of cottonwood trees (*alamo* in Spanish) that surrounded it. Led by Lieutenant William Barret Travis, the band of 187 volunteers, including border heros Davy Crockett and James Bowie, was besieged for 13 days by 3,000–5,000 Mexicans under the leadership of General Antonio López de Santa Anna. Travis refused to surrender and the Alamo was overrun by the opposing army on the morning of March 6. Only women and children among the defenders survived. The heroic action at the Alamo gave the Texans time to organize the forces necessary to save their independence movement. Six weeks after the Alamo's fall, General Sam Houston defeated and captured Santa Anna at the battle of San Jacinto (*see* SAN JACINTO DAY), forcing him to sign a treaty recognizing Texas' independence. Since 1897, this day has been celebrated as **Texas Heroes' Day**.

CONTACT:
San Antonio Convention and Visitors Bureau
121 Alamo Pl.
San Antonio, TX 78205
800-447-3372 or 210-270-8700
fax: 210-270-8782

SOURCES:
AmerBkDays-1978, p. 237
AnnivHol-1983, p. 34
Chases-1996, p. 124
DaysCustFaith-1957, p. 97
DictDays-1988, p. 2

♦ 0025 ♦ **Alaska Day**
October 18

An official holiday in America's 49th and largest state, Alaska Day commemorates the formal transfer of Alaska from Russia to the United States on October 18, 1867. The event, which took place at Sitka, was a sad one for the Russian colonists who had already made Alaska their home, and it must have seemed that Mother Nature was conspiring against them. A strong wind caught the Russian flag during the transfer ceremony, tangling it in the halyards. The seaman who was finally hoisted up to free it dropped the flag by mistake, and another gust swept it into a group of Russian bayonets. The tattered remains were presented to the weeping wife of Prince Dmitri Maksoutsoff, the last Russian governor. Today the lowering of the Russian flag and the raising of the Stars and Stripes is reenacted every year as part of this three-day festival in Sitka.

After the transfer, Alaska was eventually organized as a territory and maintained this status until it became a state on January 3, 1959 (*see also* Appendix A).

CONTACT:
Alaska Division of Tourism
P.O. Box 110801
Juneau, AK 99811
907-465-2012; fax: 907-465-2287

SOURCES:
AmerBkDays-1978, p. 935
AnnivHol-1983, p. 134
Chases-1996, p. 421
DictDays-1988, p. 3

♦ 0026 ♦ **Alaska Festival of Music**
June

A major cultural event in Alaska, held since 1956 in Anchorage. The festival, which takes place over five evenings in June, emphasizes chamber music, although a full orchestral/choral work has become the traditional finale each year. Both international and Alaskan musicians perform. There are preconcert lectures and midnight-sun receptions after the performances, giving patrons a chance to meet the artists.

CONTACT:
Anchorage Convention and Visitors Bureau
1600 'A' Street, Ste. 200
Anchorage, AK 99501
800-446-5352 or 907-276-4118
fax: 907-278-5559

SOURCES:
MusFestAmer-1990, p. 21
MusFestWrld-1963, p. 285

♦ 0027 ♦ **Albania Independence Day**
November 28

The Albanian people proclaimed their independence from the Turks on this day in 1912. The Turks had first invaded this part of Europe around 1400, but under the leadership of a brave chief named Skanderbeg, the Albanians held them off for more than 20 years. After his death, however, the Turks conquered Albania, and they continued to rule the country for more than 400 years. It wasn't until the end of the Balkan War that Turkish rule was abolished and a proclamation of independence was issued on November 28, 1912.

Independence Day is a public holiday observed throughout Albania. It is closely followed by Liberation Day on November 29, the day on which the invasions of German and Italian troops during World War II were terminated in 1944.

CONTACT:
Albanian Embassy
1511 K St., N.W., Ste. 1010
Washington, D.C. 20005
202-223-4942; fax: 202-628-7342

SOURCES:
AnnivHol-1983, p. 152
Chases-1996, p. 462
NatlHolWrld-1968, p. 210

♦ 0028 ♦ **Albania Republic Day**
January 11

This national holiday, also known as **Anniversary Day**, commemorates the founding of the Albanian republic on January 11, 1946, and the adoption of its constitution.

CONTACT:
Albanian Embassy
1511 K St., N.W., Ste. 1010
Washington, D.C. 20005
202-223-4942; fax: 202-628-7342

SOURCES:
AnnivHol-1983, p. 7

♦ 0029 ♦ **Albuquerque International Balloon Fiesta**
First full weekend in October

The world's largest gathering of hot-air balloonists. More than 500 balloons, some more than six stories high, present dizzying colors and designs in the skies of New Mexico for a nine-day fiesta that attracts about a million spectators. Besides the daytime ascensions, illuminated balloons light up the night skies. The fiesta also boasts skydivers, marching bands, and food of all sorts.

See also HOT AIR BALLOON CHAMPIONSHIP, NATIONAL

CONTACT:
New Mexico Tourism and Travel Division
491 Old Santa Fe Trail
Santa Fe, NM 87503
800-545-2040 or 505-827-7400
fax: 505-827-7402

SOURCES:
Chases-1996, p. 404

♦ 0030 ♦ **Aldeburgh Festival of Music and the Arts**
June

The English fishing village of Aldeburgh, located on the North Sea about 100 miles from London, may seem an unlikely place for an international music festival. But it was here that Benjamin Britten, the great English composer and musicologist, lived and wrote until his death in 1967. In the 1940s, Britten managed to get his fellow townspeople interested in opera by giving them some catchy tunes to sing and eventually getting them to perform his *Let's Make an Opera*. The Aldeburgh Festival, established in 1947 with the help of Britten's colleague Peter Pears, grew out of these early experiments in audience participation.

Today, the 17-day festival is still aimed at smaller audiences. Although for many years it focused on the operas of Benjamin Britten, today it includes chamber and symphonic concerts, recitals, lectures, and art exhibitions as well. Many of the performances are still held in Aldeburgh's old churches and public halls, although a new concert hall complex was built in 1969, on the site of an old malt brewery barn in the nearby village of Snape. The festival prides itself on presenting quality performances without attracting a mass audience.

CONTACT:
British Tourist Authority
551 Fifth Ave., Ste. 702
New York, NY 10176
800-462-2748 or 212-986-2200
fax: 212-986-1188

SOURCES:
GdWrldFest-1985, p. 89
IntlThFolk-1979, p. 155
MusFestEurBrit-1980, p. 42
MusFestWrld-1963, p. 21

♦ 0031 ♦ Aldersgate Experience
Sunday nearest May 24

On the evening of May 24, 1738, John Wesley (1703–1791), co-founder of the Methodist Church, visited a house on Aldersgate Street, London, to join a group reading of Martin Luther's preface to the *Epistle to the Romans*. At about quarter to nine, just as they were reading Luther's description of the change that God works in man's heart, Wesley underwent a conversion experience. "I felt my heart strangely warmed," he says in his account of the evening. From that time until his death in 1791, Wesley considered it his mission in life to tell people about his experience and to persuade them to share his beliefs. The anniversary of this event is commemorated by the Methodist Church on the Sunday nearest May 24.

SOURCES:
DaysCustFaith-1957, p. 127
RelHolCal-1993, p. 56

♦ 0032 ♦ Alexandra Rose Day
A Saturday in June

Sometimes called **Alexandra Day** or simply **Rose Day**, this day commemorates the arrival of Queen Alexandra (1844–1925), wife of the English king, Edward VII, in England on June 26, 1862. In 1902 the much-loved queen founded the Imperial Military Nursing Service, and in 1912 she started Alexandra Rose Day. The Danish-born queen died 13 years later, but the day is still celebrated by selling rose emblems to raise money for hospitals.

See also HOSPITAL DAY, NATIONAL

SOURCES:
DictDays-1988, p. 3

♦ 0033 ♦ Algeria Independence Day
July 3

On this day in 1962, more than 100 years of French rule in Algeria came to an end as France officially recognized a referendum for independence that was passed by a vote of the Algerian people on July 1. Algerians had struggled for independence, or at least equality with the French occupants of their land, with organized movements for revolution since the end of World War I. Independence Day is a legal holiday in Algeria.

Another important celebration takes place on ALGERIA NATIONAL DAY, which commemorates the day the successful revolution against the French began.

CONTACT:
Algerian Embassy
2118 Kalorama Rd., N.W.
Washington, D.C. 20008
202-265-2800; fax: 202-667-2174

SOURCES:
AnnivHol-1983, p. 88

♦ 0034 ♦ Algeria National Day
November 1

This national holiday, also known as **Revolution Day**, commemorates the day Algerians began their revolution against the French, who had ruled since 1830. Huge crowds of people celebrate in the capital city of Algiers on the Mediterranean coast.

CONTACT:
Algerian Embassy
2118 Kalorama Rd., N.W.
Washington, D.C. 20008
202-265-2800; fax: 202-667-2174

SOURCES:
Chases-1996, p. 436
NatlHolWrld-1968, p. 198

Alholland Eve
See **Halloween**

♦ 0035 ♦ All American Championships Sled Dog Races
Third weekend in January

Originally known as the **Minnesota Arrowhead Championship**, this annual racing event is held in Ely, Minnesota, on the third weekend in January, when the snow is at its deepest (or so it is hoped). Contestants come from all over Canada, Alaska, and as far east as New Hampshire to compete in the two-day event, sometimes referred to as the **Ely All-American**. Both sprints and endurance racing—which requires larger teams of dogs and much longer courses—are included in the championships. Spectators gather at crossings, checkpoints, and rest stops to watch the mushers and their teams pass. The races are run against the clock, and the fastest time for two days wins.

Ely is home to Will Steger, the man who led sled-dog-powered expeditions to the North and South Poles and who is largely responsible for the increased attention being paid to the sport. Other important sled dog races in the state include the Cannon Valley Classic, also in January, and the Beargrease Dog Sled Marathon, which runs over 500 miles from Duluth to Grand Portage and back. The latter commemorates John Beargrease, a Chippewa Indian who carried the mail by dog sled.

CONTACT:
Minnesota Office of Tourism
121 E. Seventh Pl. Metro Sq., Ste. 100
St. Paul, MN 55101
612-296-5029 or 800-657-3700
fax: 612-296-7095

SOURCES:
GdUSFest-1984, p. 95

♦ 0036 ♦ All-American Soap Box Derby
First Saturday in August

The Soap Box Derby is a youth racing program that has been run nationally since 1934. The idea came from an Ohio journalist named Myron Scott, who was assigned to cover a race of gravity-propelled cars built by young boys in his hometown of Dayton and was so impressed by the event that he began to develop a similar program on a nationwide scale. In 1935 the race was moved to Akron because of its hilly terrain, and the following year a permanent track was constructed through the efforts of the Works Progress Administration (WPA).

The World Championship finals held at Derby Downs in

Akron consist of three racing divisions: the Stock Division for girls and boys ages nine through 16 competing in simplified cars built from kits; the Kit Car Division for youngsters competing in more advanced models, although still using standardized kits and shells; and the Masters Division for girls and boys ages 11 through 16 who want to test their creativity and design skills. They can build a car from scratch or purchase and assemble a Masters Kit and shell.

Competitors arrive on the Monday before the race and spend the week working on their cars, participating in trial runs, and relaxing before the big race on Saturday. The home-built cars used in the derby today bear little resemblance to derby cars in the 1930s, many of which were actually built out of soap boxes.

CONTACT:
Akron/Summit County Convention and Visitors Bureau
77 E. Mill St.
Akron, OH 44308
800-245-4254 or 216-374-7560
fax: 216-374-7626

SOURCES:
Chases-1996, p. 330
GdUSFest-1984, p. 137

♦ 0037 ♦ Allen, Richard, Birthday of
February 14

The son of two slaves, Richard Allen (1760–1831) was born in Philadelphia on this day. By the time he was 26 years old, he had saved enough money to purchase his own freedom, and soon after that he established an African-American congregation that met on Sunday afternoons in St. George's Methodist Church. Because he didn't want his church to exist solely as an appendage to a white man's church, Allen bought some land and set up America's first African-American church in an old blacksmith shop. His followers were known as Allenites.

A new church building, completed in 1794, was dedicated by Francis Asbury, America's first Methodist bishop. Allen's work among African Americans expanded at such a rapid rate that in 1816 he organized his church on a national scale. Members of the African Methodist Episcopal (AME) Church commemorate the birth of their founder and first bishop on this day.

CONTACT:
African Methodist Episcopal Church
1134 11th St., N.W.
Washington, D.C. 20001

SOURCES:
DaysCustFaith-1957, p. 51
RelHolCal-1993, p. 63

All Fools' Day
See **April Fools' Day**

All Hallows' Day
See **All Saints' Day**

♦ 0038 ♦ All Saints' Day
November 1 in West; first Sunday after Pentecost in East

In the Roman Catholic, Anglican, and many Protestant churches, the first day of November is a celebration of all the Christian saints—particularly those who have no special feast days of their own. Also known as **All-Hallomas** or **All Hallows' Day**, the idea for this holy day goes back to the

fourth century, when the Greek Christians kept a festival on the first Sunday after PENTECOST (in late May or early June) in honor of all martyrs and saints. When the Pantheon at Rome was converted into a Christian place of worship in the seventh century, Pope Boniface IV dedicated it to the Virgin and all the martyrs, and the anniversary of this event was celebrated on May 1.

Moving the day to November 1 may have been an attempt to supplant the pagan Festival of the Dead (also known as SAMHAIN or the feast of Saman, lord of death), which had long been celebrated on November 1.

SOURCES:
AmerBkDays-1978, p. 978
BkDays-1864, vol. II, p. 520
DaysCustFaith-1957, p. 280
DictFolkMyth-1984, pp. 36, 181, 573, 1056
FestSaintDays-1915, p. 197
FestWestEur-1958, pp. 17, 47
FolkAmerHol-1991, pp. 373, 383
FolkWrldHol-1992, p. 541
RelHolCal-1993, p. 56
SaintFestCh-1904, p. 470

♦ 0039 ♦ All Saints' Day in France
November 1

Both All Saints' Day, **La Toussaint**, and ALL SOULS' DAY, *Le Jour des Morts*, are widely observed in France. Church services in memory of all the saints are held on November 1, but by evening the focus turns toward the dead. Cemeteries everywhere are crowded with people who have come to clean and decorate the family graves. All Souls' Day, November 2, is dedicated to prayers for the dead who are not yet glorified. Church services are often followed by visits to the churchyard, and families get together to pay homage to the deceased.

In Brittany, pancakes and cider are set out for the dead on the eve of All Souls' Day, and children play practical jokes in the cemeteries—such as placing lit candles inside skulls, or rattling bones in empty pails—to frighten visitors.

SOURCES:
AmerBkDays-1978, p. 981
DictFolkMyth-1984, p. 842
FestWestEur-1958, p. 47

♦ 0040 ♦ All Saints' Day in Louisiana
November 1

ALL SAINTS' DAY is celebrated in many areas of the United States where there are large Roman Catholic populations. In New Orleans, for example, it is a legal holiday where Catholics gather in local cemeteries and decorate the graves with flowers. The descendants of the French Canadian (also known as Acadian or Cajun) settlers around St. Martinsville, Louisiana, observe this day in the traditional French manner by laying wreaths and bouquets on even the most obscure graves and, as darkness falls, by lighting candles throughout the cemeteries in anticipation of ALL SOULS' DAY on November 2.

SOURCES:
AmerBkDays-1978, p. 979
DictDays-1988, p. 3

◆ 0041 ◆ All Souls' Day
November 2 in West; three Saturdays prior to
Lent and the day before Pentecost in East

People held festivals for the dead long before Christianity. It was St. Odilo, the abbot of Cluny in France, who in the 10th century proposed that the day after ALL SAINTS' DAY be set aside in honor of the departed—particularly those whose souls were still in purgatory. Today, the souls of all the faithful departed are commemorated. Although All Souls' Day is observed informally by some Protestants, it is primarily a Roman Catholic, Anglican, and Orthodox holy day.

In many Catholic countries, people attend churches, which are appropriately draped in black, and visit family graves on this day to honor their ancestors. In Shropshire and Cheshire, England, children still go out "souling" from house to house, although they are no longer given the traditional "soul cakes" that were supposed to rescue souls from purgatory. The evening of November 1 is often called **All Souls' Eve** and is a time to decorate graveyards and light candles in memory of the dead.

Orthodox Christians commemorate the dead on the three Saturdays prior to Lent and on the day before Pentecost.

In Mexico, it is a national holiday called the **Día de los Muertos** (or **Day of the Dead**). Many Spanish-Indians believe that the spirits of the dead return to enjoy a visit with their friends and relatives on this day. Long before sunrise, people stream into the cemeteries laden with candles, flowers, and food that is often shaped and decorated to resemble the symbols of death. Children eat tiny chocolate hearses, sugar funeral wreaths, and candy skulls and coffins. But the atmosphere is festive. In the United States, el Día de los Muertos is celebrated in areas such as Los Angeles, Calif., where there is a large Mexican-American population.

In many homes Indians set up *ofrendas*, or altars to the departed. These are decked with lighted candles, special foods, and whatever the dead enjoyed when they were alive. The Day of the Dead is also a popular time to see performances of the ancient Spanish drama, *Don Juan Tenorio*, about a reckless lover who kills the father of a woman he has tried to seduce and then erects a statue of his victim. The statue eventually comes alive and drags Don Juan down to hell to account for his crimes.

In Portugal, November 2 is known as **Día dos Finados** (All Souls' Day) and is observed with special masses and processions to cemeteries. Similar celebrations are held for All Souls' Day in Ecuador, El Salvador, the French West Indies, Macao, and Uruguay.

In Italy **Il Giorno dei Morti** begins at dawn with a solemn Requiem for the dead. Church bells toll and people decorate the graves of their family members with flowers and candles. But Il Giorno dei Morti is not entirely a somber occasion. In Sicily the children who have prayed for the *morti*, or souls of the departed, leave their shoes outside doors and windows, where they are filled with gifts. In Rome, it is customary for young people to announce their engagements on All Souls' Day. The man sends the engagement ring to his fiancée in a small white box, which in turn is packed in an oval container filled with *fave dei morti*, or 'beans of the dead'—little bean-shaped cakes made of ground almonds and sugar combined with eggs, butter, and flour.

SOURCES:
AmerBkDays-1978, p. 980
DaysCustFaith-1957, p. 282
DictFolkMyth-1984, pp. 38,
184, 505, 842, 1051, 1052
FestSaintDays-1915, p. 200
FestWestEur-1958, pp. 17, 47,
100
FolkAmerHol-1991, pp. 373,
384
FolkWrldHol-1992, pp. 544,
548
RelHolCal-1993, p. 57
SaintFestCh-1904, p. 472

◆ 0042 ◆ All Souls' Day at the Cochiti Pueblo
November 2

The Cochiti Pueblo Indians, who occupy the northernmost of the Keresan-speaking pueblos along the Rio Grande west of Santa Fe, refer to this day as **"Their Grandfathers Arrive from the West Feast"** (or **"Their Grandfathers Arrive from the Dead Feast"**). Converted to Catholicism by Spanish missionaries in the late 17th century, the Cochiti Indians regard ALL SOULS' DAY as an opportunity to persuade the visiting spirits of the departed that they have not been forgotten and that their kin are prospering. Each family fasts, setting out bowls of food in the corner of the house and leaving the door open for the returning spirits. The family's material goods—in the form of blankets, shawls, and jewelry—are displayed on the walls, and candles are lit so that the dead can find their way to their former homes. The men congregate in the *kiva*, or ceremonial chamber, where they spend the night singing and cutting up small pieces of food as offerings for the dead.

Similar ceremonies are held at other Indian pueblos in New Mexico. At Taos Pueblo, for example, the church bell rings all night while candles burn and food is brought to the graves in the churchyard. At the Zuni Pueblo around this same time, **Grandmothers' Day** is celebrated by making offerings of food to the dead. The men and boys spend the day going from house to house singing and receiving food.

CONTACT:
Cochiti Pueblo
P.O. Box 70
Cochiti, NM 87041
505-867-3211 or 505-465-2244

SOURCES:
AmerBkDays-1978, p. 981

All Souls' Day in France
See **All Saints' Day in France**

◆ 0043 ◆ Almabtrieb
September

The **Return from the Mountain Pasture** is an autumn festival that takes place in the German Alps on the day that the cattle are driven down from the mountain pastures to their winter shelter. The cattle are decorated with flowers and the *Sennerinnen*, or 'herd-girls', who lead them wear traditional costumes that vary from place to place. Sometimes the cattle are brought to their final destination on flower-decked boats that ferry them across the mountain lakes. Once the cattle are safely in for the winter, the farmers hold welcome-home feasts which are followed by music, dancing, and singing.

See also ALPAUFZUG and COW FIGHTS

SOURCES:
FestWestEur-1958, p. 70

♦ 0044 ♦ Alma Highland Festival and Games
May, Memorial Day weekend

Like other American cities and towns founded or settled primarily by Scots, Alma, Michigan, celebrates its Scottish heritage by holding a traditional Highland Festival for three days in late May each year. The festival was originated by a local resident who attended the Scottish games in Boston in 1962 and decided that a similar event should be held in Alma, a city founded by Scots and with a Scottish name. Activities include Scottish athletic events, border collie demonstrations, fiddling contests, an arts and crafts show, piping, drumming, and highland dancing. Participants come from all over the United States and Canada, and some even come from Scotland. The food served at the festival includes meat pies, haggis (a traditional Scottish dish made from the heart, liver, etc. of a sheep or calf, minced with suet and oatmeal, seasoned, and boiled in the stomach of the animal), bridies (hot sausage or meat rolls), and shortbread.

See also Grandfather Mountain Highland Games and Gathering of Scottish Clans, Highland Games, and Virginia Scottish Games

CONTACT:
Michigan Travel Bureau
333 S. Capitol Ave., Ste. F
Lansing, MI 48933
800-543-2937 or 517-373-0670
fax: 517-373-0059

SOURCES:
Chases-1996, p. 224
GdUSFest-1984, p. 91

♦ 0045 ♦ Aloha Week Festivals
September–October

A celebration of Hawaiian culture that was once a week long. Now it's a two-month affair that starts in Honolulu in early September and runs through the end of October, with a week of festivities on every island of Hawaii. The celebrations include canoe races between the islands of Molokai and Oahu, coronations of royal courts as commemorations of the former Hawaiian monarchy, street parties, and parades and pageantry.

CONTACT:
Hawaii Visitors Bureau
2270 Kalakaua Ave., Ste. 801
Honolulu, HI 96815
808-923-1811; fax: 808-922-8991

SOURCES:
Chases-1996, p. 374
GdUSFest-1984, p. 41

♦ 0046 ♦ Alpaufzug
May or June

An old custom in Switzerland is this springtime 'ascent to the mountains,' when goats and cows are driven to higher pasture. In the canton of Appenzell in eastern Switzerland and also in the Alpine canton of Valais, there are picturesque festivals, with herders and their families dressing in traditional costume (the Appenzell men wear red vests and yellow knicker-type pants) and everyone enjoying the Cow Fights that establish the leader of the herd. In September and October, bringing the herds back down to the valleys, known as *Alpabfahrten*, also prompts festivals, and the cow that has been the greatest milk producer is feted and decked with flowers.

See also Almabtrieb

CONTACT:
Swiss National Tourist Office
608 Fifth Ave.
New York, NY 10020
212-757-5944; fax: 212-262-6116

SOURCES:
BkHolWrld-1986, Apr 17
FestWestEur-1958, p. 229

♦ 0047 ♦ Alpenfest
Third week in July

At an altitude of 1,348 feet, Gaylord is one of the highest incorporated communities in Michigan. Five rivers rise nearby and flow in different directions. Gaylord receives nearly 150 inches of snow each year and the town's main streets are lined with Swiss-style architecture. The annual Alpenfest is basically a celebration of summer.

A highlight of the festival is the "Burning of the Boog." People write their troubles on slips of paper and place them in the "Boog"—a 300-pound, 10-foot-high monster—which is then burned, giving spectators a chance to watch their troubles literally go up in smoke. The festival also boasts a number of outdoor cafes which host "the World's Largest Coffee Break."

CONTACT:
Gaylord Chamber of Commerce
P.O. Box 513
Gaylord, MI 49735
517-732-4000

♦ 0048 ♦ Amalaka Ekadashi
February–March; 11th day of waxing half of Hindu month of Phalguna

Among Hindus, who respect all animate and inanimate things because they are manifestations of the Universal Spirit, this is a day for worshipping the Alma tree (Amalaka), where Vishnu is believed to live. An Amalaka tree is ceremonially bathed and watered, a fast is observed, and Brahmans are given gifts.

Amalaka Ekadashi also marks the beginning of the Holi or spring festival in India, where people splash each other with colored water and red powder (an aphrodisiac), indulge in eating and drinking, and generally behave in an uninhibited manner.

SOURCES:
RelHolCal-1993, p. 57

♦ 0049 ♦ Amarnath Yatra
July–August; full moon of Hindu month of Sravana

A pilgrimage to the Amarnath Cave, high in the Kashmir Himalayas, near Pahalgam in northern India. This cave holds a natural ice lingam, the Hindu phallic symbol of Lord Shiva. The trek to the cave, at an altitude of about 12,700 feet, is along narrow, winding mountain trails. The thousands of pilgrims who make this trip include everyone from *sadhus* (holy men) walking barefoot over the stones and snow to wealthy people being carried by coolies.

CONTACT:
India Tourist Office
30 Rockefeller Ave.
15 N. Mezzanine
New York, NY 10112
212-586-4901; fax: 212-582-3274

♦ 0050 ♦ **American Birkebeiner**
Three days in late February

The Birkie started in 1973 as a 55-kilometer cross-country ski race from Hayward, Wis., to Telemark Lodge in the neighboring town of Cable, with only 35 skiers competing. Now it is the largest and most prestigious cross-country ski race in North America, an event that attracts top cross-country skiers from all over the world. In addition to the 55-kilometer Birkie, there is also the Kortelopet or "short race" of 29 kilometers, which is open to competitors ages 13 and up. Other races held during the three-day festival include the Barnebirkie (for children), the Jack Rabbit 10K Classic, telemark race (cross-country skiing on a downhill slalom course), and a biathlon competition combining cross-country ski racing and target shooting. The American Birkebeiner is part of the Worldloppet, an international series of 12 marathon races held in Japan, Switzerland, Sweden, Norway, France, Germany, Austria, Finland, Italy, Canada, Australia, and the United States.

The American race was patterned after the Birkebeiner Rennet in Lillehammer, Norway. During the 13th century, a foreign invader was about to capture Norway's infant prince and heir to the throne. He was saved by two Viking warriors—called "Birkebeiners" for the birch-bark leggings they wore. These men took the child and skied 55 kilometers to safety. The baby eventually became the great Norwegian king, Haakon Haakonson.

CONTACT:
Wisconsin Division of Tourism
123 W. Washington Ave., 6th Fl.
Madison, WI 53703
800-432-8747 or 608-266-7621
fax: 608-266-3403

SOURCES:
Chases-1996, p. 107
GdUSFest-1984, p. 210

♦ 0051 ♦ **American Folklife, Festival of**
Last weekend in June to first weekend in July

Since 1967 the Festival of American Folklife has been held on the National Mall in Washington, D.C., to celebrate the richness and diversity of American and world cultures. Since that time the Festival has presented more than 15,000 musicians, craftspeople, storytellers, cooks, workers, performers, and other cultural specialists from every region of the United States and from more than 45 other nations. Recent festival programs have included musicians from the former Soviet Union, demonstrations of African-American coil basketry and Italian-American stone-carving, the performance of a Japanese rice-planting ritual, and exhibits illustrating the occupational cultures of working people—taxicab drivers, firefighters, waiters, and railway workers.

The Festival is designed to expose visitors to people and cultures who would not ordinarily be heard in a national setting. It emphasizes folk, tribal, ethnic, and regional traditions in communities throughout the U.S. and abroad. Each year the festival features a particular state (or region) and country. One year, for example, the featured region was

"Family Farming in the Heartland." More than 100 farmers from 12 Midwestern states came to the nation's capital to talk to visitors about changes in farming methods and farm life, and to demonstrate both modern and traditional farming skills. The featured country was Indonesia, and there were demonstrations of Buginese boat-building and traditional mask carving, in addition to an all-night Indonesian shadow-puppet show.

CONTACT:
Washington D.C. Convention and
    Visitors Association
1212 New York Ave., N.W., Ste.
    600
Washington, D.C. 20005
800-635-6338 or 202-789-7000
fax: 202-789-7037

SOURCES:
Chases-1996, p. 271
MusFestAmer-1990, p. 219

♦ 0052 ♦ **American Indian Day**
Various

In 1914 Red Fox James of the Blackfeet tribe rode a pony 4,000 miles to present his request—endorsed by the governors of 24 states—that a day be set aside in honor of American Indians, or Native Americans, a name many prefer. The first general American Indian Day was observed on the second Saturday in May 1916, but now the observance and its date are left to the individual states, and they vary widely. A number of states—including Illinois, Arizona, California, and Connecticut—observe it on the fourth Friday in September. Massachusetts, New York, Oklahoma, and Maine have chosen different dates, or vary the date from year to year. In South Dakota it is called **Native Americans' Day**, and is celebrated on the second Monday in October.

Although the holiday has not yet gained nationwide recognition, few would argue that the plight of American Indians today is a grim one, with unemployment, illiteracy, and high school drop-out rates among the highest in the country. Although the largest Indian populations can be found in Oklahoma, Arizona, California, New Mexico, and North Carolina, many other states have come up with ways to draw attention to their unique contribution to American culture and to the need for improving their condition. Most celebrations focus on educational and promotional events, displays of Native American art and dance, and agricultural fairs.

SOURCES:
AmerBkDays-1978, p. 863
AnnivHol-1983, p. 122
BkHolWrld-1986, Sep 23
Chases-1996, pp. 395, 418

♦ 0053 ♦ **American Royal Livestock, Horse Show and Rodeo**
Two weeks in November

Also known as the **American Royal**, or simply the **Royal**, this is the oldest and one of the largest livestock shows and rodeos in the United States. It dates back to the period just after the Civil War, when Texans returning from the battlefield discovered that their cattle herds had multiplied unchecked. They were forced to conduct massive roundups that reached as far west as Kansas City, Missouri, which soon became a center for the consignment of cattle. Meat packers started building plants there to accommodate the supply, and breeders began to show their stock. The National Hereford

Show, held in the Kansas City Stockyards in 1899, is now considered the first American Royal. Over the years the Hereford breeders were joined by breeders of other cattle as well as sheep, swine, and poultry. Draft and carriage horses were first shown at the Royal in 1903.

Although the Royal has suffered some setbacks over the years—including a fire that nearly destroyed the American Royal Building in 1922 and a serious flood in 1951—it has continued to expand and now draws more than 300,000 visitors. There are special tours and instruction for school children, 20,000 of whom come to the show to learn more about agribusiness. The **American Royal Rodeo** is the first rodeo of the season on the professional circuit, featuring over seven hundred professional riders and offering over $100,000 in prize money. There are also livestock auctions, barbecue competitions, and a parade through downtown Kansas City that has been called America's largest hometown parade.

CONTACT:
Missouri Division of Tourism
P.O. Box 1055
Jefferson City, MO 65102
800-877-1234 or 314-751-4133
fax: 314-751-5160

♦ 0054 ♦ **American West, Festival of the**
July–August

This nine-day festival was started in 1972 by Glen L. Taggart, president of Utah State University in Logan. Designed to educate people about America's pioneer and Indian cultures at the close of the 19th century, the festival includes a multimedia historical pageant; an exhibit of Western art, photographs, and engravings; a display of vintage steam tractors; an Old West parade of antique horse-drawn wagons; and demonstrations of pioneer cooking. Various celebrities—including actors Robert Redford, Peter Strauss, and James Drury—have participated in past festivals, and Jimmy Stewart did the taped narration that still accompanies festival events.

Proceeds from the yearly festival have been used to establish a center for the Outlaw-Lawman History Association at Utah State University, a Western Writers' Conference, and two Western magazines. The events are held on the USU campus and in surrounding areas.

CONTACT: SOURCES:
Utah Tourism and Travel   *GdUSFest-1984*, p. 189
Council House
Capitol Hill
Salt Lake City, UT 84114
800-200-1160; fax: 801-538-1000

♦ 0055 ♦ **America's Cup**
Held whenever the Cup is challenged, usually every 3–4 years

Named for the trophy, originally called the Hundred Guinea Cup by the Royal Yacht Squadron of Great Britain, that was won by the 100-foot schooner *America* in a race around the Isle of Wight in 1851. The America's Cup races are the world's longest-running international sporting event. The Cup was given by *America*'s owner, J. C. Stevens, to the New York Yacht Club, which successfully defended it against international challenges for 130 years. In 1984, the challenger *Australia II* defeated the American defender *Courageous* in

races off Newport, Rhode Island, marking the end of the longest winning streak in international sports. In 1987, the American challenger *Stars & Stripes*, sailing for the San Diego Yacht Club, regained the Cup in races off Perth, Australia. *Stars & Stripes* successfully defended the cup in 1988 against New Zealand, and in 1992 *America*[3] retained the Cup for the United States by defeating the Italian boat four races to one.

The race is usually held every three to four years, with challengers coming from England, Canada, France, Sweden, Italy, New Zealand, Australia, Japan, and other countries. The rules require that the defenders and challengers sail in closely matched boats built to the same general specifications, but designs have varied over the years as sailing technology has grown more sophisticated. A new class of boats, the America's Cup class, was introduced in 1991.

CONTACT: SOURCES:
Museum of Yachting   *AmerBkDays-1978*, p. 771
P.O. Box 129
Newport, RI 02840
401-847-1018

America's Discovery Day
See **Columbus Day**

♦ 0056 ♦ **Anant Chaturdashi**
August–September; 14th day of waxing half of Hindu month of Bhadrapada

Among Hindus, this is a day for worshipping and meditating on the god Vishnu. A day-long fast is observed, with offerings of fruits, sweets, and flowers to Vishnu. A thread colored in turmeric paste and having 14 knots is tied on the upper right arm while meditating in the belief that it will protect the worshipper from evil and bring prosperity and happiness. The Pandava princes in exile observed this fast on the advice of Sri Krishna and as a result, they defeated the Kauravas and regained their lost kingdom (*see* BHISHMA ASHTAMI).

                                 SOURCES:
                                 BkFest-1937, p. 160
                                 RelHolCal-1993, p. 57

♦ 0057 ♦ **Anastenaria**
May 21–23

A fire-walking ceremony in Greece, in the communes of Agia Eleni near Serres and of Langada near Thessalonike. Men and women, some holding red kerchiefs and some carrying icons of St. Constantine and St. Helen—in whose honor the ceremonies are held—dance barefooted on red-hot coals while folk musicians play. The custom is supposed to have originated in an ancient form of worship that was brought by travelers from Kosti in Eastern Thrace and adapted to Christian beliefs.

Fire walking has been practiced in many parts of the world and has been thought at times to ensure a good harvest and at other times to purify the participants.

CONTACT:
Greek National Tourist
  Organization
645 Fifth Ave.
New York, NY 10022
212-421-5777; fax: 212-826-6940

♦ 0058 ♦ **Anchorage Fur Rendezvous**
Begins second Friday in February

A 10-day city-wide celebration, also called the **Rondy** and sometimes the **Mardi Gras of the North**, held in Anchorage, Alaska. The Rondy had its origins in the days when fur trappers, joined by miners, capped off a season of trapping by carousing in Anchorage; this annual rendezvous was formalized as a winter carnival in 1936.

Highlighting the celebration is the World Championship Sled Dog Race, a 75-mile race run in three 25-mile legs on three successive days, starting and ending in Anchorage. Contestants come from throughout the United States. Other contests include one for Mr. Fur Face, obviously the man with the most luxuriant beard. Among the scores of other events and exhibits are parades, the Miners and Trappers Ball, Eskimo blanket tossing, Eskimo dances, a snowshoe baseball game, wrestling matches, and performances of an old-time melodrama. Special Alaskan foods sold include sourdough pancakes.

See also IDITAROD TRAIL SLED DOG RACE

CONTACT:
Anchorage Convention and Visitors Bureau
1600 'A' Street, Ste. 200
Anchorage, AK 99501
800-446-5352 or 907-276-4118
fax: 907-278-5559

SOURCES:
AnnivHol-1983, p. 173
Chases-1996, p. 91
GdUSFest-1984, p. 7

♦ 0059 ♦ **Andersen Festival, Hans Christian**
July–August

Sometimes referred to as the **Hans Christian Andersen Plays**, this month-long event features dramatizations of the Danish author's works at the Open Air Theater in the Funen Village in Odense, Denmark. It began in 1965 with the Danish actor Freddy Albeck, who dressed up like Andersen and did dramatic readings of his stories for children. Eventually it turned into a real theater event with both professional and child actors as well as a small orchestra. Prominent Danish producer Erik Bent Svendlund took over as manager of the festival in 1974, and he is still adapting Andersen's stories for the stage. About 50 children are chosen each year to act in the productions.

Lasting almost a month, the festival offers hour-long performances of such classic stories as *The Ugly Duckling*, *The Tinder Box*, *Little Claus and Big Claus*, and *Simple Simon*, and draws about 30,000 spectators, many of them foreign tourists.

See also CHILDREN'S BOOK DAY, INTERNATIONAL

CONTACT:
Danish Tourist Board
655 Third Ave., 18th Floor
New York, NY 10017
212-949-2333; fax: 212-983-5260

SOURCES:
GdWrldFest-1985, p. 73

♦ 0060 ♦ **Andorra National Day**
September 8

The Principality of Andorra, located in the Pyrénées Mountains between France and Spain, was founded by the Emperor Charlemagne, who recovered the region from the Muslims in 803. His son later granted part of his empire to the Spanish bishop of Urgel, and by the late 13th century the citizens of Andorra were ruled by two princes, one in Spain and one in France. Until recently, the principality had been governed jointly by the bishop of Urgel and the king, and later, president of France. On September 8, 1278, Andorra's first constitutional document, known as the ''Pareatges,'' was signed. Among other things, it stated that each of the co-rulers would receive a token tribute each year known as the Questia. Originally, the French king received $2 biennially; the bishop $8, plus six hams, six cheeses, and 12 hens in alternate years. On March 14, 1993, the people of Andorra voted to abandon this mode of government and institute a parliamentary system.

The people of Andorra celebrate their **National Day** by honoring Jungfrau von Meritxell, their patron saint. Pilgrims climb to her hilltop sanctuary near the villages of Encamp and Canillo, where her statue was found by a shepherd under an almond tree (some say a rose bush) blooming out of season. The pilgrims stop to refresh themselves with drinks that have been cooled in the nearby springs, and after the sermon, they celebrate by dancing and eating lamb grilled on slabs of slate.

CONTACT:
Andorra Bureau for Tourism and Information
6800 N. Knox Ave.
Lincolnwood, IL 60646
708-674-3091; fax: 708-329-9470

SOURCES:
AnnivHol-1983, p. 115
FolkWrldHol-1992, p. 474
NatlHolWrld-1968, p. 160

♦ 0061 ♦ **Angelitos, Los**
October 30

For the Mayan Indians of the Yucatán Peninsula in southeastern Mexico, October 30 was a day devoted to children who had died—the *angelitos*, or 'little angels.' It was customary for families to decorate their doors with flowers and to prepare special foods for the *angelitos* who would visit them that night. Los Angelitos marked the beginning of the period during which all the dead were commemorated.

Mexican Indians celebrate the Day of the Dead, or Día de los Muertos, on ALL SOULS' DAY, November 2.

SOURCES:
BkHolWrld-1986, Oct 30

♦ 0062 ♦ **Angola Independence Day**
November 11

This national holiday commemorates Angola's formal independence from Portugal on this day in 1975, after battling for autonomy since the beginning of the 20th century.

CONTACT:
Angola Embassy
1819 L Street, N.W., Ste. 400
Washington, D.C. 20036
202-785-1156; fax: 202-785-1258

SOURCES:
AnnivHol-1983, p. 145
Chases-1996, p. 447

♦ 0063 ♦ **Anjou Festival**
July–August

Festival d'Anjou, the theater, dance, art, and music festival held in Angers, France, every summer gives young artists an unparalleled opportunity to work with and learn from professionals in their fields. Approximately 50 young dancers are selected from regional dance conservatories and private dance classes to participate in a choreography workshop taught by well-established dancers. A similar workshop is held for 20 young actors from French dramatic conservatories, who learn voice, movement, diction, and interpretation skills from faculty members at the National Conservatory of Paris.

In addition to offering workshops in choreography, drama, circus, music, and the plastic arts, the festival presents concerts and performances by some of the world's best known dance and theatrical groups, including the Martha Graham Dance Company, Pilobolus Dance Theater, La Mama E.T.C., and the Great Jones Repertory Company. Most of these performances are held either outdoors or in nearby churches, abbeys, and castles.

CONTACT:
French Government Tourist Office
9454 Wilshire Blvd., Ste. 715
Beverly Hills, CA 90212
310-271-6665; fax: 310-276-2835

SOURCES:
IntlThFolk-1979, p. 98

♦ 0064 ♦ **Anna Parenna Festival**
March 15

Anna Parenna was a Roman goddess who represented the circle or ring of the year—Anna being the feminine form of *annus* (meaning 'year') and March, the month her festival was observed, being the first month of the Roman calendar. Anna was usually depicted as the old woman of the year that had just passed, while Mars was the god of the first month of the new year. According to legend, in 494 B.C. the ancient Roman *plebs,* or common citizens, fled the city to put political pressure on the patricians (aristocracy), who needed the plebs for the army. They took refuge on the Mons Sacer, a mountain near Rome. They began to run out of food and suffer starvation. Anna, an old woman from Bovillae, brought them cakes every day. When peace was reestablished, the people made her one of their deities and added *Parenna* (meaning 'enduring' or 'lasting throughout the year') to her name.

On the day of her festival, the plebs of Rome went to the Campus Martius, a large field outside the walls of the city, and lay about on the grass, often pitching tents or constructing simple huts out of stakes and branches with togas stretched across the top. They spent the day drinking, dancing, and singing, returning to the city at night in a state of deep intoxication. As they drank, they often prayed to Anna to let them live as many years as the number of cups of wine they had swallowed.

SOURCES:
ClassDict-1984, p. 48
FestRom-1981, p. 90

♦ 0065 ♦ **Annapolis Valley Apple Blossom Festival**
May–June

Nova Scotia's Annapolis Valley is widely known for its apple orchards, which begin to flower in late May or early June. The area's first Apple Blossom Festival was held in 1933 in the town of Kentville, but since that time it has grown into a five-day celebration whose events are held throughout the 60 towns and villages of the Annapolis Valley. In addition to a children's parade, sporting events, tours to view the apple blossoms, apple pie baking and eating contests, and a cook-

ing competition, the festival includes the crowning of "Queen Annapolisa," who is chosen from among 18 local princesses.

The festival is also designed to draw attention to the area's historic background as "The Land of Evangeline," the heroine of Henry Wadsworth Longfellow's long narrative poem about the expulsion of a group of Acadians and their subsequent settlement in Louisiana.

CONTACT:
Dept. of Tourism and Culture
P.O. Box 456
Halifax, Nova Scotia
Canada B3J 2R5
800-565-0000 or 902-424-5000

SOURCES:
Chases-1996, p. 234
GdWrldFest-1985, p. 44

Anniversary Day
See **Australia Day**

♦ 0066 ♦ **Annual Patriots' Weekend**
Last weekend in September

Initiated in 1975, the Annual Patriots' Weekend held in the Bethel-Redding area of Connecticut, honors all American patriots, from the Revolutionary War to the Persian Gulf War. Held at the Putnam Memorial State Park, activities include encampments of both British and American soldiers, artillery demonstrations, infantry drills, and crafts of the Revolutionary period. In the late afternoon, there is a parade to the park's Revolutionary War battlefield. This is followed by a battle reenactment that is unusual in that it does not attempt to replay the historic events. Instead both sides fight to win using the same military tactics that were used during the Revolution (but without live ammunition, of course). Spectators are kept a safe distance away, but they are encouraged to observe and ask questions. In some years, depending upon the availability of horses, there are cavalry demonstrations as well.

CONTACT:
Putnam Memorial State Park
c/o Squantz Pond State Park
178 Shortwoods Rd.
New Fairfield, CT 06810
203-797-4165

Connecticut Tourism Division
865 Brook St.
Rocky Hill, CT 06067
800-282-6863 or 860-258-4355
fax: 860-258-4275

♦ 0067 ♦ **Annunciation of the Blessed Virgin Mary, Feast of the**
March 25

This day celebrates the appearance of the Archangel Gabriel to the Virgin Mary announcing that she was to become the mother of Jesus. The date for this feast couldn't have been fixed until the date of CHRISTMAS was established, and obviously the two dates had to be nine months apart. In England, the Feast of the Annunciation is commonly called LADY DAY.

Annunciation usually falls during LENT, and is kept as a feast day in the midst of the Lenten fast. If it should happen to fall on MAUNDY THURSDAY or GOOD FRIDAY, it is transferred to a date following EASTER. According to medieval superstition, it was a bad omen when Easter and the Annunciation fell on the same day.

In Sweden it was called *Varfrudagen*, 'our Lady's Day.' Common pronunciation turned it into *Vaffeldagen*, or 'waffle day.' This is the source of heart-shaped waffle irons: the waffles commemorate the heart of the Virgin Mary.

SOURCES:
AmerBkDays-1978, pp. 4, 284
BkDays-1864, vol. I, p. 417
BkHolWrld-1986, Mar 25
DaysCustFaith-1957, p. 86
FestSaintDays-1915, p. 56
FestWestEur-1958, pp. 6, 213
FolkWrldHol-1992, p. 188
RelHolCal-1993, p. 57
SaintFestCh-1904, p. 146

♦ 0068 ♦ Annunciation of the Blessed Virgin Mary, Feast of the, in Belgium
March 25

The Feast of the Annunciation or LADY DAY is known in Belgium as **Notre Dame do la Prospérité**, due to a popular belief that seeds sown on this day are bound to germinate. This day is also associated with weather lore: traditional Belgian belief has it that a clear, starry sky before sunrise is a good omen for the next harvest.

According to legend, the Lord asked even the wild birds and animals to observe the Feast of the Annunciation with quiet meditation. When the cuckoo ignored this command and continued its loud and raucous calling, God punished the bird by dooming it to eternal wandering, without a nest of its own.

SOURCES:
FestSaintDays-1915, p. 59
FestWestEur-1958, p. 6

♦ 0069 ♦ Anthesteria
February–March

A spring festival held for three days annually in ancient Athens during the Attic month of Anthesterion (February–March). Its purpose was to celebrate the beginning of spring, the god Dionysus, and the maturing of the wine stored during the previous year. The first day was celebrated by tasting the new wine from the previous vintage. This was known as the Pithoigia, or 'opening of the casks'. The second day, the Choes, or 'pitcher feast', was a merry celebration of the marriage of the chief archon's (magistrate's) wife to Dionysus. A festival of the dead was held on the third day. This was called the Chutroi, or 'feast of pots'. This was a time of mourning to honor the dead, and to placate or expel ghosts. The three days of the Anthesteria incorporated the theme of birth-growth-death.

SOURCES:
DictFolkMyth-1984, p. 64

♦ 0070 ♦ Anthony Day, Susan B.
February 15; August 26

Susan Brownell Anthony (1820–1906) devoted her life to the temperance, anti-slavery, and women's suffrage movements. After the Civil War ended in 1865, she focused all of her energies on getting women the right to vote. That goal was achieved in 1920 with the passage of the 19th Amendment to the Constitution of the United States, sometimes called "the Anthony Amendment." She was elected to the Hall of Fame for Great Americans in 1950, and was honored in 1979 when she became the first American woman to have her likeness on a coin: the Susan B. Anthony dollar.

Tributes to Anthony take place on her birthday, February 15, in various parts of the country. Sometimes a memorial service is held in the crypt of the Capitol in Washington, D.C., where there is a statue of the pioneers in the women's suffrage movement: Anthony, Elizabeth Cady STANTON, and Lucretia Mott. Ceremonies honoring Anthony are often held at her grave in Rochester, New York, near the home where for more than 40 years she lived and frequently met with other influential reformers. Women's organizations, such as the National Organization for Women (NOW), usually play a major role in sponsoring memorial observances.

Some states observe Susan B. Anthony Day on August 26, the day on which the 19th Amendment was ratified.

CONTACT:
National Organization for Women
1000 16th St., N.W., Ste. 700
Washington, D.C. 20036
202-331-0066; fax: 202-785-8576
E-mail: now@now.org
WWW: http://now.org/now/home.html

SOURCES:
AmerBkDays-1978, p. 184
AnnivHol-1983, p. 25
Chases-1996, pp. 98, 350
DictDays-1988, p. 115

♦ 0071 ♦ Antigua and Barbuda Independence Day
November 1

Antigua and its dependency, Barbuda, became officially independent from England in 1981. Antigua had been settled by English people as early as 1632. It did not gain self-rule until 1967.

This small state also observes August 5–6 as a legal holiday known as Carnival, during which a festival celebrates the islanders' cultural heritage.

CONTACT:
Embassy of Antigua and Barbuda
3400 International Dr., N.W., Ste. 4M
Washington, D.C. 20008
202-362-5122; fax: 202-362-5225

SOURCES:
AnnivHol-1983, p. 138
Chases-1996, p. 436

♦ 0072 ♦ Antique and Classic Boat Rendezvous
Last weekend in July

Every July since 1975, classic wooden yachts of pre-1952 vintage have gathered for the annual Antique and Classic Boat Rendezvous at Mystic Seaport Museum in Mystic, Connecticut. Although some boats built as early as 1890 have participated, most date from the 1920s to the 1940s. Many are one-of-a-kind and have been kept in mint condition by their owners. More than 50 boats from throughout the Northeast participate each year, making it one of the largest gatherings of its kind.

The boats can be viewed at dockside on Friday evening and early on Saturday. Saturday afternoon the vessels begin their colorful parade down the Mystic River to Noank, led by the museum's 84-year-old steamboat, *Sabino*, with a Dixieland jazz band on board. The boats are "dressed" with brightly colored signal flags, and many carry crews in period costumes as they compete for awards in various categories.

CONTACT:
Mystic Seaport Museum Stores
47 Greenmanville Ave.
Mystic, CT 06355
800-331-2665 or 860-572-5385
fax: 860-572-8260

SOURCES:
Chases-1996, p. 304

♦ 0073 ♦ **An tOireachtas**
Early November

The original *Oireachtas*, or 'Assembly', dates back to the ancient kingdoms of seventh-century Ireland. In 1897 Conradh na Gaeilge revived the tradition of assembly and discussion that had begun centuries earlier by founding what is now Ireland's oldest annual cultural festival. An tOireachtas is a 10-day celebration of Irish culture and language, and it includes lectures, debates, literary and stage competitions, concerts, art exhibitions, storytelling, and performances of traditional Irish song, music, and dance. A highlight of the festival is the *sean-nós*, or traditional singing in the Irish language. The *sean-nós* singing competitions culminate in the Corn Uí Riada, the final competition for the coveted Ó Riada Trophy.

Sponsored by the Gaelic League, the festival is held in a different venue each year. It is similar to the EISTEDDFOD in Wales and the GAELIC MOD in Scotland.

CONTACT:
Irish Tourist Board
345 Park Ave., 17th Floor
New York, NY 10154
800-223-6470 or 212-418-0800
fax: 212-371-9052

SOURCES:
IntlThFolk-1979, p. 237

♦ 0074 ♦ **Anzac Day**
April 25

A national holiday in Australia and New Zealand, this day takes its name from the initial letters of "Australia and New Zealand Army Corps." It commemorates the landing of the Anzac troops on the Gallipoli Peninsula in European Turkey on April 25, 1915, during World War I. Like MEMORIAL DAY in the U.S., this day is celebrated with veterans' parades and church services. Observed as a holiday since 1920, Anzac Day now honors those who have died in both world wars as well as in Korea and Vietnam.

CONTACT:
Australian Tourist Commission
100 Park Ave., 25th Floor
New York, NY 10017
212-687-6300; fax: 212-661-3340

SOURCES:
AnnivHol-1983, p. 56
BkHolWrld-1986, Apr 25
Chases-1996, p. 184
DictDays-1988, p. 4

New Zealand Tourism Board
501 Santa Monica Blvd., Ste. 300
Santa Monica, CA 90401
800-388-5494 or 310-395-7480
fax: 310-395-5453

♦ 0075 ♦ **Aoi Matsuri**
May 15

One of the three major festivals of Kyoto, Japan, the **Hollyhock Festival** is believed to date from the sixth century. The festival's name derives from the hollyhock leaves adorning the headdresses of the participants; legend says hollyhocks

help prevent storms and earthquakes. The festival owes its present form to the time in the Heian period (792–1099) when imperial messengers were sent to the Kyoto shrines of Shimogamo and Kamigamo after a plague (or a flood) that came about because the shrines were neglected. Today the festival, which was revived in 1884, consists of a re-creation of the original imperial procession. Some 500 people in ancient costume parade with horses and large lacquered oxcarts carrying the "imperial messengers" from the Kyoto Imperial Palace to the shrines.

See also GION MATSURI and JIDAI MATSURI

CONTACT:
Japan National Tourist
  Organization
630 Fifth Ave., Ste. 2101
New York, NY 10111
212-757-5640; fax: 212-307-6754

SOURCES:
Chases-1996, p. 213
GdWrldFest-1985, p. 122
JapanFest-1965, p. 30

♦ 0076 ♦ **Apache Maidens' Puberty Rites**
July 4

A celebration of the coming-of-age of girls of the Mescalero Apache Tribe, held for four days and four nights around the FOURTH OF JULY in Mescalero, N.M. Besides the puberty rites, there are other events: a rodeo, a powwow with cash prizes for dancers, a parade on July 4, and the nighttime Dance of the Mountain Gods.

The rites are related to the belief that soon after the creation of the world, White Painted Woman appeared in the east as a beautiful young woman, moved to the west, and disappeared when she was old. On the first and last days of the ceremonial, the girls must run around a basket four times, symbolically going through the four stages of life (infancy, childhood, adulthood, and old age). On the last day, their faces are painted with white clay and they enact the role of White Painted Woman, taking on her qualities and preparing for a rewarding adult life. On each of the four nights, the girls dance in the Holy Lodge, which was set up on the first day, while singers sing of the creation and beat time with deer-hoof rattles. The celebrations also involve feasting and elaborate ceremonial dresses.

In the 1800s, the U.S. government forbade the Apaches to congregate, but in 1911 decreed that they could congregate on July 4 to celebrate the nation's birthday. The Apaches then chose that date for their most important cultural ritual as an insult to their conquerors.

CONTACT:
Mescalero Apache Tribal Council
P.O. Box 176
Mescalero, NM 88340
505-671-4494 or 505-671-4495

SOURCES:
DictWrldRel-1989, p. 531
IndianAmer-1989, p. 301

♦ 0077 ♦ **Apple and Candle Night**
October 31

Another name for HALLOWEEN among the children in the Swansea area of Wales. The traditional game of "Apple and Candle" is played by suspending a stick from the ceiling with an apple fastened to one end and a lit candle to the other. The object is to eat the apple without using hands and without getting burned by the swinging candle. To make the game more challenging, players are sometimes blindfolded and the stick is twirled around before the game begins.

See also MISCHIEF NIGHT

SOURCES:
AmerBkDays-1978, p. 969
DictDays-1988, p. 4
DictFolkMyth-1984, p. 869
FestSaintDays-1915, p. 192
FolkWrldHol-1992, p. 523

♦ 0078 ♦ **Appomattox Day**
April 9

The Civil War ended on April 9, 1865, in the village of Appomattox Court House, Virginia, when Lieutenant General Ulysses S. Grant of the Union army accepted the surrender of General Robert E. Lee of the Confederacy (*see* LEE DAY, ROBERT E.). The Confederate soldiers were allowed to keep their horses and return to their homes; the officers were allowed to retain their side arms and swords as well. Thus ended the bloody four-year conflict that had cost more than half a million lives.

The most widespread celebration of Appomattox Day took place in 1965 during the Civil War centennial year. Thousands of people attended the ceremonies at the Appomattox Court House National Historical Park. Participants included the Union leader's grandson, Ulysses S. Grant III, as well as Robert E. Lee IV, great-grandson of the Confederate leader. The day was noted across the country—but particularly in the South—with costumed pageants, books and articles reflecting on the war, and concerts of martial music. Although the anniversary is not observed on a yearly basis, reenactments of the historic surrender are held about once every five years.

CONTACT:
Appomattox Court House National Historical Park
P.O. Box 218
Appomattox, VA 24522
804-352-8987

SOURCES:
AmerBkDays-1978, p. 314

♦ 0079 ♦ **April Fools' Day**
April 1

There are many names for this day—including **All Fools' Day, April Noddy Day, Gowkie Day, Huntigowk Day,** and **St. All-Fools' Morn**—just as there are many practical jokes to play on the unsuspecting. One theory about its origin points to Noah as the first "April Fool." It is said that on that day he mistakenly sent the dove out to find dry land after the flood. Another points to the adoption of the Gregorian calendar in 1582, when NEW YEAR'S DAY was officially moved from March 25 to January 1. People who forgot about the change were often mocked by their friends, as they continued to make New Year visits just after the old March date.

The simplest pranks usually involve children who, for example, tell each other that their shoelaces are undone and then cry "April Fool!" when the victims glance at their feet. Sometimes the media get into the act, broadcasting fictitious news items designed to amuse or alarm the public. British television, for example, once showed Italian farmers "harvesting" spaghetti from trees. The French call it **Fooling the April Fish Day** (the fool being the *poisson d'avril*) and try to pin a paper fish on someone's back without getting caught.

In Mexico, April Fools' Day is celebrated on December 28, HOLY INNOCENTS' DAY.

SOURCES:
AmerBkDays-1978, p. 314
BkDays-1864, vol. I, p. 460
BkFest-1937, p. 17
DaysCustFaith-1957, p. 92
FestSaintDays-1915, p. 58
FestWestEur-1958, p. 34
FolkAmerHol-1991, p. 175
FolkWrldHol-1992, p. 223

Araw ng Kagitingan
See **Bataan Day**

♦ 0080 ♦ **Arbor Day**
Last Friday in April

Julius Sterling Morton (1832–1902), one of the earliest American conservationists, settled on the treeless plains of Nebraska in 1855, where he edited the Nebraska City *News* and developed a lifelong interest in new agricultural methods. Believing that the prairie needed more trees to serve as windbreaks, to hold moisture in the soil, and to provide lumber for housing, Morgan began planting trees and urged his neighbors to do the same. On April 10, 1872, when he first proposed that a specific day be set aside for the planting of trees, the response was overwhelming: a million trees were planted in Nebraska on that day alone.

All 50 states now observe Arbor Day—usually on the last Friday in April—and the idea has spread to other countries as well. Most observances take place in the public schools, where the value of trees is discussed and trees and shrubs are planted. At the White House, the president, first lady, or a presidential designate plants a special tree on the grounds each year on Arbor Day. But it is in Nebraska City, Nebraska, that Morton is best remembered as the originator of Arbor Day, with celebrations taking place on or near his birthday, April 22. A special ceremony is held at Arbor Lodge, Morton's homestead and one of the earliest known attempts at conservation and beautification in America.

Some states call this day **Bird and Arbor Day**, emphasizing the planting of trees that are attractive to birds.

CONTACT:
National Arbor Day Foundation
211 N. 12th St., Ste. 501
Lincoln, NE 68508
402-474-5655; fax: 402-474-0820

SOURCES:
AmerBkDays-1978, p. 366
AnnivHol-1983, p. 57
BkFestHolWrld-1970, p. 86
BkHolWrld-1986, Apr 24
Chases-1996, pp. 181, 186
DictDays-1988, p. 5
GdUSFest-1984, p. 109

♦ 0081 ♦ **Argentine Independence Day**
May 25

Argentina was originally one of a number of Spanish colonies controlled by the Spanish viceroy in Lima, Peru. When the colonies became too large to be controlled from one site, a separate viceroyalty was formed in 1776, with its headquarters in Buenos Aires.

On May 25, 1810, Buenos Aires declared its independence from the viceroyalty but continued to pledge loyalty to the Spanish crown. Although May 25 is observed throughout the country as Independence Day, or **Argentine National Day**, independence from Spain wasn't declared until July 9, 1816—an event that provoked a long series of civil wars in which rival political leaders fought for national control. Both days are national holidays and are observed with religious services at the cathedral and special performances at the Colón Theatre in Buenos Aires. The city's *Plaza de Mayo* (May Square) was named for the month in which independence was declared.

The Argentine flag is honored with a legal holiday on June 20, **Argentine Flag Day**.

CONTACT:
Argentina National Tourist Office
12 W. 56th St.
New York, NY 10019
212-603-0443; fax: 212-315-5545

SOURCES:
AnnivHol-1983, pp. 82, 91
Chases-1996, p. 227

♦ 0082 ♦ Argungu Fishing Festival
February

A fishing and NEW YEAR festival held along a sacred mile of the Sokoto River, a tributary of the Niger River, near Argungu in northwestern Nigeria. About 5,000 men from throughout Nigeria take part in the approximately 45 minutes of frenzied fishing. Using nets with calabashes (gourds) as floats, they can catch perch of up to 140 pounds. The largest perch are presented to the emirs, or rulers, who hold the festival.

CONTACT:
Nigerian Embassy
1333 16th St., N.W.
Washington, D.C. 20036
202-986-8400; fax: 202-775-1385

SOURCES:
BkHolWrld-1986, Feb 10

♦ 0083 ♦ Armed Forces Day in Egypt
October 6

An important national holiday in Egypt marking the surprise attack on Israel that began the October War of 1973 (also known as the YOM KIPPUR War). Egypt's ally in the war was Syria. The war ended with a cease-fire secured by the United States, and was declared a victory by Egyptian President Anwar Sadat. It strengthened his position and enabled him to seek an honorable peace with Israel. In 1974 and 1975, agreements were signed that paved the way for the return of the Sinai Peninsula to Egypt in April 1982; Israel had occupied the peninsula since the Six-Day War of 1967, in which Egypt had been crushed. In 1977 Sadat made his dramatic trip to Jerusalem to address the Israeli Knesset (Parliament); a year later, Sadat, Israeli Prime Minister Menachem Begin and United States President Jimmy Carter held talks at Camp David, Md., that led to the Israeli-Egyptian peace treaty of 1979.

The holiday is celebrated with grand parades, speeches by government officials, and fireworks. It was while reviewing a military parade on this day in 1981 that Anwar Sadat was assassinated by opponents of peace with Israel.

CONTACT:
Egyptian Tourist Authority
645 N. Michigan Ave., Ste. 829
Chicago, IL 60611
312-280-4666; fax: 312-280-4788

SOURCES:
Chases-1996, p. 408

♦ 0084 ♦ Armed Forces Day in the United States
Third Saturday in May

Before President Harry S. Truman proclaimed the third Saturday in May as Armed Forces Day in 1949, the three major branches of the United States armed forces—the Army, the Navy, and the Air Force—held elaborate celebrations on three different days during the year. Although the service units continue to celebrate their own days on April 6 (Army), October 27 (Navy), the second Saturday in September (Air Force), and November 10 (Marine Corps, part of the Navy), the purpose of Armed Forces Day is to promote the unification of the three branches under the Department of Defense (which took place in 1947) and to pay tribute to those serving in all the armed forces.

While commemorations of the individual service units are usually confined to military bases, the celebration of Armed Forces Day entails much broader participation. In addition to the huge parade held on this day each year in New York City, the armed forces often hold "open house" to acquaint the public with their facilities and to demonstrate some of the latest technological advances.

CONTACT:
American Forces Information
  Service
601 N. Fairfax St.
Carlough Plaza
Alexandria, VA 22314
703-274-4824

SOURCES:
AmerBkDays-1978, p. 454
AnnivHol-1983, p. 67
Chases-1996, p. 217
DaysCustFaith-1957, p. 137
DictDays-1988, p. 5

♦ 0085 ♦ Armenia Independence Day
September 23

On September 23, 1991, Armenia declared independence from the U.S.S.R.; it was granted independence on December 26 of that year, by which time the former Soviet Union had collapsed. Armenia had been part of the Soviet Union since the 1920s.

CONTACT:
Armenian Embassy
1660 L St., N.W., 11th Floor
Washington, D.C. 20036
202-628-5766; fax: 202-628-5769

Armenian Grape Festival
See **Blessing of the Grapes**

♦ 0086 ♦ Armenian Martyrs' Day
April 24

The day of remembrance for the one million Armenians who died in the Turkish massacre of 1915–16. On April 24, 1915, Turks arrested the Armenian political and intellectual leaders in Istanbul, killing 250 of them. That was the start of deportations, forced marches in the desert, rapes, and imprisonments that killed half the Armenian population in Turkey.

Armenian communities throughout the world observe this day. In the United States, many state governors issue proclamations of remembrance, and special programs, with speeches and prayers, are held in state capitals. There are also special services in Armenian churches.

SOURCES:
AnnivHol-1983, p. 56
Chases-1996, p. 183

Armistice Day
See **Veterans Day**

Arrival of the Tooth Relic
See **Esala Perahera**

Artistic Weeks of Budapest
See **Budapest Music Weeks**

♦ 0087 ♦ **Arts and Pageant of the Masters, Festival of**
July–August

A display of art works in arty Laguna Beach, Calif., along with breathtaking *tableaux vivants*—living pictures that recreate master art works. Since the 1940s, artists have created the tableaux to reproduce paintings by such varied masters as Leonardo da Vinci, Henri Matisse, and Winslow Homer. They don't stop there; they also transform delicate pieces of jewelry, sculptures, antique artifacts, and even scenes from postage stamps into life-size works of art. The tableaux, presented for two hours each evening at the Irvine Bowl, are created by some 300 models who have used 1,000 yards of fabric and 100 gallons of makeup. Example of a tableau: three gilded men and two gilded styrofoam horses appear in a setting that reproduces a five-inch Scythian gold comb.

CONTACT:
California Division of Tourism
801 K Street, Ste. 1600
Sacramento, CA 95814
800-862-2543 or 916-322-2881
fax: 916-322-3402

SOURCES:
GdUSFest-1984, p. 18

♦ 0088 ♦ **Asarah be-Tevet (Fast of the Tenth of Tevet)**
Between December 13 and January 10; Tevet 10

Asarah be-Tevet is a Jewish fast day commemorating the beginning of the siege of Jerusalem by the Babylonians under King Nebuchadnezzar in 586 B.C. that was a prelude to the destruction of the First Temple. The fast begins at first morning light on the 10th day of the Jewish month of Tevet.

In Israel it is also a day to remember the victims of the Holocaust. However, Jews outside Israel observe Yom ha-Shoah as HOLOCAUST DAY.

CONTACT:
Israel Ministry of Tourism
6380 Wilshire Blvd., Ste. 1700
Los Angeles, CA 90048
213-658-7462; fax: 213-658-6543

♦ 0089 ♦ **Ascension Day**
Between April 30 and June 3; forty days after Easter

Ascension Day is one of the earliest Christian festivals, dating back to the year 68. According to the New Testament, Jesus met several times with his disciples during the 40 days after his Resurrection to instruct them in how to carry out his teachings. Then on the 40th day he took them to the Mount of Olives, where they watched as he ascended to heaven.

Reflecting both Christian and pagan customs, Ascension Day celebrations include processions symbolizing Christ's entry into heaven and, in some countries, chasing a "devil" through the streets and dunking him in a pond or burning him in effigy—symbolic of the Messiah's triumph over the devil when he opened the kingdom of heaven to all believers.

Other customs attached to this day include "beating the bounds"—switching young boys with willow branches as they are driven along parish boundaries, not only to purify them of evil but to teach them the limits of their parish. This gave rise to the name **Bounds Thursday** in England, where it is also sometimes called **Holy Thursday**, though in the rest of the world that applies to MAUNDY THURSDAY.

In Germany it is sometimes called Father's Day because Protestant men have *herrenpartien*, 'outings,' on this day. In Sweden many people go out to the woods at three or four o'clock to hear the birds at sunrise. It is good luck if a cuckoo is heard from the east or west. These jaunts are called *gökotta*, or 'early cuckoo morning'.

See also BANNTAG

SOURCES:
AmerBkDays-1978, p. 422
BkFest-1937, p. 135
DaysCustFaith-1957, p. 135
DictFolkMyth-1984, pp. 49, 1156
DictWrldRel-1989, p. 65
FestSaintDays-1915, p. 113
FestWestEur-1958, pp. 64, 165, 215
FolkAmerHol-1991, p. 222
FolkWrldHol-1992, p. 280
RelHolCal-1993, p. 58

♦ 0090 ♦ **Ascension Day in Portugal**
Between April 30 and June 3; forty days after Easter

Also known as **Quinta-Feira da Espiga**, or **Ear of Wheat Thursday**, ASCENSION DAY in Portugal is associated with wishes for peace and prosperity. Traditionally, in rural communities, people make bouquets out of olive branches and sheaves of wheat with poppies and daisies. The olive and wheat are symbolic of an abundant harvest; the poppy stands for peace, and the daisy for money. A bit of wheat is usually kept in the house throughout the coming year as a symbol of prosperity. Another Ascension Day custom is to gather medicinal plants and herbs to be used later in the preparation of home remedies or magic spells.

SOURCES:
BkFest-1937, p. 268
FestWestEur-1958, p. 165

♦ 0091 ♦ **Asheville Mountain Dance and Folk Festival**
First Thursday, Friday, and Saturday in August

The oldest folk and dance festival in the country, held since 1928 in Asheville, N.C. Dedicated to traditional southern Appalachian music, it draws more than 400 performers: dulcimer sweepers, tune bow and mouth harp players, mountain fiddlers, and dancers who compete in smooth- and clog-dancing. Bluegrass and old-time bands also are on hand. ("Bluegrass" is not named for the Kentucky grass, but for the Blue Grass Boys, a band formed in 1938 by Bill Monroe, whose style of country popular music is still widely imitated; *see* BLUEGRASS FAN FEST).

Other events of the weekend include a quilt show and the

Gee Haw Whimmy Diddle World Competition at the Folk Art Center, which usually draws about 50 contestants. The whimmy diddle, an Appalachian whittled folk toy, is a notched wooden gadget with a propeller on one end; when a stick is rubbed across the notches, the propeller spins. The idea of the contest is to control the spin, to make the propeller gee (turn to the right) and haw (turn to the left). The winners of cash prizes are those who get their whimmy diddle to change the direction of rotation the most times. There is also a cash prize for the Most Unusual and World's Largest Whimmy Diddle.

CONTACT:
Asheville Area Convention and
  Visitors Bureau
P.O. Box 1010
Asheville, NC 28802
800-257-1300 or 704-258-6111

SOURCES:
Chases-1996, p. 318
MusFestAmer-1990, p. 226

♦ 0092 ♦ **Ashura**
First 10 days of Islamic month of Muharram

On the 10th of Muharram in the year 680, Muhammad's grandson Hussein (also spelled Husain) was killed in a skirmish between Sunnis and the small group of Shi'ite supporters with whom he was travelling to Iraq. They had been cut off from water and had suffered for 10 days before the men were killed and the women and children taken to Damascus, Syria, along with the heads of the men. His battlefield grave in Kerbela, about 60 miles southwest of Baghdad, became a pilgrimage site almost immediately, and to this day it remains a devotional center for Shi'ite Muslims around the world. Many aging Shi'ites settle in Kerbela or ask in their will to have their bodies carried to the holy city. So many dead have been sent to Kerbela that the town has been transformed into one vast burial ground.

This Islamic holy day, celebrated in the first month of the Islamic year, was derived by Muhammad from the Jewish fast of YOM KIPPUR; he later changed it to an optional fast day and it is so observed by modern-day Sunni Muslims. But for Shi'ites throughout Asia, the festival is dedicated to Hussein and begins on the first day of Muharram, when people put on their mourning clothes and refrain from shaving or bathing. The story of Hussein's martyrdom is recited in Muslim halls, with as much elaboration as possible. The celebration culminates on the 10th day of Muharram, in a large procession designed as a reenactment of Hussein's funeral, with many men whipping themselves bloody with whips and knives to take on the pain of Hussein. Since the early 19th century, the **Hussein Day** celebration has culminated in the performance of a *ta'ziyah*, or passion play, in which Hussein's life, death, and burial are recreated in a loose sequence of 40 to 50 scenes.

The Fatimid dynasty (969–1171) transferred Hussein's head to Cairo and built the Mosque of the Hasanain ('the two Hasans': Hasan and his brother, Hussein) over the relic. It is an especially holy place and is venerated also by Sunnis.

In India non-Shi'ites frequently take part in the processions, whereas in Iraq they would not be tolerated. Small replicas of Hussein's tomb, called *Ta ziyehs* (from the Arabic *aza*, meaning 'mourning'), are carried and buried in the local "Kerbela" grounds: India is so far from Kerbela, Iraq, that Indian Shi'ites consecrate local lands so they, too, may be buried in "Kerbela" grounds.

In Jamaica and Trinidad the festival is called HOSAY and is celebrated by Muslims and Hindus as a symbol of East Indian unity. In Guyana, it is called **Tadja** and is now celebrated by Afro- and Indo-Guyanese, after having been outlawed in the 1930s because of clashes between Muslims and Hindus when it coincided with DURGA PUJA.

In West Africa the holy day is combined with African beliefs, and ensuring prosperity is of uppermost importance: everyone eats as much as possible, inviting poor people to join them, because a full belly ensures prosperity. The Hausa give a fowl or goat's head to each member of the household, which they eat with their backs to each other. In Senegal, Guinea, and Sierra Leone, the dried head and feet of the ram killed at 'ID AL-ADHA are cooked and eaten. Symbolic bathing in rivers and purification by leaping over small fires are followed by torchlight parades and contests.

In Turkey, the 10th of Muharram is called **Yevmi Ashurer**, 'day of sweet soup or porridge' and commemorates Noah's departure from the Ark onto Mount Ararat. They must share Allah's gifts with others, so everyone makes *ashurer*, which is a sweet soup or porridge made of boiled wheat, dried currants, grain, and nuts, similar to that supposedly made by Noah and stored in the bins of the Ark. Each person is assigned a day to invite his neighbors to come and share it.

SOURCES:
AnnivHol-1983, p. 170
BkFest-1937, p. 237
Chases-1996, p. 232
FolkWrldHol-1992, pp. 369,
  370
MuhFest-1988, pp. 51, 86
RelHolCal-1993, p. 59

♦ 0093 ♦ **Ash Wednesday**
Between February 4 and March 10

The first day of LENT in the West. For 14 centuries the season of Lent has been a time for self-examination and penitence in preparation for EASTER. The name comes from the Saxon *lengten-tide*, referring to the lengthening of the days and the coming of spring. This 40-day period of abstinence recalls the fasts of Moses, Elijah, and Jesus, all of which—according to scripture—lasted 40 days. It was originally begun in the Western Church on a Sunday. But since Sundays were feast days, in the latter part of the sixth century Pope Gregory I moved the beginning of Lent ahead four days.

Gregory is also credited with having introduced the ceremony that gives this day its name. When public penitents came to the church for forgiveness, the priest would take some ash (made by burning the palms used on PALM SUNDAY of the previous year) and mark their foreheads with the sign of the cross as a reminder that they were but ashes and dust. Eventually the practice was extended to include all who wished to receive ashes.

In the East, ashes are not used, and Lent begins on the Monday before Ash Wednesday.

On Ash Wednesday in Iceland, children try to hook small bags of ashes or stones to the back of people's clothing.

See also SHROVE TUESDAY

SOURCES:
AmerBkDays-1978, p. 162
BkDays-1864, vol. I, p. 240

BkFest-1937, p. 299
DaysCustFaith-1957, p. 64
DictFolkMyth-1984, pp. 82, 535
FestWestEur-1958, p. 194
FolkAmerHol-1991, p. 101
FolkWrldHol-1992, p. 120
RelHolCal-1993, p. 58
SaintFestCh-1904, p. 115

♦ 0094 ♦ Aspen Music Festival
Late June to late August

One of the finest and most important musical events in the United States, this event was founded in 1949 in Aspen in the Colorado Rocky Mountains. Symphonic orchestra and chamber-music concerts are staged in the white-tented amphitheater designed by Finnish-born architect Eero Saarinen, and smaller presentations in a renovated opera house and a church. Programs range from baroque to modern. Each season new compositions are introduced by "composers in residence"; Virgil Thomson and Aaron Copland have been among them. A school of music operates along with the festival and has an enrollment of more than 900 students.

Aspen was a wealthy silver-mining town in the 1880s, but lost its glitter when silver prices collapsed in the 1890s. Its rebirth began in the late 1930s, largely because of the enterprise of Chicago industrialist Walter Paepcke, who thought Aspen would be suitable for a Platonic community. It is now a popular though pricey skiing resort.

CONTACT:
Colorado Office of Tourism and
 Travel
1625 Broadway, Ste. 1700
Denver, CO 80202
800-592-1939; fax: 303-592-5510

SOURCES:
Chases-1996, p. 260
GdUSFest-1984, p. 23
MusFestAmer-1990, p. 42
MusFestWrld-1963, p. 277

♦ 0095 ♦ Assumption of the Blessed Virgin Mary, Feast of the
August 15

Assumption Day, called the **Dormition of the Most Holy Mother of God** in the East, commemorates the belief that when Mary, the mother of Jesus, died, her body was not subjected to the usual process of physical decay but was "assumed" into heaven and reunited there with her soul. Like the IMMACULATE CONCEPTION, the Assumption wasn't always an official dogma of the Roman Catholic Church—not until Pope Pius XII ruled it so in 1950. It is, however, a pious belief held by most Orthodox Christians and some Anglicans. It is regarded as the principal feast day of the Virgin Mother.

This festival may be a Christianization of an earlier Artemis harvest feast, and in some parts of Europe it is still called the **Feast of Our Lady of the Harvest**. The people of Queven, France, actually reenact the Assumption by lowering a wooden angel from the tower of the church and then making her rise again toward "heaven." In Elche, Spain, a two-day enactment of the apocryphal Gospels is performed each year. It is the national holiday of the Acadians in the Maritime Provinces of Canada, and is called *tinta marre* (meaning 'a racket'). At 6 P.M. on the 15th, pots and pans are banged, whistles blown, and drums beaten. On the nearest Sunday, all boats are decorated and sail past the dock where the priest blesses the fleet. Messina, Sicily, celebrates with a two-week festival

including a human tableau of the Assumption and giant figures believed to symbolize the mythical founders of the city, Zancleo and his wife. The girl who portrays the Madonna is allowed to pardon one criminal.

In São Paulo and other parts of southern Brazil, the feast is called **Nosa Senhora dos Navegantes**, or 'Our Lady of the Navigators'. Pageants are held on decorated canoes, each carrying a captain, a purser, three musicians, and two rowers. They travel to small villages to entertain and feast. Towns may have a church procession with musicians whose costumes and demeanors depict the Three Wise Men.

See also BLESSING OF THE GRAPES

SOURCES:
AmerBkDays-1978, p. 755
BkFest-1937, p. 172
DaysCustFaith-1957, p. 206
DictFolkMyth-1984, pp. 886, 1065
FestSaintDays-1915, p. 169
FestWestEur-1958, pp. 15, 47, 184, 203
FolkAmerHol-1991, p. 309
FolkWrldHol-1992, pp. 270, 419
IndianAmer-1989, pp. 288, 321
RelHolCal-1993, p. 59

♦ 0096 ♦ Assumption of the Virgin Mary, Feast of the, in Hasselt, Belgium
Third and fourth Sundays in August, every seven years

In Hasselt, the capital of the Belgian province of Limburg, the festival known as **Virge Jesse** (Virgin of the Line of Jesse) is celebrated every seven years on the third and fourth Sundays in August. According to tradition, the image of the Virgin once stood in a tree at the crossroads near the present-day site of Hasselt. Travelers left offerings at this shrine and prayed for a safe journey. By the 14th century, reports of the image's miraculous powers had spread, and pilgrims began journeying from far away to worship at the shrine.

Today, an ancient image of the Virgin, which the townspeople claim is the same one that once stood in the tree at the crossroads, is clothed in a velvet mantle and carried in a procession through the town, passing under a series of arches commemorating important episodes in Hasselt's history.

CONTACT:
Belgian Tourist Office
780 Third Ave.
New York, NY 10017
212-758-8130; fax: 212-355-7675

SOURCES:
BkFest-1937, p. 46
FestWestEur-1958, p. 15

♦ 0097 ♦ Assumption of the Virgin Mary, Feast of the, in Italy
August 15

Colorful processions through the streets and displays of fireworks mark the celebration of the Feast of the Assumption in Italy, as they do in Italian-American communities throughout the United States. In Sicily and rural areas outside of Rome, a **Bowing Procession** is the day's main event. A statue of the Virgin Mary is carried through the town to a ceremonial arch of flowers, where a group of people holding a statue of Christ awaits her arrival. Both statues are inclined toward each other three times, and then the Christ figure precedes that of Mary back to the parish church for a special benediction. The journey to the arch symbolizes Mary's sojourn on earth, the arch itself represents the gate of heaven, and the trip back to the church represents her entrance into heaven.

CONTACT:
Italian Government Travel Office
630 Fifth Ave.
New York, NY 10111
212-245-4822

SOURCES:
AmerBkDays-1978, p. 756
DaysCustFaith-1957, p. 207

♦ 0098 ♦ Aston Magna Festival
Early July, three consecutive Saturday evenings

The oldest summer festival in the United States devoted to music performed on period instruments, the Aston Magna Festival takes place in Great Barrington, Massachusetts, just 10 miles from the well-known BERKSHIRE MUSIC FESTIVAL at Tanglewood. The festival is an outgrowth of the Aston Magna Foundation for Music, which was founded in 1972 by Lee Elman and the well-known harpsichordist Albert Fuller to study the music of the 17th and 18th centuries. For three consecutive Saturday evenings in July the works of BACH, MOZART, Haydn, Gluck, and other composers are performed on original instruments, using the techniques, tuning, and pitch of the baroque period.

The complete Bach Brandenburg Concertos were first performed in the United States at this festival, as were the first Mozart symphonies played on original instruments. The concerts are held in Great Barrington's St. James Church.

CONTACT:
Massachusetts Office of Travel
and Tourism
100 Cambridge St., 13th Floor
Boston, MA 02202
800-447-6277 or 617-727-3201
fax: 617-727-6525

SOURCES:
MusFestAmer-1990, p. 73

♦ 0099 ♦ Athens Festival
End of June through September

The ancient ruins of the Acropolis in Athens form the backdrop for a huge music, dance, and theater festival that goes on every summer. Performances are presented in the Herod Atticus Odeon, a Roman-style open-air theater that seats 6,000. Since 1955 orchestral and chamber music, classical and popular theater, opera, ballet, and modern dance have been performed there by both Greek and international artists, among them the Paris Symphony Orchestra, the Kirov Opera, the Peking Opera, the Alvin Ailey American Dance Theater, the English Bach Festival, the National Theater of Greece, the Old Vic Company, and the Bolshoi Ballet.

One of the festival's major attractions is the setting. The Herod Atticus Odeon, built in A.D. 161 by one of the city's most famous rhetoricians and philanthropists in memory of his wife, offers a breathtaking view of the Parthenon. Made of brick and stone set in concrete and built into a hillside, the original theater has been damaged by fire and war over the years but was reconstructed after World War II to its present state.

CONTACT:
Greek National Tourist
Organization
645 Fifth Ave.
New York, NY 10022
212-421-5777; fax: 212-826-6940

SOURCES:
GdWrldFest-1985, p. 101
IntlThFolk-1979, p. 192
MusFestEurBrit-1980, p. 107
MusFestWrld-1963, p. 231

♦ 0100 ♦ Ati-Atihan Festival
Third weekend in January

One of the most colorful festivals in the Philippines, held in Kalibo, the capital city of the province of Aklan. Originally falling on the Feast Day of Santo Niño (the infant Jesus), the celebration combines Christian and pre-Christian elements.

Its origins are in the 13th century, when 10 families fled Borneo and landed on the Philippine island of Panay. There the resident Ati people gave them land. The Ati (also called Negritos or Pygmies) were small dark people, and after receiving the land, the story goes, the Malayan people blackened their faces to look like the Ati. Years later, the Spanish Christians, having converted much of the country, persuaded the inhabitants to darken their skin, wear warlike clothing, and pretend they were Ati to frighten away the Muslims. They were victorious over the Muslims, and attributed their victory to Santo Niño. At that time, religion came into the festival.

Ati-Atihan means 'to make like Atis.' During the present-day festival, revelers cover their skin with soot and wear Ati costumes that are patchworks of coconut shells, feathers, and fronds. They converge on the main streets and around the town plaza and, to the beat of drums, shout "Hala Bira" ('Go on and fight!'), pound their spears, and repeatedly dance a two-step dance. From a distance, the celebrants look like a solid mass of people lurching and swinging in a frenzied rhythm.

See also DINAGYANG and SINULOG

CONTACT:
Philippine Department of Tourism
556 Fifth Ave.
First Floor Mezzanine
New York, NY 10036
212-575-7915; fax: 212-302-6759

SOURCES:
Chases-1996, p. 71
GdWrldFest-1985, p. 152
IntlThFolk-1979, p. 288

Atomic Bomb Day
See **Hiroshima Peace Ceremony**

♦ 0101 ♦ Audubon Day
April 26

John James Audubon (1785–1851) was America's foremost ornithological illustrator. After studying drawing in Paris under the French painter Jacques Louis David, Audubon struggled for many years to make a living from his art, shuttling back and forth between Europe and the United States and supplementing his income by giving drawing lessons, turning out portraits, playing the flute or violin at local dances, and at one time running a general store. In 1820 he began a flatboat excursion down the Mississippi River to seek out new varieties of birds to paint. Eventually he had enough bird portraits to publish in book form. *Birds of America*, produced with the help of the engraver Robert Havell, Jr., contains 435 hand-colored plates and was published in "elephant folio" format to accommodate the life-sized portrayals of birds on which Audubon insisted.

After his death in 1851, Audubon's wife Lucy returned to teaching to support herself. One of her students, George Bird Grinnell, became the editor of *Forest and Stream* magazine and in 1886 organized the Audubon Society for the study and protection of birds. Today there are many branches of this organization, known as the National Audubon Society, and it remains dedicated to the conservation of wildlife and natural resources. Its members honor Audubon on his birthday, April 26. In some states, Audubon Day and ARBOR DAY are celebrated together by planting trees in bird sanctuaries.

CONTACT:
National Audubon Society
700 Broadway
New York, NY 10003
212-979-3000; fax: 212-353-0508

SOURCES:
AmerBkDays-1978, p. 380
AnnivHol-1983, p. 57
BkFestHolWrld-1970, p. 93
Chases-1996, p. 185

♦ 0102 ♦ Australia Day
January 26 or following Monday

The anniversary of the first British settlement in Australia on January 26, 1788, was formerly known as **Foundation Day** or **Anniversary Day**. Captain Arthur Phillip and his company of British convicts arrived first at Botany Bay, and when that proved to be an unsuitable location they moved on to Port Jackson, where the city of Sydney was eventually established. They built a penal colony there to help relieve overcrowding in the British prisons.

First celebrated in Sydney in 1817, Australia Day has been a public holiday since 1838. It is usually observed on January 26 or the first Monday thereafter.

CONTACT:
Australian Tourist Commission
100 Park Ave., 25th Floor
New York, NY 10017
212-687-6300; fax: 212-661-3340

SOURCES:
AnnivHol-1983, p. 14
Chases-1996, pp. 76, 78
DictDays-1988, p. 7
IntlThFolk-1979, p. 11
NatlHolWrld-1968, p. 16

♦ 0103 ♦ Australian Open Tennis
January

The year's first event in the Grand Slam of tennis, followed by the FRENCH OPEN, the UNITED STATES OPEN, and WIMBLEDON. It is played on synthetic hard courts at Sydney, Australia, and Melbourne, Australia, and known officially as the **Australian Championships.** Tennis took root in Australia in 1880 at the Melbourne Cricket Club. The championship for men began in 1905, and the women's championship in 1922. The matches became an "open" (to both amateurs and professionals) in 1969.

Margaret Smith Court, an Australian known for her powerful serve and volley, is the all-time champion in the women's division of the open; she won the title 11 times between 1960 and 1973. In 1970, she was the second woman to win the Grand Slam; Maureen Connolly had swept the four tournaments in 1953, and Steffi Graf won all four in 1988.

Top multiple winners in the men's division of the Australian Open have been Roy Emerson, who took six titles (1961 and 1962–67); Jack Crawford, Ken Rosewall, and Pat Wood, who each won four; and Rod Laver, Adrian Quist, and Mats Wilander, who each won three.

In 1990, for the first time in Open Grand Slam history, the eight singles titles for men and women were won by eight different players.

CONTACT:
Australian Tourist Commission
100 Park Ave., 25th Floor
New York, NY 10017
212-687-6300; fax: 212-661-3340

♦ 0104 ♦ Austria National Day
October 26

National Day commemorates the day in 1955 when Soviet occupation forces left Austria, after taking control in 1945. The Austrian State Treaty of May 15, 1955, ensured that Austrians would regain sovereignty over their country on July 27. By October 26, it was once again a free, independent country.

Though a national holiday in Austria, people do not get the day off from school or work, mainly because of the idea that one's country is best served by working. Schools hold special presentations, and the president delivers a speech.

SOURCES:
Chases-1996, p. 430

♦ 0105 ♦ Author's Day, National
November 1

The idea of setting aside a day to celebrate American authors came from Nellie Verne Burt McPherson, president of the Bement (Illinois) Women's Club in 1928. McPherson was a teacher and an avid reader throughout her life. During World War I, when she was recuperating in a hospital, she wrote a fan letter to fiction writer Irving Bacheller, telling him how much she had enjoyed his story, "Eben Holden's Last Day A'Fishin." Bacheller sent her an autographed copy of another story, and McPherson realized that she could never adequately thank him for his gift. Instead, she showed her appreciation by submitting an idea for a National Author's Day to the General Federation of Women's Clubs, which passed a resolution setting aside November 1 as a day to honor American writers. In 1949 the day was recognized by the U.S. Department of Commerce.

Sue Cole, McPherson's granddaughter, has been largely responsible for promoting the observation of National Author's Day since her grandmother's death in 1968. She urges people to write a note to their favorite author on this day to "brighten up the sometimes lonely business of being a writer." Flying the American flag on November 1, according to Mrs. Cole, is another way of showing appreciation of the men and women who have made American literature possible.

CONTACT:
Mrs. Sue Cole
191 W. Cole St.
Macon, IL 62544

SOURCES:
Chases-1996, p. 437

♦ 0106 ♦ Autumnal Equinox
September 22–23

The sun crosses the plane of the earth's equator twice a year: on or about March 21 (*see* VERNAL EQUINOX) and again six months later, on or about September 23. On these two occasions, night and day are of equal length all over the world. In the Northern Hemisphere, September 22 is the first day of autumn.

Autumnal Equinox Day, or **Shubun-no-Hi**, is a national holiday in Japan, observed on either September 23 or 24 to celebrate the arrival of autumn and to honor family ancestors.

> **SOURCES:**
> *AmerBkDays-1978*, p. 859
> *BkDays-1864*, vol. II, p. 364
> *Chases-1996*, p. 387
> *DictDays-1988*, p. 37
> *FolkWrldHol-1992*, p. 487

♦ 0107 ♦ Avani Mulam
August or September

According to Hindu mythology, the god Indra showed his displeasure with the king of Madura by sending a drought, during which the river completely dried up. When a sudden, heavy rainfall threatened to flood the river's banks, the king ordered everyone in Madura to help build a dam to conserve the precious water. The portion of the dam assigned to one old woman was never completed, because she was too busy cooking for the other hungry laborers. One of the workmen who came to her for food was actually the god Sundara, who saved the dam from leaking by throwing a small handful of earth in the gap left by the old woman.

Although Avani Mulam is observed throughout India, the grandest celebration is in Madura, where an image of Sundara, with a golden basket and a golden spade, is carried in a procession from the river to the temple.

CONTACT:
India Tourist Office
30 Rockefeller Ave.
15 N. Mezzanine
New York, NY 10112
212-586-4901; fax: 212-582-3274

SOURCES:
BkFestHolWrld-1970, p. 107

♦ 0108 ♦ Aviation Day
August 19

National Aviation Day honors the birthday of the American inventor and early manufacturer of airplanes, Orville Wright (1871–1948), as well as the progress that has been made in manned flight since the Wright Brothers made their historic 120-foot flight at Kitty Hawk, North Carolina, in 1903 (*see* Wright Brothers' Day). President Franklin D. Roosevelt proclaimed August 19 as Aviation Day in 1939, and since that time celebrations have been sponsored in a number of states by organizations involved in aviation. Parachute jumping, glider demonstrations, films, airplane rides, and displays of new and antique aircraft are popular events on this day, and open house celebrations are often held at local airports. One of the more impressive observations of Aviation Day occurs when military aircraft fly in formation, often at lower-than-usual altitudes, over airports or other locations where celebrations are being held.

CONTACT:
International Council of Air Shows
1931 Horton Rd., Ste. 5
Jackson, MI 49203
517-782-2424; fax: 517-782-5886

SOURCES:
AmerBkDays-1978, p. 766
AnnivHol-1983, p. 108
Chases-1996, p. 343

Awa Odori
See Obon Festival

♦ 0109 ♦ Awoojoh
Various

A thanksgiving feast in the West African nation of Sierra Leone, the Awoojoh honors the spirits of the dead, who are believed to have influence over the fortunes of the living. It may be held at any time of year, and the guests include not only friends and relatives but, in a small community, the entire village. The day begins with a family visit to the cemetery, where a libation is poured over the relatives' graves and the dead are invited to join in the thanksgiving celebration. Two kola nuts, one red and one white, are split in half and thrown upon the grave, and the pattern in which they fall is believed to carry a message from the ancestors. It is essential for all family quarrels to be settled before the feast begins.

Many popular African dishes—such as fried bean cakes, fried plantains, rice bread, and "Awoojoh beans"—are served, but the highlight of the meal is an elaborate stew, a portion of which is set out for the dead ancestors or thrown to the vultures, who are believed to embody the souls of the departed. Although the practice of holding a thanksgiving feast originated with the Yoruba, who came to Sierra Leone from Nigeria, Christians and Muslims give them as well.

SOURCES:
FolkWrldHol-1992, p. 466

♦ 0110 ♦ Awuru Odo Festival
Biannually in April

Among the Igbo people of Nigeria, the Odo are the spirits of the dead, who return to the earth to visit their families every two years. They arrive sometime between September and November (*see* Odo Festival) and depart in April. Before they leave, there is a big theatrical performance known as the Awuru Odo in which masked players, representing the Odo spirits, reenact the story of their visit to the living and the agony of their departure. The performance takes place on a ritual stage in the market square.

Because the Odo festival occurs only once every two years, elaborate preparations are made to welcome the returning spirits. The masks used in the performance are refurbished or new ones are made. Fences are put up around the shrines where the Odo will worship. Many of these preparations are carried out in secrecy by the men, while the women, who are totally excluded from and can have no knowledge of the activities, are responsible for providing enough food for the celebration.

SOURCES:
FolkWrldHol-1992, pp. 218, 575

♦ 0111 ♦ Ayyam-i-Ha
February 25–March 1

Also known as **Days of Ha**, these are intercalary days (extra days inserted in a calendar) in the Baha'i calendar. The calendar is made up of 19 months of 19 days each (361 days), plus the period of four days (five in leap years) of Ayyam-i-Ha added between the 18th and 19th months, which allows for the year to be adjusted to the solar cycle. The days are set aside for rejoicing, hospitality, gift-giving, special acts of charity, and spiritually preparing for the Baha'i fast, from March 2–20. March 21 is New Year's Day, NAWRUZ, and the first day of the Baha'i calendar.

The new calendar was inaugurated by Mirza Ali Mohammad, known as the Bab, founder of the Babi religion from which the Baha'i faith emerged. Baha'is believe that the new age of unity they foresee should have a new calendar free of the associations of the older calendars.

The Baha'i observe nine days on which work connected with trade, commerce, industry, and agriculture should be suspended. These days are the first, ninth, and 12th days of the Feast of RIDVAN, Nawruz, the anniversaries of the Bab's birth, declaration, and martyrdom, and the birth and ascension of Baha'u'llah.

See also BAB, BIRTH OF THE; BAB, DECLARATION OF THE; BAB, MARTYRDOM OF THE; BAHA'U'LLAH, BIRTH OF; and BAHA'U'LLAH, ASCENSION OF

CONTACT:
Baha'is of the U.S.
Office of Public Information
866 United Nations Plaza, Ste. 120
New York, NY 10017-1822
212-803-2500; fax: 212-803-2573

SOURCES:
AnnivHol-1983, p. 29
RelHolCal-1993, p. 60

♦ 0112 ♦ **Azerbaijan Independence Days**
May 28; October 18

Azerbaijan observes two independence days. The May 28, 1918, establishment of the Democratic Republic of Azerbaijan provides the occasion for the older independence celebration. Two years later, Azerbaijan came under Soviet rule. By 1991, the growing perestroika (social and economic reform) movement in the former U.S.S.R. created the opportunity for Soviet republics to break free, which, one by one, they proceeded to do. Azerbaijan declared its intention to once again become an independent nation on August 30, 1991. Azerbaijan's new independence day commemorates the declaration of independence made by the Supreme Soviet of Azerbaijan on October 18, 1991. After the U.S.S.R. ceased to exist as a geopolitical entity in December 1991 (which became official on January 1, 1992), Azerbaijan became an official independent state on December 26, 1991.

CONTACT:
Azerbaijan Embassy
927 15th St., N.W.
Washington, D.C. 20005
202-842-0001; fax: 202-842-0004

SOURCES:
Chases-1996, p. 232

B

♦ 0113 ♦ Bab, Birth of the
October 20

A holy day in the Baha'i religion to celebrate the birthday in 1819 or 1820 of Mirza Ali Mohammad in Shiraz, Persia (now Iran). In 1844, Mirza Ali declared himself the Bab (meaning 'gate') and foretold the coming of one greater than he. The day, on which work is suspended, is a happy social occasion for Baha'is.

See also BAB, DECLARATION OF THE

CONTACT:
Baha'is of the U.S.
Office of Public Information
866 United Nations Plaza, Ste. 120
New York, NY 10017-1822
212-803-2500; fax: 212-803-2573

SOURCES:
AnnivHol-1983, p. 134
Chases-1996, p. 424
DictWrldRel-1989, pp. 86, 87
RelHolCal-1993, p. 62

♦ 0114 ♦ Bab, Declaration of the
May 23

A joyous Baha'i festival to celebrate the Bab's announcement in 1844 in Shiraz, Persia (now Iran), that he was the ''gate'' (which is the meaning of *Bab*) to the coming of the promised one of all religions. This proclamation is considered the beginning of the Baha'i faith, although the religion was founded after the Bab's death.

The Bab, who was born Mirza Ali Mohammad, founded an independent religion known as the Babi faith which grew out of Shi'ite Islam. At the time of this proclamation, the Bab also announced that it was his mission to herald a prophet who would be greater than he (paralleling St. John the Baptist as the forerunner of Jesus; *see* ST. JOHN'S DAY). After his proclamation, the Bab assembled 18 disciples.

This day is holy to Baha'is and a day on which work is suspended. Its observation begins at about two hours after sunset.

CONTACT:
Baha'is of the U.S.
Office of Public Information
866 United Nations Plaza, Ste. 120
New York, NY 10017-1822
212-803-2500; fax: 212-803-2573

SOURCES:
AnnivHol-1983, p. 60
Chases-1996, p. 223
DictWrldRel-1989, pp. 86, 87
RelHolCal-1993, p. 71

♦ 0115 ♦ Bab, Martyrdom of the
July 9

A solemn commemoration of the day in 1850 when the Bab, the first prophet of the Baha'i faith, was executed in Tabriz, Persia (now Iran). Prayers and readings mark the Baha'i holy day, and work is suspended.

After founding the Babi, a new religion growing out of Shi'ite Islam in 1844, the Bab was repeatedly exiled and imprisoned by Muslim rulers and priests who opposed the idea that the Bab would provide another avenue to the truth. They saw the Babis as revolutionaries and heterodox despoilers. A committee of priests demanded the Bab's execution, and he was led to the town square and tied to a post in front of 750 riflemen. The Baha'i's say that shots were fired, but they only severed the ropes binding him. When the smoke cleared, the Bab was found in his cell completing the work he had been doing before the volley of shots—dictating holy words to a scribe. He was taken before a second regiment of riflemen, and this time he was killed. His body was disposed of in a ditch, but was retrieved by his followers and eventually placed in a mausoleum on Mt. Carmel in Haifa, Israel, where the Baha'i headquarters is today.

CONTACT:
Baha'is of the U.S.
Office of Public Information
866 United Nations Plaza, Ste. 120
New York, NY 10017-1822
212-803-2500; fax: 212-803-2573

SOURCES:
AnnivHol-1983, p. 91
Chases-1996, p. 289
DictWrldRel-1989, pp. 86, 87
RelHolCal-1993, p. 71

♦ 0116 ♦ Babin Den
January 20

In Bulgaria the old women who helped deliver babies—much like the modern midwife—were called *baba*, or grandmother. It was widely believed that the baby received some of the *baba's* wisdom, and it was customary for the baby's parents to bring the *baba* flowers on a particular day each year, called **Grandmother's Day** or **Day of the Midwives**. Eventually the children grew up, but they would continue to visit their *baba* each year.

Most babies in Bulgaria today are born in hospitals, so the children bring flowers to the doctors and nurses who assisted at their birth. Another traditional activity on this day involves boys dunking girls in the icy waters of rivers and lakes, supposedly to bring them good health in the coming year.

See also GRANDPARENTS' DAY

SOURCES:
AnnivHol-1983, p. 12
BkFest-1937, p. 66
BkHolWrld-1986, Jan 20
Chases-1996, p. 74

◆ 0117 ◆ **Baby Parade**
Second Thursday in August

Started in 1901 by Leo Bamberger, founder of New Jersey's Bamberger's Department Store chain, the Baby Parade that takes place along the boardwalk at the seaside resort of Ocean City on the second Thursday in August each year allows children up to the age of 10 to participate and compete for prizes. There are four different divisions: Division A is for children in decorated strollers, go-carts, wagons, etc., and is further divided into three sections according to the age of the child; Division B features children in comically decorated vehicles, as well as walkers; Division C is for floats; and Division D is for larger commercial and noncommercial floats. The children are reviewed by the judges as they walk or wheel along the boardwalk from Sixth Street to Twelfth Street, and every child who enters receives a sterling silver identification bracelet. Cash prizes are given to the best entry in each division. More than 50,000 spectators are drawn to the **Ocean City Baby Parade** each year. Similar baby parades are held in August in Avalon, Sea Isle City, and Wildwood.

CONTACT:
New Jersey Division of Travel and Tourism
20 W. State St.
Trenton, NJ 08625
800-537-7397 or 609-292-2470
fax: 609-633-7418

SOURCES:
Chases-1996, p. 328
GdUSFest-1984, p. 118

Bacchanalia
See **Dionysia**

Bachelors' Day
See **Leap Year Day**

◆ 0118 ◆ **Bach Festival**
Biennially in late July for 10 days

Although the Bavarian city of Ansbach, Germany, has no particular connection to Johann Sebastian Bach, it has been the site of a biennial Bach Festival since 1947. The **Bachwoche Ansbach** festival is unique in that only music by Bach (or occasionally one of his family members) is played, and only on authentic instruments from Bach's time, such as the 1776 fortepiano. Even the concerts are held in buildings that were standing during Bach's lifetime, such as the 15th-century St. Gumbertus Church with its fine baroque organ.

Bach's motets, cantatas, organ, and orchestral works are performed in Ansbach by some of the world's best instrumental artists and ensembles. The audience can experience not only the music but the fine acoustics and period architecture of the historic sites where the festival is held. The Palace

of Carl Wilhelm Friedrich, for example, allows 500 festivalgoers to listen to Bach in its rococo-style ballroom.

CONTACT:
German National Tourist Office
122 E. 42nd St., 52nd Floor
New York, NY 10168
212-661-7200; fax: 212-661-7174

SOURCES:
MusFestEurBrit-1980, p. 95

◆ 0119 ◆ **Bach Festival, International**
June

Started in 1979 as an event that would draw tourists to Madeira Island in the Azores, Portugal, during its off-season, the International Bach Festival at Funchal now attracts world-class performers, conductors, ensembles, and soloists as well as thousands of visitors. The concerts are held in the town's 15th-century Se Cathedral and in its Municipal Theater. Although past festivals have focused primarily on the works of Johann Sebastian Bach, it has since expanded to include pieces by MOZART, Telemann, Vivaldi, Haydn, and other composers.

CONTACT:
Portuguese National Tourist Office
590 Fifth Ave., 4th Floor
New York, NY 10036
212-354-4403; fax: 212-764-6137

SOURCES:
GdWrldFest-1985, p. 155

◆ 0120 ◆ **Bachok Cultural Festival**
May

This two-week cultural festival held in Bachok, Kelantan, Malaysia, features traditional Menora and Ma'yong dance-drama troupes, who often perform on the beach. In addition to giant top-spinning and kiteflying competitions, the festival includes *wayang kulit*, or shadow plays, which are not normally seen in public but are performed privately at weddings, anniversaries, and other important celebrations. A puppeteer called *To'Dalang* (Father of the Mysteries) manipulates the puppets from inside an enclosed bamboo stage, and then their shadows are cast upon a screen in front of the audience. Most of the shadow plays are based upon either the *Ramayana* or *Mahabharata* epics from India. The plays are accompanied by a small band of five or six players with drums, a gong, a flageolet (a small, end-blown flute), and sometimes a Malay violin.

CONTACT:
Malaysian Tourism Promotion Board
818 W. Seventh St., Ste. 804
Los Angeles, CA 90017
213-689-9702; fax: 213-689-1530

SOURCES:
GdWrldFest-1985, p. 131
IntlThFolk-1979, p. 266

◆ 0121 ◆ **Bad Durkheim Wurstmarkt (Sausage Fair)**
Saturday to Tuesday of second weekend of September; Friday to Monday of third weekend of September

Germany's biggest wine festival, held in Bad Durkheim. The name is said to have originated about 150 years ago because of the immense amounts of sausage consumed. Today there are about 40 wheelbarrow stands selling sausage and also chicken and shish-kebab. The religious origins of the feast are traced to 1417, when the villagers sold sausages, wine, and bread from wheelbarrows to pilgrims going to Michelsberg (St. Michael's hill) on MICHAELMAS (St. Michael's Day).

The opening day of the festival features a concert and a procession of bands, vineyard proprietors, and tapsters of the tavern stalls with decorated wine floats. The official opening is conducted by the mayor of Bad Durkheim and the German Wine Queen, and is followed by the tapping of the first cask. The following days are a medley of fireworks, band playing, dancing, and singing through the night. At the three dozen or so tavern stalls, wine is served in glasses called *Schoppen* that hold about a pint. Before the festival is over, some half a million people will have drunk more than 400,000 Schoppen.

From July through late October, there are numerous other wine festivals, mainly in the villages of the Rhine and Moselle valleys. Among them are Rudesheim, Bernkastel-Kues, St. Goarshausen, Boppard, and Neustadt.

CONTACT:
German National Tourist Office
122 E. 42nd St., 52nd Floor
New York, NY 10168
212-661-7200; fax: 212-661-7174

♦ 0122 ♦ Bahamas Emancipation Day
First Monday in August

The English settled in the Bahamas during the mid-17th century, and brought African slaves with them to work in the cotton fields. Slavery was formally abolished in the British Empire by the Abolition Act of 1833, but it wasn't until 1838 that the slaves in the Bahamas were freed.

Emancipation Day in the Bahamas is observed on the first Monday in August. Businesses are closed, and a regatta is held at Black Point, near Staniel Cay, in the Exuma island group.

See also FOX HILL DAY

CONTACT:
Bahamas Tourist Office
150 E. 52nd St., 28th Floor N.
New York, NY 10022
800-422-4262 or 212-758-2777
fax: 212-753-6531

SOURCES:
AnnivHol-1983, p. 101
Chases-1996, p. 325

♦ 0123 ♦ Bahamas Independence Day
July 10

The Bahama Islands gained independence from Great Britain at 12:01 A.M. on this day in 1973. The islands had been a British colony for nearly 250 years, but are now a commonwealth, with their own prime minister and parliament.

Businesses are closed on the tenth, a legal holiday, but festivities go on for a week with parades and celebrations. A fireworks display at Clifford Park on July 10 tops off the week.

CONTACT:
Bahamas Tourist Office
150 E. 52nd St., 28th Floor N.
New York, NY 10022
800-422-4262 or 212-758-2777
fax: 212-753-6531

SOURCES:
AnnivHol-1983, p. 91
Chases-1996, p. 290

♦ 0124 ♦ Baha'u'llah, Ascension of
May 29

The anniversary of the death in 1892 of Mirza Husayn Ali, known as Baha'u'llah, founder of the Baha'i religion. "Ascension" is not meant literally, but is considered the ascension of the spirit. The day is one of nine Baha'i holy days on which work is suspended. It is observed by gathering together at 3:00 A.M., the time of Baha'u'llah's death in Acre, Palestine (now Israel), for prayers and sometimes readings from Baha'i historical works.

CONTACT:
Baha'is of the U.S.
Office of Public Information
866 United Nations Plaza, Ste. 120
New York, NY 10017-1822
212-803-2500; fax: 212-803-2573

SOURCES:
AnnivHol-1983, p. 72
Chases-1996, p. 233
RelHolCal-1993, p. 58

♦ 0125 ♦ Baha'u'llah, Birth of
November 12

The anniversary of the birth in 1817 of the founder of the Baha'i religion and a holy day on which work is suspended. Mirza Husayn Ali, later known as Baha'u'llah ('Glory of God'), was born in Tehran, Persia (now Iran). He was an adherent of Islam, and later a follower of the Bab, who founded the Babi faith, an independent messianic religion. Thirteen years after the Bab's execution in 1850, Husayn Ali declared himself the messenger of God, foretold by the Bab.

See also RIDVAN, FEAST OF

CONTACT:
Baha'is of the U.S.
Office of Public Information
866 United Nations Plaza, Ste. 120
New York, NY 10017-1822
212-803-2500; fax: 212-803-2573

SOURCES:
AnnivHol-1983, p. 146
Chases-1996, p. 448
DictWrldRel-1989, pp. 87, 89
RelHolCal-1993, p. 62

♦ 0126 ♦ Bahia Independence Day
July 2

The consolidation of Brazilian independence in the state of Bahia is remembered each year with a procession following the path that the Brazilians took when they defeated Portuguese troops there in 1823. Folkloric characters like the *caboclo*, who symbolizes the superiority of native strength over the colonizers, have worked their way into this primarily civic celebration.

CONTACT:
Brazilian Embassy
3006 Massachusetts Ave., N.W.
Washington, D.C. 20008
202-745-2700; fax: 202-745-2827

♦ 0127 ♦ Bahrain National Day
December 16

Bahrain is a small (260 square miles in area) country of islands in the Persian Gulf. After being a British protectorate for more than 100 years, Bahrain became independent in 1971. National Day is a legal holiday observed on December 16.

CONTACT:
Bahrain Embassy
3502 International Dr., N.W.
Washington, D.C. 20008
202-342-0741; fax: 202-362-2192

SOURCES:
Chases-1996, p. 482

Baisakhi
See **Vaisakh**

♦ 0128 ♦ **Bal du Rat Mort (Dead Rat's Ball)**
Between end of January and beginning of March;
usually the weekend before Ash Wednesday

A huge carnival and ball, concentrated in the casino of
Ostend, Belgium, but also spreading out all over the town.
The carnival began at the end of the 19th century, launched
by members of the Ostend Art and Philanthropic Circle who
named the affair for a café on Montmartre (a hilly part of
northern Paris, home to many artists) where they had whiled
away pleasant hours. People are masked at the ball, and
there's a competition for the best costume.

CONTACT:
Belgian Tourist Office
780 Third Ave.
New York, NY 10017
212-758-8130; fax: 212-355-7675

♦ 0129 ♦ **Balfour Declaration Day**
November 2

Jews, particularly those in Israel, observe Balfour Declaration
Day in memory of a turning point in modern Jewish history.
On November 2, 1917, Arthur J. Balfour, British Secretary of
State for Foreign Affairs, sent a letter to Lord Rothschild
indicating that the British government was in favor of estab-
lishing a national home for the Jewish people in Palestine.
Although this may not seem to be as significant an event as
ISRAELI INDEPENDENCE DAY, the Jewish people felt that the
British government's commitment to their cause was very
important. The day on which it was made has been kept as a
semi-holiday ever since.

SOURCES:
AnnivHol-1983, p. 141
DaysCustFaith-1957, p. 282
DictWrldRel-1989, p. 89

♦ 0130 ♦ **Baltic Song Festivals**
Summer, every five years

Massive festivals of song and dance, emphasizing folk music
and national culture, held every five years in the Baltic
countries of Estonia, Latvia, and Lithuania. These festivals
came to symbolize nationhood, especially after the countries
came under Soviet domination.

The first all-Estonian song festival, called the *Laulupidu,* was
held in Tartu in 1869 with 845 performers singing to 15,000
people. Nationalist leaders, led by J. V. Jannsen, publisher of
the first Estonian-language newspaper, had organized the
festival to demonstrate that their culture had survived its
conquerors.

In 1975 the festival drew 30,000 on stage and 200,000
spectators, and when it ended, the people rose and sang their
unofficial anthem, "My Fatherland Is My Love," as tears
streamed down their cheeks. The anthem was written during
World War II by Lydia Koidula, the daughter of Song
Festival originator Jannsen, and put to music by Gustav
Ernesaks. In 1988, as political activities heightened, there

were spontaneous song fests throughout Estonia. Recently,
the festival has been held at the Song Festival Amphitheater
outside Tallinn.

In Latvia, the first Song Festival was held in 1873 at the
Keizardarzs (the Czar's Garden), a park created in 1721 and
named for Czar Peter I. Janis Cimze began collecting the
melodies of folk songs in 1869, and these songs, some more
than 1,000 years old, were performed by thousands of singers
in huge choirs at the first and later festivals.

In Lithuania, each region has its own distinct musical style.
Northeastern Aukstaitija, for example, is known for a kind of
polyphonic round not found in any other region or in neighboring countries. The rhythms are syncopated, and the rounds
sound very dissonant.

The old town of Vilnius is the site each May of "Skamba
kankliai," performances by vocalists, instrumentalists, and
dancers.

CONTACT:
Estonian Embassy
1030 15th St., N.W., Ste. 1000
Washington, D.C. 20005
202-588-0101

Lithuanian Embassy
2622 16th St., N.W.
Washington, D.C. 20009
202-234-5860; fax: 202-328-0466

♦ 0131 ♦ **Banana Festival, International**
Mid-September

A glorification of the banana, culminating with the serving of
a one-ton banana pudding, in the twin cities of Fulton, Ky.,
and South Fulton, Tenn. The festival began in 1963 when
most bananas were still shipped by rail after being unloaded
at Gulf of Mexico ports. The twin cities were the distribution
point for 70 percent of all bananas brought to the U.S., and
also a checkpoint where the bananas were refreshed with ice
or heated, as the weather directed.

Bananas and the Fultons became associated more than a
century ago. This was an important railroad switching point,
tying New Orleans to Canada. The Illinois Central Railroad,
with major facilities in the cities, was the first railroad to
develop refrigerated cars, and it began shipping bananas out
of New Orleans in 1880. Suddenly people in the hinterlands
could have this exotic fruit that had been enjoyed only by
those in port cities. The emphasis on the banana trade in the
twin cities won the communities the title "Banana Crossroads of the United States," and, more chauvinistically,
"Banana Capital of the World."

It doesn't matter to the citizens of the twin cities that carloads
of bananas no longer arrive here. Festival events sprawl over
a period of two weeks, beginning with a Banana Princess
Pageant in the Fulton City High School. Other events include
a Banana Bake-off, a Banana Bonnet Contest, a no-hands
Banana Split Eating Contest, a model railroad show, a flea
market, an antique car show, an arts and crafts exhibit, and
on the final day, a grand parade. The parade ends with the
serving of the "World's Largest Banana Pudding." It's made
each year by about 16 people following a recipe that calls for
3,000 bananas, 250 pounds of vanilla wafers, and 950 packages of cream pudding, all prepared in a bowl three feet tall
and five feet across. Servings: 10,000.

CONTACT:
Kentucky Dept. of Travel
    Development
500 Mero St., 22nd Floor
Frankfort, KY 40601
800-225-8747 or 502-564-4930
fax: 502-564-5695

Tennessee Dept. of Tourism
    Development
P.O. Box 23170
Nashville, TN 37202
615-741-2158; fax: 615-741-7225

◆ 0132 ◆ Banff Festival of the Arts
Early June to late August

The Banff Festival grew out of the Banff Centre School of Fine Arts, which was founded in 1933 to promote the study of music, dance, opera, drama, musical theater, writing, and the visual arts. Since 1971, the school's two-and-a-half month session has culminated in the Banff Festival of the Arts, where students and faculty present their works to the public. A wide range of musical events, from orchestra and chamber concerts to opera and jazz, are performed in the Centre's modern theater facilities and at other locations throughout the town. Most of the performances are held in August, when internationally renowned artists join the students and faculty of the School of Fine Arts. There is a music, ballet, or theater performance almost every night, as well as art and photography exhibitions, seminars, and readings.

Banff, which is located in the Canadian Rockies near Lake Louise, is also known for the spectacular scenery of its National Park.

CONTACT: SOURCES:
Alberta Economic Development   *GdWrldFest-1985*, p. 28
    and Tourism   *IntlThFolk-1979*, p. 59
Commerce Place, 3rd Floor   *MusFestAmer-1990*, p. 158
10155-102 Street
Edmonton, Alberta
Canada T5J 4L6
800-661-8886 or 403-427-4321

◆ 0133 ◆ Bangladesh Independence Day
March 26

This public holiday celebrates the declaration of the existence of the state of Bangladesh on March 26, 1971. When India gained independence from Britain in 1947, the region that is now Bangladesh was part of Bengal, India. It became East Pakistan and was governed together with West Pakistan as one country. The movement for autonomy in East Pakistan began in 1949. By early 1971, differences between East and West Pakistan had led to war. India entered the war in November in support of East Pakistan, and independence was assured within a month (*see* BANGLADESH VICTORY DAY).

Bangladeshis observe their national holiday of independence with parades and other festivities.

CONTACT: SOURCES:
Bangladesh Embassy   *AnnivHol-1983*, p. 42
2201 Wisconsin Ave., N.W., Ste.   *Chases-1996*, p. 145
    300
Washington, D.C. 20007
202-342-8372; fax: 202-333-4971

◆ 0134 ◆ Bangladesh Victory Day
December 16

This public holiday in Bangladesh commemorates the official creation of the state of Bangladesh, after months of fighting and years of struggle to gain autonomy from Pakistan.

See also BANGLADESH INDEPENDENCE DAY

CONTACT: SOURCES:
Bangladesh Embassy   *AnnivHol-1983*, p. 160
2201 Wisconsin Ave., N.W., Ste.   *Chases-1996*, p. 482
    300
Washington, D.C. 20007
202-342-8372; fax: 202-333-4971

◆ 0135 ◆ Bank Holiday
Various

In England there are typically six "bank holidays"—weekdays when the banks are closed for business: NEW YEAR'S DAY, GOOD FRIDAY, EASTER MONDAY, August (or Summer) Bank Holiday, CHRISTMAS, and BOXING DAY. These official public holidays were established by law in 1871 and are traditionally spent at local fairgrounds.

In the United States, the Great Depression of 1929 had caused many people to withdraw their savings, and the banks had trouble meeting the demand. In February 1933 the Detroit banks failed and this caused a country-wide panic. President Franklin D. Roosevelt proclaimed his first full day in office (March 6, 1933) a national "Bank Holiday" to help save the country's banking system. The "holiday" actually lasted 10 days, during which "scrip" (paper currency in denominations of less than a dollar) temporarily replaced real money in many American households.

SOURCES:
AnnivHol-1983, p. 112
Chases-1996, pp. 232, 350
DictDays-1988, pp. 6, 8

◆ 0136 ◆ Banntag
Between April 30 and June 3; Ascension Day

In the canton of Basel in Switzerland, this is a day when village citizens walk the village boundaries. *Banntag* means community- or town-boundary day.

Until the Reformation, ASCENSION DAY was a time for the blessing of the fields and checking of boundary markers. The religious aspect of the day declined, and now Ascension Day, which is a national holiday, is seen as a community festival. Citizens of Basel canton, accompanied by a local official, flag bearers, and musicians, walk along the boundaries to a certain spot where the president of the town council greets them and discusses town topics. In some communities, the walk is followed by a church service and community meal.

CONTACT:
Swiss National Tourist Office
608 Fifth Ave.
New York, NY 10020
212-757-5944; fax: 212-262-6116

◆ 0137 ◆ Baptism of the Lord, Feast of the
January, Sunday following Epiphany

Jesus' baptism by John the Baptist in the River Jordan has always been considered a significant manifestation of Jesus' divinity, and has been celebrated on EPIPHANY by the Orthodox church since the end of the second century. However, in 1961 the Roman Catholic church began to celebrate it as a separate feast in its own right. The original date for the feast was January 13, but when the church calendar was reorganized in 1969, the Feast of the Baptism of the Lord was moved to the Sunday following the Epiphany. The Church omits the observance in years when it coincides with the Epiphany, especially in places like the United States, where celebration of the Epiphany has been shifted from the traditional January 6 observance to the Sunday between January 2 and 8.

See also TIMQAT

SOURCES:
AmerBkDays-1978, p. 65
AnnivHol-1983, p. 7
RelHolCal-1993, p. 60

♦ 0138 ♦ **Barbados-Caribbean Jazz Festival**
Late May

Established in 1985 to promote jazz that is distinctly Caribbean in imagery and rhythm, the Barbados-Caribbean Jazz Festival has featured musicians from Antigua, Barbados, Colombia, Cuba, Curaçao, Guadeloupe, Guyana, Jamaica, Martinique, Panama, Puerto Rico, St. Lucia, St. Vincent, Trinidad and Tobago, and Venezuela. But jazz groups and musicians from the United States and Europe have participated in the festival as well—including Ellis Marsalis (father of the jazz trumpeter Wynton and saxophonist Branford), the Dirty Dozen Dixieland Jazz Band from New Orleans, and Donald Byrd. Indoor performances are held at The Frank Collymore Hall, the island's largest musical auditorium, and at The After Dark, Barbados' top jazz club. There are also open-air concerts in Bridgetown, the island's capital. The festival is held from Thursday to Sunday in late May.

CONTACT:
Barbados Tourism Authority
800 Second Ave.
New York, NY 10017
800-221-9831 or 212-986-6516
fax: 212-573-9850

♦ 0139 ♦ **Barbados Independence Day**
November 30

After having been a British colony since the 17th century, Barbados became independent on this day in 1966. A ceremony took place near the capital city of Bridgetown, during which the British flag was lowered and replaced by the Barbados flag, and the national anthem was sung.

Today, festivities extend through the month of November with the National Independence Festival of the Creative Arts. This is a talent show of all ages in singing, dancing, writing, and acting. On Independence Day, festivities culminate with the final appearance of performers, and exhibits of art work and photography are on display.

See also BARROW DAY, ERROL

CONTACT:
Barbados Tourism Authority
800 Second Ave.
New York, NY 10017
800-221-9831 or 212-986-6516
fax: 212-573-9850

SOURCES:
AnnivHol-1983, p. 153
Chases-1996, p. 465
NatlHolWrld-1968, p. 215

♦ 0140 ♦ **Bar-B-Q Festival, International**
Mid-May

A two-day mouth-watering event in Owensboro, Ky., which calls itself the Bar-B-Q Capital of the World. In the course of the weekend, 10 tons of mutton, 3,000 chickens, and 1,500 gallons of burgoo are cooked and served. Kentucky burgoo is a thick soup made of chicken, mutton, beef, tomatoes, cabbage, potatoes, onions, and corn.

The festival had its beginnings at the turn of the century when the many Roman Catholic churches in the area had summertime picnics in their parishes. Each church had a cooking team to vie with the others in cooking the best barbecue. Eventually, the idea struck someone that there could be a city-wide barbecue if all the church barbecues were combined. Out of that grew the present festival, which now attracts more than 40,000 people. The barbecue-pit fires are lit on Friday afternoon on the banks of the Ohio River, and the chicken and meat—always mutton, not beef—is barbecued the next day when the coals are red. The Roman Catholic parish chefs still compete, but the cooking contest has expanded to be open to anyone. Events besides cooking and eating include arts and crafts exhibits, bluegrass and country music, street dancing, and contests of pie eating, keg throwing and horseshoe throwing. There are also likely to be political speeches.

CONTACT:
Kentucky Dept. of Travel
  Development
500 Mero St., 22nd Floor
Frankfort, KY 40601
800-225-8747 or 502-564-4930
fax: 502-564-5695

♦ 0141 ♦ **Barcelona Festival**
October

The month-long **International Music Festival** that takes place in Barcelona, Spain, each year began in 1963 as a showcase for young Catalan composers and performers. But since then the festival has taken on a more international flavor, with musicians and composers from other countries participating as well. The commitment of the festival's organizers to Catalan artists remains strong however, and each year the festival premieres the work of about 180 local composers.

The Barcelona Festival is always held in October as part of the Fiestas de la Merced, or the festival honoring Barcelona's patron saint, Our Lady of Mercy.

CONTACT:
Tourist Office of Spain
665 Fifth Ave.
New York, NY 10022
212-759-8822; fax: 212-980-1053

SOURCES:
GdWrldFest-1985, p. 161
MusFestEurBrit-1980, p. 134

♦ 0142 ♦ **Barnum Festival**
Late June–July 4 or 5

Bridgeport, Connecticut, was the home of Phineas Taylor Barnum (1810–1891) and the birthplace of Charles Sherwood Stratton (1838–1883), known by his circus name of "General" Tom Thumb, a 28" tall man who was the main attraction of Barnum's 19th-century circus, the Greatest Show on Earth. Barnum was also Bridgeport's mayor in 1875, and his contributions to the city included bringing in new industrial jobs and building a number of parks. Since 1949 he has been honored with a festival beginning in late June and extending through the FOURTH OF JULY. Occasionally it continues through July 5, which is Barnum's birthday. The idea behind the festival, which is sponsored by the P.T. Barnum Foundation, Inc., is to get away from Bridgeport's industrial image and to promote the city's circus heritage.

One of the highlights of the festival is the Saturday evening event known as "Champions on Parade," the largest senior drum corps competition in the Northeast. On Sunday there is a Barnum Memorial Ceremony at the cemetery where he is buried. Many of the events focus on Barnum's circus background, including entertainment by clowns and a visit to the Barnum Museum, where there is a miniature replica of his circus. The festival is preceded by the selection of an honorary Tom Thumb. There is also an honorary Jenny Lind (the Swedish-born soprano who toured the United States under Barnum's sponsorship). Other figures associated with Barnum and his circus are recognized in this way as well.

CONTACT:
Connecticut Tourism Division
865 Brook St.
Rocky Hill, CT 06067
800-282-6863 or 860-258-4355
fax: 860-258-4275

SOURCES:
AmerBkDays-1978, pp. 624.
      631
GdUSFest-1985, p. 2?

♦ 0143 ♦ **Baron Bliss Day**
March 9

Baron Bliss Day is a public holiday in Belize honoring Englishman Henry Edward Ernest Victor Bliss (1869–1926). When he died, Bliss bequeathed his entire estate to Belize City.

SOURCES:
AnnivHol-1983, p. 35
Chases-1996, p. 127

♦ 0144 ♦ **Barrow Day, Errol**
January 21

A national public holiday that honors Barbados' first prime minister. Errol Barrow was born in 1920, earned a law degree in England, then returned to Barbados. He became finance minister in 1959 and prime minister in 1961. He was reelected in 1966 and, soon after, Barbados became independent of Great Britain (*see* BARBADOS INDEPENDENCE DAY). Barrow was voted out in 1976, but regained office in 1986; he died the next year.

CONTACT:
Barbados Tourism Authority
800 Second Ave.
New York, NY 10017
800-221-9831 or 212-986-6516
fax: 212-573-9850

♦ 0145 ♦ **Bartholomew Fair**
August 24

Although **St. Bartholomew's Day** isn't really celebrated any more, for more than 700 years (1133–1855) it was the day on which the Bartholomew Fair was held at Smithfield on the outskirts of London. What began as an opportunity for buying and selling cloth eventually turned into a major national event. Almost every type of commodity could be purchased there, and a number of sideshows and other crude

sources of entertainment were available as well—earning the Fair its present-day reputation as "the Coney Island of medieval England."

Eventually the entertainment aspects of the Fair outweighed its commercial purposes, and although it was very much a part of English life there was a movement to close it down. In 1822, thousands of people rioted in protest against the threat of closing the Fair. But finally, in 1855, it was permanently abolished.

St. Bartholomew's Day is also known for the massacre of the Huguenots (Protestants) in France, which began at the instigation of Catherine de' Medici in Paris on the night of August 23–24, 1572, and spread throughout the country for two more days until between 5,000 and 10,000 had been killed.

SOURCES:
BkDays-1864, vol. II, p. 264
DaysCustFaith-1957, p. 217
DictDays-1988, p. 9
DictMyth-1962, vol. I, p. 183
FestSaintDays-1915, p. 176

Basant Panchami
See **Vasant Panchami**

♦ 0146 ♦ **Basket Dances**
October–November

Ceremonial dances by Hopi Indian women held in the plaza of their mesa villages in northeastern Arizona. The basket dances, known as the *Lakon* and the *Owaqöl*, celebrate the harvest and fertility. The women are costumed, and while they dance and sing they throw small gifts from baskets to the men.

CONTACT:
Hopi Tribal Council
P.O. Box 123
Kykotsmovi, AZ 86039
602-734-2445

SOURCES:
EncyRel-1987, vol. 10, p. 520
IndianAmer-1989, p. 266

♦ 0147 ♦ **Basque Festival, National**
First weekend in July

A sports-music-dance-barbecue celebration of the Basque heritage, held annually since 1962 in Elko, Nev. The Basque people settled in the west, largely in Nevada and Idaho, in the late 1800s, many becoming shepherds and sheep ranchers.

Participants in the festival wear the traditional red, white, and green of the Basque provinces of Spain. The men also wear the traditional Basque beret.

The festival begins on Friday with social and exhibition dancing. On Saturday there's a parade of more than 50 floats, and major contests of weightlifting, sheep hooking (sheep are hooked with a crook, dragged to a designated spot, and tied by one leg), sheepdog-working, yelling, and dancing the native *jota*. Each year, there is also a three-event contest of log chopping, weightlifting, and a strength-and-endurance event in which contestants race to pluck each of 30 beer cans (they were ears of corn in the old country) from a line and deposit them in a trash can. Some years, when contestants from Spain are present, there are pentathlons—five-event contests that largely involve lifting, dragging, and walking with enormous weights (for example, a 1,200-pound granite slab is dragged). On Sunday, the events wind up with a big barbecue of steak, marinated lamb, and spicy sausages called *chorizo*. Music and dancing are important parts of the festival, and *bertsolaris*, 'troubadours', entertain with song improvisations in the Basque language.

Other Nevada Basque festivals are held in Winnemucca on the second weekend in June and in Reno in August. Another major event is the Basque Association Picnic in Gooding, Idaho, in late July.

CONTACT:
Nevada Commission on Tourism
5151 S. Carson St.
Capitol Complex
Carson City, NV 89710
800-638-2328 or 702-687-4322
fax: 702-687-6779

SOURCES:
GdUSFest-1984, p. 112

♦ 0148 ♦ **Bastille, Festival de la**
Weekend closest to July 14

Because the storming of the Bastille on July 14, 1789 (*see* BASTILLE DAY), marked an important turning point in the history of France, members of the Club Calumet in Augusta, Maine, chose this day (or the nearest Friday, Saturday, and Sunday) to celebrate the state's French-Canadian (or Acadian) heritage. Events include entertainment by Cajun bands, French folk dancers and Maine cloggers, a huge fireworks display, and a parade through downtown Augusta.

In 1991 the festival honored 85 visitors from Paris—all members of the Sarthois Club who were in this country as part of an exchange with its sister club, Le Club Calumet. But the festival is not limited to the French or descendants of the original Acadian settlers. More than 13,000 visitors come to Augusta each year to participate in the festival. About one-fourth of Maine's current population is of Acadian descent (*see also* ACADIAN FESTIVAL).

CONTACT:
Calumet Club
West River Rd.
Augusta, ME 04330
207-623-8211

♦ 0149 ♦ **Bastille Day**
July 14

The Bastille was a 14th-century fortress that became a notorious state prison in Paris. An angry mob assaulted the Bastille—which had come to symbolize the oppression of the French monarchy—on July 14, 1789, freeing the political prisoners held there and launching the French Revolution.

Although the building itself was razed a year after the attack, the Bastille became a symbol of French independence, and July 14 has been celebrated since that time in France as **Fête Nationale**, as well as in her territories in the Pacific with parades, fireworks, and dancing in the streets. This period in French history is familiar to many through Charles Dickens's portrayal of it in *A Tale of Two Cities*.

In Tahiti and the rest of French Polynesia it is called **Tiurai** or **Heiva**, and is celebrated for most of the month. The festival includes European-type celebrations plus Polynesian competitions that include both men and women, and a play about the enthronement of a Tahitian high chief. The highlight is the nightly folklore spectacle—a competition of music and dance among groups from throughout French Polynesia who have practiced all year for the event.

CONTACT:
French Government Tourist Office
9454 Wilshire Blvd., Ste. 715
Beverly Hills, CA 90212
310-271-6665; fax: 310-276-2835

SOURCES:
AmerBkDays-1978, p. 659
AnnivHol-1983, p. 93
BkDays-1864, vol. II, p. 59
BkHolWrld-1986, Jul 14
FolkWrldHol-1992, p. 372
NatlHolWrld-1968, p. 113

♦ 0150 ♦ **Bastille Day in Kaplan, Louisiana**
July 14

The French-speaking town of Kaplan, Louisiana, where most of the inhabitants are descended from French-Canadians (Acadians), claims to hold the only community-wide celebration of BASTILLE DAY in the United States. The celebration there on July 14 includes fireworks, amateur athletic competitions, and a "fais do-do" or Acadian street dance.

The custom of observing Bastille Day was started by Eugene Eleazer, a French immigrant who became mayor of Kaplan in 1920. With the exception of a brief interruption during World War II, the town has held its fête every year since 1906. Smaller Bastille Day celebrations are held elsewhere in Louisiana, including New Orleans and Baton Rouge, where French traditions still run strong.

CONTACT:
Louisiana Office of Tourism
P.O. Box 94291
Baton Rouge, LA 70804
800-334-8626 or 504-342-8119
fax: 504-342-8390

SOURCES:
AmerBkDays-1978, p. 659

♦ 0151 ♦ **Bataan Day**
May 6

A national legal holiday in the Philippines in commemoration of the disastrous World War II Battle of Bataan in 1942, in which the Philippines fell to the Japanese. It is also known as **Araw ng Kagitingan** or **Heroes Day** in the Philippines. Also remembered on this date are the 37,000 U.S. and Filipino soldiers who were captured and the thousands who died during the infamous 70-mile "death march" from Mariveles to a Japanese concentration camp inland at San Fernando. Ceremonies are held at Mt. Samat Shrine, the site of side-by-side fighting by Filipino and American troops.

CONTACT:
Philippine Department of Tourism
556 Fifth Ave.
First Floor Mezzanine
New York, NY 10036
212-575-7915; fax: 212-302-6759

SOURCES:
AnnivHol-1983, p. 49
Chases-1996, p. 203

♦ 0152 ♦ **Bat Flight Breakfast**
Second Thursday in August

Carlsbad Caverns in southern New Mexico was proclaimed a national monument in 1923 not only for its geologic formations but for its teeming bat population. Carlsbad's summer colony of Mexican free-tailed bats, whose numbers vary from one hundred thousand to a million, migrates to the cave each spring. They eat, sleep, digest, communicate, mate, and raise their young while hanging upside-down. The accumulation of guano—a valuable source of fertilizer—can reach depths of up to 40 feet.

Although many visitors to the park witness the bats' spectacular outbound flight at sunset, when they leave the cave in a dense black cloud for their night's feeding in the Pecos River Valley, far fewer are there to witness their return—except those who attend the annual Bat Flight Breakfast. Started in the late 1950s by a group of park employees who wanted to encourage people to witness this natural phenomenon, the breakfast soon became an annual tradition. About 400 people arrive at the cave before sunrise on the second Thursday in August and eat sausages and scrambled eggs in their official yellow "bat breakfast hats" while they wait for the bats to return to their roosts. It is said that the bats generate an eerie sound as they rocket downward with folded wings.

When a television crew was there to film the event in 1989, the bats failed to return as expected. No one is sure how or when they got back into the cave, but 13 hours later, at sunset, they left in droves as usual.

CONTACT:
Carlsbad Caverns National Park
3225 National Parks Highway
Carlsbad, NM 88220
505-785-2232

♦ 0153 ♦ **Bath Festival**
Late May

Located about 100 miles west of London, the city of Bath provides one of the finest examples of 18th-century architecture in all of Europe. The residents of the Royal Crescent, a semicircular street in the heart of Bath lined with Georgian-style houses, light candles in their windows on the opening night of the 17-day music festival that has been held there since 1958. While musical events dominate the festival—there are usually two operas and a wide variety of concerts and recitals—in recent years children's events, theater, film, jazz, dance, art exhibitions, and lectures have been added. Violinist Yehudi Menuhin's 10 years as artistic director of the festival established it as one of the most important musical events in Britain. Menuhin also helped train the Bath Festival Orchestra, now recognized as one of the best small orchestras in the world (*see also* MENUHIN FESTIVAL).

Bath is known for its mineral hot springs, which were discovered by the Romans when they invaded Britain 2,000 years ago. During the 18th century it became a fashionable resort and cultural center, and festival events take place in many of its well-preserved buildings. A festival ball is held each year in one of the city's historic homes.

CONTACT:
British Tourist Authority
551 Fifth Ave., Ste. 702
New York, NY 10176
800-462-2748 or 212-986-2200
fax: 212-986-1188

SOURCES:
GdWrldFest-1985, p. 89
MusFestEurBrit-1980, p. 43
MusFestWrld-1963, p. 24

♦ 0154 ♦ **Baths of Caracalla**
First week in July to second week in August

Built in A.D. 216, the Baths of Caracalla in Rome were originally designed as a social gathering place where men could exchange ideas and hear lectures while they bathed. The first open-air opera was presented there in 1937, and since then the **Bath Operas** have become a popular summer event. With a stage that is claimed to be the largest in the world—100'

long and 162' wide—the Baths provide an ideal setting for such grand spectacles as Giuseppe Verdi's *Aida*, which is performed there every summer, complete with horses, elephants, camels, soldiers, and hundreds of costumed slaves. All of the operas staged at the Baths are produced by the Rome Opera Company. One or two ballet productions are usually performed as well.

While the acoustics are far from ideal and singers must rely on a huge amplification system to carry their voices, more than 10,000 spectators fill the bleachers (formerly the stadium seats adjoining the baths) to hear the grand Italian operas performed in a setting that cannot be duplicated anywhere in the world.

CONTACT:
Italian Government Travel Office
630 Fifth Ave.
New York, NY 10111
212-245-4822

SOURCES:
MusFestEurBrit-1980, p. 113

♦ 0155 ♦ **Battle of Britain Day**
September 15

In England, September 15, 1940, is remembered as the day of the biggest daylight bombing raid of Britain by the German Luftwaffe. The German air attacks had begun in June 1940, and beginning September 7 bombs rained on London for 57 consecutive nights. The Royal Air Force (RAF), while greatly outnumbered, had a secret advantage—radar—and the early-warning chain gave RAF pilots a half-hour's notice of German planes taking off from France. The Luftwaffe was finally defeated in April 1941, ending the first extended battle ever fought for control of the air. Winston Churchill, in a speech in August 1940, was referring to the RAF pilots when he said, "Never in the field of human conflict was so much owed by so many to so few."

SOURCES:
AnnivHol-1983, p. 119
Chases-1996, p. 377

♦ 0156 ♦ **Battle of Flowers, Jersey**
Second Thursday in August

First held in 1902 as part of the celebration honoring the coronation of Edward VII and Queen Alexandra, the **Jersey Battle of Flowers** takes place on Jersey in the British Channel Islands every August. It begins with a parade of floats covered in flowers, many of which are quite elaborate. In past years, floats have included a working windmill and large birds made completely out of flowers. Another popular theme is significant events in the island's history, including the 1871 Battle of Jersey. There is a special float for Miss Jersey, the queen of the event. After the parade is over, spectators pelt each other with blossoms.

CONTACT:
British Tourist Authority
551 Fifth Ave., Ste. 702
New York, NY 10176
800-462-2748 or 212-986-2200
fax: 212-986-1188

SOURCES:
AnnivHol-1983, p. 173
GdWrldFest-1985, p. 98

♦ 0157 ♦ **Battle of Flowers, Vienna**
Summer

The Battle of Flowers is the culmination of a huge flower

festival in the capital city of Vienna, Austria. Hundreds of floats are elaborately decorated with flowers, often to symbolize a particular aspect of Austrian history or culture. Sometimes they re-create entire scenes from Austrian operettas or ballets. The people of Vienna dress up in their best clothes and hats—similar to what Americans do on EASTER—to watch the parade, which is reviewed by government officials and the leaders of various cultural organizations.

Similar "Battles of Flowers" are held in other Austrian cities, such as Linz, Salzburg, and Innsbruck. A particularly famous one is held on a lake in south Upper Austria known as the Traun See, where barges and boats, rather than floats, are decorated with flowers.

CONTACT:
Austrian National Tourist Office
P.O. Box 1142, Times Square
New York, NY 10148
212-944-6880; fax: 212-730-4568

♦ 0158 ♦ **Battle of Germantown, Reenactment of**
First Saturday in October

In October of 1777, George Washington's battle strategy to recapture Philadelphia from the British called for an assault on the little community of Germantown to the northwest of the city. The British soldiers took refuge in a new stone house, Cliveden, that had just been built by Benjamin Chew. Although the house was pounded by cannon balls, the stone walls withstood the assault and Washington's men were eventually forced to retreat. The thick fog proved to be a decisive factor, hindering the movements of Washington's soldiers at a point where they appeared to be on the verge of winning. Although the Americans were defeated, the Battle of Germantown was considered a moral victory, especially when it was followed two weeks later by the victory of General Horatio Gates at Saratoga.

Since the early 1970s, there has been a reenactment of Washington's defeat by the British in Germantown, now a suburb of Philadelphia, on the first Saturday in October. British and American troops stage a mock battle from house to house. At Cliveden, which now belongs to the National Trust for Historic Preservation, visitors can still see the scars left by American bullets.

CONTACT:
Philadelphia Convention and Visitors Bureau
1515 Market St., Ste. 2020
Philadelphia, PA 19102
800-537-7676 or 215-636-3300
fax: 215-636-3327

♦ 0159 ♦ **Battle of New Orleans Day**
January 8

When 8,000 British soldiers attacked New Orleans on January 8, 1815, they were met by a ragtag army of militiamen, sailors, and pirates fighting from behind barricades. The defending U.S. troops were led by General Andrew Jackson, whose stunning victory—the British suffered some 2,000 casualties, while the Americans lost only eight men—made him a national hero.

This day is no longer as widely celebrated as it was before the Civil War, but it remains a legal holiday in Louisiana, where

it is also known as **Jackson Day** or, in honor of Jackson's nickname, as **Old Hickory's Day**.

See also JACKSON'S BIRTHDAY, ANDREW

SOURCES:
AmerBkDays-1978, p. 49
AnnivHol-1983, p. 6
Chases-1996, p. 60
DictDays-1988, pp. 9, 61, 84
FolkAmerHol-1991, p. 41

Battle of Pichincha Day
See **Ecuador Independence Day**

♦ 0160 ♦ **Battles of the Flowers**
Between March 10 and April 13; during Carnival

Flowers play an important role in CARNIVAL celebrations in Nice, for it is in the south of France that the flowers for French perfume are grown. During the 12 days of Carnival festivities, there are several afternoons devoted to Battles of the Flowers, where people bring their own "ammunition" and, at a predetermined signal, start throwing flowers at each other. The city streets are often knee-deep in flowers by the time these fragrant mock-battles are over.

CONTACT:
French Government Tourist Office
9454 Wilshire Blvd., Ste. 715
Beverly Hills, CA 90212
310-271-6665; fax: 310-276-2835

SOURCES:
AmerBkDays-1978, p. 43
BkFest-1937, p. 120
BkFestHolWrld-1970, p. 33
Chases-1996, p. 91
DictFolkMyth-1984, p. 192
FestWestEur-1958, p. 34

♦ 0161 ♦ **Bawming the Thorn Day**
Late June

This is the day on which the people of Appleton in Cheshire, England, celebrate the centuries-old tradition of bawming the thorn, or decorating the hawthorn tree that stands in the center of their town. Children dance around the tree after draping its branches with flowers, flags, and ribbons. The original hawthorn tree was planted there in 1125, but the custom may date back even farther to the ancient custom of worshipping trees as guardians.

CONTACT:
British Tourist Authority
551 Fifth Ave., Ste. 702
New York, NY 10176
800-462-2748 or 212-986-2200
fax: 212-986-1188

SOURCES:
AnnivHol-1983, p. 92
BkHolWrld-1986, Jun 29

♦ 0162 ♦ **Bayreuth Festival**
Late July through end of August

An internationally famous month-long festival in Bayreuth (pronounced buy-ROIT), Germany, celebrating the music of Richard Wagner. It features six to eight Wagner operas and is usually sold out a year in advance. Performances are in the Festspielhaus ('Festival Theatre') designed by Wagner himself specifically for the presentation of his works. The festival was launched with the first complete performance of the four-opera *Der Ring des Nibelungen* ('The Ring of the Nibelung'), triumphantly presented in the new Festspielhaus on Aug. 13, 14, 16, and 17, 1876. Except for wartime interruptions, the festival has been staged every year since then. Wagner had moved to Bayreuth in 1874, and lived in the house he called *Wahnfried* ('Peace from Delusion') until his death in 1883. During those years, he composed his last work, the sacred festival drama *Parsifal*, and it was produced at Bayreuth in 1882. The festival was directed after Wagner's death by his wife Cosima; their son Seigfried took over as director in 1930, and grandsons Wieland and Wolfgang Wagner revived it after World War II, in 1951.

See also PACIFIC NORTHWEST FESTIVAL and RAVELLO MUSIC FESTIVAL

CONTACT:
German National Tourist Office
122 E. 42nd St., 52nd Floor
New York, NY 10168
212-661-7200; fax: 212-661-7174

SOURCES:
Chases-1996, p. 309
GdWrldFest-1985, p. 83
MusFestEurBrit-1980, p. 97
MusFestWrld-1963, p. 47

Beale Street Music Festival
See **Memphis in May International Festival**

Bean-Throwing Festival
See **Setsubun**

♦ 0163 ♦ Bear Festival
Varies

Among the Ainu people of the northernmost islands of Japan, especially on Hokkaido, the baiting and killing of a young bear was not considered a brutal act but a ceremonial send-off to the spirit world. The "divine" cub was ceremoniously fed and cared for, then killed and arranged with fetishes. Some of his own cooked meat and a dish of his own blood, along with cakes and dried fish were laid before him. He was supposed to bring these gifts to his parents when he arrived in heaven. After a time, Ainu belief has it, he would be reincarnated and return to earth as another cub.

SOURCES:
FolkWrldHol-1992, p. 574
JapanFest-1965, p. 207

♦ 0164 ♦ Befana Festival
January 5

Sometimes referred to simply as **La Befana**, this is the TWELFTH NIGHT festival in Italy where the *Befana*, a kindly witch, plays much the same role that Santa Claus plays in the United States on CHRISTMAS EVE—giving toys and candy to the children who have been good and a lump of coal or a pebble to those who haven't. According to legend, the Befana was sweeping her house when the Magi, or Three Wise Men, stopped by on their way to Bethlehem. But when they asked her to accompany them, she said she was too busy. She later changed her mind and set out to find the Christ Child, but she got lost. Every year *la Befana* passes through Italy in her continuing search for the *Gésu Bambino*, leaving gifts for the children.

The festival begins on EPIPHANY EVE, when the Befana is supposed to come down the chimney on her broom to leave gifts in the children's stockings. In Rome, the Piazza Navona is thronged with children and their parents, who shop for toys and exchange greetings. Bands of young people march around, blowing on cardboard trumpets, and the noise level in the square can be deafening. In the countryside, bonfires are often lit on Epiphany Eve, and people try to predict the weather by watching the direction in which the smoke blows.

See also DÍA DE LOS TRES REYES

SOURCES:
AmerBkDays-1978, p. 30
BkFest-1937, p. 178
DictFolkMyth-1984, p. 131
FestSaintDays-1915, p. 16
FestWestEur-1958, p. 87
FolkWrldHol-1992, p. 14
RelHolCal-1992, p. 67

Beggar's Day
See **Martinmas**

Beheading, Feast of the
See **St. John the Baptist, Martyrdom of**

♦ 0165 ♦ Beiderbecke Memorial Jazz Festival, Bix
Last full weekend in July

Leon "Bix" Beiderbecke (1903–1931) was an American jazz cornetist and composer whose recordings of "Singin' the Blues" and "A Good Man Is Hard to Find" remain jazz classics. Since 1972 he has been commemorated in his hometown of Davenport, Iowa, with an annual jazz festival, popularly known as **Bix Jazz Fest**, featuring concerts by many of the world's top traditional jazz bands. The festival is held at LeClaire Park on the banks of the Mississippi River, where musicians perform in a bandshell, as well as indoor venues. The Bix Fest is staffed by volunteers and sponsored by the Bix Beiderbecke Memorial Society.

Beiderbecke's playing inspired a generation of jazz musicians. His life has been depicted in films and novels, such as Dorothy Baker's *Young Man with a Horn*. His compositions include "In a Mist," a piano piece inspired by the French Impressionist composers.

CONTACT:
Bix Beiderbecke Memorial Society
P. O. Box 3688
Davenport, IA 52808
319-324-7170; fax: 319-326-1732

SOURCES:
Chases-1996, p. 309
MusFestAmer-1990, p. 192

♦ 0166 ♦ Be Kind to Animals Week
First full week in May

The oldest week of its kind in the United States, Be Kind to Animals Week was first observed in 1915. Established by Dr. William O. Stillman, the leader of the American Humane Association at the time, this week was dedicated to helping animals and to publicizing the achievements of the nation's humane societies.

Today, Be Kind to Animals Week is observed by thousands of animal shelters across the country. They host special media events, promote education on the humane treatment of animals, and try to remind people of the debt that humankind owes to both wild and domestic animals.

See also HUMANE SUNDAY

CONTACT:
American Humane Association
63 Inverness Drive East
Englewood, CO 80112-5117
800-227-4645 or 303-792-0900
fax: 303-792-5333

SOURCES:
Chases-1996, p. 201

♦ 0167 ♦ Belarus Independence Day
July 27; August 25

After nearly 70 years under Soviet domination, Belarus declared its sovereignty on July 27, 1990, and issued its declaration of independence on August 25, 1991. Belarus became officially autonomous on December 26, 1991, as did other former Soviet republics.

CONTACT:
Belarus Embassy
1619 New Hampshire Ave., N.W.
Washington, D.C. 20009
202-986-1604; fax: 202-986-1805

♦ 0168 ♦ Belgian-American Days
August

Ghent, Minnesota, named after the famous city in Belgium, is the state's only predominantly Belgian community. The annual Belgian-American Days celebration gives the descendants of Ghent's original Belgian settlers an opportunity to compete in the traditional Belgian sport of *rolle bolle*, which is similar to lawn bowling or Italian bocci. The game is played on bare ground or grass, with stakes set 30 feet apart. The eight-pound disc called a *bolle* is rolled from one stake to the other. The bolle that lands closest to the stake scores. Teams usually consist of three players, and the first team to score eight points wins the game. As many as 300 bollers participate in the championship round, which is held on the third day of the four-day event.

Although rolle bolle is the biggest attraction, the festival also features a softball tournament, parades, a firemen's dinner, and a dance.

CONTACT:
Minnesota Office of Tourism
121 E. Seventh Pl. Metro Sq., Ste.
  100
St. Paul, MN 55101
612-296-5029 or 800-657-3700
fax: 612-296-7095

♦ 0169 ♦ Belgium Independence Day
July 21

This public holiday, also known as the Belgium **National Holiday,** commemorates Belgium's independence from the Netherlands on July 21, 1831. Belgians had struggled against their rulers for 15 years. A revolt began in 1830, and the next year, the state of Belgium was formed, and King Leopold I (1790–1865) was made its first king.

Belgians sing "La Brabançonne," the national anthem, and observe their independence with festivities, especially in the capital city of Brussels.

CONTACT:
Belgian Tourist Office
780 Third Ave.
New York, NY 10017
212-758-8130; fax: 212-355-7675

SOURCES:
AnnivHol-1983, p. 95
Chases-1996, p. 306
NatlHolWrld-1968, p. 119

♦ 0170 ♦ Belize Independence Day
September 21

On September 21, 1981, Belize gained independence from Britain. Belize was formerly known as British Honduras and had been internally self-governing since 1965.

Independence Day is a national public holiday in Belize.

CONTACT:
Belize Tourist Board
421 Seventh Ave., Ste. 701
New York, NY 10001
800-624-0686 or 212-563-6011
fax: 212-563-6033

SOURCES:
AnnivHol-1983, p. 121
Chases-1996, p. 384

♦ 0171 ♦ Belize National Day
September 10

A public holiday in Belize commemorating the Battle of St. George's Caye, fought in 1798 between the Spanish and the English over possession of the area. English loggers had settled in what is now Belize in the early 17th century. British pirates used to hide in the cays there waiting for opportunities to plunder passing Spanish ships. It is also known as **St. George's Caye Day.**

CONTACT:
Belize Tourist Board
421 Seventh Ave., Ste. 701
New York, NY 10001
800-624-0686 or 212-563-6011
fax: 212-563-6033

SOURCES:
AnnivHol-1983, p. 117
Chases-1996, p. 371

♦ 0172 ♦ Bella Coola Midwinter Rites
November–February

The *kusiut* was a masked dancing society of the Bella Coola, Kimsquit, and other Indian tribes of coastal British Columbia. The society performed dramatic curing dances during the midwinter ceremonial season, which began with the opening rite in November and ended in February. Most involved feats of juggling as well as masked mime. Some were used by initiates to prove that they had received a supernatural "call" to join the society.

Among the more frightening was the series of five *kusiotem* dances: the stomach-cutting dance, the beheading dance, the drowning dance, the burning dance, and the fungus dance. All involved elaborate masks and deception. The beheading dance, for example, was simulated with a false head, and the drowning dance used a dummy and a trap door.

Nowadays membership in the kusiut is open to all men, though the number of spectators is decreasing. As a result, the society's status is deteriorating.

SOURCES:
DictFolkMyth-1984, pp. 596,
  946, 963, 1186

♦ 0173 ♦ Belmont Stakes
June; fifth Saturday after Kentucky Derby

The final race of the Triple Crown of horseracing, the Belmont Stakes is traditionally run on the fifth Saturday after the KENTUCKY DERBY (the third Saturday after the PREAKNESS STAKES). Founded in 1867, it takes place at the Belmont Park Race Track in western Nassau County on Long Island, named for

August Belmont, a well-to-do German who played an important role in establishing horseracing in New York.

The horse that sweeps the Triple Crown receives a $1 million bonus in addition to the winner's share of the purses, but in years when no horse wins the Triple Crown, the bonus goes to the horse competing in all three races and scoring the highest on a 5-3-1 point system for finishing first, second, or third. The chances of a single horse winning all three races are relatively slim: in 114 years only 11 horses have managed to do it.

Many breeders pay more attention to the Belmont than they do to the other races when it comes to selecting stud prospects because they believe that in the long run, Belmont winners make better sires.

CONTACT:
Belmont Park Race Track
2150 Hempstead Turnpike
Belmont, NY 11003
718-641-4700; fax: 516-488-1396

SOURCES:
Chases-1996, p. 247

♦ 0174 ♦ **Beltane**
April 30

Beltane (also spelled **Beltine** or **Beltein**) is the Celtic name for the first day of May (see MAY DAY), which divided the ancient Celtic year in half. It was believed that each day began with the setting of the sun the night before, so Beltane was celebrated by lighting bonfires to honor the sun god. Cattle were driven through the "Beltane fire"—or between two fires—to protect them from disease before putting them out to pasture for the new season. Sometimes people followed the same ritual to forestall bad luck and to cure barrenness. Contact with the fire was symbolic of contact with the life-giving sun.

Along with LAMMAS (August 1), Hallowmas (ALL SAINTS' DAY, November 1), and CANDLEMAS (February 2), Beltane was one of the British QUARTER DAYS, or term days, when rents were due and debts were settled. The day is still observed in parts of Ireland, the Scottish Highlands, Wales, Brittany, and the Isle of Man, with most of the celebrations revolving around fire and reflecting ancient fertility rites.

See also MIDSUMMER DAY

SOURCES:
AmerBkDays-1978, p. 407
BkDays-1864, vol. I, p. 571
DictFolkMyth-1984, pp. 135, 181, 203, 304, 789
FestSaintDays-1915, p. 104
FolkAmerHol-1991, p. 188
RelHolCal-1993, p. 60

♦ 0175 ♦ **Benin Independence Day**
August 1

On August 1, 1960, Benin declared its independence from France, ending 70 years as a French colony. Independence Day is a national holiday observed throughout the country, especially in the capital city of Porto Novo.

CONTACT:
Benin Embassy
2737 Cathedral Ave., N.W.
Washington, D.C. 20008
202-232-6656; fax: 202-265-1996

SOURCES:
AnnivHol-1983, p. 101
Chases-1996, p. 317
NatlHolWrld-1968, p. 130

♦ 0176 ♦ **Bennington Battle Day**
August 16

During the Revolutionary War, Colonel Seth Warner and 350 of his Green Mountain Boys, a group of soldiers from Vermont, played a vital role in defeating the British forces who had come to capture the American supply depot at Bennington, a town in southern Vermont near the New York border. The anniversary of the fighting that took place along the Walloomsac River on August 16, 1777, is a legal holiday in Vermont, and a 306-foot tower has been erected in the town of Old Bennington, two miles west of Bennington proper. A statue of Seth Warner stands nearby. Across the state border in New York's Rensselaer County, the Bennington Battlefield State Park includes the site where the heaviest fighting took place.

SOURCES:
AmerBkDays-1978, p. 758
AnnivHol-1983, p. 108
Chases-1996, p. 338
DictDays-1988, p. 11

♦ 0177 ♦ **Berchtold's Day**
January 2

In Switzerland, the day after NEW YEAR'S DAY is known as **Berchtoldstag** and is celebrated primarily by children who hold neighborhood parties that feature nut eating and nut games followed by singing and folk dancing. A favorite game is the building of "hocks" composed of four nuts placed close together with a fifth balanced on top. The children begin gathering and hoarding nuts for the Berchtold's Day festivities in early autumn.

SOURCES:
AnnivHol-1983, p. 3
BkFest-1937, p. 316
FestWestEur-1958, p. 225

♦ 0178 ♦ **Bergen International Festival**
May–June

The Bergen International Festival is the major cultural event in Norway, and features more than 100 events in music, drama, folklore, opera, ballet, and the visual arts. Most of the musical events are held in Bergen's Viking Castle, Haakon's Hall (built in 1250), at the Grieg Concert Hall, at Edvard Grieg's home (known as "Troldhaugen"), and at Lysoen, the island home of composer and violinist Ole Bull. It was, in fact, Edvard Grieg—the composer and founder of the Norwegian nationalist school of music—who originated the idea for a musical festival and who first sponsored such a festival back in 1898. But the Bergen International Festival as it exists today didn't really get started until 1952. Although the primary attraction is music—ranging from classical to jazz, organ concerts, military band performances, and folklore opera—sometimes films and art exhibits are featured as well.

CONTACT:
Norwegian Tourist Board
655 Third Ave.
New York, NY 10017
212- 949-2333

SOURCES:
Chases-1996, p. 223
GdWrldFest-1985, p. 144
IntlThFolk-1979, p. 286
MusFestEurBrit-1980, p. 126
MusFestWrld-1963, p. 186

♦ 0179 ♦ **Bering Sea Ice Golf Classic**
Mid–March

This golfing challenge, played on a six-hole course with bright orange golf balls, takes place on the frozen Bering Sea off Nome, Alaska, at a time when the winds can be gale-strength. Par is 41, but winners have claimed scores as low as 23. Entry fees benefit the Lions Club. The tournament, not a wholly serious affair, coincides with the final days of the IDITAROD TRAIL SLED DOG RACE that starts about the first of March and ends in Nome about two weeks later.

CONTACT:
Alaska Division of Tourism
P.O. Box 110801
Juneau, AK 99811
907-465-2012; fax: 907-465-2287

SOURCES:
Chases-1996, p. 134

♦ 0180 ♦ **Berkshire Music Festival**
July–August

The 210-acre estate, donated in 1937 by Mrs. Gorham Brooks, in the Berkshire Mountains of western Massachusetts and known as Tanglewood, is the summer home of the Boston Symphony Orchestra. What is popularly known as the Berkshire or **Tanglewood Festival** originated in 1934 and in 1940 became part of the Berkshire Music Center, where advanced American and foreign musicians come to study and perform for nine weeks each summer. The festival includes concerts by the Boston Symphony and the Berkshire Music Center Orchestra as well as chamber music, jazz, choral and vocal concerts, and music theater productions. In early August there is a Festival of Contemporary Music that focuses on new works, some of which have been specially commissioned for the festival.

The grounds at Tanglewood open about two hours prior to the concerts so people can picnic on the lawns. More than 350,000 people come to Tanglewood over the course of the festival each summer.

CONTACT:
Massachusetts Office of Travel
  and Tourism
100 Cambridge St., 13th Floor
Boston, MA 02202
800-447-6277 or 617-727-3201
fax: 617-727-6525

SOURCES:
GdUSFest-1984, p. 86
MusFestAmer-1990, p. 81
MusFestWrld-1963, p. 280

♦ 0181 ♦ **Bermuda College Weeks**
March–April

College Weeks began as **Rugby Weeks** in the 1950s, when Ivy League rugby teams came to the island of Bermuda to spend their spring holidays and compete against Bermudian and British teams. But parties and socializing soon took precedence over the rugby competition, and College Weeks became a time for young people from colleges and universities all over the United States to meet in Bermuda and get an early start on the summer season.

The Bermuda government organizes and pays for all of the activities that are scheduled during this period, issuing courtesy cards that entitle college students free admission to everything from a "Get Acquainted" dance at one of the major hotels to beach parties, boat cruises, and steel band concerts. Scores of moped-riding college students take advantage of the island's hospitality, making Bermuda one of the most popular SPRING BREAK destinations.

CONTACT:
Bermuda Dept. of Tourism
310 Madison Ave., Ste. 201
New York, NY 10017
800-223-6106 or 212-818-9800
fax: 212-983-5289

SOURCES:
GdWrldFest-1985, p. 22

♦ 0182 ♦ **Bermuda Day**
May 24

Bermuda Day, formerly **Commonwealth Day,** is a public holiday, and the highlight of Bermuda Heritage Month. Since 1979, during May, there are a variety of cultural activities, including historical exhibits, musical concerts, and thanksgiving services in area churches. Festivities on May 24 include a parade starting at the Hamilton city hall. It is also a popular day for Bermudians to hit the beaches. Runners participate in a marathon race that starts at the Somerset Cricket Club and finishes up at the National Stadium. May 24 is also the beginning of dinghy-racing season—about every other Sunday the boaters race in St. George's Harbor.

CONTACT:
Bermuda Dept. of Tourism
310 Madison Ave., Ste. 201
New York, NY 10017
800-223-6106 or 212-818-9800
fax: 212-983-5289

Bermuda Race
See **Newport to Bermuda Race**

♦ 0183 ♦ **Bermuda Rendezvous Time**
December–mid-March

The winter season (December through mid-March) on the island of Bermuda is known as **Rendezvous Time,** a period during which the local Department of Tourism plans a number of special events for visitors. One of the most popular is the Skirling Ceremony held Mondays at noon at Fort Hamilton, which is a ceremonial performance by bagpipers in kilts, drummers, and dancers. Other regularly scheduled events include exhibitions of local crafts, walking tours of the 17th-century town of St. George, and visits by motorbike or ferry to the rustic village of Somerset. Bermuda also hosts an annual Festival for the Performing Arts during this period (early January to mid-February) which includes theater, dance, opera, classical, and modern music performances.

CONTACT:
Bermuda Dept. of Tourism
310 Madison Ave., Ste. 201
New York, NY 10017
800-223-6106 or 212-818-9800
fax: 212-983-5289

SOURCES:
GdWrldFest-1985, p. 22
IntlThFolk-1979, p. 50
MusFestAmer-1990, p. 157

♦ 0184 ♦ **Bettara-Ichi**
October 19

The annual **Pickle Market** or **Sticky-Sticky Fair** is held near the Ebisu Shrine in Tokyo, Japan, to supply people with what they will need to observe the Ebisu Festival on the following day, October 20. One of the seven Shinto deities of good luck and the patron deity of tradesmen, Ebisu has a limited following in Tokyo. But the fair that is held the day before is very popular. People buy wooden images of Ebisu, good-luck tokens, and most important of all, the large, white, pickled radish known as *bettara* that is so closely identified with the fair.

The Sticky-Sticky Fair was named after the way the pickled radishes were sold. Stall keepers used to dangle them from a rope so the buyer wouldn't get his hands sticky from the malted rice in which the radishes had been pickled. People would carry them home by swinging them from their ropes, calling out "Bettara! Bettara!" so that others would make way for them. But mischievous young boys would often deliberately swing the sticky pickles around in a crowd to tease the women and girls, who were all dressed up in their holiday clothes.

CONTACT:
Japan National Tourist
  Organization
630 Fifth Ave., Ste. 2101
New York, NY 10111
212-757-5640; fax: 212-307-6754

SOURCES:
BkFestHolWrld-1970, p. 114
BkHolWrld-1986, Oct 19
DictFolkMyth-1984, p. 336
JapanFest-1965, p. 200

♦ 0185 ♦ **Bhishma Ashtami**
January–February, eighth day of waxing half of Hindu month of Magha or during Hindu month of Kartika (October–November)

In Hindu mythology Bhishma was the son of King Shantanu. When his father decided he wanted to marry a beautiful young maiden named Satyavati, her parents would not permit it because it was Bhishma who was heir to the throne, and if she had sons they could not inherit the kingdom. To allow the marriage to go forward, Bhishma vowed never to marry and have children of his own, nor to accept the crown. Shantanu then married Satyavati, and she bore him two sons.

The two sons died without producing any offspring, but Satyavati had two grandchildren by a son who had been born before she married the king. Bhishma ended up raising these two and taking charge of the training of their children, who were known as the Kauravas and the Pandavas (*see also* ANANT CHATURDASHI). In the battle that was eventually fought between the two groups of offspring, Bhishma sided with the Kauravas and was so badly wounded it was said that there was barely a space of two fingers' width on his body that had not been pierced by an arrow. Since he had been allowed to choose the time of his death, he waited on his death-bed of arrows for 58 days, during which he delivered many religious discourses. He later became the model for modern ascetics who lie on nail-studded beds, and to this day is considered a great example of self-denial, loyalty, and devotion.

During the festival held in his honor, libations are offered to Bhishma with barley, sesame, flowers, and water from the sacred Ganges River.

CONTACT:
India Tourist Office
30 Rockefeller Ave.
15 N. Mezzanine
New York, NY 10112
212-586-4901; fax: 212-582-3274

SOURCES:
DictFolkMyth-1984, p. 139
RelHolCal-1993, p. 61

♦ 0186 ♦ **Bianou**
First new moon of February

A celebration of the end of the winter season in the market

town of Agadés (or Agadéz), Niger. The festivities are held for three days, and start with the sound of distant drumming and chanting of the *muzzein* calling people to prayer. As people assemble, the drummers appear. Behind them come the Tuareg nomads, wearing long blue robes and spinning around in their special dance, the *guedra*. The Tuareg turbans are folded in a way that suggests a cock's comb, since the cock is the symbol of the new season. Agadés is in northern Niger in the Sahara Desert. It was the seat of a Tuareg sultanate in the 15th century, and has been a crossroads for Fulani cattle herders, Tuareg traders, and Hausa merchants. The nomadic peoples also hold an annual gathering in Ingal town in August to take a census, at which time medical care is given by the national government.

See also CAMEL MARKET

CONTACT:
Niger Embassy
2204 R St., N.W.
Washington, D.C. 20008
202-483-4224; fax: 202-483-3169

♦ 0187 ♦ **Bible Week, National**
November, begins the Sunday before Thanksgiving

A week devoted to encouraging people to read the Bible, in the belief that it will arouse a positive spiritual force in a world plagued with problems. National Bible Week is promoted by the Laymen's National Bible Association, a nondenominational group of businessmen founded in 1940 and devoted to the application of the Golden Rule in daily life. On December 7, 1941, the group was broadcasting a program on NBC radio to kick off the first National Bible Week when the program was interrupted with the announcement that Pearl Harbor had just been bombed (*see* PEARL HARBOR DAY).

CONTACT:
Laymen's National Bible Association, Inc.
1865 Broadway, 12th Floor
New York, NY 10023
212-408-1390

SOURCES:
Chases-1996, p. 459
DaysCustFaith-1957, p. 275

♦ 0188 ♦ **Big Iron Farm Show and Exhibition**
September

The upper Midwest's largest agricultural exposition, the **Big Iron** is held at the Red River Valley Fairgrounds in West Fargo, North Dakota. Established in 1981 so that farmers would have a place where they could come to view the latest innovations in farming and agricultural equipment, the Big Iron prides itself on being a business event rather than a carnival. In the words of one organizer, "We don't distract people with music, pots and pans, and dog and pony acts." The three-day show regularly attracts more than 60,000 visitors, who come to see not only the farm equipment that is on exhibit but field demonstrations of tillage, crop-spraying, irrigation, and other equipment.

A special program for women takes place on "Ladies' Day." Seminars on such subjects as "Heirloom Art" and "The Changing Role of the Rural Woman" are offered, as well as other activities designed to inform and entertain women who participate in the running of a family farm.

CONTACT:
Fargo-Moorhead Convention and
  Visitors Bureau
P.O. Box 2164
Fargo, ND 58107
800-235-7654 or 701-282-3653
fax: 701-282-4366

Bike Week
See **Motorcycle Week**

♦ 0189 ♦ Bill of Rights Day
December 15

The first 10 amendments to the U.S. Constitution of 1787—referred to collectively as the Bill of Rights—were ratified on December 15, 1791. This landmark document protected American citizens from specific abuses by their government and guaranteed such basic rights as the freedom of religion, freedom of speech, and freedom of the press. In 1941 President Franklin D. Roosevelt designated December 15 as Bill of Rights Day and called upon Americans to observe it with appropriate patriotic ceremonies.

On December 10, 1948, the United Nations General Assembly unanimously adopted the Universal Declaration of Human Rights, and member countries of the U.N. began to observe December 10 as Human Rights Day. In the United States, the observance extended from December 10 to December 17 and was referred to as Human Rights Week. Since it encompasses December 15, the two events are now observed together and are typically celebrated with essay contests on the importance of freedom and democracy, special radio and television shows, and speeches on the themes of personal freedom and human rights.

In Massachusetts, the week of December 8–15 has been celebrated as Civil Rights Week since 1952. It honors not only the ratification of the Bill of Rights but the adoption of the state's first code of laws, the Body of Liberties, on December 10, 1641.

SOURCES:
AmerBkDays-1978, p. 1105
Chases-1996, p. 481
DaysCustFaith-1957, p. 314

♦ 0190 ♦ Billy Bowlegs Festival
First full week in June

The oldest and one of the biggest festivals in northwest Florida, held in Fort Walton Beach to commemorate the pirate William Augustus Bowles, also known as Capt. Billy Bowlegs. Bowles arrived in what's now known as the Florida panhandle in 1778 when the Spanish, English, and Americans were maneuvering for control of the Gulf shores. He put together a force of Indians and "White Banditti," created his own throne, and formed the State of Muskogee. To support it, he ran raids on the Gulf of Mexico and on the mainland. He was finally seized and imprisoned in Morro Castle in Cuba, where he starved himself to death in 1803.

This is not a particularly joyous saga, but the light-hearted affair of the Billy Bowlegs Festival goes on for a week. The festival began in 1954 and today attracts about 40,000 spectators. Activities begin with a simulated naval gun battle on Friday night. The following day, the pirate captain and his red-kerchiefed "krewe" members storm the city from the pirate ship *Blackhawk*. As events move on there are spectacular fireworks displays, a treasure hunt, a boat parade with about 300 boats, arts and crafts, numerous food vendors, concerts, and sports events that include a midnight run. More than 100 floats take part in a torchlight parade, and parade participants rain gold doubloons and assorted trinkets on the clamoring crowds.

CONTACT:
Florida Division of Tourism
126 W. Van Buren
Tallahassee, FL 32399
904-487-1462; fax: 904-921-9158

SOURCES:
Chases-1996, p. 245

Birchat Hahamah
See **Blessing the Sun**

♦ 0191 ♦ Birmingham Festival of the Arts
Third week in April

This display of performing and visual arts honors a different nation each year, and has been held since 1951 in Birmingham, Ala. A 10-day affair, the festival celebrates the chosen country's theater, literature, history, music, customs, and food with films, lectures, exhibits, and book-and-author luncheons. Traditional dance and folk music ensembles from the honored country perform, and the Alabama Symphony Orchestra presents concerts. There are also parades and street dances.

CONTACT:
Alabama Bureau of Tourism and
  Travel
P.O. Box 4927
Montgomery, AL 36103
800-252-2263 or 334-242-4169
fax: 334-242-4554

SOURCES:
Chases-1996, p. 174
GdUSFest-1984, p. 3
MusFestAmer-1990, p. 20

Bi-Shevat
See **Tu Bishvat**

♦ 0192 ♦ Bisket Jatra
April 13 or 14

The festival of the new year in Nepal, **Nava Varsa**, is celebrated with exchanges of greetings and in some areas with ritual bathing. The most important celebration is Bisket Jatra, which means the 'festival after the death of the serpent.' In Bhaktapur, the new year is celebrated by parading images of gods in chariots. The main attraction of the festival is the erection of a ceremonial pole—a lingam or phallic symbol. This is a peeled tree trunk as much as 80 feet in length that is erected using bamboo and heavy ropes while crowds watch. On New Year's Day, the pole is torn down.

There is a legend behind this ceremonial pole. The daughter of the king of Bhaktapur was insatiable and demanded a new lover every night, but she left her lovers dead by morning. Then a brave prince appeared to try his luck. He managed to stay awake through the night, and saw two thread-like wisps emerging from the princess's nostrils. These wisps turned into poisonous snakes, so the prince drew his sword and killed them. Of course the prince and princess lived happily ever after. This story is recalled with the raising of the pole of Bisket Jatra.

Most holidays in Nepal are set by the lunar calendar, but New Year's Day is an exception and always falls in the middle of April.

CONTACT:
Nepal Embassy
2131 Leroy Pl., N.W.
Washington, D.C. 20008
202-667-4550; fax: 202-667-5534

♦ 0193 ♦ **Black Christ, Festival of the**
October 21

There are two legends associated with the observance of the **Black Christ Festival** in Portobelo, Panama. One says that during a cholera epidemic on the Isthmus, the people found a crate floating on the water near the beach. When they brought it ashore and opened it, they discovered a statue of a black Christ. They brought it into the church and, within a few days, the cholera had completely disappeared from Portobelo, even though it continued to rage elsewhere.

The other legend concerns a ship carrying the black Christ statue from Spain to Cartagena, Colombia. The ship stopped for supplies in Portobelo, but when it attempted to leave, it was turned back five times by sudden storms. The crew finally threw the crate containing the statue overboard, but local residents rescued it and put it in a place of honor in their church. The image of the black Christ, which is made of dark brown coco-bolo wood, has been credited with everything from miraculous cures to helping the city win the national lottery.

The people of Portobelo honor their patron saint, El Jesús Nazarene, by carrying the statue in procession on a decorated platform through the city streets. Pilgrims come from all over Panama, as they have for more than 300 years, to celebrate with folk dancing, music, and songs.

See also BLACK NAZARENE FIESTA

CONTACT:
Panama Embassy
2862 McGill Terr., N.W.
Washington, D.C. 20008
202-483-1407; fax: 202-483-8413

SOURCES:
GdWrldFest-1985, p. 148

♦ 0194 ♦ **Black Cowboys Parade**
First Saturday in October

A salute to the black cowboys who helped settle the West, held since 1975 in Oakland, Calif. Hundreds of mounted cowboys and marching bands participate in the parade, the only one of its kind in the nation. There are also arts and crafts exhibits and food booths.

CONTACT:
Oakland Convention and Visitors
  Bureau
1000 Broadway, Ste. 200
Oakland, CA 94607
800-262-5526 or 510-839-9000
fax: 510-839-5924

♦ 0195 ♦ **Black Friday**
Various

Black Friday usually refers either to the infamous Wall Street Panic of September 24, 1869, when Jay Gould and James Fisk tried to "corner" the gold market, or to September 19, 1873,

when stock failures caused the Panic of 1873. In England, it is often used by workers to describe May 12, 1926, the day on which the General Strike was ended. It is occasionally used to refer to GOOD FRIDAY.

Shoppers and retailers in the United States sometimes refer to the day after THANKSGIVING as Black Friday because it marks the beginning of the CHRISTMAS commercial season and is traditionally a frenetic day of shopping.

SOURCES:
Chases-1996, p. 463
DictDays-1988, p. 12

♦ 0196 ♦ **Black Hills Motor Classic**
First Monday of August through following Sunday

A mammoth yearly rally of 250,000 or so motorcyclists in small Sturgis, S.D. (population 7,000). There are races, merrymaking, band music, and usually some misbehavior, including arrests for drunken driving. There tend to be numerous accidents with injuries, and sometimes, fatalities. Motorcycle drag racing runs eight days, and other official events include bike shows, a swap meet, monster truck races, Tough Man and Tough Woman Contests (the titles determined by fights in which biting and kicking but not much else are forbidden), and a fireworks show. Unofficial events are weddings; bikers find it romantic to get married during the rally, and in 1990, the 50th anniversary rally, 176 motorcycling couples exchanged vows.

The rally began in 1938 when Clarence (Pappy) Hoel, a local motorcycle dealer, invited some fellow bikers to a get-to-gether. His wife, Pearl, made hot dogs, potato salad, and iced tea for the crew. The rally has been held ever since, except for two years during World War II, and has become part of biker lore.

CONTACT:
South Dakota Dept. of Tourism
711 E. Wells Ave.
Pierre, SD 57501
800-952-3625 or 605-773-3301
fax: 605-773-3256

SOURCES:
Chases-1996, p. 325

♦ 0197 ♦ **Black Hills Passion Play**
June–August

One of Europe's oldest productions, the Passion Play—which recreates events during the last seven days of the life of Christ—was first presented on the American stage in 1932. It was brought to the United States from Germany by Joseph Meier, who continues to produce and direct the drama three nights a week from early June through the end of August in an outdoor amphitheater in Spearfish, South Dakota. Known as the Black Hills Passion Play since 1939, when the company settled in Spearfish, the huge outdoor production features Roman soldiers on horseback, a camel caravan, and pigeons escaping from cages as merchants and moneylenders are driven from the Temple. The amphitheater, which seats 6,000, was built specifically for the Passion Play and claims to have the world's largest stage. A series of permanent sets are used to portray Bethany, the home of Mary and Martha; the palace of Pontius Pilate, the Roman governor; the Temple; the Garden of Gethsemane; the Tomb; and Mount Calvary.

CONTACT:
South Dakota Dept. of Tourism
711 E. Wells Ave.
Pierre, SD 57501
800-952-3625 or 605-773-3301
fax: 605-773-3256

SOURCES:
Chases-1996, p. 240

♦ 0198 ♦ **Black History Month**
February

Black History Month grew out of **Negro History Week,** which was established in February 1926 by the African-American historian Carter G. Woodson. Expanded in 1976 to a month-long observance, this celebration of the contributions and achievements of African-Americans was initially designed to encompass the birthday of the abolitionist orator and journalist Frederick Douglass (1817–1895) on February 14 as well as Abraham Lincoln's birthday (*see* LINCOLN'S BIRTHDAY). The event is widely observed by schools, churches, libraries, clubs, and organizations wishing to draw attention to the contributions of African-Americans.

Douglass was a fugitive slave who assumed this name when, by posing as a sailor, he escaped to New Bedford, Massachusetts. His former master's wife had secretly taught him to read and write, and after his escape Douglass became a skilled orator who lectured widely in favor of abolition. He settled for a while in Rochester, New York, where he founded an anti-slavery newspaper, and eventually ended up in Washington, D.C., where he held a number of government positions. One of his former residences there now houses the Museum of African Art and the Frederick Douglass Institute.

CONTACT:
Association for the Study of
  Afro-American Life and History
1407 14th St., N.W.
Washington, D.C. 20005
202-667-2822; fax: 202-387-9802

SOURCES:
Chases-1996, p. 81

♦ 0199 ♦ **Black Madonna of Jasna Gora, Feast of the**
August 15

The most famous icon in Eastern Europe can be found at the monastery on Jasna Gora, in the city of Czestochowa, Poland. The *Czarna Madonna,* or Black Madonna, is so called because of the dark complexion in the portrait of the Virgin Mary that, according to legend, was painted by St. Luke on a linden wood tabletop built by the apprentice carpenter, Jesus of Nazareth. Each year on August 15, the feast of the ASSUMPTION, hundreds of thousands of pilgrims attend the **Feast of Our Lady of Czestochowa** to seek forgiveness for their sins, recovery from injury or illness, or to offer gratitude for a favor granted. With their rosaries in hand, the pilgrims—some on their knees—climb Jasna Gora, which means the 'Hill of Light,' to attend mass at the monastery, celebrated above them, on the high monastery walls, by priests in golden chasubles.

More than 80 miracles have been documented at the shrine, which is only one of many dedicated to the Virgin Mary throughout the country. King John II Casimir proclaimed the Virgin Mary to be the Queen of Poland in 1656 after an unlikely victory over the Swedes at Jasna Gora prevented the latter from overrunning the monastery and looting its treasures. Mary is the patron saint of Poland.

CONTACT:
Polish National Tourist Office
275 Madison Ave., Ste. 1711
New York, NY 10016
212-338-9412; fax: 212-338-9283

♦ 0200 ♦ **Black Nazarene Fiesta**
January 1–9

The **Fiesta of Quiapo District** is the largest festival in Manila, Philippines. It is held each year in honor of the Quiapo District's patron saint—the Black Nazarene, a life-size statue of Jesus carved from blackwood, whose shrine is located in Quiapo's baroque church. The traditional nine-day fiesta features nightly cultural events, band concerts, and fireworks. On the last day of the festival there is a procession of barefoot men pulling a carriage that holds the 200-year-old statue of Christ on the way to Calvary. Those members of the procession who are not pulling the carriage carry candles and circle throughout the district.

CONTACT:
Philippine Department of Tourism
556 Fifth Ave.
First Floor Mezzanine
New York, NY 10036
212-575-7915; fax: 212-302-6759

SOURCES:
AnnivHol-1983, p. 173
Chases-1996, pp. 51, 61
GdWrldFest-1985, p. 153

♦ 0201 ♦ **Black Poetry Day**
October 17

Jupiter Hammon, the first African-American poet to publish his own verse, was born on this day in 1711 and lived most of his life in the Lloyd Neck area of Huntington, Long Island. Hammon was a slave—first to the merchant Henry Lloyd, lord of the Manor of Queen's Village (now Lloyd Neck), and later to Joseph Lloyd, an American patriot who moved to Hartford, Connecticut, during the Revolution. Hammon eventually returned to Lloyd Neck as slave to Joseph's grandson, John Lloyd. Hammon learned how to read and was allowed to use his master's library. On Christmas Day, 1760, he published his first poem, "An Evening Thought," at the age of 49. He went on to publish other poems and a number of prose pieces as well.

Black Poetry Day was first proposed in 1970 by Stanley A. Ransom of Huntington, who was concerned that there were no existing celebrations to honor the contributions African-Americans have made to American life and culture. When Ransom relocated to Plattsburgh, New York, he brought Black Poetry Day with him. Although it is celebrated all over the state, it has yet to be formally proclaimed a state holiday. Oregon has already proclaimed October 17 as Black Poetry Day, and schools elsewhere have taken advantage of the opportunity to encourage African-American students to express their thoughts and feelings through poetry. Other celebrations include inviting guest poets to do readings and meet with students at SUNY-Plattsburgh. In 1985, the African-American poet Gwendolyn Brooks spoke at SUNY-Plattsburgh in honor of Jupiter Hammon's contribution to American culture. Other poets who have visited in the past for Black Poetry Day include Nikki Giovanni, Lucille Clifton, Ntozake Shange, Derek Walcott, Michael Harper, and Yusef Komunyakaa. In 1993 Rita Dove, an African-American, was named poet laureate of the United States.

CONTACT:
Black Poetry Day Committee
Affirmative Action Office
State University College
Plattsburgh, NY 12901
518-564-5250; fax: 518-564-4600

SOURCES:
Chases-1996, p. 420

♦ 0202 ♦ **Black Ships Festival**
*May 16 and 17 in Shimoda, Japan; last weekend
in July in Rhode Island*

Kurofune is what the Japanese called the black ships that
Commodore Matthew C. Perry anchored off Shimoda, Japan, on July 8, 1853. He forcefully negotiated the Treaty of
Kanagawa—the first treaty between the United States and
Japan—in 1854. The treaty opened trade between the two
countries and ended two centuries of self-imposed isolation
for Japan.

In 1934, Shimoda began commemorating the arrival of Commodore Perry and his black ships. It is the site of the first
American consulate in Japan, placed there by the Japanese to
keep the "barbarians" (Americans) away from the capital,
then called Edo. The first consul-general, Townsend Harris,
arrived in August 1856. Twenty years later, Shimoda became
the sister city to Newport, Rhode Island, where Perry was
born. In 1984, Newport celebrated a reciprocal Black Ships
Festival emphasizing Japanese art, culture, and education.
Events include Japanese tea ceremonies, ikebana (flower
arranging), origami (paper folding), kendo (martial arts),
Sumo wrestling, Japanese kite flying, and traditional Japanese performing arts. In 1986 the Black Ships Festival was
expanded to form the Japan-America Society of Rhode
Island, which now sponsors the festival and works to develop cooperation and understanding between the citizens of
Rhode Island and Japan.

CONTACT:
Rhode Island Tourism Division
7 Jackson Walkway
Providence, RI 02903
800-556-2484 or 401-277-2601
fax: 401-277-2102

Japan National Tourist
  Organization
630 Fifth Ave., Ste. 2101
New York, NY 10111
212-757-5640; fax: 212-307-6754

SOURCES:
AnnivHol-1983, p. 93
JapanFest-1965, p. 152

♦ 0203 ♦ **Blajini, Feast of the (Sarbatoarea
Blajinilor)**
April–May; second Monday after Easter

Among the peasants in Romania there is a widespread belief
in the existence of the *Blajini,* the 'Meek' or 'Kindly Ones'—a
lost race who keep to themselves, know nothing of the world
of men, and live in a fairy-land "by the Sunday-water."
They are beloved by God because of their purity and inno-
cence. On the Monday after EASTER MONDAY, Romanian wom-
en throw red Easter egg shells on running streams, since they
believe that the *Blajini* live on the banks of the river fed by all
the streams of the world. Their hope is that the *Blajini* will
find the shells and know it is time to celebrate the EASTER
feast.

SOURCES:
BkFest-1937, p. 277

FolkWrldHol-1992, p. 207

♦ 0204 ♦ **Blavatsky, Death of Helena Petrovna**
May 8

The anniversary of the death of Helena Petrovna Blavatsky
(1831–1891) is commemorated by members of the Theosophical
Society, which was founded in New York in 1875 by Blavatsky
and Henry Olcott. Theosophy, a pantheistic philosophical-
religious system that seeks to learn about reality through
mystical experience and by finding esoteric meanings in
sacred writings, is regarded as the precursor of American
Hinduism. Olcott and Blavatsky moved to India in 1878, and
the international headquarters for the Theosophical movement remains in Adyar (near Madras) today.

Blavatsky believed that she possessed extraordinary psychic
powers, although in 1884 the Indian press accused her of
concocting spiritualist phenomena. When the London Society of Psychical Research declared her a fraud the following
year, Blavatsky left India and never returned. She did, however, complete her most important work, *The Secret Doctrine*
(1888), an overview of Theosophical teachings, along with
numerous other books, before her death in 1891.

CONTACT:
Theosophical Society in America
1926 N. Main St.
Wheaton, IL 60187
800-669-1571 or 708-668-1571
fax: 708-668-4976

SOURCES:
DictWrldRel-1989, pp. 320,
  757
RelHolCal-1993, p. 70

♦ 0205 ♦ **Blessed Sacrament, Feast of the**
First weekend in August

The **Festival of the Blessed Sacrament** held annually in New
Bedford, Massachusetts, coincides with a similar festival on
the Portuguese island of Madeira. The American festival,
which was first held in 1914, celebrates the safe arrival of the
Portuguese immigrants who came to New Bedford in the
early 19th century after braving rough seas and stormy
weather en route. The descendants of these immigrants,
many of whom served aboard American whaleships, give
thanks each year by holding what they would like to think of
as the largest Portuguese feast in the world on the first
weekend in August. Preparations for the festivities go on
throughout the year, and the events include a parade, Portuguese folkloric dancers and singers, Portuguese specialties
such as *cabra* (goat) and *bacalhau* (codfish), and a colorful
procession to the Immaculate Conception Church. The festival is held at Madeira Field, although the events extend
throughout the city. New Bedford, once a thriving New
England whaling port, remains home to a large Portuguese-
American community.

CONTACT:
Massachusetts Office of Travel
  and Tourism
100 Cambridge St., 13th Floor
Boston, MA 02202
800-447-6277 or 617-727-3201
fax: 617-727-6525

SOURCES:
GdUSFest-1984, p. 87

♦ 0206 ♦ **Blessing of the Grapes (Haghoghy
Ortnootyoon)**
Sunday nearest August 15

In ancient times the people of Armenia dedicated their grape harvest to Astrik, the goddess of the hearth, in a New Year celebration called *Navasard*. Nowadays the festival is associated with the Feast of the ASSUMPTION, and is celebrated on the Sunday nearest to August 15, which is the feast day. No one is supposed to eat grapes until this day, when a tray filled with them is blessed in the church. Each member of the congregation is given a bunch of grapes as he or she leaves, and parties are held after the church ceremony in homes and in the vineyards. It is also traditional for women named Mary to entertain their friends on this, their name day.

SOURCES:
BkFest-1937, p. 27
BkFestHolWrld-1970, p. 109
BkHolWrld-1986, Aug 25
DaysCustFaith-1957, p. 207
FestSaintDays-1915, p. 172
FolkWrldHol-1992, p. 419

♦ 0207 ♦ **Blessing of the Shrimp Fleet**
June

In the coastal town of Bayou La Batre, the "Seafood Capital of Alabama," the two-day event has been celebrated since 1950. The "main street" of the town, founded in 1786, is actually the bayou, where trawlers are often tied up three- or four-deep. Shrimp is the mainstay of commercial fishing here, and more than 350 shrimp boats work out of the town, while several hundred other vessels operate in the waters off the port harvesting oysters, crab, and finfish. Seafood products landed in the port have a dockside value of $33 million annually, but the total seafood industry, including processors, is thought to produce $300 million for the local economy. Boat building and repair are also major industries.

The fleet blessing began simply: a priest went up and down the bayou blessing the boats tied to the docks. From the start, a wreath has been lowered into the bayou to honor fishermen lost at sea. Now some 25,000 people come for the highlight and final event of the weekend: the blessing ceremony by the priest of St. Margaret Roman Catholic Church and a parade of between 50 and 100 boats decorated with pennants, bunting, and papier mâché figures. Other events include contests in oyster shucking, shrimp heading, and crab picking; seafood and gumbo dinners; a land parade; a fiddler-crab race for children; and the crowning of the Fleet Queen. The affair is sponsored by St. Margaret Church.

In the port city of Biloxi, Mississippi, **Blessing of the Fleet** is a celebration of the start of the fishing season, where seafood is the major industry. It is held over the first weekend in June. The blessing began in 1924 when sailing craft made up most of the fleet. Today up to 80 boats parade past the Blessing Boat, where the pastor of St. Michael's Roman Catholic Church (known as the Church of the Fisherman) stands and bestows the blessings. The boats are decorated with flags and elaborate three-dimensional plywood constructions of such figures as mermaids, shrimp, paddlewheels, and fishnets. The blessing is the culmination of the weekend; before that, there are net-throwing and oyster-shucking contests, the crowning of a king and queen, and street dances known as *fais-do-do*. Supposedly "fais-do-do" was the song sung to children to tell them to go to sleep, and the dance got its name because adults danced when the children slept. The weekend also offers lots of local food—mullet, boiled shrimp, and Biloxi bacon.

CONTACT:
Alabama Bureau of Tourism and
 Travel
P.O. Box 4927
Montgomery, AL 36103
800-252-2263 or 334-242-4169
fax: 334-242-4554

Mississippi Division of Tourism
 Development
P.O. Box 849
Jackson, MS 39205
800-927-6378 or 601-359-3297
fax: 601-359-5757

SOURCES:
GdUSFest-1984, p. 100
RelHolCal-1993, p. 64

Blessing of the Waters Day
See **Orthodox Epiphany**

Blessing of Throats
See **St. Blaise's Day**

♦ 0208 ♦ **Blessing the Sun (Birchat Hahamah)**
*March–April; every 28 years on the first
Wednesday in Jewish month of Nisan*

According to Jewish tradition, God made the sun, the moon, and the stars on the fourth day of Creation—a Wednesday, according to ancient reckoning—and once every 28 years the sun returns to the same astronomical position that it held on that day. The Talmud says that the turning point of this 28-year sun cycle occurs at the VERNAL EQUINOX on a Tuesday evening (the first in the month of Nisan) at 6:00 P.M. in Jerusalem. But since the sun is not visible at that time in all parts of the world, the blessing isn't recited until the following morning at sunrise. The blessing is said while standing, and the sun must be visible.

The last blessing of the sun occurred on April 8, 1981, with about 50,000 Jews gathered at the Wailing Wall in Jerusalem, Judaism's holiest shrine. Similar celebrations took place on top of Israel's highest building in Tel Aviv and at the Empire State Building in New York City. The next **Blessing of the Sun** will take place in 2009.

SOURCES:
FolkAmerHol-1991, p. 182

♦ 0209 ♦ **Bloomsday**
June 16

James Joyce's novel *Ulysses* describes the events of a single day in Dublin: June 16, 1904. First published in Paris in 1922 because it had been banned elsewhere, *Ulysses* caused an uproar when it finally did appear in Ireland, and for a time, Joyce was reviled by the people of Dublin. But since 1954 Bloomsday—named after the novel's main character, Leopold Bloom—has been a Joycean feast day, observed with a number of events throughout Dublin that commemorate its illustrious author and the lives of his characters. There is a ritual pilgrimage along the "Ulysses Trail" (the path followed by Leopold Bloom), public readings from the novel, costume parties, and parades. Joyce fans can visit the Martello

Tower, where the author lived, the James Joyce Cultural Center, and Davy Byrne's Pub, where Leopold Bloom stops on his day-long odyssey. Restaurants specialize in serving the dishes that Bloom ate: kidneys for breakfast, gorgonzola cheese and burgundy for lunch.

CONTACT:
Irish Tourist Board
345 Park Ave.
New York, NY 10154
212-418-0800; fax: 212-371-9052

SOURCES:
AnnivHol-1983, p. 80
Chases-1996, p. 259
DictDays-1988, p. 13
FestEur-1992, p. 12

♦ 0210 ♦ Blowing the Midwinter Horn
December–January; beginning of Advent through Sunday after Epiphany

The custom of **Midwinterhoorn Blazen** in the province of Overijssel, Netherlands, is believed to have originated more than 2,000 years ago. The local farmers make their winter horns out of fitted sections of curving birchwood. The horns are about 45 inches long and when soaked in water, they give out a shrill, plaintive sound that carries for great distances over the frozen countryside. Although in pagan times the blowing of the horns was thought to rid the earth of evil spirits, today the horns announce the coming of Christ.

In Oldenzaal, a special melody composed by the area's champion hornblower is played from the four corners of the local church tower, beginning at dawn on ADVENT Eve and continuing until THREE KINGS' DAY (EPIPHANY).

SOURCES:
BkHolWrld-1986, Dec 15
Chases-1996, p. 468
FestWestEur-1958, p. 143

♦ 0211 ♦ Bluegrass Fan Fest
Third week in September

A festival for fans that follows a week-long trade show of the International Bluegrass Music Association, held the third week in September in Owensboro, Ky. Owensboro was the choice for the event's location because Bill Monroe (1912-1996)—the founder of the seminal bluegrass group, The Blue Grass Boys, and father of bluegrass music—was born in Ohio County, 30 miles from the city. Between 30 and 40 bluegrass groups perform, and proceeds from admission sales go to a trust fund for IBMA members.

CONTACT:
International Bluegrass Music
  Association
207 E. Second St.
Owensboro, KY 42303
502-684-9025; fax: 502-686-7863

♦ 0212 ♦ Boat Race Day in Okinawa
Fourteenth day of fifth lunar month

On Okinawa, the largest of the Ryukyu Islands southwest of Japan, the 14th day of the fifth month is both a religious festival and a sporting event. In Minatogawa, for example, this is the **Festival of the Gods of the Sea**. The villagers first go to the religious sites to make offerings and pray, and then they attend the boat races held in the estuary of the river. In Taira, it is the day on which fishing canoes from Taira race against competitors from the neighboring village of Kawata.

CONTACT:
Japan National Tourist
  Organization
630 Fifth Ave., Ste. 2101
New York, NY 10111
212-757-5640; fax: 212-307-6754

SOURCES:
FolkWrldHol-1992, p. 316

♦ 0213 ♦ Boat Race Day on the Thames
Late March or early April

This is the annual rowing race between the Oxford and Cambridge University "eights" (as the crews of the eight-oared rowing shells are called) that takes place on the Thames River in England. The race is scheduled to be held on a day when there's an incoming spring tide, which usually occurs in late March or early April. Beginning in Putney and ending four-and-a-quarter miles downriver at Mortlake, the race attracts large crowds of spectators—many of whom are hoping for the drama of an unexpected capsizing.

CONTACT:
British Tourist Authority
551 Fifth Ave., Ste. 702
New York, NY 10176
800-462-2748 or 212-986-2200
fax: 212-986-1188

SOURCES:
Chases-1996, p. 149
DictDays-1988, p. 14

♦ 0214 ♦ Boggy Bayou Mullet Festival
Third full weekend in October

A festival of seafood, folk culture, sports, and pageants held since 1976 in Niceville, Fla. It celebrates the unappreciated mullet, the underdog of seafood, and serves up 10 tons of fried and smoked mullet, plus vast quantities of "mullet dogs," mullet filets on buns. Attendance can reach upwards of 200,000.

Niceville is a small town about 50 miles east of Pensacola on the Florida panhandle. But people kept calling Niceville "Nashville", so, to publicize the town and to promote mullet the Boggy Bayou Festival was begun. Mullet, abundant in the local Gulf waters, is a cheap source of high-quality protein but has had a bad reputation among seafood fanciers because of its feeding habits. Mullet are bottom-feeding vegetarians, and they taste like what they eat. The people of Niceville know that only mullet caught from waters with clean bottoms—like those on Florida's Gulf Coast—are worth eating.

This sleepy bayou town's festival has exploded into a fully rounded affair. It has beauty pageants to name not only the Queen of the Mullet Festival but also Miss Teen Mullet Festival, Junior Miss Mullet Festival, and Little Miss Mullet Festival. Sports events include golf, rugby, and racquetball tournaments, and a canoe race; the U.S. Army Rangers bring their reptile exhibit of a six-foot alligator and rattlesnakes; free entertainment is on stage all weekend. Then there is the food. Beyond the mullet, these are samplings from the food booths: Cajun specialties like crawfish pie, gumbo, and gator sausage; American Indian staples of fried bread and *pasole*, which is like pizza; barbecued rabbit, stingray and barracuda on a stick, fried oysters, boiled shrimp, apple dumplings, strawberry pie, and Mexican fried ice cream.

CONTACT:
Florida Division of Tourism
126 W. Van Buren
Tallahassee, FL 32399
904-487-1462; fax: 904-921-9158

♦ 0215 ♦ **Bok Kai Festival**
Usually March or April; second day of second month of Chinese lunar year

A two-day event in Marysville, Calif., that began as a Chinese religious event to honor Bok Eye (or Bok I), the god who has the power to control flooding and the waters of irrigation and the rains. The festival, held since the 1880s, is now more of a cultural tribute to the Bok Kai legend.

Chinese immigrants came to northern California in the 1850s to find work in the gold fields or on the railroads being built through the Sierra Nevada mountains. When the railroads were completed, they settled in Marysville, which became the third largest Chinese community in the country, after San Francisco and Sacramento.

Between 1825 and 1862, three floods caused hundreds of fatalities in the Marysville area. In 1865, the Chinese first built a temple on the Yuba River, naming it Bok Kai Mui, meaning temple (Mui) on the north (Bok) side of the stream (Kai). (The temple was destroyed by fire and rebuilt in 1880.) Several gods were placed in the temple, but Bok Eye, meaning Northern or Dark North God, was the central deity. By building the temple in his honor, the Chinese people hoped to protect the city from future flooding.

The celebration of **Bomb Day**—Bok Eye's birthday—began in the 1880s. Today the celebration of Bomb Day with the Bok Kai Festival is a community-wide affair, drawing thousands of visitors from as far as Hong Kong. A parade is the highlight of the festival, and a 150-foot dragon is the highlight of the parade. It winds its way along the parade route on the legs of 100 volunteers, accompanied by floats and marching bands, Clydesdale horses and a Wells Fargo stagecoach—more than 100 entries in all. The current dragon is the second one to be used in the parade. The first, brought to the United States before 1900, was retired in 1937 and now rests in the temple.

Besides the parade, there are vendors' markets for foods and crafts, demonstrations of martial arts, lion dancing, art displays, and performances by celebrated Chinese artists; these have included a master of Chinese brush painting, a pianist from China, and a composer and poet.

The Bok Kai Temple in Marysville is the only religious shrine to Bok Eye outside of Asia and is a designated historical landmark.

CONTACT:
California Division of Tourism
801 K Street, Ste. 1600
Sacramento, CA 95814
800-862-2543 or 916-322-2881
fax: 916-322-3402

♦ 0216 ♦ **Bolivia Independence Day**
August 6

Bolivians proclaimed their independence from Spain in 1809, but it took 16 years of struggle to actually gain it in 1825. Spain had ruled the area since the 16th century. The country was named for its revolutionary hero, Simon Bolívar, who, with José SAN MARTIN, led the Battle of Ayacucho in 1824 that resulted in the end of Spanish rule of Bolivia and Peru.

Independence Day is a public holiday, celebrated over two

days including August 6, with parades and dancing in the streets of La Paz and Sucre.

CONTACT:
Bolivian Embassy
3014 Massachusetts Ave., N.W.
Washington, D.C. 20008
202-483-4410; fax: 202-328-3712

SOURCES:
AnnivHol-1983, p. 103
Chases-1996, p. 326
NatlHolWrld-1968, p. 134

♦ 0217 ♦ **Bologna Festival**
Last full weekend in July

In 1906 a bologna maker named T. J. Minnie set up his shop in Yale, Michigan. Over the next several decades, a number of other bologna makers settled in Yale, but today only one remains: C. Roy Inc., which produces Yale Bologna. The annual Bologna Festival, established in 1989, is designed to attract true bologna lovers with its booths serving bologna rings, bologna hot dogs, bologna and sauerkraut, and fried bologna sandwiches. A King and Queen Bologna are crowned, and they ride through town on the C. Roy float in the Big Bologna Parade wearing crowns made out of bologna rings.

CONTACT:
Michigan Travel Bureau
333 S. Capitol Ave., Ste. F
Lansing, MI 48933
800-543-2937 or 517-373-0670
fax: 517-373-0059

♦ 0218 ♦ **Bolshevik Revolution Day**
November 7

The commemoration of the October Revolution of 1917 when the Bolsheviks overthrew the Russian government by seizing power in Petrograd (formerly St. Petersburg, later named Leningrad, and in 1991, after the collapse of the Communist Party, renamed St. Petersburg). The coup took place on Nov. 7 (Oct. 25 on the Julian calendar) and through the years was celebrated as a national holiday marking the start of the Soviet regime. Celebrations were particularly lavish in Moscow, with grand military parades and fly-overs and the Soviet leadership reviewing the parade from atop the Lenin Mausoleum. In Leningrad, the Soviet Baltic fleet sailed up the Neva to drop anchor across from the Winter Palace.

All this ended in 1991. With the Soviet Union disintegrating, the state holiday was still in place, but marches and demonstrations were banned in Moscow. In the newly renamed St. Petersburg, Mayor Anatoly A. Sobchak attended Russian Orthodox services (formerly forbidden) with the Grand Duke Vladimir Kirillovich Romanov, son of a cousin of the last czar.

SOURCES:
AnnivHol-1983, p. 143
BkFest-1937, p. 286
Chases-1996, p. 443
FolkWrldHol-1992, p. 554
NatlHolWrld-1968, p. 202

♦ 0219 ♦ **Bom Jesus dos Navegantes**
January 1

In Salvador, Brazil, the festival known as Bom Jesus dos Navegantes is celebrated on NEW YEAR'S DAY. A procession of small boats decorated with flags and streamers carries a statue of the **Lord Jesus of Seafarers** from the main harbor to the outlying beach of Boa Viagem. Thousands of spectators line Salvador's beaches to catch a glimpse of the spectacle. According to legend, sailors participating in the event will never die by drowning.

A similar procession takes place on the same day in Angra dos Reis, 90 miles south of Rio de Janeiro.

CONTACT:
Brazilian Embassy
3006 Massachusetts Ave., N.W.
Washington, D.C. 20008
202-745-2700; fax: 202-745-2827

♦ 0220 ♦ Bona Dea Festival
May 1

The ancient Roman festival known as the Bona Dea, or **Maia Maiesta Festival**, was celebrated only by women; no men were allowed to observe or participate in the festivities. Variously described as the sister, daughter, or wife of Faunus, the rustic Roman fertility god, Bona Dea was a deified woman, a chaste matron who was killed by a suspicious husband. Because she revealed her prophesies only to women, Bona Dea's temple was cared for by women, and all of her rites were restricted to women.

The festival of Bona Dea was observed on May 1, the day on which her temple had been dedicated on the Aventine Hill in Rome. The ceremonies were performed by vestal virgins and a group of very respectable matrons, although the rituals associated with the festival apparently included remnants of phallic worship and the telling of indecencies which were not to be repeated to the uninitiated. The observance of the Bona Dea festival undoubtedly contributed to the Roman belief that May was an unlucky month for marriage.

See also MEGALESIA and OPALIA

SOURCES:
AmerBkDays-1978, p. 406
DictFolkMyth-1984, p. 867
FestSaintDays-1915, p. 110

♦ 0221 ♦ Bonfim Festival (Festa do Bonfim)
January

There is a church in Salvador, Bahia, Brazil, known as Our Lord of the Happy Ending (*bonfim*). It was built by the captain of a ship, wrecked off the coast of Bahia in 1875, who promised God that if his men survived, he would build Him a church in gratitude. Today during the Bonfim Festival, hundreds of Brazilian women dress in the traditional white dresses of colonial Bahia and form a procession to the church. The *bahianas* carry pots of water on their heads, perfumed with white flowers. The washing of the steps at Bonfim Basilica on the final Sunday is the highlight of this week-long festival.

CONTACT:
Brazilian Embassy
3006 Massachusetts Ave., N.W.
Washington, D.C. 20008
202-745-2700; fax: 202-745-2827

SOURCES:
BkHolWrld-1986, Jan 23
Chases-1996, p. 70
FolkWrldHol-1992, p. 27

♦ 0222 ♦ Bonfire Night
Various

There are a number of holidays that are referred to by this name. GUY FAWKES DAY (November 5) in England is sometimes called Bonfire Night, and in Scotland the name is applied to the Monday nearest May 24th, the former Empire Day (*see* COMMONWEALTH DAY). The original bonfires were actually "bone-fires" in which human or animal bones were burned to appease the gods. But nowadays bonfires are lit primarily for amusement. Other traditional bonfire nights include the eve of MIDSUMMER DAY (June 23), when fires were lit to cure disease and ward off evil spirits, and the WINTER SOLSTICE, when bonfires heralded the return of the sun.

SOURCES:
DictDays-1988, p. 14

♦ 0223 ♦ Bonneville Speed Week
Third week in August

A competition to set speed records on the Bonneville Salt Flats near Wendover, Utah. The salt flats were once under Lake Bonneville which was formed about two million years ago and covered 19,000 square miles in what are now Utah, Nevada, and Idaho. The Great Salt Lake to the east of the flats is all that remains of that prehistoric lake. Bonneville is so flat that it is the only place in the United States where the curvature of the earth can be seen. Its salt surface is as hard as concrete by summer's end, and the many miles of unobstructed space create an anomaly of nature found nowhere else in the world. These conditions are ideal for land speed racing.

Speed Week has been held since 1949. About 300 cars and motorcycles come here from all over the world to try to break land speed records. The one-mile automobile speed record was set in 1983 by Britain's Richard Noble who zipped over the flats in the Thrust 2 at 633.6 mph. The first person to set a speed record on the Bonneville Salt Flats was Teddy Tetzlaff who drove a Blitzen Benz 141 mph in 1914.

CONTACT:
Utah Tourism and Travel
Council House
Capitol Hill
Salt Lake City, UT 84114
800-200-1160; fax: 801-538-1000

♦ 0224 ♦ Boomerang Festival
Usually October

A national roundup in Hampton, Va., of throwers of boomerangs, the curved sticks that return to the thrower after being thrown. Top performers compete in a series of throwing events for speed, maximum time aloft, accuracy, consecutive catches, and other categories. The competition, which began in 1985, is topped off by an awards banquet.

The boomerang has been used in Australia for about 20,000 years as a weapon and for felling game animals. It is also believed to have been used by ancient Egyptians and American Indians. As a sport, boomeranging has grown more popular in the U.S. during the last 20 years. World championship meets are held in various countries at irregular times; in April 1991, the World Boomerang Cup Tournament was held in Perth, Australia, and American teams took the two top prizes.

CONTACT:
Virginia Dept. of Economic
  Development
Division of Tourism
901 E. Byrd St.
Richmond, VA 23219
804-786-4484; fax: 804-786-1919

♦ 0225 ♦ Boone Festival, Daniel
Eight days beginning the first Saturday in October

Held annually since 1948 in Barbourville, Kentucky, this week-long festival honors the frontiersman Daniel Boone (1734–1820), who in 1775 was the first to carve a trail through the Appalachian Mountains from eastern Tennessee all the way to the Ohio River. For 50 years Boone's "Wilderness Road" was the major route for settlers heading west.

An important part of the festival is the signing of the Cherokee Cane Treaty. Descendants of the original Cherokees who hid in the Smoky Mountains to avoid being forced to move to Oklahoma in 1838–39 sign a treaty each year that provides them with cane, which still grows along the Cumberland River, that they can use to make baskets. Other festival events include an old-fashioned barbecue featuring pioneer and American Indian foods, traditional Indian dances, a long-rifle shoot, and competitions in such activities as hog-calling, wood-chopping, and fiddling.

CONTACT:
Kentucky Dept. of Travel
 Development
500 Mero St., 22nd Floor
Frankfort, KY 40601
800-225-8747 or 502-564-4930
fax: 502-564-5695

SOURCES:
AmerBkDays-1978, p. 901

Booths, Feast of
See **Sukkot**

♦ 0226 ♦ Borrowed Days
March 29, 30, 31

According to an old Scottish rhyme, the last three days in March were "borrowed" from April, in return for which March promised to destroy three young sheep. But the weather proved to be an obstacle, and the promise was never fulfilled. Other references to the **Borrowing Days** go back even farther. Both an ancient calendar of the Church of Rome and a 1548 book known as the *Complaynt of Scotland* allude to the days at the end of March as being more like winter than spring. Whatever their origin, it seems likely that the wet, windy weather that so often comes at the end of March gave rise to the notion that this month had to "borrow" some additional time.

In the Scottish Highlands, there is an ancient belief that February 12, 13, and 14 were "borrowed" from January, and that it was a good omen for the rest of the year if the weather was as stormy as possible on these days. But if they were fair, no further good weather could be expected through the spring.

SOURCES:
BkDays-1864, vol. I, p. 448
DictDays-1988, p. 14

♦ 0227 ♦ Boston Marathon
April 19 or nearest Monday

The oldest footrace in the United States was first held on

Patriots' Day, April 19, 1897. Organized by members of the Boston Athletic Association (BAA), the race involved only 15 runners. Nowadays the Boston Marathon draws anywhere from 7,000 to more than 9,000 official starters, who must meet established qualifying times. Several thousand additional runners participate on an unofficial basis. In 1972, it became the first marathon to officially admit women runners.

The 26.2-mile course begins exactly at noon in Hopkinton, Massachusetts, includes the infamous "Heartbreak Hill" (a section of Commonwealth Avenue in Newton Centre, Massachusetts, that marks the race's 21st mile), and ends in front of the Prudential Center in downtown Boston. Well-known American winners of the Boston Marathon include the "old" John Kelley, who won twice and continues, in his 80s, to complete the race; the "young" John J. Kelley (no relation), who was the first American victor in the post-World War II era; and "Tarzan" Brown, who in 1938 took a break at the nine-mile mark for a quick swim in Lake Cochichuate. Among the women, Rosa Mota of Portugal was the first to win three official Boston Marathon titles. And few people will forget the infamous Rosie Ruiz in 1980, who many believed tried to defraud the BAA by showing up at the end of the race to capture the women's laurel wreath, the traditional symbol of victory, without having actually run the full distance; this was substantiated by television coverage of certain checkpoints. Jackie Gareau of Canada was later declared the women's winner, although Ruiz continued to insist that she'd run the race fairly.

CONTACT:
Greater Boston Convention and
 Visitors Bureau
P.O. Box 490
Boston, MA 02199
800-374-7400 or 617-536-4100
fax: 617-424-7664

SOURCES:
AmerBkDays-1978, p. 362
AnnivHol-1983, p. 53
Chases-1996, p. 171

♦ 0228 ♦ Boston Massacre Day
March 5

Celebrated in New Jersey as **Crispus Attucks Day**, March 5 marks the anniversary of the 1770 street fight between a group of colonial American protesters and a squad of British troops quartered in Boston—an event that reflected the unpopularity of the British regime in colonial America and set the stage for the American Revolution. A British sentry was pelted with stones and snowballs by a mob of about 50 people. He called for help, and Captain Thomas Preston sent several soldiers. The soldiers fired and five of the protesters were killed. One of them was Crispus Attucks, a runaway slave who'd spent 20 years as a whaleman. It was Attucks who led the crowd from Dock Square to King Street (now State Street), where the confrontation occurred, and who later became known as the first martyr of the American Revolution.

The name "Boston Massacre" was invented by the colonists and used as propaganda to force the removal of the British troops.

In Massachusetts, the anniversary of the "Boston Massacre" is observed annually with patriotic songs and speeches recalling Attucks's sacrifice. On the 200th anniversary of the massacre in 1970, and again five years later on the 200th anniversary of the outbreak of the Revolutionary War, the Charlestown Militia Company staged a reenactment of the event. In New Jersey, Crispus Attucks is often honored in conjunction with Martin Luther King, Jr. (*see* KING, JR.'S BIRTHDAY, MARTIN LUTHER).

CONTACT:
Massachusetts Office of Travel
and Tourism
100 Cambridge St., 13th Floor
Boston, MA 02202
800-447-6277 or 617-727-3201
fax: 617-727-6525

SOURCES:
AmerBkDays-1978, p. 235
AnnivHol-1983, p. 33
Chases-1996, p. 123

♦ 0229 ♦ Boston Pops
First week in May–middle of June

Henry Lee Higginson, who established the Boston Symphony Orchestra in 1881, believed that people should be exposed not only to classical music but to popular music as well. When he founded the **Music Hall Promenade Concerts** four years later, he deliberately focused on performing "light classics" and providing his listeners with refreshments to make the experience more enjoyable. It wasn't long before people started calling his summer concerts at Boston's Music Hall "the Pops," which is what they have been called ever since.

After the Music Hall was torn down in 1899, the Pops moved into the new Symphony Hall, considered to be acoustically one of the finest concert halls in the world. In 1930 Arthur Fiedler, who had already started an outdoor musical series in Boston known as the ESPLANADE CONCERTS, took over the position of conductor of the Boston Pops. He was succeeded in 1979 by composer John Williams, best known for his film scores. Keith Lockhart, former associate conductor of the Cincinnati Pops Orchestra, succeeded Williams in 1995.

The Pops continues to focus on American music and musicians, particularly popular songs, medleys, or movements from symphonic works. Soloists who have appeared there include Leontyne Price, Nell Carter, Bernadette Peters, Joel Grey, and Itzhak Perlman. Performances are given Tuesday through Sunday evenings for nine or 10 weeks during the summer, and they are often broadcast on public television.

CONTACT:
Boston Pops
301 Massachusetts Ave.
Boston, MA 02115
617-266-1492; fax: 617-638-9367

SOURCES:
MusFestAmer-1990, p. 209

♦ 0230 ♦ Botswana Independence Day
September 30–October 1

Botswana became independent from Great Britain on September 30, 1966. Since 1885, the region had been a British colony called the Bechuanaland Protectorate. The biggest Independence Day festivities are held in the capital city of Gaberones, and includes the singing of the national anthem, "Fatshe La Rona" (Blessed Country).

President's Day is another national holiday, observed on July 15.

CONTACT:
Botswana Embassy
3400 International Dr.
Intelfat Bldg., Ste. 7M
Washington, D.C. 20008
202-244-4990; fax: 202-244-4164

SOURCES:
AnnivHol-1983, p. 125
Chases-1996, p. 396
NatlHolWrld-1968, p. 179

♦ 0231 ♦ Bottle Kicking and Hare Pie Scramble, Annual
Between March 23 and April 26; Easter Monday

This 700-year-old event is the highpoint of the local calendar in the small village of Hallaton in Leicestershire, England. Opposing teams from Hallaton and the neighboring town of Medbourne scramble to maneuver two out of three small wooden beer kegs across a goal line in a game that has been described as being "unsurpassed for sheer animal ferocity." The chaos on the field may have something to do with the fact that players drop out of the game from time to time and have "a pint."

The event begins when the local rector blesses the Hare Pie—originally made of hare but now of beef. After handing out slices to some of the villagers, he scatters the remainder on the rectory lawn, where people scramble for it. Then comes the contest for the beer-filled kegs.

Where did these activities originate? According to legend, a village woman was crossing a field when she was attacked by a bull. A running hare diverted the bull's attention and she escaped. She bequeathed a field to the town in gratitude. The connection between the legend and the modern festivities is vague.

CONTACT:
British Tourist Authority
551 Fifth Ave., Ste. 702
New York, NY 10176
800-462-2748 or 212-986-2200
fax: 212-986-1188

SOURCES:
Chases-1996, p. 163

Boun Bang Fay
See **Bun Bang Fai**

♦ 0232 ♦ Boundary Walk (Grenzumgang)
Various

Boundary Walk festivals are held in many German towns. The custom dates back to the Middle Ages, when landowners and church officials, accompanied by armed men, periodically reviewed the boundaries to see that marking stones were in place and that hunting or fishing rights were observed. Eventually town and village boundaries were surveyed in the same way, with a huge feast ending the ceremony.

In Springe Deister, Lower Saxony, the Boundary Walk has been held once every 10 years since its revival in 1951. The celebration starts with morning reveille and a band concert. The band then leads a group of marchers off to the first boundary, where they are met by a delegation from an adjoining town. There is a brief ceremony, drinks are exchanged, and the group proceeds to the next boundary point. Each time the marchers are joined by more neighbors, and after their circuit has been completed, the raucous group disperses to attend the day's other festivities.

CONTACT:
German National Tourist Office
122 E. 42nd St., 52nd Floor
New York, NY 10168
212-661-7200; fax: 212-661-7174

SOURCES:
FestWestEur-1958, p. 73

♦ 0233 ♦ Boun Phan Vet
October–November; 12th lunar month

In the Laotian capital of Vientiane, national rites commemorating Lao origins and historical events are held on this day in That Luang, the temple where the Buddha's relics have traditionally been housed. Outside the capital, Boun Phan Vet is celebrated at different times in different communities to honor Prince Vessantara, an incarnation of the Buddha. There are dramatic performances, lovesong contests, cockfights, banquets, and other social gatherings at which the villagers entertain their neighbors from other villages. This is also a time for young men to be ordained into the *sangha*, or Buddhist monkhood.

CONTACT:
Lao Embassy
222 'S' St., N.W.
Washington, D.C. 20008
202-332-6416; fax: 202-332-4923

SOURCES:
FolkWrldHol-1992, p. 567

♦ 0234 ♦ **Bouphonia (Buphonia)**
End of June

An ancient Greek ceremony that was held in Athens each year as part of the festival known as **Dipolia** or **Diipolia**. Wheat and barley, or cakes made from them, were placed at the altar of Zeus on the Acropolis. Oxen were driven around the altar, and as soon as one of them nibbled on the grasses or ate the cakes, he was killed with an ax, which was then thrown into the sea. The flesh of the ox was eaten, but his hide was stuffed with straw and sewn together. Then the stuffed animal was set up and yoked to a plow.

According to legend, a man called Sopatrus killed an ox in anger after the animal had eaten some of the cereal he was offering as a sacrifice. He felt so much remorse that he buried the ox and fled to Crete. When a famine ensued, the festival known as Bouphonia was instituted. It was customary for the killing of the ox to be followed by a ceremonial trial for those who had participated in its murder, after which the knife used to slit its throat and the ax used to fell it were thrown into the sea.

SOURCES:
DictFolkMyth-1984, p. 158
NewCentClassHand-1962, pp.
   222, 410

♦ 0235 ♦ **Boxing Day**
December 26

The term 'Boxing Day' comes from the little earthenware boxes that servants, tradespeople, and others who rendered services to the public used to carry around on the day after CHRISTMAS to collect tips and year-end bonuses. Although the custom of distributing gifts (usually money) to public servants and employees has continued, it often takes place before Christmas rather than after, and boxes have nothing to do with it. But the name has remained, and Boxing Day is still observed in England, Canada, Australia, and many other nations. In South Africa, it is known as the **Day of Good Will**. If December 26 falls on a Saturday or Sunday, the following Monday or Tuesday is usually observed as a public or BANK HOLIDAY.

SOURCES:
BkDays-1864, vol. II, p. 764
BkHolWrld-1986, Dec 26
DaysCustFaith-1957, p. 322
FolkAmerHol-1991, p. 478
FolkWrldHol-1992, p. 639

NatlHolWrld-1968, p. 79

♦ 0236 ♦ **Boy Scouts' Day**
February 8

The Boy Scout movement was started by a British cavalry officer, Robert S. S. Baden-Powell, who was well-known not only for his heroic defense of Mafeking in southern Africa during the Boer War, but also for his publication of a military pamphlet, "Aids to Scouting," which emphasized the need for a strong character and outdoor survival skills among British soldiers. King George V ordered Baden-Powell to retire from the military so that he could help British boys learn about camping, hiking, signaling, plant identification, swimming, and other such activities. Baden-Powell's 1908 book, *Scouting for Boys*, was an immediate success, and he devoted the rest of his life to the task of promoting the scouting movement.

The Boy Scouts of America, the nation's largest youth organization, was founded on February 8, 1910. A Chicago publisher, William D. Boyce, who had experienced the courtesy and helpfulness of a young scout firsthand while staying in London, decided that young American boys needed the same kind of training. Two existing organizations—Dan C. Beard's Sons of Daniel Boone and Ernest Thompson Seton's "Woodcraft Indians"—had already introduced boys to the same idea, and the Sons of Daniel Boone eventually merged with the Boy Scouts of America. Cub Scout "Blue and Gold" dinners, flag ceremonies, parents' nights, shopping center demonstrations, and the presentation of advancement awards are popular ways of celebrating this day, which is part of **Boy Scout Month**, an annual anniversary celebration extending throughout February.

CONTACT:
Boy Scouts of America
1325 W. Walnut Hill Ln.
Irving, TX 75038
214-580-2000; fax: 214-580-2502

SOURCES:
AnnivHol-1983, p. 21
Chases-1996, p. 90

♦ 0237 ♦ **Boys' Dodo Masquerade**
Full moon of Islamic month of Ramadan

A children's entertainment introduced by Muslim Hausa traders during the mid-19th century, the **Dodo Masquerade** performed in Burkina Faso (formerly Upper Volta), has changed considerably over the years, and now reflects the local largely non-Muslim Mossi culture. As the RAMADAN season approaches, boys between the ages of 12 and 16 form groups consisting of a principal singer, a chorus, five or more dancers, a drummer, a few costumed wild animals based on local folklore, and a leader who dresses in military style. The boys decide on their roles and dance steps, which are usually variations on a dozen well-known patterns. Each dancer wears knee bells made from tin can tops and carries two sticks decorated by painting or peeling the bark away in special patterns.

On the night of the full moon during the Islamic month of Ramadan, the boys in their masks and costumes perform their dance for each household or compound while the chorus sings. Younger boys (seven to 12 years of age) started forming their own "Petit Dodo" groups and by the mid-1950s, little boys were dancing Dodo in many Mossi villages.

CONTACT:
Burkina Faso Embassy
2340 Massachusetts Ave., N.W.
Washington, D.C. 20008
202-332-5577

SOURCES:
FolkWrldHol-1992, p. 171

Boys' Rifle Match
See **Knabenschiessen**

♦ 0238 ♦ **Braemar Highland Gathering**
September

In the 11th century, King Malcolm held a gathering of the Scottish clans in Braemar to test their strength and to choose the hardiest soldiers. Competitors were asked to toss the caber—a pole 16' to 20' long and weighing 120 pounds—in such a way that it landed on its other end, much the way loggers used to toss logs across a river. The Braemar Gathering is still an annual event in the village of Braemar in Scotland, and the participants are still required to wear kilts and toss the caber. But the event has been expanded to include traditional Highland dancing, bagpipe music, games, and other athletic competitions as well.

See also Highland Games

CONTACT:
British Tourist Authority
551 Fifth Ave., Ste. 702
New York, NY 10176
800-462-2748 or 212-986-2200
fax: 212-986-1188

SOURCES:
AnnivHol-1983, p. 174
BkHolWrld-1986, Sep 6
Chases-1996, p. 368

♦ 0239 ♦ **Bratislava Music Festival**
October 1–15

The International Rostrum of Young Interpreters (IRI) is a project of the International Music Council in collaboration with UNESCO. It is designed to help young performers gain access to the theatrical stage or the concert platform, where they can achieve international recognition for their talents. During the first two weeks in October every year, the IRI finalists in two categories—concert (including instrumentalists and concert singers) and music theater—perform at the Bratislava Music Festival in southwestern Slovakia.

Since 1965 the festival has presented opera, symphonic concerts, chamber music, recitals, and occasionally ballet, with performances held in the city's six concert halls. But it is the focus on young artists that sets the Bratislava Festival apart.

CONTACT:
Slovakia Embassy
2201 Wisconsin Ave., N.W., Ste. 380
Washington, D.C. 20007
202-965-5161; fax: 202-965-5166

SOURCES:
GdWrldFest-1985, p. 67
IntlThFolk-1979, p. 87

♦ 0240 ♦ **Brauteln**
Between February 3 and March 9; Shrove Tuesday

The **Wooing a Bride Ceremony** in Sigmaringen, Germany, is part of a Carnival custom that dates back to 1648. After the Thirty Years' War was over, hunger and disease were widespread in Sigmaringen. This discouraged young men from marrying and starting families. The population dropped so rapidly that the mayor offered to reward the first young man brave enough to become engaged with the *Brauteln*, or bride-wooing ceremony, during which the lucky bachelor was carried at the head of a colorful procession around the town square.

Today the custom continues. On Shrove Tuesday any man who has married within the last 12 months, who has just moved into town with his wife, or who has celebrated his 25th or 50th wedding anniversary is invited to be *brautelt*. Heralds dressed in traditional costumes carry the men around the town pump to the accompaniment of drummers and pipers.

CONTACT:
German National Tourist Office
122 E. 42nd St., 52nd Floor
New York, NY 10168
212-661-7200; fax: 212-661-7174

SOURCES:
FestWestEur-1958, p. 57

♦ 0241 ♦ **Brazil Independence Day**
September 7

A declaration of independence was made by Pedro di Alcántara (1798–1834) on this day in 1822. Brazil had been a colony of Portugal since the 16th century. Alcántara, better known as Pedro I, became the first emperor of Brazil in 1823 and ruled until 1831.

Independence Day is a public holiday in Brazil, and there are celebrations in Brasilia, the capital, with parades of military personnel and floats decorated with flowers.

See also Inconfidência Week

CONTACT:
Brazilian Embassy
3006 Massachusetts Ave., N.W.
Washington, D.C. 20008
202-745-2700; fax: 202-745-2827

SOURCES:
AnnivHol-1983, p. 115
Chases-1996, p. 366
NatlHolWrld-1968, p. 158

♦ 0242 ♦ **Brazil Proclamation of the Republic Day**
November 15

November 15 is a public holiday commemorating the proclamation of the Republic of Brazil during the rule of Pedro II (1825–1891), who reigned from 1831 to 1889.

SOURCES:
Chases-1996, p. 450
NatlHolWrld-1968, p. 158

♦ 0243 ♦ **Bregenz Festival**
July–August

The Bregenz Festival held each summer in Bregenz, Austria, is perhaps best known for its floating stage, built on Lake Constance. Started in 1946 to give people some enjoyment after the end of World War II, the festival has since added a new indoor Festival House on the shore of the lake and regularly attracts as many as 100,000 visitors. It is famous for its performances of opera, operetta, plays, ballet, and symphonic concerts.

CONTACT:
Austrian National Tourist Office
P.O. Box 1142, Times Square
New York, NY 10148
212-944-6880; fax: 212-730-4568

SOURCES:
GdWrldFest-1985, p. 11
IntlThFolk-1979, p. 31
MusFestEurBrit-1980, p. 17

♦ 0244 ♦ Bridge Day
Third Saturday in October

A celebration of the New River Gorge Bridge in Fayetteville, W. Va., and a day of bliss for daredevils. The bridge, completed in 1977, is the world's longest steel-arch span and is one of the highest bridges in the nation. Its span is 1,700 feet, with a rise of 360 feet, putting it 876 feet above the New River Gorge National River. On Bridge Day, celebrated since 1980, parachutists jump from the bridge onto the river's banks below. The less bold walk over the bridge. About 200 vendors offer food, crafts, and souvenirs for sale. Attendance is about 150,000.

See also WHITEWATER WEDNESDAY

CONTACT:
West Virginia Tourism and Parks
  Division
2101 Washington St. E.
Charleston, WV 25305
304-558-2200 or 800-225-5982
fax: 304-558-0108

♦ 0245 ♦ British Open
Summer (usually July)

The oldest and one of the most prestigious international golf championship tournaments in the world. It is officially the **Open Championship of the British Isles,** but in Great Britain it is known simply as the **Open.** It began in 1860 at the then 12-hole Prestwick course in Scotland and is now rotated among select golf courses in England and Scotland. Scot Willie Park won the first tournament, which is memorable for the tourney's highest single-hole stroke total—21.

Other notable years in the Open:

In 1901, Scot James Braid, who became one of Scotland's greatest golf heroes, won the first of five Open championships.

In 1907, Arnaud Massy of France was the first player from outside Great Britain to win.

In 1910, the Open's 50th anniversary was celebrated at St. Andrews (considered by many to be the premier golf course of the world) in a tempest of a rainstorm that put some of the greens under water.

In 1914, at Prestwick, the great triumvirate of golf, Braid and Englishmen John Henry Taylor and Harry Vardon, entered the match with each having five Open titles behind them. Vardon won with a final total round of 78.

In 1921, Bobby Jones (Robert Tyre Jones Jr.), the legendary golfer and lawyer from Atlanta, Ga., lost his temper at the par-three 11th hole at St. Andrews and shredded his scorecard while the gallery gaped.

In 1926, that same Bobby Jones won the cup; it was the first time in 29 years that an amateur had won.

In 1930, Jones won and went on to sweep the UNITED STATES OPEN and the British Amateur and U.S. Amateur for golfing's Grand Slam, after which he retired. The feat hasn't been equaled. (Later, in 1958, Jones became the first American since Benjamin FRANKLIN to receive the Freedom of the Burgh of St. Andrews.)

In 1973, Gene Sarazen, celebrating his 50th anniversary of play, shot a first-round hole-in-one on the par-three, 126-yard eighth hole (known as the Postage Stamp) at Royal Troon. In the second round, he deuced the hole.

In 1975, American Tom Watson won the first of five championships.

In 1977, Watson and fellow American Jack Nicklaus left the field behind them and dueled to a dramatic final round; Watson won by a stroke with a 72-hole total score of 268.

The Open has a special cachet for golfers since Scotland is considered, if not the birthplace of golf, the place where it developed into its present form played with ball, club, and hole. (At one time, pub doors were the target). The game may actually have originated in Holland, where they called it *kolven,* but golf in Scotland goes back before 1457. That year, Scottish King James II banned "fute-ball and golfe" because they interfered with his subjects' archery practice. The ban didn't take. Golf was confined pretty much to Scotland until 1603 when King James VI of Scotland also assumed the throne of England and brought golf there, even though many English sportsmen sniffily derided it as "Scottish croquet."

CONTACT:
British Tourist Authority
551 Fifth Ave., Ste. 702
New York, NY 10176
800-462-2748 or 212-986-2200
fax: 212-986-1188

SOURCES:
Chases-1996, p. 242

♦ 0246 ♦ Broadstairs Dickens Festival
June

This eight-day festival commemorating the 19th-century novelist Charles Dickens and his association with the English town of Broadstairs features a play adapted from a different Dickens novel each year. The actors are members of the Broadstairs Dickens Players' Society, and they spend about eight months preparing for their June performance. During the festival, the entire town is transformed: people wander through the streets in Dickensian costumes, play croquet and other games popular during the 19th century, and attend bathing parties and social events with a Victorian theme. There are also concerts of Victorian music, exhibits, and lectures on Dickens.

Charles Dickens lived for many years in Bleak House, overlooking the harbor of Broadstairs. The festival was started by a later inhabitant of Bleak House, Gladys Waterer, in 1936. Although all of Dickens's works have been adapted and performed at the festival at least once, the town's nostalgia for its most famous citizen shows no signs of flagging.

CONTACT:
British Tourist Authority
551 Fifth Ave., Ste. 702
New York, NY 10176
800-462-2748 or 212-986-2200
fax: 212-986-1188

SOURCES:
Chases-1996, p. 257
GdWrldFest-1985, p. 90
IntlThFolk-1979, p. 157

Broken Needles, Festival of
See **Hari-Kuyo**

Brother and Sister Day
See **Raksha Bandhana**

♦ 0247 ♦ **Brotherhood Sunday**
Sunday nearest Washington's birthday, February 22

Every year since 1934 Brotherhood Week has been proclaimed by the president of the United States, sponsored by the National Conference of Christians and Jews, and observed by the country as a whole. The original idea was to set aside a week each year when people of all faiths would get together, discuss their differences, and reaffirm the human brotherhood that underlies the variations in their religious beliefs. Schools, churches, synagogues, civic groups, and other organizations across America celebrate this week—and, in particular, Brotherhood Sunday—by bringing together people of different faiths and backgrounds.

The decision to celebrate Brotherhood Week at the same time as WASHINGTON'S BIRTHDAY called attention to George Washington as a symbol of America's commitment to freedom from racial and religious prejudice. When Washington was president he wrote a letter to the Hebrew congregation in Newport, Rhode Island, in which he assured them that in this country there would be "to bigotry no sanction, to persecution no assistance." This quotation has become practically a slogan for the National Conference of Christians and Jews which, in addition to organizing Brotherhood Week, is engaged in a continuing effort to promote interfaith relations.

CONTACT:
National Conference of Christians
  and Jews
71 Fifth Ave, Ste. 1100
New York, NY 10003
212-206-0006; fax: 212-255-6177

SOURCES:
AmerBkDays-1978, p. 200
DaysCustFaith-1957, p. 60
DictDays-1988, p. 15

♦ 0248 ♦ **Bruckner Festival, International**
September

Linz, Austria, is the setting for a four-week festival devoted to the works of composer Anton Bruckner (1824–1896), best known for his nine symphonies and three Masses. Although a number of famous composers have lived and worked in Austria—among them Beethoven, Mahler, and Brahms—Bruckner's roots there go back to the fifth century. On the 150th anniversary of his birth in 1974, therefore, it seemed appropriate to institute a four-week festival in his honor.

The Orchestra of Linz and other well-known orchestras perform Bruckner's symphonies, piano and organ compositions, sacred choral and orchestral works, and Masses in the Brucknerhaus, a concert hall built in 1974, as well as in other locations throughout the city. Choral concerts are usually performed in the Augustinian monastery in St. Florian (near Linz) where Bruckner was organist from 1848–55 and where he is buried.

CONTACT:
Austrian National Tourist Office
P.O. Box 1142, Times Square
New York, NY 10148
212-944-6880; fax: 212-730-4568

SOURCES:
MusFestEurBrit-1980, p. 21

♦ 0249 ♦ **Brunei National Day**
February 23

Brunei is an independent sultanate on the island of Borneo in the Malay Archipelago. It had been a British protectorate since 1888. The sultanate gained independence in 1984 and observes its National Day each year on February 23.

CONTACT:
Brunei Embassy
2600 Virginia Ave., N.W., Ste. 300
Washington, D.C. 20037
202-342-0159; fax: 202-342-0158

SOURCES:
Chases-1996, p. 108

♦ 0250 ♦ **Buccaneer Days**
Last weekend in April through first weekend in May

A time when the city of Corpus Christi, Tex., by proclamation of the mayor, is under pirate rule, similar to the GASPARILLA PIRATE FESTIVAL in Tampa, Fla. Buccaneer Days began in 1940 to honor the discovery of Corpus Christi Bay by Spanish explorer Alonzo Alvarez Pineda in 1519. It has become a 10-day carnival, calling to mind the days of the early 19th century when the settlement was a hideaway for pirates, who did a brisk trade in contraband. Events of the festival include sailboat regattas, parades, sports events, concerts, a coronation and ball, and fireworks on the bayfront.

CONTACT:
Corpus Christi Convention and
  Visitors Bureau
1201 N. Shoreline Blvd.
Corpus Christi, TX 78401
800-678-6232 or 512-882-5603

Buchmesse
See Frankfurt Book Fair

♦ 0251 ♦ **Budapest Music Weeks**
September–October

Music by the Hungarian composers Bela Bartók and Franz Liszt is a standby at the four-week music festival held in Budapest from the last week in September through late October each year. But the festival was founded in 1959 to commemorate the 150th anniversary of the death of Franz Josef Haydn, the Austrian composer who spent 30 years at the Esterházy Palace as court composer to Prince Nicolaus Esterházy. The festival always includes works by Hungarians—Zoltan Kodály, Gyula Illyés, and Zsigmond Móricz as well as Bartók and Liszt—but there are works by composers from other countries as well. Performances of symphonic, chamber, and organ music are held daily, usually in the Budapest Opera House, the Erkel Theatre, the Academy of Music, and in nearby churches and castles. For one week in October, there is a "festival within a festival": the Contemporary Music Series, in which the latest works by Hungarian and foreign composers are premiered.

Held in conjunction with Budapest Music Weeks is Artistic Weeks of Budapest, which presents Hungarian and foreign plays, dance performances, films, and exhibitions.

CONTACT:
Hungarian Embassy
3910 Shoemaker St., N.W.
Washington, D.C. 20008
202-362-6730; fax: 202-966-8135

SOURCES:
IntlThFolk-1979, p. 199
MusFestEurBrit-1980, p. 109
MusFestWrld-1963, p. 145

♦ 0252 ♦ **Bud Billiken Day**
Second Saturday in August

Bud Billiken is the "patron saint" of Chicago's African-American children. Created in 1923 by Robert S. Abbott, the founder of the *Chicago Daily Defender* newspaper, Bud Billiken is a symbol of things as they should be—not necessarily as they are—and his day is primarily a children's event. There is a parade held on the second Saturday in August each year that goes on for four hours, complete with marching bands, baton twirlers, floats holding celebrities and politicians, and units from the Navy, Air Force, and National Guard. The formalities end when the parade reaches Washington Park in the Grand Boulevard area of Chicago, where families have picnics and cookouts and the children can watch swimming shows in the park's three Olympic-sized pools.

CONTACT:
Chicago Convention and Tourism
Bureau
2301 S. Lake Shore Dr.
McCormick Place On-the-Lake
Chicago, IL 60616
312-567-8500; fax: 312-567-8533

SOURCES:
AnnivHol-1983, p. 107
Chases-1996, p. 331

Buddha's Birthday
See **Vesak**

Buddhist Rains Retreat
See **Waso**

♦ 0253 ♦ **Budget Day**
April 9

As a general term, Budget Day refers to the day on which a government official presents the budget for the following year. In England, however, there is a tradition of having the Chancellor of the Exchequer carry the dispatch box containing papers relating to the government's revenues and expenditures for the coming year from the Prime Minister's residence at 10 Downing Street in London to the House of Commons on April 9.

The word "budget" originally referred to a leather wallet or bag, and the Chancellor of the Exchequer carried the government's financial papers in such a bag. The expression, "to open one's budget" meant "to speak one's mind." Eventually the word came to stand for the contents of the bag, and the Chancellor of the Exchequer was said to be "opening the budget" when he presented his annual statement to the House of Commons. The modern meaning of the word dates from the mid-18th century.

SOURCES:
AnnivHol-1983, p. 49
DictDays-1988, p. 16

♦ 0254 ♦ **Buena Vista Logging Days**
Last Saturday in February

In the 1800s the logging of Minnesota's pine forests near

Bemidji was in full swing. During the winter timber harvest, lumberjacks guided teams of Percheron horses, who hauled logs along ice-covered roads. Although the timber industry still works the woods around Bemidji, the golden days of the Minnesota logging boom only lasted 50 years. But the area continues to remember, recreate, and celebrate the skills of the old-time lumberjack by holding a festival at Buena Vista village and logging camp located north of Bemidji. Each year participants dressed in red plaid wool shirts demonstrate log scaling and compete in axe chopping and crosscut-sawing contests. They also guide teams of Percheron, Belgian, and Clydesdale draft horses in log loading and hauling demonstrations.

Visitors are transported to the logging camp aboard horse-powered sleighs and are served lumberjack camp meals all day long. Buena Vista village is also the home of the Lumberjack Hall of Fame, where up to 100 of the old lumberjacks are honored and inducted during the festival. Many of those fabled laborers of the north woods, some of whom are nearly 100 years old, attend the festival each year.

CONTACT:
Minnesota Office of Tourism
121 E. Seventh Pl. Metro Sq., Ste.
100
St. Paul, MN 55101
612-296-5029 or 800-657-3700
fax: 612-296-7095

♦ 0255 ♦ **Buergsonndeg**
February 25

On this day, young people go to hills in the countryside throughout Luxembourg to build bonfires to celebrate the sun and to signify the end of winter. Though this custom can be traced to pre-Christian times, in modern times it is associated with Lent.

CONTACT:
Luxembourg National Tourist
Office
17 Beekman Pl.
New York, NY 10022
212-935-8888; fax: 212-935-5896

SOURCES:
AnnivHol-1983, p. 36
Chases-1996, p. 95

♦ 0256 ♦ **Buffalo's Big Board Surfing Classic**
February

Two days of surfing contests at Makaha Beach, Oahu, Hawaii, where the surf is sometimes 20 feet high. The classic is a tribute to "Buffalo" Keaulana, one of the state's premiere watermen. Old-timers ride the waves on the huge wooden surfboards that were used in Hawaii's early days; other events include canoe surfing, team bodyboarding, and tandem surfing. There are also food booths and Hawaiian entertainment.

CONTACT:
Hawaii Visitors Bureau
2270 Kalakaua Ave., Ste. 801
Honolulu, HI 96815
808-923-1811; fax: 808-922-8991

SOURCES:
Chases-1996, p. 85

♦ 0257 ♦ **Bulgaria Culture Day**
May 24

This Bulgarian national holiday—formerly known as **Holy**

Day of Letters—promotes Bulgarian culture and honors two brothers, St. Cyril (c. 827–869) and St. Methodius (c. 825–884), missionaries to Moravia. St. Cyril is believed to have invented the Slavonic alphabet also known as the Cyrillic alphabet in 855 and they are both widely regarded as the country's patrons of education and culture. In 1980, Pope John Paul II declared them patrons of Europe. The brothers started out preaching Christianity in what are now the Czech and Slovak Republics, but their followers fled to Bulgaria when they were persecuted, and Cyrillic became the official alphabet there. It is still used in the former Soviet Union, Serbia, and other Slavic countries as well.

Special masses, festivals, and student parades are held throughout Bulgaria on this day, which is also known as **Saints Cyril and Methodius's Day.** An impressive High Mass, celebrated at the cathedral in Sofia, is one of the highlights.

CONTACT:
Bulgarian Embassy
1621 22nd St., N.W.
Washington, D.C. 20008
202-387-7969; fax: 202-234-7973

SOURCES:
BkFest-1937, p. 71
BkHolWrld-1986, May 24
Chases-1996, p. 225

♦ 0258 ♦ **Bulgaria Liberation Day**
March 3

Liberation Day is a public holiday in Bulgaria honoring the Russian and Romanian forces who helped Bulgarian volunteers free themselves from 500 years of Turkish Ottoman rule during the Russo-Turkish War of 1877–78. The Treaty of San Stefano in 1878 proclaimed Bulgaria's autonomy.

CONTACT:
Bulgarian Embassy
1621 22nd St., N.W.
Washington, D.C. 20008
202-387-7969; fax: 202-234-7973

SOURCES:
AnnivHol-1983, p. 33
Chases-1996, p. 121

♦ 0259 ♦ **Bulgaria National Day**
September 9

On this day in 1944, Bulgarian and Russian forces drove out German troops from Bulgaria, and Soviet rule began.

September 9 and 10 are observed as a national holiday in Bulgaria.

CONTACT:
Bulgarian Embassy
1621 22nd St., N.W.
Washington, D.C. 20008
202-387-7969; fax: 202-234-7973

SOURCES:
AnnivHol-1983, p. 116
Chases-1996, p. 371
NatlHolWrld-1968, p. 162

♦ 0260 ♦ **Bumba-meu-Boi Folk Drama**
June 13–29

The Bumba-meu-Boi is a Brazilian folk drama that is typically performed in small towns and villages. The characters in the play include a sea captain riding a wicker hobbyhorse, the Ox, the cowboys Mateus and Birico, Catarina (the pregnant mistress of Mateus), the Doctor, and the Chorus. A colorful procession announces the arrival of the players, who sometimes stage playful attacks on the spectators lining the streets. Performances usually take place in a room of the house belonging to the most important family in town, or else in front of a church or in the town's main square.

CONTACT:
Brazilian Embassy
3006 Massachusetts Ave., N.W.
Washington, D.C. 20008
202-745-2700; fax: 202-745-2827

SOURCES:
FolkWrldHol-1992, p. 326

♦ 0261 ♦ **Bumbershoot**
September, four days over Labor Day weekend

The premier festival of Seattle, Wash., held since 1971 and now a wide-ranging round-up of many arts. It started as Festival '71, but became Bumbershoot in 1973: Bumbershoot is British slang for umbrella, and the festival is supposed to be an umbrella for the arts; the word also calls to mind Seattle's rainy climate.

In recent years, Bumbershoot attractions have included Japanese Kabuki theater, Russian rock, robot art, flamenco dancing, and readings by contemporary writers. In 1991, performers included: Foday Musa Suso, a hereditary musician and oral historian of the Mandingo people of West Africa; Roger Ferguson, the former National Flat-Pick Guitar Champion, presenting bluegrass music; and the Mazeltones, singing Jewish music in Yiddish, Hebrew, and English. The food offerings yield Cajun-style salmon, Pennsylvania Dutch funnel cake, Italian calzone, Lebanese falafels, Thai beef sticks, strawberry shortcake, etc. In other words, Bumbershoot is a gallimaufry of music, dance, theater, visual and literary arts, children's activities, food, and crafts. It's held at the Seattle Center, the site of the 1962 World's Fair, and attracts about 250,000 people.

CONTACT:
Seattle-King County Convention
  and Visitors Bureau
520 Pike St., Ste. 1300
Seattle, WA 98101
360-461-5800; fax: 360-461-5855

♦ 0262 ♦ **Bun Bang Fai (Boun Bang Fay; Rocket Festival)**
April–May; full moon day of Hindu month of Vaisakha; second weekend in May

A rain ceremony celebrated in Laos and northeastern Thailand during Buddhist VESAK or Vesakha Puja, observed on the full moon day of the sixth Hindu month (Vaisakha). The Bun Bang Fai (*bun* means 'festival' in Lao) pre-dates Buddhism and is intended to insure good crops.

In Laos, this is one of the country's wildest celebrations, with music and irreverent dances, processions, and merrymaking. The celebration ends with the firing of bamboo rockets into the sky, supposedly prompting the heavens to commence the rainy season and bring water to the rice fields. Prizes go to the fastest, highest, and brightest rockets.

In Thailand, the celebration is usually on the second weekend in May and is especially festive in Yasothon, with villagers shooting off huge rockets. Before the shooting, there are beauty parades, folk dances, and ribald entertainment.

CONTACT:
Lao Embassy
222 'S' St., N.W.
Washington, D.C. 20008
202-332-6416; fax: 202-332-4923

Tourism Authority of Thailand
5 World Trade Center, Ste. 3443
New York, NY 10048
212-432-0433; fax: 212-912-0920

SOURCES:
BkHolWrld-1986, May 26
FolkWrldHol-1992, p. 308

♦ 0263 ♦ Bunka-no-Hi (Culture Day)
November 3

A Japanese national holiday on which medals are awarded by the government to those who have made special contributions in the fields of arts and sciences. The day was formerly celebrated as the birthday of Emperor Meiji, who ruled from 1868 until his death in 1912, and was the great-grandfather of Emperor Akihito (b. 1933). The years of his reign were a time of turning away from feudalism and toward Western rationalism and science, and were known as the age of *bummeikaika*—'civilization and enlightenment.'

Today, this holiday serves to promote the love of freedom, peace and cultural development.

SOURCES:
AnnivHol-1983, p. 141
Chases-1996, p. 439
JapanFest-1965, p. 205

♦ 0264 ♦ Bunker Hill Day
June 17

Observed primarily in Boston, Mass., Bunker Hill Day commemorates the Revolutionary War battle of June 1775 between 3,000 British troops under the leadership of General William Howe and half that number of Americans under Colonel William Prescott. In fact, Breed's Hill was fortified, not nearby Bunker Hill, and that is where the British attacked the rebels three times, eventually driving them out of their hastily constructed barricade, but only after losing more than 1,000 men. The American revolutionaries, who had exhausted their small store of ammunition, ended up fighting the British bayonets with the butts of their muskets.

Although the Americans were driven from their fortification and lost some 450 men, the battle boosted their confidence and has always been looked upon as one of the great heroic battles of the American Revolution. A 220-foot granite obelisk in Charlestown, just north of Boston, marks the site of the battle on Breed's Hill, which itself is only 87 feet high. This day is sometimes referred to as **Boston's Fourth of July**.

CONTACT:
Greater Boston Convention and
    Visitors Bureau
P.O. Box 490
Boston, MA 02199
800-374-7400 or 617-536-4100
fax: 617-424-7664

SOURCES:
AmerBkDays-1978, p. 563
AnnivHol-1983, p. 80
BkDays-1864, vol. I, p. 790
Chases-1996, p. 260
DictDays-1988, p. 16

♦ 0265 ♦ Burbank Day
March 7

The birthday of naturalist and plant breeder Luther Burbank (1849–1926) is observed in California in much the same way as Arbor Day is observed in other states—that is, with activities promoting the value of natural resources and the protection of trees and birds. Burbank moved from his native Massachusetts to Santa Rosa, Calif., in 1875 and spent the rest of his life there experimenting with new varieties of fruits, flowers, and vegetables. Among his other achievements, he is credited with introducing the Shasta daisy. All in all, he developed more that 800 new strains and varieties of fruits, flowers, and forage plants, drawing worldwide attention to the science of plant breeding and helping farmers learn how to use their land more productively.

Burbank was fortunate enough to be honored by the citizens of Santa Rosa during his lifetime. The Rose Carnival was held intermittently between 1894 and his death in 1926. Then, in 1950, the three-day Luther Burbank Rose Festival was instituted. This celebration, which takes place annually in mid-May, includes flower shows, music and sporting events, and a Rose Festival parade.

CONTACT:
California Division of Tourism
801 K Street, Ste. 1600
Sacramento, CA 95814
800-862-2543 or 916-322-2881
fax: 916-322-3402

SOURCES:
AmerBkDays-1978, p. 240
AnnivHol-1983, p. 34
Chases-1996, p. 125

♦ 0266 ♦ Burgoyne's Surrender Day
October 17

British General John Burgoyne (1722–1792) is best remembered for his defeat by the colonial American forces in the Saratoga campaign of 1777, during the Revolutionary War. The plan was to have British troops from the north, south, and west unite at Albany, New York, thus isolating New England from the other rebellious colonies. Burgoyne led his troops south from Canada by way of Lake Champlain, capturing Fort Ticonderoga, New York, on July 6, 1777. But they were stopped at the Hudson River by the American forces commanded by General Philip Schuyler and, later, General Horatio Gates, with the assistance of General Benedict Arnold. Burgoyne was eventually forced to surrender to Gates near Saratoga Springs, New York, on October 17, 1777. Historians regard the surrender at Saratoga as the turning point in the Revolutionary War. The Americans' victory gave them a psychological advantage and persuaded France to ally itself with the colonists against England, its traditional rival.

The anniversary of Burgoyne's surrender is observed in New York State, particularly in the communities surrounding the Saratoga National Historical Park near Stillwater, New York. A well-known painting of Burgoyne's surrender by John Trumbull hangs in the U.S. Capitol Rotunda in Washington, D.C.

CONTACT:
New York Division of Tourism
1 Commerce Pl.
Albany, NY 12245
800-225-5697 or 518-474-4116
fax: 518-486-6416

SOURCES:
AmerBkDays-1978, p. 932
AnnivHol-1983, p. 134
BkDaysAmerHist-1987, Oct 17

♦ 0267 ♦ Burial of the Sardine
Between February 4 and March 10; Ash Wednesday, the first day of Lent

The custom of burying a strip of meat as thin as a sardine on Ash Wednesday is common throughout Spain and is thought to have originated in an old fertility custom symbolizing the burial of winter in early spring. The **Entierro de la Sardinia** also symbolizes the burial of worldly pleasures and serves as a reminder that people must abstain from eating meat and eat only fish throughout the 40 days of Lent. After the burial is over, people attend Ash Wednesday church services.

Another Spanish custom is to make a figure of an ugly old woman out of stucco or cardboard or figures representing the King and Queen of Carnival and to burn or drown these personifications of Carnival on Ash Wednesday or Shrove Tuesday.

See also Carnival in Panama

SOURCES:
BkFest-1937, p. 299
DictFolkMyth-1984, p. 82
FestSaintDays-1915, p. 49
FestWestEur-1958, p. 194

♦ 0268 ♦ Burkina Faso Independence Day
August 4–5

Formerly called Upper Volta, Burkina Faso gained independence from France in 1960, an event commemorated as a national holiday during August 4–5. The area had been a French protectorate since the 1890s.

CONTACT:
Burkina Faso Embassy
2340 Massachusetts Ave., N.W.
Washington, D.C. 20008
202-332-5577

SOURCES:
AnnivHol-1983, p. 103
Chases-1996, p. 323

♦ 0269 ♦ Burkina Faso Republic Day
December 11

On this day in 1958 Upper Volta (now Burkina Faso) voted to become an independent republic within the French community. It was then internally self-governing until it achieved independence in 1960 (*see* Burkina Faso Independence Day). This is considered the most important national holiday in Burkina Faso, with many events held in the capital city of Ouagadougou.

CONTACT:
Burkina Faso Embassy
2340 Massachusetts Ave., N.W.
Washington, D.C. 20008
202-332-5577

SOURCES:
AnnivHol-1983, p. 159
NatlHolWrld-1968, p. 224

♦ 0270 ♦ Burma Independence Day
January 4

The southeast Asian country of Burma, renamed Myanmar in 1989 by its military government, was under the control of the British for more than a century. During World War II, the Japanese captured Burma and created a puppet state, which came to an end when the Japanese were driven out at the end of the war in 1945. The Burmese people were unwilling to return to British rule, and when they were given their independence on January 4, 1948, they refused to join the British Commonwealth.

The Burmese capital, Rangoon, is decorated for the Independence Day festivities. Most of the people dress in their national costume, which consists of an *aingyi* (blouse or shirt) and a *longyi* (skirt). Women draw the *longyi* to one side, fold it back to the opposite side, and tuck it in at the waist, while the men tie theirs in front. The Burmese are unusual in that they have kept their national dress longer than most other southeast Asian countries. Although men often wear regular Western shirts, on Independence Day they're more likely to put on their collarless Burmese shirts. A dish known as *panthay khowse* (noodles and chicken) is traditionally served on this day, as is *nga sak kin* (curried fish balls). The preferred beverage is tea.

CONTACT:
Myanmar Embassy
2300 'S' St., N.W.
Washington, D.C. 20008
202-332-9044; fax: 202-332-9046

SOURCES:
AnnivHol-1983, p. 4
Chases-1996, p. 56
NatlHolWrld-1968, p. 12

♦ 0271 ♦ Burning of Judas
Between March 22 and April 25; Easter

La Quema de Judas takes place throughout Venezuela on the evening of Easter. In contrast to the many solemn rituals organized by the Roman Catholic Church during Holy Week, Judas burning takes place at the village or urban neighborhood level. The preparations go on all week, beginning with the selection of an appropriate Judas—usually a public figure in the community, but sometimes an individual of state or national prominence—against whom the group has decided to stage a protest. The women construct a life-size effigy of this person, making sure to include elements of dress or appearance that leave no mistake about its identity. The men build a wooden stand in a central location where the Judas figure will be placed.

On Easter morning, the people proceed to the house where the effigy has been stored for safekeeping and demand that Judas Iscariot, the disciple who betrayed Jesus, be turned over for punishment. The Judas effigy is placed on the stand, where everyone gets a chance to slap, punch, or kick it. At dusk the leader of the group recites the list of grievances that the people have against this individual—a document known as "The Testament of Judas," which is often written in verse and quite humorous. Then the Judas is doused with gasoline or kerosene and set on fire. The drinking, dancing, and fireworks continue late into the evening.

Although no one seems to know exactly how the custom originated, accounts of it have been traced back as far as 13th-century Spain.

See also Holy Saturday in Mexico

CONTACT:
Venezuelan Tourism Association
7 E. 51st St., 4th Floor
New York, NY 10022
800-331-0100 or 212-826-1678
fax: 212-826-4175

SOURCES:
FolkWrldHol-1992, p. 204

Burning of the Witches
See May Day Eve in Czech Republic

♦ 0272 ♦ Burning the Devil
December 7

La Quema del Diablo takes place in Guatemala. Men dressed as devils chase children through the streets from the start of ADVENT until December 7. On this day, trash fires are lit in the streets of Guatemala City and other towns, and the devils' reign of terror comes to an end.

CONTACT:
Guatemala Embassy
2220 R St., N.W.
Washington, D.C. 20008
202-745-4952; fax: 202-745-1908

SOURCES:
FolkWrldHol-1992, p. 583

♦ 0273 ♦ **Burning the Moon House**
Fifteenth day of first lunar month

The festival known as **Dal-jip-tae-u-gee** in the Kyungsang Province of Korea pays tribute to the moon by watching it rise through a moon house or moon gate—a carefully constructed pile of pine twigs which are set on fire. The moon gate is usually built on the top of a hill or at the seashore, where it is easier to see the moon rise through the flames. Jumping over the flames is believed to ward off evil, and the direction in which the moon gate collapses is an indication of whether the coming year will bring good luck or bad.

In other parts of Korea, a similar moon festival known as **Dal-ma-ji** is celebrated on the eve of the first full moon of the lunar year. People climb hills and build bonfires (without the "gate") to welcome the moon. Various folkloric beliefs concerning the harvest and the weather are associated with the color and brightness of the moon on this night.

CONTACT:
Korea National Tourism Corp.
205 N. Michigan Ave., Ste. 2212
Chicago, IL 60601
312-819-2560; fax: 312-819-2563

SOURCES:
FolkWrldHol-1992, p. 72

♦ 0274 ♦ **Burns Night**
January 25

The anniversary of the birthday of Scottish poet Robert Burns, who was born in 1759 in a clay cottage that blew down a week later, and died in 1796. The day is celebrated not only in Scotland but Newfoundland, where there is a sizeable settlement of Scots, and wherever there are devotees of this lusty poet. The celebrations generally take the form of recitations of Burns's poetry ("Tam O'Shanter" is a standard), the imbibing of quantities of single-malt Scotch whiskey, and the serving of haggis, a Scottish dish made of a sheep's or calf's innards (liver, heart, etc.) cut up with suet and oatmeal, seasoned, and boiled in the stomach of the animal. At the point of the carving of the haggis, it is traditional to recite "To a Haggis," with its line, "Great chieftain o' the pudding race!"

In the course of things, the Selkirk grace is also read: *"Some hae meat, and canna eat/ And some wad eat that want it/ But we hae meat and we can eat/ And sae the Lord be thanket."*

And other favorite lines will be heard—for example, "O, my luve's like a red, red rose," and "O wad some Pow'r the giftie gie us/ To see oursels as others see us!" The evening always ends, of course, with "Auld Lang Syne."

SOURCES:
AmerBkDays-1978, p. 109
BkHolWrld-1986, Jan 25
DictDays-1988, p. 16
FolkWrldHol-1992, p. 38

♦ 0275 ♦ **Burundi Independence Day**
July 1

This national holiday commemorates Burundi's independence from Belgium on this day in 1962.

CONTACT:
Burundi Embassy
2233 Wisconsin Ave., N.W., Ste. 212
Washington, D.C. 20007
202-342-2574; fax: 202-342-2578

SOURCES:
AnnivHol-1983, p. 87
Chases-1996, p. 277
NatlHolWrld-1968, p. 97

♦ 0276 ♦ **Buskers' Festival**
Late August

"Buskers" are vagabond musicians. They were common in the streets of 14th-century Ferrara, Italy, when it was ruled by the Dukes of Este. They still roam the streets of the world's cities, although they may be difficult to find because they usually have no fixed address and no manager or agent to contact. But Stefano Buttoni, artistic director of Ferrara's Buskers' Festival, manages to track them down and persuade them to come for a seven-day celebration of music that ranges from salsa to Celtic laments, and from Mozart to New Orleans jazz. They are not paid anything, nor are they given a stage to perform on, but since 1988 hundreds of them have wandered the city's narrow streets for a week in August, improvising their own kind of music and jamming with other itinerant musicians. The buskers come from all over the world to perform in Ferrara's squares and alleyways, with its spectacular medieval and Renaissance architecture as their backdrop. The week ends with a jam session in front of the walls of the castle in the center of the town.

CONTACT:
Italian Government Travel Office
630 Fifth Ave.
New York, NY 10111
212-245-4822

♦ 0277 ♦ **Butter and Egg Days**
First weekend after last Wednesday in April

A promotional event in Petaluma, Calif., that recalls the historic days when Petaluma was the "World's Egg Basket," producing millions of eggs that were shipped all over the world. The first Butter and Egg Days was a modest affair in 1983; it now draws about 25,000 for a parade with floats, bands, bagpipers, and children dressed as such things as butter pats and fried eggs. There are also street fairs, an antiques show, an egg toss, a butter-churning contest, and the presentation of the Good Egg award to a Petaluma booster.

The seed of this event was laid in 1918 when the first Egg Day parade was held. With the food shortages of World War I, people were being urged to eat less meat, and Petalumans decided to promote the idea of eating more eggs. Petaluma had the eggs; there were more hatcheries here than anywhere else. In 1878, the incubator developer L. C. Byce had established the Petaluma Incubator Co., which allowed great numbers of baby chicks to be artificially hatched. The town became a thriving poultry center, and boasted the world's only chicken pharmacy. The Egg Days, which ran from 1918 to 1926, brought the town national attention. These were huge celebrations, with nighttime illuminations, balls, chicken rodeos, and parades with gigantic Humpty Dumptys and white leghorn chickens. The chicken-and-egg industry waned in the 1950s, and the dairy industry moved in, and is now honored along with eggs.

CONTACT:
California Division of Tourism
801 K Street, Ste. 1600
Sacramento, CA 95814
800-862-2543 or 916-322-2881
fax: 916-322-3402

◆ 0278 ◆ **Butter Sculpture Festival**
Fifteenth day of first lunar month

The celebration of the Buddhist New Year (LOSAR) in Tibet is followed by MONLAM, a two-week prayer festival. On the 15th day, everyone goes to a monastery to view the butter sculptures. The most famous are at Jokhang Monastery in Lhasa, Tibet's capital. Completed over a period of months, the huge sculptures are made out of yak butter pigmented with dyes. They are fastened to 30-foot-high frames for display purposes and illuminated by special butter lamps. Each monastery maintains a workshop where its own artists shape the cold-hardened butter into depictions of legends, or other themes, different each year. The government awards a prize to the best sculpture.

CONTACT:
India Tourist Office
30 Rockefeller Ave.
15 N. Mezzanine
New York, NY 10112
212-586-4901; fax: 212-582-3274

SOURCES:
BkHolWrld-1986, Mar 9
FolkWrldHol-1992, pp. 64, 68
RelHolCal-1993, p. 96

◆ 0279 ◆ **Butter Week in Russia**
February–March, the week preceding Ash Wednesday

CARNIVAL is known as Butter Week or **Maslyanitza** (also rendered **Maslenitza**) in Russia because so many rich foods are served before the seven-week Lenten fast. *Bliny*, which are coarse flour pancakes, are served with butter and sour cream, and people go from one meal to another as the week proceeds. Fasting begins at midnight on SHROVE TUESDAY, and oil takes the place of butter.

Around the turn of the century, the Carnival celebration in St. Petersburg ended with a ceremony in which Prince Carnival bade farewell. Ten horses harnessed in single file drew a high cart holding a drunken man sitting before a table covered with food. When the Prince left town, Carnival came to an end with a display of primitive fireworks.

SOURCES:
BkFest-1937, p. 289
FolkWrldHol-1992, p. 124

◆ 0280 ◆ **Buzzard Day**
March 15

About 75 turkey vultures, also known as turkey buzzards, return to Hinckley, Ohio, each March 15 to spend the summer. While these carrion-eating birds may lack the charm of the SWALLOWS OF SAN JUAN CAPISTRANO, thousands of people celebrate them at the Hinckley Buzzard Day Festival, held since 1958 on the first Sunday after March 15. It features a pancake breakfast, an arts and crafts display, souvenir sales, and talks by naturalists at Metro Park, where the buzzards roost.

The vultures' return was first documented by a park patrolman who logged their arrival date for 23 years. Why the birds return, however, isn't known. One theory recalls the Great Hinckley Varmint Hunt on Dec. 24, 1818, when 475 men and boys lined up along Hinckley's borders and moved inward, slaughtering predators that were killing farm animals. The tons of carrion, of course, provided fine repasts for vulturine tastes.

CONTACT:
Ohio Division of Travel and
Tourism
P.O. Box 1001
Columbus, OH 43266
800-282-5393 or 614-466-8844
fax: 614-466-6744

SOURCES:
AnnivHol-1983, p. 37
Chases-1996, p. 133
FolkAmerHol-1991, p. 118

◆ 0281 ◆ **Byblos Festival**
May–September

The ancient city of Byblos in Lebanon has hosted an international music festival since the late 1960s. Performances of orchestral, chamber music, and jazz concerts are held throughout the summer. There are also plays, operettas, ballet, and modern dance recitals. Most of the events are held in the 12th-century castle built by the Crusaders out of the stones and granite columns of ancient Roman temples and public buildings.

Byblos, also known as Jubayl or Jebeil, is one of the oldest continuously inhabited towns in the world. The precursor of the modern alphabet was developed in Byblos, and the ancient Phoenicians exported their papyrus to the Aegean through the city. The English word ''Bible'' is derived from *byblos*, the early Greek name for papyrus.

CONTACT:
Lebanese Embassy
2560 28th St., N.W.
Washington, D.C. 20008
202-939-6300; fax: 202-939-6324

SOURCES:
IntlThFolk-1979, p. 264

C

♦ 0282 ♦ Cabrillo Day
September 28

Juan Rodríguez Cabrillo was the Portuguese explorer who discovered California on September 28, 1542, when he sailed into the bay that would eventually be called San Diego. He went on to explore the upper California coast, naming both Catalina and San Clemente islands after his ships, but he failed to discover San Francisco Bay before being driven south again by a severe storm.

In the San Diego area, Cabrillo Day celebrations were relatively modest until the early 1960s, when the week-long Cabrillo Festival became a yearly event. Activities include Portuguese-American music and dancing, the placing of a wreath at the base of Cabrillo's statue on Point Loma, and a costumed reenactment of the discovery of San Diego Bay.

CONTACT:
San Diego Convention and Visitors Bureau
401 B St., Ste. 1400
San Diego, CA 92101
619-232-3101; fax: 619-696-9371

SOURCES:
AmerBkDays-1978, p. 873
AnnivHol-1983, p. 124
Chases-1996, p. 393

♦ 0283 ♦ Cactus Jack Festival
Second weekend of October

A celebration honoring the outspoken former vice president of the United States, John Nance Garner, in Uvalde, Tex., where he made his home. Garner, born in 1868, was a member of the House of Representatives from 1903 until being chosen as vice president under Franklin Delano Roosevelt. He served two terms, from 1933 to 1941, but never quite let the position go to his head: he supposedly told a reporter that the vice presidency "isn't worth a bucket of warm spit." (It has since been revealed that Garner didn't use the word spit, and that the reporter cleaned up the quote.) On another occasion, he said the vice president was "a spare tire on the automobile of government." And furthermore, he said, "Becoming vice president was the only demotion I ever had."

So much for the vice presidency.

Cactus Jack earned his nickname in 1901 when the Texas legislature was deciding on a state flower. Garner led the faction that wanted the prickly-pear cactus, but the bluebonnet won by one vote. The name Cactus Jack stuck because he was a prickly kind of person who told people what he thought.

The Ettie R. Garner Museum here is the house where Garner and his wife, the former Mariette Rheiner, lived for 37 years. She was his secretary and advisor until her death in 1948; Garner donated the home in her memory to the town. He died in 1967, just short of his 99th year.

The celebration features a parade, dance, horseshoe and washer pitching, sports events, arts and crafts, and a typical south Texas barbecue of *fajitas* (small strips of marinated beef) and tacos.

CONTACT:
Texas Department of Commerce
Tourism Division
1700 N. Congress Ave., Ste. 200
Austin, TX 78711
800-888-8839 or 512-462-9192
fax: 512-936-0089

♦ 0284 ♦ Caitra Parb
March–April; eight days before the full moon of Caitra

A Hindu festival held in Orissa, India, Caitra Parb begins eight days before the Purnima (full moon). Throughout the celebration people fast, dance, and hunt. Heads of the families pay homage to their forefathers in the presence of the village priest, or *Jani*, and family members put on festive new costumes. Animal sacrifice plays a prominent part in the celebration, which also signals the beginning of the mango season.

SOURCES:
RelHolCal-1993, p. 65

♦ 0285 ♦ Calaveras County Fair and Frog Jumping Jubilee
Third weekend in May

A four-day county fair, established in 1928, in Angels Camp, Calif. It includes the official, original frog-jumping contest based on Mark Twain's story, "The Celebrated Jumping Frog of Calaveras County," as well as a children's parade, livestock competitions, a professional rodeo, a demolition derby, fireworks, and art exhibits. About 3,500 frogs are jumped in daily contests leading up to the Grand Finals on Sunday, in which there are 75 to 100 frog contestants. Jumps are measured from starting point to the landing point of the third hop. The world's record is 21'5¾", set in 1986 by Rosie the Ribiter. There are cash prizes for winners in various divisions, and anyone breaking Rosie's world record will win $5,000.

Mark Twain wrote the story of the jumping frog in 1865 and claimed it was told to him as the true story of an episode in Angels Camp in 1849. In his story, the original frog, named Dan'l Webster, was owned by one Jim Smiley, who educated it to be a fine jumper. When a stranger came along, Smiley bet him $40 Dan'l Webster could out-jump any frog in Calaveras County. The time arrived for the contest, but the stranger had secretly filled Dan'l Webster with quail shot, and the frog couldn't move. The stranger took the money and left, saying (according to Twain), "Well, *I* don't see no p'ints about that frog that's any better'n any other frog."

CONTACT:
California Division of Tourism
801 K Street, Ste. 1600
Sacramento, CA 95814
800-862-2543 or 916-322-2881
fax: 916-322-3402

SOURCES:
AmerBkDays-1978, p. 1065
AnnivHol-1983, p. 69
BkHolWrld-1986, May 22
Chases-1996, p. 214

Calends
See **Ides**

♦ 0286 ♦ Calgary Exhibition and Stampede
July

The 10-day Calgary Exhibition and Stampede, originally called the **Calgary Stampede**, is Canada's largest rodeo event, similar to CHEYENNE FRONTIER DAYS in the United States. The stampede offers a world-class rodeo competition in saddle bronc and bareback riding, steer wrestling, calf roping, and bull riding as well as a chuck wagon race that carries a $175,000 prize. Most of the rodeo events are held in the 130-acre Stampede Park in downtown Calgary, but there's also a Wild West town called Weadickville (named for Guy Weadick from Cheyenne, Wyoming, who founded the event in 1912), an Indian Village populated by representatives of five Indian tribes from the nearby Plains, a Frontier Casino with blackjack tables and roulette wheels, and agricultural and livestock exhibits.

CONTACT:
Alberta Economic Development
  and Tourism
Commerce Place, 3rd Floor
10155-102 Street
Edmonton, Alberta
Canada T5J 4L6
800-661-8886 or 403-427-4321

SOURCES:
GdWrldFest-1985, p. 28

♦ 0287 ♦ Calico Pitchin', Cookin', and Spittin' Hullabaloo
March–April; Palm Sunday weekend

A celebration highlighting a tobacco-spitting contest and recalling the 19th-century heyday of Calico, a silver-mining

ghost town in southern California about 10 miles north of Barstow. The contest for World Tobacco Spitting Champion began in 1977 and has led to two mentions in the *Guinness Book of World Records* for distance in juice-spitting: Randy Ober of Arkansas spat a record 44'6" in 1980 and then topped that record the next year with 47'10". Other contest categories are accuracy in juice-spitting and distance in wad-spitting (wads are required to be at least half an inch in diameter). Contestants have come not only from the United States but also from Great Britain, Germany, and Japan.

The hullabaloo also features a stew cook-off and flapjack racing, plus more standard fare such as a horseshoe-pitching contest, egg-tossing, greased-pole climbing, and bluegrass music.

The date of the event recalls the time of year in 1881 when the miners arrived and named the town Calico because they thought the reds, greens, and yellows of the rock formations looked like a calico skirt. It was the location of one of the largest silver strikes in California, producing about $86 million in silver during the 20 years it flourished. When silver prices sank, so did Calico. In San Bernardino County, Calico is visited by tourists year-round.

CONTACT:
California Division of Tourism
801 K Street, Ste. 1600
Sacramento, CA 95814
800-862-2543 or 916-322-2881
fax: 916-322-3402

SOURCES:
Chases-1996, p. 169

♦ 0288 ♦ California Gold Rush Day
Weekend nearest January 24

The anniversary of James W. Marshall's discovery of gold in 1848 while overseeing the construction of a sawmill near Coloma, California, is commemorated with an annual celebration at the Marshall Gold Discovery State Historic Park on the weekend nearest January 24. An employee of John A. Sutter, a wealthy landowner and entrepreneur, Marshall noticed flakes of gold in the streambed as he was inspecting work on the mill. Although Sutter and Marshall tried to keep the discovery secret, over the next year approximately 60,000 to 100,000 gold prospectors flocked to California. The surface deposits of gold eventually dwindled, but both Sutter and Marshall had already been ruined by the gold rush they tried to forestall. Sutter died bankrupt in 1888, and Marshall died five years later, living alone in a crude cabin just a short distance from where he'd first noticed the gleam of metal.

Marshall's cabin is now part of the Marshall Gold Discovery State Historic Park, and Sutter's adobe home is part of a museum and park in Sacramento.

CONTACT:
Marshall Gold Discovery State
  Historic Park
c/o Gold Rush District
101 J St.
Sacramento, CA 95814
916-622-3470 (park)
916-445-7373 (district office)
fax: 916-327-8872 (district office)

SOURCES:
AmerBkDays-1978, p. 109
AnnivHol-1983, p. 13
Chases-1996, p. 74

♦ 0289 ♦ **Calinda Dance**
June 23

The Calinda Dance was a 19th-century voodoo ritual observed on the eve of St. John's Day in New Orleans. Performed by Sanité Dédé, a voodoo priestess who confined herself to a very small space and imitated the undulations of a snake, the Calinda was so sensual that in the frenzied group dance that followed it, the dancers tore off their clothing and engaged in an orgy.

Although most voodoo ceremonies were held in secret, the New Orleans authorities allowed slaves to dance in Congo Square on Sunday afternoons where the authorities could keep an eye on them. This marked the end of the orgy climax and resulted in a combination of the original snake dance with an African war dance. But the Calinda remained so threatening to whites that it was banned as obscene in 1843, shortly before voodoo enjoyed its greatest popularity under the leadership of Marie Laveau. Laveau presided over the gatherings in Congo Square and turned the St. John's Eve celebration into a public show to which whites and even some newspaper reporters were invited.

SOURCES:
FolkAmerHol-1991, p. 246

♦ 0290 ♦ **Cambodia Independence Day**
November 9

November 9 marks the anniversary of Cambodia's independence from France in 1955. It is observed as a public holiday.

CONTACT:
Cambodian Embassy
4500 16th St., N.W.
Washington, D.C. 20011
202-726-7742

SOURCES:
Chases-1996, p. 445
NatlHolWrld-1968, p. 204

♦ 0291 ♦ **Camel Market**
Usually July

An important annual camel-trading fair in Guelmime (also spelled Goulimime or Goulimine), Morocco, a walled town that historically was a caravan center. Located on the northwest edge of the Sahara, the market is attended by the wanderers of the desert—the Shluh (a Berber people from southern Morocco), as well as the blue-veiled Tuareg men known as the Blue Men. The Tuaregs wear a blue *litham*, a double strip of blue cloth worn over the head and covering all but the eyes, sometimes giving their faces a blue tint. They also wear blue robes over their white *djellabahs*. The story is that an English cloth merchant visited the port and trading city of Agadir in the 1500s with calico dyed indigo blue. The Tuaregs liked the blue cloth and have had a predilection for it ever since.

The camel market brings together thousands of these Blue Men and their camels. They come to sell and trade baby camels as well as animal skins and wool. Hundreds of tents are pitched, and there is constant activity and noise: camel races, shouted bartering, and, at night, performances of the erotic *guedra* dance.

See also Bianou and Cure Salée

CONTACT:
Moroccan National Tourist Office
20 E. 46th St., Ste. 1201
New York, NY 10017
212-557-2520; fax: 212-949-8148

Camel Motorcycle Week
See **Motorcycle Week**

♦ 0292 ♦ **Camel Races, International**
September, weekend after Labor Day

Possibly the only camel races in the United States, and a reminder of a peculiar 19th-century experiment. The races have been held since 1954 in Virginia City, Nev., the one-time mining town that was considered the richest place on earth in the 1860s. In 1991, a team from Alice Springs, Australia, won the races.

The town is the site of the celebrated Comstock Lode, which yielded nearly $300 million in gold and silver in the two decades after its discovery in 1859. The wealth also gave the territory strategic importance: President Abraham Lincoln wanted Nevada as a state on the side of the North to support anti-slavery amendments and he also needed the mineral riches to finance the Civil War. Nevada became a state in 1864, and gold and silver were dug from the mines—with the help, briefly, of camels.

It was thought that camels could work like mules in the mines, and camels in the Federal Camel Corps were shipped to Nevada from Texas (where they were used in the army cavalry). The army had originally brought about 120 camels to the U.S. from Africa and Asia in the mid-1850s to carry cargo from Texas to California. But they didn't last long; their hoofs didn't adapt to the rocky terrain, so they were allowed to roam wild, and apparently died out.

There are some camels kept in town today, though, and others are imported for the races. The three-day race weekend now includes a Camel Hump Ball (a dance and barbecue); a parade with about 70 units, including belly dancers and bagpipe players; and a race of ostriches pulling chariots.

When the camel race was being held in 1961, the movie *The Misfits* was being filmed nearby. Director John Huston came to the races, borrowed a camel, and won.

CONTACT:
Nevada Commission on Tourism
5151 S. Carson St.
Capitol Complex
Carson City, NV 89710
800-638-2328 or 702-687-4322
fax: 702-687-6779

♦ 0293 ♦ **Cameroon National Day**
May 20

A public holiday commemorating the people's vote to establish a united Republic of Cameroon on May 20, 1972. This day is also known as **Constitution Day**.

CONTACT:
Cameroon Embassy
2349 Massachusetts Ave., N.W.
Washington, D.C. 20008
202-265-8790; fax: 202-387-3826

SOURCES:
AnnivHol-1983, p. 68
Chases-1996, p. 221

♦ 0294 ♦ **Camp Fire Founders' Day**
March 17

The organization originally known as the Camp Fire Girls was founded on March 17, 1910, around the same time that the Boy Scout movement was getting its start in Great Britain (*see* BOY SCOUTS' DAY). Now it is coeducational and is known as Camp Fire Boys and Girls. The organization stresses self-reliance, and membership is divided into five different age levels, ranging from Sparks (pre-school) to Horizon (grades 9–12). Skilled adults work with these young people in small groups, helping them to become acquainted with nature's secrets and to learn a variety of crafts. Interaction with adults is also emphasized as a way of learning about career choices, hobbies, and other interests.

Camp Fire's founding is observed by the group's members as part of **Camp Fire Boys and Girls Birthday Week**. The Sunday nearest March 17 is **Camp Fire Boys and Girls Birthday Sunday,** and is a day when Camp Fire Boys and Girls worship together and participate in their church or temple services.

CONTACT:
Camp Fire Boys and Girls
4601 Madison Ave.
Kansas City, MO 64112
800-669-6884 or 816-756-1950
fax: 816-756-0258

SOURCES:
AnnivHol-1983, p. 38
Chases-1996, p. 135

♦ 0295 ♦ **Canada Day**
July 1

The British North America Act went into effect on July 1, 1867, uniting Upper Canada (now called Ontario), Lower Canada (now Quebec), New Brunswick, and Nova Scotia into a British dominion. Canadians celebrate this day—which was formerly known as **Dominion Day**—with parades and picnics, somewhat similar to FOURTH OF JULY festivities in the United States.

In Detroit, Michigan, and Windsor, Ontario, which are on opposite sides of the Detroit River and are connected by a vehicular tunnel and the Ambassador Bridge, this is also one of the days on which the **International Freedom Festival** is held. A salute to both countries, the festival includes a powerboat race, sky-diving exhibitions, baton-twirling and kite-flying competitions, and an old-fashioned hootenanny.

CONTACT:
Ontario Travel
Queen's Park
Toronto, Ontario
Canada M7A 2R9
800-ONTARIO or 416-314-0944

Detroit Visitor Information Center
2 E. Jefferson Ave.
Detroit, MI 48226
800-338-7648 or 313-567-1170

SOURCES:
AnnivHol-1983, p. 87
BkHolWrld-1986, Jul 1
Chases-1996, p. 277
DictDays-1988, pp. 18, 32
FolkWrldHol-1992, p. 362
GdWrldFest-1985, p. 55
NatlHolWrld-1968, p. 98

♦ 0296 ♦ **Canadian National Exhibition**
August–September

The first Canadian National Exhibition was held in 1879 in Toronto. The fair moved briefly to Ottawa, but returned to Toronto and was called the **Toronto Industrial Exhibition** until 1921, when the name was changed to reflect its nation-

wide appeal. Located on the shores of Lake Ontario, about 10 minutes from downtown Toronto, the fairgrounds occupy 350 acres of lawns, gardens, pavilions, and Victorian-style buildings. Events include an air show, a horse show, a Scottish World Festival, and celebrity appearances. The Exhibition claims to be the oldest and largest of its kind in the world.

CONTACT:
Canadian Tourism Commission
4th Floor, East Tower
235 Queen St.
Ottawa, Ontario
Canada K1A OH6
800-577-2266

SOURCES:
GdWrldFest-1985, p. 53

♦ 0297 ♦ **Canberra Day**
Third Monday in March

Canberra, the capital city of Australia, was founded on March 12, 1913. Unusual in that it is one of the few world capitals planned from the ground up, the city and its giant ornamental pond, Lake Burley Griffin, were built out of a depression in a dusty plain about 200 miles southwest of Sydney.

The city's founding is celebrated on the third Monday in March each year, which marks the end of the 10-day Canberra Festival. The festival is an outdoor community event that encompasses everything from hot-air balloon rides and a "street bed" derby (in which wheeled beds are raced through the streets), to opera and "A Tribute to Elvis Presley."

CONTACT:
Australian Tourist Commission
100 Park Ave., 25th Floor
New York, NY 10017
212-687-6300; fax: 212-661-3340

SOURCES:
AnnivHol-1983, p. 37
Chases-1996, p. 137
IntlThFolk-1979, p. 8

Candelaria
See **Candlemas**

♦ 0298 ♦ **Candlemas**
February 2

After observing the traditional 40-day period of purification following the birth of Jesus, Mary presented him to God at the Temple in Jerusalem. According to a New Testament gospel, an aged and devout Jew named Simeon held the baby in his arms and said that he would be "a light to lighten the Gentiles" (Luke 2:32). It is for this reason that February 2 has come to be called Candlemas (or **Candelaria** in Spanish-speaking countries) and has been celebrated by the blessing of candles since the 11th century. In the Eastern Church it is known as the **Feast of the Presentation of Christ in the Temple;** in the Western Church, it's the **Feast of the Purification of the Blessed Virgin Mary.** In the United States, February 2 is also GROUNDHOG DAY; in Great Britain it is said that the badger comes out to test the weather. The old rhyme is as follows:

> *If Candlemas Day be dry and fair,*
> *The half of winter's to come and mair.*
> *If Candlemas Day be wet and foul,*
> *The half of winter's gone at Yule.*

See also MIHR, FESTIVAL OF

SOURCES:
AmerBkDays-1978, p. 135
BkDays-1864, vol. I, p. 212
BkFest-1937, p. 226
DaysCustFaith-1957, p. 45
DictFolkMyth-1984, pp. 181,
  186, 787
FestSaintDays-1915, p. 27
FestWestEur-1958, p. 105
FolkAmerHol-1991, p. 65
FolkWrldHol-1992, p. 92
RelHolCal-1993, p. 104
SaintFestCh-1904, p. 90

♦ 0299 ♦ **Candlewalk**
December 31

The custom of seeing the old year out and the new year in with some type of candlelight procession or WATCH NIGHT SERVICE may have derived from pagan WINTER SOLSTICE fire rituals, but it was John Wesley, the founder of Methodism, who first brought it to America. St. George's Methodist Church in Philadelphia held the first watch night services in 1770, and in some areas members of the African Methodist Episcopal Church have continued the custom.

In rural Bladen County, North Carolina, an observance known as the Candlewalk combines pagan fertility rites with the Christian worship of the Virgin Mary. On CHRISTMAS EVE the women and girls of the church walk deep into the swamp or forest, while the men and boys are threatened with a death curse if they follow. According to local legend, this period of withdrawal is for the purpose of sexual indoctrination. When the women return, they do so in a single file procession, bearing lighted torches or candles and singing ancient hymns in an African language or pidgin English that only the congregation understands. As each woman enters the church, she extinguishes her candle. The watch-night ritual, which usually takes place right before midnight, is often followed by prayers, hymns, or sermons.

See also ALLEN, RICHARD, BIRTHDAY OF

SOURCES:
FolkAmerHol-1991, p. 482

♦ 0300 ♦ **Cannes Film Festival**
May

The **International Film Festival** held in the resort city of Cannes on the French Riviera is probably the best known of the hundreds of film festivals held all over the world each year. Sponsored by governments, industry, service organizations, experimental film groups, or individual promoters, these festivals provide filmmakers, critics, distributors, and cinema enthusiasts an opportunity to attend showings of new films and to discuss current trends in the industry. The festival at Cannes is held at the Palais des Festivals, and its founding in 1947 marked a resurgence for the film industry, which had been shattered by World War II. The festival has also been responsible for the growing popularity of foreign films in the United States.

Other important film festivals are held in Berlin, London, San Francisco, New York, Chicago, Venice, and Karlovy Vary in the Czech Republic. Some cater to the films of just one country, some to specific subjects, and some are special festivals for student filmmakers.

CONTACT:
French Government Tourist Office
9454 Wilshire Blvd., Ste. 715
Beverly Hills, CA 90212
310-271-6665; fax: 310-276-2835

♦ 0301 ♦ **Cape Verde Independence Day**
July 5

This public holiday commemorates Cape Verde's independence from Portugal on this day in 1975.

CONTACT:
Cape Verde Embassy
3415 Massachusetts Ave., N.W.
Washington, D.C. 20007
202-965-6820; fax: 202-965-1207

SOURCES:
AnnivHol-1983, p. 89
Chases-1996, p. 285

♦ 0302 ♦ **Cape Vincent French Festival**
Saturday before July 14

Cape Vincent, New York, is in the Thousand Islands, where Lake Ontario meets the St. Lawrence River, an area with a strong French heritage. At one time, there was so much feeling for Napoleon among the local residents that they built a cup-and-saucer style house (a local architectural style in which the ground floor is wider than the second floor) where they hoped he might decide to spend his exile. However, it was one of Napoleon's followers, Le Roy de Chaumont, who first settled here in the 1800s. (*See also* NAPOLEON'S DAY.)

Launched in 1968, the festival immediately drew an astounding number of visitors, many of them French Canadians. It takes place, appropriately enough, on the Saturday before BASTILLE DAY and features a wide variety of French foods as well as a pageant and a parade of decorated carts. A French mass is held at St. Vincent de Paul's Church, and the evening ends with a waterfront display of fireworks.

CONTACT:
New York Division of Tourism
1 Commerce Pl.
Albany, NY 12245
800-225-5697 or 518-474-4116
fax: 518-486-6416

SOURCES:
GdUSFest-1984, p. 123

♦ 0303 ♦ **Captain Brady Day**
Second week in July

The body of water around which the village of Brady Lake, Ohio, was built has more than aesthetic value to the residents. Captain Samuel Brady, an American frontiersman who fought in the Revolutionary War, was a scout in what was then called the Northwest Territory. He escaped a group of Wyandotte Indians by hiding under the surface of the lake and breathing through a hollow reed. The importance of this event is reflected in the fact that both the community and the lake were named after Captain Brady, and every summer (on a date that has not yet been firmly fixed), the escape is reenacted on the shores of the lake.

When the level of Brady Lake began to drop suddenly in the late 1970s, the residents pulled together to deal with the problems triggered by the water shortage rather than trying to sell their homes in anticipation of falling real estate values.

The Captain Brady Day celebration has become an important unifying event for the people of Brady Lake, who view the lake as a symbol of their solidarity and peaceful way of life.

CONTACT:
Ohio Division of Travel and
  Tourism
P.O. Box 1001
Columbus, OH 43266
800-282-5393 or 614-466-8844
fax: 614-466-6744

SOURCES:
FolkAmerHol-1991, p. 299

♦ 0304 ♦ **Carabao Festival**
Third week of May

A feast in honor of San Isidro Labrador (St. Isidore the Farmer), the patron saint of Filipino farmers, held in Pulilan, Bulacan province, the Philippines. The feast also honors the *carabao*, or water buffalo, the universal beast of burden of the Philippines. Farmers scrub their carabao, then decorate them with flowers to parade with the image of San Isidro. A carabao race is held, and at the finish line, the animals kneel and are blessed by the parish priest. The festival is also marked by exploding firecrackers and the performance of the Bamboo Dance, where dancers represent the tinikling bird, a menace to the rice crop. Among the games played is *palo sebo*—climbing a 'greased pole' to get the prize at the top.

See also SAN ISIDRO THE FARMER, FEAST OF

CONTACT:
Philippine Department of Tourism
556 Fifth Ave.
First Floor Mezzanine
New York, NY 10036
212-575-7915; fax: 212-302-6759

SOURCES:
Chases-1996, p. 212
FolkWrldHol-1992, p. 298
GdWrldFest-1985, p. 153

♦ 0305 ♦ **Caramoor Festival**
Mid-June to mid-August

In the 1930s, Walter and Lucie Rosen gave private concerts for their friends in the music room of their Mediterranean-style country estate in Katonah, New York, known as Caramoor. Their devotion to music led to the establishment of the Caramoor Festival in 1946. Small opera productions, chamber music, and children's programs are held in the estate's open-air Spanish courtyard, while the Venetian Theater, which incorporates Greek and Roman marble columns from a 15th-century Italian villa, has a stage large enough to accommodate a symphony orchestra and full-scale opera. Such world-class singers as Beverly Sills, Jessye Norman, and Charles Bressler have performed there, as have well-known instrumentalists Alicia De Larrocha, Misha Dichter, Garrick Ohlsson, and Philippe Entremont. Concerts are held Thursdays through Sundays for nine weeks during the summer. The festival is the summer home of the Orchestra of St. Luke's and St. Luke's Chamber Ensemble.

CONTACT:
New York Division of Tourism
1 Commerce Pl.
Albany, NY 12245
800-225-5697 or 518-474-4116
fax: 518-486-6416

SOURCES:
MusFestAmer-1990, p. 99

♦ 0306 ♦ **Carberry Day**
Friday the 13th

The students and faculty at Brown University in Providence, Rhode Island, celebrate the fictitious academic exploits of Professor Josiah Stinkney Carberry every Friday the 13th. It all began in 1929, when a young faculty member at Brown posted a notice saying that J. S. Carberry would give a lecture on "Archaic Greek Architectural Revetments in Connection with Ionian Phonology" at eight o'clock on a certain evening. Ben C. Clough, a retired Latin professor spotted the hoax and decided to join in the fun by inserting the word "not" between "will" and "give." After that, the joke took on a life of its own, and the ubiquitous Professor Carberry began to send postcards and telegrams with news of his latest exotic research trips. Articles under his name began appearing in scholarly journals and, in 1966, Brown gave Carberry a bona fide M.A. degree—awarded, of course, *in absentia*.

On Carberry Day, small brown jugs appear around the campus, and students and teachers fill them with change. The money goes to a book fund that Professor Carberry has set up "in memory of my future late wife, Laura."

CONTACT:
Brown University
Providence, RI 02912
401-863-1000; fax: 401-863-3700

SOURCES:
FolkAmerHol-1991, p. 42

♦ 0307 ♦ **Caricom Day**
On or near July 4

CARICOM stands for the "Caribbean Community," an organization established on July 4, 1973, for the purpose of supporting a common market, coordinating foreign policy, and promoting cooperation among the 13 member states of the Caribbean: Antigua and Barbuda, Bahamas, Barbados, Belize, Dominica, Grenada, Guyana, Jamaica, Montserrat, St. Kitts-Nevis, St. Lucia, St. Vincent, and Trinidad and Tobago. Caricom Day is celebrated on or around July 4 in Barbados, Guyana, and St. Vincent. In Antigua and Barbuda, it is celebrated on the first Saturday in June.

CONTACT:
Caribbean Community
Bank of Guyana Bldg.
P.O. Box 10827
Georgetown, Guyana
011-592-2-692-881

SOURCES:
AnnivHol-1983, p. 88
Chases-1996, p. 277

♦ 0308 ♦ **Carillon Festival, International**
Second full week in June

The only event of its kind in the world, the International Carillon Festival in Springfield, Illinois, attracts carillonneurs from France, Belgium, Germany, Brazil, New Zealand, and the Netherlands as well as from the United States. The centerpiece of the festival is the Rees Memorial Carillon, housed in a tower given to the community by Thomas Rees, publisher of the *Illinois State Register* from 1881 to 1933. Rees first became interested in the art and skill of playing bell music while visiting Holland and Belgium. The tower holds 66 bronze bells cast by a 300-year-old Dutch foundry and covering a range of five-and-a-half chromatic octaves. The bells are played manually by means of a keyboard.

The festival, instituted in 1962, features the music of BACH,

Schubert (*see also* SCHUBERTIADE HOHENEMS), MOZART, Grieg, and other composers arranged for the carillon and played by internationally acclaimed masters of the instrument. The performances take place in Springfield's Washington Park, where listeners can sit the recommended 300 or more feet away.

CONTACT:
Springfield Convention and Visitors Bureau
109 N. Seventh St.
Springfield, IL 62701
800-545-7300 or 217-789-2360
fax: 217-544-8711

SOURCES:
MusFestAmer-1990, p. 55

♦ 0309 ♦ **Carling Sunday**
Between March 8 and April 11 in West; between March 21 and April 24 in East

The fifth Sunday in LENT, also known as **Passion Sunday,** whose name possibly derives from 'care.' It is traditional in Great Britain to eat a dish of parched peas cooked in butter, called a *carling,* said to be in memory of corn Jesus' disciples picked on the Sabbath.

SOURCES:
BkDays-1864, vol. I, p. 336
BkFest-1937, p. 56
DictDays-1988, p. 19
FestSaintDays-1915, p. 53
FolkWrldHol-1992, p. 128

♦ 0310 ♦ **Carmentalia**
January 11 and 15

It was unusual in ancient Rome for a single deity to have two separate festival days only a few days apart, and a number of explanations—none of them conclusive—have been offered for why the second festival in honor of the goddess Carmenta was instituted. The only thing that is certain is that the goddess' most prominent characteristic was her gift of prophecy, and that it was primarily women who frequented her temple near the Porta Carmentalis, a gate at the foot of the southern end of the capitol. Carmenta was also a birth-goddess, and although it might seem unusual to celebrate birth in the middle of winter, January happens to be exactly nine months after April, then the most popular time for marriages.

Carmenta had her own priest, or *flamen,* whose duties on her festival days were confined to the preparation of offerings of grain or cereal. There was a taboo against animal skins in Carmenta's cult, perhaps because the slaughter of animals was antithetical to a goddess of birth. The women known as *Carmentes* were similar to midwives—wise old women whose skills and spells assisted women in childbirth, and who had the power to tell their fortunes.

SOURCES:
ClassDict-1984, p. 127
FestRom-1981, p. 62
RomFest-1925, p. 290

Carnaval de Quebec
See **Quebec Winter Carnival**

♦ 0311 ♦ **Carnaval Miami**
First two full weeks in March

The biggest event in Miami, Fla., honoring Hispanic culture. Held since 1938, it is estimated that one million people attend each year. The highlight and grand finale of the festival is the famous Calle Ocho Open House. This is non-stop, wall-to-wall entertainment along 23 blocks of Southwest Eighth Street (*Calle Ocho*): 40 stages with more than 200 troupes offering live music, dancing, and folkloric performances. There are more than 600 vendors of ethnic food. Other events are the Miss Carnaval Miami beauty contest; a grand *paseo* or parade with floats; limbo dancers, samba groups, and steel bands from the Caribbean; a footrace; a laser display; fireworks; and concerts of international stars.

CONTACT:
Greater Miami Convention and Visitors Bureau
701 Brickell Ave., Ste. 2700
Miami, FL 33131
800-933-8448 or 305-539-3000
fax: 305-539-3113

SOURCES:
Chases-1996, p. 116

♦ 0312 ♦ **Carnea (Karneia, Karnea, Carneia)**
August

The Carnea was one of ancient Sparta's three principal religious festivals—the other two being the Hyacinthia and the Gymnopaidiai—which were observed in many parts of the Peloponnesus as well as in Cyrene, Magna Graecia, and elsewhere. It was the ultimate expression of the cult of Apollo Karneios, the ram god of flocks and herds and of fertility in general. It was held during the month of Carneus (August) and dates back to 676 B.C. The Carnea was both a vintage festival and a military one, Apollo being expected to help his people both by promoting the harvest and by supporting them in battle. Young men called *staphylodromoi,* or 'grape-cluster-runners', chased after a man wearing garlands. It was considered a good omen for the city if they caught him and a bad one if they didn't.

No military operations could be held during this festival, and it is said that the Spartans might not have been defeated by the Persians at Thermopylae if the Carnea hadn't prevented the movement of their main army.

SOURCES:
DictFolkMyth-1984, pp. 67, 192
RelHolCal-1993, p. 65

♦ 0313 ♦ **Carnival**
Varying dates, from Epiphany to Ash Wednesday Eve

The period known as Carnival—probably from the Latin *caro* or *carne levara,* meaning 'to take away meat' and 'a farewell to flesh'—begins anytime after EPIPHANY and usually comes to a climax during the last three days before ASH WEDNESDAY, especially during MARDI GRAS. It is a time of feasting and revelry in anticipation of the prohibitions of LENT.

Carnival is still observed in most of Europe and the Americas. It features masked balls, lavish costume parades, torch processions, dancing, fireworks, noise-making, and of course feasting on all the foods that will have to be given up for Lent. Ordinarily Carnival includes only the Sunday, Monday and Tuesday before Ash Wednesday (*see* FASCHING), but sometimes it begins on the preceding Friday or even earlier. In Brazil, Carnival is the major holiday of the year.

See also SHROVE TUESDAY

SOURCES:
AmerBkDays-1978, pp. 43, 156
BkDays-1864, vol. I, pp. 65, 236
BkFest-1937, pp. 4, 29, 38, 54, 67, 95, 102, 111, 120, 132, 146, 166, 179, 219, 241, 249, 259, 267, 289, 298, 316, 328
DictFolkMyth-1984, pp. 105, 178, 181, 192, 193, 197, 220, 370, 397, 543, 568, 629, 747, 749, 757, 759, 787, 807, 842, 844, 947, 977, 980, 1082
FestWestEur-1958, pp. 6, 23, 34, 55, 56, 89, 124, 151, 163, 191, 211, 230
FolkAmerHol-1991, p. 84
FolkWrldHol-1992, pp. 103, 104, 106
GdUSFest-1984, pp. 5, 68, 133
GdWrldFest-1985, pp. 4, 24, 64, 96, 133, 147, 175
IntlThFolk-1979, pp. 44, 82, 278
RelHolCal-1993, pp. 65, 76, 93

♦ 0314 ♦ Carnival in Aruba
February–March; three days before Ash Wednesday

Preparations for the CARNIVAL celebration on the island of Aruba begin months before the actual event. There is a calypso competition at the end of January, followed by a steel band competition to see who gets to perform in the Carnival parade in Oranjestad. Then there's a tumba contest, "tumba" being the native music of the Netherlands Antilles. The actual celebration begins three days before ASH WEDNESDAY and ends at midnight on MARDI GRAS.

The highlight is the Carnival Main Parade, which takes eight hours to wind its way through the streets of Oranjestad. It includes elaborate floats and people in colorful costumes dancing the jump-up, a dance performed to a half-march rhythm. The three-day festival comes to an end with the Old Mask Parade, followed by the traditional burning of "King Momo."

CONTACT:
Aruba Tourism Authority
1000 Harbor Blvd.
Weehawken, NJ 07087
800-862-7822 or 201-330-0800
fax: 201-330-8757

SOURCES:
FolkWrldHol-1992, p. 106
GdWrldFest-1985, p. 4

♦ 0315 ♦ Carnival in Brazil
Between January 30 and March 5; five days preceding Ash Wednesday

CARNIVAL is the largest popular festival in Brazil, the last chance for partying before LENT. The most extravagant celebration takes place along the eight miles of Copacabana Beach in Rio de Janeiro, where, since the 1930s, the parades, pageants, and costume balls go on for four days, all accompanied by the distinctive rhythm of the samba. The whole city is decorated with colored lights and streamers, and impromptu bands play on every street corner. Banks, stores, and government offices are closed until noon on ASH WEDNESDAY.

The high point of the **Carioca** (as the natives of Rio are known) **Carnival** is the parade of the samba schools (*Escola de Samba*), which begins on Carnival Sunday and ends about midday on Monday. The samba schools are neighborhood groups, many of whom come from the humblest sections of Rio, who develop their own choreography, costumes, and theme songs. The competition among them is as fierce as the rivalry of top sports teams. A single samba school can have as many as two to three thousand participants, so the scale of the parade can only be described as massive. People spend months learning special dances for the parade, and must often raise huge sums of money to pay for their costumes, which range from a few strategically placed strings of beads to elaborate spangled and feathered headdresses. Each samba school dances the length of the Sambadrome, a one-of-a-kind samba stadium designed by Oscar Niemeyer and built in 1984 to allow 85,000 spectators to watch the samba schools dance by. Viewing the parade from the Sambadrome is usually an all-night affair.

In recent years, more and more of Carnival has moved into clubs, the Club Monte Libano being one of the most famous. The Marilyn Monroe look-alike contest held by transvestites on Sugarloaf Mountain is among the most unusual events.

CONTACT:
Brazilian Embassy
3006 Massachusetts Ave., N.W.
Washington, D.C. 20008
202-745-2700; fax: 202-745-2827

SOURCES:
AmerBkDays-1978, pp. 43, 157
BkHolWrld-1986, Feb 25
DictFolkMyth-1984, p. 193
FolkWrldHol-1992, p. 108
GdWrldFest-1985, p. 24
RelHolCal-1993, p. 65

♦ 0316 ♦ Carnival in Colombia
February–March; Friday through Tuesday before Ash Wednesday

From the Friday preceding ASH WEDNESDAY until SHROVE TUESDAY, the Colombian city of Barranquilla celebrates CARNIVAL. There are costume balls, folklore shows, water festivals, and, on the night before Ash Wednesday, the ceremonial burial of "José Carnaval," the spirit who rules over the festivities. Each barrio, or neighborhood, chooses its own beauty queen and holds informal parties, while the city's wealthier inhabitants hold pageants and formal balls, competing to see who can come up with the most ornate costume. *Ron blanco*, the local white rum, is the favored drink, and residents dance in the streets to African and Indian rhythms. The Battle of Flowers on the opening day of the festival involves many elaborate floats decorated with the country's exotic flora.

CONTACT:
Colombian Embassy
2118 Leroy Pl., N.W.
Washington, D.C. 20008
202-387-8338; fax: 202-232-8643

SOURCES:
GdWrldFest-1985, p. 64

◆ 0317 ◆ Carnival in Goa
February–March; Saturday through Tuesday
before Ash Wednesday

In Goa, a region on the southwest coast of India, CARNIVAL is known as **Intruz** because it leads into the period of LENT. Rules and regulations are relaxed, and people wearing masks go around throwing *cocotes* and *cartuchos* (small paper packets containing flour and sawdust) at one another, or squirting each other with syringes of perfumed colored water—much like what goes on during the Hindu festival of HOLI. In Panaji, the capital of Goa, there is a huge parade in honor of King Momo, the Lord of the Revels, on SHROVE TUESDAY. There are floats with dance troupes and swing bands, stilt-walkers dressed up as Walt Disney characters, tableaux, and grotesque figures in African masks. The entire procession can take as long as four hours to pass, ending at the Church of Our Lady of the Immaculate Conception. Afterward, there is dancing in the town squares, public halls, and on the beaches, with older people doing the tango and waltz while the young people dance to popular music. The Carnival celebration comes to a close at dawn on ASH WEDNESDAY, when most of the revelers attend early morning mass.

CONTACT:
India Tourist Office
30 Rockefeller Ave.
15 N. Mezzanine
New York, NY 10112
212-586-4901; fax: 212-582-3274

SOURCES:
FolkWrldHol-1992, p. 111

◆ 0318 ◆ Carnival in Hungary (Farsang)
January 6 to Ash Wednesday (February–March)

This is the time of year when most weddings are celebrated in Hungary, and when parties, balls, and entertainments are held. In some parts of the country, villagers perform the symbolic burying of King Marrow Bone, who represents life's indulgences. Prince Cibere, named after the sour bran soup eaten during LENT, begins his 40-day reign on ASH WEDNESDAY.

In southern Hungary, masks known as *buso* that are passed down from one generation to the next are worn during MARDI GRAS. They are made out of carved wood painted with ox blood, with animal skins covering the top and ram's horns emerging from either side. Although at one time only adult married men could wear these masks, young unmarried men now wear them, shaking huge wooden rattles, shooting off cannons, and teasing women with long sticks topped by sheepskin gourds, a phallic symbol. In Slovenia, these masks have dangling red tongues, and the men wearing them run around in groups carrying clubs covered at one end with the skins of hedgehogs.

SOURCES:
BkFest-1937, p. 166
FolkWrldHol-1992, p. 112

◆ 0319 ◆ Carnival in Malta
February–March; before Ash Wednesday

Five days of pre-Lenten festivities in Malta, a custom since the 1500s. There are some festivities in the villages, but the main activities are in the capital city of Valletta. Here the traditional events include a parade with floats, brass bands, and participants wearing grotesque masks, and open-air folk-dancing competitions. A King Carnival reigns over the festival.

CONTACT:
Malta National Tourist Office
350 Fifth Ave.
Empire State Bldg., Ste. 4412
New York, NY 10118
212-695-9520; fax: 212-695-8229

SOURCES:
Chases-1996, p. 200
FolkWrldHol-1992, p. 113

◆ 0320 ◆ Carnival in Martinique and Guadeloupe
January–March, till Ash Wednesday night

CARNIVAL celebrations on the French Caribbean island of Martinique and its sister island of Guadeloupe begin the Sunday after NEW YEAR'S DAY with weekend parties and dances in the larger cities and towns. But they reach a climax during the last few days before LENT. On the Sunday before Lent, there are parades with marchers in exotic costumes dancing to the beat of the *beguine*, a Congolese ritual dance. Stores and offices are closed on Monday, an official holiday that is spent singing and dancing, with masked balls that go on far into the night. SHROVE TUESDAY is a day for children to dress up in red-devil costumes and carry homemade tridents as they parade through the streets.

The celebration continues right through ASH WEDNESDAY, when thousands of masked, costumed she-devils (many of whom are men in drag) have a parade of their own. Everyone wears black and white, and dark-skinned faces are smeared with ash. Effigies of King Vaval and his alter ego, Bois-Bois, tower over the procession. That night the effigies are burned, and Vaval's coffin is lowered into the ground.

CONTACT:
French Government Tourist Office
9454 Wilshire Blvd., Ste. 715
Beverly Hills, CA 90212
310-271-6665; fax: 310-276-2835

SOURCES:
FolkWrldHol-1992, p. 113
GdWrldFest-1985, p. 133

◆ 0321 ◆ Carnival in Mexico
February–March

CARNIVAL celebrations in Mexico vary from one town or region to the next, but almost all involve folk and ritual dances. In Tepeyanco and Papalotla, Tlaxcala State, *paragueros* ("umbrella men") perform exaggerated polkas and mazurkas during Carnival, wearing headdresses shaped like an umbrella. In Santa Ana Chiautempan and Contla, also in Tlaxcala State, *los catrines*—men dressed as women, or 'dandies'—carry umbrellas as they mock high-society dances. Other dances performed during Carnival include the *moros, diablos,* and *muertos* taken over from the Spanish as well as the *arcos* and *pastoras*, which are danced with flowered arches. In Morelos, the Carnival dancers are known as *chinelos*. Although they were formerly disguised as black Africans, nowadays they wear long embroidered satin gowns, hats topped with ostrich plumes, and masks with horn-shaped black beards.

Carnival in Mexico is known for drama as well as dance. In Zaachila, Oaxaca State, there is a mock battle between priests and devils. In Huejotzingo, Puebla State, an elaborate drama staged over a period of three or four days dramatizes the exploits of the bandit Agustin Lorenzo and the woman with whom he elopes. Carnival is celebrated in Mexico City with fireworks, parades, street dancers, and costume balls.

CONTACT:
Mexican Government Tourist
  Office
405 Park Ave., Ste. 1401
New York, NY 10022
800-446-3942 or 212-755-7261
fax: 212-753-2874

SOURCES:
DictFolkMyth-1984, pp. 193,
  197, 220, 759
IntlThFolk-1979, p. 278

♦ 0322 ♦ Carnival in Panama
February–March; four days preceding Ash Wednesday

The celebration of CARNIVAL in Panama begins on the Saturday before ASH WEDNESDAY, when the Carnival Queen and her courtiers enter Panama City. They are greeted by King Momus, the god of gaiety. The Queen leads a parade through the streets, to the accompaniment of *murgas,* or walking bands. Sunday is Pollera Day, when the women bring out the brilliantly colored, hand-embroidered, multilayered *pollera* dresses that are often handed down from one generation to the next. Monday is the day where the *comparasas*—precision dance troupes dressed in elaborate costumes—compete for prizes. On Tuesday, the last day of the celebration, there is a Grand Parade of floats, walking bands, dancers, and all the groups that have performed or paraded on previous days. The festivities continue throughout the night, ending at dawn with the "burial of the fish" ceremony. A mock funeral is held for a dead fish, which is then dumped into the ocean or a swimming pool.

See also BURIAL OF THE SARDINE

CONTACT:
Panama Embassy
2862 McGill Terr., N.W.
Washington, D.C. 20008
202-483-1407; fax: 202-483-8413

SOURCES:
FolkWrldHol-1992, p. 115
GdWrldFest-1985, p. 147

♦ 0323 ♦ Carnival in Peru
February–March

In Peru, it is customary during CARNIVAL for people to throw water and flour at each other. Sometimes the flour and water are thrown from a balcony on whoever happens to be walking beneath. Groups of young people often stage battles in which the boys throw the girls into fountains or bathtubs and vice versa. At Carnival dances, even well-bred young men and women squirt water at each other from special syringes sold for this purpose. Water-throwing battles are common between sailboats on lakes and in private homes. A particularly colorful celebration is held in Cajamarca.

Although Carnival is celebrated throughout Peru, the events are not as elaborate as those in neighboring Brazil.

CONTACT:
Embassy of Peru
1700 Massachusetts Ave., N.W.
Washington, D.C. 20036
202-833-9860; fax: 202-659-8124

SOURCES:
BkFestHolWrld-1970, p. 37

♦ 0324 ♦ Carnival in Portugal
February–March; three days preceding Ash Wednesday

The pre-Lenten festivities in Portugal culminate on the last three days before ASH WEDNESDAY. There was a time when the CARNIVAL celebration in Lisbon was characterized by obscene jokes and horseplay, with battles involving eggs, oranges, flour, and water. But the present-day public festivities are more restrained. People decorate their cars with masses of flowers, and as the cars parade through town, they pelt their friends and neighbors with blossoms while the bystanders try to retaliate.

There are balls, parties, and dances in the cities, but in the provinces many of the more uninhibited Carnival traditions persist. The *folía* (literally, 'madness'), a fertility dance associated with the Portuguese Carnival celebration, is named after the furious tempo and lunatic actions of the participants. Mummers and musicians, the burial in effigy of King Carnival, and traditional folk plays are also part of these rural Carnival observances.

CONTACT:
Portuguese National Tourist
  Office
590 Fifth Ave., 4th Floor
New York, NY 10036
212-354-4403; fax: 212-764-6137

SOURCES:
BkFest-1937, p. 267
BkFestHolWrld-1970, p. 34
DictFolkMyth-1984, p. 397

♦ 0325 ♦ Carnival in St. Vincent
February–March; before Ash Wednesday

Touring musical groups, led by one or two "maskers" who act as leaders, are a primary feature of CARNIVAL celebrations on the Caribbean island of St. Vincent. The leaders are usually dressed as traditional characters—among them the Devil, Wild Indian, Bold Robber, and the hump-backed Bruise-ee-Back. Each group may perform a song written for the occasion by its leader, and usually acts out some kind of violent argument that will amuse or scare the onlookers and persuade them to donate some money. The songs are mocking or even slanderous in nature, and usually concern an individual or event associated with a particular locale. The band members typically dress in costumes based on that of their leader, but sometimes they merely blacken their faces, paint rude words and faces on white pants and T-shirts, and wear *washikongs* (tennis shoes) and unusual hats.

CONTACT:
St. Vincent and the Grenadines
  Tourist Information Office
801 Second Ave., 21st Floor
New York, NY 10017
800-729-1726 or 212-687-4981
fax: 212-949-5946

SOURCES:
FolkWrldHol-1992, p. 115

♦ 0326 ♦ Carnival in Spain
February–March; three days preceding Ash Wednesday

CARNIVAL in Spain is an occasion for feasting and partying. Bullfights, masquerade parties, weddings, and dances are held in almost every town and village. The Prado Museum in Madrid resembles a huge street fair, with masqueraders, battles of flowers, showers of confetti, and throngs of vendors. In Catalonia, the northeastern section of Spain, Carnival is observed with the *baile de cintas* or *baile del cordon,* the Spanish ribbon or Maypole dance. Another traditional Spanish dance associated with Carnival is *los seises* ("the six"), similar to the English Morris dance. When *los seises* were on the verge of being suppressed in 1685, they were preserved by papal edict for as long as the costumes lasted. With good care and numerous repairs, they have lasted to this day.

Throwing flowers and confetti at bystanders from blossom-decked cars is another Carnival tradition in Spain. Some towns even stage a battle of flowers. A particularly colorful celebration is held in Valencia, where the orange trees are in bloom at this time of year.

CONTACT:
Tourist Office of Spain
665 Fifth Ave.
New York, NY 10022
212-759-8822; fax: 212-980-1053

SOURCES:
BkFest-1937, p. 298
BkFestHolWrld-1970, p. 34
DictFolkMyth-1984, pp. 105, 178, 980
FestWestEur-1958, p. 191

♦ 0327 ♦ Carnival in Switzerland
February–March; usually the three days preceding Ash Wednesday

The Swiss actually observe CARNIVAL, or **Fastnacht**, at two different times: in the Roman Catholic cantons, it is observed according to the Gregorian calendar; the Protestant cantons follow the Julian calendar and celebrate it 13 days later.

In Basel, the lights of the city go out at 4:00 A.M., when fife and drum bands perform in the market square. Then members of the Carnival guilds, wearing wild masks and costumes, parade through the streets with lanterns on long poles or perched on their heads, to the accompaniment of pipers and drummers. Frightening masks are also worn during the Carnival celebration at Flums, where they often symbolize abstract concepts such as war, death, or disease. At Einsiedeln, "Carnival Runners" run through the streets continuously from Sunday to ASH WEDNESDAY morning, wearing grotesque false faces and enormous bells attached to their backs that clang loudly. The masks and bells found in many Swiss Carnival traditions are believed to have survived from ancient times, when people "drove out winter" with deafening noise and frightening faces.

In some parts of Switzerland it is the children who parade through the streets at Carnival, singing and carrying the national flag. The boys often masquerade in costumes that suggest their fathers' professions, while the young girls dress as fairies.

CONTACT:
Swiss National Tourist Office
608 Fifth Ave.
New York, NY 10020
212-757-5944; fax: 212-262-6116

SOURCES:
BkFest-1937, p. 316
BkHolWrld-1986, Mar 4
FestWestEur-1958, p. 230
FolkWrldHol-1992, p. 116

Carnival in the Netherlands
See **Shrove Tuesday in the Netherlands**

♦ 0328 ♦ Carnival in the U.S. Virgin Islands
Last two weeks in April

Unlike CARNIVAL in New Orleans, Brazil, and elsewhere in the world, where it is a pre-Lenten celebration, the Virgin Islands Carnival is held after EASTER, toward the end of April. It dates back to the days when Danish plantation owners gave their slaves time off to celebrate the end of the sugar cane harvest. Although the first Carnival in 1912 was a great success, it wasn't held again for four decades. Since 1952, it has been an annual event in the capital city of Charlotte Amalie on the island of St. Thomas, and nowadays the

Carnival observance in St. Thomas ranks second only to the TRINIDAD AND TOBAGO CARNIVAL.

Preliminary events begin a week or more beforehand, and the official Carnival period runs from Sunday until midnight the following Saturday. It begins with the opening of Calypso Tent, a week-long calypso song competition for the coveted title of "Calypso King." The celebrations include the crowning of a Carnival Queen, children's parades, a J'Ouvert morning tramp, steel bands, and dancing in the streets. The climax comes on Saturday with the grand carnival parade, featuring limbo dancers, masked figures, and mock stick-fights between Carib Indians and "Zulus." The celebration winds up with one of the most elaborate all-day parades in the Caribbean, featuring the Mocko Jumbi Dancers. These are colorful dancers on 17-foot stilts whose dances and customs derived from ancient cult traditions brought to the islands by African slaves.

CONTACT:
U.S. Virgin Islands Dept. of Tourism
P.O. Box 4538
Christiansted, St. Croix, VI 00822
809-773-0495

SOURCES:
AmerBkDays-1978, p. 387
AnnivHol-1983, p. 183
BkFestHolWrld-1970, p. 36
GdUSFest-1984, p. 221

Carnival in Trinidad and Tobago
See **Trinidad and Tobago Carnival**

♦ 0329 ♦ Carnival in Venice
Beginning between February 3 and March 9; ending on Shrove Tuesday night

The CARNIVAL celebration in Venice, Italy, is more sophisticated and steeped in tradition than the gaudy MARDI GRAS celebrations in New Orleans and Rio de Janeiro (*see* CARNIVAL IN BRAZIL). Costumes for the event are often drawn from the stock characters of Italian popular theater from the 16th through 18th centuries—including Harlequin, a masked clown in diamond-patterned tights; Punchinello, the hunchback; and Pierrot, the sad white-faced clown adapted by the French from the commedia dell'arte. There are also traditional costumed characters such as *La Bautta* (the domino), *Il Dottore* (the professor or doctor of law), and the Renaissance count or countess.

Italian university students, usually in more innovative costumes, pour into Venice by the trainload. As ASH WEDNESDAY draws near, the pace of the celebration picks up with a number of spectacular costume balls. The annual charity ball at Teatro La Fenice, for example, is known for attracting the rich and famous, including a number of movie stars and European aristocrats.

CONTACT:
Italian Government Travel Office
630 Fifth Ave.
New York, NY 10111
212-245-4822

SOURCES:
FolkWrldHol-1992, p. 112

♦ 0330 ♦ Carnival Lamayote
February–March; before Ash Wednesday

CARNIVAL, the biggest holiday of the year in Haiti, is distinguished from other Carnival celebrations by the preparation of wooden boxes, decorated with tissue paper and paint, known as *lamayotes*. Haitian boys put a "monster"—usually a mouse, lizard, bug, or other small animal—inside these boxes. During Carnival they dress up in masks and costumes and try to persuade people to pay them a penny for a peek inside their box.

SOURCES:
BkHolWrld-1986, Feb 9
RelHolCal-1993, p. 65

♦ 0331 ♦ **Carnival of Binche**
February–March; seven weeks preceding Shrove Tuesday

The most famous pre-Lenten carnival in Belgium and one of the most unusual in Europe. Festivities in Binche, a town of 10,000 population, begin seven weeks before LENT starts and culminate on MARDI GRAS with day-long rites of elaborately costumed, orange-throwing clowns called *Gilles*, which means roughly 'fools' or 'jesters'. Some 200,000 visitors come for the Mardi Gras weekend.

The Gilles—about 800 men and boys—wear suits stuffed with hay and decorated with appliqued rearing lions, crowns, and stars in the Belgian colors of red, yellow, and black. Heavy bells hang at their waists, and their headdresses—four feet tall and weighing up to seven pounds—are topped by ostrich plumes. In the early morning, the Gilles wear masks with green spectacles and orange eyebrows and moustaches, but these are doffed later in the day when the ostrich headdresses go on. The rites start at daybreak when the Gilles gather in the main square of Binche. To the beating of drums, they march and dance through the streets, stomping their wooden shoes and pelting spectators with oranges. Fireworks at midnight officially end the carnival, but dancing often goes on until dawn of ASH WEDNESDAY.

The most accepted legend explaining the carnival traces its origins to a fete in 1549. Spain had just conquered Peru, and Mary of Hungary, regent of the Netherlands, gave a sumptuous reception at her Binche palace for her nephew, Philip II of Spain. Supposedly, the costumes of the Gilles are patterned on the wardrobe of the Incas, and the thrown oranges represent the Incan gold. A document from 1795 is the earliest to describe the mask of the Gilles.

Some people have suggested that the English word 'binge' comes from Binche.

CONTACT:
Belgian Tourist Office
780 Third Ave.
New York, NY 10017
212-758-8130; fax: 212-355-7675

SOURCES:
AmerBkDays-1978, p. 43
BkFest-1937, p. 38
BkFestHolWrld-1970, p. 34
FestWestEur-1958, p. 6
FolkWrldHol-1992, p. 106
IntlThFolk-1979, p. 44

♦ 0332 ♦ **Carnival of Flowers**
Late September–early October

The **Toowoomba Carnival of Flowers** held in Queensland, Australia, is responsible for the city of Toowoomba being known as "Australia's Garden City." Since 1950 the eight-day event has included tours of home and city gardens, floral exhibits in all the city shops, a competition for home gardeners, and a special display of exotic and native orchids by the Toowoomba Orchid Society. The highlight of the festival is

the Floral Parade, which features thousands of flower-decorated floats and girls in floral costumes. The festival's performing and visual arts section, called the "Joy of Living," includes theater, music, children's plays, jazz, films, and arts and crafts exhibits.

CONTACT:
Australian Tourist Commission
100 Park Ave., 25th Floor
New York, NY 10017
212-687-6300; fax: 212-661-3340

SOURCES:
GdWrldFest-1985, p. 7
IntlThFolk-1979, p. 18

♦ 0333 ♦ **Carnival of Oruro**
Between end of January and early March; week preceding Ash Wednesday

The CARNIVAL celebrations in Oruro, Bolivia, continue for an entire week and include music, dancing, eating and drinking, and offerings to *Pachamama*, or Mother Earth. But the highlight is the parade that begins with a motorcade of vehicles carrying gold and silverware, jewels, fine embroideries, and old coins and banknotes. Next are the Diablos, wearing plaster-of-Paris horns, painted light bulbs for eyes, mirrors for teeth, and hair from the tails of oxen or horses. They are led by Lucifer and two Satans and surrounded by five dancing she-devils. Next are the Incas, who represent historical figures from the time of the Spanish conquest, and the Tobas, who perform war dances. The llama drivers, or *llameros*, are next, followed by the *Callahuallas*, or witch doctors, and a number of other companies, each with its own distinctive costumes and role in the procession. The parade ends with the entry of all the masked groups into the church for a mass in honor of the Virgen del Socavón.

CONTACT:
Bolivian Embassy
3014 Massachusetts Ave., N.W.
Washington, D.C. 20008
202-483-4410; fax: 202-328-3712

SOURCES:
FolkWrldHol-1992, p. 106

♦ 0334 ♦ **Carnival Thursday**
Between January 29 and March 4; Thursday before Shrove Tuesday

This was the day on which pre-Lenten celebrations, such as CARNIVAL, traditionally began, ending several days later on SHROVE TUESDAY night. These celebrations often take the form of wild revelry, which is perhaps why it was also referred to as **Mad Thursday**.

SOURCES:
DictDays-1988, pp. 19, 72

♦ 0335 ♦ **Carthage, International Festival of**
July 1–August 31

The International Festival of Carthage features classical music, jazz, folk music, theater, films, and ballet. It was founded in 1963 by the Tunisian Ministry of Cultural Affairs to bring foreign productions to Tunisia and to introduce the Tunisian public to the cultures of the West. Both Tunisian and foreign artists and ensembles—many of them from Romania, Spain, France, Germany, the Czech Republic, and the former U.S.S.R.—appear at the festival, which is held in a Roman amphitheater. Well-known American stars who have appeared there include James Brown, Joan Baez, Ray Charles, and Cab Calloway. The two-month Carthage Festival is held concurrently with the Festival of Hammamet, which also includes performances of music, dance, folklore, and theater in an open-air setting.

CONTACT:
Tunisian Embassy
1515 Massachusetts Ave., N.W.
Washington, D.C. 20005
202-862-1850; fax: 202-862-1858

SOURCES:
GdWrldFest-1985, p. 178
IntlThFolk-1979, pp. 358, 361

◆ 0336 ◆ Caruaru Roundup
September

Roundups started out as nothing more than the yearly task of bringing the cattle together in the winter for branding. But in Brazil they have developed into folkloric celebrations involving the participation of hundreds of cowboys who compete in "downing the steers." The Caruaru Roundup in the state of Pernambuco is one of the largest. In addition to steer-roping contests, viola players and *repentistas* (verse improvisers) entertain the people with their music and rhyming descriptions of the day's activities. Local food specialties are served during the three-day event.

CONTACT:
Brazilian Embassy
3006 Massachusetts Ave., N.W.
Washington, D.C. 20008
202-745-2700; fax: 202-745-2827

◆ 0337 ◆ Casals Festival
Early June

A two-week music festival held in San Juan, Puerto Rico, to celebrate the memory of Pablo Casals (1876–1973), the world-renowned Spanish-born cellist and conductor. An outspoken opponent of Fascism and the regime of Francisco Franco, he was forced to leave Spain and moved to France in 1936. Twenty years later he moved to Puerto Rico, the birthplace of his mother. There he initiated this music festival.

Through the years internationally known artists, among them Rudolf Serkin, Andrés Segovia, Arthur Rubenstein, Isaac Stern, and Yehudi Menuhin (*see also* MENUHIN FESTIVAL), have appeared at the festival. Programs offer a variety of composers, from BACH to Bartok.

CONTACT:
Puerto Rico Dept. of Culture
P.O. Box 9024184
San Juan, PR 00902-4184
809-724-0700

SOURCES:
GdUSFest-1984, p. 220
MusFestAmer-1990, p. 156

◆ 0338 ◆ Castor and Pollux, Festival of
July 8

In Greco-Roman mythology, Castor and Pollux were twin gods who helped shipwrecked sailors and received sacrifices for favorable winds. Worshipped as the Dioscuri (from the Greek *Dioskouroi*, or "sons of Zeus"), their cult was a popular one in 484 B.C., when according to legend, the twins fought on the side of the Romans in the Battle of Lake Regillus and brought word of their victory to Rome. A temple was built for them in the Forum, and it was here that the annual festival in their honor was celebrated on July 8.

Castor and Pollux were renowned for their athletic ability and are usually depicted as horsemen. They shared the same mother, Leda, but Castor was the son of Tyndareus and was therefore mortal, while Pollux was the son of Zeus and immortal. When they got into an argument with Idas and Lynceus, another set of twins, Castor was slain. Pollux was heartbroken because, as an immortal, he could not join his brother in death. Zeus finally allowed them to stay together, dividing their time between the heavens and the underworld. Eventually they were transformed into the constellation known as Gemini (The Twins), which before the invention of the compass was an important aid to navigation.

SOURCES:
AmerBkDays-1978, p. 608
NewCentClassHand-1962, p. 408
OxClassDict-1970, p. 213

◆ 0339 ◆ Castroville Artichoke Festival
Third weekend in September

One of the oldest agricultural festivals in California, held in Castroville, which calls itself the "Artichoke Center of the World." The two-day festival began in 1959 with a barbecue and parade; there is still a parade, and the lead float traditionally carries the Artichoke Queen and a huge green artichoke replica. Other events include a firefighters' muster, a coronation dinner dance, an artichoke recipe contest, and an artichoke-eating contest. Food booths offer artichoke cookies and french-fried artichokes. Attendance is about 50,000.

Castroville, founded in 1863 by Juan Bautista Castro, was an agricultural community from the start. In 1888, sugar beets became an important crop on the land west of Castro's settlement. When beet prices declined in 1921, Andrew J. Molera, the owner of the land, decided to grow artichokes, which were new to the U.S. market. He provided the plants for the first crop and leased the acreage to farmers. By 1925, more than 4,000 acres of artichokes were being cultivated, and by 1929 artichokes were the third largest cash crop of the Salinas Valley.

CONTACT:
California Division of Tourism
801 K Street, Ste. 1600
Sacramento, CA 95814
800-862-2543 or 916-322-2881
fax: 916-322-3402

Cats, Festival of the
See **Kattestoet**

◆ 0340 ◆ Cavalcata Sarda
Last Sunday of May

This famous procession—or *cavalcata*—was originally held in Sassari, Sardinia, Italy, more than 900 years ago to celebrate a victory over Saracen invaders. Today the procession consists of costumed groups from over 100 Sardinian villages. Wearing the traditional dress of their region, participants in the Cavalcata Sarda often ride through the streets in ox-drawn carts. After the procession is over, the celebration continues with singing and dancing.

CONTACT:
Italian Government Travel Office
630 Fifth Ave.
New York, NY 10111
212-245-4822

SOURCES:
BkHolWrld-1986, May 23
GdWrldFest-1985, p. 118

Celebration, Days of
See St. Genevieve, Jour de Fête à

♦ 0341 ♦ Central African Republic Independence Day
August 13; December 1

On December 1, 1958, the region now known as Central African Republic became a republic within the French Community. The republic achieved independence from France on August 13, 1960. Both days are celebrated as national holidays.

CONTACT:
Central African Republic Embassy
1618 22nd St., N.W.
Washington, D.C. 20008
202-483-7800; fax: 202-332-9893

SOURCES:
AnnivHol-1983, pp. 106, 154
Chases-1996, pp. 335, 467
NatlHolWrld-1968, p. 218

♦ 0342 ♦ Central City Summer Festival
Third weekend in August

A festival of opera, operetta, and cabaret in the one-time mining town of Central City, Colo. Performances of two operas and one American operetta are staged in the Old Opera House, built in 1878 and since restored to its original Victorian elegance. On opening night, "flower girls" present the audience with fresh flowers, which are thrown on stage to the cast at the end of the performance.

Inaugurated in 1932, the **Opera Festival** was not only the first summer opera festival in the country but also the first to espouse singing opera in English, a tradition that continues. *The Ballad of Baby Doe*, an opera that depicts the love story of the real-life silver king, Horace Tabor, who left his wife for the beautiful and much younger Baby Doe, was commissioned by Central City.

Cabaret opera is presented on Saturdays and Sundays in the historic Teller House next to the Opera House. This was once the grandest hotel in the west, built in 1872, host to President Ulysses S. Grant and other notables.

One of the presentations is *Face on the Barroom Floor*, which was commissioned on the 100th anniversary of the opera house. The saloon of the Teller House is the site of the "face" made famous in the poem by H. Antoine D'Arcy. The poem tells the story of the drunken vagabond who comes into the bar, asks for whiskey, and explains that he was once a painter who fell in love with beautiful Madeline—and that she was stolen away by his friend. "That's why I took to drink, boys," the vagabond says, and then offers to draw Madeline's portrait on the barroom floor:

> *Another drink, and with chalk in hand the vagabond began*
> *To sketch a face that well might buy the soul of any man.*
> *Then, as he placed another lock upon the shapely head,*
> *With a fearful shriek, he leaped and fell across the picture—*
> *dead.*

CONTACT:
Central City Chamber of
  Commerce
P.O. Box 249
Central City, CO 80427
800-542-2999 or 303-582-5251
fax: 303-642-0429

SOURCES:
GdUSFest-1984, p. 25
MusFestAmer-1990, p. 167

♦ 0343 ♦ Central Maine Egg Festival
Fourth Saturday in July

This one-day event in Pittsfield, Maine, was started in 1972 by two journalists who were tired of hearing about their state's potato crop and wanted to focus attention on central Maine's egg and chicken industry. Today its primary attraction is the world's largest skillet—a 300-pound teflon-coated frying pan, 10 feet in diameter, that is used to cook more than 4,000 eggs for those attending the festival breakfast. The giant skillet, designed and donated by the Alcoa Corporation, is stored in an airplane hangar.

A festival highlight is the World's Largest Egg Contest, in which only chicken eggs can be entered. Since entries come from all over the world, special tests must often be conducted to reveal imposters. The winning egg is plated with gold. Other events include parachute-jumping with chickens, a chicken-flying contest, and a chicken barbecue.

CONTACT:
Maine Office of Tourism
33 Stone St.
Augusta, ME 04333
800-533-9595 or 207-287-5711
fax: 207-287-5701

SOURCES:
Chases-1996, p. 312
GdUSFest-1984, p. 77

♦ 0344 ♦ Cerealia (Cerialia)
April 19

Ceres was the ancient Roman goddess of grain and of harvests, often identified with the Greek goddess Demeter. People held festivals in her honor in various locations, but the Cerealia originated in Rome, where she was worshipped at her temple on the Aventine Hill along with two other deities, Liber (a fertility god) and Libera, his female counterpart. The temple became a center of activity for the plebeians, or common people, who usually suffered when there was a grain shortage.

The festival known as Cerealia was observed at various locations only by Roman matrons, who, for several days preceding the festival, abstained from wine and other carnal pleasures. People who were in mourning were not allowed to appear at the celebration. For this reason, the Cerealia was not observed after the Battle of Cannae, when 50,000 Roman troops were killed by Hannibal.

There is a theory that APRIL FOOL'S DAY is a relic of the ancient Roman Cerealia, also held in April. According to legend, when Ceres's daughter Proserpine was carried off to the underworld by Pluto, Ceres heard the echo of her screams and tried to follow her voice. But it was a fool's errand, for it was impossible to locate the echo's source.

The THESMOPHORIA was a similar festival observed in ancient Greece.

SOURCES:
AmerBkDays-1978, p. 314

ClassDict-1984, p. 140
OxClassDict-1970, p. 223

Ceremony of the Car
See **Easter in Italy**

♦ 0345 ♦ **Cervantes Festival, International**
April–May

Spanish novelist, poet, and playwright Miguel de Cervantes (1547–1616) is best known for his creation of *Don Quixote* (1605), a novel that describes the adventures of an elderly knight and his pragmatic squire, Sancho Panza. Cervantes is honored in a three-week festival held in Guanajuato, Mexico, featuring orchestral music, opera, theater, dance, film, and folklore. At the festival's opening ceremony, statues of Don Quixote and Sancho Panza are lit up by fireworks.

Although most festival events are held in the Teatro Juarez and the Teatro Principal, amateur Mexican actors often give street performances of Cervantes's famous one-act plays in the Plaza de San Roque. Puppet and marionette theaters are a popular attraction, as are mimes, children's theater groups, and folkloric dance ensembles.

CONTACT:
Mexican Government Tourist
  Office
405 Park Ave., Ste. 1401
New York, NY 10022
800-446-3942 or 212-755-7261
fax: 212-753-2874

SOURCES:
GdWrldFest-1985, p. 134
IntlThFolk-1979, p. 269

♦ 0346 ♦ **Chad Independence Day**
August 11

On August 11, 1960, Chad became an independent country after struggling against the French since they first claimed Chad as a French territory in the 1890s.

Celebrations of this national holiday—including parades, dancing, and singing—are often moved to January 11 because of the heavy rains in August.

CONTACT:
Chad Embassy
2002 R St., N.W.
Washington, D.C. 20009
202-462-4009; fax: 202-265-1937

SOURCES:
AnnivHol-1983, p. 105
Chases-1996, p. 333
NatlHolWrld-1968, p. 15

♦ 0347 ♦ **Chad Republic Day**
November 28

This national holiday commemorates the establishment of the republic on this day in 1958, which afforded Chad some autonomy, though it was a French territory until it attained full independence (*see* CHAD INDEPENDENCE DAY).

CONTACT:
Chad Embassy
2002 R St., N.W.
Washington, D.C. 20009
202-462-4009; fax: 202-265-1937

SOURCES:
AnnivHol-1983, p. 152

♦ 0348 ♦ **Chakri Day**
April 6

A national holiday in Thailand to commemorate the en-

thronement of Rama I, who founded the Chakri Dynasty in 1782. He was born Chao Phraya Chakri in 1737, and had become Thailand's leading general when a palace coup took place in Thon Buri. Officials invited the general to assume the throne; he did, and one of his first acts was to move the capital across the river to Bangkok. The dynasty he established has headed the country to this day, although the end of absolute monarchy came in 1932. The king was given the title Rama after his death. Ceremonies on April 6 honor his deeds and the founding of Bangkok as the capital.

CONTACT:
Tourism Authority of Thailand
5 World Trade Center, Ste. 3443
New York, NY 10048
212-432-0433; fax: 212-912-0920

SOURCES:
AnnivHol-1983, p. 48
Chases-1996, p. 161

♦ 0349 ♦ **Chalanda Marz (First of March)**
March 1

In Engadine, located in the Inn River valley of eastern Switzerland, the arrival of spring is celebrated with the ringing of bells. Young people put on herdsmen's costumes with wide leather belts from which they hang as many cow bells as they can collect. Smaller bells hang from their necks or are strapped across their chests. These "herdsmen" are followed by other young boys with bells around their necks who represent the cows. They go from house to house, clanging their bells as loudly as possible to scare off winter and serenading people with traditional spring songs. Sometimes they are given money, but more often they are rewarded with cakes, apples, or eggs. An evening feast is made out of the food, and afterward there are games and dancing. The money goes to the village schoolmaster, who saves it for a class picnic or excursion.

SOURCES:
AnnivHol-1983, p. 32
Chases-1996, p. 118
FestWestEur-1958, p. 226

♦ 0350 ♦ **Chalk Sunday**
Between February 8 and March 14; first Sunday of Lent

In rural Ireland it was at one time customary to mark unmarried persons with chalk as they entered the church on the first Sunday of LENT. Because Roman Catholics were not permitted to hold weddings during Lent, those who were still unmarried at the beginning of the Lenten season had to remain so until EASTER—if not longer. Back when it was less common for young people to stay single well into their 20s and 30s, marking them with chalk was a way of chiding them for their unmarried status.

SOURCES:
FolkWrldHol-1992, p. 126

Chanukah
See **Hanukkah**

♦ 0351 ♦ **Chaomos**
At least seven days, including December 21, the winter solstice

The winter festival of the Kalasha (also known as Kalash

Kafir) people, who live in valleys in the northwestern corner of Pakistan, about 20 miles north of Chitral. The festival honors Balomain, a demigod who once lived among the Kalasha and did heroic deeds. Every year, his spirit comes to the valleys to count the people, collect their prayers, and take them back to Tsiam, the mythical land where the Kalasha originated, and to Dezao, the omnipotent creator god.

The celebration begins with the purification of women and girls: they take ritual baths, and then have water poured over their heads as they hold loaves of bread cooked by the men. A man waves burning juniper over the head of each woman, murmuring, "*Sooch*" ('Be pure'). On the following day, the men and boys are purified. They, too, take ritual baths and are then forbidden to sit on chairs or beds until evening when the blood of a sacrificed goat is sprinkled on their faces. The celebration continues with singing and chanting, a torchlight procession, dancing, bonfires, and festive eating of special bread and goat tripe.

Kalash means 'black,' and the people (thought to have descended from Alexander the Great) are called that because of the women's black robes. The Kalasha are among the people who live in Afghanistan in the area called Nuristan ('land of light'). This entire region was once known to the Muslims as Kafiristan ('land of infidels'), but in 1896 the Afghan Kafirs were forcibly converted to Islam. The Kalasha still maintain their old religion, a mixture of animism and ancestor and fire worship. Their pantheon of gods, besides Dezao, includes Sajigor, the "great" god, Mahandeu, the "wise" god, and Surisan, who protects cattle.

Chaomos is one of the four annual festivals of the Kalasha; others are the spring festival in mid-May, the harvest festival in mid-August, and the autumn festival that marks the walnut and grape harvest.

CONTACT:
Pakistani Embassy
2315 Massachusetts Ave., N.W.
Washington, D.C. 20008
202-939-6200; fax: 202-387-0484

♦ 0352 ♦ **Charleston Sternwheel Regatta**
August–September, 10 days ending on Labor Day

A celebration of its river-town history by Charleston, W.V. The highlights are the sternwheel and power-boat races on the Kanawha River. There are also 40 other events including concerts, parades, car shows, a distance run, and the "Anything That Floats Race." There is free nightly entertainment by internationally known artists. The regatta began in 1971 and now attracts about a million spectators.

CONTACT:
Charleston Convention and Visitors Bureau
200 Civic Center Dr.
Charleston, WV 25301
800-733-5469 or 304-344-5075

SOURCES:
Chases-1996, p. 347

♦ 0353 ♦ **Charlottetown Festival**
June–September

The Charlottetown Festival is devoted entirely to musicals by Canadians. Held from the third week in June through the third week in September on Prince Edward Island, the festival presents three full-scale musicals every year. One of these is always *Anne of Green Gables*, a story about rural life on the island at the turn of the century, written by island-born novelist Lucy Maud Montgomery. In fact, *Anne of Green Gables* was the first musical presented at the festival when it was founded in 1965.

The festival also offers plays for children, Sunday evening pop concerts, and a series of short plays and musical events. The full-scale musicals and most of the festival's events are held at the Confederation Centre of the Arts in Charlottetown, the capital of Prince Edward Island.

CONTACT:
Prince Edward Island Dept. of Tourism
Visitors Services Division
P.O. Box 940
Charlottetown, PEI
Canada C1A 7M5
800-463-4PEI or 902-368-4444

SOURCES:
GdWrldFest-1985, p. 55
IntlThFolk-1979, p. 75

♦ 0354 ♦ **Charro Days Fiesta**
Between January 31 and March 4; four days beginning the Thursday of the weekend before Ash Wednesday

The pre-Lenten festival known as Charro Days has been held each year since 1938 in the border towns of Brownsville, Texas, and Matamoros, Mexico, on opposite sides of the Rio Grande. A major border-crossing point, the two towns have a rich Spanish-Mexican heritage which is reflected in the fiesta. Male residents of the two cities wear the *charro* costume—a cross between the costume worn by the Spanish dons who once ruled Mexico and the Mexican horseman's outfit. Women wear the *china poblana*—a regional costume once worn by a little Chinese girl who was befriended by the Mexicans and has since become a kind of fairy princess to them.

Fiesta events take place in both Brownsville and Matamoros, and include a huge children's parade, costume dances in the street, rodeos, bullfights, and other events with Mexican and Latin themes. The festival has been known to attract as many as 400,000 visitors, many of whom wear costumes and participate in the events.

CONTACT:
Texas Department of Commerce
Tourism Division
1700 N. Congress Ave., Ste. 200
Austin, TX 78711
800-888-8839 or 512-462-9192
fax: 512-936-0089

SOURCES:
AmerBkDays-1978, p. 141
AnnivHol-1983, p. 174
Chases-1996, p. 114

♦ 0355 ♦ **Cheese Sunday**
Between February 8 and 28; Sunday before Lent

The week before Orthodox Christian Lent is known as Cheese or Dairy Week—especially in regions of Greece and Macedonia—because it is the last opportunity for people to eat dairy products. It is usually characterized by dancing, masquerading, and generally uninhibited behavior. At sunset on the final Sunday, people attend an evening church service during which the priest and congregation exchange mutual forgiveness for their sins. The last dish eaten on Cheese Sunday, or **Cheesefare Sunday**, is usually eggs.

Following custom, the last egg left over from the meal may be hung from a string in the middle of the ceiling. People sitting around the table hit it with their foreheads to get it swinging and then try to catch it in their mouths. Another variation of this game is to have someone hold a stick with an egg swinging from a string or thread on the end. People sit in a circle with their mouths open, trying to catch it. The popular saying, "With an egg I close my mouth, with an egg I shall open it again" refers to the hard-boiled Easter eggs that will mark the end of the Lenten fast.

In the Orthodox Church, the second Sunday before the beginning of Great Lent is called Meat Fare Sunday because it is traditionally the last day on which meat may be eaten until EASTER.

SOURCES:
BkFestHolWrld-1970, p. 35
FolkWrldHol-1992, p. 102

♦ 0356 ♦ **Cheese Week (Sirna Sedmitza)**
Between February 8 and 28; week preceding Lent

In Bulgaria, the week preceding the fast of Orthodox Christian LENT is known as Cheese Week because only cheese, milk, pure lard, and fish are eaten. It is a time for forgiving quarrels and reconciling with neighbors. Young people visit their elders, sons and daughters visit their parents, and godchildren visit their godparents—often presenting them with a lemon (if it's a man) or an orange (if it's a woman).

A favorite traditional sport during Cheese Week is to tie a piece of Turkish taffy to a string suspended from the ceiling. As the candy is set swinging, children try to bite it while holding their hands clasped behind their backs. Sometimes the same game is played with a piece of cheese or a hard-boiled egg. In some parts of Bulgaria, the evening is devoted to building bonfires. The boys jump through the fires while the girls dance around them—possibly a remnant from an ancient custom ensuring fertility.

SOURCES:
BkFest-1937, p. 67
FolkWrldHol-1992, p. 103

♦ 0357 ♦ **Chelsea Flower Show**
Late May

For more than eight decades, England's Royal Horticultural Society (RHS) has held a flower show in London on the grounds of the Royal Hospital in Chelsea. The highlight of this four-day event is the full-sized show gardens that are planted and landscaped in the space of only three weeks by some of Britain's top garden designers. There are also scientific displays of the latest advances in gardening; booths for flower arranging and garden design; and trade stands showing everything from antique garden statuary to the very latest in garden tools and machinery. Experts are also on hand to give people advice on courtyard gardens, window boxes, hanging baskets, and other less elaborate forms of gardening.

The Chelsea Flower Show is followed by other RHS-sponsored shows that span the entire calendar, among them the Hampton Court Palace Flower Show in July, the Westminster Shows held every month in the Royal Horticultural

Halls, the Harrogate Spring Flower Show in April, and the Malvern Autumn Show in late September.

CONTACT:
British Tourist Authority
551 Fifth Ave., Ste. 702
New York, NY 10176
800-462-2748 or 212-986-2200
fax: 212-986-1188

SOURCES:
GdWrldFest-1985, p. 95

♦ 0358 ♦ **Cheltenham International Festival of Music**
First week in July

Established in 1945 to give first performances of works by British composers, the nine-day Cheltenham International Festival of Music has since expanded its scope considerably. Its musical repertoire now ranges from medieval to contemporary compositions, with both British and foreign composers offering operas as well as symphonic, chamber, and choral music. The festival commissions a handful of new works each year and often highlights British works that have been neglected. Composers whose works have premiered there include Malcolm Arnold, Thea Musgrave, Alan Rawsthorne, and Sir Michael Tippett. Special master classes are also offered each year on such subjects as string quartets, piano trios, and brass instruments.

Recitals and chamber music concerts are held in the Pittville Pump Room, Cheltenham Spa's most important Regency structure. Operas are presented in the Everyman Theatre, and symphony concerts take place in the Town Hall. Other locations include local churches, abbeys, and castles. Cheltenham Spa is well known for its mineral springs, its Regency architecture, and its proximity to other attractions in the Cotswold Hills.

CONTACT:
British Tourist Authority
551 Fifth Ave., Ste. 702
New York, NY 10176
800-462-2748 or 212-986-2200
fax: 212-986-1188

SOURCES:
Chases-1996, p. 286
MusFestEurBrit-1980, p. 50
MusFestWrld-1963, p. 245

♦ 0359 ♦ **Cherokee National Holiday**
August–September, Labor Day weekend

The Cherokee National Holiday has been held since 1953 in Tahlequah, Oklahoma. To commemorate the signing of the 1839 Cherokee Constitution and the establishment of the Cherokee Nation, thousands of Cherokee Indians get together for a four-day celebration in early September. There is an all-Indian rodeo, a native dance competition, a powwow, and a parade with colorful floats and Cherokees in ceremonial dress. Native American arts and crafts—including baskets, flutes, dolls, and jewelry—are on display, and visitors can sample Native American foods. Games and sports offered at the festival include a golf tournament, a horseshoe tournament, a cornstalk shoot, a blowgun shoot, and a traditional Indian marble game.

CONTACT:
Cherokee Nation of Oklahoma
P. O. Box 948
Tahlequah, OK 74465
918-456-0671

SOURCES:
Chases-1996, p. 352
IndianAmer-1989, p. 65

♦ 0360 ♦ **Cherokee Strip Day**
September 16

September 16, 1893, was the date of the last and largest of the "land runs" that opened western Indian territories to white settlement. The Cherokee Strip encompassed more than six million acres of mostly grassy plains where white homesteaders wanted to graze their animals. Anyone who wanted to claim and settle the 160-acre parcels had to line up on the morning of September 16 and race to plant his flag at a chosen spot. The lure of free land attracted an estimated 100,000 prospective settlers, mostly young men who could withstand the harsh climate.

Cherokee Strip Day is a festival day in Oklahoma—particularly in the communities of Ponca City, Enid, and Perry—towns that sprang up as a result of the 1893 run. The celebrations last several days and include parades, picnics, dances, and rodeos.

See also OKLAHOMA DAY

CONTACT:
Oklahoma Tourism and Recreation Dept.
2401 N. Lincoln Blvd.
Will Rogers Bldg., Ste. 500
Oklahoma City, OK 73105
800-652-6552 or 405-521-2413
fax: 405-521-4883

SOURCES:
AmerBkDays-1978, p. 844
AnnivHol-1983, p. 119
Chases-1996, p. 378

♦ 0361 ♦ **Cherry Blossom Festival**
Between late March and mid-April

The **National Cherry Blossom Festival** in Washington, D.C., is held whenever the cherry trees planted around the Potomac River Tidal Basin bloom—usually between March 20 and April 15. The 3,000 trees were a gift to the city of Washington from the city of Tokyo, Japan, in 1912, and today they are the focal point of a six-day festival celebrating the friendship between the two countries. Most of the original trees died because the water in the Basin flooded their roots. Their replacements were more carefully planted and now thrive. Dates for the festival are set a year in advance to avoid coinciding with EASTER and HOLY WEEK observances.

The week-long festival has been in existence since 1948, although earlier celebrations included re-enacting the original planting and crowning a Cherry Blossom Festival Queen. Today the festivities include formal receptions for the 52 festival princesses (representing the 50 states, the District of Columbia, and the territory of Guam) and a Cherry Blossom parade through downtown Washington.

See also MACON CHERRY BLOSSOM FESTIVAL

CONTACT:
Washington D.C. Convention and Visitors Association
1212 New York Ave., N.W., Ste. 600
Washington, D.C. 20005
800-635-6338 or 202-789-7000
fax: 202-789-7037

SOURCES:
AmerBkDays-1978, p. 330
AnnivHol-1983, p. 174
GdUSFest-1984, pp. 43, 203

♦ 0362 ♦ **Cherry Blossom Festival in Hawaii**
February–April

The Cherry Blossom Festival in Hawaii is an annual Japanese cultural celebration held in Honolulu, Hawaii, usually from mid-February until the first week in April. The beauty of cherry blossoms is almost sacred in Japan, but the cherry blossoms of this festival are purely symbolic; cherry trees don't grow in Hawaii. The festival offers a variety of events: presentations of Kabuki drama, traditional Japanese dances, martial arts, and Japanese films as well as demonstrations of such arts as weaving and paper-doll making. The celebration was created in 1953 by the Honolulu Japanese community to "bridge the cultural gap by sharing with others the essence of the Japanese heritage."

See also HANAMI

CONTACT:
Hawaii Visitors Bureau
2270 Kalakaua Ave., Ste. 801
Honolulu, HI 96815
808-923-1811; fax: 808-922-8991

SOURCES:
GdUSFest-1984, p. 43

♦ 0363 ♦ **Cherry Blossom Festival in San Francisco**
April

More than 2,000 Japanese-Americans and performers from Japan participate in this seven-day festival in San Francisco's Japantown. Based on a similar event held in Japan, this celebration of Japanese culture and customs includes exhibitions of Japanese art and dancing, kimono and obi (the sash worn with a kimono) demonstrations, tea ceremonies, and bonsai exhibits. The climax of the festival is a three-hour parade from City Hall to the Japan Center at Post and Fillmore Streets. The parade includes singers and dancers, floats, Akita dogs, Taiko drummers, the Cherry Blossom Queen, and the traditional Taru Mikoshi, a portable shrine piled so high with casks of sake—an alcoholic beverage made from rice—that it takes 100 men to carry it. The festival lasts for seven days, covering two weekends in April. It was first held in 1968 to mark the official opening of San Francisco's Japan Center.

CONTACT:
San Francisco Convention and Visitors Bureau
201 Third St., Ste. 900
San Francisco, CA 94103
415-974-6900; fax: 415-227-2602

SOURCES:
GdUSFest-1984, p. 22

♦ 0364 ♦ **Cherry Festival, National**
Second week in July

An annual event since 1926, Michigan's National Cherry Festival takes place in Traverse City, "The Cherry Capital of the World," where 70 percent of the world's red cherries are grown. Traditionally held for a full week in July, the time of the cherry harvest, the festival features both traditional and offbeat events involving cherries: cherry pie-eating and cooking contests, a cherry wine competition, displays of cherries and cherry products, free tours of the cherry orchards, a cherry smorgasbord luncheon, and the weighing-in of the world's largest cherry.

The festival began in 1924 with a ceremony to bless the cherry blossoms and ensure a good crop. Now it draws upwards of half a million visitors and includes three major parades, national high school band competitions, canoe races, and a water ski tournament among the more than 100 different events. Former President Gerald R. Ford, a Michigan native, officiated at the festival in 1975.

CONTACT:
Michigan Travel Bureau
333 S. Capitol Ave., Ste. F
Lansing, MI 48933
800-543-2937 or 517-373-0670
fax: 517-373-0059

SOURCES:
AmerBkDays-1978, p. 635
Chases-1996, p. 287
GdUSFest-1984, p. 94

♦ 0365 ♦ **Chesapeake Appreciation Days**
Last weekend in October

This two-day celebration in Annapolis, Maryland, focuses on the skipjacks—the working sailboats that have dredged the Chesapeake Bay for oysters since the early 19th century. A featured event is the skipjack race which spectators can watch from the beach at Sandy Point State Park, near the twin-span Chesapeake Bay Bridge, because the boats' shallow draft and movable centerboard enable them to race close to shore. Other festival events include an oyster-cooking contest, regional arts and crafts, and an air show. But it is the skipjacks—unique to the Chesapeake—that most people come to see, as these classic sailing craft have been largely replaced by power vessels. Skipjack races are also held off Deal Island on Maryland's Eastern Shore on LABOR DAY.

CONTACT:
Annapolis and Anne Arundel
   Conference and Visitors Bureau
26 West St.
Annapolis, MD 21401
410-268-8687; fax: 410-263-9591

SOURCES:
GdUSFest-1984, p. 79

♦ 0366 ♦ **Chestertown Tea Party Festival**
Third weekend in May

When the British passed the Boston Port Act closing the Port of Boston until complete restitution had been made for the tea destroyed during the Boston Tea Party, it unleashed a wave of anger throughout the American colonies. Shortly after the news reached Chestertown, Maryland, the brigantine *Geddes* dropped anchor in Chestertown harbor on May 13, 1774. Word went out that the *Geddes* was carrying a small shipment of tea, and 10 days later a group of local residents boarded the ship and dumped the tea in the Chester River.

Every year during the Chestertown Tea Party Festival the rebellion is reenacted. The local merchants gather at the town park, where they voice their opposition to the British tax on tea. The crowd winds its way down High Street to the river, where the "colonists" board a ship—usually a reproduction of an historic vessel—and throw its cargo of tea (and some of its crew) into the river. Other festival events include a colonial parade with fife and drum corps, exhibits and demonstrations of 18th-century American crafts, walking tours of Chestertown, clog dancing and fiddling, horse-and-carriage rides, and tall ship cruises. Typical Eastern Shore foods are served, such as Maryland fried chicken, barbequed ribs, "chitlins," crab cakes, she-crab soup, and fried clams.

CONTACT:
Maryland Office of Tourism
   Development
217 E. Redwood St., 9th Floor
Baltimore, MD 21202
800-543-1036 or 410-333-6611
fax: 410-333-6643

SOURCES:
Chases-1996, p. 227

♦ 0367 ♦ **Cheung Chau Bun Festival**
*April–May; date decided by divination—usually
four days between the end of third lunar month
and 10th day of fourth lunar month*

One of the most spectacular events in Hong Kong, celebrated only on Cheung Chau (which means 'Long Island' in Chinese), one of the outlying islands of Hong Kong. It is believed that restless ghosts roam the island during the seven days of the festival. Some believe they are the spirits of islanders massacred by 19th-century pirates. Others say they are the spirits of animals killed and eaten during the year. Whatever they are, the festival is held to placate them.

Three bamboo-and-paper towers, about 45 feet high and covered with sweet pink and white buns, are dedicated to them. No meat or fish is eaten, and people burn paper replicas of houses, cars, and money.

At the island's Pak Tai Temple, rites are held to honor Pak Tai, "Supreme Emperor of the Dark Heaven." He is worshipped as a god of the sea who defeated a demon king and the king's allies, a tortoise and a serpent. The temple holds many small wooden statues of Pak Tai, all with a tortoise under one foot and a serpent under the other.

In the highlight of the festival the images of the temple gods are carried in a procession of lion and dragon dancers and children aged about five to eight, who are costumed as legendary Chinese figures. These children are carried shoulder-high so that they seem to float above the procession.

CONTACT:
Hong Kong Tourist Association
590 Fifth Ave.
New York, NY 10036
212-869-5008; fax: 212-730-2605

SOURCES:
BkHolWrld-1986, May 25
GdWrldFest-1985, p. 105
IntlThFolk-1979, p. 197

♦ 0368 ♦ **Cheyenne Frontier Days**
Last full week of July

What began in 1897 as an attempt to keep alive the sports and customs of the Old West has grown into a six-day festival that regularly attracts over 300,000 visitors. Cheyenne, Wyoming, was one of the wealthiest cattle-raising cities in the world in the 1880s, and now it celebrates its colorful history by staging one of the world's largest outdoor rodeos. The festival also includes parades of covered wagons, stagecoaches, and other old-time vehicles; ceremonial Indian dances; the crowning of a "Miss Frontier" queen; and pageants recreating events from Cheyenne's past. Cheyenne residents make pancakes for all with batter mixed in a concrete mixer.

CONTACT:
Cheyenne Area Convention and
   Visitors Bureau
P.O. Box 765
Cheyenne, WY 82003
800-426-5009 or 307-778-3133
fax: 778-3190

SOURCES:
AmerBkDays-1978, p. 682
AnnivHol-1983, pp. 121, 175
BkHolWrld-1986, Jul 28
DictDays-1988, p. 45
GdUSFest-1984, p. 215

♦ 0369 ♦ **Chhau Mask-Dance Festival**
April 11–13

Chhau is a form of dance rooted in the religious beliefs of Indian folk culture. Different regions of India practice their own unique style of Chhau, incorporating various folk, classical, and traditional elements. The masked dancers are often silent and use stylized movements to illustrate the conflict between good and evil to the accompaniment of drums, pipes, and cymbals. The dramatic situations that give shape to the dances are often drawn from episodes in the *Ramayana* and the *Mahabharata,* the two most famous epic poems of India.

The Seraikalla Chhau dance held every April in the Singhbhum District of Bihar reflects variations that are unique to the region. The influence of the martial arts can be seen in the dance, but the predominant mood is lyrical. Seraikalla is also the home of the Government Chhau Dance School, which sponsors the two-day festival.

In the Mayurbhanj Chhau Dance, also held April 11–13, the dancers do not wear masks but hold their facial expressions as still as possible, as if to imitate a mask. Unlike other forms of Indian dance, the Chhau dancers use all of the space available to them, and there are many long entrances and sweeping gestures.

CONTACT:
India Tourist Office
30 Rockefeller Ave.
15 N. Mezzanine
New York, NY 10112
212-586-4901; fax: 212-582-3274

SOURCES:
IntlThFolk-1979, p. 203

♦ 0370 ♦ Chicago Jazz Festival
August–September, four days preceding Labor Day

In the 1920s a four-block area along Chicago's State Street, known to the black community as "the Stroll," was the mecca of the jazz world. It was here that jazz took root in the city, establishing Chicago as a center for this uniquely American music. Shortly after the great composer-bandleader Duke Ellington died in 1974, a group of Chicago musicians got together to hold a concert in his honor; after that, the Ellington Concert became an annual event. A similar memorial concert was held for saxophonist John Coltrane in 1978, and the following year these two events merged with the jazz festival already being planned by the Jazz Institute of Chicago. Now it is the most extensive free jazz festival in the world, drawing an estimated audience of 400,000 and featuring such well-known artists as Sarah Vaughan, Ray Charles, Dave Brubeck, Herbie Hancock, George Benson, and Wynton Marsalis.

A number of major jazz events have occurred at the festival, such as the world premiere of Randy Weston's *African Sunrise* by Dizzy Gillespie and the Machito All-Star Orchestra in 1984, or the rendition of "Happy Birthday" sung in honor of Charlie Parker, the great jazz improviser, who was born on August 29, 1920, and died March 12, 1955.

CONTACT:
Chicago Convention and Tourism Bureau
2301 S. Lake Shore Dr.
McCormick Place On-the-Lake
Chicago, IL 60616
312-567-8500; fax: 312-567-8533

SOURCES:
MusFestAmer-1990, p. 191

♦ 0371 ♦ Chickaban
During Mayan month of Xul

The ancient Mayan feast known as Chickaban, observed at Mani in the Yucatán state of Mexico, was held in honor of the feathered serpent and storm god Kukulcán. Before the feast, the tribal chiefs spent five days fasting, dancing, and worshipping their idols. At the feast itself, offerings were made to Kukulcán, who came down from the sky to join them.

According to the myth, Kukulcán came to the Mayas from the west with 19 attendants, all bareheaded and wearing long robes and sandals. He built Chichén-Itzá, the ancient Mayan city, and ruled over the four points of the compass and the four elements of air, earth, fire, and water. Kukulcán is usually depicted with a serpent's body, a jaguar's teeth, and the long plumes of the quetzal bird. He is holding a human head in his jaws and is seated on the cross-shaped symbol of the compass.

SOURCES:
DictFolkMyth-1984, p. 594

♦ 0372 ♦ Chief Seattle Days
Third weekend in August

A three-day inter-tribal festival to honor Chief Seattle (1786–1866), for whom Seattle, Washington, is named. He was head of the Suquamish and Duwamish Indian tribes in the Puget Sound area of Washington. His name in the Lushootseed language was *See-ahth.*

The festival is held at the Port Madison Indian Reservation in Suquamish, 40 miles south of Seattle. Besides featuring traditional Indian dances and drumming and dancing contests, it has a distinctive northwestern flavor with salmon and clam bakes and canoe races. Other highlights are a horseshoe tournament, storytelling, and the election of a Chief Seattle Days Queen. The festival closes with the blessing of Chief Seattle's grave.

Chief Seattle and his father were both friendly to white settlers and helped them. He was the first to sign the Port Elliott Treaty in 1855, which set aside reservations for the Suquamish and other Washington tribes.

In a moving speech made in 1854 to a large group of Indians gathered to greet Isaac Stevens, the new United States Indian superintendent, Chief Seattle spoke of the passing away of the Indian tribes, fleeing at the approach of the White Man. "Let him be just and deal kindly with my people," he said, "for the dead are not powerless. There is no death, only a change of worlds."

It is uncertain that Chief Seattle actually uttered these words. The only known translation of Seattle's speech was made from the recollection of Dr. Harvy Smith 33 years later. The waters were made even muddier when, in 1971, Ted Perry, a screenwriter who now teaches at Middlebury College in Vermont, wrote a speech for the Chief that was included in a film on ecology. Mr. Perry knew the script was fiction, but others did not. Perry's apocryphal speech has been attributed to Chief Seattle ever since.

In 1992 a children's book based on an embellished version of Perry's script, *Brother Eagle, Sister Sky* by Susan Jeffers, made the *New York Times* Best Seller list and the great Chief Seattle slipped further into the mists of legend.

CONTACT:
Suquamish Tribal Council
P.O. Box 498
Suquamish, WA 98392
206-598-3311

SOURCES:
IndianAmer-1989, p. 215

Childermas
See **Holy Innocents' Day**

♦ 0373 ♦ **Children's Book Day, International**
April 2

This day, which is observed by countries all over the world, was first suggested by the International Board on Books for Young People (IBBY). They chose Hans Christian Andersen's birthday, April 2, because the Danish author's stories—which include "The Little Match Girl," "The Steadfast Tin Soldier," "The Ugly Duckling," and "Thumbelina"—have been favorites among children of all nationalities. The celebrations include contests in which children illustrate their favorite books, as well as the adoption of foreign pen pals. Every two years the IBBY sponsors the Hans Christian Andersen medals, which are awarded to a children's book author and a children's book illustrator for their contributions to children's literature.

See also ANDERSEN FESTIVAL, HANS CHRISTIAN

CONTACT:
International Reading Association
P.O. Box 8139
Newark, DE 19714
302-731-1600; fax: 302-731-1057

SOURCES:
AnnivHol-1983, p. 47
BkHolWrld-1986, Apr 2
Chases-1996, p. 155

♦ 0374 ♦ **Children's Day**
Various

Many countries have set aside a day on which children are allowed to participate in church services, in government, and in various cultural and recreational activities. In the United States, Children's Day was first celebrated in June 1856 at the Universalist Church in Chelsea, Massachusetts. By 1868 its date had been set on a nationwide basis as the second Sunday in June.

Children's Day is also celebrated in the Congo (Dec. 25), Iceland (on April 24), Indonesia (June 17), Japan (*see* KODOMO-NO-HI), Korea (May 5), Nigeria (May 27), and Turkey. The Turkish Children's Day on April 23 gives 400 students the educational opportunity to take seats in the national government in Ankara. The same thing takes place on a smaller scale in cities and towns all over the country.

See also URINI NAL

SOURCES:
AmerBkDays-1978, p. 555
AnnivHol-1983, pp. 56, 72, 79
BkFestHolWrld-1970, p. 80
Chases-1996, pp. 201, 239, 249
DaysCustFaith-1957, p. 157
RelHolCal-1993, p. 66

♦ 0375 ♦ **Children's Day in the former Yugoslavia**
December; three Sundays before Christmas

On the third Sunday before Christmas, known as **Dechiyi Dan** or Children's Day, parents in the former Yugoslavia tie up their children and refuse to release them until they have promised to be good.

And, although many people think that MOTHER'S DAY originated in the United States, Slavs traditionally set aside a Sunday in December to visit their mothers and bring them small gifts. Young children, on the other hand, honor their mothers by tying them up and refusing to release them until they have paid a "ransom" of sweets and goodies. Sometimes the mother hides small gifts under her mattress so that if the children tie her up before she gets out of bed in the morning, she'll have something to offer them. In view of the fact that mothers tie up their children on the previous Sunday, this custom isn't as outrageous as it seems.

The Sunday following Materitse is *Ochichi* or *Ocevi* (Father's Day). Boys and girls tie their fathers to his chair or bed. The ransom in this case is even higher, as the father must promise to buy them coats, shoes, dresses, or other expensive items before they let him go. These promises are usually fulfilled a short time later as CHRISTMAS gifts.

SOURCES:
AmerBkDays-1978, p. 439
BkFest-1937, p. 344
FolkWrldHol-1992, pp. 587, 594

Children's Party
See **Kinderzeche**

♦ 0376 ♦ **Chile Independence Day**
September 18

Chile issued its first declaration of independence on this day in 1810, but it didn't achieve complete independence from Spain until February 12, 1818, after seven years of bitter warfare. September 18, however, is the day on which the country celebrates its independence, and the president of the Republic of Chile addresses people gathered at the Plaza de la Constitución in Santiago, the capital. Folk dancers perform Chile's national dance, the *cueca*, to the accompaniment of guitars. The *huasos*, or cowboy-farmers, who come into town to join in the Independence Day celebrations may be seen wearing flat-topped brown or black sombreros, *mantas* (short capes), scarves, fringed leggings, and high-heeled black boots.

CONTACT:
Chilean Embassy
1732 Massachusetts Ave., N.W.
Washington, D.C. 20036
202-785-1746; fax: 202-887-5579

SOURCES:
AnnivHol-1983, p. 120
Chases-1996, p. 381
NatlHolWrld-1968, p. 174

♦ 0377 ♦ **Chilympiad (Republic of Texas Chili Cookoff)**
Third weekend in September

A chili cookoff in San Marcos, Tex., is called the "largest bowl o' red" competition in the world, which it probably is. From 500 to 600 chili chefs compete for the men's state championship, being judged on showmanship as much as recipes. (There is a smaller cookoff for women in Luckenbach in October.) Participation in the Chilympiad is a preliminary to entering the Terlingua Chili Cookoff in November. Besides the Chilympiad's gastronomic attractions, there are also concerts, arts and crafts, a parade, and carnival.

CONTACT:
Texas Department of Commerce
Tourism Division
1700 N. Congress Ave., Ste. 200
Austin, TX 78711
800-888-8839 or 512-462-9192
fax: 512-936-0089

◆ 0378 ◆ **China National Days**
October 1–2

This public holiday commemorates the founding of the People's Republic of China in the capital of Beijing in 1949. Observances take place on October 1–2.

CONTACT:
China National Tourist Office
350 Fifth Ave., Ste. 6413
New York, NY 10165
212-760-9700; fax: 212-760-8809

SOURCES:
AnnivHol-1983, p. 126
Chases-1996, p. 397
NatlHolWrld-1968, p. 182

◆ 0379 ◆ **Chincoteague Pony Roundup and Penning**
Wednesday before the last Thursday in July

The annual saltwater roundup of the famous wild ponies of Assateague Island off the Delmarva Peninsula. The volunteer firemen of Chincoteague Island, the largest inhabited island on the Eastern Shore of Virginia, become cowboys for a day. They ride to Assateague, round up as many as 250 or 300 foals, mares, and sires, and then guide them into the water to swim across the channel to Chincoteague. There the ponies are penned in corrals, and the next day some foals are sold at auction, and the rest of the herd swims back to Assateague.

Legend says the ponies, which are considered stunted horses rather than true ponies, are the descendants of mustangs that survived a shipwreck of a 16th-century Spanish galleon. Another story holds that the ponies were left behind by pirates who used the island as a hideout and had to leave in a hurry. Still a third (and most probable) version is that English colonists, having brought the ponies to the New World, turned them loose on Assateague and Chincoteague when they began to damage mainland crops.

The annual penning probably started with the colonists, who rounded up foals and yearlings to invigorate their workhorse supply. It took its present form in 1925 when the Chincoteague Volunteer Fire Company decided to add a fund-raising carnival to the regular pony penning.

Now a week of festivities surrounds the roundup, with midway rides, country music, and oysters and clams to eat. Tens of thousands come to watch the excitement from land and small boats.

A book featuring the event, *Misty of Chincoteague* by Marguerite Henry, was published in 1947 and became a children's classic. A movie based on the book appeared in 1960.

CONTACT:
Virginia Dept. of Economic
Development
Division of Tourism
901 E. Byrd St.
Richmond, VA 23219
804-786-4484; fax: 804-786-1919

SOURCES:
AmerBkDays-1978, p. 703
AnnivHol-1983, p. 183
Chases-1996, p. 315
GdUSFest-1984, p. 199

Chinese New Year
See **Lunar New Year**

Ching Ming Festival
See **Qing Ming Festival**

◆ 0380 ◆ **Chinhae Cherry Blossom Festival**
Early April

A festival in Chinhae, Korea, the headquarters of the Korean Navy, to enjoy the thousands of blossoming cherry trees and also to honor Korea's illustrious Admiral Yi Sun-shin. Admiral Yi defeated the Japanese in several sea battles during the latter's invasions of the late 16th century. He is famous for developing "turtle boats," the first iron-clad naval vessels, with 26 cannons on each side; though outnumbered, they proved superior to the Japanese boats. While the cherries bloom, there are daily events—a memorial service, parades, sports contests, music and dance performances, and folk games.

CONTACT:
Korea National Tourism Corp.
205 N. Michigan Ave., Ste. 2212
Chicago, IL 60601
312-819-2560; fax: 312-819-2563

◆ 0381 ◆ **Chitlin' Strut**
November, Friday and Saturday after Thanksgiving

A feast of chitlins or chitterlings (hog intestines), held in the small town of Salley, S.C. The affair features hog-calling contests, country music, arts and crafts, a parade, lots of chitlins (about 8,000 pounds are devoured each year), and chicken for those not enamored of chitlins. (Former president George Bush has said he is a chitlin fan.) Chitlins are prepared by cleaning them well, boiling them until they are tender, and then, after coating them in egg and crumbs, frying them in deep fat until they're crackling crisp.

Salley was named for Col. Dempsey Hammond Salley, who donated the site in the 19th century.

The Chitlin' Strut began in 1966 to raise money for the town's Christmas decorations. The strut now draws as many as 25,000 people, and Salley, with a population of 700, has used the revenues from it to pay for such necessities as trash cans, signs, and even a fire truck.

CONTACT:
South Carolina Division of
Tourism
1205 Pendleton St.
Columbia, SC 29201
803-734-0122; fax: 803-734-0133

SOURCES:
GdUSFest-1984, p. 171

♦ 0382 ♦ **Choctaw Indian Fair**
Begins first Wednesday after Fourth of July

Formerly known as the Green Corn Ceremony, this is a four-day annual gathering of the Mississippi band of Choctaw Indians. Held since 1949 in Philadelphia, Mississippi, it features—besides dances, crafts exhibits, and pageantry—the Choctaw Stickball World Series. Choctaw stickball, the forerunner of lacrosse, is played with long-handled sticks with pouches at the ends for carrying and pitching a leather ball. It is called the "granddaddy of games," and is thought to be the oldest field sport in America. More than 20,000 visitors usually attend the fair.

CONTACT:
Mississippi Band of Choctaw
  Indians
Route 7, Box 21
P.O. Box 6010
Philadelphia, MS 39350
601-656-5251

SOURCES:
GdUSFest-1984, p. 102
IndianAmer-1989, p. 242

♦ 0383 ♦ **Chongmyo Taeje (Royal Shrine Rite)**
First Sunday in May

A Confucian memorial ceremony held at Chongmyo Shrine in Seoul, Korea, to honor the kings and queens of the Yi Dynasty (1392–1910). The shrine, in a secluded garden in the center of Seoul, houses the ancestral tablets of the monarchs. Each year elaborate rites are performed to pay homage to them, and a number of royal descendants, robed in the traditional garments of their ancestors, take part. The rites are accompanied by court music and dance. The ceremony is a grand expression of the widespread Confucian practice of honoring ancestors, either at home or at their graves.

CONTACT:
Korea National Tourism Corp.
205 N. Michigan Ave., Ste. 2212
Chicago, IL 60601
312-819-2560; fax: 312-819-2563

♦ 0384 ♦ **Christkindlesmarkt**
Early December through Christmas Eve

The biggest and best known of the CHRISTMAS markets of Germany. The market in Nuremberg, Germany, has been held since 1697 in the city's *Hauptmarkt* ('main market'), the site of the famed 60-foot-high *Schöner Brunnen* ('beautiful fountain') and the 600-year-old redstone Church of Our Lady. More than 100 booths are set up to offer only goods directly related to Christmas—dolls, wooden soldiers, tinsel angels, picture books, and painted boxes. Food booths sell Nuremberg's specialties—*Lebkuchen*, or gingerbread, and *Zwetschgenmannlein*, which are little people-shaped confections made of prunes, figs, and raisins, with heads of painted walnuts. A post office branch is set up to cancel letters with a special stamp, and rides are offered in an old horse-drawn mail coach.

The three-week festival is inaugurated with choral singing, the pealing of church bells, and illumination of a crèche. A week or two before Christmas, some 10,000 people parade with lanterns to the Imperial Castle overlooking the city to sing carols. Other major Christmas markets are held in a number of German cities. Munich has the oldest Christmas market; it has been held annually for about 600 years, and

features daily musical programs. In Rothenburg-on-the-Tauber, the market is a month-long "Winter's Tale" of 150 events that include stagecoach rides, plays, and concerts. In Berlin, a miniature village for children is featured.

CONTACT:
German National Tourist Office
122 E. 42nd St., 52nd Floor
New York, NY 10168
212-661-7200; fax: 212-661-7174

SOURCES:
AnnivHol-1983, p. 178
BkFestHolWrld-1970, p. 129
BkHolWrld-1986, Dec 4
FestWestEur-1958, p. 80

♦ 0385 ♦ **Christmas**
December 25

The most popular of the Christian festivals, also known as the **Feast of the Nativity of Our Lord**, Christmas (from "Christ's Mass") celebrates the birth of Jesus of Nazareth. The exact date of Jesus' birth is not known, and for more than three centuries it was a movable feast, often celebrated on EPIPHANY, January 6. The Western church chose to observe it at the end of December, perhaps as a way of countering the various pre-Christian festivals celebrated around that time of year. Some believe that Pope Julius I fixed the date of Christmas at December 25 in the fourth century. The earliest reference to it is in the Philocalian Calendar of Rome in 336. Although the majority of Eastern Orthodox churches have celebrated the Nativity on December 25 since the middle of the fifth century, those that still adhere to the old Julian calendar—called Old Calendarists—mark the occasion 13 days later, on January 7. The Armenian Churches continue to celebrate OLD CHRISTMAS DAY on January 6.

The Christmas season in the church begins on Christmas Eve and ends on Epiphany, unlike the commercial season that may begin any time after HALLOWEEN.

December 25th is a holy day of obligation for Roman Catholics, who must attend one of the three masses priests are permitted to say in honor of the occasion. These services are celebrated at midnight on CHRISTMAS EVE and at dawn and mid-day on Christmas.

As a holiday, Christmas represents a strange intermingling of both Christian and the pagan traditions it replaced. Many of the secular customs now associated with Christmas—such as decorating with mistletoe, holly, and ivy; indulging in excessive eating and drinking; stringing lights in trees; and exchanging gifts—can be traced back to early pagan festivals like the SATURNALIA and ancient WINTER SOLSTICE rites. Another example is burning the YULE log, which was part of a pre-Christian winter solstice rite celebrating the return of the sun in the middle of winter. Even the Christmas tree, a German custom introduced in Britain by Queen Victoria's husband, Albert, can trace its history back to ancient times, when trees were worshipped as spirits.

One of the most universal Christmas traditions is the crèche, a model of the birth scene of Christ, with Jesus in the manger, surrounded by the Holy Family and worshipping angels, shepherds, and animals. Many families have their own crèche, with the three Wise Men set apart and moved closer each day after Christmas until they arrive at the manger on Epiphany. In Austria, the crèche is not put away until CANDLEMAS Day.

In Belgium, the manger also appears in shop windows, constructed of the material sold by the shop: bread at the bakery; silks and laces at dressmakers; a variety of materials from the hardware store; butter and cheese from dairies; and cravats and neckties at the haberdashers.

In Chile the crèche is called a *pesebre*. Some homes leave their doors open so people passing by can come in and say a brief prayer to the *Niño Lindo* (beautiful baby).

In Italy it is a *presepio*, and is placed on the lowest shelf of a *ceppo*, which is a pyramid of shelves, lit with candles, used to display secular Christmas decorations and ornaments.

In Poland, where the crèche is called a *yaselko*, it is believed to be the origin of the Christmas folk play called the King Herod play, based on Herod's order to kill all male babies in Bethlehem (*see* Holy Innocents' Day). Thirteenth-century Franciscan monks brought the crèche to Poland. Eventually the wax, clay, and wooden figures were transformed into *szopka*, puppets that performed Christmas mystery plays, which told of the mysteries of Christ's life. Later, the monks acted the parts played by the puppets and were called "living *szopka*." In time, the plays were blended with characters and events from Polish history. The performers are called "Herods" and go from house to house in their village where they are invited in to sing carols, act, and later to eat and drink with the family.

In Burkina Faso (until 1984 called Upper Volta), in western Africa, the population is mostly in Ouagadougou, the capital, and there the children make nativities (manger scenes) around the entrance to their compound. They are ready on Christmas Day so friends and neighbors can come by and, if they like them, leave a few coins in the dish provided. Some are made of paper and set on a pedestal, others of mud bricks with a thatch roof, while others are in the form of the local round house and have the bricks covered with a coat of concrete and a masonry dome instead of thatch. All of this is ornately decorated with strings of plastic packing 'peanuts,' bits of shiny metal, tinsel, plastic, and flashlight bulbs. Some are modeled after pictures of European churches, but the child who can build a multi-storied nativity is thought very clever. On the wall of the compound behind the nativity is painted a white panel on which are affixed pictures of the Holy Family, crosses, hearts, arrows, stars, and anything else that comes to the mind of the young creator.

In Japan, since the end of World War II, Christmas has become a very popular holiday, even for non-Christians. Christmas dinner is replaced with a commercial Christmas cake, called "decoration cake," (dekoreshon keki), covered with ridges and waves of frosting. Grandfather Santa Claus brings the gifts, but stockings are hung on the pipe for the bathtub stove, which is the nearest equivalent to a fireplace in Japanese homes. New Year's postcards are much more important than Christmas cards, and the most elaborate use of evergreen trees is also saved for New Year's. Christmas parties are a kind of blending with *bonenkai*, "closing of the year parties," which may only be attended by men and professional women: geishas, waitresses, entertainers. All women can attend Christmas parties, which is one of the reasons why the Japanese consider Christmas to be democratic.

Secular Christmas customs have continued to evolve. The Christmas card didn't become popular until the 19th century in England; Santa Claus's reindeer were an American invention at about the same time. Modern Christmas celebrations tend to focus on the worldly—with such "traditions" as the

office Christmas party, sending out greeting cards, and "Christmas specials" on television taking the place of church services and other religious observances for many. The movement to "put Christ back into Christmas," has not lessened the enjoyment of this holiday as much for its social and commercial events as for its spiritual significance. The way Christmas is celebrated today is actually no worse—and in many ways much less excessive—than the hedonistic medieval celebration, where the feasting and revelry often extended all the way from Christmas to Candlemas (February 2).

See also Ganna and Posadas

SOURCES:
AmerBkDays-1978, pp. 43, 1128, 1141
BkDays-1864, vol. II, pp. 733, 744
BkFest-1937, pp. 10, 11, 20, 35, 49, 62, 73, 93, 99, 108, 117, 130, 140, 150, 155, 175, 192, 216, 223, 234, 247, 254, 256, 272, 281, 287, 296, 305, 314, 323, 333, 345
DaysCustFaith-1957, pp. 319, 351
DictFolkMyth-1984, pp. 182, 193, 229, 501, 554, 571, 591, 628, 689, 761, 779, 854, 1063, 1065, 1133
FestSaintDays-1915, p. 231
FestWestEur-1958, pp. 20, 30, 53, 83, 104, 148, 158, 186, 208, 222, 241
FolkAmerHol-1991, p. 437
FolkWrldHol-1992, p. 602
RelHolCal-1993, p. 66
SaintFestCh-1904, p. 37

♦ 0386 ♦ **Christmas Eve**
December 24

Christmas Eve or the **Vigil of Christmas** represents the culmination of the Advent season. Like Christmas itself, Christmas Eve celebrations combine both religious and secular events. Perhaps the most widely anticipated by children is the arrival of Santa Claus—known as *Sinterklass* by the Dutch settlers of New York, who were the first to introduce the idea of St. Nicholas's annual appearance on this day; the original Santa Claus was the tall, saintly-looking bishop Nicholas of Metz. It wasn't until the 19th century that he became the jolly, overweight, pipe-smoking figure in a red fur-trimmed suit that children in the United States recognize today. The modern Santa Claus was largely the invention of two men: Clement Moore, who in 1822 wrote his now-famous poem, "A Visit from St. Nicholas," and Thomas Nast, a cartoonist who did numerous illustrations of Santa Claus based on Moore's description. In any case, it is on Christmas Eve that Santa Claus climbs down the chimney and fills the children's stockings that have been hung by the fireplace mantel. Before going to bed children around the world leave milk and food out for the one who brings the presents, be it Santa Claus, the baby Jesus, the Christmas elf of Denmark, the Christmas goat of Finland (called *Joulupukki*), or the Swedish *tomte*, or little man, who resembles Puck or a leprechaun.

The midnight church service celebrating the birth of Jesus

Christ is the main Christmas Eve tradition for many Christians of all denominations and even of non-believers, especially if there is a good organist, soloist, or choir. In most European countries, a large but meatless meal is eaten before church, for it is a fast day. Some families, especially those with grown children, exchange gifts on Christmas Eve rather than on Christmas day. Caroling—going from house to house singing Christmas carols—began in Europe in the Middle Ages. The English brought the custom to America, where it is still very popular.

In Venezuela after midnight on Christmas Eve, crowds of teenagers roller skate on the Avenida de los Caiboas. After an hour or so, they attend a special early mass called *Misa de Aguinaldos*, or 'Mass of the Carols', where they're greeted at the door with folk songs. Then they skate home for Christmas breakfast.

In Newfoundland and Nova Scotia, Canada, mummers, or *belsnickers*, go from house to house. Once inside they jog, tell licentious stories, play instruments and sing, and generally act up until the householder identifies the person under the mask. Then the mummer takes off his or her costume and acts like a normal visitor.

In the 19th century in what is now New Mexico bundles of branches were set ablaze along the roads and pathways. Called *farolitos* and *luminarias* these small fires were to guide the Travelers to the people's homes on Christmas eve. The residents were ready to give hospitality to anyone on that night, especially Joseph and Mary with the Christ Child. They would wait in faith for the Traveler's three knocks on their door.

But modern fire codes overtook the ancient faith and firefighters began to extinguish the small piles of burning pine branches for fear a spark would start an inferno. Small brown paper bags partially filled with sand and holding a candle eventually replaced the open fires. Inevitably merchants began to sell wires of electric lights to replace the candles, and plastic, multi-colored sleeves to imitate lunch bags, and the modern luminarias began to appear at holidays like HALLOWEEN and the FOURTH OF JULY. But it is certain that the Travelers are not looking for a place at the inn on those nights.

Last-minute shopping is another Christmas Eve tradition, and stores often stay open late to accommodate those who wait until the last minute to purchase their Christmas gifts.

In Buddhist Japan, Christmas Eve is for lovers, a concept introduced by a Japanese pop star and expanded by trendy magazines. It is a Western rite celebrated with a Japanese twist. The day should be spent doing something extra special (expensive), and should end in a fine Tokyo hotel room, most of which have been booked since the previous January; even the cheapest rooms go for exorbitant prices. Being alone on this night is comparable to being dateless on prom night in the United States.

Uncle Chimney is their version of Santa Claus. Youngsters may be treated to a $29 (or more) barrel of Kentucky Fried Chicken (10 pieces of chicken, five containers of ice cream, and salad) if their parents don't mind lining up for two hours. The reason for the chicken is that many Japanese think Colonel Sanders resembles Santa Claus. Another culinary tradition is strawberry shortcake with a plastic fir tree on top.

This was introduced 70 years ago by a Japanese confectioner as a variant of plum pudding. While the origins of this form of Christmas are unclear, many people say it dates from the 1930s, well before the United States occupation in 1945 after World War II.

See also BEFANA FESTIVAL; DÍA DE LOS TRES REYES; POSADAS; ST. NICHOLAS'S DAY

SOURCES:
AmerBkDays-1978, p. 1135
BkDays-1864, vol. II, p. 733
BkFest-1937, pp. 9, 20, 22, 35, 48, 62, 73, 92, 98, 107, 116, 129, 139, 154, 175, 191, 215, 222, 234, 252, 272, 280, 287, 296, 304, 313, 322, 333, 344
BkHolWrld-1986, Dec 24
DaysCustFaith-1957, p. 350
DictFolkMyth-1984, pp. 549, 591, 1063
FestSaintDays-1915, pp. 8, 228
FestWestEur-1958, pp. 27, 28, 50, 82, 83, 102, 120, 156, 206, 219, 239
RelHolCal-1993, p. 67

♦ 0387 ♦ **Christmas Eve, Moravian**
December 24

Members of the Moravian Church—named after Moravia, a region in the former Czechoslovakia (now part of the Czech Republic)—fled to America to escape persecution in the mid-18th century. They established a number of communities in Pennsylvania, one of which is called Bethlehem and known as "America's Christmas City." As Christmas approaches, the Moravians carry on the Old World tradition of building a Christmas "putz" (from the German word *putzen*, meaning "to decorate") or Nativity scene, which can range from a simple mantle decoration to an elaborate miniature landscape. On the afternoon of CHRISTMAS EVE, they hold a children's "love feast" consisting of music, meditation, and a simple meal—usually sweet buns and mugs of sweetened coffee—served in the church. Then after dinner, they assemble again in the church for the Christmas Eve Vigil, a service devoted almost entirely to music. The church lights are dimmed and handmade beeswax candles are distributed to the entire congregation while the children's choir sings a favorite Moravian hymn. A similar observance is held in Old Salem, North Carolina, now an historical restoration at which the Moravian way of life is preserved.

SOURCES:
AmerBkDays-1978, p. 1137

♦ 0388 ♦ **Christmas Eve in Armenia**
December 24

On Christmas Eve in Armenia it is traditional to eat fried fish, lettuce, and boiled spinach. The spinach is eaten in honor of the Virgin Mary, who is said to have eaten spinach on the night before she gave birth to the Christ child. After a morning church service on CHRISTMAS day, the men exchange brief social calls and are served coffee and sweets. On the third day after Christmas, it's the women's turn to make and receive calls.

SOURCES:
BkFest-1937, p. 22
DaysCustFaith-1957, p. 351

♦ 0389 ♦ **Christmas Eve in Bethlehem, Jordan**
December 24

Located only a few miles from Jerusalem in an area that was once part of the biblical land of Palestine, Bethlehem is known as the birthplace of Jesus and has long been regarded as a holy place by Christians. A church was eventually built on the site, and the crypt beneath it, known as the Grotto of the Nativity, is reputed to be the site of the original manger. Because there have been so many arguments over the years about which Christian church should control the sanctuary, it is jointly owned by the Armenian, Orthodox, and Roman Catholic churches. A Roman Catholic Mass is held there at midnight on CHRISTMAS EVE, and because pilgrims from all over the world attend, most of them end up watching the service on a large closed-circuit television screen in nearby Manger Square. The highlight of the service occurs when a carved wooden figure of the Christ Child is laid in a manger in the Grotto of the Nativity.

Protestants hold an outdoor service in Shepherds' Field where, according to tradition, the shepherds kept watch over the flocks on the first Christmas Eve.

CONTACT:
Jordan Information Bureau
2319 Wyoming Ave., N.W.
Washington, D.C. 20008
202-265-1606; fax: 202-667-0777

SOURCES:
AmerBkDays-1978, p. 1135

♦ 0390 ♦ **Christmas Eve in Denmark (Juleaften)**
December 24

The celebration of CHRISTMAS in Denmark actually begins on Little Christmas Eve (December 23) and continues well into the New Year. It is customary to make enough apple fritters on Little Christmas Eve to last three days. In rural areas, farmers tie a sheaf of grain to a pole in the garden so that the birds can feed from it. Even city dwellers tie bunches of grain to their balconies.

The traditional Christmas Eve dinner starts with *risengrød* (rice porridge). Like Christmas puddings elsewhere, there is an almond hidden inside the porridge. Whoever finds it receives a prize. The *risengrød* is followed by roast goose stuffed with prunes and apples and decorated with small Danish flags. After dinner, family members often dance around the Christmas tree, sing carols, and exchange gifts.

The *Julenisse*, or Christmas gnome, is a small bearded man dressed in gray with a pointed red cap who, according to Danish legend, lives in attics or barns and is responsible for bringing a family good or bad luck. On Christmas Eve the *Julenisse* is given a generous portion of *risengrød* with an extra helping of butter.

SOURCES:
AmerBkDays-1978, p. 1135
BkFest-1937, p. 98
FestWestEur-1958, p. 27

♦ 0391 ♦ **Christmas Eve in Finland (Jouluaatto)**
December 24

Before sitting down to the traditional CHRISTMAS EVE dinner, many Finns go to church and place flowers and lighted candles on the graves of deceased family members. Then the family gathers around the table and listens to the head of the household read a Christmas prayer. The meal itself includes *lipeäkala* (the Christmas fish) and ham, various breads, a kind of plum cake known as *torttuja*, and the traditional rice pudding in which an almond has been hidden. According to superstition, the boy or girl who finds it will be married before the next Christmas. The tree is trimmed with home-made paper or wooden toys, gingerbread cookies, gilded walnuts, and other treats.

SOURCES:
BkFest-1937, p. 116

♦ 0392 ♦ **Christmas Eve in France (Veille de Noël)**
December 24

CHRISTMAS EVE church services in Paris can be quite elaborate, while those in rural areas of France are usually very simple. No matter where it takes place, the Christmas Mass involves burning candles, Christmas carols, bells, and a crèche or miniature Nativity scene. Most homes also have a crèche. In Provence, the crèche includes not only the Holy Family, but small clay figures called *santons* representing traditional village characters—the butcher, baker, basket maker, flute players, etc.—who come to adore the infant Jesus. In Marseilles, there is a santons fair shortly before Christmas that is attended by people from all over Provence who want to purchase the traditional santons, made from molds that have been handed down from generation to generation.

After the midnight service is over, families return to their homes for the *réveillon*, or traditional Christmas Eve meal, which includes *pâté de foie gras*, oysters, blood sausage, pancakes, and plenty of French wine. It is customary for the newspapers to report the number of kilometers of blood sausage that have been consumed at réveillon. Many families serve goose because, according to a Provençal legend, the goose welcomed the Wise Men with its cackling as they approached the Christ Child's manger.

The children set out their shoes near the fireplace on Christmas Eve because they believe that Father Christmas, *le Père Noël*, will arrive before dawn and fill them with toys, nuts, and sweets.

Another Christmas Eve custom is the Shepherds' Mass, or Festival of the Shepherds (*Fête des Bergers*). Shepherds and shepherdesses, dressed in regional costumes, place a lamb in a two-wheeled wagon that is drawn by a ram and elaborately decorated with flowers, lighted candles, and bells. The lamb is drawn in a procession around the church, after which a young shepherd lifts it up and presents it to the priest, a symbolic offering of a new-born lamb to the Christ Child on the anniversary of his birth.

SOURCES:
BkFest-1937, p. 129
BkHolWrld-1986, Dec 24
FestWestEur-1958, p. 50

♦ 0393 ♦ **Christmas Eve in Italy (La Vigilia)**
December 24

The *presepio*, or Nativity manger, with its miniature figures of the Holy Family, angels, shepherds, and Three Kings plays a major role in the Italian observance of CHRISTMAS and is thought to have originated with ST. FRANCIS OF ASSISI more than 700 years ago. The presepio is set up on the first day of the Novena (the nine days preceding Christmas); on each subsequent morning, the family gathers before the presepio to light candles and offer prayers. Although manger figures are on sale in every market and village fair, in many families the manger is an heirloom that has been handed down for generations. The setting for the manger is usually built at home from cardboard, moss, and bits of twig, and it can be quite elaborate.

Christmas Eve is a family affair. After lighting candles before the presepio, a meatless meal known as the *cenone*, or festa supper, is served. It usually consists of some type of fish (eel is popular among the well-to-do), fowl, artichokes cooked with eggs, fancy breads, and Italian sweets such as *cannoli* (cheese-filled pastry), nougat, and other delicacies.

The YULE log plays a more important role than the Christmas tree. The children may tap it with sticks, requesting certain gifts. Few presents are given on Christmas Eve, since EPIPHANY is the time for gift-giving. The evening concludes with a church service at midnight.

In parts of Calabria and the Abruzzi, itinerant bagpipers, or *zampognari*, come down from the mountains and go from house to house playing pastoral hymns before the home-made mangers. They are given gifts of food or money.

See also BEFANA FESTIVAL

SOURCES:
BkFest-1937, p. 191
FestSaintDays-1915, p. 229
FestWestEur-1958, p. 102

♦ 0394 ♦ **Christmas Eve in Switzerland (Heiliger Abend)**
December 24

There are a number of superstitions and folk beliefs surrounding CHRISTMAS EVE in Switzerland. One is the belief that animals are blessed with the ability to speak at midnight on Christmas Eve because they were present at Jesus' birth. Farmers give their horses, cows, goats, and other animals extra food on this night, but it's considered bad luck to overhear what the animals say. Old people say that they can predict the weather for the next 12 months by peeling off 12 layers of onion skin and filling them with salt. Young lovers who want to find out whom they will marry are told to drink from nine different fountains while the midnight church bells are ringing on Christmas Eve. If they rush to the church, their future mate will be standing on the steps.

Christkindli, or the Christ Child, is the one who brings Swiss children their gifts. He makes his rounds in a sleigh drawn by six reindeer. In the area surrounding Hallwil in the canton of Lucerne, *Christkindli* is impersonated by a young girl, dressed in white with a sparkling crown and veil on her head and accompanied by white-robed children carrying lanterns and baskets of gifts. As soon as she enters a house, the Christmas

tree candles are lighted. In many homes the tree is kept hidden until after Christmas Eve supper, when the doors are finally opened and the tree is displayed in all its glory.

In Zurich, cakes known as *Tirggel* are served. Made out of flour and honey, the cakes are believed to have originated as a pagan offering. The Tirggel dough is pressed into elaborate molds representing cartoons, fairy tales, and other popular subjects, and because the finished cakes are hard and shiny, it is not uncommon for them to be kept for months or even years, and to be used as decorations around the house.

SOURCES:
BkFest-1937, p. 322
FestWestEur-1958, p. 239

♦ 0395 ♦ **Christmas Eve in the Baltics**
December 24

Many people in Estonia attend church on CHRISTMAS EVE. The holiday dinner, which follows the church service, typically includes roasted pig's head or blood sausages, turnips, and potatoes. For dessert there is cranberry soup, and of course plenty of Estonian vodka, which is made from the potatoes for which the country is famous. Many of the Christmas tree ornaments are edible, and real candles—often made by dipping a lamb's wool thread into hot sheep fat—are used to light the tree.

In Latvia, the tree is the only Christmas decoration, and it is laden with gilded walnuts, artificial snow, tinsel, small red apples, and colored candies. After the traditional Christmas Eve dinner, which consists of roast pork, goose and boar's head, and little meat-filled pastries known as *piradzini*, the candles on the tree are lighted and the gifts piled beneath it are distributed and opened.

In Lithuania, paper-thin wafers, or *plotkeles*, are broken and eaten by each member of the household on Christmas Eve as a token of peace. A bit of hay placed beneath the tablecloth recalls the manger in which the Christ child was born. The *kūcios*, or Christmas Eve supper, consists of fish soup followed by cabbage, fried and boiled fish, sauerkraut, and a huge pike served with a rich brown gravy. Dessert is *kisielius*, a kind of blanc mange made from cream of oats and served with sugar and cream.

SOURCES:
BkFest-1937, pp. 107, 215, 222

♦ 0396 ♦ **Christmas in Greece**
December 25

According to Greek folklore, supernatural beings with unusual powers are present upon earth during the 12 days between CHRISTMAS EVE and EPIPHANY. The name for these spirits is *Kallikantzaroi*, and they wander about during the Christmas season causing mischief. They are ugly and unkempt, and their favorite way of getting into the house is through the chimney, much like the traditional Santa Claus. Christmas masqueraders often dress in animal skins to represent these demons of the WINTER SOLSTICE, and their jangling bells are supposed to drive the spirits away. Children born on CHRISTMAS must be baptized immediately to rid them of the evil influence of the Kallikantzaroi.

SOURCES:
BkFest-1937, p. 154
FestSaintDays-1915, p. 230

♦ 0397 ♦ **Christmas in Norway**
December 25–26

CHRISTMAS, known as **Juledag** in Norway, is generally a quiet day. After attending morning church services, most Norwegians return home to be with their family and friends. December 26, however, is another matter. Referred to as Second Christmas Day, or *Anden Juledag*, it is spent eating, drinking, and going to parties, festivities that continue until January 13. Holiday breakfasts are popular, often accompanied by *aquavit* and other strong drinks. Traditional foods served at these Christmas get-togethers include *lutefisk* (dried cod), *lefse* (a thin potato roll served with butter or cinnamon and sugar), and *fladbröd* (a flat, hard Norwegian bread).

During the German occupation of Norway, when King Haakon was living in England, a Norwegian boat stationed there would be sent to Norway to bring back a Norway spruce each year as a gift for the king at Christmas. The custom of bringing a Norwegian tree to England was continued after the war, and every Christmas a huge Norwegian spruce stands in London's Trafalgar Square.

SOURCES:
BkFest-1937, p. 254
BkFestHolWrld-1970, p. 140
FestWestEur-1958, p. 158
FolkWrldHol-1992, p. 624

♦ 0398 ♦ **Christmas in Puerto Rico**
December 25

CHRISTMAS celebrations in Puerto Rico combine island traditions with more contemporary customs, such as Santa Claus and imported Christmas trees. Singers, often dressed as the three kings (or Magi) go from door to door singing ancient carols known as *aguinaldos* to the accompaniment of guitars. It is customary to offer gifts to the singer, and over the years, the term 'aguinaldos' has also come to stand for the gift itself. Sometimes the strolling carolers are asked inside to sample special Christmas dishes, such as roast pig and rice pudding. Christmas pageants and parties, which begin in early December, often extend right up until the Feast of the Three Kings on EPIPHANY (January 6).

On the island of Hispaniola, off the coast of Puerto Rico, a major Christmas attraction is the animated *nacimiento* (Nativity scene) at the Church of San José. This mechanized toy village features miniature trains and figures of people going about their jobs.

SOURCES:
AmerBkDays-1978, p. 1149
Chases-1996, p. 481
FolkAmerHol-1991, p. 449
FolkWrldHol-1992, p. 629

♦ 0399 ♦ **Christmas in Romania (Craciun)**
December 25

From CHRISTMAS EVE until NEW YEAR'S EVE, boys in Romania go from house to house singing carols, reciting poetry and legends, and carrying the *steaua*, which is a large wooden star covered with gilt paper, decorated with ribbons and bells, and illuminated from within by a burning candle. Dramatic performances of the story of Christ's birth can be seen in many Romanian towns and villages, with a cast of traditional characters that includes King Herod, the Magi, a clown, and a comical old man. Puppet shows are also popular.

Turte, a special kind of cake consisting of many layers of thin dough with melted sugar or honey and crushed walnuts in between, is the food most often associated with Christmas in Romania. The many-layered dough is representative of the swaddling clothes of the infant Jesus. As the housewife prepares the turte on the day before Christmas Eve, she walks into the yard followed by her husband wielding an ax. They go around to each tree in the yard, and the husband threatens to cut it down because it no longer bears any fruit. The wife intervenes, persuading the husband that the tree will be full of fruit the following summer. This custom is believed to have derived from a pagan ceremony.

SOURCES:
BkFest-1937, p. 281
BkFestHolWrld-1970, p. 142
DaysCustFaith-1957, p. 351
FolkWrldHol-1992, p. 629

♦ 0400 ♦ **Christmas in South Africa**
December 25

Because South Africa is in the Southern Hemisphere, CHRISTMAS is a summer holiday. The tinsel and evergreen boughs that decorate homes, churches, parks, and shopping malls offer a stark contrast to the weather, which encourages people to spend the day at the beach or in the shaded mountains. But Christmas traditions persist: English-speaking children hang up their stockings in anticipation of the arrival of Father Christmas, carolers sing by candlelight on CHRISTMAS EVE, and Christmas pageants are performed. One of the most popular activities for children is to produce pantomimes based on such classic tales as "Babes in the Woods." BOXING DAY, December 26, is also observed as a holiday, a time for giving boxes of food and clothing to the poor.

For the native South African, Christmas is a day for feasting and exchanging gifts. It marks the culmination of a CARNIVAL-like week of singing, dancing, and eating.

SOURCES:
BkFestHolWrld-1970, p. 152
FolkWrldHol-1992, p. 631

♦ 0401 ♦ **Christmas in Spain (Pascua de Navidad)**
December 25

The **Feast of the Birth** is observed in Spain by attending church services, feasting, and listening to Christmas music. It is a Spanish custom for public servants—such as the mail carrier and the garbage collector—to leave cards with holiday messages for their customers, a reminder of the services they have rendered in the past or hope to render in the coming year. In return, they are given *aguinaldos*, or gifts of money. In Madrid and other large cities, it is not uncommon to see a police officer directing traffic on CHRISTMAS day, surrounded by parcels of all sizes and shapes. Christmas is also a time for processions of the *gigantes,* or giant figures, which dance to the music of fife and drum.

Spanish children receive their gifts at EPIPHANY, which commemorates the coming of the Magi to Bethlehem, bearing gifts for the Christ child. Children leave their shoes on the window sill or balcony and fill them with straw and carrots or barley for the Magi's horses to eat. In Cadiz, children still observe the ancient rite of "Christmas swinging" on swings that are set up in the courtyards. At one time the custom was probably intended to help the sun in its climb to the highest point in the sky.

SOURCES:
BkFest-1937, p. 305
BkFestHolWrld-1970, p. 145
FestWestEur-1958, p. 208

♦ 0402 ♦ Christmas in Sweden (Juledagen)
December 25

Swedes rise early on CHRISTMAS to attend *Julotta,* or six o'clock church service. The church is lit with hundreds of candles and the congregation sings nativity hymns. In rural areas, lit candles are placed in farmhouse windows and people travel to church by sleigh. Each sleigh carries a torch, and when people arrive at the church they all throw their torches into a bonfire.

Unlike the American Santa Claus, the Swedish Father Christmas, or *jultomte,* is small and thin, more like a leprechaun than a jolly, white-bearded man. The *tomte,* or Little Man, is a mythical character who can be either troublesome or benevolent, depending on how well he is treated. Because midwinter was considered a dangerous season in pre-Christian times, full of evil spirits, it was important to treat the tomte well by putting out food and drink for him. Over the generations, the jultomte has become a more generous spirit who distributes gifts rather than receives them. Even when he appears in a red costume with a white beard, however, he is always depicted as being very thin.

SOURCES:
BkFest-1937, p. 314
FestWestEur-1958, p. 222
FolkWrldHol-1992, p. 632

♦ 0403 ♦ Christmas in Syria
December 25; January 01

The Syrian Santa Claus is the camel, who brings gifts to the children on NEW YEAR'S DAY. According to legend, the youngest of the three camels that carried the Magi to Bethlehem fell down, exhausted by the journey. The Christ child blessed the animal and granted it immortality. Syrian children set out water and wheat for the camel before they go to bed, and when they awake in the morning, they find gifts or, if they've been naughty, a black mark on their wrists. Another custom associated with the Magi is carried out on CHRISTMAS EVE, when vine stems are burned in the middle of the church to warm the Magi after their long journey.

CHRISTMAS itself is a family festival in Syria. A special dinner is prepared, and afterward friends and relatives pay social calls on one another. Among Syrian-Americans, it is customary to serve guests Oriental coffee and holiday cakes such as *baklawa,*

burma, and *mulabas,* as well as nuts, oranges, candies, and Syrian wines.

SOURCES:
BkFest-1937, p. 333
BkFestHolWrld-1970, p. 150
FolkWrldHol-1992, p. 635

♦ 0404 ♦ Christmas in the Marshall Islands
December 25

The United Church of Christ in the Marshall Islands of Micronesia has an unusual approach to the traditional lighting of the Christmas tree. Members of the church's Stewardship Council conceal a decorated tree inside a large wooden cross. While they are singing Christmas carols and hymns, the cross opens slowly and the tree rises from it. The singers set off firecrackers as the tree rises, and then lower their voices and sing more softly as the tree descends back into the cross. When their singing is over, the two sides of the cross come apart and the tree remains standing, symbolic of the birth, death, and resurrection of Christ.

Another Christmas custom in the Marshall Islands involves singing and dancing groups known as "Jebta"—from the English word "chapter." Each group tries to outperform the others, and the result is a celebration quite unlike the traditional religious observances of CHRISTMAS.

SOURCES:
BkFestHolWrld-1970, p. 154
FolkWrldHol-1992, p. 623

Christmas Market
See **Christkindlesmarkt**

♦ 0405 ♦ Christmas Pastorellas in Mexico
December 25–January 6

CHRISTMAS Day in Mexico is traditionally a quiet family day, especially following the POSADAS season and the midnight mass known as the *Misa de Gallo,* or 'Mass of the Cock', that many attend on CHRISTMAS EVE. But Christmas in Mexico, which extends until DÍA DE LOS TRES REYES (EPIPHANY) on January 6, is also celebrated with *pastorellas,* or pageants, showing how the Wise Men and shepherds overcame obstacles to visit Jesus in the manger in Bethlehem.

These celebrations, which date from colonial days when Spanish missionaries used pageants as a way of teaching Mexicans the story of the Nativity, are performed throughout Mexico in public squares, churches, and theaters. Most of the pageants represent a humorous mix of tradition, politics, and social affairs.

CONTACT:
Mexican Government Tourist
  Office
405 Park Ave., Ste. 1401
New York, NY 10022
800-446-3942 or 212-755-7261
fax: 212-753-2874

♦ 0406 ♦ Christmas Shooting
Christmas Eve and New Year's Eve

A very noisy custom in Berchtesgaden, Germany. About 200

marksmen gather at midnight above the Berchtesgaden valley and shoot rifles and mortars for an hour. The salvos echoing off the mountains can be heard for many miles. It is believed that the custom of making a loud racket began as a pagan rite to drive away evil spirits.

CONTACT:
German National Tourist Office
122 E. 42nd St., 52nd Floor
New York, NY 10168
212-661-7200; fax: 212-661-7174

♦ 0407 ♦ **Christ the King, Feast of**
*Last Sunday in October (Roman Catholic); last
Sunday in August (Anglican and Protestant)*

Pope Pius XI in 1925 established the last Sunday in October as the Feast of Christ the King in the Roman Catholic Church. The purpose of the feast is to place special emphasis on Jesus' earthly kingship. On this day his authority over all of humanity's political structure is asserted and homage is paid to him as the ruler of all nations. Some Protestants and churches of the Anglican Communion observe a day of the same name and for the same purpose on the last Sunday in August.

SOURCES:
AnnivHol-1983, p. 169
DaysCustFaith-1957, p. 276
RelHolCal-1993, p. 66

♦ 0408 ♦ **Chrysanthemum Festival**
*September–October, including the ninth day of
ninth lunar month*

The Chrysanthemum Festival was the last of the five sacred festivals of ancient Japan. It extended over the ninth month and sometimes into the 10th month of the Buddhist lunar calendar, although the ninth day of the ninth month was known as **Chrysanthemum Day**, primarily an occasion for paying visits to one's superiors. Also known as **Choyo**, the festival was a unique tribute to the gardening and artistic skills of the Japanese, who developed a method for growing chrysanthemums within a wire or bamboo frame in the shape of a human figure. The boughs were trained to grow in such a way that the blossoms formed only on the surface, covering the structure with a velvety coat of tiny flowers. The heads, hands, and feet of these more-than-life-size figures would be made of wax or paste, but their costumes were made entirely of chrysanthemums, with blossoms of different sizes and colors used to achieve as realistic an effect as possible.

Formerly, *kiku ningyo* exhibitions were numerous, and could still be seen in the parks of big cities in the early part of the 20th century. But the cost of growing the flowers and erecting the figures became prohibitive, and the exhibits eventually died out. In Japan, Korea, and Okinawa today, Chrysanthemum Day is a very minor holiday, observed in scattered locations by eating chrysanthemum cakes (a dumpling made from yellow chrysanthemum petals mixed with rice flour) and drinking chrysanthemum wine.

SOURCES:
DictFolkMyth-1984, p. 540
FolkWrldHol-1992, p. 495
JapanFest-1965, p. 186

♦ 0409 ♦ **Chugiak-Eagle River Bear Paw Festival**
Mid-July

A four-day community festival in the towns of Chugiak and Eagle River, near Anchorage, Alaska. Relatively new, it has established itself and achieved popularity with its Ugly Truck and Dog Contest, in which contestants compete for a combined score that rates the lack of beauty of both their vehicles and canine companions. Other events are a parade, a rodeo, arts and crafts displays, a beauty pageant, and carnival rides.

CONTACT:
Anchorage Convention and Visitors Bureau
1600 'A' Street, Ste. 200
Anchorage, AK 99501
800-446-5352 or 907-276-4118
fax: 907-278-5559

♦ 0410 ♦ **Chulalongkorn Day**
October 23

A national holiday in Thailand commemorating King Chulalongkorn (Rama V), the king who abolished slavery and introduced numerous reforms when the country was still called Siam. He succeeded to the throne in 1868 when he was 15 years old, was crowned in 1873, and ruled until his death in 1910. He had been a pupil of Anna Leonowens, who taught the young prince about Abraham LINCOLN. The story of her stay in the royal court, and her teaching of the royal children and concubines, was told in Margaret Landon's book, *Anna and the King of Siam*. The book was the basis for the popular Broadway musical, *The King and I*.

CONTACT:
Tourism Authority of Thailand
5 World Trade Center, Ste. 3443
New York, NY 10048
212-432-0433; fax: 212-912-0920

SOURCES:
AnnivHol-1983, p. 136
Chases-1996, p. 428

♦ 0411 ♦ **Chung Yeung**
*September–October; ninth day of ninth lunar
month*

A Chinese holiday, the second family-remembrance day of the year. It's customary, as on the festival of QING MING, for families to visit the graves of ancestors, tend their gravestones, and make offerings of food, which are eaten after the ceremonies are completed.

It's also traditional on this day for people to go to the hills for picnics and kite-flying. This is done because, according to an ancient legend, a scholar was warned by a soothsayer that disaster would fall on the ninth day of the ninth lunar month. He took his family up into the mountains. When the family returned to their village, they found every living thing dead. They gave thanks that they had been spared. The custom of flying kites stems from the belief that kites carry misfortune into the skies.

The day is also known as **Ch'ung Yang, Double Nine Day**, and the **Festival of High Places**. It is a public holiday in some places, including Hong Kong and Macau.

SOURCES:
AnnivHol-1983, p. 175
BkFest-1937, p. 81

BkFestHolWrld-1970, p. 117
BkHolWrld-1986, Oct 15
DictFolkMyth-1984, pp. 225, 1106
FolkAmerHol-1991, p. 336
FolkWrldHol-1992, p. 493

♦ 0412 ♦ **Ch'un-hyang Festival**
May 20–24

A celebration in Namwon, Korea, to honor Ch'un-hyang, a symbol of female virtue. She is the heroine of the ancient Korean story, *Ch'un-hyangjon,* which tells of the love between a commoner and a nobleman. During the festival, her story is reenacted, and other events include a *p'ansori,* or 'narrative song' contest, a swinging competition, traditionally enjoyed by young women, and a Miss Ch'un-hyang beauty pageant.

Ch'un-hyang was the daughter of a *kisaeng,* or female entertainer, and she and a nobleman's son, Yi Mongnyong, fell in love and were secretly married. Soon after, he was transferred from Namwon to Seoul. The new governor of Namwon was corrupt and licentious, and he wanted Ch'un-hyang. But even though she was beaten, she didn't give in to his advances. Finally Yi Mongnyong returned to Namwon as provincial inspector. He punished the governor and took Ch'un-hyang as his official bride. To Koreans, this is a favorite tale of love and fidelity and also a symbol of the resistance by common people to privileged classes.

CONTACT:
Korea National Tourism Corp.
205 N. Michigan Ave., Ste. 2212
Chicago, IL 60601
312-819-2560; fax: 312-819-2563

SOURCES:
GdWrldFest-1985, p. 128

Ch'usok
See **Mid-Autumn Festival**

♦ 0413 ♦ **Cinco de Mayo**
May 5

Cinco de Mayo or the **Fifth of May** is a national holiday in Mexico commemorating the Battle of Puebla on May 5, 1862, in which Mexican troops under General Ignacio Zaragoza defeated the invading French forces of Napoleon III. Although the battle itself represented only a temporary setback for the French, the Mexicans' victory against overwhelming odds gave them the confidence they needed to persevere until finally triumphing on April 2, 1867.

The anniversary of this event is celebrated not only in Mexico but in many American communities with large Mexican-American populations—especially in the southwestern states of Texas, Arizona, and southern California. The events include parades, patriotic speeches, bullfights, barbecues, and beauty contests. Olvera Street in Los Angeles is particularly known for its Cinco de Mayo celebration.

SOURCES:
AmerBkDays-1987, p. 421
AnnivHol-1983, p. 61
Chases-1996, p. 202
DictFolkMyth-1984, p. 1065
FolkWrldHol-1992, p. 273

♦ 0414 ♦ **Circuit Finals Rodeo, National**
Four days ending third Saturday in March

Also known as the **Dodge National Circuit Finals Rodeo,** these are the finals competitions for cowboys competing in the regional circuit system of rodeos, held since 1986 in Pocatello, Idaho. Some 200 top cowboys and cowgirls of the Professional Rodeo Cowboys Association and the Women's Professional Rodeo Association competed in 1992 for their share of a $250,000 purse and gold championship buckles. Competitions for cowboys are in saddle bronc, bull riding, calf roping, bareback riding, team roping, and steer wrestling; the women compete in barrel racing. For youngsters aged four to seven, there's mutton bustin'—riding sheep. Opening ceremonies spotlight the Pocatello Rodeo Queen and her court. Post-rodeo parties are held each night. Attendance at the finals runs about 40,000.

The circuit system was introduced to allow weekend cowboys who can't compete full-time in rodeos to compete in one of 12 regions in the United States.

See also NATIONAL FINALS RODEO

CONTACT:
Professional Rodeo Cowboys
  Association
101 Pro Rodeo Dr.
Colorado Springs, CO 80919
719-593-8840; fax: 548-4876

SOURCES:
Chases-1996, p. 138

Women's Professional Rodeo
  Association
Route 5, Box 698
Blanchard, OK 73010
405-485-2277

♦ 0415 ♦ **Circumcision, Feast of the**
January 1

The Feast of the Circumcision, which commemorates the circumcision of the infant Jesus on the eighth day after his birth, was first observed by the Eastern Orthodox and Roman Catholic churches in the sixth century or earlier, and was adopted by the Anglican church in 1549. It is known by a number of different names: Roman Catholics, who used to call it the **Octave of the Birth of Our Lord,** or the **Circumcision of Jesus,** now mark the day as the **Solemnity of Mary, the Mother of God.** Episcopalians call it the **Feast of the Holy Name of Our Lord Jesus Christ**—a reference to the fact that Jesus was officially given his name on this day. Lutherans refer to it as the **Feast of the Circumcision and the Name of Jesus.** And Eastern Orthodox churches call it the **Feast of the Circumcision of Our Lord.** Old Calendar Orthodox churches observe it 13 days later in accordance with the Julian, or Old Style, calendar.

SOURCES:
AmerBkDays-1978, p. 8
BkFest-1937, p. 326
DaysCustFaith-1957, p. 17
FolkWrldHol-1992, p. 9
RelHolCal-1993, p. 68
SaintFestCh-1904, p. 50

♦ 0416 ♦ **Círio de Nazaré**
Second Sunday in October

The Brazilian festival known as the Círio de Nazaré is a great

91

"Candle Procession," which attracts pilgrims from all over the country. The Círio de Nazaré has been celebrated since the late 18th century. It traditionally takes place on the second Sunday in October and winds through the city of Belém in the state of Pará on its way to the Nazaré Basilica. There, the statue of Our Lady of Nazaré is venerated for 15 days during the festival. The statue is carried on a wooden framework pulled by thousands of people as payment for prayers that have been answered by the saint. The origins of the festival lie in a miracle that is said to have occurred in the early 1700s, when a wooden image of the saint disappeared from someone's home and then reappeared a couple of days later in the same place. To people in Pará, this festival is on a par with CHRISTMAS, with much feasting and exchanging of gifts.

CONTACT:
Brazilian Embassy
Cultural Section
3006 Massachusetts Ave., N.W.
Washington, D.C. 20008
202-745-2700; fax: 202-745-2827

SOURCES:
Chases-1996, p. 416

♦ 0417 ♦ **Citizenship Day**
September 17

Citizenship Day is an outgrowth of two earlier patriotic celebrations. As the anniversary of the signing of the Constitution of the United States in 1787, September 17 was first observed in Philadelphia shortly after the outbreak of the Civil War as **Constitution Day**. Then in 1940 Congress set aside the third Sunday in May as **"I Am an American" Day**, which honored those who had become U.S. citizens during the preceding year. The two holidays were combined in 1952 and called Citizenship Day.

A number of states and cities hold special exercises on September 17 to focus attention on the rights and obligations of citizenship. Schools make a special effort to acquaint their students with the history and importance of the Constitution. Naturalization ceremonies, re-creations of the signing of the Constitution, and parades are other popular ways of celebrating Citizenship Day. Several states observe the entire week in which this day occurs as Constitution Week.

SOURCES:
AmerBkDays-1978, p. 850
AnnivHol-1983, p. 120
Chases-1996, p. 379
DictDays-1988, p. 21

Civil Rights Week
See **Bill of Rights Day**

♦ 0418 ♦ **Clearwater County Fair and Lumberjack Days**
Third weekend in September

An international lumberjack event that attracts loggers from throughout the world to little Orofino, Idaho (population 3,000). Goldminers came to Orofino to establish the state's

first settlements in the 1860s, and more settlers came at the turn of the century to stake out timber claims. Lumbering is now a major part of Orofino's economy. Lumberjack Days began in the early 1940s as a local contest and kept growing.

The events begin on Thursday, a children's parade is held on Friday, and the lumberjack events come on the weekend. The logging competitions include log birling, ax-throwing, chopping, chain-saw events, a speed pole climb (130 feet), jack-and-jill sawing, and a skidding, or weight-pulling, contest. The cash prizes total more than $30,000 and attendance is about 6,000.

CONTACT:
Idaho Tourism Division
700 W. State St.
Boise, ID 83720
800-635-7820 or 208-334-2017
fax: 208-334-2631

♦ 0419 ♦ **Clipping the Church Day**
August 5

The old English custom of "clipping the church" entails embracing the church by joining hands around it and performing a simple dance step, advancing and retreating three times. In Guiseley, Yorkshire, the custom is observed on St. Oswald's Day, August 5. In other areas of England, it is observed on whatever day is appropriate to the church calendar. Sometimes a "puppy-dog pie"—a round cake with almond paste on top and a small china dog inside—is baked on the day of the church-clipping ceremony.

Some observers believe that this custom dates back to the ancient pagan festival known as the LUPERCALIA, which included a sacred dance around the altar and the sacrifice of goats and young dogs—hence the puppy-dog pie. At one time it was customary for children to run through the streets after the clipping ceremony crying "Highgates!" Although the significance of the word has been lost, it is again reminiscent of the Luperci, the officiators, who dressed in goat skins ran through the streets during the Lupercalia, striking people with goatskin whips.

SOURCES:
AnnivHol-1983, p. 103
EngCustUse-1941, p. 5

♦ 0420 ♦ **Coca-Cola 600**
May, Memorial Day weekend

The longest race of the four big races of the NASCAR (National Association for Stock Car Auto Racing) Winston Cup circuit, held at the Charlotte (N.C.) Motor Speedway. The track, which opened in 1960, installed special lights in 1992 to be the first super speedway ever to have nighttime racing.

The 1992 winner of the 600 was Dale Earnhardt, who won $125,100 for his speed. This was his second win in the 600, but he had won enough other races to be the number-one leader in purses at the end of 1990, when he had collected $12,827,634.

In the week preceding the 600, the Charlotte 600 Festival offers a variety of downtown events, including a parade.

See also DAYTONA 500, WINSTON 500, and SOUTHERN 500

CONTACT:
National Association for Stock Car
  Auto Racing
P.O. Box 2875
Daytona Beach, FL 32115
904-253-0611; fax: 904-258-7646

North Carolina Travel and Tourism Division
430 N. Salisbury St.
Raleigh, NC 27603
800-847-4862 or 919-733-4171
fax: 919-733-8582

♦ 0421 ♦ **Cock Festival**
February 2

Popular throughout Castile and northern Spain, the **Fiesta
del Gallo,** or Cock Festival, usually takes place on CANDLEMAS,
and it symbolizes the renewal of life or of the harvest. It
involves two groups of young people, 12 men and 12 women,
who together comprise a kingdom, or *reinado,* with a king
and queen who officiate at this and other festivals throughout the year. Young women, dressed in white and led by the
queen, leave the church immediately after the Mass and
march to the plaza carrying a live cock. The mayor of the
village awaits them, and they must ask his permission to kill
the cock.

Just how the killing takes place varies from town to town.
Sometimes the cock is tied by the legs to a pole, and the queen
attacks it with a wooden sword. Sometimes it's buried in the
ground with just its head showing. Any young man who
wishes to try may be blindfolded, turned around several
times, and allowed to attack the cock if he can find it. In some
villages of northern Spain, blindfolded men on horseback
strike at the cock with wooden swords as it swings from a
rope that has been stretched across the street. After the cock
is killed, there is a feast.

CONTACT: **SOURCES:**
Tourist Office of Spain   *DictFolkMyth-1984,* p. 1062
665 Fifth Ave.
New York, NY 10022
212-759-8822; fax: 212-980-1053

Cock's Mass
See **Misa de Gallo**

♦ 0422 ♦ **Collop Monday**
      Between February 2 and March 8; Monday before
      Shrove Tuesday

In England, the day before SHROVE TUESDAY was called Collop
Monday, a "collop" being a slice of meat or bacon. It was
traditionally a day for getting rid of all the meat in the house
in preparation for LENT.

                        SOURCES:
                        DictDays-1988, p. 22

♦ 0423 ♦ **Colombia Independence Day**
      July 20

On the day that they celebrate their independence from
Spain, Colombians in the capital city of Bogotá often visit an
historic place known as *La Casa del Florero* (The House of the

Flowerpot). It was here, in the 19th century, that a Colombian
storekeeper was asked to lend a large flowerpot to the
Spaniards for an important occasion. Rather than let them
use it, he broke the flowerpot. A riot ensued—the beginning
of the revolt against Spain.

There are Independence Day parades throughout the country on July 20, some with uniformed cavalry performing
acrobatic feats on horseback. Schoolchildren march in their
uniforms, and dancers perform in the costumes of their
region. In the afternoon, people watch athletic games and
listen to singing groups perform their favorite folk songs.
Because July is a winter month in Colombia, almost everyone
wear *ruanas,* which are square shawls of brightly colored
wool with a slit in the center for the head, and *alpargates,* or
rope-soled canvas sandals.

When Colombia first became a republic in 1819, it included
Venezuela, Ecuador, and Panama as well. Venezuela and
Ecuador became separate states in 1830, and Panama with-
drew in 1903.

CONTACT: **SOURCES:**
Colombian Embassy   *AnnivHol-1983,* p. 95
2118 Leroy Pl., N.W.   *Chases-1996,* p. 304
Washington, D.C. 20008   *NatlHolWrld-1968,* p. 117
202-387-8338; fax: 202-232-8643

♦ 0424 ♦ **Columbus Day**
      Second Monday in October

When the Italian explorer Christopher Columbus (1451–
1506) persuaded King Ferdinand and Queen Isabella of
Spain to provide financial backing for his plan to find a new
route to the Orient by sailing west, he was confident that only
about 2,400 miles of ocean separated the two continents—a
gross underestimation, as it turned out. And when he first
landed in the Bahamas on October 12, 1492, he believed that
he'd reached the East Indies. Despite these errors in judgment, Columbus is credited with opening the New World to
European colonization, and the anniversary of his landing on
the Bahamian island of San Salvador is commemorated not
only in the United States but in Italy and most of the Spanish-
speaking nations of the world.

Also known as **Landing Day, Discoverers' Day** (in Hawaii),
DISCOVERY DAY, and in many Latin American countries as **Día
de la Raza** or **'Day of the Race',** the second Monday in
October is celebrated in this country with parades, patriotic
ceremonies, and pageants reenacting the historic landing. A
mammoth parade up Fifth Avenue in New York City is a
Columbus Day tradition.

In 1991, the spirit of political correctness affected Berkeley,
California, as Columbus Day was cancelled in favor of
Indigenous Peoples Day. Likewise, the Student Senate at the
University of Cincinnati declared that myths about Colum-
bus may not be studied or discussed—the University is "a
Columbus-myth-free-campus."

                        SOURCES:
                        AmerBkDays-1978, p. 918
                        BkDays-1864, vol. II, p. 437
                        BkFest-1937, p. 18
                        BkHolWrld-1986, Oct 12
                        Chases-1996, pp. 414, 417
                        DaysCustFaith-1957, p. 255
                        DictDays-1988, pp. 22, 31

FolkAmerHol-1991, p. 365

Coming-of-Age Day
See **Seijin-no-Hi**

♦ 0425 ♦ Common Prayer Day
Between April 18 and May 21; fourth Friday after Easter

A public holiday in Denmark, Common Prayer Day is a nationwide day of prayer which has been observed since the 18th century, when King Christian VII's prime minister, Count Johann Friedrich Struensee, decided that one great day of prayer should replace the numerous penitential days observed by the Evangelical Lutheran Church, the state church.

The eve of **Store Bededag** is announced by the ringing of church bells. In former times, it was customary for Copenhagen burghers to greet the spring by putting on new clothes and strolling around the city ramparts. Then they went home and ate *varme hveder*, a small square wheat bread, served hot. Today, people still dress in their spring finery and eat the traditional bread, but now they walk along the famous Langelinie, the boulevard that faces Copenhagen's waterfront.

SOURCES:
AnnivHol-1983, p. 175
Chases-1996, p. 197
FestWestEur-1958, p. 25

♦ 0426 ♦ Common Ridings Day
Various dates in June and July

Many Scottish border towns hold a ceremony known as **Riding the Marches** in June or July. The marches are border districts between England and Scotland and England and Wales. The custom dates back to the Middle Ages, when it was often necessary to reconfirm boundaries destroyed by fire in order to retain royal charters. Originally this was done only as the need arose, but eventually it became a yearly event.

The two main observations of Common Ridings Day occur in Selkirk and Haywick in June. In Selkirk, the event is combined with a commemoration of the 1513 Battle of Flodden, in which King James IV of Scotland and 10,000 others were killed. The Royal Burgh Standard Bearer leads a cavalcade of 200 riders around the borders of the town common.

CONTACT:
British Tourist Authority
551 Fifth Ave., Ste. 702
New York, NY 10176
800-462-2748 or 212-986-2200
fax: 212-986-1188

SOURCES:
AnnivHol-1983, p. 175

♦ 0427 ♦ Commonwealth Day
Second Sunday in March

From 1903 until 1957, this holiday in honor of the British Empire was known as **Empire Day** and was celebrated on May 24, Queen Victoria's birthday. Between 1958 and 1966, it was called **British Commonwealth Day**. Then it was switched to Queen Elizabeth II's official birthday in June (*see* Queen Elizabeth II Birthday), and the name was shortened to Commonwealth Day. Since 1977 it has been observed annually on the second Sunday in March.

In Canada it is still celebrated on May 24 (or the Monday before) and referred to as **Victoria Day**.

SOURCES:
AnnivHol-1983, p. 70
Chases-1996, pp. 129, 130
DictDays-1988, pp. 23, 36, 125
FolkWrldHol-1992, p. 301

♦ 0428 ♦ Comoros Independence Day
July 6

Comoros proclaimed its declaration of independence from France on this day in 1975, after more than 100 years under French rule. It is commemorated with a national holiday.

CONTACT:
Comoros Embassy
336 E. 45th St., 2nd Floor
New York, NY 10017
212-972-8010; fax: 212-983-4712

SOURCES:
Chases-1996, p. 286

♦ 0429 ♦ Compitalia
Early January

The Compitalia were festivals celebrated in ancient Rome in early January (between the 3rd and the 5th, according to some accounts) in honor of the *Lares*, or deities of the household farm and family. *Compita* were places where roads or farm paths crossed each other, and which were considered sacred. Small tower-like shrines were often built there, and people would hold sacrifices at the shrines at the end of the agricultural year. The shrines were left open in four directions so that the Lares had access to them. Sometimes farmers would also hang a broken plough there to indicate that a job was done.

The institution of the Compitalia is attributed to either Tarquin the Proud (also known as Tarquinius Superbus because of his proud and insolent nature) or Servius Tullius. There is some indication that the original sacrifices were human, but that Brutus, the first consul of Rome, eventually substituted dolls and the heads of poppies for human figures. Slaves enjoyed a brief period of freedom during the Compitalia, and the spirit of the ancient festival survived in Plough Monday, an occasion for servants to celebrate the completion of their ploughing.

SOURCES:
ClassDict-1984, pp. 162, 608
DictFolkMyth-1984, p. 604
FestRom-1981, p. 58
FestSaintDays-1915, p. 19

♦ 0430 ♦ Concordia Day
November 11

A public holiday on the island of St. Maarten in the West Indies, Concordia Day commemorates the 1648 agreement to divide the island between the Dutch and the French. To this day, St. Maarten is the smallest territory shared by two sovereign states, with only a stone monument and two hand-lettered signs marking the boundary.

Concordia Day celebrates the long-standing peaceful coexistence of the two countries by holding parades and a joint ceremony with French and Dutch officials at the obelisk border monument. November 11 is also the anniversary of the island's discovery in 1493 by Christopher COLUMBUS, who named it after the saint (ST. MARTIN) on whose feast day it was discovered.

CONTACT:
French Government Tourist Office
9454 Wilshire Blvd., Ste. 715
Beverly Hills, CA 90212
310-271-6665; fax: 310-276-2835

Netherlands Board of Tourism
355 Lexington Ave., 21st Floor
New York, NY 10017
212-370-7360; fax: 212-370-9507

SOURCES:
AnnivHol-1983, p. 146

♦ 0431 ♦ **Confederados Reunion**
April

The "Confederados" are the descendants of a small band of Southerners who fled the United States at the end of the Civil War to establish a new life in Brazil. Led by Colonel William Hutchinson Norris, an Alabama state senator who arrived in December 1865 and purchased a large farm about 80 miles northwest of São Paulo, the newcomers found the area's reddish soil reminiscent of Mississippi clay and the climate perfect for growing cotton and watermelons. As the word spread, thousands of Southerners followed—an estimated 2,900 a year landed in Rio de Janeiro between 1867 and 1871, and many more arrived at other Brazilian ports. They settled in a number of places, but the most successful colony was the one started by Norris. Americana, as it is known today, is a center for the textile industry in Brazil.

Many of the Americans missed their homeland and eventually returned there; the number of Confederados living in and around Americana leveled off at about 500 by the turn of the century. They hold four gatherings a year, the largest and most important of which takes place in April. In celebration of their heritage, they eat hot dogs and candied apples, drink cold beer, dance in hoop skirts and Civil War uniforms, and display the flag of the Confederate States of America. The April reunion takes place in a small local cemetery between Americana and Santa Barbara, where more than 400 of their ancestors are buried.

CONTACT:
Brazilian Embassy
3006 Massachusetts Ave., N.W.
Washington, D.C. 20008
202-745-2700; fax: 202-745-2827

♦ 0432 ♦ **Confederate Memorial Day**
Varies from state to state

Observed in memory of the Confederate soldiers who died in the Civil War, Confederate Memorial Day is widely observed in the southern United States. It grew out of a number of smaller, more localized responses to the bloodshed of the War between the States. In Vicksburg, Mississippi, for example, a group of women got together in 1865 to decorate the graves of more than 18,000 men who had been killed during the siege of Vicksburg. A similar event took place the following year in Columbus, Mississippi, where the women laid

magnolia blossoms on the graves of the enemy soldiers as well.

The dates on which Confederate Memorial Day is observed vary from state to state, and are often linked to some local historical event. In Texas it is called **Confederate Heroes Day**, and is observed on January 19, Robert E. Lee's birthday (*see* LEE DAY, ROBERT E.).

SOURCES:
AmerBkDays-1978, p. 383
AnnivHol-1983, p. 57
Chases-1996, pp. 185, 190, 206, 231
DictDays-1988, p. 23

♦ 0433 ♦ **Confucius's Birthday (Teacher's Day)**
September 28

A time to commemorate the birth of the teacher Confucius, perhaps the most influential man in China's history. In Taiwan, the day is a national holiday. In Qufu, Shandong Province, China, the birthplace of Confucius, there is a two-week-long **Confucian Culture Festival**. In Hong Kong observances are held by the Confucian Society at the Confucius Temple at Causeway Bay near this date.

Confucius, the Latinized version of the name K'ung-fu-tzu, was born in 551 B.C. during the Warring States Period and developed a system of ethics and politics that stressed five virtues: charity, justice, propriety, wisdom, and loyalty. His teachings were recorded by his followers in the *Analects* and formed the code of ethics called Confucianism that is still the cornerstone of Chinese thought. It taught filial obedience, respect, and selflessness; the Confucian "golden rule" is "Do not do unto others what you would not want others to do unto you." Confucius died at the age of 73 in 479 B.C.

During the Cultural Revolution Confucianism lost favor, and in the late 1960s Red Guards defaced many of the buildings in Qufu. They have since been restored, and the festival held there from late September into October attracts scholars from China and abroad. The festival opens with a ceremony accompanied by ancient music and dance and includes exhibitions and lectures on the life and teachings of Confucius and on Chinese customs.

Commemorations in Taiwan take the form of dawn services at the Confucian temples. The Confucius Temple in Tainan was built in 1665 by Gen. Chen Yunghua of the Ming Dynasty and is the oldest Confucian temple in Taiwan.

CONTACT:
Taiwan Visitors Association
1 World Trade Center, Ste. 7953
New York, NY 10048
212-466-0691; fax: 212-432-6436

SOURCES:
AnnivHol-1983, p. 175
BkFest-1937, p. 76
Chases-1996, p. 394
DictWrldRel-1989, p. 191

♦ 0434 ♦ **Congo Independence Day Celebration**
August 13–15

The **Three Glorious Days**, or **Trois Glorieuses**, constitute a national holiday in the Republic of Congo, commemorating the independence gained from France on August 15, 1960.

CONTACT:
Republic of Congo Embassy
4891 Colorado Ave., N.W.
Washington, D.C. 20011
202-726-0825; fax: 202-726-1860

SOURCES:
AnnivHol-1983, pp. 106, 107
Chases-1996, p. 337
NatlHolWrld-1968, p. 142

♦ 0435 ♦ Congo Republic Day
December 31

This national holiday in the Republic of Congo commemorates the establishment of the republic on this day in 1969. The Congolese Labor Party, Congo's only legal political party, was also founded on this day.

CONTACT:
Republic of Congo Embassy
4891 Colorado Ave., N.W.
Washington, D.C. 20011
202-726-0825; fax: 202-726-1860

SOURCES:
AnnivHol-1983, p. 166

♦ 0436 ♦ Connecticut Early Music Festival
First three weeks in June

The term "early music" refers to music from the medieval, renaissance, baroque, and classical periods, up to and including Beethoven and Schubert, performed on period instruments. Since 1983, when harpsichordist Igor Kipnis and flutist John Solum co-founded the Connecticut Early Music Festival, the residents of southeastern Connecticut have been able to hear the music of such composers as Purcell, Mozart, Boccherini, Telemann, Bach, Couperin, Salieri, Gluck, Corelli, Vivaldi, Monteverdi, Handel, Haydn, Schubert (*see also* Schubertiade Hohenems), and Beethoven performed on such unusual instruments as the cornet, slide trumpet, sackbut, viola da gamba, and the clavichord. The concerts are held in small rooms or churches so that the subtleties of the instruments can be heard—particularly the Noank Baptist Church in Noank and the Harkness Chapel at Connecticut College in New London. There is a special evening concert and cruise aboard the S.S. *Sabino* at Mystic Seaport Museum in Mystic.

CONTACT:
Connecticut Tourism Division
865 Brook St.
Rocky Hill, CT 06067
800-282-6863 or 860-258-4355
fax: 860-258-4275

Mystic Seaport Museum Stores
47 Greenmanville Ave.
Mystic, CT 06355
800-331-2665 or 860-572-5385
fax: 860-572-8260

SOURCES:
MusFestAmer-1990, p. 46

♦ 0437 ♦ Connecticut River Powwow
August–September, weekend before Labor Day

A two- to three-day festival organized since 1985 by the Connecticut River Powwow Society, a non-profit organization consisting of native peoples and Anglo-Americans, this is largely an educational event. The powwow was formerly held in Farmington, Conn. (the new site was not determined at this writing), and draws about 35,000 visitors.

Featured are demonstrations of the hunting ability of live birds of prey, including eagles and hawks. Other events include tribal dancing, drum playing, storytelling, a live wolf program, exhibits of Indian arts such as sculpture and pot-

tery, and talks on environmental issues. The Society sponsors a similar powwow the weekend before July 4 at the Somers Fairground in Somers, Conn.

CONTACT:
Connecticut River Powwow
 Society
P.O. Box 63
Stafford, CT 06075
860-684-6984

Constitution Day
See under individual countries

Constitution Week (U.S.)
See **Citizenship Day**

♦ 0438 ♦ Consualia
August 21 and December 15

The infamous rape of the Sabine women occurred at the first Consualia in ancient Rome. Consus, originally an agricultural deity but also regarded as the god of good counsel and the guardian of secrets, is said to have advised Romulus, the founder of Rome, to abduct the Sabine women as wives for his supporters.

The sanctuary dedicated to Consus in 272 B.C. was located on the Aventine Hill in Rome. Sacrifices were held there during his festival, and there were also horse and chariot races in the Circus Maximus, the large arena that lay between the Palatine and Aventine hills. There were actually two festivals in honor of Consus, one on August 21 and the other on December 15. During the August festival, the chariots competing in the races were drawn by mules instead of horses.

SOURCES:
AmerBkDays-1978, p. 713
DictFolkMyth-1984, p. 248

♦ 0439 ♦ Conversion of St. Paul, Feast of the
January 25

Saul of Tarsus, a highly educated, devout Jew, was converted to Christianity on the road to Damascus not long after the death of Jesus Christ. Later he was known as Paul and through his life, his teachings, and his writings became the most influential leader in the history of the church. According to tradition, he was beheaded during Nero's persecution of Christians about the year 67.

The eight-day period ending on January 25 is known as the Week of Prayer for Christian Unity. Since 1908 it has been a time for interdenominational prayer and worship. At St. Paul's Chapel in New York City, the oldest church building in Manhattan, the path through the graveyard that is routinely used as a shortcut between Broadway and Fulton Street is closed for 48 hours, beginning on the eve of the Feast of the Conversion of St. Paul.

At one time the weather on this day was linked to predictions about the coming year. Fair weather on St. Paul's day was said to presage a prosperous year; snow or rain an unproductive one. Clouds meant that many cattle would die, and a windy day was said to be the forerunner of war.

SOURCES:
AmerBkDays-1978, p. 110
BkDays-1864, vol. I, p. 157
BkFest-1937, p. 52
DaysCustFaith-1957, pp. 30,
    155
DictDays-1988, p. 105
DictWrldRel-1989, p. 563
FestSaintDays-1915, p. 22
SaintFestCh-1904, p. 80

◆ 0440 ◆ Coolidge Birthday Celebration, Calvin
July 4

The village of Plymouth Notch, Vermont, contains what many consider to be the best preserved and most authentic of all presidential homesites. It was here that Calvin Coolidge (1872–1933), 30th president of the United States, spent his boyhood and was sworn in as president by his father following the death of Warren Harding in 1923. The Coolidge Homestead was donated to the State of Vermont by John Coolidge, the President's son, in 1956. The state eventually acquired his birthplace, the general store and post office owned by his father, the homes of his mother and stepmother, his paternal grandparents' farmhouse, the family church, and the cemetery where the President and six generations of Coolidges are buried.

On the FOURTH OF JULY each year, the anniversary of Coolidge's birth, there is a noontime march from the green near the Plymouth Post Office to the Notch Cemetery, led by a Vermont National Guard colorguard with a bugler and a chaplain. The White House sends a wreath, which is laid at the President's tomb. Townspeople, tourists, and descendants of the Coolidge family listen to a brief graveside prayer service followed by the playing of taps. Next to the president's grave are those of his father and his son, Calvin Coolidge, Jr., who died at the age of 16 during his father's White House years.

CONTACT:
Vermont Dept. of Travel and
    Tourism
134 State St.
Montpelier, VT 05602
800-837-6668 or 802-828-3236
fax: 802-828-3233

SOURCES:
AmerBkDays-1978, p. 628
Chases-1996, p. 282

◆ 0441 ◆ Coptic New Year
September 11

Members of the Coptic Orthodox Church, the native Christian church in Egypt, celebrate the New Year on September 11 because it is the day on which the Dog Star, Sirius, reappears in the Egyptian sky, signalling the flooding of the Nile and the beginning of a new planting season.

To commemorate the martyrs of the church, red vestments and altar clothes are used on this day. A food of special significance on this day is the red date: red signifies the martyrs' blood, the white meat of the date symbolizes the purity of their hearts, and the hard pit represents their steadfast faith. The Coptic New Year is also celebrated by Canadians of Egyptian descent and by Egyptian communities elsewhere.

SOURCES:
FolkWrldHol-1992, p. 477

◆ 0442 ◆ Corn Palace Festival
One week in mid-September

The world's only Corn Palace was built in Mitchell, South Dakota, in 1892. It was home to the Corn Belt Exposition, designed to encourage farmers to settle in the area by displaying its corn and wheat crops on the building's exterior. A second and larger Corn Palace was built in 1905 to accommodate the growing crowds, and in 1937 a third Corn Palace was completed, this time with the addition of Moorish-looking minarets, turrets, and kiosks. The outside of the Palace is covered entirely with decorations consisting of dock, wild oats, bromegrass, blue grass, rye straw, and wheat tied in bunches. Corn of different colors, sawn in half lengthwise and nailed to the outside walls, is also used to complete the design, which changes every year. The decorating process usually begins in mid-summer and is completed in time for the festival.

Entertainment at the festival has reflected changing public tastes over the years. Stage revues in the 1920s gave way to the "big bands" of the '30s and '40s. Standup comedians and television entertainers in the '50s and '60s have yielded to country and western stars today.

CONTACT:
South Dakota Dept. of Tourism
711 E. Wells Ave.
Pierre, SD 57501
800-952-3625 or 605-773-3301
fax: 605-773-3256

SOURCES:
Chases-1996, p. 375
GdUSFest-1984, p. 173

◆ 0443 ◆ Corpus Christi
*Between May 21 and June 24; Thursday after
Trinity Sunday*

Also known as the **Feast of the Most Holy Body of Christ,** the **Day of Wreaths,** and in France as the **Fête-Dieu,** Corpus Christi is a Roman Catholic festival that has been celebrated in honor of the Eucharist since 1246. In commemoration of the Last Supper on the day before Jesus' crucifixion, worshippers receive Communion and, in some countries, the consecrated bread (or Host) is paraded through the streets, held by the priests in a monstrance. In Spain and Provence, these processions can be quite elaborate, with saints and characters from the Bible following a path decorated with wreaths and strewn with flowers.

In Portugal the feast is known as **Día de Corpo de Deus** and has been one of the major religious observances—both on the mainland and in the Azores—since medieval times. In the city of Ponta Delgada, on San Miguel in the Azores, the people make a flower-petal carpet almost three-quarters of a mile in length. Over this carpet passes a colorful procession of high-ranking clergy and red-robed priests, who are followed by a group of first communicants (those who are to receive communion for the first time)—the young boys wearing dark suits and scarlet capes and the girls wearing white dresses and veils. The climax of the ceremony comes when the bishop raises the silver monstrance and exposes the Blessed Sacrament, the Body of Christ.

CONTACT:
Portuguese National Tourist
  Office
590 Fifth Ave., 4th Floor
New York, NY 10036
212-354-4403; fax: 212-764-6137

SOURCES:
BkDays-1864, vol. I, p. 686
BkFest-1937, pp. 124, 186, 303
DaysCustFaith-1957, p. 156
DictFolkMyth-1984, pp. 253,
  747, 749, 754, 787, 980, 1065
FestSaintDays-1915, p. 131
FestWestEur-1958, pp. 67, 98,
  165, 198, 234
FolkAmerHol-1991, p. 231
FolkWrldHol-1992, p. 288
IntlThFolk-1979, pp. 275, 276
RelHolCal-1993, p. 69
SaintFestCh-1904, p. 263

♦ 0444 ♦ Corpus Christi in England
*Between May 21 and June 24; Thursday after
Trinity Sunday*

In England before the Reformation, there was a famous procession in London on Corpus Christi Day. Beginning at Cheapside, a group of clergymen would move down the street chanting the paternoster, or Lord's Prayer. Over the years they perfected their timing so that just as they reached a certain corner, they sang, "Amen." To this day, there is a street corner in London known as the "Amen Corner," and the street leading to it is known as "Paternoster Row." The procession then turned the corner and proceeded down another street, still known as "Ave Maria Lane."

Although the feast of Corpus Christi is no longer observed in England, there was a time when the city guilds were involved in processions on this day and often performed what were known as "Corpus Christi plays." These were pageants based on a scriptural subject or religious mystery, named after the *pagiante*, or large, partitioned cart in which they were presented.

SOURCES:
BkFestHolWrld-1970, p. 69
FestSaintDays-1915, p. 133

♦ 0445 ♦ Corpus Christi in Germany
(Fronleichnamsfest)
*Between May 21 and June 24; Thursday after
Trinity Sunday*

Corpus Christi Day in Germany is celebrated with colorful processions where the Sacrament and other holy symbols are carried through villages. Small-town streets are decorated with flowers and greenery, and children dressed in white and wearing wreaths of flowers accompany women in regional costume and local clergy. Sometimes people display pictures of Christ and spread carpets in front of their houses in honor of the day. The most picturesque of these processions take place in Bavaria. Some are held on lakes rather than in the streets, with flower-decked boats carrying members of the procession and worshippers across crystal clear waters. The processions at Lake Staffelsee and Lake Chiemsee in Upper Bavaria are among the most dramatic.

CONTACT:
German National Tourist Office
122 E. 42nd St., 52nd Floor
New York, NY 10168
212-661-7200; fax: 212-661-7174

SOURCES:
FestSaintDays-1915, p. 137
FestWestEur-1958, p. 67
FolkWrldHol-1992, p. 288

♦ 0446 ♦ Corpus Christi in Mexico
*Between May 21 and June 24; Thursday after
Trinity Sunday*

A Roman Catholic holiday commemorating the Eucharist, Corpus Christi is often observed in Mexico with symbolic battles between the Moors (Muslims) and the Christians, particularly in the Sierras of Puebla and Veracruz. Although costumes vary from one area to the next, the Moors can always be distinguished by their turbans and crescents, while the Christians usually wear either elaborate plumed helmets with visors or derby hats with pink masks. The battle between them may last four or five hours, at the end of which the Moors are defeated and their leader is symbolically buried.

Another spectacle that takes place on Corpus Christi is the *Danza de los Voladores*, or Flying Pole Dance, performed by the Totonac Indians in Papantla. Four dancers dressed as birds stand on a small platform atop a 70-foot tree that has been stripped of its branches. By carefully winding ropes around the tree and around themselves, they are able to hurl themselves into space and circle the tree 13 times before landing on the ground feet first. The four dancers multiplied by the 13 circles equals 52, the number of years in the ancient Aztec calendar cycle. Other versions of the Flying Pole Dance are performed in Pahuatlan and Cuetzalan, Puebla State.

Religious processions are common in Mexico on Corpus Christi, as is the *reposiar*, a small shrine or altar set up along the procession's path, covered with a lace-trimmed altar cloth and decorated with candles, flowers, and garlands. As the priest makes his rounds of the village, he stops at each of these shrines and gives his benediction. Local tradespeople set up a "mock" market along the path of the procession at which they display miniature objects of their trade. A builder, for example, makes doll houses, while restaurant owners serve small portions of food in miniature dishes and weavers make tiny blankets. The inch-long breads made by the bakers are used by the children as money to buy other miniature wares.

See also Moors and Christians Fiesta

CONTACT:
Mexican Government Tourist
  Office
405 Park Ave., Ste. 1401
New York, NY 10022
800-446-3942 or 212-755-7261
fax: 212-753-2874

SOURCES:
BkFestHolWrld-1970, p. 70
DictFolkMyth-1984, pp. 253,
  749
FolkWrldHol-1992, p. 288
IntlThFolk-1979, p. 275

♦ 0447 ♦ Corpus Christi in Switzerland
(Fronleichnamsfest)
*Between May 21 and June 24; Thursday after
Trinity Sunday*

Many of the ceremonies observed on Corpus Christi in Switzerland have come down from the Middle Ages. Although customs may vary from one canton to the next, this festival is almost always observed with elaborate processions of clergy in their best robes, people in picturesque regional costumes, and soldiers in historic uniforms. The priest who leads the procession often walks on a carpet of flowers.

In Fribourg, people decorate their houses with Gobelins (tapestries) as the Bishop of Fribourg carries the Holy Sacrament through the streets. In the canton of Appenzell, the processions include women in native costume, Capuchin monks in their robes, and young girls with white dresses and wreaths of flowers in their hair.

It is customary to throw the church doors open on Corpus Christi and to decorate the altar and aisles with garlands and greens. Outdoor village altars with flowers and candles are often erected in secluded places.

CONTACT:
Swiss National Tourist Office
608 Fifth Ave.
New York, NY 10020
212-757-5944; fax: 212-262-6116

SOURCES:
FestWestEur-1958, p. 234

♦ 0448 ♦ Cosby Ramp Festival
First Sunday in May

A festival started in 1951 to honor an obnoxious plant—the ramp. Held on Kineauvista Hill near Cosby, Tenn. (which is near Knoxville), the festival is touted as the first and largest of the ramp celebrations.

The ramp, related to the onion, is scientifically designated *Allium triccorcum lilaceae.* The name 'ramp' supposedly was a shortening of *rampson*, the name of a similar plant. Devotees of the ramp say it has a mouth-watering, sweet flavor with a hint of garlic; they also concede that it has an astoundingly strong smell—like that of a wild onion multiplied a thousand times. It was once used in medicinal tonics, the theory being that the odor was enough to ward off germs and certainly germy people. It is rich in vitamin C and was the first spring vegetable for mountain people. Ramp harvest festivals of an informal sort are an old Appalachian custom handed down from the Indians, who taught the European settlers how to cook ramps.

Several days before the festival, a group of ramp pluckers goes into the mountains to pick and clean the ramps. The festival lunch, of course, features fried ramp with eggs cooked with streaked meat, a kind of bacon. The festival music is bluegrass, gospel, and country, and the events include the crowning of the Ramp Prince and Princess and the Maid of Ramps. About 5,000 to 6,000 attend.

The Polk County Ramp Festival, a similar but smaller affair, is held in late April in Benton, Tenn. It has bluegrass music all day, and awards are given to the oldest and youngest ramp eaters, the largest family, and the person who has come the farthest distance (winners of this last have even come from outside of the U.S.).

CONTACT:
Tennessee Dept. of Tourism
  Development
P.O. Box 23170
Nashville, TN 37202
615-741-2158; fax: 615-741-7225

♦ 0449 ♦ Costa Rica Independence Day
September 15

On this day in 1821, Costa Rica achieved independence, after having been ruled by Spain since the early 1500s. EL SALVADOR, GUATEMALA, HONDURAS, and NICARAGUA also declared independence from Spain on September 15, 1821.

On the evening of September 14, the president traditionally lights a torch representing liberty in the old capital city of Cartago, and on Independence Day, gives a speech to schoolchildren. There are more speeches and dancing in San José, the modern capital.

Other national holidays are National Day on July 26 and Liberation Day, observed on January 1, NEW YEAR'S DAY.

CONTACT:
Costa Rican Embassy
2114 'S' St., N.W.
Washington, D.C. 20008
202-234-2945; fax: 202-265-4795

SOURCES:
AnnivHol-1983, p. 118
Chases-1996, p. 377
NatlHolWrld-1968, p. 163

♦ 0450 ♦ Cotton Bowl Game
January 1

This great college football game was inaugurated in 1937 and pits the Southwest Conference champion against another nationally ranked team. In 1993 Notre Dame faced Texas A&M and beat them 28-3 in the 72,000-seat Cotton Bowl stadium in Dallas, Texas.

Until 1993 the game was preceded by Cotton Bowl Week which offered a variety of activities and culminated in the Cotton Bowl Parade. Like other NEW YEAR'S DAY parades, it was a lavish display of colorful floats and marching bands. The organizers of the Cotton Bowl couldn't secure a contract for television coverage of the parade and so it and Cotton Bowl week were canceled. However, the football game continues.

CONTACT:
Cotton Bowl
P.O. Box 569420
Dallas, TX 75356
214-638-BOWL

SOURCES:
Chases-1996, p. 49

♦ 0451 ♦ Cotton Carnival
Late May through early June

A two-week salute to King Cotton in Memphis, Tenn. The carnival began in 1931 during the Great Depression as an event to cheer up the people. Its forebear was the Memphis Mardi Gras, which was started in 1872 to promote good spirits because the Civil War and a yellow-fever epidemic had just about wiped out the city. Antebellum Memphis had been the site of the largest indoor port and cotton market in the South. Mardi Gras was discontinued in 1891, and Memphis has recovered and is once again a busy port on the Mississippi. As one of the world's biggest cotton markets, more than four million bales are traded each year.

A King and Queen Cotton are crowned a month before the carnival and rule over all the events. The official opening comes with a great river pageant featuring illuminated barges carrying the king and queen and their court of some 200 princesses and ladies-in-waiting. When the king and queen debark from the barge they are greeted by municipal and cotton-industry leaders and the Maid of Cotton, a young woman who has spent the previous year traveling to promote cotton clothing. The pageant is, after all, more than fun; it is a promotion for the cotton industry.

The days of the carnival are filled with parades, art exhibits, a week-long Music Fest with star performers on six outdoor stages, sports events, and such miscellany as crayfish boils, a masked ball, and tours of antebellum houses.

CONTACT:
Memphis Convention and Visitors
  Bureau
47 Union Ave.
Memphis, TN 38103
800-873-6282 or 901-543-5300
fax: 901-574-5350

SOURCES:
AmerBkDays-1978, p. 434
AnnivHol-1983, p. 31
GdUSFest-1984, p. 175

Cotton Row on Parade
See **Crop Day**

Counting of the Omer
See **Lag ba-Omer**

♦ 0452 ♦ **Country Dionysia**
December

Like the HALOA, the Country Dionysia was an ancient Greek celebration that was originally a fertility festival with a strong phallic emphasis. Both were observed during the latter part of the month of Poseideon (December), at the time of year when the days were at their shortest. The Country Dionysia, in fact, was not tied to a single date but was celebrated all over Attica on dates that were determined by local custom. Like CHRISTMAS festivities, it was something that everyone—even slaves—participated in. It was also a time for traditional games, particularly *askoliasmos* ('standing on one leg'), which involved trying to stand on top of a goatskin that had been blown up like a beachball and then covered in grease. There were other contests that also entailed standing on one leg and jumping the longest possible distance, or trying to touch the other players with the leg that was held off the ground.

In its earlier days, the Country Dionysia included a simple procession in which someone carried a jar of wine and a vine, someone dragged a he-goat, someone held a wicker basket of raisins, and someone held a phallus. But over time, it became an elaborate event with gold vessels, expensive costumes, and teams of horses.

SOURCES:
FestAth-1977, p. 100

♦ 0453 ♦ **Country Music Fan Fair, International**
Early June

A week-long country feast of music at the Tennessee State Fairgrounds in Nashville, Tenn., also known as "Music City, U.S.A." and the home of the Grand Ole Opry. The 20th anniversary of the Fan Fair was celebrated in 1991 with a "grand ole party" attended by country music's brightest stars. Yearly attractions are 30 or more hours of stage shows and concerts, autograph-and-picture-taking sessions with big-name stars, some 300 booths and exhibits, fan-club banquet dinners, and a celebrity auction that gives bidders a chance to buy such items as Junior Sample's overalls from TV's "Hee Haw" or Dolly Parton's boots. The Grand Master Fiddling Championship is held at Opryland U.S.A., a music-theme entertainment park.

The Grand Ole Opry was founded by George Dewey Hay,

who was called "the Solemn Ole Judge," and began weekly radio broadcasts from Nashville in 1925. The music developed from ballads of rural laborers in the 1920s through the string bands and cowboy music of the 1930s into honky-tonk and rockabilly music after World War II. In 1941, the Opry was staged live at the Ryman Auditorium in Nashville, and in 1974 it moved to Opryland U.S.A. This all led to the Fan Fair, which is billed as "The Closest Thing to Hillbilly Heaven."

CONTACT:
Nashville Convention and Visitors
  Bureau
161 Fourth Ave. N.
Nashville, TN 37219
615-259-4730; fax: 615-244-6278

SOURCES:
Chases-1996, p. 251
GdUSFest-1984, p. 178
MusFestAmer-1990, p. 251

♦ 0454 ♦ **Cow, Festival of the**
January 25

The **Fiesta de la Vaca** takes place in the village of San Pablo de los Montes, in the Spanish province of Toledo, on St. Paul's Day. While the religious procession and Mass that are a traditional part of the observance of the feast of San Pablo are going on, a group of young men form a counter-procession in the opposite direction. One of them plays the role of the cow, *La Vaca*, while another is dressed as Mother Sow, *Madre Cochina*. A third is dressed as a shepherd, and there are others ringing cow bells. Every time the group passes the image of the saint, they call out, "Here goes the cow!"

After the Mass is over, the mayor and the town councilmen follow the priest to the town hall for the *correr de la Vaca*, or Race of the Cow. La Vaca and the rest of the young men in the group run from the church to the town hall, La Vaca threatening the spectators with his horns. When the Cow reaches the town hall, he is greeted by the mayor, and a celebration with wine follows. Everyone goes home when the church bells ring at noon.

It is believed that the Festival of the Cow is the remnant of a pagan festival and that it survived in opposition to the Christian festivities. Today, however, the two exist quite peacefully side by side.

CONTACT:
Tourist Office of Spain
665 Fifth Ave.
New York, NY 10022
212-759-8822; fax: 212-980-1053

SOURCES:
DictFolkMyth-1984, p. 1063

♦ 0455 ♦ **Cowboy Poetry Gathering**
January

A celebration of the old tradition of cowboy poetry—and of other cowboy art—in the buckaroo town of Elko, Nev.

Poetry by cowboys has a long history; cowboys traditionally recited poetry as they rode on cattle drives, but it was a private, little-known custom. A poem by Allen McCanless published in 1885 has these lines:

> *. . . My ceiling the sky, my carpet the grass,*
> *My music the lowing of herds as they pass*

My books are the brooks, my sermons the stones,
My parson's a wolf on a pulpit of bones . . .

The gathering, which began in 1985 with about 50 working cowboys, has become a six-day affair that now includes folk-music concerts, western dances, exhibits of cowboy gear, and workshops not only on writing but also on such topics as horse-hair braiding and photography. In 1992, the Hispanic *vaquero* (cowboy) was honored with performances and exhibits. Poetry remains the heart of the festival, and the poets—all working ranch people—include men, women, and children as young as six or eight. The poetry includes doggerel and limericks, but is mostly in ballad form with narratives like those of Rudyard Kipling's.

Close to 300 cowboys, cowgirls, and ranchers participate, and between 6,000 and 8,000 people from all over the world attend the various events. Tickets go on sale in October and are instant sell-outs. The gathering has spawned other cowboy-poetry festivals throughout the west (*see also* DAKOTA COWBOY POETRY GATHERING).

Hal Cannon, director of the Western Folklore Center in Salt Lake City, was the force behind the first gathering, and the center still sponsors it. The goals of the gathering are to represent the voice of working ranch people through their poetry, music, and folklife; to promote a dialogue between urban and rural people of the American west; and to nurture understanding between pastoral peoples throughout the world.

CONTACT:
Nevada Commission on Tourism
5151 S. Carson St.
Capitol Complex
Carson City, NV 89710
800-638-2328 or 702-687-4322
fax: 702-687-6779

♦ 0456 ♦ **Cow Fights**
April and October

Each spring the winner of the cow battles, or **Kuhkämpfe**, held in the canton of Valais, Switzerland, is crowned Queen Cow of the village herds. A championship tournament is held in October in Martigny's amphitheater after the cows are herded down the mountains for the winter (*see* ALMABTRIEB). The cow fights began in the 1920s in Martigny, and today crowds fill the streets for the event. Refreshments of choice include wine and sausages, but no beef. The Queen Cow is adorned with a flower garland between her horns and a large bell hanging from a decorated collar. The calf of a Queen Cow can fetch up to 10 times the price of a regular calf.

The term "cow fights" is a bit misleading, however; as a rule, cows don't often exhibit much aggressive behavior, though their owners do. Much of the event consists of cows standing around, grazing, drooling, or even attempting to step out of the fighting arena. Sometimes, though (with considerable prodding), some cows can be provoked into pushing another cow, letting loose with some barbarous mooing, or—on momentous occasions—butting heads. A group of animal rights activists from Austria descended on the 1993 Fights, but dropped their protest when they witnessed what actually goes on.

See also ALPAUFZUG

CONTACT:
Swiss National Tourist Office
608 Fifth Ave.
New York, NY 10020
212-757-5944; fax: 212-262-6116

SOURCES:
FestWestEur-1958, p. 228

♦ 0457 ♦ **Craftsmen's Fair**
August

Although craft fairs can be found all over New England during the summer months, the Craftsmen's Fair at Mt. Sunapee State Park in Newbury, N.H., is considered to be the oldest continuously held craft fair, dating back to 1934. Beginning on the first Tuesday in August and ending five days later, the fair features about 300 craftspeople who sell their work and display their skills through demonstrations in such diverse areas as decoy carving, printmaking, weaving and spinning, basket making, embroidering, pipe making, and blacksmithing. Visitors to the **League of New Hampshire Craftsmen's Fair** can buy clothing, pottery, leaded glass, lampshades, character dolls, marionettes, jewelry, blown glass, leather goods, and just about any other craft they can imagine. There is also a juried craft exhibit, which is open only to members of the League.

CONTACT:
League of New Hampshire
  Craftsmen
205 N. Main St.
Concord, NH 03301
603-224-3375

SOURCES:
Chases-1996, p. 322
GdUSFest-1984, p. 117

♦ 0458 ♦ **Cranberry Harvest Festival**
Two days in late September or early October

Also known as the **Massachusetts Cranberry Festival**, this annual event has celebrated the harvesting of cranberries in South Carver, Massachusetts, since 1949. The idea for the festival came from Ellis D. Atwood, founder of the Edaville Railroad, and Robert Rich of Ocean Spray Cranberries. Rides through the cranberry bogs on the old Edaville steam train are still a popular festival attraction, as are the cranberry-baking and pie-eating contests, the crowning of the Cranberry Queen, and performances by strolling musicians dressed as 17th-century sailors singing old ballads and sea chanteys. The highlight of the festival, of course, is the harvesting of the cranberries themselves, which are a traditional part of the American and Canadian THANKSGIVING feasts.

CONTACT:
Massachusetts Office of Travel
  and Tourism
100 Cambridge St., 13th Floor
Boston, MA 02202
800-447-6277 or 617-727-3201
fax: 617-727-6525

♦ 0459 ♦ **Crandall Day, Prudence**
September, Saturday of Labor Day weekend

The official celebration of Prudence Crandall Day in Canterbury, Connecticut, only dates back to 1987, but Crandall herself has been recognized for some time as a pioneer in the education of young African-American girls. Born in 1803 in Hopkinton, Rhode Island, and educated at the Friends' School in Providence, she established a private academy for girls in Canterbury in 1831. Although her school was widely recognized as one of the state's best, she lost many of her white patrons when she admitted a young African-American girl. Rather than bow to social pressure, she opened another school for "young ladies and little misses of colour"—an act for which she was socially ostracized.

Eventually the Connecticut legislature passed a Black Law (repealed in 1838), which prohibited setting up schools for nonresident African-Americans in any Connecticut city or town without the local authorities' approval. Crandall ignored the new law and was arrested, tried, and convicted. Although the verdict was reversed by the court of appeals in July 1834, this only served to strengthen the opposition of the people of Canterbury. Crandall moved to Illinois later that year with her husband, a Baptist clergyman. In a belated attempt to make amends, Connecticut provided Crandall with an annuity. She died in Kansas in 1890.

Prudence Crandall Day events include craft demonstrations from the 1830s, period children's games, and at least one activity directly relating to Crandall herself. One year, for example, an actor portraying Crandall gave an interpretation of her character. Most of the festival events are held at the Prudence Crandall Museum, located in the house where Crandall lived and taught.

CONTACT:
Prudence Crandall Museum
Routes 14 & 169
P.O. Box 58
Canterbury, CT 06331-0058
860-546-9916

♦ 0460 ♦ **Crane Watch**
March–April

There are actually two events in Nebraska that celebrate the world's largest concentration of sandhill cranes: the Crane Watch in Kearney and **Wings Over the Platte** in Grand Island. Both take place during a six-week period in March and April when 70 percent of the world's sandhill cranes—over a half million birds—crowd a 150-mile stretch of the Platte River between Grand Island and Sutherland. Arriving from west Texas, New Mexico, southern California, and central Mexico, the cranes rest and feed in the area before continuing their migration to Canada and Alaska.

The Fort Kearney State Historical Park serves as an information center for the many visitors who come to see the cranes, and there are guided tours to the most advantageous viewing areas. Events associated with the Crane Watch also include wildlife displays, outdoor photo seminars, and nature workshops.

CONTACT:
Fort Kearney State Historical Park
Rural Route 4, Box 17
Kearney, NE 68847
308-234-9513

Nebraska Travel and Tourism
  Division
700 S. 16th St.
Lincoln, NE 68508
800-228-4307 or 402-471-3794
fax: 402-471-3026

SOURCES:
Chases-1996, p. 116

♦ 0461 ♦ **Crawfish Festival**
First weekend in May during even-numbered years

A time to celebrate and eat the small crustaceans (also called crayfish and crawdads) in Breaux Bridge, La., a small Cajun village. Since 1959, by act of the state legislature, the village has been officially called the "Crawfish Capital of the World."

Crawfish is related to the lobster, and local folk say the crawfish is really the Acadian lobster that followed them to the bayou lands of southern Louisiana. The Cajuns are descendants of the French Canadians whom the British drove from the colony of Acadia (now Nova Scotia) in the 18th century. They still speak their own patois, a combination of French forms with words borrowed from American Indian, African, Spanish, English, and other languages; they often still live in small, self-contained communities.

The festival is a two-day event, featuring crawfish races (on a special circular table, with betting allowed), a parade, Cajun music night and day, a World Championship Crawfish-Peeling Contest and a World Championship Crawfish-Eating Contest. In the latter, contestants start out with a dishpan of five pounds of crawfish and eat for two hours. The record is 33 pounds. The prize is a trophy and crawfish to take home. As many as 100,000 visitors come to this village of 5,000 for the festival.

CONTACT:
Louisiana Office of Tourism
P.O. Box 94291
Baton Rouge, LA 70804
800-334-8626 or 504-342-8119
fax: 504-342-8390

SOURCES:
Chases-1996, p. 197
GdUSFest-1984, p. 66

♦ 0462 ♦ **Creek Green Corn Ceremony**
Late summer

A religious harvest festival, not open to the public, held in late summer by the Muskogee-Creek Indians on the ceremonial grounds in Okmulgee, Oklahoma. Each tribal group conducts its own Green Corn Ceremony on one of 12 such Creek ceremonial grounds in the state.

The dances for the ceremony are performed not to the beat of drums, but to the rhythm of turtle and gourd rattles. Women are designated "shell-shakers," and they dance in groups of four with shells (or sometimes today with juice cans filled with pebbles) around their ankles. Children are included in ceremonies from the earliest age: women dancers with babies carry them into the ceremonial circle. One dance, known as the ribbon dance, honors women and is performed only by women and girls.

Other elements of the festival are stickball games and cleansing ceremonies, but the affair is essentially religious. To worship the Great Spirit, Creeks perform rituals relating to wind, fire, water, and earth.

Seminoles and Yuchis in Oklahoma also celebrate the Green Corn. In some ceremonies participants purge themselves with emetics and submit to ceremonial scratching on the legs and arms.

SOURCES:
EncyRel-1987, vol. 4, p. 467

♦ 0463 ♦ **Cromm Dub's Sunday**
First Sunday in August

In Irish folklore, Cromm Dub was a famous pagan idol that was destroyed on this day. Despite this, as late as the mid-19th century, flowers were still being offered to Cromm Dub on Mount Callan in County Clare. It is for this reason that the Irish also called this day **Garland Sunday**. In ancient times, the flowers were probably preceded by more bloody sacrifices.

> SOURCES:
> *DictFolkMyth-1984*, pp. 201, 263

♦ 0464 ♦ **Cromwell's Day**
September 3

As a British general, Puritan statesman, and Lord Protector of England from 1653–58, Oliver Cromwell is remembered today more for his actions as a general and a statesman than for his efforts within the narrow field of Puritanism. Each year the Cromwell Association in England holds a special service near Cromwell's statue outside the Houses of Parliament on September 3. The date is particularly appropriate. It was on this day in 1650 that Cromwell won the battle of Dunbar, inflicting 3,000 casualties and taking 10,000 prisoners at a cost of only 20 British lives. It was on the same day a year later that he won a decisive victory at the battle of Worcester against the Scots. And it was also the day on which he died.

> CONTACT:
> British Tourist Authority
> 551 Fifth Ave., Ste. 702
> New York, NY 10176
> 800-462-2748 or 212-986-2200
> fax: 212-986-1188

> SOURCES:
> *BkDays-1864*, vol. II, p. 308
> *DictDays-1988*, p. 24

♦ 0465 ♦ **Cronia**
Midsummer

In Greek mythology, Cronus was lord of the universe before the Olympian gods took power. He was the son of Uranus, whom he eventually castrated with a sickle given to him by his mother, Gaea. Once he succeeded his father as ruler of the universe, his reign was so peaceful it was known as the Golden Age. Because he had been warned that one of his children would eventually overthrow him, Cronus swallowed his sons as they were born. But the youngest son, Zeus, managed to escape this fate and was the victor in a 10-year war against his father and the other Titan gods.

The only important festival held in honor of Cronus in classical times was the Cronia, held at Athens, Rhodes, and Thebes in midsummer and resembling the Roman Saturnalia in terms of the unrestrained behavior that accompanied it. Some say that when Cronus was defeated by Zeus, he fled to the west and established another Golden Age in Rome, where he was known as Saturn.

Cronus is usually depicted holding a curved object, perhaps the sickle he used to castrate Uranus. After the defeat of Cronus, the universe was divided among his three sons: Zeus ruled the sky, Hades the underworld, and Poseidon the sea.

> SOURCES:
> *DictFolkMyth-1984*, p. 263

NewCentClassHand-1962, p. 340

♦ 0466 ♦ **Crop Day (Cotton Row on Parade)**
First Saturday in August

A salute to the historic Cotton Row business area of Greenwood, Miss. Cotton Row, listed on the National Register of Historic Places, has the nation's largest concentration of 19th-century cotton dealers' offices. These buildings are still in use and in their original architectural state. Of the original 57 buildings on Cotton Row, 24 are currently occupied by cotton buyers and sellers, known as cotton factors. Greenwood today has one of the biggest cotton markets in the United States.

In the late 1800s, hundreds of thousands of acres of swamp land were opened for cotton production through a federal levee system. Front, Howard, and Main Streets, close to the Yazoo River, became the central point for cotton offices, banks, law offices, insurance companies, and the other businesses that supported the industry of cotton marketing and shipping.

Crop Day began in 1980 and has become the biggest outdoor event in the Mississippi Delta. It's a one-day affair, held early in August. This is a time when the cotton is high enough to fend for itself against the weeds and farmers can take a brief rest before the harvest. Activities include a street dance, a cotton-seed pulling contest, a cotton bale give-away, a bed race, a rubber duck race, a food fair, and sports events.

> CONTACT:
> Mississippi Division of Tourism
>   Development
> P.O. Box 849
> Jackson, MS 39205
> 800-927-6378 or 601-359-3297
> fax: 601-359-5757

> SOURCES:
> *Chases-1996*, p. 321

♦ 0467 ♦ **Crop Over**
Last three weeks in July–first Monday in August

This harvest festival in Barbados was originally celebrated in the 1800s by slaves at the end of the sugar-cane harvest. A procession of carts and animals decorated with flowers would bring the last load of cane to the plantation owner, who would then provide a feast for the laborers. One of the carts carried an effigy known as Mr. Harding, made from sugar-cane refuse and dressed in a black coat, top hat, and mask. The effigy represented the cruel gangdrivers and symbolized the hard times that lay ahead for the laborers until the next crop.

Today, Crop Over is a civic celebration, which was revived in 1974. It takes place during the last three weeks of July and usually ends on the first Monday in August. There are historical displays, craft shows, fairs, cane-cutting contests, open-air concerts, native dancing, and "stick licking"—a self-defense sport similar to fencing. By the last weekend of the festival, the celebration moves to the island's capital, Bridgetown, which is transformed into a huge open-air bazaar where people can shop and listen to live bands. A contest (known as the Cohobblepot) to select the Crop Over Queen is held at the National Stadium. Monday is the finale, known as the Kadooment—a public holiday—which includes the judging of costumed bands at the stadium and a five-mile procession to the Garrison Savannah, where a huge effigy of Mr. Harding is set on fire and pelted with stones.

CONTACT:
Barbados Tourism Authority
800 Second Ave.
New York, NY 10017
800-221-9831 or 212-986-6516
fax: 212-573-9850

SOURCES:
FolkWrldHol-1992, p. 444
GdWrldFest-1985, p. 17

◆ 0468 ◆ Crossing of the Delaware
December 25

What is now known as Washington Crossing State Park is the site of the historic event that took place on CHRISTMAS night in 1776, when General George WASHINGTON and the Continental Army crossed the Delaware River just before the Battle of Trenton. **Washington's Crossing of the Delaware** is reenacted on December 25 each year, beginning at Washington Crossing, Pennsylvania (formerly McKonkey's Ferry) and ending on the opposite bank at Washington Crossing, New Jersey.

St. John Terrell, an actor and producer inaugurated this observance in 1953; he played the part of George Washington himself for a number of years. The costumed actors who cross the river in a specially made Durham boat, similar to those originally used by Washington and his men, try to reproduce the scene exactly as it is depicted in the well-known painting by Emanual Leutze: Vermont's Green Mountain Boys sit in the bow, Gloucester fishermen from Massachusetts man the oars, and General Washington stands with one foot on the gunwale. The actor who portrays Lieutenant James Monroe carries the 13-star flag seen in the painting—an anachronism, since the flag had not been adopted in 1776.

CONTACT:
Washington Crossing State Park
355 Washington Crossing-Pennsylvania Rd.
Titusville, NJ 08560
609-737-0623

SOURCES:
AmerBkDays-1978, p. 1152
Chases-1996, p. 489

◆ 0469 ◆ Crow Fair
Third weekend in August

One of the biggest powwows in the U.S., held since 1918 at Crow Agency, Mont., about 65 miles southeast of Billings. The fair, held Thursday through Sunday, is hosted by the Crow tribe but attracts thousands of other Indians (Peruvian Incas and Alaskan Eskimos were among those attending in 1991) who set up more than 1,000 tepees on the camp grounds.

Dancing at the fair includes not only traditional Plains Indian dances but also the Crow Hop, which is similar to a war dance and is unique to the Crows. It was originally a men's dance, but now women also take part, and all wear clothes of buckskin, feathers, quills, and bells to add a counterpoint to the drum beats. There are rodeos with cash prizes, horse races, a relay of bareback riding, art exhibits, and demonstrations of such crafts as pipe-carving and jewelry-designing with turquoise and silver.

CONTACT:
Crow Tribal Council
P.O. Box 159
Crow Agency, MT 59022
406-638-2601

SOURCES:
GdUSFest-1984, p. 107
IndianAmer-1989, p. 33

Crucifixion Friday
See **Good Friday**

◆ 0470 ◆ Cruft's Dog Show
Three days in February

Charles Cruft was an English salesman who went to France to collect orders for "dog cakes" and so impressed the French dog breeders that they invited him to organize the canine section of the Paris Exhibition of 1878. Eight years later Cruft organized his first dog show in London, which won the patronage of Queen Victoria, an ardent dog lover. Now more than 10,000 dogs representing 150 breeds compete for the Best in Show title, and Cruft's Dog Show is considered to be the largest and most widely attended dog show in Britain.

CONTACT:
British Tourist Authority
551 Fifth Ave., Ste. 702
New York, NY 10176
800-462-2748 or 212-986-2200
fax: 212-986-1188

SOURCES:
Chases-1996, p. 132
EndlessCaval-1964, p. 32
GdWrldFest-1985, p. 94

Crystal Night
See **Kristallnacht**

◆ 0471 ◆ Cuba Independence Day
May 20

This national holiday marks Cuba's independence from Spain on May 20, 1902, when control of the island was turned over to the United States.

CONTACT:
Cuban Mission to the U.N.
315 Lexington Ave.
New York, NY 10016
212-689-7215

SOURCES:
NatlHolWrld-1968, p. 65

◆ 0472 ◆ Cuba Liberation Day
January 1; July 26

This national public holiday commemorates the overthrow of the military government of Fulgencio Batista (1901–1973) led by Fidel Castro (b. 1926) that succeeded on January 1, 1959. July 26 is **National Day**, another public holiday marking the beginning of the revolution Castro led in 1953.

CONTACT:
Cuban Mission to the U.N.
315 Lexington Ave.
New York, NY 10016
212-689-7215

SOURCES:
AnnivHol-1983, pp. 1, 97
Chases-1996, pp. 49, 311

◆ 0473 ◆ Cuisinières, Fête des la
Early August

With the possible exception of the celebration at CARNIVAL, this is the most colorful event of the year in the French West Indian island of Guadeloupe. The **Women Cooks' Festival** begins with a morning service at the cathedral and a parade of women in Creole dress. The highlight of the festival is the five-hour feast prepared by the dozen or so members of the Association of Women Chefs. The Creole dishes they prepare include *blaffs* (a fish or shellfish dish in a sauce; the name comes from the sound made by the fish as it is plunged into boiling water), *boudins* (sausage), and *crabes farcis* (stuffed crabs). It has been said that "one fistful of the tiny hot peppers that are vital to Creole cooking is generally considered enough to blow up an average European city."

CONTACT:
French West Indies Tourist Board
610 Fifth Ave.
New York, NY 10020
212-757-1125; fax: 212-247-6468

SOURCES:
Chases-1996, p. 331
GdWrldFest-1985, p. 104

♦ 0474 ♦ Cultural Olympiad
Various

As the name implies, the Cultural Olympiad is the cultural arm of the OLYMPIC GAMES. When it was first held in 1948, the **Olympic Arts Festival** took place during the games; but since the Barcelona Games in 1992, it has started immediately after the preceding summer or winter Olympic Games end and continued right up until the next Olympics. The 1992 Cultural Olympiad, for example, began immediately after the Seoul Games in 1988. Similarly, the 1996 Cultural Olympiad began in 1993 with a program called "Winterland," a tribute to the 1994 Winter Games host country, Norway. It ended on April 25, 1995, with a gathering of eight Nobel literature laureates for two days of free-wheeling discussions that covered many topics.

The 1996 Olympic Arts Festival in Atlanta, Georgia, included hundreds of performances and nearly 40 exhibitions.

CONTACT:
International Olympic Committee
Public Affairs
Chateau de Vidy
1007 Lausanne, Switzerland
011-41-21-621-6511
fax: 011-41-21-617-0313

SOURCES:
Chases-1996, p. 239

Culture Day
See **Bunka-no-Hi**

♦ 0475 ♦ Cure Salée
September–October

The Tuareg, a largely nomadic ethnic group found primarily in Algeria, Niger, Mali, and Libya, converge with their camels and cattle on a place known as Ingal just after the first rains of the season arrive. An oasis in the Sahara region of northern Niger, Ingal has palm groves and date plantations, and is a favorite grazing ground. The **Salted Cure Festival** takes its name from the salt contained in the new grass, which is essential to the animals' diet. Each Tuareg group participating in the Cure Salée follows a very specific transhumance or seasonal migration route, some traveling hundreds of miles.

In Tamacheq, the language of the Tuareg, the event is known as **Tanekert** or **Tenekert**. The return of the rains is also celebrated with dancing, singing, and camel races.

CONTACT:
Niger Embassy
2204 R St., N.W.
Washington, D.C. 20008
202-483-4224; fax: 202-483-3169

SOURCES:
BkHolWrld-1986, Sep 11

♦ 0476 ♦ Curium Festival
June–July

The ancient city of Curium on the southwest coast of Cyprus, about 12 miles west of Limassol, was buried by volcanic lava in 365. Extensive excavation in recent decades has uncovered a stadium, a basilica and sanctuary of Apollo, and a Roman amphitheater that dates from 50 to 175 A.D. Curium has been the setting for an annual drama festival since 1961. Performances are held in the restored amphitheater, which seats 2,400. Both international and Cypriot drama companies participate in the festival, which focuses on the classical Greek dramatists and Shakespeare. There are also moonlight concerts overlooking Episkopi Bay.

CONTACT:
Cyprus Tourism Organization
13 E. 40th St.
New York, NY 10016
212-683-5280; fax: 212-683-5282

SOURCES:
GdWrldFest-1985, p. 66
IntlThFolk-1979, p. 81

♦ 0477 ♦ Cynonfardd Eisteddfod
Last Saturday in April

When the Welsh began to emigrate to the United States during the latter part of the 19th century and the early years of the 20th, many were drawn to the coal-mining areas of northeastern Pennsylvania. Among them was a minister, Dr. Thomas C. Edwards, who emigrated in 1870 and established a church society designed to teach English to Welsh children by having them read and memorize music, hymns, songs, poetry, and other literary selections in the tradition of the Welsh EISTEDDFOD. This group became known as the Cynonfardd Literary Society—the Cynon being a stream in South Wales where Edwards had lived as a child. Edwards patterned the society's activities after the Welsh National Eisteddfod, and by 1889 the Cynonfardd Eisteddfod was well established.

Believed to be the oldest continuous Eisteddfod outside of Wales and the only one of its kind in the United States today, the Cynonfardd Eisteddfod was originally held on March 17, ST. PATRICK'S DAY, probably because the coal mines were closed on that day so the Irish miners could celebrate. Now it is held at the end of April, and the competition is limited to recitations and vocal and instrumental selections. Competitors range in age from under five years old to adults, and the prizes are generally modest—two dollars, for example, for the child under five years who sings the best "Twinkle, Twinkle Little Star," or $50 for the prize-winning senior citizen who sings a Welsh hymn. Literary recitations include selections from the Bible, Henry Wadsworth Longfellow, and other well-known American authors. All performers in both the poetry and music competitions must memorize their selections.

CONTACT:
Pennsylvania Office of Travel
  Marketing
453 Forum Bldg.
Harrisburg, PA 17120
800-237-4363 or 717-787-5453
fax: 717-234-4560

♦ 0478 ♦ Cyprus Independence Day
October 1

Cyprus gained independence from Great Britain on August 16, 1960. On that day, British governor Hugh Foot departed amid much ceremony, and Greek Cypriot freedom fighters landed on a plane from Athens with a heroes' welcome. The new Cypriot president, Archbishop Makarios III (1913–1977), gave a speech inspiring Cypriots to improve their new nation.

Independence Day is observed as a public holiday on October 1 each year.

CONTACT:
Cyprus Tourism Organization
13 E. 40th St.
New York, NY 10016
212-683-5280; fax: 212-683-5282

SOURCES:
AnnivHol-1983, p. 107
Chases-1996, p. 397
NatlHolWrld-1968, p. 145

♦ 0479 ♦ Czech Festival, National
First full weekend in August

Wilber, Nebraska's annual Czech Festival is held in a town that has been designated by the U.S. Congress as the "Czech Capital of America." Patterned after the well-known Pennsylvania Dutch Festival in Kutztown (*see* KUTZTOWN FAIR), the purpose of the festival is to recognize contributions of Czech immigrants and to foster Czech culture. Folk dance groups come from all over the state, and local residents wear Czech costumes and dance the *beseda*, or polka, in the streets. Foods prepared by the town's residents and served at the festival include a number of Czech specialties, such as roast duck, sauerkraut, dumplings, and *kolaches* (sweet buns). There is even a kolache-eating contest.

On the second day of the festival, awards are presented for special achievements in promoting both Nebraska and Czech culture.

CONTACT:
Nebraska Travel and Tourism
  Division
700 S. 16th St.
Lincoln, NE 68508
800-228-4307 or 402-471-3794
fax: 402-471-3026

SOURCES:
Chases-1996, p. 320
GdUSFest-1984, p. 112

♦ 0480 ♦ Czechoslovak Independence Day
October 28

The Republic of Czechoslovakia was founded on October 28, 1918, when the National Committee in Prague proclaimed independence from the Austrian Hapsburg emperors and took over the administration of an independent Czechoslovak state. They were supported in this move by President Woodrow Wilson, who sent a note to the Austro-Hungarian foreign minister urging that the various nationalities of the empire be allowed to determine their own political future.

Independence Day was widely celebrated in Czechoslovakia until the Communists seized power there in 1948 and turned it into a Soviet satellite. But it continued to be recognized in the United States with special banquets, addresses, religious services, cultural programs, and the laying of a wreath at the tomb of President Wilson at the Cathedral of St. Peter and St. Paul (also known as the National Cathedral, or Washington Cathedral) in Washington, D.C. Communities with large Czech or Slovak populations such as New York City, Los Angeles, Wilber, Nebraska, and Newark, New Jersey, also mark the occasion, but the recent division of the country into the Czech and Slovak republics has caused uncertainty about the way future celebrations will be handled.

This day should not be confused with Czechoslovak Liberation Day, a national holiday observed on May 9 to commemorate the country's liberation by the Soviet army and U.S. forces at the end of World War II.

CONTACT:
Czech Center
1109 Madison Ave.
New York, NY 10028
212-288-0830; fax: 212-288-0971
E-mail: nycenter@czech.cz

SOURCES:
AmerBkDays-1978, p. 963
AnnivHol-1983, p. 137
Chases-1996, p. 432

D

♦ 0481 ♦ Daedala
Spring

This is the name given to two festivals held in ancient Boeotia, which was a part of Greece, in honor of the reconciliation of Hera and Zeus. According to the myth, Hera and Zeus quarreled and Hera went away to Euboea and refused to return to his bed. To trick her into coming back and on the advice of Cithaeron, Zeus dressed up a carved oak-trunk to resemble a bride and let it be known that he planned to marry Plataea, the daughter of Asopus. Hera was so angry she tore the clothes from the statue, discovered the deception, and was so pleased that the two were reconciled.

The **Little Daedala**, held every six years, involved going to an ancient oak grove and cutting down trees for images. Every 60 years the **Great Daedala** was held, and all Boeotia joined in the celebration. All the images that had been collected over the years during the Little Daedala were carried to the top of Mt. Cithaeron, where they were burned on an altar along with sacrifices to Zeus and Hera.

SOURCES:
DictFolkMyth-1984, p. 273

♦ 0482 ♦ Dahlonega Gold Rush Days
October

A celebratory reminder in Dahlonega, Ga., of the town's heyday as a gold-rush town. The nation's first major gold rush was here in 1828, and the area around Dahlonega boomed; a federal mint built in 1838 operated for 23 years and coined more than $6 million. Mining continued into the beginning of the 20th century, and today visitors can pan for gold at several locations. The name of the town is pronounced dah-LON-a-gah; it is derived from the Cherokee name *Talonega*, meaning 'golden.' The festival includes arts and crafts exhibits, country cooking, and beard-growing and tobacco-spitting contests.

CONTACT:
Georgia Dept. of Industry
Trade and Tourism
285 Peachtree Center Ave., N.E.
Marquis Tower II, Ste. 1000
Atlanta, GA 30303
800-847-4842 or 404-656-3592
fax: 404-651-9063

SOURCES:
Chases-1996, p. 423

♦ 0483 ♦ Dairy Festival
July

The dairy capital of Michigan is appropriately named Elsie in honor of the cow in Borden's ads, and although it has fewer than 1,000 residents, there are 20 working dairy farms in the area. One of them is Green Meadow Farm, which boasts the largest herd of registered Holsteins in the United States.

For three days in July each year since 1986, the town of Elsie serves gallons of ice cream at bargain prices. Green Meadow Farm is open to visitors, and there are competitions in cow-milking, ice cream eating, and even milk drinking, with competitors using a baby bottle. The 14-foot-tall fiberglass Holstein in the center of town is a popular place for the festival's 20,000 visitors to have their photographs taken.

CONTACT:
Michigan Travel Bureau
333 S. Capitol Ave., Ste. F
Lansing, MI 48933
800-543-2937 or 517-373-0670
fax: 517-373-0059

♦ 0484 ♦ Dakota Cowboy Poetry Gathering
May, Memorial Day weekend

The Dakota Cowboy Poetry Gathering was founded by Bill Lowman, a cowboy poet who had attended a similar event in Nevada in 1985 (*see* COWBOY POETRY GATHERING) and decided that the badlands of North Dakota should host its own cowboy poetry festival. Two years later the first "Real Cowboy Review" was held in Medora, with 40 poets and musicians participating. The crowds drawn to the event have continued to grow, and the performers often travel long distances to share their poetry, songs, and stories inspired by life on the ranch.

The Medora gathering prides itself on featuring only "the Real Ones"—those cowboys who "have spent a lifetime looking down the top of a cow." It tries to discourage "novelty cowboys, movie cowboys, or rodeo cowboys" who don't really live the life portrayed in their poems. This burgeoning interest in cowboy poetry is largely the result of research done by folklorists who wanted to draw attention to the cowboys' passion for rhyme and tale-spinning and to keep the tradition alive.

See also MEDORA MUSICAL

CONTACT:
North Dakota Tourism
604 E. Boulevard Ave.
Liberty Memorial Bldg.
Bismarck, ND 58505
800-435-5663 or 701-328-2525
fax: 701-328-4878

SOURCES:
Chases-1996, p. 227

♦ 0485 ♦ Dalai Lama, Birthday of the
July 6

This celebration is always held on July 6 for the birthday of the Dalai Lama, the spiritual and political head of Tibet. The name Dalai means 'ocean' and was given to the ruling lama in the 16th century by the Mongol leader Altan Khan. The title suggests depth of wisdom.

The present Dalai Lama, who was enthroned in 1940 at the age of five, is the latest in the line that began in the 14th century. Each Dalai Lama is believed to be the reincarnation of the preceding one, and when a Dalai Lama dies, Tibetan lamas search throughout the country for a child who is his reincarnation.

Tibet had been a sovereign country until 1949 when China invaded eastern Tibet and sporadic warfare followed. In 1959, a popular uprising exploded at Lhasa but was suppressed, and the Dalai Lama and most of his ministers and about 100,000 Tibetans escaped across the Himalayas. The Dalai Lama has lived since then in exile in Dharmsala, India. Today there are some 80,000 Tibetans in India, 30,000 in Nepal, and 3,000 in Bhutan.

The birthday is observed today by exiles in India with incense-burning ceremonies to appease the local spirits, family picnics, and traditional dances and singing. The incense-burning is a rite pre-dating Buddhism.

See also UNIVERSAL PRAYER DAY

CONTACT:
India Tourist Office
30 Rockefeller Ave.
15 N. Mezzanine
New York, NY 10112
212-586-4901; fax: 212-582-3274

Dance of Thanksgiving
See **Whe'wahchee**

♦ 0486 ♦ Dancing Procession
Between May 12 and June 15; Whit Tuesday

The **Sprangprocession** in Luxembourg has been held on Whit Tuesday, which falls 52 days after EASTER, for the past 13 centuries. It honors St. Willibrord (St. Wilfred), the patron saint of Luxembourg, whose feast day is celebrated November 7. The dance that is performed by thousands of participants in the procession through the narrow streets of Echternach, has remained basically unchanged. It involves taking three steps forward and two back (or, according to some sources, five steps forward and three back), to the accompaniment of local bands playing the same melody that was played more than 1,300 years ago. The procession ends up in the Basilica, where the remains of St. Willibrord are buried.

There are a number of legends that attempt to explain the origin of the Dancing Procession. According to one of them, St. Willibrord came to Luxembourg from northern England to convert the people to Christianity. He saved them from a plague by promising that if they subjected themselves to physical punishment, the plague would end. The people danced to the same tune that is played today, hopping up and down until they were completely exhausted and, as promised, the plague disappeared.

Another explanation is that a crusader returned from the Holy Land to discover that his dead wife's greedy relatives had taken over his property and branded him a murderer. As he was about to be hanged, he asked permission to play one last tune on his violin. The haunting melody mesmerized the onlookers, who started dancing and were unable to stop. The condemned man walked away from the scaffold, and the procession that is held each year is penance for his unjust condemnation.

CONTACT:
Luxembourg National Tourist
Office
17 Beekman Pl.
New York, NY 10022
212-935-8888; fax: 212-935-5896

SOURCES:
BkHolWrld-1986, Jun 3
FestWestEur-1958, p. 112
GdWrldFest-1985, p. 128

♦ 0487 ♦ Dartmouth Winter Carnival
A weekend in February

The students of Dartmouth College in Hanover, New Hampshire, have been celebrating Winter Carnival since 1910, when they decided to hold their own mini-OLYMPICS to shake off the winter blues. Soon other colleges were invited to join in the athletic events, which included ski jumping and snowshoe races. By the 1920s, there were so many parties and balls associated with the weekend that it was called "The Mardi Gras of the North."

The event became even more popular after it was featured in the 1939 movie *Winter Carnival*. Students from other colleges, some as far away as Florida, came to Hanover to join in the fun, and eventually drunkenness and vandalism became a problem. Carnival events nowadays are limited to Dartmouth students and their guests. Teams from a dozen or so northeastern colleges and universities compete in Nordic and Alpine skiing, ski jumping, hockey, basketball, gymnastics, and other sports. But the highlight for many is the snow sculpture competition on the Dartmouth green. Because snow has been so scarce in recent winters, the sculptors have had to rely on snow trucked in from nearby ski areas, scraped off parking lots, and recycled from skating rinks.

CONTACT:
Dartmouth College
Main St.
Hanover, NH 03755
603-646-1110

Dasain
See **Durga Puja**

♦ 0488 ♦ **Data Ganj Baksh Death Festival**
Islamic month of Safar, days 18–19

An occasion for massive pilgrimages to the Mausoleum of Data Ganj Baksh in Lahore, Pakistan. Data Ganj Baksh, which means 'He Who Gives Generously,' was the name given to Syed Ali Abdul Hasan Bin Usman Hujwiri (also rendered Ali Hajweri or al-Hujwiri), a scholar and author who lived most of his life in Lahore and died in 1072. He wrote *Kashful Mahjub* (or *Kashf al-mahjub*), the oldest Persian treatise on Sufism. It is a text on the fundamentals of Sufism and it reviews Islamic mysticism, linking each famous master to a particular doctrine. Ali Hujwiri is one of the most popular saints in Pakistan, and every day hundreds of pilgrims pray at his shrine and ask for blessings and favors. On his *urs* (death festival), thousands throng to the shrine for celebratory activities and prayers.

CONTACT:
Pakistani Embassy
2315 Massachusetts Ave., N.W.
Washington, D.C. 20008
202-939-6200; fax: 202-387-0484

SOURCES:
DictWrldRel-1989, pp. 719, 720

♦ 0489 ♦ **Dattatreya Jayanti**
November–December; full moon day of Hindu month of Margasirsa

Dattatreya's birthday is celebrated all over India. One legend has him as the son of Anusuya, an exceptionally devoted and virtuous wife. The wives of Brahma, Vishnu, and Shiva decided to test her virtue by sending their husbands, disguised as beggars, to ask her to give them alms while in the nude. Anusuya avoided the trap by transforming them into babies and suckling them. When her husband, Atri, returned from his morning bath and discovered what had occurred, he turned them into one child with three heads and six hands. The wives begged for their husbands' return, and when Anusuya restored them to their original forms, they blessed Anusuya, Atri, and their son Dattatreya.

On Dattatreya's birthday, Hindus rise early and bathe in sacred streams, fast, and spend the day in worship and prayer. They also meditate on sacred works that include the *Avadhuta Gita* and *Jivanmukta Gita*. Recently, Dattatreya is identified with the triad of Brahma, Vishnu, and Shiva, for it is believed that portions of these deities were incarnated in him. He is usually depicted with three heads and six hands.

SOURCES:
RelHolCal-1993, p. 70

♦ 0490 ♦ **Davis Cup**
November–December

The oldest international men's tennis competition, inaugurated in 1900 and credited with drawing world attention to the game. Tennis was then a young sport; the first U.S. national championship games were played in 1881. The competition was fathered by Dwight F. Davis, who was U.S. doubles champion with Harvard teammate Holcombe Ward in 1899–1901. Davis believed international competition would boost the game's popularity, and had a 13-inch-high silver bowl crafted by a Boston silversmith; it was to be called the International Lawn Tennis Challenge Trophy but became known as the Davis Cup.

From the first, the championship was open to all nations. The first games, held at the Longwood Cricket Club in Chestnut Hill, Massachusetts, had only two contestants: a British Isles team and the American team (captained by Davis). The Americans won, 3-0. The Brits did better—but still lost—in 1902. In 1903, they won, and it was not until 1913 that the U.S. regained the cup.

There was growing interest in the cup. Four nations competed in 1919, and that number grew to 14 in 1922 and 24 in 1926. From the start, teams have consisted of two singles players and a doubles team. There are five matches—four singles and one doubles. Each match is awarded one point, and the first team to win three points wins the cup. In women's tennis, the Federation Cup, inaugurated in 1963 and played each year in the spring, is considered the equivalent of the Davis Cup.

The United States dominated the Davis Cup in the 1920s, spurred by William T. ("Big Bill") Tilden 2nd, who was a member of the Davis Cup team for 11 years. France won in 1927, and went on to win the next five years up through 1932. Great Britain was a power in the 1930s, and Australia and the United States dominated in the 1940s, 1950s, and 1960s; in the late 1970s and the 1980s the winners had a multi-national flavor. In 1980, Czechoslovakia became the first Communist country to win the Davis Cup. The United States won in 1990, but in 1991, playing in Lyons, France, the French team knocked out the champion U.S. team 3-1, and owned the cup for the first time in 59 years. The French team (led by Guy Forget, Henri Leconte, and coach Yannick Noah) kissed, hugged, leapt over the net, lay down on the court, and danced a conga line.

CONTACT:
International Tennis Federation
Palliser Rd., Barons Ct.
London W14 9EN England
011-44-71-381-8060

♦ 0491 ♦ **Davis's Birthday, Jefferson**
First Monday in June

The only president of the Confederate States of America, Jefferson Davis, was captured and imprisoned after the Civil War but never brought to trial. Since he refused to ask the federal government for a pardon, he went to his grave deprived of the rights of citizenship, including all of his former privileges and properties. It wasn't until October 17, 1978, that his citizenship was restored, posthumously, by President Jimmy Carter when he signed an Amnesty Bill designed to "finally set at rest the divisions that threatened to destroy our nation."

Davis's memory is honored by many white southerners in the United States, and his birthday (June 3) is a legal holiday in Alabama, Florida, Georgia, Mississippi, and South Carolina. In Kentucky and Louisiana, it is observed as CONFEDERATE MEMORIAL DAY, a time when the graves of Confederate soldiers are decorated and memorial ceremonies are held. At Arlington National Cemetery in Virginia, the Confederate Memorial Services are held each year on the Sunday nearest June 3, and a speaker usually pays tribute to those who died while serving the Confederacy. Another important ceremony is the Massing of the Flags, which is held at the Jefferson Davis Monument in Richmond, Virginia. The flags of the various Southern states are presented in the order in which they seceded from the nation.

CONTACT:
Virginia Dept. of Economic
  Development
Division of Tourism
901 E. Byrd St.
Richmond, VA 23219
804-786-4484; fax: 804-786-1919

SOURCES:
AmerBkDays-1978, p. 519
AnnivHol-1983, p. 75
Chases-1996, p. 241
DictDays-1988, p. 61

Day of Judgment
See **Rosh Hashanah**

♦ 0492 ♦ Day of Peace, International
Third Tuesday of September

The day of the opening session of the United Nations General Assembly, and a day proclaimed by the U.N. to promote the ideals of peace. The first official observance of the day was in September 1982, and every year since then the Secretary-General of the United Nations has set a theme for the day. In 1991, the theme was "Light a Candle for Peace."

At the United Nations the day is marked with a special message by the Secretary-General, who then rings the Japanese Peace Bell and invites people throughout the world to reflect on the meaning of peace.

Special events are organized in various countries, and in the United States, the mayors of a number of cities issue proclamations for the day.

CONTACT:
United Nations
Dept. of Public Information
New York, NY 10017
212-963-1234; fax: 212-963-4879
WWW: http://www.undp.org

SOURCES:
Chases-1996, p. 380

Day of the Blowing
See **Rosh Hashanah**

♦ 0493 ♦ Day of the Covenant, Baha'i
November 26

A Baha'i holy day, commemorating the covenant Baha'u'llah, founder of the faith, made with humanity and his followers, appointing Abdu'l-Baha as the head of the Baha'i religion who would interpret Baha'i teachings. Abdu'l-Baha chose the date when followers requested an occasion to remember his importance.

CONTACT:
Baha'is of the U.S.
Office of Public Information
866 United Nations Plaza, Ste. 120
New York, NY 10017-1822
212-803-2500; fax: 212-803-2573

SOURCES:
AnnivHol-1983, p. 151
RelHolCal-1993, p. 70

♦ 0494 ♦ Day of the Covenant in South Africa
December 16

This South African legal holiday was established on December 16, 1838, in commemoration of the victory of the Voortrekkers over Dingaan (d. 1840) and the Zulus. The "covenant" it refers to is the vow that Andries Pretorius (1798–1853) and the Voortrekkers made with God as they prepared for the Battle of Blood River: that if they were victorious, the day would be observed as a Sabbath and a church would be built in gratitude.

The original name for this holiday was **Dingaan's Day**. Then it was called **Day of the Vow** and, eventually, Day of the Covenant.

SOURCES:
AnnivHol-1983, p. 161
DictDays-1988, p. 28
FolkWrldHol-1992, p. 592

Day of the Dead
See **All Souls' Day**

♦ 0495 ♦ Day of the Enlighteners (Den na Buditelite)
November 1

A holiday in Bulgaria, this day commemorates the patriots, writers, and revolutionaries who helped to ignite the spirit of Bulgarian nationalism. Thanksgiving services are held in churches, and elsewhere patriotic speeches, parades, and folk music mark this yearly event. Also known as the **Day of the Awakeners**, it is largely observed by schools and municipalities.

CONTACT:
Bulgarian Embassy
1621 22nd St., N.W.
Washington, D.C. 20008
202-387-7969; fax: 202-234-7973

SOURCES:
BkFest-1937, p. 72

Day of the Kings
See **Día de los Tres Reyes; Epiphany**

Day of the Race
See **Columbus Day**

♦ 0496 ♦ Day of the Three Archbishops
January 30

In Greece during the 11th century there was a popular controversy going on over which of the three fourth-century archbishops—Basil the Great, Gregory the Theologian, or John Chrysostom—was the greatest saint of the Greek Orthodox church. In 1081 Bishop John of Galatia resolved the problem by reporting that the three saints had appeared to him in a vision to say that they were all equal in the eyes of God. Their equality is celebrated on this day, which is also known as the **Holiday of the Three Hierarchs**. In Greek schools special exercises are held in honor of the three, who supported the classical Greek tradition at a time when many early Christians were opposed to all non-Christian literature.

SOURCES:
BkHolWrld-1986, Jan 30

♦ 0497 ♦ Days of '76
First full weekend in August

This three-day celebration held each year in Deadwood, South Dakota, is an attempt to revive the spirit of the gold rush days. It is timed to coincide as closely as possible with the anniversaries of the deaths of "Calamity Jane" Canary (August 1, 1903) and "Wild Bill" Hickok (August 2, 1876), two of Deadwood's most famous residents. The festivities begin with a three-mile-long historical parade that includes floats portraying the various stages of, and characters in,

Deadwood's history—from the earliest settlers to the coming of industry and tourism.

A highlight of the event is the reenactment of the capture and trial of Jack McCall, who shot the much-admired U.S. Marshal James Butler "Wild Bill" Hickok in the back, and who was eventually hanged. Visitors can tour long-abandoned gold mines and the cemetery where Calamity Jane, the famous frontierswoman, Wild Bill Hickok, and the brilliant young minister Henry Weston "Preacher" Smith are buried.

CONTACT:
South Dakota Dept. of Tourism
711 E. Wells Ave.
Pierre, SD 57501
800-952-3625 or 605-773-3301
fax: 605-773-3256

SOURCES:
AnnivHol-1983, p. 176
GdUSFest-1984, p. 172

♦ 0498 ♦ **Daytona 500**
February

The richest of the four biggest NASCAR (National Association for Stock Car Auto Racing) Winston Cup races. It's the final event of the 16-day Speedweeks at Daytona International Speedway in Daytona Beach, Fla. The speedway is a 2.5-mile oval, and racers must complete 200 laps. The all-time champion of the Daytona 500 is Richard Petty, who won seven times (1964, 1966, 1971, 1973, 1974, 1979, and 1981).

The Daytona Speedway, which has a seating capacity of 102,900, has been operating since 1959, but stock-car racing at Daytona dates back to 1936, and car racing has been going on here since the early days of cars. Between 1902 and 1935, thirteen automobile speed records were set on the beach by racing greats Barney Oldfield, Sir Henry Segrave, and Sir Malcolm Campbell, who broke existing records five times.

The speedway was the creation of William H. G. (Bill) France, a mechanic and racer who moved to Daytona Beach in 1934 in the heyday of beach racing. He gave up driving to organize and promote races, and in 1947 founded NASCAR. He had the idea of building the Daytona track in 1953, but financial and political problems delayed its opening until 1959. When he died in 1992, he was known as the father of stock-car racing.

Today the Speedway presents eight weeks of racing events. Speedweeks starts with the Sunbank 24, a 24-hour endurance race; this race and the 24 Hours of Le Mans (France) are the only two 24-hour races for prototype sports cars in the world.

The "crown jewels" of the NASCAR circuit are the Daytona 500, the Winston 500, the Coca-Cola 600, and the Southern 500.

CONTACT:
National Association for Stock Car
   Auto Racing
P.O. Box 2875
Daytona Beach, FL 32115
904-253-0611; fax: 904-258-7646

SOURCES:
Chases-1996, p. 103

Florida Division of Tourism
126 W. Van Buren
Tallahassee, FL 32399
904-487-1462; fax: 904-921-9158

♦ 0499 ♦ **D-Day**
June 6

The day is also known as **Allied Landing Observances Day**. It marks the start of the Allied invasion of occupied France in 1944, which led to the final defeat of Hitler's Germany the following May. The assault, led by U.S. Gen. Dwight D. Eisenhower, was carried out by airborne forces and the greatest armada the world had ever known. About 3,000 ships transported 130,000 British, Canadian, and American troops across the English Channel to land on the beaches of Normandy, which are known historically by their invasion code names: Utah Beach, Omaha Beach, Gold Beach, Juno Beach, Sword Beach.

Airborne troops began parachuting into Normandy at 15 minutes past midnight on June 6, and Landing Craft Transports plowed through the surf to spill troops onto the beaches starting at 6:30 A.M. About 10,000 troops were killed or wounded that day. Each year, simple ceremonies at the Normandy cemeteries commemorate the men who fell.

CONTACT:
French Government Tourist Office
9454 Wilshire Blvd., Ste. 715
Beverly Hills, CA 90212
310-271-6665; fax: 310-276-2835

SOURCES:
AmerBkDays-1978, p. 527
AnnivHol-1983, p. 76
Chases-1996, p. 244
DictDays-1988, p. 29

♦ 0500 ♦ **Dead, Feast for the**
Annually or semiannually

An Iroquois Indian ceremony, the Feast for the Dead—the **'Ohgiwe**—is an attempt to placate the spirits of the dead. Sometimes the 'ohgiwe was used as a healing ceremony, for it was believed that an offended spirit could cause sickness or loss of sleep. Often it was held in the longhouse in the spring or fall as a communal ceremony.

The ceremony itself consists of two long dances, a ritual during which pieces of cloth are waved back and forth and distributed to all the singers and dancers, and the ceremonial carrying out of the kettle or drum. There are social dances after the feast is over, and a mock-struggle over special cakes that have been prepared for the dead.

SOURCES:
DictFolkMyth-1984, p. 816
EncyRel-1987, vol. 7, p. 286

Dead, Feast of the
See **Samhain**

Dead Rat's Ball
See **Bal du Rat Mort**

♦ 0501 ♦ **Decorated Horse, Procession of the**
Between May 21 and June 24; Corpus Christi

According to legend, during the Crusades the ship in which the French king was traveling and bearing the Eucharist, was wrecked on the beach at Brindisi, Italy. The local archbishop salvaged the sacred Host and carried it with him as he rode through the town on a white horse. To commemorate this event, the current Archbishop of Brindisi carries the Most Holy Sacrament in a procession that takes place on Corpus Christi each year. He rides at the head of the procession on a white horse caparisoned in gold, passing through galleries of silk draperies and a constant rain of flowers thrown by spectators. This event is sometimes referred to as the **Procession of the Caparisoned Horse.**

Corpus Christi is celebrated with flowers and colorful processions in other Italian towns and villages as well—those occurring at Genzano and Perugia being among the more spectacular.

CONTACT:
Italian Government Travel Office
630 Fifth Ave.
New York, NY 10111
212-245-4822

SOURCES:
BkFest-1937, p. 186
FestWestEur-1958, p. 98

Dedication, Feast of
See **Hanukkah**

Deepavali
See **Dewali**

♦ 0502 ♦ Deep Sea Fishing Rodeo
Weekend of July 4

The "World's Largest Fishing Rodeo," according to its promoters, and a four-day event staged from Gulfport, Miss. The Mississippi Gulf Coast area is reputed to be one of the world's best natural fish hatcheries, with an abundance of species of fresh-water, salt-water, and deep-sea game fish. The rodeo's fishing waters are the Mississippi Sound of the Gulf of Mexico, and the bayous and creeks within a range of 200 miles north of the Mississippi shoreline.

The rodeo began in 1949, and today attracts from 15,000 to 20,000 people and entrants from 48 states. Prizes are awarded for the top weight in 28 categories of fish. Besides fishing, there are also all the peripherals of a festival: arts and crafts exhibits, dances, a midway, fireworks, bands, and the coronation of a Rodeo Queen.

CONTACT:
Mississippi Division of Tourism
   Development
P.O. Box 849
Jackson, MS 39205
800-927-6378 or 601-359-3297
fax: 601-359-5757

SOURCES:
Chases-1996, p. 283

♦ 0503 ♦ Defenders' Day
September 12

Defenders' Day, a legal holiday in Maryland, celebrates the anniversary of the battle of North Point. The battle took place near Baltimore on September 12, 1814; two days later, the unsuccessful British attack on Baltimore's Fort McHenry inspired Francis Scott Key to jot down the words of "The Star-Spangled Banner." For this reason the two events are celebrated more or less in conjunction on September 12, a day that is sometimes referred to as **National Anthem Day.**

A 56-foot monument at Calvert and Fayette Streets in Baltimore commemorates the 1814 battle, and the star-shaped Fort McHenry is a national monument and an historic shrine. Defenders' Day is celebrated with a number of patriotic events, including an annual mock bombardment of the fort on the Sunday nearest September 12.

CONTACT:
Baltimore Area Convention and
   Visitors Association
100 Light St., 12th Floor
Baltimore, MD 21202
800-343-3468 or 410-659-7300
fax: 410-727-2308

SOURCES:
AmerBkDays-1978, p. 833
AnnivHol-1983, p. 117
Chases-1996, p. 373
DictDays-1988, p. 30

♦ 0504 ♦ Denmark Constitution Day
June 5

This public holiday commemorates the constitution signed on June 5, 1849, that made Denmark a constitutional monarchy, and the one signed on June 5, 1953, that created parliamentary reforms.

A parade takes place in Copenhagen, and other festivities are held in villages throughout Denmark.

CONTACT:
Danish Tourist Board
655 Third Ave., 18th Floor
New York, NY 10017
212-949-2333; fax: 212-983-5260

SOURCES:
AnnivHol-1983, p. 76
Chases-1996, p. 243
NatlHolWrld-1968, p. 33

♦ 0505 ♦ Denmark Flag Day
June 15

According to legend, the Danish King Valdemar set out to conquer the pagan Estonians and convert them to Christianity. During the night of June 15, 1219, the Estonians made a surprise attack on the Danish camp. As he raised his arms toward heaven to pray for help, the Danish archbishop discovered that as long as he could hold his arms up, the Danes were able to push back the enemy. But when they dropped from weariness, the Estonians gained ground. Eventually a red banner with a white cross floated down from the sky and, as the archbishop caught it, he heard a voice from the clouds say that the Danes would win if they raised this banner before their enemies. A messenger took the banner to King Valdemar, and the Danes won the battle.

Schools, sports organizations, and Boy Scout troops in Denmark often hold Flag Day pageants on June 15 in which they reenact the story of the *Dannebrog* (the Danish flag) and King Valdemar. The red and white flag can be seen flying everywhere on this day in honor of its miraculous first appearance.

CONTACT:
Danish Tourist Board
655 Third Ave., 18th Floor
New York, NY 10017
212-949-2333; fax: 212-983-5260

SOURCES:
AnnivHol-1983, p. 80

Den na Buditelite
See **Day of the Enlighteners**

♦ 0506 ♦ Departure of the Continental Army
Saturday nearest June 19

On December 19, 1777, George Washington and between 11,000 and 12,000 of his Continental Army soldiers marched into Valley Forge, about 18 miles north of Philadelphia to set up camp for the winter. The men were exhausted, hungry, and poorly equipped. Severe winter weather didn't make their stay at Valley Forge any easier, and they received only irregular supplies of meat and bread. Between 2,000 and

3,000 of the men died from typhus, typhoid, dysentery, and pneumonia before the winter was over.

It was largely through Washington's leadership and the efforts of Baron Friedrich von Steuben (*see* VON STEUBEN DAY) that the dispirited army was turned into a well-trained, dependable fighting force by the following summer. The anniversary of the day the Continental army marched out of Valley Forge in pursuit of the British, who were moving toward New York, is still celebrated with an historic reenactment that takes place on or near June 19 at the Valley Forge National Historical Park each year.

Other historic events observed at Valley Forge include December 19, the anniversary of the army's arrival; Washington's Birthday Encampment Week in mid-February; and May 6, the French Alliance Day celebration.

CONTACT:
Valley Forge National Historical
  Park
Valley Forge, PA 19481
610-783-1000

SOURCES:
AmerBkDays-1978, p. 1117

♦ 0507 ♦ Derby Day
Late May or early June

The most prestigious horse race in the world. The idea for the race arose at a dinner party in 1779 and was eventually named for the Earl of Derby, one of the guests who was present that evening. Derby Day is held annually at the Epsom Racecourse in Surrey, England, on the second day of the summer meeting, usually in late May or early June. Many companies in England give their employees the day off so they can join in the picnicking that takes place near the course.

Like its American counterpart, the KENTUCKY DERBY, the festivities surrounding the Epsom Derby last far longer than the race itself, which covers a mile and a half and is over in just a few minutes. Only three-year-old colts and fillies can enter, which means that the race can never be won by the same horse twice.

CONTACT:
British Tourist Authority
551 Fifth Ave., Ste. 702
New York, NY 10176
800-462-2748 or 212-986-2200
fax: 212-986-1188

SOURCES:
Chases-1996, p. 243
DictDays-1988, p. 30

♦ 0508 ♦ De Soto Celebration
Mid-March

The celebration also known as **De Soto Landing Day** in Florida is in honor of the young Spanish explorer Hernando de Soto (c. 1500–1542), who arrived on the west coast of Florida, probably near Tampa Bay and the present-day town of Bradenton in 1539. With his band of several hundred conquistadores (conquerors), de Soto set out on a 4,000-mile trek through the wilderness north to the Blue Ridge Mountains, across them, south along the Alabama River to present-day Mobile, across the Mississippi River into what is now Arkansas, and explored further to the south and west. It was the first time a European had explored the North American interior.

The De Soto Celebration held each year in mid-March in Bradenton goes back to 1939. A group of 35 costumed conquistadores reenacts de Soto's landing, coming ashore in longboats and skirmishing with the "Indians" in full view of a grandstand full of spectators. The conquest continues, with the "explorers" pressing onward until they reach Bradenton, where they raid the county courthouse. Most of the men in town grow beards for the occasion, which they then shave off in a race against time at the end of the festival.

CONTACT:
Florida Division of Tourism
126 W. Van Buren
Tallahassee, FL 32399
904-487-1462; fax: 904-921-9158

SOURCES:
AmerBkDays-1978, p. 251
GdUSFest-1984, p. 33

Detroit-Windsor International Freedom Festival
See **Canada Day**

♦ 0509 ♦ Dewali (Divali, Deepavali, Festival of Lights)
October–November; 15th day of waning half of Hindu month of Kartika

The word *dewali* means 'a row or cluster of lights', and the week-long festivities are illuminated by lamps, fireworks, and bonfires. The holiday means different things in different parts of Asia. In northern India it marks the beginning of the Hindu New Year. In Gujarat and Malaysia families clean and whitewash their homes and draw elaborate designs (called *alpanas*) on their floors with colored powder to welcome Lakshmi, the Hindu goddess of wealth and prosperity. Then they set up rows of little clay lamps, decorating their courtyards, windows, and roofs with light in the belief that Lakshmi won't bless a home that isn't lit up to greet her.

In the Punjab and Mauritius, Dewali celebrates the coronation of Rama (an incarnation of Vishnu) after his conquest of Ravana, the ruler of Sri Lanka, who had stolen his wife. In West Bengal it is a Kali festival. In Maharashtra the lights fend off King Bali, the ruler of the underworld. The Jains commemorate the death of their great hero, Mahavira, on this day called Deva Dewali, in the city of Pava in Bihar (*see* MAHAVIR JAYANTI). In Nepal it is TIHAR, a multi-holiday that celebrates the New Year and Lakshmi, sisters honor brothers, and mandalas are prepared for each member of the family.

Dewali is as important to Hindus as CHRISTMAS is to Christians. It is celebrated by the world's 500 million Hindus with gift exchanges, fireworks, and festive (typically vegetarian) meals.

SOURCES:
AnnivHol-1983, p. 176
BkFest-1937, p. 161
BkHolWrld-1986, Nov 1
FolkAmerHol-1991, p. 371
FolkWrldHol-1992, p. 530
GdWrldFest-1985, p. 110
RelHolCal-1993, p. 71

♦ 0510 ♦ Dew Treading
Between April 30 and June 3; Ascension Day

Both city and country dwellers in the Netherlands continue to observe the old folk custom known as **Dauwtrappen** ('dew treading') on ASCENSION DAY. People take their children to the fields—or, in the case of city dwellers, to the suburbs—to walk through the morning dew and gather spring flowers. According to an old superstition, the Ascension Day dew possesses supernatural growing and healing powers. In the country, it is customary for friends and neighbors to meet each other at an inn for a big breakfast afterward.

SOURCES:
FestWestEur-1958, p. 133

◆ 0511 ◆ Dhan Teras
October–November; 13th day of waning half of Hindu month of Kartika

Dhan Teras or **Dhanvantri Trayodashi** is observed two days prior to Dewali, the Hindu Festival of Lights. It is held in honor of Dhanvantri, the physician of the gods and the father of Indian medicine, whom doctors in particular worship on this day. According to Hindu mythology, the gods and the demons tried to produce the elixir known as *amrita* by churning up the ocean. Dhanvantri rose up out of the water bearing a cup filled with it. He is also credited with inventing the traditional system of Indian medicine known as Ayurveda.

On this day Hindus rise at dawn and bathe, put on new robes, and fast. In the evening, they light an earthen lamp before the door of the house and break their fast. It is considered an auspicious day to purchase new utensils.

SOURCES:
RelHolCal-1993, p. 72

Día de Corpo de Deus
See **Corpus Christi**

◆ 0512 ◆ Día de la Santa Cruz
May 3

In Mexico the **Day of the Holy Cross** is primarily observed by miners, masons, and construction workers. They make elaborately decorated crosses and place them on the buildings where they are working. Anyone who is constructing a new building must throw a party for the workers on this day. Fireworks are set off and the occasion is treated as a fiesta.

See also Exaltation of the Cross

SOURCES:
AnnivHol-1983, p. 61
BkFest-1937, p. 228
BkFestHolWrld-1970, p. 93
BkHolWrld-1986, May 3
Chases-1996, p. 198

◆ 0513 ◆ Día de los Tres Reyes
January 6

Throughout most of Latin America, Epiphany is called *el día de los tres reyes* (**Three Kings Day** or **Day of the Wise Men**). It marks the end of the Christmas season that began on December 16 with Posadas. In Mexico, on the night of January 5, children stuff their shoes with hay and leave them out for the Wise Men to fill with sweets and gifts—much as children elsewhere leave their Christmas stockings out for Santa Claus to fill on Christmas Eve. And just as letters to Santa Claus are a popular custom in the United States, Mexican children often write letters to the Magi (the three Wise Men), listing their good deeds and suggesting what gifts they would like to receive.

In Venezuela, children leave straw by their beds so that the Magi's camels will have something to eat. On the morning of January 6 they awake to find the straw gone and gifts delivered in its place.

See also Befana Festival and Twelfth Night

SOURCES:
BkFest-1937, p. 225
DictFolkMyth-1984, p. 346
FolkWrldHol-1992, p. 16

◆ 0514 ◆ Día del Puno
November 5

Many of the festivals celebrated by the Andean Indians of South America commemorate their Incan ancestors. Día del Puno, which is observed in Puno, Peru, reenacts the birth of Manco Capac and Mama Ocllo, the legendary founders of the Inca dynasty. A fleet of *balsas*—skiffs built from reeds, or *totoras*, that are discarded as soon as they become waterlogged—gathers on Lake Titicaca and moves toward Puno. A royal barge carries the two Indians who play the parts of Manco Capac and Mama Ocllo. According to legend, these two were sent by their father, the Sun, to inhabit the Isla de Titicaca, one of the 41 islands in the lake, and become the first human rulers there. A ruined temple still marks the spot where this miraculous birth took place.

On shore, the festival features Indian musicians playing flutes and panpipes in the traditional costumes of the Quechua and Aymara Indians, and dancers twirling beaded strings.

CONTACT:
Embassy of Peru
1700 Massachusetts Ave., N.W.
Washington, D.C. 20036
202-833-9860; fax: 202-659-8124

Día de San Giuseppe
See **St. Joseph's Day**

Día de San Juan
See **St. John the Baptist's Day**

◆ 0515 ◆ Día de San Lorenzo
August 10

St. Laurence of Rome was a deacon under Pope Sixtus II in the third century. According to legend, after the martyrdom of the Pope, St. Laurence was roasted alive on a gridiron. In the midst of his torture, it is said he suggested that his tormentors turn him over to ensure that he would be well-cooked. His feast day is August 10.

As the patron saint of Zinacantan, Mexico, San Lorenzo is honored with a five-day festival that takes place August 7–11 each year. The highlight is a dance performed by the *Capitanes* that involves rhythmic hops on one foot while the other is held in front of the dancer. Thousands attend the festival, which includes a huge open market and spectacular fireworks.

CONTACT:
Mexican Government Tourist
  Office
405 Park Ave., Ste. 1401
New York, NY 10022
800-446-3942 or 212-755-7261
fax: 212-753-2874

SOURCES:
AnnivHol-1983, p. 105
DaysCustFaith-1957, p. 204
DictMyth-1962, vol. II, p. 1374
FolkWrldHol-1992, p. 417
SaintFestCh-1904, p. 361

♦ 0516 ♦ **Dicing for the Maid's Money Day**
Last Thursday in January

In the 17th century, dicing (throwing dice) for money was a favorite English pastime in which large sums of money could be won or lost. However, the annual dicing competition that still takes place in Guildford, England, is for the relatively modest sum of 11 pounds, 19 shillings. In 1674 a local resident named John How established a fund of 400 pounds, which in his will he said he wanted invested and the proceeds distributed each year to a local "maid" or house servant who had served faithfully in the same position for at least two years. The will also stipulated that two servants should throw dice for the gift, and that the one who threw the highest number should receive the entire amount.

In the presence of the mayor, trustees, and assembled townspeople, the two women chosen to participate in this event each year take turns shaking the dice in a special hide-covered, silver-banded dice box which has been used for this purpose over the past century. According to the official Maid's Money receipt book, the recipients of the prize in recent years have been older women who have served faithfully in the same family for many years. But the gift was originally designed for young, unmarried women who might need the money for a dowry.

CONTACT:
British Tourist Authority
551 Fifth Ave., Ste. 702
New York, NY 10176
800-462-2748 or 212-986-2200
fax: 212-986-1188

SOURCES:
AnnivHol-1983, p. 16

♦ 0517 ♦ **Dinagyang**
Last weekend in January

A dancing-in-the-streets carnival on the island of Panay in Iloilo City, Philippines, held a week after the ATI-ATIHAN in Kalibo and the SINULOG in Cebu. Like these festivals, Dinagyang venerates the Santo Niño, or Holy Infant. In Iloilo (pronounced EE-lo-EE-lo) the participation of tribal groups adds to the festival's color, but, unlike the exuberant Kalibo crowds, the spectators in Iloilo are quiet.

CONTACT:
Philippine Department of Tourism
556 Fifth Ave.
First Floor Mezzanine
New York, NY 10036
212-575-7915; fax: 212-302-6759

♦ 0518 ♦ **Dinosaur Days**
Last week in July

A new celebration of very old bones: the dinosaur fossils that rest in Dinosaur, Colo., near Grand Junction, in the Dinosaur National Monument. About 140 million years ago, when the area of Grand Junction was semi-tropical, dinosaurs roamed here. In 1900, the remains of a brachiosaurus, one of the biggest of the dinosaurs, was found four miles west of downtown. Hence, the Dinosaur Days, which started in 1986 and consist of four days of festivities with a reptilian theme.

A foot race, called the Pterodactyl Trot for the ancient bird, starts things off and is followed by a parade of dinosaurs and cave men (anachronisms are allowed), a raft race on the Colorado River, and a street dance (with a rock band, of course) named the Stegosaurus Stomp. Other features are the

T-Rex Tee-off, a golf game played in the wilds with oversized golf balls, and Kids' Day at the dinosaur quarry, during which paleontologists explain the dinosaur digs to children and help them make plaster molds of bones.

CONTACT:
Dinosaur National Monument
4545 Highway 40
Dinosaur, CO 81610
303-374-2216

♦ 0519 ♦ **Dionysia (Bacchanalia)**
Throughout the year

A festival in ancient Greece in honor of Dionysus (also called Bacchus), the son of Zeus and god of wine, fertility, and drama. There were a series of Dionysian festivals: the Oschophoria, the rustic Dionysia, the Lenaea, the ANTHESTERIA, the urban Dionysia, and the most famous—the City or Great Dionysia.

The Great Dionysias were held in the spring (March or April) in Athens for five or six days, and their centerpieces were the performances of new tragedies, comedies, and satyric dramas. These took place in the Theater of Dionysus on the side of the Acropolis and were attended by people from throughout the country. The earliest tragedy that survives is *Persai* by Aeschylus, from the year 472 B.C. The dramatists, actors, and singers were considered to be performing an act of worship of the god, and Dionysus was thought to be present at the productions. The City Dionysias were a time of general springtime rejoicing (even prisoners were released to share in the festivities) and great pomp. The statue of Dionysus was carried in a procession that also included representations of the phallus, symbolizing the god.

Dionysus was both a merry god who inspired great poetry and a cruel god; the Greeks realistically saw wine as something that made people happy and also made them drunk and cruel. Thus, like the god, his festivals seem to have combined contrasting elements of poetry and revelry.

The small rustic Dionysia were festive and bawdy affairs held in December or January at the first tasting of new wine. Besides dramatic presentations, there were processions of slaves carrying the phallus, the singing of obscene lays, youths balancing on a full goat-skin, and the like.

The Leneae, held in Athens in January or February included a procession of jesting citizens through the city and dramatic presentations. The Oschophoria ('carrying of the grape cluster'), held in the fall when the grapes were ripe, was marked by a footrace for youths.

SOURCES:
DictMyth-1962, vol. I, pp. 170, 447
DictFolkMyth-1984, 830, 867

♦ 0520 ♦ **Dipri Festival**
March–April

A celebration held by the Abidji tribe in Gomon, Ivory Coast. The Abidjis are one of about 60 ethnic groups in the country, which became a French colony in 1893 and attained independence in 1960 (*see* IVORY COAST INDEPENDENCE DAY). First, relatives or neighbors meet on the evening before the celebration to reconcile their differences. Then, during the festival, the people go into frenzied trances as they are possessed by *sékés*—beneficient spirits—and stumble, dazed in the street. Some people, supposedly led by the spirits, plunge knives into their bodies and then, with the guidance of the *sékés*, are healed with poultices of raw eggs and herbs. This festival serves several purposes: it resolves conflicts between generations and in the community; it drives away evil spirits; it purifies the celebrants.

CONTACT:
Cote D'Ivoire Embassy
2424 Massachusetts Ave., N.W.
Washington, D.C. 20008
202-797-0300; fax: 202-483-8482

♦ 0521 ♦ **Discovery Day**
November 19; December 5

There are a number of different days referred to by this name, all of which relate to the voyages of Christopher Columbus. In Trinidad and Tobago, August 1 was Discovery Day, in honor of Columbus's discovery of the two islands on his third voyage to the Western Hemisphere. Since 1985, however, August 1 has been observed as Trinidad and Tobago Emancipation Day. In Haiti, Discovery Day is a legal holiday celebrated on December 5, commemorating its discovery by Columbus in 1492. And in Puerto Rico, which Columbus found on his second voyage in 1493, Discovery Day is celebrated on November 19.

See also Columbus Day

SOURCES:
AnnivHol-1983, pp. 102, 149, 156
BkHolWrld-1986, p. 176
Chases-1996, pp. 454, 471

♦ 0522 ♦ **Distaff Day**
January 7

After the 12-day Christmas celebration ended on Twelfth Night or Epiphany, **St. Distaff's Day** was traditionally the day on which women resumed their chores, symbolized by the distaff, a tool used in spinning flax or wool. It was also called **Rock Day**, from the German word *rocken*—"rock" being another name for the distaff. The "spear side" and the "distaff side" were legal terms used to distinguish the inheritance of male from that of female children, and the distaff eventually became a synonym for the female sex as a whole. Distaff Day was not really a church festival, but it was widely observed at one time in England.

Although the women had to return to work after Twelfth Night was over, the men apparently had plenty of time to amuse themselves by setting the flax on fire, in return for which they would get buckets of water dumped on their heads.

SOURCES:
AnnivHol-1983, p. 6
BkDays-1864, vol. I, p. 68
DaysCustFaith-1957, p. 22
DictDays-1988, pp. 32, 96
FolkWrldHol-1992, p. 21
SaintFestCh-1904, p. 57

Divali
See **Dewali**

♦ 0523 ♦ **Divine Holy Spirit, Festival of the**
May

This religious festival was first introduced in Brazil during the 16th century and is still celebrated today in many Brazilian cities. One of the most traditional celebrations takes place in Diamantina. The week-long festivities include Masses and fireworks, culminating in the "parade of the Emperor."

CONTACT:
Brazilian Embassy
3006 Massachusetts Ave., N.W.
Washington, D.C. 20008
202-745-2700; fax: 202-745-2827

♦ 0524 ♦ **Divino, Festa do**
Between May 9 and June 12; Saturday before Pentecost

Festa do Divino celebrations can be found in two of Brazil's most beautiful colonial-era towns: Alcântara and Paraty. The townspeople dress up in colonial costumes, with many playing the roles of prominent figures from Brazilian history. The climax is a visit from the "Emperor," who arrives with his servants for a procession and Mass at the church square. He frees prisoners from the town jail in a symbolic gesture of royal generosity, and strolling musicians known as *Folias do Divino* serenade the townspeople day and night.

CONTACT:
Brazilian Embassy
3006 Massachusetts Ave., N.W.
Washington, D.C. 20008
202-745-2700; fax: 202-745-2827

♦ 0525 ♦ **Djibouti Independence Day**
June 27

On this day in 1977, Djibouti gained autonomy from France, after more than 100 years under French rule. It is observed as a national holiday.

CONTACT:
Djibouti Embassy
1156 15th St., N.W., Ste. 515
Washington, D.C. 20005
202-331-0270; fax: 202-331-0302

SOURCES:
AnnivHol-1983, p. 85
Chases-1996, p. 271

♦ 0526 ♦ **Doan Ngu (Summer Solstice Day)**
May–June; fifth day of fifth lunar month

A celebration of the Summer Solstice in Vietnam. Offerings are made to spirits and ghosts and to the God of Death to fend off epidemics. Offerings are made and human effigies are burned, providing souls to staff the army of the God of Death.

CONTACT:
Vietnamese Embassy
1233 20th St., N.W., Rm. 501
Washington, D.C. 20036
202-861-0737

♦ 0527 ♦ **Doctors' Day**
March 30

Since 1933 this day has been set aside to honor America's physicians. It is the anniversary of the day in 1842 on which Dr. Crawford W. Long removed a tumor from the neck of a man while the patient was anesthetized by ether. Dr. Long was the first acclaimed American physician to use ether as an anesthetic agent in a surgical procedure.

Although Doctors' Day highlights the achievement of Dr. Long, the issue of who really discovered general anesthesia is far from clear. In addition to Dr. Long, Gardner Colton, Horace Wells, and Charles Jackson have also claimed credit for the discovery, although some used nitrous oxide gas while others used ether. It was William Thomas Morton who first demonstrated the use of ether as a general anesthetic in front of a gathering of physicians on October 16, 1846, at Massachusetts General Hospital.

The red carnation is the official flower associated with Doctors' Day.

> **SOURCES:**
> *AnnivHol-1983*, p. 44
> *Chases-1996*, p. 149

♦ 0528 ♦ Dodge City Days
Late July through early August

Dodge City's name alone is enough to conjure up memories of the Old West for the residents of Kansas and the surrounding states who come here to celebrate Dodge City Days every summer. Held annually in late July and early August, the main purpose of the festival is to keep the area's history alive. There are staged shootouts between ''Marshal Dillon'' and the bad guys, a rodeo, a horse show, and parades featuring costumed characters from the Old West on horseback.

First held in 1960, Dodge City Days now attracts crowds of up to 50,000—most of whom are tourists. In recent years the festival has featured entertainment by top country-and-western music stars, and the events have expanded to include a golf tournament, auto racing, and other decidedly non-traditional activities that have little to do with Dodge City's Old West heritage.

CONTACT:
Kansas Division of Travel and
  Tourism
700 S.W. Harrison St., Ste. 1300
Topeka, KS 66603
800-252-6727 or 913-296-2009
fax: 913-296-6988

SOURCES:
Chases-1996, p. 311
GdUSFest-1984, p. 60

Dodge National Circuit Finals Rodeo
See **Circuit Finals Rodeo, National**

♦ 0529 ♦ Dodge Poetry Festival, Geraldine R.
September, every other year

Since the first **Dodge Poetry Festival** was held in 1986, the biennial gathering has grown into a three-day event that draws upwards of 5,000 people—including television crews—for what has been described as ''a grueling but exhilarating marathon of poetry activity.'' Readings, panel discussions, and talks by some of America's most famous poets have made the restored village of Waterloo in rural southern New Jersey synonymous with the word ''poetry'' for the students, writers, and interested spectators who flock to the festival, which is sponsored by the Geraldine R. Dodge Foundation. Mrs. Dodge was a local philanthropist.

Many of the events take place outdoors and include music, food, and strolling performers, giving the whole affair the flavor of a bona fide festival rather than the typical writers' conference. Coverage of the Dodge Festival by the award-winning PBS series ''The Power of the Word,'' hosted by Bill Moyers, is thought to have contributed to the festival's broad public appeal.

CONTACT:
Geraldine R. Dodge Foundation
P.O. Box 1239
Morristown, NJ 07962
201-540-8442; fax: 201-540-1211

♦ 0530 ♦ Dog Days
July 3–August 11

The Dog Days are known as the hottest days of the year in the Northern Hemisphere and usually occur in July and early August. In ancient times, the sultry weather in Rome during these months often made people sick, and they blamed their illnesses on the fact that this was the time of year when Sirius, the Dog Star, rose at about the same time as the sun. Because Sirius was the brightest star, it was thought to add its heat to the sun, producing hot, unhealthy weather. The ancients used to sacrifice a brown dog at the beginning of the Dog Days to appease the rage of Sirius.

Although there are many different ways of calculating which days in any given year are the dog days, and how long they last, it is impossible to be precise. Nowadays it is generally assumed that they fall between July 3 and August 11—slightly later than they occurred in ancient times.

Because of their association with the Dog Star, various beliefs have sprung up involving the behavior of dogs during this period. In the 16th century it was believed that dogs went mad during the Dog Star season. Another name for this time of year, the **canicular days**, comes from the Latin word *canis* meaning ''dog.''

> **SOURCES:**
> *BkDays-1864*, vol. II, p. 5
> *Chases-1996*, p. 281
> *DictDays-1988*, p. 32
> *DictFolkMyth-1984*, p. 918

♦ 0531 ♦ Doggett's Coat and Badge Race
August 1

Established in 1716 by Thomas Doggett, an actor and one of the owners of the Drury Lane Theatre in London, the **Waterman's Derby** is an annual rowing race held on the Thames River between Old Swan Pier and Cadogan Pier. Six young boatmen who have just completed their apprenticeship must row against the tide for a distance of four and a half miles. The winner receives a new pair of breeches, an orange coat, and—because the original race was to commemorate the crowning of King George I—a badge with the Hanoverian white horse on it. There are cash prizes as well: 10 pounds for the winner, and six, five, four, three, or two pounds for the other rowers, according to the order in which they complete the race. When Doggett died in 1721, he left a legacy that would ensure the continuation of both the race and its prizes.

The race is administered by the Fishmongers' Company, of which Doggett was a member.

♦ 0532 ♦ Dogwood Festival
April

A night-and-day celebration of the pink and white dogwoods (and azaleas) blooming everywhere in Atlanta, Ga. The founders of the first festival in 1936 thought the event could make Atlanta "internationally known for its beauty during the blooming of the dogwood trees and be the beginning of an annual pilgrimage to the Gate City of the South." The festival comes close to doing that, even though it lapsed during World War II, and didn't really get going again until 1968. Now this gala event each year attracts about 100,000 people who come not only to see the trees but also for numerous concerts, a hot-air balloon race, an architectural-design competition, a kite-flying exhibition, a street festival on famed Peachtree Street, a bike tour along a trail of dogwoods, and the annual Druid Hill Homes and Garden Tour, conducted on the first day of the festival. Children's activities include parades designed and carried out by children, theatrical performances, and a kite-making workshop. Trees are spotlit at night, and special tours of the lighted Dogwood Trail are offered.

♦ 0533 ♦ Doleing Day
December 21

It was customary at one time in England on St. Thomas's Day for the poorer inhabitants of the parish to call on their wealthier neighbors and receive a gift or 'dole' of food or money. In return, they would give their benefactors a sprig of holly or mistletoe.

The custom of 'going a-gooding', as it was called, gave rise to the name **Gooding Day** in parts of Sussex; in other areas it was referred to as **Mumping (Begging) Day**, since those who had to beg were said to be 'on the mump.' The children would often spend St. Thomas's Day begging for apples.

Doll Festival
See **Hina Matsuri**

♦ 0534 ♦ Dol Purnima
February–March; full moon day of Hindu month of Phalguna

The Dol Purnima festival, celebrated throughout India by followers of Krishna, occurs on the same day as the birthday of Chaitanya Mahaprabhu (1486–1534), also known as Gauranga, the 16th-century Vishnavite saint and poet of Bengal, regarded as an incarnation of Krishna. It is therefore a significant festival for Hindus, who carry an image of Lord Krishna, covered with colored powder and placed in a swinging cradle, through the streets as they sing songs composed especially for the occasion.

♦ 0535 ♦ Dom Fair
November through Christmas

The **Hamburger Dom**, or Dom Fair, is one of the most famous Christmas fairs in the world. It was named after its original location, which was in the open square in front of the Dom, or cathedral, in Hamburg, Germany. Today the fair is held in the Heiligengeistfeld, or Holy Ghost Field, in the center of town. It features booths filled with toys, gingerbread, crafts, and other temptations for holiday shoppers. The Dom opens in November and doesn't close until just before Christmas, giving shoppers from Hamburg and the surrounding area plenty of time to buy their gifts.

♦ 0536 ♦ Dominica Independence Day
November 3

On this day in 1978, Dominica gained independence from Britain as it became a member of the Commonwealth. It is celebrated as a national holiday for three days, including November 3.

♦ 0537 ♦ Dominican Republic Independence Day
February 27

In the 1830s Juan Pablo Duarte (1813–1876)—known as "the father of Dominican independence"—organized a secret society known as *La Trinitaria* to fight the Haitians. After a long struggle, independence was finally declared on February 27, 1844. Although disorder, dictatorships, and intermittent peace characterized the Dominican Republic's history until the U.S. Marines occupied it from 1916 to 1924 to keep peace between rival political groups, February 27 is still observed as the country's Independence Day and is celebrated with parades and political meetings. The site of the proclamation, Independence Park, contains a shrine known as the *Altar de la Patria*, 'the nation's altar,' honoring the three founders of the Republic—Duarte, Ramón Mella, and Juan Sánchez Ramírez. Duarte's birthday, January 26, is also a public holiday, celebrated as Duarte Day.

CONTACT:
Dominican Republic Embassy
1715 22nd St., N.W.
Washington, D.C. 20008
202-332-6280; fax: 202-265-8057

SOURCES:
AnnivHol-1983, p. 29
Chases-1996, p. 113
NatlHolWrld-1968, p. 27

Dominion Day
See **Canada Day**

Dormition of the Mother of God
See **Assumption, Feast of the**

♦ 0538 ♦ Dosmoche
December–January; 28th day of 12th lunar month

This five-day **Tibetan New Year** festival begins with the erection of a large *dosmo*, or magical pole, decorated with pentagrams, stars, and crosses made out of string. The lamas make a food and drink offering to the Buddha and the gods after the dosmo is in place. The following day is devoted to various prayers and rituals designed to drive away evil. The *lo si-sku-rim*, or 'ceremony of the dying year,' is held, during which dancers wearing hideous demons' masks try to scare off the hostile spirits. A similar custom involves throwing *tsamba* (toasted barley or wheat flour) until everyone is covered in white—a ceremony known as *Yangdrug*, or 'the gathering of luck.' As evening falls, the dosmo is surrendered to the people, who have been waiting patiently to tear it down.

SOURCES:
FolkWrldHol-1992, p. 658

Double Seventh
See **Seven Sisters Festival**

♦ 0539 ♦ Double Tenth Day
October 10

A national holiday in Taiwan to commemorate the Chinese Revolution of October 10, 1911. The revolt marked the end of the Ching, or Qing, Dynasty that had been established in 1644 by the Manchus, and it led to the founding of the Republic of China on January 1, 1912.

It took the Ching rulers several decades to complete their military conquest of China and by 1683, when Taiwan became part of the empire, they governed all of China. The Ching Court's period of glory was in the time of the first three emperors, but after 1795 the court began a slow decline. By the end of the 19th century, Japan and the Western powers had reduced China to what Sun Yat-sen called a "sub-colony," the court was weak and corrupt, and a group of national capitalists was fomenting uprisings. Sun Yat-sen was one of the leaders of this nationalistic group; he was a Jeffersonian figure who wanted a Western-style government with a parliament and separation of powers.

In October 1911, when a revolt in Wuhan (in the province of Hubei) succeeded, supportive uprisings broke out in other cities. The fall of the Manchus followed. Sun Yat-sen, who was in Denver, Colo., at the time of the October revolt, returned to Shanghai and was elected provisional president of the new republic. He is thought of today as the father of

modern China, and his birthday on Nov. 12 is also a national holiday in Taiwan.

For several weeks before Double Tenth Day, the plaza in front of the Presidential Office Building in Taipei, Taiwan, is illuminated. Here there are massive parades and rallies on the holiday, displays of martial arts, folk dancing, and other cultural activities. One of the world's most dazzling displays of fireworks is presented over an island in the middle of the Tanshui River.

See also Sun Yat-sen's Birthday

CONTACT:
Taiwan Visitors Association
1 World Trade Center, Ste. 7953
New York, NY 10048
212-466-0691; fax: 212-432-6436

SOURCES:
AnnivHol-1983, p. 131
Chases-1996, p. 411
NatlHolWrld-1968, p. 189

Doughnut Tuesday
See **Shrove Tuesday**

♦ 0540 ♦ Dozynki Festival
August 15

For many Christians around the world, August 15 is the Feast of the Assumption. But in Poland, it is also a time for celebrating the harvest. During the wheat harvest festival known as **Dozynki Pod Debami**, or **Festival under the Oaks**, the reapers make wreaths out of grain, flowers, nuts and corn. When they present their wreaths to the master and mistress of the estate on which the wheat is grown, they are invited in for a feast, which is followed by dancing.

For Americans of Polish descent living in Orange County, New York—one of the richest onion-growing areas in the United States—the Dozynki Festival underwent a brief revival around 1940 under the name of the **Feast of Our Lady of the Flowers**. In the village of Florida, the streets were banked high with piles of onions, and there was a huge parade with floats depicting the arrival of the Polish immigrants in America and various aspects of the onion production industry. There was a costumed pageant in which the onion farmers presented the Lord and Lady of the Manor with a huge wreath of onions and flowers, followed by the Onion Dance, which had been created especially for the festival. Although a celebration of this magnitude was the exception, the Assumption had always been a holiday for the Polish onion farmers of Orange County.

SOURCES:
FolkAmerHol-1991, p. 309
FolkWrldHol-1992, p. 462

♦ 0541 ♦ Drachenstich (Spearing the Dragon)
Mid-August

The performance of an open-air play, *Drachenstich*, in Fürth, Germany, in the Bavarian Forest. The climax of the play is a battle between a knight on horseback and a huge (about 50-feet long and 10-feet tall), fire-spewing dragon. The knight, of course, wins—by thrusting his spear into the dragon's throat, thereby piercing a pig's bladder filled with ox blood. Besides the dragon-sticking, the celebrations include various merrymaking events and a street procession. The play has been performed for about 500 years, and is thought to be based on a pagan legend or to be connected with religious processions.

CONTACT:
German National Tourist Office
122 E. 42nd St., 52nd Floor
New York, NY 10168
212-661-7200; fax: 212-661-7174

♦ 0542 ♦ Dragon Boat Festival (Tuan Yang Chieh)
Fifth day of fifth lunar month

Chu'ü Yüan (328–298 B.C.) was a Chinese poet and statesman of the Chou Dynasty who drowned himself in the Tungting Lake to protest the corruption and injustice of Prince Huai's court. The colorful dragon boat races that take place on lakes and rivers throughout China on this day are a reenactment of the search for his body, which was never found. Although the shape of the boats has changed over time, most are narrow shells about 100-feet long with a dragon's head at the prow and a drummer beating out the rhythm for his crew of up to 50 rowers.

It is said that rice dumplings were cast on the water to lure fish away from the martyr's body. Chinese people in the United States, Hong Kong, and other countries celebrate the Dragon Boat Festival (also called the **Fifth Month Festival** or **Summer Festival**) by eating special dumplings made of steamed rice wrapped in banana leaves.

CONTACT:
China National Tourist Office
350 Fifth Ave., Ste. 6413
New York, NY 10165
212-760-9700; fax: 212-760-8809

SOURCES:
BkFest-1937, p. 79
BkHolWrld-1986, Jun 18
DictFolkMyth-1984, pp. 206, 225, 1130, 1185
FolkAmerHol-1991, p. 204
FolkWrldHol-1992, pp. 310, 312
GdWrldFest-1985, p. 106
IntlThFolk-1979, p. 197

♦ 0543 ♦ Dragon Boat International Races
Week after fifth day of fifth lunar month

An international boat race held in Hong Kong usually a week after the traditional Chinese DRAGON BOAT FESTIVAL that commemorates the death of the poet Chu'ü Yüan. The dragon boats are built to strict specifications, and the crew may not exceed 22 people, of whom one must be the drummer and one the steersman. Teams from throughout the world enter the races which raise money for the Community Chest of Hong Kong.

CONTACT:
Hong Kong Tourist Association
590 Fifth Ave.
New York, NY 10036
212-869-5008; fax: 212-730-2605

SOURCES:
Chases-1996, p. 275

♦ 0544 ♦ Dramatic Arts Festival at Avignon
July

The month-long **Festival Annuel d'Art Dramatique** was founded by 1947 by Jean Vilar, a well-known French actor and director. When he was invited to direct the first annual drama festival at Avignon, his approach was an innovative one, using bold movements and simplified sets on the large outdoor stage. His success at Avignon eventually led to his appointment as director of the Théâtre National Populaire.

In addition to the festival's large theatrical productions, there are performances that recall the popular pageants of the Middle Ages. Some of the events take place in the city's many historical buildings, while others overflow into the streets. The Dramatic Arts Festival has made Avignon the kind of cultural center to which other Provençal towns aspire, and it regularly attracts a cosmopolitan crowd from all over Europe.

CONTACT:
French Government Tourist Office
9454 Wilshire Blvd., Ste. 715
Beverly Hills, CA 90212
310-271-6665; fax: 310-276-2835

SOURCES:
IntlThFolk-1979, p. 99
MusFestEurBrit-1980, p. 74

♦ 0545 ♦ Drymiais
March 1–3

In Macedonia, the first three days of March are known as Drymiais and are associated with a number of superstitious beliefs. No trees are pruned or planted during this period because it is believed that they will wither. The same fate awaits trees that are pruned or planted during the last three days of March or on any Wednesday or Friday during the month.

The first day of March is traditionally considered to mark the beginning of spring. One custom is for Macedonian mothers to tie pieces of red and white yarn, twisted together, around their children's wrists on this day (*see* MARTENITZA). When they see a swallow, the children throw the skein of yarn to the bird as an offering or place it under a stone. If they lift the stone a few days later and find a swarm of ants beneath it, they can expect a healthy and prosperous year.

SOURCES:
FolkWrldHol-1992, p. 152

♦ 0546 ♦ Dukang Festival
December 15

A trade fair and festival held in Yichuan in the Henan province of China. This was the homeland of Dukang, who is supposed to have discovered alcoholic beverages 4,000 years ago (as Dionysus, in Greek mythology, invented wine). A Chinese folk tale tells of Dukang's beverage intoxicating the eight deities, and a poem contains the line, "Who other than Dukang can relieve me of my grief?" Dukang has become a synonym for liquor, and is also the name of a distillery in Yichuan.

The trade fair highlights not only wines and spirits but also cooking oil and food products, electrical appliances, dyes, and other manufactured goods. The festival features performances by opera troupes and dance ensembles.

CONTACT:
China National Tourist Office
350 Fifth Ave., Ste. 6413
New York, NY 10165
212-760-9700; fax: 212-760-8809

♦ 0547 ♦ Dulcimer and Harp Convention
Second weekend in June

Founded in 1962 by Jean and Lee Schilling, this annual festival takes place at the Folk Life Center of the Smokies in Cosby, Tenn., which is dedicated to the study and preservation of southern Appalachian folk traditions. There is a modern amphitheater on the Center's 19-acre grounds in the foothills of the Great Smoky Mountains where most of the musical demonstrations and concerts are held. There are also workshops for those who play the musical saw, jew's harp, mountain dulcimer, hammered dulcimer, autoharp, bowed psaltery, and banjo. Both renowned instrumentalists and amateurs from all over the United States attend the two-day festival, which includes jam sessions, craft displays, and special activities for children.

CONTACT:
Folk Life Center of the Smokies
P.O. Box 8
Cosby, TN 37722
615-487-5543

SOURCES:
MusFestAmer-1990, p. 228

♦ 0548 ♦ Dulcimer Days
Third weekend in May

The hammered dulcimer is a stringed musical instrument in which the strings are beaten with small hammers rather than plucked with the fingers. It is a favorite with American folk musicians, many of whom gather in Coshocton, Ohio, each year for the **Mid-Eastern Regional Dulcimer Championships**. The competition takes place near Roscoe Village, a restored 1830s canal town. In addition to the musical competition there are exhibits, workshops dealing with the hammered and mountain dulcimers—the latter being a narrow folk-zither with three to five metal strings—and jam sessions. The winners of the Dulcimer Days competition are given a chance to compete in the national competition held each year in Winfield, Kansas.

CONTACT:
Ohio Division of Travel and
    Tourism
P.O. Box 1001
Columbus, OH 43266
800-282-5393 or 614-466-8844
fax: 614-466-6744

SOURCES:
Chases-1996, p. 215

♦ 0549 ♦ Durga Puja
September–October; waxing half of Hindu month of Asvina

There are various Hindu festivals on the Indian subcontinent that celebrate the victory of good over evil.

The festival in Calcutta, India, in the state of West Bengal, India, honors Durga, who rides a lion and destroys demons. She is one aspect of the Mother Goddess and the personification of energy, and is famous for slaying the buffalo demon, Mahisasura. During the 10 days of Durga Puja, the city becomes one great festival, with deafening music and fireworks. Before the *puja* (a Sanskrit word meaning 'worship' or 'homage'), artisans have constructed clay figures over straw-and-bamboo frames, some of them 10 feet high. Stages are set up for these figures in neighborhoods throughout the city, and for four days throngs of people admire the clay tableaux, often showing Durga on a lion slaying demons. (Artist Aloke Sen's images have become famous because his demons have the faces of ordinary men and women and represent such evils as lust, anger, vanity, and greed.) On the fourth night, the images, which are genuine works of art and have cost as much as $20,000, are taken down from the stages, placed on bamboo stretchers, and carried—to the music of hundreds of bagpipers and other musicians—to the banks of the Hooghly River and tossed in. As they float toward the mouth of the Ganges, they dissolve back into clay, straw and bamboo.

Navaratri. In the states of southern India this festival is known as Navaratri (nine nights), and also involves the worship of the goddesses Lakshmi and Sarasvati. Lakshmi is linked with wealth and good luck, and Sarasvati is associated with a river of that name, as well as with fertility, wisdom, and education. The festival is a time for visiting friends and relatives, and houses are decorated with displays of toys and dolls and images of gods. In the state of Gujarat there are nine days of music and dancing devoted to the nine forms of the goddess Ambaji, as well as competitions of *garba* dancing.

Dussehra (or **Dashara**). In other parts of India the festival also celebrates the victory of Lord Rama over Ravana, and is known as Dussehra (Dashara).

During the 10 days of Dussehra, scenes from the epic poem *Ramayana* are enacted. The epic tells the story of Lord Rama who wins the lovely Sita for his wife, only to have her carried off by evil 10-headed Ravana, demon king of Lanka. Ultimately, Rama slays Ravana, and the forces of good triumph over evil. The dramatizations with music, held throughout northern India, are considered at their best in Delhi. On the 10th day, immense effigies of demon Ravana, his brother, and his son (all of them stuffed with firecrackers) explode in dramatic bursts of flame and noise.

In the northern mountains of Himachal Pradesh, the festival begins with a procession of deities to the town of Kulu from the little hill temples of neighboring villages. Accompanying the deities are villagers blowing large horns, ringing bells, and beating drums. When a deity arrives in Kulu, it is placed before Raghunathji, the presiding god of Kulu Valley, who is in an honored position in a tent. Outside, there is folk dancing and music. On the final day of the festival, a bull is sacrificed as a gift to the gods.

Mysore, in the state of Karnataka, celebrates the victory of goddess Chamundi over demon Mahisasura with regal pomp. The palace of the maharajah is illuminated, there are torchlight and daylight parades, and deities on decorated barges in a floodlit lake. On the final day, there is a grand procession of magnificently caparisoned elephants, the camel corps, the cavalry, and the infantry.

Dasain. In Nepal, the festival is called Dasain, or Bada Dasain. It comes at the end of the long monsoon period when days are clear and the rice is ready for harvesting, and lasts for 10 days.

In Nepal, Buddhists also celebrate this festival and special events are held at Buddhist shrines in Patan and Bhaktapur. The Nepalese also modify the *Ramayana* story to include the goddess Durga's victory over the forces of evil represented by the demon Mahisasura. Since Durga is bloodthirsty, there are thousands of animal sacrifices.

Before the festival begins, Nepalese clean their houses and set up ferris wheels and swings in their villages. On the first day of the festival, a water jug called a *kalash* is filled with holy water, and barley seeds are planted in cow dung on the outside of the jug. During the festival, the seeds are sprinkled with the water, and ceremonies are performed around it.

The first big day of the festival is the seventh day, Fulpati, meaning 'day of flowers.' A royal kalash holding flowers is carried by Brahmin priests from the ancestral palace in Gurkha to Katmandu. Cannons boom, the king and queen review troops, and then revere the flowers at the Hanuman Dhoka Palace, the old residence of kings.

The eighth night is known as Kalratri, or 'black night.' At midnight, at Hanuman Dhoka, eight buffaloes and 108 goats are beheaded. During the next day, thousands of buffaloes, goats, and chickens are sacrificed in temples, military posts, and homes as people ask Durga for protection. Blood is sprinkled on the wheels of vehicles, and at the airport, a goat is sacrificed for each Royal Nepal Airlines aircraft.

The 10th day, Vijaya Dashami, commemorates the day that Durga (or Rama) appeared riding a lion to slay the Mahisasura (or Ravana). On this day, people wear the fresh shoots of the barley in their hair and visit older relatives to receive the red *tika* blessing on their foreheads. In towns of the Katmandu Valley, there are masked dances and processions of priests carrying wooden swords, symbolic of the sword used to kill the buffalo demon.

Caitra Dasain, observed in the month of Caitra (March–April), is similar to Bada Dasain, but observed with less pomp. On this earlier occasion, the goddess Bhagavati is worshipped and animal sacrifices are made to her.

CONTACT:
India Tourist Office
30 Rockefeller Ave.
15 N. Mezzanine
New York, NY 10112
212-586-4901; fax: 212-582-3274

Nepal Embassy
2131 Leroy Pl., N.W.
Washington, D.C. 20008
202-667-4550; fax: 202-667-5534

SOURCES:
AnnivHol-1983, pp. 175, 176
BkFest-1937, p. 161
BkHolWrld-1986, Oct 13
DictWrldRel-1989, p. 280
FolkWrldHol-1992, p. 500
GdWrldFest-1985, p. 110
RelHolCal-1993, pp. 69, 72

Dussehra
See **Durga Puja**

♦ 0550 ♦ **Dutch Liberation Day**
May 5

Liberation Day, or **National Day**, in the Netherlands celebrates the day on which the Nazi forces were driven out of Holland by the Allies in 1945. Although the Dutch had succeeded in remaining neutral during World War I, the country was invaded by the Nazis in May 1940 and rapidly overrun. Despite the occupation, however, the Dutch managed to make a significant contribution to the Allied cause by building up an effective resistance. The liberation of Holland in 1945, in which the resistance played a leading part, was an important step leading to the subsequent defeat of the Nazis.

Many Dutch cities hold military parades and special concerts on this day. A special service of commemoration is held in Amsterdam's Dam Square on May 5 each year.

CONTACT:
Netherlands Board of Tourism
355 Lexington Ave., 21st Floor
New York, NY 10017
212-370-7360; fax: 212-370-9507

SOURCES:
AnnivHol-1983, p. 61
Chases-1996, p. 202

Dzam Ling Chi Sang
See **Universal Prayer Day**

E

♦ 0551 ♦ **Eagle Dance**
Early spring

Many North American Indians associate the eagle with supernatural powers, particularly the power to control thunder and rain. In the Jemez and Tesuque pueblos in New Mexico, the eagle dance takes place in the early spring. Two dancers, representing male and female, wear feathered caps with yellow beaks and hold wings made out of eagle feathers. They circle each other with hopping and swaying motions. The Comanches hold an eagle dance where a single dancer imitates the eagle, who according to legend is the young son of a chieftain who was turned into an eagle when he died. Dancers in the Iowa tribe's eagle dance carry an eagle feather fan in their left hands, while the Iroquois eagle dance features feathered rattles and wands.

Among some tribes, eagle feathers are believed to exert special powers. The Sioux wear them in their war bonnets for victory, while the Pawnee, Yuchi, Delaware, and Iroquois Indians use them in ceremonial fans or brushes or as ornaments.

SOURCES:
DictFolkMyth-1984, p. 333
EncyRel-1987, vol. 4, p. 466

♦ 0552 ♦ **Earth Day**
April 22

The first Earth Day was observed on April 22, 1970, for the purpose of drawing public attention to the need for cleaning up the earth's air and water and for conserving our natural resources. Since that time the idea has spread, and Earth Day is now observed regularly throughout the United States and in many other countries (though there were some years of slack observance until the late 1980s).

Typical ways of celebrating Earth Day include planting trees, picking up roadside trash, and conducting various programs for recycling and conservation. School children may be asked to use only recyclable containers for their snacks and lunches, and environmentally concerned families often try to give up wasteful habits, such as using paper towels or plastic garbage bags.

"Earth" days have been observed by other groups as well.

The day of the VERNAL EQUINOX is also observed by some as Earth Day.

SOURCES:
AnnivHol-1983, pp. 40, 55
Chases-1996, p. 181

♦ 0553 ♦ **Easter**
Between March 22 and April 25 in the West and between April 4 and May 8 in the East; first Sunday after the first full moon on or following the vernal equinox

Easter is the principal feast of the Christian year, despite the popularity and commercialization that surrounds CHRISTMAS. According to the Gospel of John, Mary Magdalene came to the cave where Jesus had been buried and found the tomb empty. An angel of the Lord told her that Jesus had risen. The anniversary of his resurrection from the dead is joyfully celebrated by Christians every year with special services, music, candlelight, flowers, and the ringing of church bells that had remained silent during LENT.

For Orthodox Christians, the sorrow of GOOD FRIDAY lifts with the service of the Holy Resurrection on Saturday night in a dimly lit church. At midnight, all lights are extinguished, the door to the altar opens and the priest, holding a lighted candle, appears and proclaims that Christ is risen. The congregants light their candles from the priest's, bells ring, people turn to each other and say, *Christos Anesti*, "Christ is risen," and receive the reply, *Alithos Anesti*, "He is risen indeed."

In Cyprus, fireworks are set off, ships in ports blow their whistles and bonfires are built to burn Judas. People go home for a late dinner starting with red-dyed hard-boiled eggs and then a special soup and often cheese pie (*tiropita*). It's customary to tap the eggs against each other; whoever cracks the other's egg will have good luck in the coming year. Often there is feasting on lamb roasted on spits over open fires; other traditional foods are *kokoretsi*, a sausage made of lamb innards and herbs, and *lambropsomo*, an Easter bread with a whole red-dyed egg in the center. In the countryside, the feasting is accompanied by fairs and dancing in regional costume. Passersby are offered lamb, red eggs, and wine and are toasted with "Christos Anesti."

Easter is a movable holiday whose day of observation has for centuries been painstakingly calculated. This is because its day of observance is determined initially by the lunar calendar, like Passover, but then must be put into terms of the solar calendar. After many centuries of controversy among Christians, Western Christendom settled on the use of the Gregorian calendar (Eastern Christians use the Julian calendar to determine Easter), decreeing that Easter shall be celebrated on the Sunday after the full moon on or following the vernal equinox. If the full moon is on a Sunday, Easter is held the next Sunday. In the East, Easter can occur between April 4 and May 8, but it must come after Passover has ended. In 1997, the World Council of Churches proposed that the Eastern and Western churches celebrate Easter on the same date.

The name for Easter may have come from *Eostre*, the Teutonic goddess of spring and fertility, whose feast was celebrated around this same time. There is also a Germanic goddess named Ostara who was always accompanied by a hare—possibly the ancestor of our modern Easter Bunny. The association of both the rabbit and eggs with Easter is probably the vestige of an ancient springtime fertility rite.

Although Easter has retained a greater religious significance than Christmas, many children in the United States think of it as a time to get new spring clothes, to decorate eggs, and to indulge in the chocolate and jelly beans that the Easter Bunny has left in their Easter baskets.

In Belgium, throughout Walloonia, the priest gives a number of unconsecrated priest's wafers to young children to sell to householders. The proceeds are given to the needy parish families, and the wafers are nailed over the front doors to protect the families from evil.

In Ethiopia, Easter is called **Fasika** and is welcomed in the capital city of Addis Ababa at dawn with a 21-gun salute.

SOURCES:
AmerBkDays-1978, p. 299
BkDays-1864, vol. I, p. 423
BkFest-1937, pp. 6, 16, 24, 30, 42, 57, 70, 87, 96, 113, 121, 133, 148, 168, 185, 211, 219, 228, 241, 249, 260, 268, 276, 287, 292, 301, 309, 317, 330, 339
DaysCustFaith-1957, pp. 108, 353
DictFolkMyth-1984, pp. 129, 181, 212, 334, 561, 628, 687, 789, 854, 947
FestSaintDays-1915, p. 73
FestWestEur-1958, pp. 9, 24, 35, 61, 95, 108, 126, 130, 152, 164, 213, 231
FolkAmerHol-1991, p. 152
FolkWrldHol-1992, p. 189
GdUSFest-1984, p. 144
IndianAmer-1989, pp. 274, 277
RelHolCal-1993, p. 73
SaintFestCh-1904, p. 162

♦ 0554 ♦ **Easter among the Yaqui Indians**
Between March 22 and April 25

Although they were originally Mexican, the Yaqui Indians

resettled in Arizona, and most of them now live near Tucson or Phoenix. During Holy Week they perform a series of dances and pageants that combine Christian, Native American, and Spanish customs. They act out their own version of the biblical events associated with Easter, using spectacular masks and costumes and incorporating the complicated symbolism of their native culture as well as such recognizable Christian figures as Jesus, the Virgin Mary, Judas, and Pilate.

When the Yaqui lived in Mexico, a group of ritual clowns known as the Chapayekas played the role of police during the Easter week celebrations. They wore masks made out of goat or wild pig skin with long earns and snouts (*chapayekas* means 'long slender noses') and huge horns. They maintained a ritual silence and communicated only by sign language. Today they still play a part in Yaqui Easter observances, performing dances during Easter processions and church services. At noon on Easter Sunday, they rush out of the church and burn all of their paraphernalia except their masks and deer-hoof belts.

CONTACT:
Pascua Yaqui Tribal Council
7474 S. Camino de Oeste
Tucson, AZ 85746
602-883-2838

SOURCES:
AmerBkDays-1978, p. 304
DictFolkMyth-1984, p. 212
IndianAmer-1989, p. 274

♦ 0555 ♦ **Easter Egg Roll**
Between March 23 and April 26; Monday following Easter

Starting in the middle of the 19th century, it was customary for young children to roll Easter eggs on the lawn of the Capitol Building in Washington, D.C. But Congress objected to the damage they inflicted on the grass and in 1878 stationed guards there to halt the practice. President Rutherford B. Hayes, who enjoyed children, said they could use the White House lawn. President Franklin D. Roosevelt stopped the custom during World War II, but then it was restored again in 1953 by President Dwight D. Eisenhower.

Today the Egg Roll takes place on the Ellipse behind the White House, and children up to age eight are invited to participate. In addition to rolling their own hard-boiled eggs, the children hunt for about 1,000 wooden eggs—many of them signed by past presidents or celebrities—that have been hidden in the grass. A crowd of up to 10,000 adults and children gathers for the annual event, and sometimes the president greets the crowd from the balcony of the White House.

CONTACT:
Washington D.C. Convention and Visitors Association
1212 New York Ave., N.W., Ste. 600
Washington, D.C. 20005
800-635-6338 or 202-789-7000
fax: 202-789-7037

SOURCES:
AmerBkDays-1978, p. 308
BkFest-1937, p. 16
Chases-1996, p. 163

♦ 0556 ♦ **Easter Festival (Osterfestspiele)**
Beginning between March 15 and April 18 through between March 22 and April 26; Palm Sunday through Easter Monday

Salzburg's Easter festival was founded by the famous conductor Herbert von Karajan (1908–1989) in 1967 to honor the works of Richard Wagner (1813–1883), and it remains one of Europe's most elite and elegant music festivals. Those who attend pay top prices, but in return they get to hear some of the world's greatest performers. The Berlin Philharmonic Orchestra is the festival's resident ensemble, and the chorus of the Vienna State Opera or the Choir of the Society of Friends of Music in Vienna perform the choral works. Von Karajan himself conducted all of the concerts, which include the works of BACH, Beethoven, Brahms, Mahler, MOZART and Verdi, until his death in 1989. Now various conductors are invited. A full-scale opera is performed twice during each nine-day festival in the *Grosses Festspielhaus* (large festival hall), which is known for its unique acoustics and seats more than 2,000.

CONTACT:
Austrian National Tourist Office
P.O. Box 1142, Times Square
New York, NY 10148
212-944-6880; fax: 212-730-4568

SOURCES:
MusFestEurBrit-1980, p. 20

♦ 0557 ♦ **Easter Fires**
March–April; Easter eve

A tradition of hillside fires on EASTER eve in Fredericksburg, Tex. The tradition is thought to have begun many years ago, soon after the town's settlement by German farmers in 1846. A pioneer mother, to calm her children, told them the fires burning on the town's hillside had been lit by the Easter Bunny to boil their Easter eggs. In reality, the fires were those of Indians who were watching the settlement—but since then, fires glow on the hillside every Easter.

SOURCES:
AmerBkDays-1978, p. 299

Easter in Bermuda
See **Good Friday in Bermuda**

♦ 0558 ♦ **Easter in Bulgaria**
Between March 22 and April 25

Although midnight church services are widespread throughout Bulgaria on **Velikden** (The Great Day), or **Vuzkresenie** (Resurrection Day), the EASTER service held in the cathedral in Sofia, the capital, is by far the most impressive. Just before midnight on Easter morning, the traditional hour of Christ's resurrection, a procession of church dignitaries in elaborate vestments follows the archbishop from the cathedral to Alexander Nevsky Square, which is already filled with thousands of worshippers carrying unlighted candles. As the midnight chimes peal, the archbishop blesses the people and the thousands of candles are lit. A service in the cathedral follows.

Easter celebrations in Bulgaria last a full week, known as *Svetla Nedelya*, or the Week of Light, because the peasants believe that the sun did not set in Jerusalem for eight days after the resurrection of Christ. A principal form of amusement during this week is the national dance known as the *Choro*, which is performed by a circle composed of equal numbers of male and female dancers who begin with a very slow movement that gradually quickens in pace.

CONTACT:
Bulgarian Embassy
1621 22nd St., N.W.
Washington, D.C. 20008
202-387-7969; fax: 202-234-7973

SOURCES:
BkFest-1937, p. 70
FestSaintDays-1915, p. 82

♦ 0559 ♦ **Easter in Germany (Ostern)**
Between March 22 and April 25

The first recorded evidence of a rabbit being associated with EASTER dates from the 16th century in Germany, although the custom may be even older. The Easter hare still brings eggs to German children and hides them in out-of-the-way places, although in the past, the stork, the fox, and the cuckoo have played the same role. In many parts of Germany, little "rabbit gardens" are built for the Easter bunny, using moss or grass as a nest for the eggs. Egg-gathering and egg-rolling are both popular activities at Easter, as are contests to see who can devour the greatest number of eggs.

Perhaps a remnant of ancient sacrificial rites, bonfires are built on high points of land in northern Germany. Although usually built out of huge piles of tar-soaked barrels and old tree roots and limbs, in the Westphalian village of Luegde, bonfires are made by tying twigs and straw to seven-foot wheels, lighting them, and rolling them down the hill. The flaming wheels, symbolic of the sun, weigh about 800 pounds each. Every time one of them reaches the bottom of the hill, the spectators shout for joy, for it is believed that this will bring a special blessing to the land and a bountiful harvest.

Water is also associated with Easter celebrations in Germany. One old custom entails girls in the Harz, Thuringia, and other regions rising at dawn to draw "Easter water" from the rivers. If they do so in complete silence and then bathe in the water, they will be blessed with beauty throughout the year. Easter morning dew is used for the same purpose.

"Easter smacks," or *Schmeckostern*, are traditional beatings that the men and women give to each other in various parts of Germany to bring them luck, to protect them from disease, and to keep them young and healthy. The men beat the women on EASTER MONDAY, and the women beat the men on Easter Tuesday. The new life contained by a green branch is supposed to be bestowed on the one who is beaten with it.

SOURCES:
BkFest-1937, p. 133
BkFestHolWrld-1970, p. 60
DictFolkMyth-1984, p. 335
FestWestEur-1958, p. 61
RelHolCal-1993, p. 74

♦ 0560 ♦ **Easter in Hollywood**
Between March 22 and April 25

The early Christians believed that on EASTER morning, the sun danced in honor of the resurrection of Christ. This led to the custom of rising before dawn to witness the phenomenon and may be the reason why sunrise services on Easter morning are common throughout the United States.

At the Hollywood Bowl, a huge outdoor amphitheater in the Hollywood Hills of Los Angeles, the Easter sunrise service is a spectacle on a scale that only Hollywood could produce. First held in 1921, the service is attended by about 30,000 people who spend the night in the stadium. Fifty thousand calla lilies decorate the stage, where a huge choir and a symphony orchestra perform the *Hallelujah* chorus from Handel's *Messiah* and traditional Easter hymns. Two hundred and fifty teenagers form a "living cross" just after dawn.

CONTACT:
Los Angeles Convention and Visitors Bureau
633 W. Fifth St., Ste. 6000
Los Angeles, CA 90071
800-228-2452 or 213-624-7300
fax: 213-624-9746

SOURCES:
BkFestHolWrld-1970, p. 59

♦ 0561 ♦ **Easter in Italy (La Pasqua)**
Between March 22 and April 25

In many Italian towns and villages sacred dramas commemorating episodes in the EASTER story or from the Bible are held in the *piazzas* on Easter day. Pastries called *corona di nove* are baked in the form of a crown; in America, these pastries are often made in the shape of rabbits instead. Other traditional foods of the season include *capretto* (lamb) and *agnello* (kid).

In Florence, the Ceremony of the Car, or *Scoppio del Carro*, is held on HOLY SATURDAY. Inaugurated by the ancient Florentine family of de'Pazzi, the custom involves a decorated wooden car filled with explosives, which is drawn into the piazza by white oxen and placed before the cathedral doors. A wire runs from the high altar inside the cathedral to the car in the piazza. As the mass ends, a dove-shaped rocket is ignited at the altar and sent shooting out along the wire. When it reaches the car, it sets fire to the explosives. Tuscan farmers believe that if the rocket does its job well, their harvests will prosper in the coming year. If it fails to ignite the *carro* or if something else goes wrong, their crops in the coming season will be poor.

CONTACT:
Italian Government Travel Office
630 Fifth Ave.
New York, NY 10111
212-245-4822

SOURCES:
BkFest-1937, p. 185
FestSaintDays-1915, p. 75
FestWestEur-1958, p. 95

♦ 0562 ♦ **Easter in Norway (Paske)**
Between March 22 and April 25

EASTER in Norway is a popular time to go to mountain resorts and enjoy winter sports. From MAUNDY THURSDAY through EASTER MONDAY, the towns and cities are deserted, but every mountain inn and hotel is packed to overflowing with those who come to ski, skate, toboggan, and enjoy watching others pursue such activities. Ice carnivals, sports competitions, dances, and concerts are also popular, and many mountain resorts hold special out-of-doors Easter services for skiers.

Norwegians who observe the holiday at home dye and decorate Easter eggs after boring small holes in the ends and blowing out the yolk and white, or by carefully cutting the shells in half and then pasting them together again with strips of paper. The decorated eggs are hidden all over the house, and on Easter morning, everyone hunts for the eggs that have been concealed for them by other family members.

SOURCES:
BkFest-1937, p. 249
FestWestEur-1958, p. 152

♦ 0563 ♦ **Easter in Poland (Wielkanoc)**
Between March 22 and April 25

After attending the EASTER church service, Polish families gather to share a cold meal, for the day is considered too sacred to light a fire. The head of the family slices a colored egg and shares it with family and guests while everyone exchanges good wishes. The meal itself usually consists of ham, sausages, salads, *babka* (the Polish national cake), and *mazurki*, or sweet cakes filled with nuts, fruit, and honey.

On EASTER MONDAY, everyone puts on old clothes and engages in a water-throwing game known as *smigus*. Children often throw decorated eggshells into a stream, in hopes that their Easter wishes will reach those who live beneath the earth.

SOURCES:
BkFest-1937, p. 260
FolkWrldHol-1992, p. 202

♦ 0564 ♦ **Easter in Russia (Paskha)**
Between April 4 and May 8

EASTER is one of the most important holidays of the Russian year. A great deal of attention is devoted to the preparation of *koulich*, a very tall Easter cake made according to a traditional recipe and a major part of the Easter meal that breaks the Lenten fast. Pillows are often placed around the pan while the dough is rising, because any jarring might cause the cake to fall. Husbands often complain that they've been kicked out of the house because their heavy footsteps are disturbing the koulich. The finished cake is usually marked with the initials X and B, which stand for the Russian words meaning "Christ is risen."

On Easter Sunday and Monday the men visit each other, but Easter Tuesday is reserved for the women to call on their friends. In rural areas it is customary for children to swing, dance, and play games and musical instruments on this day. Church bells ring throughout the Easter holiday.

SOURCES:
BkFest-1937, p. 292
Chases-1996, p. 161

♦ 0565 ♦ **Easter in Spain**
Between March 22 and April 25

After attending EASTER morning Mass, many Spanish people throng the cafes and restaurants to break their Lenten fast. In the afternoon, residents of Madrid, Seville, and other cities usually attend bullfights. In Jumilla, Alcañiz, and other villages south of Valencia, the coming of Easter is marked by a *tamborada*—three days of non-stop drumming. In Hellin, between 8,000 and 10,000 drums are beaten between Holy Wednesday and Easter Sunday.

The shop windows of confectioners and pastry cooks are filled with elaborate displays of cakes around Easter. Sometimes a farmyard is made out of pastry, with hens, cocks, and monkeys. A special pastry known as a *mona* (female monkey) contains a hard-boiled egg, and elaborate and ingenious monas are often given as Easter presents.

In the region of Spain known as Catalonia, HOLY WEEK *pasos* (tableaux) are formed by men standing on each other's shoulders to form a kind of circular pyramid, with a small child standing on the top. Easter pasos often illustrate a biblical scene, such as the Descent from the Cross.

CONTACT:
Tourist Office of Spain
665 Fifth Ave.
New York, NY 10022
212-759-8822; fax: 212-980-1053

SOURCES:
BkFest-1937, p. 301
FestSaintDays-1915, p. 84
FolkWrldHol-1992, p. 202

♦ 0566 ♦ Easter in Sweden (Påskdagen)
Between March 22 and April 25

EASTER in Sweden is a time for winter sports. Thousands of people from Stockholm and other southern cities board special excursion trains and spend the Easter holidays in the northern provinces, where winter sports are at their peak.

On either MAUNDY THURSDAY or Easter Eve, children often dress up as witches and call on their neighbors, much as children in the United States do on HALLOWEEN. Sometimes they slip a secret "Easter letter" under the door or in the mailbox. Bonfires are popular in the western provinces of Sweden, with competitions to see which village can build the biggest fire. The witches and bonfires are reminiscent of pagan ceremonies to ward off evil, and in rural areas people still hang crossed scythes in their stables or paint crosses over their doors to protect themselves against the evil spread by Easter hags flying around on their broomsticks.

SOURCES:
BkFest-1937, p. 309
FestWestEur-1958, p. 213
FolkWrldHol-1992, p. 203

♦ 0567 ♦ Easter in the Netherlands (Paschen, Paasch Zondag)
Between March 22 and April 25

The lighting of bonfires is a common occurrence on EASTER or Easter Eve in the Netherlands. The fuel is collected weeks in advance, and neighboring towns often compete with each other to see which can build the biggest fire. As the flames get higher, the villagers join hands and dance around the fire. In ancient times, bits of charred wood carried home from the bonfire were believed to protect people's houses from fire and other disasters during the year.

In the village of Denekamp, in the province of Overijssel, two young men who represent the comic characters known as Judas and Iscariot—Judas being "the clever man"and Iscariot being "the stupid man"—prepare the Easter bonfire and help set up the "Easter pole," which is a tall fir tree that has been stripped of its branches, cut down, and carried to the hill where the bonfire will be lit. Judas sets a ladder against the tree, climbs up, and starts auctioning it to the highest bidder. The crowd hoots and jeers at him and at Iscariot, who replaces him. At eight o'clock in the evening the fire is lit, and the townspeople dance and sing a very old hymn whose dialect words and meanings are understood only by local people.

In the eastern Netherlands village of Ootmarsum, the VLÖGGELEN, or "winging ceremony," held on Easter Sunday and Monday is a slow, ritualistic dance that may be the survivor of an ancient spring fertility rite. The villagers form a human chain by putting their right hand behind their back and clasping the left hand of the person behind them. The line moves forward to the constantly repeated words and melody of an ancient Easter hymn, winding through the village streets and country roads and going in and out of shops, farmhouses, and barns along the way. Since very few people know all the words by heart, it is customary to pin a copy of the song to each dancer's back. All 19 verses end with an *Alleluia* refrain.

See also EASTER MONDAY IN THE NETHERLANDS

CONTACT:
Netherlands Board of Tourism
355 Lexington Ave., 21st Floor
New York, NY 10017
212-370-7360; fax: 212-370-9507

SOURCES:
BkFest-1937, p. 241
FestWestEur-1958, pp. 126, 130

♦ 0568 ♦ Easter in the Ukraine
Between April 4 and May 8

Decorating eggs is the EASTER custom for which Ukrainians are known all over the world. The *pysanki* eggs are not cooked because the raw egg shell absorbs the color better. The initial design is drawn on the shell with a *pysar*, or small, metal-tipped writing tool, dipped in beeswax. When the egg is dipped in the first dye (usually yellow, the lightest color), the wax prevents any dye from being absorbed. When the next layer of the design is drawn on the shell, it will remain yellow while the rest of the egg is dyed a darker color (usually orange or red). This layering process continues until the desired artistic effect is achieved. Then the egg is held over a candle flame to melt off the wax and is coated with shellac or varnish. A woman who is particularly adept at decorating Easter eggs is called a *pysarka*.

The eggs are presented as gifts to friends and relatives on Easter morning. One of the decorated eggs that has been hard-boiled is shelled, sliced up, and served at the beginning of the Easter dinner to symbolize the end of the Lenten fast. Sometimes the eggs are used in a game where children try to strike each other's eggs with their own. But due to the eggs' religious significance and the work that goes into decorating them, the shells are never dropped on the ground or discarded. If broken, they are usually thrown into fire or water.

SOURCES:
FolkAmerHol-1991, p. 164
FolkWrldHol-1992, p. 203

♦ 0569 ♦ Easter Monday
Between March 23 and April 26; Monday after Easter

Although EASTER Sunday is the culmination of HOLY WEEK and the end of LENT, the following Monday (also known as **Pasch Monday**) is observed as a public holiday in 82 nations, perhaps to round off the long weekend that begins on GOOD FRIDAY. In London there is a big Easter parade in Hyde Park on this day.

A curious English tradition associated at one time with Easter Monday involved "lifting" or "heaving." Forming what children call a "chair" by crossing hands and grasping another person's wrists, the men would lift the women on Easter Monday—sometimes carrying them for a short distance down the street or to the village green—and on Easter Tuesday the women would lift the men. A similar retaliatory game involved taking off each other's shoes. This is thought to have a connection with the resurrection of Christ. Polish children play *smigus*, a water-throwing game.

CONTACT:
British Tourist Authority
551 Fifth Ave., Ste. 702
New York, NY 10176
800-462-2748 or 212-986-2200
fax: 212-986-1188

SOURCES:
AmerBkDays-1978, p. 309
BkFest-1937, pp. 16, 57, 261
Chases-1996, p. 163
DictDays-1988, pp. 8, 11, 35,
    55, 56, 122
FestSaintDays-1915, p. 91
FolkWrldHol-1992, pp. 194,
    202, 208

♦ 0570 ♦ Easter Monday in the Netherlands
Between March 23 and April 26; Monday after Easter

EASTER MONDAY, or **Paasch Maandag**, is celebrated in the Netherlands with games played with Easter eggs. *Eierrapen*, or hunting for eggs, is a favorite pastime among younger children. *Eiertikken*, or hitting hard-boiled eggs together, is a sport for children of all ages. In rural areas, the eggs are still dyed with coffee grounds, beet juice, onion skins, and other vegetable substances. Then they're packed in baskets and carried to an open field for the eiertikken contest. At a given signal, the children line up and try to break the shell of an opposing team member's egg (the two eggs must be the same color) by knocking them together. The winner keeps the opponent's egg, and the boy or girl who collects the most eggs wins.

Another Easter game, which was popular in the 16th and 17th centuries and is still played today, is called the *eiergaren*. Played by both children and adults who assemble in the main street of the village on Easter Monday, the game involves a tub of water with a huge apple floating in it. The tub is placed in the middle of the road and the local innkeeper supplies 25 eggs, which are placed at intervals of about 12 feet along the same road. One person must eat the apple with his hands tied behind his back while a second contestant has to run and gather up all the eggs in a basket before the apple is eaten. Whoever finishes his or her task first is the victor.

SOURCES:
BkFest-1937, p. 242
FestWestEur-1958, p. 131

♦ 0571 ♦ Eastern States Exposition
September, starts the second Wednesday after Labor Day

Also known as the **Big E**, an agricultural and industrial fair in West Springfield, Mass. It's sponsored by all six New England states and runs for 12 days. The first exposition in 1917 attracted 138,000 visitors; these days, attendance tops one million.

The exposition is known for its Avenue of the States, where each New England state has erected a permanent replica of its original State House. (The New Hampshire State House uses New Hampshire granite for its columns.) In the buildings are displays of state products, for example, Maine potatoes, New Hampshire maple syrup, Vermont cheese, Massachusetts cranberries, Rhode Island clam cakes, and Connecticut apples. The livestock show is the largest in the East, and the Eastern States Horse Show is one of the oldest and most prestigious equestrian events in the country. Besides hunters, jumpers, harness, and saddle horses, there are draft horses in dress harness.

CONTACT:
Massachusetts Office of Travel
    and Tourism
100 Cambridge St., 13th Floor
Boston, MA 02202
800-447-6277 or 617-727-3201
fax: 617-727-6525

SOURCES:
Chases-1996, p. 374

♦ 0572 ♦ Ecuador Independence Day
August 10

Independence, or **National, Day** in Ecuador celebrates its independence movement of 1809. Freedom from Spanish rule was finally achieved on May 24, 1822. That event is commemorated each year on May 24 with another national holiday called Battle of Pichincha Day.

Patriotic festivities are held throughout the country, but particularly in the colorful capital city of Quito.

CONTACT:
Ecuador Trade Center
2600 Douglas Rd., Ste. 401
Coral Gables, FL 33134
305-461-2363; fax: 305-446-7755

SOURCES:
AnnivHol-1983, pp. 70, 105
Chases-1996, p. 331
NatlHolWrld-1968, p. 140

♦ 0573 ♦ Eddy, Birthday of Mary Baker
July 16

This is the day on which Mary Baker Eddy (1821–1910), founder of the Church of Christ, Scientist, was born. After spending much of her early life as a semi-invalid due to a spinal malady, Eddy suffered a serious fall in 1866 and underwent a healing experience that led her to the discovery of Christian Science. Based on the largely forgotten healing aspects of Christianity, the First Church of Christ, Scientist was established in Boston in 1879, and two years later, Eddy founded the Massachusetts Metaphysical College, where she taught until 1889. She dedicated her entire life to spreading the word about Christianity's power to heal. Her most important written work was *Science and Health with Key to the Scriptures*, published in 1875.

The basic premise of Christian Science is that only mind and spirit are real; matter is an illusion, and therefore subject to decay and dissolution. Sickness and death are only real in that they seem real to humans; through prayer and spiritual development, this error can be overcome. Mary Baker Eddy's birthday is observed by Christian Science churches around the world.

SOURCES:
AnnivHol-1983, p. 94
Chases-1996, p. 298
DictWrldRel-1989, p. 168
RelHolCal-1993, p. 63

♦ 0574 ♦ Edinburgh International Festival
August–September

The capital city of Edinburgh (pronounced ED-in-bo-ro), Scotland, is transformed during the last two weeks of August and the first week of September each year, when it hosts what is probably the most prestigious arts festival in the world. Theater and dance companies, orchestras, chamber groups, and soloists from all over the world perform at the city's major venues, and there are art exhibitions and poetry readings as well. Many important new works have been commissioned specifically for the festival—one of the most famous being T.S. Eliot's *The Cocktail Party.*

A highlight of the festival, which has been held since 1947, is the traditional Military Tattoo performed nightly at Edinburgh Castle, which is perched high above the city on a rocky promontory. Marching bands from all over the world perform along with Scottish pipe bands at the tattoo, which ends with a farewell song from a lone piper standing on the floodlit battlements.

There is also a "Fringe Festival" that goes on at the same time—an arena for new talent and amateur entertainers. Although student drama and street theater predominate, the quality of the productions in recent years has sometimes made it difficult to distinguish Fringe events from the 'official' ones. The number of Fringe performances has increased dramatically as well—from only a few in 1947 to more than 9,000 in 1989. But the three defining features of the earliest Fringe events still hold true today: none of the performers are officially invited to take part; they must use small and unconventional theater spaces; and they all assume their own financial risks, surviving or sinking according to public demand.

CONTACT:
British Tourist Authority
551 Fifth Ave., Ste. 702
New York, NY 10176
800-462-2748 or 212-986-2200
fax: 212-986-1188

SOURCES:
Chases-1996, p. 334
GdWrldFest-1985, p. 99
IntlThFolk-1979, pp. 184, 185
MusFestEurBrit-1980, p. 132
MusFestWrld-1963, p. 8

♦ 0575 ♦ **Edison Pageant of Light**
Second Wednesday through third Saturday of February

Most people associate Thomas Alva Edison (1847–1931) with his famous laboratory in Menlo Park, New Jersey. But when he was 38 years old, a widower and seriously ill, his doctors sent him to Florida for a long vacation. There he discovered giant bamboo growing along the Caloosahatchee River. He established his winter home in Fort Myers and planned to use the bamboo fiber to make filaments for his new incandescent electric lamp bulbs.

The Edison Pageant of Light held annually in Fort Myers for 11 days encompassing his birthday (*see* EDISON'S BIRTHDAY), began as a three-day event in 1938. Highlights of the festival include concerts, a formal ball, coronation of the King and Queen of Edisonia, a children's parade, a high school band competition, and exhibits of Edison's various inventions. The Grand Parade of Light—a nighttime procession of more than 100 bands, floats, and marching units—is the festival's grand finale. Edison's winter home and his Florida laboratory are open to the public year-round.

CONTACT:
Edison Winter Home and
Museum
2350 McGregor Blvd.
Fort Myers, FL 33901
813-334-3614

SOURCES:
AmerBkDays-1978, p. 164
GdUSFest-1984, p. 35

♦ 0576 ♦ **Edison's Birthday, Thomas**
February 11

Although Thomas Alva Edison (1847–1931) is best known as the inventor of the incandescent electric light, his real achievement was to produce the first incandescent lamp of any

practical value—one that could be produced inexpensively and distributed widely. In 1882 Edison lost a patent infringement case to Joseph Wilson Swan, who was developing an incandescent light at the same time in England. As a compromise, the two men combined their resources and formed the Edison and Swan Electric Lamp Company.

Edison's genius is credited with a number of other important inventions, among them the carbon transmitter (which brought Alexander Graham Bell's newly invented telephone into general use and led to the development of the microphone), the dictating machine, a method for transmitting telegraphic signals from ship to ship (or ship to shore), the Kinetoscope (which made the motion picture a reality), and the phonograph. He is often quoted as saying, "Genius is one percent inspiration and 99 percent perspiration."

See also EDISON PAGEANT OF LIGHT

CONTACT:
Thomas Edison Birthplace
Museum
9 Edison Dr.
Milan, OH 44846
419-499-2135

SOURCES:
AmerBkDays-1978, p. 163
Chases-1996, p. 94

Edison Institute
Henry Ford Museum
Greenfield Village
20900 Oakman Blvd.
P.O. Box 1970
Dearborn, MI 48124
313-271-1620
WWW: http://
hfm.umd.umich.edu

♦ 0577 ♦ **Egungun Festival**
June

The Egungun is a secret society among the Yoruba people of Ede, Nigeria. The major Egungun festival takes place in June, when members of the society come to the market place and perform masked dances. The masks they wear represent ancestral spirits and may cover the whole body or just the face. It is considered dangerous to see any part of the man who is wearing the mask—an offense that was at one time punishable by death.

The masqueraders all dance simultaneously, although each has his own drum accompaniment and entourage of chanting women and girls. The festival climaxes with the appearance of Andu, the most powerful mask. It is believed that the spirits of the deceased possess the masqueraders while they are dancing, and although it promotes a feeling of oneness between the living and the dead, the festival also inspires a certain amount of fear.

CONTACT:
Nigerian Embassy
1333 16th St., N.W.
Washington, D.C. 20036
202-986-8400; fax: 202-775-1385

SOURCES:
DictFolkMyth-1984, p. 341
FolkWrldHol-1992, p. 322

♦ 0578 ♦ **Egyptian Days**
Various

Up until the 17th century in England, these were commonly thought to be unlucky days throughout the year. Popular almanacs would list them as days on which to avoid such important activities as weddings, blood letting (a standard way of treating various illnesses) and traveling. No one knew why certain days were considered unlucky. In fact, which days were Egyptian Days seems to have depended upon which almanac was consulted; apparently, there was never any standard list that was widely circulated.

Although it is not known for sure why they were referred to as the Egyptian Days, it's possible that they were first computed by Egyptian astrologers or were somehow related to the Egyptian plagues. They were also known as the **Dismal Days**, from Latin *dies mali* (meaning 'evil days').

SOURCES:
BkDays-1864, vol. I, p. 41
DictDays-1988, pp. 31, 36

♦ 0579 ♦ Egypt National Day
July 23; April 25

Also known as **Revolution Day,** this national holiday is the anniversary of the military overthrow of the monarchy on July 23, 1952. The new government formally instituted the Republic of Egypt on June 18, 1953. In Cairo on July 23, parades and other festivities take place to commemorate the republic.

April 25 is another legal holiday in Egypt, **Sinai Day,** commemorating final withdrawal of Israeli troops on this date in 1982 under the 1978 Camp David agreement between Egypt and Israel to return the Sinai Peninsula to Egypt.

CONTACT:
Egyptian Tourist Authority
645 N. Michigan Ave., Ste. 829
Chicago, IL 60611
312-280-4666; fax: 312-280-4788

SOURCES:
AnnivHol-1983, p. 96
Chases-1996, p. 308
NatlHolWrld-1968, p. 122

♦ 0580 ♦ Eight Hour Day
Various

Each of Australia's states celebrates the improvements that have been made in working conditions with its own LABOR DAY. In Western Australia and Tasmania, where it's celebrated on March 5 and called Eight Hour Day, parades and celebrations commemorate trade union efforts to limit working hours. People still chant the unions' slogan: "Eight hours' labor, eight hours' recreation, and eight hours' rest!," which, by happenstance, is the basis of St. Benedict's Rule of Life for religious orders.

In Victoria, **Labour Day** is observed on March 11. In Queensland, it's May 6; in New South Wales and the Australian Capital Territory, it's October 7; in South Australia, it's October 14. In New Zealand, Labour Day is observed on the last Monday in October.

CONTACT:
Australian Tourist Commission
100 Park Ave., 25th Floor
New York, NY 10017
212-687-6300; fax: 212-661-3340

New Zealand Tourism Board
501 Santa Monica Blvd., Ste. 300
Santa Monica, CA 90401
800-388-5494 or 310-395-7480
fax: 310-395-5453

SOURCES:
AnnivHol-1983, pp. 31, 34, 60, 131, 135
BkHolWrld-1986, Mar 5
Chases-1996, p. 123
DictDays-1988, pp. 36, 65

♦ 0581 ♦ Eisteddfod
First week in August

The **Royal National Eisteddfod of Wales** dates back to the fourth century. Its purpose is to encourage the preservation of Welsh music and literature, and only those who sing or write in Welsh may enter the competitions. The annual event opens with the blowing of trumpets, followed by all kinds of musical and literary contests—harp playing, solo and choral singing, dramatic presentations, and poetic composition. Prizes and degrees are awarded to the winners.

The National Eisteddfod is held in northern Wales one year and southern Wales the next. Other Eisteddfodau are held in Welsh communities elsewhere from May to November.

See also CYNONFARDD EISTEDDFOD

CONTACT:
British Tourist Authority
551 Fifth Ave., Ste. 702
New York, NY 10176
800-462-2748 or 212-986-2200
fax: 212-986-1188

SOURCES:
AnnivHol-1983, p. 176
BkFest-1937, p. 60
BkHolWrld-1986, Aug 3
Chases-1996, p. 323
DictFolkMyth-1984, p. 342
GdWrldFest-1985, p. 100
IntlThFolk-1979, p. 191
MusFestEurBrit-1980, p. 150

♦ 0582 ♦ Eka Dasa Rudra
Once every 100 years

A series of processions, ceremonies, and sacrifices held every 100 years at Pura Besakih, the 'mother temple' of Bali, Indonesia. The temple, which comprises about 30 separate temples honoring a great variety of Balinese and Hindu gods, was probably built about 1,000 years ago and is on the slopes of the volcanic mountain, Gunung ('Mount') Agung. On March 17, 1963, the Eka Dasa Rudra was under way when Agung catastrophically erupted and killed more than 1,500 people. Since the sacrifices were interrupted, the Eka Dasa Rudra was started again 16 years later and completed in the period from late February to early May of 1979. Images of gods were carried 19 miles down the mountain to be washed in the sea: entire villages gathered along the route. In all, it is estimated that more than 100,000 people participated in the ritual. The climax came during the Taur rites when 23 priests offered prayers and sacrificed animals—ranging from an eagle to an anteater—to appease forms of Rudra, a Hindu demonic manifestation. Thousands of pilgrims traveled by truck and foot to Besakih. The complex Balinese religion is largely a blend with Hinduism; the majority of Balinese hold to the Bali Hindu faith, also known as Agama Tirtha.

CONTACT:
Indonesian Tourist Promotion Office
3457 Wilshire Blvd., Ste. 104
Los Angeles, CA 90010
213-387-2078; fax: 213-380-4876

SOURCES:
EncyRel-1987, vol. 2, p. 48

♦ 0583 ♦ Ekadashi
Eleventh day of each waxing and waning moon

Ekadashi is the Hindi word for "eleventh." Twenty-four 11th-day fasts are observed during the course of the Hindu year, although some are more important than others. Each Ekadashi is held in honor of a different Hindu legend and has specific religious duties associated with it. Eating rice, however, is prohibited on all Ekadashi. According to legend, a demon was born of the sweat that fell from Brahma's head on this day, and Brahma instructed it to inhabit the rice grains eaten by people on Ekadashi and to turn into worms in their stomachs.

See also AMALAKA EKADASHI, NIRJALA EKADASHI, PUTRADA EKADASHI.

> SOURCES:
> *RelHolCal-1993,* p. 74

◆ 0584 ◆ Eldon Turkey Festival
Second Saturday in October

While people in most parts of the United States think about turkeys only as THANKSGIVING day approaches, it is a year-round concern for the turkey farmers of Eldon, Missouri, and the surrounding area, where over two million turkeys are raised annually. There is also a large wild turkey population, which makes turkey hunting a popular local sport. Since 1986, Eldon has held a **Turkey Festival** designed to educate the public about domestic turkey production, turkey-farming operations, and the health benefits of turkey-food products. The festival is also an opportunity for numerous conservation and turkey-hunting organizations to provide information on safe hunting practices, wild-turkey-calling techniques, and efforts to increase the wild turkey population.

Events at the October festival include turkey races (with the turkeys on leashes), a turkey egg toss, sales of turkey foods, and exhibits on the production of domestic turkeys.

> CONTACT:
> Missouri Division of Tourism
> P.O. Box 1055
> Jefferson City, MO 65102
> 800-877-1234 or 314-751-4133
> fax: 314-751-5160

◆ 0585 ◆ Election Day
Tuesday following the first Monday in November

Americans vote for their president and vice president every four years on the Tuesday after the first Monday in November, and for their state senators and representatives on the same day every two years. U.S. senators are elected every six years—one-third of them are up for reelection every two years—and representatives are elected every two years during even-numbered years.

This date was set by Congress in 1845 to correct abuses caused by having allowed each state to appoint its electors any time before the date in December set for their convening. To encourage people to vote, Election Day is either a legal holiday or half-holiday in many states and all territories, and employers in other states often give their employees the day off. But despite the easing of restrictions on who may vote and the unceasing efforts of the League of Women Voters and other civic organizations, the majority of Americans do not take advantage of what may be their most valuable privilege.

In England, the day when every constituency elects a representative is called **General Election Day.**

> SOURCES:
> *AmerBkDays-1978,* p. 991

> *AnnivHol-1983,* p. 142
> *Chases-1996,* p. 441
> *DictDays-1988,* p. 36

◆ 0586 ◆ Elephant Round-Up
Third weekend in November

An internationally famous show of 100 trained elephants held annually in the provincial capital of Surin, Thailand. The Suay people of the area have traditionally captured and trained wild elephants to work in the northern Thailand teak forests. The Round-Up gives the trainers the opportunity to demonstrate their elephants' intelligence, strength, and obedience. A tug-of-war is staged where elephants are pitted against 200 Thai soldiers. There are also log-pulling contests, a soccer game with two teams of elephants kicking a giant soccer ball, and other stunts. A highlight is the spectacular array of elephants rigged out to reenact a medieval war parade. Besides the elephant demonstrations, there are cultural performances and folk dancing.

> CONTACT:
> Tourism Authority of Thailand
> 5 World Trade Center, Ste. 3443
> New York, NY 10048
> 212-432-0433; fax: 212-912-0920
>
> SOURCES:
> *BkHolWrld-1986,* Nov 16
> *Chases-1996,* p. 451
> *GdWrldFest-1985,* p. 175

◆ 0587 ◆ Eleusinia
Every five years; the Lesser Eleusinia in early spring; the Greater Eleusinia between harvest and seed time (September 15–23)

In ancient Athens, the Eleusinia was the most celebrated of all religious ceremonies. Often referred to as the **Mysteries** because anyone who violated the secrecy surrounding the festival rites would be punished by death, the Eleusinia consisted of two celebrations: The Greater Eleusinia was observed between harvest and seed time; the Lesser Eleusinia was observed in early spring. Those who had been initiated at the lesser mysteries were allowed to participate in the greater mysteries the following year, when the secrets of the festival would be revealed to them.

The Eleusinia was based on the legend of Demeter, the corn goddess, and her daughter Persephone, who was carried off by Pluto to live in his underground kingdom. Although the secrecy that accompanied the Eleusinian mysteries has made it difficult to reconstruct exactly what went on there, it is believed that they were intended to encourage a bountiful growing season. The men and women who were initiated during these ceremonies were believed to live happier and more secure lives, and when they died, they were granted a place in the Elysian Fields, the mythical place where the souls of the virtuous went after death.

The Greater Eleusinia was held for nine days, from the 15th to the 23rd of September. Something different happened on each day. For example, the fifth day was called the "torch day," because the celebrants ran about with torches in their hands to commemorate Demeter, who searched for her daughter with a torch. The seventh day was set aside for sports, and on the ninth and final day, earthen vessels were filled with wine, which was then spilled on the ground and offered as a libation.

> SOURCES:
> *ClassDict-1984,* p. 220
> *DictFolkMyth-1984,* p. 512

DictMyth-1962, vol. I, p. 502

◆ 0588 ◆ Elfreth's Alley Fete Day
First weekend in June

Elfreth's Alley is a well-preserved street of privately owned 18th-century homes in Philadelphia. It is the only street in the city that has survived architecturally since the alley first opened in 1702. The 30 houses on the street, dating from 1713 to 1811, have all remained private residences, with the exception of the Mantua Makers House, which is now a museum open to the public.

The idea of holding an "at home" day dates back to 1934, when a group of residents formed the Elfreth's Alley Association. Now called **Fete Day**, it is a day on which many of the houses are open to visitors, with members of the Association acting as hostesses in Colonial dress. On Fete Day in 1963, the Alley's distinctive character and historical value were officially recognized by its designation as a Registered National Historic Landmark. Over the years the Elfreth's Alley Association has played an active role in renovating the street's cartway and brick sidewalks, as well as saving some of the houses from destruction.

CONTACT:
Elfreth's Alley Association
126 Elfreth's Alley
Philadelphia, PA 19106
215-574-0560

SOURCES:
GdUSFest-1984, p. 160

◆ 0589 ◆ Elfstedentocht
December, January, or February

The day of this famous ice skating race in the Netherlands depends on the weather and the thickness of the ice. In the 18th century, young men in the northern part of the country, known as Friesland, would try to skate all the canals that connected the province's 11 towns. Today the **Eleven Cities Race** covers the same 124-mile course, but increasingly mild winters have made its timing less dependable. As many as 16,000 men and women have competed in the race at one time, which takes several hours to complete.

CONTACT:
Netherlands Board of Tourism
355 Lexington Ave., 21st Floor
New York, NY 10017
212-370-7360; fax: 212-370-9507

SOURCES:
BkHolWrld-1986, Jan 22

◆ 0590 ◆ Elijah Day
July 20

Considered to be among the greatest of prophets, Elijah is commemorated on this day in both the Roman Catholic and Orthodox churches. An Old Testament Jew who is revered by Jews and Muslims as well, Elijah's story appears in chapters 17 and 18 of the first book of Kings, with the final episode appearing in Second Kings, chapter two. It tells of Elijah's sojourn in the desert, where he was fed every morning and evening by ravens. It also tells about the miracles he performed, replenishing the meal and oil supplies of a widow who fed him despite a severe famine and bringing her son back to life when he died.

The highpoint of Elijah's ministry occurred when he called the priests who worshipped Baal, the pagan fertility god, to the top of Mount Carmel and challenged them to a contest that would prove who was the true God. When the pagan priests failed in their efforts to ask Baal to set fire to their sacrifice, Elijah called on his God, who immediately consumed with fire not only the sacrifice but the altar itself and the dust and water surrounding it. When Elijah died, it is said that he was taken up to heaven in a fiery chariot by a whirlwind.

SOURCES:
DayRel-1990, p. 139
DaysCustFaith-1957, p. 187

◆ 0591 ◆ Ellensburg Rodeo
September, Labor Day weekend

The richest rodeo in the state of Washington and also one of the top 25 rodeos of the Professional Rodeo Cowboys Association. Prize money in recent years has been more than $100,000, and an estimated 20,000 people visit Ellensburg on this weekend. Events include a parade and displays of hand crafts, especially weaving and bead work, by the people of the Yakima Indian nation. Yakimas, many in feathered headdress, open each performance of the rodeo with a solemn horseback ride down a steep hill that overlooks the arena.

CONTACT:
Professional Rodeo Cowboys
  Association
101 Pro Rodeo Dr.
Colorado Springs, CO 80919
719-593-8840; fax: 548-4876

Washington State Tourism Development Division
P.O. Box 42500
Olympia, WA 98504
800-544-1800 or 360-753-5601
fax: 360-753-4470

◆ 0592 ◆ El Salvador Independence Day
September 15

El Salvador joined with other Central American countries in revolt against Spanish rule in 1821, and revolutionary leader Father José Matías Delgado declared El Salvador to be independent. On this same day, Costa Rica, Guatemala, Honduras, and Nicaragua also declared their independence.

Independence Day is a national holiday in El Salvador.

CONTACT:
El Salvadoran Embassy
2308 California St., N.W.
Washington, D.C. 20008
202-265-9671; fax: 202-332-5103

SOURCES:
AnnivHol-1983, p. 118
Chases-1996, p. 377
NatlHolWrld-1968, p. 165

◆ 0593 ◆ Elvis International Tribute Week
Week including August 16

A week-long tribute in Memphis, Tenn., to rock and roll singer Elvis Presley—"The King of Rock and Roll." The tribute takes place largely at Graceland, the 15,000-square-foot mansion that Elvis called home and which is now his gravesite, museum, and a rock and roll shrine.

Born in 1935 in a two-room house in Tupelo, Miss., Elvis moved to Memphis when he was 12, and came to fame in the 1950s with hits like "Hound Dog," "Don't Be Cruel," and "All Shook Up." As a white man singing a black sound, he swept the music world and helped create the Memphis

Sound. He was charismatic and sexy and gyrated his hips while performing in a fashion that sent the females in his audiences into a screeching frenzy. This won him the nickname, "Elvis the Pelvis." When he first appeared on television on the "Ed Sullivan Show," the hip shaking was considered too erotic, and he was photographed only from the waist up. He appeared in 33 motion pictures and made 45 recordings that sold over a million copies each. He died at Graceland of an overdose of prescription drugs on Aug. 16, 1977.

A candlelight vigil is held on the evening of Aug. 15 at Graceland. Thousands of Elvis's fans, each carrying a candle, pour through the gates and walk to the gravesite. Other events of the week include a Nostalgia Concert by singers and musicians who worked with Presley; a Sock Hop Ball for "flat-top cats and dungaree dolls," in which Elvis songs and other classics of the 1950s and 1960s are played; and an art exhibit and contest, with art depicting Elvis or his home. The Elvis Presley Memorial Karate Tournament draws about 500 competitors from all over the world and reflects Presley's interest in karate—he studied the martial arts for years and was the first movie star to use karate in films.

CONTACT:
Graceland
3734 Elvis Presley Blvd.
Memphis, TN 38116
800-238-2000 or 901-332-3322
fax: 901-344-3131

SOURCES:
AnnivHol-1983, p. 108
Chases-1996, p. 333

♦ 0594 ♦ Emancipation Day in the United States
January 1

President Abraham LINCOLN issued his famous Emancipation Proclamation freeing the slaves on January 1, 1863. Although some states have their own emancipation, or freedom, celebrations on the anniversary of the day on which they adopted the 13th Amendment, the most widespread observance takes place on January 1 because it is both a traditional and a legal holiday in all the states. In Texas, and other parts of the South and Southwest, the emancipation of the slaves is celebrated on June 19 or JUNETEENTH, the anniversary of the day in 1863 when General Gordon Granger arrived there to enforce Lincoln's proclamation.

Celebrations are more common in the southern United States, where they frequently center around public readings of the original Emancipation Proclamation, often in a rhythmic, dramatic style.

SOURCES:
AmerBkDays-1978, p. 9
AnnivHol-1983, p. 2
Chases-1996, p. 50
FolkAmerHol-1991, p. 24

♦ 0595 ♦ Ember Days
Four times a year

The Ember Days occur four times a year, at the beginning of each of the natural seasons. Traditionally they are marked by three days of fasting and abstinence—the Wednesday, Friday, and Saturday following, respectively, ASH WEDNESDAY, PENTECOST (Whitsunday), EXALTATION OF THE CROSS, and ST. LUCY'S DAY. In 1966, the Roman Catholic Church replaced them with days of prayer for various needs and withdrew the obligation to fast. The Anglican Communion still ob-

serves them. The four weeks in which these days occur are called Ember Weeks, and the Friday in each of these weeks is known as **Golden Friday**. The word "ember" itself derives from an Old English word referring to the revolution of time.

Some scholars believe that the Ember Days originated with the old pagan purification rites that took place at the seasons of planting, harvest, and vintage. The idea of fasting on these days was instituted by Pope Calixtus I in the third century. By the ninth century it was observed throughout Europe, but it wasn't until 1095 that the dates were fixed. In the Roman Catholic Church and the Church of England, since the sixth century, priests have been ordained on an Ember Saturday.

SOURCES:
BkDays-1864, vol. II, p. 687
DaysCustFaith-1957, p. 163
DictDays-1988, p. 48
DictMyth-1962, vol. I, p. 507
DictWrldRel-1989, p. 237
RelHolCal-1993, p. 74
SaintFestCh-1904, p. 253

Empire Day
See **Commonwealth Day**

♦ 0596 ♦ Encaenia Day
June

In general terms, *encaenia* (pronounced en-SEEN-ya) refers to the festivities celebrating the founding of a city or the dedication of a church. But in Oxford, England, Encaenia Day—sometimes referred to as **Commemoration Day**—is the day at the end of the summer term when the founders and benefactors of Oxford University are commemorated and honorary degrees are awarded to distinguished men and women. The ceremonies take place in the Sheldonian Theatre, designed by Christopher Wren in 1669 when he was a professor of astronomy at the university. Based on a classical amphitheater, the Sheldonian offers an exceptional and often-photographed view from its cupola of Oxford's spires and gargoyles.

SOURCES:
DictDays-1988, pp. 23, 36

♦ 0597 ♦ Enkutatash
September 11

The **Ethiopian New Year** falls on the first day of the Ethiopian month of Maskarem, which is September 11 on the Gregorian calendar. It comes at the end of the rainy season, so the wildflowers that the children gather and the tall grass that the peasants use to cover their floors on this day are plentiful. Small groups of children go from house to house, singing songs, leaving small bouquets of flowers, and hoping for a handful of *dabo*, or roasted grain, in return. In some parts of Ethiopia it is customary to slaughter an animal on this day. For traditional reasons this is either a white-headed lamb or a red chicken.

SOURCES:
AnnivHol-1983, p. 117
FolkWrldHol-1992, p. 478

Entrance of the Lord into Jerusalem
See **Palm Sunday**

♦ 0598 ♦ **Epidauros Festival**
Late June through August

Theatrical productions of ancient Greek tragedy and comedy at the theater built in the third century B.C. in Epidauros, Greece, about 90 miles southwest of Athens. This open-air theater, the best preserved in Greece, can seat 14,000, and the acoustics are so fine that those seated in the top row can hear a whisper on stage. The performances, also known as the **Festival of Ancient Drama**, are presented by the National Theater of Greece and the Northern Greece State and Art Theater. Summaries of the Greek-language plays are available to the audience in English.

CONTACT:
Greek National Tourist
  Organization
645 Fifth Ave.
New York, NY 10022
212-421-5777; fax: 212-826-6940

SOURCES:
GdWrldFest-1985, p. 102
IntlThFolk-1979, p. 193
MusFestEurBrit-1980, p. 108

♦ 0599 ♦ **Epiphany, Feast of the**
January 6

One of the oldest Christian feasts (celebrated since the end of the second century, before the establishment of the CHRISTMAS holiday), Epiphany (which means "manifestation" or "showing forth") is sometimes called Twelfth Day, THREE KINGS' DAY, DÍA DE LOS TRES REYES (in Latin America), the **Feast of Jordan** (by Ukrainian Orthodox), or OLD CHRISTMAS DAY. It commemorates the first two occasions on which the divinity of Jesus was manifested: when the three kings (or wise men or Magi) came to worship the infant Jesus in Bethlehem, and when he was baptized by John the Baptist in the River Jordan and the Holy Spirit descended in the form of a dove and proclaimed him the Son of God. The Roman Catholic and Protestant churches emphasize the visit of the Magi when they celebrate the Epiphany; the Eastern Orthodox churches focus on the baptism of Jesus. The blessing of lakes, rivers, and seas plays a central role in their celebrations.

In France **Le Jour des Rois** (the **Day of the Kings**), sometimes called the **Fête des Rois**, is celebrated with parties for children and adults alike. The highlight of these celebrations is the *galette des rois*, or 'cake of the Kings'—a round, flat cake which is cut in the pantry, covered with a white napkin, and carried into the dining room on a small table. An extra piece is always cut, which is traditionally called *le part à Dieu* ('God's share') and is reserved for the first poor person who comes to the door. The youngest person in the room oversees the distribution of the pieces of cake, one of which contains a bean or tiny china doll. The person who finds this token becomes king or queen for the evening. He or she chooses a consort, and for the remainder of the evening, every move the royal couple makes is imitated and commented upon by the other guests, who take great delight in exclaiming, for example, "The King drinks!" or "The Queen coughs!"

In many parts of France, the celebration begins on the evening of January 5 and involves collecting and distributing food and gifts for the poor (*see* EPIPHANY EVE IN FRANCE).

Now observed by a growing number of Protestants as well as Roman Catholics and Orthodox Christians, Epiphany refers not only to the day itself but to the church season that follows it—a season whose length varies because it ends when LENT begins, and that depends on the date of EASTER.

See also BEFANA FESTIVAL, FOUR AN' TWENTY DAY, ORTHODOX EPIPHANY, TIMQAT, and TWELFTH NIGHT

SOURCES:
AmerBkDays-1978, pp. 34, 37, 38, 89
BkDays-1864, vol. I, p. 62
BkFest-1937, pp. 3, 119, 144, 289, 335
BkFestHolWrld-1970, pp. 19, 20, 22
DaysCustFaith-1957, p. 20
FestSaintDays-1915, pp. 15, 17
FestWestEur-1958, p. 33
FolkAmerHol-1991, p. 27
FolkWrldHol-1992, pp. 13, 14, 23
RelHolCal-1993, p. 75

Epiphany Eve
See **Twelfth Night**

♦ 0600 ♦ **Epiphany Eve in Austria**
January 5

At one time the 12 nights between CHRISTMAS and EPIPHANY were known as "Smoke Nights" in Austria because people went through their houses and barns burning incense. Now the ceremony takes place on only one night, January 5. Also known as the **Vigil of Epiphany**, there is traditionally a special feast on this night during which an Epiphany cake is served. Three beans are concealed in the cake—two white, one black—and whoever finds a bean in his or her portion gets to dress up as one of the Three Wise Men or Holy Kings. The one with the black bean dresses up as the African king, Balthasar, by rubbing his face with soot or shoe polish. On Epiphany Day the three kings are the guests of honor at the table.

After the Epiphany Eve meal is served, to follow an old custom, the father or head of the household takes a shovelful of coal and burns incense on it. He walks through the house and outbuildings spreading smoke from the incense, followed by the oldest son, who sprinkles holy water in his path. The rest of the family follow, with the youngest child carrying a piece of chalk on a plate that has been blessed in morning mass. After each room and outbuilding has been blessed, the father takes the chalk and writes the initials of the Three Kings—C for Caspar, M for Melchior, and B for Balthasar—over every door leading to the outside. The ritual is believed to protect the household from evil in the coming year.

SOURCES:
BkFestHolWrld-1970, p. 21
FolkWrldHol-1992, p. 12

♦ 0601 ♦ **Epiphany Eve in France**
January 5

On the eve of **Le Jour des Rois** ('the Day of the Kings') it is customary in France to give food, clothing, money, and gifts to the parish poor. In Alsace, the children go from door to door dressed as the Three Kings, asking for donations of eggs, bacon, and cakes. In Normandy, the children make their neighborhood rounds carrying Chinese lanterns and empty baskets, in which they hope to collect food, clothing, and money. In Brittany, someone dressed as a beggar leads a horse, decorated with ribbons and mistletoe, through the streets. There are empty baskets hanging from the saddle in which donations are carried. In Provence and some other parts of southern France, the children go out on Epiphany Eve to meet the Three Kings, carrying cakes and figs for the hungry Magi and hay for their camels. Even though they may not meet the Three Kings on the road, they can see their statues standing near the altar of the church, where an Epiphany Mass is celebrated at night.

SOURCES:
AmerBkDays-1978, p. 30
BkFest-1937, p. 119
DictFolkMyth-1984, pp. 182, 581
FestWestEur-1958, p. 33
FolkWrldHol-1992, p. 13

♦ 0602 ♦ Epiphany in Germany (Dreikönigsfest)
January 6

Boys dressed up as the Three Kings go from house to house caroling on EPIPHANY in Germany. Because they carry a star on a pole, they are known as Starsingers, or *Sternsinger* (*see also* EPIPHANY IN SWEDEN and NEW YEAR'S DAY IN GERMANY). In western and southern Germany, salt and chalk are consecrated in church on this day. The salt is given to the animals to lick, while the chalk is used to write the initials of the Three Kings—C.M.B. for Caspar, Melchior, and Balthasar—over the house and stable doors to protect the household from danger and to keep out the evil spirits.

According to folk belief, a mysterious witch known as *Frau Perchta* (also *Berchta* or *Bertha*) wanders about the earth causing trouble between CHRISTMAS and Epiphany. In Upper Bavaria, according to tradition, peasants wearing wooden masks go around cracking whips and symbolically driving out Perchta, who is actually an ancient German fertility goddess and custodian of the dead. It is for this reason that Epiphany is also known as **Perchtennacht**. The Perchta masks, which can be terrifying in their ugliness, are often handed down from one generation to the next.

See also PERCHTENLAUF

SOURCES:
BkFest-1937, p. 131
FestSaintDays-1915, p. 9
FestWestEur-1958, p. 54
FolkWrldHol-1992, p. 13

♦ 0603 ♦ Epiphany in Labrador
January 6

The *naluyuks* that visit children on EPIPHANY in Labrador, Canada, are a combination of Santa Claus and the bogeyman. They go from house to house on January 6, their bodies covered in bearskin or an oversized coat, with a mask over their faces, a stick in their hand, and a bag of gifts that have been donated ahead of time by parents. Children regard the coming of the naluyuks with great trepidation; as an Eskimo

bogeyman figure, the naluyuks are regularly used to frighten them into good behavior. When the naluyuks enter the house, the children are expected to sing a Christmas carol or hymn for them, and the naluyuks show their approval by pounding their sticks on the floor. After the singing, the children are asked various questions regarding their behavior over the past year. If the naluyuks are pleased with the answers, they hand each child a gift from their bag.

SOURCES:
FolkWrldHol-1992, p. 12

♦ 0604 ♦ Epiphany in Portugal (Dia de Reis)
January 6

EPIPHANY plays and pageants are common in Portugal, particularly in rural areas of the country. Bands of carolers go from house to house singing and begging gifts. Sometimes family groups visit one another, standing at the door and begging to come in so they can sing to the Christ Child. After they sing their carols, the guests are entertained with wines and sweets.

It is common for parents to give parties for their children on Epiphany Day. The Epiphany Cake, or *bolo-rei*, is a favorite tradition at these parties. Baked in the shape of a crown or ring, the cake contains many small trinkets and a single dried bean. Whoever finds the bean is crowned king of the party and must promise to make the cake the following year. At adult parties, the person who finds the bean is expected to pay for the following year's cake.

Epiphany is also a time when the traditional Portuguese dances known as *mouriscadas* and *paulitos* are performed. The latter is an elaborate stick dance in which the dancers, who are usually male but may be dressed as women, manipulate sticks or staves (substitutes for swords) in two opposing lines.

CONTACT:
Portuguese National Tourist Office
590 Fifth Ave., 4th Floor
New York, NY 10036
212-354-4403; fax: 212-764-6137

SOURCES:
BkFest-1937, p. 266
DictFolkMyth-1984, pp. 346, 1082
FestWestEur-1958, p. 160

♦ 0605 ♦ Epiphany in Spain (Día de los Reyes Magos)
January 6

EPIPHANY is the day when Spanish children receive their gifts, and it is the Three Kings, rather than Santa Claus, who bring them. On Epiphany Eve the children fill their shoes with straw or grain for the Three Kings' horses to eat and place them on balconies or by the front door. The next morning, they find cookies, sweets, and gifts in their place.

In many cities throughout Spain, the Three Kings make a spectacular entry on Epiphany Eve, to the accompaniment of military bands and drummers in medieval dress. The Kings themselves usually ride horses, although in the Canary Islands they arrive by camel. One custom was for groups of people to walk out toward the city boundary to meet the Kings, some carrying ladders and some making a huge racket with horns, bells, and drums. Occasionally, those with ladders would pause in the procession while someone climbed a ladder to look for the Kings.

CONTACT:
Tourist Office of Spain
665 Fifth Ave.
New York, NY 10022
212-759-8822; fax: 212-980-1053

SOURCES:
BkFest-1937, p. 297
DictFolkMyth-1984, p. 1063
FestWestEur-1958, p. 188

♦ 0606 ♦ **Epiphany in Sweden (Trettondag Jul)**
January 6

The **Night of the Three Holy Kings** was celebrated in Sweden during the Middle Ages with ecclesiastical folk plays commemorating the Magi's finding of Jesus in the manger. It is still customary for *Stjärngossar*, or Star Boys (*see also* EPIPHANY IN GERMANY), to present pageants dramatizing the journey of the Three Kings to Bethlehem. They wear white robes and cone-shaped hats with pompons and astronomical symbols on them. They carry paper star lanterns on long poles, illuminated from within by candles.

In rural areas, the Star Boys go from house to house, accompanied by other children dressed in costumes to resemble biblical characters, singing folk songs and hymns. The group almost always includes someone dressed up as Judas, wearing a huge false nose and carrying a purse or money bag jingling with the 30 pieces of silver he received for betraying Jesus.

SOURCES:
BkFest-1937, p. 307
FestWestEur-1958, p. 210
FolkWrldHol-1992, p. 15

♦ 0607 ♦ **Equal Opportunity Day**
November 19

At the dedication of the Gettysburg National Cemetery in southern Pennsylvania on November 19, 1863, President Abraham LINCOLN delivered the GETTYSBURG Address, a 270-word speech that is considered one of the greatest in American history, though it didn't receive much attention at the time. Equal Opportunity Day is observed at Gettysburg National Cemetery each year, where ceremonies commemorating Lincoln's address are held under the sponsorship of the Sons of Union Veterans and the Lincoln Fellowship of Pennsylvania. Sometimes this day is referred to as **Gettysburg Address Day**.

CONTACT:
Pennsylvania Office of Travel
  Marketing
453 Forum Bldg.
Harrisburg, PA 17120
800-237-4363 or 717-787-5453
fax: 717-234-4560

SOURCES:
AnnivHol-1983, p. 149
Chases-1996, pp. 453, 454

♦ 0608 ♦ **Equatorial Guinea Independence Day**
October 12

On this day in 1968, Equatorial Guinea became independent from Spain after being one of its colonies for nearly 300 years. On October 12—the same day on which COLUMBUS DAY is celebrated elsewhere in the world—Equatorial Guinea celebrates its autonomy with a national holiday.

CONTACT:
Equatorial Guinea Embassy
57 Magnolia Ave.
Mount Vernon, NY 10553
914-738-9584; fax: 914-667-6838

SOURCES:
AnnivHol-1983, p. 132
Chases-1996, p. 414

♦ 0609 ♦ **Esala Perahera (Arrival of the Tooth Relic)**
June–July; during full moon of Hindu month of Asadha

A celebration in Kandy, Sri Lanka (formerly Ceylon), that lasts 14 nights and pays homage to the sacred relic believed to be a tooth of the Buddha. Kandy, originally the capital of the independent kingdom of Kandy in the Sri Lankan highlands, is the site of the Dalada Maligava, or Temple of the Tooth, where the relic is kept. The celebration originated in the fourth century when the king of Kandy declared that the tooth be paraded annually so people could honor it.

Processions are held each night for nine nights, and the tooth is paraded in an elaborate *howdah* (platform) on the back of an ornately decorated elephant. Dozens of richly caparisoned elephants follow, and there are also drummers beating big bass drums and small tom-toms, horn blowers, the famous Kandyan dancers, acrobats, and torch bearers holding aloft baskets of blazing *copra* (coconut meat). Representatives of the major Hindu temples also are part of the processions.

CONTACT:
Sri Lankan Embassy
2148 Wyoming Ave., N.W.
Washington, D.C. 20008
202-483-4025; fax: 202-232-7181

SOURCES:
AnnivHol-1983, p. 176
BkHolWrld-1986, Aug 20
DictWrldRel-1989, p. 135
FolkWrldHol-1992, p. 400
GdWrldFest-1985, p. 165
IntlThFolk-1979, p. 344

♦ 0610 ♦ **Escalade (Scaling the Walls)**
December 11

A celebration in Geneva, Switzerland, of the victory of the people of Geneva over the attacking French Savoyards. On the nights of Dec. 11 and 12 in 1602, the French soldiers tried to scale the city ramparts, but were ferociously turned back. Among the remembered defenders is Mère Royaume, who poured a pot of scalding soup on the head of a Savoyard soldier.

To mark the victory, people carrying torches and wearing period costumes and armor proceed through the old city on both banks of the Rhone River. Historic figures, like Mère Royaume, are always represented. Shops sell chocolates that look like miniature soup pots. These commemorate Royaume's courageous act. At several points on the route, the procession stops while a herald on horseback reads the proclamation of victory. The procession winds up at St. Peter's Cathedral, where the citizens sing patriotic songs and a huge bonfire concludes the celebration.

CONTACT:
Swiss National Tourist Office
608 Fifth Ave.
New York, NY 10020
212-757-5944; fax: 212-262-6116

SOURCES:
AnnivHol-1983, p. 159

♦ 0611 ♦ **Esplanade Concerts**
Early July

Arthur Fiedler (1894–1979), a violinist for the Boston Symphony Orchestra, started this outdoor concert series on July 4, 1929. The first concerts were held under a temporary wooden shell along the banks of the Charles River in Boston, which has since been replaced by the Hatch Memorial Shell, a gift presented to the city in 1940. The concerts are free, and it is not uncommon for 20,000 or more concertgoers to bring picnic suppers and relax on the grassy riverbank or listen to the concerts from boats moored in the Charles River lagoon.

During the Bicentennial celebration in 1976, the Boston Pops Esplanade Orchestra performed a spectacular rendition of Tchaikovsky's *1812 Overture*. The music was accompanied by the firing of live cannons, the ringing of nearby church bells, and a dramatic fireworks display.

See also Boston Pops

CONTACT:
Greater Boston Convention and
 Visitors Bureau
P.O. Box 490
Boston, MA 02199
800-374-7400 or 617-536-4100
fax: 617-424-7664

SOURCES:
MusFestAmer-1990, p. 211

Esther, Fast of
See **Ta'anit Esther**

♦ 0612 ♦ **Estonia Independence Day**
February 24

On this day in 1918, Estonia issued a declaration of independence from the new Soviet Russia, which was followed by war with the Soviets to maintain Estonian liberty. On February 2, 1920, the war ended with the Tartu Peace Treaty which guaranteed Estonia's independence for all time. The Soviets went on to break this pact, however, and Estonia was under Soviet control for 75 years. Following a strong independence movement during the late 1980s, Estonia officially declared its independence from the former U.S.S.R. on August 20, 1991. Latvia and Lithuania had also declared independence from the disintegrating Soviet empire. On September 6, independence was formally recognized by the former Soviet Union.

CONTACT:
Estonian Embassy
1030 15th St., N.W., Ste. 1000
Washington, D.C. 20005
202-588-0101

SOURCES:
AnnivHol-1983, p. 28
Chases-1996, pp. 110, 365

♦ 0613 ♦ **Ethiopia National Day**
September 12

The Ethiopian army brought an end to the Ethiopian Empire and Haile Selassie's rule on this day in 1974. Haile Selassie (born Ras Tafari; 1892–1975) was crowned in 1930, inheriting the throne from a long line of regents. According to tradition, he was the 111th ruler descended from King Solomon and the Queen of Sheba.

Also known as **Revolution Day**, this is a national Ethiopian holiday.

See also Haile Selassie's Birthday and Haile Selassie's Coronation Day

CONTACT:
Ethiopian Embassy
2134 Kalorama Rd., N.W.
Washington, D.C. 20008
202-234-2281; fax: 202-328-7950

SOURCES:
AnnivHol-1983, p. 117

♦ 0614 ♦ **Europalia**
September–December in odd-numbered years

Since its founding in 1969, the biennial European arts festival known around the world as Europalia has presented a comprehensive survey of the diverse cultural and artistic aspects of a specific country. The first several festivals were devoted to European cultures: Italy, the Netherlands, Great Britain, France, Germany, Belgium, Greece, Spain, and Austria. But in 1989 the decision was made to devote the festival to a major culture from outside Europe: Japan. In 1993 the festival's founders moved its focus to the American continent, devoting the three-month festival to a display of cultural events representing Mexico.

While most of the festival events take place in Brussels, other cities in the Netherlands, France, Luxembourg, and Germany also host events, which include art, photography, and craft exhibitions; theater, dance, and orchestral performances; literary and scientific colloquia; and film retrospectives. Europalia '93 Mexico, for example, offered 14 exhibitions, 76 concerts, eight ballet performances, 22 theatrical productions, 17 literary events, 187 films, and nine traditional folk events. Discussions with the well-known writers Octavio Paz and Carlos Fuentes were a highlight of the festival.

CONTACT:
Belgian Tourist Office
780 Third Ave.
New York, NY 10017
212-758-8130; fax: 212-355-7675

SOURCES:
IntlThFolk-1979, p. 45

♦ 0615 ♦ **Evacuation Day**
March 17; September 1; November 25

"Evacuation Day" has been used to describe a number of dates in history on which military forces have withdrawn from a city or country. The best-known evacuation in the United States took place on March 17, 1776, during the early part of the American Revolution. British troops were forced out of Boston, when the British commander, General Sir William Howe, conceded defeat to the American General George Washington in a move that he hoped would save the British fleet. Bostonians have been celebrating the day ever since. Because of the large Irish-American community in Boston, the popularity of this holiday is often attributed to its being coincident with St. Patrick's Day. Another well-known evacuation took place a few years later on November 25, 1783, when the British were forced out of New York City.

In England, "Evacuation Day" has also been used to refer to September 1, 1939, and the two days following, when over a million children and adults were evacuated from London and other cities considered to be likely targets for bombing during World War II.

SOURCES:
AmerBkDays-1978, pp. 264,
 1051
AnnivHol-1983, p. 38
Chases-1996, p. 135
DictDays-1988, p. 37

♦ 0616 ♦ Evamelunga
September 8

Evamelunga, which means **'The Taking Away of the Burden of Sin'** is a day of thanksgiving for Christians in Cameroon. Families put on their best clothes and flock to the thatched-roof churches, which are decorated with flowers and palm leaves for the occasion. Church choirs and school choruses sing songs expressing gratitude for the arrival of the first missionary who brought them the story of Jesus in the late 19th century. After the church services are over, the feasting and singing continue late into the evening.

SOURCES:
FolkWrldHol-1992, p. 445

♦ 0617 ♦ Exaltation of the Cross, Feast of the
September 14; formerly May 3 by Roman Catholics

So-called by the Eastern church, where it is one of the 12 great feasts, and is also known as the **Elevation, Recovery** or **Adoration of the Cross**. In the West, it is known as **Holy Cross Day** (by the Anglican Communion), the **Triumph of the Cross** (by Roman Catholics), and also the **Invention of the Cross** (from Latin *invenire,* meaning 'to find'). It commemorates three events: the finding of the cross on which Jesus was crucified, the dedication in 335 of the basilica built by Emperor Constantine enclosing the supposed site of Christ's crucifixion on Golgotha, and the recovery in 629 by Emperor Heraclius of the relic of the cross that had been stolen by the Persians.

According to tradition, St. Helena, mother of Emperor Constantine, found the cross on a visit to Jerusalem, being enabled to identify it by a miracle. Many relics from the cross were distributed among churches throughout the world. (In the late 19th century, Rohault de Fleury catalogued all the known relics in the world; he estimated that they constituted less than one-third of the size of the cross that was believed to have been used.) In addition, St. Helena discovered the four nails used in the Crucifixion, and the small plaque hung above Christ that bore the sarcastic inscription "INRI" (*Iesus Nazarenus Rex Iudaeorum,* Latin for 'Jesus of Nazareth, King of the Jews'). Two of the nails were placed in Constantine's crown, one was later brought to France by Charlemagne, and the fourth was supposedly cast into the Adriatic Sea when Helena's ship was threatened by a storm on her return journey.

On September 13, 335, bishops met in Jerusalem for the dedication of the basilica of the Holy Sepulchre built by order of Constantine. It is believed that the date was the anniversary of the discovery of the remains of the cross during excavations on the site of the Temple of Venus. On the 14th, a relic enshrined in a silver-gilt receptacle was elevated for veneration.

The relic was taken to Persia in 614 after the Persian army of King Choesroes occupied Jerusalem. When Heraclius of Constantinople defeated the Persians on the banks of the Danube in 629, he brought the sacred relic to Constantinople (now Istanbul). On September 14, 633, it was carried in a solemn procession to the Church of the Holy Wisdom (Hagia Sophia in Greek; Saint Sophia in English) where it was elevated for all to adore, recalling Christ's words, "And I, if I be lifted up from the earth, will draw all men unto me" (John 12:32).

Former names for this day are **Crouchmas (Cross Mass)**, **Holy Rood Day**, and **Roodmas**, *rood* referring to the wood of which the cross was made.

In the Philippines, there is also a nationwide celebration commemorating the discovery of the Holy Cross of Calvary by St. Helena. It is known as **Santacruzan**. Nine-day pageants are held in May with local men and women playing the parts of biblical characters. There are processions with floats of each town's patron saint, and costumed young women and their escorts parade under flower-decked arches. In Lucban, Quezon Province, multicolored rice wafers, called *kiping,* are shaped into the form of fruits and vegetables and displayed as window ornaments.

See also MASKAL and ORTHODOX EPIPHANY

CONTACT:
Philippine Department of Tourism
556 Fifth Ave.
First Floor Mezzanine
New York, NY 10036
212-575-7915; fax: 212-302-6759

SOURCES:
BkDays-1864, vol. I, p. 586; vol. II, p. 340
BkFest-1937, pp. 152, 295
BkHolWrld-1986, May 3
DaysCustFaith-1957, pp. 118, 234
FestSaintDays-1915, pp. 110, 177
FolkAmerHol-1991, pp. 197, 337
FolkWrldHol-1992, p. 270
RelHolCal-1993, p. 118
SaintFestCh-1904, pp. 224, 404

♦ 0618 ♦ Excited Insects, Feast of
On or around March 5

Known as **Kyongchip** in Korea and as **Ching Che** in China, the Feast of Excited Insects marks the transition from winter to spring. It is the day when the insects are said to awaken from their long winter hibernation. In China, it is the day when "the dragon raises his head," summoning the insects back to life, and various rituals designed to placate the insects and assist Nature in the task of restoring fertility to the earth are performed. In Korea, this is one of 24 days in the lunar calendar year that indicate a change of season. Farmers sow their rice and wheat, and families lay flowers on the graves of their ancestors to welcome spring.

SOURCES:
FolkWrldHol-1992, p. 159

F

♦ 0619 ♦ **Fairbanks Winter Carnival**
Second week in March

A week of festivities in Fairbanks, Alaska, highlighted by sled dog races. The carnival opens with the two-day Limited North American Sled Dog Race, and concludes, on the last two days, with the Open North American Sled Dog Race. Other events include dances, a parka parade, a campstove chili contest, a native potlatch, snow- and ice-sculpting contests, snowshoe races and softball, musical and dramatic presentations, and a trade fair.

CONTACT:
Fairbanks Convention and Visitors
  Bureau
550 First Ave.
Fairbanks, AK 99701
800-456-5774 or 907-456-INFO
fax: 907-452-2867

♦ 0620 ♦ **Fairhope Jubilee**
Summer, usually August

A natural phenomenon greeted by the citizens of Fairhope, Alabama, with a rush to the shores of Mobile Bay. Fairhope, on a bluff over the bay, has two miles of beach. At a certain time, when the bay is calm and there is an east wind and a certain feel to the air, bottom-dwelling fish and crustaceans are trapped between a low-oxygen water mass and the shore. They become sluggish because of the shortage of oxygen and can't swim, so townsfolk rush out with buckets, cooking pots, crab nets, long poles, and wash basins to harvest them. The harvest may include flounder, shrimp, blue crab, stingrays, eels, and smaller fish such as shiners, anchovies, and hogchokers.

It's impossible to predict when the phenomenon will occur except that it's always in the summer and usually in August. Sometimes there is more than one occurrence; sometimes it will happen five days in a row. This event depends on a number of very specific circumstances: an overcast day, a gentle wind from the east, a rising tide. Here's what happens: a deep-water pocket of very salty water stagnates and collects plant matter. This food supply and the warm temperatures cause a population explosion of microorganisms that consume great quantities of oxygen. A gentle east wind comes along and moves the upper-layer water offshore.

Then the rising tide pushes the oxygen-poor bottom water toward the shore, and the bottom sea creatures are pushed in front of it. They act as though they're in a stupor because they're trying to get oxygen; they move slowly and don't try to swim. Eels will leave the water and burrow tail-first into the moist sand, leaving their heads in the air with mouths open.

Supposedly the event got its name because the first person seeing the marine migration called out, "Jubilee!"

CONTACT:
Alabama Bureau of Tourism and
  Travel
P.O. Box 4927
Montgomery, AL 36103
800-252-2263 or 334-242-4169
fax: 334-242-4554

Fallas de San Jose (Bonfires of St. Joseph)
See **St. Joseph's Day**

♦ 0621 ♦ **Family Week**
Begins on the first Sunday in May

In America, Protestant churches, Roman Catholic churches, and Jewish congregations observe **National Family Week**. While each has its own way of celebrating this event, the emphasis is on the strength that a family can find in religion. Members of the congregation are encouraged to examine their own lives from the perspective of how they have contributed to the religious life of their families, and groups often meet to discuss how to deal with social conditions that are having an adverse effect on family life. National Family Week begins on the first Sunday in May and leads up to Mother's Day and, among Christians, to the **Festival of the Christian Home**.

Many other countries observe a **Family Day**, as well, particularly in Africa. In Angola, Family Day is observed on December 25; in Namibia, December 26. Family Day is also the name by which Easter Monday is known in South Africa.

SOURCES:
AnnivHol-1983, pp. 89, 164
Chases-1996, p. 202
DaysCustFaith-1957, p. 133

RelHolCal-1993, p. 76

♦ 0622 ♦ Farvardegan Days
March 11–20; July; August

Also known as **Farvadin** or **Farvardin**, this is a Zoroastrian festival celebrated by the followers of Zoroaster in Iran and India. In parts of India, the festival is called Khordad Sal. The 10-day **Remembrance of the Departed** commemorates the spirits of the dead (*fravashis*), who have returned to God, or Ahura Mazda, to help in the fight against evil. Parsi worshippers attend ceremonies for the dead on the hills in front of the *dakhmas* (towers of silence) and at shrines in their homes.

Farvardegan is celebrated from March 11 to 20 by the Fasli sect of the Parsis, in July by the Kadmi sect, and in August by the Shahenshai sect. Zoroaster (or Zarathushtra) was a Persian prophet and reformer in the sixth century B.C. whose teachings influenced Judaism, Christianity, and Islam. The largest Zoroastrian groups remaining today are the Parsis (or Parsees) of India and the Gabars of Iran.

> **SOURCES:**
> *AnnivHol-1983*, p. 180
> *FolkWrldHol-1992*, p. 441
> *RelHolCal-1993*, p. 101

♦ 0623 ♦ Fasching
Between February 2 and March 8; the two days before Ash Wednesday

Known in southwest Germany as **Fastnacht**, in Mainz as **Fassenacht**, in Bavaria and Austria as Fasching, as **Karneval** in the Rhineland, and elsewhere as the **Feast of Fools**. This is a Shrovetide festival that takes place on the two days immediately preceding Ash Wednesday, otherwise known as Rose Monday and Shrove Tuesday. It features processions of masked figures, and is the equivalent of Mardi Gras and the last day of Carnival. Fastnacht means 'eve of the fast,' and the wild celebrations that typically take place during this festival are a way of making the most of the last hours before the deprivations of Lent.

In the Black Forest area of southern Germany, these pre-Lenten festivities are called **Fastnet**. The celebrations date back to the Middle Ages and were developed by craftsmen's guilds. Today's carnival clubs (*Narrenzünfte*) still use the same wooden masks and traditional costumes in their parades as their ancestors did. The rites of Fasnet are distinctive: in Elzach, wooden-masked Schuddig Fools, wearing red costumes and large hats decorated with snail shells, run through the town beating people with blown-up hogs' bladders; in Wolfach, fools stroll around in nightgowns and nightcaps; in Überlinger on the Bodensee and Villingen, they crack long whips, toss fruit and nuts to the children, and wear foxes' tails and smiling wooden masks. Carnival ends with *Kehraus*, a 'sweeping out.'

See also Karneval in Cologne

CONTACT:
German National Tourist Office
122 E. 42nd St., 52nd Floor
New York, NY 10168
212-661-7200; fax: 212-661-7174

Austrian National Tourist Office
P.O. Box 1142, Times Square
New York, NY 10148
212-944-6880; fax: 212-730-4568

SOURCES:
AmerBkDays-1978, pp. 43, 157
BkFest-1937, pp. 29, 132
BkHolWrld-1986, Feb 25
Chases-1996, pp. 103, 104
DictFolkMyth-1984, pp. 192, 370, 977, 1082
FestWestEur-1958, pp. 55, 56
FolkWrldHol-1992, p. 110

RelHolCal-1993, pp. 65, 76, 110

♦ 0624 ♦ Fasinada
July 22

A commemoration of a miraculous event on the tiny island of Gospa od Skrpjela (Our Lady of the Chisels) off Montenegro (formerly in Yugoslavia). The island, according to the story, was once nothing more than a rock. One stormy night, a shipwrecked sailor clung to the rock and vowed that if he survived he would build a church to the Virgin Mary. He did survive, and sailors dumped stones there until an island was formed; in the 17th century a church was built on the pile of rocks. The festival includes a procession to the island of boats decorated with garlands of flowers and loaded with rocks. The rocks are piled up to reinforce the shores of the island, and then the participants enjoy folk dancing and country sports and games.

CONTACT:
Yugoslavia Embassy
2410 California St., N.W.
Washington, D.C. 20008
202-462-6566; fax: 202-797-9663

♦ 0625 ♦ Fast Day
Fourth Monday in April

At one time it was customary for the governors of the New England states to proclaim days of public fasting and prayer, usually around the middle of April. But after the Revolutionary War, enthusiasm for the custom began to wane. Because the day's spiritual significance had faded by the 19th century, Massachusetts abolished its Fast Day in 1895 and began to observe Patriots' Day in its place. Maine followed suit a few years later.

New Hampshire is now the only state that continues to observe Fast Day as a legal holiday, maintaining a tradition that can be traced back to 1679. No longer an occasion for abstinence, it is usually regarded as an opportunity for outdoor recreation and spring chores. Although the date is set by law, the governor of New Hampshire issues a yearly proclamation designating the day on which it will be observed.

> **SOURCES:**
> *AnnivHol-1983*, p. 57
> *Chases-1996*, p. 181
> *DictDays-1988*, p. 39

♦ 0626 ♦ Fastelavn
Between February 2 and March 8; Monday before Ash Wednesday

The Monday before Lent begins is a school holiday for children in Denmark. Early in the morning they enter their parents' bedrooms armed with "Lenten birches"—twigs covered with silk, crepe paper, or ribbon. As they poke or smack their parents they cry out, "Give buns! Give buns!"—referring to the traditional *Fastelavnsboller*, or Shrovetide buns, which their parents give them to put a stop to the beating. This custom probably has its roots in ancient purification rites, where people used to beat one another with switches to drive out evil. Various games are played with the buns, such as suspending one by string from a chandelier and trying to take a bite of it. Later in the day, the children dress up in costume and go from door to door, where they are given coins, candy, and more buns.

SOURCES:
AnnivHol-1983, p. 177
BkFest-1937, p. 95
BkHolWrld-1986, Feb 24
FestWestEur-1958, p. 23

♦ 0627 ♦ **Fastens-een**
Between February 3 and March 9; the day before Ash Wednesday

The eve or day before Ash Wednesday has been given a number of names in Scotland and northern England, including Fastens-een, **Fastens-eve, Fastens-Even,** and **Fastens Tuesday.** All refer to the Lenten season that is about to begin, "Fasten Day" being the Old English form of "Fast Day." **Fastingong** was an early English expression for Shrove Tuesday, which was also called **Fastingong Tuesday.** In certain English dialects the word "fastgong" means "fast-going" or "approaching a time of fast."

No matter what the day is called, the day before Lent begins in the West is traditionally a time for carnival-like celebrations.

See also Carnival, Collop Monday, Fasching, Shrove Tuesday

SOURCES:
AmerBkDays-1978, p. 157
BkDays-1864, vol. I, p. 236
BkFest-1937, p. 54
DictDays-1988, pp. 9, 15, 39, 42

♦ 0628 ♦ **Father's Day**
Third Sunday in June

Sonora Louise Smart Dodd from Spokane, Washington, suggested to her minister in 1910 that a day be set aside for honoring fathers. Her own father was a Civil War veteran who raised his six children on the family farm after his wife died in childbirth. The Ministerial Association and the Spokane YMCA picked up on the idea, and in 1924 Father's Day received the support of President Calvin Coolidge. But it wasn't until 1966 that a presidential proclamation established Father's Day as the third Sunday in June. Although it began as a religious celebration, today it is primarily an occasion for showing appreciation through gift-giving.

SOURCES:
AmerBkDays-1978, p. 574
AnnivHol-1983, p. 82
BkHolWrld-1986, Jun 21
Chases-1996, p. 259
DaysCustFaith-1957, p. 158
DictDays-1988, p. 39

Father's Day in the former Yugoslavia
See **Children's Day in the former Yugoslavia**

Fat Tuesday
See **Shrove Tuesday**

♦ 0629 ♦ **Faunalia**
December 15 and February 13

In Roman mythology, Faunus was a woodland deity later identified with the Arcadian god Pan. It was believed that Faunus sent his prophecies through the mysterious sounds heard in the forest. He was also the fertility god of shepherds and crops. Two celebrations were held each year in his honor, one on December 15 and the other on February 13. Goats were sacrificed, games were played, and there were libations of wine and milk.

Faunus was known as the brother, father, or husband of Bona Dea. Lupercus, the fertility god associated with the Lupercalia, was also identified with Faunus, as was Inuus, the fertilizer of cattle. Like Pan, Faunus had horns and hooves like a goat's. The Fauni, or fauns, were spirits of the forest who resembled the Greek satyrs.

SOURCES:
DictFolkMyth-1984, p. 372
NewCentClassHand-1962, p. 479
OxClassDict-1970, p. 432

♦ 0630 ♦ **Feast of Fools**
On or around January 1

A mock-religious festival popular during the Middle Ages in Europe, particularly France, the Feast of Fools had much in common with the Roman Saturnalia. During the holiday period around Christmas and New Year's Day, various classes of the clergy took turns reversing the normal procedures in the church. On January 1, the Feast of the Circumcision, for example, the priests were in charge; on Holy Innocents' Day, December 28, the choirboys held sway. The group to whom the day belonged would nominate a bishop and archbishop of fools, ordaining them in a mock ceremony and then presenting them to the people. Masked and dressed in women's clothing, they would dance and sing obscene songs, play dice or eat at the altar, burn old shoes in the censers, and engage in other activities that would normally be unthinkable. The revelry died out around the time of the Reformation.

The Feast of Fools was similar, but not identical, to the Feast of the Ass that was observed in France around Christmas time

SOURCES:
DictFolkMyth-1984, p. 374
DictMyth-1962, vol. I, p. 555
EncyRel-1987, vol. 3, p. 99; vol. 6, p. 526
FestSaintDays-1915, p. 253
SeasFeast-1961, p. 278

♦ 0631 ♦ **Feast of the Ass**
Around Christmas, December 25

This festival commemorating the flight of Joseph, Mary, and Jesus into Egypt to escape King Herod reached its peak during the Middle Ages in France. It was customary to have a girl carrying a baby and riding an elaborately decorated ass led through the streets to the church, where a mass was said. But the celebration gradually took on comic overtones, with the priest and congregation imitating the braying of an ass at appropriate times during the service and the ass itself being led into the church and given food and drink. By the 15th century the feast had obviously degenerated into a farce, and it was suppressed thereafter by the Church, although it didn't disappear entirely until much later.

See also Feast of Fools

SOURCES:
BkDays-1864, vol. I, p. 112
DictFolkMyth-1984, p. 84
EncyRel-1987, vol. 3, p. 99
FestSaintDays-1915, p. 254

♦ 0632 ♦ Feralia
February 21

This ancient Roman festival marked the culmination of a week-long celebration in honor of the *Manes*, spirits of the dead. It began on February 13 with the PARENTALIA, a private celebration in honor of deceased family members, and ended on February 21 with a public celebration known as the Feralia. This was the day on which offerings and gifts were placed on the graves of the deceased and the anniversary of the funeral feast was celebrated. The Feralia is the pagan equivalent of ALL SOULS' DAY.

SOURCES:
DictFolkMyth-1984, p. 673
FestSaintDays-1915, p. 191
OxClassDict-1970, p. 434

♦ 0633 ♦ Festa del Grillo
Between April 30 and June 3; forty days after Easter

In most European countries, ASCENSION DAY is a holiday when families go to the country to have picnics or just to spend the day outdoors. On Ascension Day in Florence, Italy, crowds gather in the Cascine—a public park along the banks of the Arno River—to celebrate the Festa del Grillo, or **Cricket Festival**, the chirping cricket being a traditional symbol of spring. Food stalls are set up in the park, and there are balloons and other souvenirs for sale.

Although people used to catch their own crickets, today they can buy them in brightly painted wood, wicker, or wire cages, where they are kept with a large lettuce leaf to sustain them. The children carry their crickets through the park and later hang the cages outside their windows. If the *grillo* sings to them, it means they'll have good luck.

SOURCES:
BkFestHolWrld-1970, p. 105
BkHolWrld-1986, May 21
FestSaintDays-1915, p. 116
FestWestEur-1958, p. 97

♦ 0634 ♦ Festival-Institute at Round Top
Late May to mid-July

This teaching institute and music festival was founded by world-renowned pianist James Dick in 1971. Dick wanted to establish a center where talented student musicians could make a smooth transition to a professional career. He started out with a 10-day workshop, but now the institute offers advanced lessons, coaching, and various seminars (the application deadline for students is March 1). The emphasis is still on pianists, but there is also instruction in strings, woodwinds, brass, chamber music, and orchestra. The faculty is composed of internationally known musicians who not only teach at the Institute but perform as soloists at the concerts given there.

Round Top is the smallest incorporated city in Texas, with a population of less than 100. It was named for a building with a rounded roof that was at one time a landmark for arriving stage coaches. Just north of the town square is the scenic 200-acre Festival Hill grounds. Concerts are held in the acoustically excellent 1,200-seat festival concert hall and the Edythe Bates Old Chapel, built in 1883. The campus is open all year to visitors and hosts various events, including an Early Music Festival during Memorial Day weekend, "August-to-April Concert Series," herb workshops, retreats and conferences, and guided tours.

CONTACT:
Festival-Institute at Round Top
P.O. Drawer 89
Round Top, TX 78954
409-249-3129; fax: 409-249-5078
E-mail: festinst@fais.net

SOURCES:
GdUSFest-1984, p. 185
MusFestAmer-1990, p. 139

♦ 0635 ♦ Festival of Flanders
April–October

The Festival of Flanders, or **Festival van Vlaanderen**, is one of the longest and most diverse music festivals in Europe. The season extends from spring to mid-autumn, with events taking place in seven cities spread over the five Flemish provinces of Belgium. In the medieval city of Bruges, for instance, the festival takes place in August and features baroque and early classical music. In Ghent, it takes place between August and October and includes opera and ballet as well as choral, chamber, and symphonic music. The festival in Antwerp is devoted to international theater, and in Mechelen it focuses on organ and carillon music. Other cities participating in the festival include Brussels-Leuven, Kortrijk, and Tongeren.

Established in 1958, the **Flanders Festival** grew out of the Brussels World Fair. The world's most famous performers, opera companies, and ensembles perform—often in more than one city—in settings that range from concert halls to abbeys and stadiums.

CONTACT:
Belgian Tourist Office
780 Third Ave.
New York, NY 10017
212-758-8130; fax: 212-355-7675

SOURCES:
GdWrldFest-1985, p. 18
IntlThFolk-1979, p. 43
MusFestEurBrit-1980, p. 30

♦ 0636 ♦ Festival of Perth
February–March

Originally designed as a program of cultural entertainment for students attending evening and summer classes at the University of Western Australia, the Festival of Perth has grown into one of Australia's major arts festivals. It offers drama, dance, music, opera, films, art exhibits, children's programs, and even sporting events at locations throughout the city. Although the focus is on Australian performing artists, international groups appear there on a regular basis, including England's Chichester Festival Theatre Company, the National Theater of the Deaf from the United States, Spain's Madrid Flamenco Company, and the Stratford National Theatre of Canada. Plays performed at the festival range from the classics to contemporary works by Australian and English dramatists. The month-long festival also features open-air folk music concerts and dancing, street theater, parades, improvisations, and other dramatic performances.

CONTACT:
Australian Tourist Commission
100 Park Ave., 25th Floor
New York, NY 10017
212-687-6300; fax: 212-661-3340

SOURCES:
GdWrldFest-1985, p. 10
IntlThFolk-1979, p. 29

Fête des Géants
See Giants, Festival of the

Fête Nationale
See Bastille Day

♦ 0637 ♦ Field Days, National
Second week of June

The largest agricultural show in New Zealand takes place for three days during the second week in June in Hamilton, and attracts visitors from more than 40 countries. There are exhibits covering every type of rural activity, demonstrations of how to use the latest farm equipment, and contests in such areas as hay-baling, wire-fencing, tractor-driving, and helicopter log-lifting.

Other agricultural shows in New Zealand include the Agricultural and Pastoral Show at Auckland in late November, featuring New Zealand's largest livestock parade; the Annual Agricultural and Pastoral Show at Hamilton in late October, the country's largest dairy cattle and pig show; and the Canterbury Agricultural and Pastoral Show in mid-November. In a country that in 1990 had more than 60 million sheep and only 3.3 million people, these regional agricultural shows attract the kind of audiences that are usually associated with major athletic competitions.

See also ROYAL SHOW DAYS

CONTACT:
New Zealand Tourism Board
501 Santa Monica Blvd., Ste. 300
Santa Monica, CA 90401
800-388-5494 or 310-395-7480
fax: 310-395-5453

SOURCES:
BkHolWrld-1986, Jun 9

♦ 0638 ♦ Fiesta sa EDSA (People Power Anniversary)
February 25

A commemoration of the bloodless People Power Revolution in the Philippines on Feb. 22–25, 1986, in which the dictatorial regime of President Ferdinand Marcos was toppled. The revolution began because Marcos and Corazon C. Aquino both claimed victory in a presidential election filled with fraud and violence. Two key government officers, Minister Juan Ponce Enrile and Armed Forces Vice Chief of Staff Fidel Ramos, rebelled in protest of Marcos's oppression and demanded his resignation. They holed up at military camps at the Epifanio de los Santos Highway (EDSA), which borders Manila on the east. Pro-Marcos forces threatened to annihilate them, but two million unarmed people surged toward the camps. With offerings of flowers, food, and prayers, they provided a human shield and overcame the military's firepower. Fourteen years of Marcos's rule ended, and Corazon C. Aquino became the first woman president of the Philippines (1986–92). The day is marked with ceremonies at the site of the revolution in Quezon City, a part of metropolitan Manila.

CONTACT:
Philippine Department of Tourism
556 Fifth Ave.
First Floor Mezzanine
New York, NY 10036
212-575-7915; fax: 212-302-6759

♦ 0639 ♦ Fifteenth of Av (Tu be-Av; Hamishah Asar B'Av)
Between July 23 and August 21; Av 15

During the time of the Second Temple in Jerusalem (dedicated between 521 and 517 B.C. and destroyed in 70 A.D.), this was a Jewish folk festival in which young women would dress in white and dance in the vineyards, where young bachelors would come to choose their brides. There are a number of explanations for why the festival was celebrated this way. According to the Talmud, the 15th day of Av was the day when members of different tribes were allowed to intermarry. It was also the day when the cutting of trees to burn on the altar ceased, because the heat of the sun was diminishing and there was some concern that the trees wouldn't dry properly. It's also possible that the holiday was adapted from an ancient SUMMER SOLSTICE festival.

Although in modern times there have been attempts by the new settlements in Israel to turn this day into one of music and folk dancing, the idea doesn't seem to have caught on. The Fifteenth of Av is marked only by a ban on eulogies or fasting.

CONTACT:
Israel Ministry of Tourism
6380 Wilshire Blvd., Ste. 1700
Los Angeles, CA 90048
213-658-7462; fax: 213-658-6543

♦ 0640 ♦ Fig Sunday
Between March 14 and April 18; Palm Sunday

The custom of eating figs on PALM SUNDAY gave rise to the name Fig Sunday, or **Fig Pudding Day**, in England, when children would buy figs and either eat them or bring them home to their mothers to make fig pudding. The name may have come from Christ's cursing of the barren fig tree on the day after his entry into Jerusalem, as told in the 11th chapter of the Gospel of Mark.

SOURCES:
DictDays-1988, p. 41

♦ 0641 ♦ Finland Independence Day
December 6

Sweden and Russia contended for Finland for almost 700 years. The Finnish people lived under Russian control beginning in 1809. The Finnish nationalist movement grew in the 1800s, and when the Bolsheviks took over Russia on Nov. 17, 1917, the Finns saw a time to declare their independence. They did so on Dec. 6 of that same year. This day is a national holiday celebrated with military parades in Helsinki and performances at the National Theater. It is generally a solemn occasion that begins with a parade of students carrying torches and one flag for each year of independence.

CONTACT:
Finnish Tourist Board
655 Third Ave., 18th Floor
New York, NY 10017
212-949-2333; fax: 212-983-5260

SOURCES:
AnnivHol-1983, p. 156
Chases-1996, p. 472
NatlHolWrld-1968, p. 221

♦ 0642 ♦ Finnish Sliding Festival
Two days in February

Patterned after the traditional event in Finland that celebrates Fat Tuesday or SHROVE TUESDAY before the beginning of LENT, the Finnish Sliding Festival, or **Laskiainen**, has been held in Aurora, Minnesota, every winter for more than 50 years. It features two large ice slides which are constructed at the edge of Loon Lake. People bring their sleds or toboggans for an exciting ride down the slide onto the frozen expanse of the lake. For those who want more thrills, there is a *vipukelka* ('wild sled') which resembles a kind of merry-go-round on ice.

Other activities at the weekend event include log-sawing contests, Finnish music and dance performances, and traditional Finnish foods such as oven pancakes and pea soup.

CONTACT:
Minnesota Office of Tourism
121 E. 7th Pl. Metro Sq., Ste. 100
St. Paul, MN 55101
612-296-5029 or 800-657-3700
fax: 612-296-7095

♦ 0643 ♦ Fire Prevention Week, National
Week including October 9

National Fire Prevention Day is October 9, the anniversary of the Great Chicago Fire of 1871, which killed 300 people, left 100,000 homeless, and destroyed more than 17,000 structures. The people of Chicago celebrated their restoration of the city by holding festivities on the anniversary of the fire, but it was the Fire Marshals' Association of North America that decided in 1911 to observe the day in a way that would raise the public's consciousness about fire prevention. President Woodrow Wilson issued the first National Fire Prevention Day proclamation in 1920, and every year since 1925 the week in which October 9 falls has been observed nationwide as National Fire Prevention Week.

Each year the National Fire Protection Association (NFPA) announces a theme for National Fire Prevention Week and sets up programs to educate the public about a particular aspect of fire prevention. In 1994, for example, the theme was the importance of keeping smoke detectors in good working order, and the theme for 1995 was avoiding the major causes of home fires—lighted cigarettes, unattended cooking equipment, and auxiliary heat sources. The NFPA provides a Community Awareness Kit each year to help communities plan their own fire prevention activities.

CONTACT:
National Fire Protection
  Association
One Batterymarch Park
Quincy, MA 02269
800-344-3555 or 617-770-3000
fax: 617-770-0700

SOURCES:
Chases-1996, p. 408

Fireworks Day
See **Guy Fawkes Day**

♦ 0644 ♦ First-born, Fast of the
Between March 26 and April 23; Nisan 14

The Fast of the First-born is the only fast in the Jewish calendar which is neither an atonement for sin nor a fast of petition. Observed only symbolically by firstborn male Jews on the day before PASSOVER, its main purpose appears to be to remind Jews of the Angel of Death's slaying of the Egyptians' firstborn sons and the miraculous escape of their own sons. The obligation to fast can be avoided by participating in a *siyyum*—the study of a particular passage of the Talmud.

SOURCES:
RelHolCal-1993, p. 76

♦ 0645 ♦ First Day of Summer in Iceland
Thursday between April 19–25

In Iceland the First Day of Summer is second in importance only to CHRISTMAS and NEW YEAR'S DAY. It is a legal holiday observed on the Thursday that falls between April 19 and April 25, a time of year that marks the end of the long northern winter. The custom of giving gifts on this day was widespread by the middle of the 19th century, although they were usually homemade articles or, in some areas, a share of the fisherman's catch.

Special foods associated with the First Day of Summer include summer-day cakes—flat rye breads up to a foot in diameter—on top of which the day's share of food for each person would be piled. Since the turn of the century it has also been a popular day for young people to give speeches, poetry readings and dramatic performances, or to engage in singing, dancing, and sports.

SOURCES:
BkHolWrld-1986, Apr 22
Chases-1996, p. 175
FolkWrldHol-1992, p. 246

♦ 0646 ♦ First-Foot Day
January 1

The custom of first-footing, or being the first to cross the threshold of a home in the early hours of NEW YEAR'S DAY, was so popular in England and Scotland during the 19th century that the streets were often more crowded between midnight and one o'clock in the morning than they would normally be at midday. If the "First-Foot," traditionally a man, was to bring the family luck, he had to arrive with his arms full of cakes, bread, and cheese for everyone to share. He should be dark-haired, not fair, and must not have flat feet.

Today the custom may still be observed in Britain and in scattered areas of the United States.

SOURCES:
AmerBkDays-1987, p. 6
BkDays-1864, vol. I, p. 27
BkFest-1937, p. 51
BkFestHolWrld-1970, p. 3
FolkAmerHol-1991, p. 13
FolkWrldHol-1992, p. 3

♦ 0647 ♦ First Fruits of the Alps Sunday
Fourth Sunday in August

The Alpine dairymen of Vissoie, Switzerland, show their appreciation to the parish priest by presenting him with cheeses known as *les prémices des Alpes,* or the "first fruits of the Alps," on the fourth Sunday in August every year. Because they live in huts and graze their herds in the mountains all summer, the dairymen rely on the priest's visits so they can attend Mass and receive the Holy Sacraments. In return, they give him all the milk their herds yield on the third day after their arrival in the mountains by making it into cheeses. At the end of August, the Justice of the Peace of Val D'Anniviers counts, inspects, and weighs the cheeses brought back to Vissoie with the returning herds. After High Mass, the dairymen of the district march in procession to the altar, each carrying his own cheese, and stand before the town's red-and-black-robed magistrates. After giving the first fruits of the Alps to the priest, the dairymen once more form a procession and march to the parsonage, where a feast is held in the courtyard.

> **SOURCES:**
> *BkFestHolWrld-1970,* p. 105
> *FestWestEur-1958,* p. 236

♦ 0648 ♦ First Monday Trade Day
Weekend of first Monday of each month

A colossal trading bazaar, originally known as **Horse Monday**, that each month brings 60,000 people to the small town of Canton, Tex. (population 2,800). This legendary affair in northern Texas had its origins in the 1860s when farmers began gathering in Canton on the first Monday of the month to sell or trade horses, hunting hounds, and other dogs. The event continued and grew. Now it starts on a Friday, runs through the weekend, and offers merchandise at 5,000 exhibition stalls.

Scottsboro, Ala., also has well-known First Monday Trade Days attended by thousands, and this custom is observed in most southern states. Commonly, the markets are held on the streets surrounding the county courthouse. Fiddling and storytelling are often part of the day's activities. The name for the event differs; in some places, it's **Court Day**. In Abingdon, Va., it's **Jockey Day** because of the horse races held along with the trading.

CONTACT:
Texas Department of Commerce
Tourism Division
1700 N. Congress Ave., Ste. 200
Austin, TX 78711
800-888-8839 or 512-462-9192
fax: 512-936-0089

Alabama Bureau of Tourism and
  Travel
P.O. Box 4927
Montgomery, AL 36103
800-252-2262 or 334-242-4169
fax: 334-242-4554

SOURCES:
Chases-1996, p. 50

♦ 0649 ♦ First Night in Boston
December 31

First Night originated in Boston as their annual NEW YEAR'S EVE celebration of the arts. This citywide festival was first held in 1976 to change the drinking and partying that have traditionally marked New Year's Eve celebrations in most American cities into a night of family entertainment. It has proved so successful that 65 other cities in the United States and Canada have followed Boston's lead.

To bring both inner city and suburban communities together,

1,000 artists in Boston offer a wide variety of artistic events and performances at 70 indoor and outdoor sites in Boston's Back Bay, Beacon Hill, South End, downtown, and waterfront areas. In recent years as many as half a million residents and visitors have been drawn to places in the city where they would not normally walk after dark.

CONTACT:
Greater Boston Convention and
  Visitors Bureau
P.O. Box 490
Boston, MA 02199
800-374-7400 or 617-536-4100
fax: 617-424-7664

SOURCES:
Chases-1996, p. 493

Fish Carnival
See **Groppenfasnacht**

♦ 0650 ♦ Flag Day
June 14

On June 14, 1777, the Continental Congress replaced the British symbols of George Washington's Grand Union flag with a new design featuring 13 white stars in a circle on a field of blue and 13 red and white stripes—one for each state. Although it is not certain, this flag may have been made by the Philadelphia seamstress Betsy Ross who was an official flagmaker for the Pennsylvania Navy. The number of stars increased as the new states entered the Union, but the number of stripes stopped at 15 and was later returned to 13.

President Woodrow Wilson issued a proclamation that established June 14 as Flag Day in 1916, but it didn't become official until 1949. This occurred as a result of a campaign by Bernard J. Cigrand and the American Flag-Day Association. It is a legal holiday only in Pennsylvania, but is observed across the country by displaying the American flag on homes and public buildings. Other popular ways of observing this day include flag-raising ceremonies, the singing of the national anthem, and the study of flag etiquette and the flag's origin and meaning.

> **SOURCES:**
> *AmerBkDays-1978,* p. 551
> *AnnivHol-1983,* p. 79
> *BkHolWrld-1986,* Jun 14
> *Chases-1996,* p. 255
> *DictDays-1988,* p. 42

Flag Day in Paraguay
See **Independence and Flag Day in Paraguay**

♦ 0651 ♦ Flagstaff Festival of the Arts
July

The major performing and visual arts festival of Arizona, held in Flagstaff on the campus of Northern Arizona University. The affair began in the early 1960s as a music camp and became a full-fledged festival in 1966. It ran one week that year, and today is a four-week festival with more than 48 events: symphonic and chamber music concerts, ballet, theater, film showings, and art exhibits. From 1966 to 1977, Izler Solomon directed and conducted the festival orchestra, which is composed of musicians from major U.S. orchestras.

CONTACT:
Flagstaff Convention and Visitors
  Bureau
211 W. Aspen Ave.
Flagstaff, AZ 86001
520-779-7611; fax: 520-556-1305

SOURCES:
MusFestAmer-1990, p. 23

♦ 0652 ♦ **Flemington Fair**
August–September, week before Labor Day

The **New Jersey State Agricultural Fair** held in Flemington for seven days at the end of August and continuing right through LABOR DAY is a traditional agricultural fair that was started by a group of local farmers in 1856, making it one of the oldest state fairs in the country. It features a statewide 4-H Lamb Show and Sale, a tractor pull, a horse and pony pull, and all types of car racing (mini-stocks, modified stocks, midgets, and super sprints). The fair also offers programs and exhibits of flowers, the 4-H organization, nurserymen, and various commercial enterprises.

CONTACT:
New Jersey Division of Travel and
  Tourism
20 W. State St.
Trenton, NJ 08625
800-537-7397 or 609-292-2470
fax: 609-633-7418

SOURCES:
Chases-1996, p. 350
GdUSFest-1984, p. 117

Flitting Day
See **Moving Day**

♦ 0653 ♦ **Float Festival**
*January–February; night of full moon in Tamil
month of Thai (Hindu month of Magha)*

A festival held at the temple city of Madurai in the state of Tamil Nadu, India, to commemorate the birth of Tirumala Nayak, a 17th-century king of Madurai. The center of the festival is the Mariamman Teppakulam pond surrounding a temple on an island. Images of the goddess Meenakshi and her consort are floated on a flower-bedecked raft to the illuminated temple, and a spectacular array of lit floats move in procession around the pond, accompanied by music and chanted hymns.

CONTACT:
India Tourist Office
30 Rockefeller Ave.
15 N. Mezzanine
New York, NY 10112
212-586-4901; fax: 212-582-3274

SOURCES:
RelHolCal-1993, p. 95

♦ 0654 ♦ **Floating Lantern Ceremony (Toro Nagashi)**
August 15

A Buddhist ceremony held in Honolulu, Hawaii, on the anniversary of the end of World War II. The festival is part of the annual Buddhist Bon season of July and August in which the spirits of departed ancestors are welcomed back to earth with prayers, dances, offerings, and by setting afloat some 2,000 colorful paper lanterns bearing the names of the dead.

See also OBON FESTIVAL

CONTACT:
Hawaii Visitors Bureau
2270 Kalakaua Ave., Ste. 801
Honolulu, HI 96815
808-923-1811; fax: 808-922-8991

SOURCES:
RelHolCal-1993, p. 77

Flood, Festival of the
See **Kataklysmos, Feast of**

♦ 0655 ♦ **Floralia**
April 28–May 3

An ancient Roman festival held in honor of Flora, the goddess of flowers and gardens, the Floralia was instituted in 238 B.C., but it was originally a movable feast whose date depended on the condition of the crops and flowers in any particular year at the end of April and beginning of May. In 173 B.C., after severe storms had proved disastrous for the cornfields and vineyards, the Roman Senate made it an annual festival extending for six days—from April 28, the anniversary of the founding of Flora's temple, through May 3. Traditionally, the first person to lay a wreath or garland on the temple's statue of Flora was destined to have good fortune in the months that followed.

From the beginning, the Floralia was characterized by wild and licentious behavior on the part of the celebrants. The games, dances, and dramatic productions involved in the celebration were usually lewd, and courtesans are said to have performed mimes in the nude. The obscene nature of the festivities was undoubtedly due to their origins in earlier pagan fertility rites designed to promote the earth's fruitfulness. But when the festival was introduced into Rome, it became a good excuse for excessive drinking and carrying on. The Floralia, which originally featured small statues of Flora that children would decorate with flowers, is believed to have been the precedent for Christian-oriented MAY DAY celebrations, which often included dolls or images of the Virgin Mary.

SOURCES:
AmerBkDays-1978, pp. 314,
  407
ClassDict-1984, p. 244
SeasFeast-1961, p. 169

♦ 0656 ♦ **Florence Musical May (Maggio Musicale Fiorentino)**
Early May–third week in June

The **Florence May Festival** was first held in 1933, and it wasn't long before it had established itself as one of the most important international festivals in Italy. It offers chamber and symphonic music, ballet, and dance, and is recognized as a pioneer in its efforts to revive rare foreign and Italian operas. Most of the larger events are held in the Teatro della Pergola or the more modern Teatro Comunale, home of the festival's resident opera company. In the past, when operas were staged outdoors, the city fathers had to ban the Vespa motor scooters that young Florentines use to get around, for fear that the noise would ruin the listening experience for festival-goers.

Many of the world's greatest singers have performed at the festival, among them Maria Callas, Renata Tebaldi, Mario del Monaco, and Boris Christoff. The festival regularly commissions new opera and dance productions, using funds received from the Ministry of Culture.

CONTACT:
Italian Government Travel Office
630 Fifth Ave.
New York, NY 10111
212-245-4822

SOURCES:
GdWrldFest-1985, p. 117
IntlThFolk-1979, p. 242
MusFestEurBrit-1980, p. 114
MusFestWrld-1963, p. 100

♦ 0657 ♦ Flores de Mayo
May 31

Flores de Mayo ('May flowers') festivals take place throughout the Philippines during the month of May. Children make floral offerings and take them to their churches in the afternoon. Processions wind through the streets of the towns and villages, with girls wearing traditional costumes followed by their relatives and friends singing Hail Marys.

The festival culminates on May 31 with fiestas everywhere. In big cities like Manila, Flores de Mayo is one of the largest festivals of the year, featuring May Queens and fancy dress balls. In the smaller towns and villages, the last day of the month is a day to celebrate the birthday of their patron saint.

CONTACT:
Philippine Department of Tourism
556 Fifth Ave.
First Floor Mezzanine
New York, NY 10036
212-575-7915; fax: 212-302-6759

SOURCES:
FolkWrldHol-1992, p. 306

♦ 0658 ♦ Floriade
Once every 10 years, April–October

Once every 10 years, the Netherlands organizes a World Horticultural Exhibition called the Floriade. The grounds for the exhibition are the Zoeteneer, outside Amsterdam. They cover 230 acres with lakes, gardens, theme pavilions, restaurants, and environmental displays—including a miniature Netherlands with dykes and canals that visitors can flood and drain at will. What has been billed as the greatest flower show on earth runs from early April through early October and attracts about three million visitors. Magnificent displays of bulbs and flowers, plants and trees, and fruits and vegetables are divided into seven thematic areas: transport, production, consumer, environment, future, world, and recreation. In addition to the many open-air activities, there are extensive indoor attractions in the numerous halls, greenhouses, and pavilions.

CONTACT:
Netherlands Board of Tourism
355 Lexington Ave., 21st Floor
New York, NY 10017
212-370-7360; fax: 212-370-9507

Flower Festival
See **Hana Matsuri**

Fool Plough
See **Plough Monday**

Fools, Feast of
See **Fasching; Feast of Fools**

♦ 0659 ♦ Footwashing Day
A Sunday in early summer

According to the Gospel of John, before the Last Supper Jesus washed the feet of his disciples and instructed them to follow his example of humility and love. In some places, this practice is an important part of the celebration of the Eucharist. Although it was originally performed on MAUNDY THURSDAY, in most American Protestant sects it takes place at other times and occasionally at more frequent intervals.

For the mountain people of Kentucky, this observance takes place only once a year, but the preparations go on for weeks beforehand. On Footwashing Day, the women take turns washing each other's feet, and on the opposite side of the church the men do the same thing. Refreshment stands have been set up so children can eat while their parents are participating in the ritual. After the service, the people who live near the church invite the rest of the participants to eat with them.

SOURCES:
FolkAmerHol-1991, p. 255
RelHolCal-1993, p. 77

♦ 0660 ♦ Forefathers' Day
December 21 or 22

Observed primarily in Plymouth, Massachusetts, and by various New England societies throughout the country, Forefathers' Day commemorates the landing of the Pilgrims, who arrived in 1620 on the *Mayflower* and established the second English colony in North America. (The first colony successfully established was in Jamestown, Virginia, in 1607.) The Old Colony Club of Plymouth was the first group to observe the anniversary in 1769, but since this was only 15 years after the New Style Calendar went into effect, there was some confusion about how many days should be added to the original December 11 date of the landing. All dates before 1700 were supposed to have 10 days added, and all dates after 1700 were supposed to have 11 days added. Somehow a mistake was made, and Old Colony Club members still celebrate Forefathers' Day on December 22. Wearing top hats and led by a drummer, they march down the main street of Plymouth. After firing a small cannon, they return to their Club for breakfast and toasts to the Pilgrims.

Transplanted New Englanders who have formed New England societies in other parts of the country, however, observe the occasion on December 21, as does the General Society of Mayflower Descendants, which sometimes refers to it as **Compact Day**. The Pilgrim Society, which was founded in 1820 by a group of people interested in the history of Plymouth, holds its annual meeting on December 21 and serves a traditional dinner of succotash, stew, corn, turnips, and beans.

CONTACT:
Massachusetts Office of Travel
  and Tourism
100 Cambridge St., 13th Floor
Boston, MA 02202
800-447-6277 or 617-727-3201
fax: 617-727-6525

SOURCES:
AmerBkDays-1978, p. 1121
AnnivHol-1983, p. 163
Chases-1996, pp. 485, 486
DictDays-1988, p. 43

Forest, Festival of the
See **Kiamichi Owa-Chito**

♦ 0661 ♦ **Forgiveness, Feast of**
August 1–2

The **Festa del Perdono,** or Feast of Forgiveness, is observed annually in Assisi, Italy, where St. Francis built his humble hermitage, known as the *Porciúncula* ('little portion'), in the 13th century. It was here on a small plot of land containing a ruined chapel that St. Francis experienced his religious conversion and began to preach and gather disciples. He restored the chapel and claimed it as his 'portion' or 'little inheritance.' In 1209 he received papal permission to establish the Franciscan monastic order, the Friars Minor, urging his followers to maintain the chapel as a sacred place. Porciúncula also refers to the plenary indulgence that used to be given to those who visited this sanctuary on August 2, the date set by Pope Honorius III in 1221. Although in the beginning the indulgence could only be gained in the Porciúncula, the privilege was eventually extended to all churches having a connection with the Franciscan order and the time for visiting the sanctuary was extended to the period between the afternoon of August 1 and sunset on August 2.

St. Francis instituted the two-day Feast of Forgiveness because it upset him that by going off to fight in the Crusades a sinful man could escape punishment in purgatory. Believing that there should be a more peaceful means to gain salvation, St. Francis received the Pope's permission for Roman Catholics to make an annual pilgrimage to Assisi to renew their relationship with the church.

The August 2 feast was brought to New Mexico by the early Spanish settlers, and it is still observed in the small town of Arroyo Hondo, about 80 miles north of Santa Fe. Although at one time it involved two processions—one beginning at the village church's main entrance and another, a quarter of a mile away, involving only members of the flagellant brotherhood—today the celebration in Arroyo Hondo that once drew large crowds has nearly died out.

See also St. Francis of Assisi, Feast of

CONTACT:
Italian Government Travel Office
630 Fifth Ave.
New York, NY 10111
212-245-4822

New Mexico Tourism and Travel
 Division
491 Old Santa Fe Trail
Santa Fe, NM 87503
800-545-2040 or 505-827-7400
fax: 505-827-7402

SOURCES:
FolkAmerHol-1991, p. 307

♦ 0662 ♦ **Fornacalia**
Around February 17

The Fornacalia, or **Feast of Ovens,** was observed no later than February 17, which was also the day of the Quirinalia festival honoring the ancient Roman god Quirinus. The Fornacalia was designed to benefit the ovens (*fornices*) that parched grain and was held to placate the goddess Fornix, who presided over them. It lasted a week, during which each household made an offering of *far,* flour of the oldest kind of Italian wheat, roasted in the oven and then crushed in an ancient mill and served in the form of cakes. The rituals involved in the Fornacalia were observed primarily by the *curiae,* or tribal divisions of Rome, and it was celebrated in February on different days—one day for the state and one for each of the curiae. According to Ovid, those who were uncertain which curia they belonged to ended up observing this festival on February 17 instead of on the proper day. At this time a general offering of cakes was made by the whole community.

SOURCES:
FestSaintDays-1915, p. 43
NewCentClassHand-1962, p.
 641
OxClassDict-1970, p. 444

♦ 0663 ♦ **Forty Martyrs' Day**
March 10

The "Forty Martyrs of Sebaste" were Roman soldiers quartered in Armenia in 320. Agricola, the governor of the province, told them that under orders of the Emperor Licinius, they would have to make a sacrifice to the Roman gods. As Christians, they refused to do so. Agricola told them to strip themselves naked and stand on the ice of a nearby pond. All died from exposure during the night. They are greatly revered in the Eastern Christian Church. This day is observed in the Orthodox church in Syria as **'Id al-Arba'in Shahid.** In Greece, special foods are prepared: cake with 40 layers of pastry, stew with 40 herbs, 40 pancakes, etc. In Romania, little cakes called *sfintisori* ('little mints') are baked and given to and received from every passer-by. *Coliva,* a cake of cooked corn and honey, is also traditional. Farm tools are readied for work, and hearth ashes are spread around the cottage to keep the serpent from entering (each home is said to have a serpent protecting it).

SOURCES:
BkFest-1937, p. 328
FolkWrldHol-1992, p. 161

♦ 0664 ♦ **Foster Memorial Day, Stephen**
January 13

Stephen Collins Foster (1826–1864) was a composer whose popular minstrel songs and sentimental ballads have found a lasting place in American music. When he died at the age of 37, suffering from poverty and alcoholism, he left behind more than 200 compositions—among them "Camptown Races," "Beautiful Dreamer," "My Old Kentucky Home," "Oh! Susanna," "Swanee River," and "Jeanie with the Light Brown Hair."

January 13, the anniversary of Foster's death, was proclaimed as Stephen Foster Memorial Day in 1951. In Florida, this day is part of Stephen Foster Memorial Week, established by the state legislature in 1935. One of the most widely known observances takes place at the Stephen Foster Center in White Springs, Florida, on the Sunday nearest January 13. The events commemorating Foster's contributions to American music include performances by musical groups from schools and universities throughout the state and daily concerts from the 97-bell carillon tower. During the preceding October, the so-called "Jeanie auditions" (named for Foster's wife, the subject of "Jeanie with the Light Brown Hair") are held to determine the winner of a music scholarship for 18- to 21-year-old Florida women. The winner often appears at the Memorial Week festivities and performs some of Foster's songs.

148

CONTACT:
Stephen Foster Center
P.O. Box G
White Springs, FL 32096
904-397-4331

SOURCES:
AmerBkDays-1978, p. 74
AnnivHol-1983, p. 8
Chases-1996, p. 64

♦ 0665 ♦ Founder's Day
May 29; April 6

Many organizations and institutions celebrate a Founder's Day. In London, the old soldiers at the Royal Hospital in Chelsea hold a Founder's Day parade on May 29, the birthday of Charles II (1630–1685), the hospital's founder and one of England's most popular monarchs. May 29 is also Royal Oak Day (*see* SHICK-SHACK DAY).

In South Africa, Founder's Day honors the founders of the nation. It is observed on April 6, the day on which Jan Van Riebeek (1619–1677) first landed at what would come to be known as Cape Town in 1652. It is also called **Van Riebeek Day**.

SOURCES:
AnnivHol-1983, p. 48
Chases-1996, p. 233

♦ 0666 ♦ Four an' Twenty Day
January 18

When England and Scotland switched from the Julian to the Gregorian calendar in 1752, eleven days were dropped to make up for the additional time that had accumulated during the use of the Julian calendar. Four an' Twenty Day (or **Old Twelfth Day**) is a Scottish expression referring to the day on which TWELFTH NIGHT used to be celebrated before the switch.

SOURCES:
DictDays-1988, p. 43

♦ 0667 ♦ Fourth of July
July 4

In Philadelphia, Pennsylvania, on July 4, 1776, the Continental Congress approved the final draft of the Declaration of Independence. John Hancock, the president of the Congress was the first to sign the document, using a clear and distinctive hand, thus giving rise to the expression "John Hancock" for one's signature.

As the most important national holiday in the U.S., Independence Day, often called the Fourth of July, is traditionally celebrated with fireworks displays, family picnics, parades, band concerts, and patriotic speeches. It is observed throughout the United States and U.S. territories.

SOURCES:
AmerBkDays-1978, p. 619
BkFest-1937, p. 18
BkHolWrld-1986, Jul 4
Chases-1996, pp. 282, 283, 284
DaysCustFaith-1957, p. 169
FolkAmerHol-1991, p. 256
GdUSFest-1984, pp. 165, 201, 220
IntlThFolk-1979, p. 90

♦ 0668 ♦ Fourth of July in Denmark
July 4

The Fourth of July celebration held in Aalborg, Denmark, each year since 1912 was started by an American of Danish descent, Dr. Max Henius of Chicago. He bought 200 acres of land in Rebild and deeded the land to King Christian X, with the stipulation that his fellow Danish-Americans be allowed to celebrate the Fourth of July there every year. The area is now a national park to which about 35,000 people come to observe America's Independence Day. A replica of the Liberty Bell is rung, the national anthems of both countries are sung by stars from the Royal Danish Opera, military bands perform, and there are bilingual readings of the Declaration of Independence and the Gettysburg Address. As a permanent shrine for Americans of Danish ancestry, there is a replica of the log cabin in which Abraham Lincoln lived as a young boy.

CONTACT:
Danish Tourist Board
655 Third Ave., 18th Floor
New York, NY 10017
212-949-2333; fax: 212-983-5260

SOURCES:
Chases-1996, p. 278
GdWrldFest-1985, p. 70

♦ 0669 ♦ Fox, Death of George
March 4

George Fox (1624–1691) was the founder of the Society of Friends, or Quakers, which he organized in 1650 to protest the overly formal religion of his time. An English preacher and missionary, Fox believed that creeds and scriptures were unimportant in religion; all that really counted was the divine light of Christ as it manifested itself in all people. Church was merely a gathering of friends who were guided by the Inner Light and who were thus able to provide guidance for each other. There was no need for an ordained ministry.

In the early days, the "Friends" set themselves apart from the rest of the world by dressing in black and speaking in biblical "thee and thou" style. They were known for their efforts in the abolition of slavery, prison reform, temperance, and education. In the United States, William Penn received a land grant that subsequently became the Quaker colony of Pennsylvania. Quakers all over the world observe the anniversary of their founder's death in their meetinghouses.

SOURCES:
DayRel-1990, p. 11
DaysCustFaith-1957, p. 71
RelHolCal-1993, p. 70

♦ 0670 ♦ Fox Hill Day
Second Tuesday in August

For over 100 years this day has been celebrated in Nassau, a seaside resort on the island of New Providence in the Bahamas, to commemorate the abolition of slavery. Most of the events take place at the Fox Hill Parade Ground about five miles from Nassau. Bahamian foods, singing, and dancing contribute to a carnival atmosphere, although there is a thanksgiving service in the local Baptist church in the morning that features gospel and Bahamian religious songs.

See also BAHAMAS EMANCIPATION DAY

CONTACT:
Bahamas Tourist Office
150 E. 52nd St., 28th Floor N.
New York, NY 10022
800-422-4262 or 212-758-2777
fax: 212-753-6531

SOURCES:
Chases-1996, p. 335
GdWrldFest-1985, p. 16

◆ 0671 ◆ Frankenmuth Bavarian Festival
Second weekend and third week in June

Religious leaders in Bavaria sent a group of 15 Franconians to Michigan's Saginaw Valley in 1845 to set up a mission for the Indians. Although the mission eventually moved elsewhere, the settlement known as Frankenmuth, meaning "courage of the Franconians," retained its Bavarian roots and soon attracted other German immigrants. In fact, for many years after the beginning of the 20th century, German remained the community's principal language.

The Frankenmuth Bavarian Festival, held in June each year to celebrate the town's German heritage, takes advantage of the town's Old-World atmosphere and Bavarian architecture, which includes a glockenspiel tower that plays traditional German melodies, while carved wooden figures depict the legend of the Pied Piper of Hamelin. There is also a replica of the 19th-century Holz Brücke, Frankenmuth's covered wooden bridge that spans the Cass River. The festival features a dance tent resembling a German *biergarten* with German dance bands and beverages, as well as farm tours, arts and crafts displays, a parade featuring the festival's Bavarian Princess, and well-known entertainers of German origin.

CONTACT:
Michigan Travel Bureau
333 S. Capitol Ave., Ste. F
Lansing, MI 48933
800-543-2937 or 517-373-0670
fax: 517-373-0059

SOURCES:
Chases-1996, p. 246

◆ 0672 ◆ Frankfurt Book Fair (Buchmesse)
Second week in October

The world's largest annual trade show for the book-publishing industry, held annually for six days in Frankfurt, Germany. It attracts exhibitors from about 90 countries, and is attended by close to 250,000 people, of whom 8,000 to 8,500 are publishers, editors, and exhibitors.

Trade fairs have been a tradition in Frankfurt for at least 800 years, and, in even earlier times, its location on the Main River in the heart of the continent made the community a crossroads of trade. Book fairs were held in Frankfurt in the 16th century, when the city had become the center of German publishing. In 1579, the book fairs came under the supervision of the imperial censorship commission, and gradually the center of publishing shifted to Leipzig. The world wars severely restricted publishing in Europe, but the industry reemerged after the war. Because Leipzig was in Soviet-controlled East Germany, the publishing trade center moved back to Frankfurt for the first time since about 1650. The book fair had been chiefly an event for German publishers before 1939, but it grew in a few years to be the world's preeminent book fair. In its present international form, the fair is officially dated to 1949.

CONTACT:
German National Tourist Office
122 E. 42nd St., 52nd Floor
New York, NY 10168
212-661-7200; fax: 212-661-7174

SOURCES:
Chases-1996, p. 401

◆ 0673 ◆ Franklin's Birthday, Benjamin
January 17

The commemoration of the birth of Benjamin Franklin—printer, scientist, inventor, statesman, diplomat, writer, editor, wit, and aphorist. Born in Boston on this day in 1706, Franklin helped write, and was a signer of, the Declaration of Independence. He also helped to frame the Constitution. The common-sense moralities of his *Poor Richard's Almanac* became catch-phrases in his time and are still quoted today. For example: "Make haste slowly"; "Fish and visitors smell in three days"; "He that goes a-borrowing, goes a-sorrowing." He invented bifocals, proposed Daylight Saving Time in 1786, and unsuccessfully recommended the wild turkey rather than the bald eagle as the national bird. When he died in 1790 in Philadelphia, he was given the most impressive funeral that city had ever seen: 20,000 people attended.

Since 1991, the Bower Award and Prize in Science—a cash prize of more than $300,000—has been presented on Jan. 17 by the Franklin Institute in Philadelphia to a person who has made a scientific contribution of a practical nature in the manner of Franklin. Also in Philadelphia, the Franklin Institute Science Museum holds a two-day "birthday bash" that often involves people dressing as Franklin. The celebration takes place on the weekend preceding Martin Luther King, Jr. Day, which is the Monday after Jan. 15 (*see* King, Jr's Birthday, Martin Luther).

CONTACT:
Franklin Institute Science Museum
20th St. & Benjamin Franklin
  Pkwy.
Philadelphia, PA 19103
215-448-1200; fax: 215-448-1235
WWW: http://sln.fi.edu

SOURCES:
AmerBkDays-1978, p. 85
AnnivHol-1983, p. 10
Chases-1996, p. 67
DictDays-1988, p. 44

◆ 0674 ◆ Fraternal Day
Second Monday in October

Fraternal Day has been a legal holiday in Alabama since 1915. The state legislature established it as a day to promote good will among people of all religions and beliefs. It is observed the same day as Columbus Day.

SOURCES:
AmerBkDays-1978, p. 920
DictDays-1988, p. 44

Freedom Festival, International
See Canada Day

◆ 0675 ◆ Freeing the Insects
Late August–early September

There is a festival in Japan on May 28 during which vendors sell insects in tiny bamboo cages. Those who purchase the diminutive pets keep them in or near the house during the summer months so that they can hear their songs in the evening. Then, on a day in late August or early September, they gather in public parks and at temples or shrines to set the insects free. When the creatures get their bearings, the former captors listen to them burst into their individual sounds.

The custom of freeing the insects, also known as the **Insect-Hearing Festival**, is more prevalent in rural areas. Although no one seems to know its exact origin, it is reminiscent of Italy's FESTA DEL GRILLO, where crickets are purchased in cages and kept as good luck tokens or harbingers of spring.

SOURCES:
FolkWrldHol-1992, p. 472
JapanFest-1965, p. 185

♦ 0676 ♦ **French Open Tennis**
May–June

Officially known as the **French Championships**, one of the four major tournaments that make up the Grand Slam of tennis. (The others are the AUSTRALIAN OPEN, the UNITED STATES OPEN, and WIMBLEDON.) The French National Championship, played at the Stade Roland Garros in Auteil, France, on red-clay courts, was instituted in 1891 but wasn't opened to players from other nations until 1925. It became an open (to both amateurs and professionals) in 1968.

In 1974, Bjorn Borg of Sweden, 18 years old, became the youngest French Open winner. He went on to become a six-time winner—1974, 1975, 1978-81—putting him ahead of the former champion, Henri Cochet, the winner in 1926, 1928, 1930, and 1932. In the women's division, the most-wins champions since 1925 have been American Chris Evert Lloyd (seven wins: 1974, 1975, 1979, 1980, 1983, 1985, and 1986) and Australian Margaret Smith Court (five wins: 1962, 1964, 1969, 1970, and 1973). In 1990, 16-year-old Monica Seles of Yugoslavia took the youngest-champion honors from Borg when she beat German Steffi Graf.

CONTACT:
French Government Tourist Office
9454 Wilshire Blvd., Ste. 715
Beverly Hills, CA 90212
310-271-6665; fax: 310-276-2835

♦ 0677 ♦ **Frisbee Festival, National**
First weekend in September

The frisbee—a disc made of rigid plastic that soars through the air when thrown with a twisting movement of the wrist—has grown from a child's toy to a national pastime. In 1947 Californians Fred Morrison and Warren Francioni designed and constructed a plastic flying disk which improved upon the pie tins of the Frisbie Pie Company of Bridgeport, Connecticut (founded 1871), which had been tossed in games of catch by Yale college students for decades. The name "Frisbee" was copyrighted by the Wham-O Manufacturing Company, although it had been in use from the days of pie tins.

At the National Frisbee Festival held on the Mall near the National Air and Space Museum in Washington, D.C., each year, enthusiasts come to watch frisbee exhibitions (including a special division for frisbee-catching dogs) and to attend workshops with more than 200 instructors and world champions. The festival was originally organized by the Smithsonian with the help of frisbee champion Larry Schindel—the idea being that such a festival would display another aspect of aerodynamics and relate to the exhibits at the Smithsonian Institution's National Air and Space Museum. But now Schindel organizes the festival himself.

One of the festival's goals has been to win a place in the *Guinness Book of World Records* by achieving "the big throw"— i.e., the largest number of frisbees in the air at once.

CONTACT:
Washington D.C. Convention and
 Visitors Association
1212 New York Ave., N.W., Ste.
 600
Washington, D.C. 20005
800-635-6338 or 202-789-7000
fax: 202-789-7037

SOURCES:
Chases-1996, p. 356

♦ 0678 ♦ **Fritter Thursday**
Between February 5 and March 11; day after Ash Wednesday

At one time in England, each day of the week during which LENT began had a special name: COLLOP MONDAY, SHROVE TUESDAY, ASH WEDNESDAY, Fritter Thursday, and Kissing Friday. Fritter Thursday took its name from the custom of eating apple fritters—fruit-filled cakes fried in deep fat—on this day.

SOURCES:
DictDays-1988, p. 45

♦ 0679 ♦ **Frost Saints' Days**
May 11, 12, 13

These three consecutive days in May mark the feasts of St. Mammertus, St. Pancras, and St. Servatus. In the wine-growing districts of France, a severe cold spell occasionally strikes at this time of year, inflicting serious damage on the grapevines. Although scientists claim that the unseasonable frost is caused by air currents blowing off a late breakup of polar ice in the north, French peasants have always believed that it is the result of their having offended one of the three saints, who for this reason are called the "frost saints."

In Germany, too, feelings toward these three saints are mixed, especially among those whose livelihood depends on agriculture. They call them "the three severe lords," and farmers believe that their crops are not safe from frost until May 13 has passed. French peasants have been known to show their displeasure over a cold snap at this time of year by flogging the statues and defacing the pictures of Mammertus, Pancras, and Servatus.

SOURCES:
DaysCustFaith-1957, p. 122
FolkWrldHol-1992, p. 295

Full Moon Day
See **Magha Puja**

♦ 0680 ♦ **Furrinalia**
July 25

Furrina (or Furina) was an ancient Roman deity whose reason for existence has been largely forgotten. She might have been associated with a spring or springs, and some experts regard her as a spirit of the darkness. Others say she was the goddess of robbers. All that is known for certain is that she possessed a grove (on the slopes of the Janiculum, a ridge near the Tiber River), a festival (the Furrinalia, on July 25), and her own *flamen*, or priest, named Furrinalis. Although Furrina belongs to the earliest of Roman religions, the

Furrinalia continued to be observed in later Roman times. It was in Furrina's grove that the Roman tribune Gaius Sempronius Gracchus ordered his slave to kill him in 121 B.C.

SOURCES:
ClassDict-1984, p. 246
DictFolkMyth-1984, p. 428
OxClassDict-1970, p. 451

♦ 0681 ♦ **Furry Day**
May 8

According to legend, there was a large stone that at one time blocked off the entrance to hell. One night Satan tried to steal the stone. But on his way through Cornwall, England, he was intercepted by the Archangel Michael, who forced him to drop the stone and flee. The town where he dropped it was called Helston (from Hellstone, or stone of hell), and for many years a large block of granite sat in the yard of a tavern there.

The people of Helston continue to celebrate the Archangel's victory, although no one is quite sure why they call this celebration "Furry Day." It may derive from the Gaelic word *fer* meaning "a fair," or from the Latin *feriae*, meaning "festival." Some think it's a corruption of "Flora's Day," a reference to the original Roman goddess of flowers (*see* FLORALIA). The day's festivities include the "Furry dance," which is performed in the streets by men in top hats and women in fancy dresses, and a trip to the woods in search of flowers and leaves. The original rock has long since been broken up into building stones and used for local construction.

CONTACT:
British Tourist Authority
551 Fifth Ave., Ste. 702
New York, NY 10176
800-462-2748 or 212-986-2200
fax: 212-986-1188

SOURCES:
BkFest-1937, p. 58
BkHolWrld-1986, May 8
Chases-1996, p. 204
DaysCustFaith-1957, p. 120
DictDays-1988, p. 45
DictFolkMyth-1984, p. 204

♦ 0682 ♦ **Fur Trade Days**
First full weekend after July 4

Chadron, Nebraska, was at one time a frontier town with a reputation for lawlessness. Shoot-outs in the local saloons were a regular occurrence. But in 1893 a local newspaper came up with a way of putting the town's high spiritedness to better use. They organized the 1,000 Mile Horse Race from Chadron to Chicago—a publicity stunt that made Chadron a household name. Nine men, including one former outlaw,

competed in the race. John Berry, the winner, reached Chicago in 13 days, 16 hours.

Today Chadron's frontier roots are celebrated in two annual events. Fur Trade Days, which takes place on the first full weekend in July after the fourth, is an attempt to recreate the excitement of the town's active trading days in the mid-1800s. Activities include a buffalo stew cookout, horseshoe pitching and buffalo chip-throwing contests, a pig roast, and a primitive rendezvous with a black powder shoot. The other event, which also takes place in mid-July, is the Buckskin Rendezvous, featuring such traditional events as tomahawk-throwing contests and demonstrations of hide tanning, flint-lock marksmanship, and various camp activities.

CONTACT:
Nebraska Travel and Tourism
   Division
700 S. 16th St.
Lincoln, NE 68508
800-228-4307 or 402-471-3794
fax: 402-471-3026

♦ 0683 ♦ **Fyr-Bål Fest**
Weekend nearest June 21

The Fyr-Bål Fest held every year in Ephraim, Wisconsin, reflects the town's Swedish and Norwegian heritage by incorporating customs traditionally associated with Scandinavian MIDSUMMER celebrations. The two-day festival is presided over by a "Viking chieftain," chosen on the basis of his contributions to the community. On the first evening the chieftain, whose identity has been kept secret, arrives by boat at Ephraim on the shores of Lake Michigan, where he is greeted by children dressed as elves. After a coronation ceremony, he proclaims the official opening of summer and lights a bonfire in which an effigy of the Winter Witch is burned. Other groups along the shores of adjacent Eagle Harbor then light their own bonfires. In addition to the bonfire, traditional Scandinavian events at the festival include folk dancing and welcome mats in doorways made out of evergreen boughs woven together. There is also a trophy race at the Ephraim Yacht Club.

CONTACT:
Wisconsin Division of Tourism
123 W. Washington Ave., 6th
   Floor
Madison, WI 53703
800-432-8747 or 608-266-7621
fax: 608-266-3403

SOURCES:
AmerBkDays-1978, pp. 584, 587

G

♦ 0684 ♦ Gable Birthday Celebration, Clark
Saturday nearest February 1

The American film actor William Clark Gable was born in Cadiz, Ohio, on February 1, 1901. For almost a quarter of a century he was Hollywood's leading male star, playing such romantic heroes as Rhett Butler in *Gone With the Wind* (1939).

The Clark Gable Foundation, Inc., was formed in the actor's hometown of Cadiz in 1985 for the purpose of preserving and promoting Gable's memory. Since 1987 it has hosted an annual celebration of Gable's birthday on or near February 1, an event that has been attended by John Clark, Gable's son; Joan Spreckles, his step-daughter; and a number of the original cast members of *Gone With the Wind*. There are booths for Gable memorabilia and showings of his films. The celebration is attended by several hundred collectors and fans.

The Foundation plans to rebuild the house in which Gable was born and to construct a theater-museum where the actor's 67 films will be shown 365 days a year.

CONTACT:
Clark Gable Foundation, Inc.
P.O. Box 65
Cadiz, OH 43907
614-942-GWTW

♦ 0685 ♦ Gabon Independence Day
August 16–18

Gabon gained official independence from France on August 17, 1960, after more than a century of domination.

August 17 is a public holiday, but celebrations extend to the days before and after Independence Day, with parades and dancing.

CONTACT:
Gabon Tourist Information Office
347 Fifth Ave., Ste. 810
New York, NY 10016
212-447-6701; fax: 212-447-1532

SOURCES:
AnnivHol-1983, p. 108
Chases-1996, p. 341
NatlHolWrld-1968, p. 146

♦ 0686 ♦ Gaelic Mod
First full week in August

Held at the end of a five-week summer session at the Gaelic College of Celtic Folk Arts and Highland Home Crafts in St. Ann's, Nova Scotia, the Gaelic Mod is patterned after a similar event observed in Scotland every October. A mod is a competition that involves Gaelic singing, highland dancing, bagpipe playing, and athletic skills—not unlike the Welsh EISTEDDFOD, although the latter is primarily a music and literary event. The Canadian Gaelic Mod includes visits by Scottish clan chiefs and performances by bagpipe bands and highland dance groups. The first mod was held in 1939 when the Gaelic College was founded. Its students teach and perform all over the world.

CONTACT:
Dept. of Tourism and Culture
P.O. Box 456
Halifax, Nova Scotia
Canada B3J 2R5
800-565-0000 or 902-424-5000

SOURCES:
AnnivHol-1983, p. 177
GdWrldFest-1985, p. 46
IntlThFolk-1979, p. 67

♦ 0687 ♦ Gai Jatra
One week beginning the day after the full moon in August

An eight-day carnival-type festival in Nepal, also known as the **Cow Festival**. The largest observances takes place in Katmandu, though Gai Jatra takes place throughout the country. It is sponsored by families who had deaths during the year and is intended to help the dead complete a smooth journey to heaven. Cows are believed to ease the journey and open the gates of heaven with their horns; therefore, during the festival, cows decorated with flowers and teenagers dressed as cows process through the streets. Dancing, singing, and performances satirizing the government and society are also part of the celebrations. These diversions stem from a legend that, after the death of a queen's child, the king sent clowns to console the queen.

CONTACT:
Nepal Embassy
2131 Leroy Pl., N.W.
Washington, D.C. 20008
202-667-4550; fax: 202-667-5534

SOURCES:
BkHolWrld-1986, Oct 8
FolkWrldHol-1992, p. 395

♦ 0688 ♦ **Gallup Inter-Tribal Indian Ceremonial**
Second week in August, Tuesday through Sunday

A major six-day inter-tribal celebration held at Red Rock State Park near Gallup, New Mexico. The ceremonial originated in 1922, and now more than 50 tribes from the United States, Canada, and Mexico participate. Average attendance is 30,000.

The ceremonial activities include competitive dancing, a barbecue, and all-Indian professional rodeos, in which cowboys compete for silver belt-buckle prizes in such events as calf-roping and bronco-riding. There are also three evenings of Indian ceremonial dancing, with the Hoop, Deer, Buffalo, and other dances performed by different tribes.

The markets here present some of the country's finest displays of Indian fine arts—Navajo rugs, katchinas, jewelry, pottery, basketry, beadwork, leatherwork, sculptures, and painting—there are also silversmiths, weavers, and potters at work on their crafts. On Saturday morning, downtown Gallup is the scene of the Ceremonial Parade, with tribal bands playing traditional and contemporary music. It is called the country's only all-Indian non-mechanized parade—all participants are walking, on horseback or in wagons. On Saturday night, a Ceremonial Queen is crowned.

CONTACT:
Intertribal Indian Ceremonial
    Association
Box 1
Church Rock, NM 87311
800-233-4528; fax: 505-722-5158

SOURCES:
Chases-1996, p. 326

♦ 0689 ♦ **Galungan**
Every 210 days

A major 10-day religious festival commemorating the Balinese New Year that is celebrated throughout the Indonesian island-province of Bali every 210 days. (The Balinese calendar followed for holidays is a 210-day cycle.) This is a Bali Hindu festival (Balinese religion is a mix of traditional Balinese and Hindu practices and beliefs), during which the gods are thought to come to earth. Balinese festivals include rituals in the temples, where small thrones are symbolic seats for the gods to occupy; cock-fights, a combination of sport and gambling; offerings of foods, fruit, and flowers to the temple by the women; and card games, music, and dancing.

Numerous temple festivals are held during the year in individual Balinese villages, but Galungan is island-wide.

CONTACT:
Indonesian Tourist Promotion
    Office
3457 Wilshire Blvd., Ste. 104
Los Angeles, CA 90010
213-387-2078; fax: 213-380-4876

SOURCES:
AnnivHol-1983, p. 177
GdWrldFest-1985, p. 112
IntlThFolk-1979, p. 218

♦ 0690 ♦ **Galway Oyster Festival**
Early September

In Galway, Ireland, the opening of the oyster season is celebrated by bringing the first shellfish ashore to the accompaniment of fiddle music. A young woman chosen to preside over the day's activities as the Queen of Connemara presents the first oyster to the mayor, who stands on Clarenbridge Pier in his scarlet robes waiting to open and taste it. Banquets are held in the evening and local pubs serve oysters by the bucketful, washed down by beer.

CONTACT:
Irish Tourist Board
345 Park Ave., 17th Floor
New York, NY 10154
800-223-6470 or 212-418-0800
fax: 212-371-9052

SOURCES:
GdWrldFest-1985, p. 114

♦ 0691 ♦ **Gambia Independence Day**
February 18

Gambia gained independence from Britain on February 18, 1965, and became a constitutional monarchy. On that day, people gathered in Bathurst for music, dancing, and the replacement of the Union Jack with the Gambian flag. A public vote in 1970 made the Republic of the Gambia a British Commonwealth.

Independence Day is a national holiday in Gambia.

CONTACT:
Gambian Embassy
1155 15th St., N.W., Ste. 1000
Washington, D.C. 20005
202-785-1399; fax: 202-785-1430

SOURCES:
Chases-1996, p. 103
NatlHolWrld-1968, p. 25

Ganden Ngamcho
See **Lights, Festival of**

♦ 0692 ♦ **Gandhi Jayanti (Mahatma Gandhi's Birthday)**
October 2

A national holiday in India to commemorate the birth of Mohandas Karamchand Gandhi, who came to be known as Mahatma ('great soul') Gandhi. At this time pilgrimages are made from throughout the country to the Raj Ghat on the banks of the Yamuna River in Delhi where Gandhi was cremated. Many communities also hold spinning and weaving sessions in his honor.

Gandhi, often pictured in a simple white cotton robe at a spinning wheel, was the leader of the movement for Indian nationalism, the 20th century's great prophet of nonviolence, and a religious innovator who encouraged a reformed, liberal Hinduism. He was born in 1869 in Porbandar, India, and educated both in India and England. He went to South Africa as a young lawyer, was shocked by the racial discrimination, and led the African Indians in a non-violent struggle against repression. Returning to India, he became a dominant political figure, and, in the struggle for independence, was jailed several times. His protests often took the form of fasts.

In the 1930s, he worked for rural people trying to eradicate discrimination against the Untouchable caste and promoting hand spinning and weaving as occupations for the poor and as a way to overcome the British monopoly on cloth. The ashram (a religious retreat center) he established near Ahmedabad became the center of his freedom movement. In the 1940s, he helped heal the scars of religious conflict in Bengal and Bihar; in 1947 his fasting put an end to the rioting in Calcutta. On January 30, 1948, on his way to an evening prayer meeting in Delhi, he was shot and killed by a Hindu fanatic. Albert Einstein was among his great admirers.

CONTACT:
India Tourist Office
30 Rockefeller Ave.
15 N. Mezzanine
New York, NY 10112
212-586-4901; fax: 212-582-3274

SOURCES:
AnnivHol-1983, p. 127
BkHolWrld-1986, Oct 2
Chases-1996, p. 401
DictWrldRel-1989, p. 271

♦ 0693 ♦ **Ganesh Chathurthi**
August–September; waxing half of Hindu month of Bhadrapada

A lively week-long festival to worship the elephant-headed Ganesh, the Hindu god of wisdom and success. He is also the remover of obstacles, so he is also called Vighnesa, or Vighneswara. The festival is especially colorful in the Indian states of Tamil Nadu, Maharashtra, Andhra Pradesh, and Karnataka, and is the best-known event in Bombay. Everyone pays homage to huge clay images of Ganesh made by highly respected artists, and he is also propitiated with street performances, competitions, processions, and yoga demonstrations. In Bombay, at the end of the week of celebration, as sacred songs are chanted, an image is taken to the sea and immersed to ensure prosperity for both land and water.

It is said that Ganesh, the son of the gods Shiva and Parvati, so annoyed his father one day that Shiva cut off his head. But Shiva then repented, and replaced his head with that of an elephant. Today people ask for Ganesh's help in undertaking new projects.

The story behind the festival in Nepal is that the day, called **Ganesh Chata**, celebrates a bitter dispute between Ganesh and the moon goddess. Therefore, the Nepalese try to stay inside on this night and close out the moonlight.

CONTACT:
India Tourist Office
30 Rockefeller Ave.
15 N. Mezzanine
New York, NY 10112
212-586-4901; fax: 212-582-3274

Nepal Embassy
2131 Leroy Pl., N.W.
Washington, D.C. 20008
202-667-4550; fax: 202-667-5534

SOURCES:
AnnivHol-1983, p. 177
BkFest-1937, p. 162
BkHolWrld-1986, Sep 5
DictFolkMyth-1984, p. 440
DictWrldRel-1989, p. 273
FolkWrldHol-1992, p. 434
RelHolCal-1993, p. 77

♦ 0694 ♦ **Ganga Dussehra**
May–June; Hindu month of Jyestha

According to Hindu mythology, the Ganges River in India originally flowed only in heaven. In the form of a goddess, Ganga, the river was brought down to earth by King Bhagiratha in order to purify the ashes of his ancestors, 60,000 of whom had been burned under a curse from the great sage Kapila. The river came down reluctantly, breaking her fall on the head of Shiva so that she wouldn't shatter the Earth. By the time she reached the Bay of Bengal, she had touched the ashes of the 60,000 princes and fertilized the entire region.

On Ganga Dussehra, the 10th day of the waxing half of the month of Jyestha, Hindus who are able to reach the Ganges take a dip in the river to purify their sins and remedy their physical ills. The largest crowds assemble at Hardwar, Garh Muktesvar, Varanasi, and other locations on the banks of the Ganges that have legendary significance. Those who live far away from the Ganges immerse themselves in whatever river, pond, or sea they can get to on this day.

Part of the Hindu faith includes the hope of bathing in the Ganges at some point during one's live. Upon death, a Hindu's body is generally cremated and the ashes are immersed in its holy water to assure peace for the soul.

See also KUMBH MELA

CONTACT:
India Tourist Office
30 Rockefeller Ave.
15 N. Mezzanine
New York, NY 10112
212-586-4901; fax: 212-582-3274

SOURCES:
DictFolkMyth-1984, p. 671
FolkWrldHol-1992, p. 318
RelHolCal-1993, p. 78

Gang Days
See **Rogation Days**

♦ 0695 ♦ **Ganna (Genna)**
January 7

The CHRISTMAS celebration in Ethiopia, which is officially called **Leddat**, takes place on January 7 (*see* OLD CHRISTMAS). But it is more popularly known as Ganna, after the game that is traditionally played by boys, young men, and occasionally elders, only on this day. According to legend, the shepherds were so happy when they heard about the birth of Jesus that they used their hooked staffs to play *ganna*—a game similar to field hockey.

SOURCES:
AnnivHol-1983, p. 6
BkFestHolWrld-1970, p. 151
BkHolWrld-1986, Jan 7
FolkWrldHol-1992, p. 22
GdWrldFest-1985, p. 74

♦ 0696 ♦ **Gansabhauet**
November 11 (St. Martin's Day)

An old and peculiar festival involving a dead goose, held only in the country town of Sursee, Switzerland. A dead goose is hung by its neck in front of the town hall, and young men draw lots to take turns trying to knock it down with a blunt saber. (*Gansabhauet* means 'knocking down goose.') The young men, blindfolded and wearing red robes and big round masks representing the sun, get only one try at the bird. While the men whack at the goose, children's games take place: they scale a stripped tree, race in sacks, and compete in seeing who can make the ugliest face.

Gansabhauet was first mentioned in 1821. Its real origin is uncertain, although it is thought that it may have something to do with the old practice of handing over payment in kind to the landlord.

CONTACT:
Swiss National Tourist Office
608 Fifth Ave.
New York, NY 10020
212-757-5944; fax: 212-262-6116

SOURCES:
Chases-1996, p. 448

♦ 0697 ♦ **Garland Day**
May 12; May 29

On May 12, or **Old May Day**, the children of the Dorset fishing village of Abbotsbury still "bring in the May." They do this by carrying garlands from door to door and receiving small gifts in return. The May garlands are woven by a local woman and her helpers, who are regarded as the town's official garland-makers. Each garland is constructed over a frame and supported by a stout broomstick, which is carried by two young people as they go about the village. Later, the garlands are laid at the base of the local war memorial.

At one time this was an important festival marking the beginning of the fishing season. Garland Day used to center around the blessing of the wreaths, which were then carried down to the water and fastened to the bows of the fishing boats. The fishermen then rowed out to sea after dark and tossed the garlands to the waves with prayers for a safe and plentiful fishing season. This ceremony is probably a carry-over from pagan times, when sacrificial offerings were made to the gods of the sea.

Another Garland Day celebration is held in Castleton, Derbyshire, on May 29 or SHICK-SHACK DAY. The Garland King (or May King) rides on horseback at the head of a procession of musicians and young girls, who perform a dance similar to the Helston Furry (see FURRY DAY). The "garland" is an immense beehive-shaped structure that fits over his head and shoulders, covered with greenery and flowers and crowned with a special bouquet called the "queen." This is laid at the war memorial in Castleton's marketplace.

CONTACT:
British Tourist Authority
551 Fifth Ave., Ste. 702
New York, NY 10176
800-462-2748 or 212-986-2200
fax: 212-986-1188

SOURCES:
AnnivHol-1983, p. 65
DictDays-1988, p. 46
RelHolCal-1993, p. 55

◆ 0698 ◆ **Gasparilla Pirate Festival**
Begins on the Monday following the first Tuesday in February

In early February a 164-foot reproduction pirate ship sails up Florida's Tampa Bay and into the Hillsborough River with its cannons booming. About 500 costumed pirates lower themselves over the side and "capture" the city of Tampa and its mayor, raising the pirate flag over city hall. Thus begins the six-day **Gasparilla Pirate Invasion**, one of the nation's largest and best-attended celebrations. The mock invasion is followed by a three-hour victory parade featuring members of a men's club known as Ye Mystic Krewe, which started the pirate festival in 1904.

The festival is named for José Gaspar, an 18th-century Spanish pirate who terrorized the Florida coast from around 1783 until his death in 1821, when he wrapped a length of anchor chain around his waist and leapt into the sea brandishing his sword rather than be captured by a U.S. Navy warship.

CONTACT:
Tampa-Hillsborough Convention
  and Visitors Association
111 Madison St., Ste. 1010
Tampa, FL 33602-4706
800-448-2672

SOURCES:
AmerBkDays-1978, p. 154
AnnivHol-1983, p. 23
BkHolWrld-1986, Feb 7
Chases-1996, p. 102
FolkAmerHol-1991, p. 72
GdUSFest-1984, p. 37

◆ 0699 ◆ **Gaspee Days**
May–June

The British revenue schooner *Gaspee* was sent to the American colonies to reinforce various British revenue laws, including the Townshend Acts of 1767. Because of these laws,

colonists had to pay taxes to the British on imported goods they bought from them. As a result, smuggling was common. The colonists at Rhode Island burned the ship on June 10, 1772, in what many regard as the first act of rebellion leading up to the Revolutionary War. Since 1966 the event has been commemorated in a 16-day festival that includes a symbolic reenactment of the burning, a colonial fife and drum muster, a parade of people in early American costumes, and a "Miss Gaspee" pageant. There are also numerous athletic events, a Colonial Ball, and a johnnycake breakfast. The events, which take place in both Cranston and Warwick, Rhode Island, were proclaimed part of the "Year of the Gaspee" in 1972, the bicentennial of this early stage in the struggle for independence.

See also RHODE ISLAND INDEPENDENCE DAY

CONTACT:
Rhode Island Tourism Division
7 Jackson Walkway
Providence, RI 02903
800-556-2484 or 401-277-2601
fax: 401-277-2102

SOURCES:
AmerBkDays-1978, p. 624
Chases-1996, p. 228
GdUSFest-1984, p. 166

◆ 0700 ◆ **Gawai Dayak**
May–June

A harvest festival of the Dayak people of Sarawak, Malaysia, on the northern coast of Borneo. The celebrations have remained essentially the same for centuries. They take place in longhouses, the bamboo-and-palm-leaf structures built on stilts that are shared by 20 or 30 families. At midnight on the eve of Gawai Dayak, a house elder or bard conducts the chief ritual: while sacrificing a white cock, he recites a poem to ask for guidance, blessings, and a long life. Other events include the selection of the most beautiful man and woman to be king and queen of the harvest, dancing, a feast of rice, eggs, and vegetables, and the serving of traditional *tuak*, 'rice wine'.

SOURCES:
BkHolWrld-1986, Jun 2
FolkWrldHol-1992, pp. 323,
  465
GdWrldFest-1985, p. 132

◆ 0701 ◆ **Gedaliah, Fast of (Tsom Gedalyah, Tzom Gedaliahu)**
Between September 8 and October 6; Tishri 3 (first day following Rosh Hashanah)

When Nebuchadnezzar, the Babylonian king, destroyed Jerusalem and the First Temple, and carried away most of the Jews into slavery in 586 B.C., he left behind a few farmers and families under the supervision of a Jewish governor named Gedaliah ben Ahikam to clean up after the army and to administer affairs in the devastated land. Eventually some Jews who had managed to hide out in the hills came back to the area and joined the thousand or so who had been left behind.

Things progressed well until a few hot-headed traitors, who accused Gedaliah of collaborating with the enemy, murdered him and the small garrison of soldiers Nebuchadnezzar had stationed there. Many of the farmers took their families and fled in terror to Egypt; the rest were either killed or taken to Babylon, bringing about Judah's final collapse. The Fast of Gedaliah commemorates the man who was assassinated at a time when he was needed most.

SOURCES:
Chases-1996, p. 378
DaysCustFaith-1957, p. 245
RelHolCal-1993, p. 76

♦ 0702 ♦ **Geerewol Celebrations**
Rainy season, late June to mid-September

Elaborate week-long festivities held by the Wodaabe people of Niger as a kind of male beauty contest. The festivities also serve the important purpose of allowing young men and women to meet prospective mates outside their circle of cousins.

There are two main dances to the celebrations, the *yaake* and the *geerewol*. The *yaake* is the dance for demonstrating charm. The men paint their faces with pale yellow powder and borders of black kohl around their eyes; they also shave their hairline to heighten the forehead. They dance in a line, leaning forward on tiptoe to accentuate their height, and contorting their faces with rolling eyes, pursed lips, and inflated cheeks. Their charm and personality is judged based on these expressions. The *geerewol* is held to select the most beautiful men. In this dance the men line up wearing beads on their bare chests and turbans adorned with ostrich feathers on their heads. For a couple of hours they chant and jump and stomp while selected young unmarried women kneel and scrutinize them. These women are the judges; eventually they walk toward the dancers and indicate their favorites by swinging their arms.

The Geerewol celebration ends at sunrise after an entire night of dancing when the host group presents the departing guests with roasted meat.

CONTACT:
Niger Embassy
2204 R St., N.W.
Washington, D.C. 20008
202-483-4224; fax: 202-483-3169

♦ 0703 ♦ **General Clinton Canoe Regatta**
May

Originally a re-creation of the historic trip down the Susquehanna River by General James Clinton during the Revolutionary War, this well-known canoe regatta now has three divisions, one for professionals and two for amateurs, based on the type of canoe used. The professional race, which has gained national recognition as the **World Championship Flat Water Endurance Race**, is the longest one-day race of its kind and covers a 70-mile stretch of the river between Cooperstown and Bainbridge, New York. When it was first held in 1962, it was a one-day affair, but now the regatta and the events associated with it extend for three and a half days over the MEMORIAL DAY weekend. There are cash prizes, and the event attracts canoeists from Canada, Michigan, Minnesota, and Wisconsin.

In addition to the races, a carnival and many other activities for spectators are held at General Clinton Park. It was, in fact, money raised by the races that enabled the Bainbridge Chamber of Commerce to purchase the riverfront land on which the park now stands.

CONTACT:
New York Division of Tourism
1 Commerce Pl.
Albany, NY 12245
800-225-5697 or 518-474-4116
fax: 518-486-6416

SOURCES:
GdUSFest-1984, p. 122

Gerna
See Ganna

♦ 0704 ♦ **Georgia Day**
February 12

Also known as **Oglethorpe Day**, February 12 commemorates the day in 1733 when James Edward Oglethorpe and 120 other Englishmen landed in Savannah, Georgia, to establish a new colony. The earliest settlers observed the day by firing salutes and offering toasts in Oglethorpe's honor. For almost 200 years thereafter, the celebrations were confined to major anniversaries of the event, and it wasn't until 1933 that February 12 became a "special day of observance" in the Georgia schools. In 1965 the anniversary of the state's founding was officially proclaimed Georgia Day and celebrated as a day-long event in Savannah.

Savannah's celebration has now grown into an eight-day event sponsored by more than 50 organizations. On February 12, there is a procession through the historic town, a number of wreath-laying ceremonies, and an Oglethorpe banquet. Since 1965 there has been a reenactment of Oglethorpe's landing, with costumed residents playing the roles of Georgia's first European settlers and of the American Indians who greeted them upon their arrival.

CONTACT:
Savannah Area Convention and
  Visitors Bureau
P.O. Box 1628
Savannah, GA 31402
800-444-2427 or 912-944-0456
fax: 912-944-0468

SOURCES:
AmerBkDays-1978, p. 174
AnnivHol-1983, p. 23
Chases-1996, p. 95
GdUSFest-1984, p. 39

♦ 0705 ♦ **Georgia Peanut Festival**
Ten days in October

A harvest festival paying tribute to Georgia's top crop is held in Sylvester, the Peanut Capital of the World. More peanuts are produced in the region around Sylvester than anywhere else in the state, and Georgia accounts for nearly half the U.S.'s peanut production and supplies five percent of the world's total production. Furthermore, Georgia's peanuts are a $2.5 billion industry. Thus Sylvester's title of Peanut Capital. In other countries, the end products of peanuts are usually oil and meal; Georgia's harvest is largely used for salted and roasted peanuts and peanut butter.

This festival, which comes at the end of the peanut harvest time, began in 1964. Highlights through the years have included an appearance by George Bush in 1979 to kick off his unsuccessful drive for the Republican presidential nomination, and the making of the World's Largest Peanut Butter and Jelly Sandwich in 1987. The sandwich measured 12½ feet by 12½ feet.

Events of the festival include a beauty pageant to choose a Little Miss Peanut, Junior Miss Peanut, and Georgia Peanut Queen; a peanut-syrup-and-pancakes eating contest; a peanut-recipe contest for school children; concerts; clogging exhibitions; a kiddy parade and a grand parade (the state's largest commodity parade) with 150 to 200 entries, including floats, horses, antique cars, and people dressed as peanuts.

CONTACT:
Georgia Dept. of Industry
Trade and Tourism
285 Peachtree Center Ave., N.E.
Marquis Tower II, Ste. 1000
Atlanta, GA 30303
800-847-4842 or 404-656-3592
fax: 404-651-9063

♦ 0706 ♦ **Georgiritt (St. George's Parade)**
April 23

St. George is honored each year at Traunstein in Upper Bavaria, Germany, and in other Bavarian villages on April 23, the day on which he is said to have been martyred in 303. The Georgiritt, or St. George's Parade, commemorates the legend of George's victory over the dragon that was threatening the pagan city of Sylene by demanding that humans be sacrificed to feed it. St. George killed the dragon, saved the king's daughter (who was next in line to be sacrificed), and converted Sylene's 15,000 citizens to Christianity.

Because St. George is usually depicted on horseback, the farmers of Traunstein decorate their own horses with garlands on April 23 and ride them across the fields and three times around the parish church. After the local priest blesses the horses and other farm animals, the procession turns toward the village. The festival ends with ritualistic sword dances that have been handed down from medieval times.

See also St. George's Day

CONTACT:
German National Tourist Office
122 E. 42nd St., 52nd Floor
New York, NY 10168
212-661-7200; fax: 212-661-7174

SOURCES:
FestWestEur-1958, p. 64

♦ 0707 ♦ **Geranium Day**
Early April

Since the 1920s this has been a day in England to collect money for the blind. It represents a joint effort by a number of charities dedicated to helping the blind and is organized by the Greater London Fund for the Blind. Although at one time real geraniums were given to those who made donations, today contributors receive a sticker with a red geranium on it. The choice of the geranium—a flower without a strong scent—seems unusual as a symbol for the blind, but it may have been chosen simply because the poppy (*see* Veterans Day) and the rose (*see* Alexandra Rose Day) were already being used for fund-raising purposes. It may also have been chosen for its symbolic meaning: consolation.

SOURCES:
DictDays-1988, p. 47

♦ 0708 ♦ **German-American Day**
October 6

Descendants of the earliest German settlers have observed October 6 as **German Pioneer Day** or **German Settlement**

Day since 1908, commemorating the day on which the first permanent German settlement in America was established at Germantown, Pennsylvania, in 1683. But it wasn't until 1987 that October 6 was formally designated German-American Day by President Ronald Reagan.

According to the 1990 census, German-Americans are the largest ethnic group in the United States, and their traditions and institutions have had a wide-ranging impact on the American way of life. This day is often observed by attending programs and events that promote an understanding of the contributions of German immigrants—for example, lectures on German history, art, music, and literature; exhibits featuring German artifacts; performances of German music and hymns; and church services that acknowledge German-American members of the congregation. Ohio observes German-American Heritage Month throughout October, and smaller celebrations are held in more than 2,000 communities across the country. In recent years, October 6 has also become a time to celebrate the reunification of Germany.

CONTACT:
Society for German-American
 Studies
University of Cincinnati
P.O. Box 20113
Cincinnati, OH 45211
513-556-1955

SOURCES:
Chases-1996, p. 408
DictDays-1988, p. 47

♦ 0709 ♦ **Gettysburg Civil War Heritage Days**
Last weekend in June and first week in July

The Battle of Gettysburg on July 1–3, 1863, marked a turning point in the American Civil War. It was here that General Robert E. Lee's Confederate army of 75,000 men and the 97,000-man Northern army of General George G. Meade met by chance when a Confederate brigade sent there for supplies observed a forward column of Meade's cavalry. The ensuing battle did not end the war, nor did it attain any major military goals for either the North or the South. But the Confederate army was turned back, and it never recovered from its losses. With 51,000 casualties and 5,000 dead horses, the Battle of Gettysburg ranks as the bloodiest battle in American history.

Every year since 1983 the anniversary of the battle has been commemorated with a nine-day festival at the Gettysburg National Military Park. Civil War reenactment groups in authentic uniforms, carrying 19th-century weapons of the type used in the battle, demonstrate infantry tactics and drill, cavalry drill, and soldiers' occupations and pastimes. There are also band concerts, a Civil War battle reenactment, lectures by nationally known historians, and a Civil War collectors' show featuring antique arms and uniforms, documents, books, photographs, and personal effects from pre-1865 American military history.

CONTACT:
Pennsylvania Office of Travel
 Marketing
453 Forum Bldg.
Harrisburg, PA 17120
800-237-4363 or 717-787-5453
fax: 717-234-4560

Gettysburg National Military Park
Gettysburg, PA 17325
717-334-1124

SOURCES:
AnnivHol-1983, p. 87
Chases-1996, p. 275

◆ 0710 ◆ **Gettysburg Day**
July 1

The Battle of Gettysburg, which began on July 1, 1863, was a turning point in the Civil War. Under the leadership of General Robert E. LEE, Confederate soldiers were advancing toward Harrisburg, Pennsylvania, when they encountered General George Meade's Union forces. On the third day of the battle, Lee ordered his men to attack the center of the Union line in an action that later came to be known as Pickett's Charge. But Meade had anticipated just such a strategy, and the rebels were forced to retreat to Virginia. The toll of missing, wounded, and dead was more than 23,000 for the North and 28,000 for the South.

On the 50th anniversary of the battle, Civil War veterans reenacted Pickett's Charge. There continued to be major observances at the Gettysburg battlefield on all the major anniversaries, although the 75th (in 1938) was the last in which surviving Civil War veterans actually participated. The annual observation takes place throughout the week of July 1 and includes speeches by distinguished guests, a military band concert, and a parade with floats illustrating historic events (*see* GETTYSBURG CIVIL WAR HERITAGE DAYS).

SOURCES:
AmerBkDays-1978, p. 609
AnnivHol-1983, p. 87
Chases-1996, p. 277

◆ 0711 ◆ **Ghana Republic Day**
July 1

Ghana's Republic Day celebration is one of the most striking in West Africa, due to the fact that the popular attire includes the brightly colored cloth known as the *kenti*. Although at one time each tribe's *kenti* had a distinctive pattern, weave, and color combination, today most are orange or yellow with a hexagonal pattern. Men wear it draped over one shoulder and around the waist, while women may wear it as a long skirt.

July 1 is the day on which Ghana became an independent republic in 1960. The people also celebrate March 6 as Independence Day—the day in 1957 when British rule ended and Ghana became the first state in the British Commonwealth to be governed by black Africans.

CONTACT:
Ghana Embassy
3512 International Dr., N.W.
Washington, D.C. 20008
202-686-4520; fax: 202-686-4527

SOURCES:
AnnivHol-1983, p. 34
Chases-1996, pp. 124, 278
NatlHolWrld-1968, p. 100

◆ 0712 ◆ **Ghanta Karna**
July–August; 14th day of waning half of Hindu month of Sravana

This day commemorates the death of Ghanta Karna, or 'Bell Ears,' a monster who wore jingling bells in his ears so that he'd never have to hear the name of Vishnu. In Hindu mythology he caused death and destruction wherever he went, until a god in the form of a frog persuaded him to leap into a well, after which the people clubbed him to death and dragged his body to the river to be cremated.

Also known as the **Festival of Boys** because young boys play a primary role in the celebration of Ghanta Karna's death, this day is observed in Nepal by erecting effigies at various crossroads and making passers-by pay a toll. After they've spent the day collecting tolls and preparing for the Ghanta Karna funeral, the boys tie up the effigy with a rope and throw it in the river. Sometimes the effigy is set on fire before being thrown in the water. Young girls hang tiny dolls on the effigy of Ghanta Karna to protect themselves from the monster.

Children also sell iron rings on this day and use the money to buy candy. It is believed that those who have iron nails in the lintels of their homes or are wearing an iron ring will be protected from evil spirits in the coming year.

SOURCES:
BkHolWrld-1986, Aug 23
FolkWrldHol-1992, p. 396

◆ 0713 ◆ **Ghent Floralies**
April or May, every five years (1995, 2000, . . .)

The famous flower festival of Ghent, Belgium, held every five years in the Flanders Expo Hall. More than 450 horticulturists from around the world show their best products to be judged for cash prizes. The showing attracts about 700,000 visitors.

Ghent is the center of a thriving horticultural industry, and the *floralies* began in 1809 at the Frascati Inn where 50 plants were arranged around a bust of Napoleon. In 1814, it is believed that John Quincy Adams and other U.S. delegates visited the flower show; they were staying in Ghent during negotiations preceding the signing of the Treaty of Ghent, which ended the War of 1812.

See also LOCHRISTI BEGONIA FESTIVAL

CONTACT:
Belgian Tourist Office
780 Third Ave.
New York, NY 10017
212-758-8130; fax: 212-355-7675

◆ 0714 ◆ **Giant Lantern Festival**
December 23–24

A highlight of CHRISTMAS in the Philippines. In San Fernando, Pampanga, giant lanterns of colored paper and *capiz* shells, some 12 feet in diameter, are lit and carried in a parade. The event attracts crowds of people from Manila and nearby provinces.

CONTACT:
Philippine Department of Tourism
556 Fifth Ave.
First Floor Mezzanine
New York, NY 10036
212-575-7915; fax: 212-302-6759

◆ 0715 ◆ **Giants, Festival of the (Fête des Géants)**
Begins on the Sunday following July 5

The huge figures that are often carried in procession through the streets of France used to be made of wicker supported by a light wooden frame, but their modern counterparts are usually made of plastic.

For three days and nights during the Fête des Géants in Douai, France, the figure of Gayant is carried through the streets to the accompaniment of drums and church bells. About 25 feet tall and wearing a military uniform, Gayant is followed by his wife, who is 20 feet high and always dressed in the latest fashion. Then come their three children—Jacquot,

Fillion, and the baby, Binbin. The giants leave their home on Rue de Lambres and go to the town hall to salute the mayor, after which they continue on to the Place D'Armes and take part in the carnival festivities.

Another famous procession of the giants takes place in the city of Lille on Whit-Monday, when more than 100 of these fabulous figures are carried through the streets of the town.

CONTACT:
French Government Tourist Office
9454 Wilshire Blvd., Ste. 715
Beverly Hills, CA 90212
310-271-6665; fax: 310-276-2835

SOURCES:
BkFestHolWrld-1970, p. 65

♦ 0716 ♦ Giants, Festival of the, in Belgium
Fourth Sunday in August

In many French and Belgian towns, people carry giants—towering figures representing various biblical, historical, or legendary characters—through the streets in their religious and other festival processions.

One of Belgium's more distinctive and colorful pageants, held in Ath (or Aat), highlights the "Marriage of the Giants." The origins of the festival are a little vague, but the giants—Goliath and his bride, strong-man Samson, a warrior named Ambiorix, and several others—are supposed to date from the mid-15th-century Procession of St. Julien. Other figures were added by local guilds over the years, and today the procession is known as **Les Vêpres de Gouyasse**, because it portrays the marriage of Goliath.

The giants, 20-foot-tall figures made of wicker and cloth, are paraded through the streets; men are underneath the figures and see where they're going by peering out through peepholes. Goliath wears a helmet and breastplate, his bride has orange blossoms in her hair, Samson carries a broken column. After they lumber through the streets to the Church of St. Julien, Goliath and his lady are married.

Along with the giants is the legendary horse, Bayard, purported to be able to change size according to the size of his rider. The medieval story has it that four brothers, the sons of Aymon, were carried by the mighty steed Bayard as they fled the wrath of Charlemagne. The horse and its riders were tracked to a high cliff above the Meuse River; the horse gave a tremendous leap and carried the riders to safety across the river. The replica of the horse weighs about three-quarters of a ton and is propelled by a dozen men while four boys ride on its back.

Besides the procession, the day is marked by the shooting of muskets, revelry, eating, drinking, and dancing.

CONTACT:
Belgian Tourist Office
780 Third Ave.
New York, NY 10017
212-758-8130; fax: 212-355-7675

SOURCES:
Chases-1996, p. 348
FestWestEur-1958, p. 16

♦ 0717 ♦ Gift of the Waters Pageant
First weekend in August

The tract of land now known as Hot Springs State Park in Thermopolis, Wyoming, originally belonged to the Shoshone and Arapahoe Indians. They sold it to the United States in 1886, receiving about $60,000 worth of cattle and food supplies in return. Within the boundaries of the land were several hot mineral springs known for their healing powers. In 1889 the Wyoming State Legislature established the site as a park, stating that one-quarter of the water from the main spring—known as Big Spring, the largest hot mineral spring in the world—was to be set aside for public use. There has been a free bathhouse there since 1902.

The highlight of the three-day event known as the Gift of the Waters Pageant is the reenactment of the signing of the treaty deeding the mineral springs to the people of Wyoming. The role of Washakie, chief of the Shoshones, was originally played by Chief Washakie's son, and later by his great-grandson.

CONTACT:
Wyoming Tourism and Marketing Division
I-25 and College Dr.
Cheyenne, WY 82002
800-225-5996 or 307-777-7777
fax: 307-777-6904

SOURCES:
Chases-1996, p. 322
GdUSFest-1984, p. 217

Giglio, Festa del
See Lily Festival

♦ 0718 ♦ Gilroy Garlic Festival
Third weekend in July

A celebration of garlic in the California town, located in Santa Clara County, that calls itself the Garlic Capital of the World. The claim is made because 90 percent of America's garlic is grown and processed in the area. Humorist Will Rogers once described Gilroy as "the only town in America where you can marinate a steak by hanging it on the clothesline."

The highlight of the festival is Gourmet Alley with about 75 food booths that use eight tons of garlic in preparing various garlic-flavored dishes, including garlic ice cream. Other events are a Great Garlic Cook-off and Recipe Contest, arts and crafts exhibits, a Tour de Garlique bicycle race, and a barn dance.

CONTACT:
California Division of Tourism
801 K Street, Ste. 1600
Sacramento, CA 95814
800-862-2543 or 916-322-2881
fax: 916-322-3402

SOURCES:
Chases-1996, p. 311

♦ 0719 ♦ Ginem
December

The Bagobo are a Malay people who live in southeastern Mindanao in the Philippines. In December each year, they observe a ceremony known as the Ginem to thank the spirits for domestic and military successes, to ward off illness, and to drive off the *buso*, a class of demons feared by the Bagobo because they eat the flesh of the dead. At one time the Bagobo went on a skull raid before the Ginem, tying the skulls to ceremonial poles. Today the poles, without skulls, are decorated and carried into the datu's, or chief's, house. A chicken is sacrificed, and offerings of clothes and knives are made in the hope that the spirits will grant a good harvest and health. There is feasting, dancing, and singing until dawn. In areas where the ceremony lasts more than one day, the feasting continues.

SOURCES:
DictFolkMyth-1984, p. 454

♦ 0720 ♦ **Ginseng Festival**
September 5–7

A celebration of ginseng in Fusong, a county in the Changbai Mountains of China and the largest ginseng grower in the country. The twisted roots of the ginseng, an herb, have for centuries been considered a cure for many ills as well as an aphrodisiac. The people of Fusong have traditionally celebrated the ginseng harvest, and in 1987 the government officially set aside three days for both a festival and a trade fair of ginseng products. The festival features performances of yangko, dragon, and lion dances; story-telling parties with a ginseng theme; art and photo exhibits; and a fireworks display. The trade fair has exhibits not only of ginseng products but also of Chinese medicines and local crafts.

CONTACT:
China National Tourist Office
350 Fifth Ave., Ste. 6413
New York, NY 10165
212-760-9700; fax: 212-760-8809

♦ 0721 ♦ **Gion Matsuri (Gion Festival)**
July 17

The best-known festival in Japan and the biggest in Kyoto. It began in the year 869 when hundreds of people died in an epidemic that swept through Kyoto. The head priest of the Gion Shrine, now called the Yasaka Shrine, mounted 66 spears on a portable shrine, took it to the Emperor's garden, and the pestilence ended. In gratitude to the gods, the priest led a procession in the streets. Except for the period of the Onin War (1467–77), which destroyed the city, the procession has been held ever since.

There are events related to the festival throughout July but the main event is the parade of elaborate, carefully preserved floats on July 17. There are 29 *hoko* (or 'spears') floats and 22 smaller *yama* ('mountains') floats. The immense hoko weigh as much as 10 tons and can be 30 feet tall; they look like wonderfully ornate towers on wheels. They are decorated with Chinese and Japanese paintings and even with French Gobelin tapestries imported during the 17th and 18th centuries. Just under their lacquered roofs musicians play flutes and drums. From the rooftops of the floats two men toss straw good-luck favors to the crowds. The hoko roll slowly on their big wooden wheels, pulled with ropes by parade participants.

Yama floats weigh only about a ton, and are carried on long poles by teams of men. Life-size dolls on platforms atop each float represent characters in the story the float depicts.

The towns of Hakata (Fukuoka Prefecture), Narita (Chiba Prefecture), and Takayama (Gifu Prefecture) have imitated the Kyoto celebration and now have their own "Gion" festivals.

See also AOI MATSURI and JIDAI MATSURI

CONTACT:
Japan National Tourist
   Organization
630 Fifth Ave., Ste. 2101
New York, NY 10111
212-757-5640; fax: 212-307-6754

SOURCES:
AnnivHol-1983, p. 177
BkHolWrld-1986, Jul 17
JapanFest-1965, p. 44

Giorno dei Morti, Il
See **All Souls' Day**

♦ 0722 ♦ **Girl Scout Day**
March 12

The anniversary of the founding of the American Girl Scouts by Juliette Gordon Low (1860–1927) in Savannah, Ga., in 1912. The day is the focal point of Girl Scout Week, which begins on the Sunday before March 12 and is observed by Girl Scout troops nationwide in various ways—with community service projects, anniversary parties, and plays. The 80th anniversary in 1992 was celebrated with various events, including the kick-off of a national service project on the environment.

CONTACT:
Girl Scouts of the U.S.A.
420 Fifth Ave.
New York, NY 10018
800-223-0624 or 212-852-8000
fax: 212-852-6517

SOURCES:
AmerBkDays-1978, p. 245
AnnivHol-1983, p. 36
Chases-1996, pp. 129, 130
DictDays-1988, p. 47

♦ 0723 ♦ **Gita Jayanti**
November–December; 11th day of waxing half of Hindu month of Margasirsa

The birthday of the *Bhagavad Gita*—a Sanskrit poem relating a dialogue between Lord Krishna and Arjuna found in the Hindu epic *Mahabharata*—is celebrated by reading and reciting passages from the *Gita* and by holding discussions on its philosophical aspects. This is also a day on which Hindus fast, worship Krishna, and resolve to put more effort into their study of the *Gita*.

Why is this day considered the *Gita's* birthday? Some texts assert that on the 11th day of the waxing half of Margasirsa, Lord Krishna taught Arjuna the sacred lore of the *Gita* on the battlefield of Kurukshetra, and thus made available to the entire human race the poem often referred to as the "Song Celestial."

SOURCES:
DictWrldRel-1989, p. 96
RelHolCal-1993, p. 79

♦ 0724 ♦ **Glorious Twelfth**
August 12, July 12

August 12 is the legal opening of grouse season in Scotland. If the 12th falls on a Sunday, **Grouse Day** is the following day. Because grouse-shooting has always played such a central role in the life of Scottish gentlemen, the occasion is referred to as the Glorious Twelfth and is observed as a social event by Scots around the world.

Another day that is sometimes referred to by this epithet is ORANGE DAY, which falls on July 12.

SOURCES:
AnnivHol-1983, p. 106
Chases-1996, p. 293
DictDays-1988, pp. 48, 51,
   103, 122

♦ 0725 ♦ Glyndebourne Festival Opera
May–August

Now considered one of the most prestigious opera festivals in the world, the Glyndebourne Festival was founded in 1934 by music lover John Christie and his wife, Audrey Mildmay, who was an opera singer. They built an opera house on the grounds of their Elizabethan estate in Glyndebourne, about 54 miles south of London, and formed an opera company. In the beginning, Christie wanted to stage only Wagnerian operas, but his wife and some of the musicians who helped him put the festival together eventually persuaded him that the emphasis should be on the operas of MOZART. The repertoire expanded even further after Christie's death in 1962, when his son George took over. During the current 11-week season, five full-length operas are presented, at least one of which is by Mozart.

The Glyndebourne Festival has a reputation for spotting and showcasing young talent. It was here that Birgit Nilsson performed in 1951, Joan Sutherland in 1956, and Luciano Pavarotti in 1964. The London Philharmonic Orchestra has been the main ensemble since 1964, and the chorus consists of young British singers who are often selected to sing major roles. The performances start at 5:30, and opera-goers are encouraged to bring a picnic dinner so they can eat outdoors and enjoy the grounds during the 75-minute intermission.

CONTACT:
British Tourist Authority
551 Fifth Ave., Ste. 702
New York, NY 10176
800-462-2748 or 212-986-2200
fax: 212-986-1188

SOURCES:
GdWrldFest-1985, p. 92
MusFestEurBrit-1980, p. 54

♦ 0726 ♦ Goddess of Mercy, Birthday of the
March–April, 19th day of third lunar month;
October–November, 19th day of 10th lunar month

A celebration of Kuan Yin, the *Bodhisattva* ('Buddha-to-be') of infinite compassion and mercy. One of the most beloved of Buddhist deities, he or she is accepted not only by Buddhists but also by Japanese, Chinese, and Koreans. This deity has been depicted as both masculine and feminine and sometimes as transcending sexual identity (with soft body contours but also a moustache). The *Lotus Sutra*, or scripture, says Avalokitesvara (the deity's Sanskrit name, meaning 'the lord who looks in every direction') is able to assume whatever form is needed to relieve suffering. He/she exemplifies the compassion of the enlightened and is known in Tibet as *Spyan-ras gzigs*, 'with a pitying look'. Kuan Yin, the Chinese name, means 'regarder of sounds,' or 'of the voices of the suffering'. The Japanese word for the deity is pronounced "Kannon".

Women especially celebrate Kuan Yin. In Malaysia, hundreds of devotees bearing joss sticks, fresh fruit, flowers, and sweet cakes gather twice a year at temples dedicated to Kuan Yin in Kuala Lumpur and Penang to pray for her benevo-

lence. (She is feminine there and in China, Korea, and Japan.) At the old temple at Jalan Pitt, Penang, puppet shows are staged in celebration of her. In Hong Kong, Kuan Yin is honored on the 19th day of the sixth lunar month at Pak Sha Wan in Hebe Haven.

See also SANJA MATSURI

CONTACT:
Malaysian Tourism Promotion
   Board
818 W. Seventh St., Ste. 804
Los Angeles, CA 90017
213-689-9702; fax: 213-689-1530

SOURCES:
DictWrldRel-1989, p. 79

♦ 0727 ♦ Going to the Fields (Veldgang)
Between April 27 and May 21; Monday before
Ascension Thursday

On Rogation Monday (*see* ROGATION DAYS), the inhabitants of the eastern Netherlands village of Mekkelhorst form a procession to the fields to ask God's blessing on all growing things. With the women and girls walking two abreast at the front of the procession, they follow the boundaries of the parish, stopping briefly at an ancient boundary oak and then proceeding to the fields to kneel before a crucifix and pray for a prosperous harvest.

Rogationtide processions like this one are believed to stem from an ancient Roman tradition. The ROBIGALIA is one example of a spring ritual designed to promote the growth of the newly sown crops and to head off diseases that might harm them. Another ancient Roman tradition was to have young maidens visit the fields at the end of May to drive out winter.

SOURCES:
FestWestEur-1958, p. 132
SeasFeast-1961, p. 220

♦ 0728 ♦ Gold Discovery Days
Five days, including the last weekend in July

This five-day festival celebrates the beauty of the Black Hills and the discovery of gold on July 27, 1874, near the present-day city of Custer, South Dakota. The scientific expedition led by General George Custer confirmed the growing speculation about gold in the area and opened the way for a steady influx of eager prospectors. The festival includes a street fair, hot air balloon rally, baseball tournament, and musical productions. But the highlight of the event is the Paha Sapa Pageant held on the fourth day (Saturday), which recreates this important era in South Dakota's history.

Part one of the pageant depicts the *Paha Sapa*, or sacred land of the Sioux Indians. Part two portrays the lure of gold and the coming of Custer's expedition. In part three the Sioux display their rich cultural heritage by performing ancient ceremonial dances. At the end of the pageant, the entire cast—many of whom have participated since they were children—reappear in special costumes to create a "living flag" of the United States.

CONTACT:
South Dakota Dept. of Tourism
711 E. Wells Ave.
Pierre, SD 57501
800-952-3625 or 605-773-3301
fax: 605-773-3256

SOURCES:
AmerBkDays-1978, p. 594
Chases-1996, p. 311

♦ 0729 ♦ **Golden Chariot and Battle of the Lumecon, Procession of the**
Between May 17 and June 20; Trinity Sunday

An ancient commemoration in Mons, Belgium, of the delivery of the town from the plague in 1349. In the morning, a golden chariot carrying a reliquary of St. Waudru is drawn by white horses through the city, followed by clerics and girls dressed in brocades and lace. In the afternoon, St. George, mounted on a steed, fights the dragon (the *lumecon*), a terrible-tailed beast called Doudou. The battle represents the triumph of good over evil. Before the fight starts, spectators sing the "Song of the Doudou" while carillons ring. Much boisterous merrymaking and feasting culminates in the evening with a pageant presented by 2,000 actors, musicians, and singers.

See also St. George's Day in Bulgaria

CONTACT:
Belgian Tourist Office
780 Third Ave.
New York, NY 10017
212-758-8130; fax: 212-355-7675

SOURCES:
Chases-1996, p. 240

♦ 0730 ♦ **Golden Days**
Third week in July

A celebration in Fairbanks, Alaska, of the discovery of gold here on July 22, 1902, and the Gold Rush days that followed. This is the largest summertime event in Alaska. Its 10 days of activities include "Fairbanks in Bloom," billed as the farthest-north flower show, a Rubber Ducky race, beard and hairy-leg contests, drag races, a golf tournament, concerts, and a grand parade.

There's also a Felix Pedro look-alike contest. Felix Pedrone (remembered as Felix Pedro) was the Italian immigrant who first found gold on a creek near what is now Fairbanks.

CONTACT:
Fairbanks Convention and Visitors
  Bureau
550 First Ave.
Fairbanks, AK 99701
800-327-5774 or 907-456-5774
fax: 907-452-2867

Golden Friday
See Ember Days

♦ 0731 ♦ **Golden Orpheus**
June

Named after the Greek god of song and poetry who, according to legend, lived in the Balkan and Rhodope mountains, the Bulgarian popular music competition known as Golden Orpheus is held every summer in Slunchev Bryag, a resort town on the Black Sea. Musicians from more than 60 countries compete in every category of popular music, including synthesizer, soul, big band, and pop. A prize is given for the best pop song by a Bulgarian composer, and there is an international competition for singers and instrumentalists. World-renowned conductors, directors, and musicologists serve as the jury for the 10-day festival.

CONTACT:
Bulgarian Embassy
1621 22nd St., N.W.
Washington, D.C. 20008
202-387-7969; fax: 202-234-7973

SOURCES:
GdWrldFest-1985, p. 27

♦ 0732 ♦ **Golden Spike Anniversary**
May 10

A reenactment of the completion of America's transcontinental railroad on May 10, 1869, at Promontory Summit, Utah, held since 1952. It is supposed to be historically accurate, but differs from accounts of the time, which greatly varied because the crowds kept the members of the press from actually seeing the ceremony. Not only this, some reporters wrote their stories days before the event occurred.

Today, preliminary events start at 10 A.M., and at 12:30 P.M. two trains—the Central Pacific's "Jupiter" and Union Pacific's "119" (reproductions of the original locomotives that were present in 1869)—steam from opposite directions on the track and meet at the site of the ceremony where men in period dress speak. Then the Golden Spike and three other spikes are tapped into a special railroad tie; at 12:47 an ordinary iron "last spike" is driven into the last tie to connect the railroads and the message "D-O-N-E" is sent by ham radio to the California State Railway Museum in Sacramento. Originally the message "D-O-N-E" was telegraphed (along lines strung beside the railroad) to San Francisco and Philadelphia. There is then much noise of train whistles, bands playing, and people shouting and hurrahing. A second reenactment is performed at 2 P.M.

There were four ceremonial spikes at the original ceremony. One was the famous Golden Spike; it was engraved on the top, "The Last Spike," and on one side, "May God continue the unity of our Country as the Railroad unites the two great Oceans of the World." That spike was made by San Francisco jewelers from $350 worth of gold supplied by David Hewes, a contractor friend of Central Pacific President Leland Stanford.

The other spikes were a second gold spike, not engraved, a silver spike from Nevada, and an iron spike from Arizona that was clad in silver and topped with gold.

There was also a polished laurel-wood tie for the ceremonial last tie. Four holes had been augured in it, and the ceremonial spikes were tapped into the holes. (Nobody tried to drive a soft gold spike into a hardwood tie.) The engraved Golden Spike and the silver spike are in the possession of Stanford University, and the iron spike from Arizona belongs to the Smithsonian Institution. The second gold spike and the hardwood tie have been lost, probably during the San Francisco Earthquake of 1906. The spikes used in the reenactments are replicas.

The building of the transcontinental railroad was a prodigious feat. It was started in 1863, with the Central Pacific working eastward from Sacramento and the Union Pacific laying tracks westward from Omaha. The Central Pacific crews faced the rugged Sierras almost immediately, and also had to have every rail, spike, and locomotive shipped around Cape Horn. Union Pacific had easier terrain, but its crews were harassed by Indians. The Union Pacific crews were Irish, German, and Italian immigrants, Civil War veterans, and ex-slaves. California's labor pool had been drained by the gold rush, so the railroad imported 10,000 Chinese who became the backbone of the labor force.

CONTACT:
Utah County Travel Council
51 S. University Ave.
Historic County Courthouse, Ste. 111
Provo, UT 84601
800-222-8824 or 801-370-8390

SOURCES:
AmerBkDays-1978, p. 441
AnnivHol-1983, p. 64
Chases-1996, p. 206

Golondrinas, Fiesta de las
See **Swallows of San Juan Capistrano**

♦ 0733 ♦ Good Friday
Between March 20 and April 23; Friday before Easter

There are several theories as to why the day commemorating Jesus' crucifixion is called ''Good'' Friday. Some scholars think it's a corruption of ''God's Friday,'' while others interpret ''good'' in the sense of ''observed as holy,'' or to signify that the act of the Crucifixion is central to the Christian view of salvation. It is called **Great Friday** by Orthodox Christians, but it's not surprising that the Friday before EASTER is sometimes referred to as **Black Friday** or **Sorrowful Friday**.

This day has been in the Christian calendar even longer than Easter. And although it was neglected for a long time by Protestant churches, Good Friday has again come into almost universal observance by Christians. From noon to three o'clock many western Christian churches in the U.S. hold the *Tre Ore* (Italian for 'Three Hours', referring to the last three hours Jesus hung on the cross), a service based on the last seven things Jesus said on the cross. Many churches also observe the day by reenacting the procession to the cross as in the ritual of the Stations of the Cross.

In every Orthodox church, the *Epitaphios*, a gold-embroidered pall representing the body of Christ, is laid on a special platform, which is smothered in flowers. During the evening service, the platform is carried out of the church in a procession. The faithful follow, carrying lighted candles and chanting hymns. At squares and crossroads, the procession stops for a prayer by the priest.

Long Friday is another name for Good Friday. In Norway, this day is called **Langfredag**; in Finland, **Pitkäperjantai** (or Long Friday) because it was a day of suffering for Christ.

See also PLEUREUSES, CEREMONY OF

SOURCES:
AmerBkDays-1978, p. 294
BkFest-1937, pp. 6, 16, 30, 41,
  56, 70, 86, 96, 103, 112, 121,
  147, 167, 184, 211, 227, 249,
  259, 275, 291, 300, 309, 330,
  338
DaysCustFaith-1957, p. 107
DictFolkMyth-1984, pp. 181,
  961, 1072
FestSaintDays-1915, p. 62
FestWestEur-1958, pp. 8, 93,
  107, 152, 212
FolkAmerHol-1991, p. 153
FolkWrldHol-1992, p. 191
RelHolCal-1993, p. 79
SaintFestCh-1904, p. 160

♦ 0734 ♦ Good Friday in Belgium (Goede Vrijdag)
Between March 20 and April 23; Friday before Easter

Belgian churches are draped in black on GOOD FRIDAY, in memory of Jesus' suffering on the cross, and a general air of sadness prevails in the cities and towns. In rural villages, peasant women often wear mourning on this day. In the afternoon, many attend the three-hour Passion service at the local church.

In Verne, there is a pilgrims' procession that stops before each of the 18 Stations of the Cross, built there in 1680, to pray and sing hymns. The distance between the different stations is said to correspond to the number of steps (5,751) taken by Christ as he went from Jerusalem to Mount Calvary. The original Stations of the Cross were sites associated with Christ's Passion in Jerusalem and the surrounding area. Pictures or carvings of the Stations of the Cross can often be seen on the walls of Roman Catholic churches.

CONTACT:
Belgian Tourist Office
780 Third Ave.
New York, NY 10017
212-758-8130; fax: 212-355-7675

SOURCES:
BkFest-1937, p. 41
BkFestHolWrld-1970, p. 54
FestWestEur-1958, p. 8

♦ 0735 ♦ Good Friday in Bermuda
Between March 20 and April 23; Friday before Easter

The custom of flying kites on GOOD FRIDAY in Bermuda dates back to the 19th century, when a teacher who was having difficulty explaining to his students how Jesus ascended into heaven took them to the highest hill on the island and launched a kite bearing an image of Jesus. When he ran out of string, he cut the line and let the kite fly out of sight. It has been an island tradition since that time for children to fly kites on Good Friday.

Breakfast on EASTER is another Bermudian tradition. It consists of salted cod that has been soaked overnight and then boiled the next day with potatoes. It is served with an olive oil and mayonnaise topping, with sliced bananas on the side.

SOURCES:
BkHolWrld-1986, Apr 10
FolkWrldHol-1992, p. 191

♦ 0736 ♦ Good Friday in England
Between March 20 and April 23; Friday before Easter

The Friday before EASTER has often been regarded as a day of ill omen by those in rural areas. In England, bread baked on GOOD FRIDAY was marked with a cross to keep the Devil away, and there was a superstition that hanging a ''hot cross bun'' in the house on this day would protect it from bad luck in the coming year. Sometimes Good Friday buns or cakes remained hanging on a rack or in a wire basket for years afterward, gathering dust and growing black with mold. A piece of Good Friday cake was supposed to be especially beneficial to sick cows.

Other Good Friday superstitions include the belief that breaking a piece of crockery on Good Friday would bring good luck because the sharp point would penetrate Judas Iscariot's body. In rural areas, boys often hunted squirrels on this day, because according to legend, Judas was turned into a squirrel.

SOURCES:
BkFest-1937, p. 56
FestSaintDays-1915, p. 63
FolkWrldHol-1992, p. 195

♦ 0737 ♦ Good Friday in Italy
Between March 20 and April 23; Friday before Easter

Folk processions with realistic images of the dead Christ displayed on platforms are common in Italian towns and villages on GOOD FRIDAY. Sometimes the platforms are accompanied by cloaked and hooded worshippers, or by large candles carried aloft on long spiked poles. Funereal music and figures of the grieving Mary and angels holding stained graveclothes accompany the procession. Other objects symbolic of the Passion include the cross, the crown of thorns, and the spear. In the afternoon, there is a church service known as *l'agonia*.

At Santa Croce and other churches in Florence, a custom known as "Thrashing Judas Iscariot" traditionally has been observed on Good Friday. Young boys bring long willow rods tied with colored ribbons to church and at a certain point in the service, they beat the benches loudly with the branches.

CONTACT:
Italian Government Travel Office
630 Fifth Ave.
New York, NY 10111
212-245-4822

SOURCES:
BkFest-1937, p. 184
FestSaintDays-1915, p. 64
FestWestEur-1958, p. 93

♦ 0738 ♦ Good Friday in Mexico (Viernes Santo)
Between March 20 and April 23; Friday before Easter

GOOD FRIDAY is a very somber day in Mexico. The churches are often darkened and draped in black. The religious processions that take place on this day represent the funeral that Jesus never had. An effigy of the dead Christ, stained with blood and wearing a crown of thorns, is carried in a glass coffin through the streets. The highlight of these processions is when the statue of Mary, also draped in black, meets the effigy of her crucified son.

The funereal atmosphere is maintained throughout the day. Running, shouting, or using profanity is discouraged, in reverence for the Lord. The mood of those attending church services is very much that of friends and neighbors paying a condolence call on the members of a bereaved family.

SOURCES:
AmerBkDays-1978, p. 297
BkFest-1937, p. 227
FolkWrldHol-1992, p. 199

♦ 0739 ♦ Good Friday in Poland (Wielki Piatek)
Between March 20 and April 23; Friday before Easter

People fast on dry bread and roasted potatoes from GOOD FRIDAY until EASTER Sunday in Poland, but housewives often spend **Great Friday** or **Holy Friday** kneading and rolling out the dough for elaborate Easter cakes. Egg-decorating is also part of the preparations for Easter, and there are three different techniques for decorating eggs: (1) *malowanki* are eggs painted in solid colors with natural substances, such as vegetable skins, roots, or grains; (2) *pisanki* are eggs that are batiked in traditional designs, usually animal or geometrical figures that have been handed down from generation to generation; and (3) *skrobanki* are eggs dyed in solid colors upon which the outlines of birds, flowers, and animals are scratched with a pointed instrument.

In Krakow and other large cities, going from church to church on Good Friday to view the replicas of Christ's body that are on display traditionally is considered to be an important social event.

See also EASTER IN THE UKRAINE

SOURCES:
BkFest-1937, p. 259

♦ 0740 ♦ Good Friday in Spain
Between March 20 and April 23; Friday before Easter

The religious processions that take place on GOOD FRIDAY in Spain are among the most impressive and elaborate in the world. They are made up of huge *pasos*, or floats, illustrating different scenes in the Passion story and carried by members of various organizations or trade guilds. The pasos are so heavy that it can take 25 or 30 bearers to carry one, and the procession must halt frequently so they can rest.

In Seville, the Good Friday procession dates back to the Middle Ages and includes 44 pasos, many of which are elaborate works of art in themselves, with platforms made out of real silver and figures wearing robes embroidered in gold. Among the more outstanding pasos are those portraying the Agony in the Garden, Christ Bearing the Cross, the Crucifixion, and the Descent from the Cross. They are carried by black-robed penitents through the streets of Seville, followed by cross-bearers, uniformed civic leaders, and clergy in magnificent robes.

CONTACT:
Tourist Office of Spain
665 Fifth Ave.
New York, NY 10022
212-759-8822; fax: 212-980-1053

SOURCES:
AmerBkDays-1978, p. 297
BkFest-1937, p. 300
BkFestHolWrld-1970, p. 54

Goombay Summer Festival
See **Junkanoo Festival**

♦ 0741 ♦ Goschenhoppen Historians' Folk Festival
Second Friday and Saturday of August

The Goschenhoppen region of Pennsylvania, in what is now Montgomery County, was settled in the early 18th century by Mennonite, Schwenkfeldian, Lutheran, Reformed, and Catholic farmers and artisans, most of whom were German immigrants. It remains one of the oldest and most "authentic" Pennsylvania German communities in America. The Goschenhoppen Historians, a group founded in 1963 to study and preserve the culture of the Pennsylvania German, also known as the Pennsylvania Dutch, and related groups, hold an annual Folk Festival at Goschenhoppen Park in East Greenville every summer to educate the public about life in this area during the 18th and 19th centuries and to preserve the traditional skills of the Pennsylvania German people.

Since 1967, when the first Folk Festival was held, the Historians have made every effort to keep the festival as educational and as non-commercial as possible. One of the most interesting aspects is the participation of schoolchildren, who are recruited as apprentices or helpers for the craft demonstrators at the festival. By actively participating in the demonstrations, young people learn traditional skills that might otherwise die out. These include: blacksmithing, fishnet making, pewtering, gunsmithing, chair caning, rope making, weaving, and thatch and tile roofing. The Historians also operate a folklife museum and country store.

See also KUTZTOWN FAIR

CONTACT:
Goschenhoppen Historical Society
P.O. Box 476
Green Lane, PA 18054
215-234-8953 or 610-367-8286

♦ 0742 ♦ Govardhan Puja
October–November; first day of waxing half of Hindu month of Kartika

This Hindu festival is observed on the day following DEWALI in northern India. It celebrates an event in Krishna's life in which he lifted the Govardhan Mountain on his little finger for seven days, to protect the cows and people of Vrindavana against the deluge of rain sent by Indra, god of the heavens and rains. People come to Vrindavana from all over India to visit and worship at Mount Govardhan on this day. Those who cannot make the trip worship at home and give gifts to Brahmans. Cows and bulls are also decorated and worshipped on this day.

CONTACT:
India Tourist Office
30 Rockefeller Ave.
15 N. Mezzanine
New York, NY 10112
212-586-4901; fax: 212-582-3274

SOURCES:
RelHolCal-1993, p. 80

Grand Duke Day
See **Luxembourg National Day**

♦ 0743 ♦ Grandfather Mountain Highland Games and Gathering of Scottish Clans
Second full weekend in July

This largest and best-known Scottish event in America, held since 1956 on Grandfather Mountain near Linville, N.C., opens with a torchlight ceremony. On Friday there's a piping concert, followed by a *ceilidh*, or concert of Scottish folk music, followed by a Scottish country dance gala. On Saturday competitions are held throughout the day for Highland dancing, piping, drumming, Scottish fiddling, track and field events, and other athletic events including tugs-of-war. Entertainment includes sheep-herding demonstrations and performances by pipe bands and Scottish performing artists. Another ceilidh and the Tartan Ball round out the day. Sunday opens with a worship service, followed by more competitions and entertainment, including the colorful Parade of Tartans.

See also ALMA HIGHLAND FESTIVAL AND GAMES, HIGHLAND GAMES and VIRGINIA SCOTTISH GAMES

CONTACT:
North Carolina Travel and Tourism Division
430 N. Salisbury St.
Raleigh, NC 27603
800-847-4862 or 919-733-4171
fax: 919-733-8582

SOURCES:
AmerBkDays-1978, p. 653

♦ 0744 ♦ Grand National
Last Saturday in March or first Saturday in April

The world-famous steeplechase, run at the Aintree race course in Liverpool, England. It was started in 1839 by William Lynn, owner of the Waterloo Hotel in Liverpool, as a means of attracting hotel patrons. The first races were at Maghull just outside Liverpool, but the course was moved to Aintree in 1864 and remained unchanged until 1961 when a railing was erected to keep spectators off the course. The next change was in 1990 when the slope at the infamously hazardous Becher's Brook jump was modified because so many horses had been killed there.

The course is four and one-half miles long and has 16 bush fences, of which 14 are jumped twice. The fences average 5'3" high. All have ditches either on the take-off or landing side. The race is limited now to 40 starters, and usually there is a full field. Of the starters, rarely do as many as half finish, and sometimes only as few as three or four. Horses have to qualify by winning three other set races in England, although any horse that wins the MARYLAND HUNT CUP is automatically eligible to run.

Probably the greatest horse to run the Grand National was Red Rum, a big, strong horse that won in 1973, 1974, and 1977. In 1973, Red Rum set a record for the fastest time—9 minutes, 1.90 seconds.

The race became widely known to the general public with the 1944 movie *National Velvet*, based on the 1935 bestseller by Enid Bagnold. It starred Mickey Rooney, playing an ex-jockey, and Elizabeth Taylor as Velvet Brown, the girl who trains "The Pi" for the Grand National steeplechase. When the jockey scheduled to ride proves unsuitable, Velvet cuts her hair and rides to victory herself, but is disqualified when it's discovered she's a girl. Only men could ride originally, but today women are eligible.

CONTACT:
British Tourist Authority
551 Fifth Ave., Ste. 702
New York, NY 10176
800-462-2748 or 212-986-2200
fax: 212-986-1188

SOURCES:
Chases-1996, p. 146
DictDays-1988, p. 50

♦ 0745 ♦ Grandparents' Day
September, first Sunday after Labor Day

Grandparents' Day is a far more recent invention than MOTHER'S DAY or FATHER'S DAY. It was fostered by Marion McQuade, and a presidential proclamation on September 6, 1979, made it official. It is observed throughout the United States on the first Sunday after LABOR DAY, except in Massachusetts, where it is observed on the first Sunday in October.

There are a number of ways in which grandparents can be honored and their day celebrated. One is to invite real or 'adopted' grandparents to school for the day, where they participate in their grandchildren's classes or special assembly programs. Gift-giving is not as widespread on this day as it is on Mother's Day or Father's Day.

See also BABIN DEN

SOURCES:
AnnivHol-1983, p. 115
Chases-1996, pp. 370, 408
DictDays-1988, p. 50

♦ 0746 ♦ Grand Prix
March to November

Formerly part of the international racing series that includes the MONACO GRAND PRIX, the first U.S. Grand Prix was held in 1959 at Sebring, Florida. After 1961 it was held at Watkins Glen, N.Y., Detroit, and then Phoenix. In 1991, however, the racing committee rejected the Phoenix site, and the Grand Prix has not been held in the U.S. Points won in this race count toward the World Championship of Drivers. More than 15 Grand Prix races are held yearly in countries around the world; the season runs from March to November.

Like other Grand Prix races, the race at Watkins Glen was for Formula One race cars, which are generally smaller and more maneuverable than the cars used in speedway racing. Engine size, fuel, and other specifications are strictly controlled by the Féderation Internationale de l'Automobile (FIA).

CONTACT:
Féderation Internationale de
  l'Automobile
8 Place de la Concorde
75008 Paris, France
011-33-14-265-9951
fax: 011-33-14-742-8731
WWW: http://www2.fia.com

♦ 0747 ♦ Grant's Bluegrass Festival
Early August

The oldest and largest bluegrass festival west of the Mississippi, held for five days near Hugo, Okla. The festival began in 1969, organized by Bill Grant as an extension of jam sessions in his home. Attendance the first year was less than 1,000; now more than 20,000 show up. There are band and instrument contests for all ages, non-stop entertainment from 10 A.M. until midnight each day, and jam sessions at all hours.

CONTACT:
Oklahoma Tourism and Recreation Dept.
2401 N. Lincoln Blvd.
Will Rogers Bldg., Ste. 500
Oklahoma City, OK 73105
800-652-6552 or 405-521-2413
fax: 405-521-4883

SOURCES:
MusFestAmer-1990, p. 248

♦ 0748 ♦ Grape Festival
September, Labor Day weekend

The highlight of the Grape Festival held each year in Nauvoo, Illinois, is the historical pageant known as the **Wedding of the Wine and Cheese**. It tells the story of a young French boy who left his unfinished lunch in a limestone cave to keep it cool and then forgot to pick it up. He returned months later and discovered that the bread had grown moldy and spread through the cheese, creating the first blue-veined Roquefort cheese. In the pageant there is a marriage ceremony celebrating the union of cheese and wine in which a magistrate reads the marriage contract, places it between the wine (carried by the bride) and the cheese (carried by the groom), and circles all three with a wooden hoop symbolizing the wedding ring. The festival also includes parades, a grape stomp, and historical tours.

In the late 1840s, Nauvoo was occupied by French and German Icarians, members of a socialist sect whose creed was "From each according to his ability and to each according to his need," which derives from the social-economic philosophy of Karl Marx. The Icarians brought wine-making to the area, and several of their original wine cellars are still used to make the blue cheese that this festival has celebrated for over 50 years. A similar festival is held in Roquefort, France.

CONTACT:
Illinois Tourism and Travel
100 W. Randolph, Ste. 3-400
Chicago, IL 60601
800-2-CONNECT; fax: 312-814-
  1800

SOURCES:
GdUSFest-1984, p. 49

♦ 0749 ♦ Grasmere Sports
Third Thursday in August

This annual event in England's Lake District began in the 1800s to encourage Cumberland and Westmorland wrestling, but it has since expanded to include other traditional lake district sports. The wrestling competitors stand chest to chest and lock arms behind each other's back. The aim of this subtle form of combat is to throw the opponent to the ground—a goal that many wrestlers struggle all day to achieve while other events are going on elsewhere. Fell running (a *fell* is a highland plateau), another traditional sport, is an all-out race to the top of the nearest mountain and back. Hound trailing, which reflects the Lake District's importance as a center for fox hunting, is done on foot with packs of hounds who run across the fells after their prey. Up until 1974, when Cumberland and Westmorland were combined to form Cumbria County, competition between the two rival counties had been fierce.

CONTACT:
British Tourist Authority
551 Fifth Ave., Ste. 702
New York, NY 10176
800-462-2748 or 212-986-2200
fax: 212-986-1188

♦ 0750 ♦ Graveyard Cleaning and Decoration Day
Between May and early September

In some Southern states—particularly Texas, Kentucky, and Tennessee—a day in summer is set aside for honoring the dead and maintaining the local cemetery. Sometimes called **Grave Day**, MEMORIAL DAY, **Decoration Day**, or **Memory Day**, it is a time for families and neighbors to get together, sharing "dinner-on-the-ground" or picnic suppers and listening to sermons. In Pleasant Grove, Kentucky, Grave Day originated as a peace-making ceremony after the Civil War had split Hardin County into two opposing factions.

Graveyard Cleaning Day is often held in July, but it may be observed any time from late May until early September.

There usually isn't any connection to official Memorial Day celebrations; the date is a matter of local choice and convenience. In New Orleans, for example, it is customary to whitewash the tombs on ALL SAINTS' DAY. All of these observations, however, harken back to the ancient Roman festival known as the PARENTALIA, an uncharacteristically somber occasion on which people decorated the graves of the deceased with flowers and left food in the cemeteries to sustain the spirits of the dead.

SOURCES:
FolkAmerHol-1991, p. 301

♦ 0751 ♦ Great American Brass Band Festival
Mid-June

A weekend re-creation of the golden age of brass bands in America, held at Centre College in Danville, Ky. About a dozen bands from throughout the country and Canada play Sousa march music, ragtime, and jazz in the New Orleans funeral-march style. A highlight is a band playing over-the-shoulder instruments of the Civil War period; the music blew to the rear of the band so it could be heard by the troops marching behind. The festival begins with a hot-air balloon race, and music then continues through the weekend.

CONTACT:
Kentucky Dept. of Travel
  Development
500 Mero St., 22nd Floor
Frankfort, KY 40601
800-225-8747 or 502-564-4930
fax: 502-564-5695

SOURCES:
Chases-1996, p. 256

♦ 0752 ♦ Great American Duck Race
Fourth weekend in August

A uniquely American event started in 1979 in Deming, N.M., just to make a little whoopee. Up to 80 live ducks race for cash prizes in an eight-lane chute. There are races which include politicians' heats and a media heat. Other events in the week preceding the duck races are a parade, a gun and knife show, dances, a Mexican rodeo, an arts and crafts exhibit, an outhouse race, a tortilla toss, a pageant of people dressed like ducks, and a duck contest in which ducks are dressed like people. Race participants come from several states; spectators now number about 20,000, almost double the population of Deming.

CONTACT:
New Mexico Tourism and Travel
  Division
491 Old Santa Fe Trail
Santa Fe, NM 87503
800-545-2040 or 505-827-7400
fax: 505-827-7402

SOURCES:
Chases-1996, p. 346

♦ 0753 ♦ Great American Smokeout
Third Thursday in November

It was the *Surgeon General's Report on Smoking and Health* that first gave impetus to grassroots efforts to discourage the smoking of cigarettes. As far back as 1971, the town of Randolph, Massachusetts, had asked its residents to give up tobacco for a day. In 1974 the editor of the *Monticello Times* in Minnesota led the first mass movement by smokers to give up cigarettes, calling it "D-Day" for "Don't Smoke." The idea spread quickly throughout Minnesota and skipped west

to California in 1977, where it became known as the Great American Smokeout. The following year it was observed nationwide for the first time, under the sponsorship of the American Cancer Society.

The Smokeout focuses attention not only on cigarette smokers but, more recently, on smokeless tobacco users as well. Activities are generally light-hearted rallies, parades, obstacle courses, contests, skits, parties, etc.—all designed to keep smokers away from their cigarettes for an entire day, in the hope that they will continue the effort on their own. The Cancer Society encourages nonsmokers to "adopt" smokers on this day and support them as they go through withdrawal from nicotine—a drug that is said to be as addictive as heroin. Schools are particularly active in observing the Smokeout, teaching young people that the easiest way to avoid the health problems associated with smoking is never to start. Businesses, hospitals, and other organizations also sponsor programs and activities designed to increase public awareness of the hazards to which both smokers and those who breathe their smoke are exposed—particularly lung cancer.

In recent years, millions of people have quit for the day, and many of them do not return to the habit.

CONTACT:
American Cancer Society
1599 Clifton Rd., N.W.
Atlanta, GA 30329
800-227-2345 or 404-320-3333
fax: 404-325-1467

SOURCES:
Chases-1996, p. 455

♦ 0754 ♦ Great Fifteenth
Fifteenth day of first lunar month

The Great Fifteenth marks the end of the New Year holiday season in Korea and is considered the last opportunity to ensure good luck for the coming year. The number nine is considered lucky on this day, and people routinely repeat their actions nine times—particularly children, who compete with each other to see how many "lucky nines" they can achieve before the day is over.

It is common to celebrate the Great Fifteenth with kite flying and kite fighting, which is done by covering the strings with glass dust and then crossing them so that they rub together as they fly. The string held by the more skillfully maneuvered kite eventually cuts through the string of the less successful kite, sending it crashing to the ground.

Another popular sport on this day is the tug-of-war. In some areas, an entire town or county is divided into two opposing teams. It is widely believed that the winning side will have a good harvest and will be protected from disease in the coming year.

SOURCES:
FolkWrldHol-1992, p. 70

Great Friday
See Good Friday

♦ 0755 ♦ Great Irish Houses Festival
First two weeks in June

Among the great Irish houses of Wicklow County that are the setting for this annual music festival is Castledown, an 18th-century Palladian-style house about 12 miles from Dublin whose Long Hall is perfectly suited to chamber music performances. The other houses are Carton House (1740), Headfort and Slane Castles (1775 and 1785), and Tullynally Castle, a 17th-century Gothic castle about 65 miles from Dublin.

Since its first season in 1970, the Great Irish Houses Festival has featured recitals and chamber music by composers ranging from Vivaldi to Elgar. Soloists who have performed there include Yehudi MENUHIN, Peter Frankl, Alicia de Larrocha, and John Ogden. Ensembles such as the Amadeus String Quartet, the New Irish Chamber Orchestra, the Gabrieli String Quartet, and the Allegri String Quartet have performed in these stately homes, which strive to duplicate the intimate and relaxed atmosphere of a private concert.

CONTACT:
Irish Tourist Board
345 Park Ave., 17th Floor
New York, NY 10154
800-223-6470 or 212-418-0800
fax: 212-371-9052

SOURCES:
MusFestEurBrit-1980, p. 110

♦ 0756 ♦ Great Lapp Winter Fair
Four days in February

The Lapps, or Samis, are a nomadic people of ancient origin who still make their living keeping reindeer herds in the northernmost regions of Norway, Sweden, and Finland, and on the Kola Peninsula of the former Soviet Union. They started holding the **Great Sami Winter Fair** in Jokkmokk, Lapland, more than 100 years ago, and have continued to hold it in February because this is the time of year when they bring their reindeer to this area. The four-day event draws many visitors who are curious about Sami culture. It includes the marking of the reindeer, reindeer roundup demonstrations, and the sale of special Sami foods and handicrafts.

CONTACT:
Scandinavian Tourist Board
655 Third Ave., 18th Floor
New York, NY 10017
212-949-2333; fax: 212-983-5260

SOURCES:
GdWrldFest-1985, p. 168

♦ 0757 ♦ Great Locomotive Chase Festival
First weekend in October

A three-day celebration in Adairsville, Ga., to commemorate the storied Civil War locomotive chase that led to the execution of six Union soldiers by the Confederates.

The chase came on April 12, 1862 (the one-year anniversary of the Confederate attack on Fort Sumter), after the Yankee spy, James J. Andrews, stole the Confederate engine named "The General," along with three boxcars and the tender. His plan was to burn the rail bridges between Atlanta and Chattanooga, in order to cut Confederate supply lines. Andrews swiped the locomotive at Big Shanty (Kennesaw), Georgia, and roared off, stopping to cut telegraph wires and tear up tracks. In due time W. A. Fuller, conductor of "The General," who had been having breakfast when his train was stolen, realized something was missing and set off in a handcar with Anthony Murphy. In Adairsville, they boarded the locomotive "Texas," and barreled after "The General" and Andrews, who was trying to reach the bridge at Resaca so he could burn it. The drivers of "The General" kept throwing things on the track to derail the "Texas," but the

"Texas" kept in pursuit. Finally, the Yankee raiders were out of fuel and had nothing left to throw on the track; arriving in Ringgold, Andrews ordered his men to jump and run. They did, but all were apprehended. Andrews and six others were tried and hanged; others were taken as prisoners until being exchanged, and later they received medals from the Union army. The Confederates won the accolades of the Army of the Confederacy.

In 1927, Buster Keaton made the movie *The General* based on the chase, and in 1956, a Disney movie, *The Great Locomotive Chase*, later retitled *Andrews' Raiders*, retold the old story.

Events of the festival include showings of the locomotive-chase movies, a grand parade, beauty pageants, fireworks, and gospel singing. There are also such contests as three-legged races, a marshmallow-spitting contest, a bean-bag toss, a balloon toss, and a tug of war. Attendance is estimated at more than 10,000.

CONTACT:
Georgia Dept. of Industry
Trade and Tourism
285 Peachtree Center Ave., N.E.
Marquis Tower II, Ste. 1000
Atlanta, GA 30303
800-847-4842 or 404-656-3592
fax: 404-651-9063

♦ 0758 ♦ Great Monterey Squid Festival
May, Memorial Day weekend

A two-day celebration of the squid industry in Monterey, Calif. The main attraction is squid prepared in every imaginable way: fried, broiled, sauteed, marinated, barbecued; Siciliano-, Cajun-, or Greek-style; as (or in) ceviche, fajitas, pizza, chowder, and empanadas. There are also numerous exhibits, films, and demonstrations to let spectators learn more than they ever wanted to know about the lives of squid, and how they are caught and prepared for eating. Squid balloons (they have lots of trailing legs) are sold, and entertainment includes music, clowns and mimes, and crafts exhibits.

Monterey is the home of Cannery Row, made famous in John Steinbeck's novel of that name, and of the Monterey Bay Aquarium, one of the largest aquariums in the world.

CONTACT:
California Division of Tourism
801 K Street, Ste. 1600
Sacramento, CA 95814
800-862-2543 or 916-322-2881
fax: 916-322-3402

SOURCES:
Chases-1996, p. 228

Great Saturday
See **Holy Saturday**

♦ 0759 ♦ Great Schooner Race
Friday following July 4

The Great Schooner race is part of a four-day festival in Rockland and Thomaston, Maine, known as **Schooner Days**. Held since 1977, the race features schooners from the Maine Windjammer Association and a number of other large sailing ships—usually 25 to 30 in all. The race begins at Isleboro Island and ends in Rockland, where the boats parade through Penobscot Bay. On land, there are arts and crafts exhibits, entertainment by musicians and storytellers, children's activities and a harbor fireworks display. Visitors can sample a variety of seafood or take a harbor cruise.

CONTACT:
Maine Office of Tourism
33 Stone St.
Augusta, ME 04333
800-533-9595 or 207-287-5711
fax: 207-287-5701

SOURCES:
Chases-1996, p. 285

Great Spring Festival of the Toshogu Shrine
See **Toshogu Haru-No-Taisai**

Great Sunday
See **Palm Sunday**

Great Thursday
See **Maundy Thursday**

♦ 0760 ♦ Greece Independence Day
March 25

A national holiday in Greece to celebrate the anniversary of the country's proclamation of independence in 1821 after four centuries of Turkish occupation. The war that followed went on until 1829 when finally the Turkish sultan recognized the independence of Greece. The day is marked with church services and military parades—an especially impressive parade is held in Athens. Greek communities in other parts of the world also observe the day. In New York City, Greece Independence Day is celebrated on the Sunday nearest to March 25 with a parade up Fifth Avenue.

CONTACT:
Greek National Tourist
  Organization
645 Fifth Ave.
New York, NY 10022
212-421-5777; fax: 212-826-6940

SOURCES:
AmerBkDays-1978, p. 285
AnnivHol-1983, p. 42
Chases-1996, p. 144
DictDays-1988, p. 50
NatlHolWrld-1968, p. 39

♦ 0761 ♦ Greenery Day
April 29

This day formerly observed the birthday of Emperor Hirohito of Japan (1901–1989), who was the world's longest ruling monarch. His reign included the attempted military conquest of Asia, the attack on the United States at Pearl Harbor, and his country's defeat after the U.S. dropped atomic bombs on Hiroshima and Nagasaki. He also oversaw Japan's postwar resurgence to a position of economic strength and influence. Hirohito renounced his divinity in 1946 and became a symbolic head of state in Japan's new parliamentary democracy.

Today this day is celebrated as Greenery Day, or **Midori-no-Hi**—with parades featuring elaborate floats, paper lanterns, traditional Japanese costumes, and fireworks. Popular places from which to observe the festivities in Tokyo include Tokyo Tower, the highest structure in the city, and Shiba Park.

CONTACT:
Japan National Tourist
  Organization
630 Fifth Ave., Ste. 2101
New York, NY 10111
212-757-5640; fax: 212-307-6754

SOURCES:
AnnivHol-1983, p. 58
BkFest-1937, p. 198
NatlHolWrld-1968, p. 52

♦ 0762 ♦ Green George Festival
April 23

Observed on St. George's Day, April 23, by Romany people (also known as gypsies) in Transylvania, the Green George Festival is a tree-spirit festival in which folkloric beliefs play a major role. A young willow is cut down, decorated with flowers and leaves, and set up in a central place where everyone can see it. Pregnant women may leave a piece of clothing under the tree; if a leaf falls on it by the next morning, they'll have an easy delivery. Sick or elderly people spit on the tree three times, praying for long life and good health. On April 24, an old custom is for a boy dressed in green leaves and flowers to take three iron nails that have spent three days and three nights in running water, hammer them into the willow, pull them out, and throw them back into the stream. In the evening, Green George appears as a leaf-clad puppet who is also thrown into the stream.

Green George is believed to be a variation on the medieval English Jack in the Green. A relic of European tree worship, Jack in the Green is associated with Pentecost and other celebrations of spring. On May Day in England, he appeared as a boy (typically a chimneysweep) encased in a framework of lath and hoops covered with ivy and holly and wearing a high headdress of leaves.

SOURCES:
DictFolkMyth-1984, pp. 534, 954

♦ 0763 ♦ Green River Rendezvous
Second Sunday in July

A reenactment in Pinedale, Wyo., of the days when mountain men, Indians, and traders came together to transact business, trade, drink, holler, and celebrate. The first rendezvous, or gathering, of trappers was held on the Green River, near the present Wyoming-Utah border. After trading posts were established, the rendezvous became less important. The last of these colorful gatherings was held in 1840. A two-hour pageant recreating these rendezvous has been presented by the Sublette County Historical Society since 1936. Celebrations are held over three days, and other events include black-powder shoots and barbecues.

The trappers, traders and explorers who came to be known as mountain men were a distinctive breed who numbered in their ranks the legendary Jim Bridger, the scout and Indian agent Kit Carson, and William Sublette, who established the area's first trading post. They were satisfying the demand for fur and especially for beaver; the beaver hat was supreme in the world of fashion at the start of the 19th century. Besides trapping beaver, they also planted the American claim to much of the territory of the American West. For most of the year, they trapped on the tributaries of the Green River, but for several weeks each summer when there was no beaver trapping, they came out of the wilderness and met at a rendezvous site. Trade goods—blankets, coffee, sugar, gunpowder, and cheap whiskey—were brought from Missouri by pack animals and trade wagons, and the trappers brought their beaver skins. It was a time of more than trading: on one occasion Jim Bridger rode around in a suit of armor that had been brought to him from Scotland. The rendezvous brought together a concentration of explorers and frontiersmen and provided a stepping stone for the settlers who followed. The rendezvous and the era of the mountain men came to an end in the 1840s when the whims of fashion shifted from beaver hats to silk hats, and the race for beaver furs was over.

See also MOUNTAIN MAN RENDEZVOUS

CONTACT:
Sublette County Historical Society
c/o Museum of the Mountain
  Man
P.O. Box 909
Pinedale, WY 82941
307-367-4101; fax: 307-367-6768

SOURCES:
GdUSFest-1984, p. 216

Green Teej
See **Teej**

Green Thursday
See **Maundy Thursday**

♦ 0764 ♦ **Greenwood Day, Chester**
First Saturday in December

Chester Greenwood (1858–1937) made his first pair of "ear protectors" when he was 15 years old. He was granted a patent in 1877 and established an entirely new industry in his hometown of Farmington, Maine, where he continued to refine the design and manufacture of what we now know as earmuffs. By 1918 he was making 216,000 pairs a year, and by 1932 checks and plaids were added to the standard black velvet covering.

Although Greenwood was involved in a number of other business ventures in Farmington and was granted his last patent—for a tempered steel lawn rake—only a few months before he died, it is for his ear protectors that he is primarily remembered. Farmington residents celebrate Chester Greenwood Day on the first Saturday in December (Greenwood was born on December 4) with a parade, flag-raising ceremony, and a foot race.

CONTACT:
Maine Office of Tourism
33 Stone St.
Augusta, ME 04333
800-533-9595 or 207-287-5711
fax: 207-287-5701

♦ 0765 ♦ **Grenada Independence Day**
February 7

This is a national holiday commemorating Grenada's independence from Britain on this day in 1974. Britain had held the island since the 18th century, when France ceded it under the Treaty of Paris.

CONTACT:
Grenada Embassy
1701 New Hampshire Ave., N.W.
Washington, D.C. 20009
202-265-2561; fax: 202-265-2468

SOURCES:
AnnivHol-1983, p. 20
Chases-1996, p. 89

♦ 0766 ♦ **Grenada National Day**
March 13

March 13 is a national holiday in Grenada that commemorates the revolution on this day in 1979 that overthrew the government of Sir Eric Gairy. The New Joint Endeavor for Welfare, Education, and Liberation Movement (JEWEL) then took over and established a socialist People's Revolutionary Government.

CONTACT:
Grenada Embassy
1701 New Hampshire Ave., N.W.
Washington, D.C. 20009
202-265-2561; fax: 202-265-2468

SOURCES:
AnnivHol-1983, p. 36

♦ 0767 ♦ **Grey Cup Day**
Mid-November

The best teams from the Eastern and Western Conferences of the Canadian Football League play against each other in an annual event similar to the SUPER BOWL in the United States. It is called Grey Cup Day after the trophy that is awarded to the winning team—a cup donated by former Canadian Governor-General Earl Grey in 1909.

Parties are held throughout the country so that fans can get together to watch the big game on television. In sports and social clubs, it is not uncommon to set up two televisions so that rival supporters can each watch their own team. Like its American counterpart, the Super Bowl, the Grey Cup is an occasion for widespread drinking and rowdiness.

CONTACT:
Canadian Tourism Commission
4th Floor, East Tower
235 Queen St.
Ottawa, Ontario
Canada K1A OH6
800-577-2266

SOURCES:
DictDays-1988, p. 50

♦ 0768 ♦ **Groppenfasnacht (Fish Carnival)**
Between March 1 and April 4; Laetare Sunday
(three weeks before Easter), every three years
(1994, 1997, . . .)

A Lenten celebration in the village of Ermatingen, Switzerland, that takes its name from the *Gropp,* a fish a few inches long caught only in the Ermatingen area. The event dates to the time when fishermen celebrated the breaking up of the ice in the spring because they could return to catching fish. Every three years a committee of villagers organizes a procession in which children dress as frogs and dwarfs and follow a float that carries a huge Gropp, while men march along carrying antique fishing implements. Smaller versions of the procession are held during the intervening years.

CONTACT:
Swiss National Tourist Office
608 Fifth Ave.
New York, NY 10020
212-757-5944; fax: 212-262-6116

♦ 0769 ♦ **Grotto Day**
August 5; July 25

In England during the late 18th and early 19th centuries, oysters were not considered the rare delicacy they are today and were, in fact, one of the common staples of fishermen's diets. The large number of oysters eaten at that time meant there were lots of shells around. On ST. JAMES's DAY, which was observed on August 5 before the Gregorian, or New Style, Calendar came into use and on July 25 thereafter, children used the shells to construct small decorative grottoes. Perhaps these were to represent the shrine of St. James in Spain. Sometimes the children begged for pennies as a reward for their efforts. Most of this grotto-building took place in London, and the custom continued right up to the 1950s. St. James the Great was one of the Apostles and brother to ST. JOHN THE EVANGELIST, and the scallop shell was his emblem.

SOURCES:
DictDays-1988, pp. 50, 85

♦ 0770 ♦ **Groundhog Day**
February 2

There was a medieval superstition that all hibernating animals—not just groundhogs—came out of their caves and dens on CANDLEMAS to check on the weather. If they could see their shadows, it meant that winter would go on for another six weeks and they could go back to sleep. A cloudy day meant that spring was just around the corner. It was the early German settlers known as the Pennsylvania Dutch who attached this superstition to the groundhog. In Germany it was the badger, and in England, France, and Canada it was the bear who was believed to make similar predictions about the weather.

The most famous forecaster in the United States is Punxsutawney Phil, a legendary groundhog in north-central Pennsylvania believed to be nearly a century old. There is a club whose members trek up to Phil's burrow on February 2 and get the news directly from him. Unfortunately, weather researchers have determined that over the years the groundhog has been correct only 28 percent of the time.

SOURCES:
AmerBkDays-1978, p. 138
BkFestHolWrld-1970, p. 29
Chases-1996, p. 84
DaysCustFaith-1957, p. 45
DictDays-1988, p. 51
FolkAmerHol-1991, p. 65

Guadalupeño, Festival
See **Our Lady of Guadalupe, Feast of, in the United States**

♦ 0771 ♦ **Gualterianas, Festas**
Four days beginning the first Sunday in August

The **Festivals of St. Walter** take place in Guimarães, the 12th-century capital of Portugal. The celebrations, which date back to 1452, include magnificent processions, fireworks, animal fairs, and displays of food and merchandise. Music, ranging from brass bands to modern jazz, can be heard all over the town.

St. Walter (or São Gualter), the town's patron, is represented by an image of a young Franciscan monk who stands in the nave of Senhor dos Passos (Our Lord of the Way of the Cross), the blue-and-white-tiled church that overlooks the town's public garden. During a Sunday night procession known as the *Procissão Gualteriana*, the image of the saint is carried from the church through the decorated streets of Guimarães while thousands of spectators gather to watch. The procession is followed by a night of fireworks, folk dancing in regional costume, and great activity at the shooting galleries and side shows that line the streets. The festival culminates on Wednesday with the *Marcha Gualteriana*, a midnight procession of 12 allegorical floats.

CONTACT:
Portuguese National Tourist Office
590 Fifth Ave., 4th Floor
New York, NY 10036
212-354-4403; fax: 212-764-6137

SOURCES:
FestWestEur-1958, p. 181

Guardian Angel, Festival of the
See **Schutzengelfest**

♦ 0772 ♦ **Guardian Angels Day**
October 2

As early as the ninth century, a day was set aside to honor angels in general and the archangel Michael in particular. This was September 29, the Feast of St. Michael and All Angels or MICHAELMAS. But some people, believing that a particular angel is assigned to watch over each human being, wanted to honor their own personal protectors or guardian angels. A feast in their honor observed in 16th-century Spain was extended to the whole church by Pope Paul V in 1608, and in 1672 Pope Clement X set October 2 as the universal day for the festival.

SOURCES:
DaysCustFaith-1957, p. 249
RelHolCal-1993, p. 80

♦ 0773 ♦ **Guatemala Independence Day**
September 15

This is the day on which Guatemala won its independence from Spain in 1821. Four other countries also declared their independence on September 15, 1821: COSTA RICA, EL SALVADOR, HONDURAS, and NICARAGUA.

It is a public holiday, during which the buildings in Guatemala City are draped in blue-and-white bunting, and there are parades with schoolchildren marching to the music of military bands. A popular holiday pastime is watching *La Conquista* (The Conquest), a traditional dance where the dancers, in wooden masks and red wigs, reenact the conquest of the Mayan Indians by the Spanish soldier Pedro de Alvarado. The Mayan civilization, which had flourished in Guatemala since 2500 B.C., began to decline after 900 A.D. Alvarado, the red-haired Spanish conquistador, began subjugating their descendants in 1523.

CONTACT:
Guatemala Embassy
2220 R St., N.W.
Washington, D.C. 20008
202-745-4952; fax: 202-745-1908

SOURCES:
AnnivHol-1983, p. 118
Chases-1996, p. 377
NatlHolWrld-1968, p. 167

♦ 0774 ♦ **Guavaween**
Last Saturday of October

A parade and block party with a Latin flavor in Ybor City, a two-square-mile area in Tampa, Fla. Ybor City grew around the cigar factory established in 1886 by Cuban Vicente Martínez Ybor. From the steps of the factory, José Martí (1853–1895), sometimes called the George Washington of Cuba, exhorted the cigar workers to take up arms against Spain. The area still has a Latin flavor, and Guavaween is an event to celebrate the culture and have a good time. The parade, with 20 to 50 bands, is led by a woman portraying the mythical "Mama Guava" doing the "Mama Guava Stumble." Many paraders wear costumes lampooning national figures. After the early evening parade, there is partying until the wee hours. Attendance is about 150,000.

CONTACT:
Tampa/Hillsborough Convention
and Visitors Association
111 E. Madison St., Ste. 1010
Tampa, FL 33602
800-448-2672 or 813-223-1111
fax: 813-229-6616

SOURCES:
Chases-1996, p. 430

♦ 0775 ♦ **Guelaguetza, La**
Third and fourth Monday of July

Also known as **Los Lunes del Cerro**, or **Mondays of the Hill**, this huge dance festival is held in Oaxaca, Mexico, on the last two Mondays of July. Costumed dancers from different *oaxaquena* tribes perform in a hilltop arena built exclusively for this event. Seats for the nationally televised festival are expensive, and many of the visiting dance groups must stay in local missions. Although the event is geared mostly to tourists, it represents a unique opportunity to see regional dances from all the Mexican states.

CONTACT:
Mexican Government Tourist
Office
405 Park Ave., Ste. 1401
New York, NY 10022
800-446-3942 or 212-755-7261
fax: 212-753-2874

SOURCES:
IntlThFolk-1979, p. 274

♦ 0776 ♦ **Guinea-Bissau Independence Day**
September 24

After more than 500 years of Portuguese rule, Guinea-Bissau (formerly known as Portuguese Guinea) declared itself an independent republic on September 24, 1973. The U.S. recognized it as such on September 10, 1974, and Portugal followed suit the same day.

September 24 is a national holiday in Guinea-Bissau.

CONTACT:
Guinea-Bissau Embassy
918 16th St.
Mezzanine Suite
Washington, D.C. 20006
202-872-4222; fax: 202-872-4226

SOURCES:
AnnivHol-1983, pp. 116, 122
Chases-1996, p. 389

♦ 0777 ♦ **Guinea Independence Day**
October 2

Guinea became an independent republic on this day in 1958, after having been a French colony since the late 19th century.

Independence Day is a national holiday celebrated all over the country with parades, dances, and sports competitions, especially in the capital city of Conakry.

CONTACT:
Guinea Embassy
2112 Leroy Pl., N.W.
Washington, D.C. 20008
202-483-9420; fax: 202-483-8688

SOURCES:
AnnivHol-1985, p. 127
Chases-1996, p. 401
NatlHolWrld-1968, p. 185

Gunpowder Plot Day
See **Guy Fawkes Day**

♦ 0778 ♦ **Guru Parab**
*October–November; full moon day of Hindu
month of Kartika*

Guru Nanak (1469–1539), was the founder of the Sikh Dharma faith (Sikhism), which was based on a belief in one god and on the rejection of idolatry and caste distinctions. In Pakistan at Nanak's birthplace, Talwandi (now Nankana Sahib, near Lahore, Pakistan), there is a shrine and a holy tank where thousands of Sikhs congregate on this day for a huge fair and festival. Here and at Sikh shrines everywhere, the holy scripture, *Guru Granth Sahib*, is read continuously and recited on Nanak's birthday. Food is distributed, and processions are common.

Nanak was followed by nine other gurus, under whom Sikhism gradually developed. Other Guru Parabs commemorate these later leaders. For example, the Guru Parab in honor of Guru Govind, or Gobind, Singh (1666–1708) is observed during the month of Pausa (December–January).

CONTACT:
Pakistani Embassy
2315 Massachusetts Ave., N.W.
Washington, D.C. 20008
202-939-6200; fax: 202-387-0484

SOURCES:
RelHolCal-1993, p. 80

♦ 0779 ♦ **Guru Purnima**
*June–July; full moon day of Hindu month of
Asadha*

In Hinduism, a guru is a personal teacher or guide who has already attained spiritual insight. The tutorial approach to religious instruction has always been emphasized in India, and in ancient times it was the guru who personally transmitted his knowledge of the Vedas, sacred Hindu books, to his student. The student often lived at the home of his guru and looked up to him with devotion.

Guru Purnima, or **Asadha Purnima,** is the day set aside for the veneration of the guru. In ancient times, when students were educated in ashrams and gurukuls, this was the day they would honor their teachers, pay their fees, and give them presents. It was customary to fast on this day and to seek the guru's blessing.

This day is also known as **Vyasa Purnima** after Rishi Vyasa (fifth? century B.C.), a famous guru who is said to have compiled the four Vedas, the *Mahabharata*, and the Puranas, a series of 18 epics dealing with creation and the gods in the form of fables, legends, and tales.

SOURCES:
RelHolCal-1993, p. 81

♦ 0780 ♦ **Gus Macker Basketball**
January–October; varies according to host city

This is 3-on-3 basketball—and party—on the streets of more than 70 cities across the United States. The **Gus Macker 3-on-3 Basketball Tournament** grew out of a low-wager backyard competition when, in 1974, Scott McNeal assembled 17 friends at his parents' house in the western Michigan city of Lowell, near Grand Rapids, to play with six teams of three people each. McNeal, apparently realizing that this kind of event could have larger popular appeal, adopted the moniker "Gus Macker" and began holding Macker tournaments once a year in Belding, Michigan. National media attention from the likes of *Sports Illustrated* and ABC's "Wide World of Sports" sparked inquiries from communities around the country, and in 1987 McNeal began taking the Macker on tour. In 1995 the Macker traveled to 72 cities where more than 200,000 people played basketball while 1.7 million watched. Several Canadian cities have begun to participate as well. In 1992 the Macker was honored by the Basketball Hall of Fame as the Official 3-on-3 Tournament. Indoor Mackers were introduced in 1994 so that the games could proceed during winter months in northern cities.

The Macker is notable for its insistence on donating proceeds to local charities (by 1994 more than $3 million had been given) and its stringent guidelines for having a positive, family-oriented event.

CONTACT:
L. Parks, Public Relations
Gus Macker Enterprises, Inc.
820 Monroe, N.W., Rm. 222
Grand Rapids, MI 49503
800-876-HOOP

SOURCES:
Chases-1996, p. 248

♦ 0781 ♦ Gustavus Adolphus Day (Gustaf Adolfsdagen)
November 6

Gustavus Adolphus (1594–1632) was the king of Sweden (1611–32) who laid the foundations of the modern Swedish state and turned the country into a major European power. By resolving the long-standing constitutional struggle between the crown and the aristocracy, he was able to achieve sweeping reforms in the fields of administrative organization, economic development, and particularly education. Among other things, he created the *Gymnasia* in 1620, which provided for secondary education in Sweden, and gave the University of Uppsala the financial support it needed to flourish.

King Gustav II was killed during the Thirty Years' War while leading a cavalry charge at the Battle of Lützen on November 6, 1632, turning a tactical victory into a national tragedy for the Swedes. The anniversary of his death is observed throughout Sweden with patriotic demonstrations—particularly in Skansen, Stockholm's outdoor museum. Enormous bonfires are built on Reindeer Mountain and processions of students carry lighted torches through the museum grounds.

CONTACT:
Swedish National Tourist Office
655 Third Ave., 18th Floor
New York, NY 10017
212-949-2333; fax: 212-983-5260

SOURCES:
BkFest-1937, p. 312
Chases-1996, p. 442

♦ 0782 ♦ Gutzon Borglum Day
August 10

On this day in 1927, sculptor John Gutzon de la Mothe

Borglum began carving the faces of four American presidents out of Mount Rushmore in the Black Hills of South Dakota. He chose this site because of its smooth-grained granite and the way it dominated the surrounding terrain. It took 14 years to bring the mountain sculpture to its present appearance, but because of delays caused by lack of funds and bad weather, only six and a half years were actually spent in carving. Gutzon Borglum died before the national memorial could be completed, but his son, Lincoln, continued to work on the project until funds ran out in 1941. Since that time no additional carving has been done, nor is any further work planned other than maintenance of the memorial.

The four presidents whose faces emerge from the granite cliffs were chosen as symbols of the birth and growth of the United States during its first 150 years. George Washington signifies the struggle for independence and the birth of the republic, Thomas Jefferson the idea of representative government, Abraham Lincoln the permanent union of the States and equality for all citizens, and Theodore Roosevelt the 20th-century role of the U.S. in world affairs.

August 10 is observed at Mount Rushmore each year with patriotic music and speeches. The 50th anniversary celebration in 1991 included a formal dedication of the monument and a summer-long extravaganza featuring appearances by former presidents, television personalities, and famous South Dakotans.

CONTACT:
Mount Rushmore Preservation
 Fund
P.O. Box 1066
Rapid City, SD 57709
605-341-8883; fax: 605-341-0433

♦ 0783 ♦ Guyana Independence Day
May 26

This public holiday marks Guyana's independence from Britain on this day in 1966.

Republic Day is another national holiday, commemorating February 23, 1970, when Guyana became a republic.

CONTACT:
Guyana Embassy
2490 Tracy Pl., N.W.
Washington, D.C. 20008
202-265-6900; fax: 202-232-1297

SOURCES:
AnnivHol-1983, pp. 28, 71
Chases-1996, p. 109

♦ 0784 ♦ Guy Fawkes Day
November 5

On the night of November 4, 1605, thirty-six barrels of gunpowder were discovered in a cellar beneath the Houses of Parliament in London. The conspirators of the so-called Gunpowder Plot, who planned to blow up King James I and his government to avenge their laws against Roman Catholics, were discovered and arrested, and on January 31 eight of them were beheaded. While Guy Fawkes didn't originate the plan, he was caught red-handed after someone tipped off the king's ministers. And he was among those whose heads were displayed on pikes at London Bridge.

The following year, Parliament established November 5 as a

national day of thanksgiving. Children still make effigies of Guy Fawkes and ask passers-by for money ("Penny for the Guy") which they spend on fireworks. The effigies are burned in bonfires that night, and fireworks traditionally fill the skies over Britain in remembrance of the failure of the Gunpowder Plot.

CONTACT:
British Tourist Authority
551 Fifth Ave., Ste. 702
New York, NY 10176
800-462-2748 or 212-986-2200
fax: 212-986-1188

SOURCES:
BkDays-1864, vol. II, p. 546
BkFest-1937, p. 61
BkHolWrld-1986, Nov 5
DaysCustFaith-1957, p. 284
DictDays-1988, pp. 51, 90, 96
FestSaintDays-1915, p. 199
FolkAmerHol-1991, p. 386
FolkWrldHol-1992, pp. 518, 551

♦ 0785 ♦ **Gynaecocratia**
January 8

The Greek title of this observance is a word that means female rule or government. This stab at feminist revolt is of long tradition in northern Greece where it is common for women to do all the household work and for most men to take life easy in cafes. Today in the villages of Komotini, Xanthi, Kilkis, and Serres, that standard is reversed for a day when Gynaecocratia is celebrated. The women gather in village cafes to socialize, while the men stay at home cleaning house, tending the babies, and generally looking after household tasks. At dusk, the men join their wives in celebrations.

SOURCES:
Chases-1996, p. 60

H

Haghoghy Ortnootyoon
See **Blessing of the Grapes**

♦ 0786 ♦ **Hagodol**
*Between end of March and mid-April; the
Sabbath before Passover*

The Sabbath just before PASSOVER is called Hagodol. It commemorates the Sabbath that preceded the escape from Egypt, of which Passover is the memorial. As recorded in the Old Testament book of Exodus, each Jewish family had been ordered by Moses to set aside a lamb to be sacrificed—an order which they carried out with considerable fear, because the lamb was held sacred by the Egyptians. As the Egyptians were preparing to punish this sacrilege, God destroyed every first-born among the Egyptians, including humans and animals. In the subsequent confusion, the Jews were able to make their famous exodus, ending more than 400 years of slavery. The day on which the miracle occurred that made their escape possible is also called the **Great Sabbath**, or the **Day of Deliverance**.

> SOURCES:
> *DaysCustFaith-1957*, p. 111

♦ 0787 ♦ **Haile Selassie's Birthday**
July 23

Haile Selassie I (1892–1975), emperor of Ethiopia from 1930 to 1974, was born Tafari Makonnen; he became Prince (or *Ras*) Tafari in 1916. Among the Jamaicans known as Rastafarians, Selassie was believed to be the Messiah, and Ethiopia was identified with heaven. Rastafarian theology and political belief was based on the superiority of the black man and the repatriation of black people to Ethiopia.

Ethiopians still celebrate Haile Selassie's birthday. During the years of his reign as emperor, Selassie would stand on the balcony of his palace in Addis Ababa and greet the thousands of well-wishers who gathered there on his birthday.

See also ETHIOPIA NATIONAL DAY and HAILE SELASSIE'S CORONATION DAY

CONTACT:
Ethiopian Embassy
2134 Kalorama Rd., N.W.
Washington, D.C. 20008
202-234-2281; fax: 202-328-7950

SOURCES:
NatlHolWrld-1968, p. 123

♦ 0788 ♦ **Haile Selassie's Coronation Day**
On or near November 15

The Rastafarians (or Ras Tafarians), members of a political-religious movement among the black population of Jamaica, worship Haile Selassie I, 'Might of the Trinity.' His original name was Tafari Makonnen (1892–1975), and he was emperor of Ethiopia under the name *Ras* (meaning 'Prince') Tafari. Rastafarians consider the Ethiopian emperor the Messiah and son of God, and the champion of their race. Their beliefs, which combine political militancy and religious mysticism, include taboos on funerals, second-hand clothing, physical contact with whites, the eating of pork, and all magic and witchcraft.

The Rastafarians' most important celebration is the anniversary of Haile Selassie's Coronation Day, which occurred on November 2, 1930. The dedication of babies to Ras Tafari, recitations, and singing are typically part of the celebrations on this day.

CONTACT:
Jamaica Tourist Board
801 Second Ave.
New York, NY 10017
800-233-4582 or 212-856-9727
fax: 212-856-9730

SOURCES:
DictWrldRel-1989, p. 601
FolkWrldHol-1992, p. 562

♦ 0789 ♦ **Haiti Independence Day**
January 1

The people of Haiti celebrate both NEW YEAR'S DAY and Independence Day on January 1, the day on which they declared their independence from the French in 1804. Thousands of people assemble in the capital city of Port-au-Prince to see the parades and to visit the National Palace on the Champs de Mars. They set off fireworks, dance in the streets, and sing the national anthem, which honors their founder, Jean-Jacques Dessalines, the hero of the anti-French revolt.

According to Haitian custom, whatever happens to someone

on January 1 is indicative of what will happen to them during the coming year, motivating even the poorest people to make an effort to put on new clothes, to visit their friends, and to give and receive gifts in the hope that these efforts will be rewarded in the coming year.

CONTACT:
Haitian Embassy
2311 Massachusetts Ave., N.W.
Washington, D.C. 20008
202-332-4090; fax: 202-745-7215

SOURCES:
Chases-1996, p. 50
FolkWrldHol-1992, p. 4
NatlHolWrld-1968, p. 6

Hajj
See **Pilgrimage to Mecca**

♦ 0790 ♦ Hakata Dontaku
May 3–4

The largest festival in Japan held in Fukuoka City (Fukuoka Prefecture) during Golden Week, the first week in May. This festival attracts more than two million spectators every year because Golden Week is a national holiday encompassing Children's Day (*see* KODOMO-NO-HI) and Japan Memorial Day (*see* JAPANESE NATIONAL FOUNDATION DAY).

The festival originated in the Muromachi Period (1333–1568) as a procession of the merchants of Hakata, an old section of Fukuoka City, paying their new year visit to the *daimyo,* or feudal lord. The name of the holiday curiously is thought to have derived from the Dutch word *Zondag,* meaning 'Sunday,' which was broadened to mean 'holiday,' and corrupted into *Dontaku.*

The festival highlight is a three-hour parade with legendary gods on horseback, floats, and musicians playing samisens (a three-stringed instrument similar to a guitar), flutes, and drums.

CONTACT:
Japan National Tourist
  Organization
630 Fifth Ave., Ste. 2101
New York, NY 10111
212-757-5640; fax: 212-307-6754

SOURCES:
JapanFest-1965, p. 147

♦ 0791 ♦ Halashashti
August–September; sixth day of waning half of Hindu month of Bhadrapada

This Hindu festival is often referred to as **Balarama Shashti,** after Krishna's older brother, Balarama, who was born on this day. Balarama's weapon was a plough, so it is also the day on which the farmers and peasants of India worship the *hala,* or plough. They apply powdered rice and turmeric to the plough's iron blade and decorate it with flowers. A small piece of ground is sanctified and plastered with cow dung, then a small pool of water is dug in the middle and branches of plum, fig, and other fruit trees are planted there. Some women fast all day in the belief that it will ensure happiness, prosperity, and longevity to their sons. When the fast is broken in the evening, there is a great feast and celebration.

SOURCES:
FolkWrldHol-1992, p. 437
RelHolCal-1993, p. 81

♦ 0792 ♦ Halcyon Days
December 14–18

The ancient Greeks called the seven days preceding and the seven days following the WINTER SOLSTICE the "Halcyon Days." According to one legend, the halcyon bird, or kingfisher, nested during this period. Because she built her nest on the water, the gods granted her a respite from storms and high seas so that she could hatch and rear her young. But Greek mythology has it that Halcyone (or Alcyone), Ceyx's wife and one of Aeolus's daughters, drowned herself when she learned her husband had drowned. The gods took pity on her and transformed them both into kingfishers, and Zeus commanded the seas to be still during these days. Thus it was considered a period when sailors could navigate in safety.

Today, the expression "halcyon days" has come to mean a period of tranquillity, often used as a nostalgic reference to times past.

SOURCES:
BkDays-1864, vol. II, p. 726
Chases-1996, p. 480
DictFolkMyth-1984, p. 475

♦ 0793 ♦ Half Moon Bay Art and Pumpkin Festival
October, weekend after Columbus Day

A festival highlighted by a Great Pumpkin Weigh-Off, held since 1971 in Half Moon Bay, Calif. The weigh-off winner gets $2,500; winning pumpkins have weighed in excess of 600 pounds. Other festival features are a Great Pumpkin Parade, arts and crafts, food concessions selling pumpkin bread, pumpkin crepes, pumpkin ice cream, and pumpkin strudel, and entertainment that includes live music, puppet shows, magicians, jugglers, clowns, and professional pumpkin carvers. There are competitions in pumpkin carving and pie eating.

Pumpkins have been grown in the Half Moon Bay area for decades but were used for cattle feed until the 1920s when two farmer brothers decided to try them as human food. That began a surge in pumpkin popularity. The pumpkin festival has also surged; attendance is estimated at 300,000.

CONTACT:
California Division of Tourism
801 K Street, Ste. 1600
Sacramento, CA 95814
800-862-2543 or 916-322-2881
fax: 916-322-3402

♦ 0794 ♦ Halifax Day
April 12

Also known as **Halifax Resolves Day, Halifax Resolutions Day, Halifax Independence Day,** or **Halifax Resolutions of Independence Day,** this is the day on which, in the spring of 1776, North Carolina's delegates to the Second Continental Congress were given permission to join with representatives from other colonies in declaring their independence from British rule. As the first official sanction of separation from Great Britain, the Halifax Resolutions laid the groundwork for the American Revolution. It is a legal holiday in North Carolina.

SOURCES:
AnnivHol-1983, p. 50

Chases-1996, p. 167
DictDays-1988, p. 54

◆ 0795 ◆ Halloween
October 31

Halloween has its ultimate origins in the ancient Celtic harvest festival, SAMHAIN, a time when people believed that the spirits of the dead roamed the earth. Irish settlers brought their Halloween customs—which included bobbing for apples and lighting jack-o'-lanterns—to America in the 1840s.

In the United States children go from house to house in costume—often dressed as ghosts, skeletons, or vampires—on Halloween saying, "Trick or treat!" Though for the most part the threat is in jest, the "Trick" part of the children's cry carries the implication that if they don't receive a treat, the children will subject that house to some kind of prank, such as marking its windows with a bar of soap or throwing eggs at it. Most receive treats in the form of candy or money. But Halloween parties and parades are popular with adults as well. Because nuts were a favorite means of foretelling the future on this night, **All Hallows' Eve** in England became known as **Nutcrack Night**. Other British names for the day include **Bob Apple Night, Duck (or Dookie) Apple Night, Crab Apple Night, Thump-the-door Night**, and, in Wales, APPLE AND CANDLE NIGHT. In the United States it is sometimes referred to as **Trick or Treat Night**.

See also MISCHIEF NIGHT

SOURCES:
AmerBkDays-1978, p. 968
BkDays-1864, vol. II, p. 519
BkFest-1937, p. 60
BkHolWrld-1986, Oct 31
DaysCustFaith-1957, p. 280
DictFolkMyth-1984, pp. 181, 869, 961
FestSaintDays-1915, p. 191
FolkAmerHol-1991, p. 373
FolkWrldHol-1992, p. 518
RelHolCal-1993, p. 81
SaintFestCh-1904, p. 468

◆ 0796 ◆ Halloween in Ireland
October 31

In Ireland, HALLOWEEN is observed with traditional foods and customs that are largely based on superstitions or folk beliefs. One of the dishes served is known as *colcannon*, or *callcannon*. It consists of mashed potatoes, parsnips, and chopped onions. A ring, a thimble, a small china doll, and a coin are mixed in, and the one who finds the ring will be married within a year. The one who finds the doll will have children, the one who finds the coin will be wealthy, and the one who finds the thimble will never marry. *Barmbrack*—a cake made with a ring concealed inside—is a variation on the same theme. Whoever gets the ring in his or her slice will be the first to marry. Sometimes there is a nut inside, and the one who finds the nut will marry a widow or widower. If the kernel of the nut is shriveled, the finder will never marry.

Nuts have traditionally played a role in Halloween celebrations in the British Isles. In England, Halloween is known as **Nutcrack Night**. In Ireland, a popular superstition involved putting three nuts on the hearth and naming them after

lovers. If one of the nuts cracked or jumped, that lover would be unfaithful; if it began to burn, it meant that he was interested. If a girl named one of the nuts after herself and it burned together with the nut named after her lover, it meant that they would be married.

The jack-o'-lantern, according to the Irish, was the invention of a man named Jack who was too greedy to get into heaven and couldn't get into hell because he had tricked the devil. The devil threw him a lighted coal from hell instead, and Jack stuck it in the turnip he was eating. According to the legend, he used it to light his way as he wandered the earth looking for a final resting place.

SOURCES:
AmerBkDays-1978, p. 969
BkDays-1864, vol. II, p. 519
BkHolWrld-1986, Oct 31
FestSaintDays-1915, p. 194
FolkWrldHol-1992, p. 520

◆ 0797 ◆ Halloween in New Orleans
October 31

A spooky and macabre celebration in New Orleans, La., when costumed revelers parade up and down Bourbon Street and actors dressed as legendary characters are on the streets to narrate their grisly histories. The sheriff's Haunted House in City Park is a standard feature, and a Ghost Train rolls through the park while costumed police officers jump out of bushes to spook the riders. The Voodoo Museum usually offers a special Halloween ritual in which people may see voodoo rites. Walking tours take visitors to such haunts as Le Pretre House, where a Turkish sultan and his five wives were murdered one night in 1792; it is said that their ghosts still have noisy parties.

On a more solemn note, the St. Louis Cathedral holds vigil services on Halloween, and several masses on ALL SAINTS' DAY. On the afternoon of that day, the archbishop leaves the cathedral for St. Louis Cemetery No. 1 to bless the newly scrubbed and decorated tombs.

CONTACT:
New Orleans Metropolitan Convention and Visitors Bureau
1520 Sugar Bowl Dr.
New Orleans, LA 70112
504-566-5011; fax: 504-566-5046

◆ 0798 ◆ Halloween in Scotland
October 31

Many of the traditional customs associated with HALLOWEEN in Scotland are described in the famous poem of that name by the Scottish poet Robert BURNS, although not all of them are still observed. "Pulling the kail" referred to the custom of sending boys and girls out into the garden (or kailyard) blindfolded. They were instructed to pull up the first plant they encountered and bring it into the house, where its size, shape, and texture would reveal the appearance and disposition of the finder's future husband or wife. It was also believed that by eating an apple in front of a mirror, a young woman could see the reflection of her future mate peering over her shoulder.

Another custom referred to by Burns was known as "The Three Dishes," or *Luggies*. One was filled with clean water, one with dirty water, and one remained empty. They were arranged on the hearth, and as people were led into the room blindfolded, they would dip their fingers into one of the bowls. Choosing the clean water indicated that one would marry a maiden (or bachelor); the dirty water indicated marriage to a widow (or widower). The empty dish meant that the person was destined never to marry.

"Dipping the shift" was another popular superstition regarding marital prospects. If someone dipped a shirt-sleeve in a south-running stream and hung it up by the fire to dry, the apparition of the person's future mate would come in to turn the sleeve.

Superstition surrounded death as well as marriage. It was customary on Halloween for each member of the family to put a stone in the fire and mark a circle around it. When the fire went out, the ashes were raked over the stones. If one of the stones was found out of place the next morning, it means that the person to whom it belonged would die within the year.

SOURCES:
AmerBkDays-1978, p. 969
BkDays-1864, vol. II, p. 520
FestSaintDays-1915, p. 193

♦ 0799 ♦ Halloween on the Isle of Man
October 31

In the early part of this century, Halloween was referred to as **Thump-the-Door Night** on the Isle of Man because boys would gather outside the house of someone they didn't like and bombard the door with turnips or cabbages until the inhabitants gave them some money to make them go away—much like the trick-or-treating that goes on in the United States. As might be expected, the game occasionally got out of control, provoking complaints and sometimes legal action. Eventually it fell out of favor.

Halloween is commonly called **Hollantide** on the Isle of Man because there was a time when it marked the beginning of the church year. This was based on the Celtic custom of beginning the year in November instead of in January.

SOURCES:
DictDays-1988, p. 120
FestSaintDays-1915, p. 196

♦ 0800 ♦ Haloa
Late December

The Haloa was an ancient Greek festival in honor of Demeter and Dionysus. It took place in Eleusis on the 25th or 26th day of the month called Poseideon, which would place it around December 31 on the Julian calendar, near the time of the WINTER SOLSTICE. The Haloa is believed to have been an attempt to restore the earth's lost fertility and also, in years when it was obvious that the crops were not growing well, to reverse the course of nature and assist the weak shoots in surviving the winter months.

Only women attended the Haloa. Although there are many theories about what went on there, most involve lewd jokes and games, and uninhibited discussions about sex and illicit love. The celebrants carried sexual organs made out of clay, and pastries made to resemble sex organs were set out on the table. It was believed that such obscene behavior encouraged fertility, and it makes sense in view of the fact that the Haloa

was held at a time of year when the fields were frozen and the growth of crops was at a temporary standstill. By manipulating sexual and agricultural symbols, by feasting and carrying on, the women attempted to "warm up" the earth and stimulate its dormant fertility.

SOURCES:
AtticFest-1981, p. 104
DictFolkMyth-1984, p. 867

♦ 0801 ♦ Hambletonian Harness Racing Classic
First Saturday in August

Harness racing's most prestigious race for three-year-old trotters, the Hambletonian is a test of both speed and stamina. Currently held at the Meadowlands Racetrack in East Rutherford, New Jersey, the race dates back to 1926. It is always held on the first Saturday in August and is preceded by a week of other races, with purses ranging from $225,000 to $600,000. The purse for the one-mile Hambletonian race is $1.2 million, and the winner usually goes on to take a divisional title.

CONTACT:
Meadowlands Racetrack
50 Highway 120
East Rutherford, NJ 07073
201-935-8500; fax: 201-460-4035

Hamishah Asar B'Av
See **Fifteenth of Av**

Hamishah Asar Bishevat
See **Tu Bishvat**

♦ 0802 ♦ Hana Matsuri (Flower Festival)
April 8

A celebration of the Buddha's birthday, observed in Buddhist temples throughout Japan. The highlight of the celebration is a ritual known as *kambutsue* ("ceremony of 'baptizing' the Buddha"), in which a tiny bronze statue of the Buddha, standing in an open lotus flower, is anointed with sweet tea. People use a small bamboo ladle to pour the tea, made of hydrangea leaves, over the head of the statue. The custom is supposed to date from the seventh century, when perfume was used, as well as tea. Festivities often include a procession of children carrying flowers.

See also VESAK

CONTACT:
Japan National Tourist
  Organization
630 Fifth Ave., Ste. 2101
New York, NY 10111
212-757-5640; fax: 212-307-6754

SOURCES:
BkFestHolWrld-1970, p. 76
Chases-1996, p. 163
JapanFest-1965, p. 62

♦ 0803 ♦ Hanami
March–April

The word *hana* means 'flower' in Japanese, and *hanami* means 'flower viewing'. However, appreciation of the cherry blossom in Japan is almost a religion, and therefore hanami has come to refer specifically to cherry blossoms. The pink-and-white blooms last for about two weeks, and during that time people swarm to the parks to picnic, play games, tell stories, and dance. Often companies organize hanami parties for their employees. The season usually starts at the end of March in Kyushu, in early April in the Tokyo area, and in late April in the north of Japan. The most famous viewing place is Yoshinoyama near Nara, where it is said 1,000 trees can be seen at a glance.

See also CHERRY BLOSSOM FESTIVAL

CONTACT:
Japan National Tourist
 Organization
630 Fifth Ave., Ste. 2101
New York, NY 10111
212-757-5640; fax: 212-307-6754

SOURCES:
AnnivHol-1983, p. 174
BkFestHolWrld-1970, p. 89
FolkWrldHol-1992, p. 220
JapanFest-1965, p. 99

♦ 0804 ♦ **Handsel Monday**
*First Monday of the year; first Monday after
January 12*

A secular holiday, Handsel Monday was important among the rural people of Scotland. 'Handsel' was something given as a token of good luck, particularly at the beginning of something; the modern house-warming gift would be a good example. Thus Handsel Monday was an occasion for gift-giving at the start of the new year, and it remained a Scottish tradition from the 14th until the 19th century. Eventually it was replaced by BOXING DAY, and the custom of giving farm laborers and public servants some extra money or a small gift on this day continues.

Because Handsel Monday was so widely celebrated among the rural population, many Scottish peasants celebrated **Auld Handsel Monday** on the first Monday after January 12, reflecting their reluctance to shift from the Old Style, or Julian, calendar to the New Style, or Gregorian, calendar.

SOURCES:
BkDays-1864, vol. I, p. 52
DictDays-1988, p. 54
DictFolkMyth-1984, p. 478

♦ 0805 ♦ **Handy Music Festival, W. C.**
First full week of August

A festival honoring the "Father of the Blues" in the Alabama Quad-Cities of Florence, Muscle Shoals, Sheffield, and Tuscumbia in the northwestern part of the state known as Muscle Shoals. William Christopher Handy, the son and grandson of ministers, was born in 1873 in Florence, took an early interest in music and went on to become a prolific composer, performer, orchestra leader, and music publisher despite his father's ministerial influence. In 1911, he wrote an election campaign song for Mayor Edward H. "Boss" Crump of Memphis, Tenn., that became known as the "Memphis Blues" and was one of the works that made him famous. Others included the classic "St. Louis Blues," "Beale Street Blues," and "Careless Love."

Handy, working in the period of transition from ragtime to jazz, fused elements of black folk music with ragtime to create distinctive blues pieces. He also organized a publishing firm, issued anthologies of black spirituals and blues and studies of American black musicians, and wrote an autobiography, *Father of the Blues*, published in 1941. He expressed his philosophy with these words: "Life is like this old trumpet of mine. If you don't put something into it, you don't get nothing out." When Handy died in 1958, a Harlem minister said, "Gabriel now has an understudy."

The festival celebrates not only Handy's musical heritage but also the musical roots of spirituals and jazz. Opening ceremonies are at the W. C. Handy Home & Museum, a log cabin housing Handy's collected papers and memorabilia. His piano and trumpet are on display.

Throughout the festival there is music by nationally known musicians night and day, street dancing, a foot race, folk art exhibits, and music workshops. Events are held in such nontraditional locations as ball fields, parks, and nursing homes, and concerts are performed in the church where Handy's father and grandfather served as pastor, and in restaurants and clubs. The small community of Muscle Shoals, where several events are held, is known in music circles for having given birth to the "Muscle Shoals Sound" through a recording studio that was set up in 1965. Artists as varied as Aretha Franklin, Peggy Lee, Liza Minelli, Bob Seger, and the Rolling Stones have recorded here.

CONTACT:
Alabama Bureau of Tourism and
 Travel
P.O. Box 4927
Montgomery, AL 36103
800-252-2262 or 334-242-4169
fax: 334-242-4554

SOURCES:
Chases-1996, p. 324

♦ 0806 ♦ **Han'gul Day**
October 9

This day commemorates the invention of the Korean alphabet by scholars under the direction of King Sejong of the Yi Dynasty in 1446.

The Han'gul system consists of 14 consonants and 10 vowels. The symbols for consonants are formed with curved or angled lines; the symbols for vowels are composed of vertical or horizonal straight lines with short lines on either side. Although Sejong made Han'gul the official writing system for the Korean language, it was not used by scholars or upper-class Koreans until after 1945, when Japanese rule came to an end and the influence of Confucianism and Chinese culture waned.

The reign of Sejong (1418–50) was a golden age in Korea, producing—besides the alphabet—the encyclopedic codification of medical knowledge and the development of new fonts of type for printing. (The technique of movable-type printing was developed in Korea in 1234, two hundred years before Johann Gutenberg's invention in Germany.)

The day is celebrated with Confucian rituals and Choson-period court dances performed at Yongnung, the king's tomb, in Yoju, Kyonggi. Yoju also stages the King Sejong Cultural Festival, which is part of a three-day Grand Cultural Festival, with chanting and processions at Shilluksa Temple, farmers' dances, games such as tug of war, and a lantern parade. In some areas, there are calligraphy contests for both children and adults.

Ceremonies are also held at the King Sejong Memorial Center near Seoul.

CONTACT:
Korea National Tourism Corp.
205 N. Michigan Ave., Ste. 2212
Chicago, IL 60601
312-819-2560; fax: 312-819-2563

SOURCES:
Chases-1996, p. 410
BkHolWrld-1986, Oct 9
FolkWrldHol-1992, p. 509

Hans Christian Andersen's Birthday
See **Children's Book Day, International**

♦ 0807 ♦ Hanukkah (Chanukah)
Between November 25 and December 26; from Kislev 25 to Tevet 2

Hanukkah commemorates the successful rebellion of the Jews against the Syrians in the Maccabean War of 162 B.C., but the military associations of this festival are played down. What is really being celebrated is the survival of Judaism. After the Jews' victory, they ritually cleansed and rededicated the Temple, then relit the menorah or 'perpetual lamp'; hence one of the other names for this celebration, the **Feast of Dedication** (Hanukkah means 'dedication' in Hebrew). The story is told that although there was only enough consecrated oil to keep the lamp burning for one day and it would take eight days to get more, the small bottle of oil miraculously lasted for the entire eight days. It is for this reason that Hanukkah is also known as the **Feast of Lights**.

Jewish families today celebrate this holiday by lighting a special Hanukkah menorah, a candelabrum with holders for eight candles, one for each day of celebration, plus a ninth, the shammash or 'server,' used to light the others. One candle is lit on the first night, two on the second, three on the third, through to the eighth night when all are lit. A special prayer is recited during the lighting, and while the candles burn it is a time for songs and games, including the four-sided toy called the dreidel. Other customs include the giving of gifts, especially to children, and decorating the home—much like the CHRISTMAS celebrations in Christian homes around this same time of year.

SOURCES:
AmerBkDays-1978, p. 1131
BkFest-1937, p. 205
BkFestHolWrld-1970, p. 134
BkHolWrld-1986, Dec 10
DaysCustFaith-1957, p. 326
DictFolkMyth-1984, p. 479
DictWrldRel-1989, pp. 155, 293
FolkAmerHol-1991, p. 421
FolkWrldHol-1992, p. 577
RelHolCal-1993, p. 82

♦ 0808 ♦ Hanuman Jayanti
March–April; Hindu month of Caitra

Hanuman, the Monkey-God and a central figure in the great Hindu epic the *Ramayana*, helped Rama rescue his wife Sita from the demon Ravana; for this Rama decreed the two always be worshipped together. He is revered by Hindus all over India in the form of a monkey with a red face who stands erect like a human. His birth anniversary is observed in the month of Caitra (March–April) with celibacy, fasting, and reading the *Hanuman-Chalisa*. Hindus visit his temples, of which there are many, to offer prayers on this day and to re-paint his image with vermilion.

SOURCES:
DictWrldRel-1989, p. 294
FolkWrldHol-1992, p. 214
RelHolCal-1993, p. 82

♦ 0809 ♦ Harbin Ice and Snow Festival
January 5–February 5

An extravaganza of ice sculptures in the port city of Harbin, the second largest city of northeast China. The sculptures, using themes of ancient legends and stories and modern historic events, depict pavilions, towers, temples, and mythic animals and persons. Located in Zhaolin Park, they shimmer in the sun by day, and at night are illuminated in a rainbow of colors. Theatrical events, art exhibitions, and a photo exhibition mark festival time, and wedding ceremonies are often scheduled at this time in the ice-filled park.

CONTACT:
China National Tourist Office
350 Fifth Ave., Ste. 6413
New York, NY 10165
212-760-9700; fax: 212-760-8809

♦ 0810 ♦ Harbor Festival
June–July

New York City's Harbor Festival is a good example of a festival that started as a one-time event—the bicentennial celebration on July 4, 1976, known as "Operation Sail," when tall ships from all over the world sailed into New York Harbor. This was so successful that local promoters decided to make it an annual event. Although the 18 tall ships that came to the city in 1976 do not return every year, there is a Great Parade of Ships that includes both military and commercial vessels sailing up the Hudson River. The festival ends on the FOURTH OF JULY with a magnificent fireworks display. The Harbor Festival's many cultural, sporting, ethnic, and maritime events take place not only in Manhattan but in Brooklyn and Staten Island as well.

Operation Sail 1992 was a celebration of the 500th anniversary of Christopher Columbus's voyage to the New World (*see* COLUMBUS DAY). Thirty-four tall ships from 24 countries, accompanied by replicas of Columbus's three ships, the *Niña*, the *Pinta* and the *Santa María*, followed the 11-mile parade route through New York Harbor. The dissolution of the Soviet Union allowed Russia to send four ships to the event, including the 400-foot *Sedov*, the longest of the tall ships. The total cost for the weekend was $12 million, but it generated $100 million in revenue for city businesses.

CONTACT:
New York Convention and Visitors Bureau
2 Columbus Cir.
New York, NY 10019
800-692-8474 or 212-484-1200
fax: 212-247-6193

SOURCES:
GdUSFest-1984, p. 127

♦ 0811 ♦ Hard Crab Derby, National
September, Labor Day weekend

The first **Hard Crab Derby** was held in 1947. A local newspaper editor dumped a few hard-shell crabs into a circle on Main Street in Crisfield, Maryland. The crab that scurried to an outer circle first was declared the winner, and its owner was awarded a trophy. There doesn't seem to have been any motivation for the race other than the wish to compete with the other derbies that had already been established for horses, automobiles, etc.

Today the National Hard Crab Derby attracts hundred of entries. The Governor's Cup Race, in which entries representing the 50 states compete, takes place on the Saturday of LABOR DAY weekend. There is also a boat-docking contest, a fishing tournament, a plastic-container-boat regatta, and a soft-crab cutting and wrapping contest. Fireworks, beauty contests, band concerts, drill team exhibitions, and professional entertainment complete the three-day festival.

CONTACT:
Maryland Office of Tourism
 Development
217 E. Redwood St., 9th Floor
Baltimore, MD 21202
800-543-1036 or 410-333-6611
fax: 410-333-6643

SOURCES:
Chases-1996, p. 353

♦ 0812 ♦ Hari-Kuyo (Festival of Broken Needles)
February 8 or December 8

A requiem service for needles held throughout Japan. The ceremony of laying needles to rest harks back to at least the fourth century A.D. Today the services are attended not only by tailors and dressmakers but also by people who sew at home. Traditionally, a shrine is set up in the Shinto style, with a sacred rope and strips of white paper suspended over a three-tiered altar. On the top tier are offerings of cake and fruit, on the second tier there is a pan of tofu, and the bottom tier is for placing scissors and thimbles. The tofu is the important ingredient; people insert their broken or bent needles in it while offering prayers of thanks to the needles for their years of service. In the Buddhist service, special sutras are recited for the repose of the needles. Afterwards, the needles are wrapped in paper and laid to rest in the sea.

A hari-kuyo is held in Kyoto at the Buddhist Temple Horinji on Dec. 8, and in Tokyo one is held at Asakusa Kannon Temple on Feb. 8.

SOURCES:
AnnivHol-1983, p. 174
Chases-1996, p. 90
FolkWrldHol-1992, p. 586

Harvard-Yale Regatta
See **Yale-Harvard Regatta**

♦ 0813 ♦ Harvest Home Festival
Autumn

Many countries celebrate the end of the summer harvest or the "ingathering" of the crops with a special feast. What became known in England as Harvest Home, or **Harvest Thanksgiving**, was called the **Kirn** in Scotland (from the churn of cream usually presented on the occasion), and probably derived from the ancient LAMMAS celebrations. Eventually it gave rise to the **Harvest Festival** in Canada and THANKSGIVING in the United States.

The autumn harvest feast was usually served in a barn, a tent, or outdoors and was preceded by a church service. Although the earliest harvest feasts were served by a farmer or landowner to his laborers, eventually one big feast for the entire parish became the norm.

See also SZÜRET

SOURCES:
AmerBkDays-1978, p. 1053
AnnivHol-1983, p. 122
BkDays-1864, vol. II, p. 376

DictFolkMyth-1984, p. 484
SaintFestCh-1904, p. 424

♦ 0814 ♦ Harvest Moon Days
Full moon nearest September 23

Harvest Moon Days refers to the period of the full moon that falls closest to the AUTUMNAL EQUINOX, around September 23. This is traditionally a time for countries in the Northern Hemisphere to hold their annual harvest festivals.

See also HARVEST HOME FESTIVAL

SOURCES:
AnnivHol-1983, p. 121
Chases-1996, p. 391

♦ 0815 ♦ Hatch Chile Festival
September, Labor Day weekend

A tribute to the green chili (as it is more commonly spelled outside of New Mexico), New Mexico's state vegetable. The small town of Hatch is the center of the chili-growing industry in the southwestern part of the state. At festival time, the aroma of freshly harvested chilis permeates the town, and a marvelous variety of chilis in all forms can be purchased: fresh green chilis—from the mildest to the hottest, dried red chilis in ornamental braids called *ristras*, red chili powder; chili bread, chili salsa, chili jelly, chili wine, and chili con carne. Besides food, the festival features the crowning of a Green Chile Queen, a skeet shoot, a fiddling contest, a cookoff, and a ristra-making contest.

CONTACT:
New Mexico Tourism and Travel
 Division
491 Old Santa Fe Trail
Santa Fe, NM 87503
800-545-2040 or 505-827-7400
fax: 505-827-7402

♦ 0816 ♦ Haxey Hood Game
January 6

This centuries-old tradition in Haxey, England, can be traced back more than 600 years, when Lady Mowbray, whose husband owned a large portion of the parish of Haxey, lost her hood to a sudden gust of wind and 13 local men struggled gallantly to retrieve it. She showed her appreciation by staging an annual reenactment of the event, which is believed by some to be the origin of rugby, an English sport that combines soccer with American football.

The game known as **Throwing the Hood**, which takes place on OLD CHRISTMAS DAY (January 6) each year, involves a Lord (who acts as umpire and master of ceremonies), 13 Plough-Boggins (presumably named for the way the original 13 men turned up the soil in their efforts to capture the hood), a Fool, and as many others as care to participate. After several warm-up rounds with sham hoods, the real contest begins. The participants wrestle over a piece of leather stuffed with straw, coins, and other fillings. The winners carry it back to their village pub, where a victory celebration takes place. Later, the Boggins go from house to house, singing and collecting money for the celebration.

CONTACT:
British Tourist Authority
551 Fifth Ave., Ste. 702
New York, NY 10176
800-462-2748 or 212-986-2200
fax: 212-986-1188

◆ 0817 ◆ Hay-on-Wye Festival of Literature
Late May

This celebration of words and language has been held in Hay-on-Wye, Wales, since 1988. It offers 10 days of comedy, theater, and musical performances in addition to conversations, debates, lectures, interviews, and readings by poets and fiction writers. The festival regularly features some of the most widely known Welsh, Irish, English, European, and American writers in the world, including Margaret Atwood, Doris Lessing, John Mortimer, William Golding, Anthony Hecht, Joseph Heller, and Jan Morris. Musical performances have included the Welsh National Opera Male Choir and the English Shakespeare Company.

A series of master classes in poetry, short story, and television screenwriting has recently been established for young writers attending the festival whose poems or stories have been published or whose plays have been produced. The master classes include a week of intensive work under the supervision of such renowned writers as Joseph Brodsky, who won the Nobel Prize for Literature in 1980, and the famous Welsh poet and short-story writer Leslie Norris.

CONTACT:
British Tourist Authority
551 Fifth Ave., Ste. 702
New York, NY 10176
800-462-2748 or 212-986-2200
fax: 212-986-1188

SOURCES:
Chases-1996, p. 226

Heaving Day
See **Easter Monday**

Heinz Southern 500
See **Southern 500**

◆ 0818 ◆ Helsinki Festival
Late August–early September

The largest cultural event in the Nordic countries is the Helsinki Festival. It grew out of the Sibelius Festival, established in 1951 to honor Finland's most famous composer, Jean Sibelius. But when the first official Helsinki Festival was held in 1967, it expanded its programming to include music from all periods—rock, jazz, opera, symphonic music, and chamber works—as well as theater, ballet, and exhibitions of paintings, sculpture, glassware, and textiles. Among the many musical events is what is known as the Festival Informal, a series where artists and visitors meet informally for "relaxed performances." Events are held in the city's parks, arcades, and hospitals as well as in the modern Finlandia Hall, the Sibelius Academy, and the Finnish National Theatre and Opera.

Ensembles that have performed at the 18-day festival include the Helsinki Philharmonic Orchestra, the Royal Philharmonic Orchestra of London, the Moscow Chamber Opera, the Beaux Arts Trio, the Alvin Ailey American Dance

Theater, the Groteska Puppet Theatre of Cracow, the Tientsin Acrobat Company of China, and the Ballet Nacional de Cuba.

CONTACT:
Finnish Tourist Board
655 Third Ave., 18th Floor
New York, NY 10017
212-949-2333; fax: 212-983-5260

SOURCES:
GdWrldFest-1985, p. 75
IntlThFolk-1979, p. 94
MusFestEurBrit-1980, p. 66

◆ 0819 ◆ Hemingway Days Festival
Week including July 21

A week-long celebration of Ernest Hemingway (1899–1961), the American novelist and short-story writer, in Key West, Fla. The festival has been held since 1980 during the week of Hemingway's birthday, July 21. Hemingway made his home in Key West at one time, and his novel, *To Have and Have Not* (1937), is set there. He was awarded the Pulitzer Prize in fiction in 1953 for his short heroic novel about an old Cuban fisherman, *The Old Man and the Sea*, and he received the Nobel Prize for Literature in 1954.

At the center of the festival is the Writer's Workshop and Conference, with a schedule of fiction, poetry, and stage and screenwriting. A short-story competition, with a first-place prize of $1,000, drew a total of 972 submissions in 1991. Lorian Hemingway, the writer's granddaughter and a writer herself, is the coordinator of the story contest. Other events include a radio trivia contest, a Hemingway look-alike contest, a storytelling competition, arm wrestling, and a party and concert at the Hemingway Home and Museum.

CONTACT:
Florida Division of Tourism
126 W. Van Buren
Tallahassee, FL 32399
904-487-1462; fax: 904-921-9158

SOURCES:
Chases-1996, p. 297

◆ 0820 ◆ Hemis Festival
Usually in June or July

A three-day Buddhist festival at the Hemis Gompa in the mountainous state of Ladakh in northern India. This is the largest *gompa* (monastery) in Ladakh and has gold statues, huge stone monuments of Buddha called *stupas* that are studded with precious stones, and an impressive collection of *thangkas*, or big scroll religious paintings. The festival celebrates the birthday of Guru Padmasambhava, the Indian Buddhist mystic who introduced Tantric Buddhism to Tibet in the eighth century. Tradition says he was a native of Swat (now in Pakistan), an area noted for magicians. Tradition also says he brought on an earthquake in Tibet to get rid of the demons who were delaying the building of a monastery.

The festival attracts people from throughout the mountain areas of Kadakh and Tibet—Muslims and Hindus as well as Buddhists, all dressed in their most colorful clothes. A fair springs up, with stalls selling confections, gems, and crafts.

The highlight of the festival is the Devil Dance of the monks (*see also* MYSTERY PLAY OF TIBET). Demon dancers are costumed as satyrs, many-eyed monsters, fierce tigers, or skeletons, while lamas portraying saints wear miters and opulent silks and carry pastoral crooks. These good lamas, ringing bells and swinging censers, scatter the bad lamas, as they all swirl about to the music of cymbals, drums, and 10-foot-long trumpets. The dance is a morality play, a battle between good and evil spirits, and also expresses the idea that a person's helpless soul can be comforted only by a lama's exorcisms.

CONTACT:
India Tourist Office
30 Rockefeller Ave.
15 N. Mezzanine
New York, NY 10112
212-586-4901; fax: 212-582-3274

SOURCES:
RelHolCal-1993, p. 83

♦ 0821 ♦ Heritage Holidays
Mid-October

A five-day celebration of the history of Rome, Ga., which, like its Italian namesake, was built on seven hills. There is also a bronze replica of the Capitoline Wolf outside City Hall. This Roman statue depicting a she-wolf nursing the legendary founders of Rome—Romulus and Remus—was given to the town in 1929 by Benito Mussolini.

Heritage Holidays, however, looks back to different times: it features a re-creation of the famous ride of John Wisdom, who has been called the Paul Revere of the South. During the Civil War, Rome was important to the Confederacy as a rail and manufacturing center. Wisdom, a native of the city who was living in Alabama, was delivering mail when he heard that Yankee soldiers were headed for his hometown. He rode the 67 miles to Rome in 11 hours, wearing out five horses and a mule. The men of Rome set up two old cannons, and the Yanks decided the town seemed too heavily fortified. They surrendered to a smaller Confederate force following them.

Features of the heritage days are a wagon train, parades, riverboat rides, concerts, and a major arts and crafts fair.

CONTACT:
Georgia Dept. of Industry
Trade and Tourism
285 Peachtree Center Ave., N.E.
Marquis Tower II, Ste. 1000
Atlanta, GA 30303
800-847-4842 or 404-656-3592
fax: 404-651-9063

♦ 0822 ♦ Hermit, Feast of the
September 1

Juan Maria de Castellano is known as a saint among the Hispanic-Americans of Hot Springs, New Mexico. He lived in a cave on a mountain peak for three years and slept on the ground. According to legend, he was responsible for a number of miraculous feats, not the least of which was producing water from a rock that had the power to cure blindness and other ills. Once when he had 12 men visit him, the very small amount of food he prepared was sufficient to feed all of them for an entire day.

In the 1930s, the members of the Asociacion de Santa Maria de Guadalupe met twice a year on Hermit's Peak. The second and more important of the two meetings was held on September 1, which came to be known as the Feast of the Hermit. People brought picnics, and some built little huts where they could spend the night. Some came to be cured, while others worked on repairing the fences and clearing the trails. They lit huge bonfires and prayed for the holy man who, like Moses, had caused water to flow from a rock and who, like Jesus, had satisfied the hunger of multitudes.

SOURCES:
FolkAmerHol-1991, p. 323

♦ 0823 ♦ Higan
March 20 or 21 and September 23 or 24

A week of Buddhist services observed in Japan at the spring and autumn equinoxes (*see* VERNAL EQUINOX and AUTUMNAL EQUINOX) when day and night are of equal length.

Both equinoxes have been national holidays since the Meiji Period (1868–1912). Before World War II, they were known as *koreisai*, 'festivals of the Imperial ancestors.' After the war, when the national holidays were renamed, they became simply spring equinox and autumn equinox.

Higan is the seven-day period surrounding the equinoxes. It means the 'other shore,' and refers to the spirits of the dead reaching Nirvana after crossing the river of existence. Thus Higan is a celebration of the spiritual move from the world of suffering to the world of enlightenment and is a time for remembering the dead, visiting, cleaning, and decorating their graves, and reciting *sutras*, Buddhist prayers. *O-hagi*, rice balls covered with sweet bean paste, and sushi are offered. It is traditional not to eat meat during this period. Emperor Heizei instituted the celebration in 806 A.D., when he ordered a week-long reading of a certain sutra for the occasion.

In Okinawa it is a home thanksgiving festival. Barley (*omugi*) or barley cakes with brown sugar are eaten with prayers for good fortune.

SOURCES:
AnnivHol-1983, p. 121
FolkWrldHol-1992, p. 486
JapanFest-1965, p. 190

High Holy Days
See **Rosh Hashanah; Yom Kippur**

♦ 0824 ♦ Highland Games
Dates vary

Originally impromptu athletic competitions carried out in the Scottish Highlands as part of a clan gathering, Highland games are now held all over the world, usually under the auspices of a local Caledonian society. Although the Jacobites put an end to the clan assemblies in 1745, the tradition of the games survived, and the first of the modern gatherings was held 90 years later at Braemar (*see* BRAEMAR HIGHLAND GATHERING). Today there are about 40 major gatherings in Scotland alone, as well as in Tauranga, New Zealand, and in several American communities such as Goshen, Connecticut, and Alexandria, Virginia, where there is a strong Anglo-Scottish presence.

Events at most Highland gatherings include flat and hurdle races, long and high jumps, pole vaulting, throwing the hammer, and tossing the weight (a round stone ball). A unique Highland event is tossing the caber, a tapered fir pole that must be thrown so that it turns end over end and comes to rest with the small end pointing away from the thrower. Competitors who toss the weight or the caber must wear the kilt or traditional Scottish costume. There are also competitions in bagpipe music and Highland dancing.

See also ALMA HIGHLAND FESTIVAL AND GAMES, GRANDFATHER MOUNTAIN HIGHLAND GAMES AND GATHERING OF SCOTTISH CLANS, and VIRGINIA SCOTTISH GAMES

CONTACT:
British Tourist Authority
551 Fifth Ave., Ste. 702
New York, NY 10176
800-462-2748 or 212-986-2200
fax: 212-986-1188

SOURCES:
AnnivHol-1983, p. 177
Chases-1996, pp. 224, 355, 364, 341, 238, 374, 429, 209, 420, 120, 313

◆ 0825 ◆ Hilaria
March 15

The ancient Romans celebrated the **Festival of Hilaria**, the "mother of the gods," each year on the IDES (15th day) of March. Part of the festival involved bringing offerings to the temple. When Christianity replaced the old pagan culture, legend has it that the Festival of Hilaria was adapted to fit the new church's needs and became known as MOTHERING SUNDAY in England. Eventually it was shifted from mid-March to MID-LENT, and it was observed as a time for young men and women living away from home to visit their parents.

SOURCES:
DaysCustFaith-1957, p. 89
FestSaintDays-1915, p. 50

◆ 0826 ◆ Hill Cumorah Pageant
Mid-July

Billed as the largest outdoor pageant in the United States, the Hill Cumorah Pageant is based on the Bible and the *Book of Mormon* and is presented by the Church of Jesus Christ of Latter-Day Saints (popularly called Mormons) in Palmyra, New York, for nine consecutive evenings (excluding Sunday and Monday) beginning on the third weekend in July. The drama, entitled "America's Witness for Christ," tells the story of the people who lived on the North American continent between 600 B.C. and 421 A.D., and how Christ taught these ancient Americans his gospel after his resurrection in Jerusalem. Presented on 25 hillside stages, each showing of the pageant can accommodate an audience of 15,000. More than 500 people participate in the pageant on a volunteer basis.

Hill Cumorah is believed to be the site where, in 1823, the angel Moroni instructed Joseph Smith, the first prophet of the Mormon Church, to look for the secret records, written upon gold plates, that told about the ancient inhabitants of North America—American Indians that the Mormons believe were descended from the Israelites via the tribe of Joseph. Smith was told that the plates were hidden in a hill named Cumorah, located between Palmyra and Manchester, New York. But it was nearly four years before Moroni gave Smith permission to remove the plates and begin their translation. They would eventually be published as the *Book of Mormon* in 1830.

An impressive feature of the pageant is the water curtain that is used during the "vision" scenes.

CONTACT:
New York Division of Tourism
1 Commerce Pl.
Albany, NY 12245
800-225-5697 or 518-474-4116
fax: 518-486-6416

SOURCES:
GdUSFest-1984, p. 129
RelHolCal-1993, p. 83

◆ 0827 ◆ Hina Matsuri (Doll Festival)
March 3

A festival for girls, celebrated in homes throughout Japan since the Edo Period (1600–1867) when doll-making became a highly skilled craft.

A set of 10 to 15 dolls (or *hina*), usually unmatched family heirlooms from various generations, is displayed on a stand covered with red cloth, the stand having at least three and up to seven steps. Dressed in elaborate antique silk costumes, the dolls represent the prince and princess, ladies-in-waiting, court ministers, musicians, and servants. Replicas of ornate furnishings are part of the display, as are miniature dishes of foods offered to the prince and princess. People visit each other's homes to admire the dolls.

In parts of Tottori Prefecture, girls make boats of straw, place a pair of paper dolls in them with rice cakes and, after displaying them with the other hina, set them afloat on the Mochigase River. This custom supposedly dates back to ancient times when dolls were used as talismans to exorcize evil; a paper doll cast into a river signified the washing away of human misfortune.

SOURCES:
BkFest-1937, p. 196
BkFestHolWrld-1970, p. 72
BkHolWrld-1986, Mar 3
DictFolkMyth-1984, p. 540
FolkAmerHol-1991, p. 117
FolkWrldHol-1992, p. 156

◆ 0828 ◆ Hippokrateia Festival
August

A celebration of Hippocrates, the "Great Physician," on Kos, the Greek island where he was born in about 460 B.C. A number of ancient manuscripts bear the name of Hippocrates; the best known of these is the *Aphorisms*, a collection of short discussions on the nature of illness, its diagnosis, prognosis, and treatment. The Hippocratic oath, an ethical code attributed to Hippocrates, is still used in graduation ceremonies at many medical schools. In it, the physician pledges to refrain from causing harm and to live an exemplary personal and professional life.

Throughout antiquity, Kos attracted the sick and infirm who came for healing at the Shrine of Asclepius, the god of medicine. Today the island is a popular resort, featuring fine beaches, the ruins of Roman baths, a Greek theater, and a museum with a huge statue of Hippocrates. The festival includes performances of ancient drama, concerts, a flower show, and a reenactment of the Hippocratic oath.

CONTACT:
Greek National Tourist
  Organization
645 Fifth Ave.
New York, NY 10022
212-421-5777; fax: 212-826-6940

SOURCES:
EncyRel-1987, vol. 6, p. 367

Hirohito's Birthday
See Greenery Day

◆ 0829 ◆ Hiroshima Peace Ceremony
August 6

A ceremony held each year since 1947 at the Peace Memorial Park in Hiroshima, Japan, in memory of the victims of the atomic bomb that devastated the city in 1945. (The day was Aug. 5 in the United States, Aug. 6 in Japan.) It was the first time in history that a weapon of such destruction had been used. The American B-29 Superfortress *Enola Gay* carried the bomb, called "Little Boy." The day is sometimes called **Atomic Bomb Day**, but this refers more accurately to the anniversary of the first atomic bomb test on July 16, 1945, at Alamogordo Air Base in New Mexico.

In announcing the bombing, President Harry S. Truman said, "The force from which the sun draws its power has been loosed against those who brought war to the Far East." The immediate death toll was 60,000, at least 75,000 more were injured, and the bomb wiped out more than four square miles—60 percent of the city. One man on the mission described its explosion as a bright, blinding flash followed by a "black cloud of boiling dust" and above it white smoke that "climbed like a mushroom to 20,000 feet." Three days later, on Aug. 9, a second A-bomb, called "Fat Man," was dropped on Nagasaki, razing the center of the city and killing 39,000. On Aug. 15, Japan surrendered, ending World War II.

The peace ceremony is held in the evening, when the city's citizens set thousands of lighted lanterns adrift on the Ota River and prayers are offered for world peace. Other memorial services are also held throughout the world at this time.

CONTACT:
Japan National Tourist
  Organization
630 Fifth Ave., Ste. 2101
New York, NY 10111
212-757-5640; fax: 212-307-6754

SOURCES:
AmerBkDays-1978, p. 722
AnnivHol-1983, p. 104
Chases-1996, p. 326
DictDays-1988, p. 56

◆ 0830 ◆ Hobart Cup Day
On or near January 23

There are a number of famous horse races in Australia each year that are observed as holidays in the states where they take place. Hobart Cup Day is a holiday in Southern Tasmania, while Northern Tasmania observes Launceston Cup Day a month later. In South Australia, Adelaide Cup Day is celebrated in May. And the MELBOURNE CUP, the country's richest handicap race, is held on the first Tuesday in November.

CONTACT:
Australian Tourist Commission
100 Park Ave., 25th Floor
New York, NY 10017
212-687-6300; fax: 212-661-3340

SOURCES:
AnnivHol-1983, p. 141
DictDays-1988, p. 75

◆ 0831 ◆ Hobart Regatta Day
February

The **Royal Hobart Regatta** is a two-day aquatic carnival that includes sailing, rowing, and swimming events as well as fireworks and parades. It is a holiday in Southern Tasmania, Australia, and is held on the Derwent River sometime in early February during Australia's summer season. Hobart is the capital of Tasmania, Australia's southernmost state.

A similar holiday in Northern Tasmania is observed on the first Monday in November and is called **Recreation Day**.

CONTACT:
Australian Tourist Commission
100 Park Ave., 25th Floor
New York, NY 10017
212-687-6300; fax: 212-661-3340

SOURCES:
AnnivHol-1983, p. 22
DictDays-1988, pp. 56, 95

Hobby Horse Parade
See **Minehead Hobby Horse Parade**

◆ 0832 ◆ Hobo Convention
Three days in August

The small, rural town of Britt, Iowa (population 2,000), seems an unlikely location for a convention of hobos—the unwashed but colorful riders of America's empty boxcars—but for three days each summer its residents play host to this diminishing segment of the population. From across the nation the hobos come to Britt, where they receive free food, sleeping accommodations in empty boxcars, and the adoration of more than 20,000 visitors who want to find out what a hobo's life is really like. There is a parade, an arts fair, carnival rides, races, and music. But the real action centers on the hobo camp set up by festival organizers on the outskirts of town, where visitors can hear the life stories of these men who have chosen to travel the country unencumbered by family or property.

The hobos are quick to distinguish themselves from tramps and bums. As one explains, "A hobo wants to wander, but he always works for his meals . . . a tramp wanders, but never does any work; a bum just drinks and wanders." The first Hobo Convention was held in Britt in 1900, and during the 1930s the event attracted hundreds of hobos. But their ranks are thinning, and today the town is lucky if 30 or 40 real hobos show up.

CONTACT:
Iowa Tourism Office
200 E. Grand Ave.
Des Moines, IA 50309
800-345-4692 or 515-242-4705
fax: 515-242-4749

SOURCES:
Chases-1996, p. 329

◆ 0833 ◆ Hocktide
Between April 5 and May 9; second Monday and Tuesday after Easter

Also known as **Hock Days**, the second Monday and Tuesday after EASTER in England was in medieval times and in Hungerford, Berkshire, till the present day, associated with collecting dues or rents and money for the church, particularly in rural areas. There were a number of traditional methods for demanding money, most of them light-hearted rather than threatening. For example, people were often tied up with ropes and had to pay for their release, giving rise to the name **Binding Tuesday**. Or rope might be stretched across the road to stop passers-by, who would then have to pay before they were allowed to continue. In parts of Berkshire, two 'Tutti-men' in top hats and morning coats—a 'tutti' being a small bouquet of flowers—would go from house to house carrying a 'tutti-pole' decorated with flowers and ribbons. There was also an orange scatterer who threw oranges to the men, old women, and children to keep them busy while the Tutti-men went from house to house demanding both money and a kiss from the lady of the house. In Yorkshire, children were still celebrating **Kissing Day** as recently as the 1950s—widely believed to have derived from hocktide customs.

Hocktide was also one of the QUARTER DAYS.

SOURCES:
AmerBkDays-1978, p. 309
BkFest-1937, pp. 16, 57
DictDays-1988, pp. 11, 55, 56,
  122
FestSaintDays-1915, p. 91
FolkHolWrld-1992, p. 208

♦ 0834 ♦ Hogmanay
December 31

In Scotland and the northern part of England, the last day of the year is known as Hogmanay. There are a number of theories as to where the name comes from—one of them being that it derives from the ancient Scandinavian name for the night preceding the feast of Yule, *Hoggu-nott* or *Hogg-night*. Another is that it comes from the French expression, *Au gui l'an neuf* ('To the mistletoe this New Year'), a reference to the ancient ceremony of gathering mistletoe (*gui* in French).

Scottish children, often wearing a sheet doubled up in front to form a huge pocket, used to call at the homes of the wealthy on this day and ask for their traditional gift of an oatmeal cake. They would call out "Hogmanay!" and recite traditional rhymes or sing songs in return for which they'd be given their cakes to take home. It is for this reason that December 31 was also referred to as **Cake Day**.

SOURCES:
BkDays-1864, vol. II, p. 788
BkFest-1937, p. 63
BkHolWrld-1986, Dec 31
DictDays-1988, pp. 56, 81, 84
DictFolkMyth-1984, pp. 181,
  499, 791
FolkWrldHol-1992, p. 651

♦ 0835 ♦ Hoi Lim Festival
January–February; 13th day of first lunar month

An alternating-song contest, held in Ha Bac Province of Vietnam. This is a courtship event, in which girls and boys of different villages carry on a singing courtship dialogue. The singers take part in what is a vocal contest with set rules; one melody, for example, can only be used for two verses of the song, and therefore there is considerable improvising. The story-lines of the songs tell of daily events. Young men and women practice them while they are at work in the rice fields or fishing.

CONTACT:
Vietnamese Embassy
1233 20th St., N.W., Rm. 501
Washington, D.C. 20036
202-861-0737

♦ 0836 ♦ Hola Mohalla
February–March

A Sikh festival celebrated in Anandpur Sahib, Punjab, India, on the day after Holi, the colorful water-tossing springtime festival. Mock battles with ancient weapons are staged, and there are also exhibitions of traditional martial arts like archery and fencing. The Sikh religion was founded in the state of Punjab in the late 15th century, and the majority of Sikhs now live there.

CONTACT:
India Tourist Office
30 Rockefeller Ave.
15 N. Mezzanine
New York, NY 10112
212-586-4901; fax: 212-582-3274

♦ 0837 ♦ Holi
*February–March; 14th day of waxing half of
Hindu month of Phalguna*

A colorful and boisterous Hindu spring festival in India. This is a time of shedding inhibitions: People smear each other with red and yellow powder and shower each other with colored water shot from bamboo blowpipes or water pistols. Restrictions of caste, sex, age, and personal differences are ignored. *Bhang*, an intoxicating drink made from the same plant that produces marijuana, is imbibed, and revelry reigns.

The name of the festival derives from the name of the wicked Holika. According to legend, an evil king had a good son, Prince Prahlad, who was sent by the gods to deliver the land from the king's cruelty. Holika, the king's sister, decided to kill the prince with fire. Believing she was immune to fire, she held the child in her lap and sat in flames. But Lord Krishna stepped in to save Prahlad, and Holika was left in the fire and burned to death. On the night before the festival, images of Holika are burned on huge bonfires, drums pound, horns blow, and people whoop.

Another tale, related to the practice of water-throwing, is that the small monkey god Hanuman (*see* Hanuman Jayanti) one day managed to swallow the sun. People were sad to live in darkness, and other gods suggested they rub color on one another and laugh. They mixed the color in water and squirted each other, and Hanuman thought this was so funny he gave a great laugh, and the sun flew out of his mouth.

There is also the story that the Mongol Emperor Akbar thought everyone would look equal if covered with color, and he therefore ordained the holiday to unite the castes.

The celebrations differ from city to city. In Mathura, Lord Krishna's legendary birthplace, there are especially exuberant processions with songs and music. In the villages of Nandgaon and Barsnar, once homes of Krishna and his beloved Radha, the celebrations are spread over 16 days. And in Besant, people set up a 25-foot pole called a *chir* to begin the celebrations and burn it at the end of the festival.

In Bangladesh the festival is called **Dol-Jatra**, the **Swing Festival,** because a Krishna doll is kept in a swinging cradle (*dol*). In Nepal it is called **Rung Khelna** 'playing with color'. They build a three-tiered, 25-foot high umbrella and at its base people light joss sticks, and place flowers and red powder. Instead of squirting water, they drop water-filled balloons from upper windows.

In Suriname it is **Holi Phagwa** and also the **Hindu New Year.**

CONTACT:
India Tourist Office
30 Rockefeller Ave.
15 N. Mezzanine
New York, NY 10112
212-586-4901; fax: 212-582-3274

SOURCES:
BkFest-1937, p. 163
BkFestHolWrld-1970, p. 8
BkHolWrld-1986, Mar 27
DictFolkMyth-1984, pp. 500,
  591, 941
FolkWrldHol-1992, p. 144
RelHolCal-1993, pp. 57, 72, 83

♦ 0838 ♦ Holland Festival
June

Since Holland (the Netherlands) didn't really have a single composer who could be honored by a festival in a specific city or town—such as the Mozart Festival in Salzburg, Austria (*see* SALZBURG FESTIVAL), or Germany's Wagner Festival in Bayreuth (*see* BAYREUTH FESTIVAL), it was decided in 1947 to have a single festival focused on three major cities—Amsterdam, Rotterdam, and the Hague/Scheveningen—that would cover a wide range of artistic and cultural activities and at the same time draw top international artists to the Netherlands. The Holland Festival lasts 23 days in June, with most of the 150 programs being held in the three large cities but with some events taking place in smaller cities and towns. The festival offers not only performances of orchestral and choral works but opera, ballet, theater, and film as well.

Each year a different country is selected as a theme. In 1992, for example, the focus was on Russian and Baltic music, and many top musicians from the former Soviet Union were invited to participate.

CONTACT:
Netherlands Board of Tourism
355 Lexington Ave., 21st Floor
New York, NY 10017
212-370-7360; fax: 212-370-9507

SOURCES:
Chases-1996, p. 236
GdWrldFest-1985, p. 141
IntlThFolk-1979, p. 283
MusFestEurBrit-1980, p. 124
MusFestWrld-1963, p. 193

♦ 0839 ♦ Hollerin' Contest, National
Third Saturday in June

Many years ago, the residents of Spivey's Corner, North Carolina, communicated with each other by calling out their greetings, warnings, and cries of distress. They also hollered for their cows, pigs, and dogs to come in. After modern technology supplanted this primitive mode of communication, a local citizen named Ermon Godwin, Jr., decided in 1969 to revive the custom of hollering by holding a day-long competition on the third Saturday in June each year. In addition to the hollering contests for people of both sexes and all ages, the event includes a pole climb, corn shucking, and a greased watermelon carry. Winners of the competition have demonstrated their skills on nationwide television.

CONTACT:
North Carolina Travel and Tourism Division
430 N. Salisbury St.
Raleigh, NC 27603
800-847-4862 or 919-733-4171
fax: 919-733-8582

SOURCES:
GdUSFest-1985, p. 133

Hollyhock Festival
See **Aoi Matsuri**

♦ 0840 ♦ Holmenkollen Day
Second Sunday in March

The Holmenkollen International Ski Meet is a week-long Norwegian winter festival held at Holmenkollen Hill outside Oslo. It is the main winter sports event of the year and it covers all types of skiing—cross-country racing and jumping as well as downhill and slalom. The world's best skiers meet here to compete for highly coveted prizes.

The high point of the festival comes on Holmenkollen Day,

when over a hundred thousand spectators, headed by the king and the royal family, gather at the famous Holmenkollen Hill to watch the ski-jumping event, which has been held here since 1892. Competitors swoop down the 184-foot jump, and the one who soars the farthest wins the coveted King's Cup.

CONTACT:
Norwegian Tourist Board
655 Third Ave.
New York, NY 10017
212-949-2333

SOURCES:
AnnivHol-1983, p. 37
Chases-1996, p. 133

♦ 0841 ♦ Holocaust Day
Between April 8 and May 6; Nisan 27

Holocaust Day, or **Yom ha-Shoah**, was established by Israel's Knesset (parliament) as a memorial to the six million Jews slaughtered by the Nazis between 1933 and 1945. It is observed on the 27th day of the month of Nisan, the day on which Allied troops liberated the first Nazi concentration camp at Buchenwald, Germany, in 1945. It is a commemoration that is observed by many non-Jewish people around the world.

CONTACT:
U.S. Holocaust Memorial Museum
100 Raoul Wallenberg Place, S.W.
Washington, D.C. 20024
202-488-0400

SOURCES:
AnnivHol-1983, p. 172
Chases-1996, p. 172
DictWrldRel-1989, pp. 325, 392
RelHolCal-1993, p. 122

♦ 0842 ♦ Holy Blood, Procession of the
Between April 30 and June 3; Ascension Day

A major religious event in Bruges, Belgium, to venerate the Holy Blood of Christ that was brought back from the Second Crusade by Thierry d'Alsace, Count of Flanders.

Thierry's bravery in Jerusalem in the battles against the Saracens was legendary. As a reward for his courage, King Baudouin entrusted the count with a vial of a few drops of blood supposed to have been from Christ's wounds and collected from under the cross by Joseph of Arimathea. When Thierry returned to Bruges on April 7, 1150, there was a great celebration: flowers were strewn in the streets, people waved the banners of the city trades, city dignitaries welcomed the heroic count, and the Holy Reliquary was taken in solemn procession to the Chapel of St. Basile.

The present procession commemorates that original one, although it was not a regular celebration until 1820. Today, the activities begin at 11 A.M. with a Pontifical Mass in the cathedral. The procession gets under way at 3 P.M., lasts about an hour and a half, and closes with a blessing by the bishop.

As the celebration gets under way, every church bell peals in this usually quiet city. Through living tableaux, the procession tells the story of the Bible from the fall of Adam and Eve, on through Abraham and Moses and to the New Testament stories of ST. JOHN the Baptist, the birth of Christ, the Last Supper, and the Crucifixion on Calvary. Some dozen groups also depict the triumphant return of Thierry d'Alsace to Bruges. When the procession has returned to Burg Square, where it began, the Bishop of Bruges lifts the relic of the Holy Blood and blesses the crowd. Visitors come to Bruges from all over the world for the procession.

See also SAN GENNARO, FEAST OF

CONTACT:
Belgian Tourist Office
780 Third Ave.
New York, NY 10017
212-758-8130; fax: 212-355-7675

SOURCES:
AnnivHol-1983, p. 63
BkFest-1937, p. 42
BkHolWrld-1986, May 21
Chases-1996, p. 214
FestWestEur-1958, p. 11
GdWrldFest-1985, p. 19

Holy Cross Day

See **Día de la Santa Cruz; Exaltation of the Cross**

Holy Day of Letters

See **Bulgaria Culture Day**

♦ 0843 ♦ Holy Family, Feast of the
Sunday after January 6, Epiphany

In the Roman Catholic Church the Holy Family—Jesus, Mary and Joseph—is thought to provide the perfect example of what the family relationship should be like. But it was not until the 17th century that the Holy Family was venerated as a family, and the feast itself was not officially instituted until 1921. Its popularity spread rapidly, and it is now celebrated by Roman Catholics all over world. Each of the three members of the sacred household at Nazareth are also honored as individuals on their own feast days.

SOURCES:
DaysCustFaith-1957, p. 37
RelHolCal-1993, p. 84

Holy Friday

See **Good Friday**

♦ 0844 ♦ Holy Ghost, Feast of the
March–July

Holy Ghost Season, or **Altura Do Espírito Santo**, has been celebrated in the Azores, Portugal, since the late 15th century. There are actually two types of celebration: the *bodo*, or banquet, and the *função*, or function. Bodos are held in rural *Impérios*—lavishly decorated buildings that are vacant all year except during the festival. The bodo is a large-scale public festival that includes a Mass; a children's procession; the ceremonial distribution of meat, bread, and wine; and a number of other activities including an auction, singing competitions and bullfights. The função is a small-scale celebration held in private homes. It represents the payment of a personal promise to the Holy Ghost and a series of ritual exchange events, culminating in the coronation of an Emperor, the distribution of gifts to the poor, and a communal meal.

Although Holy Ghost season falls primarily between EASTER and TRINITY SUNDAY, urban Impérios have extended the season to July so the same festival props—such as crowns, flags, and other costly items—can be shared among the various regions. Although observation of the feast has nearly disappeared in continental Portugal, it has been carried to Brazil, Canada, Bermuda, and the United States by Portuguese immigrants.

The Holy Ghost celebrations are based on the story of Queen Isabel of Portugal, who loved the poor and pleaded with God to help her starving people. When two ships laden with cattle and grain miraculously appeared in a Portuguese harbor, the Queen served a banquet to the poor and continued this yearly ceremony as an expression of gratitude to God.

CONTACT:
Portuguese National Tourist
    Office
590 Fifth Ave., 4th Floor
New York, NY 10036
212-354-4403; fax: 212-764-6137

SOURCES:
FolkWrldHol-1992, p. 276
GdUSFest-1984, pp. 88, 156
IntlThFolk-1979, p. 311

♦ 0845 ♦ Holy Innocents' Day
December 28

Also known as **Innocents' Day** or **Childermas**, this day commemorates the massacre of all the male children two years and under in Bethlehem as ordered by King Herod, who hoped that the infant Jesus would be among them. Not surprisingly, this day has long been regarded as unlucky—particularly for getting married or undertaking any important task. Edward IV of England went so far as to change the day of his coronation when he realized it would fall on December 28.

In ancient times, the "Massacre of the Innocents" was reenacted by whipping the younger members of a family. But over the years the tables turned, and in some countries it has become a day when children play pranks on their elders. In Mexico, Childermas is the equivalent of APRIL FOOL's DAY.

SOURCES:
AmerBkDays-1978, p. 1155
BkDays-1864, vol. II, pp. 776,
    777
BkFest-1937, pp. 49, 63, 175,
    223, 234, 347
DictFolkMyth-1984, pp. 218,
    525, 950, 951, 1018
FestSaintDays-1915, pp. 252,
    255
FestWestEur-1958, pp. 20, 84
FolkAmerHol-1991, p. 481
FolkWrldHol-1992, p. 645
IndianAmer-1989, pp. 291,
    315

♦ 0846 ♦ Holy Innocents' Day in Belgium
(Allerkinderendag)
December 28

HOLY INNOCENTS' DAY is the traditional anniversary of the slaughter of Bethlehem's male children by King Herod, who hoped that the infant Jesus would be among them. According to legend, two of the murdered children were buried in the Convent of Saint Gerard in the province of Namur, Belgium.

Many Belgian children turn the tables on their elders each year on December 28 by locking them up. Early in the morning, they collect all the keys in the house, so that whenever an unsuspecting adult enters a closet or room, they can lock the door behind him or her and demand a ransom—usually spending money, candy, a toy, or fruit. The innocent person who is being held for ransom is called a "sugar uncle" or "sugar aunt."

The tricks played by children on Holy Innocents' Day have been compared to the pranks that children in the United States and elsewhere play on APRIL FOOLS' DAY.

SOURCES:
AmerBkDays-1978, p. 1156
AnnivHol-1983, p. 165
BkFest-1937, p. 49
FestWestEur-1958, p. 20

Holy Kings' Day

See Epiphany

Holy Maries, Festival of the

See Saintes Maries, Fête des

♦ 0847 ♦ Holy Queen Isabel, Festival of the
Biennially in July

Queen Isabel of Portugal, born in 1271, is best known for the "miracle of the roses." When her husband, who was unsympathetic to his wife's frequent errands of mercy for the poor and afflicted, demanded to know what she was carrying in the folds of her robe, she told him it was roses, even though she was concealing bread for the hungry. When she opened her robe for him to inspect, the loaves of bread had been transformed into roses. She was beatified by Pope Leo X in 1516 and canonized by Urban VIII in 1625.

Historically, Queen Isabel was a strong advocate for peace in the tumultuous times in which she lived. When her husband, Dom Diniz, died in 1325, she retired to the convent of Santa Clara in Coimbra, Portugal, which she had founded. As the patroness of Coimbra, Queen Isabel is honored in early July in even-numbered years with a week of festivities that include religious processions, fireworks, speeches, concerts, and popular amusements.

CONTACT:
Portuguese National Tourist Office
590 Fifth Ave., 4th Floor
New York, NY 10036
212-354-4403; fax: 212-764-6137

SOURCES:
FestWestEur-1958, p. 170

♦ 0848 ♦ Holy Saturday
Between March 21 and April 24 in West and between April 3 and May 7 in East; the day before Easter

Saturday eve before EASTER, also called **Easter Even**, is the last day of HOLY WEEK and brings the season of LENT to a close. In the early church, this was the major day for baptisms. Many churches, especially those of the Anglican Communion, still hold large baptismal services on Holy Saturday. It is also known as the **Vigil of Easter** in reference to the fact that Jesus' followers spent this day, after his crucifixion on GOOD FRIDAY, waiting. The Easter, or Paschal, Vigil, the principal celebration of Easter, is traditionally observed the night of Holy Saturday in many churches today. Another name for this day is the **Descent into Hell**, because it commemorates Jesus' descent into and victory over hell.

Slavic Orthodox Christians bring baskets of food to the church for the Blessing of the Pascha (Easter) Baskets on Holy Saturday. The baskets are filled with the foods from which people have abstained during the Lenten fast and which will be part of the Pascha feast. For many inhabitants of Mexican descent in Los Angeles, California, Holy Saturday is the day

for a colorful ceremony known as the Blessing of the Animals, which takes place at the old Plaza Church.

CONTACT:
Los Angeles Convention and Visitors Bureau
633 W. Fifth St., Ste. 6000
Los Angeles, CA 90071
800-228-2452 or 213-624-7300
fax: 213-624-9746

SOURCES:
AmerBkDays-1978, p. 297
BkFest-1937, pp. 24, 41, 70, 87, 96, 148, 168, 184, 211, 227, 260, 275, 292, 301, 339
BkHolWrld-1986, Apr 11
DictFolkMyth-1984, p. 258
FestWestEur-1958, pp. 9, 60, 94, 108
FolkWrldHol-1992, pp. 190, 197, 199, 202
IndianAmer-1989, p. 274
SaintFestCh-1904, p. 161

♦ 0849 ♦ Holy Saturday in Mexico (Sábado de Gloria)
Between March 21 and April 24; day before Easter

In Mexico, HOLY SATURDAY is observed by burning effigies of Judas Iscariot, who betrayed Jesus for 30 pieces of silver. Street vendors sell the papier-mâché effigies, which range from one to five feet in height and make Judas look as ugly as possible. The effigies designed for children are stuffed with candies and hung in the patios of private houses. Other effigies are suspended over the streets or hung from lampposts. All have firecrackers attached, which are ignited as soon as the Mass of Glory is over. As the effigies explode, children scramble for the candies and small gifts that are hidden inside.

The church bells, which have been silent since the Wednesday before EASTER, ring on Holy Saturday, and there are folk beliefs associated with the ringing of the bells. For example, it is believed that plants or hair trimmed while the bells are ringing will grow back faster. Children are often smacked on the legs so that they'll grow taller.

See also BURNING OF JUDAS

CONTACT:
Mexican Government Tourist Office
405 Park Ave., Ste. 1401
New York, NY 10022
800-446-3942 or 212-755-7261
fax: 212-753-2874

SOURCES:
BkFest-1937, p. 227
BkHolWrld-1986, Apr 11
FolkWrldHol-1992, p. 199

♦ 0850 ♦ Holy Thursday
Between April 30 and June 3; forty days after Easter

Holy Thursday usually refers to MAUNDY THURSDAY, but in parts of rural England, it traditionally refers to ASCENSION DAY, the day on which Jesus Christ ascended into heaven. The English custom of "well dressing," which may have had its roots in a pagan festival, became associated with Holy Thursday in 1615. There was a severe drought in Derbyshire that year and most of the wells and streams dried up. The only wells that still had water were at Tissington, where people came to get water for their livestock. From that time onward, a special thanksgiving service was held there on Ascension Day, and Tissington became known as "the village of holy wells."

The well-dressing ceremony developed into a full-fledged festival in the 19th century. After delivering his sermon, the vicar would lead a procession to the wells, which were nearly hidden by screens of fresh flowers fastened to wooden frames. A simple ceremony, asking God to bless and keep the waters pure, was followed by a country fair that included Romany fortune-tellers and dancing around a Maypole.

> **SOURCES:**
> *BkDays-1864*, vol. I, p. 595
> *DaysCustFaith-1957*, p. 135
> *DictDays-1988*, pp. 6, 58
> *DictWrldRel-1989*, pp. 261,
>   468
> *RelHolCal-1993*, p. 58
> *SaintFestCh-1904*, p. 231

◆ 0851 ◆ **Holy Week**
Between March 15 and April 18 in the West and between March 28 and May 1 in East; the week preceding Easter

Holy Week, the seven days beginning with PALM SUNDAY that precede EASTER, is the most solemn week in the Christian year. It includes MAUNDY THURSDAY, GOOD FRIDAY, and HOLY SATURDAY. The Germans call Holy Week **Still Week** or **Silent Week**, and some Americans call it **Passion Week**, although the season known as Passiontide actually refers to the preceding week.

Passion Sunday or CARLING SUNDAY is the fifth Sunday in LENT (the Sunday *before* Palm Sunday), but since Holy Week was also referred to as Passion Week, this apparently led to the identification of Palm Sunday with Passion Sunday. Since 1970 the Roman Catholic Church has considered the two names to be synonymous, although in 1956 the two Sundays were designated the First Sunday and Second Sunday of the Passion. Another name for the fifth Sunday in Lent is Judica Sunday, from the Introit for the day.

See also SEMANA SANTA IN GUATEMALA

> **SOURCES:**
> *BkFest-1937*, pp. 69, 274
> *BkFestHolWrld-1970*, pp. 51,
>   53, 54
> *DaysCustFaith-1957*, pp. 103,
>   106
> *DictFolkMyth-1984*, pp. 1063,
>   1171
> *FestSaintDays-1915*, p. 67
> *FestWestEur-1958*, pp. 164,
>   192
> *FolkWrldHol-1992*, p. 196
> *GdWrldFest-1985*, p. 65
> *IntlThFolk-1979*, p. 276

◆ 0852 ◆ **Holy Week in Portugal (Semana Santa)**
Between March 15 and April 18; week before Easter

There are exhibits in the churches and street processions illustrating scenes from the Passion of Christ throughout HOLY WEEK in Portugal. In the city of Guimarães, the church of *Senhor dos Passos* shows a different Passion tableau each day of Holy Week. The processions are usually attended by bands of *anjinhos*, or children dressed as angels, with crowns on their heads and fluffy wings attached to their shoulders. The figures of Jesus, which have real hair, eyelashes, and crystal tears, are elaborately dressed in purple velvet robes. The clergy's vestments are also purple, and worshippers watching the procession throw violets at the image of the suffering Jesus.

> **CONTACT:**
> Portuguese National Tourist
>   Office
> 590 Fifth Ave., 4th Floor
> New York, NY 10036
> 212-354-4403; fax: 212-764-6137

> **SOURCES:**
> *Chases-1996*, p. 151
> *FestWestEur-1958*, p. 164

◆ 0853 ◆ **Homage to Cuauhtemoc (Homenaje a Cuauhtemoc)**
August 21

Cuauhtemoc, the last Aztec emperor, is honored each year with a festival held in front of his statue on the Paseo de la Reforma in Mexico City. After the story of his life and his struggle against the Spaniards has been recited in Spanish and native Indian languages, groups of Conchero dancers perform the dances for which they are renowned. Wearing feathered headdresses trimmed with mirrors and beads and carrying pictures of Christ or various saints, they represent the blending of Indian and Spanish cultures. Most Conchero groups have 50 to 100 dancers, and each dances in his own rhythm and to his own accompaniment. The tempo increases gradually until it reaches a sudden climax, followed by a moment of silence.

Cuauhtemoc is admired for his "bold and intimate acceptance of death," in the words of the Mexican poet Octavio Paz. Paz says that the entry of the Spanish into Mexico precipitated the extinction of the Aztec culture.

> **CONTACT:**
> Mexican Government Tourist
>   Office
> 405 Park Ave., Ste. 1401
> New York, NY 10022
> 800-446-3942 or 212-755-7261
> fax: 212-753-2874

> **SOURCES:**
> *IntlThFolk-1979*, p. 273

◆ 0854 ◆ **Homowo**
Between August and September

A harvest festival of thanks to the gods of the Ga (or Gan) people as well as the mark of the new year. *Homowo* means 'starved gods,' and the festival commemorates the good harvest the Ga were given in ancient times. This harvest came after the famine they endured while traveling to their present home in Ghana. The festival begins on Thursday and those who have moved away are called *Soobii*, 'Thursday people,' because that's the day they arrive home for the festival. The following day is the yam festival and the day of twins. All twins who are dressed in white are specially treated all day. Each day there are processions, songs, and dancing until the great day arrives: Homowo, or the **Hunger-Hooting Festival** and open house.

Most homes have enough food in them for a week during the festival. Fish are abundant in Ghana at this time of year, palm-nut soup and *kpokpoi*, or *ko*, round out the traditional menu. Ko is a kind of grits made with unleavened corn dough and palm oil. The chiefs and elders sprinkle the ko everywhere people have been buried, then go to the prison and personally feed the warders. The following day they visit friends and relatives, reconciling and exchanging New Year's greetings.

CONTACT:
Ghana Embassy
3512 International Dr., N.W.
Washington, D.C. 20008
202-686-4520; fax: 202-686-4527

SOURCES:
BkHolWrld-1986, Aug 1
FolkWrldHol-1992, p. 450

♦ 0855 ♦ Honduras Independence Day
September 15

Honduras joined four other Central American countries—
Costa Rica, El Salvador, Guatemala, and Nicaragua—in
declaring independence from Spain on September 15, 1821.
Independence Day is a national holiday and festivities are
especially colorful in the capital city of Tegucigalpa.

CONTACT:
Honduras Embassy
3007 Tilden St., N.W.
Washington, D.C. 20008
202-966-7702; fax: 202-966-9751

SOURCES:
AnnivHol-1983, p. 119
Chases-1996, p. 377
NatlHolWrld-1968, p. 169

♦ 0856 ♦ Hong Kong Arts Festival
Last three weeks in January

An annual celebration of the arts in Hong Kong, held since
1972. Artists from around the world appear for a diverse
program that includes opera, orchestral concerts, chamber
music, jazz, dance, and theater and mime. The 1992 program
scheduled a presentation of the opera *Tosca* with an international cast, as well as a performance of the 400-year-old
Kunju Opera, the oldest surviving form of theater in China,
by the Shanghai Kunju Opera Troupe.

CONTACT:
Hong Kong Tourist Association
590 Fifth Ave.
New York, NY 10036
212-869-5008; fax: 212-730-2605

SOURCES:
GdWrldFest-1985, p. 105
IntlThFolk-1979, p. 198

♦ 0857 ♦ Hong Kong Liberation Day
Last Monday in August

This public holiday commemorates the day, August 30, 1945,
when Japanese occupation during World War II came to an
end.

CONTACT:
Hong Kong Tourist Association
590 Fifth Ave.
New York, NY 10036
212-869-5008; fax: 212-730-2605

SOURCES:
AnnivHol-1983, p. 112
Chases-1996, p. 349

♦ 0858 ♦ Hope Watermelon Festival
Third weekend in August

Best known as the birthplace of U.S. President Bill Clinton,
Hope, Ark., is also "Home of the World's Largest Watermelons" and hosts the only watermelon festival featuring giant
watermelons.

They are indeed large. Hope watermelon growers have been
competing to grow the biggest since the 1920s. In 1925, Hugh
Laseter created a sensation with a record 136-pounder that
was exhibited for a few days and then sent to President
Calvin Coolidge. The watermelons kept getting bigger. The
1928 champion was 144¾ pounds and was sent to the Rexall
Corp. in Boston, Mass., where it "created quite a bit of
excitement," according to old accounts. The first 200-pound
melon was grown in 1979 by Ivan Bright and his son Lloyd;

seeds from it went for $8 each. That melon broke a 44-year
record held by O. D. Middlebrooks, who had grown a 195-
pound melon. (It was sent to actor Dick Powell.) In 1985,
Lloyd Bright's 10-year-old son Jason produced a 260-pound
watermelon that was recorded in the *1992 Guinness Book of
World Records*. These melons attain their great size because of
the quality of the soil, an early greenhouse start, and careful
pruning. Hope farmers also grow average-size watermelons, weighing 30 to 40 pounds.

The Hope Watermelon Festival originated in 1926, lapsed
with hard times, was revived in 1977, and has been held
annually ever since with attendance at about 75,000. There
has been nationwide television and press coverage because
of the colossal melons. This is a festival of real down-home
Americana: ice cream socials, a big fish fry, softball, a dog
show, tug-o'-war, juggling, sack races, arm wrestling, an air
show, horseshoe pitching, and a hula-hoop contest. The
watermelon events include a watermelon toss, a melon-
decorating competition, a melon-eating contest, a melon-
seed-spitting contest, and a melon-judging and auction.
While he was governor of Arkansas, Mr. Clinton visited the
festival to compete in the Watermelon 5K Run.

CONTACT:
Arkansas Dept. of Parks and
    Tourism
1 Capitol Mall
Little Rock, AR 72201
800-628-8725 or 501-682-7777
fax: 501-682-1364

SOURCES:
Chases-1996, p. 337

♦ 0859 ♦ Hopi Snake Dance
August or early September

The grand finale of ceremonies to pray for rain, held by
individual Hopi tribes in Arizona every two years. Hopis
believe their ancestors originated in an underworld, and that
their gods and the spirits of ancestors live there. They call
snakes their brothers, and trust that the snakes will carry
their prayers to the Rainmakers beneath the earth. Thus the
Hopi dancers carry snakes in their mouths to impart prayers
to them.

The ceremonies, conducted by the Snake and Antelope fraternities, last 16 days. On the 11th day preparations start for
the snake dance. For four days, snake priests go out from
their village to gather snakes. On the 15th day, a race is run,
signifying rain gods bringing water to the village. Then the
Antelopes build a *kisi*, a shallow pit covered with a board, to
represent the entrance to the underworld. At sunset on the
15th day, the Snake and Antelope dancers dance around the
plaza, stamping on the kisi board and shaking rattles to
simulate the sounds of thunder and rain. The Antelope priest
dances with green vines around his neck and in his mouth—
just as the Snake priests will later do with snakes.

The last day starts with a footrace to honor the snakes. The
snakes are washed and deposited in the kisi. The Snake
priests dance around the kisi. Each is accompanied by two
other priests: one holding a snake whip and one whose
function will be to catch the snake when it's dropped. Then
each priest takes a snake and carries it first in his hands and
then in his mouth. The whipper dances behind him with his
left arm around the dancer's neck and calms the snake by
stroking it with a feathered wand. After four dances around
the plaza, the priests throw the snakes to the catchers. A

priest draws a circle on the ground, the catchers throw the snakes in the circle, the Snake priests grab handfuls of them and run with them to turn them loose in the desert.

CONTACT:
Hopi Cultural Center
P.O. Box 67
Second Mesa, AZ 86043
602-734-2401

SOURCES:
BkHolWrld-1986, Aug 22

♦ 0860 ♦ Hora at Prislop
Second Sunday in August

A dancing festival held at Mount Prislop at the Transylvania-Moldavia border in Romania. The dancers of the hora carry big rings that symbolize the friendship of the people of the regions of Moldavia, Maramures, and Transylvania. The top artistic groups gather at Prislop Pass to present a parade in colorful folk costumes and then a program of songs and dances, ending with the lively peasant horas. Typical food dishes of the area are served and folk art is on display.

CONTACT:
Romanian National Tourist Office
342 Madison Ave., Ste. 210
New York, NY 10173
212-697-6971; fax: 212-697-6972

SOURCES:
GdWrldFest-1985, p. 157
IntlThFolk-1979, p. 317

♦ 0861 ♦ Horn Dance
Monday following first Sunday after September 4

The ancient Horn Dance, believed by many to have originated in Norman times or before, is performed at Abbots Bromley, a small village in Staffordshire, England, as part of the **Wakes Monday** celebration each year. Wakes Monday, the day after the first Sunday following September 4, was at one time part of the Old St. Bartholomew Fair. But the Horn Dance is all that remains of the original three-day festival. Although some believe it was once an ancient fertility dance, the Horn Dance probably had something to do with hunting rights and customs in nearby Needwood Forest.

A dozen local men, ranging in age from 12 to more than 50, dress in 16th-century foresters' costumes. Six of them carry reindeer antlers mounted on short wooden sticks. There is also a Hobby Horse, a man playing Robin Hood, a man dressed as a woman who plays the role of Maid Marian, a Fool carrying an inflated bladder on a stick, and a young archer who snaps his bow in time with the music—originally provided by a pipe and tabor but nowadays by a concertina and a triangle.

Beginning at the parish church, the men dance their way around the parish boundaries, stopping to perform at homes and farms along the way. The six deermen, three of whom carry white antlers and three black, take turns "charging" each other while the Hobby Horse prances, the Fool shakes his bladder at the spectators, and Maid Marian takes up a collection. The dancing is over by evening, when everyone adjourns to the local pub or goes home to eat Wakes Cakes, "fair rock candy"—sugar-coated sticks of candy—and brandy snap cookies.

CONTACT:
British Tourist Authority
551 Fifth Ave., Ste. 702
New York, NY 10176
800-462-2748 or 212-986-2200
fax: 212-986-1188

SOURCES:
DictFolkMyth-1984, pp. 3, 947

♦ 0862 ♦ Horse, Festival of the
October

A nine-day celebration of horses in Oklahoma City, capital of Oklahoma, which calls itself the Horse Capital of the World and boasts more horses per square mile than any other state. Highlighting the festival are the parimutuel thoroughbred races at Remington Park. Other equine events are professional rodeo at Lazy E Arena in nearby Guthrie, the world's largest indoor rodeo arena; indoor polo; a showcase of breeds; the National Miniature Horse Show; and a horse basketball tournament. Accompanying these activities are a celebrity golf tournament, a country and western concert, and other entertainment by nationally known stars.

Many of the events are hosted by the National Cowboy Hall of Fame and Western Heritage Center, which houses the 18-foot statue, *The End of the Trail,* by James Earle Fraser; a 33-foot statue of Buffalo Bill; artworks by Charles M. Russell (*see also* Russell, C.M., Auction) and Frederic Remington; and portraits of western television and movie stars, including, of course, John Wayne.

CONTACT:
Oklahoma Tourism and Recreation Dept.
2401 N. Lincoln Blvd.
Will Rogers Bldg., Ste. 500
Oklahoma City, OK 73105
800-652-6552 or 405-521-2413
fax: 405-521-4883

SOURCES:
Chases-1996, p. 412

Horse Sacrifice
See **October Horse Sacrifice**

♦ 0863 ♦ Hortobágy Bridge Fair and International Equestrian Festival
July

A showcase of Hungary's fine horses and riders on the Hortobágy, part of the Great Plain of Hungary. The festival also celebrates the famous nine-arched bridge, built in 1833, that crosses the Hortobágy River and is the longest stone bridge in the country.

The Hortobágy National Park is 150 square kilometers in the grassy *puszta* ('prairie') of the Great Plain near the historic city of Debrecen. During the Turkish occupation that began in the 14th century the area was depopulated, and in the 18th century it was used for breeding horses, cattle, and sheep. The equestrian fair is held outside the city and features the famed Lipizzaner horses (from Austrian stock) in dressage exhibitions, the *csikós* (Hungarian cowboy) in colorful embroidered riding costume, carriage parades, pulling contests for draft horses, and other equestrian events. There are also crafts fairs and a peasant market.

CONTACT:
Hungarian Embassy
3910 Shoemaker St., N.W.
Washington, D.C. 20008
202-362-6730; fax: 202-966-8135

♦ 0864 ♦ Hosay Festival
Tenth day of Islamic month of Muharram and between February and March

To Muslims in the eastern hemisphere, the **Hussein Festival** is a solemn occasion commemorating the massacre of Hussein and his brother Hassan, grandsons of the prophet Muhammad, on the 10th day of the month of Muharram in 680 (*see* Ashura). But in Trinidad and Tobago, where the Hosay (or Hussein) Festival was first celebrated in 1884, the traditional procession of mourning has been mixed with various European, African, and Indian rituals to form a celebration that is far from somber.

The most popular processions are held between February and March in the towns of St. James, Curepe, Tunapuna, Couva, and Cedros. The festival usually begins with a procession of flags symbolizing the beginning of the battle of Kerbela, in which Hussein and Hassan were killed. On the second day dancers wearing *Tadjahs*—small minaretted tombs made of bamboo, colored tissue, tinfoil, crepe paper, mirrors, and coconut leis—parade through the streets to the accompaniment of African drummers in a ritual that is reminiscent of Carnival (*see* Trinidad and Tobago Carnival).

The highlight of the festival occurs on the third night, when the large Tadjahs, some of which are six feet tall, are carried through the streets. There are also two moons, representing Hussein and his brother, carried by specially trained dancers. These large crescent-shaped structures are studded with sharp blades and carried on the dancers' shoulders. At midnight, the two moons engage in a ritual embrace to a chorus of cheers from the onlookers.

CONTACT:
Trinidad and Tobago Tourism Development Authority
25 W. 43rd St., Ste. 1508
New York, NY 10036
800-232-0082 or 212-719-0540
fax: 212-719-0988

SOURCES:
FolkWrldHol-1992, pp. 367, 368, 370

♦ 0865 ♦ **Hoshana Rabbah**
Between September 27 and October 24; Tishri 21

On each of the first six days of the Jewish Sukkot festival, a single stanza of the *Hoshanat* litany is recited (except on the Sabbath) and the congregation circles the reader's platform carrying the four species: a palm branch, citron, three myrtle twigs, and two willow branches, gathered into a bouquet. But on the seventh day, known as the **Great Hoshana**, the congregation makes seven circuits around the altar, after which the four species are laid down and a bunch of five willow branches is picked up and beaten on the ground three times to symbolize humanity's dependence on rain.

Because Hoshana Rabbah is considered the last possible day on which one can seek forgiveness for the sins of the preceding year, the morning service on this day is very solemn. According to Jewish tradition, on Yom Kippur God seals the Book of Life and thus each individual's fate for the coming year. Yom Kippur falls on the 10th day of Tishri. But since the Middle Ages, Hoshana Rabbah has been regarded as an extension of the deadline for Divine judgment. According to an old Jewish folk belief, notes fell from Heaven on this day informing people of how they had been judged. The traditional Yiddish greeting, *a gute kvitl* 'May you receive a good note', reflects this belief. There is also a popular superstition claiming that a man who doesn't see his shadow on this night is fated to die in the coming year.

SOURCES:
DaysCustFaith-1957, p. 272

♦ 0866 ♦ **Hospital Day, National**
May 12

Although Florence Nightingale (1820–1910), the famous nurse and public health activist, spent most of her life in England, it is in the United States that the anniversary of her birth has been celebrated since 1921 as National Hospital Day. Originally a day set aside in honor of the woman who made nursing a respectable profession and who revolutionized the way hospitals were run, the May 12 observance was expanded to a week-long event in 1953 so that hospitals could use it to plan and implement more extensive public information programs. Currently sponsored by the American Hospital Association, **National Hospital Week** provides an opportunity to recognize employee achievements, to educate the community about the services hospitals offer, and to keep the public up to date on technological advances in the health care field.

In 19th-century England, it was customary for each community to designate a **Hospital Saturday** and a **Hospital Sunday**—a time to collect money for local hospitals both on the streets and in the churches. Hospital Saturday later became Alexandra Rose Day.

CONTACT:
American Hospital Association
1 N. Franklin, Ste. 2700
Chicago, IL 60606
312-422-3000; fax: 312-422-4796

SOURCES:
AmerBkDays-1978, p. 445
AnnivHol-1983, p. 65
Chases-1996, p. 210
DictDays-1988, p. 58

♦ 0867 ♦ **Hostos Day**
January 11

Eugenio Maria de Hostos (1839–1903) was a Puerto Rican philosopher and patriot who became a leader of the opposition to Spanish colonial rule in the 19th century. He campaigned for the education of women in Brazil, and his books on law and education triggered reforms in other Latin American countries. He even sponsored the first railroad between Chile and Argentina, across the Andes Mountains. The anniversary of his birth is observed as a public holiday in Puerto Rico.

CONTACT:
Puerto Rico Dept. of Culture
P.O. Box 9024184
San Juan, PR 00902-4184
809-724-0700

SOURCES:
AnnivHol-1983, p. 7
BkHolWrld-1986, Jan 11
Chases-1996, p. 62

♦ 0868 ♦ **Hot Air Balloon Championships, National**
Late July–early August

The **U.S. National Hot Air Balloon Races** take place over a 10-day period in late July–early August at the campus of Simpson College in Indianola, Iowa. Their purpose is not only to select America's national champion but to select the hot air balloon team that will represent the United States in the World Hot Air Balloon Championships. When the event was first held in 1970, only 11 balloonists participated, but now there are close to 200 participants and as many as 250,000 spectators. There are several flights or "tasks" involved in each race, designed to test the pilot's skill in handling his or her balloon. New tasks are added regularly to make the sport more demanding. As a result of the races, Indianola has come to be known as the balloon capital of the nation.

CONTACT:
Iowa Tourism Office
200 E. Grand Ave.
Des Moines, IA 50309
800-345-4692 or 515-242-4705
fax: 515-242-4749

SOURCES:
Chases-1996, p. 311
GdUSFest-1984, p. 58

♦ 0869 ♦ Houses and Gardens, Festival of
March–April

One of the nation's oldest and most prestigious house tours, held from March to mid-April in Charleston, S.C. This 300-year-old city has been bombarded by land and sea, devastated by an earthquake, and battered by hurricanes, but it remains a place known for splendid wrought-iron embellished architecture. The port city has 73 pre-Revolutionary buildings, 136 late 18th-century structures, and 600 others built before the 1840s. Among the more interesting areas is Cabbage Row, the model for Catfish Row in DuBose Heyward's novel *Porgy*, on which George Gershwin's opera *Porgy and Bess* was based.

More than 100 homes and gardens, full of blooming azaleas and camellias, are usually included in the festival, which dates from 1947. It features both afternoon and evening candlelight tours, and special candlelight galas with music and wine.

CONTACT:
Charleston Area Convention and
  Visitors Bureau
P.O. Box 975
Charleston, SC 29402
800-868-8118 or 803-853-8000

SOURCES:
Chases-1996, p. 140
GdUSFest-1984, p. 168

♦ 0870 ♦ Houston Livestock Show & Rodeo
Last two weeks in February

The nation's largest livestock show, with some 20,000 entries, held in the famous Astrodome of Houston, Tex. The show is a reminder of the 19th-century days when Houston's shipping trade was based on timber, cotton, and cattle. Things get under way with a downtown parade, and the agenda then includes celebrity entertainers, a rally of hot air balloons, and a chili cookoff.

CONTACT:
Greater Houston Convention and
  Visitors Bureau
801 Congress St.
Houston, TX 77002
800-365-7575 or 713-227-3100
fax: 713-227-6336

SOURCES:
Chases-1996, p. 97

♦ 0871 ♦ Humane Sunday
First Sunday in May

Humane Sunday is dedicated to the prevention of child abuse and cruelty to animals. Observed on the first Sunday in May, it is sponsored by the American Humane Association and was the inspiration of its founder, Dr. William O. Stillman. The association encourages churches and other organizations to set aside the first Sunday in May to remember the helpless—especially children and animals—with compassion and kindness, and to observe the Golden Rule.

See also BE KIND TO ANIMALS WEEK

CONTACT:
American Humane Association
63 Inverness Drive East
Englewood, CO 80112-5117
800-227-4645 or 303-792-0900
fax: 303-792-5333

SOURCES:
AnnivHol-1983, p. 61
Chases-1996, p. 201

Human Rights Day
See **Bill of Rights Day**

♦ 0872 ♦ Human Towers of Valls
June 24

On ST. JOHN'S DAY in the city of Valls in the Catalan region of Spain, a touring acrobatic company, or *comparsa*, presents the **Xiquets de Valls**, or 'human towers of Valls.' The acrobats form human towers or pyramids with four to six men at the base and one or more children at the top. The towers can extend to eight times a man's height, and they are formed to the musical accompaniment of the *gralla*, or native oboe. There is a point during the performance at which the children on top salute, the music ceases, and the entire structure stands immobile for several seconds before collapsing gracefully to the ground.

CONTACT:
Tourist Office of Spain
665 Fifth Ave.
New York, NY 10022
212-759-8822; fax: 212-980-1053

SOURCES:
AnnivHol-1983, p. 183
FestWestEur-1958, p. 200

♦ 0873 ♦ Humor and Satire Festival, National
Late May–early June

Gabrovo, Bulgaria, may seem an unlikely place for the only festival in the world devoted to humor. This town, founded by a blacksmith in the 14th century, has a longstanding reputation for stinginess, and many jokes are told about the length to which its inhabitants will go to avoid spending money. The first humor festival was held there in 1967 in hopes of attracting tourism to the area. Now it is a 10-day event that features a procession of people dressed as their favorite comic figure, a parade of satiric floats, and competitions to see who can get the best laugh. More than a thousand participants from 50 countries—mostly cartoonists, filmmakers, sculptors, artists, and performers specializing in humor and satire—take part in the festival each year, which attracts more than 10,000 spectators.

CONTACT:
Bulgarian Embassy
1621 22nd St., N.W.
Washington, D.C. 20008
202-387-7969; fax: 202-234-7973

SOURCES:
GdWrldFest-1985, p. 26

Hundred Drums Festival
See **Wangala**

♦ 0874 ♦ Hungary National Days
March 15; August 20; October 23

Hungary celebrates three national days, according to a 1991 state mandate. The founding of Hungary is commemorated on August 20, which is also the feast day of the founder of the country, St. Stephen of Hungary (c. 975–1038). He assumed the kingship in 1000 and worked to unite the various clans into a single Christian state. In 1950 the day was changed to

Constitution Day by the communist regime, but since 1990, it has again celebrated St. Stephen.

On March 15, Hungarians observe the anniversary of the beginning of the revolution in 1848 against the Habsburg monarchy and calling for the creation of a nation-state with freedom of the press and an independent parliamentary government. In 1989, celebrations were open for the first time since the Soviet invasion, and took place all over the country.

Revolution Day is celebrated on October 23 and originally commemorated the 1956 uprising against Soviet control; on October 23, 1989, in honor of the previous revolution, Hungarians established a new republic, amending the constitution to allow multiparty politics, public assembly, and create separation of power in the government.

CONTACT:
Hungarian Embassy
3910 Shoemaker St., N.W.
Washington, D.C. 20008
202-362-6730; fax: 202-966-8135

SOURCES:
AnnivHol-1983, p. 108
Chases-1996, p. 427

Hunger-Hooting Festival
See **Homowo**

♦ 0875 ♦ **Hungry Ghosts, Festival of**
July–August; full moon or 15th day of seventh lunar month

A Buddhist and Taoist festival probably dating back to the sixth century and Confucius, observed in China as well as throughout the rest of eastern Asia. It is believed that during this month the souls of the dead are released from purgatory to roam the earth. In Taiwan the day is called "opening of the gates of Hell." This makes it a dangerous time to travel, get married, or move to a new house. Unhappy and hungry spirits—those who died without descendants to look after them or who had no proper funeral (because they were killed in a plane crash, for example)—may cause trouble and therefore must be placated with offerings. So people burn paper replicas of material possessions like automobiles, furniture, clothing, and paper money ("ghost money") believing that this frees these things for the spirits' use. Joss sticks are burned, and offerings of food are placed on tables outside people's homes. Prayers are said at all Chinese temples and at Chinese shops and homes, and *wayang* (Chinese street opera) and puppet shows are performed on open-air stages.

Families in Vietnam remember the souls of the dead by visiting their graves. It is known as **Yue Lan**, **Vu Lan Day**, **Day of the Dead**, and **Trung Nguyen**. The festival, the second most important of the year after Tᴇᴛ, is observed throughout the country in Buddhist temples and homes and offices. To remember the dead, families perform the *dan chay*, an offering of incense at graves. An altar at home is prepared with two levels—one for Buddha with offerings of incense, fruit, and rice, and one for departed relatives with rice soup, fruit, and meat. It is considered best if offerings include the *tan sinh*, three kinds of creatures—fish, meat, and shrimp—and the *ngu qua*, five kinds of fruit. Money and clothes made of votive papers are also burned at this time.

SOURCES:
AnnivHol-1983, p. 177
BkHolWrld-1986, Aug 18
Chases-1996, p. 336

DictFolkMyth-1984, pp. 225, 1051
DictWrldRel-1989, pp. 135, 581
FolkWrldHol-1992, p. 393
RelHolCal-1993, p. 84

♦ 0876 ♦ **Hunters' Moon, Feast of the**
End of September or early October

October was traditionally the time when the *voyageurs*, or traders, came to Fort Ouiatenon (in what is now Lafayette, Indiana) to trade their goods, gossip with the local French settlers, and generally relax and enjoy themselves before setting out on their next journey. Ouiatenon was home not only to the Ouiatenon Indian tribe but also to a number of French families from Canada. The Feast of the Hunter's Moon attempts to reenact as accurately as possible the events that took place there during the mid-18th century.

The two-day festival, which was first held in 1968, begins with the arrival of the voyageurs by canoe on the Wabash River. Events include Indian chants, French folk songs, demonstrations of traditional crafts, and the cooking of typical French and Indian foods over an open fire.

CONTACT:
Indiana Tourism Division
1 N. Capitol Ave., Ste. 700
Indianapolis, IN 46204
800-289-6646 or 317-232-8860
fax: 317-233-6887

SOURCES:
Chases-1996, p. 414
GdUSFest-1985, p. 53

♦ 0877 ♦ **Hurling the Silver Ball**
Sunday nearest or Monday following February 3

St. Ia (Eia, Ives) is the patron saint of St. Ives, Cornwall. She was one of a group of Celtic missionary saints believed to have reached the southwestern tip of England miraculously by crossing the Irish Sea in a millstone boat. They made a safe landing at the place where St. Ives now stands, and there are parishes and churches throughout Cornwall named after them.

St. Ives celebrates **Feast Monday**, near the Feast of St. Ia on February 3, by playing an ancient game known as hurling. In this case the ball is made of cork encased in silver, which is believed to be very old and is kept in the town clerk's office during the year. The mayor begins the game by tossing the silver ball against the side of the parish church, which is dedicated to St. Ia. Children then take over, tossing the ball back and forth in what might be described as a kind of "hand football." The game stops promptly at 12 noon, and whoever has the ball in his or her possession at that time receives a cash prize or a medal. The festivities continue in the afternoon with more sporting events, and there is a municipal ball in the evening.

CONTACT:
British Tourist Authority
551 Fifth Ave., Ste. 702
New York, NY 10176
800-462-2748 or 212-986-2200
fax: 212-986-1188

♦ 0878 ♦ **Hurricane Supplication Day**
Fourth Monday in July

Observed in the U.S. Virgin Islands—St. Croix, St. Thomas,

and St. John—Hurricane Supplication Day marks the beginning of the hurricane season. Special church services are held to pray for safety from the storms that ravage these and other Caribbean islands. The custom probably dates back to the "rogation" ceremonies which began in fifth-century England—the word *rogare*, meaning 'to beg or supplicate.' Rogations usually followed a frightening series of storms, earthquakes, or other natural disasters, although sometimes they took place annually on the Rogation Days that preceded Ascension Day.

At the end of the hurricane season in October there is a **Hurricane Thanksgiving Day**. Again, church services are held so that the islanders can give thanks for being spared the destruction of a major storm.

SOURCES:
AnnivHol-1983, pp. 95, 134
BkFestHolWrld-1970, p. 125
BkHolWrld-1986, Oct 18
Chases-1996, pp. 307, 426
FolkAmerHol-1991, pp. 296, 369

Husain Day
See **Ashura; Hosay Festival**

I

♦ 0879 ♦ Ibu Afo Festival
On or near March 20

The Igbo people of Nigeria celebrate their New Year's Eve around March 20 with a solemn ceremony marking the end of the old year and heralding the arrival of the new. The council of elders who fix the annual calendar determine the exact hour at which the year will end. When it arrives, a wailing noise signals the departing year, and children rush into their houses, lock the doors to avoid being carried away by the old year as it leaves, and bang on the doors to add to the din. As soon as the wailing dies down, the doors are thrown open and everyone greets the new year with spontaneous applause.

CONTACT:
Nigerian Embassy
1333 16th St., N.W.
Washington, D.C. 20036
202-986-8400; fax: 202-775-1385

SOURCES:
BkHolWrld-1986, Mar 18
FolkWrldHol-1992, p. 181

♦ 0880 ♦ Icelandic Festival
Late July or early August

The Icelandic Festival, or **Islendingadagurinn**, held in Gimli, Manitoba, each year is one of the oldest ethnic festivals in Canada, dating back to 1890. The Icelandic settlers who emigrated to Canada after their homes in Iceland were destroyed by volcanic eruptions in 1875 wanted to do something to preserve their heritage and customs, and the current festival continues to reflect this interest in Icelandic culture. The events include theater programs, choral singing, song writing, and poetry competitions. Participants dress in native Icelandic costumes and eat traditional foods such as smoked lamb and *skyr*, which is similar to yogurt. In recent years a regatta and air show have been added to the more traditional events, which extend over a three-day period during the last week of July or the first week in August.

CONTACT:
Travel Manitoba
155 Carlton St., 7th Floor
Winnipeg, Manitoba
Canada R3C 3H8
800-665-0040 or 204-945-3777

SOURCES:
GdWrldFest-1985, p. 33
IntlThFolk-1979, p. 63

♦ 0881 ♦ Iceland Independence Day
June 17

Iceland was proclaimed an independent republic on June 17, 1944. Sometimes referred to as **National Day**, the anniversary of this event is also the birthday of Jon Sigurdsson, the nation's 19th-century leader. A varied program of parades, sporting competitions, outdoor concerts and shows, speeches, and amusements culminates in the evening with dancing in the streets of Reykjavik and other towns.

Another National Day was December 1, the anniversary of the 1918 treaty recognizing Iceland as an independent state under the Danish crown. This is now largely a student celebration.

CONTACT:
Icelandic Tourist Board
655 Third Ave., 18th Floor
New York, NY 10017
212-949-2333; fax: 212-983-5260

SOURCES:
AnnivHol-1983, p. 80
Chases-1996, pp. 260, 467
NatlHolWrld-1968, p. 85

♦ 0882 ♦ Ice Worm Festival
Weekend after first Friday in February

A zany mid-winter festival to celebrate the emergence of the ice worm in Cordova, Alaska, where the winters are long and dark and give rise to thoughts of things like ice worms. The highlight of the three-day festival is the procession of a 150-foot-long ice worm (it has a dragon's head) followed by 500 or so paraders. Other events include variety shows, skeet shooting, ski events, a survival-suit race, a beard-growing contest, beauty pageants, and dances.

The celebration began in 1961 as a way to shake off the winter blahs, and the legend was born then that an ice worm hibernates during the winter in the Cordova Glacier but starts to hatch or wake up in early February. The worm has gained international fame, and the festival draws great crowds of people.

CONTACT:
Alaska Division of Tourism
P.O. Box 110801
Juneau, AK 99811
907-465-2012; fax: 907-465-2287

SOURCES:
BkFestHolWrld-1970, p. 31
Chases-1996, p. 84
GdUSFest-1984, p. 8

◆ 0883 ◆ **Idaho Regatta**
Last weekend in June

A full-throttle three-day event on the Snake River at Burley, Idaho. Burley's population of 9,000 is doubled for the regatta which is a qualifying race for the American Power Boat Association Western Divisional Championship. A hundred speedboats in 11 inboard limited classes compete for a share of $35,000 in cash prizes—and a mink coat. The regatta has been held since the 1970s, and each year, a coat has been donated as a prize by Lee Moyle, one of the founders of the regatta, and an owner of the Don and Lee Moyle Mink Farm. Boats are entered from throughout the country. They include seven-liter, hydroplanes, super-stock, pro-stock, KRR flat-bottoms, Comp Jets, and stock hydros.

CONTACT:
Idaho Tourism Division
700 W. State St.
Boise, ID 83720
800-635-7820 or 208-334-2017
fax: 208-334-2631

SOURCES:
Chases-1996, p. 273

◆ 0884 ◆ **Idaho Spud Day**
Third week in September

A celebration of the potato in Shelley, Idaho. The potato has come to be thought of as *the* crop of Idaho, but the state actually has a number of other important crops: wheat, hay, oats, barley, beans, peas, sugar beets, and fruits. Nonetheless, the spud gets the hurrahs with a six-day festival (even though it's called Spud "Day") that began in 1928 and includes a parade, potato-picking and horseshoe-throwing contests, and, of course, potatoes fried, baked, scalloped, mashed, etc. Five thousand free baked potatoes are given to visitors.

CONTACT:
Idaho Tourism Division
700 W. State St.
Boise, ID 83720
800-635-7820 or 208-334-2017
fax: 208-334-2631

◆ 0885 ◆ **'Id al-Adha (Feast of Sacrifice; Eid)**
Tenth through twelfth days of Islamic month of Dhu al-Hijjah

This most important feast of the Muslim calendar is the concluding rite of those performing the Hajj or PILGRIMAGE TO MECCA. It is also known as **'Id al-Kabir**, the **Great Feast**. For those not on pilgrimage, 'Id al-Adha is a three-day festival celebrating Ibrahim's (Abraham's) willingness to obey Allah by killing his son, believed by Muslims to be Ishmael, and not Isaac as written in the Old Testament. Muslims consider Ishmael to be the forefather of the Arabs. According to the Qu'ran, Ibrahim had an ax poised over the boy when a voice from Heaven told him to stop. He was allowed to sacrifice a ram instead. Many Muslim families reenact this show of faith by sacrificing a cow, a ram, or a lamb on this day, using a portion of it for the family feast and donating one- or two-thirds to the poor. In Turkey this day is called the **Kurban** 'sacrificial' **Bayram**. In northern Central Africa it is called **Tabaski**. It is an official government holiday in Chad and Cameroon.

SOURCES:
BkFest-1937, p. 238

BkFestHolWrld-1970, p. 80
BkHolWrld-1986, Aug 28
Chases-1996, p. 190
DictWrldRel-1989, pp. 290, 569
FolkWrldHol-1992, p. 328
RelHolCal-1993, p. 84

◆ 0886 ◆ **'Id al-Fitr (Eid)**
First day of Islamic month of Shawwal

Also known as the **Feast of Fast-Breaking**, or the **Lesser Feast**, 'Id al-Fitr marks the end of the month-long fast of RAMADAN and the beginning of a three-day feast. It is the second most important Islamic holiday after 'ID AL-ADHA. The 'Id prayer is performed by the whole community at an outdoor prayer ground (*musalla*) or mosque. Then people put on new clothes, children are given presents, and everyone visits relatives and friends. It is the time when everyone asks pardon for all the wrongs of the past year. Village squares have carnival rides, puppet shows, and candy vendors. It is called **Lebaran** or **Hari Raya** by Indonesians, Thais, and Malaysians. In Turkey, where it is called the **Candy Festival**, or **Seker Bayrami**, this is the day on which children are given candy or money wrapped in handkerchiefs. In Pakistan the special treat associated with this day is *saween*, a spaghetti cooked in milk and sugar, and sprinkled with almonds, pistachios, and dates. In Malaya, where it is called Hari Raya, they hold open houses. It is the new custom to have one's non-Muslim friends visit to foster more understanding between the different ethnic groups. Muslims in turn will visit Chinese friends during LUNAR NEW YEAR, Hindus during DEWALI, and Christians at CHRISTMAS.

In West Africa, a Mande feast of the virgins has been added to this feast. In western Guinea, young men and women parade all night with floats of animals and boats, singing and dancing; small children sing for presents.

SOURCES:
BkFest-1937, p. 238
BkFestHolWrld-1970, pp. 80, 113
BkHolWrld-1986, Jun 27
Chases-1996, p. 105
DictWrldRel-1989, p. 597
FolkWrldHol-1992, pp. 162, 173
RelHolCal-1993, p. 85

◆ 0887 ◆ **Ides**
Various

In the ancient Roman calendar, the ides fell on the 15th day of March, May, July, and October, and on the 13th day of the other months. The Roman emperor Julius Caesar was assassinated on the Ides of March in 44 B.C., and Shakespeare's famous reference to this day in his play *Julius Caesar*— "Beware the Ides of March"—is probably the best-known use of the term.

The ancient Romans specified a particular day in the month by relating it to the next calends, ides, or nones. For example, "six days before the Ides of June" meant June 8, since the ides in June fell on the 13th.

Calends, sometimes spelled 'kalends', refers to the first day of the month, from which the days of the preceding months were counted backward. The order of the days in each month were publicly proclaimed on the calends. For example, "the sixth of the calends of April" meant March 27, or the sixth day before the first day of April (counting April 1 as the first day.)

The Greeks didn't use the term, which is why the phrase 'on (or at) the Greek calends' is a synonym for 'never.' Occasionally calends was used to mean Settlement Day, since the first of the month was usually the day on which debts were settled.

The nones fell on the ninth day before the ides. In March, May, July, and October, the nones occurred on the seventh of the month because the ides fell on the 15th. In all the other months, the nones occurred on the fifth day because the ides fell on the 13th.

SOURCES:
AnnivHol-1983, p. 37
Chases-1996, p. 133
DictDays-1988, p. 18

♦ 0888 ♦ **Iditarod Trail Sled Dog Race**
Early March

The world's longest and toughest sled dog race, across the state of Alaska from Anchorage on the south-central coast to Nome on the south coast of the Seward peninsula on the Bering Sea just south of the Arctic Circle. It commemorates a 650-mile mid-winter emergency run to take serum from Nenana to Nome during the 1925 diphtheria epidemic. The race, which began in 1973, follows an old frozen-river mail route and is named for a deserted mining town along the way.

About 70 teams compete each year, and the winner is acclaimed the world's best long-distance dog musher. The race is completed in about two weeks. In 1985, Libby Riddles, age 28, was the first woman to win the race, coming in three hours ahead of the second-place finisher. It took her 18 days. Susan Butcher won in 1986, and again in 1987, 1988, and 1990. In 1991, Rick Swenson battled a howling blizzard on the last leg to win and become the first five-time winner (1977, 1979, 1981, 1982). His prize money was $50,000 out of the $250,000 purse. The 1992 winner, Martin Buser, set a record time of 10 days, 19 hours, and 17 minutes.

Mushers draw lots for starting position at a banquet held in Anchorage a couple of days before the race. Each musher, with a team of eight to 18 huskies, can expect to face 30-foot snowdrifts and winds of up to 60 miles an hour.

A number of events are clustered around the running of the race. At Wasilla, near Anchorage, Iditarod Days are held on the beginning weekend of the race, and feature softball, golf on ice, fireworks, and snow sculptures. Anchorage stages an International Ice Carving Competition that weekend, with ice carvers from around the world creating their cold images in the city's Town Square. At Nome, the BERING SEA ICE GOLF CLASSIC, a six-hole golf tournament, is played on the frozen Bering Sea during the second week of the race.

CONTACT:
Alaska Division of Tourism
P.O. Box 110801
Juneau, AK 99811
907-465-2012; fax: 907-465-2287

SOURCES:
BkHolWrld-1986, Mar 24
Chases-1996, p. 120

♦ 0889 ♦ **Iemanjá Festival**
February

A major festival in the Rio Vermelho district of Brazil. *Maes-de-santo* and *filhas-de-santo* (men and women mediums, or followers of the saints) sing and dance from daybreak on, summoning *Iemanjá* (the goddess of the ocean) to the festival. Offerings are placed in boats and carried down to the sea, where they are set afloat. Thousands of people flock to the coast for the festivities.

See also NEW YEAR'S EVE IN BRAZIL.

CONTACT:
Brazilian Embassy
3006 Massachusetts Ave., N.W.
Washington, D.C. 20008
202-745-2700; fax: 202-745-2827

♦ 0890 ♦ **Igbi**
Sunday nearest February 5

Because February 5 is the day that the sun, it is hoped, will shine for the first time of the year on the village of Khora, and then on Shaitli in the Dagestan region of Russia, the Tsezy (Didoitsy) people celebrate this event marking the middle of winter with a festival known as Igbi. The name comes from the plural of the Tsezian word *ig*—a ring-shaped bread similar to a bagel—and the baking of these ritual breads plays a central role in the celebration, which involves a number of masked and costumed characters playing traditional roles. Six *botsi*, or wolves, carrying wooden swords go from house to house collecting the igbi that the women have been baking in preparation for their arrival. The bagels are strung on a long pole known as the *giri*, and those who fail to cooperate are hit with the swords or have their shoes filled with wet snow and ice. The children get up early on this day, which is now observed on the Sunday nearest February 5 so they don't have to miss school, and go through the village collecting the igbi that have been made especially for them.

Igbi is also a day of reckoning. All through the year the young organizers of the feast have kept notes of the good and bad deeds of the villagers. Now after all the igbi have been collected, there is a ceremony in the center of the village in which the *kvidili*—a traditional figure wearing an animal-skin mask resembling no known animal; lately it looks like a horse with horns and a big mouth like a crocodile—reads out the names of those who have committed a transgression (such as public drunkenness) during the year. The unlucky ones are dragged to the river and immersed up to their knees through a hole in the ice. Those who are congratulated for their good deeds are handed an ig. At the end of the festival, the kvidili is symbolically slain with a wooden sword.

CONTACT:
Russian Travel Information Office
610 Fifth Ave.
Rockefeller Center, Ste. 603
New York, NY 10020
212-757-3884; fax: 212-459-0031

SOURCES:
FolkWrldHol-1992, p. 97

♦ 0891 ♦ **I Madonnari Italian Street Painting Festival**
May, Memorial Day weekend

An ancient Italian tradition of street painting, brought to Santa Barbara, Calif., in 1987. Some 200 professional and amateur artists create chalk "paintings"—both reproductions of old masters and original designs—on the Old Mission courtyard. Artist Kurt Wenner has been known for his *trompe l'oeil* paintings in which he transforms sidewalks into fountains or chasms. In 1988, his *Dies Irae*, or 'Day of Wrath,' was a maelstrom of struggling bodies. He used 200 sticks of chalk for *Dies Irae*.

In Italy in the 17th century, vagabond artists created sidewalk works of chalk art. Because they often painted the Madonna, they were known as *madonnari*. Artists still follow the tradition in the Italian village of Grazie di Curtattone, and Santa Barbara's "I Madonnari" is considered the village's "sister festival." The art works, masterful as they are, are gone in a week's time.

CONTACT:
California Division of Tourism
801 K Street, Ste. 1600
Sacramento, CA 95814
800-862-2543 or 916-322-2881
fax: 916-322-3402

♦ 0892 ♦ **Imbolc (Imbolg)**
February 2

One of the "Greater Sabbats" during the Wiccan year, Imbolc celebrates the coming of spring and the recovery of the Earth Goddess after giving birth to the Sun God at Yule. "Wicca" is the name used by many believers in modern Neopagan witchcraft because it doesn't carry the stigma that the terms "witch" or "pagan" carry.

The Greater Sabbats (or Sabbaths) take place four times a year, on February 2, April 30, July 31, and October 31 (*see* Samhain). In ancient days, they were huge get-togethers that involved dancing, singing, and feasting which went on all night. Revolving around the changing of the seasons and the breeding of animals, they served as a way to give thanks for the bounties of the earth. Other names for Imbolc include the **Feast of Pan, Feast of Torches, Feast of Waxing Lights,** and **Oimelc.**

SOURCES:
Chases-1996, p. 84

♦ 0893 ♦ **Immaculate Conception, Feast of the**
December 8

Theological controversy surrounded this festival for centuries, though popular celebration of it dates to at least the eighth century. The argument hinged on the meaning of the word "immaculate," which in this context refers to the belief that Jesus' mother Mary was conceived without original sin, the basic inclination toward wrongdoing that originates from the sin of Adam. Many leading theologians, including St. Thomas Aquinas, questioned the Immaculate Conception. Although for many years it remained open for debate, in 1854 Pope Pius IX proclaimed it to be an essential dogma of the Roman Catholic Church, and since that time the Feast of the Immaculate Conception has celebrated God's choice of Mary to give birth to his Son. This is also a pious belief held by many Anglicans. In Guam, this is a legal holiday also known as Our Lady of Camarin Day, commemorating a statute of Mary that a fisherman found floating off the coast.

CONTACT:
Guam Visitors Bureau
401 Pale San Vittores Rd.
Tumon, Guam 96911
011-671-646-5278 or 011-671-646-8516
fax: 011-671-646-8861

SOURCES:
AmerBkDays-1978, p. 1084
BkFest-1937, pp. 190, 271
BkFestHolWrld-1970, p. 131
BkHolWrld-1986, Dec 8
DaysCustFaith-1957, p. 308
DictWrldRel-1989, p. 338
FolkWrldHol-1992, p. 585
RelHolCal-1993, p. 85
SaintFestCh-1904, p. 14

♦ 0894 ♦ **Immaculate Heart of Mary, Feast of the**
May–June; second Saturday following the second Sunday after Pentecost

It was St. John Eudes who initiated the worship of the Holy Heart of Mary in 1648 by composing a Mass and Office, although the feast failed to be approved by the Congregation of Rites in 1669. Repeated requests over the years for official recognition of the feast were reinforced in 1917 when the Virgin Mary appeared at Fátima, Portugal, and expressed her wish that the devotion be established so that Russia would be saved. On October 31, 1942, the 25th anniversary of the appearance at Fátima, Pope Pius XII consecrated the entire human race to the Immaculate Heart of Mary, and two years later, a feast under that name was established for August 22, octave of the Feast of the Immaculate Conception. (*See also* Our Lady of Fátima Day.) It was moved to its present day in 1969. Roman Catholics observe this day in honor of Mary and to obtain her intercession for world peace and the practice of virtue.

SOURCES:
RelHolCal-1993, p. 85

♦ 0895 ♦ **Impruneta, Festa del**
Late October

The fair held at Impruneta, outside Florence, Italy, is one of the largest and noisiest of the autumn harvest festivals held all over Tuscany in October.

For weeks before the festival begins, the walls of Florence are covered with posters announcing when the fair will be held. Dating back three centuries, the *festa* originally celebrated the figure of the Virgin Mary which was believed to have been painted by St. Luke. But now it is primarily a celebration of the harvest and a last opportunity before winter to indulge in the area's special foods and the wines of the Elsa and Pesa valleys.

Chickens, pigeons, and suckling pigs are roasted on spits, and there are tables heaped with home-cured hams and loaves of country-style bread. Other foods associated with the fair include the paper-thin anise cookies known as *brigidini* and almond toffee, which is boiled in iron cauldrons.

CONTACT:
Italian Government Travel Office
630 Fifth Ave.
New York, NY 10111
212-245-4822

♦ 0896 ♦ **Inauguration Day**
January 20

From 1789 until 1933, the day on which the newly elected president of the United States began his term of office was March 4—now known as **Old Inauguration Day.** The day was changed to January 20 when the 20th Amendment to the Constitution was passed in 1933. When Inauguration Day falls on a Sunday, the oath of office is administered privately, but the public ceremonies are usually postponed until the following day.

The swearing-in of the president has been held at the east portico of the Capitol building since 1817. At noontime, the chief justice of the United States administers the oath of office to the president, who then delivers an Inaugural Address. This is followed by a colorful Inauguration Parade through the streets of Washington, D.C. Inauguration festivities are usually somewhat more modest when a president is elected for a second term or when a change in the presidency does not involve a change in the ruling political party.

In the evening inaugural balls are held in a number of different locations, and the president and the first lady try to make a brief appearance at each of them. William Henry Harrison was the first American president to dance at his own inaugural ball, but the exertion proved too much for him. Already suffering from his exposure to the stormy weather during his record-breaking inaugural address (one hour and 45 minutes), he later developed pneumonia and died within a month.

CONTACT:
Washington D.C. Convention and
  Visitors Association
1212 New York Ave., N.W., Ste.
  600
Washington, D.C. 20005
800-635-6338 or 202-789-7000
fax: 202-789-7037

SOURCES:
AmerBkDays-1978, p. 96
AnnivHol-1983, p. 11
Chases-1996, p. 122
DictDays-1988, p. 59

♦ 0897 ♦ **Inconfidência Week**
April

The *Inconfidência* was a colonial uprising for Brazilian independence from Portugal at the end of the 18th century (*see also* BRAZIL INDEPENDENCE DAY). It is celebrated today by paying tribute to Joaquim José da Silva Xavier—also known as **Tiradentes** ('tooth-puller') because of his occasional practice of extracting teeth—who became a martyr for independence when the uprising was put down and he was executed.

The Inconfidência Week festivities include performances by orchestras, bands and choirs, and athletic competitions. The city of Ouro Preto is honorarily restored to its former position as state capital of Minas Gerais during the festival.

CONTACT:
Brazilian Embassy
3006 Massachusetts Ave., N.W.
Washington, D.C. 20008
202-745-2700; fax: 202-745-2827

SOURCES:
AnnivHol-1983, p. 54
Chases-1996, p. 179
NatlHolWrld-1968, p. 159

♦ 0898 ♦ **Incwala**
December or January

The most sacred of the national ceremonies of the independent kingdom of Swaziland. Held in the royal village of Lobamba, it is a six-day ritualized festival of song, dance, folklore, and martial display, focusing on the king as the source of fertility and the symbol of power and unity. During the main ceremony, warriors dance and chant to persuade the king (who has secluded himself) to return to his people. He finally appears wearing a black-plumed headdress,

dances the king's dance, eats part of a pumpkin, and throws away the remainder as a symbol of the harvest.

The main musical instruments of the Swazis are rattles, buckhorn whistles, long reed flutes, and the shield, used for percussion.

CONTACT:
Swaziland Embassy
3400 International Dr., N.W., Ste.
  3M
Washington, D.C. 20008
202-362-6683; fax: 202-244-8059

SOURCES:
BkHolWrld-1986, Dec 22
FolkHolWrld-1992, p. 467

Independence Day
See under individual countries

Independence Movement Day (Korea)
See **Samil-jol**

India Independence Day
See **India Republic Day**

♦ 0899 ♦ **Indianapolis 500**
May, Sunday of Memorial Day weekend

The "Greatest Spectacle in Racing," popularly known as the **Indy 500**, is actually the culmination of a month-long event. It begins the first week in May with the Mayor's Breakfast and parade around the Indianapolis Motor Speedway, the two-and-a-half-mile oval track on which the race takes place. Then there are qualifying races to determine who will participate in the final **Indianapolis 500 Mile Race**, which is held on the Sunday before MEMORIAL DAY. On the day before the big race, there is a 500 Festival Memorial Parade that draws more than 300,000 spectators to the streets of downtown Indianapolis and features floats, musical groups, and celebrities. The race itself, which has been held in Indianapolis since 1911, regularly attracts about 450,000 spectators to the 559-acre speedway, in addition to 4,000 media people and a nationwide television audience. The Indy is said to be the largest one-day sporting event in the world. The official track record belongs to Robert Guerrero whose one-lap speed was 232.482 mph. This speed won Guerrero the pole position for the start of the 1992 race, but he crashed into a wall during a warm-up lap and had to leave the race.

The Indy racing car is fueled with a blend of fuels (such as methanol and nitromethane) and usually powered by a turbo-charged engine. Officially, the Indy 500 is a testing-ground for devices that will eventually be used in passenger cars. The annual race has been credited with such automotive improvements as the rearview mirror, balloon tires, and ethyl gasoline.

CONTACT:
Indianapolis Convention and Visitors Association
200 S. Capitol Ave.
1 RCA Dome, Ste. 100
Indianapolis, IN 46225
800-323-4639 or 317-639-4282
fax: 317-639-5273

SOURCES:
Chases-1996, p. 230
GdUSFest-1984, p. 52

◆ 0900 ◆ Indian Market
Third weekend in August

A showplace for traditional and contemporary Indian art, held on the Plaza of Santa Fe, N.M. The market is the oldest and largest juried competition among Indian artists. It originated as part of the 1922 Fiesta de Santa Fe and continued and grew out of concern that the art forms of the Indian pueblos (villages) were disappearing.

Today more than 800 Indians enter the competition, largely from the 19 New Mexico pueblos and the Apache, Navajo, Hopi, and Ute tribes of the Southwest. Besides the booths of art works, there are numerous food booths, offering such Indian specialties as green chile on fried bread. Indian dances are performed at the courtyard of the Palace of the Governors. A poster-signing ceremony and a benefit art auction precede the market days.

CONTACT:
Southwest Association of Indian
  Artists
509 Camino de Los Marquez,
  Ste. 1
Santa Fe, NM 87501
505-983-5220

SOURCES:
GdUSFest-1984, p. 119

◆ 0901 ◆ India Republic Day
January 26

An important national festival in India celebrating the day in 1950 when India's ties with Britain were severed and the country became a fully independent republic. The holiday is marked with parades and much celebration in all the state capitals, but the celebration in Delhi is especially grand. There is a mammoth parade with military units, floats from each state, dancers and musicians, and fly-overs. The festivities in Delhi actually last for about a week, with special events of all sorts in auditoriums and hotels.

England's Queen Victoria had been proclaimed Empress of India in 1877, and it wasn't until 1947 that India won its long fight for freedom. The India Independence Act was passed by the British Parliament in July 1947, and by August 15 the Muslim nation of Pakistan and the Hindu nation of India had become independent dominions. Lord Mountbatten served as governor-general during the transition period. When a new constitution came into effect in 1950 his governor-generalship ended, and India stood fully independent. Independence Day on Aug. 15 is also a national holiday, but is observed chiefly with speech-making and none of the grandeur of Republic Day.

CONTACT:
India Tourist Office
30 Rockefeller Ave.
15 N. Mezzanine
New York, NY 10112
212-586-4901; fax: 212-582-3274

SOURCES:
AnnivHol-1983, pp. 14, 107,
  173
Chases-1996, p. 76
GdWrldFest-1985, p. 111
IntlThFolk-1979, p. 205
NatlHolWrld-1968, p. 18

◆ 0902 ◆ Indonesia Independence Day
August 17

Indonesia had been a Dutch colony for 300 years when a group of revolutionaries declared independence on August 17, 1945. Indonesians endured four more years of struggle before their independence was formally granted by Queen Juliana of the Netherlands.

This national holiday is celebrated throughout Indonesia with parades, athletic events, and a multitude of cultural and performing arts festivals.

CONTACT:
Indonesian Tourist Promotion
  Office
3457 Wilshire Blvd., Ste. 104
Los Angeles, CA 90010
213-387-2078; fax: 213-380-4876

SOURCES:
AnnivHol-1983, p. 108
Chases-1996, p. 341
IntlThFolk-1979, p. 227
NatlHolWrld-1968, p. 147

◆ 0903 ◆ Indra Jatra
*September–October; end of Hindu month of
Bhadrapada to early in the Hindu month of
Asvina*

The most important festival of Nepal, combining homage to a god with an appearance by a living goddess. The festival, lasting for eight days, is a time to honor the recently deceased and to pay homage to the Hindu god Indra and his mother Dagini so they will bless the coming harvests. It furthermore commemorates the day in 1768, during an Indra Jatra (*jatra* means 'festival'), that Prithwi Narayan Shah (1730–1775) conquered the Katmandu Valley and unified Nepal.

Legend says that Indra, the god of rain and ruler of heaven, once visited the Katmandu Valley in human form to pick flowers for his mother. The people caught him stealing flowers. Dagini, the mother, came down and promised to spread dew over the crops and to take those who had died in the past year back to heaven with her. The people then released Indra and they have celebrated the occasion ever since.

Before the ceremonies start, a 50-foot tree is cut, sanctified, and dragged to the Hanuman Dhoka Palace in Katmandu. It represents Shiva's lingam, the phallic symbol of his creative powers and shows he's come to the valley. As the pole is erected, bands play and cannons boom. Images of Indra, usually as a captive, are displayed, and sacrifices of goats and roosters are offered.

Three gold chariots are assembled in Basantpur Square, outside the home of the Kumari, the living goddess and vestal virgin. She is a young girl who was selected to be a goddess when she was about three years old, and she will be replaced by another girl when she begins to menstruate. This indicates she is human. Two boys playing the roles of the gods Ganesh and Bhairab emerge from the Kumari's house to be attendants to the goddess. Then the goddess herself appears in public for the first time, walking on a carpet so her feet don't touch the ground. The crowds go wild. The king bows to the Kumari, and the procession moves off to the palace where it stops in front of the 12-foot mask of the Bhairab. This is the fearsome form of Shiva in Nepal and is displayed only at this time. The Kumari greets the image and rice beer pours from its mouth. Those who catch a drop of the beer are blessed, but even more are those who catch one of the tiny live fish in the beer.

In the following days the procession moves from place to place around Katmandu. Masked dancers perform every night at the Hanuman Dhoka square dramatizing each of the earthly incarnations of Vishnu. On the final day of the festival the great pole is carried to the river.

CONTACT:
Nepal Embassy
2131 Leroy Pl., N.W.
Washington, D.C. 20008
202-667-4550; fax: 202-667-5534

SOURCES:
FolkWrldHol-1992, p. 438

Innocents' Day
See **Holy Innocents' Day**

♦ 0904 ♦ **International Day for the Elderly**
October 1

The United Nations General Assembly decided to set aside October 1 as International Day for the Elderly in 1990, at which time it asked its member nations to contribute to the Trust Fund for Ageing, which supports projects in developing countries that benefit the elderly. Two years later, in 1992, the General Assembly adopted a set of global targets for meeting the needs of the elderly by the year 2001.

By designating a day when governments are supposed to focus on what they can do to provide for the elderly, the U.N. hopes not only to forestall problems related to the aging of the population but to focus attention on the promise that a maturing population holds for social, economic, cultural, and spiritual undertakings. The United Nations has set aside the year 1999 as the International Year of Older Persons.

CONTACT:
United Nations
Dept. of Public Information
New York, NY 10017
212-963-1234; fax: 212-963-4879
WWW: http://www.undp.org

SOURCES:
Chases-1996, p. 400

♦ 0905 ♦ **International Day for the Elimination of Racial Discrimination**
March 21

International Day for the Elimination of Racial Discrimination is observed annually on March 21, the anniversary of the day in 1960 when, at a peaceful demonstration against the apartheid "pass laws" in Sharpeville, South Africa, police opened fire and killed 69 black South Africans. The observation of this day was initiated by the United Nations General Assembly in 1966, when it called on the international community to redouble its efforts to eliminate all forms of racial discrimination and to remember "the victims of Sharpeville and those countless others in different parts of the world who have fallen victim to racial injustice."

CONTACT:
United Nations
Dept. of Public Information
New York, NY 10017
212-963-1234; fax: 212-963-4879
WWW: http://www.undp.org

SOURCES:
Chases-1996, p. 140

♦ 0906 ♦ **International Day of Disabled Persons**
December 3

The years 1983–92 marked the United Nations Decade of Disabled Persons, a period during which great strides were made in raising awareness and enacting laws to improve the situation of individuals with disabilities. At the conclusion of this 10-year observance, December 3 was proclaimed the International Day of Disabled Persons. The U.N. General Assembly appealed to its members to observe this day with activities and events designed to promote the advantages of integrating disabled persons in every area of social, economic, and political life.

CONTACT:
United Nations
Dept. of Public Information
New York, NY 10017
212-963-1234; fax: 212-963-4879
WWW: http://www.undp.org

SOURCES:
Chases-1996, p. 470

♦ 0907 ♦ **International Literacy Day**
September 8

Established by the United Nations to encourage universal literacy, this day has been observed since 1966 by all countries and organizations that are part of the United Nations system. It was a direct outgrowth of the World Conference of Ministers of Education in Tehran, Iran, which first called for the eradication of illiteracy throughout the world. Observances are sponsored primarily by UNESCO (United Nations Educational, Scientific and Cultural Organization) and include the awarding of special literacy prizes.

Prizes are also awarded by the International Reading Association and the Japanese publisher Shoichi Noma to literacy programs that have made a significant difference. For example, in 1984 the Noma Prize was given to the Bazhong District in the People's Republic of China, where the literacy rate had been raised from 10 percent to 90 percent over a 35-year period.

CONTACT:
United Nations
Dept. of Public Information
New York, NY 10017
212-963-1234; fax: 212-963-4879
WWW: http://www.undp.org

SOURCES:
AnnivHol-1983, p. 116
BkHolWrld-1986, Sep 8
Chases-1996, p. 370

♦ 0908 ♦ **Inti Raymi Fiesta**
June 24

The **Inti Raymi Festival**, also known as the **Inti Raymi Pageant**, **Sun Festival**, or **Feast of the Sun**, is an ancient MIDSUMMER DAY festival celebrated by the Incans in Peru on June 24. The ancient Indians, whose empire at one time extended along the Pacific coast of South America from the northern border of modern Ecuador to the Río Maule in central Chile, believed that their land lay at the center of the earth. They honored Inti Raymi, their sun god, at the foot of La Marca Hills, not far from where the actual equator is now known to be. Their religion embraces both Christian and Indian elements, and they still believe that the sun and moon have god-like powers.

The original Inti Raymi celebration involved animal sacrifices performed by the shaman or priest at the top of the hill of La Marca when the sun reached its zenith at the solstice. Today the main celebration takes place in Cuzco, the 12th-century Incan capital, where there is a special procession and mock sacrifice to the sun, followed by a week-long celebration involving folkloric dances, tours of archeological ruins, and regional arts and crafts displays. Bonfires are still lit in the Andes Mountains to celebrate the rebirth of the sun, and people burn their old clothes as a way of marking the end of the harvest cycle.

CONTACT:
Embassy of Peru
1700 Massachusetts Ave., N.W.
Washington, D.C. 20036
202-833-9860; fax: 202-659-8124

SOURCES:
AnnivHol-1983, p. 84
DictFolkMyth-1984, pp. 526, 1032, 1055
FolkWrldHol-1992, p. 339
GdWrldFest-1985, p. 149

Invention of the Cross
See **Exaltation of the Cross**

♦ 0909 ♦ **Iowa State Fair**
Eleven days through last Sunday in August

One of America's foremost state fairs, celebrating agriculture and featuring a life-size cow sculpted out of 600 pounds of sweet butter. Held for 11 days at the fairgrounds in Des Moines, and attracting close to a million people each year, the fair is famous for having inspired the Phil Stong novel, *State Fair*, and three movies based on the novel. Will ROGERS starred in the first movie. The second and third were musicals by Rodgers and Hammerstein and included the now-standard songs "It Might as Well Be Spring" and "It's a Grand Night for Singing."

The fair is also famous for its cow made out of butter. The breed represented varies from year to year. It's kept in a display case cooled to 40 degrees. The most frequently asked question at the fair information booth is, "Where's the butter cow?" (Answer: in the Agriculture Building.)

Sheep are an important feature at the fair, reflecting the fact that Iowa has more sheep farms than any other state. Sheepshearing contests are popular; champions can shear a sheep in 90 seconds. The big boar contest is also popular; the winning animal always weighs in at more than half a ton. There are other competitions as well: checker playing, horseshoe pitching, fiddling, and rolling-pin throwing.

The first Iowa state fair was held in 1854. Memorable moments in the intervening years include the spectacular crash of two trains, one labeled Roosevelt and the other Hoover, which were throttled up at opposite ends of a track. They roared down on each other, crashed, and exploded. The year was 1932, when the presidential candidates were Herbert Hoover and Franklin D. ROOSEVELT.

The fair underwent a period of rapid change between 1880 and 1930, expanding to encompass such activities as horse and auto racing, biplane stunt-flying, high-diving horses, and auto-to-airplane transfers. The American aviator Charles Lindbergh visited the fair in 1927, soon after his triumphant nonstop solo flight across the Atlantic.

CONTACT:
Iowa Tourism Office
200 E. Grand Ave.
Des Moines, IA 50309
800-345-4692 or 515-242-4705
fax: 515-242-4749

SOURCES:
Chases-1996, p. 328

♦ 0910 ♦ **Ironman Triathlon Championships**
Saturday nearest the full moon in October

An extraordinarily grueling international athletic contest held since 1978 in Kailua-Kona on Hawaii Island. It consists of a 2.4-mile swim, a 112-mile bicycle race, and, for the final leg, a standard 26.2-mile marathon run. Close to 2,000 stout-hearted men and women participate, preceding the races with a Thursday-night party in which they stoke up on carbohydrates. Originally, contestants swam, biked, and ran for the fun and challenge of the event, but cash prizes are now awarded at a banquet the day after the triathlon. The event is scheduled for the Saturday nearest the full moon in October so that more beach is exposed at low tide, and there is more light from the moon at night. This is the original, but no longer the toughest such contest: double ironmen now challenge triathletes.

CONTACT:
Hawaii Visitors Bureau
2270 Kalakaua Ave., Ste. 801
Honolulu, HI 96815
808-923-1811; fax: 808-922-8991

♦ 0911 ♦ **Iroquois White Dog Feast**
First quarter moon in January

The White Dog Feast was the traditional midwinter ceremony of the Iroquois Indians in Canada and the United States. Dedicated to Teharonhiawagon, the Master of Life, it was based on the belief that the sacrifice of a dog and an offering of tobacco were necessary to ensure the return of spring and the rebirth of life. A white dog was strangled so that no blood was shed or bones broken. It was decorated with ribbons, feathers, and red paint and hung from a cross-pole for four days. On the fifth day, it was taken down and carried to the longhouse or assembly hall, where it was placed on the altar and burned. A basket containing tobacco was also thrown on the fire, its smoke rising as incense.

The Great Feather Dance was performed on the sixth day as a way of giving thanks to the Creator for the crops. The False Face Dance, during which a pair of masked "uncles" would visit Iroquois homes and scatter ashes, was also performed during the White Dog Feast. It was a popular time to play traditional games of chance involving bones, fruit stones, or buttons made of deer horn.

SOURCES:
BkHolWrld-1986, Jan 10
DictFolkMyth-1984, p. 835
FolkAmerHol-1991, p. 43

♦ 0912 ♦ **Irrigation Festival**
First full weekend in May

The oldest continuous festival in Washington, held since 1896 in Sequim. Originally known as "May Days," the festival celebrated the opening of the first ditch to bring water from the Dungeness River to the arid Sequim prairie. In the early days there were horse races, dancing, a keg of beer hidden in the brush, and tables loaded with food. After a few years, Maypole dances with girls in frilly dresses were a big attraction. The first queen of May Day was chosen in 1908; the first parade was held in 1918; the first queen's float was built in 1948; and a descendant of a pioneer family has been honored as the festival's Grand Pioneer since 1960.

Today, thousands come for a week of activities: a grand parade, a loggers' show, a high-school operetta, crafts and flower exhibits, dances, a horseshoe-pitching tournament, music, and the Ditchwalkers Clam and Spaghetti Dinner.

CONTACT:
Sequim Chamber of Commerce
P.O. Box 907
Sequim, WA 98382
360-683-6197

Islamic New Year
See **Nawruz**

♦ 0913 ♦ **Israel Festival**
September

This three-week festival, founded in 1961, is primarily dedicated to Israeli arts and culture, although guest conductors and performers from other countries are featured as well. There are symphony and choral concerts, opera, ballet and modern dance, theater, jazz, folklore, films, and art exhibitions at several locations in Haifa, Tel Aviv, and Jerusalem, and at the Roman amphitheater in Caesarea. The Israel Philharmonic Orchestra has performed with guest conductors like Zubin Mehta and Leonard Bernstein, and Israeli dance groups offer both traditional and modern programs. Pablo CASALS and Isaac Stern have played there, Rudolf Nureyev and Merce Cunningham have danced at the festival, and Sir John Gielgud has read Shakespeare there. The En Gev Festival, primarily a music festival, is considered part of the Israel Festival and is held concurrently on the shores of the Sea of Galilee.

CONTACT:
Israel Ministry of Tourism
6380 Wilshire Blvd., Ste. 1700
Los Angeles, CA 90048
213-658-7462; fax: 213-658-6543

SOURCES:
GdWrldFest-1985, p. 115
IntlThFolk-1979, p. 238
MusFestWrld-1963, p. 259

♦ 0914 ♦ **Israeli Independence Day**
Between April 16 and May 14; Iyyar 5

Known in Hebrew as **Yom ha-Atzma'ut**, this day commemorates the proclamation of independence by Palestinian Jews and the establishment of a provisional government in Israel on May 14, 1948 (5 Iyyar 5708 on the Jewish calendar). It is observed with parties, performances, and military parades as well as religious rituals, which include the reading of Psalms. In the United States, Jews celebrate Israeli Independence Day by attending concerts, films, parades, Israeli fairs, and other public events. An "Israeli Day Parade" is held in New York City, but it doesn't always take place on the fifth day of Iyyar.

A popular custom on this day for Israelis is to walk at least a short distance somewhere in the country where they have never walked before.

CONTACT:
Israel Ministry of Tourism
6380 Wilshire Blvd., Ste. 1700
Los Angeles, CA 90048
213-658-7462; fax: 213-658-6543

SOURCES:
AnnivHol-1983, p. 66
Chases-1996, p. 183
NatlHolWrld-1968, p. 60

New York Convention and Visitors Bureau
2 Columbus Cir.
New York, NY 10019
800-692-8474 or 212-484-1200
fax: 212-247-6193

♦ 0915 ♦ **Istanbul Festival**
June–July

Since the first **International Istanbul Festival** was held in 1973, the Istanbul Foundation for Culture and the Arts has used this event to bridge the cultures of East and West and to promote Turkey's rich cultural heritage. The only criterion used in selecting the traditional and contemporary theater, dance, and musical groups that perform at the festival is the contribution that the artist or the work of art makes to world peace. The Istanbul Foundation seeks the advice of embassies, cultural offices, and international artistic agents in choosing festival participants, many of whom have won awards at international competitions in their fields. Locations for performances include the Rumelihisar Open-Air Theatre, a 15th-century Ottoman fortress, and St. Irene Church, a fourth-century Byzantine basilica.

CONTACT:
Republic of Turkey Embassy
1714 Massachusetts Ave., N.W.
Washington, D.C. 20036
202-659-8200; fax: 202-659-0744

SOURCES:
GdWrldFest-1985, p. 180
IntlThFolk-1979, p. 369

♦ 0916 ♦ **Isthmian Games**
First month of spring

Athletic competitions held in ancient times at Corinth in Greece. They were held during alternate years beginning in 581 B.C., with contests in various events, including gymnastics, horse racing, and poetry (the last was open to both men and women). The prize was a crown of celery.

There are differing stories as to the origin of the games; one legend says they were founded by Theseus after he killed the robber chief Sinis. The games were one of the four great national Greek festivals, the others being the Olympic, Pythian, and Nemean games. The Isthmian games were especially popular because they offered more amusements than the other three festivals.

See also NEMEAN GAMES, OLYMPIC GAMES, and PYTHIAN GAMES

SOURCES:
OxClassDict-1970, p. 556

♦ 0917 ♦ **Italian Festival**
Late May

A weekend festival in McAlester, Okla., in Pittsburg County, a coal-rich area that drew miners of Italian heritage in the 1880s. The town began as a tent store owned by J. J. McAlester, who discovered and mined the coal here. He was later lieutenant governor of the state. The descendants of the Italian miners celebrate their heritage with folk music, dances, costumes, arts and crafts, and, of course, food, lots of it: 12,000 meatballs, 6,000 sausages, and 200 gallons of spaghetti and sauce.

CONTACT:
Italian Festival
Box 1212
McAlester, OK 74502
918-423-8822 or 918-426-2055

♦ 0918 ♦ **Italy Liberation Day**
April 25

Liberation Day is a national holiday commemorating the

Allied invasion of Italy in 1943 that led to the overthrow of Mussolini's Fascist rule during World War II.

CONTACT:
Italian Government Travel Office
630 Fifth Ave.
New York, NY 10111
212-245-4822

SOURCES:
AnnivHol-1983, p. 56

◆ 0919 ◆ Italy Republic Day
June 2

This national holiday, also known as **Constitution Day**, commemorates the people's vote on this day in 1946 to transform Italy into a republic rather than continue to be ruled by the monarchy.

Republic Day is observed with parades—in Venice, gondolas parade in the canals—and other festivities all over Italy.

CONTACT:
Italian Government Travel Office
630 Fifth Ave.
New York, NY 10111
212-245-4822

SOURCES:
AnnivHol-1983, p. 75
Chases-1996, p. 240
NatlHolWrld-1968, p. 80

◆ 0920 ◆ Itul
Early December

This highly regarded ritual is a ceremonial dance performed by the Kuba people who live in the Congo. It takes place on an infrequent basis, not only because the costs and preparation involved are so extensive but also because it can only be held with the king's authorization; the only sponsors (and funders) may be the children of a king. An itul performed for a king is held in the dance area of the palace and is considered more refined because the king's wives are professional dancers and singers. If the itul is open to the public, it takes place in the plaza in front of the palace. Although it is usually held in December, the dates can vary.

The preparations can take up to several months, but the dance itself lasts only a few hours. The villain's role is danced by someone dressed as an animal, and the plot on which the dance is based combines both traditional episodes and those that have been adapted to whatever animal is chosen. The dance is performed in two parts over two consecutive days. The first part mourns the destruction caused by the enemy-animal, and the second part deals with its capture and killing. There is a chorus of women kneeling in the center who perform the songs and provide a rhythmical accompaniment by beating calabashes or gourd drums on the ground. The dancers move counterclockwise around the chorus, and the king watches the spectacle from a special shelter set off to one side.

The Itul is considered so important that once the word

spreads that the ceremony is taking place, Kuba people from all over rush to attend it. It is revived from time to time by kings who fear that their traditional power is being threatened by modern secular life.

CONTACT:
Republic of Congo Embassy
4891 Colorado Ave., N.W.
Washington, D.C. 20011
202-726-0825; fax: 202-726-1860

SOURCES:
FolkWrldHol-1992, p. 584

◆ 0921 ◆ Ivory Coast Independence Day
December 7

Ivory Coast was granted independence from France on August 7, 1960. As a French colony since the 1893, it has also been known as Côte d'Ivoire.

Independence Day is a national holiday in Ivory Coast, celebrated with parades, dancing, and fireworks on December 7 each year.

CONTACT:
Cote D'Ivoire Embassy
2424 Massachusetts Ave., N.W.
Washington, D.C. 20008
202-797-0300; fax: 202-483-8482

SOURCES:
AnnivHol-1983, p. 157
Chases-1996, p. 474
NatlHolWrld-1968, p. 139

◆ 0922 ◆ Ivy Day
October 6

October 6 is the anniversary of the death of Charles Stewart Parnell (1846–1891), the famous Irish statesman and leader of the Home Rule Party. He entered the House of Commons when he was only 29 and quickly established a reputation for hostility to England and all things English. He became a hero to the Irish poor, many of whom would try to touch his clothes or kiss his hands and knees when he walked through a crowd.

Parnell fell out of public favor somewhat when he became involved in a divorce case in 1890, and the trauma of rejection by so many of his countrypeople is thought to have contributed to his early death in 1891. But he is a symbol of Irish pride and independence, and his name appears frequently in Irish literature, particularly the poetry of William Butler Yeats and the short story in James Joyce's *Dubliners* called "Ivy Day in the Committee Room." It is somewhat ironic that the sprig of green ivy traditionally worn on this day—chosen by Parnell himself as an emblem—is a color he apparently intensely disliked.

SOURCES:
Chases-1996, p. 408
DictDays-1988, p. 60

J

♦ 0923 ♦ **Jackalope Days**
Late June

Four days of celebration in Douglas, Wyo., to honor the jackalope, an elusive animal that is a cross between a jackrabbit and an antelope (according to the legends of Wyoming's Converse County). The jackalope might be mistaken for a large rabbit except for its antlers, and it might be identified as a small deer, except for its rabbit-like shape. The jackalope was first seen in 1829 by Roy Ball, a trapper, who was denounced as a liar. Some people still doubt its existence, despite the evidence of numerous stuffed heads on barroom walls. The jackalope is rarely seen because it is a shy animal and comes out of hiding only for breeding with the commonly seen and hornless females, called does, which look like ordinary rabbits. But it breeds only during electrical storms, at the precise moment of the flash when most people are not out wandering around. A 10-foot replica of a jackalope in Centennial Jackalope Square in Douglas attests to the cultural importance of this critter.

Events of Jackalope Days include a downtown carnival, rodeos, a street dance, a parade, the crowning of a rodeo queen, and sports competitions.

CONTACT:
Wyoming Tourism and Marketing
 Division
I-25 and College Dr.
Cheyenne, WY 82002
800-225-5996 or 307-777-7777
fax: 307-777-6904

Jackson Day
See **Battle of New Orleans Day**

♦ 0924 ♦ **Jackson's Birthday, Andrew**
March 15

Andrew Jackson (1767–1845), the seventh president of the United States (1829–37), became a national hero during the War of 1812 when he successfully fought the British at New Orleans, despite the fact that he was so sick he could barely stand without assistance, and no one knew that a peace treaty had been signed two weeks earlier. His soldiers thought he was as "tough as hickory," resulting in his nickname, "Old Hickory." The anniversary of his birth is a special observance in Tennessee, and the president of the United States usually brings or sends a wreath to be placed on Jackson's grave in the garden at his home, The Hermitage, near Nashville.

Other tributes paid to Jackson during this week include radio speeches and newspaper editorials, school essay contests, and Jackson Day dinners sponsored by the Democratic party, of which he is considered one of the founders. Sometimes these celebrations are held on January 8, BATTLE OF NEW ORLEANS DAY. In Virginia, Jackson's birthday is celebrated in January along with those of Martin Luther King, Jr. and Robert E. Lee (*see* KING, JR.'S BIRTHDAY, MARTIN LUTHER and LEE DAY, ROBERT E.).

SOURCES:
AmerBkDays-1978, p. 252
Chases-1996, p. 133

♦ 0925 ♦ **Jacob's Pillow Dance Festival**
June–August

The second oldest dance festival in the United States (after the Bennington Dance Festival), the Jacob's Pillow Dance Festival takes place for 10 weeks every summer at the historic Ted Shawn Theatre near Lenox, Massachusetts. Edwin Myers ("Ted") Shawn was an innovative modern dancer and cofounder, with his wife Ruth St. Denis, of Denishawn, the first American modern dance company. In 1933, at his farm named Jacob's Pillow, he founded the Jacob's Pillow Dance Festival as a summer residence and theater for his male dancers. After the group disbanded, Shawn turned Jacob's Pillow into a dance center of international importance—a place where not only ballet but modern and ethnic dance could be presented. Top dancers from all over the world give regular performances throughout the summer to packed houses.

CONTACT:
Jacob's Pillow Dance Festival
Box 287
Lee, MA 01238
413-637-1322

SOURCES:
GdUSFest-1984, p. 85

♦ 0926 ♦ Jamaica Festival
Late July through first Monday in August

Originally called the **Independence Festival of Jamaica** because it ended on the first Monday in August, JAMAICA INDEPENDENCE DAY, the five-day event now known as the Jamaica Festival emphasizes the cultural roots, conservation, and revival of traditional art forms by ethnic groups—particularly folk music, folk dances, and folk games of African origin. Competitions to determine who will perform at the festival begin in May at the local level. After regional and national competitions are held, the best in each category are selected to participate in the final festival programs, which include exhibitions, street dances, concerts, plays, and readings. The festival has been held in Kingston, Montego Bay, and elsewhere on the island since 1963. A film festival was added in 1977.

CONTACT:
Jamaica Tourist Board
801 Second Ave.
New York, NY 10017
800-233-4582 or 212-856-9727
fax: 212-856-9730

SOURCES:
GdWrldFest-1985, p. 121

♦ 0927 ♦ Jamaica Independence Day
First Monday in August

The island of Jamaica became an independent nation with loose ties to the British Commonwealth on August 6, 1962. Before that it had been a founding member of the Federation of the West Indies, a group of Caribbean islands that formed a unit within the Commonwealth of Nations. Allegiance to the British gradually gave way to the emergence of a national identity, and the federation was dissolved.

A public holiday throughout the island, Independence Day is celebrated with traditional music and dancing, and agricultural, arts and crafts exhibits, and other events as part of the JAMAICA FESTIVAL.

CONTACT:
Jamaica Tourist Board
801 Second Ave.
New York, NY 10017
800-233-4582 or 212-856-9727
fax: 212-856-9730

SOURCES:
AnnivHol-1983, p. 102
Chases-1996, p. 325
NatlHolWrld-1968, p. 136

♦ 0928 ♦ Jamestown Day
May 14

Jamestown, Virginia, is the site of the first permanent English settlement in America. A group of 105 settlers sponsored by the London Company (sometimes called the Virginia Company) disembarked about 50 miles from the mouth of the James River on May 14, 1607, and spent a difficult few years fighting famine and disease. Eventually they initiated the tobacco trade that allowed Virginia to become economically self-sufficient. Jamestown is also credited with establishing the first representative government on the continent, bringing the first African slaves to the colonies, and building America's first Anglican (Episcopal) church.

On the Sunday nearest May 14, which is officially known as Jamestown Day, a commemorative service is held at the historic site of the original settlement. There are speeches, readings, and choral selections; addresses by British and American officials; and a procession to the Memorial Cross, which marks the town's earliest cemetery, followed by a wreath-laying ceremony.

CONTACT:
Colonial National Historical Park
P.O. Box 210
Yorktown, VA 23690
804-898-3400

SOURCES:
AmerBkDays-1978, p. 447
AnnivHol-1983, p. 65
Chases-1996, pp. 208, 212

♦ 0929 ♦ Jamhuri (Kenya Independence Day)
December 12

The biggest of the national holidays in Kenya, observed to commemorate the full independence of Kenya from the British in 1963. A year later, the country became a republic with Jomo Kenyatta (c. 1894–1978) the first president. The day is celebrated nationwide but with special events in Nairobi—speeches by the president and other officials, parades, fireworks, and *ngomas* ('dances') performed in public plazas.

CONTACT:
Kenya Tourist Office
424 Madison Ave.
New York, NY 10017
212-486-1300; fax: 212-688-0911

SOURCES:
AnnivHol-1983, p. 159
Chases-1996, p. 479
NatlHolWrld-1968, p. 226

♦ 0930 ♦ Jamshed Navaroz (Jamshed Navroz)
March 21

The **Zoroastrian New Year** is observed at the VERNAL EQUINOX among the Parsis in India, who are the descendants of the original Zoroastrian immigrants from Iran (formerly Persia). It is traditional for men to dress in white, while women wear colored clothing. Ritual bathing, worship, and the exchange of gifts are part of the celebration.

See also NAWRUZ

SOURCES:
FolkWrldHol-1992, p. 186
RelHolCal-1993, p. 85

Janai Purnima
See **Raksha Bandhana**

♦ 0931 ♦ Janaki Navami
April–May; ninth day of waxing half of Hindu month of Vaisakha

Sita, heroine of the Hindu epic poem *Ramayana*, is supposed to have sprung on this day from a furrow in a field plowed by King Janaka. He named her Sita, which means "furrow of the earth," and raised her as his own child. She was actually the goddess Lakshmi, sent to the earth to bring about the destruction of Ravana and other demons. Many Hindus believe that Sita represents the ideal Indian woman as an embodiment of self-sacrifice, purity, tenderness, fidelity, conjugal affection, and other virtues. Some believe that she appeared in King Janaka's field on the eighth day of the waning half of Phalguna (February–March), and fast on that day instead of the ninth day of Vaisakha.

SOURCES:
DictWrldRel-1989, p. 695
RelHolCal-1993, p. 86

◆ 0932 ◆ Janmashtami (Krishnastami; Krishna's Birthday)
August–September; new moon day of Hindu month of Bhadrapada

One of the most important Hindu festivals, celebrating the birthday of Lord Krishna, the eighth incarnation of Vishnu and the hero of both rich and poor. Throughout India it is a fast day until the new moon is sighted. Then there are ceremonies and prayers at temples dedicated to Krishna. Rituals include bathing the statue of the infant Krishna and then placing his image in a silver cradle with playthings.

In Mathura, where Krishna was born, there are performances of Krishna Lila, the folk dramas depicting scenes from Krishna's life. In the state of Tamil Nadu, oiled poles called *ureyadi* are set up, a pot of money is tied to the top, and boys dressed as Krishna try to shinny up the pole and win the prize while spectators squirt water at them. In Maharashtra, where the festival is known as *Govinda*, pots containing money and curds and butter are suspended high over streets. Boys form human pyramids climbing on each others' shoulders to try to break the pot. These climbing games reflect stories of Krishna, who as a boy loved milk and butter so much they had to be kept out of his reach.

In Nepal, a religious fast is observed on Krishnastami, and Krishna's temple at Lalitpur is visited by pilgrims. People parade in a procession around the town and display pictures of Krishna.

Numerous rich legends tell of Krishna's life. He is supposed to have been adored as a child for his mischievous pranks— tricking people out of their freshly churned butter or stealing the clothes of the cow maidens, called *gopis*, while they bathed in the river. Later, he used his flute to lure the gopis to amorous dalliances. He also defeated the 100-headed serpent Kaliya by dancing it into submission. Paintings, sculpture, and classical dances depict the many episodes of his life. Portraits of him as a child often show him dancing joyously and holding a ball of butter in his hands. Most often he is shown as the divine lover, playing the flute and surrounded by adoring women.

CONTACT:
India Tourist Office
30 Rockefeller Plaza
15 N. Mezzanine
New York, NY 10112
212-586-4901; fax: 212-582-3274

Nepal Embassy
2131 Leroy Pl., N.W.
Washington, D.C. 20008
202-667-4550; fax: 202-667-5534

SOURCES:
AnnivHol-1983, p. 178
BkFest-1937, p. 160
BkHolWrld-1986, Aug 26
DictFolkMyth-1984, pp. 590, 924
DictWrldRel-1989, p. 304
FolkWrldHol-1992, p. 439
RelHolCal-1993, p. 86

◆ 0933 ◆ Japanese Emperor's Birthday
December 23

This is a national holiday in Japan honoring the birth of Emperor Akihito (b. 1933). He and his family typically appear on the Imperial Palace balcony to greet visitors, who are invited to enter the grounds on this day.

CONTACT:
Japan National Tourist
  Organization
630 Fifth Ave., Ste. 2101
New York, NY 10111
212-757-5640; fax: 212-307-6754

SOURCES:
Chases-1996, p. 487

◆ 0934 ◆ Japanese National Foundation Day and Constitution Memorial Day
February 11; May 3

The nationwide holiday known as **Kenkoku Kinen-no-Hi** commemorates the accession to the throne of Jimmu Tenno, Japan's first human emperor, in the year 660 B.C. He was believed to be a direct descendant of the gods and is credited with founding the Japanese empire. In fact, this day was originally known as **Empire Day** back in 1872, when the Japanese government first designated it as a national holiday. It was abolished after World War II, then revived as National Foundation Day in 1966. It is observed throughout Japan with fireworks and speeches on Japan's position in the world. One of the most elaborate celebrations takes place in Tokyo, where special rites are performed at the Imperial Sanctuary. The Emperor and Empress, the Prime Minister, and other high officials attend the ceremony.

Constitution Memorial Day, or **Kempo Kinen-Bi**, is observed as a national holiday on May 3 and commemorates the adoption of the democratic constitution in 1947.

CONTACT:
Japan National Tourist
  Organization
630 Fifth Ave., Ste. 2101
New York, NY 10111
212-757-5640; fax: 212-307-6754

SOURCES:
AnnivHol-1983, pp. 22, 60
BkFest-1937, p. 196
Chases-1996, pp. 94, 198
DictWrldRel-1989, p. 382

◆ 0935 ◆ Jayuya Festival of Indian Lore
Mid-November

The **Jayuya Indian Festival** was started in 1969, when new traces of the Taino Indian culture were discovered in and around Jayuya, Puerto Rico. The town of Jayuya was once a center of Taino Indian activity, and many Taino stone carvings can still be seen in nearby caves, even though the tribe itself is extinct. The annual festival is held in mid-November and is timed to coincide with the anniversary of the first sighting of Puerto Rico by COLUMBUS on November 19, 1493.

Festival events include Indian ceremonies and dances as well as concerts featuring *fotutos* (conch shells) as instruments. There is a ceremonial Taino ball game that resembles soccer, and a village (*yukayeque*) of thatched-roof huts that enables visitors to see how the Indians lived. Visitors can attend lectures on the Taino language and customs or take a tour of the caves containing the Indian drawings. Although Indian arts and crafts are on sale and there are kiosks serving food typical of the island's indigenous population, the Jayuya Indian Festival also has a serious scholarly purpose, which is to educate people about the Taino culture and to encourage more research in this area. Awards are presented each year at the festival to those who have done scholarly work on Puerto Rico's pre-Columbian cultures.

CONTACT:
Puerto Rico Dept. of Culture
P.O. Box 9024184
San Juan, PR 00902-4184
809-724-0700

SOURCES:
GdUSFest-1984, p. 219

♦ 0936 ♦ Jefferson's Birthday, Thomas
April 13

Unique among American presidents, Thomas Jefferson (1743–1826) was not only a statesman but a scholar, linguist, writer, philosopher, political theorist, architect, engineer, and farmer. In Europe, he was praised as the foremost American thinker of his time. In the United States, he is remembered primarily as the author in 1776 of the Declaration of Independence. After retiring from government service, Jefferson founded the University of Virginia, which opened in 1825. He died on July 4, 1826, the 50th anniversary of the signing of the Declaration of Independence.

As one of the founders of the Democratic party, along with Andrew JACKSON, he has been honored since 1936 by the Democratic National Committee, which sponsors official dinners in various locations across the country known as "Jefferson-Jackson Day Dinners." Sometimes these dinners are held on January 8, the anniversary of the BATTLE OF NEW ORLEANS.

At the University of Virginia at Charlottesville, April 13 was observed for many years as **Founder's Day**, but in 1975 the date was shifted to early fall. There is a formal academic procession, after which an address is given by a nationally known figure. This is also the day on which the Thomas Jefferson Award is give to a leading member of the university community.

SOURCES:
AmerBkDays-1978, p. 348
AnnivHol-1983, p. 51
Chases-1996, p. 169

♦ 0937 ♦ Jerash Festival
Mid-August

Jordan's Queen Noor (Lisa Najeb Halaby, b. 1951) played an important role in establishing the visual and performing arts festival that is now held in Jerash every August. Since 1981 visitors have come to the 2,000-year-old ruins where a Graeco-Roman city once stood to hear Jordanian music, to see folkloric dances performed by Jordanian and other Arab groups, and to watch Arab plays and puppet shows. King Hussein and Queen Noor open the nine-day festival by lighting a symbolic flame in the city forum.

In addition to the music, dance and theater events, the Jerash Festival also includes an Arab book fair, with titles in both Arabic and English, sponsored by the Jordan Department of Libraries, Documentation, and National Archives.

CONTACT:
Jordan Information Bureau
2319 Wyoming Ave., N.W.
Washington, D.C. 20008
202-265-1606; fax: 202-667-0777

SOURCES:
GdWrldFest-1985, p. 125

Jerez de Frontera Festival
See **Vendimia, Festa de la**

♦ 0938 ♦ Jeshn (Afghan Independence Day)
Late August

A week-long celebration of Afghanistan's independence from British control, observed throughout the country but with special ceremonies in Kabul. The Treaty of Rawalpindi, signed on August 8, 1919, gave Afghanistan the right to conduct its own foreign affairs. It was the formal conclusion of the brief Third Anglo-Afghan War, which actually ended in May 1919, but August is a slack agricultural period in Afghanistan and therefore a time when more people can celebrate a holiday.

The holiday is observed with parades, dancing, games, music, and speeches by government figures. For example, at Nawruz, buzkashi matches (the Afghan version of polo) are played, and customarily there are also wrestling matches and tent-pegging contests, based on cavalry maneuvers of past centuries. Often the period of Jeshn is used for major policy announcements. In 1959, one of the more significant events of modern Afghanistan occurred during Jeshn. Prime Minister Mohammad Daoud and other ministers and cabinet and royal-family members appeared on the reviewing stand with their wives and daughters exposing their faces. This was a highly dramatic event; until then, women in public always wore the *chadri* (an ankle-length tent-like gown and veil that totally covers the head and face, with only a mesh slit to see through). This marked the beginning of abolishing the required chadri, and now most urban upper-class women go about without a veil.

Despite the unsettled conditions in Afghanistan, since the withdrawal of the Soviet military, the independence day celebrations continue.

CONTACT:
Afghanistan Embassy
2341 Wyoming Ave., N.W.
Washington, D.C. 20008
202-234-3770; fax: 202-328-3516

SOURCES:
Chases-1996, p. 342
NatlHolWrld-1968, p. 71

♦ 0939 ♦ Jidai Matsuri (Festival of the Ages)
October 22

One of the three great festivals of Kyoto, Japan, and also one of the more recent, commemorating the founding of the city as capital in the year 794. A procession of more than 2,000 picturesquely costumed people depict the epochs or ages in Kyoto's history. They parade from the Imperial Palace to the Heian Shrine, which was built in the 18th century as a dedication to the emperors who established Kyoto (then called Heian-kyo) as the capital. The capital was moved in 1868 to Tokyo, and the festival stems from that time. Among the paraders is one representing Gen. Toyotomi Hideyoshi, a patron of the arts under whom Kyoto flourished. He reunified the country after a period of civil war in the Azuchi-Momoyama Period (1573–1600). Wearing full armor, he reenacts an official visit to the Emperor.

See also AOI MATSURI and GION MATSURI

CONTACT:
Japan National Tourist
    Organization
630 Fifth Ave., Ste. 2101
New York, NY 10111
212-757-5640; fax: 212-307-6754

SOURCES:
AnnivHol-1983, p. 135
JapanFest-1965, p. 37

◆ 0940 ◆ Jizo Ennichi
Twenty-fourth day of each month

It is customary for Japanese Buddhists to express their devotion to Kshitigarba Jizo on the 24th day of each month in a devotional practice known as Jizo Ennichi.

Kshitigarba Jizo is a Bodhisattva, or 'Buddha-to-be,' who is highly regarded by Buddhists in Japan as well as in China, where he is known as Ti-t'sang. Among Japanese Buddhists, Kshitigarba is known for helping children, women in labor, and the wicked. He is also believed to play a role in receiving and welcoming the faithful when they die. He is usually depicted in monk's robes, holding a staff with six rings in his right hand (symbolizing the six dimensions of existence in the realm of desire) and an orb or pearl in his left hand whose symbolic meaning is not known. His statue is most often found outside the temple, where he can guide both the dead and the living. Shrines in his honor are often set up along the roadside, since he protects travelers as well.

SOURCES:
DictWrldRel-1989, p. 418

◆ 0941 ◆ Joan of Arc, Feast Day of
May 30; May 9

The second patron saint of France (the first is St. Denys) and one of the best known of all the saints, Joan of Arc—whom the French refer to as Jeanne d'Arc, the "Maid of Orleans," for the role she played in saving the city of Orleans from the British in the 15th century—was a young, pious peasant girl from the village of Domremy. In 1428 she heard voices she identified as St. Michael, St. Catherine, and St. Margaret telling her to help the Dauphin, Charles VII, recover his kingdom from the British. Her mission was accomplished within 15 months, but Joan was captured by the king's enemies, tried for witchcraft and heresy, and burned at the stake in Rouen on May 30, 1431.

St. Joan's Day is celebrated on May 30 everywhere except in the city of New Orleans, Louisiana, where she is honored on May 9, the day after the anniversary of her dramatic rescue of the French city for which New Orleans was named. In France, the **Fête de Jeanne d'Arc** is observed with special ceremonies in Rouen and Orleans, where the streets are decorated with banners, garlands, and portraits of the teenage girl who was canonized in 1920, five centuries after she led the French forces to victory and brought about the coronation of Charles VII at Reims.

CONTACT:
French Government Tourist Office
9454 Wilshire Blvd., Ste. 715
Beverly Hills, CA 90212
310-271-6665; fax: 310-276-2835

New Orleans Metropolitan Convention and Visitors Bureau
1520 Sugar Bowl Dr.
New Orleans, LA 70112
504-566-5011; fax: 504-566-5046

SOURCES:
AnnivHol-1983, p. 73
BkFest-1937, p. 123
BkHolWrld-1986, May 11
Chases-1996, p. 235
DaysCustFaith-1957, p. 130
DictMyth-1962, vol. II, p. 881
DictWrldRel-1989, p. 383

◆ 0942 ◆ Jodlerfests (Yodeling Festivals)
Summer (end of May through September)

Regional festivals of the art of yodeling are held in the summer months throughout the northern German region of Switzerland. Every two years a national Jodlerfest is held. In 1991, it was in Engelberg and brought together not only yodelers from all over the country but also about 150 players of the Alphorn, a 10- to 15-foot wooden horn with a haunting sound.

The regular annual festivals are held outdoors and feature yodeling clubs, and sometimes solists, who usually yodel without musical accompaniment. The themes of the songs are related to the mountains, the cows and the herdsman's life and loves.

Technically, yodeling is a type of singing in which high falsetto and low chest notes alternate. It is supposed to have originated in Switzerland as a way for Alpine cowherds to call from meadow to meadow or to urge on their cows. However, yodeling is also found in other mountain areas in China and North and South America, and among the Aboriginal people of Australia as well as various ethnic groups in Africa which Westerners have referred to as Pygmies.

CONTACT:
Swiss National Tourist Office
608 Fifth Ave.
New York, NY 10020
212-757-5944; fax: 212-262-6116

◆ 0943 ◆ Johnny Appleseed, Birthday of
September 26

John Chapman—better known as Johnny Appleseed for his lifelong dedication to planting apple seedlings all over the American Midwest—was born on this day in 1774. While some frontier settlers thought he was a saint, or at the very least a religious fanatic, with his tin pot hat and coffee-sack tunic, the Indians regarded him as a great medicine man since he planted herbs as well as apples.

Since 1962 Johnny Appleseed's birthday has been observed in his hometown of Leominster, Massachusetts, on the first Saturday in June as **Johnny Appleseed Civic Day**. There is usually a ceremony at the monument that marks the site of Chapman's birthplace. In 1966 the day was celebrated with a ceremony marking the issue of a commemorative stamp bearing an image of the pioneer horticulturalist. His birthday is also honored in Ashland, Ohio, where he lived for more than 25 years, and at harvest festivals in apple-growing regions throughout the United States. In fact, the last week in September has been observed as Johnny Appleseed Week in Ohio since 1941.

See also JOHNNY APPLESEED FESTIVAL

CONTACT:
Massachusetts Office of Travel
    and Tourism
100 Cambridge St., 13th Floor
Boston, MA 02202
800-447-6277 or 617-727-3201
fax: 617-727-6525

SOURCES:
AmerBkDays-1978, p. 868
BkHolWrld-1986, Sep 26
Chases-1996, p. 391
DictFolkMyth-1984, p. 555

♦ 0944 ♦ **Johnny Appleseed Festival**
Third weekend in September

A legend in his own time, John Chapman—better known as "Johnny Appleseed"—was born in Leominster, Massachusetts, on September 26, 1774. Although facts about his early life are hard to come by, there is a story that he fell in love with a woman named Dorothy Durand and that the families of the two lovers were bitter enemies. When Dorothy's family moved West, Johnny followed. But she died of a broken heart before he found her, the legend says, and many years later he returned to place apple blossoms on her grave.

Chapman knew that there was money to be made in the apple nursery business. By the 1790s he was planting apple trees in western Pennsylvania, and by the turn of the century, he'd moved on to Ohio. He had an uncanny knack for selecting the most advantageous spot near a new settlement, begging or leasing a plot of land to plant his trees, and then selling the saplings to frontier farmers. Ironically, his trees and apples were never of the best quality, because he refused to improve his stock by grafting superior branches onto his seedlings. One settler in Fort Wayne, Indiana, where Chapman arrived in 1834, complained that his apples were "so sour they would make a pig squeal." It was supposedly in Fort Wayne that he died in 1845, although no one is certain exactly where he is buried.

Chapman has been commemorated in Fort Wayne since 1974 with a two-day fall festival held at Johnny Appleseed Park. The festival includes traditional music and entertainment, demonstrations of pioneer arts and crafts, visits to the alleged gravesite, and discussions with "The Living Lincoln," who talks with visitors about the social issues of the period in history he shared with Johnny Appleseed.

CONTACT:
Fort Wayne/Allen County Convention and Visitors Bureau
1021 S. Calhoun St.
Fort Wayne, IN 46802
800-767-7752 or 219-424-3700
fax: 219-424-3914

♦ 0945 ♦ **Jonquil Festival**
Third weekend in March

A three-day (Friday through Sunday) festival to enjoy about 10,000 jonquils in Old Washington Historic State Park in the town of Washington, Ark. The first of these jonquils and daffodils were planted by pioneer families who came here along the Southwest Trail that ran from Missouri to Texas. Washington was the home of the state government after Union troops took Little Rock, Ark., during the Civil War. It is also where James Black, a blacksmith, forged the original Bowie knife for James Bowie in the 1830s.

This festival focuses on the history of Washington; the Pioneer Washington Restoration Foundation, established in 1958, has restored buildings that recreate the period of the early 1800s. Tours are given of these historic buildings. Other events are folk-music concerts, food vendors selling funnel cakes (round, greasy, flat cakes made by pouring dough through a funnel onto a grid and sprinkled with powdered sugar) as well as hot dogs and lemonade, an arts and crafts show, blacksmithing, and a special worship service on Sunday morning. The festival attracts about 60,000 visitors.

CONTACT:
Arkansas Dept. of Parks and Tourism
1 Capitol Mall
Little Rock, AR 72201
800-628-8725 or 501-682-7777
fax: 501-682-1364

Jordan, Feast of
See **Epiphany**

♦ 0946 ♦ **Jordan Independence Day**
May 25

A treaty signed on this day in 1946 established the constitutional monarchy of the Hashemite Kingdom of Jordan and independence from Great Britain.

Parades through the capital city of Amman mark the celebrations of this national holiday.

CONTACT:
Jordan Information Bureau
2319 Wyoming Ave., N.W.
Washington, D.C. 20008
202-265-1606; fax: 202-667-0777

SOURCES:
AnnivHol-1983, p. 71
Chases-1996, p. 228
NatlHolWrld-1968, p. 69

♦ 0947 ♦ **Jordbruksdagarna**
Last full weekend in September

The town of Bishop Hill, Illinois, was founded in 1846 by a group of Swedes fleeing religious persecution in the Old World. Their leader, Erik Jansson, sailed across the Atlantic with 1,200 followers, crossed the Great Lakes on steamers, and walked 150 miles to form the colony named with the English translation of Jansson's birthplace in Sweden. Cholera took its toll on the settlers, but their biggest setback was Jansson's murder in 1850. Without his leadership, the colony entered a period of rapid decline and, since it was bypassed by the main railroad line, time stood still there for about a century. As a result, many of the historic buildings remained undisturbed, and in 1984 Bishop Hill was designated a National Historic Landmark.

Many of the descendants of the original colonists still live in Bishop Hill or nearby towns, and they continue to celebrate a number of traditional Swedish holidays. One of these is Jordbruksdagarna, or **Agricultural Days**, a two-day celebration featuring harvest demonstrations, 19th-century crafts and children's games, and ample servings of Colony Stew. The residents of Bishop Hill also celebrate Lucia Nights (*see* ST. LUCY'S DAY), when young women dressed as "Lucias" serve refreshments in the shops and museums.

CONTACT:
Bishop Hill Arts Council
P.O. Box 47
Bishop Hill, IL 61419
309-927-3899

Jour des Rois, Le
See **Epiphany**

♦ 0948 ♦ **Jousting the Bear**
March 10

Although jousting normally involves two knights charging

213

each other on horseback with lances, the custom has been changed somewhat in Pistoia, Italy, where **La Giostra dell' Orso** is held in March each year. Twelve horsemen representing the town's four districts join in a procession to the Cathedral Square, each accompanied by a group of costumed attendants. They compete against each other in pairs, racing at a gallop toward the effigies of two bears holding targets in their outstretched paws. Points are won by hitting the targets, and the most successful knight is proclaimed Knight of the Golden Spur of Pistoia.

CONTACT:
Italian Government Travel Office
630 Fifth Ave.
New York, NY 10111
212-245-4822

♦ 0949 ♦ Jousting Tournament
Third Saturday in June and second Sunday in October

A tournament for "knights" on horseback sponsored by the National Jousting Hall of Fame and held since 1823 in Mount Solon, Va. It's reputed to be America's oldest continuous sporting event. The tourney, recalling the knights of old, is held at the Natural Chimneys Regional Park, where rock formations resemble castle towers.

Jousting contestants gallop full-tilt down an 80-yard course as they try to spear and pluck with their lances three steel rings from crossbars; this exercise is called "running at the ring." The rings are as small as ¼" in diameter. Jousting has been practiced in the United States since the 17th century. Tournaments are also held in Maryland, South Carolina, Virginia, and West Virginia, but the Virginia spectacle is the oldest and the most prestigious. Accompanied by parties, these are high social points of the year. About 150 jousters run at the rings at the Mount Solon tournaments.

CONTACT:
National Jousting Association
c/o Sandy Izer
P.O. Box 14
Mount Solon, VA 22843
301-223-9468

SOURCES:
AmerBkDays-1978, p. 756
Chases-1996, p. 258

♦ 0950 ♦ Joust of the Quintain
Second weekend in September

In the 17th century a tournament known as the Joust of the Quintain was held in Foligno, Italy, to commemorate both the equestrian exercises of the early Roman legionnaires and the Joust of the Ring that was popular throughout Europe during the Middle Ages. The tournament was revived in 1946, adhering as closely as possible to the original rules. The celebration begins on the evening of the second Saturday in September, when the townspeople gather to hear the First Magistrate announce the event. Early Sunday morning there is a parade of people in Renaissance dress, accompanied by musicians and dancers. Ten "knights" representing the city's 10 districts compete on horseback in the actual tournament, which involves galloping past the statue of Mars and trying to remove the ring in its outstretched hand by spearing it with the tip of a lance. The winner receives an ornamental cloak, and a torchlight parade concludes the day's events.

CONTACT:
Italian Government Travel Office
630 Fifth Ave.
New York, NY 10111
212-245-4822

SOURCES:
Chases-1996, p. 369
IntlThFolk-1979, p. 243

♦ 0951 ♦ Juhannus (Midsummer Day)
Saturday nearest June 24

A celebration in Finland of the Summer Solstice and of the feast of St. John. Like a medieval holiday, people celebrate at the lake shores where they build bonfires and dance all night. Since this is near the longest day of the year, special late performances are held at open-air theaters in many towns. There are also dances at hotels.

Many customs are remnants of pagan times. In earlier times, the bonfire was supposed to reveal the future. Birch-tree branches are brought into the homes to insure future happiness. Even buses and office buildings are adorned with birch branches. On the Aland Islands, tall poles are decorated with flowers and leaves, and supper tables are decorated with birch and garlands of flowers. The church made the festival St. John's Day, but the celebration has more pagan overtones than Christian.

See also Midsummer Day; St. John's Day

CONTACT:
Finnish Tourist Board
655 Third Ave., 18th Floor
New York, NY 10017
212-949-2333; fax: 212-983-5260

SOURCES:
AnnivHol-1983, p. 96
FolkWrldHol-1992, p. 335

♦ 0952 ♦ June Festival, International
May–June

Originally called the Zurich May Festival, this international music, dance, and theater festival in Switzerland was founded in 1909 by Alfred Reucker, director at the time of the Zurich Opera House, because the opera season usually ended in April, and singers and actors needed more work. It was patterned after the Bayreuth Festival, with the primary emphasis on opera, but since that time it has expanded to include orchestral and chamber music, vocal and instrumental recitals, ballet, and art exhibits. Recent performers at the festival have included the Royal Shakespeare Company, Tokyo's Red Buddha Theatre, the Netherlands Dance Theatre, Belgium's Ballet of the 20th Century, and the Abafumi Company of Uganda. Exhibits in city museums are set up to coincide with the festival, and there are master classes for young musicians.

CONTACT:
Swiss National Tourist Office
608 Fifth Ave.
New York, NY 10020
212-757-5944; fax: 212-262-6116

SOURCES:
GdWrldFest-1985, p. 172
IntlThFolk-1979, p. 356

♦ 0953 ♦ Juneteenth
June 19

Although President Abraham Lincoln signed the Emancipation Proclamation on January 1, 1863, it wasn't until two years later that the word reached the slaves in Texas. General Gordon Granger arrived in Galveston on June 19, 1865, with the intention of forcing the slave owners there to release their slaves, and the day has been celebrated since that time in eastern Texas, Louisiana, southwestern Arkansas, Oklahoma and other parts of the Deep South under the nickname "Juneteenth."

Observed primarily in African-American communities, Juneteenth festivities usually include parades, picnics, and baseball games. Although Juneteenth observances can be found as far west as California, many blacks who originally came from east Texas and surrounding areas choose to return home on the weekend nearest the 19th of June.

See also EMANCIPATION DAY

SOURCES:
AnnivHol-1983, p. 81
BkHolWrld-1986, Jun 19
Chases-1996, p. 262
DictDays-1988, p. 36
FolkAmerHol-1991, p. 243

♦ 0954 ♦ **Junkanoo Festival**
December 26; January 1

The **Junkanoo Parade and Festival**, held in Nassau's native quarter combines elements of MARDI GRAS, mummer's parades, and ancient African tribal rituals. It is held on December 26, BOXING DAY, and January 1, NEW YEAR'S DAY. Masqueraded marchers wearing colorful headpieces and costumes that have taken months to prepare dance to the beat of an Afro-Bahamian rhythm called Goombay, which refers to all Bahamian secular music. The music is played by a variety of unusual native instruments, including goat skin drums, lignum vitae sticks, pebble-filled "shak-shaks," and steel drums. The name comes from a number of sources. Historically, it referred to the drumbeats and rhythms of Africa, which were brought to the Bahamas by slaves. The term was used during jump-in dances, when the drummer would shout "Gimbey!" at the beginning of each dance. The Ibo tribes in West Africa have a drum they call Gamby, from which the name goombay probably derived. The Junkanoo parade, which begins at four o'clock in the morning and continues until sunrise, is followed by the judging of costumes and awarding of prizes. There are Junkanoo parades in Freeport and the Family of Out Islands as well.

In Belize and parts of Guatemala the Junkanoo masqueraders dance from house to house. Their wire-screen masks are painted white or pink, have staring eyes, red lips, black eyebrows, and thin moustaches for men; they are accompanied by two drums and a women's chorus.

In Jamaica, Junkanoo is featured also at political rallies and Independence Day celebrations. There are "root" and "fancy dress" troupes, the latter being more sedate. Their procession contains Courtiers; a King and Queen preceded by a Flower Girl; Sailor Boy who uses a whip to keep the audience in line; Babu, an East Indian cowboy with a long cattle prod; and Pitchy Patchy, the latter three being more boisterous than the courtiers. The "root" Junkanoo parade features Amerindians and Warriors, the former dancing with a throbbing rhythm and more body movement; Whore Girl who raises skirts or Belly Woman who shakes her belly in time with the music; and Cowhead and other animal characters who butt the crowd to keep it in line. "Root" Junkanoo is usually found in remote villages far from large towns or cities.

There are a number of theories as to where the name "Junkanoo" came from. One is that the festival was started

by a West African named Jananin Canno, or from a folkloric figure known in the West Indies, John or Johnny Canoe. Another is that it comes from the French expression *gens inconnus,* or 'unknown people,' which would seem to refer to the masked dancers.

SOURCES:
Chases-1996, p. 489
DictFolkMyth-1984, p. 554
FolkWrldHol-1992, p. 639
GdWrldFest-1985, p. 16

♦ 0955 ♦ **Juno Caprotina, Festival of**
July 7

Juno was the ancient Roman goddess of women and marriage, identified with the Greek goddess Hera. As the highest deity in the Roman pantheon next to Jupiter, her brother and husband, she ruled all aspects of women's lives, including sexuality and childbirth, and served as a kind of guardian angel for women. Along with Jupiter and Minerva, she shared a temple on the Capitoline Hill in Rome; together they were known as the Capitoline Triad. This temple contained Juno's sacred geese, whose cackling, according to Plutarch, saved Rome from the Gauls in 390 B.C.

The two most important festivals in honor of Juno were the Juno Caprotina (or **Nonae Caprotinae**) and the MATRONALIA. The former was held under a wild fig tree in the Campus Martius, or Field of Mars, a floodplain of the Tiber River. The kalends or first day of every month were sacred to Juno, and she was also associated with the ancient ceremony of announcing at the new moon the date of the nones (*see* IDES).

The month of June, named after the goddess Juno, is still considered the most popular month for getting married.

SOURCES:
AmerBkDays-1978, p. 608
OxClassDict-1970, p. 569

♦ 0956 ♦ **Juturnalia**
January 11

According to Virgil, Juturna is the sister of Turnus, king of the Rutuli. In return for her virginity, Jupiter gave her immortality. Afterwards she was turned into a fountain of the same name near the Numicus, the river where Aeneas' dead body was found. The waters from this fountain were used in sacrifices, particularly those in honor of the Roman goddess Vesta, and were believed to have curative powers. On January 11, a festival in honor of Juturna was observed by men working on aqueducts and wells. She was also celebrated at the VULCANALIA on August 23 as a protectress against fire.

SOURCES:
ClassDict-1984, p. 312
DictFolkMyth-1984, p. 564

♦ 0957 ♦ **Juul, Feast of**
December 21 or 22

The Feast of Juul was a pre-Christian festival observed in Scandinavia at the time of the WINTER SOLSTICE. Fires were lit to symbolize the heat, light, and life-giving properties of the returning sun. A YULE (or Juul) log was brought in with great ceremony and burned on the hearth in honor of the Scandinavian god, Thor. A piece of the log was kept as both a token of good luck and as kindling for the following year's log. In England and in many parts of Germany, France, and other European countries, the Yule log was burned until nothing but ash remained; then the ashes were collected and either strewn on the fields as fertilizer every night until TWELFTH NIGHT or kept as a charm and useful medicine. French peasants believed that if the ashes were kept under the bed, they would protect the house against thunder and lightning, as well as prevent chilblains on the heels during the winter.

The present-day custom of lighting a Yule log at CHRISTMAS is believed to have originated in the bonfires associated with the Feast of Juul.

SOURCES:
DaysCustFaith-1957, p. 352
RoundYr-1950, p. 196
StoryWrldHol-1924, p. 312

◆ 0958 ◆ Juvenalia
Three days in June

During the Juvenalia festival each year in Cracow, Poland, the students of Jagiellonian University take over the city for three days. After the mayor hands over the keys to the city, they dress up in costumes and masks and parade through the streets making fun of anything they choose. This celebration goes back to a medieval tradition, when new students at the university had to pay a tax to older ones as part of their ritual entry into college life—much like the "hazing" that goes on in fraternities and sororities at American colleges.

CONTACT:
Polish National Tourist Office
275 Madison Ave., Ste. 1711
New York, NY 10016
212-338-9412; fax: 212-338-9283

SOURCES:
BkHolWrld-1986, Jun 4

◆ 0959 ◆ JVC Jazz Festival
Mid-August

Known for many years as the **Newport Jazz Festival**, this event was moved to New York in 1972 and later returned to Newport, Rhode Island, as the JVC Jazz Festival. One of the most important jazz festivals in the world, it features legendary jazz performers as well as up-and-coming new stars and some of the most outstanding big bands, jazz combos, and instrumental and vocal soloists in the country. Dizzy Gillespie, Woody Herman, Ella Fitzgerald, Miles Davis, and Sarah Vaughan have performed there, as have Wynton Marsalis and Spyro Gyra. The first evening's event is usually held at the Newport Casino in the International Tennis Hall of Fame. Subsequent concerts during the three-day festival are held outdoors in Fort Adams State Park, where visitors are encouraged to picnic and relax on the lawn as they listen.

CONTACT:
Rhode Island Tourism Division
7 Jackson Walkway
Providence, RI 02903
800-556-2484 or 401-277-2601
fax: 401-277-2102

SOURCES:
MusFestAmer-1990, p. 200

◆ 0960 ◆ Jyestha Ashtami
May–June; eighth day of waxing half of Hindu month of Jyestha

This Hindu festival is celebrated by the people of Khir Bhawani in Kashmir in honor of their patron goddess, also named Khir Bhawani. People from the adjoining hill areas assemble at the shrine, offer prayers and worship at the foot of the goddess, and sing hymns and songs in her praise. *Khir* (rice boiled in milk) is prepared on this day as a food offering. The marble shrine to Bhawani, located about 25 kilometers from Srinagar, India, overlooks a pool formed by spring waters known for their changing colors. Hundreds of Kashmiri Hindus visit the shrine daily.

SOURCES:
RelHolCal-1993, p. 87

◆ 0961 ◆ Jyvaskyla Arts Festival
June–July

This 10-day cultural festival in Finland was started in 1955 by three well-known figures in the music world: Professor Timo Makinen, composer Seppo Nummi, and Professor Paivo Oksala. It has now expanded beyond musical events to include film, theater, art exhibits, and seminars designed to promote understanding among different national and ethnic traditions. The festival includes a summer Academy of Chamber Music and performances by world-renowned chamber music groups such as the Bartok Quartet and the London Early Music Group. Organized around a different theme each year, festival events are held throughout the city in local churches, museums, theaters, and parks.

CONTACT:
Finnish Tourist Board
655 Third Ave.
New York, NY 10017
212-949-2333

SOURCES:
Chases-1996, p. 252
GdWrldFest-1985, p. 76
IntlThFolk-1979, p. 95

K

Kadooment
See **Crop Over**

♦ 0962 ♦ **Kalakshetra Arts Festival**
December–January

The Kalakshetra Foundation in Tiruvanmiyur, Madras, is one of India's most outstanding cultural institutions. It was founded in 1936 and directed for many years by Rukmini Devi Arundale, an Indian woman who married an Englishman and devoted herself to the rejuvenation of Indian dance, music, sculpture, and crafts. Rukmini Devi is also known for choreographing 25 dance-dramas, a traditional Indian art form.

The Kalakshetra Arts Festival, which has been held annually for eight days in December–January since 1951, takes place at the Foundation's College of Fine Arts, a school that specializes in teaching the *Bharatanatyam* and other traditional styles of Indian dance. There are folk dance performances, vocal and instrumental recitals, and of course the famous dance-dramas choreographed by Rukmini Devi and based on themes from *puranas*, or Hindu epics.

CONTACT:
India Tourist Office
30 Rockefeller Ave.
15 N. Mezzanine
New York, NY 10112
212-586-4901; fax: 212-582-3274

SOURCES:
IntlThFolk-1979, p. 215

♦ 0963 ♦ **Kalevala Day**
February 28

The *Kalevala* is Finland's national epic poem, researched and transcribed by Dr. Elias Lönnrot. In the 19th century, Lönnrot and his assistants traveled throughout the country, asking people to tell them whatever they could remember about the folklore surrounding Kalevala, the "Land of Heroes." On February 28, 1835, after years of research, Lönnrot signed the preface to the first edition of the poem. Its more than 20,000 verses brought to life the adventures of such characters as the warrior Lemminkäinen and the blacksmith Ilmarinen, who played a part in the creation of the world when he forged the "lids of heaven." This event marked a turning point in Finnish literature; up to this point, little had been written in the Finnish language. Lönnrot is honored with parades and concerts on this day.

CONTACT:
Finnish Tourist Board
655 Third Ave.
New York, NY 10017
212-949-2333

SOURCES:
AnnivHol-1983, p. 29
BkFest-1937, p. 111
BkHolWrld-1986, Feb 28

♦ 0964 ♦ **Kallemooi**
Between May 10 and June 13; Saturday before Pentecost

Observed in the North Coast Islands of the Netherlands, the custom known as Kallemooi represents the fishermen's welcome to spring. A tall pole with a transverse arm near the top is erected in the center of the village. A live cock—usually one that has been "borrowed" from a nearby farm—is suspended in a basket from the apex of the crosspiece. An empty bottle is hung from either arm of the structure, which is decorated at the top with the Dutch flag, a green branch, and a placard bearing the word "Kallemooi." For three days and three nights before PENTECOST, or Whitsunday, people feast, make merry, and play Whitsun games. After the fun is over, the rooster is released and returned to its owner.

There has been much speculation about the origin of the word Kallemooi. Some say it can be translated as "calling the May," while others claim it is derived from the word *kalemei*, meaning a "tree without branches" or a bare tree. During the festival, a special drink known as "Kallemooi bitters" is served by all the local inns.

CONTACT:
Netherlands Board of Tourism
355 Lexington Ave., 21st Floor
New York, NY 10017
212-370-7360; fax: 212-370-9507

SOURCES:
FestWestEur-1958, p. 134

♦ 0965 ♦ **Kamakura Matsuri (Snow Hut Festival)**
February 15–17

Held in northern Japan in the Akita Prefecture, at the time of year when there is usually deep snow on the ground. The original purpose of the festival was to offer prayers for a good rice crop to Suijin-sama, the water god.

In Yokote and other towns of the region, children build *Kamakura*, snow houses about six feet in diameter resembling Eskimo igloos. They furnish the huts with tatami mats and a wooden altar dedicated to Suijin-sama and have parties in them, while families gather to drink sweet sake and eat rice cakes and fruits. The rice cakes are made in the shape of cranes and turtles, traditional symbols of longevity, and of dogs called *inukko*, thought to guard against devils.

A similar Kamakura Festival is held in Tokamachi in Niigata Prefecture on Jan. 14.

CONTACT:
Japan National Tourist
  Organization
630 Fifth Ave., Ste. 2101
New York, NY 10111
212-757-5640; fax: 212-307-6754

SOURCES:
BkHolWrld-1986, Feb 15
FolkWrldHol-1992, p. 136

Kamehameha Day
See **King Kamehameha Day**

◆ 0966 ◆ Kan-Ben
August–September; waning half of Cambodian month of Photrobot

The 15-day period known as **Prachum-Ben** in Cambodia is dedicated to rituals for the dead. It occurs during the rainy season when skies are usually overcast, and the darkness seems an appropriate time for Yama, the Hindu God of the Underworld, to let the souls of the dead visit their families. The traditional offering to the dead consists of *ben*—special cakes made of glutinous rice mixed with coconut milk and other ingredients—arranged on a platter around a centerpiece and placed on a pedestal. Sometimes the rice is formed into a cone called *bay bettbor*, with flags, flowers, and joss sticks used to decorate the top. During this time a monk says prayers at the tombs of the dead.

SOURCES:
FolkWrldHol-1992, p. 426

Karnea
See **Carnea**

◆ 0967 ◆ Karneval in Cologne
November 11 until Ash Wednesday

Pre-Lenten activities are especially festive in Cologne, Germany. The celebration begins officially on the 11th day of the 11th month at 11:11 P.M., when CARNIVAL societies throughout Germany begin their public activities with singers submitting their latest songs and speakers telling funny tales. The date was originally the end of a fasting period ordered by the church.

During the period from early January until the beginning of LENT, the festival calendar is filled with 300 costume balls, performances of original songs and humorous speeches, and numerous smaller affairs sponsored by such special interest groups as skittle clubs and a rabbit breeders' association. The humorous talks began in 1829, and today audiences clap hands in a slow rhythm to show their approval and whistle to express their disapproval.

These events lead up to the final "crazy days" (Tolle Tage) just before ASH WEDNESDAY. During this time, the Lord Mayor of Cologne receives the Triumvirate of Carnival—Prince Carnival, the Cologne Virgin (who, according to tradition, is played by a man), and the Cologne Peasant. The prince represents the prince of joy, the peasant the valor of the men of the town, and the virgin the purity of the city of Cologne, whose city walls the enemy never breached. The prince gets the keys to the city and rules the city until Carnival ends. On *Weiberfastnacht*, or 'Women's Carnival,' the Thursday before Ash Wednesday, women take control and cut off the ties of any men within reach. This is revenge—women were excluded from Karneval in the 19th century. On Sunday, there are school and suburban parades. ROSE MONDAY is the day of Carnival's mammoth parade with decorated floats, giant figures, and bands. Police from surrounding districts are on duty and join the crowds in singing and dancing. On SHROVE TUESDAY, there are more parades, and crowds cheer the prince and his attendants. That evening, the Carnival season ends with a ball in Gürzenich Hall, the city's 15th-century festival hall. The prince returns the keys of the city, and normalcy is back. On Ash Wednesday, people traditionally eat a fish dinner, and so the restraint of Lent begins.

See also FASCHING

CONTACT:
German National Tourist Office
122 E. 42nd St., 52nd Floor
New York, NY 10168
212-661-7200; fax: 212-661-7174

SOURCES:
AmerBkDays-1978, p. 43

◆ 0968 ◆ Kartika Purnima
October–November; full moon day of Hindu month of Kartika

Hindus celebrate Kartika Purnima in honor of the day when God incarnated himself as the Matsya Avatar in fish form. According to Hindu mythology, the purpose of this incarnation was to save Vavaswata, the seventh Manu and progenitor of the human race, from destruction by a deluge. Good deeds done on this day are believed to earn high religious merit. Bathing in the Ganges or in other holy water is considered to be of special religious significance. Hindus spend the day fasting, meditating, and performing charitable acts.

It is also believed the Shankara killed the demon Tripurasura on this day, for which he is also called the Tripurari. Shiva is worshipped on this occasion, and giving a bull (Shiva's mount) as a gift to a Brahman is considered to be an appropriate and significant act. For this reason, it is common to hold cattle fairs on this day.

SOURCES:
RelHolCal-1993, p. 87

◆ 0969 ◆ Kartika Snan
October–November; Hindu month of Kartika

The Hindu months of Vaisakha (April–May), Kartika (October–November), and Magha (January–February) are regarded as especially sacred and therefore the most suitable for acts of piety. Throughout the month of Kartika, Hindus bathe in a sacred river, stream, pond, or well early in the morning. On the sacred rivers, such as the Ganges and the Yamuna in India, a month-long bathing festival is held.

People set up tents on the riverbank for this purpose, have regular morning baths, eat only a single meal each day, and spend their time in prayer, meditation, and other acts of devotion.

Hindu women in villages and towns get up early in the morning and visit the sacred streams in groups, singing hymns. After their baths, they visit the nearby temples. They also fast and hang lamps in small baskets around their houses or on the tops of the bamboo along the river. These lamps are kept burning throughout the month. The women also worship the Tulsi plant, which is considered sacred and is cultivated in homes and temples. When Tulsi leaves are put into any water, it becomes as holy as water from the Ganges. Tulsi leaves offered to Vishnu during the month of Kartika are said to please him more than the gift of a thousand cows.

CONTACT:
India Tourist Office
30 Rockefeller Ave.
15 N. Mezzanine
New York, NY 10112
212-586-4901; fax: 212-582-3274

SOURCES:
RelHolCal-1993, p. 88

♦ 0970 ♦ **Kartini Day**
April 21

An Indonesian holiday commemorating the birth in 1879 of Raden Ajeng Kartini, one of the country's national heroes and a pioneer in the emancipation of Indonesian women. Throughout Indonesia women wear their national dress to symbolize their unity and the nation enjoys parades, lectures, and various school activities.

Lady Kartini, the daughter of a Javanese nobleman who worked for the Dutch colonial administration, was exposed to Western ideas when she attended a Dutch school. When she had to withdraw from school because she was of noble birth, she corresponded with Dutch friends telling of her concern both for the plight of Indonesians under colonial rule and for the restricted lives of Indonesian women. She married in 1903 and began a fight for the right of women to be educated and against the unwritten but all-pervading Javanese law, *Adat*. She died in 1904 at the age of 25, after the birth of her first child. Her letters were published in 1911 under the title, *Door duisternis tot licht* ('Through Darkness into Light'), and created support for the Kartini Foundation, which opened the first girls' school in Java in 1916.

CONTACT:
Indonesian Tourist Promotion Office
3457 Wilshire Blvd., Ste. 104
Los Angeles, CA 90010
213-387-2078; fax: 213-380-4876

SOURCES:
BkHolWrld-1986, Apr 21
Chases-1996, p. 180

♦ 0971 ♦ **Karwachoth**
October–November; fourth day of waning half of Hindu month of Kartika

Observed by married women in Hindu families, the Karwachoth festival is a day-long fast in honor of the Hindu god Shiva and goddess Parvati, whom they hope will bring prosperity and long life to their husbands. It is also a time for mothers to bless their married daughters and present them with gifts. Virgins and widows are not allowed to participate in the celebrations, which begin at dawn when the women bathe

and put on new clothes. The day is devoted to worshipping Shiva and Parvati, and the fast is broken at night when the moon rises.

See also VATA SAVITRI

SOURCES:
FolkWrldHol-1992, p. 533
RelHolCal-1993, p. 88

♦ 0972 ♦ **Kasone Festival of Watering the Banyan Tree**
Mid-April to May; full moon day of Burmese month of Kasone

The most important of the 12 Burmese festivals of the months, **Kasone Full Moon Day**—sometimes known as **Buddha Day**—celebrates the birth and the enlightenment of the Buddha at the foot of the banyan tree. Buddhists gather at monasteries and precept halls to practice meditation, to make charitable donations, and to observe the precepts of Buddhism. Another ritual associated with this day is the pouring of water, both individually and collectively, to celebrate the preservation of the banyan tree. Because Kasone is a hot, dry month, fish are often transferred from streams, ponds, and tanks to places where there is more water.

CONTACT:
Myanmar Embassy
2300 "S" St., N.W.
Washington, D.C. 20008
202-332-9044; fax: 202-332-9046

SOURCES:
AnnivHol-1983, p. 183
FolkWrldHol-1992, p. 141

♦ 0973 ♦ **Kataklysmos, Feast of (Festival of the Flood)**
Between May 10 and June 13; coincides with Christian Pentecost

A religious and popular festival celebrated only on Cyprus, with its roots in both the Bible and Greek mythology. The Greek word *kataklysmos*, meaning 'flood,' refers to the Bible's story in the book of Genesis, and a Greek creation story.

In Genesis 6:5-9:1, God decided all humankind was corrupt and that he would bring a flood to destroy all life—except for Noah, his wife, their sons and their sons' wives, and male and female specimens of every beast and fowl. Noah built an ark for this menagerie, and they all lived on it while it rained for 40 days and 40 nights, eventually landing, it is thought, on Mt. Ararat. (*See also* ASHURA.) When the flood ended, God told Noah and his family to be fruitful and replenish the earth.

In the Greek story, Zeus decided to destroy the earth because of human wickedness. Floods covered the earth, leaving only a spot of dry land on top of Mt. Parnassus. After it had rained nine days and nine nights, a great wooden chest drifted to the spot. Within it were Deucalion, the son of Prometheus, and his wife Pyrrha. Prometheus, knowing the flood was coming, had told his son to build the chest and embark in it.

Coming down from the mountain into a dead world, Deucalion and Pyrrha heard a voice telling them to "cast behind you the bones of your mother." They realized the earth was the mother, and stones her bones. They began to throw the stones, and the stones took human shape. They were called Stone People, and rescued the earth from desolation.

Biblical scholars have suggested that the flood described in Genesis is based on the one from ancient Mesopotamian literature, especially in the Gilgamesh Epic, whose hero is called Ut-Napishtim. In this story, the gods bring on the flood because mankind is so noisy they cannot sleep. After the flood, Ut-Napishtim is made a god.

The Kataklysmos festivities, held in seaside towns, usually last from Saturday through Monday. They include games, folk dancing, boat races, swimming competitions, feasting, and the singing of *tchattista*, improvised verses sung in competition. The most popular custom is throwing water at one another on Monday to symbolize the purification of both body and soul. Larnaca is especially known for its celebration of Kataklysmos, and other celebrations are held in Limassol, Paphos, Polis, Agia Napa, and Paralimni.

CONTACT:
Cyprus Tourism Organization
13 E. 40th St.
New York, NY 10016
212-683-5280; fax: 212-683-5282

SOURCES:
BkHolWrld-1986, Jun 8
FolkWrldHol-1992, p. 324
IntlThFolk-1979, p. 86

◆ 0974 ◆ Kataragama Festival
June–July; 10 days and nights prior to full moon day of Hindu month of Asadha

Kataragama is considered one of the 16 holiest pilgrimage sites in Sri Lanka and is venerated not only by Hindus but by Buddhists and even Muslims. There is a shrine there dedicated to Skanda, the Hindu god of war, and his consort Valli. Their union is commemorated by taking the god's yantra, or icon, from his temple to the temple dedicated to Valli at the opposite end of the town square. It is carried on the back of an elephant to the accompaniment of conch shells and the clamor of thousands of pilgrims, both Hindu and Buddhist, who gather in Kataragama to watch and to undergo penances. The climax of the festival is the fire-walking ceremony, where devotees walk across a bed of red-hot embers without burning their feet. Other pilgrims walk on shoes with interior spikes, pull carts with lines attached to hooks in their flesh, or dance until they are completely exhausted.

The festival, which is also known as the **Perahära**, concludes at the exact hour of the full moon with a water-cutting ceremony. The priest, along with Skanda's yantra, is lowered into the river. He draws a mandala in the riverbed with a sword and then bathes the god's image. After this symbolic exercise, the pilgrims plunge themselves into the sacred stream in the belief that it will wash away their sins.

CONTACT:
Sri Lankan Embassy
2148 Wyoming Ave., N.W.
Washington, D.C. 20008
202-483-4025; fax: 202-232-7181

SOURCES:
DictWrldRel-1989, p. 569
IntlThFolk-1979, p. 345
RelFestSriLank-1982, p. 302

◆ 0975 ◆ Kattestoet (Festival of the Cats)
Second Sunday in May

A peculiar celebration to commemorate an event involving cats, held in Ypres, Belgium. There are different stories about how the festival began. One story says that in 962, Baudoin III, count of Flanders, threw several live cats from his castle tower to show that he wasn't awed by cats. The animals had historically been worshipped as creatures related to witches, and Baudoin, a recent Christian convert, was demonstrating that he didn't believe in such pagan ideas.

Another story is that cats in great numbers were needed in the Middle Ages to battle mice and rats. The Cloth Hall, where yearly sales of cloth and garments were held, attracted mice, and cats were set free to devour the mice. But once the sales were over, the rodent problem disappeared and there was a cat problem. The solution seemed to be to hurl the live cats from the belfry.

In the celebration today, about 2,000 people, dressed as cats, witches, and giants, march in a parade to the tune of bagpipes. Floats depict the history of the town and of feline figures—Puss in Boots, the Egyptian cat-headed goddess Bast, and others. The climax of the celebration comes when a jester throws toy witches and stuffed cloth cats from the town belfry.

CONTACT:
Belgian Tourist Office
780 Third Ave.
New York, NY 10017
212-758-8130; fax: 212-355-7675

SOURCES:
BkHolWrld-1986, May 12
Chases-1996, p. 107
GdWrldFest-1985, p. 21

◆ 0976 ◆ Kaustinen Folk Music Festival
Third week in July

Scandinavia's largest international festival of folk music and dance, Finland's Kaustinen Folk Music Festival was founded in 1968 to preserve Finnish folk music, dance, and art. Only Finnish amateur groups participated in the beginning, but now the festival includes performances by groups from Japan, Greenland, Canada, the United States, and other foreign countries. There are scheduled performances in local banquet halls as well as impromptu sidewalk jam sessions and open air competitions among musicians and dancers. Special events include the Kaustinen Cavalcade, a display of local musicians' talents, and a grand folk music parade on the last day of the week-long festival.

CONTACT:
Finnish Tourist Board
655 Third Ave.
New York, NY 10017
212-949-2333

SOURCES:
Chases-1996, p. 295
GdWrldFest-1985, p. 77
IntlThFolk-1979, p. 95

◆ 0977 ◆ Keaw Yed Wakes Festival
Sunday of or following August 24

Keaw Yed means 'cow's head' in Lancastrian dialect, and *Wakes* refers to the annual feast held in Westhoughton, Lancashire, on the Sunday of or following St. Bartholomew's Day, August 24 (*see* BARTHOLOMEW FAIR). Dating back more than 400 years, the Wakes started out as a religious festival featuring a grand rushbearing procession in which a cart filled with new rushes, to replace those used in the church pews, moved through the town, ending up at the church where special services were held. After the sermon, the children were given "rush money" to spend at the fair. But over time, the rushbearing ceremony faded and the festival became primarily an opportunity for merrymaking. The foods traditionally served at the festival included pork pasties and frumenty (often called furmenty or furmety), a porridge made from boiled wheat seasoned with sugar, cinnamon, and raisins. Today it is more common to find pies made of chicken, beef, or pork—often with a small china doll baked inside—and brandy snaps, or paper-thin wafers rolled into small hollow cylinders and served with tea.

There have been several attempts to explain the association

of the cow's head with the Wakes. One story says that some of the town's wealthier citizens donated a cow to be publicly roasted and distributed to the poor. But rivalry between two factions in town led to a brawl, and the cow's head went to the victors, who were then referred to as "Keaw Yeds" by their rivals.

CONTACT:
British Tourist Authority
551 Fifth Ave., Ste. 702
New York, NY 10176
800-462-2748 or 212-986-2200
fax: 212-986-1188

SOURCES:
YrbookEngFest-1954, p. 114

♦ 0978 ♦ **Keiro-no-Hi (Respect-for-the-Aged Day)**
September 15

A national holiday in Japan set aside as a day to honor the elderly. At community centers entertainments are held and the guests are given small keepsakes and gifts of food—for example, rice cakes dyed red and white, the traditional Japanese colors of happiness.

SOURCES:
AnnivHol-1983, p. 119
Chases-1996, p. 377
FolkWrldHol-1992, p. 480

♦ 0979 ♦ **Keller Festival, Helen**
Last weekend in June

A three-day festival in Tuscumbia, Ala., to honor Helen Keller and her remarkable life. Born in Tuscumbia in 1880, she was left blind, deaf, and mute by illness at the age of 19 months. After Helen's parents appealed to Alexander Graham Bell for help in educating the child, 20-year-old Anne Mansfield Sullivan, partially blind and a graduate of the Perkins School for the Blind in Boston, arrived and taught the child by pressing objects and a manual alphabet into Helen's palm. Helen learned to read and write and later graduated cum laude from Radcliffe College. She became widely known for her writings, and toured the world to promote opportunities for other blind and deaf persons. Samuel L. Clemens (Mark Twain) was so moved by her spirit that he likened Miss Keller to JOAN OF ARC.

Festival events include art exhibits, stage shows, musical entertainment, sports tournaments, a parade, and historic tours. At Miss Keller's birthplace, Ivy Green, visitors can see the pump at which Helen learned her first word, "water." The house contains a library of Braille books, a Braille typewriter, and other mementos.

The Miracle Worker, the play by William Gibson about Helen Keller and Anne Sullivan, has been presented since 1962 on Friday and Saturday nights in late June and July on the grounds of Ivy Green. The play opened in New York in 1959, won the Pulitzer Prize in 1960, and was made into a movie in 1962.

CONTACT:
Alabama Bureau of Tourism and Travel
P.O. Box 4927
Montgomery, AL 36103
800-252-2263 or 334-242-4169
fax: 334-242-4554

SOURCES:
AmerBkDays-1978, p. 598
Chases-1996, p. 273

♦ 0980 ♦ **Kelly Clown Festival, Emmett**
Early May

Houston, Missouri, is the hometown of Emmett Kelly, who was the world's most famous clown. Kelly was born on December 9, 1898, in Sedan, Kansas, but his Irish father moved the family to a farm near Houston when he was six years old. Kelly developed an interest in cartooning, and by the time he left Houston to seek work in Kansas City at the age of 19, he had gained a reputation as an entertainer with his "chalk talk" act, which involved telling a story while sketching on paper with colored chalk. Best known for his role as "Weary Willie," a sad-faced tramp dressed in tattered clothes who was originally one of his cartoon characters, Kelly worked for a number of circuses and in 1952 made his motion picture debut in *The Greatest Show on Earth*. He died in Sarasota, Florida, on March 28, 1979—opening day for the Ringling Bros. and Barnum & Bailey Circus in New York.

Houston's Emmett Kelly Clown Festival is still relatively new (1988), and is timed to coincide with the opening of the circus season in May. Among the 700 or 800 clowns who participate in the two-day festival are Emmett Kelly's son (Emmett Kelly, Jr.) and grandson (Joseph Kelly), both of whom continue the "Weary Willie" tradition. In addition to the clown parade and performances of clown stunts and skits, there are a number of "chalk talk" storytelling events.

CONTACT:
Missouri Division of Tourism
P.O. Box 1055
Jefferson City, MO 65102
800-877-1234 or 314-751-4133
fax: 314-751-5160

♦ 0981 ♦ **Kent State Memorial Day**
May 4

When students at Kent State University in Ohio decided to hold a rally to protest the incursion of U.S. military forces into Cambodia during the Vietnam War, no one thought it would end in a national tragedy or that it would mark a turning point in public opinion about the war. But when the Ohio National Guard started firing indiscriminately at the crowd, four Kent State students were killed and nine were wounded—one of whom was paralyzed from the waist down. The next year, three students were convicted on rioting charges, but the eight guardsmen involved in the tragic incident were never tried. A lawsuit brought by the parents of the slain and wounded students ended in an out-of-court settlement.

A candlelight vigil takes place at the Kent State campus every year on May 4, the anniversary of the 1970 shootings. It begins at midnight on May 3, when a candlelight procession winds its way around the campus and stops in a parking lot near the university's Prentice Hall. There, for the next 12 hours, rotating teams of sentinels stand in the places where Allison Krause, Sandy Scheuer, Bill Schroeder, and Jeff Miller were killed. The vigil is coordinated by the May 4 Task Force, a group led by a Kent State graduate and dedicated to promoting campus awareness and preventing a repetition of the violence. Although the university refused to discuss the tragedy for 10 years after it occurred, nowadays it is commemorated openly—to the point where the May 4 Memorial is featured prominently in the college catalog and a course is offered on "May 4th and its Aftermath." There are four permanent scholarships named for the dead.

CONTACT:
Kent State University
Kent, OH 44242
216-672-2121

SOURCES:
AnnivHol-1983, p. 61
Chases-1996, p. 199

♦ 0982 ♦ Kentucky Derby
First Saturday in May

The greatest and most glamorous horse race in America, run since 1875 in Louisville, Ky. Also known as the **Run for the Roses** because of the garland of roses draped on the winning horse, it is a one-and-one-quarter-mile race for three-year-old thoroughbreds and is the first race in the Triple Crown; the others are the PREAKNESS and the BELMONT STAKES. The site of the race is hallowed Churchill Downs, the track known for its twin spires, built in 1895.

The race is usually run in slightly over two minutes, but in 1964, Northern Dancer was the first to win the Derby in two minutes flat. In 1973, the great Secretariat, fondly known as Big Red, won in 1:59 2/5. That remains the only time the Derby was raced in less than two minutes. Ridden by Ron Turcotte, Secretariat then went on to take the Triple Crown, exploding from the pack to win the Belmont by an unprecedented 31 lengths.

The Derby took its name from the English horse race that was started in 1780 by the twelfth Earl of Derby, and Kentuckians hoped to duplicate the social panache of the Epsom Derby (*see* DERBY DAY). They did, in a different way. The Derby became Louisville's major social occasion of the year; women to this day wear their most stylish hats to the racetrack, and there are numerous lavish Derby breakfasts and parties. Traditional food includes Kentucky ham and beaten biscuits. And, of course, the Derby wouldn't be the Derby without mint juleps, the bourbon-and-mint drink served in cold silver julep cups or in special iced commemorative glasses at the track. Parties are not confined to Louisville; throughout the country and the world, Derby parties are held to watch the race on television. Stephen Foster's "My Old Kentucky Home," the official state song, is played as the horses parade to the post, and spectators in Louisville and far away stand and sing and (sometimes) dab their eyes.

Attendance at Churchill Downs is usually 120,000 to 130,000 people—most of them watching what they can from the infield and a select few, often including royalty, from Millionaires Row high in the clubhouse.

Derby Day is the finale of the 10-day Kentucky Derby Festival—a series of events that include a sternwheel steamboat race on the Ohio River, a Pegasus parade, fireworks, concerts, and a coronation ball.

Landmark events of past Derbies:

The first win by a filly, Regret, was in 1915. She paid $7.30 to win. The only other filly to win was Genuine Risk in 1980; the pay-out was $28.60.

The first woman to ride the Derby was Diane Crump in 1970; fourteen years later, P. J. Cooksey was the second woman jockey.

In 1978, Steve Cauthen, an 18-year-old wunderkind known as The Kid, rode to the roses on Affirmed, the latest Triple Crown winner.

Incidental information: the two most winning jockeys have been Eddie Arcaro and Bill Hartack, who have each won five Derbies. Aristides was the name of the horse who won the first Derby.

CONTACT:
Churchill Downs
700 Central Ave.
Louisville, KY 40208
502-636-4400; fax: 505-636-4430

SOURCES:
AmerBkDays-1978, p. 414
AnnivHol-1983, p. 60
Chases-1996, p. 199
FolkAmerHol-1991, p. 205
GdUSFest-1984, p. 63

Kenya Independence Day
See **Jamhuri**

♦ 0983 ♦ Keretkun Festival
Late autumn

The Chukchi people of northeastern Siberia hold a two- or three-day celebration in late autumn known as the Keretkun Festival, in honor of the "owner" of all the sea animals on which they depend for their livelihood. The purpose of the festival is to symbolically return all the animals that had been killed during the hunting season to the sea, thus replenishing the resource that had been plundered. Objects used in the celebration include a special net made out of reindeer tendons, painted oars, statues of birds, and a small wooden image of Keretkun, which is burned at the end of the festival.

A similar festival is held by the Koryak people, another group that depends upon sea animals for survival. The **Seal Festival** is held at the end of the hunting season in November, and the participants plead with the animals they've killed to return to the sea and let themselves be caught again next year. The dead animals are represented by stylized likenesses made out of seaweed.

CONTACT:
Russian Travel Information Office
Rockefeller Center
610 Fifth Ave., Ste. 603
New York, NY 10020
212-757-3884; fax: 212-459-0031

SOURCES:
FolkWrldHol-1992, pp. 536, 540

♦ 0984 ♦ Keukenhof Flower Show
Late March–late May

The world's largest flower show takes place in Lisse, Holland, at the Keukenhof, a former 15th-century estate and hunting lodge that has been turned into a park dotted with lakes. As many as five or six million bulbs blossom here between late March and the end of May, either in hothouses or in the flowerbeds that border the ponds and fountains. There is a museum in Lisse devoted to the history and cultivation of bulbs, and young girls (*meisjes*) in 15th-century dress sell guidebooks to help acquaint visitors with the 800 varieties of tulips, hyacinths, and daffodils that fill the 70-acre park with color. Thousands of people flock to the gardens each spring, although some prefer to view the bulbs from the windows of the Leyden-Haarlem train.

CONTACT:
Netherlands Board of Tourism
355 Lexington Ave., 21st Floor
New York, NY 10017
212-370-7360; fax: 212-370-9507

SOURCES:
GdWrldFest-1985, p. 142

♦ 0985 ♦ **Kewpiesta**
Third weekend in April

The Kewpie doll, which was very popular in the 1920s and 1930s, was the creation of Rose O'Neill, a writer, artist, and sculptor from the Ozark region of Missouri. Modeled on her baby brother, the kewpie doll had a pointed tuft of hair at the top of the head. The annual four-day event known as Kewpiesta is held in Branson, about 10 miles south of O'Neill's homestead. Planned and sponsored by members of the National Rose O'Neill Club, the festival includes tours of O'Neill's birthplace, a Kewpie doll look-alike contest, and special displays in store windows. It is held in April, which is the month during which O'Neill died in 1944 as well as the start of the tourist season in the Ozarks.

CONTACT:
Missouri Division of Tourism
P.O. Box 1055
Jefferson City, MO 65102
800-877-1234 or 314-751-4133
fax: 314-751-5160

SOURCES:
GdUSFest-1984, p. 104

♦ 0986 ♦ **Khamis al-Amwat**
Between March 26 and April 29; Thursday after Easter

Also known as **Dead Remembrance Thursday**, the observation of this day by Muslims was instituted by Saladin the Magnificent (1137–1193) to offset the widespread celebration in Jordan of EASTER by the Christians and of PASSOVER by the Jews. It is a day to visit cemeteries and to give colored eggs to children. Before World War II, it became a three-day holiday, which included **Ziyarit al-Nabi Musi**, a visit to the shrine of Moses, or simply **al-Ziyara**, 'the Visit'.

In Jerusalem on Saturday of HOLY WEEK (*see* HOLY SATURDAY), Muslims hold the feast of Nebi Mousa for the same reason. Peasants from the countryside arrive in great numbers and go to the mosque near the Dome of the Rock. Old green war banners are unfurled and there is a parade to the shrine of Moses near the Dead Sea which can last for several hours.

CONTACT:
Jordan Information Bureau
2319 Wyoming Ave., N.W.
Washington, D.C. 20008
202-265-1606; fax: 202-667-0777

SOURCES:
FolkWrldHol-1992, p. 197

♦ 0987 ♦ **Khordad Sal**
March 21; July 13; August 15

The Parsis of India, descendants of the original Zoroastrian immigrants from Iran (formerly Persia), celebrate the birthday of their founder on this day. Zoroaster (or Zarathushtra, or Zarathustra; c. 628 B.C.–c. 551 B.C.) was a Persian prophet and religious reformer whose ideas combined both monotheism and dualism in the worship of Ahura Mazda, the Wise Lord, and his evil opponent, Ahriman. The largest group of Zoroastrians today can be found in India, where they are known as Parsis (or Parsees), although there are still isolated groups of Zoroastrians in Iran.

Zoroaster's birth is observed on March 21 by the Fasli sect of the Parsis, on July 13 by the Kadmi sect, and on August 15 by the Shahenshai sect.

See also FARVARDEGAN DAYS

SOURCES:
AnnivHol-1983, p. 178
FolkWrldHol-1992, p. 441

♦ 0988 ♦ **Kiamichi Owa-Chito (Festival of the Forest)**
Third weekend in June

A celebration of southeastern Oklahoma's forestry industry and of the culture of the Choctaw Indians of the area, held in Beavers Bend State Park near Broken Bow. Shortleaf and loblolly pines are abundant in the region, which is the heart of Oklahoma's timberland. The mistletoe, Oklahoma's state flower, also flourishes here. The Forest Heritage Center in the park has exhibits that include petrified logs, tools of the forestry industry, and dioramas.

Sporting events of the festival include canoe races, archery, horseshoe throwing, and log birling (log rolling). Other activities range from contests in tobacco spitting and turkey and owl calling to a photography show and musical entertainment—gospel singing, fiddling, and bluegrass.

CONTACT:
Oklahoma Tourism and Recreation Dept.
2401 N. Lincoln Blvd.
Will Rogers Bldg., Ste. 500
Oklahoma City, OK 73105
800-652-6552 or 405-521-2413
fax: 405-521-4883

SOURCES:
Chases-1996, p. 262
GdUSFest-1984, p. 144

♦ 0989 ♦ **Kiddies' Carnival**
Between January and March; the week before Carnival

Trinidad and Tobago, in the West Indies, is the only country that sponsors a CARNIVAL celebration specifically for children, based on the pre-Lenten Carnival celebrations for adults. The week before Carnival begins, there is a big parade in which groups of children choose a theme (such as "Arabian Nights") and dress up in costumes illustrating their theme. They sing and dance to calypso or do the "jump-up," a freestyle dance that originated here.

CONTACT:
Trinidad and Tobago Tourism Development Authority
25 W. 43rd St., Ste. 1508
New York, NY 10036
800-232-0082 or 212-719-0540
fax: 212-719-0988

SOURCES:
BkHolWrld-1986, Feb 19

♦ 0990 ♦ **Kiel Week**
Last week of June

An international sailing regatta in Kiel, Germany, at which the world's leading yachters compete. Craft of all sorts—sail, motor, and muscle-powered—race on the waters of the Kiel Fjord. Kiel, once the chief naval port of Germany, is a center of inshore and deep-sea fishing, and was host for the sailing races of the 1972 OLYMPIC GAMES.

CONTACT:
German National Tourist Office
122 E. 42nd St., 52nd Floor
New York, NY 10168
212-661-7200; fax: 212-661-7174

SOURCES:
IntlThFolk-1979, p. 142

♦ 0991 ♦ **Killing the Pigs, Festival of**
September

In rural areas of Estonia, the Festival of Killing the Pigs traditionally has been celebrated sometime in September. Each village has a few men who are skilled in time-honored methods of slaughtering animals and preparing the meat. On the day of the festival, the wife prepares a meal of pork, vodka, and "blood bread"—flour mixed with the animal's blood that is boiled and, then, often fried before eaten. After the meal is over, neighbors get together and spend the evening singing and dancing.

SOURCES:
BkFest-1937, p. 106

♦ 0992 ♦ **Kinderzeche (Children's Party)**
Saturday before the third Monday of July

A festival in Dinkelsbühl, Bavaria, Germany, to honor the children who saved the town during the Thirty Years' War of 1618–48. In 1632, according to legend, the Swedish commander, a Colonel Sperreuth, threatened destruction of the town (which endured eight sieges during the war). The town council was debating its response, when a gatekeeper's daughter named Lore proposed gathering a group of children together to appeal to Sperreuth. The council agreed to let her try. As the Swedish troops rode into town, the children sang, and Lore with her small band of children appeared before the commander, knelt, and asked his mercy. The commander's heart softened; he spared the town, and told the citizens, "Children are the rescuers of Dinkelsbühl. Always remember the debt of thanks you owe them."

The celebration today is a reenactment of the event, with participants (most of them Dinkelsbühl residents) in the costume of 17th-century town councilors and soldiers. Highlights of the festival are the parade of the Dinkelsbühl Boys' Band and a performance of a medieval sword dance, in which dancers stand on top of a pedestal of crossed blades. About 300,000 visitors attend the festival.

Dinkelsbühl is about 20 miles from Rothenburg-on-the-Tauber, Germany, which also commemorates an event of the Thirty Years' War.

See also MEISTERTRUNK PAGEANT

CONTACT:
German National Tourist Office
122 E. 42nd St., 52nd Floor
New York, NY 10168
212-661-7200; fax: 212-661-7174

SOURCES:
BkHolWrld-1986, Jul 16
IntlThFolk-1979, p. 137

♦ 0993 ♦ **King, Jr.'s Birthday, Martin Luther**
Federal holiday: third Monday in January;
birthday: January 15

In 1955 Rosa Parks, a black seamstress in Montgomery, Alabama, refused to obey a bus driver's order to give up her seat to a white male passenger. She was fined $14 for her defiance of the Jim Crow (segregationist) law that required blacks to sit in the rear of buses, and if the bus were crowded, to give up their seat to a white. The incident led to a citywide bus boycott and raised its leader, the young black Baptist minister Dr. Martin Luther King, Jr., to national prominence.

King went on to establish the Southern Christian Leadership Conference, to win the Nobel Peace Prize, and to play an active role in the civil rights movement of the 1960s. He was in Memphis, Tennessee, on April 4, 1968, organizing a strike of the city's predominantly black sanitation workers when he was shot to death at the age of 39 by James Earl Ray.

Martin Luther King Day is a federal holiday, the only one for a person who was not a president; federal government offices are closed on that day. It has become a focal point for recognition of African-American history and the American civil rights movement led by Dr. King. It is also a legal holiday in some states—among them Connecticut, Illinois, Kentucky, Maryland, Massachusetts, Michigan, New Jersey, New York, and Ohio—although it is sometimes moved to the nearest Monday. New Hampshire observes this day as **Civil Rights Day.** In Alabama it became **Martin Luther King and Robert E. Lee's Birthday**, observed on the third Monday in January. The same day in Virginia is called **Lee-Jackson-King Day**, combining Dr. King's birthday with those of Robert E. Lee and Andrew "Stonewall" Jackson (*see also* LEE DAY, ROBERT E. and JACKSON'S BIRTHDAY, ANDREW). In schools, the day is often observed with special lessons and assembly programs dealing with Dr. King's life and work.

SOURCES:
AmerBkDays-1978, p. 77
AnnivHol-1983, p. 9
BkHolWrld-1986, Jan 15
Chases-1996, p. 65
DictDays-1988, p. 73
DictWrldRel-1989, p. 407
RelHolCal-1993, p. 63

♦ 0994 ♦ **Kingdom Days**
Last weekend in June

This annual festival in Fulton, Missouri, is based on a Civil War confrontation between a Union general and the local militia. On July 28, 1861, there was a battle near Calwood that left 19 dead and 76 wounded. In an effort to spare Callaway County any further bloodshed, Colonel Jefferson Jones sent a letter to General John B. Henderson, commander of the Union military forces in northeastern Missouri. Jones requested that the county be left alone to conduct its own business and to control its own destiny. Henderson, perhaps fearing stiff resistance, agreed to the truce and signed the treaty that designated Callaway County a "kingdom," separate from both the U.S. and the Confederacy. No shots were fired, no one was injured, and the disagreements between the two military units were settled peacefully.

This event is only one of the historic reenactments that take place during the annual Kingdom Days festival. Others are more humorous, such as the "shotgun" Civil War-era wedding that took place in 1991. Other events include bed races, a "baby derby" in which babies up to 18 months old crawl 10 feet to the finish line, a hot air balloon rally, and a pig-kissing contest.

CONTACT:
Kingdom of Callaway Chamber of
Commerce
409 Court St.
Fulton, MO 65251
314-642-3055

◆ 0995 ◆ King in Nepal, Birthday of His Majesty the
December 28

A public holiday to celebrate the birthday of Nepal's present ruler, King Birendra Bir Bikram Shah Dev, born in 1945. People from all over the country gather for a huge parade and rally on the Tundikhel parade grounds of Katmandu, Nepal. Troupes perform songs and dances in traditional costumes, and fireworks round off the festivities.

CONTACT:
Nepal Embassy
2131 Leroy Pl., N.W.
Washington, D.C. 20008
202-667-4550; fax: 202-667-5534

SOURCES:
Chases-1996, p. 491

◆ 0996 ◆ King Kamehameha Celebration
June 11

A state holiday in Hawaii to celebrate the reign of the island state's first king, and the only public holiday in the United States that honors royalty.

King Kamehameha I, known as 'the Great' (1758?–1819) was the son of a high chief. At his birth it was prophesied that he would defeat all his rivals. He originally was named Paiea, which means 'soft-shelled crab'. When he grew to manhood he took the name Kamehameha, meaning 'the very lonely one' or 'the one set apart'. By 1810 he had united all the Hawaiian islands and until his death was the undisputed ruler. He promulgated the *mamalahoe kanawai,* or 'law of the splintered paddle,' which protected the common people from the brutality of powerful chiefs, and he outlawed human sacrifice. He made a fortune for his people with a government monopoly on the sandalwood trade. After his death, he was succeeded by his son, Kamehameha II.

Celebrations extend several days beyond the actual public holiday. Leis (Hawaiian floral necklaces) are draped on the king's statue across from Iolani Palace, formerly the home of Hawaii's monarchs and now the state capitol in Honolulu, and there is another lei-draping at Kapaau, North Kohala. A floral parade travels from downtown Honolulu to Waikiki; it features a young man who depicts the king wearing a replica of the golden amo-feather cloak and Grecian-style helmet (the originals are kept in Honolulu's Bernice P. Bishop Museum and are displayed on this day). The parade also includes floats and princesses on horseback wearing the *pa'u,* satin riding dresses in the color of their island home. Other events include demonstrations of arts and crafts, a competition of chants and hulas, and a luau, or Hawaiian cookout.

CONTACT:
Hawaii Visitors Bureau
2270 Kalakaua Ave., Ste. 801
Honolulu, HI 96815
808-923-1811; fax: 808-922-8991

SOURCES:
AmerBkDays-1978, p. 545
AnnivHol-1983, p. 78
Chases-1996, p. 251
DictDays-1988, p. 63
GdUSFest-1984, p. 44

◆ 0997 ◆ King's Birthday in Belgium
November 15

King Leopold I (1790–1865) of Belgium was named after Sᴛ. Lᴇᴏᴘᴏʟᴅ, whose feast is celebrated on this day. He was the first leader of Belgium after it achieved independence from the Netherlands in 1831, and reigned until his death. Also known as **Dynasty Day**, or **Fête de la Dynastie**, the day is a national public holiday.

CONTACT:
Belgian Tourist Office
780 Third Ave.
New York, NY 10017
212-758-8130; fax: 212-355-7675

SOURCES:
AnnivHol-1983, p. 147
Chases-1996, p. 450

◆ 0998 ◆ King's Birthday in Denmark
March 11

Though no longer observed, the birthday of Frederick IX of Denmark (1899–1972) was a national holiday in that country, marked by patriotic speeches and parades. Soldiers in uniform would march down the main street of Copenhagen, the capital, accompanied by military bands. This was also an occasion for singing Denmark's two national anthems, "Kong Kristian Stod Ved Hojen Mast" ("King Kristian Stood Beside the Lofty Mast") and "Der Er Et Yndigt Land" ("This is a Lovely Land"). The words of the former were written by Johannes Ewald and translated into English by the well-known American poet, Henry Wadsworth Longfellow.

Frederick IX became king of Denmark in 1947 and ruled until his death in 1972. He is remembered for the encouragement he gave to the Danish resistance movement against the German occupation during World War II. In fact, from 1943–45 he was imprisoned by the Germans along with his father, Christian X.

SOURCES:
NatlHolWrld-1968, p. 32

◆ 0999 ◆ King's Birthday in Thailand
December 5

A national holiday to celebrate the birthday of Thailand's King Bhumibol Adulyadej (b. 1927), who has been the largely symbolic chief of state since 1950. Bangkok blooms with decorations, which are especially lavish in the area of the floodlit Grand Palace. Full dress ceremonies, including a Trooping of the Colors by Thailand's elite Royal Guards, are performed at the palace.

CONTACT:
Tourism Authority of Thailand
5 World Trade Center, Ste. 3443
New York, NY 10048
212-432-0433; fax: 212-912-0920

SOURCES:
Chases-1996, p. 471
NatlHolWrld-1968, p. 219

◆ 1000 ◆ Kingsburg Swedish Festival
Third weekend in May

A tribute to the Swedish heritage of Kingsburg, Calif. The event began in 1924 as a luncheon to commemorate the midsummer celebration of the harvest in Sweden. Today it's a full-fledged festival running from Thursday through Sunday of the third weekend in May and attracts about 25,000 visitors. Traditional Swedish costumes are worn, and Swedish food is eaten—Swedish pancakes, Swedish pea soup, a smorgasbord. Events include a Parade of Trolls, raising of the May Pole, folk dancing, arts and crafts displays, a horse trot, and live entertainment.

CONTACT:
California Division of Tourism
801 K Street, Ste. 1600
Sacramento, CA 95814
800-862-2543 or 916-322-2881
fax: 916-322-3402

♦ 1001 ♦ Kiribati Independence Day
July 12

This island group in the middle of the Pacific Ocean was known as the Gilbert Islands until its independence from Britain on July 12, 1979. Independence Day is observed as a national holiday.

CONTACT:
Republic of Kiribati Honorary
  Consulate
850 Richards St., Ste. 503
Honolulu, HI 96813
808-521-7703

SOURCES:
AnnivHol-1983, p. 92
Chases-1996, p. 293

♦ 1002 ♦ Kissing Day
January 1

In the 19th century, Chippewa Indians of Minnesota observed NEW YEAR'S DAY by giving and receiving a kiss or a cake—a custom they apparently picked up from the French-Canadians. The Puritan missionaries who came to Minnesota to convert the Indians to Christianity were aghast when the natives attempted to greet them in this way on New Year's Day, and eventually convinced them to receive gifts and sing a New Year's hymn instead.

SOURCES:
FolkAmerHol-1991, p. 12

Kite Flying
See **Tako-Age**

♦ 1003 ♦ Kiwanis Kids' Day
Fourth Saturday in September

The National Kids' Day Foundation and Kiwanis International first came up with the idea of setting aside a day to focus on children and their welfare in 1949. Kiwanis International eventually assumed responsibility for the program and re-named it Kiwanis Kids' Day.

On the fourth Saturday in September, local Kiwanis clubs sponsor activities designed to show the community's appreciation of and pride in its children. The actual program for the day varies from one club to the next, but some of the more popular activities include parades, picnics and field days, theater parties, free admission programs, poster contests, fishing derbies, talent shows, and youth recognition banquets. The idea is to show youngsters that they are an important part of the community and that the community wants them to be good citizens.

CONTACT:
Kiwanis International Foundation
3636 Woodview Trace
Indianapolis, IN 46268
317-875-8755; fax: 317-879-0204

SOURCES:
Chases-1996, p. 394
DictDays-1988, p. 63

♦ 1004 ♦ Klo Dance
Autumn

A harvest celebration among the Baoulé people of the Ivory Coast in western Africa, the *klo* dance takes place during the fall harvest season and is similar to HALLOWEEN in the United States. Groups of young boys dressed from head to toe in strips of palm leaves go from house to house, dancing to the accompaniment of sticks beaten together. They ask for "treats"—yams, manioc, or peanuts—and sing a song of thanks if they are given any. But if they are refused, their "trick" is to sing teasing songs and to scold the woman of the house for being stingy. Afterward, the boys take their treats into the bush to eat them.

SOURCES:
FolkWrldHol-1992, p. 453

♦ 1005 ♦ Klondike Days Exposition
Late July

For 10 days in late July every year since 1962, the city of Edmonton, Alberta, has commemorated the Gold Rush of 1898 and its impact on what was originally a small agricultural town. People dress up in Klondike costumes—long dresses, stockings, and lace-up boots for the women, frontier wear for the men. A two-hour parade through the city's downtown area kicks off the festivities, followed by a band competition at Clark Stadium. There is a Sourdough Raft Race on the North Saskatchewan River and a daily gold-panning competition at the Chilkoot Gold Mine. Local theater groups perform melodramas typical of the Klondike era, and gambling at Klondike-style casinos is a popular diversion. Klondike garden parties and pancake breakfasts are held throughout the city, which was once the starting point for the overland trip to the Yukon.

CONTACT:
Alberta Economic Development
  and Tourism
Commerce Place, 3rd Floor
10155-102 Street
Edmonton, Alberta
Canada T5J 4L6
800-661-8886 or 403-427-4321

SOURCES:
Chases-1996, p. 300
GdWrldFest-1985, p. 30

♦ 1006 ♦ Klondike Gold Discovery Day
Third weekend in August

On August 17, 1896, George Washington Carmack discovered gold at Bonanza Creek in northwestern Canada's Yukon Territory. His discovery triggered a huge gold rush and an enormous influx of American miners and traders. More than 30,000 poured into the Klondike region over the next couple of years, sparking the formation of Dawson and the construction of the Yukon narrow-gage railway. But the Klondike boom was short-lived, and by 1900 most of the miners had given up and were replaced by companies using mechanical mining techniques. To this day, mining remains the area's most important industry.

Also known as **Discovery Day**, this important event in Canada's history is observed as a holiday in the Yukon.

CONTACT:
Tourism Yukon
P.O. Box 2703
Whitehorse, Yukon
Canada Y1A 2C6
403-667-5340

SOURCES:
AnnivHol-1983, p. 108
Chases-1996, p. 338

◆ 1007 ◆ Klondike International Outhouse Race
September, Sunday of Labor Day weekend

First held in 1977, the Klondike International Outhouse Race takes place annually in the gold rush city of Dawson in Canada's Yukon Territory. A serious athletic event for some—and an opportunity for less serious competitors to indulge in what can only be described as "bathroom humor"—the race involves four-person teams, each pulling an outhouse on wheels. Many of the teams compete in outrageous costumes and cover their outhouses with appropriate graffiti or equip them with such modern-day comforts as telephones and carpeted seats.

There are two basic types of competitors: the serious runners, who train rigorously for the event and are sent off in the first heat of the three-kilometer race; and those who never make it any further than the first bar on the course, or who reach the finish line from the wrong direction. There are awards for the best dressed as well as the fastest, and the grand trophy is a wooden outhouse with an engraved plaque.

CONTACT:
Tourism Yukon
P.O. Box 2703
Whitehorse, Yukon
Canada Y1A 2C6
403-667-5340

SOURCES:
Chases-1996, p. 358

◆ 1008 ◆ Knabenschiessen (Boys' Rifle Match)
Second weekend in September

A marksmanship contest in Zurich, Switzerland, for boys aged 12 to 16. The custom dates to the 17th century when all boys were required to practice their shooting during summer holidays. The final rifle match was a kind of examination. Today, the boys use rifles like those they will be issued in the army. Prizes are awarded, and the winner is named King of the Marksmen. A huge amusement park is set up for the Knabenschiessen, and there is a parade and market.

CONTACT:
Swiss National Tourist Office
608 Fifth Ave.
New York, NY 10020
212-757-5944; fax: 212-262-6116

◆ 1009 ◆ Kneeling Sunday
Between May 24 and June 27; fifty days after Easter

In Orthodox Christianity, PENTECOST (or Whitsunday) is known as Kneeling Sunday. After the liturgy, the congregation kneels while the priest makes three invocations, one of which is a prayer for the repose of the dead. In some rural parts of Greece, the worshippers place flowers from their gardens on the ground in front of them as they kneel, and they burn candles to light the way for the souls of the departed. Sometimes they cover their eyes with rose petals, believing that if their eyes are open when the souls of their loved ones pass by, they will be recognized, and the grief that accompanies this recognition will make it impossible for the soul to leave the earth.

SOURCES:
BkFestHolWrld-1970, p. 66

◆ 1010 ◆ Kodomo-no-Hi (Children's Day)
May 5

A national holiday in Japan that was known as **Boys' Day** from the ninth century, but became a day for both boys and girls in 1948. Today the day is observed largely with family picnics, but some still practice the old custom of flying wind socks in the shape of carp, a common Japanese food fish. Households with sons erect tall bamboo poles outside the home and attach streamers in the shape of carp for each son. The carp supposedly represents the strength, courage, and determination shown in its upstream journeys. The festivities are part of **Golden Week**.

SOURCES:
BkFest-1937, p. 199
BkFestHolWrld-1970, p. 93
BkHolWrld-1986, May 5
Chases-1996, p. 201
DictFolkMyth-1984, p. 540
FolkAmerHol-1991, p. 203
FolkWrldHol-1992, p. 274

◆ 1011 ◆ Kojagara
September–October; full moon day of Hindu month of Asvina

The word "Kojagara" is a combination of two terms, "Kah" and "jagara," which means "who is awake?" This is what the goddess Lakshmi says when she descends to the earth on the night of the full moon in the month of Asvina. She blesses all those who are awake with wealth and prosperity, so the festivities go on all night. Kojagara is a harvest festival and is celebrated throughout India.

There is a folk tale about a king who fell into dire financial straits. When his queen observed the fast and night vigil in honor of Lakshmi, the goddess of wealth, their fortunes were reversed and prosperity returned to them.

CONTACT:
India Tourist Office
30 Rockefeller Ave.
15 N. Mezzanine
New York, NY 10112
212-586-4901; fax: 212-582-3274

SOURCES:
RelHolCal-1993, p. 88

◆ 1012 ◆ Koledouvane
December 24–25

Koledouvane is the ritual singing of CHRISTMAS carols that takes place in Bulgaria each year on December 24 and 25. The *koledari*, or 'carol singers,' go from house to house and wish people good health and prosperity. Although their dress and ornaments differ from region to region, the *koledarka*, a long oak stick covered with elaborate carving, is a traditional accessory.

A similar ritual, called *Sourvakari*, is carried out on NEW YEAR'S DAY. Those who go from house to house wishing people a Happy New Year carry a decorated cornel (dogwood) twig, which they use to tap people on the back as they deliver their good wishes. The near coincidence of the two customs can probably be explained by the switch from the Julian to the Gregorian calendar. They have survived as separate celebrations, even though they are closely related in meaning.

SOURCES:
BkFest-1937, p. 73

♦ 1013 ♦ Kopenfahrt (Barrel Parade)
Between February 3 and March 9; Shrove Tuesday

The **Kope Festival** on SHROVE TUESDAY has been observed by the salt miners of Lüneburg, Germany, since the 15th century. Originally the *Kope*, a wooden barrel filled with stones, was dragged through the narrow streets of the town by *Salzjunker*, or young journeymen salters, on horseback. They were followed by a long procession of local officials, salt mine laborers, and townspeople. Today the **Kope Procession** has become a folk, rather than a historical, event. As the riders attempt to guide the Kope through the streets, trumpeters blast their instruments as loudly as possible in an attempt to unnerve the horses. Once the Kope is brought to the mouth of the salt mine, it is set on a huge pile of wood and burned. Following the bonfire is a ceremony initiating the Salzjunker into the Guild of Master Salters.

Some believe that the Kopenfahrt bonfire was originally a pagan ceremony symbolizing the Sun God's triumph over the forces of darkness. In any case, the festival was revived in 1950 and is now a regular part of the old mining town's annual CARNIVAL celebration.

CONTACT:
German National Tourist Office
122 E. 42nd St., 52nd Floor
New York, NY 10168
212-661-7200; fax: 212-661-7174

SOURCES:
FestWestEur-1958, p. 56

Korea Independence Movement Day
See **Samil-jol**

♦ 1014 ♦ Korea Liberation Day
August 15

A Korean commemoration of the surrender of Japan to the Allies in 1945, liberating Korea from Japan's 35-year occupation. The day also commemorates the formal proclamation of the Republic of Korea in South Korea in 1948, but it is a national holiday in both Koreas.

See also SAMIL-JOL

CONTACT:
Korea National Tourism Corp.
205 N. Michigan Ave., Ste. 2212
Chicago, IL 60601
312-819-2560; fax: 312-819-2563

SOURCES:
AnnivHol-1983, p. 107
Chases-1996, p. 337
NatlHolWrld-1968, p. 144

♦ 1015 ♦ Korea National Foundation Day
October 3

A national holiday in the Republic of Korea (South Korea), also known as **Tangun Day**, to commemorate the legendary founding of the Korean nation in 2333 B.C. by Tangun.

Prince Hwan-ung left heaven to rule earth from Mt. T'aebaek. In his kingdom were a bear and a tiger who wished to become humans. Hwan-ung told them that if they remained in a cave for 100 days eating nothing but mugwort and garlic, they would become like people. The tiger got bored, but the bear lasted it out and became a beautiful woman. She and Hwan-ung bore a son called Tangun Wanggom, meaning Sandalwood King. When he grew up, he built his own city at the present site of P'yongyang (now the capital of North

Korea) and called his new kingdom Choson, meaning 'morning freshness' or 'morning calm.' The book *Samguk Yusa*, written in 1289, records this story. The myth is important in that it links the Korean people with a heavenly origin.

The holiday is celebrated with ceremonies at the ancient rock altar of Tangun, on the summit of Mt. Mani on Kanghwa Island, about 25 miles west of Seoul.

CONTACT:
Korea National Tourism Corp.
205 N. Michigan Ave., Ste. 2212
Chicago, IL 60601
312-819-2560; fax: 312-819-2563

SOURCES:
AnnivHol-1983, p. 127
Chases-1996, p. 402

Krishna's Birthday
See **Janmashtami**

♦ 1016 ♦ Kristallnacht (Crystal Night)
November 9–10

When a 17-year-old Jew named Herschel Grynszpan assassinated the Third Secretary at the German embassy in Paris on November 7, 1938, to avenge the expulsion of his parents and 15,000 other Polish Jews to German concentration camps, it gave the German Nazis the excuse they had been looking for to conduct a *pogrom*, or 'organized massacre.' Crystal Night, or **Night of the Broken Glass**, gets its name from the shattered glass that littered the streets two nights later, when the windows of Jewish-owned shops and homes were systematically smashed throughout Leipzig and other German and Austrian cities in a frenzy of destruction that resulted in the arrest and deportation of about 30,000 Jews.

Crystal Night marked the beginning of the Nazis' plan to rob the Jews of their possessions and to force them out of their homes and neighborhoods. Although the so-called "Final Solution" (to kill all European Jews) had not been suggested at this point, the Nazis' actions on this night left little doubt as to what the fate of German Jews would be if war broke out. Today Jews everywhere observe the anniversary of this infamous event by holding special memorial services.

In Germany, Kristallnacht coincides with the anniversary of another famous, if very recent, event: the breaching of the Berlin Wall in 1989. The coincidence of the two observances is seen by many as symbolic of the conflicts of German history.

SOURCES:
AnnivHol-1983, p. 144
Chases-1996, p. 445
DictWrldRel-1989, p. 202

♦ 1017 ♦ 'Ksan Celebrations
Friday evenings in July and August

Dances and accompanying songs held by the 'Ksan Indians in a longhouse in the Indian Village in Hazelton, British Columbia, Canada. They are generally a celebration of the important things of life, such as breathing and being at one with the cosmos.

The dances are said to go back to pre-history; they were revived in 1958, and the 'Ksan dancers have since performed in New York City, San Francisco, Seattle, Kansas City, Missouri, and even Australia.

Box-shaped skin drums provide the beat for the dances.

Songs, besides being about cosmic events, are sometimes songs of marriage, songs of divorce, or what are known as "happy heart songs" about almost anything. Performers must be *Git 'Ksan*, meaning 'People of the 'Ksan.' (The 'Ksan is a river in the area.)

Because the homeland of the Git 'Ksan is far inland, it was overlooked by the Spaniards and Russians who explored the coast in the 1700s, and fur traders didn't stay here because the climate is too humid for good fur. As a result, the 'Ksan culture has been maintained without outside influences.

CONTACT:
Tourism British Columbia
Parliament Buildings
Victoria, B.C.
Canada V8V 1X4
800-663-6000 or 604-663-6000

Kuhio Day
See **Prince Kuhio Day**

♦ 1018 ♦ **Kumbh Mela (Pitcher Fair)**
Every 12 years on a date calculated by astrologers (1989, 2001, . . .)

Mass immersion rituals by Hindus near the city of Allahabad (the ancient holy city of Prayag) in north-central India. Millions of pilgrims gather to bathe at the confluence of the Ganges and Yamuna Rivers, which is also where the mythical river of enlightenment, the Saraswati, flows. The bathers wash away the sins of their past lives and pray to escape the cycle of reincarnation. *Sadhus*, or holy men, carry images of deities to the river for immersion, and the most ascetic sadhus, naked except for loincloths, their faces and bodies smeared with ashes, go in procession to the waters, escorting images borne on palanquins. The Ganges is not only a sacred river but is the source of all sacred waters. The junction of the three rivers at Allahabad is called the *sangam* and is considered by some the holiest place in India.

The *mela* ('fair') is thought to be the largest periodic gathering of human beings in the world; a vast tent city appears, temporary water and power lines are installed, and 10 pontoon bridges are laid across the Ganges. Movies of Hindu gods and heroes are shown from the backs of trucks, and plays recounting Hindu mythology are performed. Merchants lay out all manner of goods.

The story behind the mela is that Hindu gods and *asuras*, or 'demons,' fought for a *kumbh*, or 'pitcher,' carrying *amrit*, the nectar of immortality. The god who seized the kumbh stopped at Prayag, Hardwar, Nasik, and Ujjain on his way to paradise. The journey took 12 days (which are longer than earthly days), and therefore the mela follows a 12-year cycle.

A purification bathing ceremony called the *Magh Mela* is also held each spring in Allahabad. It is India's biggest yearly religious bathing festival. Although the Magh Mela attracts a million people, more or less, the Kumbh Mela dwarfs it!

See also GANGA DUSSEHRA

CONTACT:
India Tourist Office
30 Rockefeller Ave.
15 N. Mezzanine
New York, NY 10112
212-586-4901; fax: 212-582-3274

SOURCES:
AnnivHol-1983, p. 179
DictWrldRel-1989, p. 305
RelHolCal-1993, p. 92

♦ 1019 ♦ **Ku-omboko**
February or March

Ku-omboko, which means 'getting out of the water,' is a floodtime festival observed by the Lozi people of Zambia. When the Zambezi River begins its annual flooding of the Barotzé flood plains, thousands of boats and canoes, led by the chief on his royal barge, make their way to higher ground. When the Lozi reach their new seasonal home at Limulunga, they celebrate with singing and dancing. In July, when the floods have receded, they return to the lowlands.

CONTACT:
Zambia National Tourist Board
237 E. 52nd St.
New York, NY 10022
212-308-2155; fax: 212-758-1319

SOURCES:
BkHolWrld-1986, Feb 18
FolkWrldHol-1992, p. 149
GdWrldFest-1985, p. 188

♦ 1020 ♦ **Kupalo Festival**
June 24; Midsummer's day and night

A Ukrainian festival, dating back to pagan days, that traditionally is celebrated by young unmarried men and women and boys and girls. The festival takes its name from the god of summer and fertility: Kupalo sleeps in the winter and each spring awakens and shakes the tree he's been under, making the seeds fall as a sign of the year's harvest. During the day and night of the celebration, boys and girls decorate a sapling tree with flowers, seeds, and fruit, call it Kupalo, and dance and sing special songs to please this image of the god.

In other events of the day, young women gather flowers to make a wreath that is tossed into a river; the spot where the wreath reaches the shore indicates the family the girl will marry into. Another custom for girls is to make an effigy of Marena, the goddess of cold, death, and winter. After singing special songs, they burn or drown the effigy to cut the goddess's power over the coming winter; winters in Ukraine are very harsh.

Young men sometimes go into the forest to look for a special fern that only blooms (according to the legend) on the night of MIDSUMMER. They take with them a special cloth, white powder, and a knife. If they find the fern and are strong enough to ward off the enticements of wood nymphs, they draw a circle with the white powder and sit and wait for the fern to bloom. When it does, they cut the blossom with the knife and put the flower in the special cloth. They must never, ever, tell anyone they have found the fern, or they will lose the luck and power it gives. The people's rationale behind this story is that it explains why some people have more talent and luck than others.

The celebrations to a greater or lesser degree are popular in both Ukraine and among Ukrainians in the United States.

CONTACT:
Ukraine Embassy
3350 M St., N.W.
Washington, D.C. 20007
202-333-0606; fax: 202-333-0817

♦ 1021 ♦ **Kutztown Fair**
Five days including 4th of July weekend

The **Pennsylvania Dutch Folk Festival** in Kutztown, Pennsylvania, is an annual celebration of Pennsylvania Dutch foods, crafts, and customs. Although many people identify the "Pennsylvania Dutch" with the Amish people, the Mennonites or with the Holland Dutch, the name actually came from the Yankee pronunciation of *deutsch,* meaning 'German.' But the Pennsylvania Dutch are not simply transplanted Germans, either. Their folk culture is peculiarly American, and they encompass a number of national and religious groups.

The Kutztown Fair, sponsored by Franklin and Marshall College, acquaints visitors with all aspects of Pennsylvania Dutch culture. There are special foods—such as apple butter, *rivvel* soup (rivvels are like dumplings), and the fruit pies which the Pennsylvania Dutch claim to have originated. Traditional artisans featured at the fair include tinsmiths, pretzel-makers, candlemakers, cigarmakers, weavers, potters, and quilters. There are reenactments of a Pennsylvania Dutch funeral feast and demonstrations of *nipsi*—a complicated game that involves batting a piece of wood and then "bidding" the number of hops that the opposing team will require to get from where the wood landed back to home base. There is even a seminar on Pennsylvania Dutch cooking. One of the fair's most interesting figures is the *Fraktur* painter, who illuminates birth and baptismal records and book plates with bright colors and flowing scrollwork.

CONTACT:
Franklin and Marshall College
P.O. Box 3003
Lancaster, PA 17604
717-291-3911; fax: 717-399-4437

SOURCES:
AmerBkDays-1978, p. 600
AnnivHol-1983, p. 178
Chases-1996, p. 275
GdUSFest-1984, p. 158

♦ 1022 ♦ Kuwait Independence Day
June 19

On this day in 1961, Kuwait gained full independence from Britain. Though internally governed by the Sabah family (*see* Kuwait National Day), Britain had handled its foreign affairs since 1899.

CONTACT:
Kuwait Embassy
2940 Tilden St., N.W.
Washington, D.C. 20008
202-966-0702; fax: 202-966-0517

SOURCES:
AnnivHol-1983, p. 81
NatlHolWrld-1968, p. 87

♦ 1023 ♦ Kuwait National Day
February 25

This national holiday in Kuwait commemorates the accession of Sheikh Saad'Abdallah as-Salim Sabah (1895–1965).

CONTACT:
Kuwait Embassy
2940 Tilden St., N.W.
Washington, D.C. 20008
202-966-0702; fax: 202-966-0517

SOURCES:
AnnivHol-1983, p. 28
Chases-1996, p. 112

♦ 1024 ♦ Kwanzaa
December 26–January 1

An African-American celebration of family and black culture, thought to be observed by five million Americans and perhaps 10 million others in Africa, Canada, the Caribbean, and parts of Europe. The holiday was created in 1966 by Maulana Karenga, chairman of the Black Studies Department at California State University in Long Beach.

In Swahili, Kwanzaa means 'first fruits of the harvest,' and first-fruit practices common throughout Africa were adapted by Karenga for the celebration.

Each day of the seven-day festival is dedicated to one of seven principles: *umoja* (unity), *kujichagulia* (self-determination), *ujima* (collective work and responsibility), *ujamaa* (cooperative economics), *nia* (purpose), *kuumba* (creativity), and *imani* (faith). Families gather in the evenings to discuss the principle of the day, and then light a black, red, or green candle and place it in a seven-branched candleholder called a *kinara* to symbolize giving light and life to the principle. On the evening of Dec. 31, families join with other members of the community for a feast called the *karamu*. Decorations are in the red, black, and green that symbolize Africa, and both adults and children wear African garments. Increasingly, colleges and museums are holding Kwanzaa events during some of the days. For example, in Chicago, an African Market is held on Dec. 28 by the Ujamma Family, a black self-help group. In New York City the American Museum of Natural History celebrates Kwanzaa with an African Marketplace, poetry, folktales, and music.

CONTACT:
Chicago Convention and Tourism
 Bureau
2301 S. Lake Shore Dr.
McCormick Place On-the-Lake
Chicago, IL 60616
312-567-8500; fax: 312-567-8533

American Museum of Natural
 History
Central Park W. & 79th St.
New York, NY 10024
212-769-5000; fax: 212-769-5233

SOURCES:
AnnivHol-1983, p. 164
Chases-1996, p. 489
FolkWrldHol-1992, p. 641
RelHolCal-1993, p. 89

L

♦ 1025 ♦ Labor Day
First Monday in September

Although workers' holidays had been observed since the days of the medieval trade guilds, laborers in the United States didn't have a holiday of their own until 1882, when Peter J. McGuire, a New York City carpenter and labor union leader, and Matthew Maguire, a machinist from Paterson, N.J., suggested to the Central Labor Union of New York that a celebration be held in honor of the American worker. Some 10,000 New Yorkers paraded in Union Square, New York, on September 5 of that year—a date specifically chosen by McGuire to fill the long gap between the FOURTH OF JULY and THANKSGIVING.

The first Labor Day observance was confined to New York City, but the idea of setting aside a day to honor workers spread quickly, and by 1895 Labor Day events were taking place across the nation. Oregon, in 1887, was the first state to make it a legal holiday, and in 1894 President Grover Cleveland signed a bill making it a national holiday. The holiday's association with trade unions has declined, but it remains important as the day that marks the end of the summer season for schoolchildren and as an opportunity for friends and families to get together for picnics and sporting events.

Labour Day is celebrated in England and Europe on May 1. In Australia, where it is called EIGHT HOUR DAY, it is celebrated at different times in different states, and commemorates the struggle for a shorter working day. In Antigua and Barbuda, Labor Day is observed on May 6; in the Bahamas, it's June 7; in Bermuda, Sept. 2; in Jamaica, May 23; and in Trinidad and Tobago, June 19. Labor Day is observed on the first Monday in September throughout the United States, in Canada, and in Puerto Rico. In Japan, November 23 is **Labor Thanksgiving Day**, or **Kinro Kansha-no-Hi**, a legal holiday set aside to honor working people and productivity.

SOURCES:
AmerBkDays-1978, p. 817
AnnivHol-1983, pp. 59, 114
BkFest-1937, p. 18
BkHolWrld-1986, Sep 7
Chases-1996, p. 361
DaysCustFaith-1957, p. 248
DictDays-1988, p. 65

FolkAmerHol-1991, p. 325

Labour Day
See **Eight-Hour Day**

♦ 1026 ♦ Ladouvane
December 31; June 24

Ladouvane, or the **Singing to Rings**, is a Bulgarian fertility ritual. Traditionally, young girls drop their rings, together with oats and barley (symbols of fertility) into a cauldron of spring water. The rings are tied with a red thread to a bunch of ivy, crane's bill, basil, or some other perennial plant, and the cauldron is left out overnight. Ritual dances are performed around the cauldron and the girls' fortunes are told.

In western Bulgaria, the Central Balkan Range, and along the Danube River, Ladouvane is observed on NEW YEAR'S EVE. In the rest of the country, it is observed on MIDSUMMER DAY.

CONTACT:
Bulgarian Embassy
1621 22nd St., N.W.
Washington, D.C. 20008
202-387-7969; fax: 202-234-7973

♦ 1027 ♦ Lady Day
March 25

The name in England for the Feast of the ANNUNCIATION. This day was originally called **Our Lady Day**, a name that applied to three other days relating to the Virgin Mary: the IMMACULATE CONCEPTION (December 8), the NATIVITY OF THE VIRGIN (September 8), and the ASSUMPTION OF THE BLESSED VIRGIN MARY (August 15). It commemorates the archangel Gabriel's announcement to Mary that she would give birth to Jesus, and is often referred to simply as The Annunciation. Lady Day is one of the QUARTER DAYS in England and Ireland when rents are paid and tenants change houses. In France it is called **Nôtre Dame de Mars** ('Our Lady of March').

SOURCES:
AnnivHol-1983, p. 42
BkDays-1864, vol. I, p. 417
DaysCustFaith-1957, p. 86
DictDays-1988, pp. 4, 85, 93

FestSaintDays-1915, p. 59
FolkWrldHol-1992, p. 188
RelHolCal-1993, pp. 57, 105

Laetare Sunday
See **Mothering Sunday**

◆ 1028 ◆ Lag ba-Omer
Eighteenth day of the Jewish month of Iyyar, or the 33rd day of the 50 days that separate Passover and Shavuot

The name of this Jewish holiday means "thirty-three omer," an *omer* being a sheaf of barley or wheat. In the book of Leviticus, the people were commanded by Jehovah to make an offering of a sheaf of barley on each of the 50 days between Passover and Shavuot. After the evening service, the number of the day was solemnly announced, and in time this ceremony came to be known as "the counting of the omer."

Why the 33rd day of this period was singled out may have something to do with an ancient pagan festival of the forest that was celebrated at this same time. Another story claims that the plague that had been decimating the students of Rabbi Akiba in the second century suddenly and miraculously stopped on this day. In any case, the mid-harvest festival of Lag ba-Omer represents a break in the otherwise solemn season between Passover and Shavuot.

SOURCES:
BkFest-1937, p. 207
DaysCustFaith-1957, p. 137
DictWrldRel-1989, p. 155
FolkWrldHol-1992, p. 268
RelHolCal-1993, p. 69

◆ 1029 ◆ Lajkonik
Between May 21 and June 24; first Thursday after Corpus Christi

The most popular folk festival in Krakow, Poland, Lajkonik (or the **Horse Festival**) has lost touch with its medieval roots, but is believed to commemorate the horseman who carried the news of the Tartar defeat during the 13th-century Tartar invasions. A group of 18 costumed people gathers in the courtyard of the Norbertine Monastery in a suburb of Krakow. They include a standard-bearer in the traditional dress of a Polish nobleman, a small band of musicians, and a bearded horseman in oriental costume riding a richly draped but rather small wooden hobby-horse. This is the Lajkonik, originally called the Horse or the 'Zwierzyniec Horse,' named for the town where the monastery is located, and now the unofficial symbol of Krakow.

After performing a ceremonial dance for the vicar and the nuns, the procession leaves the monastery and moves in the direction of the city. The horseman collects money from the crowds lining the streets, striking each contributor lightly with his baton to bring them good luck; they then join the procession. Eventually the parade ends up in the market square for the most important part of the ceremony. The city officials await the horseman on the steps of the town hall. He performs a dance for them and is rewarded with a purse full of money and a glass of wine, which he drinks to the health of the city.

The festival was first sponsored by the guild that furnished wood to Krakow and the salt mines. Today the actors are from the Boatman Congregation who, since the Middle Ages, have floated timber down the Vistula River to Krakow.

CONTACT:
Polish National Tourist Office
275 Madison Ave., Ste. 1711
New York, NY 10016
212-338-9412; fax: 212-338-9283

SOURCES:
BkFest-1937, p. 262
FolkWrldHol-1992, p. 293

◆ 1030 ◆ Lakshmi Puja
September–October; Hindu month of Asvina

The annual festival in honor of the Hindu goddess Lakshmi is held in the autumn, when Hindus of all castes ask for her blessings. Lights shine from every house, and no one sleeps during the celebrations.

Lakshmi is traditionally associated with wealth, prosperity, and good luck. In later Hindu literature, she appears as the dutiful wife of the god Vishnu and is typically portrayed massaging his feet while he rests on the cosmic serpent, Shesa. She remains a popular Hindu goddess to this day in India, where she is worshipped especially by merchants, who ask her to grant them wealth and success.

SOURCES:
BkFest-1937, p. 161
DictWrldRel-1989, p. 280

◆ 1031 ◆ Lammas
August 1

This was one of the four great pagan festivals of Britain and was originally called the festival of the **Gule of August**. It celebrated the harvest, and was the forerunner of America's Thanksgiving and Canada's Harvest Festival. In medieval England, loaves made from the first ripe grain were blessed in the church on this day—the word *lammas* being a short form of "loaf mass." Lammas Day is similar in original intent to the Jewish Feast of Weeks, also called Shavuot or Pentecost, which came at the end of the Passover grain harvest. A 15th-century suggestion was that the name derived from 'lamb' and 'mass,' and was the time when a feudal tribute of lambs was paid.

In the Scottish Highlands, people used to sprinkle their cows and the floors of their houses with menstrual blood, which they believed was especially potent against evil on this day. It was also one of the Quarter Days in Scotland, when tenants brought in the first new grain to their landlords.

Along with Candlemas, Walpurgis Night, and Halloween, Lammas is an important day in the occult calendar.

A phrase used from the 16th to the 19th century, "at Latter Lammas Day," meant 'never.'

SOURCES:
BkDays-1864, vol. II, p. 154
DaysCustFaith-1957, p. 199
DictDays-1988, pp. 51, 66
DictFolkMyth-1984, pp. 601, 961
FestSaintDays-1915, p. 163
FolkWrldHol-1992, p. 412
RelHolCal-1993, pp. 64, 89

SaintFestCh-1904, p. 349

♦ 1032 ♦ Landing of d'Iberville
Last weekend in April

A commemoration of the landing in 1699 of Pierre LeMoyne d'Iberville at a spot on Biloxi Bay that is now Ocean Springs, Miss. The arrival of d'Iberville and 200 colonists established the Louisiana Colony for King Louis XIV of France; the territory stretched from the Appalachians to the Rocky Mountains and from Canada to the Gulf of Mexico. D'Iberville built Fort Maurepas here, the first significant structure erected by Europeans on the Gulf Coast.

A replica of the fort is the backdrop for the reenactment of the landing. This pageant boasts a costumed cast representing both the notables of d'Iberville's fleet as well as the welcoming Biloxi Indians. The part of d'Iberville is always played by a celebrity, usually from the political world. However, in 1984, Col. Stuart A. Roosa, an Apollo 14 astronaut, played the explorer. In the reenactment, d'Iberville with his officers debarks and wades ashore, plants a cross in the sand, and claims the land for Louis XIV. The Indians, at first wary, invite the French to their village to smoke a peace pipe. The reenactment was first staged in 1939.

The celebration begins on Friday night with a covered dish supper at the civic center. On Saturday night, there is a formal-dress historic ball and pageant, with the presentation of d'Iberville, his officers, and the Cassette Girls. These were young orphan women who had been taught by Catholic nuns in Paris; they made the long trip to the Gulf Coast to become the brides of the men settled in the territory. They were called Cassette Girls because of the cases each carried that contained their trousseaus. The reenactment takes place on Sunday and is followed by a grand parade. There are also exhibits and street and food fairs.

CONTACT:
Mississippi Division of Tourism
  Development
P.O. Box 849
Jackson, MS 39205
800-927-6378 or 601-359-3297
fax: 601-359-5757

♦ 1033 ♦ Landsgemeinden
Last Sunday of April

An open-air meeting to conduct cantonal business, held once a year in Appenzell, in the canton of Appenzell Inner-Rhoden in Switzerland. At the meeting, citizens vote on representatives for cantonal offices and on budget and tax proposals. Voting is by raised hands.

The assembly is a tradition that dates back to the very early days of the Swiss state. Women may wear richly embroidered national costumes and men wear their swords. Other districts in central and eastern Switzerland also have these assemblies, each with distinct customs. In Stans, for example, the blowing of a horn signals the time to walk to the meeting place outside the town; the horn is a reminder of the ancient call to battle.

Landsgemeinden has echos in the town meetings of the United States (*see* Town Meeting Day).

CONTACT:
Swiss National Tourist Office
608 Fifth Ave.
New York, NY 10020
212-757-5944; fax: 212-262-6116

♦ 1034 ♦ Landshut Wedding
Late June and early July, every three years (1998, 2001, . . .)

A pageant in Landshut, Bavaria, Germany, that recreates a lavish 15th-century wedding—that of Duke George the Rich of Bavaria and Polish Princess Hedwig, which took place in 1475. There were 10,000 guests, and records state that they ate 333 oxen, 275 fat pigs, 40 calves, and 12,000 geese.

Today the festivities are spread over three weeks, with the wedding reenactments on weekends—a play and dances on Saturdays; the historical wedding procession, followed by a concert, on Sundays. During the week, historical dances are performed, and some 1,000 residents dressed as medieval burghers roam the streets. There are also jesters parading, armored knights on horseback, and wandering minstrels.

CONTACT:
German National Tourist Office
122 E. 42nd St., 52nd Floor
New York, NY 10168
212-661-7200; fax: 212-661-7174

SOURCES:
GdWrldFest-1985, p. 85

♦ 1035 ♦ Lantern Festival (Yuan Hsiao Chieh)
January–February; 15th day of first lunar month, fourth day of first lunar month in Tibet

A festival of lights that ends the Lunar New Year, or Chinese New Year, celebrations and marks the first full moon of the new lunar year.

In China, it's traditional for merchants to hang paper lanterns outside their shops for several days before the full-moon day. On the night of the festival, the streets are bright with both lanterns and streamers, and people go out in throngs to see the displays. The most popular lanterns are cut-outs of running horses that revolve with the heat of the candles that light them. Other customs include eating round, stuffed dumplings and solving "lantern riddles"—riddles that are written on pieces of paper and stuck to the lanterns. In many areas, children parade with lanterns of all shapes and sizes. It's also thought to be a good night for young women to find husbands. In Penang, Malaysia, single women in their best dresses stroll along the city's promenade, and some parade in decorated cars followed by musicians.

Tibetan Buddhists celebrate the day as Monlam, or Prayer Festival, and in Lhasa, the butter sculptures of the monks are famous (*see* Butter Sculpture Festival). In China's Gansu Province, the Lhabuleng Monastery is the site of sculptured butter flowers made by the lamas and hung in front of the main scripture hall. On the day before the full moon, a dance is performed by about 30 masked lamas to the music of drums, horns, and cymbals. The protagonists are the God of Death and his concubines; they dance with others who are dressed as skeletons, horned stags, and yaks.

In 1990, the Taipei Lantern Festival was first held in Taiwan's capital city. It's held at the Chiang Kai-shek Memorial Hall and features high-tech lanterns with mechanical animation, dry-ice "smoke," and laser beams. In recent years, theme lanterns were modeled after the Chinese zodiacal animals for those years. Sculptor Yuyu Yang has produced elaborate structures for the festival, including a dragon that was 40 feet high with a skin of a stainless-steel grid and 1,200 interior light bulbs that shone through to make it look like a gigantic hand-made paper lantern. Laser beams shot from the dragon's eyes, and red-colored smoke spewed from the mouth. Another year, he created three 33-foot high goats made of acrylic tubes with colored lights shining from the inside.

The festival also offers musical and folk-art performances, a procession of religious and folk floats, and troupes of performers entertaining with martial-arts demonstrations, stilt-walking, and acrobatics.

In Hong Kong, anyone who has had a son during the year brings a lantern to the Ancestral Hall, where the men gather for a meal.

The Lantern Festival is supposed to have originated with the emperors of China's Han dynasty (206 B.C.–221 A.D.), who paid tribute to the universe on that night. Because the ceremony was held in the evening, lanterns were used to illuminate the palace. The Han rulers imposed a year-round curfew on their subjects, but on this night the curfew was lifted, and the people, carrying their own simple lanterns, went forth to view the fancy lanterns of the palace.

Another legend holds that the festival originated because a maid of honor (named Yuan Xiao, also the name of the sweet dumpling of this day) in the emperor's household longed to see her parents during the days of the Spring Festival. The resourceful Dongfang Shuo decided to help her. He spread the rumor that the god of fire was going to burn down the city of Chang-an. The city was thrown into a panic. Dongfang Shuo, summoned by the emperor, advised him to have everyone leave the palace and also to order that lanterns be hung in every street and every building. In this way, the god of fire would think the city was already burning. The emperor followed the advice, and Yuan Xiao took the opportunity to see her family. There have been lanterns ever since.

SOURCES:
BkFestHolWrld-1970, p. 9
BkHolWrld-1986, Feb 27
Chases-1996, pp. 122, 123
DictFolkMyth-1984, p. 603
FolkWrldHol-1992, p. 73
GdWrldFest-1985, p. 63
RelHolCal-1993, p. 89

♦ 1036 ♦ Lanterns Festival
End of Islamic month of Ramadan

A trader known as Daddy Maggay introduced the custom of parading with lanterns in Freetown, Sierra Leone, during the 1930s. The original lanterns were simple hand-held paper boxes, lit from within and mounted on sticks. They were carried through the streets of Freetown in celebration of the 26th day of RAMADAN, also known as the **Day of Light** or **Lai-Lai-Tu-Gadri**, when the Qu'ran was sent to earth by Allah (*see* LAYLAT AL-QADR).

As the years passed, the celebration—and the lanterns—grew larger. Heavy boots, originally worn as protection from the crowds, came to be used to produce drum-like rhythmical beats on the paved streets since some Muslims discourage using drums. Maggay's group was called *bobo*, the name for

their distinctive beat. Neighborhood rivalries, based on competition in lantern-building, often erupted in violence. By the 1950s the Young Men's Muslim Association had taken over the festival in hopes of reducing the violence through better organization. The lanterns—which by that time were elaborate float-like structures illuminated from within and drawn by eight-man teams or motor vehicles—were divided into three categories for judging: Group A for ships; Group B for animals and people; and Group C for miscellaneous secular subjects. Prizes were awarded to the top three winners in each group, based on creativity and building technique.

CONTACT:
Sierra Leone Embassy
1701 19th St., N.W.
Washington, D.C. 20009
202-939-9261; fax: 202-483-1793

SOURCES:
FolkWrldHol-1992, p. 169

♦ 1037 ♦ Larentalia
December 23

In ancient Rome, the *lares* were the beneficent spirits of household and family. Along with the *penates* (the gods of the storeroom) and the *manes* (spirits of the dead), they were worshipped privately within the home. Eventually they came to be identified with the spirits of the deceased. Each household had its own *lar*, to whom a prayer was addressed every morning and for whom special offerings were made at family festivals.

During the Larentalia, observed on December 23, offerings were made to the dead, especially at the shrine of Acca Larentia, the nurse of Romulus and Remus, the legendary founders of Rome. A sacrifice was offered on the spot where Acca Larentia was said to have disappeared.

See also COMPITALIA, FERALIA, PARENTALIA

SOURCES:
DictFolkMyth-1984, p. 604
NewCentClassHand-1962, p. 625

♦ 1038 ♦ Latter-Day Saints, Founding of the Church of
April 6

April 6, 1830, is the day on which Joseph Smith formally established the Church of Jesus Christ of the Latter-Day Saints (also known as Mormons) in Fayette, New York. Three years later the anniversary of the Church's founding was celebrated for the first time, with a meeting of about 80 people on the Big Blue River in Jackson County, Missouri. After that, there were no "birthday" celebrations until 1837, when a "general conference" was held to conduct church business and to observe the anniversary. Eventually the idea of holding an annual conference became an established custom, and it was always scheduled to encompass the April 6 founding date.

CONTACT:
Church of Jesus Christ of Latter-
Day Saints
15 E. North Temple St.
Salt Lake City, UT 84150
801-240-1000; fax: 801-240-2033

SOURCES:
Chases-1996, p. 160
DaysCustFaith-1957, p. 94
DictWrldRel-1989, p. 423
FolkAmerHol-1991, p. 179
RelHolCal-1993, p. 77

Launceston Cup Day
See **Hobart Cup Day**

♦ 1039 ♦ **Law Day**
May 1

It was the American Bar Association that persuaded President Dwight D. Eisenhower in 1958 to set aside a special day to commemorate the role of law in the United States and to remind people of the contrast between democratic government under the law and the tyranny of Communism. But it wasn't until 1961 that a joint resolution of Congress designated May 1 as Law Day, and President John F. Kennedy asked Americans to display the flag and observe the occasion with appropriate programs—typically mock trials, courthouse tours, special radio and television programs, library exhibits, and essay contests. Most Law Day exercises today are sponsored by the American Bar Association in cooperation with state and local bar associations.

The first of May was previously known as LOYALTY DAY, another attempt to play up the virtues of democracy and to cast Communism in a negative light. It is no coincidence that in the former U.S.S.R., MAY DAY is the great holiday for massive military reviews and other demonstrations of armed power.

CONTACT:
American Bar Association
750 N. Lake Shore Dr.
Chicago, IL 60611
312-988-5000; fax: 312-988-6281
WWW: http://www.abanet.org

SOURCES:
AmerBkDays-1978, p. 411
AnnivHol-1983, p. 59
Chases-1996, p. 194
DictDays-1988, p. 67

♦ 1040 ♦ **Laylat al-Miraj**
Twenty-seventh day of Islamic month of Rajab

Laylat al-Miraj commemorates the ascent of the Prophet Muhammad into heaven. One night during the 10th year of his prophecy, the angel Gabriel woke Muhammad and traveled with him to Jerusalem on the winged horse, Burak. There he prayed at the site of the Temple of Solomon with the Prophets Abraham, Moses, Jesus and others. Then, carried by Gabriel, he rose to heaven from the rock of the Temple Mount, where the Dome of the Rock sanctuary now stands. Allah instructed him regarding the five daily prayers that all Muslims must observe. Muslims today celebrate the evening of the 27th day of Rajab with special prayers. This day is also known as the **Night Journey,** or the **Ascent.**

SOURCES:
AnnivHol-1983, p. 170
BkHolWrld-1986, Apr 29
Chases-1996, p. 476
FolkWrldHol-1992, p. 101
RelHolCal-1993, p. 89

♦ 1041 ♦ **Laylat al-Qadr**
One of the last 10 days of Islamic month of Ramadan

Laylat al-Qadr commemorates the night in 610 during which Allah revealed the entire Qu'ran (Muslim holy book) to Muhammad. It was then that the angel Gabriel first spoke to him, and was thus the beginning of his mission. These revelations continued throughout the remainder of his life. Children begin studying the Qu'ran when they are very young, and they celebrate when they've read all 114 chapters for the first time. Many adults try to memorize the entire Qu'ran. The common belief that this day occurred on the 26th or 27th of Ramadan has no Islamic base. It seems to have originated in Manicheism where the death of Mani is celebrated on the 27th of the fasting month. This day is also known as the **Night of Power** or **Night of Destiny**.

See also LANTERNS FESTIVAL

SOURCES:
AnnivHol-1983, p. 171
BkHolWrld-1986, Jun 23
Chases-1996, p. 93
DictWrldRel-1989, p. 661
FolkWrldHol-1992, pp. 163, 167, 169, 171, 172

♦ 1042 ♦ **Lazarus Saturday**
Between March 27 and April 30; Saturday before Palm Sunday

In Russia and in all Eastern Orthodox churches, the Saturday before PALM SUNDAY (or Willow Sunday) is set aside to honor Lazarus, whom Jesus raised from the dead. Pussywillows are blessed at the evening service in the Russian Orthodox Church, and the branches are distributed to the worshippers, who take them home and display them above their icons. It was an ancient folk custom for people to beat their children with willow branches—not so much to punish them as to ensure that they would grow up tall and resilient like the willow tree.

On this day in Greece, Romania, and the former Yugoslavia, one custom is for groups of children to carry willow branches from house to house and sing songs and act out the story of Christ raising Lazarus from the dead. In return, they receive gifts of fruit and candy. They believe the resurrection of Lazarus is symbolic of the renewal of spring, which is why the *Lazarouvane* (the celebration of ST. LAZARUS'S DAY in Bulgaria) focuses on fertility and marriage.

SOURCES:
AnnivHol-1983, p. 178
BkFest-1937, pp. 290, 337
FolkWrldHol-1992, p. 129

♦ 1043 ♦ **Leap Year Day**
February 29

The earth actually takes longer than 365 days to complete its trip around the sun—five hours, 48 minutes, and 45 seconds longer, to be precise. To accommodate this discrepancy, an extra day is added to the Gregorian calendar at the end of February every four years (but not in "century" years unless evenly divisible by 400, e.g., 1600 and 2000, but not 1700). The year in which this occurs is called Leap Year, probably because the English courts did not always recognize February 29, and the date was often "leaped over" in the records. There's an old tradition that women could propose marriage to men during Leap Year. The men had to pay a forfeit if they refused. It is for this reason that February 29 is sometimes referred to as **Ladies' Day** or **Bachelors' Day.** Leap Year Day is also **St. Oswald's Day,** named after the 10th-century archbishop of York, who died on February 29, 992.

See also SADIE HAWKINS DAY

SOURCES:
AmerBkDays-1978, p. 217
BkHolWrld-1986, Feb 29
Chases-1996, p. 115
DaysCustFaith-1957, p. 59
DictDays-1988, pp. 8, 67
FolkAmerHol-1991, p. 82
FolkWrldHol-1992, p. 140
RelHolCal-1993, p. 90

♦ 1044 ♦ Lebanon National Day
November 22

Also known as **Independence Day**, this national holiday commemorates Lebanon's independence from France on this day in 1943.

CONTACT:
Lebanese Embassy
2560 28th St., N.W.
Washington, D.C. 20008
202-939-6300; fax: 202-939-6324

SOURCES:
AnnivHol-1983, p. 150
Chases-1996, p. 456
NatlHolWrld-1968, p. 209

♦ 1045 ♦ Lee, Birthday of Ann
February 29

Ann Lee (1736–1784) founded the religious movement known as Shakerism, leaving England to establish Shaker communities throughout New England and New York state, as well as in Kentucky, Ohio, and Indiana. "Mother Ann," as she was known to her followers, believed that she was Christ in female form and that sexual activity was the cause of sin. Shaker communities were known for their inventions (which include the flat broom and the clothespin), their architecture, and their furniture design as well as their commitment to celibacy, communal ownership of property, prayer, and separation from the world. They were pioneers in scientific stock breeding, crop rotation, and food preservation. The only active Shaker community that remains today is at Sabbathday Lake in Poland Spring, Maine.

Since there are less than a dozen Shakers alive, Ann Lee's birthday is no longer celebrated on a large scale, but there are numerous events commemorating the history of the Shaker movement that take place at the many sites and museums devoted to Shakerism, including a SHAKER FESTIVAL held each July in Auburn, Ky.

CONTACT:
Friends of the Shakers
Sabbathday Lake
Poland Spring, ME 04274
207-926-4597

SOURCES:
AmerBkDays-1978, p. 218
AnnivHol-1983, p. 30
Chases-1996, p. 115
DictWrldRel-1989, p. 674

♦ 1046 ♦ Lee Day, Robert E.
Third Monday in January

The Confederate General Robert Edward Lee was born on January 19, 1807. He was in charge of the military and naval forces of Virginia during the Civil War, building a reputation as a brilliant military strategist and a man who inspired great loyalty among his troops. By the time he was appointed general-in-chief of all the Confederate armies, the South's defeat was imminent. Lee's subsequent surrender to General Ulysses S. Grant at the Appomattox Court House in 1865 marked the end of the war (*see* APPOMATTOX DAY).

In 1889 Georgia became the first state to make Lee's birthday a legal holiday. Other states observing Lee's birthday each year include Alabama, Arkansas, Florida, Kentucky, Louisiana, Mississippi, North Carolina, South Carolina, and Tennessee. While Texas observes Lee's birthday as **Confederate Heroes Day**, in Virginia it is combined with the birthdays of Andrew "Stonewall" Jackson and Martin Luther King (*see* KING, JR.'S BIRTHDAY, MARTIN LUTHER and JACKSON'S BIRTHDAY, ANDREW) and called **Lee-Jackson-King Day**.

SOURCES:
AnnivHol-1983, pp. 10, 11
Chases-1996, pp. 65, 69, 72
DictDays-1988, pp. 73, 96

♦ 1047 ♦ Lei Day
May 1

This is a celebration of Hawaii's state symbol of friendship. In 1928 Mrs. John T. Warren came up with the slogan, "Lei Day is May Day," and the holiday has been held there ever since. The events of the day include state-wide lei competitions. Leis are garlands made of flower blossoms, seeds, leaves, ferns, and pods. There is the crowning of a Lei Queen in Honolulu, and assorted exhibits and hula performances. The queen's coronation is accompanied by chanting and the blowing of conch shells.

On the day after the celebration, leis from the state-wide competitions are ceremoniously placed on the graves of Hawaii's royalty at the Royal Mausoleum in Nuuanu Valley.

CONTACT:
Hawaii Visitors Bureau
2270 Kalakaua Ave., Ste. 801
Honolulu, HI 96815
808-923-1811; fax: 808-922-8991

SOURCES:
AmerBkDays-1978, p. 412
AnnivHol-1983, p. 59
Chases-1996, p. 194
DictDays-1988, p. 67

♦ 1048 ♦ Leif Erikson Day
October 9

The Viking explorer known as Leif the Lucky or Leif Erikson (because he was the son of Eric the Red) sailed westward from Greenland somewhere around the year 1000 and discovered a place he named Vinland after the wild grapes that grew there. No one really knows where Vinland was, but some historians believe that Erikson landed in North America 488 years before COLUMBUS sailed into the New World. The only evidence that this may have happened are a few Viking relics found in Rhode Island, Minnesota, and Ontario. In 1960, the site of a Norse settlement was discovered at L'Anse aux Meadows, at the northern tip of Newfoundland. The site dates from about the year 1000, but it has not been definitively linked to Leif Erikson's explorations.

Because the date and place of Erikson's "discovery" of North America were uncertain, members of the Leif Erikson Association arbitrarily chose October 9 to commemorate this event—perhaps because the first organized group of Norwegian emigrants landed in America on October 9, 1825. But it wasn't until 1964 that President Lyndon B. Johnson proclaimed this as Leif Erikson Day.

States with large Norwegian-American populations—such as Washington, Minnesota, Wisconsin, and New York—often hold observances on this day, as do members of the Sons of Norway, the Leif Erikson Society, and other Norwegian-American organizations. October 9 is a commemorative day in Iceland and Norway as well.

SOURCES:
AmerBkDays-1978, p. 909
AnnivHol-1983, p. 130
Chases-1996, p. 410
FolkAmerHol-1991, p. 363

♦ 1049 ♦ Le Mans Motor Race
June

The motor racing circuit in the city of Le Mans, capital of the Sarthe department of France, has been the scene of important races since 1914, although it wasn't until 1923 that the first 24-hour sports car race for which the course is now famous was held. Over the years the **Le Mans 24-Hour Grand Prix d'Endurance** has had a significant impact on the development of sports cars for racing, resulting in some prototype sports cars that are not far behind Formula I racing cars in terms of power and speed. The original course was rough and dusty, with a lap distance of just under 11 miles. Eventually the road surface was improved, the corners were eased, and the lap distance was reduced to just over eight miles. Part of the course is still a French highway, now flanked by permanent concrete stands for spectators and the pits, where refueling and repairs are done. A serious accident at Le Mans in 1955, in which a French driver and 85 spectators died, led to a number of course improvements.

The all-night racing at Le Mans is a favorite spectacle for motor racing fans. One of the major attractions is the opportunity to watch what goes on in the pits. Although most Grand Prix races can now be run without refueling or tire changing, the highly efficient work of the teams' mechanics still plays an important part in long-duration races like the one at Le Mans.

CONTACT:
French Government Tourist Office
9454 Wilshire Blvd., Ste. 715
Beverly Hills, CA 90212
310-271-6665; fax: 310-276-2835

♦ 1050 ♦ Lemuralia
May 9, 11, 15

In ancient Rome the *lemures* were the ghosts of the family's dead, who were considered to be troublesome and therefore had to be exorcized on a regular basis. The lemures were generally equated with larvae or evil spirits, although some people believed that the lemures included the *lares*, or 'good spirits', as well (*see* LARENTALIA).

The Lemuralia or **Lemuria** was a yearly festival held on the ninth, 11th, and 15th of May to get rid of the lemures. Supposedly introduced by Romulus, the legendary founder of Rome, after he killed his twin brother Remus, this festival was originally called the **Remuria**. Participants walked barefoot, cleansed their hands three times, and threw black beans behind them nine times to appease the spirits of the dead. On the third day of the festival, a merchants' festival was held to ensure a prosperous year for business. The period during which the Lemuralia was held—the entire month of May—was considered to be an unlucky time for marriages.

SOURCES:
AmerBkDays-1978, p. 406
DictFolkMyth-1984, pp. 123, 613
FestSaintDays-1915, p. 110

♦ 1051 ♦ Lent
Begins between February 4 and March 10 in West and between February 15 and March 21 in East. Forty-day period, beginning on Ash Wednesday in the West and on the Monday seven weeks before Easter in the East; ends on Easter eve, Holy Saturday

Self-denial during a period of intense religious devotion has been a long-standing tradition in both the Eastern and Western churches. In the early days, Christians prepared for EASTER with a strict fast only from GOOD FRIDAY until Easter morning. It wasn't until the ninth century that the Lenten season, called the **Great Lent** in the East to differentiate it from the ADVENT fast called Little Lent, was fixed at 40 days (with Sundays omitted)—perhaps reflecting the biblical importance attached to the number 40: Moses had gone without food for 40 days on Mt. Sinai, the children of Israel had wandered for 40 years with little sustenance, Elijah had fasted 40 days, and so did Jesus, between his baptism and the beginning of his ministry. In the Western church further extensions led to a no-longer-existing "pre-Lent" season, with its Sundays called Septuagesima (roughly 70 days before Easter), Sexagesima (60), and Quinquagesima (50)—all preceding the first Sunday of Lent, QUADRAGESIMA (40).

The first day of Orthodox Lent is called Clean Monday.

For centuries the Lenten season has been observed with certain periods of strict fasting, and with abstinence from meat, and in the East, also from dairy products, wine, and olive oil, as well as giving up something—a favorite food or other worldly pleasure—for the 40 days of Lent. Celebrations such as CARNIVAL and MARDI GRAS offered Christians their last opportunities to indulge before the rigorous Lenten restrictions.

See also ASH WEDNESDAY, CHEESE SUNDAY, MOTHERING SUNDAY, SHROVE TUESDAY

SOURCES:
BkFest-1937, pp. 68, 308
DaysCustFaith-1957, p. 65
DictFolkMyth-1984, pp. 181, 212, 851
DictWrldRel-1989, pp. 154, 175, 425
FestWestEur-1958, p. 211
FolkWrldHol-1992, p. 122
IndianAmer-1989, p. 273
RelHolCal-1993, p. 90
SaintFestCh-1904, p. 115

♦ 1052 ♦ Leonhardiritt (St. Leonard's Ride)
November 6 or nearest weekend

A celebration of St. Leonhard, the patron saint of horses and cattle, observed in various towns of Bavaria, Germany. Traditionally, processions of elaborately harnessed horses draw decorated wagons to the local church. Some people also bring their cattle to be blessed. A contest of whip-cracking usually follows the procession. Among the towns where Leonard's Ride is held are Bad Tölz, Rottenbuch, Bad Fussing, Waldkirchen, and Murnau. November 6 is the name-day of the saint and the traditional day of the procession, but some towns now hold their rides on a weekend near that date.

CONTACT:
German National Tourist Office
122 E. 42nd St., 52nd Floor
New York, NY 10168
212-661-7200; fax: 212-661-7174

SOURCES:
BkFest-1937, p. 138
BkHolWrld-1986, Nov 6
FestWestEur-1958, p. 75

♦ 1053 ♦ Lesotho Independence Day
October 4

Formerly Basutoland, the Kingdom of Lesotho was formally granted its independence from Great Britain on this day in 1966. It had been a British colony since the 1860s.

Before the flag-changing ceremonies at midnight to symbolize Lesotho's new autonomy, a colorful procession took place as King Moshoeshoe II (b. 1938) paraded in full regalia leading 100 chiefs into the capital city of Maseru.

CONTACT:
Lesotho Embassy
2511 Massachusetts Ave., N.W.
Washington, D.C. 20008
202-797-5533; fax: 202-234-6815

SOURCES:
AnnivHol-1983, p. 128
Chases-1996, p. 403
NatlHolWrld-1968, p. 186

♦ 1054 ♦ Leyden Day
October 3

In 1574 the Dutch city of Leyden (or Leiden) was besieged by the Spaniards. Thousands were dying from disease and hunger, but when a group of desperate citizens pleaded with the Burgomaster to surrender, he replied that he had sworn to keep the city safe and that it was better to die of starvation than shame. His stubbornness heartened the people, and on October 2 he had the river dikes cut so that the navy could sail in over the flooded fields and save the city. A statue of the heroic Burgomaster, Adrian van der Werff, was later erected in Leyden's Church of Saint Pancras.

According to legend, the first person to emerge from the besieged city on October 3, 1574, was a young orphan boy. In the deserted Spanish camp, he discovered a huge pot of stew that was still hot. He summoned the townspeople, who enjoyed their first hot meal in several months. Known as *Hutspot met Klapstuk*, the mixture of meat and vegetables is still served on this day, along with bread and herring.

SOURCES:
AnnivHol-1983, p. 128
BkFest-1937, p. 244
BkHolWrld-1986, Oct 3
Chases-1996, p. 402
FestWestEur-1958, p. 139

♦ 1055 ♦ Liberalia
March 17

Liber and Libera were ancient Roman fertility gods, worshipped along with Ceres. The triad of Ceres, Liber, and Libera were identified with the Greek deities Demeter, Dionysus, and Persephone. At the festival held in honor of Liber and Libera on March 17, young Roman boys who had come of age wore the *toga virilis* for the first time. In the ancient Italian town of Lavinium, a whole month was consecrated to Liber. The various rituals carried out during this time were designed to ensure the growth of newly planted seeds.

See also CEREALIA

SOURCES:
DictFolkMyth-1984, p. 618

NewCentClassHand-1962, p. 641

Liberation Day
See under individual countries

♦ 1056 ♦ Liberia Independence Day
July 26

This especially important Liberian holiday is celebrated with a parade, a party for the diplomatic corps in Monrovia, and a grand ball in the evening. Similar events are held throughout the country. The day commemorates the signing of the Declaration of Independence in 1847 by the various settlements of the country, establishing the first independent black republic in Africa. The nation that is now Liberia was settled in the early 1800s by freed American slaves under the auspices of the American Colonization Society. The capital city, Monrovia, is named after U.S. President James Monroe. The first settlers arrived on Providence Island in 1822. Other settlers followed, and they united in 1838. After independence, elections were held, and Joseph Jenkins Roberts was elected the first president in January 1848.

CONTACT:
Liberia Tourist Information
5303 Colorado Ave., N.W.
Washington, D.C. 20011
202-723-0437; fax: 202-723-0436

SOURCES:
AnnivHol-1983, p. 97
Chases-1996, p. 311
NatlHolWrld-1968, p. 124

♦ 1057 ♦ Libya Independence Day
December 24

Libya, first settled by the Phoenicians and then by the Greeks, was part of the Ottoman Empire until 1911, when the Italians took over the coastal provinces. During World War II, the British ruled two of the three Libyan provinces and the French ruled the third. After the war, Libya's future status was left up to the United Nations, which resolved that it should become independent by 1952. Independence was declared on December 24, 1951.

Schools, offices, and most stores are closed on this day, and the public buildings are decorated with streamers and flags. Members of the armed forces and various youth organizations march down the streets of the capital, Tripoli.

CONTACT:
Libyan Mission to the U.N.
309 E. 48th St.
New York, NY 10017
212-752-5775

SOURCES:
NatlHolWrld-1968, p. 229

♦ 1058 ♦ Libya National Day
September 1

This national holiday commemorates the revolution, led by Col. Muammar Qaddafi (b. 1938) that ousted King Idris I (Muhammad Idris el-Senussi, 1890–1983) who had ruled since 1952, and established a republic known as the People's Arab Jamahiriyah on this day in 1969.

CONTACT:
Libyan Mission to the U.N.
309 E. 48th St.
New York, NY 10017
212-752-5775

SOURCES:
AnnivHol-1983, p. 113
Chases-1996, p. 359

◆ 1059 ◆ Li Ch'un
February

In China, Li Ch'un means "Spring is here." The festival heralding the arrival of spring features a procession of dancers, singers, and musicians led by a huge ox and his driver, known as the Meng Shan (spirit driver). Both the ox and the driver are made out of stiff paper painted in five colors—red, black, white, green, and yellow—representing the five elements of nature (metal, wood, fire, water, and earth). The effigies are dressed according to what the newly issued *T'ung Shu*, the famous long-consulted Chinese almanac, says about the agricultural prospects for the coming year. If the head of the ox is painted yellow, for example, it means that the summer will be hot. If it is green, there will be a lot of sickness in the spring. Red indicates drought, black means rain, and white means high winds and storms. The way the Meng Shan dresses also provides clues about the weather: a hat means rain, shoes indicate heavy rain, and no shoes means there will be a drought. If he is dressed warmly, it means the year will be a cold one; light clothing means milder-than-usual weather.

People place a large piece of hollow bamboo filled with chicken feathers in front of their houses. The sight of feathers floating in the breeze means that spring has officially arrived.

CONTACT:
China National Tourist Office
350 Fifth Ave., Ste. 6413
New York, NY 10165
212-760-9700; fax: 212-760-8809

SOURCES:
AnnivHol-1983, p. 178
BkFestHolWrld-1970, p. 91
DictFolkMyth-1984, pp. 225, 618

◆ 1060 ◆ Lighting of the National Christmas Tree
A Thursday in December

On a selected Thursday night in December, the president of the United States lights the national Christmas tree at the northern end of the Ellipse in Washington, D.C., to the accompaniment of orchestral and choral music. The lighting ceremony marks the beginning of the two-week **Pageant of Peace**, a huge holiday celebration in the nation's capital that includes seasonal music, caroling, a nativity scene, 50 state Christmas trees, and a burning YULE log.

CONTACT:
Washington D.C. Convention and
Visitors Association
1212 New York Ave., N.W., Ste. 600
Washington, D.C. 20005
800-635-6338 or 202-789-7000
fax: 202-789-7037

SOURCES:
GdUSFest-1984, p. 205

Lights, Feast of
See **Hanukkah**

◆ 1061 ◆ Lights, Festival of
Late November through early January

The biggest event of the year in Niagara Falls, New York, is its Festival of Lights, which is held for six weeks during the CHRISTMAS holiday season. The falls themselves are illuminated, as are displays throughout the town featuring more than 200 life-size storybook characters in dozens of animated scenes. There is an arts and crafts show, a toy train collectors' show, a boat show, a doll show, and magic shows. Musical events include performances by internationally known singers, gospel choirs, bell choirs, steel drum bands, jazz groups, and blues bands. During the festival more than half a million lights adorn the city, which was the site of the world's first commercial hydroelectric plant in 1895.

CONTACT:
Niagara Falls Convention and
Visitors Bureau
310 Fourth St.
Niagara Falls, NY 14303
800-421-5223 or 716-285-2400
fax: 716-285-0809

◆ 1062 ◆ Lights, Festival of (Ganden Ngamcho)
Twenty-fifth day of 10th Tibetan lunar month (usually November–December)

A festival in Tibet to commemorate the birth and death of Tsongkhapa (1357–1419), a saintly scholar, teacher, and reformer of the monasteries, who enforced strict monastic rules. In 1408 he instituted the Great Prayer, a New Year rededication of Tibet to Buddhism; it was celebrated without interruption until 1959 when the Chinese invaded Tibet. He formulated a doctrine that became the basis of the Gelug (meaning 'virtuous') sect of Buddhism. It became the predominant sect of Tibet, and Tsongkhapa's successors became the Dalai Lamas, the rulers of Tibet.

During the festival, thousands of butter lamps (dishes of liquid clarified butter called *ghee*, with wicks floating in them) are lit on the roofs and window sills of homes and on temple altars. At this time people seek spiritual merit by visiting the temples.

CONTACT:
India Tourist Office
30 Rockefeller Ave.
15 N. Mezzanine
New York, NY 10112
212-586-4901; fax: 212-582-3274

SOURCES:
FolkWrldHol-1992, p. 529

Ligo Svetki
See **St. John's Eve and Day in Latvia**

◆ 1063 ◆ Lily Festival (Festa del Giglio)
Sunday following June 22

The Lily Festival in Nola, Italy, honors San Paolino (St. Paulinus), the town's patron saint. Legend has it that the festival began in the fourth century as a "welcome home" celebration when Paolino, who had placed himself in slavery to release a local widow's son, returned from Africa. Eight tradesmen representing the town greeted him by strewing flowers at his feet. Eventually the eight tradesmen were represented by sticks covered in lilies, and over the years the lily sticks (*gigli* in Italian) grew longer and more ornate. Today they are from 75 feet to nearly 100 feet high. Since they weigh about 50 tons, it takes 40 men to carry each one. After a traditional blessing is given, the crowd throws flowers into the air and begins a costumed procession that meanders through the narrow streets of the town, led by a boat carrying a statue of San Paolino and featuring the eight huge *gigli*, each of which is surrounded by its own symphony orchestra.

CONTACT:
Italian Government Travel Office
630 Fifth Ave.
New York, NY 10111
212-245-4822

SOURCES:
AnnivHol-1983, p. 82
BkHolWrld-1986, Jun 28
DaysCustFaith-1957, p. 150
GdWrldFest-1985, p. 118

♦ 1064 ♦ Limassol Wine Festival
Early September

An annual 10-day celebration of the wine of Cyprus, held in the Municipal Gardens of Limassol, the center of the wine-making industry. Wineries there compete to create the most original and decorative booths, and every evening pour out from barrels free samples of their wine. People sitting at picnic tables may watch exhibits of traditional wine pressing. There are also concerts and dance performances.

CONTACT:
Cyprus Tourism Organization
13 E. 40th St.
New York, NY 10016
212-683-5280; fax: 212-683-5282

SOURCES:
GdWrldFest-1985, p. 67
IntlThFolk-1979, p. 82

♦ 1065 ♦ Lincoln's Birthday
February 12

Abraham Lincoln, the 16th president of the United States, also called the Great Emancipator, the Rail Splitter, and Honest Abe, was born on Feb. 12, 1809. President throughout the Civil War, he is known for his struggle to preserve the union, the issuance of the Emancipation Proclamation (*see* Emancipation Day), and his assassination less than two weeks after the Confederate surrender at Appomattox Court House in 1865 (*see* Appomattox Day).

A wreath-laying ceremony and reading of the Gettysburg Address at the Lincoln Memorial in Washington D.C., are traditional on Feb. 12. Because the Republican party reveres Lincoln as its first president, Republicans commonly hold Lincoln-Day fund-raising dinners, as the Democrats hold Jackson-Day dinners.

Lincoln's actual birthday, Feb. 12, is a legal holiday in 14 states: California, Connecticut, Florida, Illinois, Indiana, Kansas, Kentucky, Maryland, Michigan, Missouri, New Jersey, New York, Vermont, and West Virginia. In Arizona, Lincoln's Birthday is observed on the second Monday in February. In 15 states, Lincoln's and Washington's birthdays are combined for a legal holiday on the third Monday in February called either Presidents' Day or Washington-Lincoln Day. **Washington-Lincoln Day** is observed in New Mexico on the third Monday in January.

SOURCES:
AmerBkDays-1978, pp. 168,
 1073
AnnivHol-1983, p. 23
BkFest-1937, p. 15
BkHolWrld-1986, Feb 12
Chases-1996, pp. 88, 95
DictDays-1988, p. 68

♦ 1066 ♦ Lindenfest
Second weekend in July

A 600-year-old linden tree in Geisenheim, Germany, is the center of this annual festival celebrating the new wine. As the oldest town in the Rhineland region, Geisenheim is renowned for its vineyards, and during the **Linden Tree**

Festival people come from all over the world to taste the wine, visit the vineyards, and make pilgrimages to Marienthal, a Franciscan shrine in a nearby wooded valley. The ancient linden tree is decorated with lights for the three-day festival, and folk dancing and feasting take place beneath its branches.

CONTACT:
German National Tourist Office
122 E. 42nd St., 52nd Floor
New York, NY 10168
212-661-7200; fax: 212-661-7174

SOURCES:
FestWestEur-1958, p. 68

♦ 1067 ♦ Lithuania Independence Day
February 16; March 11

This is a national holiday in Lithuania marking the declaration of independence from Austrian, Prussian, and Russian occupation on February 16, 1918. Soviets occupied Lithuania in 1940. The people voted for self-rule in February 1990, and the Lithuanian Supreme Council declared independence from the U.S.S.R. on March 11, 1990—an event that is also commemorated in Lithuania.

CONTACT:
Lithuanian Embassy
2622 16th St., N.W.
Washington, D.C. 20009
202-234-5860; fax: 202-328-0466

SOURCES:
Chases-1996, p. 100

♦ 1068 ♦ Little Big Horn Days
Weekend nearest June 25

A commemoration in Hardin, Mont., of the Old West and particularly of the most famous Indian-U.S. cavalry battle in history, Custer's Last Stand. An hour-long reenactment of that battle, known as the Battle of Little Big Horn, is staged each night of the three-day festival near the actual site of the original battle which occurred June 25, 1876. The battle reenactment is performed by more than 200 Indian and cavalry riders. Among them are descendants of the Indian scouts who rode with Colonel George Armstrong Custer, who led more than 200 men to battle and to death. The pageant is based on the notes and outline prepared by Joe Medicine Crow, a tribal historian, and was originally sponsored by the Crow Agency, administrator of the Crow Reservation. The first presentation of the drama was in 1964. It continued for a number of years before lapsing and then being restored to life in 1990.

Other events of the weekend are a historical symposium, traditional Indian dances, a black-powder shoot, a street dance, Scandinavian dinners, and a parade.

CONTACT:
Montana Travel Promotion
 Division
1424 Ninth Ave.
Helena, MT 59620
800-847-4868 or 406-444-2654
fax: 406-444-1800

SOURCES:
AmerBkDays-1978, pp. 591,
 593
Chases-1996, p. 265

♦ 1069 ♦ Little League World Series
Late August

Little League baseball began in 1939 with only three teams. It was incorporated under a bill signed into law by President Lyndon B. Johnson in 1964. Ten years later the law was amended to allow girls to join Little League teams. It is now played by over 2.5 million boys and girls between the ages of nine and twelve in 48 countries. The field is a smaller version of the regulation baseball diamond, with bases 60 feet apart and a pitching distance of 46 feet.

Every year in August the Little League World Series is held at Howard J. Lamade Field in Williamsport, Pennsylvania, location of the International Headquarters of Little League Baseball and home of the Little League Museum. First-round games are held on Monday, Tuesday, and Wednesday, with every team guaranteed a minimum of three games. Those who advance to the championship game end up playing as many as five games. The U.S. and International Championships are on Thursday, and Friday remains an open date, in case of rain. The series finale is played on Saturday.

World Series games are also held in August for Pony League Baseball (ages 13–14), Colt League (ages 15–16), and Palomino League (ages 17–18).

CONTACT:
Little League Baseball
Box 3485
Williamsport, PA 17701
717-326-1921; fax: 717-326-1074

SOURCES:
Chases-1996, p. 343

♦ 1070 ♦ Living Chess Game (La Partita a Scácchi Viventi)
Second weekend in September in even-numbered years

Every two years the main piazza in Marostica, Italy, is transformed into a giant chessboard. More than 500 townspeople wearing elaborate medieval costumes portray chessmen and act out a living game: knights in shining armor ride real horses, castles roll by on wheels, and black and white queens and kings march from square to square to meet their destinies. Thousands of spectators watch from bleachers, cheering loudly when a castle is lost and moaning when there is an impending checkmate. The local players begin rehearsing in March for the two-and-a-half hour performances. Some start out as pawns and over the years work their way up to become knights, kings, and queens.

The basis for the game is an incident that took place in 1454, when Lionora, the daughter of the lord of the castle, was being courted by two rivals. They challenged each other to a deadly duel but were persuaded to engage in a game of chess instead. Even today, the moves in the game are spoken in an ancient dialect, including the final *scácco matto!* (checkmate).

CONTACT:
Italian Government Travel Office
630 Fifth Ave.
New York, NY 10111
212-245-4822

♦ 1071 ♦ Llama Ch'uyay
July 31

The Llama Ch'uyay in Bolivia is the ritual force-feeding of "medicine" to llamas. On the eve of August 1, which the Andean Indians believe to be the day when the earth is at her most sensitive, the llamas are gathered together in a corral and, one at a time, they are forced to drink bottles of *hampi*, a medicine made from *chicha* and *trago* (two kinds of liquor), sugar, barley mash, soup broth, and special herbs. A large male may consume more than five bottles, while baby llamas usually drink only half a bottle. Three bottles is considered a

normal dose. After the animals drink their medicine, they are decorated with colored tassels made out of yarn. While men are feeding the llamas, women continually serve them chicha and trago. After the feeding, whole containers of chicha are thrown onto the herd. A similar ritual is performed for horses on July 25, the feast of Santiago (*see* St. James's Day).

SOURCES:
FolkWrldHol-1992, p. 409

♦ 1072 ♦ Lochristi Begonia Festival
Last weekend in August

A colorful celebration of the national flower of Belgium, held in Lochristi (six miles from Ghent), where 30 to 33 million flowering tubers are produced each year on more than 400 acres. For the festival, residents create enormous three-dimensional floral tableaux for the Floral Parade of Floats. These depict a different theme each year—for example, the world's favorite fairy tales. Besides the tableaux, arrangements of millions of yellow, red, orange, and white blossoms on beds of sand turn the town's main street into a carpet of flowered pictures. Other events are band concerts and tours to the begonia fields.

The tuberous begonia was originally a tropical plant. It takes its name from Michel Bégon, a French amateur botanist who was an administrator in the West Indies at the time of Louis XIV. The plant reached England in 1777, and Belgium began cultivating the begonia in the middle of the 19th century. Because the commercial value of the begonias comes from their tubers, or underground stems, the farmers of Lochristi discarded the blossoms before the festival was begun in 1946 and put them to good use.

See also Ghent Floralies

CONTACT:
Belgian Tourist Office
780 Third Ave.
New York, NY 10017
212-758-8130; fax: 212-355-7675

SOURCES:
GdWrldFest-1985, p. 21

♦ 1073 ♦ Loi Krathong
Usually mid-November; full moon night of twelfth lunar month

An ancient festival held under a full moon throughout Thailand, considered to be the loveliest of the country's festivals. After sunset, people make their way to the water to launch small lotus-shaped banana-leaf or paper boats, each holding a lighted candle, a flower, joss sticks, and a small coin. Loi means 'to float' and Krathong is a 'leaf cup' or 'bowl'.

There are several legends linked to the origins of this festival. One holds that the festival began about 700 years ago when King Ramakhamhaeng of Sukhothai, the first Thai capital, was making a pilgrimage on the river from temple to temple. One of his wives wanted to please both the king and the Lord Buddha, so she created a paper lantern resembling a lotus flower (which symbolizes the flowering of the human spirit), put a candle in it, and set it afloat. The king was so delighted he decreed that his subjects should follow this custom on one night of the year. Fittingly, the ruins of Sukhothai are the backdrop on the night of Loi Krathong for celebrations that include displays of lighted candles, fireworks, folk dancing, and a spectacular sound-and-light presentation.

A second legend traces the festival to the more ancient practice of propitiating the Mother of Water, Me Khongkha. The aim is to thank Me Khongkha and wash away the sins of the past year. The coins in the lotus cups are meant as tokens to ask forgiveness for thoughtless ways.

In yet another story, the festival celebrates the lotus blossoms that sprang up when the Buddha took his first baby steps.

A similar celebration is held in Washington, D.C., at the reflecting pool near the Lincoln Memorial. Dinner and participation are by paid ticket, but anyone passing can watch the adult, child, and teen dances and the exhibition of martial arts; and after dark, the floating candles.

CONTACT:
Tourism Authority of Thailand
5 World Trade Center, Ste. 3443
New York, NY 10048
212-432-0433; fax: 212-912-0920

Washington D.C. Convention and
  Visitors Association
1212 New York Ave., N.W., Ste.
  600
Washington, D.C. 20005
800-635-6338 or 202-789-7000
fax: 202-789-7037

SOURCES:
AnnivHol-1983, p. 178
BkHolWrld-1986, Nov 17
FolkWrldHol-1992, p. 568
GdWrldFest-1985, p. 173
RelHolCal-1993, p. 90

♦ 1074 ♦ London, Festival of the City of
July in even-numbered years

First held in 1963, the Festival of the City of London was designed to show off the historic "square mile" in the heart of the city. The churches, cathedrals, halls, and other landmarks in this area have served as the setting for the festival's concerts, operas, and theater productions ever since. An open-air production of Gilbert and Sullivan's *Yeoman of the Guard*, staged in the Tower of London to commemorate its 900th anniversary during the festival's first year, has since become a regular event.

Concerts are given by both British and international artists, orchestras, and chamber music groups. There are band concerts, dance recitals, prose and poetry readings, art and photographic exhibits, and a series of ethnic cultural events. Street theater and traveling miracle plays round out the festival's offerings.

CONTACT:
British Tourist Authority
551 Fifth Ave., Ste. 702
New York, NY 10176
800-462-2748 or 212-986-2200
fax: 212-986-1188

SOURCES:
GdWrldFest-1985, p. 94
IntlThFolk-1979, p. 163

♦ 1075 ♦ London Bridge Days
First full week in October

Given its location, this is one of the stranger and more unexpected festivals in all of the United States. Held in Lake Havasu City in the Arizona desert, the festival is a week-long celebration of all things English and of the London Bridge that spans a channel of the Colorado River. This London Bridge was built in 1831 to span the River Thames in London, England. Opening festivities at the time included a banquet held on the bridge and a balloon ascending from it. Like its predecessor mentioned in the nursery rhyme, which was completed in 1209, this bridge was falling down until Robert P. McCulloch, Sr., of the McCulloch Oil Corp., bought 10,000 tons of the granite facing blocks, transported them from foggy Londontown to sunny Arizona, rebuilt the bridge stone by stone, and dedicated it on Oct. 10, 1971. The Bridge Days are a commemoration of that re-opening.

A replica of an English village next to the bridge is the center of festival activities. There are English costume contests, a parade, a ball, musical entertainment, arts and crafts exhibits, and a "quit-rent" ceremony (*see* PAYMENT OF QUIT RENT). Lake Havasu City is a planned community and resort on the banks of Lake Havasu, which is fed by the Colorado River and impounded by the Parker Dam.

CONTACT:
Arizona Office of Tourism
1100 W. Washington St.
Phoenix, AZ 85007
800-842-8257 or 602-542-8687
fax: 602-542-4068

SOURCES:
Chases-1996, p. 426
GdUSFest-1985, p. 11

♦ 1076 ♦ Long Day, Huey P.
August 30

Huey Long was the colorful and often controversial governor of Louisiana from 1928 until 1932. Although he was impeached only a year after he'd been elected, he refused to yield the governorship to his lieutenant governor, a political enemy, and held on to the office until someone he liked better was elected. By then he'd been elected to the U.S. Senate, where he took what many considered to be an extreme stand on the redistribution of wealth, and openly rebelled against the administration of Franklin D. ROOSEVELT, a fellow Democrat.

In 1934–35 Long reorganized the Louisiana state government and set up what amounted to a dictatorship for himself. He exercised direct control over the judiciary, the police, firefighters, schoolteachers, election officials, and tax assessors while still serving as a U.S. Senator. As he was leaving the state capitol building on September 8, 1935, he was shot and killed by Dr. Carl Weiss, the son-in-law of one of his many political enemies.

Despite his controversial political activities, Long was revered by the rural people of the state, who supported his Share-Our-Wealth Society promising a minimum income for every American family. His birthday, August 30, has been observed as a legal holiday in Louisiana since 1937.

SOURCES:
AmerBkDays-1978, p. 790
AnnivHol-1983, p. 112
Chases-1996, p. 353
DictDays-1988, p. 58

Longest Day
See Summer Solstice

Long Friday
See Good Friday

♦ 1077 ♦ Looking Glass Powwow
August

A powwow held by the Nez Perce Indians each August in Kamiah, Idaho, to celebrate the memory of Chief Looking Glass, who was killed in the Nez Perce War of 1877. Nez Perce (meaning 'pierced nose' and pronounced NEZ-purse) is the name given by the French to a number of tribes that practiced the custom of nose-piercing. The term is used now to designate the main tribe of the Shahaptian Indians who, however, never pierced their noses.

Other major annual powwows of the Nez Perce are the Epethese Powwow, held the first weekend in March in Lapwai, Idaho, to decide war dance championships; the Mat-Al-YM'A Powwow and Root Feast in Kamiah the third weekend in May, with traditional dancing; the Warriors Memorial Powwow the third weekend in June in Lapwai, honoring Chief Joseph and his warriors; and the Four Nations Powwow, held in October in Lapwai.

CONTACT:
Nez Perce Executive Committee
P.O. Box 305
Lapwai, ID 83540
208-843-2253

SOURCES:
IndianAmer-1989, p. 126

Lord Krishna's Birthday
See **Janmashtami**

♦ 1078 ♦ Lord Mayor's Show
Second Saturday in November

The second Friday in November is **Lord Mayor's Day** in London, the day on which the city's Lord Mayor is admitted to office. The following day is the Lord Mayor's Show, a series of civic ceremonies that culminate in a parade to the Law Courts. At one time the Lord Mayor rode on horseback or traveled by state barge along the Thames, but today he rides from Guildhall to the Law Courts in a scarlet and gold coach drawn by six matched horses. This is the only time the mayoral coach is used; the rest of the time it is kept in the Museum of London.

Accompanying the coach is an honor guard of musketeers and pikemen in period dress, as well as many bands and numerous floats decorated to reflect the interests or profession of the new Lord Mayor. This colorful pageant dates back to the 13th century, when King John gave the citizens of London a charter stating that the Mayor was to be elected on September 29 and that he was to present himself either to the King or to the Royal Justices to be officially installed.

CONTACT:
British Tourist Authority
551 Fifth Ave., Ste. 702
New York, NY 10176
800-462-2748 or 212-986-2200
fax: 212-986-1188

SOURCES:
AnnivHol-1983, p. 144
BkDays-1864, vol. II, p. 561
BkHolWrld-1986, Nov 12
Chases-1996, p. 445
DictDays-1988, p. 69

♦ 1079 ♦ Losar
February–March; first day of first Tibetan lunar month

The new year in Tibet, according to the Tibetan calendar, which is in use throughout the Himalayan region; the date is determined by Tibetan astrologers in Dharmsala, India.

Before the new year, bad memories from the old year must be chased away, so houses are whitewashed and thoroughly cleaned. A little of the dirt collected is thrown away at a crossroads where spirits might dwell. A special dish called *guthuk* is prepared; in it are dumplings holding omens: a pebble promises life as durable as a diamond; cayenne pepper suggests a temperamental personality; a piece of charcoal would mean the recipient has a black heart. On the

last day of the old year, monks conduct ceremonies to drive out evil spirits and negative forces. In one such ritual, the monks, in grotesque masks and wigs and exotic robes, perform a dance in which they portray the struggle between good and evil (*see* Mystery Play of Tibet).

On the first day of the year, people arise early to place water and offerings on their household shrines. In the three days of the celebration, much special food and drink is prepared. This is a time of hospitality and merrymaking, with feasts, dances, and archery competitions.

Tibet was invaded by the Chinese in 1949, and the Dalai Lama, the spiritual and political head of Tibet, has been in exile since 1959. Much of the Tibetan culture has been suppressed, but festivals are still observed in a modest way in Tibet and by Tibetans in exile.

Tibetan exiles in India celebrate Losar by flocking to the temple in Dharmsala where the Dalai Lama lives. On the second day of the new year, he blesses people by touching their heads and giving them a piece of red-and-white string. People tie the blessed string around their necks as a protection from illness.

In Bodhnath, on the eastern side of Katmandu, Nepal, crowds of Tibetan refugees visit the *stupa* there to watch lamas perform rites. Copper horns are blown, there are masked dances, and a portrait of the Dalai Lama is displayed.

See also Dalai Lama, Birthday of the; Lunar New Year; Oshogatsu; Songkran; Tet; and Thingyan

CONTACT:
India Tourist Office
30 Rockefeller Ave.
15 N. Mezzanine
New York, NY 10112
212-586-4901; fax: 212-582-3274

Nepal Embassy
2131 Leroy Pl., N.W.
Washington, D.C. 20008
202-667-4550; fax: 202-667-5534

SOURCES:
BkHolWrld-1986, Feb 23
DictFolkMyth-1984, p. 777
FolkWrldHol-1992, pp. 61, 62
RelHolCal-1993, p. 90

♦ 1080 ♦ Lotus, Birthday of the
Twenty-fourth day of sixth lunar month

Although the Chinese celebrate the birthday of flowers in general (on the 12th or 15th day of the second lunar month) and honor Wei Shen, the protectress of flowers (on the 19th day of the fourth lunar month), the lotus is singled out for special attention because of its connection with Buddhism. The Birthday of the Lotus is observed at the time when lotuses bloom in the ponds and moats around Beijing, and people flock to the city to see them—much as they do in Japan and in Washington, D.C., during cherry blossom time (*see* Cherry Blossom Festival). Their blooms are a sign that prayers to the Dragon Prince have been answered and the summer rains will soon start. Special lanes for rowboats are cut through the thick layer of lotus blossoms that cover the lakes of the Winter Palace in Beijing.

CONTACT:
China National Tourist Office
350 Fifth Ave., Ste. 6413
New York, NY 10165
212-760-9700; fax: 212-760-8809

SOURCES:
FolkWrldHol-1992, p. 353

◆ 1081 ◆ Louisiana Shrimp and Petroleum Festival
September, Labor Day weekend

A celebration of an old industry and a newer one in Morgan City, La., which once called itself the Jumbo Shrimp Capital of the World. In 1947, oil was discovered offshore, and it was decided to combine the tribute to shrimp with a tribute to oil.

The celebration was originally known as the **Shrimp Festival and Blessing of the Fleet**. It began in 1937 as a revival of the Italian custom of blessing fishing fleets before they set out to sea, but from the first it also included boat races, a dance, a parade, and free boiled shrimp. After the world's first commercial offshore well was drilled in the Gulf of Mexico below Morgan City, the shrimp industry was outstripped in economic importance by the petroleum industry, and petroleum seeped into the festival. The highlight, though, is still the Blessing of the Fleet and a water parade, with hundreds of boats taking part. Other events of this festival, one of the state's premier affairs, are fireworks, an outdoor Roman Catholic Mass, arts and crafts displays, Cajun culinary treats, the coronation of the festival King and Queen, and a parade with floats.

CONTACT:
Louisiana Office of Tourism
P.O. Box 94291
Baton Rouge, LA 70804
800-334-8626 or 504-342-8119
fax: 504-342-8390

SOURCES:
Chases-1996, p. 352
GdUSFest-1984, p. 67

◆ 1082 ◆ Louisiana Sugar Cane Festival
Last weekend in September

A tribute to this important crop in New Iberia, La., which lies on the Bayou Teche. The Teche country is known as the "Sugar Bowl of Louisiana." The festival, which began in 1937 and now is participated in by 13 of the 17 sugar-producing parishes of the area, begins on Friday with a Farmers' Day. Highlights of the day are agriculture, homemaking and livestock shows, and a boat parade down Bayou Teche. On Saturday, there's a children's parade and the crowning of Queen Sugar at a ball, and on Sunday, the new Queen Sugar and King Sucrose reign over a parade. Other features are a blessing of the crops and a *fais-do-do*, a dance party.

CONTACT:
Louisiana Office of Tourism
P.O. Box 94291
Baton Rouge, LA 70804
800-334-8626 or 504-342-8119
fax: 504-342-8390

◆ 1083 ◆ Low Sunday
Between March 29 and May 2; Sunday after Easter

The Sunday following the 'high' feast of EASTER, it is also known as **Quasimodo Sunday**, **Close Sunday**, or **Low Easterday**. "Low" probably refers to the lack of "high" ritual used on Easter, and not to the low attendance usual on this day. The name Quasimodo Sunday comes from the Introit of the Mass which is said on this day. In Latin it begins with the phrase *Quasi modo geniti infantes*—'As newborn babes . . .' The famous character Quasimodo in Victor Hugo's novel, *The Hunchback of Notre Dame*, is said to have been found

abandoned on this day, which marks the close of Easter week.

SOURCES:
DictDays-1988, pp. 21, 70, 93
FestSaintDays-1915, p. 92
RelHolCal-1993, p. 106

◆ 1084 ◆ Loyalty Day
May 1

The U.S. Veterans of Foreign Wars designated the first day of May as Loyalty Day in 1947. The intention was to direct attention away from the Communist Party in the United States, which was using U.S. MAY DAY rallies to promote its doctrines and sign up new members. The idea caught on, and soon Loyalty Day was being celebrated throughout the country with parades, school programs, patriotic exercises, and speeches on the importance of showing loyalty to the United States. In Delaware, for example, Loyalty Day was marked by a special ceremony at Cooch's Bridge, where the Stars and Stripes were first displayed in battle. And in New York City, the Loyalty Day parade routinely attracted tens of thousands of participants.

Dissent over American intervention in Vietnam eventually eroded the popularity of Loyalty Day, and in 1968 only a few thousand marchers turned out for the traditional parades in Manhattan and Brooklyn, while 87,000 people participated in the Vietnam peace march in Central Park. Loyalty Day was later replaced by LAW DAY.

SOURCES:
AmerBkDays-1978, p. 411
AnnivHol-1983, p. 60
Chases-1996, p. 194

◆ 1085 ◆ Lucerne International Festival of Music
Mid-August to mid-September

The first **Lucerne Festival** was held in 1938, when Arturo Toscanini was persuaded by the city of Lucerne, Switzerland, to conduct a concert at the Tribschen estate, formerly the home of composer Richard Wagner and recently turned into the Wagner Museum.

Because cultural life in Switzerland was not interrupted by World War II, the festival was able to attract many famous conductors and performers who were war refugees. In addition to Toscanini, other well-known participants in the early days of the festival include Bruno Walter, Vladimir Horowitz, Fritz Busch, Arthur Schnabel, Pablo CASALS, Herbert von Karajan, and Rudolf Serkin.

Ernest Ansermet, Fritz Busch, and Bruno Walter formed the Swiss Festival Orchestra in 1943, and it has been the festival's mainstay ever since. Comprised of the best musicians in Switzerland who come together specifically for the Lucerne Festival and cannot be heard elsewhere, the orchestra is joined by other national groups—among them the Lucerne Festival Choir, the Lucerne Festival Strings, and the Lucerne Vocal Soloists—as well as internationally known orchestras from other countries. The program offers a balance of symphonic and chamber music as well as master classes, young artists' matinees, and a concert for seniors and persons with disabilities. Each year the four-week festival takes a different country's music as its theme.

CONTACT:
Swiss National Tourist Office
608 Fifth Ave.
New York, NY 10020
212-757-5944; fax: 212-262-6116

SOURCES:
Chases-1996, p. 341
GdWrldFest-1985, p. 169
MusFestEurBrit-1980, p. 141
MusFestWrld-1963, p. 207

Luciadagen

See **St. Lucy's Day**

♦ 1086 ♦ Ludi
Various

Ludi was the word used for public games in ancient Rome. These were holidays devoted to rest and pleasure. The **Ludi Megalenses** were held every year from April 4–10 from 191 B.C. onwards in honor of Cybele, the Roman Mother Goddess, whose image had been brought to Rome in 204 B.C. (*see also* MEGALESIA). The **Megalensian Games** were followed by the **Ludi Ceriales** in honor of Ceres, the ancient corn goddess, from April 12–19. Then came the **Ludi Florales** in honor of Flora, the goddess of flowers, from April 28–May 3. The Ludi Florales were followed by a period of hard work in the fields, and the next games didn't occur for seven weeks. The **Ludi Apollinares**, held in honor of Apollo, went on from July 6–13. The **Ludi Romani**, instituted in 366 B.C., lasted from September 4–19. And the **Ludi Plebei**, which were first held somewhere between 220 and 216 B.C., were held from November 4–17.

All in all, there were 59 days devoted to these traditional games in the Roman calendar before the time of Sulla who became dictator of the Roman Republic in 82 B.C. They were considered to be the *dies nefasti*—days on which all civil and judicial business must be suspended for fear of offending the gods.

SOURCES:
AmerBkDays-1978, pp. 313, 794

♦ 1087 ♦ Lúgnasad (Lúgnasa)
August 1

The Lúgnasa was a pre-Christian festival in Ireland associated with hilltops and with water. Occurring at the beginning of the harvest season, the Lúgnasa was a time for gathering berries and other early fruits of the season. Many of the hilltop sites where people came to pick berries were later taken over by the Roman Catholic Church and turned into pilgrimage sites. This is the case in County Mayo, where on the last Sunday in July thousands of pilgrims still climb to the summit of "the Reek," or Croagh Patrick, Ireland's holiest mountain. That day is known as REEK SUNDAY, and a series of masses are held in a small oratory on the top of Croagh Patrick. This is where St. Patrick is said to have spent the 40 days of LENT, and it was from this mountaintop that he is said to have driven all the venomous serpents into the ocean, thus explaining why there are no snakes in Ireland.

Lúgnasa was also a popular time to hold fairs. There was at one time a huge fair held at Teltown on the River Boyne called the **Lúgnasad**—*Lu'g* being the sun god in Irish mythology and *nasad* bearing a close relationship to the words

meaning "to give in marriage." From ancient times to as late as the 19th century, the fair seems to have been an opportunity for marriage contracts to be negotiated. Single men and women would come to the fair and sit in separate groups while their parents arranged marriages between them.

See also ST. PATRICK'S DAY

SOURCES:
Chases-1996, p. 317
DictFolkMyth-1984, pp. 202, 652
FestSaintDays-1915, p. 165
FolkWrldHol-1992, p. 413
RelHolCal-1993, p. 91

♦ 1088 ♦ Luilak
Between May 9 and June 12; Saturday before Pentecost

Luilak, or **Lazybones Day**, is a youth festival celebrated in Zaandam, Haarlem, Amsterdam, and other towns in the western Netherlands. The celebration begins at four o'clock in the morning on the Saturday before PENTECOST, when groups of young people awaken their neighbors by whistling, banging on pots and pans, and ringing doorbells. Any boys or girls who refuse to get up and join the noise-making are referred to as *Luilak*, or 'Lazybones', a name that is said to have originated in 1672 when a watchman named Piet Lak fell asleep while French invaders entered the country. Thereafter he was referred to as *Luie-Lak*, 'Lazy Lak.' In many parts of the country *Luilakbollen*, or 'Lazybones Cakes,' traditionally baked in the shape of fat double rolls and served with syrup, are a specialty of the season.

Children often celebrate Luilak by making little wagons, often shaped like boots and decorated with branches and thistles, known as *luilakken*. Pulling the wagons over the cobblestone streets often generates enough friction to set the wheels smoking. The children then either watch while their luilakken go up in flames or else dump them in the canals.

In Haarlem, Luilak marks the opening of the celebrated Whitsun flower market in the Grote Markt at midnight (*see* MERCHANTS' FLOWER MARKET).

SOURCES:
BkFest-1937, p. 243
BkFestHolWrld-1970, p. 66
FestWestEur-1958, p. 134
FolkWrldHol-1992, p. 284

♦ 1089 ♦ Lumberjack World Championships
Last weekend in July

At the turn of the century Hayward, Wisconsin, was one of the most active logging towns in the northern United States. Nowadays Hayward is known primarily as the site of the largest lumberjack competition in the country. Lumberjacks and logrollers from New Zealand, Australia, Canada, England, and the United States come to Hayward to compete in one- and two-man buck sawing, power sawing, a variety of chopping events, and the speed climbing contest, where loggers climb up and down a 90-foot fir pole in less than 30 seconds. There is also a lumberjack relay race, with teams consisting of one speed climber, one "river pig" (logroller), two-man crosscut saw partners, and one standing-cut chopper.

The three-day event takes place at the end of July in the Lumberjack Bowl, a large bay of Lake Hayward that was once used as a giant holding pond for the North Wisconsin Lumber Company and is now used for the World Logrolling Championships. The sport of "birling" or logrolling originated in New England and then moved west. Lumberjacks in overalls, woolen shirts, and high boots learned to maneuver a floating carpet of logs, using their pike poles to break up log jams. A working skill soon became a pastime and then a sporting event. Today's competitors dress in shorts and t-shirts or bathing suits and wear special birling shoes. Competitors stand on a floating log and try to roll each other off balance and into the water.

CONTACT:
Wisconsin Division of Tourism
123 W. Washington Ave., 6th
  Floor
Madison, WI 53703
800-432-8747 or 608-266-7621
fax: 608-266-3403

SOURCES:
GdUSFest-1984, p. 211

♦ 1090 ♦ **Lunar New Year**
January–February; first day of first lunar month

The Lunar New Year has certain variations from country to country, but they all include offerings to the household god(s), housecleaning and new clothes, a large banquet, ancestor worship, and firecrackers.

It is the most important and the longest of all Chinese festivals, celebrated by Chinese communities throughout the world. The festival, believed to date back to prehistory, marks the beginning of the new lunar cycle. It is also called the **Spring Festival**, since it falls between the WINTER SOLSTICE and VERNAL EQUINOX. It is the day when everyone becomes one year older—age is calculated by the year not the date of birth.

Activities begin in the 12th month, as people prepare food, clean their houses, settle debts, and buy new clothes. They also paste red papers with auspicious writings on the doors and windows of their homes.

On the 24th day of the 12th month, each Kitchen God leaves earth to report to the Jade Emperor in heaven on the activities of each family during the past year. To send their Kitchen God on his way, households burn paper money and joss sticks and give him offerings of wine. To make sure that his words to the Jade Emperor are sweet, they also offer *tang kwa*, a dumpling that finds its way into the mouths of eager children.

The eve of the new year is the high point of the festival when family members return home to honor their ancestors and enjoy a great feast. The food that is served has symbolic meaning. Abalone, for example, promises abundance; bean sprouts, prosperity; oysters, good business.

This is also a night of colossal noise; firecrackers explode and rockets whistle to frighten away devils. An old legend says that the lunar festival dates from the times when a wild beast (a *nihn*; also the Cantonese word for 'year') appeared at the end of winter to devour many villagers. After the people discovered that the beast feared bright lights, the color red, and noise, they protected themselves on the last day of the year by lighting up their houses, painting objects red, banging drums and gongs, and exploding bamboo "crackers." The explosions go on till dawn, and continue sporadically for the next two weeks. In Hong Kong, it is traditional after the feast to visit the flower markets. Flowers also have symbolic meaning, and gardeners try to ensure that peach and plum trees, which signify good luck, bloom on New Year's Day.

On the first day of the new year, household doors are thrown open to let good luck enter. Families go out to visit friends and worship at temples. Words are carefully watched to avoid saying anything that might signify death, sickness, or poverty. Scissors and knives aren't used for fear of "cutting" the good fortune, and brooms aren't used either, lest they sweep away good luck. Dragon and lion dances are performed, with 50 or more people supporting long paper dragons. There are acrobatic demonstrations and much beating of gongs and clashing of cymbals.

An ancient custom is giving little red packets of money (called *hung-pao* or *lai see*) to children and employees or service-people. The red signifies good fortune, and red is everywhere at this time.

On the third day of the holiday, families stay home, because it's supposed to be a time of bad luck. On the fourth day, local deities return to earth after a stay in heaven and are welcomed back with firecrackers and the burning of spirit money. According to legend, the seventh day is the anniversary of the creation of mankind, and the ninth day is the birthday of the Jade Emperor, the supreme Taoist deity. He is honored, not surprisingly, with firecrackers.

In most Asian countries, people return to work after the fourth or fifth day of celebration. In Taiwan, New Year's Eve, New Year's Day, and the two days following are public holidays, and all government offices, most businesses, restaurants, and stores are closed. The closings may continue for eight days.

By the 13th and 14th days, shops hang out lanterns for the Yuen Siu or LANTERN FESTIVAL, the day of the first full moon of the new year and the conclusion of the celebration.

In Chinese, the lunar new year is known as **Ch'un Chieh**, or 'Spring Festival.' It was formerly called **Yuan Tan**, 'the first morning', but the name was changed when the Gregorian calendar was officially adopted by the Republic of China in 1912. To differentiate the Chinese new year from the Western new year, January 1 was designated *Yuan Tan*. Today in China and in other Eastern nations, January 1 is a public holiday, but the Spring Festival is the much grander celebration.

Celebrations vary from country to country and region to region. In some towns in the countryside of Yunnan province in China, for example, an opera is performed by the farmers. The Chinese communities in San Francisco and New York City are especially known for their exuberant and ear-splitting celebrations. In China, celebrations were banned from the onset of the Cultural Revolution in 1966 until 1980 when dragons and lions once again appeared on the streets.

In Vietnam, where the holiday is called TET, the ancestors are believed to return to heaven on the fourth day, and everyone has to return to work. On the seventh day, the *Cay Nev* is removed from the front of the home. This is a high bamboo pole that was set up on the last day of the old year. On its top are red paper with inscriptions, wind chimes, a square of woven bamboo to stop evil spirits from entering, and a small basket with betel and areca nuts for the good spirits.

In Taiwan it is called **Sang-Sin**. Small horses and palanquins are cut from yellow paper and burned to serve as conveyances for the kitchen god.

The New Year's feast is first laid before the ancestor shrine. About seven o'clock, after the ancestors have eaten, the food is gathered up, reheated, and eaten by the family. The greater the amount of food placed before the shrine, the greater will be the reward for the new year.

After the banquet, oranges are stacked in fives before the ancestor tablets and household gods. A dragon-bedecked red cloth is hung before the altar. The dragon is the spirit of rain and abundance, and the oranges are an invitation to the gods to share the family's feasting.

In Korea **Je-sok**, or **Je-ya**, is the name for New Year's Eve. Torches are lit in every part of the home, and everyone sits up all night to "defend the New Year" from evil spirits. In modern Seoul, the capital, the church bells are rung 33 times at midnight. While the foods may vary, everyone, rich and poor alike, has *duggook* soup, made from rice and containing pheasant, chicken, meat, pinenuts, and chestnuts.

Many games are played. Among the most unusual is girls seesawing. In early times Korean men stopped some of the sterner sports and forbade women to have any outdoor exercises. Korean girls then took to using a seesaw behind their garden walls. But they do it standing up—so as to get a possible glimpse of their boyfriends, as they fly up and down.

In Okinawa's villages there is the custom of new water for **Shogatsu**, the new year. About five o'clock in the morning youngsters bring a teapot of fresh water to the homes of their relatives. There a cupful is placed on the Buddhist god shelf, or the fire god's shelf in the kitchen, and the first pot of tea is made from it.

See also Losar, Narcissus Festival, Oshogatsu, and Tet

SOURCES:
AmerBkDays-1978, pp. 146, 148
BkFest-1937, pp. 75, 77
DictFolkMyth-1984, pp. 224, 626, 706, 790
FolkAmerHol-1991, p. 46
FolkWrldHol-1992, pp. 43, 56
GdWrldFest-1985, p. 62
IntlThFolk-1979, p. 197
RelHolCal-1993, p. 117

♦ 1091 ♦ **Lu Pan, Birthday of**
Usually July; 13th day of sixth lunar month

A commemoration of the birth of the Taoist patron saint of carpenters and builders. Said to have been born in 507 B.C., Lu Pan, a versatile inventor, is sometimes called the Chinese Leonardo da Vinci. In Hong Kong, people in the construction industry observe the day with celebratory banquets to give

thanks for their good fortune in the past year and to pray for better fortune in the year to come. They also pay their respects at noon at the Lu Pan Temple in Kennedy Town.

Lu Pan, an architect, engineer, and inventor, is credited with inventing the drill, plane, shovel, saw, lock, and ladder. His wife is said to have invented the umbrella. Because his inventions are indispensable to building, it is common practice at the start of major construction projects for employees to have feasts, burn incense, and offer prayers to Lu Pan so that he may protect them and the construction work from disaster.

SOURCES:
BkHolWrld-1986, Jul 18
Chases-1996, p. 313

♦ 1092 ♦ **Lupercalia**
February 15

This was an ancient Roman festival during which worshippers gathered at a grotto on the Palatine Hill in Rome called the Lupercal, where Rome's legendary founders, Romulus and Remus, had been suckled by a wolf. The sacrifice of goats and dogs to the Roman deities Lupercus and Faunus was part of the ceremony. Luperci (priests of Lupercus) dressed in goatskins and, smeared with the sacrificial blood, would run about striking the women with thongs of goat skin. This was thought to assure them of fertility and an easy delivery. The name for these thongs—*februa*—meant "means of purification" and eventually gave the month of February its name. There is some reason to believe that the Lupercalia was a forerunner of modern Valentine's Day customs. Part of the ceremony involved putting girls' names in a box and letting boys draw them out, thus pairing them off until the next Lupercalia.

SOURCES:
AmerBkDays-1978, pp. 132, 178
BkHolWrld-1986, Feb 14
DaysCustFaith-1957, p. 54
DictDays-1988, p. 70
FestSaintDays-1915, p. 34

♦ 1093 ♦ **Luxembourg National Day**
June 23

This public holiday is also known as **Grand Duke Day**, since it is the birthday of Jean, the Grand Duke of Luxembourg. It is also the day on which the country celebrates its independence. Although formerly ruled by the Netherlands and Belgium, the grand duchy raised its own flag for the first time in 1890. It remained politically neutral until after its liberation from the Germans at the end of World War II, when it joined the North Atlantic Treaty Organization.

On the eve of the national holiday, Dudelange hosts a torchlight procession, and the castle at Wiltz hosts a fête in the courtyard. In Esch-sur-Alzette, there are athletic competitions, and other festivities. Fireworks, parades, special religious services, public concerts and dancing comprise the elaborate celebration in the capital city of Luxembourg.

On National Day people assemble in the capital city of

Luxembourg, not only to celebrate their independence but also to observe the official birthday of the Grand Duke, who succeeded his mother, the Grand Duchess Charlotte, in 1964. Although Luxembourg covers less than a thousand square miles, the people there identify strongly with their country and speak their own language, known as Luxembourgeois.

CONTACT:
Luxembourg National Tourist
  Office
17 Beekman Pl.
New York, NY 10022
212-935-8888; fax: 212-935-5896

SOURCES:
AnnivHol-1983, p. 83
Chases-1996, p. 268
NatlHolWrld-1968, p. 88

♦ 1094 ♦ **Lyon International Festival**
June–July

The city of Lyon, France, was known as Lugdunum in Roman times, and the Théâtre Romain de Fourvière, a huge outdoor arena with seating for 3,000, is still used for some of the events associated with the Lyon International Festival. The four-week festival of music, theater, and dance was known as the Festival de Lyon-Charbonnières when it was started in 1946 by Georges Bassinet, because it was sponsored by the casino at the nearby summer resort of Charbonnières. The name was changed in 1960, when the city of Lyon became the official sponsor.

Musical events featured at the festival include symphonic, choral, and chamber concerts; recitals; and international competitions for organ, piano, and jazz improvisations. Most of the orchestral works are performed by the Lyon Orchestra under the direction of Serge Baudo, although the Moscow Chamber Orchestra, the Orchestre de Paris, and other international orchestras have performed there. There are also theater productions, operas, and ballets. Events are held in the ancient Roman arena, the Maurice Ravel Auditorium, the Théâtre des Célestins, the Grand Théâtre de l'Opéra, and the Théâtre de l'Eldorado.

CONTACT:
French Government Tourist Office
9454 Wilshire Blvd., Ste. 715
Beverly Hills, CA 90212
310-271-6665; fax: 310-276-2835

SOURCES:
GdWrldFest-1985, p. 80
IntlThFolk-1979, p. 112
MusFestEurBrit-1980, p. 79

M

♦ 1095 ♦ **MacArthur Day**
January 26

Douglas MacArthur (1880–1964), five-star general and supreme commander of the Allied forces in the Southwest Pacific during World War II, was born on this day in Little Rock, Arkansas. Although MacArthur retired from the U.S. Army in 1937, he was recalled to active duty in July 1941. Promoted to general in December 1944, he was appointed commander of all U.S. army forces in the Pacific four months later. After the U.S. dropped an atomic bomb on Hiroshima on August 6, 1945, it was MacArthur who supervised the surrender ceremony in Tokyo. As Allied commander of the Japanese occupation from 1945–51, MacArthur directed the demobilization of Japanese military forces and the drafting of a new constitution.

Many people felt that MacArthur was imperious and egotistical, while to others he appeared warm, courageous, and even humble. Everyone seemed to agree that he possessed superior intelligence and a rare ability to command. His birthday is observed in his home state of Arkansas, where he is widely remembered as one of the state's most famous sons.

> SOURCES:
> *AnnivHol-1983*, p. 14
> *Chases-1996*, p. 76

♦ 1096 ♦ **McClure Bean Soup Festival**
September

When a group of Civil War veterans met on the second floor of the Joseph Peters Blacksmith Shop in Bannerville, Pennsylvania, in 1883 to organize a Grand Army of the Republic Post, they probably had no idea that their actions might some day lead to a bean soup festival. But when they served a special bean soup at their first meeting, it was such a hit that they eventually invited the public to a "real Civil War bean soup dinner" in 1891. Today, thousands of gallons of bean soup are prepared in 35-gallon kettles, 16 of which can be heated simultaneously over a special battery of wood-fire furnaces set up for the occasion. The cooks, all of whom wear Civil War uniforms, take turns stirring the soup with wooden ladles for 180-minute shifts.

As the Civil War veterans died out, their sons took over the festival, which is now held at the Henry K. Ritter Camp Sons of the Union War Veterans. It takes place for two full days and five nights, usually a Tuesday through Saturday in September, and includes political speeches, exhibits, parades, nightly entertainment, and amusement rides. The recipe for the soup is based on the original Civil War recipe, and it is served to over 35,000 people.

CONTACT:
Pennsylvania Office of Travel
  Marketing
453 Forum Bldg.
Harrisburg, PA 17120
800-237-4363 or 717-787-5453
fax: 717-234-4560

SOURCES:
GdUSFest-1984, p. 159

♦ 1097 ♦ **Macon Cherry Blossom Festival**
Mid-March

A celebration of the blooming (traditional date of full bloom is March 23) of the Yoshino cherry trees in Macon, Ga., which calls itself the Cherry Blossom Capital of the World. Cherry trees in Macon date back to 1952 when William A. Fickling discovered a mystery tree on his lawn. It was identified as a Yoshino flowering cherry, a native of Japan. Fickling learned to propagate the trees, and began giving them to the community; today Macon has 170,000 Yoshino cherry trees given by the Fickling family—30 times more than the number in Washington, D.C. The festival honors Fickling, known as 'Johnny Cherry seed,' and has as its themes love and international friendship.

The 10-day celebration, started in 1982, includes the 10-mile Cherry Blossom Trail, and now offers about 250 activities. Among the events are parades, a coronation ball, a fashion show, fireworks, concerts, a bed race, a cherry-dessert contest, and the fire department's Pink Pancake Breakfast. Macon has many antebellum mansions spared by Gen. William T. Sherman on his Civil War march to the sea so there are house and garden tours, a flower show, and a tea put on by the Federated Garden Clubs.

The city continues donating trees: about 15,000 are given to area residents for planting each spring.

See also CHERRY BLOSSOM FESTIVAL

CONTACT:
Georgia Dept. of Industry
Trade and Tourism
285 Peachtree Center Ave., N.E.
Marquis Tower II, Ste. 1000
Atlanta, GA 30303
800-847-4842 or 404-656-3592
fax: 404-651-9063

SOURCES:
Chases-1996, p. 133

♦ 1098 ♦ Madagascar Independence Day
June 26

This national holiday commemorates Madagascar's independence from France on this day in 1960. **Republic Day** is another public holiday in Madagascar, held on December 30, the day the new constitution went into effect. The country became a republic in 1975.

CONTACT:
Madagascar Embassy
2374 Massachusetts Ave., N.W.
Washington, D.C. 20008
202-265-5525; fax: 202-483-7603

SOURCES:
AnnivHol-1983, pp. 84, 166
Chases-1996, p. 270
NatlHolWrld-1968, p. 89

♦ 1099 ♦ Madam Lou Bunch Day
Third Saturday in June

An annual reminder of the rowdy gold-mining days of Central City, Colorado, held to honor the town's last madam. The event features bed races, a Madams and Miners Ball, and the selection of a Madam of the Year. In addition, there are tours of old mining rigs and trains that take visitors into the heart of the mountains to see colorful veins of ore.

Central City was settled in the Gold Rush of 1859 and became known as the Richest Square Mile on Earth—some $75 million in gold was mined there. One of the miners was a man named John Gregory who dug up a fortune. New York newspaper editor Horace Greeley heard about Gregory Gulch and went west to take a look, after which he supposedly wrote, "Go west, young man." The phrase isn't found in his writings, because this advice was first given by John Babsone Soulé in an article for Indiana's *Terre Haute Express*. Greeley reprinted the article in his *New York Tribune* under Soulé's byline; nevertheless Greeley has been remembered for the inspiring phrase and both Gregory and Soulé have faded into history.

CONTACT:
Central City Casino Association
P.O. Box 773
Central City, CO 80427
303-582-5322; fax: 303-582-5326

SOURCES:
Chases-1996, p. 257
DictDays-1988, p. 70

♦ 1100 ♦ Madeleine, Fête de la
July 22

The **Magdalene Festival** is observed in St. Baume, a forested region of Provence, France, on the anniversary of the death of Mary Magdalene, according to repudiated traditions the sister of Martha and Lazarus. An unfounded ninth-century legend has it that she set out from Palestine in a small boat and miraculously arrived on the shores of Provence. Wandering eastward from Les Saintes-Maries-de-la-Mer, she came to *la fôret de la Baume*, 'the forest of the Cave,' a grotto where she spent 33 years living on wild roots and berries doing penance for her sins.

Thousands of pilgrims have visited *la Sainte Baume*, the holy cave, since the 13th century. Although July 22 is the most popular pilgrimage date, the shrine is visited throughout the year. At one time a journey to the grotto was considered especially important for engaged couples, who went there to ensure a fruitful marriage. More recently, young girls have scrambled up the wooded hillside to ask for the Magdalene's help in finding a husband.

CONTACT:
French Government Tourist Office
9454 Wilshire Blvd., Ste. 715
Beverly Hills, CA 90212
310-271-6665; fax: 310-276-2835

SOURCES:
AnnivHol-1983, pp. 95, 179
FestWestEur-1958, p. 45

♦ 1101 ♦ Magellan Day
March 6

The island of Guam, largest and southernmost of the Mariana Islands in the Pacific Ocean, about 3,000 miles west of Hawaii, was found on this date in 1521 by the Portuguese navigator Ferdinand Magellan. He named the island Ladrones, meaning 'thieves,' because of the way, according to Magellan, the inhabitants behaved. The island was formally claimed by Spain in 1565, and was later ceded to the United States as a prize at the end of the Spanish-American War. Today, Guam is the site of major U.S. military installations.

Guamanians celebrate their island's founding on or near March 6 with fiestas and sailboating. This day is also known as **Discovery Day**.

CONTACT:
Guam Visitors Bureau
401 Pale San Vittores Rd.
Tumon, Guam 96911
011-671-646-5278 or 011-671-
  646-8516
fax: 011-671-646-8861

SOURCES:
AnnivHol-1983, p. 31
Chases-1996, p. 124

♦ 1102 ♦ Magha Puja (Maka Buja, Full Moon Day)
March–April; full moon night of third lunar month

An important Buddhist holy day celebrated in India, and in Laos (as **Makha Bouxa**) and Thailand, where it is a national holiday. The day commemorates the occasion when 1,250 followers ordained by the Buddha arrived by coincidence at Veluvan Monastery in Rajagriha, India, to hear him lay down monastic regulations and predict his own death and entry with Nirvana in three months' time. On this day there are sermons in the temples throughout the day, and monks spend the day chanting. The people perform acts of merit-making, such as offering food to monks, and freeing captive birds and fish. After sunset, monks lead followers in walking three times around the chapels of monasteries. Each person carries flowers, glowing incense, and a lighted candle in homage to the Buddha. In Laos, the ceremonies are especially colorful at Vientiane and at the Khmer ruins of Wat Ph near Champasak.

SOURCES:
BkHolWrld-1986, Mar 6
FolkWrldHol-1992, p. 142

♦ 1103 ♦ **Magha Purnima**
*January–February; full moon day of Hindu month
of Magha*

Like KARTIKA PURNIMA, this is a Hindu bathing festival. Magha is considered to be one of the four most sacred months, and Hindus believe that bathing in the Ganges on this day is a great purifying act. When they cannot get to the Ganges, they bathe in the sea or in any holy stream, river, or tank (a pool or pond used to store water). Great bathing festivals are held at various places along the banks of the Yamuna, Sarayu, Narmad, and other holy rivers, and people walk for miles to have a bath. There is a large tank that is considered holy at Kumbhkonam, near Madras, which is also a popular destination since Hindus believe that on this particular day, the Ganges flows into the tank.

Magha Purnima is a day for fasting and charities. Early in the morning, libations are offered to dead ancestors, while donations of food, clothes, and money are given to the poor. Then Brahmans are fed and given *dan-dakshina* (offerings) according to one's means and capacity.

SOURCES:
RelHolCal-1993, p. 91

♦ 1104 ♦ **Magh Sankranti**
January–February; Hindu month of Magha

In celebration of the sun's movement back toward the Northern Hemisphere, the people of Nepal visit holy bathing spots during this festival in the Hindu month of Magha. Some actually bathe in the shallow water, but the weather is usually quite chilly and most are content to splash water on their hands and faces and sprinkle it on their heads. People also spend the day sitting in the sun, massaging each other with mustard oil, which is also used by mothers to bless their children. Foods traditionally served on this day include *khichari*, a mixture of rice and lentils; sesame seeds; sweet potatoes; spinach; and home-made wine and beer. Traditional gifts for the priests are a bundle of wood and a clay fire pot.

SOURCES:
FolkWrldHol-1992, p. 79

♦ 1105 ♦ **Magna Charta (Carta) Day**
June 15

The Magna Charta was the "great charter" of English liberties, which the tyrannical King John I was forced by the English nobility to sign on June 15, 1215. Although this day does not appear in the official calendar of any church, it is a day of great religious significance throughout the English-speaking world. One of the 48 personal rights and liberties guaranteed by the Magna Charta was freedom of worship; in fact, the opening words of the document were, "The Church of England shall be free."

The Magna Charta is regarded as one of the most important documents in the history of political and human freedom. Although it may seem remote to Americans, who sometimes take freedom for granted, for the English this date marks the first time that the basic belief in the value of the individual was recognized by the ruling government.

SOURCES:
AnnivHol-1983, p. 80
Chases-1996, p. 258
DaysCustFaith-1957, p. 148
RelHolCal-1993, p. 92

Mahatma Gandhi's Birthday
See **Gandhi Jayanti**

♦ 1106 ♦ **Mahavir Jayanti**
*March–April; 13th day of waxing half of Hindu
month of Caitra*

A major Jain festival in India, dedicated to Vardhamana (c. 599–527 B.C.), who came to be known as Mahavira, meaning 'great hero' of the Jains. The festival celebrates his birthday, and is marked with prayers, fasting, and recitations. The holiday is observed with special fanfare by eastern Indians at Pawapuri in the state of Bihar, where Mahavira was born near the modern town of Patna. Another large celebration is held at the Parasnatha temple in Calcutta.

Mahavira, a contemporary of the Buddha, is regarded by the Jains as the 24th and last in a series of *Tirthankaras*, or enlightened teachers or 'ford-makers', and present-day Jainism is traced to his life and teachings. For 12½ years, he was an ascetic, wandering about, begging for food, and wearing little. Then he found enlightenment, became a *Jina*, or 'conqueror,' and a Tirthankara. He taught for 30 years before he died. Jainism today continues to be an ascetic religion, practiced by about 3.5 million people. They reject any action that could harm a living being, and some, therefore, wear masks over their mouths to prevent the chance of breathing in and thus killing of an insect. Jains, with a strong literary tradition, have played an important role in conserving the writings of non-Jain Hindu authors.

See also DEWALI

CONTACT:
India Tourist Office
30 Rockefeller Ave.
15 N. Mezzanine
New York, NY 10112
212-586-4901; fax: 212-582-3274

SOURCES:
AnnivHol-1983, p. 179
DictWrldRel-1989, p. 451
FolkWrldHol-1992, p. 215
RelHolCal-1993, p. 92

Maidens' Fair on Mount Gaina
See **Tirgul de fete de pe muntele Gaina**

♦ 1107 ♦ **Maifest**
Third weekend in May

The original Maifest in Hermann, Missouri, was a children's festival founded in 1874. The festival was revived in 1952 as a German ethnic festival for people of all ages. Held the third weekend in May, the festival offers German folklore, songs, music, and food in celebration of the arrival of spring. Black beer, cheese, sausage, crackers, and bratwurst are served, and there are band concerts and musical shows. One of the festival's highlights is the house tour, which covers six historic homes and buildings in Hermann, most of which date from the mid-19th century. One of these, the Stone Hill Winery, is now a national registered historic landmark.

CONTACT:
Missouri Division of Tourism
P.O. Box 1055
Jefferson City, MO 65102
800-877-1234 or 314-751-4133
fax: 314-751-5160

SOURCES:
GdUSFest-1984, p. 105

♦ 1108 ♦ **Maimona (Maimuna)**
Between March 28 and April 25; day after Passover

Jews in North Africa commemorate the philosopher and rabbi, Moses Maimonides (1135 or 1138–1204), on the evening of the last day of Passover and the day that follows. Since the news of Maimonides's death in 1204 reached many Jews during Passover, they were not able to mourn his passing, as custom would normally dictate, by eating bread and an egg. So they postponed it until the following day.

In Libya on this day, each family member receives the *maimona* (from an Arabic word meaning 'good fortune')—a small loaf of bread with an egg baked inside, which they eat with slices of lamb. In Morocco, people dress up or wear costumes. Special displays of food are arranged on tables, including pitchers of milk and bowls of flour with eggs, broad green beans, stalks of wheat, and dates. Surrounding the bowls are honey, fruit, nuts, cookies, lettuce, wine, and a type of pancake known as *muflita*. After going to the synagogue, people stop to bless their friends and sample the refreshments at each home. A lettuce leaf, representing prosperous crops, is dipped in honey, symbolizing sweetness, and given to each guest. Wherever possible, people dip their feet in streams, rivers, or the sea.

SOURCES:
DictWrldRel-1989, p. 494
FolkWrldHol-1992, p. 238

♦ 1109 ♦ **Maine Lobster Festival**
Four days including first weekend in August

Claiming to be the "Original Lobster Festival," the four-day event known as the Maine Lobster Festival has been held in the fishing port of Rockland since 1948. The festival's emphasis is on marine foods and exhibits, with special events such as lobster crate- and trap-hauling races, a Maine cooking contest, the crowning of a Maine Sea Goddess, and a lobster-eating competition.

Although many towns in Maine hold annual lobster festivals, some have gone bankrupt by offering visitors all the lobster they can eat for a ridiculously low price. Although the prices have gone up, the lure of an inexpensive lobster meal remains one of the primary reasons people attend these festivals. At the Rockland festival, the price of the lobster meal is based on the current market price. But the lobster is fresh, and it is steamed in the world's largest lobster cooker.

CONTACT:
Maine Office of Tourism
33 Stone St.
Augusta, ME 04333
800-533-9595 or 207-287-5711
fax: 207-287-5701

SOURCES:
Chases-1996, p. 318
GdUSFest-1984, p. 78

♦ 1110 ♦ **Maine Memorial Day**
February 15

The American battleship *Maine*, which had been sent to Cuba

to rescue any Americans who might be endangered by the Cubans' unrest under Spanish rule, was blown up while sitting at anchor in Havana harbor on February 15, 1898. Many in the United States assumed that the Spanish were responsible for the ship's destruction, since American sympathies were clearly with the Cubans. But despite the fact that 260 men died, the question of responsibility for the explosion was never really settled. The Spanish-American War was declared in April, and "Remember the Maine!" is the slogan that has been associated with it ever since.

February 15 was observed for many years by the U.S. Navy and by Spanish-American War veterans' associations in Havana and the United States. Some naval units still participate in local observances, but only Maine, Massachusetts, and Connecticut observe the day officially, sometimes calling it **Battleship Day** or **Spanish-American War Memorial Day**.

SOURCES:
AmerBkDays-1978, p. 187
AnnivHol-1983, p. 25
Chases-1996, p. 99
DictDays-1988, p. 10

Maka Buja
See **Magha Puja**

♦ 1111 ♦ **Making Happiness Festival**
Ninth day of first lunar month

The **Tso-Fu Festival**, or 'making happiness' festival, is celebrated in Taiwan soon after the Lunar New Year. The Happiness Master, headman, chief medium, and other villagers "invite the gods." They collect a number of gods who normally dwell in various shrines and private homes and bring them to the temple, accompanied by a hired band, children, gongs, and banners. Mothers of newborn sons pay their respects to the Heaven God by presenting *hsin-ting ping*, or 'new male cakes.' The following day they distribute these cakes to every household except those occupied by other new mothers. Elaborate sacrificial rites are performed in the temple on this day and a special feast is held for villagers over 60, other important guests, and women who have given birth to sons during the year. At the end of the festival, the gods that have been brought to the temple are returned to their shrines.

CONTACT:
Taiwan Visitors Association
1 World Trade Center, Ste. 7953
New York, NY 10048
212-466-0691; fax: 212-432-6436

SOURCES:
FolkWrldHol-1992, p. 67

♦ 1112 ♦ **Malawi Republic Day**
July 6

Also known as **Independence Day,** this national holiday commemorates Malawi's independence from Britain on this day in 1966. The area had been known as Nyasaland. At midnight on July 5–6, 1966, forty thousand people cheered the changing of the flag at Central Stadium, ushering in Malawi's autonomy.

CONTACT:
Malawi Embassy
2408 Massachusetts Ave., N.W.
Washington, D.C. 20008
202-797-1007; fax: 202-265-0976

SOURCES:
AnnivHol-1983, p. 90
Chases-1996, p. 287
NatlHolWrld-1968, p. 111

Malaysia National Day
See **Merdeka Day**

♦ 1113 ♦ Malcolm X Day
Third Sunday in May

Malcolm X, whose original name was Malcolm Little (1925–1965), was an outspoken leader in the black nationalist movement of the 1960s. He converted to the Black Muslim faith while serving time in prison for burglary, and upon his release began touring the country on behalf of the Nation of Islam, led by Elijah Muhammad. In 1964 he was suspended from the sect and started his own religious organization. But hostility between Malcolm's followers and the rival Black Muslims escalated. He was assassinated at a rally in Harlem shortly after his PILGRIMAGE TO MECCA.

Because during most of his career Malcolm X advocated violence (for self-protection) and had a reputation for fanaticism and racism, his leadership was rejected by most other civil rights leaders of his day. But, as reflected in his *The Autobiography of Malcolm X, as Told to Alex Haley*, his pilgrimage to Mecca changed his outlook. After performing the pilgrimage rites, Malcolm composed and sent a letter back home. It read, in part: "For the past week, I have been utterly speechless and spellbound by the graciousness I see displayed all around me by people *of all colors. . . .* There were tens of thousands of pilgrims . . . from blue-eyed blonds to black-skinned Africans. But we were all participating in the same ritual, displaying a spirit of unity and brotherhood that my experiences in America had led me to believe never could exist between the white and the non-white."

His birthday, May 19, is still observed in most major American cities with a large African-American population. In Washington, D.C., the celebration takes place on the third Sunday in May at Anacostia Park and regularly draws 50,000 to 75,000 people. There is a showcase for local African-American talent and a commemorative ceremony with a speech. A community service award is given to a local citizen who has made a significant contribution to promoting racial harmony.

CONTACT:
Washington D.C. Convention and
  Visitors Association
1212 New York Ave., N.W., Ste.
  600
Washington, D.C. 20005
800-635-6338 or 202-789-7000
fax: 202-789-7037

SOURCES:
Chases-1996, p. 220

♦ 1114 ♦ Maldives Independence Day
July 26

This group of islands in the Indian Ocean had been under British control since 1887 until its full independence on this day in 1965. Independence Day is a national holiday in Maldives.

Maldives became a republic on November 11, 1968, an event commemorated with another national holiday, **Republic Day**. Festivities are held for two days, including November 11.

CONTACT:
Maldives Mission to the U.N.
820 Second Ave., Ste. 800-C
New York, NY 10017
212-599-6195; fax: 212-972-3970

SOURCES:
AnnivHol-1983, pp. 97, 145
Chases-1996, p. 311
NatlHolWrld-1968, p. 126

♦ 1115 ♦ Mali Independence Day
September 22

Mali gained its independence from France on September 22, 1960. As a colony since the 1890s, it was known as French Sudan. In ancient and medieval times Mali had a prominent role in a series of illustrious empires that spanned western Africa.

Also known as **Republic Day**, this is an important national holiday in Mali.

CONTACT:
Mali Embassy
2130 R St., N.W.
Washington, D.C. 20008
202-332-2249; fax: 202-332-6603

SOURCES:
AnnivHol-1983, p. 121
Chases-1996, p. 387
NatlHolWrld-1968, p. 177

♦ 1116 ♦ Mallard Ceremony
Every hundred years

The **Mallard Feast** or **Mallard Day** ceremony held once every 100 years at All Souls College in Oxford commemorates the college's founding in 1437. Henry Chichele, archbishop of Canterbury at the time, wanted to establish a college at Oxford in memory of those who had perished in the wars between England and France. While he was considering where such a college might be located, he had a dream that when the foundations were being dug, a fattened mallard was found stuck in the drain or sewer. He decided to heed the omen and, when the digging began at the location specified in his dream, a huge mallard was indeed found—a sure sign that his college would flourish.

Although no one is sure exactly when the first commemoration of this event was held, the ceremony itself has remained unchanged. The Fellows of the college nominate the Lord of the Mallard. He in turn appoints six officers, who march before him carrying white staves and wearing medals with the image of the mallard engraved on them. When the Lord is seated in his chair, the officers carry him around the quadrangle three times and sing a traditional song. After that, they climb up to the college roof in a torchlight procession and sing the song again, loudly enough for most of the town to hear. Eventually they retire to their common rooms to drink wine and continue their merrymaking.

SOURCES:
BkDays-1864, vol. I, p. 113

♦ 1117 ♦ Malta Independence Day
September 21

A nationwide celebration of Malta's independence achieved on this day in 1964. Malta was under the control of various political entities from its earliest days. In the early 19th century, the Maltese acknowledged Great Britain's sovereignty, but through the years various constitutions were in force, and in the 20th century, self-government was repeatedly granted and suspended. Malta's heroic stand against the Axis in World War II won a declaration that self-government would be restored at the end of the war, and indeed self-government under another constitution was granted in 1947. It was revoked in 1959, restored in 1962, and independence was finally granted in 1964. Ten years later, on Dec. 13, 1974, Malta became a republic—December 13 is a national holiday commemorating that event.

Independence Day is celebrated with parades and festivities throughout the country.

See also VICTORY DAY

CONTACT:
Malta National Tourist Office
350 Fifth Ave.
Empire State Bldg., Ste. 4412
New York, NY 10118
212-695-9520; fax: 212-695-8229

SOURCES:
AnnivHol-1983, p. 121
Chases-1996, p. 386
NatlHolWrld-1968, p. 176

♦ 1118 ♦ Mamuralia
March 14

According to one Roman myth, Mamurius was a smith who was run out of the city because the shields he had made for the Roman soldiers failed to protect them when they were substituted for the sacred shield that had fallen from heaven. Another explanation for the ceremonies held on this day is that Mamurius, whose name was a variation of Mars, represented the old year, which had to be driven away on the day preceding the first full moon of the new Roman year. In any case, the rite that took place on March 14 involved leading a man wearing only animal skins through the streets of Rome. He was pursued and beaten with long white rods until he was driven out of the city.

The Mamuralia was unusual in that no other Roman festival occurred on an even-numbered day. One explanation is that the festival was originally held on the IDES of March, but was moved back a day so that people could attend both the horse-races known as the Equirria and the ANNA PARENNA FESTIVAL held on March 15.

SOURCES:
FestRom-1981, p. 89
RomFest-1925, p. 44

♦ 1119 ♦ Mandi Safar
During Islamic month of Safar

A Muslim bathing festival unique to Malaysia. This holiday, which is observed during the month of Safar, was originally believed to commemorate the last time Muhammad was able to bathe before his death. Muslims wearing bright colors visited beaches for a religious cleansing of the body and soul with water. There is no mention of the rite in the Qu'ran (the Muslim holy book), and orthodox Muslims consider it nothing more than a picnic. It continues as a merry holiday. The best-known gathering places are the beaches of Tanjong Kling near Malacca and of Penang.

CONTACT:
Malaysian Tourism Promotion
  Board
818 W. Seventh St., Ste. 804
Los Angeles, CA 90017
213-689-9702; fax: 213-689-1530

SOURCES:
BkHolWrld-1986, Aug 7

♦ 1120 ♦ Manitoba Sunflower Festival
Last weekend in July

The Mennonites were members of an evangelical Protestant sect that originated in Europe in the 16th century and was named for Menno Simon, a Dutch priest. They began emigrating to North America in the late 17th century and lived primarily as farmers, retaining their German language. A number of Russian Mennonites settled in Manitoba, Canada, where their heritage is still celebrated in the towns along the so-called Mennonite Trail.

Because the Mennonites were the first to extract the oil from sunflower plants, the city of Altona in southern Manitoba has chosen to honor its Mennonite heritage with an annual **Sunflower Festival** during the last weekend in July. Since 1965 the festival has attempted to revive the Mennonite culture by offering performances of "low German" humor and by serving a number of Mennonite foods such as *schmaunfat, veriniki, pluma moose, borscht,* and *rollkuchen*. A special sunflower ice cream is made especially for the festival. Less "authentic" activities include the Great Ping Pong Ball Drop, motorcross races, pancake breakfasts, and a huge farmers' market.

CONTACT:
Travel Manitoba
155 Carlton St., 7th Floor
Winnipeg, Manitoba
Canada R3C 3H8
800-665-0040 or 204-945-3777

SOURCES:
AnnivHol-1983, p. 182

♦ 1121 ♦ Marbles Tournament, National
Late June

The annual National Marbles Tournament began in 1922, when Macy's Department Store in Philadelphia sponsored a promotional tournament. The Scripps-Howard Newspapers sponsored the event until 1955, when the city of Wildwood, New Jersey, and a group of volunteers interested in preserving the game decided to sponsor the event jointly. Traditionally held for five days near the end of June in this New Jersey seaside resort town, the tournament features a competition among champions selected in elimination contests throughout the country. The national boy and girl champions each receive a trophy and a plaque as well as a $2,000 scholarship.

Although there are many games that can be played with marbles—such as Potsies, Poison, Passout, Chassies, Puggy, Black Snake, and Old Boiler (reportedly a favorite with Abraham Lincoln)—the game played in the national tournament is called Ringer. It is played by placing 13 marbles in the form of a cross in a 10-foot circle. The marbles inside the circle are called "migs" or "miggles." Players alternate shots using a "shooter" or "taw," and the winner is the first one to shoot seven miggles out of the ring.

CONTACT:
New Jersey Division of Travel and
  Tourism
20 W. State St.
Trenton, NJ 08625
800-537-7397 or 609-292-2470
fax: 609-633-7418

♦ 1122 ♦ Mardi Gras
February–March; two weeks before Ash Wednesday

The most flamboyant of Mardi Gras (from the French for 'fat

Tuesday') celebrations in North America, culminating in a riot of parades and throngs of laughing, drinking, dancing people in the streets of New Orleans, La.

The Mardi Gras celebrations symbolize New Orleans, "The City that Care Forgot," to most people. The festivities actually start on Jan. 6 (EPIPHANY) with a series of private balls. The tempo picks up in the last two weeks of the Carnival season, when the streets ring with 30 separate parades organized by committees called *krewes*. The parades consist of marching jazz bands and lavishly decorated two-story floats carrying the costumed and masked krewe royalty who toss "throws" to pleading spectators; these are beads or bonbons or the coveted Mardi Gras doubloons. Each of the parades has 15 to 20 floats, all decorated to express a certain theme. Two of the biggest and most elaborate parades, the Krewe of Endymion and the Bacchus parade, take place on the weekend before Mardi Gras. On the day of Mardi Gras, designated the "Day of Un-Rule," the traditional parades spotlight Rex, King of Carnival and Monarch of Merriment, in the morning, and Comus, God of Revelry, by torchlight at night. On that same evening the private balls of Rex and Comus are held. At midnight, the madness of Carnival ends, and LENT begins, and a million or so spectators and participants face sobriety.

New Orleans had its first organized Mardi Gras parade in 1857. It consisted of two floats and was presented by the first Carnival society, the Mistick Krewe of Comus, its name alluding to John Milton's masque, *Comus*. The parade was apparently well received; it was one of the first local institutions revived after the Civil War.

Mardi Gras in New Orleans is the best known, but not the oldest Mardi Gras. A two-week pre-Lenten celebration in Mobile, Ala., stands alone as the oldest celebration of Mardi Gras in the country. It was first observed in 1703 by the French who had founded the port city the year before. When the Spanish occupied Mobile in 1780, they moved it to the eve of the TWELFTH NIGHT of CHRISTMAS and paraded in grotesque costumes and masks. The celebrations were suspended during the Civil War, but were revived in 1866 by Joe Cain, a town clerk who togged himself out as an Indian chief and rode through the streets in a charcoal wagon. The old Mardi Gras societies reappeared, and new ones evolved.

Today a different mystic society parades each evening in the two weeks before Lent, and balls are held that are open to everyone. Mardi Gras itself, the day before ASH WEDNESDAY, is a legal holiday in the city of Mobile.

Galveston, Texas, has a 12-day period of whoop-de-do leading up to the actual day of **Fat Tuesday** in this barrier-island city of Texas. About 200,000 spectators are attracted to the Mardi Gras festival, which was first held here in 1867. Though it died out at the turn of the century, it was revived in 1985. Growing bigger every year, this celebration features masked balls, royal coronations, Cajun dances, jazz performances, and, of course, numerous parades with dramatic floats.

See also CARNIVAL and SHROVE TUESDAY

CONTACT:
New Orleans Metropolitan Convention and Visitors Bureau
1520 Sugar Bowl Dr.
New Orleans, LA 70112
504-566-5011; fax: 504-566-5046

SOURCES:
AmerBkDays-1978, pp. 43, 157, 158
AnnivHol-1983, p. 179
BkFestHolWrld-1970, p. 32
Chases-1996, pp. 102, 106
DictFolkMyth-1984, p. 193

FolkAmerHol-1991, p. 84
GdUSFest-1984, p. 5
RelHolCal-1993, pp. 65, 93

◆ 1123 ◆ **Mardi Gras in France**
Between February 3 and March 9; Tuesday before Ash Wednesday

MARDI GRAS (Fat Tuesday) is the last day of CARNIVAL, the three-day period of uninhibited celebration that precedes LENT. The festivities in France are particularly colorful in southern cities like Cannes, Menton, and Grasse, where people go out in the streets in costume and indulge in all sorts of noisy pranks, such as tooting tin horns and pelting passers-by with confetti and flowers. Each town, in fact, has its own *bataille de fleurs* (battle of flowers) right before Lent, with flower-decked cars and floats driving for hours along the streets and boulevards, throwing flowers at each other.

One of the great celebrations of Europe is the carnival at Nice, where grotesque, caricatured figures parade down the Avenue de la Gare—among them giant cabbages and carrots, gnomes, devils on horseback, nymphs, and fairies. King Carnival, dressed in striped hose and a slashed doublet, leads the parade from his throne on a float draped with purple velvet. On the night of Mardi Gras, the King Carnival effigy is burned at the stake.

In Paris and some other French cities, butchers observe Carnival with the fête of the *Boeuf Gras*, or Fat Ox. An ox decked with garlands of greenery, flowers, and ribbons is led through the streets in procession, followed by a triumphal cart bearing a young boy known as the "King of the Butchers." The crowd pays tribute to him by blowing horns and throwing confetti, flowers, and sweets.

See also NICE CARNIVAL

CONTACT:
French Government Tourist Office
9454 Wilshire Blvd., Ste. 715
Beverly Hills, CA 90212
310-271-6665; fax: 310-276-2835

SOURCES:
BkFest-1937, p. 120
BkFestHolWrld-1970, p. 33
Chases-1996, p. 91
FestWestEur-1958, p. 34

◆ 1124 ◆ **Marino Wine Festival**
First weekend in October

The Italian town of Marino is located in the area southeast of Rome known as the Castelli Romani, after the numerous castles, palaces, and Renaissance villas that dot the landscape. Marino is known as a wine town, and there are about a hundred *cantine*—small, nondescript taverns where tourists and residents can buy the local wine, which is often siphoned from a large vat and poured into an empty mineral water bottle, for a very low price. It's not surprising, then, that during the town's wine festival in early October the new grape harvest is celebrated by letting the previous year's wine gush freely from the town's fountains. Crowds of Romans eager to escape the city descend upon Marino with jugs, bottles, and thermoses to fill. The wine is free for the taking and is the perfect accompaniment to a *porchetta* sandwich, the filling made by slowly roasting pig over a woodfire with fresh garlic, rosemary, and olive oil.

CONTACT:
Italian Government Travel Office
630 Fifth Ave.
New York, NY 10111
212-245-4822

◆ 1125 ◆ Marion County Ham Days
Late September

A weekend celebration of the famous Kentucky smoked ham, held in Lebanon (Marion County), Ky., since 1969. The affair started with a simple country ham breakfast served to about 300 people on the street; now about 50,000 folks show up. Breakfast (ham cured in Marion County, eggs, biscuits with local honey, fried apples) is still served on Saturday and Sunday, but there is more: a "Pigasus Parade" with more than 100 floats, a Pokey Pig 10-kilometer run, a crafts and antiques show, a hog-calling contest, a hay-bale toss, and a hot air balloon race.

CONTACT:
Kentucky Dept. of Travel
  Development
500 Mero St., 22nd Floor
Frankfort, KY 40601
800-225-8747 or 502-564-4930
fax: 502-564-5695

SOURCES:
Chases-1996, p. 394

◆ 1126 ◆ Mariposa Festival
Last week in June

Known until 1980 as the **Mariposa Folk Festival**, this three-day folk music festival is the oldest in Canada, where it has served as a model for many smaller festivals. Since 1961 the festival has presented a broad spectrum of folk music—from Kentucky blues to Indian chanting—by performers from all over Canada, the United States, Britain, Africa, and Australia. The events are held on the grounds of Molson Park, about 40 miles north of Toronto.

The Mariposa Festival helped pioneer the workshop concept, emphasizing the importance of establishing a dialogue between the artist and the audience. In addition to the workshops hosted by festival musicians, there is a "folkplay" area where a family can work with a particular performer, who shares his or her special talents with both children and their parents.

CONTACT:
Ontario Travel
Queen's Park
Toronto, Ontario
Canada M7A 2R9
800-ONTARIO or 416-314-0944

SOURCES:
IntlThFolk-1979, p. 74
MusFestAmer-1990, p. 232

◆ 1127 ◆ Maritime Day, National
May 22

The day chosen to commemorate the contribution of American commercial shipping is, appropriately, the day on which the *Savannah* left its home port in Georgia in 1819 to attempt the first steam-propelled crossing of the Atlantic. So unusual was it to see a steam-powered vessel in those days that when the *Savannah* passed the naval station at Cape Clear, Ireland, the authorities thought she was on fire and quickly dispatched a royal cutter to assist her. In reality, the *Savannah* was equipped with sails and only relied on her engines for about 90 hours of the journey.

It was President Franklin D. Roosevelt who first proclaimed May 22 as National Maritime Day in 1933. Since that time observations of this day have grown in popularity, particularly in American port cities. Ships are opened to the public, maritime art and essay contests are held, and parades and band concerts are common. Environmentalists sometimes take advantage of the attention focused on the country's maritime heritage on this day to draw attention to pollution and deterioration of maritime environments, particularly in large commercial ports like New York City.

CONTACT:
United States Maritime
  Administration
Office of Congressional and Public
  Affairs
400 Seventh St., S.W., Rm. 7219
Washington, D.C. 20590
202-366-5807; fax: 202-366-5063

SOURCES:
AmerBkDays-1978, p. 475
AnnivHol-1983, p. 69
Chases-1996, p. 223

Marksmen's Festival
See **Schutzenfest**

◆ 1128 ◆ Marlboro Music Festival
Mid-July to mid-August

It was the noted violinist Adolf Busch who came up with the idea of establishing a summer community for musicians that would free them from the pressures and restrictions of concert life. Every summer since 1951, a group of artists from all over the world has gathered in Marlboro, Vermont, to exchange musical ideas. The Marlboro Music School, which holds an eight-week session each summer, is primarily a place where students or those who are just starting out on their professional careers can study contemporary and classical chamber music. During the five-week festival, the general public has an opportunity to hear the results of their collaborations. But the primary emphasis at Marlboro is on rehearsing the works that the participants themselves have selected, rather than on performing them for the public.

Although many noted musicians have been associated with Marlboro, perhaps the best known is Pablo Casals, the world-famous cellist who conducted the Marlboro Festival Orchestra and taught master classes there from 1960 to 1973 (*see also* Casals Festival).

CONTACT:
September–June 15:
Marlboro Music School
135 S. 18th St.
Philadelphia, PA 19103
215-569-4690; fax: 215-569-9497

June 15–August 15:
Marlboro Music School
Box K
Marlboro, VT 05344
802-254-2394; fax: 802-254-4307

SOURCES:
MusFestAmer-1990, p. 142

◆ 1129 ◆ Maroon Festival
January 6

When Jamaica was a Spanish territory in the 16th century, African slaves were brought in to work the plantations. The Spanish, disappointed by the lack of gold on the island, eventually left and the former slaves fled to the mountains. During the 17th and 18th centuries, the island's British inhabitants were often harassed or attacked by the descendants of these well-armed and organized fugitive slaves, who were called Maroons (having been marooned or deserted by their owners). By 1738 the Maroons had been given permission to settle in the northern part of the island.

The annual Maroon Festival is held at Accompong on January 6, and commemorates the 1759 signing of the peace treaty with the English and establishment of the town of Accompong. It is celebrated with traditional dancing and singing, maroon feasts and ceremonies, the blowing of the *abeng*, and the playing of maroon drums.

CONTACT:
Jamaica Tourist Board
801 Second Ave.
New York, NY 10017
800-233-4582 or 212-856-9727
fax: 212-856-9730

SOURCES:
Chases-1996, p. 58

♦ 1130 ♦ Marriage Fair
September

A mass engagement and marriage *moussem*, or 'festival', held in the remote village of Imilchil in the Atlas Mountains of Morocco. As many as 30,000 people of the Ait Hadiddou tribe, a Berber clan, gather for the three days of the moussem. This is a combined trade fair and pageant of public courtship, instant engagement, and the immediate exchange of marriage vows. The festival solves the problem of meeting a mate in a society where isolation is the norm: the men spend half a year moving with their flocks to upland pastures, while the women stay in the villages, planting crops and weaving rugs.

Families and their herds of sheep and donkeys stream onto the Imilchil plateau at dawn of the first day. They sell or barter their wool, meat, grain, and vegetables, while tradesmen set up tents of pottery, rugs, and tools. Musicians beat tambourines, games are played, and acrobats perform. The center of their Islam-influenced devotions is the tomb of the holy man Sidi Mohammed el Merheni. It's not certain when he lived but it's known that the marriages he blessed were happy.

The courtship proceeds with women wearing a peaked headdress and striped wool capes over white dresses. Their eyes are outlined with kohl and their cheeks are rouged. The prospective grooms, wearing white robes and turbans, weave in pairs through the clusters of brides-to-be. A man speaks to a woman, the woman nods assent, and if the family approves, the couple will enter the wedding tent to seek approval from a representative of the Ministry of Justice in Rabat. Brides who have not been previously married will leave the moussem with their fathers, and be welcomed by their grooms' families with a feast later in the year. Women who are divorcées or widows will go directly to live with their husbands. (Ait Hadiddou women are free to divorce and remarry.)

When a woman consents to marriage, she tells her suitor, "You have captured my liver." The Ait Hadiddou consider the liver to be the soul of love because it aids digestion and well-being.

CONTACT:
Moroccan National Tourist Office
20 E. 46th St., Ste. 1201
New York, NY 10017
212-557-2520; fax: 212-949-8148

Marriage of Goliath
See Giants, Festival of the, in Belgium

♦ 1131 ♦ Martenitza
March 1

Every year on March 1, people in Bulgaria present each other with *martenitzas*—two joined tassels of red-and-white woolen thread resembling a simple CHRISTMAS decoration symbolizing health and happiness. The custom originated with the ancient Thracians, and the first martenitzas had silver or gold coins attached to them. Today it is most widespread in Bulgaria, although the Martenitza is also celebrated in southern Romania, Albania, Greece, and Cyprus.

The rites are varied. In some regions, women dress completely in red on this day. In northeastern Bulgaria, the lady of the house traditionally tosses a red cloth over a fruit tree, or spreads a red woolen cloth on the fields for fertility. In stock-breeding areas, a red-and-white thread is tied to the cattle. Bulgaria is the only country where this particular fertility custom seems to have survived. In Greece the "March" is tied to the wrist or big toe of children to protect them from the March sun. They remove it when they see the first swallow or stork, signs of springtime. On Cyprus it is hoped that one's skin will be as red (healthy) as the string. In Canada, Bulgarian-Macedonians throw the string out for the first robins to use in their nests.

See also DRYMIAIS

SOURCES:
FolkWrldHol-1992, p. 151

♦ 1132 ♦ Martinmas
November 11

This is the feast day of St. Martin of Tours (c. 316–397), one of the most popular saints of the Middle Ages. It is said that when he heard that he had been elected Bishop of Tours, he hid himself in a barn. A squawking goose gave away his hiding place, and the day is still celebrated with roast goose dinners. Another popular legend involves St. Martin's cloak, which he divided with his sword, giving half to a shivering beggar.

In Germany and northern Europe, Roman Catholics commemorate St. Martin while Protestants commemorate Martin Luther's baptismal day (*see* MARTINSFEST).

For rural people, Martinmas comes at a happy time of year: the crops are in, the animals have been slaughtered, the new wine is ready, and the hard work of summer and autumn is over. It's no surprise, then, that St. Martin is the patron saint of tavern keepers, wine-growers, and drunkards. There is a good deal of weather-lore associated with this day. Spells of mild autumn weather that Americans refer to as "Indian summer" are called "St. Martin's summer" or "a Martinmas summer" in Europe and England. It was once a QUARTER DAY. Nowadays, in England, this day is more remembered as Armistice Day (*see* VETERANS' DAY).

In Belgium, where it is called **Sint Maartens Dag**, St. Martin's Day is a favorite holiday among the children. Like ST. NICHOLAS, St. Martin visits them on the feast day eve bringing them gifts. On November 11 apples and nuts are tossed into children's rooms while they stand with their faces turned to the wall. *Gauffres*, little waffle cakes, are particularly popular on St. Martin's Day.

This day is also an important festival in the Netherlands. There it is known as **Beggar's Day**, and boys and girls serenade their neighbors and beg for goodies. In many towns the children light a bonfire and dance and shout around it. Then they march in processions with lanterns made from scooped-out turnips, carrots, or beets.

In other European countries, St. Martin's Day is regarded as a time to give thanks for the harvest and is often observed with feasting. Goose is the traditional meal. In Sweden, November 11 is known as **Martin's Goose Day (Marten Gas)**. In France, *mal de Saint Martin* ('St. Martin's sickness') is the name given to the upset stomach that often follows overindulgence. There is also an impressive ceremony at St. Martin's shrine in Tours on this day.

See also ST. MARTIN'S DAY IN PORTUGAL

CONTACT:
French Government Tourist Office
9454 Wilshire Blvd., Ste. 715
Beverly Hills, CA 90212
310-271-6665; fax: 310-276-2835

SOURCES:
AmerBkDays-1978, p. 1013
BkDays-1864, vol. II, p. 567
BkFest-1937, p. 107
DaysCustFaith-1957, p. 286
DictFolkMyth-1984, p. 682
FestSaintDays-1915, p. 204
FestWestEur-1958, pp. 18, 27, 48, 101, 140, 185, 216
FolkWrldHol-1992, p. 556
SaintFestCh-1904, p. 481

◆ 1133 ◆ Martinmas in Ireland
November 11

There are a number of superstitions and folk beliefs associated with MARTINMAS in Ireland. One is that you must have roast goose for dinner or risk eating no more goose in the coming year. (According to legend, when St. Martin heard that he had been elected Bishop of Tours, he hid himself in a barn but was given away by a squawking goose.) In any case, it is traditional to kill a sheep, lamp, kid, pig, calf, or cow on St. Martin's Eve and eat the meat on **St. Martin's Day**, after sprinkling the animal's blood in the four corners of the house as well as on the walls, threshold, and floor. A dot of blood is even smeared on the forehead of each family member in the belief that it will protect them from evil for one year. The shedding of blood may also be a survival of the time when animals were killed right before winter because it was difficult to find fodder.

On the Aran Islands off the western coast of Ireland, there is a legend that when St. Martin stopped at the house of a poor woman and asked for something to eat, she sacrificed her child because she had no meat to offer him. But when he left the house, the woman found her child still asleep in his cradle. Aran Islanders sacrifice an animal on Martinmas in memory of this miracle, and feed roast cock or goose to any beggar who comes to the door on November 11.

Fishermen in Ireland will not go fishing on Martinmas, believing that if they do, they will meet a horseman riding over the sea, followed by a terrible storm. It is also considered bad luck to turn a wheel of any kind—car, mill, or spinning—on this day.

SOURCES:
BkDays-1864, vol. II, p. 568
DaysCustFaith-1957, p. 287
DictFolkMyth-1984, p. 682
FolkWrldHol-1992, p. 557

◆ 1134 ◆ Martin's Day in Estonia (Mardi Päev)
November 29

Traditionally, children in Estonia go from door to door at dusk on Martin's Day in much the same way that American children trick-or-treat on HALLOWEEN. Their refrain is "Please let us in because Mardi's fingers and toes are cold," and if they are not welcomed into the house and given treats, they retaliate by singing rude and uncomplimentary songs. Usually they're ushered into the kitchen, where such delicacies as apples, nuts, cookies, and raisin bread are handed out. Turnips—one of the few winter vegetables in Estonia—are another prized gift, as is *viljandi kama*, a kind of meal comprised of 15 different grains and dried vegetables mixed with sour milk, sugar, and cream that is regarded as a special treat. Well-to-do families give children bags of viljandi kama on Martin's Day to show how prosperous they are.

SOURCES:
BkFest-1937, p. 107

◆ 1135 ◆ Martinsfest
November 10–11

Martin's Festival in Germany honors both St. Martin of Tours (*see* MARTINMAS and ST. MARTIN'S DAY IN PORTUGAL) and Martin Luther (1483–1546), the German theologian and leader of the Protestant Reformation (*see* REFORMATION DAY). In Düsseldorf, a man dressed as St. Martin rides through the streets followed by hundreds of children. Many carry lanterns made from hollowed-out pumpkins. It is thought that the rites associated with St. Martin's Day may have originated as an early thanksgiving festival in honor of Freya, the ancient German goddess of plenty.

While German Roman Catholics honor St. Martin on this day, Protestants honor Martin Luther, who was born on November 10, 1483, and baptized on the 11th. In Erfurt, where Martin Luther attended the university, there is a procession of children carrying lanterns. This ends in the plaza in front of the cathedral and the Severi Church. With their lanterns the children form the "Luther rose," or the escutcheon of Martin Luther.

CONTACT:
German National Tourist Office
122 E. 42nd St., 52nd Floor
New York, NY 10168
212-661-7200; fax: 212-661-7174

SOURCES:
AnnivHol-1983, p. 145
BkFest-1937, p. 138
BkFestHolWrld-1970, p. 122
DictWrldRel-1989, pp. 440, 606
FestWestEur-1958, p. 77
RelHolCal-1993, p. 63

◆ 1136 ◆ Martyrdom of Joseph and Hyrum Smith
June 27

Members of the Church of Jesus Christ of Latter-Day Saints, also known as Mormons, commemorate the day on which their founder, Joseph Smith, and his brother, Hyrum, were murdered in the city jail in Carthage, Illinois, in 1844. Joseph Smith had announced his candidacy for the U.S. presidency earlier that year, and he had been attacked by a group of Mormon dissenters for his political ambition and his alleged polygamy: There is evidence that he may have married as many as 50 wives, although he acknowledged only his first. As the mayor of Nauvoo, Ill., Smith saw to it that the press used to print the opposition newspaper was destroyed. Threats of mob violence followed, and Smith and his brother were eventually jailed on charges of treason. Although the brothers had been promised protection by the governor, a mob of men with blackened faces stormed the jail on June 27 and killed them, thus elevating them to the status of martyrs.

CONTACT:
Church of Jesus Christ of Latter-
  Day Saints
15 E. North Temple St.
Salt Lake City, UT 84150
801-240-1000; fax: 801-240-2033

SOURCES:
Chases-1996, p. 272
DictWrldRel-1989, p. 424
RelHolCal-1993, p. 93

♦ 1137 ♦ **Martyrs of North America, Feast of the**
October 19

The **Feast of the North American Martyrs** commemorates the death of eight priests who were killed by the Iroquois, mortal enemies of the Huron Indians, with whom the priests had been working for 34 years. There was a great deal of missionary activity being carried out in what is now Canada and upstate New York during the 1600s, and many of the devoted missionaries who worked among the Indians in the area extending from Nova Scotia to the Great Lakes met with torture and often cruel death. The eight who are remembered on this day are John de Brébeuf and his companions, French Jesuits who died in 1649. They were canonized together in 1930, and a shrine was built for them at Auriesville, New York.

SOURCES:
AnnivHol-1983, p. 123
DaysCustFaith-1957, p. 242

♦ 1138 ♦ **Marya**
July–August; third day of waning half of Hindu month of Sravana

When Gautama sat down under the Bo tree to await Enlightenment, Mara, the Buddhist Lord of the Senses and satanic tempter, tried a number of strategies to divert him from his goal. Disguised as a messenger, Mara brought the news that one of Gautama's rivals had usurped his family's throne. Then he scared away the other gods who had gathered to honor the future Buddha by causing a storm of rain, rocks, and ashes to fall. Finally, he sent his three daughters, representing thirst, desire, and delight, to seduce Gautama—all to no avail.

In the city of Patan, Nepal, a procession on this day commemorates the Buddha's triumph over Mara's temptations. A procession of 3,000 to 4,000 people, carrying gifts—usually butter lamps—for Lord Buddha, moves through the city from shrine to shrine. Some wear masks and others play traditional Nepalese musical instruments. The devil dancers and mask-wearers in the parade often pretend to scare the children who line the streets by suddenly jumping out at them.

CONTACT:
Nepal Embassy
2131 Leroy Pl., N.W.
Washington, D.C. 20008
202-667-4550; fax: 202-667-5534

SOURCES:
FolkWrldHol-1992, p. 402

♦ 1139 ♦ **Maryland Day**
March 25

Maryland Day, or **Founder's Day**, commemorates the land-

ing of the first colonists there in 1634, and the first Roman Catholic Mass they celebrated. Named after Henrietta Maria, the consort of King Charles I of England, Maryland was the first proprietary colony on the American mainland. George Calvert, Lord Baltimore was appointed by the king as proprietor, and as a Catholic he hoped to establish a refuge for other Catholics who had been persecuted in Anglican England. He was succeeded as head of the colony by his son, Cecilius Calvert, the second Lord Baltimore, who brought 200 more colonists over from England.

SOURCES:
AmerBkDays-1978, p. 287
AnnivHol-1983, p. 42
Chases-1996, p. 144
DictDays-1988, p. 74

♦ 1140 ♦ **Maryland Hunt Cup**
Last Saturday in April

A steeplechase that has been run in Maryland since 1894 and is considered the premier such horse race in America and one of the toughest steeplechases in the world. It's a timber race: the jumps are over stout post-and-rail fences rather than hedges as in the English GRAND NATIONAL. Since 1922, it has always been held in Glyndon, the locale of the Green Spring Valley Hounds, a hunt club. The course is four miles long and has 22 fences, none of which is jumped twice. The highest fence is the 16th at 4'10", while the most spectacular, causing the most spills, is the 4'6" third fence, near the beginning of the race before the horses are well warmed up.

The first race was held to settle a dispute between two hunt clubs, Green Spring Valley Hounds and the Elkridge Hunt, over which had the better fox-hunting horses. Originally only for club members, the race was opened to all comers in 1903, and a rivalry between Pennsylvania and Maryland horses began and still endures. At the first race, a silver cup and $100 were awarded to the winner. Today there is still a cup, but the award has grown—$25,000 is now split among the top four finishers. Memorable horses have been Mountain Dew, a three-time winner in the 1960s; Jay Trump, also a three-time winner in the 1960s and the winner of the English GRAND NATIONAL in 1965; and Ben Nevis, twice a winner, who took seven seconds off the course record in 1978, a record that still stood in 1991. Ben Nevis, who also won the English Grand National, was a small horse but a spectacular athlete.

The Hunt Cup was originally only for men, but women were allowed to enter in the late 1970s, and in 1980 Joy Slater was the first woman to take the prize.

Tailgate parties are held before the race, and a hunt ball after it is attended by riders, trainers, jockeys, owners, and members of the two local hunt clubs. It's considered the social event of the season.

CONTACT:
Maryland Office of Tourism
  Development
217 E. Redwood St., 9th Floor
Baltimore, MD 21202
800-543-1036 or 410-333-6611
fax: 410-333-6643

♦ 1141 ♦ **Maryland Kite Festival**
Last Saturday in April

Inspired by a kite festival they'd seen in Carmel, California,

Baltimore residents Valerie and Melvin Govig started the Liberty Road Kite Festival in 1967. As the competition grew and was opened up to the entire state, the name was changed to the Maryland Kite Festival. Still held in Baltimore, the festival accepts more than 300 entries in various age categories, which are then judged on the basis of design and ingenuity, craftsmanship, beauty (on the ground as well as in the air), launch, control, and retrieval. Bonus points are awarded for duration of flight. Cash prizes and trophies are awarded for the wittiest kite, the most ingenious kite breakdown and assembly, the largest kite, the best-flying miniature kite (three inches or smaller), and the youngest and oldest entrants. Special events often include maneuverability and kite-dueling exhibitions by champions, and lessons in the arts of kite flying.

CONTACT:
Baltimore Area Convention and
  Visitors Bureau
100 Light St., 12th Floor
Baltimore, MD 21202
800-343-3468 or 410-659-7300
fax: 410-727-2308

SOURCES:
GdUSFest-1984, p. 80

♦ 1142 ♦ **Marymass Fair**
Third or fourth Monday in August

Like many festivals, the Marymass Fair held in Irvine, Ayrshire, Scotland, has both Christian and pagan roots. It takes its name from the Feast of the ASSUMPTION, which is observed on August 15 in honor of the Blessed Virgin Mary. This day also coincides with Old Lammas Day on the Julian calendar. LAMMAS, which is observed on August 1 according to the Gregorian calendar, was one of the four great pagan festivals of Britain, and it was celebrated in Scotland with dancing around bonfires and other pagan rites.

The Marymass Fair, which dates back to at least the 12th century, is famous for its horse races, believed to be the oldest in Europe.

CONTACT:
British Tourist Authority
551 Fifth Ave., Ste. 702
New York, NY 10176
800-462-2748 or 212-986-2200
fax: 212-986-1188

SOURCES:
RelHolCal-1993, p. 94

♦ 1143 ♦ **Marzas**
February 28–March 1

On the last night of February and the first of March in Spain, young *marceros*, or March serenaders, wander through the streets singing songs to their lovers or girlfriends and asking for donations of food and sweets to celebrate the arrival of spring. The term *marzas* refers both to the traditional songs they sing and to the gifts they receive. Although the songs themselves vary, they always mention the month of March and the coming of spring, leading many to believe that the tradition has its roots in pagan rituals celebrating the passing of winter.

SOURCES:
DictFolkMyth-1984, p. 1063

♦ 1144 ♦ **Marzenna Day**
Saturday or Sunday nearest March 21

A festival day along the Vistula River in Poland, Marzenna

Day is a spring ritual particularly enjoyed by young people. A *Marzenna* is a straw doll about three or four feet tall and dressed in rags, a striped shirt, a hat, and lots of ribbons. On this day near the first day of spring (*see* VERNAL EQUINOX), the townspeople, dressed in costume, accompany the Marzenna to the river and throw her in. Not only is this act a final farewell to winter, but it also recalls an old legend about a young man whose faith in one god was so great that he was able to save a girl who was about to be sacrificed to appease the gods of storms and floods. After the doll is thrown into the water, the people welcome spring with singing and dancing.

SOURCES:
AnnivHol-1983, p. 40
BkHolWrld-1986, Mar 23

♦ 1145 ♦ **Masi Magham**
February–March; full moon day

The Masi Magham festival is observed every 12 years during the full moon in February or March, although a smaller festival takes place annually. Hindus flock to Kumbakonam in southern India to bathe in the Maha-Magha tank, where the waters of nine holy rivers are said to be mixed: the Ganges, the Yumma, the Godavari, the Saraswati, the Narmada, the Cauvery, the Kumari, the Payoshni, and the Sarayu. Bathing in the sacred tank (or pool) purifies them of their sins.

The Masi Magham festival is also a time for gift-giving, particularly in support of charitable institutions. One way of measuring the size of one's gift to the poor is to give one's weight in gold, a custom known as *Tulabhara*. Sometimes the gold collected in this way is used to renovate the 16 temples that have been built over the years near the site of the sacred tank.

In Malaysia, the Masi Magham is a two-day festival celebrated by the Chettiyar (a Tamil merchant caste) community in Malacca. The image of Subramanya, a Hindu god, is taken in procession to the temple known as Sannasi Malai Kovil, formerly the home of a famous ascetic who had the power to heal. Oratorical contests are held and dramas are staged at the temple, and at the end of the day, the statue is taken back through the streets of Malacca to Poyyatha Vinayagar Kovil, where it remains for another year.

CONTACT:
India Tourist Office
30 Rockefeller Ave.
15 N. Mezzanine
New York, NY 10112
212-586-4901; fax: 212-582-3274

Malaysian Tourism Promotion
  Board
818 W. Seventh St., Ste. 804
Los Angeles, CA 90017
213-689-9702; fax: 213-689-1530

SOURCES:
BkFestHolWrld-1970, p. 91
FolkWrldHol-1992, p. 147

♦ 1146 ♦ **Maskal**
September

A Christian festival in Ethiopia to commemorate the finding of the True Cross, the cross on which Christ was crucified. (*Maskal* means 'cross.') The celebration comes at the end of the rainy season in the Ethiopian spring, when fields are blooming with yellow flowers known as the maskal flowers. In communities throughout the nation, a tall pole called a *demara* is set up and topped with a cross. Families place smaller demaras against the big one, and in the evening they are made into a huge bonfire. Religious ceremonies are performed around the bonfire, with songs and dancing. The ashes of the burned-out fire are considered holy, so the people place the powder of the ashes on their foreheads.

See also EXALTATION OF THE CROSS

SOURCES:
AnnivHol-1983, p. 124
BkHolWrld-1986, Sep 27
FolkWrldHol-1992, p. 490
GdWrldFest-1985, p. 75

Master Draught Pageant
  See **Meistertrunk Pageant**

♦ 1147 ♦ Master's Golf Tournament
First full week in April

Known to golf fans everywhere as **The Masters**, this annual tournament has been held at the exclusive Augusta National Golf Club in Georgia since it was first started there in 1934 by Bobby Jones, who designed the course. It has long been associated with names like Ben Hogan, Sam Snead, Arnold Palmer, and Jack Nicklaus. Former U.S. President Dwight Eisenhower often played the course and stayed in a cottage to the left of the 10th tee that is still called "Ike's Cottage."

The qualifying rounds are held on Thursday and Friday of the four-day tournament, and the top 44 finishers participate in the final round. The top 24 finishers are automatically invited back the next year and do not have to qualify over again. In addition to the cash prize, the winner of the tournament, which has been referred to as "golf's rite of spring," receives a trophy and a green blazer. Each year on the Tuesday night before the tournament, there is a Champions Dinner attended by past winners and hosted by the defending champion—all of them wearing their distinctive green jackets.

It wasn't until September 1990 that the Augusta National Golf Club admitted its first black member, Ron Townsend, president of the Gannett Television Group. Had the Club refused to admit a black man, it is likely that the Masters would no longer have been held there, since the PGA (Professional Golfers' Association) now has rules forbidding discriminatory membership practices.

CONTACT:
Augusta-Richmond County Con-
    vention and Visitors Bureau
32 Eighth St.
Augusta, GA 30901
800-726-0243 or 706-823-6600

♦ 1148 ♦ Matralia
June 11

The Matralia was an ancient Roman festival in honor of Mater Matuta, who is often confused with the Greek dawn-goddess, Leucothea. Modern authorities describe Mater Matuta, who has no mythology but whose cult was widespread in ancient times, as a goddess of the dawn's light and of childbirth—the dawn being a lucky time to give birth. She

was also a deity of matrons, and only matrons and freeborn women were allowed to participate in the festival held at her shrine in the round temple known as the Forum Boarium.

Not much is known about what went on during the Matralia, but it appears that only the wife of a first marriage was allowed to decorate the image of the goddess. No female slaves were allowed in the temple—except for one, who was driven out after being slapped on the face. The women offered prayers primarily on behalf of their nieces and nephews; their own children were considered to be of secondary importance. They made offerings of flowers and often arrived at the temple carrying their relatives' children in their arms.

SOURCES:
ClassDict-1984, p. 360
DictFolkMyth-1984, p. 693
FestRom-1981, p. 150
RomFest-1925, p. 154

♦ 1149 ♦ Matronalia
March 1

Also known as the **Matronales Feriae**, the Matronalia was an ancient Roman festival in honor of Juno, the goddess of women. It was observed on March 1, the day on which her temple was dedicated. The cult of Juno was established by the king of the Sabines, Titus Tatius, and the Matronalia celebrated not only the sacredness of marriage as an institution but the peace that followed the first marriages that took place between Roman men and Sabine women.

It was customary for married women to form a procession to Juno's temple, where offerings were made to the goddess. At home, women received gifts from their husbands on this day and held feasts for their female slaves. They also prayed for marital peace and harmony.

SOURCES:
OxClassDict-1970, p. 569

♦ 1150 ♦ Matsu, Birthday of
Twenty-third day of third lunar month

A celebration of the birthday of the Chinese deity Matsu (or Ma-cho or Mazu), the Goddess of the Sea who is venerated by fishermen for protecting them from storms and disasters at sea. People pay homage to her on her birthday at the Meizhou Mazu Temple on Meishou Island, Fujian Province, China, on Taiwan, and in other Chinese communities.

One Chinese legend says that the goddess was born in about 960 and, because she never cried in the first month of her life, was named Lin Moniang, *moniang* meaning 'quiet girl.' She began to read when she was eight, studied Buddhist and Taoist scriptures, became a believer in Buddhism at 10, studied magic arts when she was 12, and at 28 achieved nirvana and became a goddess. She is worshipped because she is believed to have performed many miracles during her life. Courts in successive dynasties issued decrees to honor her with such titles as "Holy Princess" and "Holy Mother."

In Taiwan, the story is that Matsu, a girl from Hokkien Province in China, took up the fishing trade to support her mother after her fisherman father died. One day she died at sea, and because of her filial devotion, she came to be worshipped as a deity. During World War II, when American planes started to bomb Taiwan, many women prayed to Matsu, and it is said that some women saw a girl dressed in red holding out a red cloth to catch the falling bombs.

She is known as A-Ma, or the Mother Goddess, on Macao. The legend there says A-Ma was a beautiful young woman whose presence on a Canton-bound ship saved it from disaster. All the other ships in the fleet, whose rich owners had refused to give her passage, were destroyed in a storm.

Whatever the story, people whose lives depend on the sea visit the goddess' temples on her birthday.

On Taiwan, the most famous celebration site is the Chaotien Temple in Peikang. Built in 1694, it is Taiwan's oldest, biggest, and richest Matsu temple. A carnival-like atmosphere prevails during the **Matsu Festival**, with watermelon stalls, cotton candy stalls, and sling-shot ranges set up along roadsides. There are parades of the goddess and other gods through village streets, where altars bearing sacrifices of food and incense have been set up. Hundreds of thousands of people pour out of buses and arrive on foot at Peikang. Many of them make pilgrimages from the town of Tachia about 60 miles north, spending a week visiting about 16 Matsu temples along the route. Peikang becomes so crowded it's hard to move, and the firecrackers are deafening. It has been estimated that 75 percent of all firecrackers manufactured on Taiwan are exploded in Peikang during the Matsu Festival; afterwards the remnants of the firecrackers lie two inches deep on the streets.

See also TIN HAU FESTIVAL

CONTACT:
China National Tourist Office
350 Fifth Ave., Ste. 6413
New York, NY 10165
212-760-9700; fax: 212-760-8809

Taiwan Visitors Association
1 World Trade Center, Ste. 7953
New York, NY 10048
212-466-0691; fax: 212-432-6436

SOURCES:
FolkWrldHol-1992, p. 212

♦ 1151 ♦ **Maundy Thursday**
Between March 19 and April 22 in West and between April 1 and May 5 in East; Thursday before Easter

Also known as **Green Thursday** in Germany from the practice of giving a green branch to penitents as a sign that their penance was completed; **Shere** or **Sheer Thursday**, meaning 'free from guilt'; **Paschal Thursday, Passion Thursday,** or **Holy Thursday**, it is the day preceding GOOD FRIDAY. It commemorates Jesus' institution of the Eucharist during the Last Supper, celebrated by Christians since the middle of the fourth century. The practice of ceremonial foot-washing in imitation of Jesus, who washed his disciples' feet before the Last Supper as a sign and example of humility and love, has been largely discontinued in Protestant churches. However, the Roman Catholic Church and the Anglican Communion still celebrate the rites of Maundy Thursday, which may include handing out special coins known as "Maundy mon-

ey" to the aged and the poor, instead of foot washing. Also on this day, the sacramental Holy Oils, or chrism, are blessed.

The name "Maundy" probably comes from the Latin *mandatum*, or 'commandment', referring to Christ's words after he washed the feet of his disciples: "A new commandment I give unto you, that you love one another as I have loved you." (John 13:34)

SOURCES:
AmerBkDays-1978, p. 291
BkDays-1864, vol. I, p. 411
BkFest-1937, pp. 56, 183, 227, 329
DaysCustFaith-1957, p. 106
DictFolkMyth-1984, pp. 694, 1163
FestSaintDays-1915, p. 61
FestWestEur-1958, pp. 8, 60, 93, 212
FolkAmerHol-1991, p. 152
FolkWrldHol-1992, pp. 190, 193, 197, 199, 203
SaintFestCh-1904, p. 158

♦ 1152 ♦ **Mauni Amavasya**
January–February; 15th day of waning half of Hindu month of Magha

Complete silence is observed on the day known to Hindus as Mauni Amavasya. Because bathing during Magha, one of the most sacred Hindu months, is considered to be a purifying act, many Hindus camp out along the banks of the Ganges River throughout the month and bathe daily in the sacred river. But the bathing and fasting end with the observance of Mauni Amavasya, a day for worshipping Lord Vishnu and circumambulating the peepal (a type of ficus) tree, which is mentioned in the *Bhagavad Gita* and is regarded as holy.

For many Hindus, the celebration takes place at Prayag, a well-known pilgrimage center where the Ganges, Yamuna, and Saraswati rivers flow together. Some live here for a full month, practicing rituals and ceremonial sacrifices known as *Kalpa-Vas*. Religious discourses and services are held daily, and the worshippers who come here eat only one meal a day or confine their diet to fruit and milk.

SOURCES:
RelHolCal-1993, p. 94

♦ 1153 ♦ **Mauritania Independence Day**
November 28

This national holiday commemorates Mauritania's independence from France on November 28, 1960, after more than 50 years under French rule.

CONTACT:
Mauritania Embassy
2129 Leroy Pl., N.W.
Washington, D.C. 20008
202-232-5700; fax: 202-966-0983

SOURCES:
AnnivHol-1983, p. 152
Chases-1996, p. 462
NatlHolWrld-1968, p. 211

♦ 1154 ♦ **Mauritius Independence Day**
March 12

This national holiday commemorates the day in 1968 when

Mauritius gained independence from Britain, after being under its rule since the early 19th century.

CONTACT:
Mauritius Government Tourist Information Service
8 Haven Ave., Ste. 227
Port Washington, NY 11050
516-944-3763; fax: 516-944-8458

SOURCES:
AnnivHol-1983, p. 36
Chases-1996, p. 130

♦ 1155 ♦ Maverick Sunday Concerts
Sundays in July to early September

Hervey White, a novelist, poet and architect, purchased a piece of farmland he named "Maverick" just outside of Woodstock, New York, around the turn of the century. Within a few years, White had built a "music chapel" there and organized a Sunday afternoon concert series designed to give professional orchestral musicians an opportunity to play chamber music during the off-season. The series was under way by 1916, making the Maverick Sunday Concerts the oldest continuous chamber music series in the United States.

The concerts, which take place on Sunday afternoons from July to early September, are held in an unusual rustic concert hall made of locally cut and milled oak, pine, and chestnut. There are 56 paned windows in the front gable, a huge porch along one side, and seating for an audience of 400. The programming runs the gamut from traditional music for quintets, quartets, trios, and duos to the very latest contemporary compositions. Many of the works performed there in the past were composed by Alexander Semmier, who directed the Maverick concerts from 1954 to 1969. There have also been world premieres by noted Hudson Valley composers and performances by the Tokyo String Quartet, the Dorian Woodwind Quintet, the Beaux Arts Quartet, the Manhattan String Quartet, and the Cremona Arts Trio.

CONTACT:
New York Division of Tourism
1 Commerce Pl.
Albany, NY 12245
800-225-5697 or 518-474-4116
fax: 518-486-6416

SOURCES:
MusFestAmer-1990, p. 103

♦ 1156 ♦ Mawlid al-Nabi (Maulid al-Nabi; Prophet's Birthday)
Twelfth day of the Islamic month of Rabi al-Awwal

Mawlid al-Nabi celebrates the birth of Muhammad, the founder of Islam. Born in Mecca around 570, he was a shepherd and a trader who began to receive revelations from God when he was 40 years old. Over the next 23 years he not only established a religion but brought an unprecedented political unity to Arab tribes. Muhammad's birth began to be observed as a public holiday about the 12th century, except by conservative sects such as the Wahhabis who do not celebrate any human. They believe that to do so would detract from the worship of God. It is celebrated with the recitation of litanies in mosques, and with firecrackers and gift-giving throughout the Middle East. In Libya it is an official holiday; in Burkina Faso it is called **Damba** and in Indonesia, **Sekartan.**

SOURCES:
AnnivHol-1983, p. 170
BkFest-1937, p. 237
BkFestHolWrld-1970, p. 79
BkHolWrld-1986, Dec 3
DictWrldRel-1989, pp. 365, 348, 468, 498
FolkWrldHol-1992, p. 482
RelHolCal-1993, pp. 63, 94

♦ 1157 ♦ May Day
May 1

Many of the customs associated with the first day of May come from the old Roman FLORALIA, or festival of flowers. These include the gathering of branches and flowers on MAY DAY EVE or early May Day morning, the choosing and crowning of a May Queen, and dancing around a bush, tree, or decorated pole, the Maypole. The sports and festivities that are held on this day symbolize the rebirth of nature as well as human fertility. In fact, the ritual drinking and dancing around the Maypole in colonial America so horrified the Pilgrim Fathers that they outlawed the practice and punished the offenders. This is probably why May Day has remained a relatively quiet affair in this country.

In Communist countries, May Day has been transformed into a holiday for workers, marked by parades that are an occasion for displaying military strength. The May Day Parade in Red Square, Moscow, has long been a spectacular example though less so in recent years with the dissolution of the Soviet Union and the resulting relaxation of Cold War tensions. Perhaps in reaction to such displays, Americans instituted LOYALTY DAY and LAW DAY on this same date. In Great Britain, May 1 is LABOR DAY. More than 50 other countries also celebrate Labor Day in honor of workers on May 1.

See also PREMIER MAI and VAPPU

SOURCES:
AmerBkDays-1978, p. 407
BkDays-1864, vol. I, p. 570
BkFest-1937, pp. 17, 58, 88, 113, 122, 186, 261, 278, 310
DaysCustFaith-1957, p. 115
DictFolkMyth-1984, pp. 129, 202, 203, 534, 695, 750, 866, 946, 1064
FestSaintDays-1915, pp. 102, 105, 109
FestWestEur-1958, p. 37
FolkAmerHol-1991, p. 189
FolkWrldHol-1992, p. 262
RelHolCal-1993, p. 95

♦ 1158 ♦ May Day Eve in Ireland
April 30

According to Irish legend, the fairy people fight among themselves on the eve of MAY DAY. Every seven years, the combat is especially intense, for they compete with one another for the crops, taking the best ears of wheat, barley, and oats as their prize. By mixing the barley with dew gathered from a mountain top at midnight, they make a strong liquor. One drink is believed to set them dancing for 24 hours without pausing to rest.

The custom of celebrating May Day Eve with bonfires or with a May bush decorated with candles can be traced back to the pagan feast of BELTANE, which marked the summer's end. In Ireland, a horse's skull was often burned in the bonfire. On November Eve (October 31) in County Cork, a procession led by a man called "The White Mare," who was dressed in a white robe and carried a symbolic horse's head, went from house to house soliciting contributions of money and food. Because fairies and the spirits of the dead were believed to roam around on this night, food was left out to ward off their mischief.

SOURCES:
DictFolkMyth-1984, p. 202
FolkWrldHol-1992, p. 252

♦ 1159 ♦ May Day Eve in Italy
April 30

In Modena, Italy, if tradition is followed, the boys of the town sing May songs under the village windows on the eve of MAY DAY. A talented musician is often asked to sing to the sweethearts of the others, and the boys compete with one another to see who can compose the most persuasive lyrics. On the Sunday following, it is customary for the boys to appear with empty baskets at the houses they have serenaded. The families fill the baskets with things to eat.

May Day itself, or *Calendimaggio*, bears little resemblance to the original pagan spring festival once celebrated in ancient Rome. Modern-day Italians attend horse races, fireworks exhibitions, and various types of competitions and lotteries which are held throughout the country on May 1.

SOURCES:
BkFest-1937, p. 186

♦ 1160 ♦ May Day Eve in Switzerland (Maitag Vorabend)
April 30

Certain villages in the Seeland and Burgdorf regions of the canton of Bern in Switzerland still observe the ancient custom of planting the *Maitannli*, or May pine tree. Boys from the village steal into the forest after dark on May Day Eve, April 30, and cut down small pine trees, which they deck with flowers and ribbons and plant under their sweethearts' bedroom windows, at the front gate, or occasionally on the roof. The young man who plants the symbolic tree is usually welcomed and entertained by the girl and her family. Girls who have a reputation for being arrogant or unpopular sometimes find a grotesque straw puppet in place of the traditional Maitannli.

SOURCES:
BkFest-1937, p. 318

♦ 1161 ♦ May Day Eve in the Czech Republic
April 30

According to an old Czech superstition, witches try to enter people's homes on the eve of MAY DAY and do them harm. At one time it was customary to sprinkle sand or grass on the doorstep, in the belief that the witches had to count the grains or blades before entering the house. Now the "Burning of the Witches" ceremony is observed in some parts of the country by building bonfires on the mountain tops. Brooms that have been dipped in pitch are plunged into the fire and then held aloft like torches.

In Postupice, Bohemia, a Maypole and Burning of the Witches Festival is held April 30–May 1 every year. The young men put up a Maypole, decorated with ribbons and colored wreaths, in the village square on the afternoon of April 30. The next day, both men and women dress up in peasant costumes, weaving the ribbons in and out as they dance around the Maypole and celebrate the coming of spring. The burning of the witches takes place afterward, when the villagers throw their broomsticks into the bonfire and burn the witches in effigy. People gather around the bonfire to drink brandy or beer and roast sausages as they watch the witches burn.

SOURCES:
BkFest-1937, p. 88
GdWrldFest-1985, p. 68

♦ 1162 ♦ May Day in Scandinavia
May 1

In Scandinavia, the celebration of MAY DAY actually begins on April 30, WALPURGIS NIGHT. But the big event of the day is a mock battle between summer and winter, usually represented by two husky young men. Summer always wins, and winter is buried in effigy.

In the Swedish university town of Uppsala, students wearing white caps gather together to hear songs and speeches. Huge bonfires, also associated with Walpurgis Night, are popular in many areas of Sweden. Political speeches, parades of labor organizations, and public demonstrations take place on May 1 as well.

There is a superstition in Norway, dating back to pre-Christian times, about hearing the cuckoo's first call in spring: If the call comes from the south, the year will be good; if it is heard from the north, one will become ill or die in the coming year; if it comes from the west, one will be successful; and if it comes from the east, one will be lucky in love. For this reason, traditional Norwegian calendars show a bird perched in a tree on the mark for May 1.

<table>
<tr><td>CONTACT:
Swedish National Tourist Office
655 Third Ave., 18th Floor
New York, NY 10017
212-949-2333; fax: 212-983-5260</td><td>SOURCES:
BkFest-1937, p. 310
DaysCustFaith-1957, p. 116
FolkWrldHol-1992, p. 265</td></tr>
</table>

♦ 1163 ♦ May Day in Spain
May 1

Most Spanish MAY DAY customs have pagan origins (*see* FLORALIA). At the end of April, young people (in some villages, only bachelors) choose a tall pine tree to use as a Maypole and set it up in the plaza. They decorate it with ribbons, beads, and eggshells, and as they dance around it they sing May songs. The ceremonies around the tree continue for several days, and on the last day of the month the tree is sold to raise money for refreshments or a dinner.

La Maya refers to both the girls who take part in the May Day celebrations and to the May Queen. It is traditional for a group of boys and girls to choose a queen, sit her on a couch or chair, and dance around her on May Day. They sing love songs, or *coplas*, in which they ask for food and money from everyone who passes by, and then use the contributions for a feast or banquet. In some areas, the May Queen has been replaced by a *Cruz de Mayo*, or May Cross. An altar is set up with candles, a white cloth, and a cross decorated with flowers and ribbons. There is dancing around the altar and requests for food and money. Sometimes young girls carry the wooden May Crosses through the streets, asking for contributions. It is possible that this custom resulted from the confusion of May Day with the Feast of the Holy Cross, formerly observed by Roman Catholics on May 3 (*see* EXALTATION OF THE CROSS).

CONTACT:
Tourist Office of Spain
665 Fifth Ave.
New York, NY 10022
212-759-8822; fax: 212-980-1053

SOURCES:
DictFolkMyth-1984, p. 1064
FolkWrldHol-1992, p. 265

♦ 1164 ♦ **May Day in the Czech Republic (Prvého Máje)**
May 1

The traditional Maypole associated with MAY DAY in western Europe, the United States, and elsewhere plays a central role in the celebration of May 1 in the former Czechoslovakia (now the countries of the Czech Republic and Slovakia). On May Day Eve, boys traditionally plant Maypoles underneath their girlfriends' windows, so that the girls will wake up and see them first thing in the morning. In some villages, it is customary to raise a Maypole beneath the window of the most popular girl in town. The Maypole is said to represent the girl's life; the taller it is, the longer she will live. Sometimes it is a small tree, decorated with ribbons and colored eggshells.

Bands give concerts in village squares on May Day, and musicians go from house to house, singing. As a traditional spring festival, May Day has been a time for Czechs and Slovaks to sing, dance, and take pleasure in the beauty of the season.

See also MAY DAY EVE IN THE CZECH REPUBLIC

SOURCES:
BkFest-1937, p. 88

♦ 1165 ♦ **Mayfest, International**
May

A five-day celebration of the arts—performing, visual, and literary—held in Tulsa, Okla. One of the largest festivals in the state, the event features a juried art fair and theatrical presentations. In the past, these varied works have been staged: *Three Penny Opera*, *Our Town*, and *Revenge of the Space Pandas*. There is also a variety of musical entertainment and ethnic foods from all corners of the globe.

CONTACT:
Tulsa Convention and Visitors
Bureau
616 S. Boston, Ste. 100
Tulsa, OK 74119
800-558-3311 or 918-585-1201
fax: 918-592-6244

♦ 1166 ♦ **May Festival, International**
May

Germany's second oldest music festival (after the BAYREUTH FESTIVAL) is the **Wiesbaden May Festival**, founded in 1896. Kaiser Wilhelm II came to Wiesbaden, which is about 26 miles west of Frankfurt, to officiate at the grand opening. The

month-long festival offers eight or nine full-length operas performed in the original language, symphonic concerts, ballet, drama, experimental theater, and mime. Most of the festival events are held in the rococo-style Hessian State Theater, the Kleines Haus (a small auditorium for plays), and the Kurhaus (for symphonic concerts). Among the world-renowned groups that have been invited to perform at the festival are the Netherlands Dance Theatre, Japan's Red Buddha Theatre, the Salzburg Marionettes, the Hamburg State Opera, the Berlin State Opera, the Zurich Opera, the Welsh Philharmonic Orchestra Cardiff, and the Greek National Ballet.

CONTACT:
German National Tourist Office
122 E. 42nd St., 52nd Floor
New York, NY 10168
212-661-7200; fax: 212-661-7174

SOURCES:
GdWrldFest-1985, p. 87
IntlThFolk-1979, p. 151
MusFestEurBrit-1980, p. 106

♦ 1167 ♦ **May Musical of Bordeaux, International**
Begins first week in May

Bordeaux, the wine capital of France and its fourth largest city, has been the setting for a 17-day spring music festival since 1950. Aimed at the ordinary festival-goer as opposed to the cultural elite, the International May Musical downplays contemporary works in favor of the standard classical repertoire. In addition to symphonic and chamber concerts, there are also art exhibits, operas, ballets, theater, and film. Performances are staged at historical locations throughout the city, including the Grand Théâtre, considered to be one of the most beautiful classic-style theaters in Europe, the Gothic St. André Cathedral, and several area wine chateaux.

In additional to its offerings in the areas of instrumental music, vocal recitals, opera, and dance, an interesting feature of the May Musical is its emphasis on the art of mime. Both Ladislav Fialka and Marcel Marceau have performed there.

CONTACT:
French Government Tourist Office
9454 Wilshire Blvd., Ste. 715
Beverly Hills, CA 90212
310-271-6665; fax: 310-276-2835

SOURCES:
GdWrldFest-1985, p. 79
IntlThFolk-1979, p. 102
MusFestEurBrit-1980, p. 78
MusFestWrld-1963, p. 131

♦ 1168 ♦ **Mayoring Day**
May

In England, this is the day on which the new mayor of a town or borough parades through the streets. If it takes place on a Sunday, it is often called **Mayor's Sunday** and is celebrated with a church service. In Rye, Sussex, the old tradition of the "hot-penny scramble" is carried out on this day. The new mayor throws hot pennies to the children, who then scramble to pick them up. This custom probably dates back to the time when Rye minted its own coins, and they were distributed while still hot from the molds.

SOURCES:
AnnivHol-1983, p. 70
DictDays-1988, p. 75

♦ 1169 ♦ **Maytime Festival, International**
Third week in May

A festival center since the 12th century, the city of Dundalk in County Louth, Ireland, is the home of the International Maytime Festival and also of the International Amateur

Theatre Association. It is the festival's aim to improve amateur theater standards and to bring together outstanding amateur theater groups from all over the world. Over 200 events are presented each year in the Dundalk Town Hall auditorium. There are also a number of "fringe" events, such as a children's afternoon theater and a lunchtime theater, that are presented in other locations.

Amateur theater groups wishing to participate in the International Maytime Festival are judged on the basis of their work by the International Amateur Theatre Association's center in their own country. Theaters throughout the British Isles, the United States, and eastern Europe have appeared at the festival in recent years.

CONTACT:
Irish Tourist Board
345 Park Ave., 17th Floor
New York, NY 10154
800-223-6470 or 212-418-0800
fax: 212-371-9052

SOURCES:
IntlThFolk-1979, p. 233

Meat Fare Sunday
See **Cheese Sunday**

♦ 1170 ♦ **Mecklenburg Independence Day**
May 20

The citizens of Mecklenburg County, North Carolina, would like to think that their ancestors were the first to call for independence from the British when they adopted the Mecklenburg Declaration of Independence on May 20, 1775. But historians now believe that the resolutions calling for independence that had been sent to the Second Continental Congress in Philadelphia were never actually presented there—and, in fact, they question that the meeting ever took place.

Even though the Mecklenburg patriots may not have been the first to declare their independence from British rule, their actions represent an important step on the road to the American Revolution, and **Mecklenburg Declaration of Independence Day**, sometimes referred to simply as **Mecklenburg Day**, is still observed as a legal holiday in North Carolina.

SOURCES:
AnnivHol-1983, p. 68
Chases-1996, p. 221
DictDays-1988, p. 75

♦ 1171 ♦ **Medora Musical**
June–September, Labor Day

Theodore ("Teddy") Roosevelt, the 26th president of the United States, spent two years ranching in the Dakota Territory as a young man. When the Spanish-American War was declared in 1898, Roosevelt resigned his position as assistant secretary of the Navy under President William McKinley and organized the First Volunteer Cavalry, nicknamed the "Rough Riders," and took them to Cuba. His colorful exploits, particularly in the Battle of Santiago, made him a national hero.

Every night from mid-June through Labor Day in Medora, North Dakota, there is a musical extravaganza known as the Medora Musical—a patriotic song-and-dance salute to Teddy Roosevelt and his Rough Riders. The musical is performed in a natural amphitheater featuring an outdoor

escalator to get people to their seats. The colorful buttes and ravines of the Bad Lands form a dramatic backdrop for the Broadway-class variety show.

See also Dakota Cowboy Gathering

CONTACT:
North Dakota Tourism
604 E. Boulevard Ave.
Liberty Memorial Bldg.
Bismarck, ND 58505
800-435-5663 or 701-328-2525
fax: 701-328-4878

SOURCES:
Chases-1996, p. 246

♦ 1172 ♦ **Meenakshi Kalyanam**
Between March and May; during Hindu months of Caitra or Vaisakha

The marriage of the goddess Meenakshi, an incarnation of Parvati, and Lord Sundereswarar (also known as Lord Shiva), celebrated in Madurai, Tamil Nadu, India. The rituals are observed at the Meenakshi Temple, one of the biggest temple complexes in India, most of it built between the 12th and 18th centuries. There is a huge procession, with chariots carrying the temple images, dressed in special robes and jewels, through the streets. The people, in celebrating the marriage of the deities, also commemorate their own marriages.

In Malaysia and Singapore it is called **Panguni Uttiram** and also celebrates the marriage of Subramanya to Theivani, adopted daughter of Indra. In Malaysia, food is free to anyone all day. In Singapore, at the Sri Mariamman Temple, there is a fire-walking ceremony. A couple of days later there is a dancing procession led by a man balancing a flower-bedecked pot of yellow-colored water.

CONTACT:
India Tourist Office
30 Rockefeller Ave.
15 N. Mezzanine
New York, NY 10112
212-586-4901; fax: 212-582-3274

SOURCES:
BkHolWrld-1986, May 10
DictWrldRel-1989, pp. 482, 570
FolkWrldHol-1992, p. 216
RelHolCal-1993, p. 65

Singapore Tourist Promotion
  Board
590 Fifth Ave., 12th Floor
New York, NY 10036
212-302-4861; fax: 212-302-4801

♦ 1173 ♦ **Megalesia**
April 4

The cult of the Phrygian goddess Cybele (also known as Kybele, the Great Mother or Magna Mater; *see also* Bona Dea and Opalia) was established in Rome on this day in 204 B.C., when her image was installed in the temple of Victory on the Palatine Hill. Eventually her own temple was built on the same hill, but April 4 continued to be set aside as a commemoration of the foreign goddess' arrival in Rome.

Her festival was given a Greek name, the Megalesia, and in the beginning, no Roman citizens were allowed to take part in it. But over time it spread to the streets of Rome, where Cybele's image was carried in a chariot drawn by lions with her castrated priests leaping and gashing themselves in a frenzy of devotion. The procession went from the Palatine to the Circus, where games known as LUDI and plays known as *ludi megalenses* were held. The task of keeping the festival under Phrygian control—and within the bounds of propriety—eventually proved to be difficult, and the Megalesia became little more than a holiday celebrated in honor of the Magna Mater.

SOURCES:
AmerBkDays-1978, p. 313
EncyRel-1987, vol. 4, p. 185
NewCentClassHand-1962, p. 689
SeasFeast-1961, p. 185

♦ 1174 ♦ **Meiji Setsu**
November 3

This was formerly observed as the birthday of the Emperor Meiji (1852–1912), who ruled Japan from 1868 until his death. Meiji Tenno abolished feudalism, raised the people's standard of living, and secured Japan's reputation as a great world power. It was during his reign that Japan made rapid progress toward becoming a modern nation by using Western institutions, technology, and learning as its model. It was during this period that a constitution was adopted, a parliament was convened, civil and criminal laws were codified, and an educational system was established. Railways were built, and electric lights and telephones were put into use.

Today, November 3 is still a national holiday, but it is known as Bunka-no-Hi, or Culture Day.

CONTACT:
Japan National Tourist
  Organization
630 Fifth Ave., Ste. 2101
New York, NY 10111
212-757-5640; fax: 212-307-6754

SOURCES:
BkFest-1937, p. 200
JapanFest-1965, pp. 204, 217

♦ 1175 ♦ **Meistertrunk Pageant (Master Draught Pageant)**
Between May 8 and June 11; Pentecost

A celebration in the medieval town of Rothenburg-on-the-Tauber, Germany, to commemorate a gargantuan drinking feat in 1631. The pageant is staged for the four days ending on Whit-Monday, and the play itself, *Meistertrunk*, is also performed on various occasions during the summer. The best known of the Bavarian history plays, *Meistertrunk* dramatizes a chronicled event of the Thirty Years' War: the town was threatened with destruction by Imperial troops led by the famed general, Johann Tserclaes Tilly. The general saw the state wine beaker and decided to play a game with the town's life at stake. If a council member could drink off the entire beaker of wine—about a gallon—in one draught, Tilly promised to spare the town. Burgomaster George Nusch accepted the challenge and emptied the beaker in one mighty gulp and the town was saved.

The play is performed out of doors with the entire town a stage. Tilly's troops are camped outside the city walls, and in the market square costumed children plead with the general. The same beaker that Nusch drained in 1631 is used in the reenactment.

A parade precedes the play, and the "Shepherds' Dance" is performed after it in the market square. The dance, dating to 1516, is in honor of St. Wolfgang, the patron saint of shepherds, and recalls the time a member of the shepherds' guild raced from his pastures to warn the city of the approach of an enemy.

CONTACT:
German National Tourist Office
122 E. 42nd St., 52nd Floor
New York, NY 10168
212-661-7200; fax: 212-661-7174

SOURCES:
FestWestEur-1958, p. 66
GdWrldFest-1985, p. 87

♦ 1176 ♦ **Meitlisunntig**
Second Sunday in January

In the Seetal district of Aargau, Switzerland, the girls of Meisterschwanden and Fahrwangen hold a procession on the second Sunday in January known as Meitlisunntig. They dress in historical uniforms and stage a military parade before an all-female General Staff. The custom dates from the Villmergen War of 1712, a conflict in which the women of Meisterschwanden and Fahrwangen played a vital role in achieving victory. The military procession is followed by a popular festival.

CONTACT:
Swiss National Tourist Office
608 Fifth Ave.
New York, NY 10020
212-757-5944; fax: 212-262-6116

SOURCES:
AnnivHol-1983, p. 8
Chases-1996, p. 65

♦ 1177 ♦ **Melbourne Cup Day**
First Tuesday in November

The only public holiday in the world dedicated to a horse race, Melbourne Cup Day has been observed in Melbourne, Victoria, Australia, since the first Cup race was held there in 1867. The event actually features seven races, including the grueling handicap race of just under two miles, which is run by some 20 thoroughbreds for a purse worth about $2 million. The story of Phar Lap, the legendary New Zealand thoroughbred who won the Cup in 1930 after nearly being shot by unscrupulous gamblers, was made into a movie—*Far Lap* (1984), directed by Simon Wincer—that made the Cup an event familiar to people all over the world.

Cup Day is not only a legal holiday in the state of Victoria, but is observed throughout the world in offices where Australians work. For those who attend, it is a particularly glamorous event. The champagne flows, huge sums of money are wagered, and the women wear lavish hats while the men turn out in grey top hats and dark morning suits. There are similar races held in other Australian states (*see* Hobart Cup Day), but the Melbourne Cup is still the number one classic of the Australian horseracing circuit.

CONTACT:
Australian Tourist Commission
100 Park Ave., 25th Floor
New York, NY 10017
212-687-6300; fax: 212-661-3340

SOURCES:
AnnivHol-1983, p. 141
DictDays-1988, p. 75

♦ 1178 ♦ **Memorial Day**
Last Monday in May

A legal holiday, formerly known as **Decoration Day**, proclaimed annually by the president to honor U.S. citizens who have died in war. Since 1950, by congressional request, the day is also set aside to pray for permanent peace. Memorial Day is observed in every state but Alabama, which instead celebrates Confederate Memorial Day on the fourth Monday of April. (In all, eight states observe the Confederate holiday, and a ninth, Texas, makes Confederate Heroes Day a state holiday.)

Both religious services and patriotic parades mark the day's celebrations. In the national official observance, a wreath is placed on the Tomb of the Unknown Soldier in Arlington National Cemetery in Virginia. One of the more moving observances is at the Gettysburg National Cemetery in Pennsylvania, where schoolchildren scatter flowers over the graves of unknown soldiers of the Civil War.

The practice of decorating graves of war dead began before the close of the Civil War. However, an officially set day was established in 1868 when Gen. John A. Logan, commander-in-chief of the Grand Army of the Republic, issued an order naming May 30 as a day for "strewing with flowers or otherwise decorating the graves of comrades who died in defense of their country during the late rebellion." The day became known as Decoration Day, but as it was extended to include the dead of all wars, it took the name Memorial Day.

CONTACT:
Arlington National Cemetery
Arlington, VA 22211
703-697-2131; fax: 703-697-4967

Gettysburg National Military Park
c/o Eisenhower National Historic
  Site
P.O. Box 1080
Gettysburg, PA 17325
717-334-1124

SOURCES:
AmerBkDays-1978, p. 501
AnnivHol-1983, p. 73
BkFest-1937, p. 18
BkHolWrld-1986, May 30
Chases-1996, p. 231
DaysCustFaith-1957, p. 132
DictDays-1988, p. 30
FolkAmerHol-1991, p. 214

♦ 1179 ♦ **Memphis in May International Festival**
May

This month-long festival in Memphis, Tenn., focuses on a different nation's culture each year, with exhibitions, lectures, films, performing arts presentations, sporting events, and student exchange programs. Beginning on the first weekend in May (sometimes on April 30 to encompass May 1 and 2), the festival opens with a salute to the nations honored in past festivals and an international marketplace offering merchandise from around the world. The second festival weekend features a fiddlers' convention, the third weekend an international barbecue competition, and the fourth weekend is the Beale Street Music Festival—Beale Street being "the birthplace of the blues." There is also a Fine Arts Festival with opera, performing arts, and music. Festival events take place at Memphis' riverfront park, museums, botanical gardens, galleries, hospitals, theaters, shopping malls, and universities. The festival ends with the Memphis Symphony Orchestra's rendition of Tchaikovsky's *1812 Overture*, complete with live cannons and an impressive display of fireworks.

CONTACT:
Memphis Convention and Visitors
  Bureau
47 Union Ave.
Memphis, TN 38103
800-873-6282 or 901-543-5300
fax: 901-574-5350

SOURCES:
GdUSFest-1984, p. 176

♦ 1180 ♦ **Menuhin Festival**
Three weeks in August

The fashionable resort town of Gstaad, Switzerland, is the setting for an annual summer music festival founded in 1956 by the world-renowned violinist Yehudi Menuhin (b. 1916). Menuhin's name and status have attracted internationally known soloists, orchestras, and chamber music groups to the

festival—among them the Zurich Chamber Orchestra, the Chamber Music Ensemble of the Academy of St. Martin-in-the-Fields, and the Zurich Collegium Musicum. Students from the Menuhin School in London and the International Menuhin Music Academy in Gstaad are also invited to perform at least one concert each season. Menuhin's sister, Hepzibah, and son, Jeremy, have performed as soloists at the festival.

Although the emphasis is usually on chamber music and solo recitals, large orchestral pieces are occasionally performed as well. Chamber music concerts are given in the cone-roofed chapel at Saanen.

CONTACT:
Swiss National Tourist Office
608 Fifth Ave.
New York, NY 10020
212-757-5944; fax: 212-262-6116

SOURCES:
MusFestEurBrit-1980, p. 143

♦ 1181 ♦ **Merchants' Flower Market**
Between May 10 and June 13; the seventh Sunday after Easter

Whitsunday, or PENTECOST, in the Dutch city of Haarlem is the day on which the famous flower market opens in the *Grote Markt* (Great Market). Flower merchants arrive in the afternoon or early evening to set up displays of their flowers on tables and carts. When all the flowers have been arranged, the lights are turned off. As midnight approaches, the market square fills with people. As the bells begin to ring in the steeple of St. Bavo's Church, floodlights go on and thousands of tulips, daffodils, irises, and geraniums appear as if by magic. The festival continues all night until eight o'clock in the morning, with dancing to the sound of barrel organs. People buy herring, pastries, and ice cream from food vendors as well as flowers to place in their windows or on their dining-room tables in celebration of Whitsuntide.

See also LUILAK

CONTACT:
Netherlands Board of Tourism
355 Lexington Ave., 21st Floor
New York, NY 10017
212-370-7360; fax: 212-370-9507

SOURCES:
BkFestHolWrld-1970, p. 65
FestWestEur-1958, p. 135

♦ 1182 ♦ **Merdeka Day**
August 31

A national holiday in Malaysia to commemorate its *merdeka*, or 'independence', from the British in 1957. Parts of Malaysia were under the rule of various foreign powers for centuries, but by the 1920s all the states eventually comprising Malaysia were ruled by Britain. The Federation of Malaya was founded in 1957 and Malaysia was formed in 1963.

The streets of towns and cities are decorated on this day, and there are numerous parades, exhibitions, and stage shows.

CONTACT:
Malaysian Tourism Promotion
  Board
818 W. Seventh St., Ste. 804
Los Angeles, CA 90017
213-689-9702; fax: 213-689-1530

SOURCES:
AnnivHol-1983, p. 112
Chases-1996, p. 356
GdWrldFest-1985, p. 131
IntlThFolk-1979, p. 267

♦ 1183 ♦ **Merrie Monarch Festival**
March–April; week after Easter

A week of festivities in Honolulu honoring Hawaii's King David Kalakaua (1836–1891), who reigned from 1874 to 1891, and gave the United States exclusive rights to maintain a naval station at Pearl Harbor. The week's events, starting on Easter, close with the world's largest hula competition on the last three nights. The top hula schools (*hula halau*) compete in ancient and modern hula.

CONTACT:
Hawaii Visitors Bureau
2270 Kalakaua Ave., Ste. 801
Honolulu, HI 96815
808-923-1811; fax: 808-922-8991

SOURCES:
Chases-1996, p. 162

♦ 1184 ♦ **Messiah Festival**
March–April; eight days during Easter week

The first Messiah Festival in Lindsborg, Kansas, was held in 1882 by a group of Swedish immigrants under the leadership of Dr. and Mrs. Carl Swensson. Using the voices of local townspeople, the Swenssons established what is now known as the Bethany Oratorio Society, a group of 400 singers that includes faculty and students from Bethany College and a 50-member symphony orchestra. Other groups that perform at the annual festival include the Bethany College Choir and the Bethany Community Symphony Orchestra.

The program consists primarily of choral works, oratorios, and solo recitals, often by guest soloists such as Barbara Hocher, D'Anna Fortunato, Ronald Corrado, and Susan von Reichenback. All concerts are held at the college's Presser Auditorium. Lindsborg's Messiah Festival is often referred to as the "Oberammergau of the Plains." (*See also* Oberammergau Passion Play.)

CONTACT:
Bethany College
421 N. First St.
Lindsborg, Kansas 67456
913-227-3311

SOURCES:
MusFestAmer-1990, p. 61

♦ 1185 ♦ **Mevlana, Festival of**
Mid-December

This nine-day festival is held in Konya, Turkey, the home of the religious sect known as the Mevlevi. Sometimes referred to as the "Order of the Whirling Dervishes" for the prominent role that ritual dance plays in their weekly observance of *sama* (congregational music), the sect was founded in the 13th century by Mevlana Celaleddin Rumi, one of Turkey's greatest poets and mystics. Their practices were banned in the early part of this century, but in 1954 Konya was given permission to revive the ritual dances. For nine days each year in December, the dervishes dance to the accompaniment of chanting and the music of flute, zither, and drums. Their turning and whirling motions are supposed to represent communion with the Divine.

The Mevlana Festival also offers lectures on the Mevlevis and special exhibits of art that date back to the 11th century.

CONTACT:
Republic of Turkey Embassy
1714 Massachusetts Ave., N.W.
Washington, D.C. 20036
202-659-8200; fax: 202-659-0744

SOURCES:
DictWrldRel-1989, p. 632
GdWrldFest-1985, p. 181
IntlThFolk-1979, p. 370

♦ 1186 ♦ **Mexico Festival of Independence**
September 15–16

The **Fiesta Patrias** celebrates the anniversary of Mexico's independence. Although the festival itself goes on for the greater part of a week, it comes to a dramatic climax at 11 o'clock on the night of September 15 in Mexico City as crowds of merrymakers wait for the president to appear on the balcony of the National Palace and proclaim the famous *Grito de Dolores* (the 'cry of Dolores')—the 'call to freedom' that the priest Miguel Hidalgo y Costilla (1753–1811) of the town of Dolores used to rouse the peasant population to fight for their independence in 1810. The people respond by cheering *Viva México!* and shooting off pistols and fireworks.

The Festival of Independence is celebrated in smaller communities throughout Mexico in much the same way, with the local mayor reciting the *Grito de Dolores* at precisely 11 o'clock.

The following day is Independence Day, which is celebrated with fireworks, the ringing of cathedral bells, and a huge military parade. One of the big events on Independence Day is the drawing for the National Lottery. Tickets are inexpensive, and the winner becomes an instant millionaire. Almost everyone watches the drawing on television or listens to the radio to see who wins.

CONTACT:
Mexican Government Tourist Office
405 Park Ave., Ste. 1401
New York, NY 10022
800-446-3942 or 212-755-7261
fax: 212-753-2874

SOURCES:
AnnivHol-1983, p. 119
BkFest-1937, p. 229
Chases-1996, p. 379
GdWrldFest-1985, p. 135
NatlHolWrld-1968, p. 172

♦ 1187 ♦ **Mi-Carême**
Between March 8 and April 11; fourth Sunday in Lent

This break from the strictness of Lent is observed in France, Belgium, and various islands of the French West Indies—including Guadeloupe, St. Barthélemy, and Martinique. In Paris, it is celebrated with the **Fête des Blanchisseuses**, or laundresses, who choose a queen from each of the various metropolitan districts. The district queens and the queen of queens chosen by them ride through the streets on a float, followed by their costumed courtiers and ladies-in-waiting. Traditionally, there is a colorful ball for the washerwomen that night.

In Belgium, **Mid-Lent** or **Half-Vasten** is the day when someone dresses up as the Count of Mid-Lent and distributes gifts to children.

CONTACT:
French Government Tourist Office
9454 Wilshire Blvd., Ste. 715
Beverly Hills, CA 90212
310-271-6665; fax: 310-276-2835

SOURCES:
BkFest-1937, pp. 40, 121
FestSaintDays-1915, p. 52
FestWestEur-1958, p. 35

♦ 1188 ♦ **Michaelmas**
September 29 in the West; November 8 in the East

The **Feast of the Archangel Michael**, or the **Day of St. Michael and All Angels**, is a traditional feast day in the Roman Catholic, Anglican Communion, and Orthodox churches. The cult of St. Michael, traditionally regarded as the leader of the heavenly host of angels, probably originated in the East, then spread to the West by the fifth century. The Roman Catholic feast honors the archangels Michael, Gabriel, and Raphael, while in the East and the Anglican communion, Michael and all the angels are honored.

Churches dedicated to Michael can be found in Asia and throughout coastal Europe, usually in places where Michael is reputed to have saved the community from the threat of a monster or giant. The ninth-century abbey Mont St. Michel, off the coast of Normandy, France, once held the shield worn by Michael in his fight against the dragon.

There is an old saying that if you eat goose on Michaelmas you won't have to worry about money for a year. When tenants paid their rent on this day (*see* QUARTER DAYS), it was customary to include "one goose fit for the lord's dinner." Feasting on goose dinners is still part of the Michaelmas tradition, particularly in Ireland.

> **SOURCES:**
> *AmerBkDays-1978*, p. 876
> *BkDays-1864*, vol. II, p. 387
> *BkFest-1937*, p. 153
> *DaysCustFaith-1957*, p. 242
> *DictFolkMyth-1984*, pp. 504, 716
> *FestSaintDays-1915*, p. 180
> *FestWestEur-1958*, p. 155
> *FolkWrldHol-1992*, p. 491
> *RelHolCal-1993*, p. 95
> *SaintFestCh-1904*, p. 428

♦ 1189 ♦ Michaelmas in Norway
September 29

In Norway, **Mikkelsmesse** is the time of year when cows and goats are herded down from the mountain farms, or *sæters*, to the valley homesteads. Almost all farms of any importance have sæters, which are similar to summer camps and are normally operated by women. Cattle and other animals are put out to pasture in the lush mountain meadows, and the girls—usually the eldest daughters of the family—milk and tend the animals and make butter, goat's cheese, and other dairy products for sale or for use on the farms throughout the winter. When the girls return to their family homes in late September with their tubs of butter and well-fed animals wearing garlands of flowers, it is an occasion for dancing, singing, and feasting.

> **SOURCES:**
> *AmerBkDays-1978*, p. 878
> *FestWestEur-1958*, p. 155

♦ 1190 ♦ Michigan Brown Trout Festival
Third through fourth weekend in July

You don't have to be a professional charter captain or even a local fisherman to participate in the Michigan Brown Trout Festival, which has been held in Alpena on the shores of Lake Huron since 1975. The main event is the two-day Super Tournament, which pits boat against boat. It was won recently by someone who had never fished in the area before. Cash prizes are awarded to those who catch the largest fish (by weight) in each of five divisions—brown trout, salmon, lake trout, steelhead, and walleye—each day and over the course of the week-long festival.

Tens of thousands of people come to Alpena to enjoy not only the fishing competitions but the sailboat races, entertain-

ment, and other festival events. The lucky person who catches Big Brownie, a specially-tagged brown trout, during the festival wins a $50,000 savings bond. But the luck that is familiar to fishermen everywhere has plagued those attending the festival as well: no one has ever collected.

Michigan is also home to the National Trout Festival, which dates back to 1933. About 40,000 fishermen and visitors come to the small town of Kalkaska, which has 275 miles of trout streams and 85 lakes stocked with brown, brook, rainbow, and lake trout. This festival is timed to coincide with the opening of trout season, which is the last Saturday in April throughout Michigan.

CONTACT:
Alpena Convention and Visitors
 Bureau
P.O. Box 65
Alpena, MI 49707
800-4-ALPENA or 517-354-4181
fax: 517-356-3999

Greater Kalkaska Area Chamber
 of Commerce
353 S. Cedar
Kalkaska, MI 49646
800-487-6880 or 616-258-9103
fax: 616-258-6155

♦ 1191 ♦ Michigan Renaissance Festival
August–September for seven consecutive weekends

Visitors who walk through the turreted gates of the annual Renaissance Festival in Holly, Michigan, are made to feel as if they're stepping back into the 16th century. The festival has a permanent, 200-acre site which is set up to resemble a European village. Festival activities, which are designed to entertain as well as to educate, include theater, games, and equestrian events as well as displays and demonstrations of Renaissance crafts and cooking. The entire event, which takes place over seven consecutive weekends beginning in mid-August, is based on the theme of a harvest celebration in which visitors are encouraged to participate. They can try their hand at archery or dueling, sample roasted turkey drumsticks, observe the arts of glassblowing, pewter casting, and blacksmithing, and witness a Tournament of Chivalry in which costumed knights on horseback joust on the gaming field.

The popularity of Renaissance festivals began with their introduction in California during the 1960s. Such events are now held in Detroit, Minneapolis, Kansas City, Kansas, and Largo and Sarasota, Florida, and in many other cities across the country. Attendance at the Holly festival has grown to more than 150,000 since it was first held in 1980.

CONTACT:
Michigan Travel Bureau
333 S. Capitol Ave., Ste. F
Lansing, MI 48933
800-543-2937 or 517-373-0670
fax: 517-373-0059

SOURCES:
Chases-1996, p. 331

♦ 1192 ♦ Mid-Autumn Festival
Full moon nearest September 15; fifteenth day of eighth lunar month

This festival to honor the moon goddess is a national holiday in China and a day celebrated throughout the Far East and in Asian communities all over the world. It is also known as the **Moon Cake Festival**. In Korea, it is called **Hangawi** or **Ch'usok**; in Vietnam **Trung Thursday**; in Hong Kong **Chung Ch'iu**; and in Taiwan **Tiong-chhiu Choeh**.

Family reunions are traditional on this day, giving it some resemblance to the American THANKSGIVING. People travel long distances to be together for exchanging presents, feasting, and eating moon cakes. The ingredients of the cakes and the celebration vary according to the region.

In Taiwan, people have picnics and climb mountains to have a better view of the moon. Besides eating moon cakes, people eat pomelos, or grapefruit. The Chinese word for grapefruit is *yu*, which sounds like the Chinese word for protection, and this is a time for praying to the moon god for protection, family unity, and good fortune. It's also a time for lovers to tryst.

In Malaysia, Vietnam, and other areas, it is a children's festival. They parade through the streets on the night of the festival with candle-lit paper lanterns, some of them white and round like the moon, others like all sorts of animals. Dancers parade with dragons made of paper and cloth, and firecrackers are lit after the parades. In Hong Kong children also carry paper lanterns, and many people spend the evening on the beaches watching the moon and the many bonfires that are lit on this night.

In Suzhou, China, a celebration is held in the Museum of Chinese Drama and Opera, with spectators seated at small porcelain tables where they eat moon cakes, drink jasmine tea, and watch a program of Chinese classical music, ballad-singing, acrobatics, and comic scenes from operas.

In Japan, the custom of *tsukimi*, or 'moon-viewing,' is observed at the same time as the Chinese festival—at the time of the full moon nearest September 15. People set up a table facing the horizon where the moon will rise, and place offerings on the table to the spirit of the moon. These would include a vase holding the seven grasses of autumn, cooked vegetables, and *tsukimi dango*, moon-viewing dumplings made of rice flour. Moon-viewing festivals are held at Hyakkaen Garden, Mukojima, Tokyo, and on Osawa at Daikakuji Temple in Kyoto, where the moon is watched from boats with dragons on their bows.

There are 20 to 30 varieties of moon cakes, which in their roundness are symbolic of family unity. Some are made of lotus seed paste, some of red bean paste, some with mixed nuts, and some have a duck egg in the center. In some regions, the moon cakes are crusty, while in others they are flaky.

There are also varying versions of the origins of the festival, which is thought to go back to the ninth century. One version has it that the Chinese, looking at the dark side of the full moon, saw a hare or rabbit, which was able to make a potion for immortality. The festival was the rabbit's birthday, and people sold rabbits on the streets. Moon cakes were made to feed the rabbits. Another version says that the day marks the overthrow of the Mongol overlords in ancient China; the moon cakes supposedly hid secret messages planning the overthrow.

The more accepted version is that the day is a harvest festival at a time when the moon is brightest. At this time of year, as the weather gets colder, people want a day to rest and enjoy life.

SOURCES:
BkFest-1937, p. 81
BkFestHolWrld-1970, p. 115
BkHolWrld-1986, Sep 16
DictFolkMyth-1984, pp. 191, 225, 231
FolkWrldHol-1992, p. 428
GdWrldFest-1985, p. 158
IntlThFolk-1979, p. 198

♦ 1193 ♦ Mid-Autumn Festival in Singapore
Full moon nearest September 15

The MID-AUTUMN FESTIVAL, sometimes known as the **Mooncake Festival**, is observed by Chinese communities around the world. In Singapore, the mooncakes served during the festival recall a 14th-century uprising against the Mongols, when word of the revolt was spread by concealing the message in cakes that were then smuggled out to compatriots. Today the cakes are often sold along with lanterns and are filled with either a sweet bean paste or with melon and lotus seeds, and may be flavored with orange peels, egg yolks, or other spices. On the night of the Mid-Autumn Festival, children all over Singapore have parades so they can show off their lighted lanterns. There are also lantern-making contests, Chinese costume-making competitions, lion and dragon dances, and concerts.

CONTACT:
Singapore Tourist Promotion Board
590 Fifth Ave., 12th Floor
New York, NY 10036
212-302-4861; fax: 212-302-4801

SOURCES:
GdWrldFest-1985, p. 158

♦ 1194 ♦ Middfest International
Three days in late September–early October

Middletown, Ohio, is home to the annual festival of international culture known as Middfest. Designed to promote world understanding, friendship and peace, the festival highlights the culture of a different country each year. Performers, artists, and dignitaries from the featured country come to Middletown and stay with local families. During the week preceding the three-day festival, they perform in nearby communities, give talks, and demonstrate their art and skills. Countries that have been invited to participate since the festival's inception in 1981 include Luxembourg, Mexico, Egypt, Brazil, Japan, Switzerland, Canada, Italy, India, and Ireland. Included in the celebration are museum-quality exhibits, ethnic dances, and menus from all over the world. Lectures, workshops, films, and special interest activities are also scheduled throughout Middfest weekend.

CONTACT:
Middfest International
One City Centre Plaza
Middletown, OH 45042
513-425-7707

♦ 1195 ♦ Mid-Lent in Italy
Between March 8 and April 7; fourth Sunday in Lent

In Italy **Mezza Quaresima**, or Mid-Lent, is a day of respite from the otherwise severe restrictions of LENT. Parties, dances, and street celebrations take place throughout the country, and many feature effigies of *Quaresima* that resemble a lean, witch-like old hag—in stark contrast to the fat man who represents CARNIVAL.

In Abruzzi, according to custom, the effigy of Quaresima is pierced with seven feathers and suspended on a rope stretched across the street. On each Saturday in Lent the villagers pluck out one feather to signify the end of one of the seven weeks of the Lenten season.

CONTACT:
Italian Government Travel Office
630 Fifth Ave.
New York, NY 10111
212-245-4822

SOURCES:
FestSaintDays-1915, p. 52
FestWestEur-1958, p. 92

♦ 1196 ♦ Midnight Sun Festival
June 21

Celebrations of the SUMMER SOLSTICE in Nome, Alaska, where the sun shines for better than 22 hours a day in the peak of summer. In Nome, the longest day of the year is feted on two days with a street dance, blanket toss, barbecue, Monte Carlo night (gambling), Eskimo dances, a parade, and a mock bank hold-up and jail. A river raft race has been held at midnight on June 21 since the 1960s. Various homemade rafts paddle down a one- to two-mile course on the Nome River, and the winning team claims a fur-lined honey bucket, which is passed on from year to year. A softball tournament, with about 20 men's and women's teams competing for trophies, precedes the day of the solstice. Games start at about 10 P.M.

Various places in Alaska celebrate the midnight sun in various ways: Skagway throws a dance, and at Tok in 1990, the Frigid Poets Society began the practice of climbing a mountain to watch the sun not set.

In Fairbanks, a midnight baseball game is played without artificial lights. The home team, Fairbanks Goldpanners (the name recalls the gold-rush days of early Fairbanks), is reputed to be one of the best semi-pro teams in the nation. The solstice is also marked with department store sales. On the day before the baseball game, there is a Midnight Sun Run, a 10-kilometer race attracting local and national runners, with refreshments and entertainment at the finish.

This excessive activity at midnight may be at least partly explained by the function of the pineal gland. In humans, this pinecone-shaped gland is thought to produce the hormone melatonin that circulates through the body and triggers two reactions—drowsiness and reduced sex drive. Light inhibits melatonin production and thus makes it easier to do with less sleep when the sun shines. Hence, baseball games at midnight. (It is also a fact that 72 percent of Alaska babies are conceived between May and September.)

CONTACT:
Fairbanks Convention and Visitors
  Bureau
550 First Ave.
Fairbanks, AK 99701
800-327-5774 or 907-456-5774
fax: 907-452-2867

SOURCES:
AmerBkDays-1978, p. 587
Chases-1996, pp. 265, 267

♦ 1197 ♦ Midsummer Day
June 24, or nearest Friday

This ancient pagan festival of the SUMMER SOLSTICE, originally kept on June 21, is celebrated in Europe and Scandinavian countries in much the same way as BELTANE is celebrated in Ireland. Bonfires are still lit in some places on **Midsummer Eve** as a way of driving out evil and renewing reproductive powers. At one time it was believed that all natural waters had medicinal powers on this day, and people bathed in streams and rivers to cure their illnesses. Midsummer Day is also sacred to lovers. Shakespeare's romantic comedy, *A Midsummer Night's Dream,* reflects the traditional spirit associated with this festival.

The Swedish begin their **Midsommar** celebration on the Friday before Midsummer Eve and continue through Sunday. Every town and village sets up a maypole, or *Majstang*, which is decorated with flowers, leaves, and flags. In Rattvik, Sweden, on Lake Siljan, the festivities are held on a pier. The province of Dalarna, where some of Sweden's oldest wooden cottages have been preserved is a popular place to spend the Midsommar festival weekend.

The Swedes call Midsommar "the day that never ends," because the sun doesn't begin to set until 10:00 P.M. and it rises again at 2:00 A.M. In areas of Norway and Sweden that lie above the Arctic Circle, the sun shines brightly 24 hours a day for six weeks.

When June 24 was designated ST. JOHN'S DAY by the church, the fires that had been associated with the pagan festival were reinterpreted to symbolize St. John, whom the Lord had once called "a burning and shining light." But the pre-Christian elements surrounding Midsummer Day never really disappeared, and the Feast of St. John has long been associated with solstitial rites. This day is also one of the official QUARTER DAYS in England.

In Estonia, St. John's Eve is a national holiday known as **Voidupuha**, or **Victory Day**, commemorating the 1919 Battle of Vonnu in which Estonia regained control from Baltic-German rule; because celebrations extend into the night, the next day, June 24, is also a public holiday.

See also CALINDA DANCE, INTI RAYMI FESTIVAL, JUHANNUS, KUPALO, ST. HANS FESTIVAL

CONTACT:
Swedish National Tourist Office
655 Third Ave., 18th Floor
New York, NY 10017
212-949-2333; fax: 212-983-5260

Estonian Embassy
1030 15th St., N.W., Ste. 1000
Washington, D.C. 20005
202-588-0101

SOURCES:
AmerBkDays-1978, p. 582
BkDays-1864, vol. I, p. 814
BkFest-1937, pp. 32, 59, 125,
  136, 213, 220
DaysCustFaith-1957, pp. 151
DictFolkMyth-1984, pp. 105,
  157, 168, 202, 203, 253, 486,
  606, 629, 723, 747, 754, 789,
  866, 871, 930, 961, 966, 1032,
  1172
FestWestEur-1958, pp. 13, 27,
  43, 68, 153, 167, 199, 235
FolkWrldHol-1992, p. 336
RelHolCal-1993, pp. 64, 95
SaintFestCh-1904, p. 301

♦ 1198 ♦ Midumu Ceremony
June–October

The Midumu ceremony is a masked dance ritual celebrating the end of the three-year initiation period for Makonde boys and girls. Although the Makonde originally lived in Malawi, Zambia and Zimbabwe, they have migrated to Tanzania and Mozambique as well. Between June and October, the dry season, some of the Makonde men tell their families that they have been "called" to make a long journey. There is a public farewell ceremony, and then they disappear for 10 to 15 days. During this time they go from one village to the next and perform the masked dances of the Midumu ceremony, visiting the house of each new initiate and, after portraying various mythical stories in dance, receive honey, meat, jewelry, and occasionally money in return.

The Midumu ceremony always begins at night during the time when the moon moves from the quarter to the half phase. It usually follows a happy event—such as a successful hunt, a good haul of fish, or a bountiful harvest.

SOURCES:
FolkWrldHol-1992, p. 468

♦ 1199 ♦ **Midwinter Bear Society Dance**
Varied

This Native American ritual dance was performed by the Bear Society, an Iroquois Indian group known for its ability to cure the victims of "bear sickness," a type of mental illness of which the victim was aware, but which he or she could not control. The illness was caused by the bear spirit, and ceremonial foods that would please the spirit were an important part of the ritual. The dance was held in the patient's home under the supervision of a shaman. As part of the ritual, members of the society would blow berry juice on the patient.

There were actually two dances: one was a curing rite, and the other could be performed at any time, even without a patient present. The first consisted of slow chants, a round dance with a stomp step, and finally the pairing of dancers. Patients cured by the ritual became members of the society.

SOURCES:
DictFolkMyth-1984, p. 724

♦ 1200 ♦ **Mihr, Festival of**
February 5; forty days after Christmas

The Church of Armenia, proud of its ancient lineage and determined to retain its national character, has made it a point to keep a number of pagan ceremonies alive by investing them with Christian significance. This seems to be the case with the Festival of Mihr, the ancient god of fire. This pagan spring festival was originally observed by lighting fires in Mihr's honor in the marketplace, and by lighting a lantern that burned throughout the year in the temple. When Christianity was introduced in Armenia early in the third century, fires were lit on this day in the church courtyards, and people danced around them or jumped through the flames.

The modern-day Armenian celebration of the Presentation of Christ in the Temple or CANDLEMAS retains many elements of the pagan Festival of Mihr. In fact, the Armenian name for the month of February, *Mihragan,* is a reflection of the extent to which this ancient god and his festival have survived.

SOURCES:
BkFest-1937, p. 23

♦ 1201 ♦ **Milan Trade Fair**
April

The Milan Trade Fair was originally started in 1920 to allow

Italy and other European countries to display their products. Since then it has grown into a 10-day event hosting 35,000 manufacturers from 110 countries, 25 of whom have their own pavilions. There are also buildings devoted to the products of the various regions of Italy, with displays of leathercrafts, jewelry, textiles, graphic arts, fashions, and ceramics. Although the trade fair is a boost for Milan's economy, the city was chosen primarily because of its geographical proximity to the rest of Europe.

CONTACT:
Italian Government Travel Office
630 Fifth Ave.
New York, NY 10111
212-245-4822

SOURCES:
GdWrldFest-1985, p. 117

♦ 1202 ♦ **Mille Miglia**
Early May

The three-day endurance rally in Italy for vintage racing cars known as the Mille Miglia, or **Thousand Miles,** began in 1927 as an all-out race, and it took about 20 hours to cover the course. By 1938, the roads had improved to the point where it took only about 12 hours, and the all-time record of 10 hours, seven minutes, 48 seconds was set in 1955. This meant that the driver had to average nearly 100 miles per hour on roads that drivers normally would hesitate to traverse at 40. A tragic accident in 1957, in which one of the racers, his navigator, and 11 spectators were killed, led to a ban against racing on public roads and brought the Mille Miglia to an abrupt halt.

The event was reorganized in 1977 with different rules. Although it still features vintage racing cars from the 1920s through the 1950s and the same roads, drivers are given three days—rather than 10 hours—to cover the thousand miles. Driving in ordinary traffic, the competitors have to average a set number of miles per hour on 34 timed sections of the course, 19 of which are driven over particularly challenging and scenic stretches of road.

The route begins in Brescia, goes east to Verona, and then southeast to Ferrera, where the drivers spend the night. Early the next morning they leave for Ravenna, follow the coast to Rimini, and then head into the mountains, where they must cover some of the most serpentine and beautiful roads in the world. The drivers spend the second night in Rome and on the third day make a 12-hour dash back to Brescia via Viterbo, Siena, Florence, and Bologna.

CONTACT:
Italian Government Travel Office
630 Fifth Ave.
New York, NY 10111
212-245-4822

♦ 1203 ♦ **Minehead Hobby Horse Parade**
April 30–May 1

In England and Wales, hobby horses have been a part of celebrations welcoming spring as far back as anyone can remember. In the waterfront town of Minehead, Somerset, the "sailors' horse" has a boat-shaped frame seven to 10 feet long, which is carried on the shoulders of a man whose body is concealed by a canvas curtain that hangs to the ground. His head is covered by a painted tin mask and a tall dunce cap. Through a slit in the canvas, he can reach out his hand for contributions from spectators. Hundreds of rainbow-colored ribbons stream from the top of the horse, fluttering in the wind as he cavorts about town to the accompaniment of a drum and an accordion. Most of the money that is collected by the hobby horse and his companions is spent in the local pub afterwards, although some of it is supposed to go to charitable causes.

On MAY DAY Eve the horse sets out promptly at midnight, ending up at Whitecross (a crossroads to the west of town, the former site of a Maypole) on May Day morning. Later in the afternoon the group goes to the nearby village of Dunster and pays its respects to the lord of the local castle. The hobby horse performs again in the square at Dunster that evening.

A similar ceremony is held in Padstow, Cornwall, where "Old 'Obby 'Oss" is a ferocious-looking monster with snapping jaws and sharp teeth. During the dance that represents the culmination of the Padstow ceremony, the horse goes through a ritualistic death and rebirth—an indication, perhaps, of the ceremony's roots in ancient fertility rites driving out winter and welcoming spring.

CONTACT:
British Tourist Authority
551 Fifth Ave., Ste. 702
New York, NY 10176
800-462-2748 or 212-986-2200
fax: 212-986-1188

SOURCES:
BkHolWrld-1986, May 2
YrBookEngFest-1954, pp. 48, 51

♦ 1204 ♦ Minstrels' Carnival
January 1–10

The **Annual Minstrels' Carnival** in Cape Town, South Africa, was inspired by the animated singing and dancing of African-American musicians and singers of the United States. Bands are organized during the year, money is raised to purchase the materials needed for their costumes, and on NEW YEAR'S DAY, Second New Year (January 2), and the week or so that follows, the bands take over the city, displaying their costumes and performing their music in the streets.

This roisterous carnival is offset by string bands, the members of which are decorously dressed and parade with great dignity while playing sacred and other songs during the CHRISTMAS–New Year season.

CONTACT:
South African Tourism Board
500 Fifth Ave.
New York, NY 10110
800-822-5368 or 212-730-2929
fax: 212-764-1980

SOURCES:
FolkWrldHol-1992, p. 10

♦ 1205 ♦ Miramichi Folk Song Festival
Late June

Miramichi, a timber port along the St. Lawrence River in Canada, also refers to a type of ballad or narrative song associated with Canadian lumber camps. The Miramichi Folk Song Festival, held at Newcastle for three days in late June, is devoted entirely to songs and ballads in the miramichi "come all ye" style that tell stories of adventure, tragedy, and romance. While most of the songs are performed without accompaniment, they are often followed by tunes played on the fiddle, mouth organ, accordion, or guitar. There are also step-dancing and tap-dancing contests.

Founded in 1958 and sponsored by the Miramichi Historical Society, a Newcastle radio station, and the local tourism bureau, the festival features local folk singers and musicians as well as groups from all over Canada and the United States.

CONTACT:
Tourism New Brunswick
P.O. Box 12345
Fredericton, NB
Canada E3B 5C3
800-561-0123

SOURCES:
GdWrldFest-1985, p. 38
IntlThFolk-1979, p. 65

♦ 1206 ♦ Misa de Gallo
December 16–24

The start of the CHRISTMAS season in the Philippines, blending Christian tradition with the harvest thanksgiving of the ancient Filipinos.

As the first cockcrows are heard at dawn on Dec. 16, bells of the Roman Catholic churches ring, brass bands parade through towns, children fire small bamboo cannons, and skyrockets burst—all to awaken people for the Misa de Gallo, called **Cock's Mass** in English and **Simbang Gabi** in Tagalog. Each morning of the festival families walk to churches for mass at dawn. Then, on Dec. 24, there is a midnight mass. After the services, people congregate in food stalls that have been set up around church patios or go home for traditional breakfasts of rice cakes and ginger tea or cocoa.

Legend says the Cock's Mass started in the 1700s when a Spanish priest thought that blending native custom with Catholic ritual would help spread the faith. Filipinos had long celebrated good harvests with festivals of thanksgiving, and the priest called the farmers together at harvest time to thank God for good fortune and to pray for a good harvest in the coming year.

SOURCES:
AnnivHol-1983, p. 161
BkFestHolWrld-1970, pp. 144, 154
Chases-1996, p. 482
FolkWrldHol-1992, pp. 593, 627
GdWrldFest-1985, p. 151
IntlThFolk-1979, p. 289

Misa de Aguinaldos
See **Christmas Eve**

♦ 1207 ♦ Mischief Night
November 4

The idea of letting children have a "lawless night" originated in England, and was often celebrated on MAY DAY EVE (April 30) or on HALLOWEEN. But in the mid-17th century, when GUY FAWKES DAY (November 5) became a national holiday, Guy Fawkes Eve became the most popular night for mischief in England, Australia, and New Zealand, where it is sometimes called **Mischievous Night** or **Danger Night**.

SOURCES:
AnnivHol-1983, p. 142
BkHolWrld-1986, Nov 4
Chases-1996, pp. 434, 441

DictDays-1988, pp. 26, 77

♦ 1208 ♦ Misisi Beer Feast
October; Twamo

The ritual harvest feast known as the **Misisi** takes place in Uganda after the millet harvest each year. The Sebei people make a beer out of the *misisi* ('grain that is left on the ground') after the millet stalks have been gathered and placed in granaries. Misisi also refers to the cobs of maize that are too small to be worth storing. In addition to beer, the feast includes maize meal, steamed plantains, and a bullock, ram or chickens. A special group of close relatives is invited to the feast, and the host's father (or some other elder) pours the beer from a libation gourd or *mwendet* and offers it to a friend, saying, "Please accept this beer; I am still alive and let us enjoy it together." Libations are poured with the right hand, inside the house or *kraal,* naming the host's father, brothers, mother, mother's brothers, grandparents, father-in-law, brothers-in-law, and all deceased members of the clan who still have living descendants. Libations are poured for the evil spirits with the left hand, outside the kraal, naming deceased relatives who are jealous because they never had children, or those who cursed them in life.

The Misisi Beer Feast is usually held during the month called Twamo, which is around the same time as the month of October. Mukutanik, an adaptation of Misisi, is held at CHRISTMAS. In areas of Uganda where the millet ripens sooner, it is held earlier.

SOURCES:
FolkWrldHol-1992, p. 470

♦ 1209 ♦ Miss America Pageant
September, week after Labor Day

What began in 1921 as an attempt by the Business Men's League of Atlantic City, New Jersey, to keep tourists in town after LABOR DAY has developed into an American institution. The week-long event that begins when the winners of the 50 state pageants arrive on Monday includes evening gown, swimsuit, and talent competitions; a parade along Atlantic City's famous boardwalk; and, on Saturday evening, final judging of the 10 semifinalists and five finalists, culminating in the crowning of the new Miss America shortly before midnight. Bert Parks, who hosted the pageant on television for 25 years, was renowned for his patented rendition of "There She Goes," the song that is traditionally sung as the new Miss America walks down the runway in Convention Hall for the first time. In addition to a year of travel and lucrative personal appearances, the winner receives a $25,000 scholarship.

The Miss America Pageant has had its ups and downs over the years—notably the 1968 protests by members of the Women's Liberation Movement, who lit a symbolic fire in a trashcan and threw in a brassiere, some fashion magazines, and make-up—giving rise to the labeling of feminists as "bra-burners." Vanessa Williams, the first African American to win the pageant, was also the first to be dethroned when it was revealed in July of 1984 that she had once posed nude for *Penthouse* magazine. But many former Miss Americas have gone on to achieve successful careers as models,

actresses, or television personalities, or in public service—among them Phyllis George (Miss America 1971), Mary Ann Mobley (1959), and Bess Myerson (1945).

CONTACT:
Greater Atlantic City Region Tourism Council
P.O. Box 7457
Atlantic City, NJ 08404
609-441-2706

SOURCES:
AmerBkDays-1978, p. 821
Chases-1996, pp. 369, 375

♦ 1210 ♦ Miwok Acorn Festival
Usually weekend after fourth Friday of September

An annual two-day event of the Miwok (which means 'people') Indians, held at the Indian Grinding Rock State Historic Park near Sacramento, Calif. The park was a gathering place for Indians for thousands of years until Europeans settled there in 1848 at the time of the Gold Rush. This is an ancient harvest festival, largely religious, with ceremonial rites and traditional dances. It celebrates the acorn, just as Indians in the east have harvest festivals for the turkey, and in the south and southwest for corn. Acorns were a staple of the California Indians' diet, and were ground to make soup and meal for bread.

CONTACT:
Indian Grinding Rock State Historic Park
Calaveras District
c/o Columbia State Historic Park
P.O. Box 151
Columbia, CA 95310
209-296-7488 or 209-532-0150
fax: 209-532-5064

SOURCES:
IndianAmer-1989, p. 346

Kule Loklo Miwok Indian Village
(near Olema, California)
415-663-1092

♦ 1211 ♦ Mix Roundup, Tom
July

Tom Mix (1880–1940) was the first of the "rhinestone cowboys." He made more than 370 movies, most of them silent, and at the peak of his career in the Depression years he was earning $17,000 a week. He performed all of his own stunts, used real bullets when filming his movies, and was an expert knife thrower. When silent movies were replaced by "talkies," Mix's popularity declined somewhat because he had a speech impediment as a result of being shot in the neck during the Boer War.

In 1986 the site of Tom Mix's birthplace, a small house overlooking the Bennett Branch of the Sinnemahoning Creek about six miles from the village of Driftwood, Pennsylvania, was purchased by Ray Flaugh. Flaugh and his wife are restoring the house to its original state and have established a Tom Mix Park by selling one-inch-square plots of the Tom Mix Homestead to the public. One of the first purchasers was former President Ronald Reagan.

The Tom Mix Roundup is a three-day event that has been held in the towns of Sinnemahoning, Driftwood, and Mix Run since 1986. The events include a wagon train, live country music, appearances by the national Tom Mix look-alike, and various sharpshooting competitions.

CONTACT:
Pennsylvania Office of Travel
  Marketing
453 Forum Bldg.
Harrisburg, PA 17120
800-237-4363 or 717-787-5453
fax: 717-234-4560

♦ 1212 ♦ Mnarja (Imnarja; Feast of St. Peter and St. Paul)
June 29

The principal folk festival of Malta and a public holiday there, thought to have been originally a harvest festival. It is held in Buskett Gardens, a park with extensive vineyards and orange and lemon orchards not far from Mdina, Malta's medieval capital. The name of the festival is a corruption of Italian *luminaria*, meaning 'illumination,' since in long-ago times, the bastions around Mdina were illuminated by bonfires for the event. At one time, Mnarja was such a popular and important feast that a husband traditionally promised his bride on their wedding day that he would take her to Buskett on Mnarja-day every year.

Festivities begin on the eve of Mnarja with an agricultural show that continues through the next morning and folk-singing (*ghana*) and folk-music competitions. The traditional food of the evening is fried rabbit. On the following day, bareback horse and donkey races bring the feast to an end. The winners receive *palji*, or 'embroidered banners', which they donate to their town church.

See also St. Paul's Shipwreck, Feast of; Sts. Peter and Paul's Day

CONTACT:
Malta National Tourist Office
350 Fifth Ave.
Empire State Bldg., Ste. 4412
New York, NY 10118
212-695-9520; fax: 212-695-8229

SOURCES:
AnnivHol-1983, p. 85
FolkWrldHol-1992, p. 345

♦ 1213 ♦ Mochi No Matsuri
Eighth day of 12th lunar month

The **Rice Cake Festival** is a minor public holiday native to Okinawa. The rice cakes are red or white and cylindrical, about four inches long and one inch in diameter. They are wrapped in the leaf of the *sannin* plant or in sugar cane leaves. On the morning of the eighth day of the 12th lunar month, the cakes are placed on a special shelf while prayers are said. Then they are served to guests or hung by string around the room.

SOURCES:
FolkWrldHol-1992, p. 654

♦ 1214 ♦ Mohawk Trail Concerts
Weekends from mid-July to mid-August

The Mohawk Trail is a stretch of 67 miles along Route 2 from Greenfield in northern Massachusetts to the New York boundary. It was originally an Indian path, then a route for covered wagons and stagecoaches. Nowadays it is favored by tourists, particularly during the New England fall foliage season.

The Mohawk Trail Concerts began in 1970 as a series of chamber music performances by musicians who spent the summer in and around Charlemont, a rural area 120 miles northwest of Boston. One of the founding musicians, violinist-composer Arnold Black, eventually became the artistic director for what soon became a weekend concert series extending from mid-July to mid-August, with a special fall foliage concert presented in October. Performances are given in the Federated Church of Charlemont, where the audiences hear both well-known musicians and young artists in a varied program of classical, contemporary, jazz, and folk music. The Friday night concerts are generally casual, while the Saturday night concerts are more formal.

CONTACT:
Mohawk Trail Concerts
P. O. Box 843
Greenfield, MA 01302
413-774-3690

SOURCES:
MusFestAmer-1990, p. 77

♦ 1215 ♦ Mohegan Homecoming
Third Sunday in August

The Mohegan Homecoming, which takes place in and around Norwich, Connecticut, on the third Sunday in August each year, is a modern festival that has evolved from the pre-Columbian thanksgiving ceremony held by the Indians to thank their creator for the corn harvest. Up until 1941 the Mohegans held a Green Corn Festival, also known as the Wigwam Festival, but since that time the event has been billed as a "homecoming"—a time for Mohegan Indians living in all parts of the world to come home and renew their roots. It is an opportunity to conduct tribal business, such as the installation of new chieftains and medicine women, and to update one another on tribal matters. Foods served at the festival include succotash, clam chowder, and other New England specialties.

CONTACT:
Connecticut Tourism Division
865 Brook St.
Rocky Hill, CT 06067
800-282-6863 or 860-258-4355
fax: 860-258-4275

♦ 1216 ♦ Mollyockett Day
Third Saturday in July

Mollyockett was a Pequawket Indian who lived among the early settlers of western Maine. Born between 1730 and 1740, she lived in the area now known as Bethel after 1770 and made frequent trips throughout the Androscoggin Valley and into northern New Hampshire, Vermont, and Quebec. She was known as an "Indian doctress" who treated the white settlers of New England as well. One of her most famous patients was the infant Hannibal Hamlin, whom she found near death and cured with warm cow's milk. He grew up to become Abraham Lincoln's vice president. Mollyockett was also known as a storyteller, famous for her tales of buried Indian treasure.

The local festival that is currently known as Mollyockett Day in Bethel, Maine, started out in the 1950s as a fundraising event for families in need of assistance. In 1970 the name was changed in honor of the Indian woman whose generosity and self-reliance have become legendary. The festival includes a horseshoe tournament, parade, lumberjack competition, and frog-jumping contest.

CONTACT:
Mollyockett Day
Bethel Lions Club
Bethel, ME 04217

♦ 1217 ♦ Monaco Grand Prix
May

One of the last true road circuits, the Monaco GRAND PRIX winds through the streets of Monte Carlo, along the harbor, and through a tunnel. It is a Formula One motor race, which refers to very specific rules governing the car's weight, maximum number of cylinders, fuel, and engine cylinder capacity. First run in 1929, the Monaco Grand Prix has a lap distance of 1.95 miles with an unusually high number of corners, which demand constant gear-changes and maximum concentration from the drivers. In 1955 an Italian car skidded and ended up in the harbor, underscoring the dangerous and unusual nature of this race.

Formula One cars are single-seaters, although prior to the 1920s the mechanic rode in the car as well. The engine is located in the rear and the driver, protected by special clothing, a crash helmet and goggles, steers with a very small wheel from a reclining position, to reduce air drag to a minimum. Grand Prix races are held all over the world and are approximately 200 miles in length. But most are now run on specially constructed courses designed to simulate road conditions.

CONTACT:
Monaco Government Tourist and
   Convention Office
845 Third Ave.
New York, NY 10022
800-753-9696 or 212-759-5227
fax: 212-754-9320

SOURCES:
GdWrldFest-1985, p. 137

♦ 1218 ♦ Monkey God, Birthday of the
February 17 and September 12

A celebration by Chinese Taoists of Tai Seng Yeh, the popular Monkey God, who sneaked into heaven and acquired miraculous powers; he is thought to cure the sick and absolve the hopeless. He is the godfather of many Chinese children.

In Singapore, Taoist mediums go into a trance to let the god's spirit enter their bodies; then, possessed, they howl and slash themselves with knives, and scrawl symbols on scraps of paper that are grabbed by devotees. There are also puppet shows and Chinese street opera performances at Chinese temples.

CONTACT:
Singapore Tourist Promotion
   Board
590 Fifth Ave., 12th Floor
New York, NY 10036
212-302-4861; fax: 212-302-4801

SOURCES:
BkHolWrld-1986, Sep 17
FolkWrldHol-1992, p. 433
GdWrldFest-1985, p. 158

♦ 1219 ♦ Monlam (Prayer Festival)
Usually February; 4th–25th days of first Tibetan lunar month

The greatest festival in Tibet follows the Tibetan New Year

(LOSAR) celebrations, and commemorates the miraculous powers of Buddha. The two-week festival was started in the 14th century by Tsongkhapa, the great reformist monk, to ensure that the new year would be successful and prosperous. It is a time to attend examinations of and make offerings to monks, to light butter lamps, and above all to socialize, get the latest news, and watch sports events such as wrestling, archery, and horse racing. On the 15th day celebrants throng to Lhasa's famous Jokhang temple, where monks have created enormous butter sculptures. (*See* BUTTER SCULPTURE FESTIVAL.) A procession around the Barkor, the old city of Lhasa, carried a statue of Maitreya, the future Buddha.

When the Chinese denounced religious observances in 1959, the festival died. It was revived again in 1986, and has been observed since, although not with the grandeur of earlier days.

CONTACT:
India Tourist Office
30 Rockefeller Ave.
15 N. Mezzanine
New York, NY 10112
212-586-4901; fax: 212-582-3274

SOURCES:
BkHolWrld-1986, Mar 9
FolkWrldHol-1992, pp. 64, 68
RelHolCal-1993, p. 96

♦ 1220 ♦ Monterey Jazz Festival
Third weekend in September

A three-day celebration of jazz held since 1958 outside Monterey, Calif., at the Monterey Fairgrounds where there is seating for 7,000. Jimmy Lyons, a West Coast disc jockey, is credited with starting the first festival, and since then it has attracted top jazz artists. Among the many who have appeared are Dizzy Gillespie, Woody Herman, Thelonius Monk, Gerry Mulligan, Odetta, and Pee Wee Russell. The festival has boasted a number of world premieres: Duke Ellington's *Suite Thursday*, Lalo Schifrin's *Gillespiana*, and Charles Mingus's *Meditations on Monterey* are a few of them.

The atmosphere is jazzy and cosmopolitan. Booths outside the arena sell food for every taste, from sweet-potato pies to tacos to beef teriyaki.

CONTACT:
California Division of Tourism
801 K Street, Ste. 1600
Sacramento, CA 95814
800-862-2543 or 916-322-2881
fax: 916-322-3402

SOURCES:
Chases-1996, p. 384
GdUSFest-1984, p. 21
MusFestAmer-1990, p. 184

♦ 1221 ♦ Montreal Jazz Festival
June–July

What has been called the most important cultural event in Canada and the largest jazz festival in the world, the **Festival International de Jazz de Montréal** has attracted some of the greatest names in jazz—including Miles Davis, Pat Metheny, Ray Charles, and Dizzy Gillespie. Close to a million people come to the festival, about one-fourth of them from outside Montreal. Although the first festival in 1980 featured only about 20 performances, a recent event had 2,000 artists performing in 300 concerts, which were recorded and broadcast in 25 foreign countries.

Montreal's streets are closed for the 10 days of the festival to make room for the outdoor performances, which take place rain or shine, and represent a mix of traditional, modern, and innovative jazz.

CONTACT:
Tourisme Quebec
C.P. 979
Montreal, Quebec
Canada H3C 2W3
800-363-7777 or 514-873-2015

♦ 1222 ♦ Montreux International Jazz Festival
Early July

The most widely known jazz festival in Europe is held in Montreux, Switzerland, for 16 days in July. There are big band, blues, country and western, jazz rock, folk jazz, and avant garde jazz concerts, most of which are held inside the Montreux Casino, which is situated on the shores of Lake Leman. Other concerts and jam sessions are held on the terrace and in the gardens of the Casino or on a boat cruising the lake. Most of the bands, combos, and soloists who have appeared at Montreux are American: Oscar Peterson, Dizzy Gillespie, Ella Fitzgerald, Count Basie, Miles Davis, Ray Charles, and Buddy Rich, to name just a few. Attention is also paid to up-and-coming talent, sometimes from countries as far away as Japan and Brazil. The Montreux Festival has been an annual event since 1966, and there is now a Montreux-Detroit Jazz Festival held in Michigan on LABOR DAY weekend.

CONTACT:
Swiss National Tourist Office
608 Fifth Ave.
New York, NY 10020
212-757-5944; fax: 212-262-6116

SOURCES:
Chases-1996, p. 353
GdWrldFest-1985, p. 170
MusFestEurBrit-1980, p. 145

Detroit Visitor Information Center
2 E. Jefferson Ave.
Detroit, MI 48226
800-338-7648 or 313-567-1170

♦ 1223 ♦ Moon Day
July 20

The first man to walk on the moon was American astronaut Neil Armstrong. On July 20, 1969, he and his fellow astronaut, Edwin E. "Buzz" Aldrin, left the command module *Columbia* and landed the lunar module *Eagle* in the moon's Sea of Tranquillity. Armstrong's first words as he stepped out on the lunar surface were seen and heard by an estimated 600 million television viewers around the world: "That's one small step for a man, one giant leap for mankind."

Air Force Lieutenant Colonel Michael Collins, pilot of the *Columbia*, continued to circle the moon for the 21½ hours during which Armstrong and Aldrin conducted their experiments. The information they collected about the moon's soil, terrain, and atmospheric conditions made an enormous contribution to knowledge of the universe and future space exploration. The Apollo 11 mission was completed eight years after President John F. Kennedy told Congress he believed that the United States could put a man on the moon before the decade ended.

CONTACT:
NASA
Washington, D.C. 20546
800-424-9183 or 202-358-0000
fax: 202-358-0071
WWW: http://
    www.gsfc.nasa.gov

SOURCES:
AnnivHol-1983, p. 95
Chases-1996, p. 305

♦ 1224 ♦ Moore Days, Billy
Second weekend in October

A celebration of the pioneer who established a stage stop, general store, and saloon in what became Avondale, Ariz. Avondale and the other Tri-City towns of Goodyear and Litchfield Park commemorate Billy Moore with a carnival, arts and crafts fair, golf and softball tournaments, a nighttime five-kilometer run, a street dance, and a 100-unit parade in which assorted politicians and the Arizona Maid of Cotton take part. The celebration has been held since 1954.

Billy Moore's story is surrounded by legend. He is supposed to have belonged to the gang of guerrillas led by William Clarke Quantrill, but historians think he was a young blacksmith with the gang, not one of the pillagers. Whatever he was, he was exiled by the governor of Missouri for his part in the Quantrill gang, and he headed out for Arizona Territory in 1867. Before setting up business, he either had a run-in with an outlaw or was attacked by Apaches; in any event, he was seriously injured, and a Yaqui Indian woman who later became his wife nursed him back to health. In the late 1880s Moore bought 280 acres of land at the stage stop known as Coldwater for 25 cents an acre under the Desert Lands Act of 1877. He became a justice of the peace and was postmaster at the Coldwater station until 1905, when the post office was moved to a different location because liquor and the mail were being distributed from the same station in violation of the law. Billy Moore died in 1934 at the age of 92.

CONTACT:
Arizona Office of Tourism
1100 W. Washington St.
Phoenix, AZ 85007
800-842-8257 or 602-542-8687
fax: 602-542-4068

♦ 1225 ♦ Moors and Christians Fiesta
April 22–24

Moors and Christians fiestas are celebrated throughout the year all over Spain to commemorate various battles between the two groups. But it is the **Fiesta of Alcoy** in the province of Alicante that is one of the most colorful. Coinciding with the feast day of St. George (*see* ST. GEORGE'S DAY) on April 23, the fiesta commemorates the victory of the Christians over the Moorish leader al-Azraq in 1276.

The three-day event begins on the morning of April 22 with the ceremonial entry of the Christians, symbolizing the forces that assembled to defend the town of Alcoy in the 13th century. The Moors arrive in the afternoon, dressed in exotic Oriental costumes. On April 23 the relic of St. George is carried in procession from his temple to the parish Church of Santa Maria, where a mass is sung. On the third day the battle is reenacted and an apparition of St. George appears on the battlements of the castle.

In the 15th, 16th, and 17th centuries, fiestas of Moors and Christians were danced. It is believed that this type of celebration eventually crossed the sea to England and became the familiar Morris dance.

CONTACT:
Tourist Office of Spain
665 Fifth Ave.
New York, NY 10022
212-759-8822; fax: 212-980-1053

SOURCES:
FolkWrldHol-1992, p. 249
IntlThFolk-1979, p. 332

♦ 1226 ♦ **Moreska Sword Dance**
July 27; every Thursday from July–September

A ritual dance of the medieval knights that has been performed every July 27 for centuries in Korcula, the main town of the island of Korcula off the coast of the former Yugoslavia. The dance-cum-pageant, with many clashes of steel, symbolizes the battle against the Turks when Korcula was under the control of the kings of Bosnia in the late 14th century. A spirited and athletic dance, it has been performed in other parts of Europe, but only by men and the one woman in the pageant, all of whom were born on Korcula. Originally performed only on July 27, it is now presented regularly during the tourist season.

From the 15th century, Korcula was under the control, successively, of Venice, Austria, France, Britain, again Austria, and Italy, until being ceded to Yugoslavia after World War I. It was under Italian occupation in World War II and liberated by Yugoslavian partisans in 1944–45. Marco Polo is supposed to have been born on Korcula.

CONTACT:
Atlas Tourism and Travel
60 E. 42nd St., Ste. 2235
New York, NY 10165
800-528-5275 or 212-697-6767
fax: 212-697-7678

SOURCES:
IntlThFolk-1979, p. 390

♦ 1227 ♦ **Moriones Festival**
Beginning between March 15 and April 18; Holy Week

One of the more popular and colorful of the many passion plays performed before EASTER in the Philippines. Held in Marinduque with participants wearing masks and costumes of Roman soldiers, Moriones focuses not on Jesus but tells the story of the legendary Roman centurion, Longinus, who is said to have been blind in one eye. As he pierced the side of the crucified Jesus, a drop of the blood cured his blindness. The first thing he saw with both eyes was Christ's passage to heaven. According to the legend Longinus announced this good news. The Roman warriors, however, wanted to stop this report and captured him. The beheading of Longinus is the climax of the play.

CONTACT:
Philippine Department of Tourism
556 Fifth Ave.
First Floor Mezzanine
New York, NY 10036
212-575-7915; fax: 212-302-6759

SOURCES:
Chases-1996, p. 157
GdWrldFest-1985, p. 152
IntlThFolk-1979, p. 289

♦ 1228 ♦ **Mormon Pioneer Day**
July 24

After their founder, Joseph Smith, was murdered in 1844, the Mormons—members of the Church of Jesus Christ of Latter-Day Saints—moved westward from their settlement in Nauvoo, Illinois, under the leadership of Brigham Young. When Young surveyed the Salt Lake Valley on July 24, 1847, he proclaimed, "This is the right place." Thousands of Mormon pioneers followed him over the next two decades, many of them pushing their belongings in handcarts. The original 40-acre plot with log houses where the Mormons settled is the modern Salt Lake City and the day on which Young chose the site is celebrated not only in Utah but in surrounding states with significant Mormon populations, such as Idaho,

Arizona, Nevada, Wyoming, and California. Other states observe their own **Pioneer Day** at different times of the year.

SOURCES:
AmerBkDays-1978, p. 686
AnnivHol-1983, p. 96
Chases-1996, pp. 308, 309
DictDays-1988, p. 89
FolkAmerHol-1991, p. 282

♦ 1229 ♦ **Morocco Independence Day**
November 18

Independence Day, also known as **Fete de l'Independence**, is a national holiday commemorating Morocco's independence from France on November 18, 1927; a secret treaty in 1904 had divided Morocco between France and Spain.

Throne Day, March 3, is also a public holiday, commemorating the anniversary of King Hassan II's accession in 1961. It is the most important holiday in Morocco and is celebrated with parades, fireworks, and dances.

Other public holidays in Morocco include: January 11, commemorating the manifesto of independence; May 23, National Day; August 14, Allegiance of Wadi-Eddahab; August 20, Anniversary of the King's and People's Revolution; and November 6, the anniversary of the Green March in 1975 when, in order to claim the Western Sahara for Morocco, more than 300,000 Moroccans marched into the territory, which the Spanish still controlled; Spanish troops left the area by early 1976.

CONTACT:
Moroccan National Tourist Office
20 E. 46th St., Ste. 1201
New York, NY 10017
212-557-2520; fax: 212-949-8148

SOURCES:
AnnivHol-1983, p. 32
Chases-1996, p. 121
NatlHolWrld-1968, p. 30

♦ 1230 ♦ **Moro-Moro Play**
April or May

The term *moro-moro* refers to a type of folk drama performed in villages throughout the Philippines, usually during fiestas. Although each village's *moro-moro* is a little different in terms of treatment, all are full of romance and melodrama, and the highpoint is always a battle between Muslims and Christians. Local people write the script, which is in verse, and some performances include quite elaborate scenery and costumes. Music and dance are also part of the production.

One of the most notable *moro-moros* is held in San Dionisio in Rizal Province, where the drama is performed in the church and the village square every spring, usually in April or May.

See also MOORS AND CHRISTIANS FIESTA

CONTACT:
Philippine Department of Tourism
556 Fifth Ave.
First Floor Mezzanine
New York, NY 10036
212-575-7915; fax: 212-302-6759

SOURCES:
IntlThFolk-1979, p. 290

♦ 1231 ♦ **Morris Rattlesnake Roundup**
Second weekend in June

In 1956, when the first **Rattlesnake Roundup** was held in Morris, Pennsylvania, more than 400 of the poisonous snakes were caught and sold to leather craftsmen and zoos. But their numbers have dwindled since that time, and the trend has been toward the protection of endangered species—even poisonous ones. Now only about 25 to 35 snakes are found each year, and by law they must be returned to the wild. The roundup is sponsored by the local fire department and about 80 hunters participate, catching the snakes with tongs and forked sticks. Most of the snakes are 30"–45" long.

CONTACT:
Pennsylvania Office of Travel
  Marketing
453 Forum Bldg.
Harrisburg, PA 17120
800-237-4363 or 717-787-5453
fax: 717-234-4560

♦ 1232 ♦ Moshoeshoe's Day
March 12

Moshoeshoe (also called **Mshweshwe** or **Moshesh**, and pronounced mow-SHOO-shoo; c. 1790–1870) was a leader in South Africa who organized a group of tribes to fight the Zulu warlord, Shaka. He called his followers the Basotho (or Basuto) people, and although they succeeded in fending off the Zulu, they were eventually drawn into a war with the Europeans who started settling their territory. Moshoeshoe and the Basotho retreated into the mountains, and from this position they were able to keep the European invaders at bay. In 1868 the Basotho nation became a British protectorate known as Basutoland, and in 1966 it became the independent kingdom of Lesotho within the British Commonwealth (*see* LESOTHO INDEPENDENCE DAY).

The Basotho people continue to honor their founder on this day with sports and traditional music and dancing.

CONTACT:
Lesotho Embassy
2511 Massachusetts Ave., N.W.
Washington, D.C. 20008
202-797-5533; fax: 202-234-6815

SOURCES:
AnnivHol-1983, p. 36
BkHolWrld-1986, Mar 12
Chases-1996, p. 130

♦ 1233 ♦ Most Precious Blood, Feast of the
Formerly July 1

In the Roman Catholic Church, July was the month of the Most Precious Blood—referring to the blood of Jesus, which ever since the time of the Last Supper has been regarded by Christians as possessing redemptive power. But it wasn't until 1849 that a specific day was chosen for general observance of this festival. At that time Pope Pius IX was forced into exile while Rome was under attack by the French. One of his companions, who happened to be a general officer of the Fathers of the Most Precious Blood, tried to convince the Pope to promise that if he regained his papal lands he would establish this festival as a universal observance. The Pope, of course, said he didn't want to bargain with God, but that he would extend the festival to the whole church anyway. Since he reached this decision on the day before the first Sunday in July, it was originally the first Sunday that was dedicated to the Most Precious Blood. But Pius X moved the feast to the first day of July. In 1969 it was suppressed altogether and is no longer on the church calendar.

SOURCES:
DaysCustFaith-1957, p. 166
RelHolCal-1993, p. 96

♦ 1234 ♦ Mothering Sunday
March–April; fourth Sunday in Lent

It was the custom in 17th-century England for Christians to pay their respects on the fourth Sunday in LENT to the "Mother Church" where they had been baptized. Also known as **Misers**, or **Mid-Lent, Sunday,** this day usually included a visit to one's parents—to "go a-mothering," as it was called back then. It was common practice to bring a cake or trinket for the mother of the family. In England the favorite gift was the simnel cake, a saffron-flavored fruitcake topped with almond paste.

In the Roman Catholic Church and the Anglican Communion, the fourth Sunday in Lent is known as **Laetare Sunday**. The Introit of the Mass begins with the word "Rejoice" (*laetare* in Latin), marking a slight respite in the solemn Lenten season, hence the terms Mid-Lent Sunday and **Refreshment Sunday**. Priests may wear rose-colored vestments to Mass, instead of the usual purple for Lent, so the day is also called **Rose Sunday**. Also on this day the Pope blesses the Golden Rose, an ornament resembling a spray of roses, symbolizing spiritual joy.

SOURCES:
BkDays-1864, vol. I, p. 335
BkFest-1937, p. 55
DaysCustFaith-1957, p. 89
DictDays-1988, pp. 76, 78, 95, 112
DictFolkMyth-1984, pp. 752, 1013
FestSaintDays-1915, p. 50
FolkWrldHol-1992, p. 127
RelHolCal-1993, p. 96
SaintFestCh-1904, p. 143

♦ 1235 ♦ Mother-in-Law Day
Fourth Sunday in October

Modeled on the celebration of MOTHER'S DAY and FATHER'S DAY, **Mother-in-Law's Day** was first celebrated on March 5, 1934, in Amarillo, Texas, where it was initiated by the editor of the local newspaper. The observance was later moved to the fourth Sunday in October.

Mothers-in-law have never enjoyed the widespread respect and devotion that mothers have received over the years, and the rising divorce rate has given the whole concept of in-laws a less permanent place in the national imagination. This may be part of the reason why Mother-in-Law Day has failed to catch on like MOTHER'S DAY, FATHER'S DAY, and even GRANDPARENTS' DAY. But many people feel that mothers-in-law deserve a special day of their own, if for no other reason than for their good humor in enduring the many jokes that have been told about them.

SOURCES:
Chases-1996, p. 432

♦ 1236 ♦ Mother's Day
Second Sunday in May

The setting aside of a day each year to honor mothers was the suggestion of Anna M. Jarvis of Philadelphia, Pennsylvania, whose own mother had died on May 9, 1906. She held a memorial service and asked those attending to wear white carnations—a gesture that soon became a tradition. By 1914 President Woodrow Wilson had proclaimed a national day in honor of mothers, and some people still wear carnations on the second Sunday in May—pink or red for mothers who are living and white for those who have died.

Sometimes Mother's Day is confused with Mothering Sunday, an English holiday that falls on the fourth Sunday in Lent. But Mother's Day is now observed in England as well, and the traditions associated with Mothering Sunday have been largely forgotten. A number of Protestant churches have designated this day as the **Festival of the Christian Home.**

SOURCES:
AmerBkDays-1978, p. 439
AnnivHol-1983, p. 64
BkHolWrld-1986, May 14
Chases-1996, p. 210
DaysCustFaith-1957, p. 133
DictDays-1988, p. 78
FolkAmerHol-1991, p. 211

Mother's Day in the former Yugoslavia
See **Children's Day in the former Yugoslavia**

♦ 1237 ♦ Motorcycle Week (Camel Motorcycle Week; Bike Week)
First week in March

The largest motorcycle meet in the world, held for 10 days in Daytona Beach, Fla. The event began in 1937, as an outgrowth of automobile races. These had been started years earlier on Daytona's Ormond Beach by Henry Ford, who had a mansion and was testing cars there. It was suspended for a few years during World War II, but the 50th anniversary was celebrated in 1991, with half a million people attending.

The highlight of the week is the Daytona 200 race, which attracts competitors from all over the world and is considered one of the most prestigious motorcycle road races in the world. Other race events include a three-hour U.S. Endurance Championship race and vintage motorcycle races on Classics Day. The events take place in the Daytona Beach Municipal Stadium, with a quarter-mile banked oval track, and on the Daytona International Speedway.

Motorcyclists come from around the world, and most bring their motorcycles with them. A popular feature of the week is a mammoth parade of over 5,000 motorcycles. Parade watchers include large contingents of elderly people, some of whom hold signs saying "Grandmothers Love Biking" and other slogans. Concerts and trade shows are held throughout the week.

CONTACT:
Florida Division of Tourism
126 W. Van Buren
Tallahassee, FL 32399
904-487-1462; fax: 904-921-9158

SOURCES:
Chases-1996, p. 116

♦ 1238 ♦ Mountain Man Rendezvous
September, Labor Day weekend

A celebration of 19th-century history at Fort Bridger, Wyo. This town was founded in 1842 as a trading post by mountain men Jim Bridger and Louis Vasquez. It was established as a stronghold by Mormons in 1853, and taken over by the U.S. Army in 1959. In the great westward migration, streams of wagon trains passed through Fort Bridger for points west.

The Mountain Man Rendezvous began in 1973 and today attracts about 45,000 visitors over four days. The days of 1820–1840 are reenacted with people in calico and buckskins, furs and feathers. A tepee village is set up where campers wear clothing of the period, and there is a traders' row where replicas of pre-1840 items are for sale. Other activities include competitions in tomahawk throwing and archery, costume and cooking contests, black-powder shoots, and Indian tribal dances.

See also Green River Rendezvous

CONTACT:
Wyoming Tourism and Marketing
  Division
I-25 and College Dr.
Cheyenne, WY 82002
800-225-5996 or 307-777-7777
fax: 307-777-6904

♦ 1239 ♦ Mountain State Forest Festival
Late September through early October

A two-week celebration of the timber industry—one of West Virginia's biggest industries—in the small town of Elkins. The 55th annual festival was held in 1991, but the event actually has its origins in the 1930 three-day "fall homecoming" held to call attention to the area's scenic attractions. The festival was suspended during World War II. Today attendance tops 100,000.

A highlight of the festival is the crowning of Queen Silvia, who wears an elaborate embroidered velvet gown. Usually the governor crowns the queen, but in 1936, President Franklin D. Roosevelt did the honors. After his address, a pageant was presented that was based on the ancient Egyptian myth of creation.

Events today salute the timber industry but also include non-timber events. Hence, there are forestry and wood-products exhibits and lumberjack contests along with a pet show, horseshoe tournaments, archery and turkey-calling contests, a bed race, a cross-country motorcycle race, arts and crafts exhibits, hot air balloon rides, and a mammoth buckwheat-cake and sausage feed. Buckwheat cakes are a local favorite. There are additionally several parades, including a fireman's parade with antique and modern fire equipment.

CONTACT:
West Virginia Tourism and Parks
  Division
2101 Washington St. E.
Charleston, WV 25305
800-225-5982 or 304-558-2200
fax: 304-558-0108

SOURCES:
AmerBkDays-1978, p. 881
Chases-1996, p. 394
GdUSFest-1984, p. 209

♦ 1240 ♦ Mount Cameroon Race
Last Sunday in January

The annual "mad race" up and down Mt. Cameroon (13,353 ft.) in the central African country of Cameroon. The race is the most difficult in Africa; the course is so steep that runners have to carry poles, and temperatures can vary from a humid 80 degrees F. at the start of the race to freezing at the summit. On the night before the race, local people make sacrifices to appease the mountain spirits. Thousands of spectators watch the race, in which about 250 runners usually participate; the winner's time can be under four hours.

CONTACT:
Cameroon Embassy
2349 Massachusetts Ave., N.W.
Washington, D.C. 20008
202-265-8790; fax: 202-387-3826

♦ 1241 ♦ Mount Ceahlau Feast
Second Sunday in August

A folk event that has ancient roots, held at Durau, Romania, at the foot of Mount Ceahlau. The mountain was considered sacred to the Dacians, the ancestors of the present Romanians, and was the scene of their annual celebrations. In those days, people climbed to the summit to greet the sun with religious ceremonies and feasts. Today there are demonstrations of such sports as wrestling and foot racing, and exhibits and sales of folk art.

CONTACT:
Romanian National Tourist Office
342 Madison Ave., Ste. 210
New York, NY 10173
212-697-6971; fax: 212-697-6972

♦ 1242 ♦ Mount Fuji Climbing Season, End of
On or near August 26

Climbing Mount Fuji is such a popular sport in Japan that the climbing season has a formal opening and closing. It begins on July 1, when the six most popular routes for the journey up the mountain are opened for the summer, and ends with a fire festival at Yoshida on or near the evening of August 26. Huge torches more than 10 feet high and several feet in circumference are set up along the streets, and families pile up firewood in front of their houses. At about 6:30 P.M., a portable shrine is brought down from the mountain and carried through the main street of Yoshida. About an hour later, all the torches and family bonfires are lit simultaneously. The flames continue long past midnight, and thousands of spectators flock to the town to witness the spectacle.

CONTACT:
Japan National Tourist
 Organization
630 Fifth Ave., Ste. 2101
New York, NY 10111
212-757-5640; fax: 212-307-6754

SOURCES:
BkFestHolWrld-1970, p. 110

♦ 1243 ♦ Moving Day
May 1; May 25

The idea of packing up one's belongings and changing residences on a particular day has been a tradition in many countries. In 19th-century America, May 1st was the normal day for the inhabitants of Boston and New York to change their place of residence, since leases normally expired on this day.

In Scotland, it was called **Flitting Day** and took place on May 25. The decision of whether to "sit or flit" was up to the tenant, but "flitting" seemed to be more common. On Flitting Day they had to vacate their houses by noon, which often meant a great upheaval for the family during the preceding day or two. But apparently the novelty value of "flitting" outweighed the boredom of "sitting." In some parts of Scotland, this occurs on May 1, and is also called **Term Day**.

In Norway, Moving Day or **Flyttedag** takes place sometime during the autumn months. But rather than being a day for changing residences, it is a day when servants searching for employment flock to the larger towns and cities dressed in the costumes of their native villages. Sometimes they ride in small carts or wagons, piled high with painted trunks or bundles of clothing and other possessions. While city residents take advantage of this opportunity to interview their help for the coming year, the servants seeking employment often try to sell their produce, farm animals, and handicrafts on the street.

SOURCES:
BkDays-1864, vol. I, p. 679
BkFest-1937, p. 252
DictDays-1988, p. 42
FestWestEur-1958, p. 155
FolkWrldHol-1992, p. 265

♦ 1244 ♦ Moxie Festival
Second Saturday in July

Moxie, originally a nerve tonic, was invented in 1876 by Dr. Augustine Thompson of Union, Maine. In 1884 it became a carbonated beverage whose main ingredient was gentian root. The Moxie Festival in Lisbon, Maine, began as an autograph session for Frank Potter, the author of *The Moxie Mystique,* in 1982. Within a few years the event had grown to include a pancake breakfast, parade, car show, craft fair, chicken barbecue, and firemen's muster.

Although Moxie is no longer widely available, those who remember it describe it as a kind of precursor to Coca Cola. The drink can still be found in Maine, where it is quite popular. About 10,000 people attend the festival each year.

CONTACT:
Maine Office of Tourism
33 Stone St.
Augusta, ME 04333
800-533-9595 or 207-287-5711
fax: 207-287-5701

♦ 1245 ♦ Mozambique Independence Day
June 25

This national holiday commemorates Mozambique's independence from Portugal, attained on this day in 1975 after 10 years of warfare and nearly half a century of Portuguese rule.

CONTACT:
Mozambique Embassy
1990 M St., N.W., Ste. 570
Washington, D.C. 20036
202-293-7146; fax: 202-835-0245

SOURCES:
AnnivHol-1983, p. 84
Chases-1996, p. 270

♦ 1246 ♦ Mozart, Wolfgang Amadeus, Birthday of
January 27

Wolfgang Amadeus Mozart was born in Salzburg, Austria, on this day in 1756 and died only 35 years later, on December 5, 1791. An extraordinarily precocious child, he began performing at the age of three and was composing by the age of five. Mozart represents the high point of the late 18th-century Viennese Classical style, and his achievements in composing operas, chamber music, symphonies, and piano concerti have earned him a reputation as one of the greatest musical geniuses of all time.

Mozart's birthday is observed by musical societies all over the world, who often give concerts of his music on this day.

The city of his birth also honors him every summer with the SALZBURG FESTIVAL, which has become so closely identified with him that it is often referred to as ''The Mozart Festival,'' and the end of January with MOZART WEEK.

SOURCES:
AnnivHol-1983, p. 14
Chases-1996, p. 77

♦ 1247 ♦ Mozart Festival (Mozartfest)
June

The only time Wolfgang Amadeus Mozart (1756–1791) spent in Würzburg was when he stopped there for some coffee while traveling between Salzburg and Frankfurt, but the German city has hosted a three-week Mozart Festival in June each year since 1922, with the exception of a nine-year interruption during and after World War II. Daily concerts of Mozart's symphonies, concertos, sonatas, motets, sacred vocal works, and operas are performed each year, with little repetition due to the vast number of such works. Würzburg's churches, palaces, and fortresses often serve as locations for the concerts, the most impressive being Prince Bishop's Residence, considered one of Europe's most stunning baroque palaces. Mozart's *Eine kleine Nachtmusik* is performed on Saturday evenings in the torchlit garden of the Residence, while indoor concerts are given in the elaborate baroque *Kaisersaal* (Imperial Hall), which has a ceiling fresco painted by Teipolo, the great 18th-century Italian artist.

Musical groups that have performed at past festivals include the Würzburg Philharmonic Orchestra, the Bambert Symphony Orchestra, the Prague Chamber Orchestra, and the Amadeus Quartet.

CONTACT:
German National Tourist Office
122 E. 42nd St., 52nd Floor
New York, NY 10168
212-661-7200; fax: 212-661-7174

SOURCES:
MusFestEurBrit-1980, p. 102

♦ 1248 ♦ Mozart Week (Mozartwoche)
Last week in January

Wolfgang Amadeus Mozart was born on January 27, 1756. Every January since 1956, his birthday has been celebrated by the people of Salzburg, Austria, where he was born, with a nine-day music festival devoted entirely to his works. Along with his chamber music and symphonies, Mozart's operas are often given in concert form. The festival also prides itself on presenting many of his lesser known works, which are seldom performed elsewhere.

The principle ensembles for the festival are the Vienna Philharmonic Orchestra and the Mozarteum Orchestra, under the leadership of both native and guest conductors. The concerts are given in a number of sites associated with Mozart's life, including the Mozarteum Building, St. Peter's Church, the Salzburg Cathedral, and even Mozart's home.

CONTACT:
Austrian National Tourist Office
P.O. Box 1142, Times Square
New York, NY 10148
212-944-6880; fax: 212-730-4568

SOURCES:
MusFestEurBrit-1980, p. 22

Muhammad's Birthday
See **Mawlid al-Nabi**

♦ 1249 ♦ Mule Days
May, Memorial Day weekend

A raucous salute in Bishop, Calif., to that workhorse of the ages, the mule. Bishop is an outfitting point for pack trips and lies between California's two highest mountain ranges. The entire region depends on mules to transport people and gear into the High Sierra.

Mule Days was started in 1969 by mule-packers who wanted to have a good time and initiate their summer packing season. Now about 50,000 people show up in Bishop (population 3,500) for the Thursday-through-Monday celebration. A highlight is the Saturday morning 250-unit parade, billed as the world's largest non-motorized parade. It includes pack strings from local pack stations and national parks, a sheep-drawn wagon, llamas (used for sheepherding), and a rider on a Brahma steer. The pack loads demonstrate how mules haul such various necessities as machinery, wood, and outhouses into remote areas. Other events include mule-shoeing contests and such muleback cowboy events as steer roping and barrel racing. The weekend's wildest events are ''packers' scrambles'', where about 50 packers scramble to catch mules, pack and saddle them, and race away with horses and cattle. About 40 horses, two dozen cattle, and 80 mules raise the dust in the arena during the scrambles.

Draft horses and miniature horses also put in appearances, and there are mule shows and sales, western art, barbecues, and country dances. Motels are booked solid a year in advance. Ronald Reagan attended Mule Days in 1974 when he was California's governor.

Mules are the sterile progeny of male asses or donkeys and mares (female horses). The rarer offspring of male horses and female donkeys are called hinneys. Mules have been beasts of burden for at least 3,000 years.

CONTACT:
California Division of Tourism
801 K Street, Ste. 1600
Sacramento, CA 95814
800-862-2543 or 916-322-2881
fax: 916-322-3402

SOURCES:
GdUSFest-1984, p. 15

Mummers' Parade
See **New Year's Day**

♦ 1250 ♦ Munich Opera Festival
July

Although Munich, Germany, may be best known for its OKTOBERFEST, it is also the home of one of the world's great opera festivals. The focus is on three composers who were associated with the city in some way: Richard Strauss, who was born there; Richard Wagner, some of whose operas premiered there; and Wolfgang Amadeus MOZART, some of whose operas were first performed in the rococo Residenz Theater, a former royal palace. But other operas have been staged there as well, particularly those by Donizetti, Rossini, Leoncavallo, Mascagni, and other Italian composers. Six or seven operas are normally presented during the 25-day festival, along with one or two ballets and a few recitals.

Most of the operas are staged in the Nationaltheater, home of the Bavarian State Opera. Some of the events take place in the Cuvilliés-Theater, a horseshoe-shaped rococo theater that was destroyed in World War II and then rebuilt according to its original plan. There is an hour-long intermission to allow patrons time to eat dinner.

CONTACT:
German National Tourist Office
122 E. 42nd St., 52nd Floor
New York, NY 10168
212-661-7200; fax: 212-661-7174

SOURCES:
GdWrldFest-1985, p. 85
MusFestEurBrit-1980, p. 103

♦ 1251 ♦ **Muñoz–Rivera Day**
July 17

Luis Muñoz–Rivera was born on this day in 1859 in Barranquitas, Puerto Rico. A statesman, journalist, and patriot who devoted his life to the cause of Puerto Rican independence, Muñoz–Rivera was instrumental in obtaining Puerto Rico's charter of home rule from Spain in 1897 and served as secretary of state and later president of the first autonomist cabinet. However, when the United States put an end to his country's short-lived experiment with home rule, Muñoz–Rivera resigned. He eventually went to live in the U.S., where he continued to advocate Puerto Rican independence by publishing a magazine to acquaint North Americans with the plight of his homeland. He died in 1910 just before the passage of the Jones Bill, which gave Puerto Rico a large measure of self-government.

Muñoz–Rivera's birthday is a public holiday in Puerto Rico. His hometown of Barranquitas holds a three-day crafts fair every July that is timed to coincide with the birthday anniversary celebration. The fair tries to keep traditional skills and crafts alive by passing them on to the young.

CONTACT:
Puerto Rico Dept. of Culture
P.O. Box 9024184
San Juan, PR 00902-4184
809-724-0700

SOURCES:
AnnivHol-1983, p. 94
Chases-1996, p. 299
GdUSFest-1984, p. 218

♦ 1252 ♦ **Mushroom Festival**
First weekend in May

Richmond, Missouri, isn't the only town that claims to be the "mushroom capital of the world." Kennett Square, Pennsylvania, and Stover, Missouri, share this distinction as well. But Richmond is known for its highly prized morel mushrooms, which resemble a deeply pitted or folded cone-like sponge at the top of a hollow stem. The highlight of the annual Mushroom Festival, which has been held in Richmond since 1980, is the Big Morel Contest. Mushroom hunters flock to the town's wooded areas in search of the morel, known as the "Golden Fleece of mushrooms" because it is hard to find and has never been successfully cultivated.

Widespread morel hunting during the festival has necessitated an informal code of ethics among hunters. The rules include asking permission to hunt on privately owned lands, avoiding damage to the delicate fungi by inadvertently "stomping" small morels concealed by leaves, and dividing the day's booty with one's fellow "morellers." Above all, the hunters must refrain from revealing where they found their prize-winning specimens.

CONTACT:
Missouri Division of Tourism
P.O. Box 1055
Jefferson City, MO 65102
800-877-1234 or 314-751-4133
fax: 314-751-5160

SOURCES:
Chases-1996, p. 198

♦ 1253 ♦ **Music and Dance Festival, International**
June–July

One of the most important music and dance festivals in Europe, the festival in Granada, Spain, has been held for more than 40 years. It features an array of international orchestras and performers in settings of incomparable grandeur, such as the Alhambra (a 14th-century palace built for the Moorish kings), the adjoining Renaissance palace of Charles V, and the theater of the Generalife Gardens.

CONTACT:
Tourist Office of Spain
665 Fifth Ave.
New York, NY 10022
212-759-8822; fax: 212-980-1053

SOURCES:
GdWrldFest-1985, p. 162
IntlThFolk-1979, p. 337
MusFestEurBrit-1980, p. 136
MusFestWrld-1963, p. 165

♦ 1254 ♦ **Mut l-ard**
May 17

This is believed to be the first day of summer in Morocco, and the word *mut l-ard* means 'death of the earth.' Various rituals performed on this day by different tribes are designed to ward off evil and danger. For example, it is believed that rising at dawn and taking a bath will strengthen the body, and there is a taboo against sleeping, which is believed to result in a loss of courage. A special dish made from barley, fresh milk or buttermilk, and the root of a plant called *bûzeffur* is prepared and eaten on this day in the belief that it will make the people strong and ward off evil. In some areas it is believed that a husband's affections will waver on this day, and that the wife should therefore make herself as attractive as possible by using cosmetics.

SOURCES:
FolkWrldHol-1992, p. 300

♦ 1255 ♦ **Mystery Play of Tibet**
February–March; last day of Tibetan year

Originally performed by a devil-dancing cult to drive out the old year along with its demons and human enemies, this annual dramatic presentation was known to Tibetans as the **Dance of the Red-Tiger Devil** and to Europeans as the **Pageant of the Lamas** or the Mystery Play of Tibet. Under Buddhist influence, it was seen as symbolizing the triumph of the Indian missionary monks, led by Padmasambhava (*see also* HEMIS FESTIVAL and PARO TSHECHU), over pagan devils, and more recently, it has been changed to represent the assassination of Lang-darma, the king who tried to rid Tibet of Lamaism. Despite its many transformations over the years, however, the play continues to retain the devil-dancing features of its earliest form.

It is performed on the last day of the year in the courtyards of Buddhist temples or monasteries and continues for two days. A group of priests in black miters is confronted by one group of demons after another, which they manage to exorcize. On the second day, a dough effigy representing the enemies of Tibet and Lamaism is dismembered and disemboweled. Pieces of the effigy are thrown to the audience, who eat them or keep them to use as talismans. The play is followed by a burnt offering and a procession.

See also LOSAR

CONTACT:
India Tourist Office
30 Rockefeller Ave.
15 N. Mezzanine
New York, NY 10112
212-586-4901; fax: 212-582-3274

SOURCES:
DictFolkMyth-1984, p. 777

N

◆ 1256 ◆ **Naag Panchami**
July–August; waxing half of Hindu month of Sravana

A Hindu festival celebrated throughout India and Nepal, dedicated to the sacred serpent, Ananta, on whose coils Vishnu rested while he was creating the universe. According to Hindu belief, snakes can bring wealth and rain, and unhappy ones can cause a home to collapse. Therefore milk and flowers are offered to snakes, especially cobras; snake deities; or painted snake images at shrines. Because snakes are also worn by Shiva, hundreds of snakes are released at the Indian Shiva temples in Ujjain, where Shiva lived after destroying a demon, and in Varanasi, considered the religious capital of the Hindu faith. In Jodhpur, India, huge cloth *naags*, or 'cobras', are displayed.

CONTACT:
India Tourist Office
30 Rockefeller Ave.
15 N. Mezzanine
New York, NY 10112
212-586-4901; fax: 212-582-3274

Nepal Embassy
2131 Leroy Pl., N.W.
Washington, D.C. 20008
202-667-4550; fax: 202-667-5534

SOURCES:
BkFest-1937, p. 159
BkHolWrld-1986, Aug 8
DictFolkMyth-1984, pp. 671, 921
DictWrldRel-1989, p. 431
FolkWrldHol-1992, p. 403
RelHolCal-1993, p. 97

◆ 1257 ◆ **Nadam**
July 11; July 20–26

This Mongolian festival spotlights three major sports events. Its history goes back to the 13th century when Marco Polo described a gathering of 10,000 white horses. Mongolian chieftains, after meeting for parleys, competed in horse racing, archery, and wrestling, the "three manly games" for a Mongolian. Later, the fairs included women and were held in July or August when the pastures were lush and the horses well-fed. Today Nadam is held on July 11 (Revolution Day, a legal holiday in Mongolia) in provinces throughout the country. The chief Nadam is in the stadium in Ulan Bator, the capital. In Inner Mongolia (the Inner Mongolia Autonomous Region of China), Nadam is celebrated on July 20–26 on the Gogantala Pasture and at Lake Salim in the prefecture of Xinjiang. Other Nadams are held as people desire.

The fairs bring together the nomadic people who pitch a city of *yurts*, cone-shaped felt tents. Wrestling is usually the first event; at Ulan Bator, several hundred participants make a grand entrance in special tight-fitting costumes that leave the chest bare, proving the wrestler is male. A legend has it that long ago many men were once defeated by a woman. Titles awarded to top wrestlers are Falcon, Elephant, Lion, and Titan, and their prizes are silk scarves and horses. The second sport is archery, a sport of great antiquity—sixth-century Mongols hunted hares with bows and arrows while riding at full speed. Modern contests are both on foot and horseback. The last of the traditional sporting events is horse racing. In the National Nadam, the featured race is for children aged seven to 12 who cover a 20-mile cross-country course. When night falls, a bowed stringed instrument called a *matouqin* is played, and people sit by their yurts talking, dancing, and drinking aromatic butter tea and *kumys*, a drink made of fermented mare's milk.

CONTACT:
Mongolian Embassy
2833 M St., N.W.
Washington, D.C. 20007
202-333-7117; fax: 202-298-9227

SOURCES:
AnnivHol-1983, p. 92
Chases-1996, p. 291
FolkWrldHol-1992, p. 364

◆ 1258 ◆ **Nagoya City Festival**
October 10–20

An annual secular festival in Nagoya, Japan, started by the city's merchants to give thanks for their prosperity. It features a parade of about 700 participants depicting historical figures in period costume, among them Oda Nobunaga, Toyotomi Hideyoshi, and Tokugawa Ieyasu, the three feudal warlords who unified the country at the end of the 16th century.

CONTACT:
Japan National Tourist
Organization
630 Fifth Ave., Ste. 2101
New York, NY 10111
212-757-5640; fax: 212-307-6754

♦ 1259 ♦ **Nanakusa Matsuri (Seven Herbs or Grasses Festival)**
January 7

A Japanese ceremony dating back to the ninth century, also called **Wakana-setsu** or **'Festival of Young Herbs,'** or **Jin-jitsu 'Man Day'** because it occurs on the zodiacal day for "man." After an offering to the clan deity in the morning, participants partake of *nanakusa gayu*, a rice gruel seasoned with seven different herbs that is said to have been served for its medicinal value to the young prince of the Emperor Saga (ruled 810–824). The herbs are shepherd's-purse, chickweed, parsley, cottonweed, radish, as well as herbs known as *hotoke-no-za* and *aona* in Japanese.

SOURCES:
Chases-1996, p. 59
DictFolkMyth-1984, p. 540
FolkWrldHol-1992, p. 65

♦ 1260 ♦ **Napoleon's Day**
May 5

Napoleon Bonaparte, emperor of France from 1804–15, is one of the most celebrated individuals in European history and still has many admirers in France. Often referred to as "Le Corse" (from Corsica, where he was born) or "Le Petit Caporal" (the little corporal) for his short stature, Napoleon is best known for the zeal with which he pursued the military expansion of France and for his reforms, which left a lasting mark on the judicial, financial, administrative, and educational institutions of not only France, but much of western Europe.

After finally abdicating in favor of his son on June 22, 1815, Napoleon was exiled to the island of St. Helena in the southern Atlantic with a small group of followers. He died there on May 5, 1821, at the age of only 51. But his legend grew, and in 1840 his remains were taken from St. Helena back to Paris, where a magnificent funeral was held. He was finally entombed under the gold-plated dome of the Church of Saint-Louis, one of the buildings in the compound of the Hôtel des Invalides, where his descendants and admirers still congregate on May 5 each year to attend a commemorative mass.

See also CAPE VINCENT FRENCH FESTIVAL

CONTACT:
French Government Tourist Office
9454 Wilshire Blvd., Ste. 715
Beverly Hills, CA 90212
310-271-6665; fax: 310-276-2835

SOURCES:
AnnivHol-1983, p. 62

♦ 1261 ♦ **Narak Chaturdashi**
October–November; 14th day of waning half of Hindu month of Kartika

The day after DHAN TERAS is celebrated by Hindus as Narak Chaturdashi. It is dedicated to Yama, the god of Naraka or Hell. Bathing at dawn on this day is considered essential; in fact, those who bathe after the sun has risen risk losing their religious merit. After bathing, Hindus offer libations to Yama three times in the hope that he will spare them the tortures of hell. A fast is observed and in the evening, lamps are lit in Yama's honor.

SOURCES:
RelHolCal-1993, p. 97

♦ 1262 ♦ **Narcissus Festival**
January or February

A celebration in Honolulu, Hawaii, to usher in the Chinese or LUNAR NEW YEAR. There is a queen pageant and a coronation ball, Chinese cooking demonstrations, food booths, and arts and crafts exhibits. A parade features lion dances and fireworks. The first Narcissus Festival was held in 1950, narcissus blossoms being chosen as a symbol of hope that Chinese culture would have a renaissance in Hawaii.

CONTACT:
Hawaii Visitors Bureau
2270 Kalakaua Ave., Ste. 801
Honolulu, HI 96815
808-923-1811; fax: 808-922-8991

SOURCES:
BkFestHolWrld-1970, p. 26
GdUSFest-1984, p. 42

♦ 1263 ♦ **Narsimha Jayanti**
April–May; 14th day of waxing half of Hindu month of Vaisakha

According to Hindu mythology, this is the day on which Vishnu appeared as the Narsimha, or Man-Lion, to free the world from the demon king, Hiranyakasipu. The king, who had forbidden the worship of anyone but himself, was very annoyed to discover that his own son, Prahlad, was an ardent devotee of Vishnu. He tortured Prahlad in an attempt to convert him, but the child remained unmoved in his devotion. Then the king tried to kill him by having him trampled by elephants and thrown off precipices, but again without success. Eventually Hiranyakasipu became so enraged that he rushed to kill Prahlad with his own sword, asking the child, "Where is your savior?" It was at this moment that Vishnu stepped from behind a nearby pillar in the form of Narsimha—half-lion, half-man—and tore the king to pieces.

On this day, Hindus fast, meditate, and pray for the spiritual fortitude of Prahlad. Sometime they demonstrate the depth of their devotion by giving cows, grain, gold, robes, and other goods to the poor and the Brahmans as acts of charity.

SOURCES:
RelHolCal-1993, p. 98

♦ 1264 ♦ **Natchez Spring and Fall Pilgrimages**
March and October

These events, held since 1932 in Natchez, Miss., attract about 75,000 people to tour the county's antebellum houses. Women in hoop skirts welcome visitors to the mansions and their gardens of azaleas, camellias, olive trees, and boxwood hedges.

Natchez, situated on 200-foot bluffs overlooking the Mississippi River, was named for the Natchez Indians. It was founded by the French in 1716, and was the first European settlement on the river. It had a golden era in the 60 years after Mississippi became a territory in 1798. The town was an important river port, and wealthy citizens had vast plantations and built magnificent homes. Thirty of these, some owned by descendants of the original families, are open for tours. They include such spectacular homes as Longwood, the largest octagonal house remaining in the United States, and Auburn, an imposing mansion with a free-standing stairway to the second floor.

Besides the tours, there are candlelight dinners in Magnolia

Hall, a mansion that houses a costume museum, and presentations four times a week of the "Confederate Pageant," a lavish musical with local performers in costume presenting vignettes of the Old South. A satire of the pilgrimage, "Southern Exposure," is presented four times a week. "Southern Road to Freedom," presented by the Holy Family Choir, is a musical tribute to the struggles and victories of African Americans in Natchez from colonial days to the present, and is performed three times a week.

During a month-long fall celebration in October, there is another mansion tour. During the three-week Natchez Fall Pilgrimage there are 24 homes open to tours. October also brings theatrical performances of classic melodrama, the Great Mississippi River Balloon Race, a street dance, and arts and crafts exhibits.

CONTACT:
Mississippi Division of Tourism
  Development
P.O. Box 849
Jackson, MS 39205
800-927-6378 or 601-359-3297
fax: 601-359-5757

SOURCES:
Chases-1996, pp. 128, 407
GdUSFest-1984, p. 101

♦ 1265 ♦ **National and International Festivals of Amateur Puppeteers**
June–July

The art of making and performing with puppets has enjoyed a resurgence in the decades since World War II—particularly in the Czech Republic, where puppet ensembles proliferated after 1945. Every summer since 1951, a nationwide festival of puppeteers has been held in Chrudim in June and July. Every fifth year, puppeteers from other countries are invited to participate in an International Festival of Amateur Puppeteers. In addition to the performances of puppet theaters, there are discussions and seminars on the art of puppetry. Puppeteers from as many as 11 foreign countries participate in the International Festival, while the National Festival focuses on the work of Czech puppeteers.

Other international puppet festivals are held in Barcelona, Spain (April–May); Braunschweig, Germany (March during odd-numbered years); Bielski-Biala, Poland (May–June during even-numbered years); Bialystok, Poland (March during odd-numbered years); and Bochum, Germany (May–June).

CONTACT:
Czech Center
1109 Madison Ave.
New York, NY 10028
212-288-0830; fax: 212-288-0971
E-mail: nycenter@czech.cz

SOURCES:
IntlThFolk-1979, p. 88

National Anthem Day
See **Defenders' Day**

♦ 1266 ♦ **National Finals Rodeo**
Starting on first Friday in December

Rodeo's premier event, sometimes called the Super Bowl of rodeos, a 10-day affair held since 1985 in Las Vegas, Nev. The National Finals Rodeo, which offered a record $2.45 million in prize money in 1991, is reserved for the top 15 contestants in each of seven events: bareback riding, steer wrestling, team roping, saddle bronc riding, calf roping, women's

barrel racing, and bull riding. The winners are considered the world champions in their event. There is also a world all-around champion. Twenty-two-year-old Ty Murray who made more than half a million dollars in three years as a Professional Rodeo Cowboy Association competitor, was a recent all-around champ.

The national finals debuted in 1959 in Dallas, moved to Los Angeles in 1962 and to Oklahoma City in 1965, where it stayed until its move to Las Vegas 20 years later. Attendance is about 85,000.

The rodeo is preceded by the Miss Rodeo America Pageant. Events during the 10 days of rodeo include a Professional Rodeo Cowboy Association convention and trade show, horsemanship competitions, the National Finals Rodeo Christmas Gift Show, a hoedown, cowboy poetry gatherings, style shows, a golf invitational, fashion shows, and dances. The World Champions Awards Banquet is the grand finale.

See also Circuit Finals Rodeo

CONTACT:
Professional Rodeo Cowboys
  Association
101 Pro Rodeo Dr.
Colorado Springs, CO 80919
719-593-8840; fax: 548-4876

SOURCES:
Chases-1996, p. 473
GdUSFest-1984, p. 146

Las Vegas Convention and Visitors Authority
3150 Paradise Rd.
Las Vegas, NV 89109
800-332-5333 or 702-892-0711
fax: 702-892-2824

♦ 1267 ♦ **Nations, Festival of (Minnesota)**
Last weekend in April

Minnesota's largest ethnic celebration, the Festival of Nations takes place in St. Paul, a city of great ethnic diversity. As many as 65 different ethnic groups participate in this event, which has been held since 1932 and features costumes, folk craft demonstrations, and cultural exhibits. Folk dance and music performances run continuously and showcase performers from Greece, Egypt, Ireland, Polynesia, Norway, Ecuador, Armenia, and many other countries. Spectators can also take 20-minute language lessons in Russian, Swedish, Lao, Italian, and other tongues. Another festival event is the naturalization ceremony for new citizens.

Food is one of the festival's main attractions. There is sausage with kraut (Czech), chicken schnitzel in pita (Israeli), fafaatoo and sambusa (Oromo people of Ethiopia and Kenya), fatiah spinach pie (Syrian), strawberry mousse with kirsch (French), and maple syrup tarts (Canadian). Visitors who are thirsty can find mango milk shakes (Indian), green tea (Japanese), and egg coffee (Finnish). Sidewalk cafes serve authentic food from more than four dozen countries.

CONTACT:
St. Paul Convention and Visitors
  Bureau
55 E. Fifth St.
Norwest Center, Ste. 102
St. Paul, MN 55101
800-627-6101 or 612-297-6985
fax: 612-297-6879

SOURCES:
Chases-1996, p. 197
GdUSFest-1984, p. 97

◆ 1268 ◆ Nations, Festival of (Montana)
Starting first Saturday of August for nine days

A celebration of the multi-ethnic heritage of Red Lodge, Mont. In its early days, Red Lodge was a coal-mining town where miners who came from a number of European nations established their own communities. This festival began in 1961 to honor the different ethnic traditions. Today there is dancing, singing, and eating. Special foods are served by representatives of England, Scotland, Ireland, Wales, Germany, Finland, the Scandinavian countries, Italy, and the several nationalities that made up the former Yugoslavia. Nine days of events wind up with an All Nations Parade followed by a street dance.

CONTACT:
Montana Travel Promotion
  Division
1424 Ninth Ave.
Helena, MT 59620
800-847-4868 or 406-444-2654
fax: 406-444-1800

SOURCES:
Chases-1996, p. 322
GdUSFest-1984, p. 108

Native American Day
See **American Indian Day**

Nativity of Our Lord, Feast of the
See **Christmas**

◆ 1269 ◆ Nativity of the Blessed Virgin Mary, Feast of the
September 8

Only three births are celebrated in the whole Christian calendar: the Virgin Mary's, Sᴛ. Jᴏʜɴ's on June 24, and Jesus Christ's on December 25. Although it is not known where the September 8 date of Mary's birth originated, it seems to have been established by the end of the seventh century. In the Coptic and Abyssinian churches, the first day of every month is celebrated as the birthday of the Virgin Mary.

There are a number of legends describing the Virgin Mary's birth. Most early works of art show Mary and her mother, Anne, surrounded by elaborate furnishings and ancient Hebrew decorations, with a choir of angels hovering overhead. There are more festivals in honor of Mary than of any other saint—among them the Feasts of the Iᴍᴍᴀᴄᴜʟᴀᴛᴇ Cᴏɴᴄᴇᴘᴛɪᴏɴ the Aɴɴᴜɴᴄɪᴀᴛɪᴏɴ, the Purification or Cᴀɴᴅʟᴇᴍᴀs, and the Vɪsɪᴛᴀᴛɪᴏɴ.

In Malta there is a regatta in the capital, Valletta, in celebration of the defeat of the Turks by the Knights of St. John of Jerusalem on this day in 1565, and the end of the Axis siege in 1943.

In northern Europe, the **Feast of the Nativity of Our Lady** functioned as a traditional harvest festival—a time to give thanks to Mary for the bounty of the fields and to ask her to protect the crops until they were harvested. Native Americans in the United States often observe September 8 with traditional Indian harvest dances in Mary's honor, following Mass in the local Roman Catholic mission church.

CONTACT:
Malta National Tourist Office
350 Fifth Ave.
Empire State Bldg., Ste. 4412
New York, NY 10118
212-695-9520; fax: 212-695-8229

SOURCES:
AmerBkDays-1978, p. 822
DaysCustFaith-1957, p. 232
FestWestEur-1958, p. 70
FolkWrldHol-1992, p. 475
IndianAmer-1989, pp. 289, 301
RelHolCal-1993, p. 98
SaintFestCh-1904, p. 400

◆ 1270 ◆ Nativity of the Theotokos
September 8

The Greek word *theotokos* means 'god-bearer,' or 'mother of God.' The feast known as the **Nativity of Our Most Holy Lady, the Theotokos** (or simply as the Nativity of the Theotokos) is observed in Orthodox Christian churches on September 8. Western Christian churches celebrate the feast on the same day, but call it the Nᴀᴛɪᴠɪᴛʏ ᴏF ᴛʜᴇ Bʟᴇssᴇᴅ Vɪʀɢɪɴ Mᴀʀʏ.

The feast of Mary's nativity is believed to have originated in the East, probably in Syria or Palestine, some centuries ago. It was already a major celebration in Jerusalem by the end of the fifth century, and by the seventh century it had become established in the Roman liturgy. By the 11th century, the observation of this feast had spread throughout the Christian world.

Mary was declared to be *Theotokos* as a result of the Council of Ephesus, held in 431. A major item on the Council's agenda was the theological controversy over Mary: Was she the mother of the incarnate Son of God, or had she given birth to a human being who was later united to the Son of God? The Council condemned the latter viewpoint as heretical.

SOURCES:
AmerBkDays-1978, p. 822

◆ 1271 ◆ Nativity of the Virgin, Feast of, in Germany
September 8

Farmers of the Black Forest region of Germany customarily bring their horses to St. Märgen on this day to be blessed by the local priest. The horses wear traditional harnesses with well-polished brass, which are decorated with flowers. Streamers of ribbon are woven into their manes and tails. Both the farmers and their wives may wear the traditional costumes of the Black Forest valley.

Long known as the center of a famous horse-breeding area, St. Märgen is especially noted for the sturdy horses that work the neighboring farms. September 8, the Feast of the Nᴀᴛɪᴠɪᴛʏ ᴏF ᴛʜᴇ Bʟᴇssᴇᴅ Vɪʀɢɪɴ Mᴀʀʏ, is known in the Black Forest region as **Pferdeweihe**, or the **Blessing of Horses**.

SOURCES:
FestWestEur-1958, p. 70

◆ 1272 ◆ Naumberg Orchestral Concerts
Sunday before Memorial Day, July 4, July 31, and Labor Day

When Elkan Naumburg decided in 1905 that Central Park would be the ideal place to stage free concerts for the people of New York, the park provided a far more pastoral setting than it would today. Naumburg sponsored a symphony orchestra and held the concerts in the existing pagoda-shaped bandstand. In 1923 he gave the city a new bandstand, and concerts were held in the Mall at Central Park continuously until 1980. Since 1981, they have been held at Lincoln Center's Damrosch Park Bandshell.

Although the Naumburg Concerts were originally held on three holiday evenings—MEMORIAL DAY, the FOURTH OF JULY, and LABOR DAY—a fourth concert was added on July 31, the approximate date of Naumburg's death in 1924. In 1976 the schedule was changed to the Sunday afternoon preceding these four days. The concerts themselves offer vocal and instrumental recitals, light opera, and symphonic and chamber music. The Empire Brass Quintet has performed often at the series, as have many other well-known ensembles.

CONTACT:
New York Convention and Visitors Bureau
2 Columbus Cir.
New York, NY 10019
800-692-8474 or 212-484-1200
fax: 212-247-6193

SOURCES:
MusFestAmer-1990, p. 107

♦ 1273 ♦ **Nauru Independence Day**
January 31

This island in the Pacific Ocean gained independence from Great Britain on January 31, 1968. It had been governed by Australia. Independence Day is a national holiday in Nauru.

CONTACT:
Republic of Nauru Honorary Consulate
841 Bishop St., Ste. 506
Honolulu, HI 96813
808-523-7821

SOURCES:
AnnivHol-1983, p. 16
Chases-1996, p. 80
NatlHolWrld-1968, p. 19

♦ 1274 ♦ **Navajo Nation Fair at Window Rock**
Early September

A five-day gala billed as the "World's Largest American Indian Fair," held in Window Rock, Ariz., the capital of the Navajo Nation. More than 100,000 visitors attend the fair, which dates back to 1947. It features a parade through the Window Rock area and a rodeo with more than 900 cowboys and cowgirls from eight different Indian rodeo associations. Other events include horse races, an inter-tribal powwow, a Miss Navajo Nation competition, an Indian fry-bread contest, a baby contest, country and western dances, Indian song and dance competitions, and agricultural and livestock exhibits. Arts and crafts exhibits are also part of Navajo fairs: the Navajos are famous for turquoise-and-silver jewelry, sand paintings, and woven rugs. The art of weaving was taught to Navajo women, their lore says, by Spider Woman, one of the Holy People from the underworld.

The Navajo Reservation covers 17.5 million acres and is the largest in the United States. Other fairs are the Eastern Navajo Fair held in Crownpoint, New Mexico, in late July; the Central Navajo Fair, Chinle, Ariz., in late August; Southwestern Navajo Fair, Dilcon, Ariz., in mid-September; the Northern or SHIPROCK NAVAJO NATION FAIR, Shiprock, New Mexico, in early October; Western Navajo Fair, Tuba City, Ariz., in mid-October; and the Utah Navajo Fair in Bluff, Utah, the second week in September.

CONTACT:
Navajo Tribal Council
P.O. Box 308
Window Rock, AZ 86515
602-871-4941

SOURCES:
AmerBkDays-1978, p. 832
AnnivHol-1983, p. 179
IndianAmer-1989, p. 289

Navratri
See **Durga Puja**

♦ 1275 ♦ **Nawruz (Naw roz; No Ruz; New Year)**
Beginning about March 21 for 13 days

The first day of spring and the first day of the Islamic new year (*nawruz* means 'new day') celebrated by all religious groups in Iran and Afghanistan. In India, it is celebrated by the Parsis as JAMSHED NAVROZ. The holiday is pre-Islamic, a legacy of Zoroastrian Persia. It is also called **Ras al-Am**. In Afghanistan it is celebrated as **Nauroz**; in Kashmir as **Nav Roz**; and in Turkmenistan, it's **Novrus Bairam.**

The origins of Nawruz are obscure, but it is generally thought to have been a pastoral festival marking the change from winter to summer. Legends have grown up around the holiday. In Afghanistan, where it is also **Farmer's Day**, an ugly old woman named Ajuzak is thought to roam around when Nawruz begins. If it rains on Nawruz, she is washing her hair and the spring plantings will thrive. The Achaemenid kings (559 B.C.–330 B.C.) are known to have celebrated Nawruz, probably with gift-giving.

Farmers decorate their cows and come into the city for an annual agricultural fair with prizes. Betting on kite flying is a sport for later in the day.

A special event, *jandah bala kardan* ('raising of the standard'), is held on Nawruz at the tomb of Hazrat Ali in Mazar-I-Sharif in northern Afghanistan. The *jandah*, or 'standard,' is raised in the courtyard of the shrine, and stays there for 40 days. Thousands visit the shrine to touch the staff to gain merit, and the sick and crippled touch it hoping for cures. The standard comes down at a time when a distinct kind of red tulip blooms and then soon fades; at this time, people visit friends and wish each other long lives and many children.

Buzkashi, the national game of Afghanistan, is usually played on Nawruz, especially in Mazar-I-Sharif. *Buzkashi* means 'goat-grabbing,' and the object of the game is for a team of horse riders to grab the carcass of a goat placed in a pit, carry it around a goal post, and put it back in the pit. The game is supposed to have developed on the plains of Mongolia and Central Asia, sometimes using a prisoner-of-war instead of a goat; now a dead calf is usually used. It's a ferocious game occasionally producing fatalities; there are several hundred horsemen (*chapandaz*) on each team, and they gallop at breakneck speed, lashing at horses and each other with special buzkashi whips.

Special Afghan dishes on Nawruz are *samanak*, a dessert made of wheat and sugar, and *haft-mewah* ('seven fruits')—a compote of walnuts, almonds, pistachio nuts, red and green raisins, dried apricots, and a fruit called *sanjet*.

In Iran, Nawruz is an event lasting 13 days, during which people wear new clothes, give gifts, and visit friends and relatives. Banquet tables traditionally hold seven foods starting with the letter S. Plates with sprouting wheat symbolize fertility, as do eggs, which are colored. Other symbols on the table are a mirror, candlesticks, and a bowl of water with a green leaf in it. The 13th day after No Ruz is Sizdah-Bedar or '13th day out' and everyone picnics in the country or on rugs in city parks. The idea is to get out of their houses, taking any bad luck with them.

For the Baha'i, the day also marks the end of the 19-day fast, from March 2–20, when Baha'i abstain from food and drink from sunrise to sunset as a reminder that one's true nature is spiritual rather than material.

See also AYYAM-I-HA

SOURCES:
BkFestHolWrld-1970, p. 7
BkHolWrld-1986, Mar 21
Chases-1996, p. 140
FolkWrldHol-1992, pp. 186, 187

♦ 1276 ♦ NEBRASKAland DAYS
Third week in June

This week-long celebration of Nebraska's western heritage is held in North Platte, the home of Colonel William "Buffalo Bill" Cody. This famous buffalo hunter, U.S. Army scout, and Indian fighter eventually became a touring showman, organizing his first Wild West exhibition in 1883. His stars included Annie Oakley (*see* OAKLEY FESTIVAL, ANNIE) and Chief Sitting Bull. Since 1965 the NEBRASKAland DAYS celebration has honored North Platte's most famous citizen by bestowing the Buffalo Bill Award on a well-known Western film star. Past winners have included Andy Devine, Gene Autry, Henry Fonda, Slim Pickens, and Wilford Brimley.

Other highlights of the festival include the Buffalo Bill Rodeo; the Frontier Revue, which tells the story of the West in song and dance; entertainment by top country and western performers; an equestrian show; and a Chuckwagon Pork Breakfast.

CONTACT:
NEBRASKAland DAYS
P.O. Box 706
North Platte, NE 69103
308-532-7948

SOURCES:
AmerBkDays-1978, p. 225
Chases-1996, p. 260

♦ 1277 ♦ Nebuta Matsuri
August 2–7

The main festival of Aomori Prefecture in Japan, featuring processions of huge, elaborately painted papier-mâché figures called *nebuta*. The festival supposedly originated when Sakanoue-no-Tamuramaro (758–811) was sent here to put down a rebellion. He won by raising dummy soldiers along the skyline, making the enemy think his army was bigger than it was. Today in the capital city of Aomori, the nebuta figures, up to 60 feet wide and 30 feet high, depict birds and animals, fabulous creatures, and ferociously scowling warriors. Illuminated from within by candles, they glow as they are carried through the streets at nightfall. Spectators wear hats made of flowers and dance in the streets.

A similar but smaller festival is held in Hirosaki Aug. 1–7. Here, the nebuta are fan-shaped and depict warriors on one side and beautiful women on the other.

CONTACT:
Japan National Tourist Organization
630 Fifth Ave., Ste. 2101
New York, NY 10111
212-757-5640; fax: 212-307-6754

SOURCES:
JapanFest-1965, p. 174

♦ 1278 ♦ Nemean Games
Probably August

Ancient Greek games, one of four ancient Greek festivals involving games, held every second year in the sanctuary of Zeus in the valley of Nemea in the northeastern part at the Greek Peloponnesus. Little is known of these games before 573 B.C. Legend says they may have been originated by Hercules after he slew the lion of Nemea—one of his 12 labors. He killed the lion by driving it into a cave and strangling it. The games consisted of gymnastic, equestrian, and musical contests. Winners were crowned with a garland of wild celery.

See also ISTHMIAN GAMES, PYTHIAN GAMES, and OLYMPIC GAMES

SOURCES:
ClassDict-1984, p. 399
GdAnctWrld-1986, p. 427

♦ 1279 ♦ Nemoralia
August 13

The Nemoralia was an ancient Roman festival in honor of the goddess Diana held at Nemi, in the territory of Aricia about 16 miles southeast of Rome. As the goddess of the hunt, Diana presided over the forests of Aricia. There was a grove, or *nemus*, there that adjoined a famous shrine dedicated to the goddess, and her priest was known as *rex nemorensis*, or 'king of the grove.' By custom, the rex nemorensis was a runaway slave who attained his royal office by murdering his predecessor.

Diana was worshipped throughout Rome and Latium (now western Italy) on August 13, the day on which her temple on the Aventine Hill had been dedicated by Servius Tullius. But her most famous cult was in Aricia, where the Nemoralia was observed to protect the vines and the fruit trees as well as to celebrate Diana's power. Some experts believe that the Christian Feast of the Dormition, or ASSUMPTION on August 15, eventually incorporated the harvest-blessing element of the ancient Nemoralia: It is still common in some parts of the Orthodox Christian Church for worshippers to make offerings of new wheat and cakes to the Theotokos on that day.

SOURCES:
ClassDict-1984, p. 400
FestSaintDays-1915, p. 173
GdAnctWrld-1986, pp. 64, 427
RomFest-1925, p. 198

♦ 1280 ♦ Nenana Ice Classic
Late February

Alaska's oldest tradition, a legal game that allows people to bet on when the massive ice cover on the Tanana River will break up. The Classic is kicked off in late February in Nenana (which has a population of about 570) with a winter carnival known as Tripod Days. At this time, a 1,500-pound spruce tripod is set into the ice of the Tanana River with a rope leading to a watchtower and clock. Two to three months later when the ice starts to move, a siren will sound, and when the tripod has moved 100 feet downstream, a meat cleaver stops the hands of the clock. This becomes the official time of the breakup. This setup of tripod, tower, clock, and cleaver has been the same since 1936 and has never failed.

Throughout Alaska, people place $2 bets in red gas cans with their predictions on the month, day, and hour of the ice's breakup. In early April, Nenana residents collect and sort the tickets. The earliest breakup ever recorded was April 20, 1940, at 3:27 A.M., and the latest May 20, 1964, at 11:41 A.M.

Wagering on the Nenana River ice began informally in 1906 when Jimmy Duke, owner of a roadhouse on the banks of the Tanana, started wagering with his chum Adolph "Two Cord" Nelson on the breakup day. In 1913, railroad engineers surveying the site for a bridge got in on the betting, and a pool started. In 1917, they started keeping records, and that year has been marked as the first official year of the Nenana Ice Classic. Now it's part of Alaskan lore, and the red betting cans are sometimes called the first spring flower. In 1990, 152,000 tickets were sold, and after deductions for taxes and expenses, the purse was $138,000.

CONTACT:
Alaska Division of Tourism
P.O. Box 110801
Juneau, AK 99811
907-465-2012; fax: 907-465-2287

SOURCES:
Chases-1996, p. 110

♦ 1281 ♦ Nepal National Day
February 18; November 8; January 11

Also known as **Rashtriya Prajatantra Divas**, or **National Democracy Day**, this holiday commemorates the introduction of a democratic system of government in Nepal, which had been ruled by the Rana family since the mid-19th century.

Two other national holidays in Nepal are **Unity Day**, January 11—celebrating the unification of the various principalities into one country more than 200 years ago—and **Constitution Day**, November 8—observing the adoption of a new Nepalese constitution in 1990.

CONTACT:
Nepal Embassy
2131 Leroy Pl., N.W.
Washington, D.C. 20008
202-667-4550; fax: 202-667-5534

SOURCES:
AnnivHol-1983, p. 26
NatlHolWrld-1968, p. 26

♦ 1282 ♦ Neri-Kuyo
August 16, every three years (1996, 1999, . . .)

A Buddhist ceremony held every three years at Joshinji Temple in Tokyo, Japan, to celebrate the coming to earth of the Bodhisattvas. They are Buddhas-to-be who have undertaken a quest for enlightenment and have vowed to save all beings before they attain Buddhahood.

One of the best-known vows taken by a Bodhisattva is this:

> *Living beings are countless—*
> *I vow to save them all.*
> *Passions are inextinguishable—*
> *I vow to extinguish them all.*
> *Dharma truths are measureless—*
> *I vow to master them all.*
> *The Buddha-way is unexcelled—*

I vow to attain it.

For the Neri-Kuyo in Tokyo, a curved wooden bridge is erected between two of the temple buildings, and local people dressed as Amitabha Buddha and 24 other Bodhisattvas file slowly across the bridge and back again. Wearing golden masks and haloes and fanned by attendants, they repeat this ceremony three times a day.

CONTACT:
Japan National Tourist
  Organization
630 Fifth Ave., Ste. 2101
New York, NY 10111
212-757-5640; fax: 212-307-6754

SOURCES:
DictWrldRel-1989, p. 112

Nevada Day
See **Appendix A: Admission Days and Facts about the States and Territories**

♦ 1283 ♦ Nevis Tea Meeting
Full moon night in summer

The pageant known as the **Tea Meeting** held on the island of Nevis in the West Indies probably developed from church fund-raising events in the 19th century. The characters include a King, his Queen, and their court. The King and Queen sit on a stage while costumed members of the audience get up and perform for them—singing, dancing, reciting poetry, or giving a speech. Tea (or some other hot drink) is served and ceremonial fruit, cakes, and kisses from the King and Queen are auctioned off. Then the King and Queen and their court give ironic speeches, followed by more audience acts. If there is enough participation from the audience, the pageant can go on all night. It is common for scoffers in the back of the room to make loud and obscene comments throughout the performance.

CONTACT:
St. Kitts and Nevis Embassy
3216 New Mexico Ave., N.W.
Washington, D.C. 20016
202-686-2636

SOURCES:
FolkWrldHol-1992, p. 408

♦ 1284 ♦ Newala
December–January

A first fruits ceremony, before which the people are forbidden to eat certain new crops, the Newala ceremony in Swaziland takes place at the end of the year. It is a combination harvest and New Year's festival. It is also a celebration of kingship, since according to tradition the king of Swaziland—the Ngwenyama, or 'Lion'—has mystical powers and is believed to embody the nation's prosperity and fertility, thus he must have many wives and sire many children.

Events taking place during the ceremony, which lasts nearly a month, include the gathering of foam from the tops of waves and the collection of water from the major rivers by a group of *bemanti*, or Swazi water officials. The day before they leave, the king goes into seclusion. Young boys from all over the country who have reached puberty gather *lusekwane*, a type of acacia that is considered sacred, and bring it to the cattle pen. The climax of the Newala occurs when warriors, chanting sacred songs, dance around the *nhlambelo*, the king's sacred enclosure, persuading him to rejoin his people. The king feigns reluctance but eventually emerges: his face is blackened with medicines, he wears a headdress of large black plumes and a silver monkey skin belt, and bright green grass covers his body. He improvises a dance before his people, and at one point he eats part of a special pumpkin known as the *luselwa* and throws the rest to one of his warriors. This is a signal that the new crops may now be eaten. The Newala ends with a huge bonfire which represents the burning of the past year. It is believed that rain will fall to quench the flames.

CONTACT:
Swaziland Embassy
3400 International Dr., N.W., Ste. 3M
Washington, D.C. 20008
202-362-6683; fax: 202-244-8059

SOURCES:
FolkWrldHol-1992, p. 467

♦ 1285 ♦ New Church Day
June 19

New Church Day refers to the Church of the New Jerusalem, founded in London in the late 18th century by the disciples of Emanuel Swedenborg, the Swedish scientist, philosopher, and theologian. In 1817, the General Convention of the New Jerusalem in the U.S.A. was founded in Philadelphia.

Swedenborg's followers believe that in 1757 there was a great judgment in the spiritual world, and that as a result the evil spirits were separated from the good and a new heaven was established. At that time Jesus called his apostles together and told them to preach the new doctrines in the new heaven, just as he had told them to do 16 centuries earlier on earth. All of this took place on June 19 and 20. June 19 is also the date on which Swedenborg's disciples met in 1770 to organize the Church of the New Jerusalem. Every year on this day members of the New Church, called Swedenborgians, meet to conduct important church business and to commemorate the church's founding.

CONTACT:
Swedenborgian Church
48 Sargent St.
Newton, MA 02158

SOURCES:
DaysCustFaith-1957, p. 148
DictWrldRel-1989, p. 728
RelHolCal-1993, p. 98

♦ 1286 ♦ New England Folk Festival
Third weekend in April

The first New England Folk Festival was held in 1944, and for 25 years it was held in different locations throughout New England. Now its permanent home is in Natick, Massachusetts, and all of the festival's events are held in and around Natick High School. The emphasis is on folk dancing: Morris dancing teams from all over the country perform at the festival, and there are square and contra dances, folk dance workshops, and many other events for folk dance enthusiasts. There are also instrumental jam sessions, national food booths, and displays of ethnic crafts, such as Ukrainian EASTER eggs and colored scrimshaw. The festival is unusual in that those who attend are encouraged to participate by bringing along their musical instruments and joining in any impromptu or scheduled jam sessions or workshops. Attendees are also encouraged to dance with any group they choose.

CONTACT:
New England Folk Festival
1950 Massachusetts Ave.
Cambridge, MA 01241
617-354-1340

SOURCES:
MusFestAmer-1990, p. 224

♦ 1287 ♦ New Fire Ceremony
Every 52 years

Among the ancient Aztec people of what is now Mexico, the year was divided into 18 months of 20 days each, plus a five-day "unlucky" period. There was also a ritualistic period of 260 days, which was composed of 13 months with 20 named days in each month. When one cycle was superimposed on the other, it resulted in a "century" of 52 years. Although festivals were observed each month, the most impressive and important occurred at the end of the 52-year cycle, when people feared that the world would be destroyed. It was known as the New Fire Ceremony because the old altar fire was extinguished and a new one was lit, symbolizing the new lease on life that the dawn of a new cycle represented.

Just before dusk on the day of the ceremony, all fires in the Valley of Mexico were put out. Huge crowds of people followed their priests from Mexico City to a temple several miles away on the Hill of the Star. Because the hill permitted them to view the heavens in all directions, it was here that the priests waited for a celestial sign telling them that the world would end or that a new century would begin. If the constellation known as the Pleiades passed the zenith, life would continue as it had. But if it failed to do so, the sun and stars would be changed into wild beasts who would fall to the earth and devour all the people, after which an earthquake would complete the destruction.

As soon as the heavenly signal received a favorable interpretation, burning torches were carried by runners throughout the valley to relight the fires in each house.

SOURCES:
DictFolkMyth-1984, p. 713

♦ 1288 ♦ New Jersey Offshore Grand Prix
Four days in mid-July

Formerly known as the **Benihana Grand Prix Power Boat Regatta** and before that as the **Hennessy Grand Prix**, this four-day race is not only one of the largest offshore power boat races in the country but a festival as well, with a beauty pageant, band concerts, and fireworks taking place at the popular beach resort of Point Pleasant. The race itself takes place on a Wednesday and runs along the Atlantic coast of New Jersey from Asbury Park to Barnegat attracting more than 250,000 spectators to the state's beaches.

When the regatta was first held in 1964, it covered a 265-mile course around Long Island. But it was eventually moved to the Jersey shore, where there were more open beaches and clear waterways. In addition to the large number of onshore spectators, about 3,000 power boats watch the race from the water.

CONTACT:
New Jersey Division of Travel and Tourism
20 W. State St.
Trenton, NJ 08625
800-537-7397 or 609-292-2470
fax: 609-633-7418

SOURCES:
GdUSFest-1984, p. 119

♦ 1289 ♦ New Orleans Jazz and Heritage Festival
Late April to early May

A 10-day feast for the ears, the eyes, and the stomach, held in New Orleans "Crescent City," Louisiana. The festival's forerunner was the New Orleans International Jazz Fest organized in 1968 to celebrate the city's 250th anniversary. Among the jazz greats on hand were Louis Armstrong and Duke Ellington. After it disbanded, George Wein, the founder of the famed Newport Jazz Festival (*see* JVC JAZZ FESTIVAL), urged the initiation of a festival to celebrate the regional culture of New Orleans, and in 1970 it was under way. A high spot in the festival was the evening when Eubie Blake, then 95 years old, was honored as a ragtime and jazz pioneer; he played several of his own tunes, including "I'm Just Wild About Harry" and "Memories of You."

Today it brings together more than 4,000 musicians, artisans, and cooks who do their thing for more than a quarter of a million visitors. The concerts feature not only traditional and contemporary jazz, but also other music forms developed in New Orleans: ragtime, country, Cajun, zydeco, gospel, folk, and Latin. Food tents serve a multitude of indigenous foods, such as jambalaya, andouille, crawfish bisque, gumbo, frog legs, and so on. Hundreds of artisans also display their crafts.

CONTACT:
New Orleans Metropolitan Convention and Visitors Bureau
1520 Sugar Bowl Dr.
New Orleans, LA 70112
504-566-5011; fax: 504-566-5046

SOURCES:
Chases-1996, p. 186
GdUSFest-1984, p. 71
MusFestAmer-1990, p. 194

♦ 1290 ♦ Newport Harbor Christmas Boat Parade
December 17–23

A week-long nightly parade of boats at Newport Beach, Calif., which has one of the largest concentrations of pleasure craft in the world—more than 9,000 boats are docked at the harbor. About 200 boats of all kinds, wildly decorated with lights that depict Santa Claus, snowmen, snowflakes, and other symbols of winter, join the parade. Some boats carry huge inflated figures (an enormous Grinch in an engineer's cap appeared in 1990) and many play music. The vessels range from rowboats to tugs to elegant yachts.

The floating parades actually started in 1908 as a FOURTH OF JULY spectacular. (The Fourth parades are no more.) John Scarpa, a real-estate broker was trying to sell some property, and to promote it he lit up a gondola and eight canoes with Japanese lanterns and paraded around the harbor. This developed into the **Illuminated Water Parade**, and was a highlight of the Fourth for years. In 1946, the city got a barge, put a tree and carolers on it, and towed it around the harbor, and that began the current December parades. They are considered the "granddaddy" of water parades, the biggest in the nation. About a million spectators watch them during the festival's seven days.

CONTACT:
California Division of Tourism
801 K Street, Ste. 1600
Sacramento, CA 95814
800-862-2543 or 916-322-2881
fax: 916-322-3402

Newport Jazz Festival
See JVC Jazz Festival

♦ 1291 ♦ Newport Music Festival
Two weeks in mid-July

In 1969 the Metropolitan Opera in New York City decided to establish its summer home in Newport, Rhode Island. The fog and humidity, however, played havoc with the artists' delicate instruments, and it quickly became apparent that Newport wasn't the place for outdoor opera. But the grand rooms of its famed waterfront mansions provided an ideal setting for chamber music. Using members of the Metropolitan Opera Orchestra, the festival in its infancy paved the way for the "Romantic revival," which soon spread worldwide.

The Newport Music Festival still offers music of the Romantic era (1825–1900) but in recent years it has expanded its offerings and now presents a wide spectrum of composers and performers. Dozens of world premieres of forgotten or lost minor masterpieces by well-known composers, such as the four-handed *Andante Cantabile* by Debussy, have taken place here, as have the North American debuts of many now-famous international and American artists, such as the young Dimitris Sgouros. Up to 45 concerts are presented during the two-week festival, which has developed a reputation for programs so rare and varied that they draw music-lovers from thousands of miles away.

CONTACT:
Rhode Island Tourism Division
7 Jackson Walkway
Providence, RI 02903
800-556-2484 or 401-277-2601
fax: 401-277-2102

SOURCES:
Chases-1996, p. 287
GdUSFest-1984, p. 167
MusFestAmer-1990, p. 134

♦ 1292 ♦ Newport to Bermuda Race
June in even-numbered years

One of the oldest sailing races in the international calendar, the race from Newport, Rhode Island, to Bermuda was initiated by Thomas Fleming Day, editor and founder of *Rudder* magazine. At the time, most existing ocean races were for yachts of more than 100 feet, and Day wanted to see a race for smaller yachts (less than 40 feet overall). The first such race, in 1904, was run from Brooklyn, New York, to Marblehead, Massachusetts, a distance of 330 nautical miles. The following year it went from Brooklyn to Hampton Roads, Virginia (250 miles). In 1906, the finish was in Bermuda.

The Bermuda races died out in 1910, but they were revived in 1923 under the sponsorship of the Cruising Club of America (CCA). Since 1924 the race has been sailed biennially in June. The starting point was moved from New London, Connecticut, to Montauk, Long Island. But since 1936 the race has been run from Brenton Reef Tower off Newport to Mount Hill Light on St. David's Head, Bermuda—a distance of 635 miles. Sponsored jointly by the CCA and the Royal Bermuda Yacht Club, the Newport to Bermuda Race is now part of the Onion Patch trophy series, which consists of this and three local, unnamed races.

CONTACT:
Cruising Club of America
P.O. Box 227
North Branford, CT 06471

♦ 1293 ♦ New Yam Festival
End of June

Celebrated by almost every ethnic group in Nigeria, the New

Yam festival is observed annually at the end of June. It is considered taboo to eat the new yam before this festival. The high priest sacrifices a goat and pours its blood over a symbol representing the god of the harvest. Then the carcass is cooked and a soup is made from it, while the yams are boiled and pounded to make *foofoo*. After the priest has prayed for a better harvest in the coming year, he declares the feast open by eating the pounded yam and the soup. Then everyone joins in, and there is dancing, drinking, and merrymaking. After the festival is over, new yam may be eaten by anyone in the community.

Among the Igbo people, the yam crop is considered sacred, and anyone who steals yam is banished. This is because the original yam is believed to have grown out of the flesh of two children who had been sacrificed so that the other Igbo children wouldn't starve. At the New Yam Festival, each household places four or eight new yams on the ground and cuts small pieces off the head and the tail. The yams are then cooked with palm oil and chicken, and the meal is considered to be a symbolic reenactment of the original sacrifice.

Among the Yoruba people, where the New Yam Festival is known as **Eje**, the celebration is more elaborate. It takes place over two days and consists of purification rites, presentation rites, divining rites, and thanksgiving rites. In one divination rite, a recently harvested yam is divided into two parts. They are thrown on the ground, and if one lands face up and the other face down, this is considered a positive sign for the life of the community and the success of crops in the coming year. If both fall face down or face up, problems lie ahead.

CONTACT:
Nigerian Embassy
1333 16th St., N.W.
Washington, D.C. 20036
202-986-8400; fax: 202-775-1385

SOURCES:
FolkWrldHol-1992, p. 455

♦ 1294 ♦ New Year's Day
January 1

Celebrating the first day of the year on the first day of January is a relatively modern practice. Although the Romans began marking the beginning of their civil year on January 1, the traditional springtime opening of the growing season and time for major military campaigns still held on as the popular New Year celebration.

William the Conqueror decreed that the New Year commence on January 1, but practice in England was still variable. Even after the Gregorian calendar was adopted by all Roman Catholic countries in 1582, Great Britain and the English colonies in America continued to begin the year on March 25 in accordance with the old Julian calendar. It wasn't until 1752 that Britain and its possessions adopted the New Style (Gregorian) calendar and accepted January 1 as the beginning of the year. New Year's Day is a public holiday in the U.S. and in many other countries, and is traditionally a day for receiving visitors and recovering from New Year's Eve festivities. A favorite pastime in the United States is watching football games on television—especially the Rose Bowl game in Pasadena, California, the Cotton Bowl in Dallas, Texas, the Sugar Bowl in New Orleans, Louisiana, and the Orange Bowl in Miami, Florida. A number of parades are also televised on New Year's Day, one of the most famous being the Mummers' Parade in Philadelphia, Pennsylvania. New Year's is a time

for making resolutions for the coming year—promises that are loudly proclaimed and then often forgotten.

See also Hogmanay; Lunar New Year; Oshogatsu; St. Basil, Feast of; Sol

SOURCES:
AmerBkDays-1978, p. 2
BkDays-1864, vol. I, p. 27
BkFest-1937, pp. 3, 14, 22, 29, 37, 51, 65, 77, 84, 94, 101, 110, 118, 131, 143, 157, 165, 178, 194, 203, 210, 218, 236, 240, 248, 266, 273, 288, 297, 307, 316, 326, 335
DaysCustFaith-1957, pp. 17, 355
DictFolkMyth-1984, pp. 181, 790, 791, 950, 1063
FestSaintDays-1915, pp. 1, 2, 4, 7
FestWestEur-1958, pp. 3, 22, 32, 54, 87, 105, 121, 150, 160, 188, 210, 225
FolkAmerHol-1991, p. 1
FolkWrldHol-1992, p. 1, 225

♦ 1295 ♦ New Year's Day in Denmark (Nytaarsdag)
January 1

In towns and cities throughout Denmark, the New Year marks the beginning of one of the most important social seasons in the calendar. Men and women attend church services and later call on relatives and friends to wish them a Happy New Year. These social calls only last about a half hour, but they go on for almost two weeks. Wine and small cookies are usually served during these visits.

Young people usher in the New Year by banging loudly on their friends' doors and throwing pieces of broken pottery that they have collected during the year against the sides of their houses.

SOURCES:
BkFest-1937, p. 94
BkFestHolWrld-1970, p. 2
FestWestEur-1958, p. 22

♦ 1296 ♦ New Year's Day in France
January 1

Known as **Le Jour de l'An** or **Le Jour des Étrennes** for the gifts that are exchanged on this day, New Year's Day in France is a time for family reunions, visits, and greeting cards or letters. Tradespeople send their errand boys or girls to deliver gifts to their patrons. The baker, for example, might send a *brioche*, while the butcher might send a chicken and the dairyman some eggs. Those who deliver the gifts are usually given wine or money. Servants and clerks often receive an extra month's pay as a New Year's gift, while family and friends give each other chocolates, flowers, preserved fruit, and *marrons glacés*, or candied chestnuts.

In the afternoon, men pay social calls on their women friends and young people visit their elders. In the evening, a formal dinner is usually held at the home of the family's eldest member. Since relatives come from far and wide to attend these reunions, they are usually very large and festive affairs.

SOURCES:
BkFest-1937, p. 188
FestWestEur-1958, p. 32
FolkWrldHol-1992, p. 2

♦ 1297 ♦ New Year's Day in Germany
January 1

According to German folk tradition, **Neujahr** is a time of new beginnings, and the first day of the year must be lived as you hope to live during the next 12 months. Housewives put forth an extra effort to make sure their homes are in order, and everyone wears new clothes. People avoid unpleasant tasks and try not to spend money, although they often jingle the coins in their pockets for good luck. People exchange greeting cards, but the giving of gifts is confined to those who have served the family throughout the year—for example, the mail carrier, janitor, and cleaning person.

In the Bavarian town of Oberammergau, a "star singer" (*see also* EPIPHANY IN GERMANY) carrying a large illuminated star on a long pole leads a NEW YEAR'S EVE procession that lasts for several hours. He sings a song that summarizes the events of the past year and extends good wishes for the year to come, accompanied by members of the Passion Play orchestra.

See also OBERAMMERGAU PASSION PLAY

CONTACT:
German National Tourist Office
122 E. 42nd St., 52nd Floor
New York, NY 10168
212-661-7200; fax: 212-661-7174

SOURCES:
BkFest-1937, p. 131
BkFestHolWrld-1970, p. 3
FestWestEur-1958, p. 54

♦ 1298 ♦ New Year's Day in Portugal (Ano Novo)
January 1

In Portugal, the New Year begins with special church services. Sometimes the service takes the form of Holy Communion, and people make promises about how they will live their lives in the coming year. Afterward, friends and relatives visit each other's houses, greeting each other with "Boas Festas" ('Happy Holidays') and exchanging good wishes. In northern Portugal, the children go through the neighborhood singing old songs called *janeiras* ('January songs'), which are thought to bring luck in the coming year. Sometimes a band of local musicians will go through the streets, stopping to play a special selection when they pass the house of someone they know.

There are many traditions and folk beliefs concerning NEW YEAR'S DAY. People tend to mind their manners, believing that how they conduct themselves on this day foreshadows their behavior for the coming year. If they should pay off a debt on New Year's Day, they are likely to end up paying for the next 12 months. It is the custom in Portugal on NEW YEAR'S EVE to choose 12 grapes from a bunch, and to eat them one after another just as the clock strikes 12, offering New Year's wishes to everyone in the room. This act will guarantee happiness in the coming year.

SOURCES:
BkFest-1937, p. 266
BkFestHolWrld-1970, pp. 3, 5
FestWestEur-1958, p. 160

♦ 1299 ♦ New Year's Day in Romania (Anul Nou)
January 1

Children welcome the New Year in Romania with an ancient fertility rite called *samanatul*, or 'sowing.' Children stuff their pockets with corn and go from house to house, throwing corn at people and greeting them with wishes for a long life. In some parts of Romania, the *sorcova*—a stick to which flowers are tied—is used instead of corn. The flowers are from twigs plucked on ST. ANDREW'S EVE and forced into blossom by CHRISTMAS. Rather than throwing corn at people, the children brush their faces lightly with the sorcova. This custom may be a survival from ancient Roman times, when people saluted one another with laurel branches.

Romanians also celebrate NEW YEAR'S DAY by exchanging gifts. Servants, the poor, and the young often receive gifts of money.

SOURCES:
BkFest-1937, p. 273

♦ 1300 ♦ New Year's Day in Switzerland (Neujahrstag)
January 1

The Swiss celebrate NEW YEAR'S DAY with amateur dramatic performances, visits with friends, and feasting on roast goose with chestnut stuffing, New Year's bread, and *birewegge*, or pear pie, which looks like a shiny loaf of bread and has a rich filling of pears and raisins. Goose necks filled with ground giblets, seasoning, and other ingredients are a favorite delicacy when sliced thin and served as a between-meal snack. Although the holiday is generally a quiet one, children often hide on New Year's morning, startling their parents when they jump out to greet them with "Happy New Year!"

According to Swiss folklore, the first day of January is full of omens and predictions. A red sky, for example, signifies storms, fire, and war in the coming year. Meeting a woman the first thing on New Year's Day is thought to bring bad luck, while encountering a man or a child is looked upon as a good sign.

SOURCES:
BkFest-1937, p. 316
FestWestEur-1958, p. 225

♦ 1301 ♦ New Year's Day in the former Soviet Union
January 1

NEW YEAR'S DAY has largely replaced CHRISTMAS as the major winter festival in the former Soviet Union (*see* RUSSIAN WINTER FESTIVAL). This was the day on which Grandfather Frost visited, bringing gifts for the children. Within the walls of Moscow's Kremlin, there was a huge party at the Palace of Congresses attended by as many as 50,000 children. Entertainment at the party included the arrival of *D'yed Moroz*, or Grandfather Frost, wearing a white beard, red robe, and a hat trimmed in white fur and riding a Sputnik-drawn sleigh or some other outlandish vehicle. There were also troops of folk dancers, magicians, clowns, and tumblers who performed for the children. Older Muscovites celebrated New Year's by attending dances at schools, clubs, theaters, and union halls. Outside of Moscow, the same festivities took place on a more modest scale.

Caviar, smoked fish, roast meats, and other treats were served in honor of the holiday. Among the many cakes and sweets served were *babka,* a yeast coffee cake made in a round pan, and *kulich,* a fancy fruitbread of Ukrainian origin made in three tiers to symbolize the Trinity.

SOURCES:
BkFest-1937, p. 288
Chases-1996, p. 52
FolkWrldHol-1992, p. 7

♦ 1302 ♦ New Year's Day in the Netherlands (Nieuwjaarsdag)
January 1

The first day of the New Year in the Netherlands is spent eating holiday cakes, breads, and waffles, visiting friends, and drinking *slemp,* a traditional New Year's hot beverage made with milk, tea, sugar, and spices. Traditional baked specialties include *knijpertjes,* or 'clothespins,' which have been popular since the Middle Ages, and a long decorative loaf known as *duivekater.* These and other holiday cakes and pastries are served with slemp, which was originally sold to skaters from stalls on the ice-covered canals.

In Zeeland, Overijssel, and other areas, boys go from house to house ringing bells and wishing people a Happy New Year. Sometimes they bang on a homemade drum called a *rommelpot,* or 'rumble pot,' and beg for pennies. It is possible that the rommelpot was originally intended to frighten away evil spirits at the start of the New Year.

SOURCES:
BkFest-1937, p. 240
FestWestEur-1958, p. 121

♦ 1303 ♦ New Year's Eve
December 31

The last day of the year is usually greeted with mixed emotions—joy and anticipation on the one hand, melancholy and regret on the other. Some celebrate by attending midnight church services, while others congregate in public places like Times Square in New York City, or Trafalgar Square in London, Glasgow's George Square or Edinburgh's Iron Kirk to count down the closing seconds of the old year. In the United States, people congregate at parties, some lasting all night, and many people spend New Year's Eve in front of the television watching other people celebrate. In recent years, celebrations in time zones other than Eastern have also been televised, so viewers nationwide can celebrate four times in one night, if they wish.

In Scotland, December 31 is known as **Old Year's Night**, or HOGMANAY. Although there are a number of theories about the derivation of the name, the tradition it refers to involves handing out pieces of oat-cake to poor children, who go from door to door calling out "Hogmanay!" In the United States, the Scottish song "Auld Lang Syne," with lyrics by poet Robert BURNS, is sung at almost every New Year's Eve celebration, while in London, the Scots at St. Paul's Churchyard toast and sing.

In Denmark the New Year is "shot in" with a thunderous explosion of fireworks, rockets, and Chinese pistols. In the villages, young people play pranks such as those done on HALLOWEEN in the United States.

Iceland has bonfires to clean up trash, and elf dances because elves are believed to be about on this night and might want to stop and rest on their way.

Neapolitans believe it brings luck to throw pots and dishes out the windows at midnight.

On the last two days of the year in Japan, a fire watch is implemented to prepare for the New Year, their most important holiday. Young men gather into groups then go to separate parts of the towns. They carry a clapper which they sound every few yards, crying out, "take care with fire."

Armenian families spend the night at home feasting. During the celebration, the neighbors, one at a time, lower a basket of presents down the chimney, then it is the recipients' turn to go to their neighbors.

Romanian boys used to go around to their neighbors with a *plugusorul,* a little plough, which is a remnant of the Roman OPALIA, the festival to the goddess of abundance, Ops. Later they changed to a homemade drum that sounds like a bull, which is what pulls the plough through the meadow. They ring cow bells and crack whips and recite hundreds of verses of their country story at the top of their lungs.

See also FIRST NIGHT and OMISOKA

SOURCES:
AmerBkDays-1978, p. 1166
BkDays-1864, vol. II, p. 787
BkFest-1937, pp. 63, 99, 117, 306, 335
DaysCustFaith-1957, p. 325
DictFolkMyth-1984, pp. 12, 842, 1100
FestSaintDays-1915, p. 256
FestWestEur-1958, pp. 21, 30, 84, 149, 159, 187, 209, 242
FolkAmerHol-1991, p. 1
FolkWrldHol-1992, p. 647
GdWrldFest-1985, p. 168

♦ 1304 ♦ New Year's Eve in Brazil
January 31

One of the most exotic NEW YEAR'S EVE celebrations in the world takes place along the beaches of Brazil—particularly Copacabana Beach in Rio de Janeiro, where thousands of believers in Umbanda, a religion practiced in Brazil, meet to pay homage to the ocean goddess Iemanjá (or Yemanjá). Dressed in white and carrying fresh flowers, candles, and *cachaça* (sugarcane alcohol), they flock to the beach around 10 o'clock and lay out tablecloths surrounded by candles and covered with gifts for the goddess. Animal sacrifices are not uncommon.

The ceremony reaches its peak at midnight, when everyone rushes into the water—shrieking, sobbing, or singing—carrying their flowers and gifts for Iemanjá. If the waves carry their gifts out to sea, it means that the goddess was satisfied and they can go home happy. It is considered an ill omen if the ocean throws back their gifts.

See also IEMANJÁ FESTIVAL

CONTACT:
Brazilian Embassy
3006 Massachusetts Ave., N.W.
Washington, D.C. 20008
202-745-2700; fax: 202-745-2827

♦ 1305 ♦ New Year's Eve in Ecuador
December 31

Many Ecuadorians celebrate the Old Year, Año Viejo, on December 31 by stuffing an old shirt and pair of pants with straw and sewing them together to make an effigy of a man. With a hat on his head, a pipe in his mouth, and a cane in his hand, the scarecrow figure sits in a chair in front of the house, sometimes under an arch made of cypress branches. Someone draws up a mock "last will and testament" listing various family members' faults that must be done away with. At midnight, or earlier if there are small children in the house, someone reads the will aloud and everyone makes jokes about its contents. Then the straw figure is lit with a match, and the faults of the Old Year go up in flames. Sometimes the old man's "widow" goes from house to house, dressed in black and begging for contributions to charity.

After the straw men have burned and the widows have come in from the streets, everyone sits down to enjoy the spiced foods typically served on this night. The most popular is a crisp fried pastry in the shape of a doughnut, which is dipped into a brown sugar syrup.

SOURCES:
BkFestHolWrld-1970, p. 16
BkHolWrld-1986, Dec 31

♦ 1306 ♦ New Year's Eve in Germany (Silvesterabend)
December 31

In different areas of Germany, it is considered lucky to eat certain foods on the last night of the old year. Carp is served frequently, not only in homes but in fashionable city restaurants. Another favorite is *Silvesterabend* punch, a hot drink made from red wine flavored with cinnamon and sugar. *Feuerzangenbowle*, or 'fire tongs punch,' has special cones of sugar, soaked in liquor, suspended over the punch bowl. When they are set aflame, the alcoholic sugar drips into the hot wine below. In Baden, a special dried pea soup is considered to bring good luck when served on New Year's Eve. Along the lower Rhine, "little New Year" yeast cookies are baked in the form of spiral wreaths, pretzels, or circles. Everyone leaves a bit of each food served on his or her plate until after midnight in the belief that it will ensure a well-stocked pantry in the coming year.

According to ancient Germanic folk belief, the only way to drive out demons, devils, and other evil spirits on the last night of the year is by making noise. Grown men can be seen riding hobby horses up and down the streets of German villages on New Year's Eve at midnight, and *Buttenmandl* ('Little Butten Men'), who are peasants dressed in straw clothing and deerskin animal masks, ring bells and drag clanking chains through the streets in an effort to drive out evil spirits. In the Bavarian Alps, shooting parties are still popular. Sometimes members of shooting societies will climb a mountain and shoot off 500 or more old mortars in unison. (*See* Christmas Shooting.)

New Year's pranks are common in Germany, such as chocolates with mustard inside, sugar lumps with spiders inside, and firework dogs that produce a string of black, sausage-like material when burned. Among young people, "lead-pouring" parties are popular. They drop a little melted lead

into a bowl of cold water and read each other's fortunes by interpreting the shapes the metal assumes.

SOURCES:
AmerBkDays-1978, p. 1166
FestWestEur-1958, p. 84
FolkWrldHol-1992, p. 648

♦ 1307 ♦ New Year's Eve in Spain
December 31

In Spain, it is customary for families to gather on New Year's Eve in small groups to celebrate the coming of the New Year. Shortly before midnight, bags or bunches of grapes are distributed. When midnight arrives, everyone eats one grape for each stroke of the clock. Eating all 12 grapes before the clock is finished striking ensures good luck in the New Year. The grapes are usually washed down with muscatel wine. So firmly entrenched is the grape-eating custom that in theaters and cinemas, the show is often interrupted at midnight on New Year's Eve so that the audience can eat the grapes and drink the wine they've brought with them.

New Year's Day is spent visiting family and friends, feasting, and exchanging cards and gifts. Eating and drinking well on this day is believed to guarantee an abundance of food and drink in the coming year.

SOURCES:
BkFest-1937, p. 297
DictFolkMyth-1984, p. 1063
FestWestEur-1958, p. 188
FolkWrldHol-1992, p. 6

♦ 1308 ♦ New York City Marathon
First Sunday in November

The New York City Marathon began in 1970 as a race four times around Central Park. But in 1976, Fred Lebow and the New York Road Runners Club, the world's largest running club and the race's sponsor, decided to get corporate support, invite top runners from all over the world, and to run the course through all five New York boroughs. Unlike the Boston Marathon, which is run primarily through the countryside and small towns, the New York course is urban, beginning at the tollbooth plaza at the end of the Verrazano-Narrows Bridge on Staten Island and progressing across the bridge through Brooklyn, Queens, Manhattan, and the Bronx before finishing in Manhattan's Central Park. About 25,000 runners compete in the race—including a number of handicapped competitors in wheelchairs—and over a million New Yorkers turn out to watch. In addition to cash prizes ranging from $20,000 for the first-place finishers to $2,500 for fifth place, more than $200,000 in bonuses are handed out each year.

The marathon has had a positive effect on New York City's public image, which has suffered because of its high crime rate and frequent clashes between ethnic groups. The runners who compete regularly in New York say that the crowds are enthusiastic and friendly, and city dwellers look upon it as a time to forget racial and ethnic differences and cheer the runners on.

Like most things in New York City, its marathon is amazing. Rosie Ruiz, well known for being disqualified for cheating in the Boston Marathon, was thrown out in New York for taking the subway to the finish line.

Then there's race organizer Fred Lebow: although an avid runner he had never run New York until he was struck by brain cancer. Then in 1992, the cancer in remission, this 60-year-old Romanian-born escapee from the Holocaust finally ran the 26.2 mile course. His companion on his heroic run was his good friend and nine-time New York winner, Grete Waitz of Norway. Lebow's time: 5 hours 32 minutes 34 seconds.

In 1992 Australian-born Lisa Ondieki set a new women's course record of 2:24:40 and won a $30,000 bonus in addition to the standard $20,000 purse and Mercedes-Benz automobile. Willie Mtolo, a 28-year-old Zulu from South Africa, won his first major international marathon in 1992. This was a special victory for him since he had been unable to compete outside his homeland until this year: South African athletes had suffered a 21-year political embargo. Mtolo's time: 2 hours 9 minutes 29 seconds.

CONTACT:
New York Convention and Visitors Bureau
2 Columbus Cir.
New York, NY 10019
800-692-8474 or 212-484-1200
fax: 212-247-6193

SOURCES:
Chases-1996, p. 440

♦ 1309 ♦ Nganja, Feast of
April

A harvest festival in Angola, the Feast of Nganja is primarily celebrated by children. On a day in April, when the harvest is ripe, they go out to their family fields and gather some fresh corn. In small groups they go to the woods, where they build campfires and roast their corn on the cob. But the real excitement of the feast lies in the game that is played while the corn is being cooked. Without warning, a child from one group may jump up and steal the corn from another. The robbing and plundering is good-natured, although there are always a few children who end up with no corn at all.

A similar children's feast held in Angola during the harvest months of February, March, and April is known as the Feast of Okambondondo. This all-night celebration is held indoors, with the girls doing all the cooking and the meal itself being served in the kitchen just before dawn.

SOURCES:
FolkWrldHol-1992, p. 444

♦ 1310 ♦ Nicaragua Independence Day
September 15

Nicaragua shares its independence day with four other Central American countries—Costa Rica, El Salvador, Guatemala, and Honduras—all of which declared their independence on September 15, 1821. There is a parade in the capital city of Managua, and the president and other public officials give speeches. Nicaraguans also celebrate Independence Day by attending cockfights and bullfights. But unlike bullfights in other countries, the Nicaraguan matador does not kill the bull. Instead, he tries to mount it and ride it rodeo-style.

CONTACT:
Nicaragua Embassy
1627 New Hampshire Ave., N.W.
Washington, D.C. 20009
202-939-6570; fax: 202-939-6542

SOURCES:
AnnivHol-1983, p. 119
Chases-1996, p. 378
NatlHolWrld-1968, p. 170

♦ 1311 ♦ Nice Carnival
Twelve days beginning between January 22 and February 25, ending on Shrove Tuesday

Dating back to the 14th century and deriving, some believe, from ancient rites of spring, the Carnival celebration in Nice, France, is one of the Mediterranean resort town's most picturesque spectacles. It actually begins about three weeks before Shrove Tuesday with the arrival of King Carnival. The next two Saturdays and Sundays are filled with processions, confetti battles, fireworks, and masked balls. The procession of floats, each accompanied by marchers or riders on horseback wearing elaborate costumes, draws the largest crowd. On Shrove Tuesday, King Carnival is burnt in effigy on a pyre.

CONTACT:
French Government Tourist Office
9454 Wilshire Blvd., Ste. 715
Beverly Hills, CA 90212
310-271-6665; fax: 310-276-2835

SOURCES:
AmerBkDays-1978, p. 43
BkFest-1937, p. 120
BkFestHolWrld-1970, p. 33
BkHolWrld-1986, Feb 20
Chases-1996, p. 91
DictFolkMyth-1984, p. 192
FestWestEur-1958, p. 34

♦ 1312 ♦ Nigeria National Day
October 1

Also known as **Independence Day**, this national holiday commemorates the new autonomy of Nigeria that officially began October 1, 1960, after being under British control since 1900. Nigeria became a federal republic with a new constitution on October 1, 1963. In 1966 some military officers staged a coup and ruled until other army officers overthrew them in 1975. Civilian rule was restored on the anniversary of freedom, October 1, 1979.

CONTACT:
Nigerian Embassy
1333 16th St., N.W.
Washington, D.C. 20036
202-986-8400; fax: 202-775-1385

SOURCES:
Chases-1996, p. 400
NatlHolWrld-1968, p. 183

♦ 1313 ♦ Niger Republic Day
December 18

On August 3, 1960, Niger gained full independence from France, after having been a colony since 1922. Niger had voted to become a republic on December 18, 1958. August 3 is a national holiday celebrating **Independence Day**, while December 18 observes Republic Day.

CONTACT:
Niger Embassy
2204 R St., N.W.
Washington, D.C. 20008
202-483-4224; fax: 202-483-3169

SOURCES:
AnnivHol-1983, pp. 102, 162
Chases-1996, p. 484
NatlHolWrld-1968, p. 228

♦ 1314 ♦ Night of the Radishes
December 23

A festival that dates from the 19th century that combines art, agriculture, and religion. It is held in the *zócalo*, or main square, in Oaxaca, Mexico, 300 miles south of Mexico City. The radish made its first appearance here during the Spanish colonial period, and in commemoration Oaxaqueños carve them into elaborate shapes and display them on **La Noche de Ratanos**. The radishes, the same red-skinned, white-fleshed roots commonly eaten in salads, grow to yam-size here and are each uniquely shaped by growing through the rocky soil.

Indian families harvest these vegetables, combine and sculpt them into elaborate forms and complex scenes depicting biblical scenes, especially the nativity of Jesus. Historical and Aztec themes are also represented. After the awarding of cash prizes and ribbons, a fireworks display caps the night.

During the festival and throughout the CHRISTMAS season, another custom is observed: people buy small pottery bowls filled with sweet fried dough called *buñuelos.* After they eat the dough, they fling the bowl violently to the ground. The walks become thick with pottery shards.

CONTACT:
Mexican Government Tourist
  Office
405 Park Ave., Ste. 1401
New York, NY 10022
800-446-3942 or 212-755-7261
fax: 212-753-2874

SOURCES:
BkHolWrld-1986, Dec 23
Chases-1996, p. 487
IntlThFolk-1979, p. 274

♦ 1315 ♦ Night of the Shooting Stars
Visibility peaks around August 10–12

Meteors, also called shooting stars or falling stars, are seen as streaks of light in the sky that result when a small chunk of stony or metallic matter enters the Earth's atmosphere and vaporizes. A meteor shower occurs when a number of meteors enter the Earth's atmosphere at approximately the same time and place. The shower's name is usually derived from the constellation (or a star within it) from which the shower appears to originate.

Since the year 830 there has been an annual meteor shower known as the **Perseids** (because it appears to originate in the constellation Perseus) that is most observable during the nights of August 10–12. Observers everywhere except the South Pole can see as many as 60 meteors an hour streak across the sky on what is often referred to as the "Night of the Shooting Stars."

SOURCES:
BkHolWrld-1986, Aug 11
Chases-1996, p. 330

♦ 1316 ♦ Night Watch
July 13

La Retraite aux Flambeaux, or the Night Watch, is a half-holiday in France that is celebrated on the eve of BASTILLE DAY. The lights in Paris are darkened in remembrance of the day in 1789 when the Bastille fell. Colorful processions of soldiers, patriotic bands, and people bearing torches and Chinese lanterns march through the streets, followed by crowds of spectators. The procession usually ends at the home of a prominent citizen, who offers the torch- and lantern-bearers something to drink.

CONTACT:
French Government Tourist Office
9454 Wilshire Blvd., Ste. 715
Beverly Hills, CA 90212
310-271-6665; fax: 310-276-2835

SOURCES:
AnnivHol-1983, p. 93
BkFest-1937, p. 125
Chases-1996, p. 295

♦ 1317 ♦ Niman Festival
July

The Niman, or **Going Home Ceremony,** takes place in the

Hopi Indian pueblos of northeastern Arizona. After entering the pueblos in February, the *katchinas,* or ancestral spirits (impersonated by men wearing elaborate masks), leave again in July. During the six months when they are present in the pueblo (*see* POWAMÛ FESTIVAL), the katchinas appear in a series of dances, of which the Niman is the last. For the Going Home Ceremony, up to 75 dancers representing katchinas spend an entire day singing and dancing. They give bows, arrows, and other gifts to the boys and katchina dolls to the girls before returning to their mountain homes.

CONTACT:
Hopi Tribal Council
P.O. Box 123
Kykotsmovi, AZ 86039
602-734-2445

SOURCES:
BkHolWrld-1986, Jul 26, 178
DictFolkMyth-1984, p. 566,
  793
EncyRel-1987, vol. 10, p. 520

♦ 1318 ♦ Nine Imperial Gods, Festival of the
First nine days of ninth lunar month

As celebrated today in Singapore, the Festival of the Nine Imperial Gods derives from an ancient Chinese cleansing ritual. The festival begins with a procession to a river or the sea to invite the Nine Imperial Gods to descend from the heavens into an urn filled with burning benzoin. The urn is then carried to the temple and put in a place where only Taoist priests and Buddhist monks are allowed to enter. Nine oil lamps representing the gods are hung from a bamboo pole in front of the temple. They are lowered and then raised again to signify that the gods have arrived. The ground below the lamps is purified every morning and afternoon with holy water. Worshippers enter the temple by crossing a specially constructed bridge, symbolizing the belief that they are leaving the evils of the past year behind.

Chinese operas known as *wayang* shows—some of which take two or more days to complete—are often performed during the nine days of the festival. On the ninth day, the sacred urn with the burning ashes is brought out of the temple and taken in procession back to the water's edge, where it is placed in a boat. The observers wait for the boat to move, indicating that the gods have departed—but what often happens is that other boats turn on their engines to churn up the water and send the gods on their way.

CONTACT:
Singapore Tourist Promotion
  Board
590 Fifth Ave., 12th Floor
New York, NY 10036
212-302-4861; fax: 212-302-4801

SOURCES:
FolkWrldHol-1992, p. 497

♦ 1319 ♦ Nippy Lug Day
*Between February 6 and March 12; Friday
following Shrove Tuesday*

A "lug" at one time referred to the ear-flap of a man's cap, but in Scotland and northern England it became a synonym for the ear itself. In 19th-century Scotland, schoolchildren called their teachers "nip-lugs" because they often pulled their pupils' ears as a disciplinary measure. In Westmorland, England, it was traditional at one time for children to pinch each other's ears on the Friday following SHROVE TUESDAY, giving rise to the name Nippy Lug Day.

SOURCES:
DictDays-1988, p. 82

♦ 1320 ♦ **Nirjala Ekadashi**
May–June; 11th day of waxing half of Hindu month of Jyestha

Of the 24 Ekadashi or 11th-day fasts observed during the course of the Hindu year, Nirjala Ekadashi is one of the more important. No food or even water is taken on this day, which is an act of extreme devotion since the month of Jyestha is very hot. Both men and women observe a strict fast and offer *puja* (worship) to Vishnu to ensure happiness and forgiveness of their sins. *Panchamrata* is prepared by mixing together milk, ghee (clarified butter), curds, honey, and sugar. It is then offered to the image of Vishnu, which has been draped in rich clothing and jewels, with a fan placed beside it. Hindus meditate on Vishnu as the Lord of the Universe and worship the deity with flowers, lamps, water, and incense.

Some Hindus believe that faithful observance of the fast and other rituals on Nirjala Ekadashi ensures happiness, salvation, longevity, and prosperity. Those who can afford to do so give clothes, grains, umbrellas, fans, and pitchers filled with water to the Brahmans.

See also Amalaka Ekadashi

SOURCES:
RelHolCal-1993, p. 99

♦ 1321 ♦ **Nisei Week**
August

An annual Japanese-American festival in the Little Tokyo area of Los Angeles, Calif. Little Tokyo is the social, cultural, and economic center for the Japanese and Nisei community of southern California. The Nisei are people of Japanese descent born and raised in the United States. Held since the 1940s, this festival features a parade, a carnival, Japanese folk dancing, celebrity appearances, and a prince and princess pageant. There are special exhibits of bonsai, flower arranging, doll making, tea ceremonies, and other Japanese arts. Sports competitions and demonstrations include jiu-jitsu and karate. Attendance is about 50,000.

CONTACT:
Los Angeles Convention and Visitors Bureau
633 W. Fifth St., Ste. 6000
Los Angeles, CA 90071
800-228-2452 or 213-624-7300
fax: 213-624-9746

Noc Swietego Andreja
See **St. Andrew's Eve**

Nones
See **Ides**

♦ 1322 ♦ **Nordic Fest**
Last full weekend in July

The Nordic Fest held annually in Decorah, Iowa, prides itself on preserving the area's Norwegian heritage without resorting to commercialism. From Friday night through Sunday of the last full weekend in July, the festival offers arts and crafts displays, lectures, concerts, sporting events, dances, and museum visits. Both the Norwegian-American Museum and the Porter House Museum are open to visitors, and there is a walking tour of the Home of the Trolls—a troll being the Norwegian version of the pixie or elf. The festival begins with a parade and Norse Fire Celebration, and the events that follow are all designed to highlight a particular aspect of Decorah's Norwegian heritage. Scandinavian dancers perform, Norse plays are put on for the children, and special Norwegian and English church services are held.

The festival has been held annually in Decorah since 1967. The Luther College Women's Club had sponsored a Scandinavian Festival Day since 1936, and eventually it was expanded to the present three-day event.

CONTACT:
Iowa Tourism Office
200 E. Grand Ave.
Des Moines, IA 50309
800-345-4692 or 515-242-4705
fax: 515-242-4749

SOURCES:
GdUSFest-1984, p. 55

♦ 1323 ♦ **Norsk Høstfest**
October

All five Scandinavian countries—Denmark, Finland, Iceland, Norway, and Sweden—are represented at the annual Scandinavian heritage festival known as Norsk Høstfest that has been held in Minot, North Dakota, since 1978. The festival includes performances by top entertainers, one of whom is selected by the previous year's ticketholders as the "People's Choice" and many of whom are either Scandinavian or Americans of Scandinavian descent. There are also Swedish accordion players, Scandinavian folk dancers, and Lakota flute players, who perform at the Høstfest complex on North Dakota's state fairgrounds in Minot. The complex includes five stages, 40 food booths, and dozens of demonstration areas for craftsmen and artisans—among them the highly skilled *rosemalers*, or 'folk painters'. The Viking Age Club sets up an authentic encampment to show how the North Plains Scandinavian settlers lived.

Food is a big part of the five-day festival, which features traditional Scandinavian delicacies. More than 60,000 visitors come to Minot to sample Swedish sweet bread, *søt suppe* (fruit soup), *potet klub* (potato dumpling), Icelandic cake, *rømmergrøt* ('red porridge', a rhubarb pudding), Danish kringle (pretzel-shaped cookie), *lefse* (a thin, sweet cake spread with butter and cinnamon and folded over), and *lutefisk* (boiled cod). A similar Scandinavian festival, the Hjemkomst Festival, is held in June in Fargo.

CONTACT:
North Dakota Tourism
604 E. Boulevard Ave.
Liberty Memorial Bldg.
Bismarck, ND 58505
800-435-5663 or 701-328-2525
fax: 701-328-4878

SOURCES:
Chases-1996, p. 418

♦ 1324 ♦ **North American Indian Days**
Second week in July

One of the largest gatherings of United States and Canadian

Indian tribes, held in Browning, Montana, the hub of the Blackfeet Indian Reservation in the northwest mountains of the state. Teepees are pitched on the powwow grounds for four days of traditional Indian dancing, games, sports events, and socializing. There are also exhibits of arts and crafts—beadwork, quill and feather work, moccasins and other leather goods.

CONTACT:
Blackfeet Nation
P.O. Box 850
Browning, MT 59417
406-338-7276

SOURCES:
IndianAmer-1989, p. 23

♦ 1325 ♦ **Northern Games**
Mid-July

A showcase for traditional Inuit and Indian sports and culture, the Northern Games are held in the Northwest Territories of Canada for four days in July each year. They feature traditional dances, drumming competitions, arts and crafts displays, and the "Good Woman" Contest, which gives Northern women a chance to demonstrate their skill in such areas as animal skinning and bannock baking. The games are held in a different part of the Northwest Territories each year, and draw competitors from Alaska, Yukon Territory, and Labrador as well.

CONTACT:
Northwest Territories Tourism
P.O. Box 1320
Yellowknife, NWT
Canada X1A 2L9
800-661-0788 or 403-873-7200

SOURCES:
GdWrldFest-1985, p. 42

♦ 1326 ♦ **North Pole Winter Carnival**
Early March

A weekend to celebrate winter in North Pole, Alaska, a suburb of Fairbanks. North Pole was named by Con Miller, a man who bought a Fairbanks trading post in 1949. When he cleaned it out, he found a Santa Claus suit and started wearing it on trips to the interior to buy furs and sell supplies. A few years later he built a new trading post southeast of Fairbanks, called it Santa Claus House, and named the town around it North Pole. The town now has a government and a post office. It also has the winter carnival which features the North Pole Championship Sled Dog Race, a dog weight-pulling contest, carnival rides and games, food booths, crafts bazaars, and live entertainment.

CONTACT:
Fairbanks Convention and Visitors
  Bureau
550 First Ave.
Fairbanks, AK 99701
800-327-5774 or 907-456-5774
fax: 907-452-2867

♦ 1327 ♦ **Northwest Folklife Festival**
May, Memorial Day weekend

An international four-day festival started in 1972 in Seattle,

Wash., that draws performers and artisans from Washington, Oregon, Idaho, Alaska, and the province of British Columbia. The emphasis is on amateur performers and ethnicity with some 55 ethnic groups represented. Events include music and dance on 20 stages; demonstrations by artisans of such skills as leather tanning, boatbuilding, blacksmithing, and broom making; and an Ethnic Food Village that offers food from more than 30 nations.

The festival spans the Memorial Day weekend, starting on Friday and winding up on Monday.

CONTACT:
Seattle-King County Convention
  and Visitors Bureau
520 Pike St., Ste. 1300
Seattle, WA 98101
360-461-5800; fax: 360-461-5855

SOURCES:
Chases-1996, p. 226
MusFestAmer-1990, p. 230

♦ 1328 ♦ **Norway Constitution Day**
May 17

May 17, 1814, marks both Norway's declaration of independence from Sweden and the day on which its constitution was signed. At that time however, the king of Sweden still ruled Norway and true independence didn't come until 1905, when the union with Sweden was dissolved and Norway chose its own king. Nevertheless this day remains the great spring festival in Norway, and today it is celebrated primarily by young people. The children's procession in Oslo, the capital city, is the largest of many school parades throughout the country. Marching behind their school bands and banners, the children pass under the balcony of the Royal Palace in salute to the King. Students who are about to graduate from secondary school and enter college cheer and spin their tasseled caps in the air on bamboo canes. In the afternoon, many neighborhoods have celebrations of their own so that children who are too young to participate in the school parades may march near their homes. Everyone joins in the procession, waving Norwegian flags, leading dogs, and pushing baby carriages. Eventually they congregate in the town square to listen to patriotic speeches and play games.

May 17 has been celebrated since the 1820s and is sometimes referred to as **Norway's National Day** or **Norway's Liberation Day**.

CONTACT:
Norwegian Tourist Board
655 Third Ave., 18th Floor
New York, NY 10017
212-949-2333; fax: 212-983-5260

SOURCES:
AnnivHol-1983, p. 67
BkHolWrld-1986, May 17
Chases-1996, p. 216
NatlHolWrld-1968, p. 64

♦ 1329 ♦ **Nuestra Senora de Peñafrancia, Feast of**
Third week of September

A grand fiesta devoted to Our Lady of Peñafrancia, held in Naga City on the Bicol peninsula in the Philippines. Some 200 years ago a Spanish official attributed the recovery of his ill daughter to the lady and built a shrine to her in Naga City, starting the devotion to her that has lasted into the present.

This is the biggest festival of the Bicol region; it starts with a nine-day novena at the Naga Cathedral. A procession then carries the image of the Virgin to a pagoda on a festooned barge, which is surrounded by a flotilla of smaller boats. The people on the smaller boats chant prayers and hymns as they proceed along the river. Meanwhile, on the shore, pilgrims from other Bicol provinces kneel and pray as the barge passes by. When the water-borne pagoda has finished its journey, there are shouts of "Viva la virgen!" and the image is taken back to its shrine.

CONTACT:
Philippine Department of Tourism
556 Fifth Ave.
First Floor Mezzanine
New York, NY 10036
212-575-7915; fax: 212-302-6759

◆ 1330 ◆ **Nyambinyambi**
Spring

The annual planting festival called the **Rain-Calling Ceremony**, or Nyambinyambi, is observed by the Kwangali people of Namibia, who believe that the land must be cleansed before the rain can fall and the fields can be planted. The chief sends his grandson out to cut down a tree, which is erected at the entrance gate to the village. The people lay their planting tools, seeds, pumpkins, and hunting weapons at the base of the tree and pray to the god known as Karunga, or Kalunga, to bring them a plentiful harvest and a good hunting season. In the Songhay's region of Niger, this is called **Genji Bi Hori**, 'Black Spirit Festival'. They also pray that rain will fall soon after the ceremony, which is believed to rid the country of bad luck.

The Songhay rain-bringing ceremony is held at the end of the hot-dry season. Known as **Yenaandi** ('the act of cooling off') or the **Rain Dance**, it is usually held on a Thursday, the *Tooru* ('gods') sacred day, and is addressed to the four principal Tooru deities: Dongo, the god of thunder; Cirey, the god of lightning; Moussa Nyori, the god of clouds and wind; and Hausakoy, the god of blacksmithing.

CONTACT:
Niger Embassy
2204 R St., N.W.
Washington, D.C. 20008
202-483-4224; fax: 202-483-3169

SOURCES:
FolkWrldHol-1992, p. 226

◆ 1331 ◆ **Nyepi**
About March 21

The people of Bali in Indonesia celebrate the Vernal Equinox and the New Year by driving the devils out of the villages and then observing a day of stillness, known as Nyepi or Njepi. It is believed that when spring arrives and the rainy season ends, the Lord of Hell, Yama, sweeps the devils out of Hades, which then fall on Bali making it necessary to purify the entire island. First the evil spirits are lured out of their hiding places with an elaborate offering of food, drink, money, and household utensils. Samples of every seed and fruit and of every animal used as food are all laid out in an eight-point star representing the Rose of the Winds. Then the evil spirits are driven out of the village by the strong incantations and curses of the priests, and by the people who run through the streets with their faces and bodies painted, lighting firecrackers, carrying torches, beating the trees and the ground, and banging drums, tin cans, and anything else they can find to make noise to drive the demons away. Cockfighting plays an important role in the ceremony, because blood is believed to cleanse the impure earth.

The following day, Nyepi, marks the start of the New Year and the arrival of spring. It is observed with the suspension of all activity: no cooking or fires, no sexual intercourse, and no work of any kind are permitted.

CONTACT:
Indonesian Tourist Promotion
    Office
3457 Wilshire Blvd., Ste. 104
Los Angeles, CA 90010
213-387-2078; fax: 213-380-4876

SOURCES:
FolkWrldHol-1992, p. 184

O

♦ 1332 ♦ Oakley Festival, Annie
Last full week in July

The legendary markswoman known as Annie Oakley was born Phoebe Ann Moses near Willow Dell, Ohio, on August 13, 1860. Her father died when she was very young, and Annie learned to shoot game for her family with her father's rifle. At the age of 15 she was invited to participate in a shooting match in Cincinnati with Frank Butler, a champion marksman. She won the match and married Butler a year later. Together they toured the country with their shooting act, "Butler and Oakley," and in 1884 they joined Buffalo Bill's Wild West Show. They performed with the show throughout Europe and the United States for 17 years, including a command performance for Queen Victoria during her Jubilee year (1887). Annie and Frank returned to Ohio in the 1920s to be near their family and friends. She died in Greenville on November 3, 1926, and he died 18 days later.

The Annie Oakley Festival in Greenville commemorates "Little Miss Sure Shot" (as she was dubbed by the great Sioux Indian chief, Sitting Bull) with eight days of shooting and sports competitions and demonstrations of hide tanning, knife throwing, bead working, and other activities associated with the Old West. There is a tour of Annie Oakley's gravesite and a Miss Annie Oakley Shooting Contest for young girls. A highlight of the festival is the Annie Oakley Days Parade on the last day.

CONTACT:
Ohio Division of Travel and
  Tourism
P.O. Box 1001
Columbus, OH 43266
800-282-5393 or 614-466-8844
fax: 614-466-6744

SOURCES:
Chases-1996, p. 309

♦ 1333 ♦ Oath Monday
July

A centuries-old custom in Ulm, Germany, that combines politics and pageantry. Each year in July, the burgomaster, or mayor, gives a policy speech in the market square, listens to the public discussions, and then, after the ringing of a bell, takes an oath swearing to stand "for rich and poor" in all matters "of the public weal."

Events then shift to the Danube River and a waterborne parade called the *Nabada*. Rafts and boats are decorated with tableaux of papier-mâché figures that satirize local and regional politics. With them are floating bands and private boats. Later, back on land, a medieval pageant is presented.

The oath-taking began in 1397 when the city was on the verge of bankruptcy. The nobles, who had been running the city, agreed to sit down with representatives of the guilds— groups of merchants and craftsmen. At the close of the negotiations, the guilds had a majority on the city council, the citizens had the right to a hearing before major city decisions were made, and the Solemn Oath was established, ending the privileges of the aristocracy.

CONTACT:
German National Tourist Office
122 E. 42nd St., 52nd Floor
New York, NY 10168
212-661-7200; fax: 212-661-7174

♦ 1334 ♦ Oberammergau Passion Play
May through September, once every decade in
years ending in zero

The most famous of Passion Plays, held since the 17th century in the small woodcarving village of Oberammergau, Germany, in the Bavarian Alps.

The play, depicting the story of Christ's suffering, crucifixion, and resurrection, is presented in six hours by a cast of about 1,500. All performers are villagers, and the 600 with speaking parts are required to have been born in Oberammergau. The role of Mary is traditionally played by an unmarried woman. Close to half a million people attend the productions, which are staged in an open-air theater seating 5,000.

Legend says that the play was first performed in 1634 in fulfillment of a vow. The plague was sweeping Europe, and the Oberammergau elders swore to God that they would reenact the Passion of Christ if he would spare the remaining villagers; already a fifth of the population had been lost. The plague passed by, and the play has been performed since then (shifting to decennial years in 1700), except in 1870 during the Franco-Prussian War and during World War II.

In modern times, the play has aroused protests that the 1860 text has anti-Semitic overtones.

CONTACT:
German National Tourist Office
122 E. 42nd St., 52nd Floor
New York, NY 10168
212-661-7200; fax: 212-661-7174

SOURCES:
GdWrldFest-1985, p. 86
IntlThFolk-1979, p. 146

◆ 1335 ◆ Obon Festival
July 13–15; August 13–15

Also called the **Festival of the Dead**, this is the time when the dead revisit the earth, according to Japanese Buddhist belief. Throughout Japan, in either July or August, depending on the area, religious rites and family reunions are held in memory of the dead. On the first evening of the festival, small bonfires are lit outside homes to welcome the spirits of ancestors. A meal, usually vegetables, rice cakes, and fruit, is set out for the spirits, and for two days they are spoken to as though they were present. On the final day (July 15 or Aug. 15), farewell dumplings are prepared, and another bonfire is lit outside the house to guide the spirits back. The climax is the *Bon-Odori*, or 'Dance of Rejoicing,' folk dances held in every town by the light of paper lanterns, to comfort the souls of the dead. Some Bon-Odori dances are especially famous—one being the **Awa Odori** of Tokushima, which is accompanied by puppet shows and groups of musicians parading night and day.

At midnight some families gather the left-over rice cakes and food and take them to the waterfront. They are placed in a two- or three-foot-long boat made of rice straw with a rice straw sail; a lit paper lantern is on the bow and burning joss sticks at the stern. The breeze carries the boats, sustaining the spirits on their outward trip.

Obon celebrations are also held in Japanese communities throughout the world. About 500 people usually take part in the Bon-Odori in Chicago in July, and there are noted celebrations in several California cities.

CONTACT:
Japan National Tourist
Organization
630 Fifth Ave., Ste. 2101
New York, NY 10111
212-757-5640; fax: 212-307-6754

SOURCES:
AmerBkDays-1978, p. 501
BkFest-1937, pp. 80, 200
BkHolWrld-1986, Jul 13
DictFolkMyth-1984, pp. 154,
    155, 541, 542, 730, 812, 1051
DictWrldRel-1989, pp. 31,
    135, 374
FolkAmerHol-1991, p. 273
FolkWrldHol-1992, p. 389
IntlThFolk-1979, p. 261
RelHolCal-1993, p. 99

◆ 1336 ◆ Obzinky
Late August or early September

There are two harvest celebrations in the Czech and Slovak Republics. One of them, known as **Posviceni**, is the church consecration of the harvest. The other, Obzinky, is a secular festival where the field workers celebrate the end of the harvest by making a wreath out of corn, ears of wheat or rye, and wildflowers. Sometimes the wreath is placed on the head of a pretty young girl, and sometimes it is placed in a wagon along with decorated rakes and scythes and pulled in procession to the home of the landowner. The laborers present the wreath and congratulate their employer on a good harvest, after which they are invited to participate in dancing and feasting at the farm owner's expense. Foods served at the feast traditionally include roast pig, roast goose, and *Kolace*—square cakes filled with plum jam or a stuffing made from sweetened cheese or poppy seed. Beer and *slivovice*, a prune liquor, accompany the food.

The woman who binds the last sheaf is known as the *Baba*, or 'old woman', in some areas. In others, the Baba is a doll made from the last sheaf of grain and decorated with ribbons and flowers. Like the wreath, the Baba is carried in procession to the landlord's home, where it occupies a place of honor until the next harvest.

A similar harvest festival, known as the **Nubaigai**, is held in Lithuania. Here, too, a Baba is borne in procession to the farm; sometimes the worker who bound the last sheaf is wrapped up in it. But the harvest wreath is carried on a plate covered with a white linen cloth, and as the procession advances, the reapers sing an old song about how they rescued the crop from a huge bison that tried to devour it.

SOURCES:
BkFest-1937, p. 90
FolkWrldHol-1992, p. 447

◆ 1337 ◆ Octave of Our Lady, Consoler of the Afflicted
April–May; begins fifth Sunday after Easter

The Octave of **Notre Dame la Consolatrice des Affligés** is observed in Luxembourg beginning on the fifth Sunday after EASTER and lasting from eight to 15 days. Since 1666, when Luxembourg-Ville was dedicated to the patronage of Mary the Consolatrice and the keys of the city were entrusted to her statue in the cathedral, she has been regarded as the capital city's protector, and her festival is the country's most outstanding religious celebration. Colorful banners are hung across the streets, and the route of the procession is lined with fir trees. Brass bands, Boy Scouts, Girl Guides, school and church groups, and small children dressed as priests, bishops, and cardinals start the procession, scattering rose petals. The image of the Virgin follows, dressed in dark blue velvet embroidered with gold and jewels. The symbolic key of Luxembourg-Ville hangs from one of her wrists.

According to legend, the statue was discovered in a hollow oak in 1624 by some Jesuit students. They took it to the Jesuit college church (now the cathedral) and placed it on the altar. That night the figure vanished mysteriously and was later found in the oak. The same thing occurred a second time, at which point the church fathers realized that the Virgin wished to remain outside the fortress walls. They built a tiny chapel for the image in 1625, which became a pilgrimage center. The chapel was destroyed in the French Revolution, but the image was miraculously saved and eventually installed in the cathedral's main altar. When Napoleon I made his triumphal entry into the fortress after the Revolution, a little girl officially presented him with the keys on a crimson cushion. "Take them back," he told her. "They are in good hands."

CONTACT:
Luxembourg National Tourist
Office
17 Beekman Pl.
New York, NY 10022
212-935-8888; fax: 212-935-5896

SOURCES:
FestWestEur-1958, p. 109

♦ 1338 ♦ **October Horse Sacrifice**
October 15

In ancient Rome, a chariot race was held in the Field of Mars on October 15. After the race was over, the right-hand horse of the winning chariot was killed as a sacrifice to Mars. The head was cut off first, and there was a fight between the inhabitants of two different quarters of the city to see who could seize the head and place it in a designated spot. As soon as the tail was cut off, it was rushed to the king's hearth so that the blood would fall on the hearth. The rest of the blood was preserved until April 21, when it was mixed with other blood in a special ceremony and given to shepherds to burn, since they believed that the smoke would purify their flocks (*see* PARILIA).

The symbolic elements of the October Horse Sacrifice—the race, the choice of the right-hand horse, the blood, the hearth, and the necklace of loaves that was hung around the horse's head—all have strong associations with fertility. Although the horse sacrifice may have started out as a fertility rite, however, it later became a martial one.

SOURCES:
DictFolkMyth-1984, p. 811

♦ 1339 ♦ **October War of Liberation Anniversary**
October 6

In Syria, the anniversary of the Arab-Israeli War of 1973 is celebrated on October 6, the day the hostilities started with a surprise attack by Syrian and Egyptian forces that caught the Israelis off guard during the Jewish fast of YOM KIPPUR. Although the Arab armies were turned back, they inflicted heavy casualties on Israel and reclaimed some of the land they had lost in the Six-Day War. Also known as **Tishrin**—after the month of October in which the war started—the celebration tends to play up the Arab soldiers' role in the war with special television broadcasts glorifying the conflict, art exhibits, plays, films, concerts, rallies, and wreath-laying ceremonies. No mention is made of the fact that 6,000 Syrians died in the conflict, or that Israeli troops reached the outskirts of Damascus.

In Egypt, October 6 is ARMED FORCES DAY, commemorating the Egyptians' role in the October War. Anwar Sadat, the hero of that war, was assassinated on October 6, 1981, while viewing the Armed Forces Day parade.

CONTACT:
Syrian Embassy
2215 Wyoming Ave., N.W.
Washington, D.C. 20008
202-232-6313; fax: 202-234-9548

♦ 1340 ♦ **Odo Festival**
December–August, biannually

The Odo festival marks the return of the dead (*odo*) to visit the living in the northern Igbo villages of Nigeria. Lasting in some places from December until August, the festival has three distinct stages: the arrival of the odo, their stay with the living, and their departure. The first stage is observed with ritual celebrations and festivities welcoming the returning spirits of the dead. Then there is a stretch of six or more months during which the spirits of the dead interact with their living relatives and visit their ancestral homes. Their final departure is a very emotional affair (*see* AWURU ODO FESTIVAL), since they will not return for two more years.

Odo plays, featuring certain stock characters identified by their costumes and the manner in which they interact with the audience, are usually performed at the return and staying stages of the odo journey. Most of the roles are played by men, while the women function as chorus members and sometimes as spectators. The performers wear costumes traditionally made from plant fiber, leaves, beads, and feathers, although more durable cloth costumes are becoming more common in contemporary Odo plays. A musical accompaniment, featuring xylophones, drums and rattles, is known as *obilenu* music, meaning 'that which lies above.'

CONTACT:
Nigerian Embassy
1333 16th St., N.W.
Washington, D.C. 20036
202-986-8400; fax: 202-775-1385

SOURCES:
FolkWrldHol-1992, pp. 218, 575

♦ 1341 ♦ **Odwira**
September

A celebration of national identity by the Ashanti (or Asante) people of Ghana, once known as the Gold Coast. The festival originated centuries ago as a time for people to assemble after the yam harvest, and was inaccurately called the Yam Festival by non-Africans.

The kingdom of Ashanti, which is now the region of Ashanti, became rich and powerful in the late 1600s under its first ruler, Asantehene ('King') Osei Tutu. He is believed to have initiated the festival with the additional purpose of reinforcing the loyalty of the subjugated chiefs. The nation he built up withstood the British until 1901. He built a palace at Kumasi, and to further strengthen the nation, he and a priest, Okomfo Anokye, introduced the legendary Golden Stool. Supposed to have been brought down from heaven, it was thought to enshrine the nation's soul and became a symbol of the bond between all Ashanti people. Tutu also set down laws for life and religion. Much of this culture still survives.

During Odwira, the national identity is reinforced with purification ceremonies: a priest in each town prepares a purification bundle of certain tree branches and shoots, and in the evening carries it out of town and buries it. The Golden Stool is carried in a procession and placed on a throne without touching the ground. Huge umbrellas to protect participants from the sun add to the color of the procession. Drums and horns provide music.

CONTACT:
Ghana Embassy
3512 International Dr., N.W.
Washington, D.C. 20008
202-686-4520; fax: 202-686-4527

SOURCES:
BkHolWrld-1986, Sep 19
FolkWrldHol-1992, pp. 448, 449

♦ 1342 ♦ **Offering Ceremony**
January, April, July, August

Offering ceremonies are an important practice in some Javanese religious groups, and are often observed by fishermen in various Indonesian coastal towns as their way of giving thanks to the sea god for their livelihood and of asking for his protection during the coming year. At Banyuwangi, East Java, the ceremony is held in July and preceded by a night of cultural events as well as rowing, sailing, and fishing contests. Similar offering ceremonies are observed at Pangandaran in West Java in January, at Pelabuhan Ratu and at Parang Kusuma (Jogjakarta District) in April, and at Tasikmalaya and Pantai Charita in July.

The offering ceremony held every August in Tegal is in many ways characteristic. There is a feast and a puppet show the night before the ceremony. In the morning, the fishermen bring their offerings down to the beach. A convoy of decorated boats sets out to sea, and the offerings—which often include food, flowers, or a bull's head—are thrown into the water.

CONTACT:
Indonesian Tourist Promotion
  Office
3457 Wilshire Blvd., Ste. 104
Los Angeles, CA 90010
213-387-2078; fax: 213-380-4876

SOURCES:
IntlThFolk-1979, p. 223

♦ 1343 ♦ **Ohio River Sternwheel Festival**
September, weekend after Labor Day

A sternwheeler is a boat propelled by a paddle wheel at the stern or rear of the vessel. At one time they were a common sight along the Ohio River, although many have fallen into decay or have been turned into floating restaurants. The riverfront town of Marietta, Ohio, is home to two of the sternwheelers that remain in working order and is the site of an annual Sternwheel Festival celebrating the heyday of the riverboat during the nineteenth century. Anywhere from 18 to 25 sternwheelers arrive in Marietta during the first week in September for the festival, which begins on the Friday after LABOR DAY. Outdoor concerts, calliope music, entertainment by singers and dancers, and the crowning of Queen Genevieve of the River take place on Saturday, and on Sunday there are sternwheel races. Two of the largest and best-known sternwheelers, the *Delta Queen* and the *River Queen*, participate in the festival every year.

CONTACT:
Ohio Division of Travel and
  Tourism
P.O. Box 1001
Columbus, OH 43266
800-282-5393 or 614-466-8844
fax: 614-466-6744

SOURCES:
Chases-1996, p. 365

♦ 1344 ♦ **Oklahoma Day**
April 22

After forcing the Indians to move west of the Mississippi River during the early decades of the 19th century, Congress set aside a vast area including all of what is now Oklahoma and called it the Indian Territory, telling them the land would be theirs forever. But eventually the U.S. government reneged on its policy in response to pressure from railroad companies and land-hungry homesteaders. Part of the Indian Territory was opened to white settlement by allowing "land runs" in which homesteaders raced across the border to stake their claim to 160-acre plots offered free of charge. Those who managed to sneak across the line before the official opening were called "sooners," which is how Oklahoma came to be nicknamed "the Sooner State." The land run of April 22, 1889, paved the way for the organization of the Oklahoma Territory in 1890, and for Oklahoma's statehood in 1907.

Also known as **Oklahoma 89ers Day**, the celebrations on April 22 focus on the town of Guthrie, the site of the original land office about 80 miles from the starting border. In 1915, the "89ers," as the original participants came to be called, reenacted the land rush, and each year Guthrie observes its anniversary with an 89ers festival. Elsewhere in Oklahoma, the day is celebrated with parades, rodeos, and events based on the land rush theme.

See also CHEROKEE STRIP DAY

CONTACT:
Oklahoma Tourism and Recreation Dept.
2401 N. Lincoln Blvd.
Will Rogers Bldg., Ste. 500
Oklahoma City, OK 73105
800-652-6552 or 405-521-2413
fax: 405-521-4883

SOURCES:
AmerBkDays-1978, p. 369
Chases-1996, p. 181

♦ 1345 ♦ **Oklahoma Historical Day**
October 10

The early history of Oklahoma is replete with stories about a French family named Chouteau. Major Jean Pierre Chouteau and his half-brother René Auguste monopolized the fur trade with the Indians, and in 1796 Chouteau established the first permanent non-Indian settlement within the boundaries of what is now Oklahoma when he built a cabin to serve as a headquarters and trading post in Salina. Chouteau's birthday, October 10, became a legal holiday known as Oklahoma Historical Day in 1939, and a major annual celebration is held in Salina each year.

CONTACT:
Oklahoma Tourism and Recreation Dept.
2401 N. Lincoln Blvd.
Will Rogers Bldg., Ste. 500
Oklahoma City, OK 73105
800-652-6552 or 405-521-2413
fax: 405-521-4883

SOURCES:
AnnivHol-1983, p. 131
Chases-1996, p. 411

♦ 1346 ♦ **Okmulgee Pecan Festival**
Third weekend in June

A nutty festival in Okmulgee, Okla., that made the *Guinness Book of World Records* in 1988 for the world's largest pecan pie. The pie had a diameter of 40 feet, and it weighed about 16½ tons. Even with the help of the culinary arts department of the Oklahoma State University Technical Branch in Okmulgee, this was an enormous task. So in 1990 the big event was a pecan cookie with a diameter of 32 feet and a weight of 7,500 pounds. That was a bit of a chore, too. In 1991, it was decided to keep it simple and celebrate with the "World's Largest Pecan Cookie and Ice Cream Party." More than 15,000 cookies and 5,000 single servings of vanilla ice cream were served.

Okmulgee, a name that means 'bubbling waters' in the Creek language, is the capital of the Creek Nation. It is also an area that raises a lot of pecans; some 600 acres near Okmulgee are devoted to growing pecans. The festival began in 1984 and has been voted one of the top 10 festivals in the state. Besides large pecan concoctions, it offers a carnival, a pecan bake-off, a pie-throwing booth, arm-wrestling contests, the crowning of a Pecan Prince and Princess, and a turtle race.

CONTACT:
Oklahoma Tourism and Recreation Dept.
2401 N. Lincoln Blvd.
Will Rogers Bldg., Ste. 500
Oklahoma City, OK 73105
800-652-6552 or 405-521-2413
fax: 405-521-4883

◆ 1347 ◆ Okpesi Festival
September

The Igbo people of Nigeria believe that failure to perform this annual rite will bring bad luck not only to the individual but to the entire community. It must be carried out by every male child whose father has died, for it is a ceremony in honor of the Igbo ancestors, or *ndioki*. Also known as **Itensi**, the ritual begins with a blood sacrifice of cocks, after which the blood is spread on wooden altars built specifically for the purpose. The sacrifice is followed by a feast during which communion is achieved both among the living and between the living and the dead.

See also ODO FESTIVAL

> **SOURCES:**
> *FolkWrldHol-1992*, p. 473

◆ 1348 ◆ Oktoberfest
September–October

The first Oktoberfest was held on October 17, 1810, in honor of the marriage of Crown Prince Ludwig of Bavaria to Princess Therese von Saxe-Hildburghausen. Since that time it has become, above all else, a celebration of German beer. The Lord Mayor of Munich, Germany, opens the first barrel, and the 16-day festival begins. Both citizens and tourists flock to this event, which is marked by folk costume parades in which brewery horses draw floats and decorated beer wagons through the streets. Oktoberfest celebrations modeled on the German festival are also held in cities throughout the United States.

CONTACT:
German National Tourist Office
122 E. 42nd St., 52nd Floor
New York, NY 10168
212-661-7200; fax: 212-661-7174

SOURCES:
AnnivHol-1983, p. 180
BkFest-1937, p. 137
BkHolWrld-1986, Sep 21
FestWestEur-1958, p. 72
GdWrldFest-1985, p. 86

◆ 1349 ◆ Old Christmas Day
January 6 or 7

In addition to being the Feast of the EPIPHANY, January 6 is known as Old Christmas Day. When England and Scotland switched over from the Julian to the Gregorian calendar in 1752, eleven days were dropped to make up for the calendar discrepancy that had accumulated with the use of the Julian calendar. In all subsequent years, CHRISTMAS arrived 11 days early. Many people, especially in rural areas, had trouble accepting the loss of these 11 days, and continued to recognize the holidays of the Julian calendar as Old Christmas, Old CANDLEMAS, Old MIDSUMMER DAY, etc. Ukrainians celebrate this holiday on January 7.

See also RUSSIAN ORTHODOX CHRISTMAS

> **SOURCES:**
> *Chases-1996*, p. 60
> *FolkWrldHol-1992*, p. 23

◆ 1350 ◆ Old Fiddler's Convention
Second week in August

A three-day concert in the small town of Galax, Va., that spotlights old-time music in an outdoor setting. The convention was organized in 1935 as a fund-raising event by members of Moose Lodge No. 753 and was dedicated to "keeping alive the memories and sentiments of days gone by." About 25,000 people now attend.

Hundreds of contestants take part, competing for cash prizes and trophies in categories that include guitar, mandolin, dulcimer, dobro, clawhammer and bluegrass banjo, clog or flatfoot dancing, and folk singing.

CONTACT:
Virginia Dept. of Economic Development
Division of Tourism
901 E. Byrd St.
Richmond, VA 23219
804-786-4484; fax: 804-786-1919

SOURCES:
Chases-1996, p. 328
MusFestAmer-1990, p. 252

Old Hickory's Day
See **Battle of New Orleans Day**

◆ 1351 ◆ Old Pecos Bull and Corn Dance
August 2

On the **Feast of Porcingula** (named after the shrine of their patron saint, Santa Maria de los Angeles, in Portiuncula, Italy), Indians at the Jemez Pueblo in New Mexico hold a celebration that combines both traditional Indian and Roman Catholic elements. On August 1, the day before the feast, six Indian priests wearing white shirts and trousers with red headbands and sashes come out of the ceremonial kiva and circle the plaza, chanting. Then the dancers are summoned to the kiva to prepare for the next day's corn dance.

On August 2, a Mass is sung in honor of Santa Maria de los Angeles, after which the priest of Jemez accompanies her image to the shrine that has been set up for her in the plaza. The Pecos "bull," named after the people who were forced to abandon the Pecos Pueblo in favor of Jemez in 1838, is really a dancer carrying a framework that resembles a bull. Throughout the two days of the festival, the bull is prodded with sticks and tormented in mock bullfights. The men and boys who play the role of matador are less than flattering in their imitations of white men, which usually draw laughs from the spectators. There is a feast for the bull and the bullfighters, and after that the corn dance is performed before Santa Maria's shrine.

CONTACT:
Jemez Pueblo
P.O. Box 78
Jemez Pueblo, NM 87024
505-834-7359; fax: 505-834-7331

SOURCES:
AmerBkDays-1978, p. 718
IndianAmer-1989, p. 300

◆ 1352 ◆ Old Saybrook Torchlight Parade and Muster
Second Saturday night in December

In 1970 the Colonial Saybrook Fifes and Drums, under the

leadership of Bill Reid, revived the tradition of a CHRISTMAS torchlight parade. In early December each year, in colonial America, the village militia would muster with their fifes and drums and march to the town green carrying torches and lanterns. When they heard the fifes and drums pass, the townspeople would follow behind the militia, also carrying torches and lanterns, to the green where a community meeting and carol sing would take place. It is thought that the event originally commemorated ADVENT.

Old Saybrook, Connecticut (population 10,000), is located at the mouth of the Connecticut River on Long Island Sound and was settled in 1635. It is the only community in the United States that is known to have revived this tradition.

The modern-day procession follows the traditional ritual with no less than 58 fife and drum corps from as far away as Virginia, New Jersey, and New York made up of 35 people per unit on average, plus support groups. The corps are sometimes led by Santa Claus himself and the marchers often augment their colonial-style costumes with seasonal decorations. For example, Christmas lights sparkle on tricornered hats, and silver tinsel hangs from flintlock rifles. The fifes and drums play not only colonial martial music but also the joyous and peaceful songs of Christmas. Citizens of the town and thousands of visitors join the march carrying torches and lanterns to the town green for a community carol sing led by the high school band.

CONTACT:
Connecticut Tourism Division
865 Brook St.
Rocky Hill, CT 06067
800-282-6863 or 860-258-4355
fax: 860-258-4275

♦ 1353 ♦ **Old Silvester**
December 31, January 13

The custom known as **Silvesterklausen** in the small town of Urnäsch in Appenzell Canton, Switzerland, is performed both on December 31, *New* Silvester Day (ST. SYLVESTER'S DAY), and on January 13, or *Old* Silvester Day. (The two dates reflect the change from the Julian, or Old Style, calendar to the Gregorian, or New Style, calendar in 1582.) The men of the village, wearing masks, costumes, and heavy harnesses with bells, traditionally walk in groups from house to house— or, in the surrounding countryside, from one farm to the next—singing wordless yodels. The friends and neighbors who receive them offer them a drink before they move on to the next house. The yodelers are usually so well disguised that their neighbors don't recognize them.

SOURCES:
FestWestEur-1958, p. 242
FolkWrldHol-1992, p. 653
GdWrldFest-1985, p. 168

♦ 1354 ♦ **Old Spanish Days**
Around the full moon in August

This five-day fiesta held in Santa Barbara, California, around the time of the August full moon draws heavily on the area's Spanish-American heritage. It begins with the Fiesta Pequeña, or 'Little Festival,' on the steps of the Santa Barbara Mission, the 10th of the 21 Spanish missions built in California by Fray Junípero Serra and his successors. The opening ceremonies include Spanish and Mexican songs and dances, the tradi-

tional fiesta blessing, and the introduction of ST. BARBARA, who is portrayed by a local citizen. The next few days are filled with flamenco guitarists, Mexican folklore dancers, and other performances at the Lobero Theatre, the site of the first Old Spanish Days festival in 1924. The highlight of the week is the historical parade, featuring floats that depict various episodes in Santa Barbara's history, marching bands and precision drill teams, costumed flower girls, and horses in ornate silver trappings. Other popular events include the *cabalgata* (cavalcade) of costumed riders, the children's historical parade, the rodeo and stock horse show, and the street dance.

CONTACT:
California Division of Tourism
801 K Street, Ste. 1600
Sacramento, CA 95814
800-862-2543 or 916-322-2881
fax: 916-322-3402

SOURCES:
AmerBkDays-1978, p. 750

♦ 1355 ♦ **Old-Time Country Music Contest and Festival, National**
September, Labor Day weekend

Created by Bob Everhart as part of America's bicentennial celebration in 1976, the National Old-Time Country Music Contest and Festival in Avoca, Iowa, is now the largest gathering of public domain music-makers and listeners in the United States. Sponsored by the National Traditional Country Music Association, the festival's purpose is to preserve the music that, in Everhart's words, has been "prostituted, violated, diluted, and in many instances altered so dramatically that it is no longer recognizable as a traditional American art form." There are more than 30 competitions in such varied musical genres as ragtime, polka, Cajun, mountain, folk, cowboy, Western, swing, yodeling, and gospel. The festival also includes songwriting contests and the National Bluegrass Band Championships. Non-musical events include a railroad spike-driving contest and a recreation of an 1840s fur-trading village.

CONTACT:
National Traditional Country Music Association
P.O. Box 438
Walnut, IA 51577
712-784-3001

♦ 1356 ♦ **Old-Time Fiddlers' Contest, National**
Third week in June

A major musical event in the United States, held for a full week in Weiser, Idaho, where fiddling was first heard in 1863. A way station was established that year at Weiser, and people traveling through in covered wagons stopped for rest and recreational fiddling. In 1914, the first fiddling contest was held, but interest petered out until 1953 when Blaine Stubblefield, a fiddle fan and member of the local chamber of commerce, initiated a fiddling competition. In 1963, in conjunction with Idaho's Centennial, the competition officially became the National Old-Time Fiddlers' Contest. Awards are given for the national champion in several categories; this is big-time fiddling, with contestants having won their spot through competitions in other states. Besides music, there are all-you-can-eat breakfasts, a parade, old-fashioned melodrama, street dancing, and sing-alongs; another attraction is the National Fiddlers' Hall of Fame here. Attendance is about 10,000.

CONTACT:
Idaho Tourism Division
700 W. State St.
Boise, ID 83720
800-635-7820 or 208-334-2017
fax: 208-334-2631

SOURCES:
GdUSFest-1984, p. 45
MusFestAmer-1990, p. 241

◆ 1357 ◆ Old Time Fiddlers Jamboree and Crafts Festival
Weekend near July 4

Acclaimed enough to have been the subject of an hour-long documentary on national television, the Jamboree and Crafts Festival held every year on a weekend near the FOURTH OF JULY in Smithville, Tennessee, celebrates the style of country music popularly known as bluegrass. Musical competitions are held in 21 different categories, including fiddle, banjo, mandolin, guitar, dulcimer, harmonica, gospel singing, folk singing, buck dancing, and clog dancing. There are also musical performances, both formal and impromptu, as well as more than 200 booths where working artists and craftspeople display their work. Most of the events are held on a stage set up in front of the DeKalb County Courthouse. The highlight of the festival is a head-to-head contest between the best of the fiddlers. The winner receives a cash prize and the Berry C. Williams Memorial Trophy, named after the festival's founder.

CONTACT:
Tennessee Dept. of Tourism
Development
P.O. Box 23170
Nashville, TN 37202
615-741-2158; fax: 615-741-7225

SOURCES:
Chases-1996, p. 285
GdUSFest-1984, p. 179

◆ 1358 ◆ Ole Time Fiddlers' and Bluegrass Festival
May, Memorial Day Weekend

A festival for genuinely old-time fiddlers, held in Union Grove, N.C. The festival was organized in 1970 by Harper A. Van Hoy as a serious musical venture, and admission is limited to 5,000 people to attract those who want to hear what Van Hoy has called the "purest mountain music this side of the Mississippi."

A special contest category is for fiddlers who must meet these criteria: they are over 55 years old, have had no formal musical training, and have learned from fiddlers older than themselves. There are competitions for all the major instruments of traditional American music, including autoharp, banjo, fiddle, harmonica, and mandolin. Workshops are conducted for most of the instruments played in competition, as well as in shape-note singing, storytelling, clog dancing, and children's folk music. Additionally, there are arts and crafts and food.

CONTACT:
North Carolina Travel and Tourism Division
430 N. Salisbury St.
Raleigh, NC 27603
800-847-4862 or 919-733-4171
fax: 919-733-8582

SOURCES:
MusFestAmer-1990, p. 246

◆ 1359 ◆ Olympic Games
Winter Games every four years (1998, 2002, . . .);
Summer Games every four years (1996, 2000, . . .)

The world's oldest sports spectacular, the first known Olympiad was held in 776 B.C. in Olympia, Greece. It is believed the festivals began before 1400 B.C. The modern games, which until recently were held roughly every four years in different countries, were revived in 1896 by Baron Pierre de Coubertin of France. Those 1896 summer games took place in Athens, with 13 nations sending about 300 male athletes to compete in 42 events and 10 different sports. Now about 160 nations send thousands of male and female athletes to the Summer Olympics, and hundreds of millions watch the events on television. Some winter sports were included in early years of the modern Olympics, but the Winter Games as a separate event didn't begin until 1924. Now about 1,200 male and female athletes, representing some 60 nations take part in them.

In ancient Greece, four national religious festivals—the OLYMPIC GAMES, the PYTHIAN GAMES, the NEMEAN GAMES, and the ISTHMIAN GAMES—were major events; the Olympic Games, honoring Zeus, were especially famous. Records tell of Olympic Games every four years from 776 B.C. to 217 A.D. when, with Greece under Roman domination, the games had lost their religious purpose and the athletes vied only for money. They were abolished by the Roman emperor, Theodosius I. It is generally believed, however, that the festival consisted not only of sporting contests, but of the presentation of offerings to Zeus and other gods. At first, these were simple foot races; later the long jump, discus- and javelin-throwing, wrestling, boxing, *pancratium* (a ferocious combination of boxing and wrestling), and chariot racing were added. Poets and dramatists also presented works. The games opened with trumpet fanfares and closed with a banquet.

Modern Olympics comprise Summer Games, held in a large city, and Winter Games, held at a resort. Since 1994, the games are still on a four-year cycle, but two years apart: Winter Games in 1998, 2002, etc., and Summer Games in 1996, 2000, etc. There are 23 approved sports for the Summer Games and from 15 to 23 may be included. The Winter Games consist of seven approved sports, and all are included.

Today, the opening ceremonies highlight a parade of the athletes led by those from Greece, in honor of the original Games, followed by the athletes from the other nations, in alphabetical order according to the spelling in the country's language; the host country enters last.

After the Games are declared open, the dramatic lighting of the Olympic flame occurs. A cross-country relay runner, carries a torch first lit in Olympia, and ignites the flame that burns for the 15–16 days of the games. Thousands of runners, representing each country between Greece and the host country, take part in the four-week torch relay. This is followed by a spectacular production of fireworks, strobe lights, fly-overs, music, dance, and assorted entertainment.

The Winter Games of 1992, held in Albertville, France, were historic in their reflection of dramatic political changes. The Soviet Union had broken up in August 1991, and athletes from five former Soviet republics competed as representatives of the Commonwealth of Independent States or United Team, and the Olympic flag, not that of the U.S.S.R., was raised for the winners.

The first- and second-place medals are both made of silver but the first place has a wash of gold; the third-place medal is bronze.

The Olympics are supposed to be nonpolitical but have been marked (and marred) by politics. In 1936, Adolf Hitler, who called blacks an inferior race, opened the Olympics in Berlin, Germany, as a propaganda show. It was thus a great triumph for humanity when Jesse Owens, a black man from Ohio State University, won four gold (first place) medals. He won the 100- and 200-meter dashes and the running broad jump, and was on the winning 400-meter relay team. Hitler ducked out of the stadium so he wouldn't have to congratulate Owens.

In 1972, the Games in Munich, Germany, were struck with horror when 11 Israeli athletes were killed by Arab terrorists.

The 1980 Games were opened in Moscow by Communist Party chairman Leonid I. Brezhnev, but athletes from the United States, Canada, West Germany, Japan and 50 other countries didn't participate. Their countries boycotted the event in protest of the Soviet invasion of Afghanistan.

Prominent Olympics participants have included:

Jim Thorpe, an American Indian and one of the greatest all-round athletes of all time, won gold medals for the decathlon and pentathlon in 1912. The following year, he was stripped of the medals when an investigation showed he had played semiprofessional baseball. He died in 1953, and the medals were restored to his family in 1982.

Paavo Nurmi, known as the "Flying Finn," won nine gold medals in long-distance running in three Olympics—in 1920, 1924, and 1928. On an extremely hot day at the Paris Summer Games in 1924, Nurmi set Olympic records in the 1,500-meter and 5,000-meter runs. Two days later he won the 10,000-meter cross-country race. In 1928, he set a record for the one-hour run, covering 11 miles and 1,648 yards. His 1924 wins were considered the greatest individual performance in the history of track and field.

The Norwegian skater Sonja Henie, won three gold medals—in 1928, 1932, and 1936. In 1924, at the age of 11, she was the youngest Olympian contestant ever (she finished last that year). She thrilled crowds by incorporating balletic moves into what had been standard skating exercises.

Emil Zatopek, a Czech long-distance runner, won three gold medals in 1952 and set Olympic records for the 5,000- and 10,000-meter races and for the marathon.

Jean-Claude Killy, known as "Le Superman" in his native France, won three gold medals in Alpine ski events at Grenoble, France, in 1968.

Mark Spitz, a swimmer from California, became the first athlete to win seven gold medals in a single Olympics (1972). He set world records in four individual men's events, and won the remaining medals in team events. These teams also set world records. Spitz, 22 at the time, was so popular for a while that his photo was a pinup poster.

CONTACT:
International Olympic Committee
Public Affairs
Chateau de Vidy
1007 Lausanne, Switzerland
011-41-21-621-6511
fax: 011-41-21-617-0313

SOURCES:
BkHolWrld-1986, Aug 5
Chases-1996, p. 160, 302

♦ 1360 ♦ **Omak Stampede and Suicide Race**
Second weekend in August

Three days of professional rodeo in Omak, Wash. What makes this different from other rodeos is the World Famous Suicide Race which has been featured on the television program, "Ripley's Believe It or Not." This is a terrifying hoof-thundering gallop by 20 mounted horses down an almost vertical hill, across the Okanogan River, and then into the rodeo arena. Four of these races are held, one after each rodeo performance.

The rodeos top off a week of activities which include Indian ceremonies, dances, and stick games, a type of gambling, at an Indian teepee village. (Much of the town of Omak is on the Colville Indian Reservation; the name Omak comes from the Indian word *omache*, meaning 'good medicine.') Other events are a Not Quite White Water Raft Race, a western art show, a grand parade, a kiddies' parade, and dances. Attendance is 20,000 to 30,000.

CONTACT:
Colville Business Committee
P.O. Box 150
Nespelem, WA 99155
509-634-4711

SOURCES:
IndianAmer-1989, p. 203

♦ 1361 ♦ **Omisoka**
December 31

New Year's Eve in Japan is observed by settling financial accounts (*kake*), eating a special noodle dish known as *okake*, which is hot soup over noodles, and taking a hot bath followed by a well-earned rest. Widely celebrated on December 31, Omisoka marks the end of the preparations for New Year's celebrations, which go on for the next three days. It is a popular time for visitors to drop in to exchange New Year's greetings over cups of hot sake and decorated *mochi* cakes.

The city of Ashikaga, 50 miles north of Tokyo, is the site of the 1,200-year-old Saishoji temple, headquarters for the Akutare Matsuri, the 'naughty festival,' or 'festival of abusive language'. On New Year's Eve there, participants walk (or take a bus) up a dark mountain road led by a man blowing a *horagai*, a shell that is supposed to fend off bad tidings. Some carry lanterns and wear cardboard hats bearing the picture of Bishamonten, one of the seven gods of fortune in Japanese Buddhism. The Saishoji temple was built in honor of this god.

The festival originated more than 200 years ago so repressed workers could let off steam; therefore this is not simply a midnight stroll. Those hiking toward the temple atop the 1,000-foot-high hill scream curses into the night. They curse politicians, teachers, bad grades, low pay, and any other complaints of modern daily life in Japan. They release pent-up frustrations with words they ordinarily would not say directly to anyone. *Bakayaro* is one of the words most frequently heard. It means, roughly, 'you idiot'.

After the 40-minute walk the crowd storms into the temple, the bell is rung, prayers are offered, and of course the cursing continues. But when the new year arrives at midnight the curses end and more typical celebration begins. Then the celebrants turn to another unique ceremony: when the priest calls the name of each worshipper, the individual kneels with a wide red lacquer bowl at his or her lips. Sake is then poured onto the person's forehead, runs across his or her face, into the bowl and is consumed. All this occurs while the priest reads the worshipper's personal wishes for the new year to the pounding of a taiko drum. This ceremony is supposed to ensure that happiness will flow in the new year.

See also OSHOGATSU

CONTACT:
Japan National Tourist
  Organization
630 Fifth Ave., Ste. 2101
New York, NY 10111
212-757-5640; fax: 212-307-6754

SOURCES:
AnnivHol-1983, p. 166
BkFest-1937, p. 201
DictFolkMyth-1984, pp. 123, 1100
FolkWrldHol-1992, pp. 42, 649

♦ 1362 ♦ Omizutori Matsuri (Water Drawing Festival)
March 1–14

Religious rites that have been observed for 12 centuries at the Buddhist Todaiji Temple in Nara, Akita Prefecture, Japan. During this period of meditative rituals, the drone of recited sutras and the sound of blowing conchs echo from the temple. The high point comes on March 12, when young monks on the gallery of the temple brandish burning pine-branch torches, shaking off burning pieces. Spectators below try to catch the sparks, believing they have magic power against evil.

At 2 A.M. on March 13, the ceremony of drawing water is observed to the accompaniment of ancient music. Buckets are carried to a well, and the first water of the year is drawn and offered to the Buddha. Then the monks perform a final dramatic fire dance to the beating of drums.

For many Japanese, the Omizutori signals the start of spring.

CONTACT:
Japan National Tourist
  Organization
630 Fifth Ave., Ste. 2101
New York, NY 10111
212-757-5640; fax: 212-307-6754

SOURCES:
AnnivHol-1983, p. 180
Chases-1996, p. 116
RelHolCal-1993, p. 100

♦ 1363 ♦ Ommegang
First Thursday in July

A medieval pageant presented on the Gran' Place of Brussels, Belgium, and one of Belgium's most popular attractions. The pageant in its present form dates only from 1930, the year of the centenary of Belgium, but it is a reenactment of the Ommegang of 1549. And that Ommegang had gone back at least to 1359, when it was first recorded.

The word *ommegang* is from the Flemish words *om* 'around' and *gang* 'march', and was a word used for processions around monuments. The present Brussels Ommegang is linked to the story of Béatrice Soetkens.

The year was 1348. Béatrice, a poor but honest woman, was told by the Virgin Mary to go to Antwerp to get a miracle-making statue. Béatrice ordered her husband to start rowing his boat to take her to Antwerp, and there she was able to get the statue, despite the interference of the sexton. On the way back to Brussels, her husband, exhausted, had to stop rowing, but the drifting boat safely arrived in Brussels at a spot where archers practiced. A church was built there, and every year the statue was carried around under the protection of the "Grand Serment," the Archery Guild.

That was the start of the Ommegang. At first wholly religious, in time profane elements were mingled. The royal princes were admirers of the Ommegang, and details of the 1549 Ommegang are known through the works of Juan Christobal Calvete de Estrelle, the chronicler of Philippe II, son of Charles V. The 1549 Ommegang was dedicated to Charles.

The Ommegang disappeared after 1810, but has been the same since its 1930 revival. It is preceded by strolling musicians, followed by a parade of people representing the magistrate and various city officials; the court of Marie of Hungary, with pages, ladies-in-waiting, and a hunting group of dogs and falcons; and the Court of Charles V, with mounted knights bearing banners. Many of those representing the court figures are descendants of the original noble families.

Then the actual procession takes place led by the Knight of Peace and the Theban trumpets. Participants include trade groups with floats, archers and crossbowmen, and stilt walkers and groups of dancers and Gilles (clowns) dancing around symbolic animals: the legendary horse Bayard and the four sons of Aymon (*see* GIANTS, FESTIVAL OF THE, IN BELGIUM) surrounded by eagles, a pelican, unicorn, dragon, lion, and serpent.

CONTACT:
Belgian Tourist Office
780 Third Ave.
New York, NY 10017
212-758-8130; fax: 212-355-7675

SOURCES:
BkHolWrld-1986, Jul 2
Chases-1996, p. 282

♦ 1364 ♦ Onam
August–September

A harvest festival and a celebration of ancient King Mahabalia in the state of Kerala in India. This is Kerala's biggest festival, lasting 10 days and featuring dancing, feasting, and displays of elaborately designed carpets of flowers. It's famous for the races of the so-called snake boats held at Champakulan, Aranmula, and Kottayam. The boats are designed in all shapes—with beaks or kite tails—and have crews of up to 100 men who row to the rhythm of drums and cymbals.

The festival honors King Mahabalia, who was sent into exile in the nether world when gods grew jealous of him. He's allowed to return to his people once a year, and the boat races, cleaned homes, carpets of flowers, clapping dances by girls, and other events are the welcome for him.

CONTACT:
India Tourist Office
30 Rockefeller Ave.
15 N. Mezzanine
New York, NY 10112
212-586-4901; fax: 212-582-3274

SOURCES:
AnnivHol-1983, p. 180
BkHolWrld-1986, Sep 15
GdWrldFest-1985, p. 111
RelHolCal-1993, p. 100

Onion Market
See Zibelemarit

♦ 1365 ♦ Onwasato Festival
August

Observed by the Igbo people of Nigeria, the Onwasato Festival marks the beginning of the harvest season and is celebrated by feasting on the new crops, particularly yams. The highlight of the festival is the thanksgiving ritual in which the senior member of each family kills a fowl in the

Obu (the father's sitting-house), sprinkles the blood on the Okpensi (the family symbol), and gives thanks to the family's ancestors. The feathers are then removed and scattered on the threshold of the compound—a sign that the people have forsaken all evil for the coming season. Of all the many fowl that are killed, one is roasted and set aside, while the others are used for the first day's feasting. On the second day of the festival, all the members of the extended family meet in the senior member's Obu and share the fowl that has been set aside in a ritual known as the 'handing round of fowl,' or *Inya Okuku*.

SOURCES:
FolkWrldHol-1992, p. 456

♦ 1366 ♦ Opalia
December 19

The ancient Roman fertility goddess Ops was known by several different names—among them Rhea, Cybele, BONA DEA, Magna Mater (*see* MEGALESIA), Thya, and Tellus. She married Saturn and was the mother of Jupiter, and was usually portrayed as a matron, with a loaf of bread in her left hand and her right hand opened as if offering assistance. There were actually two festivals in her honor. The Opalia was observed on December 19, when it is believed that a sacrifice to Ops was made in the temple of Saturn. On August 25, the Opiconsivia, the sacrifice took place in the Regia or king's house.

Not much is known about what actually took place during the Opalia. There is even some disagreement as to whether Ops was the wife of Saturn or the wife of Consus. The fact that the Opalia was held four days after the CONSUALIA on December 15, and that the Opiconsivia was held four days after the festival in honor of Consus on August 21 has been used to support the theory that Ops was actually the wife of Consus. In any case, it appears that women played an important role in the festival. Because Ops was a fertility goddess, she was often invoked by touching the earth.

SOURCES:
ClassDict-1984, p. 424
DictFolkMyth-1984, p. 825
FestRom-1981, pp. 180, 207
RomFest-1925, pp. 212, 273

Opening of Parliament
See State Opening of Parliament

♦ 1367 ♦ Open Marathon, International
Mid-October

A modern-day marathon in Greece run by men and women athletes of all ages. The race retraces the course of the Greek soldier, Pheidippides, who ran from the battlefield at Marathon to Athens to bring news of the Athenian victory over the Persians, a distance of about 25 miles. The starting line today is in the village of Marathon and the finish line is at the Olympic Stadium in the heart of Athens.

A mound in Marathon marks the grave of 192 Athenian soldiers killed in the 490 B.C. victory.

CONTACT:
Greek National Tourist
  Organization
645 Fifth Ave.
New York, NY 10022
212-421-5777; fax: 212-826-6940

Opiconsivia
See Opalia

♦ 1368 ♦ Orange Bowl Game
January 1

One of the older post-season college football games, first played in 1935, in which the champion of the Big-Eight Conference meets another nationally ranked team at the 74,224-seat stadium in Miami, Florida. The game is preceded by a NEW YEAR'S EVE King Orange Jamboree Parade along Biscayne Boulevard. A parade more on the satirical side is the King Mango Strut held each year near Jan. 1 in Coconut Grove, Florida.

CONTACT:
Orange Bowl Committee
601 Brickell Key Dr., Ste. 206
Miami, FL 33131
305-371-4600

SOURCES:
Chases-1996, p. 50

Greater Miami Convention and
  Visitors Bureau
701 Brickell Ave., Ste. 2700
Miami, FL 33131
800-933-8448 or 305-539-3000
fax: 305-539-3113

♦ 1369 ♦ Orange Day (Orangemen's Day)
July 12

Sometimes referred to simply as **The Twelfth** or **The Glorious Twelfth**, this is the anniversary of the Battle of Boyne, which took place in Ireland on July 1, 1690, when the old Julian calendar was still in use. Ireland was under English rule at the time, and the trouble began when James II, who was Roman Catholic, was deposed in 1668 and his throne was given to William of Orange, a Protestant. Each side raised an army of about 30,000 men, and the two clashed on the banks of the Boyne River. The Protestants won a decisive victory, but that was hardly the end of the conflict. The Catholics formed underground societies designed to restore the line of James, and the Protestants countered by forming the Orange Order, committed to maintaining the link with Protestant England. As Irishmen left Ireland and England for the New World, lodges of Orangemen were formed in Canada and the United States, where Orange Day is still observed by Protestant Irish.

SOURCES:
AnnivHol-1983, p. 92
Chases-1996, p. 293
DaysCustFaith-1957, p. 178
DictDays-1988, p. 84

♦ 1370 ♦ Orthodox Epiphany
January 6

The celebration by the Eastern Orthodox Christian churches of the baptism of Jesus in the River Jordan and the manifestation of his divinity when a dove descended on him. For Orthodox Christians around the world it is called **Blessing of**

the Waters Day. In honor of the baptism of Christ, the church's baptismal water is blessed, and small bottles of the holy water are given to parishioners to take home. In many American cities, the priest leads the congregation to a local river which he blesses. Many places throughout the world mark the day with a blessing of the waters and immersion of a cross in seas, lakes, and rivers. At the port of Piraeus, Greece, the local priest throws a cross into the sea, and the diver who retrieves it is thought to be blessed with good luck in the coming year.

In pre-revolutionary Russia, priests and church officials led a procession to the banks of streams or rivers, breaking the ice and lowering a crucifix into the water. Those brave enough to jump into the icy waters to recover the crucifix were thought to be especially blessed. In the north, diving for the cross is frequently done on September 14 (*see* EXALTATION OF THE CROSS), when the water is warmer.

The holy day of the EPIPHANY is celebrated in colorful fashion in Tarpon Springs, Fla., at one time a sea sponge center with the largest sponge market in the world. The community has a strong Greek influence, going back to the beginning of the 20th century when sponge divers from Greece came here to take part in the growing sponge industry. On Epiphany, up to 100 young men from Greek Orthodox churches compete in diving for a gold cross. The cross has been tossed in the bayou by the chief celebrant from the town's St. Nicholas Greek Orthodox Church, and the person who retrieves it will be specially blessed.

Events of this holiday begin the day before with a blessing of the sponge fleet. The next morning, after Mass and a blessing of the waters, there is a parade of school and civic groups led by ecclesiastical dignitaries in their vestments. Many of the paraders wear Greek costume. After the parade, when the cross has been retrieved, the day becomes festive, with bouzouki music, dancing, and feasting, especially on roast lamb. Epiphany has been observed in this manner at Tarpon Springs since 1904, and now attracts about 30,000 people.

In Greece, Epiphany is one of the country's most important church days, especially in the port towns where diving for the cross takes place. After Mass, on the eve of Epiphany in Cyprus, priests visit houses to cleanse them from demons known as *Kalikandjiari*. According to Cypriot tradition, these evil spirits appear on earth at CHRISTMAS, and for the next 12 days play evil tricks on people. On the eve of their departure, people appease them by throwing pancakes and sausages onto their roofs, which is where the demons dwell.

See also EPIPHANY, FEAST OF THE

SOURCES:
AmerBkDays-1978, pp. 34, 37, 38, 89
BkFest-1937, pp. 3, 144, 289, 335
DictWrldRel-1989, p. 237
FestSaintDays-1915, p. 17
FolkAmerHol-1991, pp. 27, 35
FolkWrldHol-1992, pp. 13, 14, 23
RelHolCal-1993, p. 75

♦ 1371 ♦ **Osaka International Festival**
April

Founded in 1958 as a meeting place for Eastern and Western cultures, the Osaka International Festival presents classical music performed by orchestras, chamber ensembles, and solo artists from Japan and other countries. The program also includes dance, drama, and opera, with performances given in the 3,000-seat Osaka Festival Hall, one of the largest and most modern in the Far East. The Comedie Française, Vienna Burgtheater, and Théâtre de France Renaud-Barrault have performed there, as have the New York City Ballet, the Alwin Nikolais Dance Theatre, and the Ballet Aztlan de Mexico.

Every Osaka Festival features classical Japanese Noh dance-dramas and Kabuki theatrical performances. The Bunraku Puppet Theatre also presents traditional Japanese dramas using dolls that are two-thirds human size. The 18-day festival is scheduled to take place in April, which is cherry-blossom time in Osaka.

CONTACT:
Japan National Tourist
  Organization
630 Fifth Ave., Ste. 2101
New York, NY 10111
212-757-5640; fax: 212-307-6754

SOURCES:
GdWrldFest-1985, p. 124
IntlThFolk-1979, p. 258
MusFestWrld-1963, p. 264

♦ 1372 ♦ **Oshogatsu (New Year's Day)**
January 1

This is the "festival of festivals" in Japan, also known as **Ganjitsu**, actually celebrated for several days. Government offices, banks, museums and most businesses are closed from NEW YEAR'S DAY, a national holiday, through January 3.

From the middle of December, streets are decorated with pine and plum branches, bamboo stalks, and ropes festooned with paper. Traditional home decorations are small pine trees with bamboo stems attached, which are placed on either side of the front entrance to represent longevity and constancy. For weeks before New Year's, people clean house and purchase new clothes for the children; this is also a time for exchanging gifts, sending greeting cards, and paying off personal debts.

On NEW YEAR'S EVE or OMISOKA, people wearing kimonos fill the streets as they go to visit shrines. But millions watch the "Red and White Song Contest" on the Japanese publicly owned television station. This marathon song festival, first organized in 1950, has become an indispensable ritual of the New Year. The show, lasting up to 4½ hours, has had more than 50 performers in recent years, including an orchestra playing Mozart, a group singing Okinawan folk music, and a female singer in a gown of feathers that made her look like a bird; as she finished her song she flapped her arms and flew away, suspended by a wire. Each performer is a member of a team. The Red team is comprised of women, the White team men. When the performances are over, the audience and a panel of judges decide which team won.

The TV show ends shortly before midnight in time for an older tradition: the tolling of the great bells in Buddhist temples at midnight. Priests strike the bells 108 times, a reminder of the 108 human frailties or sins in Buddhist belief. By the end of the 108 strokes of the bell, the impure desires of the old year have been driven away.

An ancient folk ritual of a very different sort is observed on the Oga Peninsula, Akita Prefecture, on New Year's Eve. Young men play the part of hairy devils called *Namahage*, dressing in grotesque red and blue masks and straw cloaks. They stomp through the streets shouting, "Any wicked people about?" and then pound on people's doorways, the idea being to frighten children and newly married women so that they won't be lazy. After being admitted to a home, they sit down for rice cakes, first scaring the wits out of children with stories of what will happen to them if they are naughty.

On New Year's Day, it's traditional to pray at the household altar and to eat special foods, for example, steamed rice that has been pounded into small, round, gooey cakes called *mochi*. Herring roe is eaten for fertility, black beans for health, dried chestnuts for success, and porgy and prawns are omens of happiness.

Business resumes on Jan. 4, and the holiday period is over on Jan. 7 when decorations come down as part of the festival of Nanakusa Matsuri.

SOURCES:
BkFest-1937, p. 194
BkFestHolWrld-1970, pp. 2, 14
DictFolkMyth-1984, pp. 181, 540, 730, 790, 871
DictWrldRel-1989, p. 374
FolkWrldHol-1992, pp. 45, 50
RelHolCal-1993, p. 79

♦ 1373 ♦ Our Lady Aparecida, Festival of
October 12

Brazil's patron saint, the Virgin Mary *Aparecida* ('she who has appeared'), is honored with a 10-day festival in the city near São Paulo that bears her name. Legend has it that after a poor day's catch, fishermen cast their nets into the Paraiba do Sul River and pulled up a small statue of the Virgin Mary, carved out of black wood. When they cast their nets again, they came up full of fish. This was the first miracle attributed to the saint, and the city of Aparecida with its beautiful church built to house the statue is now the destination of many pilgrimages.

Nossa Senhora de Aparecida is celebrated during the month of October, but the 12th is a legal public holiday in Brazil to honor the saint.

CONTACT:
Brazilian Embassy
3006 Massachusetts Ave., N.W.
Washington, D.C. 20008
202-745-2700; fax: 202-745-2827

Our Lady of Camarin
See **Immaculate Conception, Feast of the**

♦ 1374 ♦ Our Lady of Carmel, Feast of
July 16

Our Lady of Carmel (the *Madonna del Carmine*) is the patroness of the city of Naples, Italy. Her festival is celebrated with dancing, singing, and magnificent firework displays. Brightly decorated wax replicas of human body parts used to be sold at booths near the church, and people suffering from various physical ailments appealed to the Madonna to restore their health by offering her these replicas of the diseased portions of their bodies.

Her feast is also observed by Italian Americans in the United States. In New York City, novenas, anointing of the sick, processions, and special masses are held at the Church of Our Lady of Mount Carmel beginning on July 4 and ending with High Mass and a procession on the 16th.

CONTACT:
Italian Government Travel Office
630 Fifth Ave.
New York, NY 10111
212-245-4822

SOURCES:
BkFest-1937, p. 188

♦ 1375 ♦ Our Lady of Fátima Day
July 13

This Portuguese holiday commemorates the appearance of the Virgin Mary to three children, aged 10 to 13, from the village of Fátima in 1917. The first appearance to the dos Santos children—Lucia, and her cousins, Jacinto and Francisca—took place on May 13, 1917, when they heard the sound of thunder and "a young girl" appeared to them from the top of a nearby tree. No one really took their story seriously, however, until the same thing began to occur on the 13th of every month. Each time the children went to see the Virgin, they were accompanied by an increasingly large crowd of adults. She appeared to them for the last time on October 13, in the presence of about 70,000 onlookers, when she revealed she was Our Lady of the Rosary. She told them to recite the rosary daily, and asked that a church be built for her.

Eventually the cult of Our Lady of Fátima spread, a basilica was built, and pilgrimages to the isolated shrine became common. Two great pilgrimages take place each year on May 13 and October 13, with smaller groups making their way to Fátima around the 13th day of each month in between. July 13 is considered Our Lady of Fátima Day because it was two months after the Virgin's first appearance that a large number of adults witnessed the same miracle: the sun seemed to dance, tremble, and finally fall. It took 20 years for the event to be investigated, authenticated, and the cult granted acceptance by the Pope.

CONTACT:
Portuguese National Tourist
  Office
590 Fifth Ave., 4th Floor
New York, NY 10036
212-354-4403; fax: 212-764-6137

SOURCES:
AnnivHol-1983, p. 92
Chases-1996, p. 210
DaysCustFaith-1957, p. 179
DictWrldRel-1989, p. 254
FestWestEur-1958, p. 161

♦ 1376 ♦ Our Lady of Guadalupe, Feast of, in the United States
December 12

The Feast of Our Lady of Guadalupe is celebrated by Roman Catholics in the southwestern United States, where the Spanish influence is still strong. At the pueblo just north of Taos, New Mexico, there is an impressive torchlight procession on December 12. At the Jemez Pueblo, *Matachines* (clowns or buffoons) perform a variety of Indian ceremonial dances. At churches and plazas throughout New Mexico, Texas, and Arizona, such traditional Indian dances as the arc and arrow, gourd, braid, feather, palm, owl, and snake dances are performed on this day.

Several masses are held on this day at Our Lady of Guadalupe Church in San Diego, California, where the *mañanitas*, or 'good morning song', is sung to the Virgin Mary, and *mariachis*, or strolling musicians, perform in the Virgin's honor. San Antonio, Texas, also has a church dedicated to Our Lady of Guadalupe. What began there as a street procession followed by Indian dances was expanded in 1970 to a citywide event known as the **Festival Guadalupeño**. On the Sunday nearest

December 12 at the Convention Center's Hemisfair Arena, there is a solemn mass followed by mariachis, Mexican dances, and other forms of entertainment.

SOURCES:
AmerBkDays-1978, p. 1097
FolkAmerHol-1991, p. 430
IndianAmer-1989, pp. 300, 303

♦ 1377 ♦ Our Lady of Guadalupe, Fiesta of
December 12

Nuestra Señora de Guadalupe is the patron saint of Mexico, and on December 12 thousands of pilgrims flock to her shrine at the famous Church of Guadalupe outside Mexico City. This great religious festival commemorates the appearance of the Virgin Mary on Tepeyac hill just north of present-day Mexico City. According to legend, she identified herself to an Indian convert named Juan Diego in the early morning of December 9, 1531, and told him to tell the bishop to build her a shrine there. When the bishop refused to believe the story, the Virgin filled Diego's homespun blanket with Castillian roses, which did not normally grow in Mexico, as proof of his vision. When Juan opened the blanket to show the bishop the roses, they had vanished. In their place was an image of Mary on the blanket. It soon adorned the newly built shrine and has hung there for four centuries without any apparent deterioration or fading of colors.

The story of Juan Diego and the Virgin is reenacted in a puppet show each year, and relics of Our Lady of Guadalupe are sold in the streets. It is said that only the French shrine at Lourdes and the one at Fátima attract as many pilgrims (*see* OUR LADY OF FÁTIMA and OUR LADY OF LOURDES).

She is the patron saint of Peruvian students, and of all of Central and South America. In El Salvador, it is called *Día del Indio* ('Day of the Indian').

CONTACT:
Mexican Government Tourist
Office
405 Park Ave., Ste. 1401
New York, NY 10022
800-446-3942 or 212-755-7261
fax: 212-753-2874

SOURCES:
AmerBkDays-1978, p. 1097
BkFest-1937, p. 232
DaysCustFaith-1957, p. 311
DictFolkMyth-1984, p. 258
DictWrldRel-1989, p. 569
FolkAmerHol-1991, p. 430
FolkWrldHol-1992, p. 588
IndianAmer-1989, pp. 290, 300, 303
IntlThFolk-1979, p. 272

♦ 1378 ♦ Our Lady of Lourdes, Feast of
February 11

The Feast of Our Lady of Lourdes commemorates the first of 17 appearances of the Virgin Mary to a 14-year-old French peasant girl, Bernadette Soubirous. The young girl's visions occurred between February 11 and July 16, 1858, near the town of Lourdes. The Virgin led her to a nearby grotto, and the miraculous spring that appeared there has been associated ever since with the power to heal.

Pilgrimages to the grotto were authorized in 1862, and the Feast of Our Lady of Lourdes was extended to the entire Roman Catholic Church in 1907. Some four million people a year make the pilgrimage to Lourdes, making it one of the world's major pilgrimage sites. Many of them are sick, and the cures they report are reviewed by a special medical bureau. As of 1976, the Church had accepted only 63 of these cures as miraculous.

CONTACT:
French Government Tourist Office
9454 Wilshire Blvd., Ste. 715
Beverly Hills, CA 90212
310-271-6665; fax: 310-276-2835

SOURCES:
AnnivHol-1983, pp. 25, 52
BkHolWrld-1986, Feb 11
DaysCustFaith-1957, p. 50
DictWrldRel-1989, p. 439

♦ 1379 ♦ Our Lady of Nazaré Festival
September 8–18

Nazaré has been called "the most picturesque town in Portugal," and thousands of tourists flock here every summer to paint, film, and photograph the quaint fishing village. The Church of Our Lady of Nazareth was built near the place where the Virgin Mary is said to have saved the life of Fuas Roupinho, who was pursuing a white deer when a sudden sea mist arose and caused him to lose his bearings. The Virgin halted his horse in its tracks—a hoof-print is still visible—and, as the mist cleared, Roupinho discovered that he was on the brink of a cliff, 300 feet above the ocean. Today the town is built on two levels, the lower one extending along the beach. A pilgrimage chapel overlooks the town from the upper level.

The name *Nazaré* comes from a statue of the Virgin brought back here from Nazareth, the childhood home of Jesus, by a monk in the fourth century. The annual 10-day festival that takes place in the town's main square begins on September 8, the anniversary of the miracle, and includes bullfights, musical concerts, and folk dancing. Some of the best and most dangerous fishing in all of Portugal goes on here. Fishermen have to negotiate a treacherous barrier reef with a difficult swell that often capsizes entire boats with their crews. Therefore, the Nazaré fishermen, who carry the Virgin's statue on their shoulders in three festive processions, are the focus of the event.

CONTACT:
Portuguese National Tourist
Office
590 Fifth Ave., 4th Floor
New York, NY 10036
212-354-4403; fax: 212-764-6137

SOURCES:
FestWestEur-1958, p. 184

♦ 1380 ♦ Our Lady of Sorrows Festival
Friday, Saturday, and Sunday closest to August 20

The pilgrimage to the church of Our Lady of Sorrows, or **Nossa Senhora da Agonia**, in Viana do Castelo, Portugal, is one of the country's most colorful religious festivals. Sometimes called the **Pardon of Our Lady of Sorrows**, it includes a procession in which the image of the Virgin Mary is carried over carpets of flowers. Participants also enjoy fireworks on the River Lima, a parade of carnival giants and dwarfs, bull-running through the barricaded streets, and regional singing and folk dancing.

CONTACT:
Portuguese National Tourist
Office
590 Fifth Ave., 4th Floor
New York, NY 10036
212-354-4403; fax: 212-764-6137

SOURCES:
IntlThFolk-1979, p. 314

Our Lady of Victories Day
See **Victory Day**

♦ 1381 ♦ **Outback Festival**
August in odd-numbered years

In 1895 A. B. "Banjo" Patterson wrote "Waltzing Matilda," the song that is most closely identified with the Australian outback. The song was based on an incident that occurred at Dogworth Station near Winton, Queensland, and it was in Winton that the ballad was first sung in public. Today, Winton is host to the biennial Outback Festival, which celebrates Australia's pioneer traditions. There are parades, picnics, historic tours, safaris, rodeos, sheep-shearing and whip-cracking demonstrations, pigeon races, and sports competitions at the 10-day festival, which is held in August, at the end of the Australian winter.

The Bronze Swagman Award is presented at the festival for the best "Bush verse"—similar to cowboy poetry in the United States (*see* Cowboy Poetry Gathering). Entries are accepted from all over the world, but the poems must be written in English and must portray an "Australian Bush" theme.

CONTACT:
Australian Tourist Commission
100 Park Ave., 25th Floor
New York, NY 10017
212-687-6300; fax: 212-661-3340

SOURCES:
IntlThFolk-1979, p. 19

♦ 1382 ♦ **Oxi Day**
October 28

A national holiday in Greece to commemorate the Greeks saying *"oxi"* (Greek for *no,* pronounced "O-hee," with guttural h-sound) in 1940 to Italy's attempted incursion ordered by its Fascist dictator, Benito Mussolini. The day is observed with military and school parades.

On the morning of Oct. 28 in 1940, the Italian ambassador to Greece called on Gen. Ioannis Metaxas, the self-appointed prime minister, to demand that Italian troops be allowed to occupy certain strategic areas in Greece. Metaxas curtly responded, "Oxi." The Italians invaded, but were routed by the Greeks.

CONTACT:
Greek National Tourist
   Organization
645 Fifth Ave.
New York, NY 10022
212-421-5777; fax: 212-826-6940

SOURCES:
Chases-1996, p. 432

♦ 1383 ♦ **Ozark Folk Festival**
First week in November

An off-the-beaten-track affair in Eureka Springs, Ark., first held in 1948 to preserve the music and folklore of the Ozarks. For two or three days, musicians, mostly nonprofessional, gather to play mountain music on fiddles, banjos, jackass jawbones, harmonicas, dulcimers, and other non-electrified instruments. Only traditional Ozark music is allowed, and that means it must be at least 70 years old. Some of the music dates back to Elizabethan times. Also on the menu are performances by jig, clog, and square-dance groups, crafts displays, a Gay Nineties costume parade, and a Festival Queen contest.

Eureka Springs, about 50 miles north of Fayetteville, is the oldest health spa in the Ozarks, and the winding streets and houses are much the same as they were in the 1880s.

CONTACT:
Arkansas Dept. of Parks and
   Tourism
1 Capitol Mall
Little Rock, AR 72201
800-628-8725 or 501-682-7777
fax: 501-682-1364

SOURCES:
MusFestAmer-1990, p. 218

P

◆ 1384 ◆ **Pacific Northwest Festival**
August

Most opera companies shy away from Richard Wagner's *Der Ring des Nibelungen* because of the technical difficulties involved in staging the work and because it is assumed that only audiences in Wagner's native Germany will have the stamina to sit through the entire four-opera cycle. But in 1975 the Seattle Opera proved not only that the *Ring* could be staged, but that it could draw huge audiences. Under the direction of Glenn Ross, the Seattle Opera started its annual Wagner festival, performing the uncut *Ring* cycle in German the first week and in English the second week with an augmented orchestra. All operas are performed in the Seattle Opera House, which had been remodeled for the 1962 World's Fair.

Some of the world's finest Wagnerian performers have participated in the Pacific Northwest Festival over the years, among them Herbert Becker, Ingrid Bjoner, Philip Booth, Ute Vinzing, Paul Crook, and Malcolm Rivers. When General Director Speight Jenkins decided in 1985 to stage an entirely new production of *Die Walkure*, one of the operas in the *Ring* cycle, he was booed for his innovative approach by those who preferred the more traditional production.

See also BAYREUTH FESTIVAL and RAVELLO MUSIC FESTIVAL

CONTACT:
Seattle-King County Convention
  and Visitors Bureau
520 Pike St., Ste. 1300
Seattle, WA 98101
360-461-5800; fax: 360-461-5855

◆ 1385 ◆ **Padi Harvest Festival**
May 30–31

A festival and public holiday in Labuan Territory and the state of Sabah in Malaysia. The festival is celebrated by the Kadazan people (also known as the Dusun), the largest indigenous ethnic group in Sabah, which lies on the northern tip of Borneo. Originally headhunters, they were the first native group in Borneo to use the plow. Irrigated (not flooded) rice is their principal crop, and the harvest is a ritual dedicated to the *Bambaazon*, or rice spirit. If the harvest has

been good, this is a thanksgiving, and if it has been poor, the ritual is an appeasement of the spirit. The Kadazans believe that spirits reside in natural objects, and rituals are conducted by shamanist priestesses. Besides the solemn aspects of the festival, there is much merrymaking and free flowing of rice wine.

CONTACT:
Malaysian Tourism Promotion
  Board
818 W. Seventh St., Ste. 804
Los Angeles, CA 90017
213-689-9702; fax: 213-689-1530

Padstow Hobby Horse Parade
See **Minehead Hobby Horse Parade**

◆ 1386 ◆ **Paine Day, Thomas**
Sunday nearest January 29

Thomas Paine (1737–1809) was a propagandist and humanitarian whose influential pamphlet, *Common Sense*, is credited with persuading the American colonies to declare their independence from Great Britain. Six months after the publication of *Common Sense* in January 1776, the Declaration of Independence was signed. While Paine was serving in George Washington's army during the Revolutionary War, he wrote his inspirational tract, *The Crisis*, whose opening line was the famous, "These are the times that try men's souls."

On the Sunday nearest January 29, Paine's birthday, he is honored by members of the Thomas Paine National Historical Association in New Rochelle, New York. They lay a wreath at his monument in the Thomas Paine Memorial Building, a museum housing some of his letters and personal effects. The museum is located on Paine's former farmland, and the cottage in which he lived is only a short walk away. This day is also known as **Common Sense Day**, to encourage the use of good sense in protecting the rights of all people.

CONTACT:
Thomas Paine National Historical
  Association
983 North Ave.
New Rochelle, NY 10804
914-632-5376

SOURCES:
AmerBkDays-1978, p. 121
AnnivHol-1983, p. 15
Chases-1996, p. 79

♦ 1387 ♦ **Pakistan Day**
March 23

This national holiday is also known as **Republic Day,** and is the anniversary of a 1940 resolution calling for a Muslim country for Muslim Indians. On the same day in 1956, Pakistan became an Islamic republic within the British Commonwealth.

Pakistan Day is celebrated with parades and fairs.

CONTACT:
Pakistani Embassy
2315 Massachusetts Ave., N.W.
Washington, D.C. 20008
202-939-6200; fax: 202-387-0484

SOURCES:
AnnivHol-1983, p. 41
Chases-1996, p. 143
NatlHolWrld-1968, p. 37

♦ 1388 ♦ **Pakistan Independence Day**
August 14

On this day in 1947, Pakistan gained independence from Britain. Pakistan had been part of the immense British colony of India since the 18th century.

Independence Day is a national holiday observed in much the same way as PAKISTAN DAY.

CONTACT:
Pakistani Embassy
2315 Massachusetts Ave., N.W.
Washington, D.C. 20008
202-939-6200; fax: 202-387-0484

SOURCES:
AnnivHol-1983, p. 106
NatlHolWrld-1968, p. 37

♦ 1389 ♦ **Palio, Festival of the**
July 2, August 16

The **Palio of the Contrade** is a horse race that has been held in Siena, Italy, twice a year since the 13th century. Each of Siena's 17 *contrade*, or 'ward organizations'—which now are social clubs but in the Middle Ages were rival military companies—hires a professional jockey and selects his attendants. Each contrade also has its own animal symbol, flag, color, museum, church, and motto. In medieval costume and with banners flying, the riders form a procession which carries the *Palio*, or silk standard painted with an image of the Virgin Mary, through the city streets.

The race itself is run in the city's main square, the Piazza del Campo. There is intense rivalry, distrust, cheating, fixing, and bribery and frequent fights. The jockeys ride bareback, each holding a whip which he can use on his opponents' horses as well as on his own. Riders for the finalist contrade race three times around the Piazza, and the winning contrade receives the Palio to hang on its church until the next festival. Revelry and merrymaking continue until dawn, and the winning jockey is honored with a victory dinner.

The second big race, held on August 16, is known as **Madonna del Voto Day** in honor of the Virgin Mary.

CONTACT:
Italian Government Travel Office
630 Fifth Ave.
New York, NY 10111
212-245-4822

SOURCES:
AnnivHol-1983, pp. 88, 108
BkFest-1937, p. 187
BkHolWrld-1986, Aug 16
FestWestEur-1958, p. 98
GdWrldFest-1985, p. 119

♦ 1390 ♦ **Palio of the Goose and River Festival**
June 28–29

In the Middle Ages the Leap of the Goose was a test of swimming skill for the local boatmen in Pavia, Italy. Now it is a combined rowing and swimming relay race held at the end of June each year. Competitors leap from a raft at the end of the race and try to reach a goose suspended in air. Geese apparently played an important part in the city's history, acting as sentries when Pavia was besieged by the Gauls. In the procession through the streets of Pavia that precedes the competition, live geese are carried in cages.

There is also a Tournament of the Towers in which teams of six men from each of the city's nine wards try to knock down each other's wooden towers in a mock battle. A final battle involves the Beccaria Tower, which can only be approached by gangplanks. The winners set the tower on fire.

CONTACT:
Italian Government Travel Office
630 Fifth Ave.
New York, NY 10111
212-245-4822

♦ 1391 ♦ **Palm Sunday**
Between March 15 and April 18 in the West and between March 28 and May 1 in the East; the Sunday before Easter

During the Jewish PASSOVER celebration Jesus rode into Jerusalem and was given a hero's welcome by the people, who had heard of his miracles and regarded him as the leader who would deliver them from the domination of the Roman Empire. They carried palm branches, a traditional symbol of victory, and spread them in the streets before him, shouting "Hosanna, glory to God" (John 12:12,13). Palms are still used in church services on this day, which is the beginning of HOLY WEEK, and Jesus' triumphal entry into Jerusalem is often reenacted with a procession—the most impressive being the one in Rome, where the Pope, carried in St. Peter's chair, blesses the palms (*see* ST. PETER'S CHAIR, FESTIVAL OF).

At the beginning or end of the service, the palms are distributed to the congregation. In some countries, where palms are not available, branches of other trees—particularly pussy willow, olive, box, yew, and spruce—are used. They are later hung up in houses for good luck, buried to preserve crops, or used to decorate graves. Other names for this day include **Passion Sunday**, FIG SUNDAY, **Willow Sunday**, **Branch Sunday**, **Blossom Sunday**, and, in France, **Rameaux**.

SOURCES:
AmerBkDays-1978, p. 278
BkDays-1864, vol. I, p. 395
BkFest-1937, pp. 183, 300, 337
DaysCustFaith-1957, p. 104
DictFolkMyth-1984, pp. 181, 841, 954, 1171
FestSaintDays-1915, p. 54
FestWestEur-1958, pp. 59, 92, 107, 125, 163, 192
FolkAmerHol-1991, p. 152
FolkWrldHol-1992, pp. 131, 193
RelHolCal-1993, p. 101

♦ 1392 ♦ **Palm Sunday in Austria**
Between March 15 and April 18; the Sunday before Easter

PALM SUNDAY commemorates Jesus' entry into Jerusalem, where he was greeted by people waving palm branches. In

Austria and the Bavarian region of Germany, farmers make *Palmbuschen* by attaching holly leaves, willow boughs, and cedar twigs to the tops of long poles. After the Palmbuschen have been blessed in the local church, the farmers set them up in their fields or barns to ward off illness, to protect their crops from hail and drought, and to preserve their families from other disasters. The Palmbuschen are kept there throughout the year.

See also PALM SUNDAY IN GERMANY

SOURCES:
AmerBkDays-1978, p. 280
BkHolWrld-1986, Apr 5
FestWestEur-1958, p. 59

♦ 1393 ♦ Palm Sunday in Finland
Between March 15 and April 18; the Sunday before Easter

Instead of the traditional palm branches used in PALM SUNDAY observances elsewhere, willow switches or birch branches are used in rural areas of Finland. Children may gather the branches in the woods and decorate them with paper flowers and cloth streamers. According to custom, on the Saturday or Sunday before EASTER, known as **Willowswitch Saturday** and **Willowswitch Sunday**, they go from house to house and spank the woman of the house lightly while reciting a Finnish refrain wishing her good health. The woman then uses a switch on her livestock in the same way. The switches are eventually collected and saved, to be used again the first time the cattle are driven to pasture in the new year. The children return on Easter to receive a treat.

Pussywillow or birch branches are also used to foretell the arrival of spring. Once they are cut, the days are counted until the buds on the branches open; this is how many weeks it will take for the trees in the forest to bud.

SOURCES:
BkFest-1937, p. 112
FolkWrldHol-1992, p. 193

♦ 1394 ♦ Palm Sunday in Germany (Palmsonntag)
Between March 15 and April 18; the Sunday before Easter

Although PALM SUNDAY customs vary from one part of Germany to the next, all celebrate the resurgence of life as symbolized by the arrival of spring. In the Black Forest, people decorate tall poles with pussywillows, heart or cross motifs, and long multicolored ribbon streamers. They set the decorated poles up in front of their houses and later carry them in procession to the local church, where they are blessed by the priest.

In Bavaria, branches from 12 different kinds of wood are cut, then bent and fastened to long poles in a semicircular shape and decorated with glass beads to resemble glittering trees. The trees are carried in procession to the church, blessed by the priest, and then set up in the farmers' fields to protect the crops and ensure a bountiful harvest.

One of the more unusual Palm Sunday customs in Germany is the *Palm Esel*, or wooden Palm Donkey, symbolic of the ass upon which Jesus entered Jerusalem. This survival of an ancient folk custom is carried to the village church. People believe that if they touch the Palm Donkey, they will share in

the blessing that emanated from the humble ass that once carried Jesus.

See also PALM SUNDAY IN AUSTRIA

SOURCES:
FestWestEur-1958, p. 59

♦ 1395 ♦ Palm Sunday in Italy (Domenica delle Palme)
Between March 15 and April 18; the Sunday before Easter

On PALM SUNDAY the piazzas in front of most small Italian churches are filled with people dressed in spring clothes and vendors selling olive and palm branches. The olive branches are often gilded or painted silver, and the palms are braided into crosses and decorated with roses, lilies, or other flowers. After the palms have been blessed in the church, they are often exchanged as a peace offering or sign of reconciliation between those who have quarreled. In Rapallo, a center for the silk industry, silkworms' eggs are taken to church on Palm Sunday to be blessed.

The most impressive Palm Sunday observance, however, takes place in Rome. The Pope, carried in St. Peter's chair on the shoulders of eight men, comes out of St. Peter's basilica to bless the palms. (*See* ST. PETER'S CHAIR, FESTIVAL OF.) After the service, the golden palms are distributed among the clergy and the olive branches are distributed to the congregation. Then the thousands of worshippers who have gathered in St. Peter's Square march through the basilica and around the portico, emerging from one door and re-entering through another to symbolize the entry of Jesus into Jerusalem. The procession eventually makes its way to the high altar, where Mass is said. Some of the palm branches are saved and later burned to make the next year's ASH WEDNESDAY ashes. The rest are given to the people to take home, where they are treasured as protection against evil, particularly lightning and storms.

CONTACT:
Italian Government Travel Office
630 Fifth Ave.
New York, NY 10111
212-245-4822

SOURCES:
AmerBkDays-1978, p. 280
BkFest-1937, p. 183
BkFestHolWrld-1970, p. 50
DaysCustFaith-1957, p. 104
FestSaintDays-1915, p. 55
FestWestEur-1958, p. 92

♦ 1396 ♦ Palm Sunday in the Netherlands (Palm Zondag)
Between March 15 and April 18; the Sunday before Easter

The *Palmpaas*, or 'Easter palm,' in the Netherlands is a stick between 18" and 54" long to which a hoop has been attached. The hoop is covered with boxwood and decorated with colored paper flags, eggshells, sugar rings, oranges, raisins, figs, chocolate eggs, and small cakes. There are figures of swans or cocks on top that are made out of baked dough. Sometimes there are contests for the most elaborate Palmpaas. Children in rural areas of the Netherlands go from one farm to the next with their Palmpaas, singing nonsense verses in which they ask for Easter eggs, sometimes for use in the popular Easter sport of *eiertikken*, or egg tapping.

With its egg and bird decorations, it seems likely that the Palmpaas was originally a fertility symbol that represented the arrival of spring in the village and the resurgence of life after winter. In some Roman Catholic areas, the Palmpaas are blessed by the local priest and then saved as protection against lightning and sore throats during the coming year.

SOURCES:
FestWestEur-1958, p. 125
FolkWrldHol-1992, p. 131

♦ 1397 ♦ Palm Sunday in the United States
Between March 15 and April 18; the Sunday before Easter

Programs of sacred music are performed in many American towns and cities on PALM SUNDAY. They are often sponsored by and held in churches, but may be part of the musical community's regular concert series. These programs usually begin on or before Palm Sunday and may continue throughout HOLY WEEK. Some of the more popular pieces performed at these concerts include Bach's *St. John Passion* or *St. Matthew Passion,* Handel's *Messiah,* Gounod's *La Rédemption,* Haydn's *Seven Last Words,* Beethoven's *Christ on the Mount of Olives,* and Sir John Stainer's *Crucifixion.* Bethany College's MESSIAH FESTIVAL in Lindsborg, Kansas, has been held during Holy Week for over 100 years.

In addition to musical performances, plays or pageants dealing with Holy Week themes are often performed on Palm Sunday as well. The same group that performs the BLACK HILLS PASSION PLAY in South Dakota all summer portrays the last seven days in the life of Christ during Holy Week at an amphitheater near Lake Wales, Florida.

In St. Augustine, Florida, the Blessing of the Fishing and Shrimp Fleet takes place on Palm Sunday. Shrimp trawlers and other fishing boats, as well as many privately owned vessels, circle past the City Yacht Pier to receive the local priest's blessing.

In Buffalo, New York, the palm branches that have been blessed in the churches on Palm Sunday are placed behind religious pictures and statues in homes, stores, and restaurants.

CONTACT:
Florida Division of Tourism
126 W. Van Buren
Tallahassee, FL 32399
904-487-1462; fax: 904-921-9158

SOURCES:
AmerBkDays-1978, p. 280
FolkAmerHol-1991, p. 152

♦ 1398 ♦ Panama Independence Days
November 3; November 28

Panama celebrates two Independence Days: November 28, the anniversary of freedom from Spain, and November 3, the anniversary of independence from Colombia. Both are national holidays. After gaining independence from Spain on November 28, 1821, Panama joined the Republic of Greater Colombia. For 50 years, Panama struggled for complete autonomy. In 1903, Colombia and Panama disagreed on whether to let the U.S. build a canal at Panama. With U.S. backing, Panama broke away on November 3, 1903, and the canal was built.

November 3 is celebrated with parades and fireworks in Panama City.

CONTACT:
Panama Embassy
2862 McGill Terr., N.W.
Washington, D.C. 20008
202-483-1407; fax: 202-483-8413

SOURCES:
AnnivHol-1983, pp. 142, 152
Chases-1996, pp. 440, 462
NatlHolWrld-1968, p. 200

♦ 1399 ♦ Pan American Day
April 14

April 14, 1890, is the day on which the First International Conference of American States adopted a resolution forming what is now known as the Organization of American States (OAS). The member countries include Argentina, Bolivia, Brazil, Chile, Colombia, Costa Rica, Cuba, the Dominican Republic, Ecuador, El Salvador, Guatemala, Haiti, Honduras, Mexico, Nicaragua, Panama, Paraguay, Peru, the United States, Uruguay, and Venezuela. The purpose of the OAS, which has remained basically unchanged since that time, is to strengthen peace and security in the Western Hemisphere by promoting understanding among the various countries of North, Central, and South America. The International Union of American Republics (now called the Pan American Union)—the central permanent agency and general secretariat of the OAS—designated April 14 as Pan American Day in 1930, and it was first observed the following year.

Although each member country holds its own celebration, it is at the Pan American Union building in Washington, D.C., that one of the largest observances takes place. Students from all over the Western Hemisphere travel to Washington where, against a backdrop of flags in the courtyard of the House of the Americas, they perform a program of folk songs and dances. Ceremonies are also held in Miami and in other cities with large populations from Latin American countries.

CONTACT:
Washington D.C. Convention and
   Visitors Association
1212 New York Ave., N.W., Ste.
   600
Washington, D.C. 20005
800-635-6338 or 202-789-7000
fax: 202-789-7037

SOURCES:
AmerBkDays-1978, p. 353
AnnivHol-1983, p. 51
BkHolWrld-1986, Apr 14
Chases-1996, p. 171
DictDays-1988, p. 87

♦ 1400 ♦ Panathenaea
July or August

The most important of the ancient Greek festivals, celebrated in Athens in honor of Athena, the patron goddess of that city. The lesser festival was held every year, and the Great Panathenaea every fourth year with much greater pomp. The date was the 28th of the Attic month of Hecatombaeon (July or August).

In the yearly celebrations, there were musical and athletic contests, animal sacrifices, and a procession. The procession of the Great Panathenaea was an especially grand affair and is pictured on a frieze of the Parthenon. The *peplus,* a garment with an embroidered depiction of the battle of the gods and the giants, was rigged like a sail on a ship with wheels and carried through the city to the Acropolis. The procession included priests leading a train of animals that would be sacrificed, maidens carrying sacrificial implements, warriors, old men with olive branches, and horses. The festival ended with the sacrifice of oxen and a banquet.

SOURCES:
DictMyth-1962, vol. II, p. 1231

♦ 1401 ♦ Pancake Day
Between February 3 and March 9; Shrove Tuesday

For the people of Olney, England, and Liberal, Kansas, Pancake Day is more than another name for Shrove Tuesday. The old custom of making pancakes on the Tuesday preceding Ash Wednesday has survived in the form of a Pancake Race. Ladies of both towns run a 415-yard course, flipping pancakes as they go. Participants must wear a skirt, an apron, and a headscarf, and must toss their pancakes in the air three times as they run. The winner of the Kansas race is announced by a transatlantic phone call to Olney immediately after it is over.

The Olney race dates back to 1445. According to the legend, a housewife who was making pancakes heard the bell summoning her to church and was in such a hurry that she ran along the road with the frying pan still in her hand. The Liberal, Kansas, race has been run since 1950. It only lasts about a minute, but it draws a good deal of media attention and is followed by pancake-eating contests, a parade, and children's races.

CONTACT:
Kansas Division of Travel and
  Tourism
700 S.W. Harrison St., Ste. 1300
Topeka, KS 66603
800-252-6727 or 913-296-2009
fax: 913-296-6988

British Tourist Authority
551 Fifth Ave., Ste. 702
New York, NY 10176
800-462-2748 or 212-986-2200
fax: 212-986-1188

SOURCES:
AmerBkDays-1978, p. 158
AnnivHol-1983, p. 180
BkHolWrld-1986, Feb 25
Chases-1996, p. 106
DictDays-1988, p. 87
DictFolkMyth-1984, p. 842
GdWrldFest-1985, p. 96

♦ 1402 ♦ Panchadaan
August–September, third day of waning half of Hindu month of Bhadrapada; July–August, eighth day of waxing half of Hindu month of Sravana

The **Alms Giving Festival** in Nepal is based on the Dangatha chapter of Kapidawdan, an ancient Buddhist text, stating that those who donate food and clothing to beggars on this day will be blessed with seven great gifts: health, happiness, longevity, wisdom, wealth, fame, and children. All Buddhists, rich or poor, go from door to door in large groups begging for alms. They are usually well-received in Nepalese homes—even non-Buddhist people give food or money to the Buddhist beggars on this day.

In Patan and elsewhere in Nepal, Panchadaan is observed on the eighth day of the waxing half of Sravana. In Katmandu and Bhadgaon, it is observed on the third day of the waning half of Bhadrapada.

SOURCES:
FolkWrldHol-1992, p. 442

♦ 1403 ♦ Panguni Uttiram
March–April; 10 days including full moon day of Hindu month of Caitra

The full moon day of Caitra is the day on which the Hindu god Shiva married the goddess Meenakshi at Madura, Indonesia. The 10-day Hindu festival that follows also celebrates the marriage of Subramanya to Theivanai, adopted daughter of Indra.

Panguni Uttiram is a popular festival in Malaysia, where the worship of Subramanya is widespread. There are fairs on the temple grounds and processions in which Hindu gods and goddesses are carried through the streets in chariots. In Kuala Lumpur, Subramanya and his consort are taken from the Sentul temple in an elaborately decorated chariot through the city streets. Free meals are served throughout the day to visitors.

In Singapore, Panguni Uttiram is a two-day festival held at the Sri Veeramakaliamman Temple. There is a procession of Subramanya on the first day, and special *pujas* (worship ceremonies) are held at the temple on the second day. At Bukit Mertajam, a fire-walking ceremony is held on this day.

In India, this festival is known as Meenakshi Kalyanam.

CONTACT:
Malaysian Tourism Promotion
  Board
818 W. Seventh St., Ste. 804
Los Angeles, CA 90017
213-689-9702; fax: 213-689-1530

Singapore Tourist Promotion
  Board
590 Fifth Ave., 12th Floor
New York, NY 10036
212-302-4861; fax: 212-302-4801

SOURCES:
FolkWrldHol-1992, p. 216

♦ 1404 ♦ Papua New Guinea Independence Day
September 16

This national holiday celebrates Papua New Guinea's independence from Australia on this day in 1975.

CONTACT:
Papua New Guinea Embassy
1615 New Hampshire Ave., N.W.,
  3rd Floor
Washington, D.C. 20009
202-745-3680; fax: 202-745-3679

SOURCES:
AnnivHol-1983, p. 119
Chases-1996, p. 379

♦ 1405 ♦ Paraguay Independence and Flag Day
May 14 and 15

Paraguayans set aside two days to celebrate their independence from Spain, which they won on May 14, 1811, after a bloodless revolution led by Dr. José Gaspar Rodríguez Francia (1766–1840). Dr. Francia was also instrumental in the design of Paraguay's flag, which is the only national flag in the world that is different on both sides.

The most elaborate Independence Day parade is in the capital, Asunción. People may wear traditional clothes as they stroll down the streets: for the men, fancy shirts, broad-brimmed straw hats, ponchos, a *faja* (sash) around the waist, and full trousers known as *bombachas*; for the women, blouses with lace inserts and brightly colored embroidery, full skirts with many layers of petticoats underneath, and a *rebozo* or shawl similar to the Spanish mantilla. *Sopa Paraguay*, a traditional Independence Day dish, is served on this day because it is only on special occasions that the poor can afford to buy the eggs and cheese that go into the soup.

CONTACT:
Paraguayan Embassy
2400 Massachusetts Ave., N.W.
Washington, D.C. 20008
202-483-6960; fax: 202-234-4508

SOURCES:
AnnivHol-1983, p. 65
Chases-1996, p. 213
NatlHolWrld-1968, p. 62

♦ 1406 ♦ Pardon of Nossa Senhora dos Remédios
Early September

Both religious and secular activities play a part in the pilgrimage to the Sanctuary of Our Lady of the Remedies in Lamego, Portugal, a small town known for its port wine and smoked ham. Great numbers of pilgrims climb the monumental staircase up to the baroque church, but the highlight of the festival is the Triumphal Procession on the last day, in which thousands of country people in local costume participate. There is also a battle of flowers, a folklore festival, fireworks, sports contests, and handicraft exhibitions.

CONTACT:
Portuguese National Tourist
  Office
590 Fifth Ave., 4th Floor
New York, NY 10036
212-354-4403; fax: 212-764-6137

SOURCES:
IntlThFolk-1979, p. 308

♦ 1407 ♦ Pardon of Ste. Anne D'Auray
Last weekend in July

In the 17th century in Brittany, the story goes, St. Anne, mother of the Virgin Mary, appeared to a peasant named Yves (or Yvon) and told him that she wanted to see her ruined chapel rebuilt. Yves reported this to his bishop, who at first refused to believe him, but eventually changed his mind. Soon afterward, a broken image of St. Anne was found in a field nearby, and people started making contributions so that the effigy could be enshrined. A church was built in Auray and soon it became a place of pilgrimage for believers all over France.

The **Pardon of St. Anne** remains one of Brittany's most picturesque festivals. On their knees, 20,000 devout Roman Catholics mount the *Scala Santa,* or sacred stairway leading to the chapel containing St. Anne's statue. Many Bretons attending the festival wear the ornate headdresses and embroidered costumes for which their province is famous. They come to pay homage to St. Anne and pray she will grant their requests.

CONTACT:
French Government Tourist Office
9454 Wilshire Blvd., Ste. 715
Beverly Hills, CA 90212
310-271-6665; fax: 310-276-2835

SOURCES:
AmerBkDays-1978, p. 695
BkFest-1937, p. 126
BkHolWrld-1986, Jul 25
FestWestEur-1958, p. 46
FolkWrldHol-1992, p. 382

♦ 1408 ♦ Parentalia
February 13

This was an ancient Roman festival held in honor of the *Manes,* or souls of the dead—in particular, deceased relatives. It was a quiet, serious occasion, without the rowdiness that characterized other Roman festivals. Everything, including the temples, closed down for a week, and people decorated graves with flowers and left food—sometimes elaborate banquets—in the cemeteries in the belief that it would be eaten by the spirits of the deceased. The last day of the festival, known as the **Feast of Peace and Love,** was devoted to forgiveness and the restoration of friendships broken during the preceding year.

SOURCES:
DaysCustFaith-1957, p. 53
DictFolkMyth-1984, p. 673
FestSaintDays-1915, p. 31

♦ 1409 ♦ Parilia (Palilia)
April 21

This ancient Roman festival was held in honor of Pales, the protector of shepherds and their flocks—although some say it was named after *pario,* meaning 'to bear or increase.' Pales was sometimes regarded as male, and therefore similar to Pan or Faunus, and sometimes as female, and therefore related to Vesta, or Anna Parenna (see ANNA PARENNA FESTIVAL). In any case, the Parilia was a pastoral rite that was observed not only in rural areas but in Rome, where it coincided with the city's founding in 753 B.C. In fact, it is believed that Romulus, one of the legendary founders of Rome, played a significant role in the cleansing and renewal rituals associated with the Parilia.

Although no sacrifices were offered, lustrations (purifying ceremonies) were carried out with fire and smoke. The blood that had been preserved from the OCTOBER HORSE SACRIFICE six months earlier was burned, as were bean shells and the ashes of the cattle sacrificed at the CEREALIA. The stables were purified with smoke and swept out with brooms. There were also offerings to Pales of cheese, boiled wine, and millet cakes. In rural areas, heaps of straw were set ablaze, and shepherds and their flocks had to pass over or through them three times. The festival ended with a huge open-air feast.

SOURCES:
AmerBkDays-1978, p. 313
ClassDict-1984, p. 437
DictFolkMyth-1984, p. 845

♦ 1410 ♦ Paris Air and Space Show
June in odd-numbered years

The biennial **Salon Internationale de l'Aéronautique et de l'Espace** is held at Le Bourget Airport just outside of Paris—the airfield where Charles Lindbergh landed after his historic nonstop flight from New York in 1927. It attracts more than half a million visitors who come to see exhibits of aircraft, launching and ground equipment, missile propulsion units, navigational aids, anti-aircraft detection devices, and other aeronautic equipment.

On the last day of the 11-day event there is a special flying demonstration which has occasionally been marred by spectacular crashes. In 1989, for example, a Soviet MiG-29 flying only 580 feet above the ground in a maneuver designed to display its slow-speed handling suddenly plummeted earthward, burying its needle-shaped nose eight feet into the rain-softened turf before bursting into flames. The pilot was fortunate enough to have ejected in time and sustained only minor injuries.

The 39th biennial Paris Air Show was held in 1991, just a few months after the Persian Gulf War, and a worldwide recession had threatened to scuttle the event. But the role played by high technology aircraft in the Allied victory over Saddam Hussein attracted a record number of exhibitors—approximately 1,700 from 38 countries—and spectators.

CONTACT:
French Government Tourist Office
9454 Wilshire Blvd., Ste. 715
Beverly Hills, CA 90212
310-271-6665; fax: 310-276-2835

SOURCES:
GdWrldFest-1985, p. 81

♦ 1411 ♦ Paris Autumn Festival (Festival d'Automne)

Mid-September through the end of December

The Autumn Festival marks the return of Parisians from their August holidays and the start of the city's cultural season. When it was founded in 1972, the festival incorporated two existing events—Semaines Musicales Internationales and the Festival of International Dance—with theater and art exhibitions. It now encompasses film, photography, and other contemporary arts on an international scale.

Most of the theater presentations are experimental in some way, and they have included productions by Richard Foreman's Ontological Hysteric Theatre from the United States, Peter Stein's Schaubuhne am Halleschen Ufer from West Berlin, Denmark's Odin Teatret, Poland's Teatr Cricot 2, and Taganka Theatre from the former U.S.S.R. Composers whose works have been performed there include Pierre Boulez, György Ligeti, John Cage, and Iannis Zenakis. Martha Graham's, Merce Cunningham's, and Maurice Béjart's dance companies have performed at the festival, as have the New York Philharmonic, the London Sinfonietta, and the Orchestre de Paris. Events are held in over 45 locations throughout Paris, among them the Pompidou Center, the Théâtre de Chaillot, and the Théâtre des Champs Elysées.

CONTACT:
French Government Tourist Office
9454 Wilshire Blvd., Ste. 715
Beverly Hills, CA 90212
310-271-6665; fax: 310-276-2835

SOURCES:
IntlThFolk-1979, p. 116
MusFestEurBrit-1980, p. 86

♦ 1412 ♦ Paris Festival Estival

Mid-July to mid-September

Also known as the **Summer Festival of Paris**, this two-month summer music festival was founded in 1967 to provide the city with a more active cultural life during the normally quiet months of July and August, when many Parisians are away on vacation. More than 100 different events take place during the festival, which focuses on symphonic, chamber, vocal, and contemporary music as well as exhibits and discussion groups devoted to the theme of the festival or to a certain composer. Concerts are held throughout the city in such well-known sites as Sainte Chapelle, Notre Dame Cathedral, the church at Saint-Germain des Pres, the Palace of Chaillot, and the Conciergerie. A 90-minute audio-visual program about the history of Paris is presented nightly in the courtyard of the Palais Royal, accompanied by a 100-piece orchestra.

CONTACT:
French Government Tourist Office
9454 Wilshire Blvd., Ste. 715
Beverly Hills, CA 90212
310-271-6665; fax: 310-276-2835

SOURCES:
GdWrldFest-1985, p. 82
IntlThFolk-1979, p. 118
MusFestEurBrit-1980, p. 87

♦ 1413 ♦ Paro Tshechu

Early spring on a date set by the lamas, or 10th–15th days of second lunar month

One of the most popular festivals of Bhutan, a principality northeast of India in the Himalayas, is held in the town of Paro. (*Tshechus* means 'tenth day' and relates to the birth of the Buddha. It is used as 'festival' is used in English.)

The Paro festival is held over five days to commemorate the life and deeds of Padmasambhava (*see also* MYSTERY PLAY OF TIBET). Known in Bhutan as Guru Rinpoche, he was a mystic who lived in the eighth century and brought Buddhism to Bhutan from Tibet. The purpose of this festival is to exorcize evil influences and to ensure good fortune in the coming year. The highlight of Paro events comes before dawn on the last day when a huge appliqued scroll known as the *Thongdrel* is unfurled from the top of the wall of the *Dzong* (the monastery and district center). It is displayed to onlookers in the courtyard until just before the first rays of the sun touch it. The Thongdrel is said to have the power to confer blessings and provide respite from the cycle of existence. It is a type of *thangka* (a religious scroll of any size) and is so big that it covers the three-story wall of the Dzong, and it depicts the life of the Guru Rinpoche, his various peaceful manifestations, and his consorts.

Dressed in their best clothes, people bring dried yak meat and *churra*, a puffed rice dish, to the Dzong and watch masked dancers. A series of dances, called *cham*, are performed for the festival. One of these, the Black Hat Dance, tells of the victory over a Tibetan king who tried to wipe out Buddhism; those who watch the dance are supposed to receive great spiritual blessings. The Dance of the Four Stags commemorates the vanquishing of the god of the wind by Guru Rinpoche. The god rode on a stag, and the guru commandeered the stag as his own mount. Another dance, the Deer Dance, tells the story of Guru Rinpoche teaching Buddhism while traveling through the country on the back of a deer. The dances are performed by monks who play the roles of deities, heroes, and animals dressed in brilliantly colored silks and brocades. They wear carved wooden or papier mâché masks symbolizing the figure they portray.

The dances are accompanied by the music of drums, bells, gongs, conch-shell trumpets, and horns. Some horns are so long that they touch the ground.

Other activities include folk dancing and singing and lewd performances by clowns called *atsaras*. Many of the dances and performances are typical of Tibetan Buddhist traditions also observed in Tibet and the Ladakh area of India.

CONTACT:
Kingdom of Bhutan Consulate
 General
2 U.N. Plaza, 27th Floor
New York, NY 10017
212-826-1919; fax: 212-826-2998

SOURCES:
BkHolWrld-1986, Apr 20

♦ 1414 ♦ Parshurama Jayanti

April–May; third day of waxing half of Hindu month of Vaisakha

According to Hindu mythology, it was Parashurama (Rama with an Ax) who destroyed the evil Kshatriya kings and princes 21 times, including the thousand-armed warrior, Arjuna. His birthday, Parashurama Jayanti, is therefore observed with fasting, austerities, and prayer. It is also a day to worship Lord Vishnu, of whom Parashurama is believed to be the sixth incarnation. To Hindus, Parashurama represents filial obedience, austerity, power, and brahmanic ideals.

Parashurama's story is told in the *Mahabharata* and in the Puranas, or Hindu epics. He also appears in the *Ramayana*, where he challenges Ramachandra, the seventh avatar or incarnation of Vishnu, to a test of strength. When it becomes apparent that he is losing, Parashurama pays homage to Ramachandra and retires to the Himalayas. The Malabar region on the southwest coast of India is believed to have been founded by Parashurama.

SOURCES:
DictFolkMyth-1984, p. 844
RelHolCal-1993, p. 101

Partita a Scácchi Viventi, La
See **Living Chess Game**

♦ 1415 ♦ Partridge Day
September 1

This is traditionally the day on which the partridge-hunting season opens in England. Just as Grouse Day in Scotland (*see* GLORIOUS TWELFTH) was often referred to as St. Grouse's Day, Partridge Day was sometimes called **St. Partridge's Day**.

SOURCES:
DictDays-1988, p. 87

♦ 1416 ♦ Paryushana
August–September; Hindu month of Bhadrapada

Like most other Jaina festivals, the Paryushana festival is observed by focusing on the 10 cardinal virtues: forgiveness, charity, simplicity, contentment, truthfulness, self-restraint, fasting, detachment, humility, and continence. Believers ask those whom they may have offended to forgive them, and friendships that have lapsed during the year are restored.

The Paryushana festival is observed all over India in the month of Bhadrapada (August–September), but on different dates. The Svetambara Jainas observe it for eight days, and then the 10-day celebration of the Digambara Jainas begins.

SOURCES:
FolkWrldHol-1992, p. 443
RelHolCal-1993, p. 101

Pasch Monday
See **Easter Monday**

♦ 1417 ♦ Pascua Florida Day
On or near April 2

Although no one knows for certain the date on which Ponce de León (1460–1521) landed at Florida in 1513, it is widely believed that he first stepped ashore somewhere between St. Augustine and the mouth of the St. Johns River on April 2. He named the land Pascua Florida because it was Eastertime. *Pascua* is a Spanish word meaning 'Easter,' and *Florida* means 'flowering' or 'full of flowers.' (In Scotland and northern England, another name for EASTER was Pasch Day; among Orthodox Christians it is called Pascha.)

The Florida state legislature designated April 2 **Florida State**

Day in 1953, but when it falls on a Saturday or Sunday, the holiday is observed on the preceding Friday or the following Monday. The week ending on April 2 is known as Pascua Florida Week, a time when both school children and adults are encouraged to attend special programs devoted to the area's discovery and history.

SOURCES:
AmerBkDays-1978, p. 316
AnnivHol-1983, p. 47
Chases-1996, p. 155
DictDays-1988, p. 87

♦ 1418 ♦ Passion Play at Tzintzuntzan
Between March 19 and April 22; Thursday and Friday before Easter

The *Penitentes*, or penitents, are a lay brotherhood of religious flagellants. In Mexico on GOOD FRIDAY, they often participate in passion plays dramatizing the events of the closing days in the life of Christ. One of the most complete and colorful passion plays is the one staged in Tzintzuntzan. Performed in an olive grove near the church, the play begins at noon on the Thursday preceding EASTER with a representation of the Last Supper and continues until midnight on Good Friday. The penitents wear black loincloths and face-coverings, lashing their own bare backs and wearing chains that bite into the flesh of their ankles. They carry heavy crosses in imitation of Jesus. In passion plays elsewhere in Mexico, the penitents hold bundles of cacti on their shoulders while candles burn into the palms of their hands.

CONTACT:
Mexican Government Tourist Office
405 Park Ave., Ste. 1401
New York, NY 10022
800-446-3942 or 212-755-7261
fax: 212-753-2874

SOURCES:
DictFolkMyth-1984, p. 851
IntlThFolk-1979, p. 277

Passion Plays
See **Black Hills Passion Play; Oberammergau Passion Play**

Passion Saturday
See **Holy Saturday**

♦ 1419 ♦ Passover
Begins between March 27 and April 24; Nisan 15–21 (or 22)

Also known as **Pesah, Pesach,** or the **Feast of Unleavened Bread,** Passover is an eight-day celebration (seven days in Israel and by Reform Jews) of the deliverance of the Jews from slavery in Egypt. It is one of the three PILGRIM FESTIVALS (*see also* SHAVUOT and SUKKOT). According to the book of Exodus, when Pharaoh refused to let Moses lead the Jews out of Egypt, God sent a number of plagues—including locusts, fire, and hailstones—but Pharaoh still was unmoved. A 10th and final plague, during which the Angel of Death was sent to kill the Egyptians' first-born sons, finally persuaded Pharaoh to relent. All the Jews had been instructed to sacrifice a lamb and sprinkle the blood on their doorposts so that the Angel would "pass over" and spare their sons.

Jewish families today eat a ceremonial dinner called the *Seder* at which they retell the story of the Exodus from Egypt and eat various symbolic foods—including meat of the paschal lamb, bitter herbs (recalling the harsh life of slavery) and wine (symbolizing the fruitfulness of the earth). The *matzoh*, a flat, unleavened bread, is meant to symbolize the haste with which the Jews left: they didn't have time to let their bread rise before baking it. In strictly religious Jewish homes today, all foods made with leavening are prohibited during this season.

See also HAGODOL; FIRST-BORN, FAST OF THE

SOURCES:
AmerBkDays-1978, p. 362
BkFest-1937, p. 207
BkFestHolWrld-1970, pp. 52, 63
BkHolWrld-1986, Apr 4
DaysCustFaith-1957, p. 112
DictWrldRel-1989, pp. 155, 390, 560, 668
FolkAmerHol-1991, p. 145
FolkWrldHol-1992, p. 235
RelHolCal-1993, p. 102

Patrickmas
See **St. Patrick's Day**

♦ 1420 ♦ Patriots' Day
Third Monday in April

The battles of Lexington and Concord, Massachusetts, marked the beginning of the American Revolution on April 19, 1775. This is a legal holiday in Massachusetts and Maine. Although no one really knows who fired the first shot on the Lexington green—"the shot heard 'round the world," in the words of Ralph Waldo Emerson—the British proceeded from Lexington to Concord, where there was a second bloody confrontation at North Bridge.

Residents of Maine and Massachusetts have observed Patriots' Day since the 18th century with costume parades, flag-raising ceremonies, and reenactments of the battles and the famous rides of Paul Revere and William Dawes, who were sent to warn their comrades in Concord of the British troops' approach. The BOSTON MARATHON, one of the most famous of the world's marathon races, is run each year on Patriot's Day from Hopkinton, Massachusetts, to the Back Bay section of Boston. Sometimes this day is referred to as **Lexington Day** or **Battles of Lexington and Concord Day**.

CONTACT:
Massachusetts Office of Travel and Tourism
100 Cambridge St., 13th Floor
Boston, MA 02202
800-447-6277 or 617-727-3201
fax: 617-727-6525

SOURCES:
AmerBkDays-1978, p. 359
AnnivHol-1983, p. 53
Chases-1996, p. 172
DictDays-1988, pp. 68, 88

♦ 1421 ♦ Paul Bunyan Show
First full weekend in October

Paul Bunyan is the mythical hero of lumberjacks in the United States, and many tall tales have been passed down about his adventures with Babe the Blue Ox and Johnny Inkslinger. Among other things, these tales describe how he created Puget Sound and the Grand Canyon, and how his hotcake griddle was so large that it had to be greased by men

using sides of bacon for skates. The first Bunyan stories were published in 1910, and within 15 years he had become a national legend.

Since 1952 the **Paul Bunyan Festival**, sponsored jointly by the Ohio Forestry Association and Hocking College in Nelsonville (which grants an Associate Degree in Forestry) has focused on wood products and forestry conservation. It is the lumber industry's opportunity to familiarize visitors with the journey wood takes from the forest to finished products and an opportunity for both professional and student lumberjacks to test their skills in chopping and sawing. Teams of draft horses compete in a log-skidding contest—an operation that is performed today by heavy machines—and turn-of-the-century steam logging equipment is on display. Billed as the largest live forestry exposition in the East, the show gives visitors an opportunity to see both traditional and modern logging techniques in action.

CONTACT:
Hocking Technical College
3301 Hocking Pkwy.
Nelsonville, OH 45764
614-753-3591; fax: 614-753-4097

SOURCES:
Chases-1996, p. 403

Ohio Division of Travel and Tourism
P.O. Box 1001
Columbus, OH 43266
800-282-5393 or 614-466-8844
fax: 614-466-6744

♦ 1422 ♦ Payment of Quit Rent
September 29

One of London's oldest and most unusual events, the annual payment of the Quit Rent takes place at the Royal Courts of Justice on MICHAELMAS, September 29. The ceremony symbolizes the city of London's payment to the Crown for two parcels of land: the first, known as The Forge, is thought to have been the old tournament ground for the Knights of the Templars, who rented it in 1235 for an annual payment of horseshoes and nails. The second, a piece of land in Shropshire known as The Moors, came into the city's possession during the reign of Henry VIII and was rented from the Crown for an annual payment of a bill-hook and a hatchet.

During the first part of the ceremony, the City Solicitor counts out six huge horseshoes from Flemish war horses and 61 nails. He gives them to the Queen's Remembrancer, who keeps them in his office until the following year. During the second part, the City Solicitor demonstrates how sharp the blades of the bill-hook and hatchet are by cutting up a bundle of twigs. These, too, are presented to the Queen's Remembrancer, who is dressed in his wig and ceremonial robes.

CONTACT:
British Tourist Authority
551 Fifth Ave., Ste. 702
New York, NY 10176
800-462-2748 or 212-986-2200
fax: 212-986-1188

SOURCES:
YrbookEngFest-1954, p. 137

♦ 1423 ♦ Payson Rodeo
Mid-August

A rodeo and parade and general wild-west three-day weekend in the cowboy-and-cattle country of Payson, Ariz.

The first Payson rodeo was held in 1885, and it's been held ever since with no interruptions, not even for war, making it the world's oldest continuous Professional Rodeo Cowboys Association rodeo. Events of the weekend include the parade with floats, dancers, and cowboys, country music, a chili cookout, and arts and crafts. Total attendance is usually about 30,000.

CONTACT:
Professional Rodeo Cowboys
    Association
101 Pro Rodeo Dr.
Colorado Springs, CO 80919
719-593-8840; fax: 719-548-4876

Arizona Office of Tourism
1100 W. Washington St.
Phoenix, AZ 85007
800-842-8257 or 602-542-8687
fax: 602-542-4068

SOURCES:
Chases-1996, p. 340

♦ 1424 ♦ **Peanut Festival, National**
Mid-October

A two-week festival in Dothan, Ala., honoring the peanut, a multimillion-dollar crop in Alabama. A highlight is the Goober Parade, for which the streets are paved with peanuts by a giant cement mixer that moves along the line of march throwing out a ton of peanuts, while parade watchers scramble for them. It is said the parade attracts as many as 350,000 spectators. Other events include the selection of Peanut Farmer of the Year, a cooking contest of peanut dishes, crafts exhibits, fireworks, a beauty pageant, and a greased-pig contest, with the pigs coated with peanut oil, of course.

The festival began in 1938, was discontinued during World War II, and resumed in 1947. Revenues from the festival help the economy not only of Dothan but of neighboring areas of Florida and Georgia. Plains, Ga., the home of peanut farmer and former President Jimmy Carter, is just over the state border.

The peanut and its potential became nationally if not internationally known because of the work of George Washington Carver, who in 1896 became head of agricultural research at Tuskegee Institute in Tuskegee, Ala. His research program ultimately developed 300 derivative products from peanuts, including cheese, flour, inks, dyes, soap, and cosmetics. The research was crucial to the South's economy; the peanut crop freed farmers of their dependence on cotton, which depleted the soil and could be wiped out by boll weevils. When Carver arrived in Tuskegee, the peanut was not recognized as a crop; within the next 50 years, it became the South's second largest cash crop after cotton.

CONTACT:
Alabama Bureau of Tourism and
    Travel
P.O. Box 4927
Montgomery, AL 36103
800-252-2263 or 334-242-4169
fax: 334-242-4554

SOURCES:
GdUSFest-1984, p. 4

♦ 1425 ♦ **Pearl Harbor Day**
December 7

The anniversary of the Japanese raid on Pearl Harbor in 1941, bringing the United States into World War II and widening the European war to the Pacific.

The bombing, which began at 7:55 A.M. Hawaiian time on a Sunday morning, lasted little more than an hour but devastated the American military base on the island of Oahu in the Hawaiian Islands. Nearly all the ships of the U.S. Pacific Fleet were anchored there side by side, and most were damaged or destroyed; half the bombers at the army's Hickam Field were destroyed. The battleship USS *Arizona* sank, and 1,177 sailors and Marines went down with the ship, which became their tomb. In all, the attack claimed more than 3,000 casualties—2,403 killed and 1,178 wounded.

On the following day, President Franklin D. ROOSEVELT addressed a solemn Congress to ask for a declaration of war. His opening unforgettable words: "Yesterday, December 7, 1941—a date which will live in infamy—the United States of America was suddenly and deliberately attacked by naval and air forces of the Empire of Japan." War was declared immediately with only one opposing vote, that by Rep. Jeannette Rankin of Montana.

In the months that followed, the slogan "Remember Pearl Harbor" swept America, and radio stations repeatedly played the song of the same name with these lyrics:

> *Let's remember Pearl Harbor, as we go to meet the foe,*
> *Let's remember Pearl Harbor, as we did the Alamo.*
> *We will always remember, how they died for liberty,*
> *Let's remember Pearl Harbor, and go on to victory.*

Many states proclaim a Pearl Harbor Remembrance Day, and each year, services are held on December 7 at the *Arizona* Memorial in Pearl Harbor. The marble memorial, built over the sunken USS *Arizona* and dedicated in 1962, was designed by architect Albert Preis, a resident of Honolulu who was an Austrian citizen in 1941 and was interned as an enemy alien.

In 1991, on the 50th anniversary of the attack, commemorations were held over several days in Hawaii.

The observations began on Dec. 4, designated as Hawaii Remembrance Day. Ceremonies recalled the death of civilians in downtown Pearl Harbor. One of them was Nancy Masako Arakaki, a nine-year-old Japanese-American girl killed when anti-aircraft shells fell on her Japanese-language school.

On Dec. 5, Survivors Day, families of those present in Pearl Harbor in 1941 attended ceremonies at the *Arizona* Memorial. Franklin Van Valkenburgh, the commanding officer of the USS *Arizona*, was among those remembered; he posthumously won the Medal of Honor for his heroism aboard ship.

Dec. 6 was a Day of Reflection, intended to focus on the gains since the war rather than on the losses of the day.

On Pearl Harbor Day itself, former President George Bush, who received the Distinguished Flying Cross for heroism as a Navy pilot in the Pacific during World War II, spoke at ceremonies beginning at 7:55 A.M. at the *Arizona* Memorial. Other dignitaries were all Americans; no foreign representatives were invited, out of political prudence. Other events included a parade, a flyover by jet fighters, an outdoor concert by the Honolulu Symphony presenting the premiere of *Pearl Harbor Overture: Time of Remembrance* by John Duffy, and a wreath-laying service at the National Memorial Cemetery of the Pacific in the Punchbowl overlooking Honolulu. And finally, at sunset on Pearl Harbor Day, survivors and their families gathered at the Arizona Visitors Center for a final service to honor those who died aboard the battleship in 1941.

CONTACT:
Hawaii Visitors Bureau
2270 Kalakaua Ave., Ste. 801
Honolulu, HI 96815
808-923-1811; fax: 808-922-8991

SOURCES:
AmerBkDays-1978, p. 1082
AnnivHol-1983, p. 157
Chases-1996, p. 474

♦ 1426 ♦ Pendleton Round-Up and Happy Canyon
Second full week in September

One of the best-known rodeos in the West, held since 1910 in the small ranch town of Pendleton, Ore. The home of internationally known saddle makers, Pendleton is also the heart of Oregon's wheat-producing region. The week-long round-up started as a celebration of the end of the wheat harvest. Happy Canyon was inaugurated four years later when two local men decided the entertainment at a local fair was of poor quality and too expensive. The Happy Canyon shows at first depicted historical episodes and evolved into the present-day Happy Canyon Pageant, a presentation by Northwest Indian tribes that features a teepee encampment and ceremonial dancing. Nowadays, each day of the rodeo begins with a cowboy breakfast (ham, eggs, flapjacks) at Stillman Park and ends with the pageant.

In between, the rodeo features the standard competitions approved by the Professional Rodeo Cowboys Association—bronco riding, bareback riding, Brahma bull riding, steer wrestling, and calf and steer roping. Additionally, there are wild-horse and stagecoach races and wild-cow milking.

CONTACT:
Oregon Tourism Division
775 Summer St., N.E.
Salem, OR 97310
800-547-7842 or 503-986-0000
fax: 503-986-0001

SOURCES:
AmerBkDays-1978, p. 846
Chases-1996, p. 372

♦ 1427 ♦ Pennsylvania Day
On or near October 24

The state of Pennsylvania was named for William Penn, who was born in London on October 24, 1644. As a young man he joined the Quakers, who were at that time considered a radical religious group, and eventually he used his inheritance from his father to establish a Quaker colony in the New World. He put a great deal of thought and planning into how his colony would be governed, and insisted that the colonists treat the Indians with respect. The colony thrived, its population growing from about 1,000 in 1682 to more than 12,000 seven years later.

Pennsylvanians have always held large celebrations on major anniversaries of Penn's birth, and in 1932 the governor proclaimed October 24 as **William Penn Commemoration Day**, or simply **Penn Day**. This day was also commemorated with a special pageant held in Jordans, Buckinghamshire, England, where Penn and his family are buried. Since that time celebrations have tended to be local rather than statewide. In recent decades, the week of October 24 has been celebrated as **Pennsylvania Week**.

Any observation using his name would undoubtedly have made William Penn turn over in his grave, as he was outspo-ken in his opposition to the practice of naming streets, cities, states, or anything else after people.

SOURCES:
AmerBkDays-1978, p. 951
BkDays-1864, vol. II, p. 60
DictDays-1988, p. 91
DictWrldRel-1989, p. 564

♦ 1428 ♦ Pennsylvania Dutch Days
Last week in July

This week-long celebration of the arts, crafts, customs, and folklore of Pennsylvania's early German settlers was founded in 1949 by the members of an evening class studying the Pennsylvania-Dutch dialect. It started out as a one-day exhibition in Hershey, but was extended by popular demand to six days. It is now considered the oldest and largest of the many Pennsylvania Dutch celebrations that take place annually.

One of the festival's most outstanding features is the display of more than 300 handmade quilts—the largest exhibit of its kind in the world. There are demonstrations of flax handling, oak basketmaking, glassblowing, cigarmaking, candle dipping, bookbinding, and the painting of "hex signs"—the bright, circular designs often seen on Pennsylvania Dutch houses and barns. There are also lectures and seminars on the origins, arts, and folk customs of the Pennsylvania Dutch, a church service and hymn sing in Pennsylvania Dutch dialect, and an extensive display of farm buildings and implements. Traditional foods served at the festival include pretzels, apple butter, shoo-fly pie, and the traditional "seven sweets and seven sours" (pickles).

CONTACT:
Pennsylvania Office of Travel
Marketing
453 Forum Bldg.
Harrisburg, PA 17120
800-237-4363 or 717-787-5453
fax: 717-234-4560

SOURCES:
AmerBkDays-1978, p. 776

♦ 1429 ♦ Pentecost
Between May 10 and June 13 in West and between May 24 and June 27 in East; seventh Sunday after Easter

As recorded in the New Testament in Acts 2, it was on the 50th day after EASTER that the Apostles were praying together and the Holy Spirit descended on them in the form of tongues of fire. They received the "gift of tongues"—the ability to speak in other languages—and immediately began to preach about Jesus Christ to the Jews from all over the world who had flocked to Jerusalem for the Feast of SHAVUOT. (Pentecost, from the Greek word meaning 'fiftieth,' is also one of the names for the second of the three Jewish PILGRIM FESTIVALS.) Christian Pentecost thus became not only a commemoration of the Holy Spirit's visit but is the birth of the Christian Church. Interestingly, it was on roughly this same day, centuries earlier, that Moses received the Ten Commandments on Mt. Sinai and the Jewish religious community got its start.

The English call it **White Sunday**, or **Whitsunday**, after the white garments worn on Pentecost by the newly baptized. Although it is not certain when Pentecost began to be observed by Christians, it may have been as early as the first century. The period beginning with the Saturday before Whitsunday and ending the following Saturday is known as **Whitsuntide,** or in modern times simply as **Whitsun.**

Whitsunday has been linked to pagan spring rites, such as the English custom of Morris dancing and the drinking of "Whitsun ale." In Scotland, Whitsunday was one of the QUARTER DAYS. In Estonia and Finland eggs are dyed as at Easter because their hens don't lay until this time. In Germany it is called **Pfingsten,** and pink and red peonies, called *Pfingstrosen,* or 'Whitsun roses', are the symbols along with birch trees. Some churches lower a carved dove into the congregation and call this "swinging the Holy Ghost." Cattle are decorated and an overdressed person is said to be "dressed like a Whitsun ox." A holdover pagan game is called 'hunting the green man', or *Laubmannchen*—a young man dressed in leaves and moss hides, and children hunt him.

See also PINKSTER DAY

SOURCES:
AmerBkDays-1978, pp. 461, 464
BkDays-1864, vol. I, p. 629
BkFest-1937, pp. 97, 135, 244, 268
DaysCustFaith-1957, pp. 161, 354
DictFolkMyth-1984, pp. 629, 750, 1127, 1175, 1176
FestSaintDays-1915, p. 118
FestWestEur-1958, pp. 26, 42, 65, 153, 165, 215, 233
FolkAmerHol-1991, p. 226
FolkWrldHol-1992, p. 282
SaintFestCh-1904, p. 245

People Power Anniversary
See **Fiesta sa EDSA**

♦ 1430 ♦ **Peppercorn Ceremony**
Day near April 23

This ceremony has been a tradition on the island of Bermuda since 1816, when a lease to the State House in St. George (the seat of Bermuda's government from 1620–1815) was granted to the mayor, aldermen, and common council of St. George in trust by the members of the Masonic Lodge for the annual rent of one peppercorn. The date for the annual rent payment was originally December 27, the feast of ST. JOHN THE EVANGELIST, but it was changed to the most suitable day nearest April 23, ST. GEORGE'S DAY, in honor of the patron saint for whom the town is named.

On the day of the Peppercorn Ceremony, the governor of Bermuda arrives at the State House with great pomp in a horse-drawn carriage, is welcomed by the mayor of St. George, and receives a key to the State House for the purpose of holding a meeting of Her Majesty's Executive Council, which upholds the conditions of the lease. The rent of one peppercorn is delivered on a velvet pillow and members of the Executive Council proceed to the State House for their meeting.

The old State House building, with mortar made of turtle oil and lime, was constructed in 1619 and is believed to be the first stone building in Bermuda. Until the capital was moved to Hamilton in 1815, Parliament met there. Bermuda's Parliament is the third oldest in the world (after Iceland and England).

CONTACT:
Bermuda Dept. of Tourism
310 Madison Ave., Ste. 201
New York, NY 10017
800-223-6106 or 212-818-9800
fax: 212-983-5289

SOURCES:
AnnivHol-1983, p. 56
Chases-1996, p. 182

Perahera Procession
See **Esala Perahera**

♦ 1431 ♦ **Perchtenlauf**
January 6

The Perchtenlauf in Austria is usually held on EPIPHANY, but in some areas it is celebrated at a later date. The *Perchten* are old masks, usually of witches and fearsome animals, that have been handed down from generation to generation. People wearing the masks run through the village beating drums, ringing bells, singing, shouting, and making as much noise as possible to scare winter away—an ancient custom that can be traced back to pre-Christian times. Another tradition associated with the Perchtenlauf is the cracking of whips—again, an attempt to drive out winter.

Dancing also plays a part in the celebration. The *Perchtentanz* takes place when the procession of masked figures stops in the main square of the village and everyone begins to dance wildly, making even more noise than before. The Perchten dances of Imst and Thaur in Tirol are particularly well known for their brightly colored old masks.

See also EPIPHANY IN GERMANY

CONTACT:
Austrian National Tourist Office
P.O. Box 1142, Times Square
New York, NY 10148
212-944-6880; fax: 212-730-4568

SOURCES:
DictFolkMyth-1984, p. 346

♦ 1432 ♦ **Peru Independence Day**
June 28–29

Peru had been a colony of Spain for nearly 300 years when Simon Bolívar (1783–1830), along with José SAN MARTÍN (1778–1850), led the Battle of Ayacucho in 1824 that resulted in the end of Spanish rule of Bolivia and Peru. Bolívar then became the ruler of Peru (*see also* BOLIVIA INDEPENDENCE DAY).

Celebrated all over Peru, Independence Day is a public holiday. In the south, festivities also take place on July 25, St. James's Day.

CONTACT:
Embassy of Peru
1700 Massachusetts Ave., N.W.
Washington, D.C. 20036
202-833-9860; fax: 202-659-8124

SOURCES:
AnnivHol-1983, p. 98
Chases-1996, p. 313
NatlHolWrld-1968, p. 127

♦ 1433 ♦ **Peyote Dance (Híkuli Dance)**
January

To the Tarahumara and Huichol Indians of northern Mexico, peyote, or *híkuli,* is the mescal button, derived from the tops of a cactus plant and used as a stimulant or hallucinogen during religious ceremonies. In October and November, they make long journeys to eastern Chihuahua to gather híkuli.

Upon their return, they sacrifice a sheep or a goat and paint their faces with symbolic designs. Then they perform the híkuli dance to the accompaniment of deer-hoof rattles or two notched deer bones rubbed together. They jump and twist their bodies, making jerky movements in a counter-clockwise direction around the shaman and a ceremonial fire.

Híkuli is identified with the deer, and the híkuli dance is performed after the first deer hunt in January. It is designed not only to induce a supernatural state in the dancers, but also to encourage the growth of crops. The dancers often paint their faces with grains of corn, squash vines, fruit, and rain symbols.

CONTACT:
Mexican Government Tourist Office
405 Park Ave., Ste. 1401
New York, NY 10022
800-446-3942 or 212-755-7261
fax: 212-753-2874

SOURCES:
DictFolkMyth-1984, p. 861

♦ 1434 ♦ Pffiferdaj
First Sunday in September

An Alsatian festival of medieval origin, Pffiferdaj—also known as the **Day of the Strolling Fiddlers,** or **Fiddlers' Festival**—is celebrated in the city of Ribeauvillé, France, an area widely known for its wines. In the Middle Ages the Ribeaupierre family started a musicians' union here, and every September the musicians of Alsace gathered to pay homage to the lord of Ribeaupierre by forming a procession to the church of Notre Dame du Dusenbach.

Today the custom continues. Wine flows freely from the fountain in front of the town hall, and a procession of fiddlers and other musicians, often playing old instruments, makes its way through the town. Their costumes and floats recall life in the Middle Ages.

CONTACT:
French Government Tourist Office
9454 Wilshire Blvd., Ste. 715
Beverly Hills, CA 90212
310-271-6665; fax: 310-276-2835

SOURCES:
BkHolWrld-1986, Sep 9

♦ 1435 ♦ Phagwa
Full moon day in March

The Hindu festival of Phagwa celebrates the VERNAL EQUINOX and the start of the Hindu New Year (*see* VAISAKH). In Trinidad and Tobago, a Carnival spirit has gradually pervaded the festivities, which now combine both secular and religious elements and are no longer confined to Hindus. The celebration includes bonfires (to symbolize the destruction of Holika, the evil sister of King Hiranya Kashipu; *see also* HOLI) and Chowtal-singing competitions, which mix religious and secular music and are heavily influenced by calypso. The spraying of *Abeer* powder, a red vegetable dye made into a bright fuchsia liquid, gives everyone's hair and skin a tie-dyed effect.

Band competitions, similar to those held at Carnival (*see* TRINIDAD AND TOBAGO CARNIVAL), are held at several locations throughout the island. There are also reenactments of the legend of Holika, complete with oriental costumes, crowns, jewelry, and flowers.

CONTACT:
Trinidad and Tobago Tourism Development Authority
25 W. 43rd St., Ste. 1508
New York, NY 10036
800-232-0082 or 212-719-0540
fax: 212-719-0988

♦ 1436 ♦ Philippines Independence Day
June 12

As a result of the Spanish-American War, the United States became involved in the Filipino struggle for independence at the end of the 19th century. The Americans called back Emilio Aguinaldo (1869–1964), the exiled rebel leader, and helped him bring centuries of Spanish rule to an end. Aguinaldo declared the islands independent on June 12, 1898. But the U.S. acquired the Philippines after signing the Treaty of Paris in 1899, and it wasn't until July 4, 1946, that the islands were granted full independence.

For many years, Filipinos set aside July 4 to celebrate their own independence and to acknowledge their longstanding ties to the United States. But in 1962, President Diosdada Macapagal changed the date to June 12, the anniversary of Aguinaldo's initial declaration of independence from Spain. The U.S. ambassador often speaks at Independence Day ceremonies in Manila, which include a military parade and the pealing of church bells. After the official ceremonies are over, Filipinos devote the remainder of the day to recreation. There are games and athletic competitions, fireworks displays, and Independence Day balls. In Hawaii, which has a large Filipino population, there is often a Fiesta Filipina with music, folk dancing, games, and Philippine pageantry.

CONTACT:
Philippine Department of Tourism
556 Fifth Ave.
First Floor Mezzanine
New York, NY 10036
212-575-7915; fax: 212-302-6759

Hawaii Visitors Bureau
2270 Kalakaua Ave., Ste. 801
Honolulu, HI 96815
808-923-1811; fax: 808-922-8991

SOURCES:
AmerBkDays-1978, p. 547
AnnivHol-1983, p. 78
Chases-1996, p. 252
NatlHolWrld-1968, p. 83

♦ 1437 ♦ Phra Buddha Bat Fair
March

An annual festival at the Phra Buddha Bat temple (the Shrine of the Holy Footprint), a hill temple near Saraburi, Thailand, where the Holy Footprint of the Buddha is enshrined. This is one of the most sacred places in Thailand, and pilgrims throng here during the festival to pay homage. The festival features performances of folk music and a handicraft bazaar.

CONTACT:
Tourism Authority of Thailand
5 World Trade Center, Ste. 3443
New York, NY 10048
212-432-0433; fax: 212-912-0920

Pichincha Day
See **Ecuador Independence Day**

◆ 1438 ◆ **Pickle Festival**
Third weekend in August

The small town of Linwood, Michigan, is a center for pickle growing and processing. Since 1977 it has hosted a three-day festival in honor of its native product. Because so many local residents grow their own cucumbers and develop their own pickling recipes, there is a pickle-canning contest. Another popular event is the pickle-eating contest. Competitors are timed to see how long it takes them to unwrap and eat a pickle. The first one who is able to whistle afterward wins.

CONTACT:
Pickle Festival
Linwood Park Board
P.O. Box 386
Linwood, MI 48634
517-697-3868

◆ 1439 ◆ **Pied Piper Open Air Theater**
Sundays, June through mid-September

A dramatization of the legend of the Pied Piper of Hamelin, presented on an open-air stage in Hamelin (or Hameln), Germany.

According to the legend, in 1284 Hamelin was infested with rats. A stranger appeared, wearing an outlandishly colored (pied) coat, and he promised to free the town of its plague of vermin if they would pay him a set sum of money. The town agreed, and the piper began playing his pipes, and all the rats and mice came out of the houses and gathered around the piper. He led them to the Weser River, walked into it, and they followed him and were drowned. But the citizens refused to pay the piper. He left, angry. On June 26, he returned, dressed as a hunter and wearing a red hat. He played his pipes, and this time children followed him. He led 130 children out of the town and to the Koppenberg hill where they disappeared—forever. Only two children remained behind. One was blind, and couldn't see where the children went, and one was dumb.

Research tends to discredit the legend. One theory is that the ratcatcher was Nicholas of Cologne, who led thousands of German children on the disastrous Children's Crusade in 1212. Another holds that the story stemmed from the arrival of a labor agent who lured many young men to Bohemia with the promise of good wages.

Fortunately, the people of Hamelin don't let research get in the way of a good story. Today, the children of Hamelin are the principal performers in the play, and their number is limited to 130 in keeping with the legend.

Robert Browning, the English poet who wrote the poem, "The Pied Piper of Hamelin," to amuse a sick child, described the vermin this way:

Rats!
They fought the dogs and killed the cats,
And bit the babies in the cradles,
And ate the cheeses out of the vats,
And licked the soup from the cooks' own ladles . . . "

When the piper arrived and began to play, Browning wrote,

. . . out of the houses the rats came tumbling.

Great rats, small rats, lean rats, brawny rats,
Brown rats, black rats, gray rats, tawny rats . . .
Brothers, sisters, husbands, wives—
Followed the Piper for their lives."

And then when the piper led the children off to Koppenberg, a portal opened wide, the piper and the children entered, and—

When all were in to the very last,
The door in the mountain-side shut fast.

CONTACT:
German National Tourist Office
122 E. 42nd St., 52nd Floor
New York, NY 10168
212-661-7200; fax: 212-661-7174

SOURCES:
BkHolWrld-1986, Jul 22

◆ 1440 ◆ **Pig Festivals**
Various

For the Bundi people of Papua New Guinea, the Pig Festival is an event of enormous importance that encompasses dozens of social ceremonies and political events. Among other things, it is a time when tribe members must settle their debts. There are many behind-the-scenes discussions and debates involving money, as well as opportunities to trade and exchange goods. Marriage ceremonies, initiation ceremonies, bride-price payments, menstruation and courtship ceremonies also take place during the period of the Pig Festival. The *kanam,* a Bundi dance performance that depicts the life of the animals and birds that live in the forest, is frequently performed at pig festivals.

CONTACT:
Papua New Guinea Embassy
1615 New Hampshire Ave., N.W.,
  3rd Floor
Washington, D.C. 20009
202-745-3680; fax: 202-745-3679

SOURCES:
FolkWrldHol-1992, p. 461

◆ 1441 ◆ **Pig's Face Feast**
Sunday following September 14

A number of explanations have been offered for the custom of eating pig's face, or pork-chop, sandwiches on the Sunday following Holy Cross Day (September 14; *see* EXALTATION OF THE CROSS) in the Cotswold village of Avening, England. One involves the love of Matilda, who later became the wife of William the Conqueror, for Brictric, Lord of Gloucester. When Brictric refused to reciprocate, Matilda married William and then, as Queen, ordered Brictric's imprisonment and, eventually, his death. She later repented and built a church at the place where Brictric had once ruled as lord of the manor. The church was completed on September 14, Holy Cross Day, and the Queen is said to have held a boar's head dedication feast. The wild boars were so delicious that the people of Avening continued to celebrate their church dedication by eating the same meat. Another legend says that the feast commemorates the slaying of a troublesome wild boar, which took place on or around this date.

Today there is an evening anniversary service in the church at Avening, after which the villagers participate in an 11th-century banquet headed by Queen Matilda and other historic characters in period costume. Pork sandwiches are also served in the local pubs.

CONTACT:
British Tourist Authority
551 Fifth Ave., Ste. 702
New York, NY 10176
800-462-2748 or 212-986-2200
fax: 212-986-1188

SOURCES:
DictDays-1988, p. 89
YrbookEngFest-1954, p. 128

♦ 1442 ♦ Pike Festival, National
May–June

The National Pike Festival is literally the "world's longest festival"—300 miles of events along Route 40 in southwestern Pennsylvania, western Maryland, and parts of West Virginia and Ohio. The original section of the road (or "pike," as in turnpike road) from Baltimore to Cumberland, Maryland, was Thomas Jefferson's idea in 1806. The section between Cumberland and Wheeling, West Virginia, was the first road to receive federal funding in 1811.

Since 1974 the festival has commemorated America's first transportation link from the East to the western frontier. It was originally designed as a Bicentennial event in Pennsylvania, but the idea caught on quickly, and towns along Route 40 in nearby states were eager to add their own events. The festival begins on a weekend in mid-May in western Maryland and southwestern Pennsylvania and continues for four successive weekends in Wheeling, West Virginia; Belmont County, Ohio; Guernsey County, Ohio; and Muskingham County, Ohio. Wagon trains travel along the route known as the National Road or "the road that made the nation." When they set up camp for the night, there are bonfires and other entertainment to which the public is invited. Inns, taverns, toll-houses, and other historic buildings along the route host tours and special ceremonies. A Pony Express rider often meets the wagon train as it pulls into town.

CONTACT:
Laurel Highlands Visitors Bureau
120 E. Main
Town Hall
Ligonier, PA 15658
800-925-7669

Washington County Tourism
144-A McClelland Rd.
Canonsburg, PA 15315
412-746-2333

SOURCES:
Chases-1996, p. 218

♦ 1443 ♦ Pilgrimage of the Dew
*Between May 8 and June 11; Friday before
Pentecost to Tuesday following*

This colorful procession, known as the **Romería del Rocío**, or Pilgrimage of the Dew, begins during the week preceding Whitsunday, or Pentecost, in the towns and villages of Andalusia, Spain. The pilgrims' destination is the church of El Rocío in Almonte, where a small statue of the Virgin known as *La Blanca Paloma* ('the White Dove') resides. They travel in two-wheeled, white-hooded farm carts, drawn by oxen wearing bells, flowers, and ribbon streamers. Some of the carts are set up as moving shrines to the Virgin, and the pilgrims themselves are dressed in regional costumes.

On Pentecost the pilgrims file past the church of El Rocío and pay homage to La Blanca Paloma. There are fireworks at midnight, followed by dancing and singing until dawn. On Monday the image of the Virgin is carried in solemn procession through the streets of Almonte. Being chosen to bear the

statue on one's shoulders is considered a special privilege, eagerly sought by those who wish to receive special indulgence during the coming year. The procession is accompanied by the chanting of priests and the shouts of the pilgrims, who call out "Viva la Blanca Paloma!" as they wend their way through the town.

See also ROMERÍA OF OUR LADY OF VALME

CONTACT:
Tourist Office of Spain
665 Fifth Ave.
New York, NY 10022
212-759-8822; fax: 212-980-1053

SOURCES:
FestWestEur-1958, p. 196
FolkWrldHol-1992, p. 511

♦ 1444 ♦ Pilgrimage to Mecca (Hajj)
*Eighth–thirteenth days of Islamic month of Dhu
al-Hijjah*

At least once in a lifetime, every Muslim man or woman (if she is accompanied by a male protector) with the means and the opportunity to do so is expected to make a pilgrimage to Mecca, the city in Saudi Arabia where Muhammad was born. It is one of the "five pillars" (fundamental duties) of Islam, and must be performed during the special pilgrimage season. The Qu'ran (Muslim holy book) says the founder of this pilgrimage was Abraham. The pilgrims wear two sheets of seamless white cloth and perform elaborate rites at the Grand Mosque of Mecca and in the immediate vicinity, which require about six days to complete. The focal point is the Kaaba, a 15-foot high stone structure that stands in the center court of the Grand Mosque of Mecca. In one corner of the court is the Black Stone, believed to have been brought by the angel Gabriel to Moses when he was rebuilding the Kaaba. It is a symbol of eternity because of its durability. These are not worshipped, but are a sanctuary consecrated to God, and toward which all Muslim prayers are oriented. Among the stages of the Pilgrimage are walking around the Kaaba seven times, sacrificing a ram, ox, or camel, gathering at the Mount of Mercy and "standing before God" from noon to sunset, and throwing pebbles at three pillars at Mina, which represent Satan's tempting Abraham not to sacrifice his son. (*See* 'ID AL-ADHA.)

It is not uncommon for two million or more Muslims to participate in the pilgrimage, which has forced Saudi Arabia and other countries to explore new methods for freezing, preserving, and distributing the meat that is produced by so many sacrifices. At the end of the pilgrimage, it is customary to visit the tomb of Muhammad at Medina before returning home.

Returning pilgrims, wearing the green scarf of the Hajj, are met by family and friends who have rented taxis and decorated them with palm branches and the families' best rugs. The pilgrim's house has been decorated with palm-leaf arches, and sometimes outlined with lights. In Kurdish and Egyptian villages, the doorways will also have designs suggesting the journey. Then a feast and party finish the welcome home.

CONTACT:
Saudi Arabian Embassy
601 New Hampshire Ave., N.W.
Washington, D.C. 20037
202-342-3800; fax: 202-337-3233

SOURCES:
AnnivHol-1983, p. 171
BkHolWrld-1986, Aug 27
Chases-1996, p. 190
DictWrldRel-1989, pp. 290,
    569

FolkWrldHol-1992, pp. 328, 332
RelHolCal-1993, p. 81

♦ 1445 ♦ Pilgrimage to Moulay Idriss
Late August or September

The most important *moussem*, or 'festival,' in Morocco is held in the holy city of Moulay Idriss. Moulay Idriss I was the eighth-century imam (Muslim prayer leader) who united the Berbers and founded the city of Fez and the first dynasty of Morocco; he is supposed to have had 500 wives, 1,000 children, and 12,000 horses. His burial place is the white Mausoleum of Moulay Idriss. The town named for him grew up around the tomb after his death.

This moussem consists of several weeks, alternating prayers and celebrations. A feature is the *fantasia*, a great charge of horses and costumed riders who fire their rifles into the air and perform equestrian stunts as they gallop. There are also bazaars and singing and dancing.

CONTACT:
Moroccan National Tourist Office
20 E. 46th St., Ste. 1201
New York, NY 10017
212-557-2520; fax: 212-949-8148

♦ 1446 ♦ Pilgrimage to Shrine of Father Laval
September 8

An annual pilgrimage by thousands of people of all faiths to the shrine of Roman Catholic priest Père Jacques Désiré Laval in Port Louis, Mauritius. Father Laval came to Mauritius in 1841 and devoted himself to the spiritual improvement of the emancipated slaves until his death in 1864. The pilgrimage is held on the day of his death. It originated on the day the priest was buried, when more than 30,000 weeping people followed his bier as he was taken for burial opposite the Ste. Croix Church. A monument to him has since been erected there. Many masses are celebrated at the shrine on the memorial day, starting early in the morning. A vigil ends the day. Miracles of healing are attributed to Father Laval, who was beatified in 1979 in Rome by Pope John Paul II.

CONTACT:
Mauritius Government Tourist Information Service
8 Haven Ave., Ste. 227
Port Washington, NY 11050
516-944-3763; fax: 516-944-8458

♦ 1447 ♦ Pilgrim Festivals
Various

The ancient Israelites were expected to celebrate three pilgrim festivals: PASSOVER, SHAVUOT, and SUKKOT. They are referred to in Hebrew as the *shalosh regalim*, 'three (foot) pilgrimages', because the Bible commanded that they be observed "in the place the Lord your God will choose." Adult males over the age of 13 traditionally made a pilgrimage to Jerusalem on these three occasions. But after the Temple there was destroyed, the law requiring pilgrimages lapsed. The obligation to rejoice on the three pilgrim festivals—by eating meat, drinking wine, and wearing new clothes—continued.

Today, Jews come from all over the world to spend these festivals in Jerusalem. But now they tend to be sorrowful voyages, made for the purpose of mourning the destruction of the Temple. It is for this reason that Jews traditionally gather at the Wailing Wall—the only remaining retaining wall of the Temple Mount, site of the First and Second Temples, built during the first century B.C. in the reign of Herod.

CONTACT:
Israel Ministry of Tourism
6380 Wilshire Blvd., Ste. 1700
Los Angeles, CA 90048
213-658-7462; fax: 213-658-6543

♦ 1448 ♦ Pilgrim Progress Pageant
Every Friday during August

It was on Plymouth Rock in what is now Plymouth, Massachusetts, that the Pilgrims landed in December 1620 to found their first permanent settlement north of Virginia. More than half of the 102 people who sailed on the *Mayflower* to the New World died of exposure, illness, and hunger by the end of the first winter.

Each Friday in August at 5:00 P.M., a group of men, women, and children dressed as Pilgrims form a procession up Leyden Street to the site of the former Fort-Meetinghouse on Burial Hill, now the Church of the Pilgrimage on Main Street. When they reach the site of the old fort, they reenact the church service that was held by the survivors at the end of that first winter in 1621. The pageant has been held every August since 1921.

CONTACT:
Massachusetts Office of Travel and Tourism
100 Cambridge St., 13th Floor
Boston, MA 02202
800-447-6277 or 617-727-3201
fax: 617-727-6525

SOURCES:
GdUSFest-1984, p. 88

♦ 1449 ♦ Pilgrim Thanksgiving Day in Plymouth
Last Thursday in November

Ten thousand visitors flock to Plymouth, Massachusetts, on THANKSGIVING Day to watch the annual procession from Plymouth Rock to the First Parish Church, where the congregation sings the same psalms sung by the original Pilgrims more than three and a half centuries ago. Each marcher represents one of the men, women, and children who survived the 1620 trip from England aboard the *Mayflower* to form the settlement known as Plimoth Plantation.

At 11 o'clock on Thursday morning in front of Memorial Hall, the crowds line up for the first seating of the town's traditional public Thanksgiving dinner, modeled after the 1621 harvest meal shared by the town's earliest settlers. About 1,400 people participate in the four successive dinners put on by the Plymouth Chamber of Commerce, which serves up one ton of turkey, 500 pounds of mashed potatoes, 500 pounds of squash, and 400 pounds of Indian pudding.

The modern-day Plimoth Plantation is an outdoor living-history museum that recreates life in a 1627 Pilgrim village. Costumed actors and historians carry out many of the same activities performed by the original Pilgrims, such as sheep-shearing, building houses, planting crops, weeding gardens, and cooking.

CONTACT:
Massachusetts Office of Travel
  and Tourism
100 Cambridge St., 13th Floor
Boston, MA 02202
800-447-6277 or 617-727-3201
fax: 617-727-6525

SOURCES:
AmerBkDays-1978, p. 1053
GdUSFest-1984, p. 89

Pi Mai
See **Songkran**

♦ 1450 ♦ Pinkster Day
*Between May 10 and June 13; fifty days after
Easter*

When PENTECOST (Whitsunday) became part of the Christian calendar in northern Europe, the name underwent numerous transformations. In Germany it became *Pfingsten*, and the Dutch called it *Pinkster*. When the Dutch settled in New York, they called the feast of Pentecost "Pinkster Day."

By the beginning of the 19th century, Albany had become a center for this celebration, which took place on Capitol, or "Pinkster," Hill and consisted of a week-long carnival dominated by the city's African-American population. It is said that their African-inspired dancing and music horrified the staid Dutch settlers, and by 1811 Pinkster Day had been legally prohibited by the New York state legislature.

SOURCES:
BkFest-1937, p. 244
DaysCustFaith-1957, p. 162
DictDays-1988, p. 89
FolkAmerHol-1991, p. 226

Pioneer Day
See **Mormon Pioneer Day**

♦ 1451 ♦ Pirates Week
Last week in October

A Cayman Islands festival celebrating the history of Grand Cayman, at one time a favorite haunt for pirates and buccaneers. The entire island is transformed into a pirate encampment for the week-long festival. There is a mock invasion of George Town, parades, pageants, and the crowning of a pirate queen. Everyone dresses up in costumes, and the singing, dancing, and food fairs that are held throughout the island all revolve around a pirate theme.

The Cayman Islands—from the Spanish *caimán*, meaning 'alligator'—were apparently unoccupied when first sighted by COLUMBUS in 1503. Although frequented by Spanish, English, and French ships, they were not claimed by anyone until they were ceded to the British in 1670 and settlers started arriving. Before long, the islands' remote location made them an ideal stopover for pirates.

CONTACT:
Cayman Islands Dept. of Tourism
3440 Wilshire Blvd., Ste. 1202
Los Angeles, CA 90010
213-738-1968; fax: 213-738-1829

SOURCES:
GdWrldFest-1985, p. 61

Pitcher Fair
See **Kumbh Mela**

♦ 1452 ♦ Pitra Visarjana Amavasya
*September–October; waning half of Hindu month
of Asvina*

During this two-week festival in India, no male family member is allowed to shave, nor is it permissible to cut hair, pare nails, or wear new clothes. It is a time for honoring ancestors by making special offerings of food and water, especially *khir*, or rice boiled in milk. Brahmans (priests, members of the highest Hindu caste) are often invited to partake of these special foods in the belief that they will ensure that the offerings reach the souls of departed family members. It is usually the eldest son or senior member of the family who performs the rituals associated with this festival.

SOURCES:
BkFest-1937, p. 160
FolkWrldHol-1992, p. 503
RelHolCal-1993, p. 103

♦ 1453 ♦ Pjodhatid
Early August

A three-day "people's feast," celebrated in the Vestmannaeyjar area of Iceland. The festival commemorates the granting of Iceland's constitution on July 1, 1874, which permitted the nation, long under the control of Denmark, to handle its own domestic affairs. Because of foul weather, the island people of Vestmannaeyjar weren't able to attend the mainland celebration, so they held their own festival at home a month later. They've been holding this month-late celebration ever since.

Most of the festivities take place in Herjolfsdalur on Heimaey Island. Enormous bonfires are built, there are sporting events, dancing, singing, and eating and drinking. People come from the mainland for this event, so the island is filled with campers.

CONTACT:
Scandinavian Tourism, Inc.
P.O. Box 4649
New York, NY 10163-4649
212-949-2333; fax: 212-983-5260

♦ 1454 ♦ Plague Sunday
Last Sunday in August

When the plague reached the village of Eyam, Derbyshire, England, in 1665, three-fourths of the town's population was wiped out. But under the leadership of Vicar Mompesson, the villagers displayed both courage and selflessness, voluntarily isolating themselves from other villages in the parish and requesting that their food and medical supplies be dropped off at a point outside the village. The disease eventually became so virulent that the vicar had to hold open-air services for his dwindling congregation in a place up in the hills known as Cucklet Dell.

Every year on the last Sunday in August, a procession of clergy, standard bearers, choir members, and musicians forms at Eyam's parish church and slowly proceeds up the road leading toward the Dell. Hundreds of villagers, tourists, hikers, cyclists, and parents with baby carriages fall in behind them, finding seats on the grassy slopes of the Dell's natural amphitheater. A simple sermon pays tribute to the plague victims and the 35 villagers who survived.

CONTACT:
British Tourist Authority
551 Fifth Ave., Ste. 702
New York, NY 10176
800-462-2748 or 212-986-2200
fax: 212-986-1188

SOURCES:
DictDays-1988, p. 89
YrbookEngFest-1954, p. 116

♦ 1455 ♦ Pleureuses, Ceremony of

Between March 20 and April 23; Friday before Easter

A GOOD FRIDAY ceremony at the Church of Romont in Switzerland. Held since the 15th century, the ceremony begins with a reading from the Bible of the Passion of Christ (the last seven days of his life). The congregation then begins its procession through the village streets. The weepers or mourners (the *Pleureuses*) are veiled in black attire resembling nuns' habits, and walk slowly behind a young girl portraying the Virgin Mary. She walks behind a penitent wearing a black hood and carrying a large cross. The mourners carry the symbols of the Passion on scarlet cushions: a crown of thorns, a whip, nails, a hammer, tongs, and St. Veronica's shroud (Veronica was a woman in the crowd who, as Christ passed her carrying the cross, wiped his face and his image was, according to legend, imprinted on the cloth). During the procession, the town resounds with chants and prayers.

CONTACT:
Swiss National Tourist Office
608 Fifth Ave.
New York, NY 10020
212-757-5944; fax: 212-262-6116

♦ 1456 ♦ Plough Monday

January, first Monday after Epiphany

An ancient rustic English holiday, also called **Fool Plough** or **Fond Plough**, or **Fond Pleeaf**, of obscure origins that survived into the late 1800s. It is thought to have started in the days of the medieval Roman Catholic Church, when farmers, or ploughmen, kept candles called plough-lights burning in churches before the images of saints. Once a year, on the Monday after EPIPHANY (before ploughing begins), or sometimes at the end of LENT (to celebrate the end of ploughing), they gathered in villages to ask for money to pay for the plough-lights. The Reformation of the 16th century ended this homage to saints, but not the day's celebration as a time to return to labor after the CHRISTMAS festivities. By the 19th century, the day was observed with music, dancing, processions, and collecting money through trick-or-treat type means. "The Bessy"—a man dressed up to look ridiculous in women's clothing—and "The Fool," wearing animal skins or a fur cap and tail, solicited money from door to door so they could buy food and drink for their merrymaking. The ploughmen dragged a beribboned plough from house to house, shouting "God speed the plough," and if a home owner failed to make a contribution, they ploughed up his front yard. The money collected was spent not on plough-lights but on ale in the public houses. The custom of blessing the plough on the prior day, Plough Sunday, was still observed in some areas in the 20th century.

SOURCES:
BkDays-1864, vol. I, p. 94
DaysCustFaith-1957, p. 38
DictDays-1988, p. 90

DictFolkMyth-1984, pp. 138, 410
FestSaintDays-1915, p. 19
FolkWrldHol-1992, p. 20
RelHolCal-1993, p. 103
SaintFestCh-1904, p. 63

♦ 1457 ♦ Plow, Festival of the

June 25

Saban Tuy, or the Festival of the Plow, celebrates the founding of the Tatar Autonomous Soviet Socialist Republic on this date in 1920. Originally a Mongolian spring farming celebration, the festival is held in Kazan on the Volga River in what is now Russia. The events include climbing a greased pole to reach a cock in a cage on top and "smashing the crocks," a variation of Pin-the-Tail-on-the-Donkey in which a blindfolded player who has been spun around several times tries to smash a set of earthenware crocks containing prizes. The highlight of the festival is a horse race across the plains in which the riders are blindfolded.

CONTACT:
Russian Travel Information Office
Rockefeller Center
610 Fifth Ave., Ste. 603
New York, NY 10020
212-757-3884; fax: 212-459-0031

SOURCES:
BkHolWrld-1986, Jun 25
FolkWrldHol-1992, p. 344

♦ 1458 ♦ Polar Bear Swim Day

January 1

Since 1920 a group of hardy swimmers has celebrated NEW YEAR'S DAY by plunging into the frigid waters of Vancouver's English Bay. As crazy as it sounds, the custom has spread to the United States, where chapters of the American Polar Bear Club have established themselves in a number of states known for their cold winter weather. In Sheboygan, Wisconsin, more than 300 daring swimmers—many of them in costume—brave the ice floes of Lake Michigan to take their New Year's Day swim. About 3,000 to 4,000 spectators stay bundled up on the beach and watch. The Sheboygan event has gradually expanded into a day-long festival, with a brat-fry, a costume contest, and live entertainment.

CONTACT:
Tourism British Columbia
Parliament Buildings
Victoria, B.C.
Canada V8V 1X4
800-663-6000 or 604-663-6000

Wisconsin Division of Tourism
123 W. Washington Ave., 6th
  Floor
Madison, WI 53703
800-432-8747 or 608-266-7621
fax: 608-266-3403

SOURCES:
AnnivHol-1983, p. 2
Chases-1996, p. 52

♦ 1459 ♦ Polish Constitution Day

May 3

May 3, known in Poland as **Swieto Trzeciego Maja**, is a patriotic legal holiday honoring the nation's first constitution, adopted in 1791. It introduced fundamental changes in the way Poland was governed, based on the ideas of the French Revolution, and represented an attempt to preserve the country's independence. Although the May 3rd Constitution (as it was called) represented a great advance for the

Polish people, it also aroused the anxieties of neighboring countries and eventually led to the Second Partition two years later.

CONTACT:
Polish National Tourist Office
275 Madison Ave., Ste. 1711
New York, NY 10016
212-338-9412; fax: 212-338-9283

SOURCES:
AnnivHol-1983, p. 60

♦ 1460 ♦ Polish Independence Day
November 11

This national holiday commemorates the re-creation of the state of Poland at the end of World War I. On November 11, 1918, Poland was granted independence after having been partitioned under the rule of Prussia, Austria, and Russia for more than 100 years.

CONTACT:
Polish National Tourist Office
275 Madison Ave., Ste. 1711
New York, NY 10016
212-338-9412; fax: 212-338-9283

♦ 1461 ♦ Polish Liberation Day
July 22; January 17

A national holiday in Poland, July 22 marks the day on which the KRN (National Home Council) established the Polish Committee of National Liberation (PKWN) in 1944, the first people's government in the country's thousand-year history. The PKWN manifesto issued on this date proclaimed that complete liberation from the Nazis and the freeing of ancient Polish lands on the Baltic Sea and Odra River were its first priorities, as well as the democratization of the country's social and political life.

In the city of Warsaw, January 17 is observed as Liberation Day. It was on this day in 1945 that the city was freed from Nazi oppression by Soviet troops. Special ceremonies are held at the Monument to the Unknown Soldier in Warsaw's Victory Square.

CONTACT:
Polish National Tourist Office
275 Madison Ave., Ste. 1711
New York, NY 10016
212-338-9412; fax: 212-338-9283

SOURCES:
AnnivHol-1983, p. 95
Chases-1996, p. 68
NatlHolWrld-1968, p. 121

♦ 1462 ♦ Polish Solidarity Day
August 31

This marks the day in 1980 when the Polish labor union Solidarnosc (Solidarity) was formed at the Lenin Shipyards in Gdansk. Under the leadership of Lech Walesa, an electrician at the shipyard, 17,000 workers had staged a strike earlier in the year to protest rising food prices. An agreement was finally reached between the Gdansk strikers and the Polish Communist government, allowing free unions to be formed, independent of the Communist Party. Solidarity was formally founded on September 22 and consists of about 50 labor unions. But when the union stepped up its demands, staging a series of controlled strikes throughout 1981 to pressure the government for free elections and economic reforms, Premier Wojciech Jaruzelski was subjected to even greater pressure from the Soviet Union to put a stop to the group's activities. On December 13, 1981, martial law was declared, the fledgling union's legal status was terminated,

and Walesa was put under arrest. He was released in November 1982, and martial law was lifted six months later.

After almost a decade of struggle, Solidarity was finally granted legal status on April 17, 1989, clearing the way for the downfall of the Polish Communist Party. The Polish labor union's successful struggle marked the beginning of similar changes in other Communist-bloc countries in Europe, many of whom overthrew their Communist leaders and took the first steps toward establishing more democratic forms of government. Solidarity's founding is celebrated not only in Poland but by Polish-Americans in the United States, with demonstrations and programs in support of Polish workers.

CONTACT:
Polish National Tourist Office
275 Madison Ave., Ste. 1711
New York, NY 10016
212-338-9412; fax: 212-338-9283

SOURCES:
AnnivHol-1983, p. 145
Chases-1996, p. 356

♦ 1463 ♦ Polka Festival, National
Early August

The National Polka Festival that has been held annually since 1977 in Hunter, New York, features the polkas of Poland, Slovenia, Czech Republic, Slovakia, Germany, and the Ukraine. More than 60 polka bands from the United States, Canada, and Europe compete at the festival, which is held at a resort area known as Hunter Mountain. The music is continuous from 11:00 A.M. to midnight for three or four days, with the bands performing under a blue-and-white tent the size of a football field. There are also lessons in how to dance the polka, craft demonstrations, the crowning of a Polka Queen, and European puppet shows.

CONTACT:
National Polka Festival
Box 295
Hunter, NY 12442
518-263-3800

SOURCES:
GdUSFest-1984, p. 125

♦ 1464 ♦ Pongal
December–January; Hindu month of Pausa

A colorful three-day harvest and thanksgiving celebration in southern India, honoring the sun, the earth, and the cow. It is called Pongal in the state of Tamil Nadu; in Andhra Pradesh, Karnataka, and Gujarat, it is known as **Makara Sankranti**.

The first day is called Bhogi Pongal and is for cleaning everything in the house. On the second day, freshly harvested rice and *jaggery* ('palm sugar') are put to boil in new pots. When the mixture bubbles, people cry out, "Pongal!" ('It boils.') The rice is offered to Surya, the sun god, before people taste it themselves, thus the second day is called Surya Pongal. On the third day, called Mattu Pongal (Festival of the Cow), village cows and oxen are bathed, decorated with garlands of bells, beads, and leaves, and worshipped. In villages near Madurai, the festival of Jellikattu takes place. Bundles containing money are tied to the sharpened horns of bulls. The animals are paraded around the village and then stampeded. Young men who are brave enough try to snatch the money from the bulls' horns.

In Ahmedabad in the state of Gujarat, the celebration is a time of competitive kite-flying, and is termed the **International Kite Festival**. The skies are filled with kites, and kite makers come from other cities to make their multicolored kites in all shapes. As darkness falls, the battle of the kites ends, and new kites soar aloft, each with its own paper lamp, so that the sky is filled with flickering lights.

CONTACT:
India Tourist Office
30 Rockefeller Ave.·
15 N. Mezzanine
New York, NY 10112
212-586-4901; fax: 212-582-3274

SOURCES:
AnnivHol-1983, p. 179
BkHolWrld-1986, Jan 14
FolkWrldHol-1992, p. 80
RelHolCal-1993, pp. 93, 103

♦ 1465 ♦ Pony Express Ride
August

When the Pony Express riders made their first run between St. Joseph, Missouri, and Sacramento, California, on April 3, 1860, carrying mail on horseback was already routine between eastern Pennsylvania and the "frontier" settlements of Greensburg and Pittsburgh. Since 1788 postal patrons in Armstrong and Butler counties had been paying a minimum of eight cents and a maximum of 35 cents to mail a single-page letter, depending on the distance. Although the image of the Pony Express popularized by Hollywood includes Indians and bandits in hot pursuit, its reality in Pennsylvania was the opposite. It was a low-paying and often boring occupation whose main hazards were bad roads and cutthroat competition from stage lines.

Since 1989 a group of Pennsylvania towns once linked by the post riders has staged a two-day re-creation of the event known as the **Crooked Creek Pony Express Ride**. The route starts in Adrian and ends in Kittanning, with about 10 stops at post offices along the way. A brief ceremony is held at each post office to swear in the rider and to commemorate the history of the early days of postal delivery. The 33 riders chosen to participate are judged for the authenticity of their costumes and tack at the end of the 80-mile route. These "post riders" should not be confused with the later legendary Pony Express riders of the American West.

CONTACT:
Pennsylvania Office of Travel
 Marketing
453 Forum Bldg.
Harrisburg, PA 17120
800-237-4363 or 717-787-5453
fax: 717-234-4560

Pony League World Series
See **Little League World Series**

♦ 1466 ♦ Pooram
April–May; Hindu month of Vaisakha

One of the most spectacular festivals of southern India, this is a 10-day celebration in Trichur, Kerala, dedicated to Lord Shiva. People fast on the first day of the festival and the rest of the days are devoted to fairs, processions, and fireworks displays. The highlight of the pageantry comes when an image of the deity Vadakkunathan is taken from the temple and carried in a procession of about 100 temple elephants ornately decorated with gold-plated mail. The Brahmans riding them hold colorful ceremonial umbrellas and whisks of yak hair and peacock feathers. The elephants lumber through the pagoda-shaped gateway of the Vadakkunathan temple and into the village while drummers beat and pipers trill. Fireworks light the skies until dawn.

CONTACT:
India Tourist Office
30 Rockefeller Ave.
15 N. Mezzanine
New York, NY 10112
212-586-4901; fax: 212-582-3274

SOURCES:
RelHolCal-1993, p. 104

Poppy Day
See **Veterans Day**

Porciúncula
See **Forgiveness, Feast of**

♦ 1467 ♦ Pori International Jazz Festival
Mid-July

Pori, Finland, is 150 miles northwest of Helsinki—far enough north to guarantee 19 hours of daylight during the four-day summer jazz festival that has been held there since 1966. It offers 10 major concerts as well as jam sessions, films, a children's program, and many informal musical events in the city's cafes, restaurants, jazz clubs, and art galleries. All styles of jazz—from traditional to contemporary, dixieland, blues, and swing—are represented. Performers at past festivals have included Herbie Hancock, Chuck Mangione, Ornette Coleman, Dizzy Gillespie, Sonny Rollins, and B.B. King as well as Scandinavian jazz artists. The major concerts are held in an outdoor amphitheater on Kirjurinluoto Island, a natural park in the heart of the city. There are also lectures, films, and exhibitions on jazz and its influence.

CONTACT:
Finnish Tourist Board
655 Third Ave.
New York, NY 10017
212-949-2333

SOURCES:
Chases-1996, p. 295
GdWrldFest-1985, p. 77
MusFestEurBrit-1980, p. 69

♦ 1468 ♦ Portland Rose Festival
June

A 26-day salute to the rose in Portland, Ore., and certainly one of the sweetest-smelling festivals anywhere.

The "City of Roses" has been putting on a rose festival since 1907 and claims now to produce the biggest celebration of the rose in the world. To justify such a claim, the festival offers more than 60 events. These include an air show, band competitions, fireworks, a hot air balloon race, tours and cruises on visiting U.S. and Canadian Navy ships, and boat, ski, and Indy-class car races. The salute starts with the coronation of the Rose Queen, and continues with parade after parade, including a starlight parade, called the second largest lighted parade in the United States, the largest children's parade, and the climax—a grand floral parade, with dozens of rose-bedecked floats. On the final days of the festival, the Portland Rose Society stages the Rose Show, the oldest and largest rose show in the country, with about 20,000 individual blossoms exhibited.

Portland is thought to have started its life as a rose city in the early 19th century, when traders brought with them seeds of the wild rose of England. It flourished as the Oregon Sweet Briar. Settlers brought more roses, and then in 1888, Mrs. Henry L. Pittock held a rose show in her front yard, and that evolved into today's festival.

The parade is one of two major floral parades in the country, the other being the better known Tournament of Roses in Pasadena, Calif., every New Year's Day.

CONTACT:
Portland Rose Festival Association
220 N.W. Second Ave.
Portland, OR 97209
503-227-2681
WWW: http://
    www.rosefestival.org./rose/

SOURCES:
AmerBkDays-1978, p. 525
Chases-1996, p. 235
GdUSFest-1984, p. 151

♦ 1469 ♦ Portugal Liberation Day
April 25

Liberation Day, or **Liberty Day**, is a public holiday commemorating the military coup on this day in 1974 that removed Marcello Caetano (1906–1980) from power, reflecting the opposition of many Portuguese to their government's military policies and wars in Africa.

CONTACT:
Portuguese National Tourist
    Office
590 Fifth Ave., 4th Floor
New York, NY 10036
212-354-4403; fax: 212-764-6137

SOURCES:
AnnivHol-1983, p. 56
Chases-1996, p. 184

♦ 1470 ♦ Portugal National Day
June 10

Also known as **Camões Memorial Day** and **Portugal Day**, this national holiday observes the death anniversary of Luis Vas de Camões (1524–1580), Portugal's national poet. His epic work, *The Lusiads* (1572), was based on the voyage to India of Portuguese explorer Vasco de Gama.

This national holiday is observed with patriotic speeches, games, and costumed citizens in the capital city of Lisbon.

CONTACT:
Portuguese National Tourist
    Office
590 Fifth Ave., 4th Floor
New York, NY 10036
212-354-4403; fax: 212-764-6137

SOURCES:
AnnivHol-1983, p. 77
Chases-1996, p. 251
NatlHolWrld-1968, p. 82

♦ 1471 ♦ Portugal Republic Day
October 5

This national holiday commemorates the establishment of the Portuguese Republic on this day in 1910, which ended over two centuries of the monarchical rule of the Portuguese royal family, the House of Braganca.

CONTACT:
Portuguese National Tourist
    Office
590 Fifth Ave., 4th Floor
New York, NY 10036
212-354-4403; fax: 212-764-6137

SOURCES:
AnnivHol-1983, p. 128

♦ 1472 ♦ Portugal Restoration of Independence Day
December 1

This public holiday commemorates the restoration of Portugal's independence from Spain on December 1, 1640. Philip II (1527–1598) of Spain assumed control of Portugal in 1580 upon the death of Henry, prince of Portugal, and the "Spanish captivity" lasted for 60 years. Revolution began in Lisbon, and in 1640, the Portuguese dethroned Philip IV (1605–

1665; grandson of Philip II) and reclaimed independence for Portugal.

CONTACT:
Portuguese National Tourist
    Office
590 Fifth Ave., 4th Floor
New York, NY 10036
212-354-4403; fax: 212-764-6137

SOURCES:
Chases-1996, p. 468

♦ 1473 ♦ Posadas
December 16–24

This nine-day Christmas celebration in Mexico commemorates the journey Mary and Joseph (the parents of Jesus) took from Nazareth to Bethlehem. Reenacting the couple's search for shelter (*posada* in Spanish) in which the infant Jesus might be born, a group of "pilgrims" will knock on someone's door and ask the owner to let them in. Although they may initially be refused, the master of the house finally invites them to enter, and the Posadas party begins. The children are blindfolded and given a chance to break the *piñata* (a clay or papier-mâché animal that hangs from the ceiling and is filled with candy and toys) by swinging at it with a stick. The posadas are repeated for nine evenings, the last occurring on Christmas Eve.

The *Misa de Gallo*, or Mass of the Cock (so-called because it's held so early in the day), ends after midnight, and then there are fireworks and, in some towns, a special parade with floats and *tableaux vivants* representing biblical scenes.

In small Mexican villages, there is often a procession led by two children bearing images of Joseph and Mary riding a burro. The adult members of the group carry lighted tapers and sing the Litany of the Virgin as they approach each house. There is also a famous posadas celebration on Olvera Street in Los Angeles.

CONTACT:
Mexican Government Tourist
    Office
405 Park Ave., Ste. 1401
New York, NY 10022
800-446-3942 or 212-755-7261
fax: 212-753-2874

Los Angeles Convention and Visitors Bureau
633 W. Fifth St., Ste. 6000
Los Angeles, CA 90017
800-228-2452 or 213-624-7300
fax: 213-624-9746

SOURCES:
BkFest-1937, p. 232
BkFestHolWrld-1970, pp. 137, 155
BkHolWrld-1986, Dec 16
FolkAmerHol-1991, p. 436
FolkWrldHol-1992, p. 623
RelHolCal-1993, p. 89

♦ 1474 ♦ Poson
May–June; full moon day of Hindu month of Jyestha

This festival, also called **Dhamma Vijaya** and **Full Moon Day**, celebrates the bringing of Buddhism to Sri Lanka (formerly Ceylon). It is second in importance only to Vesak. The story of this day is that King Devanampiya Tissa was chasing a deer in the forest of Mihintale when someone called out his name. He looked up and saw a figure in a saffron-colored robe standing on a rock with six companions. The robed figure was the holy patron of Sri Lanka, Arahat Mahinda, the son of Emperor Asoka of India, who was a convert to Buddhism from Hinduism. He had sent his son and companions as missionaries to Ceylon in about 251

B.C. Mahinda converted King Devanampiya Tissa and the royal family, and they in turn converted the common people. Mahinda, who propagated the faith through works of practical benevolence, died in about 204 B.C.

While the holiday is celebrated throughout Sri Lanka, the major ceremonies are at the ancient cities of Anuradhapura and Mihintale. There, historical events involving Mahinda are reenacted, streets and buildings are decorated and illuminated, and temples are crowded. In Mihintale, people climb to the rock where Arahat Mahinda delivered his first sermon to the king. An important part of the festival is paying homage to the branch of the Bodhi Tree brought to Sri Lanka by Mahinda's sister, Sanghamita (*see* Sanghamita Day). This is the tree that Gautama sat under until he received enlightenment and became the Buddha.

CONTACT:
Sri Lankan Embassy
2148 Wyoming Ave., N.W.
Washington, D.C. 20008
202-483-4025; fax: 202-232-7181

♦ 1475 ♦ Potato Days
October

In Norway during the fall potato harvest, it was customary to give children a week off school to help in the fields. Norwegian farmers would put in a request for a certain number of children and feed them during their week of employment. Although this arrangement is no longer as common as it was up until the 1950s, children still help harvest the potatoes on their families' farms, and the traditional fall vacation is still known as the potato vacation, or *potetserie*.

A similar arrangement can be found in the United States, especially in states where there are many small farms producing a single crop. In northern Maine, children also harvest potatoes, and in Vermont some schools give their students time off to help pick apples.

SOURCES:
BkHolWrld-1986, Oct 28
FolkWrldHol-1992, p. 461

♦ 1476 ♦ Powamû Festival
February

The Hopi Indians believe that for six months of the year ancestral spirits called the *katchinas* leave their mountain homes and visit the tribe, bringing health to the people and rain for their crops. The Hopi who live at the Walpi Pueblo in northeastern Arizona celebrate the entry of the Sky Father (also known as the Sun God) into the pueblo in February by dramatizing the event in a festival known as Powamû. The Sky Father, represented by a man wearing a circular mask surrounded by feathers and horsehair with a curved beak in the middle, is led into the pueblo from the east at sunrise. There he visits the house and *kiva* (underground chamber used for religious and other ceremonies) of the chief, performing certain ceremonial rites and exchanging symbolic gifts.

A similar sequence of events is performed in July during the Niman Festival. At this time the Sky Father is ushered out of the pueblo. In the intervening months, it is assumed that he remains in the village or nearby, making public appearances in masked dances from time to time.

CONTACT:
Hopi Tribal Council
P.O. Box 123
Kykotsmovi, AZ 86039
602-734-2445

SOURCES:
DictFolkMyth-1984, pp. 123, 566, 883
EncyRel-1987, vol. 10, p. 520
FolkAmerHol-1991, p. 70

Prayer Festival
See Monlam

♦ 1477 ♦ Preakness Stakes
Third Saturday in May

The 10-day **Preakness Festival** or **Maryland Preakness Celebration** culminates in the running of the Preakness Stakes, the "middle jewel of the Triple Crown" of horseracing—the other two being the Kentucky Derby and the Belmont Stakes. Held at Baltimore's Pimlico Race Course, the Preakness was first run on May 27, 1873. The festival leading up to the race includes hundreds of recreational, educational, and cultural events—including a hot air balloon competition, a schooner race in Baltimore Harbor, and a celebrity golf tournament.

CONTACT:
Baltimore Area Convention and
  Visitors Bureau
100 Light St., 12th Floor
Baltimore, MD 21202
800-343-3468 or 410-659-7300
fax: 410-727-2308

SOURCES:
Chases-1996, pp. 219, 231
GdUSFest-1984, p. 81

♦ 1478 ♦ Premier Mai
May 1

In France the celebration of May Day is inextricably linked to flowers. It is considered good luck to wear lilies-of-the-valley on this day, and it is believed that any wishes made while wearing the flowers are bound to come true. Sometimes sprays of pressed lilies are sent to distant friends and loved ones. In southern France the flower vendors sell lilies-of-the-valley on every street corner.

The **First of May** has political overtones in France as well, and many working people assert their freedom by taking it as a holiday even though their employers do not officially recognize it as such. Political demonstrations, speeches, and parades are common on this day—similar to May Day celebrations in England, Russia, and other countries.

See also Vappu

CONTACT:
French Government Tourist Office
9454 Wilshire Blvd., Ste. 715
Beverly Hills, CA 90212
310-271-6665; fax: 310-276-2835

SOURCES:
BkDays-1864, vol. I, p. 579
BkFest-1937, p. 122
BkFestHolWrld-1970, p. 85
DictFolkMyth-1984, p. 696
FestWestEur-1958, p. 37
FolkWrldHol-1992, p. 262

♦ 1479 ♦ Presentation of the Blessed Virgin Mary, Feast of the
November 21

The Feast of the Presentation of the Blessed Virgin was first celebrated by the Greeks in about the eighth century and was not adopted by the Roman Catholic Church until the later Middle Ages; no one is quite sure when this festival was first introduced. As related in the apocryphal Book of James, it commemorates the presentation of the three-year-old Mary in the Temple to consecrate her to the service of God. Many have confused this festival with the Feast of the Presentation of Christ in the Temple, otherwise known as CANDLEMAS.

SOURCES:
FolkWrldHol-1992, p. 564
RelHolCal-1993, p. 104
SaintFestCh-1904, p. 493

◆ 1480 ◆ **Presidents' Day**
Third Monday in February

The passage of Public Law 90-363 in 1968, also known as the "Monday Holiday Law," changed the observance of WASHINGTON'S BIRTHDAY from February 22 to the third Monday in February. Because it occurs so soon after LINCOLN'S BIRTHDAY, many states—such as Hawaii, Minnesota, Nebraska, Wisconsin, and Wyoming—combine the two holidays and call it Presidents' Day or **Washington-Lincoln Day**. Some regard it as a day to honor all former presidents of the United States.

See also Appendix B

SOURCES:
AnnivHol-1983, p. 25
Chases-1996, p. 105
DictDays-1988, p. 91

◆ 1481 ◆ **Pretzel Sunday**
Between March 8 and April 7; fourth Sunday in Lent

On **Bretzelsonndeg** in Luxembourg, it is the custom for boys to present their sweethearts with decorated pretzel-cakes. If a girl wants to encourage the boy, she reciprocates with a decorated egg on EASTER Sunday. If the pretzel-cake is large, the egg must be large also; a small cake warrants a small egg.

The custom is reversed during Leap Year (*see* LEAP YEAR DAY), when girls give cakes to boys on Pretzel Sunday, and boys return the favor with eggs at Easter. Married couples often participate in the exchange of cakes and eggs as well.

SOURCES:
Chases-1996, p. 135
FestWestEur-1958, p. 106

◆ 1482 ◆ **Primrose Day**
April 19

Benjamin Disraeli, Earl of Beaconsfield, novelist, and twice prime minister of England, died on this day in 1881. When he was buried in the family vault at Hughenden Manor, near High Wycombe, Queen Victoria came to lay a wreath of primroses, his favorite flower, on his grave. Two years later the Primrose League was formed to support the principles of Conservatism which Disraeli had championed. Although the League has lost much of its influence since World War I, it still has a large membership. Primrose Day is observed in honor of Disraeli and his contribution to the Conservative cause.

SOURCES:
DictDays-1988, p. 91

◆ 1483 ◆ **Prince Kuhio Day**
March 26

Prince Jonah Kuhio Kalanianaole (1871–1921) was a young man when the Hawaiian monarchy was overthrown in 1893.

As a member of the royal family, he fought for the restoration of the monarchy and spent a year as a political prisoner. He lived abroad for a number of years after his release, but eventually returned to his native land and was elected as the first delegate to represent the Territory of Hawaii in the U.S. Congress in 1903. He was reelected and served 10 consecutive terms until his death in 1921.

Because he worked so hard to preserve the old Hawaiian customs and traditions and to take care of the dwindling number of Hawaiian natives, Prince Kuhio has been revered by his people. His birthday is commemorated on the island of Kauai, where he was born, with a week-long Prince Kuhio Festival during the latter part of March. The festival pays tribute to him by featuring such traditional Hawaiian events as outrigger canoe races, hula dancing, and performances of Hawaiian music.

CONTACT:
Hawaii Visitors Bureau
2270 Kalakaua Ave., Ste. 801
Honolulu, HI 96815
808-923-1811; fax: 808-922-8991

SOURCES:
AmerBkDays-1978, p. 293
AnnivHol-1983, p. 42
BkHolWrld-1986, Mar 26
Chases-1996, p. 145

◆ 1484 ◆ **Prince's Birthday**
August 15

A national holiday in Liechtenstein. This 62-square-mile country (population around 30,000) gets almost 25 percent of its revenue from selling postage stamps. The country is a constitutional monarchy headed by Prince Franz Joseph II, who turned over actual power to his son, Hans-Adam, in 1984. It was founded at the end of the 17th century when Johann Adam von Liechtenstein, a wealthy Austrian prince, bought land in the Rhine valley from two bankrupt counts. In 1719 he obtained an imperial deed creating the country. That date is considered the official birth of the nation. Members of the Liechtenstein family have ruled the country ever since.

Franz Joseph II was born on Aug. 16, 1905, but his birthday is celebrated on Aug. 15, the day of the Feast of the ASSUMPTION. Celebrations take place in the capital city of Vaduz. People come from the countryside for the festivities which include an open house at the prince's home and castle, Schloss Vaduz; dancing in the streets; special food in the cafes; and fireworks in the evening.

CONTACT:
Swiss National Tourist Office
608 Fifth Ave.
New York, NY 10020
212-757-5944; fax: 212-262-6116

SOURCES:
Chases-1996, p. 337

◆ 1485 ◆ **Prinsjesdag**
Third Tuesday in September

The state opening of Parliament in the Netherlands takes place on the third Tuesday in September at the 13th-century Ridderzaal, or Knights' Hall, in The Hague. Queen Beatrix rides to Parliament in a golden coach drawn by eight horses. She is received by the two houses of Parliament—the Upper House and the Lower House, corresponding to the Senate and the House of Representatives in the United States—to whom she addresses her speech outlining the government's intended majority program for the coming year.

A similar ceremony is observed in Great Britain (*see* STATE OPENING OF PARLIAMENT).

CONTACT:
Netherlands Board of Tourism
355 Lexington Ave., 21st Floor
New York, NY 10017
212-370-7360; fax: 212-370-9507

SOURCES:
Chases-1996, p. 380

♦ 1486 ♦ Procession of the Penitents in Belgium
Last Sunday in July

A religious procession in Veurne (or Furnes), Belgium, in which penitents in coarse robes and hoods walk barefoot through town, many carrying heavy wooden crosses. The procession, to the sound of drumbeats, is interspersed with scenes depicting biblical events. In some, costumed people dramatize Old and New Testament characters. In others there are carved wooden figures on platforms. At the end of the procession bishops parade carrying the Sacred Host, and as the Sacrament passes, spectators quietly kneel. After the procession is over there is a *kermess*, or fair, in the market-place. The celebration traditionally draws large crowds.

Two legends account for the origins of the procession. One says that it dates back to 1099 when crusader Count Robert II of Flanders returned from Jerusalem with a fragment of the True Cross. The other traces it to 1644 when townsfolk carried crosses in a reenactment of the last walk of Jesus before his crucifixion. The procession was to seek intercession against the plague and an outbreak of war between the Spanish and French.

CONTACT:
Belgian Tourist Office
780 Third Ave.
New York, NY 10017
212-758-8130; fax: 212-355-7675

SOURCES:
BkHolWrld-1986, Jul 27
FestWestEur-1958, p. 14

♦ 1487 ♦ Procession of the Penitents in Spain
Between May 3–June 6; the week preceding Pentecost

During the week before PENTECOST on the Spanish side of the Pyrénées near the French border, a procession of penitents, covered from head to toe in black except for their eyes, makes its way from the village of Burguets to the Abbey of Roncesvalles. With heavy wooden crosses tied to their backs, they struggle up the steep two-mile path that leads to the abbey, chanting a doleful *Miserere*. After attending Mass there, the penitents make their confessions without removing the black hoods that hide their faces.

Since the penitents come from five surrounding villages, each parish performs its own penitential march over a five-day period. According to legend, the procession originated as an act of penance among 23 families seeking atonement for the sins they had committed during the year.

CONTACT:
Tourist Office of Spain
665 Fifth Ave.
New York, NY 10022
212-759-8822; fax: 212-980-1053

SOURCES:
FestSaintDays-1915, p. 112
FestWestEur-1958, p. 196

♦ 1488 ♦ Procession of the Swallow
March 1

The Procession of the Swallow takes place in Greece on March 1 as a celebration of the arrival of spring. Children go from house to house in pairs, carrying a rod from which a basket full of ivy leaves is hung. At the end of the rod is an effigy of a bird made of wood with tiny bells around its neck. This is the "swallow," the traditional harbinger of spring. As they proceed through the village, the children sing "swallow songs" that go back more than 2,000 years. The woman of the house takes a few ivy leaves from the basket and places them in her hen's nest in the hope that they will encourage the hen to produce more eggs. The children receive a few eggs in return, and they move on to the next house. The ivy, which is green all year round, is symbolic of growth and fertility, and it is believed to have the power to bring good health to hens and other animals.

SOURCES:
BkFestHolWrld-1970, p. 71
DictFolkMyth-1984, p. 1091

♦ 1489 ♦ Professional Secretaries' Day
Wednesday of the last full week of April

Professional Secretaries Week was started in 1952 by Professional Secretaries International (PSI), an organization devoted to the education and professional development of secretaries, executive assistants, information specialists, and office managers. It takes place during the last full week in April, with Professional Secretaries' Day observed on Wednesday. Many PSI chapters sponsor special events throughout the week—such as educational seminars or luncheons with guest speakers for secretaries and their bosses—but Wednesday is the day when managers and executives are supposed to give their office support staff a special token of their appreciation.

How do secretaries want to be recognized on this day? According to a PSI survey, most of them want a bonus, a raise, or time off. What do they get? Lunch or dinner is the most common form of recognition, followed by flowers, gifts, and gift certificates.

CONTACT:
Professional Secretaries
 International
10502 N.W. Ambassador Dr.
Kansas City, MO 64153
816-891-6600; fax: 816-891-9118

SOURCES:
AnnivHol-1983, p. 55
Chases-1996, pp. 180, 183
DictDays-1988, p. 109

Prophet's Birthday
See **Mawlid al-Nabi**

♦ 1490 ♦ Puck's Fair
August 10–12

A traditional gathering that dates back hundreds of years, Puck's Fair is a three-day event held in Killorglin in County Kerry, Ireland. A large male goat is decorated with ribbons and paraded through the streets on the first day, which is known as Gathering Day. The goat, known as King Puck, presides over the fair from his "throne," an enclosure on a three-story platform in the town square. The main event of the second day, known as Puck's Fair Day, is a livestock show. On the third day, known as Scattering Day or Children's Day, King Puck is led out of town to the accompaniment of traditional Irish music. Gypsies in large numbers have attended the fair, selling, trading, telling fortunes, and playing wonderful Irish music.

CONTACT:
Irish Tourist Board
345 Park Ave., 17th Floor
New York, NY 10154
800-223-6470 or 212-418-0800
fax: 212-371-9052

SOURCES:
FolkWrldHol-1992, p. 418

♦ 1491 ♦ Puerto Rico Constitution Day
July 25

The anniversary of the day on which Puerto Rico changed from a territory to a commonwealth and adopted its new constitution in 1952. Sometimes referred to as **Commonwealth Day**, July 25 is a legal holiday throughout the island. It is celebrated with parades, speeches, fireworks, speedboat races, and parties.

The most interesting thing about the relationship between Puerto Rico and the United States is its voluntary nature. Under the commonwealth arrangement, islanders elect a governor and a legislature as well as a resident commissioner who is sent—with a voice but not a vote—to the U.S. Congress in Washington, D.C. The relationship remains permanent for as along as both parties agree to it, but it can be changed at any time by mutual consent. The reason Puerto Rico became a commonwealth rather than an independent republic or a state is that the election of 1948 failed to produce a majority vote in favor of either of these alternatives.

CONTACT:
Puerto Rico Dept. of Culture
P.O. Box 9024184
San Juan, PR 00902-4184
809-724-0700

SOURCES:
AmerBkDays-1978, p. 694
AnnivHol-1983, p. 97
Chases-1996, p. 310

♦ 1492 ♦ Pulaski Day
October 11; first Monday in March

Count Casimir Pulaski was already a seasoned fighter for the cause of independence when he first arrived in America in 1777 to help General George WASHINGTON and the Continental Army overthrow the British. While still a teenager he had fought to preserve the independence of his native Poland, and when he was forced to flee his country he ended up in Paris. There he met Benjamin FRANKLIN and Silas Deane, who were impressed by his military background and arranged for him to join the American revolutionaries.

Although he was put in charge of the mounted units and given the title Commander of the Horse, Pulaski had trouble maintaining his soldiers' respect. He spoke no English and was unwilling to take orders from anyone, including Washington. Eventually he resigned from the army and raised an independent cavalry corps, continuing his fight for the colonies' independence. It was on October 11, 1779, that the Polish count died while trying to free Savannah, Georgia, from British control.

The president of the United States proclaims October 11 as Pulaski Day each year, and it is observed with parades and patriotic exercises in communities in Georgia, Indiana, Nebraska, and Wisconsin. It is a legal holiday in Illinois, observed on the first Monday in March. The biggest Pulaski Day parade takes place in New York City on the Sunday nearest October 11, when more than 100,000 Polish-Americans march up Fifth Avenue.

SOURCES:
AmerBkDays-1978, p. 913

AnnivHol-1983, p. 131
Chases-1996, pp. 122, 412

♦ 1493 ♦ Punky (Punkie) Night
Last Thursday in October

In the English village of Hinton St. George, Somerset, it is traditional for both children and adults to walk through town carrying "punkies," or lanterns made from carved-out mangel-wurzels, or mangolds (a variety of beet), with candles in them. Some say that the custom originated when parish women made crude vegetable lanterns to guide their husbands home after a long evening at the local pub. October 28 was traditionally the date for the Chiselborough Fair, and it was not uncommon for the men to drink too much and get lost in the fields on their way home.

Although this custom is observed in other English towns, the celebration at Hinton St. George is by far the best established. There is a procession of children carrying punkies through the streets, begging for money, and singing the "punky song." A prize is given out for the best carved punky. There is no evidence that the name "punky" came from "pumpkin," but the custom is very similar to what takes place on HALLOWEEN in the United States, where carved, candlelit pumpkins are displayed in windows and on doorsteps.

SOURCES:
AnnivHol-1983, p. 138
DictDays-1988, p. 92
FolkWrldHol-1992, p. 517

Purification of Mary, Feast of the
See **Candlemas**

♦ 1494 ♦ Purim
Between February 25 and March 25; Adar 14

Six hundred years before the Christian era, most Jews were slaves in Persia. The Persian prime minister Haman, who generally hated Jews and particularly hated a proud Jew named Mordecai, persuaded King Ahasuerus (Xerxes I) to let him destroy the empire's entire Jewish population. Haman cast lots (*pur* is Akkadian for 'lot') to find out which day would be the most auspicious for his evil plan, and the lots told him that things would go especially well on the 14th of Adar. This is why Purim is also called **The Feast of Lots**.

The king did not realize that his own wife, Esther, was Jewish, and that Mordecai was her cousin, until she pleaded with him to spare her people. Haman was hanged, and his position as prime minister was given to Mordecai.

Ahasuerus granted the Jews an extra day to vanquish Haman's supporters, so the rabbis decreed that in Jerusalem and other walled cities, Purim should be celebrated on 15 Adar and called *Purim Shushan*, Hebrew for 'Susa', the Persian capital. In leap year, the 14th (or 15th in Jerusalem) Adar is known as *Purim Katan*, 'the lesser Purim.'

The Old Testament Book of Esther, is read aloud in synagogues on the eve and morning of Purim, and listeners drown out every mention of Haman's name by jeering and stamping their feet. Purim is also a time for sharing food with friends and for charity to the poor.

See also PURIMS, SPECIAL

SOURCES:
AmerBkDays-1978, p. 281
BkFest-1937, p. 206
DaysCustFaith-1957, p. 68
DictFolkMyth-1984, p. 477
DictWrldRel-1989, pp. 155, 588
FolkAmerHol-1991, p. 103
FolkWrldHol-1992, p. 139
RelHolCal-1993, p. 105

♦ 1495 ♦ Purims, Special
Various

Just as Jews throughout the world celebrate their escape from the evil plot of the Persian prince Haman (*see* PURIM), many individual Jewish communities commemorate their deliverance from specific calamities by observing their own Purims. The **Padua Purim**, for example, observed on 11 Sivan, celebrates Jews' deliverance from a major fire in Padua, Italy, in 1795. The **Baghdad Purim**, observed on 11 Av, celebrates the conquest of Baghdad by the Arabs and the defeat of the Persians. The **Snow Purim**, observed on 24 Tevet, celebrates the major snowstorm in Tunis that caused extensive damage and injury elsewhere but left the Jewish quarter of the city untouched. And the **Hitler Purim**, observed in Casablanca, Morocco, on 2 Kislev, commemorates the city's escape from German domination during World War II.

SOURCES:
AmerBkDays-1978, p. 281
RelHolCal-1993, p. 105

♦ 1496 ♦ Purple Spring
October

Señor de los Milagros was a nameless black artist who painted an image of Christ on the adobe wall of the brotherhood to which he belonged in Lima, Peru. A violent earthquake struck the area in 1655, and although many buildings were destroyed and lives were lost, the wall with the image of Christ remained unscathed. An even stronger earthquake in 1687 destroyed most of the city, but when the wall with Señor de los Milagros's painting was carried through the streets, the shaking stopped. Since that time, two processions with the painting take place every October.

The honor of carrying the litter is by invitation only, but bystanders show their devotion by wearing purple, the color of the black brotherhood that is in charge of the fiesta. A copy of the original painting, which remains in the small church of Las Mazarenas in the center of Lima, is used for the processions. Some of the participants walk backward so as not to turn their backs on the painted image of Christ. When the procession reaches the Plaza de Armas, the president of Peru comes out on his balcony and kneels until the image passes.

Springtime in Peru arrives in October, which is often referred to as "the purple month"—not only because the devotees of Señor de los Milagros wear purple in October, but because it is the month when the jacaranda trees burst into their purple bloom.

CONTACT:
Embassy of Peru
1700 Massachusetts Ave., N.W.
Washington, D.C. 20036
202-833-9860; fax: 202-659-8124

SOURCES:
BkFestHolWrld-1970, p. 95

♦ 1497 ♦ Pushkar Mela
October–November; full moon day of Hindu month of Kartika

A camel fair and one of the best known of the Hindu religious fairs of India, held at Pushkar, the place where it is said a lotus flower slipped out of Lord Brahma's hands. Water sprang up where the petals fell and created the holy waters of Pushkar Lake. A temple to Brahma on the shore of the lake is one of the few temples in India dedicated to Brahma. Pushkar is in the state of Rajasthan, a vast desert area dotted with oases and populated with wild black camels.

The commercial side of the fair features the sale of about 10,000 camels. Sheep, goats, horses, and donkeys are also sold there. Countless stalls offer such camel accouterments as saddles and blankets embellished with mirrors, bangles, brass utensils, and brass-studded belts. Camel races are a highlight. In the "camel rush" people jump onto camels, and the camel that holds the most people wins a prize.

On the night of the full moon (*Kartika Purnima*), devotees bathe in the waters of the lake and then make offerings of coconut and rice at the Brahma temple.

CONTACT:
India Tourist Office
30 Rockefeller Ave.
15 N. Mezzanine
New York, NY 10112
212-586-4901; fax: 212-582-3274

SOURCES:
BkHolWrld-1986, Oct 21
GdWrldFest-1985, p. 112

♦ 1498 ♦ Putrada Ekadashi
July–August; 11th day of waxing half of Hindu month of Sravana

The Hindu EKADASHI, or 11th-day fast known as Putrada Ekadashi, is observed primarily by sterile parents who want to produce a son. A fast is observed, Vishnu is worshipped and meditated upon, and the Brahmans are fed and presented with robes and money. Fasting and piety on this day are believed to ensure the conception of a boy, especially for those who sleep in the same room where Vishnu has been worshipped.

Would-be parents are also expected to observe the Ekadashi that falls in the waning half of the month of Sravana. It is known as Kamada Ekadashi, or the wish-fulfilling Ekadashi.

SOURCES:
RelHolCal-1993, p. 105

♦ 1499 ♦ Pythian Games
Mid-August

The ancient Greek games considered next in importance to the OLYMPIC GAMES. From 586 B.C., they were held every four years on the plain near Delphi. Competitions in instrumental music, singing, drama, and recitations in verse and prose were primary, but there were also athletic and equestrian contests modeled on those at Olympia. The prize was a crown of bay leaves.

See also ISTHMIAN GAMES, NEMEAN GAMES, OLYMPIC GAMES

SOURCES:
DictFolkMyth-1984, p. 67

Q

♦ 1500 ♦ **Qatar Independence Day**
September 3

This national holiday celebrates Qatar's full independence from Britain on this day in 1971.

CONTACT:
Qatar Embassy
600 New Hampshire Ave., N.W.,
Ste. 1180
Washington, D.C. 20037
202-338-0111; fax: 202-337-2989

SOURCES:
AnnivHol-1983, p. 114
Chases-1996, p. 362

♦ 1501 ♦ **Qing Ming Festival (Ching Ming Festival)**
Fourth or fifth day of third lunar month

A day for Chinese throughout the world to honor their dead. *Ching Ming* means 'clear and bright,' and refers to the weather at this time of year. It is a Confucian festival that dates back to the Han Dynasty (206 B.C. to 221 A.D.), and it is now a Chinese national holiday. It is computed as 105 days after the WINTER SOLSTICE, Tong-ji. The day is observed in the countryside with visits to ancestral graves to sweep, wash, repair, and paint them. Offerings of food, wine, incense, and flowers are made, firecrackers are set off, and paper money is burned at the graveside, so that the ancestors will have funds to spend in the afterworld. (The Chinese traditional belief is that the afterlife is quite similar to this life, and that the dead live a little below ground in the Yellow Springs region.) In ancient China, people spent Qing Ming playing Chinese football and flying kites. Today, they picnic and gather for family meals. In the cities, though, it has been changed to a day of patriotism with placement of memorial wreaths only to Chinese revolution heroes in a few state-run public cemeteries.

The day is also called **Cold Food Day** (in Korea, **Han Sik-il**; in Taiwan, **Han Shih**) because, according to an ancient legend, it was taboo to cook the day before.

In Taiwan, yellow paper strips about 3 x 2 inches, are stuck in the ground of the grave, as is shingling. This symbolically maintains the home of one's ancestors. Then the prayers and food offerings are done.

See also HUNGRY GHOSTS, FESTIVAL OF; THANH-MINH

SOURCES:
AmerBkDays-1978, p. 501
BkFestHolWrld-1970, p. 87
BkHolWrld-1986, Apr 6
Chases-1996, p. 159
DictFolkMyth-1984, pp. 225, 228, 478, 789
FolkWrldHol-1992, p. 233
RelHolCal-1993, p. 105

♦ 1502 ♦ **Quadragesima Sunday**
Between February 8 and March 14; first Sunday in Lent in West

The name for the first Sunday in LENT is derived from the Latin word meaning 'fortieth.' The first Sunday of the Lenten season is 40 days before EASTER. The other "numbered" Sundays, all before Lent, are Quinquagesima ('fiftieth'), Sexagesima ('sixtieth'), and Septuagesima ('seventieth'). These are reckoned by an approximate number of days before Easter; only Quadrigesima is close to the actual count. These names, as well as "Pre-Lent," are no longer used, the calendar now referring to the number of Sundays after EPIPHANY, e.g. first Sunday after Epiphany, second Sunday after Epiphany, and so on until ASH WEDNESDAY, then, first Sunday in Lent.

SOURCES:
DictDays-1988, p. 93
DictMyth-1962, vol. I, p. 249
FestWestEur-1958, p. 8
RelHolCal-1993, pp. 64, 105
SaintFestCh-1904, p. 97

♦ 1503 ♦ **Quadrilles of San Martin**
November 11

Every year on San Martin's Day (*see* MARTINMAS), the Quadrilles of St. Martin—often described as an "equestrian ballet"—have been held in the old Colombian town named after the saint. Forty-eight expert riders, all male and mounted on Creole horses, divide into four groups and take their place at the four corners of the town's large square. Each group of riders is dressed to represent a different ethnic group that has played a part in Colombia's past: The Moors (Arabs) wear turbans and white, Oriental-looking robes and carry scimitars; the Spaniards wear black riding jackets, white breeches, tall boots, and cowboy hats and carry sabers; the Blacks wear exotic African headgear and animal skins and carry long machetes; and the Indians wear feather headdresses, breastplates, and elaborate necklaces and are armed with bows and arrows. The performances reenact various events in Colombia's history, including the battles between the Spanish and the Moors and the wars of independence waged against Spain. Although the acts themselves are carefully staged, they often involve improvisation requiring fast riding and split-second timing.

After the Quadrilles are over, residents and visitors gather in the square's open-air cafes to drink *aguardiente*, the local anise-flavored liquor, to eat *ternara a la llanera*, or barbecued baby beef, and to watch the fireworks displays that are set off over the city. Participation in the Quadrilles is an honor that is handed down from one generation to the next among the city's oldest families.

See also MOORS AND CHRISTIANS FIESTA

CONTACT:
Colombian Embassy
2118 Leroy Pl., N.W.
Washington, D.C. 20008
202-387-8338; fax: 202-232-8643

SOURCES:
GdWrldFest-1985, p. 65

♦ 1504 ♦ **Quarter Days**
Various

The four traditional quarter days in England, Northern Ireland, and Wales are LADY DAY (March 15), MIDSUMMER DAY (June 24), MICHAELMAS (September 29), and CHRISTMAS Day (December 25). They mark off the four quarters of the year and the times at which rents and other payments are due. It was also customary to move into or out of a house on a quarter day.

In Scotland the quarter days are CANDLEMAS (February 2), PENTECOST (or Whitsunday, the seventh Sunday after Easter), LAMMAS (August 1), and MARTINMAS (November 11).

SOURCES:
DictDays-1988, pp. 18, 66, 73, 75, 93, 131
DictFolkMyth-1984, p. 601
FestSaintDays-1915, pp. 163, 166, 204
FolkWrldHol-1992, pp. 188, 492, 557
RelHolCal-1993, pp. 95, 105

♦ 1505 ♦ **Quebec Winter Carnival**
Ten days in early February

Winter carnivals are common throughout Canada, but the celebration of winter that has been held since the mid-1950s in Quebec City ranks among the great carnivals of the world. It begins with the Queen's Ball at the Château Frontenac, a hotel resembling a huge medieval castle in the center of the city, and a parade of illuminated floats. The International Ice Sculpture Contest, featuring artists from several northern countries, is held at Place Carnaval. More than 40,000 tons of snow are trucked in to construct a large snow castle, which is illuminated at night and which serves as a mock jail for those who fail to remain smiling throughout the celebration. Bonhomme Carnaval, the festival's seven-foot-high snowman mascot dressed in a red cap and traditional sash, roams the

streets teasing children and looking for people to lock up in the Ice Palace. The festival drink is caribou, a blend of white alcohol and red wine.

An unusual festival event is the hazardous race of steel-bottomed boats on the semi-frozen St. Lawrence River. Each boat has a team of five, and its members must maneuver around ice floes and occasionally drag their boats over large patches of ice.

Other events include a motorcycle race on ice and a snowmobile competition. The festival is also the setting for the International Pee-Wee Hockey Tournament, in which teams from all over Canada and the United States compete.

An interesting feature of this festival is the way it is financed. A principal source of income for the Carnaval Association is the candle, or "bougie," sale. People who buy the bougies increase the chances that their representative "duchess" (and there are a number of duchesses chosen from all over Quebec) will be selected as Carnaval Queen. They also get a chance to participate in a giant lottery. More than 10,000 people participate in the sale and distribution of candles on "Bougie Night."

CONTACT:
Tourisme Quebec
C.P. 979
Montreal, Quebec
Canada H3C 2W3
800-363-7777 or 514-873-2015

SOURCES:
FolkWrldHol-1992, p. 109
GdWrldFest-1985, p. 56

♦ 1506 ♦ **Quecholli**
280th day of the Aztec year; end of 14th month

Mixcoatl was the Aztec god of the chase, also known as the Cloud Serpent. He had deer or rabbit characteristics, was identified with the morning star, and, as one of the four creators of the world, made fire from sticks just before the creation of man. The festival in his honor, known as Quecholli, was observed with a ceremonial hunt. According to the civil cycle of the Aztec calendar—which consisted of 18 months of 20 days each, plus five unlucky days—Quecholli was celebrated at the end of the 14th month. This was also the day on which weapons were made.

SOURCES:
DictFolkMyth-1984, p. 734

♦ 1507 ♦ **Queen Elisabeth International Music Competition**
May

One of the world's most prestigious music competitions and the largest musical event in Brussels takes place throughout the month of May each year. Open to 75 competitors from around the world, ranging in age from 17 to 30, the competition focuses on violinists one year, pianists the next, composers the third year, with the fourth year set aside as a rest period. It is timed to coincide with the birthday of Queen Elisabeth of Belgium, who supported and encouraged violinist-composer Eugéne Ysaye when he started the event in 1937.

Although billed as a competition, the public is invited to attend every stage of the contest, from the initial tests at the Royal Conservatory of Music to the winner's performance with full orchestra at the Beaux Arts Palace. Members of the jury, many of whom are past winners of the competition, also perform for the public one evening during the month-long competition, and a distinguished musician is invited to give the opening concert.

CONTACT:
Belgian Tourist Office
780 Third Ave.
New York, NY 10017
212-758-8130; fax: 212-355-7675

SOURCES:
MusFestEurBrit-1980, p. 33

♦ 1508 ♦ Queen Elizabeth II Birthday
June 15

Queen Elizabeth II was born on April 21, 1926, but her birthday is officially observed on June 15 by proclamation each year (it may be changed if the weather is really foul). A good explanation for the discrepancy in dates is that the April weather is notoriously bad in London.

The celebration includes Trooping the Colour. The "colour" referred to here is the regimental flag. When British soldiers went to battle, it was important that they be able to recognize their flag so they could rally around it. "Trooping the Colour" was a marching display put on for new recruits so they would know what their regiment's flag looked like.

In 1805 the ceremony became an annual event to celebrate the king or queen's official birthday. Today, a different regiment is chosen each year to parade its flag before Queen Elizabeth II, who sits on horseback and inspects the troops in their brightly colored uniforms as they pass before her in London's Horseguards Parade, a large open space in Whitehall. Then she rides in a carriage back to Buckingham Palace. Although the event attracts thousands of tourists, many Londoners turn out for the traditional ceremony as well.

Queen's Birthday is a national holiday in Australia, where it is celebrated on June 15 as well. It was first observed there in 1788, not long after the country was settled. June 4, the birthday of King George III, was set aside at that time as a holiday for convicts and settlers. After George V died in 1936, the date of his birth, June 3, was set aside to honor the reigning king or queen. Bermuda holds an annual military parade on Hamilton's Front Street in honor of the queen.

CONTACT:
British Tourist Authority
551 Fifth Ave., Ste. 702
New York, NY 10176
800-462-2748 or 212-986-2200
fax: 212-986-1188

SOURCES:
AnnivHol-1983, pp. 78, 79
BkHolWrld-1986, Jun 13
Chases-1996, p. 248
DictDays-1988, p. 112
NatlHolWrld-1968, p. 78

♦ 1509 ♦ Queen Juliana's Birthday
April 30

Juliana Louise Emma Marie Wilhelmina, born on this day in 1909, was queen of the Netherlands from 1948 until 1980, when she voluntarily abdicated in favor of her oldest daughter, Beatrix. Although she has aroused controversy from time to time—especially by employing a faith healer in the 1950s and by letting two of her four daughters marry foreigners, she was a popular monarch whose birthday is still celebrated throughout the Netherlands with parades, fun fairs, and decorations honoring the queens of the House of Orange.

CONTACT:
Netherlands Board of Tourism
355 Lexington Ave., 21st Floor
New York, NY 10017
212-370-7360; fax: 212-370-9507

SOURCES:
AnnivHol-1983, p. 58
Chases-1996, p. 192
NatlHolWrld-1968, p. 54

♦ 1510 ♦ Queen Margrethe's Birthday
April 16

The birthday of Queen Margrethe II (b. 1940) is observed in the capital city of Copenhagen, where people congregate in the courtyard of Amalienborg, the royal palace. Carrying small Danish flags, children cheer and sing for the Queen, refusing to go home until she comes out to greet them. She often appears on the balcony at lunchtime and makes a speech, which is followed by a changing of the Royal Guard in its scarlet dress uniforms.

CONTACT:
Danish Tourist Board
655 Third Ave., 18th Floor
New York, NY 10017
212-949-2333; fax: 212-983-5260

SOURCES:
BkHolWrld-1986, Apr 16
Chases-1996, p. 172

♦ 1511 ♦ Queen's Birthday in Thailand
August 12

A nationwide celebration in Thailand of the birthday of Her Majesty Queen Sirikit (b. 1932). Throughout the country, buildings are decorated to honor the queen, but the most splendid are in Bangkok, where buildings and streets are brilliant with colored lights.

CONTACT:
Tourism Authority of Thailand
5 World Trade Center, Ste. 3443
New York, NY 10048
212-432-0433; fax: 212-912-0920

SOURCES:
AnnivHol-1983, p. 105
Chases-1996, p. 335

♦ 1512 ♦ Queen's Day in England
November 17

This is the day on which Queen Elizabeth I ascended to the throne in 1558 upon the death of her sister, Queen Mary I. Often referred to as the Virgin Queen because she never married, Elizabeth reigned for 44 years—a period that came to be known as the Elizabethan Age because it marked England's rise as a major European power in commerce, politics, and the arts.

The anniversary of her coronation was celebrated for more than 300 years after her reign ended, primarily as a holiday for those working in government offices. After the Gunpowder Plot was exposed in 1605, two years following Elizabeth's death, the day was marked by anti-papal demonstrations, which included burning the Pope in effigy. **Queen Elizabeth's Day** eventually merged with the celebration of GUY FAWKES DAY.

SOURCES:
Chases-1996, p. 452
DictDays-1988, p. 93

♦ 1513 ♦ Queenship of Mary
August 22

Mary, the mother of Jesus, was identified with the title of "Queen" at least as early as the 13th century. Artists often depicted her as wearing a crown or being crowned as she was received into heaven. When Pope Pius XII solemnly defined the dogma of the Assumption of Mary in 1950, he stated that she was raised body and soul to heaven, "to shine resplendent as Queen at the right hand of her Son." On October 11, 1954, during the Marian year that marked the centenary of the proclamation of the dogma of the Immaculate Conception of Mary, Pope Pius XII established the feast of the Queenship of Mary on May 31. After the Second Vatican Council, the feast (classified as an obligatory memorial) was changed to August 22 so that it would follow the Feast of the Assumption on August 15.

See also Immaculate Conception, Feast of the

SOURCES:
RelHolCal-1993, p. 106

♦ 1514 ♦ Quilt Festival, National
August–September

Silver Dollar City, the site of the National Quilt Festival, is a theme park built in 1960 near Branson, Missouri. It is set up to resemble a late 19th-century working community, with a resident colony of craftspeople, street performers and musicians, shops, and restaurants. It is home to more than 14 different festivals and special events throughout the year, including the National Crafts Festival (September–October) and the American Folk Music Festival (June).

The National Quilt Festival takes place for two weeks in late August and early September. In addition to displays and demonstrations by some of America's premier quiltmakers, there is an antique quilt auction, a "wearable art" competition, hands-on workshops and seminars for student quilters, and sales and displays of the latest in quilting equipment and supplies. The festival, which has been held at Silver Dollar City since 1982, also features a "Wallhanging Challenge" in which a select group of quiltmakers from across the United States are asked to design and produce a wall quilt working within a prescribed size limit and using a specially chosen group of fabrics.

CONTACT:
Missouri Division of Tourism
P.O. Box 1055
Jefferson City, MO 65102
800-877-1234 or 314-751-4133
fax: 314-751-5160

Quinquagesima Sunday
See Quadragesima Sunday

♦ 1515 ♦ Quintaine, La
Second Sunday in November

St. Leonard, the patron saint of prisoners, is honored each year in the French town of St.-Léonard-de-Noblat by a ceremony in which 30 men carry the *quintaine,* a three-foot-high box painted to resemble a prison, to the church to be blessed. Afterward they mount it on a post and strike it with mallets as they gallop by on horseback. Fragments of the smashed *quintaine* are said to bring good luck and to make hens lay eggs.

CONTACT:
French Government Tourist Office
9454 Wilshire Blvd., Ste. 715
Beverly Hills, CA 90212
310-271-6665; fax: 310-276-2835

SOURCES:
BkHolWrld-1986, Nov 8

♦ 1516 ♦ Quirinalia
February 17

Quirinus was an ancient Roman deity who closely resembled Mars, the god of war. His name is associated with that of the Quirinal, one of the seven hills on which Rome was built and the site of an ancient Sabine settlement that was the seat of his cult. Eventually Quirinus was identified with Romulus, one of the legendary founders of Rome, and his festival on February 17, the Quirinalia, coincided with the date on which Romulus was believed to have been deified. This festival was also associated with the advent of spring warfare, when the shields and weapons of the army which had been purified and retired for the winter, were brought out. The temple dedicated to Quirinus on the hill known as the Quirinal was one of the oldest in Rome.

SOURCES:
AmerBkDays-1978, p. 223
DictFolkMyth-1984, p. 916
DictMyth-1962, vol. II, p. 1314

R

♦ 1517 ♦ Race Relations Sunday
Sunday nearest February 12

This day is observed on the Sunday nearest Abraham LIN-COLN'S BIRTHDAY because of the role he played in freeing the slaves during the Civil War. Up until 1965 it was sponsored by the National Council of Churches, but since that time, sponsorship has been taken over by individual denominations within the National Council. A number of Roman Catholic groups observe Race Relations Sunday as well, and some Jewish organizations observe it on the preceding Sabbath. Although it was originally conceived in 1924 as an opportunity to focus on improving relations among all races, the longstanding racial conflict between whites and African-Americans in the United States has made this the focal point in recent decades.

There are a number of other observances dealing with race relations at this same time in February. The NAACP (National Association for the Advancement of Colored People) was established on Lincoln's Birthday in 1909, and members of this organization combine the observance of Race Relations Sunday with their organization's founding and with the birthday of the black abolitionist and early human rights activist Frederick Douglass on February 7, 1817.

See also BROTHERHOOD SUNDAY

SOURCES:
AmerBkDays-1978, p. 168
Chases-1996, p. 97
DaysCustFaith-1957, p. 60

♦ 1518 ♦ Race Unity Day
Second Sunday in June

A day observed worldwide by Baha'is and others with meetings and discussions. The day was begun in 1957 by the Baha'i National Spiritual Assembly in the United States, with the purpose of focusing attention on racial prejudice.

The Baha'is see racism as a major barrier to peace, and teach that there must be universal recognition of the oneness of all humans to achieve peace.

CONTACT:
Baha'is of the U.S.
Office of Public Information
866 United Nations Plaza, Ste. 120
New York, NY 10017-1822
212-803-2500; fax: 212-803-2573

SOURCES:
AnnivHol-1983, p. 79
Chases-1996, p. 250
RelHolCal-1993, p. 106

♦ 1519 ♦ Radha Ashtami
August–September; eighth day of waning half of Hindu month of Bhadrapada

This Hindu holiday celebrates the birth of Radha, who was the mistress of the god Krishna during the period of his life when he lived among the cowherds of Vrindavana. Although she was the wife of another *gopa* (cowherd), she was the best-loved of Krishna's consorts and his constant companion. Some Hindus believe that Radha is a symbol of the human soul drawn to the ineffable god Krishna, or the pure, divine love to which the fickle, human love returns.

Images of Radha are bathed on this day and then dressed and ornamented before being offered food and worship. Hindus bathe in the early morning and fast all day to show their devotion to Radha.

SOURCES:
RelHolCal-1993, p. 106

♦ 1520 ♦ Ragbrai
Mid-July

A bicycle ride (not race) across the state of Iowa that is billed as the oldest, longest, and largest bicycle-touring event in the nation and possibly the world. The sponsor from the start has been the *Des Moines Register*, and "Ragbrai" stands for **Register's Annual Great Bicycle Ride Across Iowa**. The field is limited to 7,500, and participants are chosen through a drawing.

The ride began in 1973 when Don Kaul, a *Register* columnist who worked out of Washington D.C., was challenged by another columnist, John Karras, to bicycle across the state to learn about Iowa. The challenge was accepted, and both decided to ride. Karras wrote an article telling about the plan and inviting readers to go along: at the start of the race, there were 300 riders, and 115 rode the distance. One of these was

83-year-old Clarence Pickard, who rode a woman's bike from border to border.

The ride was intended as a one-time event, but interest was such that it continued the next year . . . and the next, when it got the Ragbrai name. The route is different each year but always from west to east. Distances average 462 miles; the longest was the 540 miles of Ragbrai XIII in 1985. According to tradition, riders dip their rear tires in the Missouri River at the start of the tour and seven days later dip their front tires in the Mississippi River when they finish. Multi-day touring rides have been organized in other states since Ragbrai started.

CONTACT:
Greater Des Moines Convention
   and Visitors Bureau
601 Locust St., Ste. 222
Des Moines, IA 50309
800-451-2625 or 515-286-4960
fax: 244-9757

SOURCES:
AnnivHol-1983, p. 181
Chases-1996, p. 307

♦ 1521 ♦ Ragtime and Traditional Jazz Festival, National
Mid-June

The American folk music known as ragtime was born in Sedalia, Missouri, when Scott Joplin played his famous "Maple Leaf Rag" at the Maple Leaf Club in 1899. Joplin's move to St. Louis a few years later made that city the focus of ragtime's boom years. Its popularity continued until the beginning of World War I, when musical tastes shifted toward New Orleans and traditional jazz. But it was revived in the early 1960s with the formation of the Saint Louis Ragtimers, six young jazz musicians who wanted to preserve pure ragtime and traditional jazz. One of them bought an old boat, *Goldenrod*, which served as the site of a ragtime festival in 1965. The *Goldenrod* has hosted the National Ragtime and Traditional Jazz Festival ever since.

The five-day festival includes performances by ragtime and traditional jazz performers and bands from all over the world, including Banu Gibson and the New Orleans Hot Jazz Orchestra, the Salty Dogs from Chicago, the Bix Beiderbecke Memorial Jazz Band, the Storyville Dandies from Japan, the South Frisco Jazz Band, the Jazz Incredibles, David Reffkin's Ragtime String Ensemble, and of course the Saint Louis Ragtimers. The boat's decks, dining rooms, and lounges are used for festival performances, as are nearby barges. The music goes on from 6:00 P.M. until 1:00 A.M., with after-hours levee sessions that carry on until dawn.

CONTACT:
St. Louis Convention and Visitors
   Commission
10 S. Broadway, Ste. 1000
St. Louis, MO 63102
800-325-7962 or 314-421-1023
fax: 314-421-0039

SOURCES:
MusFestAmer-1990, p. 197

♦ 1522 ♦ Raksha Bandhana
*July–August; full moon of Hindu month of
Sravana*

A day, sometimes also referred to as **Brother and Sister Day,** celebrated in northern India by brothers and sisters to reaffirm their bonds of affection, as well as to perform a ritual of protection. A sister ties a bracelet, made of colorful threads and amulets, called *raksha bandhana* ("thread of protection") on her brother's wrists. The brother in turn may give his sister gifts—a piece of jewelry or money—while promising to protect her.

In Nepal it is a festival for both Hindus and Buddhists, which they may even attend in each others' temples. The Brahmins put the golden threads around everyone's wrist; it is worn until DEWALI.

SOURCES:
AnnivHol-1983, p. 181
BkFest-1937, p. 159
BkHolWrld-1986, Nov 3
EncyRel-1987, vol. 6, p. 362;
   vol. 15, p. 480
FolkWrldHol-1992, pp. 398,
   399
RelHolCal-1993, pp. 106, 107

♦ 1523 ♦ Ramadan
Ninth month of the Islamic year

The month of Ramadan traditionally begins with the actual sighting of the new moon, marking the start of the ninth month in the Islamic lunar calendar. Authorities in Saudi Arabia are relied upon for this official sighting. With the exception of children, the sick, and the very old, devout Muslims abstain from food, drink, smoking, sex, and gambling from sunrise to sunset during this period.

This holiest season in the Islamic year commemorates the time when the Qu'ran, the Islamic holy book, is said to have been revealed to Muhammad. This occurred on LAYLAT AL-QADR, one of the last 10 nights of the month. Fasting during the month of Ramadan is one of the Five Pillars (fundamental religious duties) of Islam. It is a time for self-examination and increased religious devotion—similar to the Jewish period from ROSH HASHANAH to YOM KIPPUR and the Christian LENT.

Many West Africans have a two-day carnival, similar to SHROVE TUESDAY, before Ramadan starts.

Because it is based on the Islamic lunar calendar, which does not use intercalated days to stay aligned with the solar calendar's seasons, Ramadan moves through the year, occurring in each of the seasons over time.

The **Fast of Ramadan** ends when the new moon is again sighted and the new lunar month begins. It is followed by the 'ID AL-FITR, Festival of Breaking Fast, which lasts for three days and is marked by feasting and the exchange of gifts.

SOURCES:
AnnivHol-1983, p. 170
BkFest-1937, p. 238
BkFestHolWrld-1970, pp. 80,
   112
BkHolWrld-1986, May 29
DictDays-1988, p. 94
DictWrldRel-1989, pp. 65,
   365, 597, 661
FolkWrldHol-1992, p. 162
RelHolCal-1993, p. 107

♦ 1524 ♦ Rama Leela Festival
*September–October; near the 10th day of waxing
half of Asvina*

The Hindu festival of Dussehra (*see* DURGA PUJA), observed on the 10th day of the waxing half of Asvina, celebrates the victory of the legendary hero Rama over the demon Ravana. The Rama Leela (or Ramalila) is a cycle of pageant plays based on the Hindu epic, *Ramayana*, which details the life and heroic deeds of Rama. Around the time of Dussehra, therefore, the Rama Leela is performed in towns and cities through northern India—most notably at Agra, Allahabad, Rama Nagar, and Varanasi. The performances last between seven and 31 days, during which the *Ramayana* is constantly recited to the accompaniment of music.

Perhaps the most important of these performances takes place for 31 days in Rama Nagar, where the scenes are enacted at various set locales in the form of processions depicting various scenes from the *Ramayana*.

See also RASA LEELA FESTIVAL

CONTACT:
India Tourist Office
30 Rockefeller Ave.
15 N. Mezzanine
New York, NY 10112
212-586-4901; fax: 212-582-3274

SOURCES:
IntlThFolk-1979, p. 216
RelHolCal-1993, p. 73

♦ 1525 ♦ **Ramanavami (Ram Navami)**
March–April; ninth day of waxing half of Hindu month of Caitra

The Hindu festival of Ramanavami celebrates the birth of Rama, who was the first son of King Dasaratha of Ayodhya. According to Hindu belief, the god Vishnu was incarnated in 10 different human forms, of which Rama was the seventh. He and his wife, Sita, are venerated by Hindus as the ideal man and wife. Because Rama is the hero of the great religious epic poem, the *Ramayana*, Hindus observe his birthday by reciting stories from it. They also flock to the temples, where the image of Rama is enshrined, and chant prayers, repeating his name as they strive to free themselves from the cycle of birth and death.

SOURCES:
BkFest-1937, p. 164
BkHolWrld-1986, Apr 18
DictFolkMyth-1984, p. 923
DictWrldRel-1989, pp. 304, 597
FolkWrldHol-1992, p. 217
RelHolCal-1993, p. 107

♦ 1526 ♦ **Ramayana Ballet**
May through October; four successive full moon nights in each month of the dry season

The most spectacular dance-drama on the island of Java, Indonesia, is held on an open-air stage at the Prambanan Temple near Jogjakarta. The ballet is a contemporary abbreviated version of the Hindu epic, the *Ramayana*, unfolding over the four nights to tell the story of Prince Rama banished from his country to wander for years in the wilderness. More than 100 dancers and players of *gamelans* ('percussion instruments') present spectacles of monkey armies, giants on stilts, and clashing battles. The rich carvings—lions and *Ramayana* scenes—of the Prambanan temple complex in the background are spotlighted by the moon.

CONTACT:
Indonesian Tourist Promotion Office
3457 Wilshire Blvd., Ste. 104
Los Angeles, CA 90010
213-387-2078; fax: 213-380-4876

SOURCES:
GdWrldFest-1985, p. 113
IntlThFolk-1979, p. 225

♦ 1527 ♦ **Rand Show**
April–May; during Easter season

Formerly known as the **Rand Easter Show**, this South African industrial, commercial, and agricultural show is similar to what a huge state fair is like in the United States. The Rand Show is sponsored by the Witwatersrand Agricultural Society and is considered to be the most important event of its kind in South Africa. It features agricultural, industrial, and livestock exhibitions, equestrian shows, and an amusement park. The most popular feature is the consumer goods display.

Although at the time of its founding in 1895 the show was held in March, during the schools' traditional Easter holiday, it has since shifted to reflect the change in the scheduling of school holidays. More than a million people attend the Rand Show each year, which is held at Milner Park in Johannesburg.

CONTACT:
South African Tourism Board
500 Fifth Ave.
New York, NY 10110
800-822-5368 or 212-730-2929
fax: 212-764-1980

SOURCES:
GdWrldFest-1985, p. 160

♦ 1528 ♦ **Rara (Ra-Ra)**
February–April; weekends in Lent

In Haiti the celebration of CARNIVAL is known as Rara for the groups of people who come down from the hills to dance in processions on the weekends throughout LENT and particularly during EASTER week. It begins by calling on Legba, who appears as Carrefour, the guardian of thresholds and crossroads. Each Rara band consists of a musical group, a band chief, a queen with attendants, a women's choir, and vendors selling food. The group's leader often dresses like a jester and twirls a long baton known as a *jonc*. On SHROVE TUESDAY night, the Rara bands perform a Bruler Carnival in which they carry out the ritual burning of various carnival objects then make a cross on their forehead with the ashes. Rara has deep ties with voodoo and its resemblance to other Carnival celebrations is only superficial.

CONTACT:
Haitian Embassy
2311 Massachusetts Ave., N.W.
Washington, D.C. 20008
202-332-4090; fax: 202-745-7215

SOURCES:
BkHolWrld-1986, Apr 9
FolkWrldHol-1992, p. 111
RelHolCal-1993, p. 65

♦ 1529 ♦ **Rasa Leela Festival**
August–September; Hindu month of Bhadrapada

JANMASHTAMI is the birthday of Krishna, the eighth incarnation of the Hindu god Vishnu, which is observed on the new moon day of the month of Bhadrapada. In the city of Mathura, an important center of Indian art and the birthplace of Krishna, a month-long festival is held during Bhadrapada. The Rasa Leela play cycle, a traditional operatic ballet based on the Krishna legend, is performed throughout the month. In other Indian cities, such as Manipur, the festival has been shortened. The Rasa Leela (or Ras-Lila) Festival takes its name from the *ras*, or dance, of Krishna, the divine flute-player, and his consort, Radha.

See also RAMA LEELA FESTIVAL

CONTACT:
India Tourist Office
30 Rockefeller Ave.
15 N. Mezzanine
New York, NY 10112
212-586-4901; fax: 212-582-3274

SOURCES:
DictFolkMyth-1984, p. 924

♦ 1530 ♦ **Rath Yatra**
July–August; Hindu month of Sravana

An outpouring of tens of thousands of pilgrims to honor Jagannath, Lord of the Universe, in Puri in the state of Orissa, India. Jagannath, worshipped primarily in Orissa, is a form of Krishna (though the term applies also to Vishnu), and the Jagannath Temple in Puri is one of the largest Hindu temples in the country. During the festival, wooden images of Jagannath, his brother, Balbhadra, and his sister, Subhadra, are taken in procession in three huge chariots or carts that look like temples and are called *raths*. They go from the Jagannath Temple to be bathed at Gundicha Mandir, a temple about a mile away; the gods are installed there for a week before being brought back to the Jagannath Temple. This is such a popular festival because all castes are considered equal, and everyone has to eat the food prepared by low caste men at the shrine.

The main chariot has a striped yellow-and-orange canopy 45 feet high with 16 wheels, each seven feet in diameter. It is occupied by scores of riders and pulled by thousands of devotees. Because the moving chariot becomes an inexorable force that could crush anything in its path, the name of the god entered the English language as "**Juggernaut.**"

The festival is also known as the **Jagannath Festival**, or **Car Festival**. Others are held in Varanasi, in Serompore, near Calcutta, and other areas, but the most impressive Rath Yatra is at Puri.

CONTACT:
India Tourist Office
30 Rockefeller Ave.
15 N. Mezzanine
New York, NY 10112
212-586-4901; fax: 212-582-3274

SOURCES:
BkHolWrld-1986, Jul 12
DictFolkMyth-1984, p. 537
DictWrldRel-1989, pp. 304,
  368
RelHolCal-1993, p. 108

♦ 1531 ♦ **Ratification Day**
January 14

Most people associate the end of the Revolutionary War with the surrender of Lord Cornwallis at Yorktown, Virginia, in 1781. But it was almost two years later that the Treaty of Paris was signed. It then had to be ratified by the Continental Congress and returned to England within six months. As members of the Congress arrived in Annapolis, Maryland, to ratify the treaty, it became apparent that they needed delegates from two more states to constitute a quorum. With prodding from Thomas JEFFERSON, the delegates from Connecticut finally arrived, and South Carolina Congressman Richard Beresford was dragged from his sickbed in a Philadelphia hotel room. Once everyone was assembled, the treaty was quickly ratified on January 14, 1784, and the American Revolution was officially ended. But it was still too late to get it back to England by the March deadline, since an

ocean crossing took at least two months. Fortunately, Britain was willing to forgive the delay.

The Old Senate Chamber in Maryland's historic State House at Annapolis has been preserved exactly as it was when the ratification took place. On January 14, the same type of flag that was displayed in 1784—with 12 stars in a circle and the 13th in the center—flies over the State House and many other buildings in Annapolis. The ceremony that takes place inside varies from year to year, but it often revolves around a particular aspect of the original event. One year, for example, the original Treaty of Paris was put on display in the rotunda.

CONTACT:
Annapolis and Anne Arundel
  Conference and Visitors Bureau
26 West St.
Annapolis, MD 21401
410-268-8687; fax: 410-263-9591

SOURCES:
AmerBkDays-1978, p. 76
AnnivHol-1983, p. 9
Chases-1996, p. 64

♦ 1532 ♦ **Rato (Red) Machhendranath**
April–May; Hindu month of Vaisakha

This chariot procession is the biggest event in Patan, Nepal. The festival honors Machhendranath, the god of rain and plenty, who is worshipped by both Hindus and Buddhists in different incarnations, and has shrines at both Patan and in the village of Bungamati, a few miles south of Patan. The festival, held when the monsoon season is approaching, is a plea for plentiful rain.

The image of the god, a carved piece of red-painted wood, is taken from the shrine in the Pulchowk area at the start of the festivities and paraded around the city in several stages on a wheeled chariot. The chariot is a huge wooden wagon that is towed by hundreds of devotees. Finally, after a month of being hauled about, the chariot is dismantled, and the image is conveyed to Bungamati to spend six months at the temple there.

A similar but shorter festival, the Sweta (or White) Machhendranath, is held in Katmandu in March or April. The image of the god is taken from the temple at Kel Tole, placed on a chariot and pulled from one historic location to another. When it arrives in the south of the city, the chariot is taken apart, and the image is returned to its starting place.

CONTACT:
Nepal Embassy
2131 Leroy Pl., N.W.
Washington, D.C. 20008
202-667-4550; fax: 202-667-5534

SOURCES:
GdWrldFest-1985, p. 138

♦ 1533 ♦ **Rat's Wedding Day**
Nineteenth day of first lunar month

The Rat's Wedding Day is observed in some Chinese households on the 19th day of the first moon. It is customary to go to bed early so that the rats have plenty of time to enjoy themselves. Food is left out for them in the hope that it will dissuade the more ravenous rodents from disturbing the householder's kitchen. If a very large rat takes up residence in a house, it is regarded as the "Money Rat" and is treated well on this day, for its arrival indicates that the householder will prosper.

SOURCES:
FolkWrldHol-1992, p. 78

♦ 1534 ♦ Ravello Music Festival
First week in July

When German composer Richard Wagner (1813–1883) visited the famous Villa Rufolo in Ravello, Italy, in 1880 he was so impressed by its beauty that he used it as the setting for *Parsifal,* his final opera. Fifty years after his death, the residents of Ravello held a commemorative concert at the Villa, and 20 years later, in 1953, another commemorative concert of Wagnerian music was given. Since then the concerts have been held annually. They last for only four or five days and focus entirely on music composed by Wagner, by composers who influenced (or were influenced by) him, and by composers with whom he had some connection. Most take place in the gardens of the 13th-century Villa Rufolo, the church of Santa Maria Gradillo, and the park, with its view of the Bay of Naples.

See also BAYREUTH FESTIVAL and PACIFIC NORTHWEST FESTIVAL

CONTACT:
Italian Government Travel Office
630 Fifth Ave.
New York, NY 10111
212-245-4822

SOURCES:
MusFestEurBrit-1980, p. 116

♦ 1535 ♦ Ravinia Festival
June–September

Chicago's 12-week festival of classical music, theater, and dance takes place in Highland Park, one of the city's northern suburbs. Although today the festival can boast performances by some of the world's most distinguished conductors, soloists, symphony orchestras, and dance companies, its history since 1904 has been punctuated by periodic financial crises and, in the 1940s, a fire that destroyed the Ravinia Park pavilion. But since that time the festival has rebounded, expanding to include pop, jazz, and folk music as well as several weeks of theater performances. Nearly half a million people attend the festival each year.

CONTACT:
Chicago Convention and Tourism
  Bureau
2301 S. Lake Shore Dr.
McCormick Place On-the-Lake
Chicago, IL 60616
312-567-8500; fax: 312-567-8533

SOURCES:
GdUSFest-1984, p. 48
MusFestAmer-1990, p. 56
MusFestWrld-1963, p. 292

♦ 1536 ♦ Red Earth Native American Cultural Festival
First weekend in June

One of the largest such events in the country, held in Oklahoma City and drawing participants from more than 100 American Indian tribes. The three-day festival features arts and crafts, dancing, parades, foot races, and seminars.

The name Oklahoma means 'red people,' being derived from two Choctaw words, *okla*, meaning 'people,' and *humma*, meaning 'red.' Thirty-five tribes with tribal councils now live in Oklahoma. Their population is more than 175,000, the second largest of any state in the nation.

CONTACT:
Oklahoma Tourism and Recreation Dept.
2401 N. Lincoln Blvd.
Will Rogers Bldg., Ste. 500
Oklahoma City, OK 73105
800-652-6552 or 405-521-2413
fax: 405-521-4883

SOURCES:
Chases-1996, p. 246

♦ 1537 ♦ Redentore, Festa del
Third Sunday in July

The **Feast of the Redeemer** is celebrated in Venice, Italy—one of only two remaining provincial religious festivals surviving in Venice. (The other is at the church of the Salute on the Grand Canal, which also commemorates deliverance from the plague, but is more religious in nature.) It commemorates the end of the plague in the late 16th century, when the people of Venice dedicated a church on Guidecca Island to Jesus the Redeemer and vowed to visit it every year. They continue to keep their promise by building a bridge of boats across the Guidecca and Grand canals, across which worshippers can walk back and forth during the celebration. At dawn, the boats all go out to the Lido to watch the sun rise over the Adriatic Sea. During the festival the cafes, shops, canals, and the church are decorated with lights. When the bridge of boats closes at around nine o'clock, a fireworks display begins.

Services inside the Church of the Redentore, which include Masses commemorating the redeeming power of Jesus, are quite solemn in comparison to what is going on outside—a festival that has been described as the "Venetian Bacchanal."

CONTACT:
Italian Government Travel Office
630 Fifth Ave.
New York, NY 10111
212-245-4822

SOURCES:
BkHolWrld-1986, Jul 19
Chases-1996, p. 306
GdWrldFest-1985, p. 120

♦ 1538 ♦ Red Waistcoat Festival
First or second weekend in July

The **Festa do Colete Encarnado**, or Red Waistcoat Festival, celebrates the *campionos*—the cowboys who watch over the bulls in the pasturelands of the Ribatejo in Portugal, and who traditionally wear red vests, green stocking caps, blue or black trousers, and red sashes. Supposedly the best bulls for bullfighting are those that have been allowed to roam freely in the vast, rich pastures for which this part of the country is famous, and bullfights play a big part in the festival. But unlike bullfighting elsewhere, no one gets hurt and it's against Portuguese law to kill the bull.

A highlight of the festival is the traditional running of the bulls through the streets of Vila Franca de Xira, which is about 20 miles from Lisbon. In addition to bullfighting, there are folk dances, fireworks, and various competitions for the campionos, including the Ribatejan fandango, a competitive dance for men only.

CONTACT:
Portuguese National Tourist Office
590 Fifth Ave., 4th Floor
New York, NY 10036
212-354-4403; fax: 212-764-6137

SOURCES:
FestWestEur-1958, p. 180
GdWrldFest-1985, p. 156
IntlThFolk-1979, p. 314

◆ 1539 ◆ Reed Dance
Late August

The Reed Dance is the culmination of a week-long coming-of-age ceremony for young girls in Swaziland. They gather in the royal city of Lobamba and spend several days along the riverbank gathering reeds for the Queen Mother. They use the reeds to rebuild the screens that surround the Queen Mother's *kraal*, or enclosure. The Reed Dance is performed for the Queen Mother near the end of the ceremony, when the girls, dressed in bead skirts and beautiful jewelry, perform complicated steps done in perfect time, tossing reeds high into the air. Since the Reed Dance, also known as **Umhlanga**, is not a sacred ceremony, visitors are welcome to watch.

CONTACT:
Swaziland Embassy
3400 International Dr., N.W., Ste. 3M
Washington, D.C. 20008
202-362-6683; fax: 202-244-8059

SOURCES:
AnnivHol-1983, p. 93
BkHolWrld-1986, Aug 21
FolkWrldHol-1992, p. 425

◆ 1540 ◆ Reek Sunday
Last Sunday in July

The pre-Christian festival known in Ireland as Lúghnasa was associated with various rites involving hilltops and water. As late as the 19th century, people continued to visit hilltop sites for berry-picking or picnicking on August 1, the original date for celebrating the mid-point of the summer half of the year and the start of the harvest season.

In some parts of Ireland, Lúghnasa has been turned into a religious festival. For example, in County Mayo, thousands of pilgrims climb Croagh Patrick on the last Sunday in July to pray on the spot where Ireland's patron saint, St. Patrick, is believed to have started his ministry. Some who scale the 2,510-foot mountain, known locally as The Reek, do so in bare feet, and many visit the small chapel at the top where Masses are celebrated.

CONTACT:
Irish Tourist Board
345 Park Ave., 17th Floor
New York, NY 10154
800-223-6470 or 212-418-0800
fax: 212-371-9052

SOURCES:
AnnivHol-1983, p. 97
FolkWrldHol-1992, p. 413
RelHolCal-1993, p. 108

◆ 1541 ◆ Reformation Day
October 31

When Martin Luther (1483–1546), a German monk and religious reformer, nailed his 95 "theses" (or propositions) to the church door in Wittenberg on October 31, 1517, his only intention was to voice his opinions about certain practices and customs in the Roman Catholic Church, in the hope that someone would engage him in a public debate. Instead, so many people agreed with his ideas that they spread throughout western Europe and touched off a religious revolt known as the Reformation. As a result, many Christians broke their centuries-old connection with the Roman Catholic Church and established independent churches of their own, prime among them being the Lutheran Church. October 31 is observed by most Protestant denominations as Reformation Day, and the preceding Sunday is known as **Reformation Sunday**. In Germany, the day is sometimes referred to as **Luther's Theses Day**.

SOURCES:
AmerBkDays-1978, p. 974
BkFest-1937, p. 106
DaysCustFaith-1957, p. 277
DictWrldRel-1989, p. 606
RelHolCal-1993, p. 109

Regatta, Harvard and Yale
See Yale-Harvard Regatta

◆ 1542 ◆ Regatta of the Great Maritime Republics
First Sunday in June

The great maritime republics of Italy for which this event is named are Pisa, Genoa, Amalfi, and Venice. Although they no longer enjoy the wealth and power of medieval days, the four cities commemorate their former greatness with a friendly battle for supremacy of the seas off the coast of Pisa. The contest takes the form of a historic regatta in which longboats representing each of the republics race for a prize.

Another event held on this day in Pisa is the *Giuoco del Ponte*, or 'Battle for the Bridge', which goes back to the 13th century. Following a medieval procession, two teams in full costume take part in a traditional competition which involves a reversal of the usual tug-of-war. Twenty-four men from each team line up behind a mechanism on rails and push. The first team to make a "goal" on the opposing side wins, and this is repeated five times.

CONTACT:
Italian Government Travel Office
630 Fifth Ave.
New York, NY 10111
212-245-4822

◆ 1543 ◆ Reggae Sunsplash
August

The largest reggae event in the world takes place for four nights each August at the Bob Marley Centre in Montego Bay, Jamaica. Described as the "Jamaican version of Woodstock," the annual festival features the world's best-known reggae performers as well as salespeople hawking such island specialties as curried goat, bammy and fish, sugarcane, and jelly coconut. Held since 1978, **Sunsplash** has been plagued by organizational problems. But it still qualifies as one of the world's premier musical events, attracting up to 50,000 people.

Reggae originated as the music of the Jamaican poor, reflecting social discontent and the Rastafarian movement. Jamaican-born reggae star Bob Marley, who died of brain cancer at the age of 36, transformed the island-bred music into an international craze. He is venerated in Jamaica much as Elvis Presley is in the United States, and his former house and studio in Kingston, called Tuff Gong, is still a center for some of the more serious reggae music being produced today. One of the festival's most memorable moments occurred in 1981, when American superstar Stevie Wonder sang a moving tribute to Bob Marley following his death earlier that year.

CONTACT:
Jamaica Tourist Board
801 Second Ave.
New York, NY 10017
800-233-4582 or 212-856-9727
fax: 212-856-9730

♦ 1544 ♦ Reindeer Driving Competition
Third week in March

The Lapp, or Sami, people who live in the northern part of the Scandinavian countries round up their herds of reindeer between December and March every year to count, sort, slaughter, and mark their animals in much the same way that cattle and sheep are rounded up in the United States and elsewhere. Round-ups usually last from one to three days and often include athletic competitions. During the third week of March in Inari, Finland, men and women compete on cross-country skis as they try to herd 100 reindeer over a 3¼-mile course. The fastest time wins the competition.

CONTACT:
Finnish Tourist Board
655 Third Ave., 18th Floor
New York, NY 10017
212-949-2333; fax: 212-983-5260

SOURCES:
BkHolWrld-1986, Mar 15

Repotini
See **Ropotine**

♦ 1545 ♦ Repudiation Day
November 23

The Stamp Act of 1765 forced the American colonies to pay a tax on various official documents and publications, such as legal papers, liquor permits, lawyers' licenses, and school diplomas. The tax on newspapers and pamphlets was particularly burdensome, as it was based on the number of printed sheets and advertisements in each publication. The tax had to be paid in British pounds sterling, which made it even more expensive. In defiance of the new law, the court of Frederick County, Maryland, declared that it would carry on its business without the tax stamps required by the Act. In March 1766, the Act was rescinded by Parliament.

The date on which the Stamp Act was repudiated, November 23, has been observed for many years as a half-holiday in Frederick County to commemorate this courageous act. It is customary for the Daughters of the American Revolution (DAR) to meet in the courthouse on this day and to listen while the clerk of the circuit court reads the original 1765 decision.

CONTACT:
Maryland Office of Tourism
 Development
217 E. Redwood St., 9th Floor
Baltimore, MD 21202
800-543-1036 or 410-333-6611
fax: 410-333-6643

SOURCES:
AmerBkDays-1978, p. 1045
AnnivHol-1983, p. 152
Dict Days-1988, p. 95

Respect-for-the-Aged Day
See **Keiro-no-Hi**

Resurrection Day
See **Easter**

♦ 1546 ♦ Return Day
November, the Thursday after Election Day

In the early 19th century, the rural residents of Sussex County, Delaware, had to travel all the way to Georgetown, the county seat, to cast their ballots on ELECTION DAY. The roads were rough, the weather was often bad, and many of the men were uneasy about leaving their families behind. In 1828 the General Assembly adopted new election laws establishing polling places in the "hundreds," as the political subdivisions of the county were called (probably referring to the early English "group of 100 hides," the number of land units necessary to support one peasant family). While this spared voters from having to travel, they had no way of finding out the results of the election because there were no county newspapers. The tabulations were rushed to Georgetown by couriers, and the results were read two days later from the courthouse steps. Many of the farmers in the surrounding areas would take a day off and travel to Georgetown with their families to hear the announcement and to join in the festivities, which included cockfights, band concerts, and open-air markets. The winning candidates were often carried around the town green in an impromptu victory celebration.

Of course, there is no longer any need to wait two days to hear election results. But the residents of Georgetown continue the tradition, which includes a formal announcement of the results on the Thursday after the Presidential Election Day. There are parades, picnics, military displays, and, of course, politicking. Both the winners and the losers circulate among their supporters. Street vendors sell roast oxen, which has been cooked on a spit, and there is a parade down Market Street reminiscent of the days when farmers would arrive in town in their wagons and ox-drawn carts.

CONTACT:
Delaware Tourism Office
99 Kings Highway
Dover, DE 19901
800-441-8846 or 302-739-4271
fax: 302-739-5749

SOURCES:
Chases-1996, p. 443
FolkAmerHol-1991, p. 390

♦ 1547 ♦ Reversing Current, Festival of the (Water Festival)
Late October or early November

A festival to celebrate a natural phenomenon in Cambodia. Tonle Sap, a lake, is connected to the Mekong River by the Tonle Sap River, which normally flows south from the lake. But during the rainy season, from mid-May to mid-October, the flood-swollen Mekong backs up and flows backward through the Tonle Sap River into the lake. The depth of the lake jumps from seven feet to 35 feet, and the total surface quadruples. The normal southward flow returns when the dry season starts. (Because of the phenomenon, the Tonle Sap lake is an extremely rich source of freshwater fish.)

The festival, held at the time when the Tonle Sap returns to its normal direction, is a time of fireworks, merrymaking and races of pirogues, or long canoes, at Phnom Penh.

CONTACT:
Cambodian Embassy
4500 16th St., N.W.
Washington, D.C. 20011
202-726-7742

SOURCES:
FolkWrldHol-1992, p. 553

♦ 1548 ♦ Reykjavik Arts Festival (Festspillene I Reykjavik)
June in even-numbered years

Originally called the **North Atlantic Festival**, this 16-day festival highlights the performing and visual arts. Vladimir Ashkenazy, the famous pianist and an Icelandic citizen, founded the festival with Ivar Eskeland, former director of the Nordic House in Reykjavik. While Eskeland was primarily interested in establishing a Nordic arts festival, Ashkenazy wanted it to be international in scope. The two men combined their goals, and the first festival was held in 1970. Since that time the festival has seen performances by violinist Yehudi Menuhin, flutist James Galway, conductor André Previn, bass Boris Christoff, and the London Sinfonietta. Artists and companies from Austria, Denmark, Germany, France, Greenland, Norway, Sweden, and the United States have also performed there. The festival is well attended not only by local people but by tourists as well.

CONTACT:
Scandinavian Tourism, Inc.
P.O. Box 4649
New York, NY 10163-4649
212-949-2333; fax: 212-983-5260

SOURCES:
GdWrldFest-1985, p. 108
IntlThFolk-1979, p. 201

♦ 1549 ♦ Rhode Island Independence Day
May 4

Rhode Island was the first and only state to declare its independence from England entirely on its own. Relations between the colony and its British rulers had deteriorated rapidly after the 1772 incident in which Rhode Island colonists boarded and burned the British revenue cutter, the *Gaspee*, which had been patrolling the coastal waters in search of local smugglers (*see* Gaspee Days). On May 4, 1776, both houses of the General Assembly renounced the colony's allegiance to Great Britain—a full two months before the rest of the colonies followed suit on July 4 (*see* Fourth of July). Rhode Islanders celebrate this event during May, which is Rhode Island Heritage Month, with flag-raising ceremonies, cannon salutes, and parades of local patriotic, veterans', and scouting organizations.

CONTACT:
Rhode Island Tourism Division
7 Jackson Walkway
Providence, RI 02903
800-556-2484 or 401-277-2601
fax: 401-277-2102

SOURCES:
AmerBkDays-1978, p. 419
AnnivHol-1983, p. 61
Chases-1996, p. 200

♦ 1550 ♦ Rice-Planting Festival at Osaka
June 14

There are many rituals associated with the growing of rice in Japanese farming communities. June marks the beginning of the rainy season, and transplanting usually takes place during June and July. In many rural celebrations, young women in costume perform rituals including planting seedlings while singing rice-planting songs to the accompaniment of pipes and drums. Sometimes women light fires of rice straw and pray to the rice god. Shinto priests are often asked to offer prayers for a good harvest season.

On June 14 in Osaka, thousands congregate to observe a group of young kimono-clad women plant rice and sing in the sacred fields near the Sumiyoshi Shrine. Working rhythmically to the music, the young women appear to be participating in a dance rather than the hard work of planting.

CONTACT:
Japan National Tourist
  Organization
630 Fifth Ave., Ste. 2101
New York, NY 10111
212-757-5640; fax: 212-307-6754

SOURCES:
BkHolWrld-1986, Jun 7
Chases-1996, p. 256
JapanFest-1965, pp. 92, 158

♦ 1551 ♦ Ridvan, Feast of
April 21–May 2

A Baha'i celebration to commemorate the 12-day period in 1863 when the Baha'i founder, Baha'u'llah (which means 'Glory of God'; *see* Baha'u'llah, Birth of), made the declaration that he was God's messenger for this age—the one foreseen by the Bab to be a prophet of the same rank as Abraham, Moses, Jesus, Muhammad, Buddha, Krishna, and Zoroaster. The first, ninth, and 12th days of the period are holy days when work is suspended. The celebration starts at sunset, April 20, the eve of Ridvan.

When he made his declaration, Baha'u'llah was staying outside Baghdad, Iraq, at a garden he called *Ridvan*, meaning Paradise. On the first day, he declared his manifestation to his family and close associates. On the ninth day other followers joined him, and the declaration of his station became public knowledge. On the 12th day, he left the garden.

Nineteen years earlier, the Bab had prophesied that one greater than he would come (*see* Bab, Declaration of the); Baha'u'llah's proclamation stated that he was the "promised one." He set forth the form of the Baha'i religion, teaching the unity of all religions and the unity and brotherhood of all mankind. He wrote more than 100 works of sacred literature.

CONTACT:
Baha'is of the U.S.
Office of Public Information
866 United Nations Plaza, Ste. 120
New York, NY 10017-1822
212-803-2500; fax: 212-803-2573

SOURCES:
AnnivHol-1983, p. 54
Chases-1996, p. 179
DictWrldRel-1989, pp. 87, 89
RelHolCal-1993, p. 109

♦ 1552 ♦ Riley Festival, James Whitcomb
Early October

James Whitcomb Riley (1849–1916), a poet best known for his nostalgic dialect verse, is honored in his hometown of Greenfield, Indiana, with a three-day festival held around his birthday on October 7 each year. Most of the events are held near the Riley Birthplace Museum, the house where the poet spent his childhood, although there are poetry contests, programs in the local schools, and parades through the streets of downtown Greenfield as well.

The festival was started in 1911 by Minnie Belle Mitchell, an author who wanted schools and literary clubs to observe the poet's birthday. The governor of Indiana proclaimed October 7 as **Riley Day** soon afterward, and Riley attended the celebration in 1912, finding himself smothered in bouquets of flowers as his car paraded down the street.

Today Riley is best remembered for such poems as "When the Frost is on the Punkin," "The Raggedy Man," and "Little Orphan Annie," which later inspired both the Raggedy Ann and Andy dolls as well as the Orphan Annie comic strip, which was successfully brought to Broadway as the musical *Annie.*

CONTACT:
Indiana Tourism Division
1 N. Capitol Ave., Ste. 700
Indianapolis, IN 46204
800-289-6646 or 317-232-8860
fax: 317-233-6887

SOURCES:
Chases-1996, pp. 402, 409
GdUSFest-1984, p. 51

♦ 1553 ♦ Rishi Panchami
*August–September; fifth day of waxing half of
Hindu month of Bhadrapada*

Hindus devote this day to the Sapta Rishis, also known as the seven seers or mental sons of Brahma: Bhrigu, Pulastya, Kratu, Pulaha, Marichi, Atri, and Vasistha. An earthenware or copper pitcher filled with water is placed on an altar sanctified with cow dung. The seven seers are then worshipped with betel leaf, flowers, camphor, and lamps. Only fruits are eaten on this day.

Rishi Panchami is primarily a women's festival, but men may observe it for the well-being and happiness of their wives. Devi Arundhati, the wife of Rishi Vasistha and a model of conjugal excellence, is also worshipped on this day.

SOURCES:
RelHolCal-1993, p. 109

♦ 1554 ♦ River Kwai Bridge Week
Last week in November

A commemoration in Kanchanaburi, Thailand, of World War II's infamous Death Railway and the River Kwai (Khwae Noi) Bridge. Between 1942 and 1945, more than 16,000 Allied prisoners of war and 49,000 impressed Asian laborers were forced by the Japanese to build a railway through the jungle from Bangkok, Thailand, into Burma, and it is said that one person died for every railway tie on the track. At the Kanchanaburi War Cemetery, commemorative services are held every April 25 for the 6,982 American, Australian, British, and Dutch prisoners of war buried there.

The bridge became known as a symbol of the horrors and futilities of war through the novel, *The Bridge Over the River Kwai,* by Pierre Boulle and the movie based on it, *The Bridge on the River Kwai.* During the week-long events, the reconstructed bridge (it was bombed during the war) is the setting for sound-and-light presentations, and there are also historical exhibitions and rides on World War II-era trains.

CONTACT:
Tourism Authority of Thailand
5 World Trade Center, Ste. 3443
New York, NY 10048
212-432-0433; fax: 212-912-0920

♦ 1555 ♦ Rizal Day
December 30

A national holiday in the Philippines commemorating the execution of the national hero, Dr. José Rizal, on this day in 1896. Flags fly at half-mast throughout the country, and special rites are led by the president at the 500-foot obelisk that is the Rizal Monument in Manila.

Rizal, born in 1861 in the Philippines, was a doctor who studied medicine in Spain, France, and Germany. He was also a botanist, educator, man of letters, and inspiration for the Philippine nationalist movement. Writing from Europe and denouncing the corrupt ruling of the Philippines by Spanish friars, he became known as a leader of the Philippine reform movement. He wrote the novel, *Noli me tangere* (1886; *The Lost Eden,* 1961), for which the Spanish administration deported him, shortly after he had returned to the Philippines in 1887. He again returned to the Philippines in 1892 and founded a nonviolent reform movement, as a result of which he was exiled to the Philippine island of Mindanao, where he established a school and hospital. Rizal had no direct role in the nationalist insurrection; nevertheless, he was arrested, tried for sedition, and executed by a firing squad. On the eve of his execution, he wrote the poem "Mi Ultimo Adiós," meaning 'My Last Farewell.' The poem, in the original Spanish and translated into other languages, is transcribed on a marble slab near the Rizal Monument.

CONTACT:
Philippine Department of Tourism
556 Fifth Ave.
First Floor Mezzanine
New York, NY 10036
212-575-7915; fax: 212-302-6759

SOURCES:
AnnivHol-1983, p. 166
Chases-1996, p. 493

♦ 1556 ♦ Road Building
April

In areas of Nigeria where the Igbo live, especially Mbaise, there is a festival in April known as **Emume Ibo Uzo,** or Road Building. It is a time for everyone in the community to get together and maintain the major thoroughfares by clearing and leveling them. This festival was particularly important in the days before government-sponsored road building became common.

SOURCES:
FolkWrldHol-1992, p. 221

♦ 1557 ♦ Robigalia
April 25

The ancient Romans knew how much damage certain fungi could do to their crops, but they attributed these diseases to the wrath of the gods. Robigus was the Roman god who personified such blights, and the annual festival known as the Robigalia was designed to placate him. It was believed that prayers and sacrifices made on this day, April 25, would head off the mildew, rust, wilt, and other blights that so often devastated their crops.

SOURCES:
AmerBkDays-1978, p. 313
DictFolkMyth-1984, p. 916
DictMyth-1962, vol. II, p. 1343

Rocket Festival
See **Bun Bang Fai**

♦ 1558 ♦ **Rodgers Festival, Jimmie**
Last full week in May

A country music festival in Meridian, Miss., to salute the life and music of Jimmie Rodgers on the anniversary of his death on May 26, 1933. Rodgers was born in Meridian in 1897 and left school at 14 to work on the Mississippi and Ohio Railroad; later, during his singing career, he was known as the "Singing Brakeman." He learned to play the guitar and banjo, and learned the blues from black railroad workers. Mr. Rodgers's music blended blues with the sounds of country, work, hobo, and cowboy songs. In 1925, because tuberculosis prevented him from working any longer for the railroad, he became a performer, and quickly a best-selling recording artist. Today he is considered the Father of Country Music. Among his recordings that had a lasting influence on popular singers were "Blue Yodel No. 1," "Brakeman's Blues," and "My Time Ain't Long." The Jimmie Rodgers Memorial and Museum in Meridian has exhibits of his guitar, concert clothing, and railroad equipment he used.

The week-long festival highlights top musical stars and features a talent contest and a beauty contest.

CONTACT:
Jimmie Rodgers Foundation
P.O. Box 2170
Meridian, MS 39302
601-483-5763

♦ 1559 ♦ **Rogation Days**
Between April 30 and June 3; Monday, Tuesday,
and Wednesday preceding Ascension Day

Since medieval times the three days before ASCENSION DAY (called HOLY THURSDAY in Great Britain) have been known as Rogation Days (from *rogare*, 'to pray'). Both the Roman Catholic and Protestant churches set them aside as days of abstinence and prayer, especially for the harvest. In many churches in the United States **Rogation Sunday**, the fifth Sunday after EASTER, has been known as **Rural Life Sunday** or **Soil Stewardship Sunday** since 1929—a day when the religious aspects of agricultural life are emphasized. It is also known as **Cantate Sunday** because the Latin Mass for this day begins with the first words of Psalm 98, *Cantate Domino*, 'Sing to the Lord.'

The Rogation Days also had a secular meaning at one time in England, where they were called **Gang Days** or **Gange Days**—from the Saxon word *gangen*, meaning 'to go'. There was a custom of walking the parish boundaries during the three days before Holy Thursday (Ascension Day), the procession consisting of the priests and prelates of the church and a select number of men from the parish. Later these Rogation Days were set aside for special local celebrations. In 19th-century Dorsetshire, for example, a local festival called the Bezant was held each year on Rogation Monday.

SOURCES:
BkDays-1864, vol. I, p. 582
DaysCustFaith-1957, p. 135
DictDays-1988, pp. 19, 46, 96
FestSaintDays-1915, p. 99
FolkWrldHol-1992, p. 279
RelHolCal-1993, p. 109

SaintFestCh-1904, p. 227

♦ 1560 ♦ **Rogers Day, Will**
November 4

The birthday of America's "cowboy philosopher" is observed as a legal holiday in Oklahoma, where he was born on November 4, 1879, when it was still the Indian Territory (*see* OKLAHOMA DAY). After his first appearance as a vaudeville entertainer in 1905 at Madison Square Garden, he developed a widespread reputation as a humorist. He went on to become a writer, a radio performer, and a motion-picture star, best loved for his gum-chewing, homespun image.

Will Rogers died in a plane crash on August 15, 1935, while flying with the well-known aviator, Wiley Post. A monument to the two men was erected at the site of the crash near Point Barrow, Alaska. Rogers's birthday was first observed in 1947, with a celebration at the Will Rogers Memorial near the town of Claremore where he was born. Beneath the statue of Rogers at the memorial is printed the statement for which he is best remembered: "I never met a man I didn't like."

SOURCES:
AmerBkDays-1978, p. 994
Chases-1996, p. 441

♦ 1561 ♦ **Rogers Festival, Roy**
First weekend in June

With his wife Dale Evans, Roy Rogers was one of America's best-known singing cowboys. The couple starred in a popular television series, "The Roy Rogers Show," which ran from 1951 to 1957, and featured his horse, Trigger, and dog, Bullet. Since 1984 Rogers has been honored in his hometown of Portsmouth, Ohio, with an annual festival sponsored by the Roy Rogers-Dale Evans Collectors Association. The four-day event includes displays of Roy Rogers memorabilia, tours of Roy Rogers's boyhood home, and special performances by old-time Western stars such as the late Lash LaRue, "King of the Bullwhip." There are showings of Roy Rogers's films and television programs, and Western memorabilia collectors set up booths to sell and exchange their wares. Proceeds from the annual event go into a Roy Rogers Scholarship Fund that pays for a needy student to attend Shawnee State University in Portsmouth. Rogers's son, Roy (Dusty) Rogers, Jr., a cowboy singer in his own right, often attends the festival.

CONTACT:
Ohio Division of Travel and
 Tourism
P.O. Box 1001
Columbus, OH 43266
800-282-5393 or 614-466-8844
fax: 614-466-6744

♦ 1562 ♦ **Romania National Day**
December 1

The national holiday of Romania celebrated since 1990, after the fall of Romanian Communist Party head Nicolae Ceausescu, with military parades, speeches and a holiday from work. This day marks the unification in 1918 of Romania and Transylvania and the formation of the Romanian state within its present-day boundaries. Romania's full independence had been recognized in 1878, but Transylvania had remained outside the new state. On December 1, a Romanian assembly passed the resolution of unity celebrated on National Day.

CONTACT:
Romanian National Tourist Office
342 Madison Ave., Ste. 210
New York, NY 10173
212-697-6971; fax: 212-697-6972

SOURCES:
Chases-1996, p. 468

♦ 1563 ♦ **Romería of Our Lady of Valme**
October 17

The Romería (pilgrimage) of Our Lady of Valme involves a cross-country pilgrimage. The image of Our Lady of Valme is kept in the parish church of Dos Hermanas, but on this day she is carried in an elaborate procession to the shrine of Valme, on a hill overlooking Seville, Spain. Legend has it that King Ferdinand III stopped here on his way to free Seville from the Moors. He prayed to the Virgin Mary, *"valme"* ('bless me'), and promised a sanctuary for her if he were successful.

Accompanied by children in carriages, decorated floats, local men on horseback carrying silver maces, and Andalusian cavaliers and their ladies in regional dress, the cart bearing the statue of the Virgin Mary dressed in a blue velvet cloak is drawn by oxen with gilded horns and garlands of flowers around their necks. The pilgrims walk behind, and there is laughter, hand-clapping, and singing with tambourine accompaniment. Every so often fireworks are set off so the pilgrims in Valme can judge the progress of the procession. It takes about three hours to reach the sanctuary, then the cavaliers open the gates, everyone rushes inside, the statue is carried in at shoulder height, and the Mass begins. Afterwards, there is dancing, singing, and drinking until sunset, when the image is escorted back to Dos Hermanas.

Other well-known romerías in Spain include the Virgen de la Cabeza (Andalusia, late April), the Virgen de la Pena (Huelva, last Sunday in April), the Romería del Rocio (*see* PILGRIMAGE OF THE DEW), the Romería of Pedro Bernardo (Ávila, September 5–17), and La Dandelada (Ávila, second Sunday in September).

CONTACT:
Tourist Office of Spain
665 Fifth Ave.
New York, NY 10022
212-759-8822; fax: 212-980-1053

SOURCES:
FolkWrldHol-1992, p. 511

♦ 1564 ♦ **Roosevelt Day, Franklin D.**
January 30

Franklin Delano Roosevelt (1882–1945) was the 32nd president of the United States and the only one elected to four terms of office. He was stricken with polio in 1921 but regained partial use of his legs. His administration extended from the darkest days of the Great Depression to the Japanese attack on Pearl Harbor. He never lived to see the final Allied victory at the end of World War II, however; he was stricken with a massive cerebral hemorrhage and died at the Little White House in Warm Springs, Georgia, on April 12, 1945.

Roosevelt's birthday is observed by family members, friends, and representatives of various organizations at his home at Hyde Park, New York. The ceremony begins at 11:00 A.M., when a color guard from the U.S. Military Academy at West Point marches into the rose garden where the President is buried and takes its place before his grave. Wreaths are laid, and a family member places cut flowers on the grave. The superintendent of the military academy presents the "President's Wreath," a prayer is offered, and the event concludes with three volleys from a ceremonial firing squad.

CONTACT:
Franklin D. Roosevelt National
  Historic Site
519 Albany Post Rd.
Hyde Park, NY 12538
914-229-9115

SOURCES:
AmerBkDays-1978, p. 122
AnnivHol-1983, p. 16
Chases-1996, p. 79
DictDays-1988, p. 44

♦ 1565 ♦ **Ropotine (Repotini)**
Between April 7 and May 18; third Tuesday after Easter

This Romanian festival is celebrated exclusively by women, who take advantage of this day to turn the tables on their husbands. It is the one day of the year when women are the masters: they feast all day, and they can punish men for any slights they may have suffered. The spring ceremony known as Ropotine can be traced back to the ancient Roman festival known as Repotia, although no one seems to know where the custom of treating men harshly on this day got started. Traditionally, women get together and make household utensils out of straw and clay, particularly a shallow baking dish for bread, known as the *tzesturi*, used to bake rolls and cakes which they hand out to children and the poor "to keep away wars."

SOURCES:
FolkWrldHol-1992, p. 210

♦ 1566 ♦ **Rosary, Festival of the**
First Sunday in October

The rosary is a string of beads used by Roman Catholics to count a ritual series of prayers consisting of 15 paternosters ('Our Fathers,' the Lord's Prayer), and 150 *Ave Marias*, or 'Hail Marys'. The rosary is divided into 15 decades—each decade containing one paternoster marked by a large bead and 10 Ave Marias marked by 10 smaller beads. As the prayers are recited, the beads are passed through the fingers, making it easier to keep track of the sequence.

The festival, observed on the first Sunday in October, was established by Pope Pius V under the name of Santa Maria de Victoria (St. Mary of Victory). But the name was changed by Gregory XIII to Festival of the Rosary. Among the events for which the faithful in the former Yugoslavia give thanks on this day is the victory of Prince Eugene over the Turks at Belgrade in 1716.

SOURCES:
BkDays-1864, vol. II, p. 402
DictWrldRel-1989, p. 630
RelHolCal-1993, p. 94
SaintFestCh-1904, p. 438

♦ 1567 ♦ **Rose Bowl Game**
January 1

The oldest and best known of the post-season college-football bowl games, held in Pasadena, Calif., the home of the TOURNAMENT OF ROSES. The first Rose Bowl game was played in 1902 between Michigan and Stanford; the Michigan Wolverines, coached by Fielding H. "Hurry Up" Yost, demolished the

Indians, 49-0. Yost was known for his "point-a-minute" teams, and the Michigan 11 had racked up 550 points in 11 winning games, unscored on and untied, before the bowl encounter. Willie Heston, one of the great all-time backs, led the team to victory.

Football gave way to chariot races after that first game, but football came back to stay in 1916. Among the notable highlights in the years since then was the wrong-way run in 1929. The University of California was playing Georgia Tech. Roy Riegels, the center and captain of California's Golden Bears, picked up a Tech fumble, started toward the Tech goal line, and then, facing a troop of Tech defenders, cut across the field and started toward his own goal line, 60 yards away. Players on both sides gaped. Finally Benny Lom, a Bears halfback, ran after Riegels and grabbed him at the three-yard line. Tech players bounced him back to the one. California tried a punt, but it was blocked and the ball rolled out of the end zone. The officials declared a safety, and Georgia Tech won the contest by one point.

Since 1947, the Rose Bowl has brought together the champions of the Midwest Big Ten and Pac Ten (Pacific Ten) Conferences. Numerous other bowl games have come along since 1902: the Orange Bowl in Miami, the Sugar Bowl in New Orleans, the Cotton Bowl in Dallas, Tex., started games in the mid-1930s, and by the 1980s there were 16 bowl games in late December or on New Year's Day.

CONTACT:
Pasadena Tournament of Roses
391 S. Orange Grove Blvd.
Pasadena, CA 91184
818-449-4100; fax: 818-449-9066

SOURCES:
AmerBkDays-1978, p. 16
BkFestHolWrld-1970, p. 3
BkHolWrld-1986, Jan 1
Chases-1996, p. 52
DictDays-1988, p. 97
FolkAmerHol-1991, p. 10

♦ 1568 ♦ **Rose Festival**
May–June

According to legend, a Persian trader brought rose bush cuttings to the Balkans hundreds of years ago to provide attar for his lady's perfume. Bulgaria still supplies 90 percent of the world's rose attar, and roses are raised for food and medicinal purposes as well. The 10-day festival that celebrates Bulgaria's role in the cultivation and export of roses is held in Kazanluk, a small town in what is known as the Valley of the Roses. It begins with a procession of farmers and young people dressed in native costume and carrying baskets for the ritual picking of the rose petals. Even the queen of the pageant is selected not for her beauty but for her rose-picking ability. After she is crowned, she leads a long chain dance into Kazanluk, where her arrival is the signal to begin the Parade of Roses. Rose-decorated floats, costumed paraders, and folk dancers follow a route that winds through all the nearby towns. Afterward, there are picnics featuring Bulgarian foods. Folk dance and song programs complete the festival activities.

The Rose Festival is always held in late May and early June, the blooming season for roses. It takes 3,300 pounds of rose petals to make two pounds of rose attar.

CONTACT:
Bulgarian Embassy
1621 22nd St., N.W.
Washington, D.C. 20008
202-387-7969; fax: 202-234-7973

SOURCES:
GdWrldFest-1985, p. 27

♦ 1569 ♦ **Rose Monday**
Between February 2 and March 8; Monday before Lent

Germany is famous for its Carnival celebrations, which reach a climax on Rose Monday, the day before Shrove Tuesday. More than 400 Carnival balls are held in Munich alone, and Rose Monday celebrations are held in Cologne, Düsseldorf, Mainz, Münster, and Berlin as well. In addition to balls and parades, which take place in small towns as well as the cities, the day is observed by singing songs, often with haunting tunes, that have been composed especially for Carnival.

Because it is the last time for hi-jinks before Lent, **Rosenmontag** is characterized by a free-for-all atmosphere in which the normal rules of behavior are relaxed. It is not uncommon, for example, for people to go up to strangers on the street and kiss them.

The German name for the day, *Rosen Montag*, or 'Roses Monday', is a mispronunciation of the original name *Rasen Montag*, meaning 'rushing Monday' or 'live-it-up Monday.'

CONTACT:
German National Tourist Office
122 E. 42nd St., 52nd Floor
New York, NY 10168
212-661-7200; fax: 212-661-7174

SOURCES:
AmerBkDays-1978, pp. 43, 157
BkFest-1937, p. 132
DictFolkMyth-1984, pp. 192, 370, 977, 1082
FestWestEur-1958, pp. 55, 56
FolkWrldHol-1992, p. 110
RelHolCal-1993, pp. 65, 76, 110

♦ 1570 ♦ **Rose of Tralee Beauty Contest**
Late summer

The village of Tralee in County Kerry is famous for a festival that is unique in Ireland: the annual beauty contest for the "Rose of Tralee." Lasting for a week in late summer, the festivities begin with the playing of a harp by a woman belonging to a Kerry family in which harp-playing has been a traditional occupation for generations. There are also horse races and competitions in singing, dancing, and storytelling, but it is the beauty contest that draws the most attention. Contestants come from Ireland, Britain, the United States, and even Australia, although the winner must be of Kerry descent.

"The Rose of Tralee," a popular Irish ballad, was written by William Pembroke Mulchinock, who lived just outside the village of Tralee and fell in love with a girl who was a servant in one of the nearby houses. To put a stop to the relationship, his family sent him to India, where he served as a soldier for three years. He returned to Tralee just in time to see the funeral procession of the girl he loved, who had died of a broken heart. In the public park just outside of Tralee there is a memorial to the ill-fated lovers.

CONTACT:
Irish Tourist Board
345 Park Ave., 17th Floor
New York, NY 10154
800-223-6470 or 212-418-0800
fax: 212-371-9052

SOURCES:
GdWrldFest-1985, p. 114
IntlThFolk-1979, p. 236

Rose Sunday
See **Mothering Sunday**

◆ 1571 ◆ **Rosh Hashanah**
Between September 6 and October 4; Tishri 1 and 2

Rosh Hashanah marks the beginning of the **Jewish New Year** and the first two of the 10 High Holy Days that conclude with YOM KIPPUR, the Day of Atonement. Unlike the secular NEW YEAR'S DAY observance, this is a solemn season during which each person is subject to review and judgment for the coming year. It is a time of prayer and penitence, and is sometimes called the **Day of Remembrance** or the **Day of Blowing the Shofar**. The story of Abraham is read in the synagogue, and the blowing of the *shofar* ('ram's horn') serves as a reminder that although Abraham, in obedience to God, was willing to sacrifice his son, Isaac, God allowed him to sacrifice a ram instead. The plaintive sound of the shofar is also a call to penitence.

Orthodox Ashkenazim (Jews whose ancestors came from northern Europe) observe the ceremony of Tashlikh, a symbolic throwing of one's sins into a body of water, on the first day of Rosh Hashanah; Kurds jump into the water; kabbalists shake their garments to "free" themselves from sin. All debts from the past year are supposed to be settled before Rosh Hashanah, and many Jews ask forgiveness from friends and family for any slights or transgressions of the concluding year.

Jews celebrate the New Year by eating a special rounded loaf of challah bread, symbolic of the continuity of life, as well as apples dipped in honey, symbols of sweetness and health.

SOURCES:
AmerBkDays-1978, p. 884
BkFest-1937, p. 203
BkHolWrld-1986, Sep 18
DaysCustFaith-1957, pp. 244, 331, 337
DictDays-1988, pp. 27, 56, 97, 134
DictFolkMyth-1984, p. 1009
DictWrldRel-1989, pp. 155, 390, 630
FolkAmerHol-1991, p. 350
FolkWrldHol-1992, p. 476
RelHolCal-1993, p. 110

◆ 1572 ◆ **Rousa, Feast of**
Between April 29 and June 2; the 25th day after Easter

In parts of Greece, the **Feast of Mid-Pentecost**, which occurs on the 25th day after EASTER, is called the Feast of Rousa (or Rosa). On this day a special ceremony is performed to ward off scarlatina, or scarlet fever. The children bake rolls out of flour, butter, honey, sesame oil, and other ingredients which they have collected from their neighbors. Along with other foods, these are eaten at a children's banquet, which is followed by singing and dancing. Central to the ceremony, however, is the baking of special ring-shaped cakes, which can only be made by a girl whose name is unique in the neighborhood and which must be baked in a specially built oven.

After the banquet is over, these ring-shaped cakes are divided among the children and hung up to dry. If any of the children who participated in the feast come down with scarlet fever or any similar disease, a piece of the cake is pounded and sprinkled over their skin, which has already

been smeared with molten sugar, honey, or sesame oil. This is believed to be an infallible cure.

While the name of this feast is widely believed to come from the crimson rash that accompanies scarlet fever, it may also be a remnant of the old Roman festival known as Rosalia, or Feast of the Roses.

SOURCES:
FolkWrldHol-1992, p. 209

◆ 1573 ◆ **Rousalii**
Between May 17 and June 20; Trinity Sunday

In Romania, TRINITY SUNDAY is better known as Rousalii, after the three daughters of an emperor who were ill-treated during their lives on earth and, when they became goddesses, set out to cause misery and mischief wherever they could. Traditional Romanian belief holds that during the period from Trinity Sunday to ST. PETER'S DAY (June 29), the Rousalii roam over the earth, causing high winds and storms. People may be caught up in whirlwinds, or children may be snatched from the arms of their mothers if they venture outdoors or travel any distance from home.

On the eve of Rousalii, it is traditional to place a twig of wormwood under your pillow. Because medicinal herbs supposedly lose their potency for several weeks after Rousalii, it is considered unwise to gather any herbs from the fields until at least nine weeks have passed.

SOURCES:
FolkWrldHol-1992, p. 286

◆ 1574 ◆ **Royal Ascot**
Mid-June

The racecourse on Ascot Heath in Berkshire, England, is the site of a world-famous horse race also called the **Royal Meeting**, that was initiated in 1711 by Queen Anne. The Royal Ascot race meeting goes on for four days in June each year and culminates in the event known as the **Ascot Gold Cup**, an almost-two-mile race for horses more than three years old. Although the Gold Cup race was established in 1807, the original cup was stolen 100 years later.

A major social and fashion event as well as a sporting one, the Royal Ascot race is usually attended by the British sovereign and receives widespread media coverage. It has even given its name to a type of broad neck-scarf traditionally worn by well-dressed English gentlemen at the races.

CONTACT:
British Tourist Authority
551 Fifth Ave., Ste. 702
New York, NY 10176
800-462-2748 or 212-986-2200
fax: 212-986-1188

◆ 1575 ◆ **Royal Easter Show**
March–April; Easter holiday

The largest and best-attended of the Australian agricultural fairs, the Royal Easter Show was first held in 1822 as a way of promoting the country's agricultural industry and helping people sell their products. Now it attracts more than a million visitors each year and has expanded to include sports competitions, fashion and flower shows, and celebrity performances, in addition to the usual agricultural and industrial exhibits.

The show has been held at the Moore Park Showground in Sydney every year since 1882, although it was canceled during the 1919 influenza epidemic and during World War II, when the showground was occupied by the Australian army. Sponsored by the Royal Agricultural Society of New South Wales, the Royal Easter Show attracts more than 600 exhibitors each year and is similar to some of the larger American state fairs, such as the IOWA STATE FAIR and the EASTERN STATES EXPOSITION.

See also ROYAL SHOW DAYS

CONTACT:
Australian Tourist Commission
100 Park Ave., 25th Floor
New York, NY 10017
212-687-6300; fax: 212-661-3340

SOURCES:
GdWrldFest-1985, p. 6

Royal Oak Day
See **Shick-Shack Day**

♦ 1576 ♦ Royal Ploughing Ceremony
Early May

An ancient Brahman ritual held on a large field near the Grand Palace in Bangkok, Thailand. It celebrates the official start of the annual rice-planting season and is believed to ensure an abundant rice crop. The king presides over the rituals, in which the participants wear scarlet and gold costumes and oxen wear bells.

The Brahmans are a small Hindu group in Thailand, numbering only a few thousand families, but they have considerable influence. Royal and official ceremonies are almost always performed by them. The national calendar is prepared by Brahmans and the royal astrologers. Brahman rites blend with those of Buddhism, the dominant Thai religion.

CONTACT:
Tourism Authority of Thailand
5 World Trade Center, Ste. 3443
New York, NY 10048
212-432-0433; fax: 212-912-0920

SOURCES:
AnnivHol-1983, p. 180

♦ 1577 ♦ Royal Show Days
April, July, August, September, October

More than 500 agricultural shows are held in Australia each year, but the annual Royal shows, held in each of the state capitals, are famous for their outstanding livestock, agricultural, and industrial exhibits as well as their competitive events. More than four and one-half million people visit the **Royals** each year.

The **Brisbane Royal Show**, noted for its unusual display of tropical plants and flowers from all over the state of Queensland, is held in August. The **Hobart Royal Show** is held in mid-October. The **Royal Melbourne Show,** the **Royal Adelaide Show,** and the **Perth Royal Show** are held in September. The ROYAL EASTER SHOW, held at Sydney's 71-acre show grounds in early to mid-April, is the most popular of the country's Royal shows. All of the Royals feature attractions such as sheepdog trials, wood chopping, and tree-felling contests, and the uniquely Australian camp drafts—

an unusual rodeo event in which cattle are driven over a course that tests both horse and rider.

Other agricultural show days include **Alice Springs Show Day, Tennant Creek Show Day, Katherine Show Day**, and **Darwin Show Day**—all observed in the Northern Territory during the month of July.

CONTACT:
Australian Tourist Commission
100 Park Ave., 25th Floor
New York, NY 10017
212-687-6300; fax: 212-661-3340

SOURCES:
DictDays-1988, p. 56

Royal Shrine Rite
See **Chongmyo Taeje**

♦ 1578 ♦ Ruhr Festival
May–June

Germany's Ruhr Valley is known as a coal-mining and industrial center, and the annual cultural festival celebrated in Recklinghausen continues to reflect the needs and issues of the area. The festival grew out of an informal arrangement in 1946 between the artists of the Hamburg State Opera and the people of the mining town of Recklinghausen. In return for desperately needed coal to keep their theater's heating system from freezing, performers from Hamburg would go to Recklinghausen to perform their plays and operas. A new theater was built there in 1965 with the motto, "Coal I Gave for Art—Art I Gave for Coal."

The vast majority of the people who attend the festival's theater productions, concerts, and exhibitions are industrial workers, and the local trade unions lend their financial support. Events at the Ruhr Festival often address an economic or industrial theme, and there are scientific and political seminars covering new technological developments and their implications for working people.

CONTACT:
German National Tourist Office
122 E. 42nd St., 52nd Floor
New York, NY 10168
212-661-7200; fax: 212-661-7174

SOURCES:
IntlThFolk-1979, p. 148

♦ 1579 ♦ Rukmani Ashtami
December–January; eighth day of waning half of Hindu month of Pausa

Vaishnavite Hindus believe that Rukmani, Lord Krishna's principal wife and queen, was born on this day. According to the *Harivansha Purana*, she fell in love with Krishna but was already betrothed to Shishupala, king of Chedi. As she was going to the temple on her wedding day, Krishna carried her off in his chariot. They were pursued by Shishupala and Rukmin, her brother, but Krishna defeated them and eventually married her.

The fast known as Rukmani Ashtami is observed by women, both married and unmarried. Rukmani, Krishna, and Pradyumna, their son, are worshipped. A Brahman priest is also fed and given *dan-dakshina*, or charitable gifts, on this day. Many middle-class Hindus believe that observance of this fast ensures conjugal happiness and prosperity, and that it will help them find good husbands for unmarried girls.

SOURCES:
RelHolCal-1993, p. 110

♦ 1580 ♦ **Runeberg, Johan Ludvig, Birthday of**
February 5

Johan Ludvig Runeberg (1804–1877) is widely regarded as Finland's greatest poet. His work embodied the patriotic spirit of his countrymen and, because it was written in Swedish, exerted a great influence on Swedish literature as well. One of his poems, "Vartland" ("Our Country"), became the Finnish national anthem.

Schools throughout Finland are closed on Runeberg's birthday. Busts and pictures of him are displayed in shop windows, particularly in Helsinki, with rows of white candles placed in the foreground. A special ceremony is observed at Runeberg's monument in the Esplanade, where his statue is decorated with garlands of pine and spruce, suspended between four huge torches. Students lay wreaths of flowers at the foot of the monument and sing the national anthem. At night the torches are lit, and lighted candles burn in the windows of houses and apartments.

CONTACT:
Finnish Tourist Board
655 Third Ave., 18th Floor
New York, NY 10017
212-949-2333; fax: 212-983-5260

SOURCES:
BkFest-1937, p. 110

♦ 1581 ♦ **Running of the Bulls in Mexico**
Sunday following August 15

The running of the bulls that takes place on the Sunday following the Feast of the ASSUMPTION in Huamantla, Mexico, is considered to be far more dangerous than the famous running of the bulls in Pamplona, Spain, during the SAN FERMIN FESTIVAL. This is because the bulls are released from cages in nine different locations, making it almost impossible for those who are trying to outrun the bulls to anticipate the direction from which they are coming or the path that they are likely to follow through the maze of streets that lead to the arena. In Pamplona, the bulls are all released in one location, and they follow a well-known route to the bullring.

This particular running of the bulls dates back to the time when the Spanish conquistadores first brought cattle to Mexico, and the custom of running the bulls through the streets of Huamantla was observed every year until it began to fade around 1700. A group of local people revived the tradition in the 1920s as part of the **Assumption Fiesta.**

CONTACT:
Mexican Government Tourist
Office
405 Park Ave., Ste. 1401
New York, NY 10022
800-446-3942 or 212-755-7261
fax: 212-753-2874

SOURCES:
GdWrldFest-1985, p. 135

♦ 1582 ♦ **Rushbearing Festival**
*Saturday nearest July 26; Saturday nearest
August 5*

The custom of rushbearing in England dates back more than 1,000 years, perhaps to an ancient Roman harvest festival. Young girls would cover the floor of the parish church with rushes and fasten elaborate flower garlands to the walls. After the invention of floor coverings eliminated the need for rushes, the original ceremony gradually evolved into a flower festival, similar to MAY DAY celebrations, with sports, folk dancing, and floral processions.

Modern-day rushbearing ceremonies still take place in Musgrave, Ambleside, Grasmere, and Warcop in Westmorland, although Grasmere claims to be the only community where the rushbearing tradition has remained unbroken since ancient times. The poet William Wordsworth was largely responsible for keeping the custom alive there during the early 19th century. He and his sister, Dorothy, lived at Dove Cottage in Grasmere from 1799 until 1808.

Most rushbearing festivals begin with a procession of children carrying flower garlands and wood-framed bearings with rushes woven into traditional designs and ecclesiastical emblems. When they reach the parish church, they scatter rushes over the floor and arrange the garlands and bearings around the altar and against the church walls. There is a religious service, after which the entire village participates in sports, Maypole dancing, and other festivities. Most rushbearing events take place in July and August, usually on the Saturday nearest ST. ANNE'S DAY (July 26) or St. Oswald's Day (August 5).

CONTACT:
British Tourist Authority
551 Fifth Ave., Ste. 702
New York, NY 10176
800-462-2748 or 212-986-2200
fax: 212-986-1188

SOURCES:
AnnivHol-1983, p. 103
FolkCal-1930, p. 164
YrbookEngFest-1954, pp. 95,
  101, 108

♦ 1583 ♦ **Russell, C. M., Auction**
Third weekend in March

An art auction, a celebration of western artist Charles M. Russell, and a western-style good time in Great Falls, Mont., where Charley Russell had his home and studio. The affair began in 1969 to raise money for the C. M. Russell (as he signed his paintings) Museum, which was then just getting started. Events include seminars, dance demonstrations by the Blackfeet Indians, an exhibit of paintings and sculpture of western artists and an auction of their works, and a Quick Draw, in which artists have 30 minutes to draw any subject they want. Their quick draws are then auctioned. There is also a chuckwagon brunch and a Charley Russell Birthday Party (he was born March 19, 1864, and died in 1926).

Charley Russell, a cowboy artist who was also the author of a collection of stories and sketches, *Trails Plowed Under*, depicted the early days of cowpunchers and Indians in Montana and Wyoming. In an introduction to *Trails Plowed Under*, Will ROGERS wrote that there will never be "the Real Cowboy, Painter and Man, combined that old Charley was . . ." Charley Russell wrote about himself: "I am an illustrator. There are lots better ones, but some worse." His paintings now are coveted by collectors and worth millions.

CONTACT:
Montana Travel Promotion
  Division
1424 Ninth Ave.
Helena, MT 59620
800-847-4868 or 406-444-2654
fax: 406-444-1800

SOURCES:
Chases-1996, p. 138

♦ 1584 ♦ **Russian Orthodox Christmas**
January 7

This celebration of the birth of Christ is observed by the

Russian Orthodox Church under the Julian calendar. The calendar trails behind the Gregorian calendar by 13 days.

Before the 1917 Revolution, the Orthodox Christmas was widely observed in Russia, Ukraine, Byelorussia (Belarus), and Georgia. After the Revolution, churches were closed and people practicing religion were persecuted. In 1991, after the Soviet Union had been officially dissolved, Christmas was observed openly and as a state holiday in Russia for the first time in 70 years.

In Moscow, banners were strung up and Nativity scenes were displayed in Red Square. On radio and television, there were nonstop programs telling the Christmas story and showing villagers wearing embroidered folk costumes and carrying tambourines as they made the rounds to offer Christmas bread at every house. On Christmas Eve, tens of thousands jammed Red Square for performances by choirs and bellringers and gala fireworks over the multi-colored onion domes of St. Basil's Cathedral. Midnight masses were celebrated in churches. At the Kremlin, a Christmas charity ball was held to raise money for orphan children.

Before the Revolution, Christmas in Russia was a great feast celebrated with decorated trees, strolling carolers, and gifts. There was a legend of "Father Frost" or "Grandfather Frost," who wore a red robe and black boots and had a long white beard. Tchaikovsky's "Nutcracker Suite" was, of course, associated with the holiday. When Joseph Stalin was in power some aspects of the old Christmas, such as the tree and the gifts from Father Frost, were added to the New Year's celebrations. Then January 7 became a holiday observed only by those who dared to go to church.

See also Old Christmas Day; Russian Winter Festival

SOURCES:
BkFest-1937, p. 296
BkFestHolWrld-1970, p. 142
Chases-1996, p. 60
DictFolkMyth-1984, p. 230

FolkWrldHol-1992, p. 636

♦ 1585 ♦ **Russian Winter Festival**
December 25–January 5

A festival of arts and a time of holiday partying largely in Moscow, Russia, and somewhat less grandly in other cities of the former Soviet Union. In Moscow, there are circuses, performances of Russian fables for children, and other special theatrical presentations as well as traditional outdoor parties with troika (sled) rides, folk games, and dancing around fir trees. On New Year's Eve, children wait for gifts from "Father Frost" or "Grandfather Frost"—who wears a red robe and black boots and has a white beard—and his helper, Snow Girl.

In the past, Father Frost was associated with Christmas, but religious holidays were stamped out after the 1917 Revolution. In 1992, old traditions were being revived after the dissolution of the Soviet Union, and Father Frost may again become a Christmas figure.

CONTACT:
Russian Travel Information Office
Rockefeller Center
610 Fifth Ave., Ste. 603
New York, NY 10020
212-757-3884; fax: 212-459-0031

SOURCES:
AnnivHol-1983, p. 2
Chases-1996, p. 52
GdWrldFest-1985, p. 183
IntlThFolk-1979, p. 375

♦ 1586 ♦ **Rwanda Independence Day**
July 1

This national holiday celebrates Rwanda's independence from Belgium on July 1, 1962, after nearly 50 years of Belgian rule.

CONTACT:
Rwanda Embassy
1714 New Hampshire Ave., N.W.
Washington, D.C. 20009
202-232-2882; fax: 202-232-4544

SOURCES:
AnnivHol-1983, p. 87
Chases-1996, p. 279
NatlHolWrld-1968, p. 102

S

♦ 1587 ♦ Saba Saba Day
July 7

July 7 marks the day when the ruling party of Tanzania, known as TANU (Tanganyika African National Union), was formed in 1954. The TANU Creed is based on the principles of socialism as set forth in the TANU Constitution. Also known as **Saba Saba Peasants' Day** or **Farmers' Day**, it is officially celebrated in a different region of the country each year with traditional dances, sports, processions, rallies, and fairs.

Tanzania, perhaps best known as the home of Mt. Kilimanjaro, was formed in 1964 when Tanganyika merged with Zanzibar.

CONTACT:
Tanzanian Embassy
2139 R St., N.W.
Washington, D.C. 20008
202-939-6125; fax: 202-797-7408

SOURCES:
AnnivHol-1983, p. 90
Chases-1996, p. 288

♦ 1588 ♦ Sacaea
Five days, including the vernal equinox, March 21 or 22

This was an ancient five-day Babylonian New Year festival associated with Anaitis, the Syrian war goddess identified with the Greek goddess Athena. It was characterized by drunkenness and licentious behavior as well as a reversal of the usual customs and relationships. Slaves ruled their masters throughout the festival, and a mock king was selected from among the criminals. After being feasted and honored for five days, the mock king was executed, thereby serving as a surrogate for the real king, who was supposed to die each New Year when a new king was born.

The festival was instituted by Cyrus, king of the Persians, when he marched against the Sacae, or people of Scythia. In order to detain the enemy, he set out tables laden with delicacies to which they were unaccustomed. While they lingered over the food, he was able to destroy them.

SOURCES:
ClassDict-1984, p. 43
DictMyth-1962, vol. II, p. 1357

♦ 1589 ♦ Sacred Heart of Jesus, Feast of the
Between May 22 and June 25; Friday after Corpus Christi

The Feast of the Sacred Heart of Jesus is a solemnity (meaning a festival of the greatest importance) in the Roman Catholic Church celebrated on the Friday after CORPUS CHRISTI. It is devoted to the symbol of Jesus' love for all humanity and is a significant holiday in Colombia.

SOURCES:
AnnivHol-1983, p. 181
DictWrldRel-1989, p. 637
RelHolCal-1993, p. 111
SaintFestCh-1904, p. 273

Sacrifice, Feast of
See 'Id al-Adha

♦ 1590 ♦ Sadie Hawkins Day
Usually first Saturday in November

A day when spinsters can legitimately chase bachelors; if caught, the men are obliged to marry their pursuers. Artist Al Capp invented the unpretty but hopeful Sadie Hawkins and her day in his comic strip, *L'il Abner*, some time in the 1930s. In the following decades, Sadie Hawkins Days, usually featuring dances to which males were invited by females, were popular on school campuses. Celebrations are rarer now.

Capp's long-running *L'il Abner*, named for its good-looking but not-too-bright hero, injected the hillbilly characters of Dogpatch into American culture.

SOURCES:
AnnivHol-1983, p. 144
Chases-1996, p. 439
DictDays-1988, p. 100

♦ 1591 ♦ Safari Rally
March–April; Easter weekend

This grueling four-day auto race takes place on a 2,550-mile circuit over unpaved roads. Starting outside Nairobi, Kenya, the route is considered the toughest in the world; the roads climb in and out of the Great Rift Valley, and there are severe changes in climate. Furthermore, it's the rainy season when the race is held, and the roads can turn into virtual swamps. There are usually about 100 entrants, and fewer than 10 to 20 finish.

The rally began as part of the celebrations marking the coronation of Queen Elizabeth II in 1953 and was called the **Coronation Rally**. It generated such interest that it was continued and renamed the **East African Safari**, with Kenya, Uganda, and Tanzania on the route. Since 1974, it has been confined to Kenya. Nairobi gets rally fever at this time of year. The city is hung with flags, and cars sprayed to look like rally cars zoom around the streets. Thousands of spectators watch the race at various points along the route.

CONTACT:
Kenya Tourist Office
424 Madison Ave.
New York, NY 10017
212-486-1300; fax: 212-688-0911

SOURCES:
GdWrldFest-1985, p. 126

♦ 1592 ♦ **Saffron Rose Festival**
Last Sunday in October

Saffron, the world's most expensive condiment, is harvested from the stigmas of the autumn-flowering *Crocus sativus*. Much of the world's saffron comes from Spain's La Mancha region, and it is used to flavor French bouillabaisse, Spanish paella, cakes, breads, cookies, and the cuisines of East India, the Middle East, and North Africa. It takes 35,000 flowers to produce one pound.

The Saffron Rose Festival held in the town of Consuegra each year celebrates this exotic crop, which must be harvested by hand so that the valuable stigmas are not crumpled. Hosted by a national television personality, the celebrations include parades and contests, traditional folk dancing, and the crowning of a pageant queen. Costumed characters from Cervantes's 17th-century novel, *Don Quixote*, stroll among the crowds who flock to Consuegra for the fiesta (*see also* CERVANTES FESTIVAL, INTERNATIONAL).

CONTACT:
Tourist Office of Spain
665 Fifth Ave.
New York, NY 10022
212-759-8822; fax: 212-980-1053

♦ 1593 ♦ **Sahara National Festival**
November–December

The Tunisian city of Douz is considered the gateway to the Sahara Desert. It is also the site of the annual Sahara National Festival, when nomads and Bedouins from all over the country gather to compete in camel races and to perform traditional music. There is also a poetry contest, a traditional wedding ceremony, and greyhound racing. The time of the week-long festival—which celebrates the date harvest—varies according to the weather, but usually takes place in November or December. A date marketplace is set up during the festival, usually on a Thursday, and fresh dates as well as *lagmi* (the juice of the date palm, fermented in the sun) are sold. Other items for sale at the market, which draws as many tourists as tribesmen, include camels, incense, ebony, rugs, desert flowers, caftans, and Berber tapestries.

CONTACT:
Tunisian Embassy
1515 Massachusetts Ave., N.W.
Washington, D.C. 20005
202-862-1850; fax: 202-862-1858

SOURCES:
GdWrldFest-1985, p. 178

Sailors' Day
See **Sjomannadagur**

♦ 1594 ♦ **St. Agatha Festival**
February 3–5

Sant' Agata is especially revered in Catania, Sicily, where her relics are preserved in a silver casket. The beautiful young Sicilian virgin was put to death in the third century because she refused to yield to the advances of a Roman prefect. Among the tortures she is said to have endured was having her breasts cut off, and to this day she is the patron saint of nursing mothers and women suffering from diseases of the breast.

On February 3, 4 and 5 each year, a silver bust of St. Agatha wearing a jewel-encrusted crown is carried in procession from the cathedral to Catania's various churches. Included in the procession are the *ceri*, huge wooden replicas of candlesticks which are carved with episodes from the saint's martyrdom. The streets are lined with streamers and flowers, and illuminated by strings of colored lights after dark. The festival ends with a fireworks display in the piazza.

CONTACT:
Italian Government Travel Office
630 Fifth Ave.
New York, NY 10111
212-245-4822

SOURCES:
DictMyth-1962, vol. II, p. 1362
FestSaintDays-1915, p. 32
FestWestEur-1958, p. 90

♦ 1595 ♦ **St. Agnes's Eve**
January 20

The eve of St. Agnes's Day (January 21) has long been associated with various superstitions about how young girls might discover the identity of their future husbands. According to one such belief, a girl who went to bed without any supper on this night would dream of the man she was to marry. John Keats used this legend as the basis for his well-known poem, "The Eve of St. Agnes," in which a young maid dreams of her lover and wakes to find him standing at her bedside.

St. Agnes herself was martyred sometime during the fourth century, when she may have been only 12 or 13 years old, because she had consecrated herself to Christ and refused to marry. She was later named the patron saint of young virgins. In art St. Agnes is often represented with a lamb or sometimes with a dove with a ring in its beak.

SOURCES:
AmerBkDays-1978, p. 97
BkDays-1864, vol. I, p. 140
BkFest-1937, p. 180
BkHolWrld-1986, Jan 21
DaysCustFaith-1957, p. 28
DictDays-1988, p. 100
DictFolkMyth-1984, p. 28
FestSaintDays-1915, p. 20
SaintFestCh-1904, p. 75

♦ 1596 ♦ St. Alban's Day
June 22

St. Alban is the first and best known of all the English saints and martyrs. He was a soldier living as a pagan in the town of Verulamium, probably during the third century, when a Christian priest named Amphibalus, pursued by Roman persecutors, begged for refuge in his house. Alban took him in and was soon converted by him and baptized. When he could conceal Amphibalus no longer, Alban changed clothes with him and gave himself up as the priest. The deception was soon discovered, however, and Alban was brought before the governor, condemned, and beheaded.

There are a number of legends concerning St. Alban's execution. One is that when the crowd that gathered to watch the beheading was too large to get across the small bridge leading to the execution place, St. Alban said a prayer and caused the waters to divide. Another is that when he asked for a drink of water, a spring gushed forth from the ground in front of him. Supposedly, the soldier who was appointed to kill St. Alban refused to do so, and was beheaded along with the saint.

A shrine was later erected in Verulamium, and the town was renamed St. Alban's.

> SOURCES:
> *BkDays-1864*, vol. I, p. 808
> *DaysCustFaith-1957*, p. 149
> *DictMyth-1962*, vol. II, p.
>   1362

♦ 1597 ♦ St. Andrew's Day
November 30

St. Andrew, the brother of St. Peter, was the first apostle called by Christ, but he is primarily known today as the patron saint of Scotland, though he was also chosen to be patron saint of Russia. According to the apocryphal and unreliable Acts of St. Andrew, he went to Greece, and having converted the proconsul's wife there, he was condemned to be crucified. Fastened to an X-shaped cross by cords rather than nails, he eventually died of thirst and starvation.

St. Andrew's association with Scotland didn't come about until four centuries after his death, when some of his relics were brought there. Although there are a number of churches throughout England and Scotland that bear St. Andrew's name, many associate it with the famous St. Andrew's golf course near Dundee. Some Scots continue the custom of wearing a "St. Andrew's cross" on November 30, which consists of blue and white ribbons shaped like the letter X. The tradition for this form of a cross began no earlier than the 13th century.

This is also a major feast in Lapland and a time for weddings and meeting new people.

> SOURCES:
> *AmerBkDays-1978*, p. 1063
> *BkDays-1864*, vol. II, p. 635
> *BkFest-1937*, pp. 62, 174
> *DaysCustFaith-1957*, p. 296
> *DictFolkMyth-1984*, p. 55
> *FestSaintDays-1915*, p. 216
> *FolkWrldHol-1992*, p. 566

♦ 1598 ♦ St. Andrew's Eve (Noc Swietego Andreja)
November 29

The Eve of St. Andrew's Day is a special night for young Polish girls who want to find husbands. They play *Andrzejki*, or 'Andrew's games,' a kind of fortune-telling. Young girls break off dry branches from cherry trees, place them in wet sand, and tend them carefully for the next few weeks. If the branch blooms by Christmas, it is believed that they will marry within the year. Pouring liquid wax into cold water is another popular method of foretelling their romantic futures. The shapes into which the wax hardens often provide clues with which they can read their fate. The boys try to foretell their own futures on St. Catherine's Eve (*see also* St. Catherine's Day, November 25).

The patron saint of both Russia and Scotland, St. Andrew's name means "manly" or "courageous," making him an appropriate target for the appeals of young girls seeking lovers. Andrzejki are popular among Polish-Americans as well, where they include peeling apples to see what letter the apple-peel forms when thrown over the peeler's left shoulder.

Austrian peasant women also forced fruit tree branches, but they brought them to Christmas Mass and believed they gave them the ability to see all the witches in the congregation.

> SOURCES:
> *AnnivHol-1983*, p. 152
> *FolkAmerHol-1991*, p. 395

♦ 1599 ♦ St. Anne's Day
July 26

In 1650 a group of Breton sailors built a tiny frame church at the place where the town of Beaupré, Quebec, now stands in honor of St. Anne, the traditional name for the mother of the Virgin Mary and wife of Joachim or St. Joseph (the apostle James names her in his Letter). The sailors had been caught in a vicious storm at sea and vowed that if St. Anne would save them, they would build her a sanctuary at the spot where their feet first touched land. In 1658 the people of the village built a new and larger church, and it was then that the first of St. Anne de Beaupré's miraculous cures took place, when a local man suffering from rheumatism came to the church and walked away in perfect health. Since that time thousands of cures have been reported at the Basilica of Sainte Anne de Beaupré, which has been called the "Lourdes of the New World" after the famous shrine in France.

St. Anne is the patron saint of Canada. The pilgrimage to her shrine in Beaupré is one of the major pilgrimages on the North American continent. Romanies from Canada and the United States also arrive to celebrate Santana ('St. Anna'). They camp on the church property, prepare a *slava* feast of special foods for and prayers to St. Anne, and visit their families (*see* Pardon of Ste. Anne D'Auray).

> SOURCES:
> *AmerBkDays-1978*, p. 695
> *AnnivHol-1983*, p. 97
> *DaysCustFaith-1957*, p. 192
> *FolkWrldHol-1992*, p. 381

♦ 1600 ♦ St. Anthony of Padua, Feast of
June 13

St. Anthony of Padua (1195–1231) is the patron saint of

people who lose things and of children. He has also become, like St. Francis of Assisi, a patron saint of animals. In the days before automobiles, people in Rome sent their horses and mules to St. Anthony's Church to be blessed on this day. The Feast of St. Anthony is also celebrated by many Puerto Rican communities, as well as by American Indians in the southwestern United States. In New Mexico, for instance, traditional Indian dances are held on **San Antonio's Day** in the pueblos at Taos, San Juan, Santa Clara, San Ildefonso, Sandia, Cochiti, and elsewhere.

One of the most outstanding celebrations is held in New York City's Greenwich Village. St. Anthony's Shrine Church on West Houston and Sullivan Streets, in the heart of one of the original 'Little Italy' sections of New York, boasts the oldest Italian Roman Catholic congregation in the city and is the site of a 10-day festival that combines religious observance and the carnival atmosphere of a street fair. Masses are held all day on June 13, and a procession bearing the statue of St. Anthony through the streets begins at seven o'clock that evening. Thousands of people are drawn to the festival, which extends from the weekend before the actual feast day through the weekend following it.

In the village of El Pinar, Spain, a novena ends with the Rosary on St. Anthony's eve. Then a fiesta begins with a parade of huge papier-mâché heads of historical and imaginary characters (called *gigantes* 'giants' and *cabezudos* 'bigheads'), on 10-foot-tall wire frames and dressed in long robes. This parade is accompanied by a band playing *pasodobles* (a quick, light march often played at bullfights). Boys toss firecrackers, small children hide in terror, fireworks are set off, street dancing begins, and carnival booths are set up. On the 13th, the parade begins at 9 A.M. After a noon High Mass, the statue of St. Anthony is paraded through the village for three hours. The band plays and pairs of men in two lines dance the *jota* (a complex dance using the rhythm of bootheels and castanets). When the dancers tire, they are replaced by eager onlookers. At their return to the church, they block the door to keep St. Anthony from going in so the dancing can go on. Parishioners lay money at the feet of the statue for the support of the church for the coming year.

St. Anthony of Padua was born in Lisbon, Portugal, in 1195, and is the patron saint of Portugal. The festivities held here in his honor begin on the evening of June 12 with an impressive display of *marchas*, walking groups of singers and musicians, who parade along the Avenida da Liberdade. The celebration continues the next day with more processions and traditional folk dancing.

Throughout the month of June, children in Lisbon prepare altars in the saint's honor, covering boxes and tables with white paper and decorating them with candles and pictures of St. Anthony. They beg "a little penny for San António" from passersby, but the money—once used to restore the church of San António da Sé after its destruction by an earthquake in 1755—is now put toward a children's feast.

Because he is considered the matchmaker saint, St. Anthony's Eve is a time when young people write letters asking António for help in finding a mate. Another custom of the day is for a young man to present the girl he hopes to marry with a pot of basil concealing a verse or love letter.

SOURCES:
AmerBkDays-1978, p. 549

BkFest-1937, p. 187
Chases-1996, p. 254
DaysCustFaith-1957, p. 144
DictWrldRel-1989, p. 42
FestWestEur-1958, p. 166
FolkAmerHol-1991, p. 234
FolkWrldHol-1992, pp. 267, 325
IndianAmer-1989, pp. 286, 288, 301, 303, 306, 309, 312, 315, 319

♦ 1601 ♦ St. Anthony the Abbot, Feast of
January 17

St. Anthony the Abbot was one of the earliest saints. And, if St. Athanasius's biography of him is correct, Anthony lived more than 100 years (251–356). Living as a hermit, Anthony nonetheless attracted disciples and ventured out occasionally to become involved in the doctrinal controversies of his day. Eventually he came to be regarded as a healer of animals as well as of people. The order of Hospitallers of St. Anthony, founded during the 12th century, endeavored to keep animals in good health by hanging bells around their necks. His feast day is celebrated in Mexico and other parts of Latin America by bringing household pets and livestock into the churchyard, where the local priest blesses them with holy water. All the animals are carefully groomed and often decorated with ribbons and fresh flowers.

In some Latin American cities, the **Blessing of the Animals** takes place on a different day—often on Holy Saturday, the day before Easter. People of Hispanic descent living in the United States often celebrate the Blessing of the Animals on this day as well. In Los Angeles, the procession of animals to Our Lady of the Angels Church follows a cobblestone path that was laid by Mexican settlers more than 200 years ago.

CONTACT:
Los Angeles Convention and Visitors Bureau
633 W. Fifth St., Ste. 6000
Los Angeles, CA 90017
800-228-2452 or 213-624-7300
fax: 213-624-9746

SOURCES:
AmerBkDays-1978, p. 84
BkFest-1937, pp. 225, 298
Chases-1996, p. 68
DictMyth-1962, vol. II, p. 1362
FestWestEur-1958, pp. 189, 226
RelHolCal-1993, p. 64

♦ 1602 ♦ St. Augustine of Hippo, Feast of
August 28

St. Augustine's career as a Christian got off to a slow start. The son of a pagan father and a Christian mother, he spent most of his youth in dissipation and promiscuity. He was 32 years old when he converted to Christianity in 386 after undergoing conflicts within himself on how he was living and what he believed; hearing St. Ambrose preach was said to have influenced him as well. A few years later he became Bishop of Hippo in North Africa. For the next 40 years he was a teacher, writer, preacher, and theologian who exerted a profound influence on the development of Christian doctrine. He is best known for his spiritual autobiography, the *Confessions*, which detail the excesses of his youth, his career as a teacher of rhetoric, his years as a believer in Manicheism and Platonism, and his belated conversion to Christianity. It is primarily for his writings that he is known as the patron saint of theologians and scholars and one of the "Four Latin Fathers" of the Christian Church.

St. Augustine also typifies the Christian who has been converted slowly, as exemplified by his well-known prayer, "O God, make me pure—but not yet." When a company of Spanish soldiers landed on the coast of Florida on St. Augustine's Day in 1565, they named the U.S.'s oldest European community after him.

SOURCES:
AnnivHol-1983, p. 111
Chases-1996, p. 351
DaysCustFaith-1957, p. 221
DictMyth-1962, vol. II, p. 1364
DictWrldRel-1989, p. 77
SaintFestCh-1904, p. 384

♦ 1603 ♦ St. Barbara's Day
December 4

Scholars doubt that St. Barbara existed as more than a legend that emerged during the second century. The story is that her father locked her away in a tower to prevent her from ever marrying. When she became a Christian he tried to kill her, then turned her in to the pagan authorities. Then he was killed by a bolt of lightning.

In parts of France, Germany, and Syria, St. Barbara's Day is considered the beginning of the CHRISTMAS season. In southern France, especially in Provence, it is customary to set out dishes holding grains of wheat soaked in water on sunny window sills. There is a folk belief that if the "St. Barbara's grain" grows quickly, it means a good year for crops. But if it withers and dies, the crops will be ruined. On CHRISTMAS EVE, the grain is placed near the crèche as a symbol of the coming harvest. There is a similar custom in Germany and the Czech and Slovak republics, where cherry branches are placed in water and tended carefully in the hope that they will bloom on Christmas Eve. In Syria, St. Barbara's Day is for feasting and bringing food to the poor.

In Poland, St. Barbara's Day is associated with weather prophecies. If it rains, it will be cold and icy on Christmas Day; if it's cold and icy, Christmas will be rainy.

SOURCES:
BkFest-1937, p. 128
DaysCustFaith-1957, p. 305
DictFolkMyth-1984, p. 950
DictMyth-1962, vol. II, p. 1364
FestWestEur-1958, p. 49
FolkAmerHol-1991, p. 425
FolkWrldHol-1992, p. 578

♦ 1604 ♦ St. Barnabas's Day
June 11

Before England adopted the Gregorian calendar in 1752, June 11 was the day of the SUMMER SOLSTICE. In addition to being the longest day of the year, it was also St. Barnabas's Day (or **Barnaby Day**), and this association gave rise to the old English jingle, "Barnaby bright, Barnaby bright, the longest day and the shortest night." It was customary on this day for the priests and clerks in the Church of England to wear garlands of roses and to decorate the church with them. Other names for this day were **Long Barnaby** and **Barnaby Bright**.

SOURCES:
BkDays-1864, vol. I, p. 769
DaysCustFaith-1957, p. 143
DictDays-1988, pp. 9, 69, 100
DictMyth-1962, vol. II, p. 1364

♦ 1605 ♦ St. Basil, Feast of
January 1

NEW YEAR'S DAY and the feast day for Agios Vasilis (St. Basil) are one and the same in Greece and Cyprus, and for all Orthodox Christians. Celebrations begin on NEW YEAR'S EVE when Agios Vasilis is believed to visit each house, blessing the people and their belongings and animals, and bringing presents to the children. Nowadays, the parish priest goes around and blesses the homes of his flock.

On New Year's Day, a cake called the *Vassilopita,* or 'St. Basil's bread', is ceremoniously sliced, according to varying traditions going back to Byzantine times. Usually the first slice is cut for Jesus Christ, the next is for the house, and the following for absent family members. A coin has been baked in the cake, and the person finding the coin will be the luckiest member of the family that year.

St. Basil was a monk and church father who left many influential writings, including a defense of the study of pagan writings by Christians. He was born about the year 329 and was declared a saint soon after his death on Jan. 1 of the year 379 in Caesarea (in present-day Israel).

SOURCES:
BkFest-1937, pp. 3, 143, 273, 288
BkFestHolWrld-1970, p. 4
Chases-1996, p. 52
DictMyth-1962, vol. II, p. 1364
DictWrldRel-1989, p. 93
FolkWrldHol-1992, p. 11

♦ 1606 ♦ St. Blaise's Day
February 3

The association of St. Blaise (or **Blase,** or **Blasius**) with the blessing of throats can be traced to a number of sources. According to one story, as he was being led to his own execution in 316, he miraculously cured a child who was suffering from a throat infection. Another story has it that he saved the life of a boy who was choking on a fishbone. In any case, St. Blaise, since the sixth century in the East, has been the patron saint of people who suffer from throat afflictions, and celebrations on this day in the Roman Catholic Church often include the blessing of throats by the priest. In Paraguay, the religious services are followed by a holiday festival.

Among the many tortures said to have been suffered by this saint was having his body torn by iron combs similar to those used at one time by wool-combers in England. St. Blaise thus became the patron saint of wool-combers as well, and his feast day has traditionally been celebrated in English towns where the woolen industry is important.

In Spain they bake small loaves, called *tortas de San Blas* ('San Blas's loaves') or *panecillos del santo* ('little breads of the saint'). They are blessed during Mass, and each child eats a bit to prevent him or her from choking during the year.

SOURCES:
BkDays-1864, vol. I, p. 219
DaysCustFaith-1957, p. 46
DictDays-1988, p. 100
DictMyth-1962, vol. II, p. 1365
FestSaintDays-1915, p. 31
FolkAmerHol-1991, p. 69
FolkWrldHol-1992, p. 96

♦ 1607 ♦ **St. Brendan's Day**
May 16

St. Brendan, who lived in the sixth century, is one of the most popular Irish saints. In addition to founding a number of monasteries, including the one at Clonfert in Galway, Ireland, he was alleged to be the author of *Navigatio Brendani*, the story of his journey with a crew of four monks to a land across the ocean (the tale, however, is thought to have been written in the 10th century). No one, including St. Brendan himself, knew exactly where he had been when he returned, but a number of legends concerning the journey developed over the centuries—one of which claims that he actually reached the American continent.

In 1977 an Irishman named Tim Severin built a boat out of leather like the one described in *Navigatio* and set out to follow St. Brendan's instructions. After 50 days at sea, he ended up in Newfoundland, giving credence to the theory that St. Brendan reached America 1,000 years before COLUMBUS.

SOURCES:
AnnivHol-1983, p. 66
BkHolWrld-1986, May 16
DaysCustFaith-1957, p. 124
DictMyth-1962, vol. II, p. 1365

♦ 1608 ♦ **St. Bridget's Day**
February 1

St. Bridget (or **Brigid**, or **Bride**) is the female patron saint of Ireland. She has also been identified with an ancient pagan goddess. Her feast day, February 1, was traditionally the first day of spring and of the new year in rural Ireland because it marked the start of the agricultural season. Legends about Bridget associate her with abundance and fertility; her cows, for example, allegedly gave milk up to three times a day. She is credited with an almost endless number of miracles and was buried in the same church at Downpatrick where the bodies of ST. PATRICK and ST. COLUMBA lie. She lived during the sixth century and probably established the first Irish convent, around which the city of Kildare eventually grew.

Many old customs and folk beliefs are associated with St. Bridget's feast day. For example, people would not perform any work on this day that involved turning or twisting, or that required the use of a wheel. It was also customary on the eve of the saint's day for the oldest daughter of the family to bring a bundle of rushes to the door. Playing the role of St. Bridget, she would distribute the rushes among the family members, who would make crosses from them and, after the crosses were sprinkled with holy water, hang them throughout the house. Because St. Bridget is said to have woven the first cloth in Ireland, a cloth known as the *Brat Bhride*, or 'Bridget's cloak', was left outside on the steps, and during the night it was believed to acquire special healing powers.

The custom of having women propose marriage to men during Leap Year (*see* LEAP YEAR DAY) can also be traced to St. Bridget who, legend has it, complained to St. Patrick about the fact that men always took the initiative and persuaded him to grant women the right to do so during one year out of every four. Then Bridget proposed to Patrick, who turned her down but softened his refusal by giving her a kiss and a silk gown.

SOURCES:
BkDays-1864, vol. I, p. 206
BkFest-1937, p. 53
DaysCustFaith-1957, p. 43
DictFolkMyth-1984, pp. 165, 966
FestSaintDays-1915, p. 24
FolkWrldHol-1992, p. 89
RelHolCal-1993, p. 64
SaintFestCh-1904, p. 89

♦ 1609 ♦ **St. Catherine's Day**
November 25 (suppressed in 1969 in the Roman Catholic Church)

St. Catherine is now thought to have been a writer's invention rather than a historical person; for that reason, her feast day is no longer observed in the Roman Catholic Church calendar. According to apocryphal writings, St. Catherine of Alexandria was sentenced to death by Emperor Maxentius for her extraordinary success in converting people to Christianity in the fourth century. He placed her in a torture machine that consisted of wheels armed with sharp spikes so that she would be torn to pieces as the wheels revolved. She was saved from this grim fate by divine intervention, but then the Emperor had her beheaded. The "Catherine Wheel" in England today is a type of firework that revolves in pinwheel fashion. In the United States, the "cartwheels" performed regularly by aspiring gymnasts repeat the motion of St. Catherine on the wheel of torture.

In 18th-century England, young women in the textile districts engaged in merry-making or "catherning" on this day, which is sometimes referred to as **Cathern Day**. As the patron saint of old maids, St. Catherine is still celebrated in France by unmarried women under 25, especially those employed in the millinery and dressmaking industries. They wear "Catherine bonnets" on November 25—homemade creations of paper and ribbon. The French expression *coiffer Sainte Catherine*, 'to don St. Catherine's bonnet', is used to warn girls that they are likely to become spinsters.

SOURCES:
BkFest-1937, p. 128
DaysCustFaith-1957, p. 295
DictDays-1988, pp. 19, 101
DictFolkMyth-1984, pp. 197, 1168
FestSaintDays-1915, pp. 213, 215
FestWestEur-1958, p. 48
FolkWrldHol-1992, p. 565

♦ 1610 ♦ **St. Cecilia's Day**
November 22

Not much can be said with confidence about St. Cecilia's life. According to her apocryphal acts, which date from the fifth century, she was a Roman from a noble family who was put to death in the second or third century for her Christian beliefs. How she became the patron saint of music and musicians is not exactly known, but according to legend she played the harp so beautifully that an angel left heaven to come down and listen to her. In any case, the Academy of Music in Rome accepted her as its patron when it was established in 1584.

In 1683, a musical society was formed in London especially for the celebration of St. Cecilia's Day. It held a festival each year at which a special ode was sung. The poet John Dryden composed his "Ode for St. Cecilia's Day" in 1687 for this purpose. By the end of the 17th century it was customary to hold concerts on November 22 in St. Cecilia's honor—a practice which has faded over the years, but there are still many choirs and musical societies that bear her name.

SOURCES:
AnnivHol-1983, p. 150
BkDays-1864, vol. II, p. 604
Chases-1996, p. 457
DaysCustFaith-1957, p. 293
DictDays-1988, p. 101
FolkAmerHol-1991, p. 394
SaintFestCh-1904, p. 494

♦ 1611 ♦ **St. Charlemagne's Day**
January 28

Charlemagne wasn't actually a saint at all; he was an emperor and the first ruler of the Holy Roman Empire, crowned in 800 by Pope Leo III. But because of his great interest in education, French college students refer to him as a saint and a hero. Although he was never able to read and write himself, Charlemagne, whose name means "Charles the Great," founded the University of Paris. In fact, his reign was marked by a huge cultural revival, including significant advances in scholarship, literature, and philosophy.

St. Charlemagne's Day is still celebrated by college students in France, who hold champagne breakfasts at which professors and top students recite poems and give speeches.

SOURCES:
AnnivHol-1983, p. 15
DaysCustFaith-1957, p. 34
DictMyth-1962, vol. I, p. 314

♦ 1612 ♦ **St. Charles's Day**
January 30

Charles I, crowned king of England in 1625, was illegally executed on Jan. 30, 1649, primarily for defending the Anglican Church. His body was secretly buried in Windsor Castle. He was widely acclaimed as a martyr. A royal decree ordered a special service on this day to be in the Book of Common Prayer from 1662 to 1859. It also ordered it to be a day of national fasting. The anniversary of this event is commemorated by the Society of Charles the Martyr with an annual service at the site of his execution. Commemorative services are also held at the Church of St. Martin-in-the-Fields and in Trafalgar Square in London on or near February 2. St. Charles is the only post-Reformation figure to be honored in this way by the Church of England.

See also SAINTS, DOCTORS, MISSIONARIES AND MARTYRS DAY

CONTACT:
British Tourist Authority
551 Fifth Ave., Ste. 702
New York, NY 10176
800-462-2748 or 212-986-2200
fax: 212-986-1188

SOURCES:
AnnivHol-1983, p. 15
BkDays-1864, vol. I, p. 189
DaysCustFaith-1957, p. 35
DictDays-1988, p. 19
SaintFestCh-1904, p. 87

♦ 1613 ♦ **St. Christopher's Day**
May 9 in the East and July 25 in the West

The lack of reliable information about St. Christopher's life led the Roman Catholic Church to lessen the significance of his feast in its universal calendar in 1969. But he is still widely venerated—especially by travelers, of whom he is the patron saint. According to the most popular legend, Christopher became a ferryman, carrying people across a river on his strong shoulders while using his staff for balance. One day he carried a small child across, but the weight was so overwhelming that he almost didn't make it to the other side. When he did, the child revealed himself as Christ, explaining his great weight by saying, "With me thou hast borne the sins of the world." The name Christopher means 'Christ-bearer.'

St. Christopher's Day is observed by members of the Christopher movement in the United States, whose mission is to encourage individual responsibility and positive action. Founded by a member of the Roman Catholic Maryknoll order, the movement has its headquarters in New York City and embraces people of other denominations as well.

In Nesquehoning, Pennsylvania, St. Christopher's Day is the occasion for the **Blessing of the Cars**. The custom began in 1933, when the pastor of Our Lady of Mount Carmel Church started blessing automobiles on the feast day of the patron saint of travelers because he himself had been involved in three serious car accidents. Sometimes it takes an entire week to bless all the cars that arrive in Nesquehoning from throughout Pennsylvania and other nearby states. In recent years other Catholic churches in the area have taken up the custom and perform their own blessing ceremonies. (*See also* ST. FRANCES OF ROME.)

SOURCES:
AmerBkDays-1978, p. 692
AnnivHol-1983, p. 96
BkDays-1864, vol. II, p. 122
DaysCustFaith-1957, p. 190
DictMyth-1962, vol. II, p. 1367
FestSaintDays-1915, p. 156
FolkAmerHol-1991, p. 295

♦ 1614 ♦ **St. Clare of Assisi, Feast of**
August 11

There were a number of women who joined the Second Order of St. Francis, but the first and most famous was St. Clare (c. 1194–1253). The daughter of a wealthy and noble family, she heard St. Francis preach about his rule of poverty and penance and, at the age of 18, left home to dedicate herself to the Franciscan way of life. She was joined 16 days later by her sister, Agnes. Other women, referred to as the Poor Ladies, were eventually drawn to the hard life that Clare had chosen, and the religious order that she and Francis founded is known today as the Poor Clares (*see also* ST. FRANCIS OF ASSISI, FEAST DAY OF).

Clare outlived Francis, who died in 1226, by 27 years. Although she was ill and confined to her bed for most of this time, she was a tireless proponent of the so-called "Primitive Rule," which calls for perpetual fasting except on Sundays and Christmas. In addition to their vows of poverty, chastity, and obedience, the Poor Clares also take a vow of enclosure, which means that they never leave the convent.

Clare died in 1253 and was canonized on August 12, 1255. Her feast day, which was observed for centuries by Roman Catholics and some Episcopalians, was eventually moved to August 11, the date of her death according to the revised Roman Catholic calendar and some other calendars.

SOURCES:
AmerBkDays-1978, p. 747
AnnivHol-1983, p. 105
Chases-1996, p. 334

◆ 1615 ◆ St. Columba's Day
June 9

Along with St. Bridget and St. Patrick, St. Columba (c. 521–597), also known as **Colm Cille, Columeille,** or **Columcille,** is a patron saint of Ireland. Although he led an exemplary life, traveling all over Ireland to set up churches, schools, and monasteries, he is chiefly remembered for his self-imposed exile to the island of Iona off the Scottish coast. According to legend, Columba felt that he was responsible for the battle of Cuildremne, where 3,000 men were killed, and resolved to atone for his actions by winning 3,000 souls for Christ. He landed at Iona on the eve of Pentecost, and proceeded to found a monastery and school from which he and his disciples preached the gospel throughout Scotland. Although he had been forbidden to see his native country again, he returned several years later, allegedly blindfolded, to save the poets of Ireland, who were about to be expelled because they had grown so arrogant and overbearing.

St. Columba is also associated with the story of how the robin got its red breast. When Columba asked the robin who landed on his window sill to sing him a song, the robin sang the story of the crucifixion and how he had pulled the thorns out of Christ's forehead and, in doing so, had been covered with his blood.

See also St. Bridget's Day; St. Patrick's Day

SOURCES:
AnnivHol-1983, p. 77
DaysCustFaith-1957, p. 142
DictMyth-1962, vol. II, p. 1367

◆ 1616 ◆ St. Crispin's Day
October 25

According to legend, Crispin and his brother Crispinian traveled from Rome to the French town of Soissons, where they preached and earned a living as shoemakers, offering shoes to the poor at a very low price and using leather provided by angels. The people of Soissons built a church in their honor in the sixth century, and since that time they have been known as the patron saints of shoemakers and other workers in leather. People who wore shoes that were too tight were said to be "in St. Crispin's prison."

This is also the day on which the French and English armies fought the battle of Agincourt in the middle period of the Hundred Years War (1415). The association between the feast day and the battle is so strong that writers sometimes use "St. Crispin's Day" as an expression meaning "a time of battle" or "a time to fight." This day is also called the **Feast of Crispian, St. Crispian, Crispin's Day, Crispin Crispian,** and the **Day of Crispin Crispianus**.

SOURCES:
BkDays-1864, vol. II, p. 492
BkHolWrld-1986, Oct 25
DaysCustFaith-1957, p. 267
DictDays-1988, p. 101
DictFolkMyth-1984, p. 261
DictMyth-1962, vol. II, p. 1367
FestSaintDays-1915, p. 188
FolkWrldHol-1992, p. 514

◆ 1617 ◆ St. David's Day
March 1

The patron saint of Wales, St. David was a sixth-century priest who founded an austere religious order and many monasteries and churches, and eventually became primate of South Wales. His day is observed not only by the people of Wales but by Welsh groups all over the world. There are large communities of Welsh throughout the United States—particularly in Pennsylvania, Ohio, Wisconsin, and Florida—who celebrate St. David's Day with performances of choral singing, for which the Welsh are noted (*see also* Eisteddfod). The St. David's Society of New York holds an annual banquet on March 1, and the Welsh Society of Philadelphia, which was established in 1802, celebrates with eating, drinking, and songs.

The leek, Wales' national symbol, is often worn on St. David's Day. According to legend, when St. David was leading his people to victory against the Saxons, he commanded them to wear leeks in their hats to avoid being confused with the enemy. In the United States, the daffodil has replaced the leek.

SOURCES:
AmerBkDays-1978, p. 223
BkDays-1864, vol. I, p. 315
BkFest-1937, p. 55
BkHolWrld-1986, Mar 1
DaysCustFaith-1957, p. 70
DictFolkMyth-1984, p. 612
FestSaintDays-1915, p. 37
FolkAmerHol-1991, p. 115
FolkWrldHol-1992, p. 153

◆ 1618 ◆ St. Demetrius's Day
October 26 in the East and October 8 in the West

St. Demetrius is the patron saint of Salonika (Thessalonike) in northeastern Greece, near where he was martyred, perhaps during the fourth century. His feast day marks the beginning of winter for farmers, and a spell of warm weather after October 26 is often called "the little summer" or "the summer of St. Demetrius." It is a day for opening and tasting the season's new wines. St. Demetrius is also the patron saint of soldiers.

October 26 is also the anniversary of the liberation of Salonika from the Turks in 1912.

SOURCES:
DictFolkMyth-1984, p. 867
FolkWrldHol-1992, p. 515

GdWrldFest-1985, p. 103
IntlThFolk-1979, p. 196

♦ 1619 ♦ St. Denis's Day
October 9

Also known as St. Dionysius, St. Denis is the patron saint of France. According to legend, Pope Clement sent him to what is now France to establish the Church there, during the reign of Emperor Decius (249–251), but the pagans who greeted him did not treat him well. When he came to Paris as their first bishop, they threw him to the wild beasts, but the beasts licked his feet. Then they put him in a fiery furnace, but he emerged unharmed. The most widely repeated legend is that they beheaded him on Martyr's Hill—the place now known at Montmartre in Paris—but he miraculously picked up his head and carried it for two miles before expiring at the site where the Church of St. Denis was later built.

Denis has also been identified with St. Dionysius the Areopagite, legendarily portrayed as a convert of St. Paul.

SOURCES:
DaysCustFaith-1957, p. 253
DictMyth-1962, vol. II, p. 1367
SaintFestCh-1904, p. 443

♦ 1620 ♦ St. Dismas's Day
March 25; second Sunday in October

According to the Bible, two thieves were crucified with Jesus. The one on his right, traditionally called Dismas, repented and was promised, "Today thou shalt be with me in Paradise" (Luke 23:43). He is therefore the patron saint of persons condemned to death. In the United States, the National Catholic Prison Chaplains' Association, by special permission from Rome, observes the second Sunday in October as **Good Thief Sunday** and holds masses in American prisons in honor of St. Dismas. March 25 is also the Feast of the ANNUNCIATION.

SOURCES:
DaysCustFaith-1957, p. 88
DictDays-1988, pp. 33, 49
DictMyth-1962, vol. II, p. 1368
RelHolCal-1993, p. 57

♦ 1621 ♦ St. Dominique's Day
January 22

In Macedonia, St. Dominique's Day is known as **Midwife Day**, and only women of child-bearing age participate in the celebrations, which honor the midwife and not the saint. They bring their local midwife food, wine, and gifts useful in her work. Each woman must kiss the *schema*—a phallic-shaped object usually made from a large leek or sausage. While the visiting women kiss and weep over the schema, the midwife sits on a makeshift throne wearing flowers, necklaces made out of currants, dried figs, and carob-beans, and a single large onion in place of a watch. A banquet follows, at which it is considered acceptable for the women to get drunk. Afterward, the midwife is drawn on a carriage through the village streets to the public fountain, where she is sprinkled with water. The songs and jokes of the women who accompany her are often lewd, and most men try to spend the day indoors.

SOURCES:
FolkWrldHol-1992, p. 35

♦ 1622 ♦ St. Dunstan's Day
May 19

St. Dunstan (c. 909–988) was the archbishop of Canterbury. According to legend, St. Dunstan was such a good man that Satan felt his activities had to be watched all the time. One day, when Dunstan was working at the monastery forge, he looked up and saw the devil peering at him through the window. He quickly pulled the red-hot tongs from the coals and grabbed the devil's nose with them, refusing to let go until he promised not to tempt him any more. Howling in pain, Satan ran and dipped his nose in nearby Tunbridge Wells to cool it off, which is why the water there is sulphurous. St. Dunstan is buried in Canterbury Cathedral. He is the patron saint of blacksmiths, jewelers, and locksmiths.

SOURCES:
BkDays-1864, vol. I, p. 653
DaysCustFaith-1957, p. 126
DictMyth-1962, vol. II, p. 1368

♦ 1623 ♦ St. Dymphna's Day
May 15

According to legend St. Dymphna was the daughter of a seventh-century Irish king. She fled with her priest to Gheel, Belgium, to escape her pagan father's demand for an incestuous marriage. There she was found by the king, who killed her and the priest.

St. Dymphna came to be known as the patron saint of the insane, and for centuries mental patients were brought to the site of her relics in Gheel, where the townsfolk looked after them. An infirmary was eventually built next to the Church of St. Dymphna, and by 1852 Gheel was placed under state medical supervision. Today there is a large, well-equipped sanatorium for the mentally ill in Gheel, known throughout the world for its "boarding out" system, which allows harmless mental patients to be cared for as paying guests in the homes of local citizens. On May 15 special church services are held and a religious procession moves through the streets carrying a stone from St. Dymphna's alleged tomb—a relic that at one time was applied to patients as part of their therapy.

CONTACT:
Belgian Tourist Office
780 Third Ave.
New York, NY 10017
212-758-8130; fax: 212-355-7675

SOURCES:
AnnivHol-1983, p. 66
BkFest-1937, p. 42
DaysCustFaith-1957, p. 123
DictMyth-1962, vol. II, p. 1368
FestWestEur-1958, p. 11

♦ 1624 ♦ St. Elizabeth, Feast of
July 8

The **Fiesta de Santa Isabel** in Huaylas, Peru, takes place on July 8 rather than July 2, St. Elizabeth's traditional feast day. This is because at one time the fights that broke out between the whites and the *indios* (or Indians) were so vicious that the Indians were ordered to hold their own celebration on July 8. Eventually the whites' celebration died out because the Indians' fiesta was so much more lively. Most of the festivities center around musical contests and dancing in the streets.

Bullwhip fights were a popular part of the festival until the 1930s.

St. Elizabeth was the mother of John the Baptist (*see* St. John's Day) and a cousin of the Virgin Mary. The Fiesta de Santa Isabel in Huaylas celebrates Mary's visit to her cousin after finding out that she was to become the mother of Jesus (*see* Visitation, Feast of the), rather than the feast day honoring Elizabeth and her husband, Zechariah, which is November 5 in the Roman Catholic calendar.

CONTACT:
Embassy of Peru
1700 Massachusetts Ave., N.W.
Washington, D.C. 20036
202-833-9860; fax: 202-659-8124

SOURCES:
FolkWrldHol-1992, p. 363

♦ 1625 ♦ St. Elizabeth Ann Seton, Feast of
January 4

The first native-born American to be declared a saint, Elizabeth Ann Seton (1774–1821) was canonized in 1975. She was the founder of the first religious community for women in the United States, the American Sisters of Charity, and she was responsible for laying the foundations of the American Catholic school system. She also established orphan asylums, the forerunners of the modern foundling homes and child-care centers run today by the Sisters of Charity.

Special services commemorating Elizabeth Ann Seton's death on January 4, 1821, are held on major anniversaries at the Chapel of St. Joseph's Provincial House of the Daughters of Charity in Emmitsburg, Maryland, the headquarters for her order of nuns, and at Trinity Episcopal Church in New York City, of which she was a member before her conversion to Roman Catholicism in 1805. More than 100,000 people attended her canonization ceremony at St. Peter's Basilica in Rome. On that same day, over 35,000 pilgrims flocked to Emmitsburg, where six masses were said in honor of the new saint.

SOURCES:
AmerBkDays-1978, p. 23
AnnivHol-1983, p. 4
RelHolCal-1993, p. 96

♦ 1626 ♦ St. Elmo's Day
June 2

The day that is known as St. Elmo's Day is actually St. Erasmus's Day, in honor of a third-century Italian bishop who is thought to have suffered martyrdom around the year 304. Erasmus was a patron saint of sailors and was especially popular in the 13th century. He is often referred to as Elmo, a variation of Erasmus.

Sometimes at sea on stormy nights, sailors will see a pale brushlike spray of electricity at the top of the mast. In the Middle Ages, they believed that these fires were the souls of the departed, rising to glory through the intercession of St. Elmo. Such an electrical display is still referred to as "St. Elmo's Fire."

SOURCES:
AnnivHol-1983, p. 75
DaysCustFaith-1957, p. 140
DictMyth-1962, vol. II, p. 1369

♦ 1627 ♦ Saintes Festival of Ancient Music
Early July

Saintes, an ancient Roman city about 16 miles inland from the Atlantic coast of southwest France, is the setting for a week-long festival of medieval and Renaissance music in early July. Concerts are held in some of the town's most famous sites, including Abbaye aux Dames, built in the 11th century, and St. Eutrope Church, with its ancient Roman crypts. Although the artists who perform there are not always as well known as those who perform at the Festival of International Contemporary Arts, which takes place at the same time only 40 miles away in La Rochelle, performers at Saintes have included the Ensemble Vocal and Instrumental of Nantes, the Ensemble Polyphonique de Paris, and Le Collectif de Musique Ancienne de Paris. For music lovers whose tastes span the centuries, the combination of the two festivals is ideal.

CONTACT:
French Government Tourist Office
9454 Wilshire Blvd., Ste. 715
Beverly Hills, CA 90212
310-271-6665; fax: 310-276-2835

SOURCES:
MusFestEurBrit-1980, p. 89

♦ 1628 ♦ Saintes Maries, Fête des
May 24–25

According to a French legend, St. Sarah, patron saint of gypsies, was the Egyptian handmaid of Sts. Mary Jacoby and Mary Salome, and all three were shipwrecked off the Provençal coast of France. The three holy women supposedly died in the small Provençal village of Les Saintes Maries-de-la-Mer, where their remains are said to be preserved in the 15th-century church of Les Saintes-Maries. The relics of St. Sarah are deeply venerated by the Romanies, or gypsies, of southern France, who try to worship at her shrine at least once during their lives.

The highlight of the service held at the church during the **Festival of the Holy Maries** occurs when the flower-decked reliquary of the Maries is lowered slowly through a trap door in the ceiling. On the second day of the festival, there is a procession down to the sea for the blessing of the painted wooden vessel known as the "Bark of the Saints." The bark holds a silver urn which it is believed also contains some of the bones of the saints. Thousands of devout pilgrims make the journey to Les Saintes Maries-de-la-Mer each year.

CONTACT:
French Government Tourist Office
9454 Wilshire Blvd., Ste. 715
Beverly Hills, CA 90212
310-271-6665; fax: 310-276-2835

SOURCES:
AnnivHol-1983, p. 70
BkFest-1937, p. 123
DictFolkMyth-1984, p. 954
FestWestEur-1958, p. 38
FolkWrldHol-1992, p. 302

♦ 1629 ♦ St. Evermaire, Game of
May 1

The **Spel van Sint Evermarus**, or the Game of St. Evermaire, is a dramatic reenactment of the slaying of eight pilgrims in Roussen, Belgium, on their way to the Holy Land in 699. After spending the night at a farmhouse, the story goes, the saint and his seven companions were murdered by a robber. This event is portrayed by the townspeople of Roussen, Belgium, each year on the first day of May in the meadow near the Chapel of St. Evermaire. Following a procession around the casket believed to contain the saint's bones, costumed villagers representing St. Evermaire and his companions are attacked by 50 "brigands" riding heavy farm horses and led by Hacco, the legendary assailant. By the end of the drama, the saint and the seven pilgrims lie dead.

Although the event was not commemorated for 200 years after its occurrence, the inhabitants of Roussen have faithfully presented their play for the past 10 centuries.

CONTACT:
Belgian Tourist Office
780 Third Ave.
New York, NY 10017
212-758-8130; fax: 212-355-7675

SOURCES:
Chases-1996, p. 193
FestWestEur-1958, p. 9

◆ 1630 ◆ St. Frances Cabrini, Feast of
December 22; November 13

The first American citizen to be proclaimed a saint of the Roman Catholic Church, Francesca Xavier Cabrini (1850–1917) was born in Italy. After serving as a nurse and a teacher in her native country, and seeing the miserable conditions under which so many orphans lived, she became a nun and was appointed superior of the orphanage at Codogno. Known thereafter as Mother Cabrini, she founded the Missionary Sisters of the Sacred Heart in 1880 and established a number of other schools and orphanages. Nine years later she and six of her nuns landed in New York, where they had been sent to help the Italian immigrants. She went on to establish orphanages, schools, and hospitals in many American cities, as well as in Europe and South America. She was canonized on July 7, 1946, and her feast day is December 22.

St. Frances Cabrini's feast day is commemorated in many places, but particularly at Mother Cabrini High School in New York City, in whose chapel she is buried. November 13, the day on which she was beatified, is also observed at every establishment of the Missionary Sisters of the Sacred Heart.

CONTACT:
New York Convention and Visitors Bureau
2 Columbus Cir.
New York, NY 10019
800-692-8474 or 212-484-1200
fax: 212-247-6193

SOURCES:
AmerBkDays-1978, p. 1019

◆ 1631 ◆ St. Frances of Rome, Feast of
March 9

St. Frances of Rome (1384–1440), also known as Francesca Romana or Frances the Roman, was a model for housewives and widows. In her 40 years of marriage to Lorenzo Ponziano, it is said there was never the slightest dispute or misunderstanding between them. Despite the death of her children, her husband's banishment, and the confiscation of their estates, she continued to nurse the sick, care for the poor, and settle disputes wherever she went. Eventually she founded a society of women who pledged to offer themselves to God and to serve the poor. Known at first as the Oblates of Mary, they were afterwards called the Oblates of Tor de Specchi, after the building in which they were housed. When she died, St. Frances's body was removed to Santa Maria Nuova in Rome, which is now known as the church of Santa Francesca Romana. She is the patron saint of widows.

St. Frances's feast day is observed on March 9, the date on which she died. Because she is also the patron saint of motorists—although no clear reason for this is given—it is customary for Italian drivers to flock to the Colosseum in Rome for the blessing of their cars. Crowds also visit Tor de Specchi and Casa degli Esercizi Pii (formerly her home, the Palazzo Ponziano), whose rooms are opened to the public on this day.

See also St. Christopher's Day

CONTACT:
Italian Government Travel Office
630 Fifth Ave.
New York, NY 10111
212-245-4822

SOURCES:
AnnivHol-1983, p. 35
Chases-1996, p. 128

◆ 1632 ◆ St. Francis of Assisi, Feast of
October 3–4

The most important festival of the Franciscan calendar in Assisi, Italy, the feast of St. Francis (1181–1226) commemorates the saint's transition from this life to the afterlife. For two days the entire town is illuminated by oil lamps burning consecrated oil brought from a different Italian town each year. A parchment in St. Francis's handwriting, believed to be the saint's deathbed blessing to his follower, Brother Leo, is taken to the top of the Santa Maria degli Angeli basilica—built in the 16th century around St. Francis's humble hermitage known as the *Porciúncula*—and the people are blessed by the Pope's representative (*see* Forgiveness, Feast of).

In the United States, it is not uncommon for children to bring their pets to the church to be blessed on St. Francis's feast day, because of his love for animals as expressed in his *Canticle of Creatures*.

See also St. Anthony the Abbot

CONTACT:
Italian Government Travel Office
630 Fifth Ave.
New York, NY 10111
212-245-4822

SOURCES:
AmerBkDays-1978, p. 892
BkFestHolWrld-1970, p. 111
BkHolWrld-1986, Oct 4
DaysCustFaith-1957, p. 251
DictWrldRel-1989, p. 266
FolkAmerHol-1991, p. 359
IndianAmer-1989, pp. 257, 289, 302

◆ 1633 ◆ Ste. Genevieve, Jour de Fête à (Days of Celebration)
Second weekend in August

Ste. Genevieve became the first permanent settlement in the state of Missouri when the French arrived in 1725. At one time it rivaled St. Louis in size and importance, and the town still prides itself on its authentic 18th- and 19th-century architecture. The annual Jour de Fête that has been held in mid-August each year since 1965 not only celebrates the area's French heritage but is a German and Spanish festival as well. Historic homes dating back to 1770 are opened to the public, schoolchildren parade in ethnic costumes, and there's an International Kitchen that serves Spanish, French and German dishes—among them the French *andouille*, a highly seasoned sausage of minced tripe; the Spanish *barbacoa*, or barbecue, in the form of peppery pork steaks; and the German *leberknaefle*, or liver dumpling.

CONTACT:
Missouri Division of Tourism
P.O. Box 1055
Jefferson City, MO 65102
800-877-1234 or 314-751-4133
fax: 314-751-5160

SOURCES:
Chases-1996, p. 331
GdUSFest-1984, p. 106

♦ 1634 ♦ St. Gens, Festival of (La Fête de St. Gens)

Sunday following May 15; first weekend in September

St. Gens, patron saint of the fever-afflicted, was born in Monteux, France, which he is said to have saved from a great drought in the 12th century. He is honored twice annually in his native Provence: first, at Monteux on the Sunday following May 15, and again, at Beaucet, on the first Saturday and Sunday in September. The ceremonies held on both occasions are similar, consisting of a procession with the saint's image, prayers for the sick, and supplications for rain.

According to legend, St. Gens retired to a desert place near Mont Ventoux, where he worked the land with a team of oxen. One day a wolf attacked and ate one of the oxen. St. Gens made the wolf pay by hitching him with the remaining ox and forcing him to plow the land.

CONTACT:
French Government Tourist Office
9454 Wilshire Blvd., Ste. 715
Beverly Hills, CA 90212
310-271-6665; fax: 310-276-2835

SOURCES:
FestWestEur-1958, p. 37

♦ 1635 ♦ St. George's Day

April 23; February 25

Nothing much is known for certain about St. George, but the patron saint of England is popularly known in medieval legend for slaying a vicious dragon that was besieging a town in Cappadocia. After being fed two sheep a day, they became scarce and people had to be given instead—beginning with the king's daughter. She was on her way to the dragon's den to be sacrificed when she met St. George, who insisted on fighting the dragon and, according to another legend, eventually stunned it with his spear. Making a leash out of the princess's sash, he let her lead the monster back to the city like a pet dog. When the people saw what had happened, they were converted to Christianity. To this day, St. George is often depicted with a dragon.

St. George's Day, sometimes referred to as **Georgemas**, has been observed as a religious feast as well as a holiday since the 13th century. In the United States, there are St. George's societies in Philadelphia, New York City, Charleston, S.C., and Baltimore, Maryland, dedicated to charitable causes that hold annual dinners on this day. In the former Soviet Union, St. George's Day is celebrated on February 25 in Georgia. A festival is held at the cathedral of Mtskheta, the old capital and religious center of Georgia.

See also ST. GEORGE'S DAY IN BULGARIA; GOLDEN CHARIOT AND BATTLE OF THE LUMECON, PROCESSION OF THE

SOURCES:
AmerBkDays-1978, p. 373
BkDays-1864, vol. I, p. 539
BkFest-1937, pp. 58, 104, 169, 330

DaysCustFaith-1957, pp. 98, 287
DictDays-1988, pp. 46, 102
FestSaintDays-1915, p. 93
FestWestEur-1958, pp. 63, 231
FolkWrldHol-1992, p. 247

♦ 1636 ♦ St. George's Day in Bulgaria

February 25

ST. GEORGE'S DAY, or **Georgiovden,** is one of the most important celebrations in Bulgaria. It marks the start of the stock-breeding season. The sheep are turned out to graze on the eve of this day because the dew is believed to have curative powers. Special foods are served the following day, traditional songs are sung, and both livestock and their pens are decorated with blossoming willow twigs.

Traditional rural Bulgarian belief holds that someone who is born on this day is blessed with wisdom and beauty. In some areas a lamb is slaughtered, and the door sill is smeared with its blood to protect the house from witches, illness, and other forms of bad luck.

SOURCES:
BkFest-1937, p. 71

♦ 1637 ♦ St. George's Day in Syria ('Id Mar Jurjus)

April 23

In Syria, where he is known as Mar Jurjus, St. George is honored not only by Christians but by Muslims, who know him as al-Khidr and at one time identified him with the prophet Elijah. There are shrines dedicated to St. George throughout the country, and several monasteries mark sites where the saint is said to have revealed himself. One of the most important is the monastery at Humeira, near Tripoli, Syria, where both Christians and Muslims from all over Syria attend a folk festival each year on ST. GEORGE'S DAY, April 23.

CONTACT:
Syrian Embassy
2215 Wyoming Ave., N.W.
Washington, D.C. 20008
202-232-6313; fax: 202-234-9548

SOURCES:
BkFest-1937, p. 330
BkFestHolWrld-1970, p. 81

♦ 1638 ♦ St. Gregory's Day

March 12

St. Gregory was a sixth-century monk who became a pope. He is said to have invented the Gregorian chant. Popular legend attributes many acts of kindness to St. Gregory. One is that he freed frogs from the ice of early spring. Another is that he loved beggars and fed them at his own table with food served on golden plates.

St. Gregory is also the patron saint of school children and scholars. In Belgium, school children rise early on March 12 and parade through the streets dressed as "little soldiers of St. Gregory." They carry a big basket for gifts and are accompanied by a noisy drummer. One of them is dressed as Pope Gregory in gaudy vestments and a gold paper crown. The young girls in the procession wear big shoulder bows that resemble the wings of a butterfly. They march from house to house, pausing at each door to sing a song and to ask for treats.

The procession always includes a group of angels, because

the legend says that when Gregory was walking through the slave market at Rome, he saw a group of handsome young English youths. Upon learning their nationality, he exclaimed, "Were they but Christians, they would truly be *angeli* [angels], not *Angli* [Anglo-Saxons]!"

SOURCES:
DictMyth-1962, vol. II, p.
1371
FestWestEur-1958, p. 5

St. Grouse's Day
See **Glorious Twelfth**

♦ 1639 ♦ St. Gudula's Day
January 8

St. Gudula (or Gudule) is the patron saint of Brussels, Belgium. According to legend, Satan was so envious of her piety and influence among the people that he often tried to extinguish her lantern as she returned from midnight Mass. But as she prayed for help, an angel would re-light the candle.

She died in 712, and her relics were moved to Brussels in 978. Since 1047 they have remained in the church of St. Michael, thereafter named the Cathedral of St. Gudula. Her feast day is observed with great solemnity in Brussels, particularly at the cathedral that bears her name.

SOURCES:
BkDays-1864, vol. I, p. 73
BkFest-1937, p. 38
Chases-1996, p. 60
DictMyth-1962, vol. II, p.
1371
FestWestEur-1958, p. 4
SaintFestCh-1904, p. 58

♦ 1640 ♦ St. Hans Festival
June 24

Like other MIDSUMMER DAY celebrations, the St. Hans (St. John) Festival in Norway combines both pagan and Christian customs. This festival was originally held in honor of the sun god, for the ancients believed that the sun's change of course at the SUMMER SOLSTICE was an important event. The gates of the upper and lower worlds stood wide open at this time, and supernatural beings such as trolls and goblins roamed the earth.

After Christianity was introduced, the Norwegian midsummer festival was linked to the birth of John the Baptist (*see* ST. JOHN'S DAY), and it became known as **Sankt Hans Dag,** or **St. John's Day**. But some of the ancient customs and superstitions surrounding Midsummer Day have persisted. Only a century ago it was still common for Norwegians to hide their pokers and to carve a cross on their broomsticks as a way of warding off witches who might otherwise use these household items for transportation. The present-day custom of decorating with birch boughs also has its roots in ancient times, when the foliage was considered a symbol of the life force that awakens in Nature in the spring and early summer.

The festival of St. Hans is still celebrated in Norway much as it has been for hundreds of years. On *Jonsok,* or St. John's Eve, Norwegians who live near the fiords head out in their boats, which are decorated with green boughs and flowers, to get the best possible view of the St. John's bonfires on the mountains.

CONTACT:
Norwegian Tourist Board
655 Third Ave.
New York, NY 10017
212-949-2333

SOURCES:
AmerBkDays-1978, pp. 583,
586
Chases-1996, p. 268
FestWestEur-1958, p. 153
FolkWrldHol-1992, p. 339

♦ 1641 ♦ St. Hilary's Day
January 13

St. Hilary of Poitiers (c. 315–c. 367) was a French theologian who, as bishop of Poitiers, defended the divinity of Christ against Arianism, which affirmed that Christ was not truly divine because He was a "created" being. The so-called "Hilary term" beginning in January at Oxford and Dublin universities, is named after him. At one time the phrase also referred to a term or session of the High Court of Justice in England. According to tradition St. Hilary's Day—observed on January 13 by Anglicans but on January 14 by Roman Catholics—is the coldest day of the year.

SOURCES:
AnnivHol-1983, p. 8
DictDays-1988, p. 103

♦ 1642 ♦ St. Hubert de Liège, Feast of
November 3

St. Hubert (d. 727) is the patron saint of hunters, of dogs, and of victims of rabies. His feast day is especially honored at the church named for him in the little town of St. Hubert, Luxembourg. People who live in the Forest of Ardennes bring their dogs to the church to be blessed, and St. Hubert's Mass marks the official opening of the hunting season. In some places special loaves of bread are brought to the mass to be blessed, after which everyone eats a piece and feeds the rest to their dogs, horses, and other domestic animals to ward off rabies.

According to legend, St. Hubert was once more interested in hunting than he was in observing church festivals. But on GOOD FRIDAY one year, while he was hunting, he saw a young white stag with a crucifix between his antlers. The vision was so powerful that he changed his ways, became a monk, and was eventually made bishop of Liège. The site of this event is marked by a chapel about five miles from St. Hubert.

Thousands of pilgrims visit St. Hubert's shrine at the Church of St. Hubert each year. Among the artifacts there are his hunting horn and mantle, supposedly given to him by the Virgin Mary—a thread of which, when placed on a small cut on the forehead, is supposed to cure people who suffer from rabies. His relics are enshrined at the cathedral in Liège.

CONTACT:
Luxembourg National Tourist
  Office
17 Beekman Pl.
New York, NY 10022
212-935-8888; fax: 212-935-5896

SOURCES:
AnnivHol-1983, p. 141
BkFest-1937, p. 46
DaysCustFaith-1957, p. 283
DictMyth-1962, vol. II, p.
1371
FestWestEur-1958, pp. 17, 118
FolkWrldHol-1992, p. 549
SaintFestCh-1904, p. 473

♦ 1643 ♦ St. Ignatius Loyola, Feast of
July 31

St. Ignatius Loyola (1491–1556) founded the Society of Jesus, the Roman Catholic religious order whose members are known as Jesuits. Now the largest single religious order in the world, the Jesuits are known for their work in education, which St. Ignatius believed was one of the best ways to help people. In the United States, which currently has more Jesuits than any other country, they train hundreds of thousands of high school, college, and university students every year. St. Ignatius is the patron saint of retreats and those who attend retreats.

The Feast of St. Ignatius is celebrated by Jesuits everywhere, but particularly in the Basque region of Spain where he was born. The largest Basque colony in North America, located in Boise, Idaho, holds its annual **St. Ignatius Loyola Picnic** on the Sunday nearest July 31—an event often referred to as the **Basque Festival**. (*See also* Basque Festival, National.) The first Basques settled in America in 1865.

CONTACT:
Tourist Office of Spain
665 Fifth Ave.
New York, NY 10022
212-759-8822; fax: 212-980-1053

Idaho Tourism Division
700 W. State St.
Boise, ID 83720
800-635-7820 or 208-334-2017
fax: 208-334-2631

SOURCES:
AmerBkDays-1978, p. 709
BkDays-1864, vol. II, p. 148
BkHolWrld-1986, Jul 31
Chases-1996, p. 316
DictMyth-1962, vol. II, p. 1371
DictWrldRel-1989, p. 336

♦ 1644 ♦ St. Isidore, Festival of
Mid-May

Although pagan fertility rites were outlawed when Mexico was conquered by the Spaniards and converted to Catholicism, a few pre-Hispanic pagan festivities have survived—often overlaid with Christian meaning. One of these is the Festival of St. Isidore in Metepec, where farmers honor their patron saint around the time of his feast day, May 15. The men dress up as women and accompany their plows and oxen, which have been decorated with flowers, in a procession to the fields.

In Acapantzingo, Morelos State, there is a sowing festival in mid-May that includes a folk play and ritual dances, while in Matamoros, Tamaulipas State, there is a procession in honor of St. Isidore followed by dances that depict the events of the Spanish conquest.

See also San Isidro the Farmer, Feast of

CONTACT:
Mexican Government Tourist
  Office
405 Park Ave., Ste. 1401
New York, NY 10022
800-446-3942 or 212-755-7261
fax: 212-753-2874

SOURCES:
IntlThFolk-1979, p. 272

♦ 1645 ♦ St. James's Day
July 25; April 30

The Apostle James the Great (d. 44) was martyred by Herod. Also known as Santiago, he is the patron saint of Spain. His feast day is celebrated in the Western church on July 25, the anniversary of the day on which, according to Spanish

tradition, his body was miraculously discovered in Compostela, Spain, after being buried there for 800 years. A church was built on the site, which later became the town of Santiago de Compostela, once a place of pilgrimage second only to Jerusalem and Rome. St. James's Day is still celebrated in Compostela with a week-long festival that features a mock-burning of the 12th-century cathedral and an elaborate fireworks display.

The Indian pueblos of New Mexico, which were the target of early Spanish missionary efforts, also observe St. James's Day. At the Fiestas de Santiago y Santa Ana, held annually in the Taos Pueblo on July 25 and 26 (or the nearest weekend), the corn dance is performed in honor of both St. James and St. Anne, the mother of the Virgin Mary, whose feast day follows Santiago Day. Ritual dances also take place in the Santa Ana, Laguna, and Cochiti pueblos. At Acoma Pueblo, Santiago's Day is celebrated by holding a rooster pull.

In Loíza, Puerto Rico, the **Fiesta of St. James the Apostle** or **Fiesta de Santiago Apóstol** is the biggest celebration of the year. It focuses on three images of the saint—the *Santiago de los Muchachos* (St. James of the Children), the *Santiago de los Hombres* (St. James of the Men), and the *Santiago de las Mujeres* (St. James of the Women)—which are carried from the homes of the *mantenedoras* (keepers) who have kept guard over them all year to a place near the sea known as *Las Carreras*, 'the racetracks'. Santiago de los Hombres begins the procession, stopping in front of the house where another Saint is kept. This second image joins the first and the procession continues until all three end up at Las Carreras, where the traditional ceremony of racing with the flags of the Saints takes place. Farm workers and fishermen dress in traditional costumes and perform music and dances of African origin. St. James's Day is also a popular choice for baptisms and marriages.

His feast day in the Eastern church is April 30.

CONTACT:
Tourist Office of Spain
665 Fifth Ave.
New York, NY 10022
212-759-8822; fax: 212-980-1053

Puerto Rico Dept. of Culture
P.O. Box 9024184
San Juan, PR 00902-4184
809-724-0700

SOURCES:
AmerBkDays-1978, p. 694
DaysCustFaith-1957, p. 189
DictFolkMyth-1984, pp. 963, 971, 1063, 1111
FestSaintDays-1915, p. 152
FestWestEur-1958, p. 202
FolkAmerHol-1991, p. 290
FolkWrldHol-1992, p. 380
IndianAmer-1989, pp. 287, 309, 319

St. Januarius
See **San Gennaro, Feast of**

St. Joan
See **Joan of Arc, Feast Day of**

♦ 1646 ♦ St. John's Day
June 24

It is unusual for a saint's day to commemorate his birth rather than his death, but John the Baptist (d. c. 29) and the Virgin Mary are the exceptions here. (*See* Nativity of the Virgin Mary, Feast of the). Roman Catholics, Eastern Orthodox Christians, Anglicans, and Lutherans honor St. John on the anniversary of his birth; the Roman Catholic and Orthodox churches commemorate his death as well, on August 29 (*see* St. John the Baptist, Martyrdom of).

John was the cousin of Jesus, born in their old age to Zechariah and Elizabeth, a kinswoman of the Virgin Mary. John was the one chosen to prepare the way for the Messiah. It is a pious belief of many that he was sanctified—that is, freed from original sin—in his mother's womb when he was visited by Mary. (*See* Visitation, Feast of the.) He lived as a hermit in the wilderness on a diet of honey and locusts until it was time to begin his public ministry. He preached repentance of sins and baptized many, including Jesus. (*See* Epiphany.) He denounced King Herod and his second wife, Herodias, and it was she who vowed revenge for John's condemnation of her marriage, and who had her daughter, Salome, demand the Baptist's head on a platter.

Many St. John's Day customs date from pre-Christian times, when June 24 was celebrated as Midsummer Day. Celebrations in some areas still bear the hallmarks of the old pagan Summer Solstice rites, such as bonfires, dancing, and decorating with flowers. For the French in Canada, the **Feast of the Nativity of St. John the Baptist** is one of the biggest celebrations of the year, especially in Quebec. The **San Juan Fiesta** in New York City takes place on the Sunday nearest June 24 and is the year's most important festival for Hispanic Americans.

St. John's Day (**Día de San Juan**) is a major holiday throughout Mexico. As the patron saint of waters, St. John is honored by decorating fountains and wells and by bathing in local streams and rivers. The bathing begins at midnight—often to the accompaniment of village bands—and it is customary for spectators to throw flowers among the bathers. In Mexico City and other urban centers, the celebration takes place in fashionable bath-houses rather than rivers, where there are diving and swimming contests as well. Street vendors sell small mules made out of cornhusks, decorated with flowers and filled with sugar cane and candy.

A family of yellow-flowered plants, commonly called St.-John's-wort, is used by voodoo conjurors and folk medicine practitioners to ward off evil spirits and ensure good luck. In the southern United States, all species of the plant are called John the Conqueror root, or "John de Conker," and all parts of it are used: the root, leaves, petals, and stems. The plant's imagery is often mentioned in African-American folklore and blues music.

The leaves, and often the petals, contain oil and pigment-filled glands that appear as reddish spots when held to the light. According to legend, these spots are John the Baptist's blood, and the plant is most potent if rituals are performed on his birthday.

See also St. Hans Festival

SOURCES:
AmerBkDays-1978, p. 587
BkDays-1864, vol. I, p. 814
BkFest-1937, p. 229
BkFestHolWrld-1970, p. 98
BkHolWrld-1986, Jun 24
DaysCustFaith-1957, pp. 151, 222
DictFolkMyth-1984, pp. 1063, 1082
DictWrldRel-1989, p. 384
FestSaintDays-1915, p. 140
IndianAmer-1989, pp. 287, 296, 312, 319

♦ 1647 ♦ **St. John's Day, Puerto Rican Celebrations of**
June 24

Wading or bathing in the water on St. John's Day is a tradition that many see as symbolic of John the Baptist baptizing Jesus. In Puerto Rico, **San Juan Day** is observed by gathering at the beaches to eat, dance, drink, build bonfires, and bathe in the Caribbean. At midnight, the revelers take a swim in the ocean, a tradition based on the biblical scene in which John, the cousin of Jesus, baptizes him. Over the years, the religious significance of the event has been overshadowed, and today bathing in the water is believed to bring good luck in the coming year.

The annual St. John the Baptist Day parade in Camden, New Jersey, has been going on since the 1950s, not long after the first Puerto Ricans began migrating there to take jobs in the Campbell Soup factory. Billed as the only organized parade in the city, the event is eagerly anticipated by the area's 15,000 Hispanic-Americans, many of whom line the parade route from Cooper and Second Streets to Wiggins Park along the waterfront. There is a competition for the best float and a steady procession of salsa dancers, folk dancers, and beauty queens. The parade marks the culmination of a week of festivities—including a banquet, art exhibits, and a flag-raising ceremony—that honor the area's Hispanics.

In Hartford, Connecticut, a **San Juan Bautista Festival** has been held on the Saturday nearest June 24 since 1979. Sponsored by the San Juan Center, Inc., it includes Puerto Rican food and entertainment, particularly bands that play Puerto Rican music and use traditional Puerto Rican instruments. Although the Hartford festival is designed to give the area's Puerto Rican population an opportunity to celebrate their heritage, it draws many other people as well. Attendance at the most recent festival was more than 15,000.

SOURCES:
AmerBkDays-1978, pp. 582, 590
AnnivHol-1983, p. 83
FolkAmerHol-1991, p. 249

♦ 1648 ♦ **St. John's Day in Portugal**
June 24

Both St. John's Day and St. John's Eve (*see also* Midsummer Day) are widely celebrated in Portugal with parades, pageants, bullfights, fireworks, and other popular amusements. Many of the traditional rites connected with fire, water, and love are still observed here as well. Young people dance around bonfires and couples often leap over these fires, holding hands. Mothers sometimes hold their children over the burning embers, and cattle and flocks are driven through the ashes—all to take advantage of the curative powers of St. John's fires. Similar traditions focus on water, which on St. John's Eve is supposed to possess great healing power.

One of the most interesting St. John's Day celebrations takes place in Braga and is known as the *Dança de Rei David*, or Dance of King David. The role of King David is always performed by a member of a certain family living near Braga, and the dance itself probably dates back to medieval times. The King is dressed in a tall crown and voluminous cape. Ten shepherds or courtiers who accompany him wear velvet coats in brilliant colors and turban-style hats. Shepherds play ancient tunes on their fiddles, flutes, and triangles. As they parade through town this group stops frequently to perform the ritualistic Dance of King David.

CONTACT:
Portuguese National Tourist
   Office
590 Fifth Ave., 4th Floor
New York, NY 10036
212-354-4403; fax: 212-764-6137

SOURCES:
Chases-1996, p. 268
DictFolkMyth-1984, p. 1082

♦ 1649 ♦ St. John's Eve and Day in Latvia (Janu Vakars)
June 23–24

The three-day MIDSUMMER festival known as **Ligo Svetki** is Latvia's greatest feast of the year. It begins on St. John's Eve, when boys and girls meet in the village squares. The boys chase the girls and, in accordance with an ancient custom, beat them with cattail switches. Then the young people gather flowers, herbs, and grasses to make wreaths that will be used in ceremonies the following day. They also practice *Ligo* songs, which are based on the traditional Latvian *daina*, a short, unrhymed song in which epic and lyric elements are mixed. Sometimes the songs take the form of singing contests in praise or blame of the various men in town who are named Janis (or John): One group of singers praises a certain Janis for the prosperity of his farm and livestock, while another points out that his garden is full of weeds, his barnyard is littered with rubbish, and his servants are lazy. These songs serve as a reminder to everyone that their homes must be ready for the guests who will arrive on the following night— the boys and girls who arrive armed with their wreaths and place them on the heads of Janis and his wife.

As in many other countries, lighting bonfires is a tradition in Latvia on St. John's Night. Young people jump over the fires in the belief that it will ensure a good harvest. Others wave Ligo torches and perform typical Latvian folk dances, such as the *Trisparu deja*, the *Jandalins*, the *Ackups*, and the *Sudmalinas*. In some Latvian towns, arches made from birch branches and wildflowers are placed in front of the houses, and the ceremonies associated with the Ligo feast are performed beneath these fragrant canopies.

CONTACT:
Latvia Embassy
4325 17th St. N.W.
Washington, D.C. 20011
202-726-8213; fax: 202-726-6785

SOURCES:
BkFest-1937, pp. 213, 214
DictFolkMyth-1984, p. 606
FolkWrldHol-1992, p. 337

♦ 1650 ♦ St. John's Eve in Denmark
June 23

Known in Denmark as **Sankt Hans Aften**, St. John's Eve occurs near the longest day of the year and therefore is an occasion for national rejoicing. Huge bonfires, often topped with tar barrels or other flammable materials, light up the night sky for miles around. Sometimes an effigy of a witch, perhaps a pagan symbol of winter or death, is thrown on the fire. Along the coast, fires are built on the beach or shore. People go out in their boats to watch them burn and to sing romantic songs. Sometimes there are speeches, singing games, dances, and fireworks as well.

Midsummer Eve is also a popular time for Danes to leave their year-round homes and go to vacation cottages on the coast.

CONTACT:
Danish Tourist Board
655 Third Ave., 18th Floor
New York, NY 10017
212-949-2333; fax: 212-983-5260

SOURCES:
AmerBkDays-1978, p. 583
BkFestHolWrld-1970, p. 101
Chases-1996, p. 268
FestWestEur-1958, p. 27

♦ 1651 ♦ St. John's Eve in France (La Vielle de la Saint Jean)
June 23

The custom of lighting bonfires on the eve of St. John's Day originated with the ancient Druids, who built fires at the SUMMER SOLSTICE in honor of the sun god. Bonfires are still an important part of the festivities on St. John's Eve in France, where participants contribute something to burn. Traditionally, the village priest often lights the fire and leads the townspeople in the singing of hymns and the chanting of prayers. In upper Brittany, St. John's fires are built around tall poles, which are set on the hilltops. A boy named Jean or a girl named Jeanne provides a bouquet or wreath for the pole and kindles the fire. Then the young people sing and dance around it while it burns. Sometimes the fire is replaced by a burning torch thrown skyward or by a wagon wheel covered with straw, set ablaze, and rolled downhill. At sea, Breton fishermen put old clothing in a barrel, hoist it up the mainmast, and set it afire so that other ships in the fishing fleet can share the celebration.

There are many folk beliefs associated with St. John's Eve. One is that strewing the ashes from the St. John's fires over the fields will bring a good harvest. Another is that leaping over the dying embers guarantees that the crops will grow as high as the jumper can jump. In the sheep-raising Jura district, shepherds drive their flower-decked animals in a procession and later nail the flower wreaths to their stable doors as a protection against the forces of evil.

CONTACT:
French Government Tourist Office
9454 Wilshire Blvd., Ste. 715
Beverly Hills, CA 90212
310-271-6665; fax: 310-276-2835

SOURCES:
AmerBkDays-1978, p. 582
BkFest-1937, p. 125
FestWestEur-1958, p. 43
FolkWrldHol-1992, p. 336

♦ 1652 ♦ St. John's Eve in Germany (Johannisnacht)
June 23

The SUMMER SOLSTICE, or *Sommersonnenwende*, in Germany is observed by lighting the *Johannisfeuer*, or St. John's fire. Young boys often try to leap through the flames, and young lovers join hands and try to jump over the fire together in the belief that if they succeed, they will never be parted. Cattle driven through the bonfire's ashes are believed to be safe from danger and disease in the coming year.

According to German folklore, the water spirits demanded a human victim on MIDSUMMER DAY. But contrary to the danger this implies, people often went out and bathed on St. John's Eve in streams or rivers to cure disease and strengthen their legs. In Thuringia, wreaths were hung on the doors because it was believed that St. John the Baptist walked through the streets on this night, and that he would bow to any door with a wreath on it.

SOURCES:
BkFest-1937, p. 136
DictFolkMyth-1984, p. 723
FestWestEur-1958, p. 68

FolkWrldHol-1992, p. 337

♦ 1653 ♦ St. John's Eve in Greece
June 23

A custom still practiced in some rural Greek villages on Sᴛ. Jᴏʜɴ's Dᴀʏ is a procession of young boys and girls escorting the *Kalinitsa*, or the most beautiful girl in the neighborhood. On St. John's Eve, the young people gather at the Kalinitsa's house and dress her up as a bride, with a veil and a garland of flowers around her neck. The procession itself is led by a young boy holding a rod. He is followed by the Kalinitsa, who is in turn followed by four "ladies in waiting" and a little girl holding a parasol over the Kalinitsa's head. Other girls and boys accompany them, and they go around the village singing a song about drawing water for the sweet basil. If they should encounter a procession from another neighborhood at a crossroad, the parasols are lowered over the Kalinitsas' faces so they won't set eyes on each other. On the following day, June 24, the children gather at the Kalinitsa's house for a party.

Another old Greek custom, known as the *Erma*, is for two people who have chosen each other for friends to plant some seeds in a basket and raise them in darkness a few weeks before St. John's Day. On St. John's Eve they exchange plants and pledge their friendship by shaking hands three times over a fire.

SOURCES:
BkFestHolWrld-1970, p. 99
FestSaintDays-1915, p. 146

♦ 1654 ♦ St. John's Eve in Ireland
June 23

The Irish still celebrate St. John's Eve with bonfires, dancing, omens and prayers. People build fires on the hillsides and feed the flames with fragrant boughs. As the fires burn low, both old and young people customarily join hands and jump over the embers in the belief that it will bring an abundant harvest. Young Irish girls used to drop melted lead into water on St. John's Eve. They would then look for clues about their future in whatever shape the lead assumed.

According to Irish folklore, the soul leaves the body on this night and wanders about until it reaches the place where death will eventually strike. This belief was so widespread at one time that people routinely sat up all night on St. John's Eve to keep their souls from making the trip.

SOURCES:
BkDays-1864, vol. I, p. 815
BkFest-1937, p. 59

♦ 1655 ♦ St. John's Eve in Paraguay
June 23

On the eve of the **Fiesta de San Juan** in Paraguay, many rituals associated with foretelling the future are carried out. Placing a cross of laurel leaves under the pillow is believed to bring a dream about one's future lover. Planting corn and beans on this day yields further information about whom a young woman will marry: If the corn grows, she will marry a foreigner; if the beans grow, he will be Paraguayan. Similarly, when a blindfolded girl plucks a green lime from a tree, it means she will marry a young husband. A ripe lime means she will marry an old man. In rural areas, people still foretell the future by dripping molten lead or candle wax into a pan of water. Clues about what the future will bring can be found in the shapes formed by the wax or lead.

See also Sᴀɴ Jᴜᴀɴ ᴀɴᴅ Sᴀɴ Pᴇᴅʀᴏ Fᴇsᴛɪᴠᴀʟs

SOURCES:
FolkWrldHol-1992, p. 339

♦ 1656 ♦ St. John's Eve in Spain
June 23

La Víspera de San Juan in Spain is dedicated to water and fire. Fireworks displays are common and *bogueras*, or bonfires, are lighted in the villages, hilltops, and fields. In the Pyrénées, folk beliefs surround the bonfires and their charred remains, which are considered protection from thunderstorms. Cinders from the fires can also be mixed with the newly sown crops or put in the garden to ensure rapid growth. In other places people believe that cabbages planted on St. John's Eve will come up within 24 hours, and that beans will be ready by Sᴛ. Pᴇᴛᴇʀ's Dᴀʏ, six days later. Folkloric beliefs also focus on water. Walking through the dew or bathing in the sea on this day is believed to promote beauty and health.

Young girls traditionally believe that San Juan will help them see into their future. By placing a bowl of water outside the window and breaking an egg into it at midnight on St. John's Eve, they think they can read their destiny in the shape the egg assumes. Similarly, pouring melted lead into a bowl of water at noon gives clues as to what kind of man they will marry.

In the province of Asturias, a dance known as the *corri-corri* is performed on Sᴛ. Jᴏʜɴ's Dᴀʏ by six women with one man pursuing them. The sexual motif of the dance links it to the fertility rites associated with Mɪᴅsᴜᴍᴍᴇʀ Dᴀʏ in ancient times. In the Basque region, men perform the *bordón-danza*, or sword dance, in two facing lines, wearing white shirts and breeches, red sashes and berets, and carrying long sticks in place of the traditional swords. The fact that this dance is performed most commonly on St. John's Day suggests a connection with ancient sᴜᴍᴍᴇʀ sᴏʟsᴛɪᴄᴇ rites.

Pastry shops in Spain sell special cakes shaped like the letter J on St. John's Eve, which may be decorated with pink sugar roses and elaborate scrolls.

CONTACT:
Tourist Office of Spain
665 Fifth Ave.
New York, NY 10022
212-759-8822; fax: 212-980-1053

SOURCES:
DictFolkMyth-1984, pp. 157, 253
FestWestEur-1958, p. 199
FolkWrldHol-1992, p. 336

♦ 1657 ♦ St. John the Baptist, Martyrdom of
August 29

St. John the Baptist was beheaded by King Herod because he had denounced Herod's marriage to Herodias, the wife of his half-brother Philip (Luke 3:19,20), an illegal union according to Jewish law. Herodias' daughter by a former marriage, by legend called Salome, pleased Herod so much with her dancing that he swore to give her whatever she wanted. At her mother's urging she asked for the head of John the Baptist on a platter (Matthew 14:3-12). Herod, grief-stricken over having let himself be maneuvered into killing a good and innocent man, later had the head concealed within the palace walls to spare it any further indignities. It remained there until after the discovery of the holy cross by St. Helena, an event which drew many pilgrims to Jerusalem. Two of them found the head after St. John appeared to them in a vision.

The Martyrdom of St. John the Baptist—also known as the **Feast of the Beheading** in the Eastern Orthodox Church— has been celebrated by Christians since the fourth century. The observance started at Sebaste (Samaria), where the Baptist was believed to have been buried.

See also EXALTATION OF THE CROSS; ST. JOHN'S DAY

SOURCES:
AmerBkDays-1978, p. 588
AnnivHol-1983, p. 111
Chases-1996, p. 351
DaysCustFaith-1957, p. 152

♦ 1658 ♦ St. John the Evangelist's Day
December 27

John the Evangelist, also called **St. John the Divine,** was thought to be not only the youngest of the Apostles but the longest-lived, dying peacefully of natural causes at an advanced age. Although he escaped actual martyrdom, St. John endured considerable persecution and suffering for his beliefs. He is said to have drunk poison to prove his faith (so he is the patron saint of protection against poison), been cast into a cauldron of boiling oil, and at one point banished to the lonely Greek island of Patmos, where he worked among the criminals in the mines. He remained healthy, vigorous, and miraculously unharmed throughout these trials and returned to Ephesus where it is believed he wrote the Gospel according to John. He is also believed to be the author of the New Testament Book of Revelation, though many scholars disagree.

See also ST. STEPHEN'S DAY

SOURCES:
AmerBkDays-1978, p. 1154
BkDays-1864, vol. II, p. 771
DaysCustFaith-1957, p. 323
FolkWrldHol-1992, p. 644

♦ 1659 ♦ St. Joseph's Day
March 12–19

The feast of the foster-father of Jesus, known as **Dia de San Giuseppe** is widely observed in Italy as a day of feasting and sharing with the poor, of whom he is the patron saint. Each village prepares a "table of St. Joseph" by contributing money, candles, flowers, or food. Then they invite three guests of honor—representing Jesus, Mary, and Joseph—to join in their feast, as well as others representing the 12 Apostles. They also invite the orphans, widows, beggars, and poor people of the village to eat with them. The food is blessed by the village priest and by the child chosen to represent Jesus; then it is passed from one person to the next. The **Feast of St. Joseph** is celebrated by Italians in the United States and in other countries as well.

It is a week-long festival in Valencia, Spain, called **Fallas de San Jose (Bonfires of St. Joseph).** It has its roots in medieval times, when on St. Joseph's Eve, the carpenters' guild made a huge bonfire out of the wood shavings that had accumulated over the winter—St. Joseph being their patron saint. This was considered the end of winter and the last night on which

candles and lamps would have to be lighted. In fact, the carpenters often burned the *parot,* or wooden candelabrum, in front of their shops. One year the parot was dressed up as a local gossip and burned in effigy.

Nowadays the parots have become *fallas,* or huge floats of intricate scenes made of wood and papier-mâché, satirizing everything from the high cost of living to political personalities. On St. Joseph's Eve, March 18, the fallas parade through the streets. At midnight on March 19, the celebration ends with the spectacular ceremony known as the *crema,* when all the fallas are set on fire. One *Ninot,* or 'doll', from each falla is chosen, and before the fire the best one is selected and preserved in a special museum. Another highlight is the *crida,* which consists of a series of public announcements made from the Torres de Serrano by the Queen of the Fallas and the city mayor. The festival is said to reflect the happy and satirical nature of the Valencians.

See also SWALLOWS OF SAN JUAN CAPISTRANO

CONTACT:
Italian Government Travel Office
630 Fifth Ave.
New York, NY 10111
212-245-4822

Tourist Office of Spain
665 Fifth Ave.
New York, NY 10022
212-759-8822; fax: 212-980-1053

SOURCES:
BkFest-1937, pp. 181, 299
BkHolWrld-1986, Mar 19
DaysCustFaith-1957, p. 82
FestWestEur-1958, p. 90
FolkAmerHol-1991, p. 129
FolkWrldHol-1992, p. 180
GdUSFest-1984, p. 72
NatlHolWrld-1968, p. 36

♦ 1660 ♦ St. Joseph the Worker, Feast of
May 1

A public holiday in Malta, celebrated with festivities throughout the country. In Valletta, a highlight of the Mass conducted by the archbishop in St. John's Cathedral is the blessing of the tools and products of laborers and craftsmen.

St. Joseph, the husband of the Virgin Mary, was a carpenter who taught Jesus his craft. He is the patron saint of workers, laborers, carpenters, cabinetmakers, and joiners. In 1955, Pope Pius XII established the Feast of St. Joseph the Worker on May 1 as a counter-celebration to the Communists' MAY DAY celebrations honoring workers.

CONTACT:
Malta National Tourist Office
350 Fifth Ave.
Empire State Bldg., Ste. 4412
New York, NY 10118
212-695-9520; fax: 212-695-8229

♦ 1661 ♦ St. Jude's Day
October 28

Because St. Jude is believed to have been martyred with St. Simon in Persia, where they had gone to preach Christianity, their feast is celebrated jointly on October 28, thought to be the date on which their relics were moved to old St. Peter's basilica. Aside from the fact that they were both apostles, little is known about Simon and Jude. The New Testament refers to "Judas, not Iscariot" to distinguish Jude the Apostle from the Judas who betrayed Jesus.

As the patron saint of hopeless causes, St. Jude's Day is observed particularly by students, who often ask for his help on exams. St. Jude and St. Joseph are the most important saints to Roman Catholics in Buffalo, New York, where people buy St. Jude medals to help them win over impossible odds or achieve the unachievable.

SOURCES:
AnnivHol-1983, p. 137
Chases-1996, p. 433
DaysCustFaith-1957, p. 269
FolkAmerHol-1991, p. 370

♦ 1662 ♦ St. Knut's Day
January 13; January 19

Tjugondag Knut, or St. Knut's Day, marks the end of the Yuletide season in Sweden. King Canute (or Knut) ruled Denmark, England, and Norway in the 11th century; his feast day is January 19. Rather than letting the holidays fade quietly, Swedish families throughout the country hold parties to celebrate the final lighting (and subsequent dismantling) of the Christmas tree. After letting the children eat the cookies and candies used to decorate the tree, and after packing the ornaments away in their boxes, it is customary to hurl the tree through an open window.

In Norway, January 13 is known as **Tyvendedagen**, or **Twentieth Day**, since it is the 20th day after Christmas. It is observed in much the same way, with parties and the dismantling of the Christmas tree. But instead of throwing the tree out the window, it is customarily chopped up and burned in the fireplace.

SOURCES:
AnnivHol-1983, p. 8
BkFest-1937, p. 308
BkHolWrld-1986, Jan 13
FestWestEur-1958, pp. 151, 211
FolkWrldHol-1992, p. 28

♦ 1663 ♦ St. Lazarus's Day
Between March 27 and April 30; Saturday before Palm Sunday

In Bulgaria, St. Lazarus's Day (**Lazarouvane** or **Lazarovden**) is the great Slavic festival of youth and fertility and doesn't have much to do with Lazarus himself. The day takes its name from a series of ritual games and songs studied in advance by young girls during LENT. Although there are many versions of the ritual, they all have a common focus, which is the "coming out" of girls who are ready to be married. Particular attention is paid to dress, which usually involves colorful traditional costumes and heavy jewelry. In former times, the people of Bulgaria believed that the more elaborate the rituals devoted to marriage, the better the chances for happiness, long life, and a house full of children.

See also LAZARUS SATURDAY

SOURCES:
AnnivHol-1983, p. 178
Chases-1996, p. 152
FolkWrldHol-1992, p. 129

♦ 1664 ♦ St. Leopold's Day
November 15

St. Leopold (1073–1136), the patron saint of Austria, was buried in the abbey he had established in Klosterneuburg. His feast day is observed there with the ceremony known as **Fasselrutschen**, or the **Slide of the Great Cask**, in the abbey's wine cellar. Participants climb the narrow staircase that leads to the top of the cask, which was sculpted by a famous Viennese woodcarver and holds 12,000 gallons of wine, and then slide down its smooth surface to a padded platform at its base. The faster the trip down, according to tradition, the better luck the person will have in the coming year.

St. Leopold's Day is also known as **Gaense Tag**, or **Goose Day**, because the traditional evening meal served on this day is roast goose. November 15 marks the beginning of the new wine season, and all over Austria there are wine-drinking picnics and parties on this day.

CONTACT:
Austrian National Tourist Office
P.O. Box 1142, Times Square
New York, NY 10148
212-944-6880; fax: 212-730-4568

SOURCES:
AnnivHol-1983, p. 147
BkFest-1937, p. 33

♦ 1665 ♦ St. Lucia Independence Day
February 22

The West Indies island of St. Lucia celebrates its national independence holiday on February 22. On that day in 1979 it gained full independence from Britain. St. Lucia had been a British colony since 1814.

CONTACT:
St. Lucia Tourist Board
820 Second Ave., 9th Floor
New York, NY 10017
800-456-3984 or 212-867-2950
fax: 212-370-7867

SOURCES:
AnnivHol-1983, p. 27
Chases-1996, p. 108

♦ 1666 ♦ St. Lucy's Day
December 13

According to tradition, St. Lucy, or Santa Lucia, was born in Syracuse, Sicily in the third or fourth century. She was endowed with a fatal beauty that eventually attracted the unwanted attentions of a pagan nobleman, to whom she was betrothed against her will. She is the patron saint of the blind because in an attempt to end the affair, she supposedly cut out her eyes, which her suitor claimed "haunted him day and night." But God restored her eyes as a reward for her sacrifice. She was then probably killed by a sword thrust through her throat. Because of this she is the patron saint for protection from throat infections.

St. Lucy allegedly blinded herself on the shortest, darkest day of the year (*see* WINTER SOLSTICE), and she later became a symbol of the preciousness of light. Her day is widely celebrated in Sweden as **Luciadagen**, which marks the official beginning of the CHRISTMAS season. Lucy means "light," and to the sun-starved inhabitants of Scandinavia, she often appears in a shining white robe crowned by a radiant halo. It is traditional to observe Luciadagen by dressing the oldest daughter in the family in a white robe tied with a crimson sash. Candles are set into her crown, which is covered with lingonberry leaves. The younger girls are also dressed in white and given haloes of glittering tinsel. The boys—called *Starngossar*, or Star Boys—wear white robes and tall cone-shaped hats, made of silver paper, and carry star-topped scepters. The "Lucia Bride" with her crown of burning candles, followed by the Star Boys, younger girls, and dancing children, called *tomten*, or 'gnomes', wakens each member of the household on the morning of December 13 with a tray of coffee and special saffron buns or ginger cookies.

Although this is a family celebration, the Lucia tradition nowadays is observed in schools, offices, and hotels as well. Specially chosen Lucias and their attendants visit hospitals to cheer up the sick and elderly. The largest public celebration in Sweden takes place in Stockholm, where hundreds of girls compete for the title of "Stockholm Lucia."

From Sweden the Lucy celebrations spread to Finland, Norway, and Denmark. Swedish immigrants brought St. Lucy's Day to the United States, and the Swedish customs survive in Swedish-American communities throughout the country. The Central Swedish Committee of the Chicago Area holds a major citywide festival at the downtown Chicago Civic Center on the afternoon of December 13 each year. Nearly every Swedish club and organization in the city chooses its own Lucia bride, and one is chosen by lot to be crowned at this festival with a golden crown made by hand in Sweden. A similar celebration takes place at the American Swedish Historical Museum in Philadelphia, with Swedish Christmas songs, folk dances, and a Lucia procession. In Rockford, Illinois, the St. Lucy's Day program is staged by the Swedish Historical Society at the Erlander Home Museum. The young woman chosen as Lucia on this day has to meet certain criteria, such as participation in Swedish classes, contributions to Swedish culture, or membership in one of Rockford's many Swedish societies.

At Bethany College in Lindsborg, Kansas, freshmen in the women's dormitories traditionally are awakened at three o'clock in the morning by a white-clad Lucia bearing coffee and baked goods. St. Lucy's Day is also observed by Swedish Americans in Minneapolis-St. Paul, Seattle, and San Diego.

SOURCES:
BkDays-1864, vol. II, p. 687
BkFest-1937, pp. 191, 312
BkFestHolWrld-1970, pp. 132, 133
DaysCustFaith-1957, p. 313
FestWestEur-1958, pp. 101, 217
FolkAmerHol-1991, p. 434
FolkWrldHol-1992, pp. 589, 590
GdWrldFest-1985, p. 166
RelHolCal-1993, p. 91
SaintFestCh-1904, p. 20

♦ 1667 ♦ **St. Marinus Day**
September 3

This is the official foundation day of the Republic of San Marino, a landlocked area of less than 30 square miles on the Adriatic side of central Italy. The oldest independent country in Europe, San Marino takes its name from St. Marinus, who lived in the fourth century. According to legend, he was a deacon and stonemason working on an aqueduct one day when a woman wrongly identified him as the husband who had deserted her. She pursued him into the mountains, where he barricaded himself in a cave until she eventually gave up. He spent the rest of his life on Monte Titano as a hermit. The present-day city of San Marino was built on the site where his original hermitage was believed to be.

CONTACT:
San Marino Honorary Consulate General
1899 L St., N.W., Ste. 500
Washington, D.C. 20036
202-223-3517

SOURCES:
AnnivHol-1983, p. 114
Chases-1996, p. 362

♦ 1668 ♦ **St. Mark, Fair of (Feria de San Marcos)**
Ten days, beginning April 25

The Fair of St. Mark, which is held annually for 10 days in Aguascalientes, dates back to the early 17th century and remains one of Mexico's most famous fiestas. It is primarily a showcase for the country's more than 200 forms of ritual and folk dance, each of which has its own meaning, mythology, history, and pageantry. There are also commercial and art exhibits, cockfights, bullfights, sports competitions, parades, and a battle of flowers. The wandering musicians known as *mariachis* give concerts, and regional folk dance groups from all over Mexico perform in the San Marcos Garden.

CONTACT:
Mexican Government Tourist Office
405 Park Ave., Ste. 1401
New York, NY 10022
800-446-3942 or 212-755-7261
fax: 212-753-2874

SOURCES:
IntlThFolk-1979, p. 267

♦ 1669 ♦ **St. Mark's Day**
April 25

Although he is often assumed to be one of the Apostles, Mark was much too young at the time to be more than a follower of Jesus. He is known primarily as the author of one of the four Gospels, which biblical scholars believe is based on what he learned from his close friend and traveling companion, Sᴛ. Pᴇᴛᴇʀ. St. Mark the Evangelist is also associated with Venice, Italy, where the church bearing his name was built over the place where his relics were taken in 815.

In England, it was believed that if you kept a vigil on the church porch from 11 o'clock on St. Mark's Eve until one o'clock in the morning, you would see the ghosts of all those who would die in the coming year as they walked up the path and entered the church. Young girls believed that if they left a flower on the church porch during the day and returned for it at midnight, they would see a wedding procession, including an apparition of their future husband, as they walked home. Because it involved an all-night vigil, St. Mark's Day eventually came to be associated with various forms of licentious behavior, which is why the parochial clergy in the Middle Ages decided that the day should be one of abstinence.

SOURCES:
BkDays-1864, vol. I, p. 549
DaysCustFaith-1957, p. 101
DictDays-1988, p. 104
FestSaintDays-1915, p. 98

♦ 1670 ♦ **St. Mark's Day in Hungary**
April 25

In Hungary, St. Mark's Day is also known as **Buza-Szentelo** or the **Blessing of the Wheat**, during which people follow their priest or minister in a procession to the wheat fields where the crop is blessed. They return to the village carrying spears of the blessed wheat which some believe has healing powers. The fields are again blessed when harvesting begins on June 29, Sts. Peter and Paul's Day.

SOURCES:
BkFest-1937, p. 169
FolkWrldHol-1992, pp. 250, 279

♦ 1671 ♦ St. Martha's Day
Last Sunday in June; July 29

Martha was the sister of Mary and of Lazarus, whom Jesus raised from the dead (*see also* Lazarus Saturday and St. Lazarus's Day). She is best known for her role in the Lord's visit to the house she shared with her two siblings in Bethany. While Mary sat and listened to their guest, Martha was busy serving and cleaning up. When she complained, Jesus told her that what Mary was doing was just as important as housework. For this reason, Martha is known as the patroness of housewives, cooks, and laundresses.

Martha's second, and legendary, claim to fame is that she killed a dragon who was ravaging the Provençal countryside, hiding on the wooded banks of the Rhone and periodically feeding on flocks and men. She overcame the beast by sprinkling holy water on him, then she bound him with her belt and led him into town, where the townspeople stoned him to death. A church was built on the site of this alleged event in what is now known as Tarascón in Provence, France. Every year on the last Sunday in June and on July 29 a procession takes place there that commemorates St. Martha's power. In the first procession, eight men representing those devoured by the dragon walk inside its spiked body and manipulate the tail and jaws, which snap at the crowd of spectators. In the second procession, the dragon trots along behind a young girl representing St. Martha. Traditionally, she is dressed in white and leads the dragon leashed on her crimson ribbon belt.

CONTACT:
French Government Tourist Office
9454 Wilshire Blvd., Ste. 715
Beverly Hills, CA 90212
310-271-6665; fax: 310-276-2835

SOURCES:
AnnivHol-1983, p. 98
DaysCustFaith-1957, p. 194
DictMyth-1962, vol. II, p. 1375
FestWestEur-1958, p. 44
SaintFestCh-1904, p. 345

St. Martin's Day in Colombia
See **Quadrilles of St. Martin**

♦ 1672 ♦ St. Martin's Day in Portugal
November 11

In many European countries, the celebration of St. Martin's Day is associated with slaughtering animals, and Portugal is no exception. On the **Feast of São Martinho** people roast chestnuts, drink red Portuguese wine, and butcher the family pig. There is a St. Martin's Day Fair at Golegã, in Ribatejo, that features a famous horse show at which some of the country's finest thoroughbreds are displayed. Another well-known St. Martin's Day Fair is held at Penafiel, in Trás-os-Montes. The parades and celebrations that are held in towns and villages throughout Portugal on this day are usually more secular than Christian in flavor.

See also Martinmas

CONTACT:
Portuguese National Tourist Office
590 Fifth Ave., 4th Floor
New York, NY 10036
212-354-4403; fax: 212-764-6137

SOURCES:
FestWestEur-1958, p. 185
FolkWrldHol-1992, p. 557

♦ 1673 ♦ St. Mary's County Maryland Oyster Festival
Second weekend in October

Oyster festivals are common in areas where the oyster industry has survived. But the festival that has been held at the start of the oyster season in Leonardtown, Maryland, since 1967 has a special significance for those skilled in the fine art of oyster shucking. The highlight of the October festival is the National Oyster Shucking Championship to see who can open the most oysters as quickly and neatly as possible. The winner of this contest goes on to compete in the Galway Oyster Festival in Ireland the following year.

The season's new oysters are served in every imaginable way: raw on the half-shell with sauce, steamed, fried, and stewed in a broth. The two-day festival also offers exhibits of oyster-opening knife collections, oyster shell collections, and films on the history, geography, and culture of southern Maryland.

CONTACT:
Maryland Office of Tourism Development
217 E. Redwood St., 9th Floor
Baltimore, MD 21202
800-543-1036 or 410-333-6611
fax: 410-333-6643

SOURCES:
Chases-1996, p. 424
GdUSFest-1985, p. 83

♦ 1674 ♦ St. Médardus's Day
June 8

St. Médardus, or Médard, who lived from about 470 to 560, was the bishop of Vermandois, Noyon, and Tournai in France. Because he was the patron saint of farmers and good weather, he has come to play a role in weather lore similar to that of the English St. Swithin (*see* St. Swithin's Day). In Belgium he is known as the rain saint, and there is an old folk rhyme that says, "If it rains on St. Médard's Day, it will rain for 40 days."

SOURCES:
BkFest-1937, p. 43
DictMyth-1962, vol. II, p. 1377
FestWestEur-1958, p. 13
FolkAmerHol-1991, p. 233

♦ 1675 ♦ St. Mennas's Day
November 11

There are actually two different saints by the name of Mennas. One was born in Egypt and enlisted in the Roman army. He hid in a mountain cave in Phrygia to avoid persecution, but then boldly entered the arena at Cotyaeum and announced that he was a Christian—an act of courage for which he was beheaded in 295. The second St. Mennas was a Greek from Asia Minor who became a hermit in the Abruzzi region of Italy and died in the sixth century.

In Greece, St. Mennas's Day is observed by shepherds. Because he has the power to reveal where lost or stolen objects lie, his name is invoked by shepherds who have lost their sheep, or who wish to protect their flocks from wolves. Shepherds' wives refrain from using scissors on St. Mennas's Day. Instead, they wind a thread around the points of the scissors—a symbolic action designed to keep the jaws of wolves closed and the mouths of the village gossips shut. St. Mennas's Day is also regarded as the beginning of the winter season.

SOURCES:
BkFestHolWrld-1970, p. 124
FolkWrldHol-1992, p. 559

♦ 1676 ♦ St. Michael's Day
September 29 in the West and November 8 in the East; first Sunday in October

Coming at the end of the harvest season, St. Michael's Day has traditionally been a day for giving thanks and for celebrating the end of the season of hard work in the fields. In Finland, **Mikkelin Paiva** is observed on the first Sunday in October. In the countryside, servants are hired and next year's labor contracts signed. The harvesters celebrate the end of their labors on Saturday night by holding candle-light dances. The observation of Mikkelin Paiva replaced an earlier festival known as **Kekri**, which was celebrated by each landowner as soon as his crops were safely in the barns. The "Kekri" or spirits of the dead were rewarded with a feast for their help with the farm work. The Kekri festival was probably a remnant of some form of ancestor worship.

In Ethiopia, where St. Michael's Day is observed on November 8, people attend services at any churches consecrated to *Mika'el*. The celebrations include chanting and dancing by the clergy, and a procession carrying the holy ark, or *tabot*, out of the church and then, later in the day, returning it. The services are followed by singing and dancing, an occasion for young men to possibly find a bride.

See also MICHAELMAS; TIMQAT

CONTACT:
Ethiopian Embassy
2134 Kalorama Rd., N.W.
Washington, D.C. 20008
202-234-2281; fax: 202-328-7950

SOURCES:
AmerBkDays-1978, p. 876
BkHolWrld-1986, Sep 29
DaysCustFaith-1957, p. 242
DictFolkMyth-1984, pp. 203, 504, 716
FestWestEur-1958, p. 71
FolkAmerHol-1991, p. 393
FolkWrldHol-1992, pp. 32, 491, 504, 555

♦ 1677 ♦ St. Modesto's Day
December 18

St. Modesto is the patron saint of farmers in Greece. His feast day is celebrated with various rituals in honor of farm animals. Sometimes a special Mass is said for the cattle. In Lemnos, *kollyva* (cooked wheat berries) and holy water are mixed with their fodder, while in Lesbos, the holy water is sprinkled on the fields to ward off locusts and disease. For horses and oxen, December 18 is a day of rest.

The Eastern Orthodox church reserves this day to commemorate St. Modestus who was patriarch of Jerusalem from 631 to 634. He had been abbot of St. Theodosius's Monastery in the desert of Judah, and was administrator of Jerusalem during the captivity of St. Zacharias in Persia.

Modestus is known for a sermon he preached on the bodily ASSUMPTION of the Virgin Mary into heaven.

SOURCES:
FolkWrldHol-1992, p. 595

♦ 1678 ♦ St. Nicholas's Day
December 6

Very little is known about St. Nicholas's life, except that in the fourth century he was the bishop of Myra in what is now Turkey. One of the legends surrounding him is that he saved three sisters from being forced into prostitution by their poverty-stricken father by throwing three bags of gold into their room, thus providing each of them with a dowry. This may be the source of St. Nicholas's association with gift-giving. On December 6 in the Netherlands, St. Nicholas, or *Sinterklass*, still rides into town on a white horse, dressed in his red bishop's robes and preceded by "Black Peter," a Satanic figure in Moorish costume who switches the bad children while the good are rewarded with candy and gifts. (*See* CHRISTMAS EVE.) He is the patron saint of sailors, and churches dedicated to him are often built so they can be seen off the coast as landmarks.

The American Santa Claus, a corruption of 'St. Nicholas,' is a cross between the original St. Nicholas and the British "Father Christmas." The political cartoonist Thomas Nast created a Santa Claus dressed in furs and looking more like King Cole—an image that grew fatter and merrier over the years, until he became the uniquely American figure that adorns thousands of cards, decorations, and homes throughout the CHRISTMAS season. Although Americans open their gifts on Christmas or Christmas Eve, in the Netherlands, Switzerland, Germany, and some other European countries, gifts are still exchanged on December 5, St. Nicholas's Eve, or December 6, St. Nicholas's Day.

CONTACT:
Netherlands Board of Tourism
355 Lexington Ave., 21st Floor
New York, NY 10017
212-370-7360; fax: 212-370-9507

SOURCES:
AmerBkDays-1978, p. 1079
BkDays-1864, vol. II, p. 661
BkFest-1937, pp. 34, 48, 129, 190, 245
DaysCustFaith-1957, p. 306
FestSaintDays-1915, p. 219
FestWestEur-1958, pp. 19, 49, 81, 118, 144
FolkAmerHol-1991, p. 426
FolkWrldHol-1992, p. 579
RelHolCal-1993, p. 67
SaintFestCh-1904, p. 11

♦ 1679 ♦ St. Nicholas's Day in Italy
May 7–8

The **Festa di San Nicola** is celebrated in Italy on May 7 and 8, the anniversary of the transfer of the saint's relics by a group of 11th-century sailors from Bari, who risked their lives to rescue St. Nicholas's body from Muslims who threatened to desecrate his tomb at Myra in Asia Minor. This is the same St. Nicholas who is associated with CHRISTMAS and the giving of gifts to children. Therefore he is the patron saint of children.

Thousands of pilgrims come to the Romanesque Church of San Nicola in Bari to worship at the saint's tomb and to ask for his help. Nicholas is also the patron saint of sailors. There is a procession on this day in which a group of Barese sailors take the saint's image down to the water, where it is placed on a flower-decked boat and taken out to sea. Hundreds of small craft carrying pilgrims and fishermen accompany the vessel, and at night the statue is returned to its place of honor on the altar of San Nicola's crypt.

CONTACT:
Italian Government Travel Office
630 Fifth Ave.
New York, NY 10111
212-245-4822

SOURCES:
BkDays-1864, vol. II, p. 663
BkFest-1937, p. 190
FestSaintDays-1915, p. 224
FestWestEur-1958, p. 96

◆ 1680 ◆ St. Olaf's Day
July 29

The feast day of St. Olaf (995–1030), also known as **Olsok**, was at one time observed throughout Norway, although today the primary celebration takes place in Trondheim. It commemorates the death of Olaf Haraldsson—the second King Olaf—at the Battle of Stiklestad in the year 1030. By 1070, work had begun on Nidaros Cathedral, which was erected over King Olaf's grave and drew crowds of pilgrims during the annual Olsok days throughout the Middle Ages. Although it is said that King Olaf did not display many saintly qualities during his reign (1015–28), he was responsible for introducing Christianity, and legend has embellished his reputation over the years, so that today he is also considered the champion of national independence.

St. Olaf is the patron saint of Norway, and his name is identified with the highest Norwegian civilian decoration. The anniversary of his death is still marked by religious services, fireworks, and public merry-making. Every year the battle in which he died is reenacted by a large and colorful cast, occasionally drawing a well-known actor such as Liv Ullman, during the **St. Olaf Festival** in Trondheim.

In the Faroe Islands, this is known as **Olavsoka**, or 'St. Olaf's Wake,' their national holiday. Parliament opens on the 29th, but the festivities—that include dancing, rock concerts, sports events, speeches, drinking, a parade of members of *Logting* (parliament) to the church for a sermon then back for the opening session—begin the night before and continue into the early hours of the 30th.

CONTACT:
Norwegian Tourist Board
655 Third Ave., 18th Floor
New York, NY 10017
212-949-2333; fax: 212-983-5260

SOURCES:
AnnivHol-1983, p. 99
BkHolWrld-1986, Jul 29
Chases-1996, p. 314
FestWestEur-1958, p. 154
FolkWrldHol-1992, p. 383
RelHolCal-1993, p. 100

◆ 1681 ◆ St. Patrick's Day
March 17

The patron saint of Ireland, St. Patrick, was born about 390 in Roman Britain—scholars disagree as to exactly where—and and died around 461. His grandfather was a Christian priest, and his father a deacon and an official of the Roman Empire in Britain. He is said to have been kidnapped at the age of 16 by Irish raiders and sold into slavery in Ireland; he escaped after six years, and received his religious training in continental monasteries. After being consecrated a bishop, he returned to Ireland about 432 as a missionary. The association of St. Patrick with the shamrock stems from his supposed use of its three-part leaf to explain the concept of the Holy Trinity to his largely uneducated listeners (*see* TRINITY SUNDAY).

St. Patrick's Purgatory has been a famed site of pilgrimage since the early 13th century. It is on Station Island in Lough Derg in County Donegal where St. Patrick had a vision promising that all who came to the sanctuary in penitence and faith would receive an indulgence for their sins. Additionally, if their faith remained strong, they would be allowed a glimpse of the tortures of the damned and the joys of the redeemed.

The **Feast of St. Patrick** is celebrated by Roman Catholics, the Anglican Communion, and Lutherans on March 17. The day is also popularly celebrated, particularly in the U.S., by "the wearing of the green," with many people of Irish and other extractions wearing some item of green clothing. Parties featuring corned beef and cabbage, and even the drinking of beer dyed green with food coloring are also part of this celebration of Irish heritage. The St. Patrick's Day Parade in New York City, which dates back to 1762, is the largest in the United States, and a major event for Irish Americans. As many as 125,000 marchers participate, stopping at St. Patrick's Cathedral on Fifth Avenue for the blessing of the archbishop of New York. In Boston the St. Patrick's Day Parade goes back even farther, to 1737. In fact, during the siege of Boston which forced the British evacuation on March 17, 1776, General George Washington used "Boston" as the day's secret password and "St. Patrick" as the appropriate response (*see* EVACUATION DAY).

See also ST. PATRICK'S DAY PARADE IN SAVANNAH

CONTACT:
New York Convention and Visitors Bureau
2 Columbus Cir.
New York, NY 10019
800-692-8474 or 212-484-1200
fax: 212-247-6193

Greater Boston Convention and Visitors Bureau
P.O. Box 490
Boston, MA 02199
800-374-7400 or 617-536-4100
fax: 617-424-7664

SOURCES:
AmerBkDays-1978, p. 262
BkDays-1864, vol. I, p. 382
BkFest-1937, pp. 15, 55
BkHolWrld-1986, Mar 17
Chases-1996, pp. 132, 133, 134, 136
DaysCustFaith-1957, p. 78
DictWrldRel-1989, p. 563
FestSaintDays-1915, p. 38
FolkAmerHol-1991, p. 124
FolkWrldHol-1992, p. 178
RelHolCal-1993, p. 111

◆ 1682 ◆ St. Patrick's Day Encampment
Weekend nearest March 17

The winter of 1779–80 was a time of discouragement and despair for the Continental Army. General George WASHINGTON set up camp in Morristown, New Jersey, that year so he could rest and reassemble his men. The soldiers' winter routine was bleak and monotonous. There was so much work to be done that they did not even celebrate CHRISTMAS. General Washington did, however, grant his men a holiday on March 17, ST. PATRICK'S DAY. A good portion of the American army was Irish, and political changes taking place in Ireland at the time found a sympathetic following among the American revolutionaries.

The St. Patrick's Day Encampment of 1780 is reenacted each year at the Jockey Hollow Encampment Area in Morristown. Thirty to 40 men and their camp followers set up camp for the weekend and perform more or less the same chores and activities that Washington's men performed, although the trend toward milder winters has robbed the event of some of its authenticity. The original March 17 encampment was not the first St. Patrick's Day celebration in America; the first celebration took place in Boston in 1737.

CONTACT:
New Jersey Division of Travel and
  Tourism
20 W. State St.
Trenton, NJ 08625
800-537-7397 or 609-292-2470
fax: 609-633-7418

♦ **1683** ♦ **St. Patrick's Day in Ireland**
  March 17

The observation of ST. PATRICK'S DAY is universal but less frenzied in Ireland than it is in the United States. Instead of the massive parades, rowdy parties, and commercialism of the U.S. celebration, the Irish spend the day attending Mass, wearing sprigs of real shamrock, and hailing each other with the traditional St. Patrick's Day greeting: "Beannacht na feile Padraig oraibh"—"May the blessings of St. Patrick be with you." They may attend sporting events or stay home and watch the New York St. Patrick's Day parade on television, but they don't drink green beer, wear green derbies (an English invention), or put green carnations in their lapels. Because it falls during LENT, St. Patrick's Day is anticipated as a reprieve from the deprivations of the period preceding EASTER. It is a time when children can gorge themselves on sweets and adults can indulge in "a pint" at the local pub. A traditional St. Patrick's Day dinner usually includes colcannon—a dish made of mashed potatoes, butter, onions, and kale.

SOURCES:
BkFest-1937, p. 55
BkFestHolWrld-1970, p. 74
BkHolWrld-1986, Mar 17
Chases-1996, p. 135
DaysCustFaith-1957, p. 81
FolkAmerHol-1991, p. 124
FolkWrldHol-1992, p. 178
NatlHolWrld-1968, p. 34

♦ **1684** ♦ **St. Patrick's Day Parade in Savannah**
  March 17

One of the oldest and biggest parades in the country, held since 1824 in Savannah, Ga., a city with a long Irish history. The oldest Irish society in the United States, the Hibernian Society, was formed in Savannah in 1812 by 13 Irish Protestants. The next year they held a private procession which was a forerunner to the present St. Paddy's parade. The first public procession is recorded in 1824, and public parades have been held ever since. There have been only six lapses of this parade: for wars, sympathy for the Irish Revolution, and for an unrecorded reason. The first floats appeared in 1875; according to reports of the time, one carried two women representing Ireland and America, and another had 32 women for the 32 counties of Ireland.

Today the parade, which follows a route through the city's historic district, comprises between 200 and 300 separate units, including family groups, commercial floats, Georgia and out-of-state high school bands, and military bands and marching units. The day begins with Mass at the Cathedral of St. John the Baptist. Members of the Fenian Society of Savannah, formed in 1973, start things off with a members' breakfast of green grits before they form a marching unit. The other main activity is eating. The fare is predominately

green—grits, beer, doughnuts, etc. Crowds are estimated at anywhere from 300,000 to 500,000.

See also ST. PATRICK'S DAY

CONTACT:
Savannah Area Convention and
  Visitors Bureau
P.O. Box 1628
Savannah, GA 31402
800-444-2427 or 912-944-0456
fax: 912-944-0468

SOURCES:
Chases-1996, p. 132

St. Paul
  See **Conversion of St. Paul, Feast of the**

♦ **1685** ♦ **St. Paul's Shipwreck, Feast of**
  February 10

A commemoration in Malta of the shipwreck of St. Paul there in 60 A.D., an event told about in the New Testament. Paul, the story says, was being taken as a prisoner aboard ship to Rome where he was to stand trial. When storms drove the ship aground, Paul escaped and was welcomed by the "barbarous people" (meaning they were not Greco-Romans). According to legend, he got their attention when a snake bit him on the hand but did him no harm, and he then healed people of diseases. Paul stayed for three months in Malta, converting the people to Christianity (Acts 27:1–28:11). Paul is the patron saint of Malta and snakebite victims.

The day is a public holiday, and is observed with family gatherings and religious ceremonies and processions.

See also MNARJA

CONTACT:
Malta National Tourist Office
350 Fifth Ave.
Empire State Bldg., Ste. 4412
New York, NY 10118
212-695-9520; fax: 212-695-8229

SOURCES:
FolkWrldHol-1992, p. 99

♦ **1686** ♦ **St. Paul Winter Carnival**
  Last week of January–first week of February

This 10-day winter festival was established in 1886 in response to a newspaper story from the East that described St. Paul, Minnesota, as "another Siberia, unfit for human habitation." A group of local businessmen set out to publicize the area's winter attractions, and the first winter carnival featured an Ice Palace in St. Paul's Central Park constructed by a Montreal contractor. Since that time, an entire legend has developed about the founding of St. Paul. This legend is reenacted each year. The main players are Boreas, King of the Winds, the Queen of the Snows, and the fire god, Vulcanus, who storms the Ice Palace but is persuaded by the Queen to submit to Boreas and let the people enjoy their carnival celebration.

A highlight of the carnival is the 500-mile snowmobile race from Winnipeg, Canada, to St. Paul. There are also ice skating and ice fishing contests, ski and sled dog races, softball on ice, and a parade featuring antique sleighs and cutters. On Harriet Island in the Mississippi River there is a display of snow sculptures by master craftsmen from Hokkaido, Japan—home of the SAPPORO SNOW FESTIVAL.

CONTACT:
St. Paul Convention and Visitors
  Bureau
55 E. Fifth St.
Norwest Center, Ste. 102
St. Paul, MN 55101
800-627-6101 or 612-297-6985
fax: 612-297-6879

SOURCES:
Chases-1996, p. 75
GdUSFest-1984, p. 98

♦ 1687 ♦ St. Peter's Chair, Festival of

January 18

It ancient times it was the custom in many dioceses for Roman Catholics to observe the anniversary of the date on which the diocese first received a bishop. Perhaps the only remaining observance of this type takes place at the Vatican in Rome, where St. Peter is honored as Bishop of Rome and the first Pope. The current Pope, wearing his triple crown and vestments of gold cloth, is carried in his chair of state on this day in a spectacular procession up the nave of St. Peter's Basilica. He is deposited behind the altar on a richly decorated throne that enshrines the plain wooden chair on which St. Peter is believed to have sat. The ceremony dates back to at least 720 and is regarded as one of the most magnificent ecclesiastical observances to be held at St. Peter's.

CONTACT:
Italian Government Travel Office
630 Fifth Ave.
New York, NY 10111
212-245-4822

SOURCES:
BkDays-1864, vol. I, p. 130
DaysCustFaith-1957, p. 24
SaintFestCh-1904, p. 71

♦ 1688 ♦ St. Peter's Day in Belgium

June 29

Sint Pieter (as he is called in Belgium), who walked across the water to reach Jesus, is honored each year on June 29 by Belgian fishermen, mariners, and others who are exposed to the dangers of the sea. The **Blessing of the Sea** ceremony is performed at Ostend, Blankenberge, and other seaport towns on the Sunday following the saint's day. After a special church service is held, a procession of clergy, church dignitaries, and seamen carry votive offerings, flowers, and garlands down to the shore. Then the priests board the boats and go out to bless the waves.

Although the custom has died out in all but a few rural areas, the building of bonfires is traditional on St. Peter's Day in Belgium. Years ago, children trundled wheelbarrows from one farm to the next in search of wood for St. Peter's fires. As the flames grew higher and higher, the children danced in a ring around the bonfire. People still light candles on this night and say the rosary in commemoration of St. Peter.

CONTACT:
Belgian Tourist Office
780 Third Ave.
New York, NY 10017
212-758-8130; fax: 212-355-7675

SOURCES:
BkFest-1937, p. 44
BkFestHolWrld-1970, p. 102
FestWestEur-1958, p. 14

♦ 1689 ♦ St. Peter's Fiesta

Weekend nearest June 29

As the patron saint of fishermen, **St. Peter's Day** is celebrated in fishing villages and ports all over the world. Perhaps the largest American celebration takes place in Gloucester, Massachusetts, where St. Peter's Fiesta has been celebrated by the Italian-American fishing community for several decades.

The life-sized statue of St. Peter donated by an Italian-American fishing captain in 1926 provided a focal point for the celebration, and the Sunday morning procession carrying this statue from the St. Peter's Club to an outdoor altar erected on the waterfront is still the highlight of the two-day festival. The Mass that follows is usually celebrated by the Roman Catholic archbishop of Boston, who also officiates at the Blessing of the Fleet that afternoon.

Other festival events include fishing boat races, concerts, fireworks, and a "greasy-pole" contest in which competitors try to retrieve a red flag from the end of a well-greased spar suspended over the water.

CONTACT:
Massachusetts Office of Travel
  and Tourism
100 Cambridge St., 13th Floor
Boston, MA 02202
800-447-6277 or 617-727-3201
fax: 617-727-6525

SOURCES:
AmerBkDays-1978, p. 603
BkFestHolWrld-1970, p. 102

♦ 1690 ♦ St. Placidus Festival

July 11

Sankt Placidusfest is a religious procession held on July 11 at Disentis, Switzerland, in honor of St. Placidus, who was murdered near the Benedictine abbey that he and St. Sigisbert helped establish there in 614. A wealthy landowner, Placidus donated the ground, joined the religious order as a monk, and was later beheaded for defending the abbey's ecclesiastical rights.

Every year the relics of St. Placidus and St. Sigisbert are carried in a solemn procession from the abbey to the parish church and back through the village to the abbey. Traditionally, during the ceremonies, parishioners in colorful folk costumes chant the old, and very long, "Song of St. Placidus."

CONTACT:
Swiss National Tourist Office
608 Fifth Ave.
New York, NY 10020
212-757-5944; fax: 212-262-6116

SOURCES:
BkFest-1937, p. 320
FestWestEur-1958, p. 236

♦ 1691 ♦ St. Polycarp's Day

February 23 (formerly January 26)

St. Polycarp (c. 69–c. 155) was a disciple of Sᴛ. Jᴏʜɴ ᴛʜᴇ Eᴠᴀɴɢᴇʟɪsᴛ and one of the earliest fathers of the Christian Church. He became bishop of Smyrna in 96 and, when the persecution of Christians was ordered by the Roman emperor, Marcus Aurelius, he was condemned to be burned at the stake. But according to legend, the fire formed an arch over his head and his body was left unharmed. When a spear was plunged into his heart, so much blood poured out that it quenched the flames. He finally succumbed, although the date of his martyrdom has been questioned, with some asserting it took place sometime between 166 and 169. That would have made him an astonishing 120 years old. Scholars believe there are good reasons for the original date of 155, however, which would have made him 86 when he was martyred.

Polycarp's friends and fellow Christians got together afterward to discuss how they might best carry on his memory. In fact, it was the martyrdom of St. Polycarp that gave rise to one of Christianity's richest traditions: the annual commemoration of the anniversary of a saint's death, a practice that didn't become universal until the third century. The earliest of these observances consisted of a memorial banquet, but by the fourth century they included a vigil service followed by celebration of the Eucharist.

SOURCES:
AnnivHol-1983, p. 27
DaysCustFaith-1957, p. 33
DictWrldRel-1989, p. 463
SaintFestCh-1904, p. 81

♦ 1692 ♦ St. Roch's Day
August 16

Also known as Roque or Rock, St. Roch (c. 1350–c. 1380) was a Frenchman who went on a pilgrimage to Rome. The plague struck while he was there, and, legend has it, he spent his time healing the afflicted by miraculous means. Eventually he contracted the disease himself and retreated to a forest to die alone. But his faithful dog brought him food every day, and he recovered enough to return to his home in Montpellier. He had changed so much, however, that no one recognized him. He was arrested as a spy and died in prison.

Known as the patron saint of the sick and the plague-stricken, St. Roch is honored annually throughout Italy. In Florence there is a flower festival that includes a 14th-century historical costume parade, races, and competitions. In Realmonte, the saint's poverty is recalled with a procession of people dressed in rags who carry a shabby picture of the saint. In Spain, a San Roque Festival is held every August in Betanzos, La Coruna Province. It features the traditional dances of farmers and seamen, a procession in honor of St. Roch, and a boat tour of the countryside that ends in a battle of flowers among the boats.

CONTACT:
Italian Government Travel Office
630 Fifth Ave.
New York, NY 10111
212-245-4822

Tourist Office of Spain
665 Fifth Ave.
New York, NY 10022
212-759-8822; fax: 212-980-1053

SOURCES:
BkFest-1937, p. 188
DictDays-1988, p. 106
DictMyth-1962, vol. II, p. 1380
IntlThFolk-1979, p. 334

♦ 1693 ♦ St. Rose of Lima's Day
August 23 (formerly August 30)

St. Rose was the first canonized saint of the New World, born in Lima, Peru, in 1586. She is the patron saint of Central and South America and the Philippines. When her parents tried to persuade her to marry, she began a self-imposed exile in the summerhouse of the family garden, where she lived as a Dominican nun and inflicted severe penances on herself. She died in 1617 and was canonized in 1671.

On her feast day the people of Lima take the statue from her shrine in the Church of Santo Domingo and carry it, covered with roses, to the city's cathedral. The children wear white robes and sing hymns, while the adults wear purple robes and carry lit candles. St. Rose's Day is a public holiday throughout Peru.

CONTACT:
Embassy of Peru
1700 Massachusetts Ave., N.W.
Washington, D.C. 20036
202-833-9860; fax: 202-659-8124

SOURCES:
AnnivHol-1983, p. 109
BkHolWrld-1986, Aug 30
Chases-1996, p. 354
SaintFestCh-1904, p. 388

♦ 1694 ♦ Saints, Doctors, Missionaries, and Martyrs Day
November 8

Since the Reformation the Church of England has not added saints to its calendar. Although there have certainly been many candidates for sainthood over the past 450 years, and many martyrs who have given their lives as foreign missionaries, the Church of England has not canonized them, although a few are commemorated on special days. Instead, since 1928 it has set aside November 8, exactly one week after ALL SAINTS' DAY, to commemorate "the unnamed saints of the nation."

See also ST. CHARLES DAY

SOURCES:
AnnivHol-1983, p. 143
DaysCustFaith-1957, p. 284
RelHolCal-1993, p. 112

♦ 1695 ♦ St. Sarkis's Day
January 21

In Armenia St. Sarkis is associated with predictions about love and romance. It is customary for young lovers put out crumbs for birds and watch to see which way the birds fly off, for it is believed that their future spouse will come from the same direction. It is also traditional to leave some *pokhint*—a dish made of flour, butter, and honey—outside the door on St. Sarkis's Day. According to legend, when St. Sarkis was battling the Georgians, the roasted wheat in his pocket miraculously turned into pokhint.

SOURCES:
FolkWrldHol-1992, p. 34

♦ 1696 ♦ St. Sava's Day
January 14 in the West and December 5 in the East

St. Sava (1174–c. 1235) was a Serbian noble of the Nemanya dynasty who renounced his right to the throne and chose instead to become a monk. While his brother was crowned king, Sava became archbishop of Serbia and the cultural and spiritual leader of his people. He was the founder of the Serbian Orthodox Church and played a central role in education and the beginnings of medieval Serbian literature.

As the patron saint of the former Yugoslavia, St. Sava, or Sveti Sava, is commemorated on the anniversary of his death with special church services, speeches, and choral singing. School children sing, dance, and recite poems in his honor.

SOURCES:
AnnivHol-1983, p. 9
BkFest-1937, p. 336

♦ 1697 ♦ Sts. Cosmas and Damian Day
September 26 (formerly September 27)

Not much is known about Cosmas (also Cosme or Cosmo) and Damian, whose legend has them as twin brothers from Syria who were brought up in the Christian faith and who devoted their lives to medicine. As doctors they would not accept any pay for their services, but asked those who benefited from their healing miracles to believe in Christ. What can be reasonably asserted is that they probably lived and were martyred in Syria during or before the fifth century.

In Brazil, Cosmas and Damian are regarded as the patron saints of children, and on September 27 everyone gives children candy—often by the truckload. Brazilians of African descent sometimes serve children a dinner of okra, a vegetable that is associated with a pair of sacred twins in Yoruban folklore who are often identified with Cosmas and Damian.

SOURCES:
BkFest-1937, p. 151
BkHolWrld-1986, Sep 27
DictMyth-1962, vol. II, p. 1367

◆ 1698 ◆ St. Sebastian's Day
January 20

St. Sebastian is known as the patron saint of archers for reasons that are all too obvious: legend has it that when his two brothers were imprisoned for being Christians, he went to visit them and to encourage them to stand by their faith, converting many of the other prisoners and their visitors in the process. His actions drew attention to his own beliefs, however, and he was condemned to die by being tied to a stake and shot with arrows until his body resembled a pincushion. When a Christian woman came to claim his body for burial, she discovered that he was still alive and nursed him back to health. Undaunted, he confronted his persecutors again. This time they succeeded in killing him, and his body was thrown into the great sewer of Rome in 288. All that is known with reasonable surety is that Sebastian lived, was an early martyr, and was buried on the Appian Way in Rome.

In Zinacantan, Mexico, there is a nine-day celebration in honor of St. Sebastian, extending from January 17 to January 25, that marks the transfer of authority from the Big Alcalde (or chief magistrate) to his successor. At the end of the festival, the outgoing Big Alcalde is escorted with his articles of office to the house of the incoming Big Alcalde. There is an elaborate ritual during which he hands over the sacred pictures of San Sebastian and other symbols of his authority. The festival also features a jousting pantomime, dancing to the rhythm of a small sacred drum, two enormous ritual meals, and a mock curing ceremony. The connection between the **Día de San Sebastián** festivities and the martyrdom of St. Sebastian, however, remains obscure.

People in Rio de Janeiro, Brazil, celebrate the feast day of their patron saint with church services, colorful religious processions, and other festivities.

CONTACT:
Mexican Government Tourist
  Office
405 Park Ave., Ste. 1401
New York, NY 10022
800-446-3942 or 212-755-7261
fax: 212-753-2874

Brazilian Embassy
3006 Massachusetts Ave., N.W.
Washington, D.C. 20008
202-745-2700; fax: 202-745-2827

SOURCES:
AnnivHol-1983, p. 11
DaysCustFaith-1957, p. 27
DictMyth-1962, vol. II, p. 1381
FolkWrldHol-1992, p. 33

◆ 1699 ◆ Sts. Peter and Paul's Day
June 29

It is said that St. Peter and St. Paul were both martyred on June 29, and for this reason their names have been linked in various observances around the world. In Malta, the feast of St. Peter and St. Paul is a harvest festival known as MNARJA. In Peru, the **Día de San Pedro y San Pablo** is celebrated in fishing villages because St. Peter is the patron saint of fishermen. Processions of decorated boats carrying an image of the saint are common, and sometimes a special floating altar is set up, with decorations made out of shells and seaweed. In Valparaiso, Chile, this sort of procession has been going on since 1682. In Trinidad fishermen first go out to catch fish to give to the poor and as they return, the Anglican priest blesses them and the sea. Then the partying begins. After the priest leaves, bongo and bele dances are done to honor St. Peter.

SOURCES:
AmerBkDays-1978, p. 603
BkFest-1937, pp. 7, 151, 171, 294, 331
Chases-1996, p. 270
DaysCustFaith-1957, p. 155
DictWrldRel-1989, pp. 563, 566
FestWestEur-1958, p. 14
FolkWrldHol-1992, pp. 345, 346
SaintFestCh-1904, p. 308

◆ 1700 ◆ St. Spyridon (Spiridion) Day
December 12 in the East and December 14 in the West

St. Spyridon is the patron saint of Corfu, Zakynthos, and Kephalonia; these are among the Ionian Islands located off the western coast of Greece. Although he was born a shepherd in Cyprus, he became bishop of Tremithus and was renowned for his rustic simplicity. He supposedly attended the Nicene Council (325) and defended the Apostolic faith against the Arians. After his death in c. 348, his relics were brought from Cyprus to Constantinople and then to Corfu in 1456. Every year a sacred relic of the saint, dressed in costly vestments, is carried through the streets on his feast day. Colorful folk festivities complete the day-long celebration. This day is celebrated on December 14 in the Roman Catholic Church.

CONTACT:
Greek National Tourist
  Organization
645 Fifth Ave.
New York, NY 10022
212-421-5777; fax: 212-826-6940

SOURCES:
AnnivHol-1983, p. 160
BkFest-1937, p. 154
FolkWrldHol-1992, p. 591

◆ 1701 ◆ St. Stephen's Day
December 26

On this day in about the year 35, St. Stephen became the first Christian martyr. The New Testament book of Acts records that Stephen was chosen by the Apostles as one of the first seven deacons of the church in Jerusalem. He was later denounced as a blasphemer by the Sanhedrin, the Jewish council in ancient Palestine, and stoned to death. St. Stephen is the patron saint of brick-layers.

December 26, 27, and 28, otherwise known as St. Stephen's Day, St. JOHN THE EVANGELIST'S DAY, and HOLY INNOCENTS' DAY, are considered examples of the three different degrees of martyrdom. St. Stephen's death is an example of the highest class of martyrdom—that is to say, both in will and in deed.

St. John the Evangelist, who showed that he was ready to die for Christ but was prevented from actually doing so, exemplifies martyrdom in will, but not in deed. And the children who lost their lives in the slaughter of the Innocents provide an example of the martyrdom in deed but not in will.

In many countries, St. Stephen's Day is celebrated as an extra Christmas holiday. In England, it is known as Boxing Day. In Austria, priests bless the horses because St. Stephen is their patron. In Poland tossing rice at each other symbolizes blessings and recalls Stephen's stoning. And in Ireland, boys with blackened faces carrying a paper wren, go about begging and "hunting the wren." The hunting of the wren is most likely a carryover from an old belief that the robin, symbolizing the New Year, killed the wren, symbolizing the Old, at the turning of the year.

> **SOURCES:**
> *AmerBkDays-1978*, p. 1151
> *BkDays-1864*, vol. II, p. 763
> *BkFest-1937*, p. 35
> *DaysCustFaith-1957*, p. 321
> *DictFolkMyth-1984*, p. 950
> *FestSaintDays-1915*, p. 249
> *FestWestEur-1958*, p. 104
> *FolkAmerHol-1991*, p. 478
> *FolkWrldHol-1992*, p. 642
> *SaintFestCh-1904*, p. 40

◆ 1702 ◆ St. Swithin's Day
July 15

When Swithin, the bishop of Winchester, England, died in 862, he was buried according to his wish, outside the cathedral in the churchyard, in a place where the rain from the eaves poured down. Whether this request was prompted by humility on his part or a wish to feel "the sweet rain of heaven" on his grave, it was reversed after his canonization, when clerical authorities tried to move his remains to a site within the church. According to legend, the heavens opened and there was a heavy rainfall—a show of the saint's displeasure that made it impossible to remove his body. This led to the popular belief that if it rains on St. Swithin's Day it will rain for 40 days; but if it is fair, it will be dry for 40 days. Swithin is the patron saint of rain, both for and against it.

> **SOURCES:**
> *AmerBkDays-1978*, p. 665
> *BkDays-1864*, vol. II, p. 61
> *BkFest-1937*, p. 60
> *DaysCustFaith-1957*, p. 181
> *DictDays-1988*, p. 106
> *FestSaintDays-1915*, p. 150
> *FolkAmerHol-1991*, p. 277
> *FolkWrldHol-1992*, p. 375
> *SaintFestCh-1904*, p. 328

◆ 1703 ◆ St. Sylvester's Day
December 31

St. Sylvester (d. 335) was pope in the year 325, when the Emperor Constantine declared that the pagan religion of Rome was abolished and that Christianity would henceforth be the official religion of the Empire. Although it is unclear exactly what role, if any, St. Sylvester played in this important event, he is always given at least some of the credit for stamping out paganism.

Because St. Sylvester's Day is also New Year's Eve, it is celebrated in Switzerland by lighting bonfires in the mountains and ringing church bells to signal the passing of the old year and the beginning of the new. It is a day for rising early, and the last to get out of bed or to reach school are greeted with shouts of "Sylvester!" In some Swiss villages, grain is threshed on specially constructed platforms to ensure a plentiful harvest in the coming year (*see also* Old Silvester).

St. Sylvester's Eve is celebrated in Austria, Hungary, and Germany. It is not uncommon in restaurants and cafes for the owner to set a pig loose at midnight. Everyone tries to touch the pig because it is considered a symbol of good luck. In private homes, a marzipan pig may be hung from the ceiling and touched at midnight.

> **SOURCES:**
> *AmerBkDays-1978*, p. 1167
> *BkFest-1937*, pp. 36, 49, 141,
> 176, 323, 347
> *BkHolWrld-1986*, Jan 13
> *DaysCustFaith-1957*, p. 325
> *FestWestEur-1958*, pp. 21, 84,
> 242
> *FolkWrldHol-1992*, p. 653
> *SaintFestCh-1904*, p. 48

◆ 1704 ◆ St. Tammany's Day
May 12

During the Revolutionary War, the American troops were amused by the fact that the "Redcoats" (i.e., the British) had a patron saint: St. George, who had a reputation for protecting English soldiers (*see* St. George's Day). So they decided to adopt a patron saint of their own, and chose for the purpose a disreputable 17th-century Delaware Indian chief named Tammanend. They dubbed him "St. Tammany" or "St. Tamina," chose May 12 for his festival, and celebrated the day with pompous and ridiculous ceremonies.

After the revolution Tammany Societies were eventually formed in many cities and towns, representing middle-class opposition to the power of the aristocratic Federalist Party. In the early 19th century the Society of Tammany became identified with the Democratic party. But the society's tendency to dole out gifts to the poor and to bribe political leaders—among them the notorious "Boss" Tweed of New York City—made the name "Tammany Hall" (the building in which the organization had its headquarters in New York City) synonymous with urban political corruption.

> **CONTACT:**
> Dr. Nicholas Varga
> Loyola College
> Baltimore, MD 21210

> **SOURCES:**
> *AnnivHol-1983*, p. 60
> *DaysCustFaith-1957*, p. 122
> *DictMyth-1962*, vol. II, p.
> 1530
> *FolkAmerHol-1991*, p. 195

◆ 1705 ◆ St. Teresa's Day
October 15

St. Teresa of Ávila (1515–1582) was a Spanish Carmelite nun and reformer who recognized that the discipline in convents had relaxed to the point where they were little more than social clubs. In 1562, amidst intense opposition, she withdrew from the big convent she had entered in 1535 and established a small house with only 13 members known as the Reformed, or Discalced, Carmelites. Teresa's nuns devoted themselves to a rigorous way of life that had been largely forgotten in most monastic orders. They never left the convent, they maintained almost perpetual silence, they lived in austere poverty, and, as a symbol of their humility, they wore sandals instead of shoes—thus the designation ''discalced,'' which means 'barefoot.' Before she died, Teresa had established 17 such communities. She was canonized by Pope Gregory XV in 1622.

Every year in Ávila, Spain, there is a huge celebration in honor of St. Teresa on October 15. The day is filled with religious services, parades, dances, games, and feasts, and the streets are decorated with banners and flowers. St. Teresa of Ávila is often colloquially referred to as ''Big St. Teresa'' to distinguish her from St. Teresa of Lisieux, a 19th-century Carmelite nun and author.

CONTACT:
Tourist Office of Spain
665 Fifth Ave.
New York, NY 10022
212-759-8822; fax: 212-980-1053

SOURCES:
AmerBkDays-1978, p. 929
AnnivHol-1983, p. 133
DaysCustFaith-1957, p. 259
DictWrldRel-1989, p. 753
SaintFestCh-1904, p. 450

♦ 1706 ♦ **St. Thomas's Day**
December 21 by Malabar Christians and Anglicans; July 3 by Roman Catholics; October 6 in the East

St. Thomas the Apostle was dubbed ''Doubting Thomas'' because, after the Resurrection, the other Apostles told him that they had seen Jesus, and he wouldn't believe them until he had touched Jesus' wounds for himself. When the Apostles left Jerusalem to preach to the people of other nations, as Jesus had instructed them to do, tradition says Thomas traveled eastward toward India. In Kerala, the smallest state in India, the Malabar Christians (or Christians of St. Thomas) claim St. Thomas as the founder of their church. For them his feast day is a major celebration. Thomas is the patron saint of India and Pakistan.

In Guatemala on this day, Mayan Indians honor the sun god they worshipped long before they became Christians with a dangerous ritual known as the *palo voladore*, or 'flying pole dance.' Three men climb to the top of a 50-foot pole. As one of them beats a drum and plays a flute, the other two wind a long rope attached to the pole around one foot and jump. If they land on their feet, it is believed that the sun god will be pleased and that the days will start getting longer—a safe bet in view of the fact that St. Thomas's Day coincides with the WINTER SOLSTICE. The Roman Catholic Church celebrates St. Thomas's Day on July 3; the Orthodox Church on October 6.

CONTACT:
India Tourist Office
30 Rockefeller Ave.
15 N. Mezzanine
New York, NY 10112
212-586-4901; fax: 212-582-3274

Guatemala Embassy
2220 R St., N.W.
Washington, D.C. 20008
202-745-4952; fax: 202-745-1908

SOURCES:
AmerBkDays-1978, p. 1123
BkDays-1864, vol. II, p. 723
BkFest-1937, p. 246
BkHolWrld-1986, Dec 21
DaysCustFaith-1957, p. 317
FestSaintDays-1915, p. 224
FolkWrldHol-1992, p. 597

♦ 1707 ♦ **St. Thorlak's Day**
December 23

Thorlak Thorhalli (1133–1193) was born in Iceland and, after being educated abroad, returned there to become bishop of

Skalholt in 1177 or 1178. He was canonized by the Icelandic parliament five years after his death, even though the Roman Catholic Church has never officially confirmed the cult. His day traditionally marks the climax of CHRISTMAS preparations for Icelanders. It is associated with housecleaning and clotheswashing, as well as the preparation of special foods. The *hangiket*, or smoked mutton, for Christmas was usually cooked on this day, and in the western fjords, the ammonia-like smell of skate hash cooked on St. Thorlak's Day is still considered a harbinger of the holiday season.

SOURCES:
FolkWrldHol-1992, p. 601

♦ 1708 ♦ **St. Urho's Day**
March 16

St. Urho, whose name in Finnish means 'hero,' is credited with banishing a plague of grasshoppers that was threatening Finland's grape arbors. His legend in the United States was popularized in the 1950s, largely through the efforts of Professor Sulo Havumaki of Bemidji State University in Minnesota. After being celebrated as a ''joke holiday'' for several years in the Menagha-Sebeka area, the idea spread to other states with large Finnish populations, and now the governors of all 50 states have issued official proclamations stating that March 16 (or the nearest Saturday) is St. Urho's Day.

The actual celebrations, which are largely confined to Finnish communities, include wearing St. Urho's official colors—Nile green and royal purple—drinking grape juice, and chanting St. Urho's famous words, ''Grasshopper, grasshopper, go away,'' in Finnish. In some areas there is a ceremonial ''changing of the guard''—in this case, two makeshift guards carrying pitchforks or chainsaws (to cut down the giant grasshoppers) who meet and exchange clothing, including humorous or unusual undergarments.

The similarities between this day and ST. PATRICK'S DAY, observed on March 17, can hardly be overlooked. St. Patrick, who is believed to have driven the snakes out of Ireland, is widely regarded as a rival to St. Urho and his grasshoppers. There is some evidence that native Finns who have visited friends and relatives in the U.S. are taking the St. Urho's celebration back to Finland with them.

CONTACT:
Minnesota Office of Tourism
121 E. 7th Pl. Metro Sq., Ste. 100
St. Paul, MN 55101
612-296-5029 or 800-657-3700
fax: 612-296-7095

SOURCES:
AnnivHol-1983, p. 38
Chases-1996, p. 135

♦ 1709 ♦ **St. Vaclav's Day**
September 28

Also known as **St. Wenceslas** (c. 907–929), St. Vaclav was a Bohemian prince who became the patron saint of the former Czechoslovakia. He was raised a Christian and eventually took over the government, encouraging the work of German missionaries who were trying to Christianize Bohemia. His zeal antagonized his non-Christian opponents, his brother among them, and he was eventually murdered by his brother or his brother's supporters. A few years later, his remains were transferred to the Church of St. Vitus in Prague, which became a popular pilgrimage site in the medieval period.

St. Vaclav's Day is a holiday throughout the Czech Republic. The virtues of "Good King Wenceslas" have been memorialized by the popular 19th-century Christmas carol of that name, though it rests on no historical basis.

CONTACT:
Czech Center
1109 Madison Ave.
New York, NY 10028
212-288-0830; fax: 212-288-0971
E-mail: nycenter@czech.cz

SOURCES:
AnnivHol-1983, p. 123
BkFest-1937, p. 90
DictWrldRel-1989, p. 803
FolkAmerHol-1991, p. 398

♦ 1710 ♦ St. Vincent Independence and Thanksgiving Day
October 27

A group of islands in the West Indies, St. Vincent and the Grenadines gained independence from Britain on October 27, 1979, and citizens celebrate their freedom with this national holiday.

CONTACT:
St. Vincent and the Grenadines
  Tourist Information Office
801 Second Ave., 21st Floor
New York, NY 10017
800-729-1726 or 212-687-4981
fax: 212-949-5946

SOURCES:
AnnivHol-1983, p. 137
Chases-1996, p. 432

♦ 1711 ♦ St. Vincent's Day
January 22

São Vicente is the patron saint of Lisbon, Portugal. One story has it that he was murdered by Saracens (Islamic Arabs) from the Algarve region of Spain in 1173 (according to legend, the boat carrying the saint's coffin was guided up the river Tagus to Lisbon by two ravens, an event which is depicted in Lisbon's coat of arms). St. Vincent of Saragossa, however, was a deacon who, arrested along with Bishop Valerius, was tortured and martyred in Spain under Diocletian's authority around the year 304; his feast day is January 22.

In any case, St. Vincent's Day is celebrated with processions and prayers in Lisbon, but there are a number of folk traditions associated with this day in the surrounding rural areas. Farmers believe that by carrying a resin torch to the top of a high hill on January 22, they can predict what the coming harvest will be like. If the wind extinguishes the flame, the crops will be abundant; if it continues to burn, a poor growing season lies ahead.

CONTACT:
Portuguese National Tourist
  Office
590 Fifth Ave., 4th Floor
New York, NY 10036
212-354-4403; fax: 212-764-6137

SOURCES:
Chases-1996, p. 73
FestWestEur-1958, p. 161

♦ 1712 ♦ St. Vitus's Day
June 15

According to legend, St. Vitus was raised as a Christian by his nurse and his foster father. All three suffered persecution and were eventually put to death for their beliefs around 303, when Vitus was still a young boy. A chapel was later built in his honor at Ulm, Germany, and it was believed that anyone who danced before his shrine there on June 15, St. Vitus's Day, would be assured of good health in the coming year. Whether the motions of the enthusiastic dancers resembled the symptoms of those suffering from any of the diseases known as chorea, or whether people who suffered from disorders of the nervous system were often miraculously cured at the shrine is not known for certain, but chorea is commonly referred to as "St. Vitus's dance" for the violent motions that accompany the disease. St. Vitus is the patron saint not only of those suffering from epilepsy and other disorders of the nervous system, but of actors and dancers as well.

SOURCES:
AnnivHol-1983, p. 80
DaysCustFaith-1957, p. 145
DictMyth-1962, vol. II, p. 1383
SaintFestCh-1904, p. 290

♦ 1713 ♦ Sallah (Salah) Festival
Tenth day of Islamic month of Dhu al-Hijjah

An occasion of much pomp and ceremony in Nigeria, celebrating the culmination of the Muslim PILGRIMAGE TO MECCA and a day of communal prayer. People throng together in their best regalia. Processions of nobles on horseback are led by the emir to the prayer grounds. After a prayer service, the emir, dressed in white and carrying the historic Sword of Katsina, is seated in state on a platform. Groups of men take turns galloping up, reining in so their horses rear up at the last moment, and salute the emir. He raises the sword in response. Later, there is entertainment by musicians, acrobats, jesters, and dancers. Niger and some other African countries also celebrate the day with elaborate festivities.

CONTACT:
Nigerian Embassy
1333 16th St., N.W.
Washington, D.C. 20036
202-986-8400; fax: 202-775-1385

Niger Embassy
2204 R St., N.W.
Washington, D.C. 20008
202-483-4224; fax: 202-483-3169

SOURCES:
FolkWrldHol-1992, p. 332

♦ 1714 ♦ Salvation Army Founder's Day
April 10

April 10 is the day on which William Booth (1829–1912), founder of the international religious and charitable movement known as the Salvation Army, was born in Nottingham, England. His work as a pawnbroker in London acquainted Booth with all forms of human misery and economic suffering, and his conversion to Methodism led to a career as a Methodist lay preacher and eventually as an independent evangelist. With the help of his wife, Catherine Mumford, he established the East London Revival Society, which soon became known as the Christian Mission and later the Salvation Army, characterized by its military ranks, uniforms, flags, bands, and regulation books. Booth's work encompassed social reform as well as religious conversion, and he set up children's and maternity homes, food and shelter stations, and agencies for helping discharged criminals. The Salvation Army expanded to the United States in 1880, and today it has outposts in more than 80 countries.

Although Booth's birthday is observed to varying degrees at Salvation Army outposts around the world, a major celebration was held on the organization's centennial in 1965. In the

United States there were open houses at Salvation Army institutions, special commemorative religious services, and other anniversary events. In London, a centennial congress was held in the Royal Albert Hall. The Salvation Army regards 1865 as the year of its founding because on July 2 that year, William Booth first preached at an open-air meeting in London's East End, a slum district notorious for its poverty and crime rate.

CONTACT:
Salvation Army
P.O. Box 269
Alexandria, VA 22313
703-684-5500; fax: 703-684-3478

SOURCES:
AmerBkDays-1978, p. 337
AnnivHol-1983, p. 50
Chases-1996, p. 165
DictWrldRel-1989, p. 646
RelHolCal-1993, p. 112

♦ 1715 ♦ Salzburg Festival
July–August

Although the city of Salzburg, Austria, did little to honor its most famous native son during his lifetime, it has been making up for the oversight ever since. The Salzburg Festival is so closely identified with Wolfgang Amadeus Mozart that it is often referred to simply as the **Mozart Festival**. Although it features musical events by a wide variety of composers and performances by internationally celebrated musicians, conductors, singers and instrumentalists, the festival has always paid special homage to Mozart—especially so in 1991 during the Mozart bicentennial celebration.

The festival takes place at the end of July and through most of August at different venues throughout the city. Most of the operatic and large orchestral pieces are performed in the Festspielhaus, while other performances take place in the Landestheater. Some concerts and sacred music, such as Masses, are presented in the Salzburg Cathedral, which boasts a 4,000-pipe organ, or in the Abbey of St. Peter's. The finest church music can be heard at the Franziskanerkirche, where Masses are performed on Sundays with orchestra and choir. Chamber music concerts are usually given in the hall of the Mozarteum, and the Residenz is the scene for serenade concerts held by candlelight. Visits to Mozart's birthplace at Getreidegasse 9 are especially popular during the festival.

See also MOZART FESTIVAL; MOZART WEEK; and MOZART, WOLFGANG AMADEUS, BIRTHDAY OF

CONTACT:
Austrian National Tourist Office
P.O. Box 1142, Times Square
New York, NY 10148
212-944-6880; fax: 212-730-4568

SOURCES:
AnnivHol-1983, p. 181
GdWrldFest-1985, p. 13
IntlThFolk-1979, p. 39
MusFestEurBrit-1980, p. 25
MusFestWrld-1963, p. 79

♦ 1716 ♦ Samhain (Samain)
November 1

This ancient Celtic harvest festival honored Saman, the lord of the dead, at the beginning of winter. According to Celtic folklore, this was the day when the souls of all those who had died in the previous year would gather—thus giving rise to the fears about ghosts and goblins that we now associate with HALLOWEEN, or Samhain Eve. On this day the entrances to burial caves were left open to allow the spirits to come out for an airing. In Celtic mythology, this is the day in which winter giants expelled the fertility gods.

SOURCES:
AmerBkDays-1978, p. 968

BkHolWrld-1986, Oct 31,
Nov 1
DictFolkMyth-1984, pp. 202,
968
FestSaintDays-1915, p. 191
FolkWrldHol-1992, p. 524
RelHolCal-1993, pp. 64, 112

♦ 1717 ♦ Samil-jol (Independence Movement Day)
March 1

A national holiday in Korea to celebrate the anniversary of the independence demonstrations in 1919 protesting the Japanese occupation. (*Samil* means 'three-one,' signifying third month, first day.) Japan had taken over Korea in 1910, depriving Koreans of many of their freedoms. The March 1 movement was a turning point; an estimated two million people took to the streets in peaceful demonstrations, and a declaration of independence was read at a rally in Seoul. The demonstrations were met with thousands of arrests, and close to 23,000 Koreans were killed or wounded. Independence leaders formed a provisional government abroad, and there were major anti-Japanese rallies in the 1920s, but independence didn't come until 1945 with Japan's surrender and the end of World War II. The day is marked with the reading of the 1919 Declaration of Independence at Pagoda Park in Seoul.

See also KOREA LIBERATION DAY

CONTACT:
Korea National Tourism Corp.
205 N. Michigan Ave., Ste. 2212
Chicago, IL 60601
312-819-2560; fax: 312-819-2563

SOURCES:
AnnivHol-1983, p. 31
Chases-1996, p. 117

♦ 1718 ♦ San Antonio, Fiesta
Ten days including April 21

A 10-day extravaganza of events held since 1901 in San Antonio, Tex., including SAN JACINTO DAY, April 21. The fiesta celebrates the 1836 Battle of San Jacinto that won Texas' independence from Mexico, and is much more than a simple independence celebration. The distinctive highlight of the fiesta is the Battle of Flowers Parade alongside the Alamo. Merrymakers originally pelted each other with flowers, but now people crush *cascarones*, decorated eggshells filled with confetti, on each others' heads. Another focal event is "A Night in Old San Antonio," which brings thousands into La Villita—'the little town,' the earliest residential area of the city, now restored—for block dancing and more than 200 booths selling all kinds of ethnic foods. Some 150 other events include concerts, flower and fashion shows, art fairs, a *charreada* (Mexican rodeo), dances and pageants with people in lavish costume, torchlit floats in the Fiesta Flambeau Parade, and decorated barges in the San Antonio River Parade.

CONTACT:
San Antonio Convention and Visitors Bureau
121 Alamo Pl.
San Antonio, TX 78205
800-447-3372 or 210-270-8700
fax: 210-270-8782

SOURCES:
AmerBkDays-1978, p. 365
Chases-1996, p. 176
GdUSFest-1984, p. 186

♦ 1719 ♦ **Sandcastle Days**
Usually July

A cash-prize arts competition in the most ephemeral of media, sand and water, held since 1981 in Imperial Beach, Calif. Close to 250,000 spectators come for the parade, the food booths, the fireworks, the band concert—and the sandcastle building. This is no child's play; about 400 amateur and professional contestants compete for cash prizes totaling $19,000. Professionals make money building huge sand castles in malls and hotels.

There are specific rules regarding the construction of the castles: no adhesives can be used, but water spray rigs are allowed to keep the art works from drying out and blowing away; teams can number up to 10, but no substitutions are permitted.

In the past, the sand sculptures have represented assorted animals from the nearby San Diego Zoo, including hippos, lions, elephants, and creatures of the sea. One "castle" was a sand sofa with a sand man seated on it, a sand dog by his side, a sand television set, and a sand beer can. The sculpting is always scheduled for a Sunday, and by Sunday night the elaborate works of art, some 14 feet long, are lost to high tide.

The date of the festival is set through checking oceanographic tide tables to make sure the sculpting happens on a day when the tide is lower than normal. Events preceding the Sunday competition are a casual-dress Sandcastle Ball on Friday night, a community breakfast, parade, children's sand-sculpting contest, art exhibits, and fireworks. On Sunday, there's nothing but sculpting and live music.

CONTACT:
California Division of Tourism
801 K Street, Ste. 1600
Sacramento, CA 95814
800-862-2543 or 916-322-2881
fax: 916-322-3402

Sandhill Crane Migration
See **Crane Watch**

♦ 1720 ♦ **San Estevan, Feast of**
September 2

A harvest dance and annual feast day in the Indian pueblo of Acoma in New Mexico. Acoma is a cluster of adobes atop a barren mesa 367 feet above a valley. It was established in the 12th century and is the oldest continuously inhabited community in America. Only about 50 people now live there year-round, but Acoma people from nearby villages return for feast days and celebrations.

The mesa is dominated by the mission church of San Estevan del Rey, which was completed in 1640 under the direction of Friar Juan Ramirez. All the building materials, including massive logs for the roof, had to be carried from the valley below. Supposedly Friar Juan had gained both the confidence of the Acoma people and access to the mesa by saving an infant from a fall off the mesa's edge. His delivery of the child back to the mother was considered a miracle.

A mass and procession begin the feast day. The statue of the patron saint, ST. STEPHEN (San Estevan in Spanish) is taken from the church to the plaza where the dances are performed

from 9:00 A.M. to 5:00 P.M. There are 15 or so different dances—Bear, Butterfly, and Rainbow are some of them.

Acoma also has two rooster pulls, one in June and one in July. These are religious sacrificial ceremonies, during which prayers are offered for rain, for persons who need help, and for the country. Animal rights activists have protested the sacrificial aspect of these rites.

CONTACT:
Acoma Pueblo
P.O. Box 309
Acomita, NM 87034
505-552-6604

SOURCES:
IndianAmer-1989, pp. 288, 294
RelHolCal-1993, p. 113

♦ 1721 ♦ **San Fermin Festival**
July 6–14

The festivities surrounding this well-known festival in Pamplona, Spain, honoring the city's bishop, begin with a rocket fired from the balcony of the town hall. Bands of *txistularis* (a Basque word pronounced chees-too-LAH-rees)—with dancers, drummers, and *txistu* players (a musical instrument like a flute)—and bagpipers march through the town and its suburbs playing songs announcing the "running of the bulls," an event that has taken place here for 400 years. Each morning, young men, dressed in typical Basque costumes, risk their lives running through the streets of Pamplona ahead of the bulls being run to the bullring where the bullfights will be held. Perhaps the best-known portrayal of this scene occurs in Ernest Hemingway's novel, *The Sun Also Rises*.

CONTACT:
Tourist Office of Spain
665 Fifth Ave.
New York, NY 10022
212-759-8822; fax: 212-980-1053

SOURCES:
AnnivHol-1983, p. 90
BkHolWrld-1986, Jul 7
FestWestEur-1958, p. 201
GdWrldFest-1985, p. 163

♦ 1722 ♦ **San Francisco's Day in Lima, Peru**
August 4 and October 4

On Santo Domingo's Day, August 4, and again on St. Francis's (San Francisco's) Day on October 4, there is a fiesta in Lima where the two saints and their churches exchange greetings. A procession sets out from each church, complete with its own music, major-domo, and image of the saint carried on a litter. The two groups meet in the plaza under a decorated triumphal arch, at which point the litters are lowered in commemoration of the historical meeting between the two men, who died only five years apart in the 13th century. Church bells ring and fireworks are set off, with elaborate banquets to follow at the monasteries of the saint whose day is being celebrated.

See also ST. FRANCIS OF ASSISI, FEAST DAY OF

CONTACT:
Embassy of Peru
1700 Massachusetts Ave., N.W.
Washington, D.C. 20036
202-833-9860; fax: 202-659-8124

SOURCES:
BkFestHolWrld-1970, p. 111
DictMyth-1962, vol. II, pp. 1368, 1369

♦ 1723 ♦ **San Gennaro, Feast of**
September 19

San Gennaro, or St. Januarius, fourth-century bishop of

Benevento, is the patron saint of Naples. According to legend, he survived being thrown into a fiery furnace and then a den of wild beasts, but was eventually beheaded during the reign of Diocletian. His body was brought to Naples, along with a vial containing some of his blood. The congealed blood, preserved since that time in the Cathedral of San Gennaro, is claimed to liquefy on the anniversary of his death each year—an event that has drawn crowds to Naples since 1389. Scientists have recently come up with a possible explanation for the phenomenon: certain substances, including some types of mayonnaise, are normally thick gels that can be liquefied instantly by shaking or stirring. Left standing, such liquids soon revert to gels. The answer may never be known because, to date, the Roman Catholic Church has forbidden opening the vial and analyzing its chemical nature.

The Society of San Gennaro in New York City's "Little Italy" section has been holding its own San Gennaro festival on Mulberry Street since 1925. The 11-day event attracts up to three million spectators. It includes a procession carrying a bust of St. Januarius from the society's storefront headquarters to a shrine on the corner of Hester and Mulberry streets as well as a street fair. One of the goals of the event is to find a mate for the festival queen, who more often than not has married within two years after her festival reign.

See also HOLY BLOOD, PROCESSION OF THE

CONTACT:
Italian Government Travel Office
630 Fifth Ave.
New York, NY 10111
212-245-4822

New York Convention and Visitors Bureau
2 Columbus Cir.
New York, NY 10019
800-692-8474 or 212-484-1200
fax: 212-247-6193

SOURCES:
AnnivHol-1983, p. 120
Chases-1996, p. 383
DaysCustFaith-1957, p. 238
DictMyth-1962, vol. II, p. 1372
FolkAmerHol-1991, p. 345
GdUSFest-1984, p. 125

♦ 1724 ♦ **San Geronimo Feast Day**
September 29–30

The feast day for St. Jerome, the patron saint of Taos Pueblo, probably the best known of the 19 Indian pueblos (villages) in New Mexico. For 1,000 years, the Tiwa-speaking Taos Indians have lived at or near the present pueblo. In the 1540s, Spanish soldiers arrived, thinking they had discovered one of the lost cities of gold. The gold-brown adobe, multi-story structures are the largest existing pueblo structures of their kind in the U.S., unchanged from the way they looked to the Spaniards, and are still the home of about 1,500 residents.

The feast day commences on the evening of Sept. 29 with a sundown dance, followed by vespers in the San Geronimo Mission. On the following day, there are foot races in the morning, and in the afternoon, frightening looking "clowns" with black-and-white body paint and wearing black-and-white costumes climb a pole; the act has secret religious significance to the Taos. An Indian trade fair offers Indian crafts and foods for sale.

The Taos pueblo is also known for its CHRISTMAS celebrations, lasting from Christmas Eve through Dec. 29. On CHRISTMAS EVE, there is a pine torch procession from the church through the plaza, and on Christmas Day, the Deer Dance is often performed.

CONTACT:
Taos Pueblo
P.O. Box 1846
Taos, NM 87571
505-758-8626

SOURCES:
Chases-1996, p. 395
IndianAmer-1989, pp. 289, 319

♦ 1725 ♦ **Sanghamita Day**
May–June; full moon of Hindu month of Jyestha

Observed by Buddhists in Sri Lanka (formerly Ceylon), this day celebrates the arrival of Sanghamita, daughter of Emperor Asoka of India, in 288 B.C. According to legend, Buddhism was first brought to Sri Lanka by a group of missionaries led by Mahinda, Asoka's son. Mahinda later sent for his sister, Sanghamita, who arrived with a branch from the Bodhi tree at Gaya, sacred to Buddhists as the tree under which the Buddha was sitting when he attained Enlightenment. The sapling was planted in the royal city of Anuradhapura, where Sanghamita founded an order of nuns. Buddhists still make pilgrimages to the city on this day to see what is believed to be the oldest documented tree in the world.

See also POSON

CONTACT:
Sri Lankan Embassy
2148 Wyoming Ave., N.W.
Washington, D.C. 20008
202-483-4025; fax: 202-232-7181

SOURCES:
BkHolWrld-1986, Dec 2

♦ 1726 ♦ **Sango Festival**
Early November

Sango has an extremely prominent cult among the Oyo people of Nigeria. Because Sango, a former Oyo ruler, is identified with thunder and lightning, the festival held in his honor takes place toward the end of the rainy season in early November and features various ceremonies connected with rain magic.

On the first day of the seven-day festival, women form a procession to the river, where they sink a hollow calabash gourd filled with special medicines to mark the beginning of the dry season. The *Timi*, or king, meets the worshippers at a place near the river, accompanied by drummers, trumpeters, and a huge crowd of onlookers. The women of the palace put on a special musical performance praising all the tribe's rulers throughout its history. The remainder of the week is devoted to similar performances of music and dance before the Timi, although their real purpose is to please and entertain the god Sango. The main performer each day dances in a self-induced trance-like state, during which it is believed that he speaks with the voice of Sango and is impervious to pain. The festival concludes on the seventh day with a procession of fire in which a worshipper carries a large pot containing a sacred flame that brings blessing to all parts of the village.

CONTACT:
Nigerian Embassy
1333 16th St., N.W.
Washington, D.C. 20036
202-986-8400; fax: 202-775-1385

SOURCES:
FolkWrldHol-1992, p. 534

♦ 1727 ♦ **San Isidro of Seville, Feast of**
April 4

St. Isidore (c. 560–636), bishop of Seville was born in Cartagena, Spain, and eventually succeeded his brother, St. Leander, as bishop of Seville. Among his accomplishments were the founding of schools throughout the country and the compilation of a 20-volume encyclopedia of all the knowledge available at that time in Europe, the *Etymologies*. His feast day is celebrated not only in Spain, but in many Latin American countries as well.

In Río Frío, Colombia, the beginning of April is usually the end of the dry season. On San Isidro's feast day, April 4, the saint's image is carried through town with all the townspeople following and singing his praises, in the hope that he will produce a much-needed rainfall, or at least a shower, before the procession is over. To give the saint as much time as possible to work his miracle, those participating in the procession take two steps forward and one backward. If, after several trips around the town, it has still not started to rain, the people who were chanting his praises begin to reproach him. The procession continues, and eventually the reproaches turn to loud complaints and often profanity. If the entire day passes without rain, San Isidro is returned to his niche for another year.

CONTACT:
Colombian Embassy
2118 Leroy Pl., N.W.
Washington, D.C. 20008
202-387-8338; fax: 202-232-8643

SOURCES:
FolkWrldHol-1992, p. 231

♦ 1728 ♦ San Isidro the Farmer, Feast of
May 15

The **Feast of St. Isidore the Ploughman** is celebrated in Madrid, Spain, with eight days of bullfighting at the Plaza de Toros, colorful parades, and many artistic, cultural, and sporting events. Street vendors sell pictures of the saint, small glass or pottery bells believed to ward off harm from thunder and lightning, and whistle-stemmed glass roses, which provide a noisy accompaniment to the feasting and dancing that go on.

San Isidro (c. 1070–1130) is the patron saint of Madrid and also of farmers. He worked on a farm outside Madrid. According to legend, one day, as his master was spying on him to see how hard he was working, an angel and a yoke of white oxen appeared at Isidro's side. He was canonized in 1622, and local farmers still attend a special mass on his feast day, May 15. The Festival of San Isidro is celebrated in other Spanish towns as well, particularly Leon and Alicante.

San Isidro is also the patron saint of Saipan, capital of the Northern Mariana Islands in the western Pacific Ocean near Guam. While dance groups practice, men form hunting and fishing parties to provide food, and youth organizations clean and prepare the festival site. The fiesta begins at the end of a novena (nine days of prayers and special religious services). It features games of skill and traditional dances with prizes for the winners, and a great variety of foods.

Philippine towns and villages also commemorate St. Isidro. They bathe and scrub their water buffalo (*carabaos*), manicure the animals' hooves, braid their tails with ribbons, and decorate their bodies with bunting and more ribbons. The water buffalo are brought to the plaza in front of the church and kneel (having been taught by their owners) for the priest's blessing. Then everyone goes to the fiesta site for carabao races and tricks, and lots of food and fun. In Quezon Province ornaments made from rice meal dyed in bright colors, called *kiping*, are attached to the fronts of houses. Townspeople and the priest parade through town and when that's over, the kiping are eaten.

See also CARABAO FESTIVAL and ST. ISIDORE, FESTIVAL OF

CONTACT:
Tourist Office of Spain
665 Fifth Ave.
New York, NY 10022
212-759-8822; fax: 212-980-1053

SOURCES:
BkFest-1937, p. 302
FestWestEur-1958, p. 195
FolkWrldHol-1992, p. 298
GdWrldFest-1985, p. 153
IntlThFolk-1979, p. 272

♦ 1729 ♦ San Jacinto Day
April 21

Fresh from his March 1836 victory at the Battle of the Alamo (*see* ALAMO DAY), General Antonio López de Santa Anna (1795?–1876) of Mexico proceeded eastward until he encountered the Texan army general, Samuel Houston (1793–1863), at a place called San Jacinto, about 22 miles east of the present-day city of Houston. Raising the now familiar cry of "Remember the Alamo!" Houston's 900 soldiers defeated the Mexican force of nearly 1,600 in a battle that lasted only 18 minutes. Santa Anna was taken prisoner and forced to sign a treaty pledging his help in securing independence for Texas, which was annexed by the United States in 1845.

A legal holiday in Texas, San Jacinto Day is celebrated throughout the state but particularly in San Antonio, where the highpoint of the 10-day SAN ANTONIO FIESTA is the huge Battle of Flowers parade winding through miles of the city's downtown streets.

CONTACT:
Texas Department of Commerce
Tourism Division
1700 N. Congress, Ste. 200
Austin, TX 78711
800-888-8839 or 512-462-9191
fax: 512-936-0089

SOURCES:
AmerBkDays-1978, p. 364
AnnivHol-1983, p. 54
Chases-1996, p. 181
DaysCustFaith-1957, p. 97
DictDays-1988, p. 108

♦ 1730 ♦ Sanja Matsuri (Three Shrines Festival)
Weekend near May 18

One of the most spectacular festivals in Tokyo, Japan, honoring Kannon, the goddess of mercy (known as Kuan Yin in Chinese), and three fishermen brothers who founded the Asakusa Kannon Temple in the 14th century. *Sanja* means 'three shrines,' and, according to legend, after the brothers discovered a statue of Kannon in the Sumida River, their spirits were enshrined in three places. The festival has been held each year since the late 1800s on a weekend near May 18. Activities are focused on the Asakusa Temple and Tokyo's "Shitamachi," or downtown area.

More than 100 portable shrines called *mikoshi*, which weigh up to two tons and are surmounted by gold phoenixes, are paraded through the streets to the gates of the temple. Carrying them are men in *happi* coats—the traditional short laborers' jackets—worn to advertise their districts. There are also priests on horseback, musicians playing "sanja-bayashi" festival music, and dancers in traditional costume. On Sunday, various dances are performed.

See also GODDESS OF MERCY, BIRTHDAY OF THE

CONTACT:
Japan National Tourist
  Organization
630 Fifth Ave., Ste. 2101
New York, NY 10111
212-757-5640; fax: 212-307-6754

SOURCES:
JapanFest-1965, p. 152

♦ 1731 ♦ San Juan and San Pedro Festivals
June 24; June 29

The celebrations of St. John's Day (June 24) and St. Peter's Day (June 29) in Paraguay have much in common. The religious part of both celebrations involves a mass (and, a religious procession on St. Peter's Day), but it is the games that are played on these two days that set them apart from other religious festivals in Paraguay. There is a simulated bullfight in which the *toro candil* (a man wearing a hide-covered frame with a bull's skull attached to the front) chases the *cambá,* people with drums and flutes who taunt the bull and play their instruments. His horns are covered in kerosene-soaked rags and set on fire, so that when darkness falls and he chases spectators through the streets, the flaming horns make the game more exciting.

Two other costumed figures that play a part in the game include a *ñandú guazú* (a rhea, which is similar to an ostrich) and someone playing the role of a Guaycurú Indian dressed in rags with a blackened face. The *ñandú*—actually a child inside a small cage covered with leaves to represent feathers and a long stick for a neck—follows the bull around, bobbing its neck up and down and pecking at the toro from behind. The Guaycurú chases the women around and pretends to kidnap them. Other participants in the festival chase women with blazing torches—a remnant, perhaps, of the ancient festivals observed on June 24 with bonfires and the practice of walking barefoot over live coals (*see also* Midsummer Day and St. John's Eve in Paraguay).

CONTACT:
Paraguayan Embassy
2400 Massachusetts Ave., N.W.
Washington, D.C. 20008
202-483-6960; fax: 202-234-4508

SOURCES:
FolkWrldHol-1992, pp. 339,
  345

San Juan Bautista Festival
See St. John's Day, Puerto Rican Celebrations of

San Juan Day
See St. John's Day, Puerto Rican Celebrations of

♦ 1732 ♦ San Juan Pueblo Feast Day
June 24

A day to honor St. John the Baptist, the patron saint of the San Juan Pueblo, near Espanola, New Mexico. The pueblo, where the first New Mexican capital was founded by the Spaniards in 1598, is headquarters today for the Eight Northern Indian Pueblos Council.

The San Juan feast day observations, like those of other New Mexican pueblos, combines Roman Catholic ritual with traditional Indian ceremonies.

The celebration begins on the evening of June 23 with vespers and mass in the Church of St. John the Baptist. After the services, St. John's statue is carried to a shrine prepared for it in the pueblo's plaza. This procession is followed by a one-mile run in which anyone can participate; a "sing" by the pueblo war chiefs, or officers; a procession of singers and runners; and two Buffalo dances, each presented by two men and one woman wearing buffalo costumes.

The actual feast day begins with a mass, and is followed by an assortment of dances, which usually include Buffalo, Comanche, and Green Corn (harvest) dances. Men beat drums and chant as the dancers, arrayed in long lines and wearing body paint and elaborate costumes with feathers and beads, move slowly and rhythmically to the beat. Vendors sell jewelry, crafts, and assorted souvenirs, and a carnival with a ferris wheel and carousel is also part of the celebration.

See also St. John's Day

CONTACT:
San Juan Pueblo
P.O. Box 1099
San Juan Pueblo, NM 87566
505-852-4400 or 505-852-4213

SOURCES:
AmerBkDays-1978, p. 590
FolkAmerHol-1991, p. 250
IndianAmer-1989, pp. 286,
  312

♦ 1733 ♦ San Martín Day
August 17

This national holiday in Argentina commemorates the death of José Francisco de San Martín, who died on this day in 1850.

Spain had ruled what is now Argentina, as well as nearly all the rest of South and Central America, since the 16th century. Born in 1778 in a town called Yapeyú, San Martín, formerly a soldier in the Spanish army in Europe, came home in 1812 to fight in the revolution against Spain. He led forces across the Andes—an unprecedented accomplishment—to defeat the Spanish in Chile and Peru. The victories he led assured independence from Spain for much of the region.

After passing the torch to Simon Bolívar, another famous South American revolutionary leader (*see also* Bolivia Independence Day), San Martín resigned in 1822. He left Argentina in 1824, and lived out his life in exile in France.

CONTACT:
Argentina National Tourist Office
12 W. 56th St.
New York, NY 10019
212-603-0443; fax: 212-315-5545

SOURCES:
AnnivHol-1983, p. 108

♦ 1734 ♦ San Miguel, Fiesta de
September 29

On St. Michael's Day in Taypi, Bolivia, there is a fiesta that demonstrates the importance of both maintaining and crossing the boundaries that exist between communities. Two dance groups—one from Taypi and the other from Ranikera, about three hours walking distance away—meet in the town square for religious ceremonies and dance performances, although the two groups perform simultaneously rather than together. Throughout the fiesta the two groups socialize, eat, and rest separately, withdrawing to opposite corners of the square in order to be as far away from each other as possible. Five communal meals are served, with dancing in between, while spectators from the adjoining towns watch from outside the adobe wall surrounding the square.

CONTACT:
Bolivian Embassy
3014 Massachusetts Ave., N.W.
Washington, D.C. 20008
202-483-4410; fax: 202-328-3712

SOURCES:
FolkWrldHol-1992, p. 491

Santacruzan
See **Exaltation of the Cross**

♦ 1735 ♦ **Santa Fe, Fiesta de**
September, weekend after Labor Day

A religious and secular festival said (without much argument) to be the oldest such event in the country. It dates to 1712 and recalls the early history of Santa Fe, New Mexico.

The Spanish *conquistadores* were ousted from Santa Fe in 1680 in a revolt by the Pueblo Indians. Led by Don Diego de Vargas, the Spanish peacefully regained control in 1693. Vargas had promised to honor *La Conquistadora*, the small statue of the Virgin Mary that is now enshrined in St. Francis Cathedral, if she granted them success. The first procession was held in 1712 to fulfill that promise.

The festivities start with a mass early on the Friday morning after LABOR DAY. Then comes the grand procession: Vargas and the fiesta queen, *la reina*, lead the way on horseback to the town plaza, escorted by the *Caballeros de Vargas*, Vargas's guards or manservants who are also on horseback.

Friday night brings the burning of Zozobra, or Old Man Gloom, a 44-foot-high fabric and wood effigy whose yearly immolation began in 1926. Thousands watch and shout "Burn him!" when the effigy groans and asks for mercy. Fireworks announce the end of Gloom, and then spectators make their way to the plaza for the start of two days of dancing, street fairs, a grand ball, and a parade with floats satirizing local politicians. The fiesta ends Sunday night with a mass of thanksgiving and a candlelight procession to the Cross of Martyrs overlooking Santa Fe.

CONTACT:
Santa Fe Convention and Visitors
  Bureau
P. O. Box 909
Santa Fe, NM 87504
800-777-2489 or 505-984-6760
fax: 505-984-6679

SOURCES:
AmerBkDays-1978, p. 800
RelHolCal-1993, p. 113

♦ 1736 ♦ **Santa Fe Chamber Music Festival**
June–August, seven weeks

A festival in Santa Fe, N.M., that started in 1973 and has since produced a range of musical programs from the baroque to the modern. The festival began impressively: the acclaimed cellist Pablo CASALS was the first honorary president, and artist Georgia O'Keeffe produced the first of her now-famous posters and program covers. Fourteen artists presented six Sunday concerts that first year; now about 70 musicians of international acclaim take part. Youth concerts, open rehearsals, in-state tours to Indian reservations and small communities, out-of-state tours, and National Public Radio broadcasts have expanded the audiences.

Santa Fe, with its ancient tri-ethnic culture, has a great roster of historic buildings, and from time to time they serve as concert halls. For instance, chamber music concerts have been presented in the Romanesque Cathedral of St. Francis,

built in 1869; the Palace of the Governors, in continuous use since 1610; and the 18th-century Santuario de Nuestra Señora de Guadalupe, where altar bells rather than dimming lights signal the end of intermissions.

CONTACT:
Santa Fe Convention and Visitors
  Bureau
P. O. Box 909
Santa Fe, NM 87504
800-777-2489 or 505-984-6760
fax: 505-984-6679

SOURCES:
Chases-1996, p. 289
GdUSFest-1984, p. 121
MusFestAmer-1990, p. 95

♦ 1737 ♦ **Santa Fe Opera Festival**
July–August

An internationally acclaimed opera festival that began in 1957, survived the burning of the opera house in 1967, and is now staged in an open-air opera "house" atop a mesa outside Santa Fe, New Mexico. The stage is seven miles from Santa Fe, and the city lights are so distinct in the clear mountain air that they sometimes become part of the operatic scenery. Old classics, rarely performed old operas, and premieres are all presented.

The Gala Opening Celebration includes an Opera Ball to benefit apprentice programs for young artists, and, on opening night, a festive reception, tailgate parties (with tablecloths and caviar and people in formal dress) and, after the performance, waltzing for the entire audience.

CONTACT:
Santa Fe Convention and Visitors
  Bureau
P. O. Box 909
Santa Fe, NM 87504
800-777-2489 or 505-984-6760
fax: 505-984-6679

SOURCES:
GdUSFest-1984, p. 121
MusFestAmer-1990, p. 172
MusFestWrld-1963, p. 273

♦ 1738 ♦ **Santa Isobel, Fiesta of**
July 4

Santa Isobel is the great fiesta of the Yaqui Indians of southern Arizona and Mexico, observed on July 4. It features the coyote dance—a ceremonial dance performed for soldiers, chiefs, and pueblo officials who have died, as well as at certain specific fiestas. Three men, each wearing the head and hide of a coyote and holding a bow which they strike with a piece of cane, perform a slow step in a crouching position, stamping the ground with the flat of their feet to the accompaniment of a water drum. All night long the dancers advance toward and retreat from the drum, their motions mimicking those of a coyote. Just before dawn, a plate of meat is placed in front of each of the dancers. Each man picks the meat up in his teeth, just as a coyote would, and delivers it to the drum.

CONTACT:
Pascua Yaqui Tribal Council
7474 S. Camino de Oeste
Tucson, AZ 85746
602-883-2838

SOURCES:
DictFolkMyth-1984, p. 258

♦ 1739 ♦ **Santander International Festival of Music and Dance**
July–August

Santander, a resort town in northern Spain on the Atlantic coast, is not only a popular summer vacation destination but the home of an international music and dance festival that has been held there since 1951. The 37-day festival offers symphonic, choral, and chamber music; recitals; classical and Spanish dance; and jazz. Although the programs are chosen more for their broad appeal than for their adventurousness, some of the great international ensembles of the world have performed at Santander. Symphony orchestra and dance concerts are held in the floodlit Porticada Plaza in the center of the town, where a huge tent is set up for the festival and seating for 3,000 is available. Smaller concerts and recitals are held in the 14th-century Gothic cloister of the Cathedral of Santander.

CONTACT:
Tourist Office of Spain
665 Fifth Ave.
New York, NY 10022
212-759-8822; fax: 212-980-1053

SOURCES:
GdWrldFest-1985, p. 163
IntlThFolk-1979, p. 341
MusFestEurBrit-1980, p. 137
MusFestWrld-1963, p. 169

♦ 1740 ♦ Sant' Efisio, Festival of
Early May

Although nearly every town and village in Sardinia, Italy, has its own festival, one of the most important is the **Sagra di Sant' Efisio** at Cagliari, which commemorates the martyrdom of a third-century Roman general who was converted to Christianity. In early May a procession accompanies a statue of St. Efisio, Sardinia's patron saint, through the streets of Cagliari to the church of Pula, the town where he suffered martyrdom. Three days later the statue returns to Cagliari. Several thousand pilgrims on foot, in carts, or on horseback, wearing costumes that date from the 17th century and earlier, take part in the procession, which culminates in a parade down Cagliari's main avenue that is said to rival the parade on ST. PATRICK'S DAY in New York City.

CONTACT:
Italian Government Travel Office
630 Fifth Ave.
New York, NY 10111
212-245-4822

SOURCES:
Chases-1996, p. 193
IntlThFolk-1979, p. 241

Santo Domingo's Day
See **San Francisco's Day in Lima, Peru**

♦ 1741 ♦ Sao Tome and Principe National Independence Day
July 12

On this day in 1975, Sao Tome and Principe gained official independence from Portugal, and became a democratic republic. July 12 is a national holiday in Sao Tome and Principe.

CONTACT:
Sao Tome and Principe Embassy
122 E. 42nd St., Rm. 1604
New York, NY 10168
212-697-4211; fax: 212-687-8389

SOURCES:
AnnivHol-1983, p. 92
Chases-1996, p. 293

♦ 1742 ♦ Sapporo Snow Festival (Yuki Matsuri)
February 5–11 (or February 6–12 if February 11 falls on a Saturday or Sunday)

An exuberant celebration of snow and ice held since 1950 in Sapporo, the capital city of the Japanese island of Hokkaido. In 1974 the first international Snow Statue Contest was held. The week's activities feature a colorful parade and competi-

tive events in winter sports. What particularly draws more than two million tourists, though, is the display of colossal ice sculptures along the main street and snow statues in Odori Park.

Because of the shortage of snow in the festival area, thousands of tons of snow are trucked in from the suburbs. The sculptures are spectacular—intricately carved and often several stories high. About three weeks before the festival the work begins: a wooden frame is built and packed with snow; after the snow has hardened the frame is removed and the carving begins. A different theme is chosen each year for the sculptures.

CONTACT:
Japan National Tourist
   Organization
630 Fifth Ave., Ste. 2101
New York, NY 10111
212-757-5640; fax: 212-307-6754

SOURCES:
AnnivHol-1983, p. 182
BkHolWrld-1986, Feb 6
Chases-1996, p. 90
JapanFest-1965, p. 125

♦ 1743 ♦ Sarasota Circus Festival and Parade
First week in January

Colossal! Spectacular! Non-stop circus for the first days of the year in the capital of the circus world, Sarasota, Fla. The festival begins on NEW YEAR'S DAY at the Sarasota County Fairgrounds and continues for several days, the highlight being a parade in downtown Sarasota usually held on the first Sunday in January.

During the week, events include hourly shows of magic, juggling, clowning, dog stunts, knife throwing, and various other acts all day long. In addition, there are outdoor "thrill shows"—performers on high sway poles, on high wires, and on motorcycles on high wires. And there are displays of miniature circuses, arts and crafts, and a circus art and photography show. On two days, there are circus performances under the big top, in which performers compete against one another for cash prizes.

Sarasota was put on the circus map in 1927 when John Ringling, one of the founding Ringling brothers, decided to make Sarasota the winter headquarters for the Ringling Bros. and Barnum & Bailey Circus. They moved in 1960 to nearby Venice, but Sarasota was by then established as a circus mecca, and many circus people now make their year-round homes there. Furthermore, the city is home to the Circus Hall of Fame and the Ringling Museum of the Circus. John Ringling's palatial home, Ca' d'Zan, completed in 1925, can be seen there, along with the John and Mabel Ringling Museum of Art, which has a fine collection of the art work of Peter Paul Rubens.

CONTACT:
Florida Division of Tourism
126 W. Van Buren
Tallahassee, FL 32399
904-487-1462; fax: 904-921-9158

♦ 1744 ♦ Saratoga Festival
June–September

The Saratoga Performing Arts Center in Saratoga Springs, New York, is the summer home of the New York City Ballet, the Philadelphia Orchestra, and the Spa Summer Theater. The festival held there every summer includes not only performances by these groups but a four-week summer school program for talented high school students interested in dance, orchestra studies, and theater. Ballet and orchestral performances take place in a partially enclosed amphitheater, and visitors often arrive a few hours early to picnic on the grass and enjoy the spacious grounds of the Saratoga Spa State Park, where the center is located.

The Saratoga Festival has seen a number of world premieres, among them the 1976 premiere of Gian Carlo Menotti's first symphony (*see* SPOLETO USA) and the 1974 world premiere of the ballet, *Coppelia*. The summer theater performs both classical and contemporary plays in the center's 500-seat theater.

CONTACT:
Saratoga Performing Arts Center
Saratoga Springs, NY 12866
518-587-3330 (box office)
518-584-9330 (administration)
fax: 518-584-0809
  (administration)

SOURCES:
GdUSFest-1984, p. 130
MusFestAmer-1990, p. 110

Sarbatoarea Blajinilor
See **Blajini, Feast of the**

♦ 1745 ♦ Saturnalia
December 17–23

This ancient Roman WINTER SOLSTICE festival began on December 17 and lasted for seven days. It was held in honor of Saturn, the father of the gods, and was characterized by the suspension of discipline and reversal of the usual order. Grudges and quarrels were forgotten; businesses, courts, and schools closed down; wars were interrupted or postponed; slaves were served by their masters; and masquerading or change of dress between the sexes often occurred. It was traditional to offer gifts of imitation fruit (a symbol of fertility), dolls (symbolic of the custom of human sacrifice), and candles (reminiscent of the bonfires traditionally associated with pagan solstice celebrations). A mock king was chosen, usually from among a group of slaves or criminals, and although he was permitted to behave in an unrestrained manner for the seven days of the festival, he was usually killed at the end. Not surprisingly, the Saturnalia eventually degenerated into a week-long spree of debauchery and crime—giving rise to the modern use of the term *saturnalia* meaning 'a period of unrestrained license and revelry.'

SOURCES:
AmerBkDays-1978, p. 1069
BkDays-1864, vol. II, p. 745
DaysCustFaith-1957, p. 315
DictFolkMyth-1984, pp. 941, 974
DictWrldRel-1989, p. 182
FestSaintDays-1915, p. 232
RelHolCal-1993, p. 113
SaintFestCh-1904, p. 36

Sausage Fair
See **Bad Durkheim Wurstmarkt**

Sausage Festival
See **Wurstfest**

♦ 1746 ♦ Savitri-Vrata (Savitri Vow)
May–June; Hindu month of Jyestha

This day is observed by Hindu women in honor of the legendary princess Savitri, who loved her husband, Satyavan, so much that she refused to leave him when he died, eventually persuading Yama, King of Death, to give him back. Women whose husbands are alive spend the day fasting and praying, anointing their husbands' foreheads with sandalwood paste, and showering them with gifts of food and flowers. Women whose husbands have died beg to be delivered from the miseries of widowhood in a future existence. The *vrata*, or vow, is a ritual practice observed by Hindu women for a period of 14 years to obtain their wish.

SOURCES:
BkFest-1937, p. 158
FolkWrldHol-1992, p. 320
RelHolCal-1993, p. 120

♦ 1747 ♦ Savonlinna Opera Festival
July

A month-long music festival in Savonlinna, Finland. Considered one of Europe's most important musical events, it began in 1967 with a performance of Beethoven's *Fidelio*. In 1992, for its 25th anniversary, *Fidelio* was presented again, as well as George and Ira Gershwin's *Porgy and Bess*, produced by Opera Ebony of New York and conducted by Estonian maestro Eri Klas.

The main site of the festival is the Olavinlinna Castle, the best-preserved medieval fortress in Finland. It was built in 1475 and named by Swedes and Finns on the lookout for raiding Russian armies.

CONTACT:
Finnish Tourist Board
655 Third Ave., 18th Floor
New York, NY 10017
212-949-2333; fax: 212-983-5260

SOURCES:
Chases-1996, p. 286
GdWrldFest-1985, p. 78
MusFestEurBrit-1980, p. 70

Scaling the Walls
See **Escalade**

♦ 1748 ♦ Schäferlauf
August 24

St. Bartholomew's Day is celebrated in Markgröningen and other towns in the Swabia district of Germany with a barefoot race among the shepherds and shepherdesses of the Black Forest. The competition originally began as a demonstration that they could run faster than any sheep who might go astray. Today the boys and girls still race barefoot, and the winning shepherd and shepherdess are given a sheep or a large mutton roast. After the race there are other pastoral activities, such as a shepherds' dance and a water-carriers' race in which contestants must balance a pail of water on their heads and pour it into a tub at the finish line.

CONTACT:
German National Tourist Office
122 E. 42nd St., 52nd Floor
New York, NY 10168
212-661-7200; fax: 212-661-7174

SOURCES:
BkHolWrld-1986, Aug 24
FestWestEur-1958, p. 69

♦ 1749 ♦ Schemenlauf
Between January 26 and March 3; week preceding Ash Wednesday

The Schemenlauf, or **Running of the Spectres**, takes place during the CARNIVAL season at Imst, Austria, in the Tirolean Alps. The roots of this traditional Austrian celebration can be traced back to the Middle Ages, when people believed that the densely wooded mountain slopes were populated by good and evil spirits with the power to prevent or promote the growth of seeds in the ground. To ward off the evil spirits, they resorted to mummery and wore frightening masks (*see* PERCHTENLAUF) as they danced through the village making as much noise as they could. Originally the festival may have been a way of welcoming spring.

Only men are allowed to participate in the Schemenlauf at Imst. About 400 *Schemen* ('spectres') join the procession, often stopping to invite spectators to join them in the traditional circular dance. Visitors come from all over the world to see this colorful festival, which is followed by a night of revelry reminiscent of MARDI GRAS celebrations elsewhere.

CONTACT:
Austrian National Tourist Office
P.O. Box 1142, Times Square
New York, NY 10148
212-944-6880; fax: 212-730-4568

SOURCES:
BkFest-1937, p. 29

♦ 1750 ♦ Schiller Days
May

J. C. Friedrich von Schiller (1759–1805) was a leading German dramatist and poet, best known for such dramas as *Die Rauber* (The Robbers), the *Wallenstein* trilogy, *Maria Stuart*, and *Wilhelm Tell*. Every May since 1978, theater companies from Eastern and Western Europe have gathered in Mannheim, Germany, where Schiller's first play, *Die Rauber*, premiered in 1782, to present his works for the theater. The performances of Schiller's plays go on for five days, with several companies often producing the same work, giving both audiences and Schiller scholars an opportunity to compare and contrast differing interpretations.

See also TELL PLAY AT ALTDORF

CONTACT:
German National Tourist Office
122 E. 42nd St., 52nd Floor
New York, NY 10168
212-661-7200; fax: 212-661-7174

SOURCES:
IntlThFolk-1979, p. 143

♦ 1751 ♦ Schubertiade Hohenems
Mid-June for 16 days

When Austrian composer Franz Schubert (1797–1828) participated in concerts put on for a small group of friends and fans, these intimate gatherings became known as "Schubertiads." Since 1976, the 16-day festival in honor of Schubert's music known as Schubertiade Hohenems has attempted to recreate this tradition. Under the artistic direction of Hermann Prey, a 10-year cycle of Schubert's symphonies, songs, and piano concertos has been performed in the exact order in which they were composed, with chamber music, choral music, and operas performed in between. The concerts are given at the Palace of Hohenems in Hohenems, Austria, with the Alps rising in the background. A number of ensembles known for their interpretations of Schubert's work have participated in the festival, including the Brandeis Quartet, the Franz Schubert Quartet, the Amadeus Quartet, and the Vienna Philharmonic Orchestra.

CONTACT:
Austrian National Tourist Office
P.O. Box 1142, Times Square
New York, NY 10148
212-944-6880; fax: 212-730-4568

SOURCES:
MusFestEurBrit-1980, p. 27

♦ 1752 ♦ Schutzenfest (Marksmen's Festival)
July

This event in Germany is a tradition going back 400 years. There are a number of marksmen's festivals held during the summer months. The biggest of these, in Hanover, is held for 10 days at the beginning of July and attracts about 200,000 spectators. It features merry-go-rounds, other carnival rides, and food booths, many serving sausage. The fair is highlighted by Europe's longest festival procession. There are marksmen's brass-and-pipe bands, paraders in folk costumes, floats, and horse-drawn carriages. Other notable marksmen's festivals are in Düsseldorf in July and in Biberach in Upper Swabia in June or July. The Biberach festival has been celebrated every year since 1649 and features a procession of more than 1,000 costumed children.

CONTACT:
German National Tourist Office
122 E. 42nd St., 52nd Floor
New York, NY 10168
212-661-7200; fax: 212-661-7174

SOURCES:
AnnivHol-1983, p. 181
FestWestEur-1958, p. 74

♦ 1753 ♦ Schutzengelfest (Festival of the Guardian Angel)
Second Sunday in July

A religious and social occasion in northern Switzerland observed since the 17th century. Its setting is *Wildkirchli*, or 'chapel in the wild', a cave in the Alpstein mountain range in the Appenzell Innerrhoden Canton. A Capuchin monk decided in 1621 that the cave, which is now renowned for prehistoric finds, was an ideal place for a mountain worship service. In 1679, Paulus Ulmann, a priest in nearby Appenzell, set up a foundation to ensure that services would continue.

The festival starts at 10 A.M. when a priest or monk from Appenzell conducts the worship service. Then, a yodelers' choir gives a festive concert, and participants start walking to the villages of Ebenalp or Aescher for feasting and dancing.

CONTACT:
Swiss National Tourist Office
608 Fifth Ave.
New York, NY 10020
212-757-5944; fax: 212-262-6116

♦ 1754 ♦ Schwenkfelder Thanksgiving
September 24

The Schwenkfelders who now live in the Pennsylvania Dutch country are the descendants of a small Protestant sect that sprang up in Germany around the time of the Reformation. They were followers of Kaspar Schwenkfeld (1490–1561), a Silesian Reformation theologian who founded the movement called "Reformation by the Middle Way." He and his followers separated themselves from orthodox Protestant circles and formed the small societies and brotherhoods that still survive in the United States as the Schwenkfelder Church, or 'Confessors of the Glory of Christ.'

In 1733 a handful of Schwenkfelder's followers arrived in Philadelphia, and a second group emigrated from Germany on September 22, 1734. On September 24, two days after their arrival, they went to the state house as a group, swore their allegiance to the British king, and spent the rest of the day expressing their gratitude to God for having delivered them from persecution. In the Pennsylvania Dutch counties where Schwenkfelders still live, this day is observed as a special THANKSGIVING Day.

SOURCES:
Chases-1996, p. 390
DaysCustFaith-1957, p. 241

♦ 1755 ♦ Seafair
July–August for three weeks

Seafair is an annual summer festival for residents of and visitors to the Greater Puget Sound region of northwest Washington state. The three-week festival features over 55 educational, cultural, and sporting events, most of which are water-related. It begins with the Pirates' Landing at Alki Beach in West Seattle and includes concerts, a torchlight parade, a hydroplane race on Lake Washington, a relay swim team marathon, and Bon Odori (Japanese folk dancing) performances (*see also* OBON FESTIVAL). Local businesspeople are honored by being named Commodores, and scholarships are awarded to the festival Queen and Sea Princesses. Seafair claims to be one of the largest festivals in the United States, attracting more than 54 million visitors annually.

CONTACT:
Seattle-King County Convention
 and Visitors Bureau
520 Pike St., Ste. 1300
Seattle, WA 98101
360-461-5800; fax: 360-461-5855

SOURCES:
Chases-1996, p. 293
GdUSFest-1984, p. 208

♦ 1756 ♦ Sealing the Frost
Early May

The Cuchumatan Indians of Santa Eulalia in Guatemala, believe that the frost "lives" in a rocky cliff outside of town. Once a year the Indian prayer makers lead a procession of villagers up to the cliff, where one of them is lowered over the edge with a rope around his waist. He seals a crack in the rock with cement so the frost can't get out and ruin the young corn plants. Afterward he is pulled up again, and the procession returns to the village.

SOURCES:
BkHolWrld-1986, Apr 8

Seaman's Day
See **Sjomannadagur**

♦ 1757 ♦ Sea Music Festival
First week in June

The only event of its kind in the Western Hemisphere, the annual Sea Music Festival takes place during the first week in June at Mystic Seaport Museum in Mystic, Connecticut. Since 1980 the ships and exhibits representing a 19th-century maritime village along the Mystic River have been the backdrop for more than 40 musicians and chantey (pronounced

SHANT-ee) singers from around the world. The festival, attracting about 10,000 visitors, is a tribute to the music that has been an integral part of shipboard life since the 16th century.

The festival offers performances of chanteys, or sailors' work songs, as well as "forebitters"—songs sung for entertainment. Most of the lyrics and melodies are of British or Irish origin, although many incorporate American fiddle tunes, African-American minstrel ditties, older ballads, and the popular music of the time. Chanteys helped the sailor maintain the rhythm of a tedious job. In fact, it was considered bad luck to sing a chantey when no work was being done.

The event features daytime and evening concerts Thursday through Saturday, symposia, workshops, and a dance. There is also a special preview concert for museum members that highlights a well-known performer each year.

CONTACT:
Mystic Seaport Museum Stores
47 Greenmanville Ave.
Mystic, CT 06355
800-331-2665 or 860-572-5385
fax: 860-572-8260

SOURCES:
Chases-1996, p. 246

♦ 1758 ♦ Sebring 12 Hour Race/Automobile Hall of Fame Week
Third week in March

The **International Grand Prix Sports Car 12-Hour Endurance Race** held every year on the third Friday and Saturday in March ranks with the INDIANAPOLIS 500 and LE MANS as one of the three great auto races in the world. Held in Sebring, Florida, since 1950, the event draws more than 55,000 spectators and has featured such world-renowned drivers as Mario Andretti, Juan Fangio of Argentina, and Stirling Moss of England.

Holding Automobile Hall of Fame Week just before the Sebring 12-Hour Race is a fairly recent addition to the event. The week-long celebration of auto racing includes a parade, golf and tennis tournaments, boat races, ski exhibitions, and an awards ceremony at the Automobile Hall of Fame honoring men and women who have earned a lasting name for themselves in the auto industry or in auto racing.

CONTACT:
Florida Division of Tourism
126 W. Van Buren
Tallahassee, FL 32399
904-487-1462; fax: 904-921-9158

SOURCES:
GdUSFest-1984, p. 36

♦ 1759 ♦ Sechselauten
Third Monday of April and preceding Sunday

A colorful springtime festival in Zurich, Switzerland, that ushers in spring by exploding the *Böögg* ('snowman'), the symbol of winter. *Sechselauten* means the 'six-o'clock ringing,' and the present custom stems from the 14th-century practice of ringing the cathedral bells at six in the evening (instead of wintertime seven) to proclaim the earlier end of the spring and summer work day. The first ringing of the six o'clock bell was a good excuse for a celebration.

Festivities begin with a children's parade on Sunday, with the children in historical costumes and accompanied by the *Böögg*, which is stuffed with cotton wadding and firecrackers. On Monday, members of the guilds (formerly associations of craftsmen, but now social groups) parade through the flag-festooned city in medieval costumes, accompanied by bands. Everyone converges at Sechselautenplatz on the shore of Lake Zurich at six that evening, the bells ring, groups on horseback gallop around the *Böögg* to the music of a hunting march, and then the *Böögg* explodes and burns. Torchlight parades go on into the night, and feasts are held at guild halls.

CONTACT:
Swiss National Tourist Office
608 Fifth Ave.
New York, NY 10020
212-757-5944; fax: 212-262-6116

SOURCES:
AnnivHol-1983, p. 53
BkFest-1937, p. 317
BkHolWrld-1986, Apr 19
FestWestEur-1958, p. 227

♦ 1760 ♦ **Seged**
November; 29th day of eighth lunar month

This is a religious festival of unclear origin observed only by Ethiopian Jews known as the Falashas. It begins with a procession up the hill to the place where the ritual will be held. The participants wear clean, preferably white, clothes with colored fringe, symbolic of the state of purity in which they have kept themselves by avoiding sexual intercourse and bodily contact with non-Falashas for seven days. The priests, who lead the procession, sing prayers and carry the *Orit* (the Jewish scriptures in Geez—an ancient local language—written on parchment) and other holy books wrapped in colored cloth. Everyone who climbs the hill carries a stone, which is placed on an already existing circular wall marking the holy area where the Orit will be placed.

The ceremony itself includes a commemoration of the dead, where those who wish to honor their deceased relatives place a seed of grain on the stone wall for each relative and say a special prayer. There are also readings from the Orit and donations of money to the priests. After the service is over, the procession moves back down the hill to the prayerhouse, where food for the communal meal—usually *indjära* (bread), *kay wot* (meat stew), and *t'alla* (beer)—is distributed. The remainder of the day is spent in non-religious festivities, especially singing and dancing to the music of *masänqos* (one-stringed bowed lutes).

CONTACT:
Ethiopian Embassy
2134 Kalorama Rd., N.W.
Washington, D.C. 20008
202-234-2281; fax: 202-328-7950

SOURCES:
FolkWrldHol-1992, p. 537

♦ 1761 ♦ **Seijin-no-Hi (Adults Day; Coming-of-Age Day)**
January 15

A national holiday in Japan honoring those who reached their 20th birthday (voting age) in the previous year. Gatherings, usually with speakers, are held in community centers where the honorees show off their new adult finery. A traditional archery contest is held on this day at Sanjusangendo Temple in Kyoto, with people from throughout Japan participating.

SOURCES:
AnnivHol-1983, p. 9
Chases-1996, p. 65
FolkWrldHol-1992, p. 30

♦ 1762 ♦ **Semana Santa in Guatemala**
Between March 15 and April 18; Palm Sunday to Easter

Semana Santa, or HOLY WEEK, is without doubt the biggest occasion of the year in Antigua, the old colonial capital of Guatemala, and one of the largest EASTER celebrations in the New World. Thousands of tourists and believers come to the city to witness this massive display of religious theater. The entire Passion Play, beginning with Christ's entry into Jerusalem on PALM SUNDAY and ending with his Resurrection on Easter, is reenacted in the streets of Antigua—complete with armor-clad Roman soldiers on horseback, who charge through the town early on GOOD FRIDAY looking for Jesus. Men in purple robes and accompanied by Roman soldiers take turns carrying *andas* ('floats') through the streets.

CONTACT:
Guatemala Embassy
2220 R St., N.W.
Washington, D.C. 20008
202-745-4952; fax: 202-745-1908

SOURCES:
FolkWrldHol-1992, p. 196

♦ 1763 ♦ **Semik**
May–June; seventh Thursday after Easter

In pre-revolutionary Russia, Semik—from *semy*, meaning 'the seventh'—took place on the seventh Thursday after EASTER and was observed primarily by young girls. They would go to the woods and pick birch branches, decorating them with ribbons and wreaths. Then they would throw the wreaths into the nearest brook or river. If the wreath stayed on the surface, it meant that they would be married in a year, but if it sank, it meant that they would remain single—or, if married, would soon be widowed. In some areas the wreaths were hung on trees, and as long as they remained there, the girls would have good fortune. Another custom associated with the Semik was the performance of traditional songs and dances by young girls and boys in the forest, often around a decorated birch tree.

In pagan times, the Semik was the feast of a wood-god, celebrated at the time of year when the new leaves first appeared on the trees. Since it was the young girls who spent most of their time in the forest picking berries and mushrooms while the women worked in the fields, it is likely that the wreaths hung on the trees were at one time an offering to the wood-god.

See also WIANKI FESTIVAL OF WREATHS

SOURCES:
FolkWrldHol-1992, p. 291

♦ 1764 ♦ **Sending the Winter Dress**
October–November; first day of 10th lunar month

This is the day on which the Chinese send winter garments to the dead. They are not real items of clothing but paper replicas packed in parcels bearing the names of the recipients. The gift packages are first exhibited in the home; the actual sending of the garments takes place in a courtyard or near the tomb, where they are burned.

This is the third occasion of the year for visiting ancestral tombs. The other two are CHUNG YEUNG and QING MING.

SOURCES:
FolkWrldHol-1992, p. 528

♦ 1765 ♦ Senegal Independence Day
April 4

Senegal celebrates its independence from France on April 4, 1960. France gradually had been gaining control over the area since the 17th century.

This national holiday is celebrated all over the country, but festivities are particularly grand in the capital city of Dakar.

CONTACT:
Senegal Tourist Office
1350 Avenue of the Americas
New York, NY 10019
800-443-2527 or 212-757-7115
fax: 212-737-7461

SOURCES:
AnnivHol-1983, p. 47
Chases-1996, p. 157
NatlHolWrld-1968, p. 46

Septuagesima Sunday
See **Quadragesima Sunday**

♦ 1766 ♦ Serreta, Festa da
September 8–15

The Festa da Serreta that has been held annually since 1932 in Gustine, California, is based on a similar festival held on the island of Terceira in the Azores, from which many of Gustine's residents emigrated. It is held in honor of *Nossa Senhora dos Milagres*, 'Our Lady of Miracles', for whom a 16th-century priest built a small chapel in the Azorean village of Serreta.

The week-long festival attracts thousands of visitors. Highlights include the *Bodo do Leite* ('Banquet of Milk') freshdrawn from the cows as is the practice in the Azores. There are also *cantorías ao desafio* (extemporaneous song contests), which draw contestants from all over California and even some Azoreans. The image of *Nossa Senhora* is carried in a procession from the church to a portable chapel, or *capela*, that is brought out specifically for use on this occasion. A group of women sit in the chapel and watch over the donations of money that are left there. Another festival event is the traditional bullfight, which takes place in a rectangular arena. The bull is held by a long rope, his horns are padded, and the men do not so much fight him as play with him.

CONTACT:
California Division of Tourism
801 K Street, Ste. 1600
Sacramento, CA 95814
800-862-2543 or 916-322-2881
fax: 916-322-3402

SOURCES:
FolkAmerHol-1991, p. 332
RelHolCal-1993, p. 76

Portuguese National Tourist
Office
590 Fifth Ave., 4th Floor
New York, NY 10036
212-354-4403; fax: 212-764-6137

♦ 1767 ♦ Setsubun (Bean-Throwing Festival)
February 3 or 4

A ceremony observed in all major temples throughout Japan to mark the last day of winter according to the lunar calendar. People throng temple grounds where the priests or stars such as actors and sumo wrestlers throw dried beans to the crowd who shout, "Fortune in, Devils out!" Some people also decorate their doorways with sardine heads, because devils don't like their smell. Beans caught at the temple are brought home to drive out devils there.

CONTACT:
Japan National Tourist
Organization
630 Fifth Ave., Ste. 2101
New York, NY 10111
212-757-5640; fax: 212-307-6754

SOURCES:
AnnivHol-1983, p. 18
BkFest-1937, p. 196
BkHolWrld-1986, Feb 3
Chases-1996, p. 86
DictFolkMyth-1984, p. 541
FolkWrldHol-1992, p. 91

Seven-Five-Three Festival
See **Shichi-Go-San**

Seven Herbs or Grasses Festival
See **Nanakusa Matsuri**

♦ 1768 ♦ Seven Sisters Festival
July–August; seventh day of seventh lunar month

A celebration for would-be lovers, observed in China, Korea, Taiwan, and Hong Kong. It is based on an ancient Chinese legend and is also known as the **Maiden's Festival**, **Double Seventh**, **Chhit Sek**, and **Chilsuk**. In the legend, an orphaned cowherd is forced from his home by his elder brother and sister-in-law, who give him only a broken-down cart, an ox, and a tiny piece of land. The ox, called Elder Brother the Ox, takes pity on the cowherd, and tells him that on a certain day seven girls will visit earth from heaven to bathe in a nearby river. If the young man steals the clothes of any one of the girls, she will marry him.

The cowherd steals the clothes of the Seventh Maiden. They fall in love, marry, and live happily for three years, when she is ordered back to heaven by the gods. When the cowherd dies, he becomes immortal, but the Queen Mother of the Western Heaven keeps the two apart by drawing a line across the sky—the Silver River, or Milky Way. They can cross this only once a year, on the seventh day of the seventh month, on a bridge formed by thousands of magpies.

On the sixth day of the seventh month, unmarried men pay homage to the cowherd, and on the seventh day, young unmarried women make offerings of combs, mirrors, paper flowers, and powder puffs to the Seventh Maiden. The festival is celebrated chiefly at home, but in Hong Kong young women also visit Lover's Rock on Bowen Road on Hong Kong Island to burn *joss* ('incense') sticks, lay offerings at the rock, and consult soothsayers.

See also TANABATA

SOURCES:
BkFest-1937, p. 79
BkHolWrld-1986, Aug 10
DictFolkMyth-1984, p. 216
FolkWrldHol-1992, p. 384

♦ 1769 ♦ Seville Fair
Six days in April

Over the past century, the Seville Fair, also known as the **April Fair**, has developed into one of Spain's major spectacles. Originally a market for livestock, the fair with its multicolored tents, wreaths, and paper lanterns now transforms the city of Seville. The singing, dancing, and drinking go on for six days, and a sense of joyousness pervades the city. The week's activities include a parade of riders and a number of bullfights held in the Plaza de la Maestranza (equestrian parade ground)—now considered the "cathedral" of bullfighting.

CONTACT:
Tourist Office of Spain
665 Fifth Ave.
New York, NY 10022
212-759-8822; fax: 212-980-1053

SOURCES:
FestWestEur-1958, p. 194
GdWrldFest-1985, p. 163
IntlThFolk-1979, p. 342

♦ 1770 ♦ Seward's Day
Last Monday in March

When William Henry Seward, secretary of state for President Andrew Johnson, signed the treaty authorizing the purchase of Alaska from Czarist Russia for $7 million on March 30, 1867, most Americans thought he was crazy. They called it "Seward's folly," "Seward's icebox," and "Johnson's polar bear garden." But public opinion quickly changed when gold was discovered in the region.

Since that time, Alaska's natural resources have paid back the initial investment many times over. Its natural gas, coal, and oil reserves, in addition to its seafood and lumber industries, have proved to be far more valuable than its gold. Unfortunately, Seward did not live to see his foresight commemorated as a legal holiday in the state of Alaska. The purchase of Alaska is now widely regarded as the crowning achievement of both William Seward and President Johnson. (*See* ALASKA DAY.)

SOURCES:
AmerBkDays-1978, p. 309
AnnivHol-1983, p. 44
BkHolWrld-1986, Mar 30
Chases-1996, p. 144
DictDays-1988, p. 109

Sexagesima Sunday
See **Quadragesima Sunday**

♦ 1771 ♦ Seychelles Independence Day
June 29

Also known as **Republic Day**, this national holiday commemorates Seychelles' transition to an independent republic on this day in 1976. It had been a British colony since 1903. Before that, it was a dependency of Mauritius, which was ruled by France.

When Seychelles became independent, the people had a three-month-long party.

CONTACT:
Seychelles Tourist Office
820 Second Ave., Ste. 900F
New York, NY 10017
212-687-9766; fax: 212-922-9177

SOURCES:
AnnivHol-1983, p. 85

♦ 1772 ♦ Seychelles Liberation Day
June 5

Less than a year after gaining independence (see above), a coup overthrew the government. Two major political parties had developed in Seychelles, the Seychelles Democratic Party (SDP) and the Seychelles People's United Party (SPUP). James Mancham, the leader of the SDP party, which won the majority vote, became president, and France Albert Rene became prime minister. Rene's supporters led the overthrow

and ousted Mancham on June 5, 1977, the event commemorated as a national holiday on Liberation Day.

CONTACT:
Seychelles Tourist Office
820 Second Ave., Ste. 900F
New York, NY 10017
212-687-9766; fax: 212-922-9177

SOURCES:
AnnivHol-1983, p. 76

♦ 1773 ♦ Shab-Barat
Night of the 15th day of Islamic month of Sha'ban

Shab-Barat (or **Shab-I-Barat, Shaaban**) is a time when Muslims—particularly those in India and Pakistan—ask Allah to forgive the people they know who have died. They often spend the night in mosques praying and reading the Qu'ran, and they visit graveyards to pray for the souls of their friends and ancestors. They also celebrate Allah's mercy by setting off fireworks, illuminating the outsides of their mosques, and giving food to the poor.

Also known as **Laylat al-Bara'ah**, or the **Night of Forgiveness**, Shab-Barat is a time of intense prayer in preparing for RAMADAN, for it is believed that this is the night on which God fixes the destinies of humans for the coming year and sins are absolved.

SOURCES:
BkHolWrld-1986, May 13
FolkWrldHol-1992, p. 154
RelHolCal-1993, p. 113

♦ 1774 ♦ Shah Abdul Latif Death Festival
Fourteenth–sixteenth days of Islamic month of Safar

A celebration of the death of poet-musician Shah Abdul Latif (1689–1752) at Bhit Shah, Sind, Pakistan. He was one of the most beloved of Pakistan's mystic Sufi poet-musicians who founded a music tradition based on popular themes and using folk melodies. He was the author of the *Risalo*, the best-known collection of romantic poetry in the Sindhi language; its heroes and heroines have become symbols of the oppression of Sind by foreign occupiers.

At Latif's *urs*, or 'death festival', a huge fair takes place outside the poet's shrine. There are wrestling matches (a popular entertainment in Sind), transvestite dancing, a circus, theater, and numerous food and souvenir booths. Inside the shrine the atmosphere is quiet, and there is devotional singing by well-known Sind groups. The main event of the urs is a concert at which the annual Latif Award is presented to the best performers.

CONTACT:
Pakistani Embassy
2315 Massachusetts Ave., N.W.
Washington, D.C. 20008
202-939-6200; fax: 202-387-0484

♦ 1775 ♦ Shaheed Day
February 21

Shaheed or **Shaheel Day** is a national day of mourning in Bangladesh. Before becoming an autonomous country in 1971 (*see* BANGLADESH INDEPENDENCE DAY), this land had been East Pakistan ever since all of India gained independence from Britain in 1947. As East Pakistan, the country was poorer and less powerful than West Pakistan (now Pakistan), where the central government was. East Pakistan paid its taxes to West Pakistan, which gave East Pakistan little economic support in return. In addition, West Pakistan wanted to make its language, Urdu, the only official language of both Pakistans. Most of the people in East Pakistan spoke Bengali (some of the Indian region of Bengal became East Pakistan in 1947), and they were strongly opposed to the restriction of the use of their language in government and commerce.

In 1952 university students held protests which erupted in violence. Lives were lost, and as a memorial, people form a procession from the Azimpur graveyard on February 21 each year.

CONTACT:
Bangladesh Embassy
2201 Wisconsin Ave., N.W., Ste. 300
Washington, D.C. 20007
202-342-8372; fax: 202-333-4971

SOURCES:
AnnivHol-1983, p. 26
Chases-1996, p. 107

♦ 1776 ♦ **Shaker Festival**
Begins second Thursday in July

A 10-day event staged by the Shaker Museum in South Union, Ky., to tell the story of this last western Shaker community, which survived from 1807 to 1922. A nightly outdoor drama, *Shakertown Revisited*, combines Shaker songs, dances, and the relating of history. Meals are served using Shaker recipes, and there are demonstrations of Shaker crafts. The festival was first held in 1962.

Shakers are members of the United Society of Believers in Christ's Second Appearing, a celibate sect founded in 1772 in England by Ann Lee; it is a Quaker offshoot (*see* LEE, BIRTHDAY OF ANN). They adopted ritual practices of shaking, shouting, dancing, whirling, and singing in tongues. Communal settlements were established in the United States by Ann Lee, known as Mother Ann and believed to be the reincarnation of Jesus, who came to America in 1774 and founded the first church in what is now Watervliet, N.Y. The movement later spread throughout New England, Kentucky, Ohio, and Indiana. The simplicity of Shaker craftsmanship had a significant impact on American furniture design. They also invented the screw propeller, rotary harrow, and common clothespin, among other items. The Shaker movement reached its peak in the 1840s, when there were about 6,000 members; by 1905, there were only some 1,000. Today, a small group of people live as Shakers in Sabbathday Lake, Me.

CONTACT:
Shaker Museum
Highway 68-80
South Union, KY 42283
502-542-4167

SOURCES:
GdUSFest-1984, p. 65

♦ 1777 ♦ **Shakespeare Festival**
April–December

In what has been called the longest festival in the world, the Royal Shakespeare Company offers the plays of William Shakespeare in repertory performed by some of the best actors in Great Britain from April through December every year. The 18th-century actor, producer, and co-manager of the Drury Lane Theatre, David Garrick, was the first to try to

establish a Shakespeare festival, but the idea apparently died with him in 1779. Another festival was started in 1864 by Charles Edward Flower, who raised the necessary funds and contributed the riverside site for the original theater in Stratford-upon-Avon, Shakespeare's birthplace. The first Shakespeare Memorial Theatre opened there in 1879, but it burned down in 1926. A new theater opened in 1932, and it became the home of the first permanent Royal Shakespeare Company in Stratford. Now there are two companies—one that is resident in Stratford and one that tours. In 1960 the Aldwych Theatre became the company's London home, and in 1970 it moved into its own London theater.

See also STRATFORD FESTIVAL

CONTACT:
British Tourist Authority
551 Fifth Ave., Ste. 702
New York, NY 10176
800-462-2748 or 212-986-2200
fax: 212-986-1188

SOURCES:
Chases-1996, p. 147
GdWrldFest-1985, p. 97
IntlThFolk-1979, p. 177

♦ 1778 ♦ **Shakespeare's Birthday**
April 23

No one really knows the exact date of William Shakespeare's birth, although he was baptized on April 26, 1564, and died on April 23, 1616. April 23 is also ST. GEORGE'S DAY, and this may be why it was decided to observe the birth of England's greatest poet and dramatist on the feast day of England's patron saint. Special pageants are held at Stratford-upon-Avon in Warwickshire, where Shakespeare was born and where thousands of tourists go each year to see his plays performed. The bells of Holy Trinity Church ring out, and the Mayor of Stratford leads a procession there to lay flowers on Shakespeare's grave.

CONTACT:
British Tourist Authority
551 Fifth Ave., Ste. 702
New York, NY 10176
800-462-2748 or 212-986-2200
fax: 212-986-1188

SOURCES:
AmerBkDays-1978, p. 375
BkDays-1864, vol. I, p. 542
Chases-1996, p. 182
DictDays-1988, p. 109

♦ 1779 ♦ **Shalako Ceremonial**
Late November or early December

One of the most impressive of the Pueblo Indian dances, held at the Zuni Pueblo in southwestern New Mexico. In this ceremony of all-night dancing and chants, houses are blessed, the dead are commemorated, and prayers are offered for good health and good weather in the coming year. The dance features towering masked figures with beaks who represent messengers from the rainmakers. They make clacking noises as they approach designated houses, and once inside the houses, they remove their masks, chant, and share food. Other figures taking part in the ceremonial are rain gods, warriors carrying whips, and the fire god, who is depicted by a young boy. The dancing goes on all through the cold night. The following morning, there are foot races.

CONTACT:
Zuni Pueblo
P.O. Box 339
Zuni, NM 87327
505-782-4481

SOURCES:
DictFolkMyth-1984, pp. 566, 589, 1001
IndianAmer-1989, pp. 290, 321
RelHolCal-1993, p. 113

♦ 1780 ♦ **Sham el-Nesim**
Between April 5 and May 9; Monday after Coptic Easter

A national holiday and folk festival in Egypt, observed for thousands of years as a day to smell the breezes and celebrate spring. *Nesim* means 'zephyr,' the spring breeze, and *sham* means 'to breathe in.' While the date is set by the Coptic calendar, the holiday is now a non-religious national holiday observed by everyone as a family affair. Traditionally, people pack picnics to have outings along the Nile River or in parks. Certain food is specified for the occasion: the main dish is *fessikh*, a kind of salted fish, and it's also traditional to have *mouloukhiya* (stuffed vine leaves) and eggs with decorated, colored shells. The foods are believed to prevent disease, and the eggs symbolize life. Vast numbers of fish are eaten in Cairo on Sham al-Nesim. Other traditions call for placing freshly cut flowers at doors and windows, and putting a clove of garlic at the head of each bed to prevent boredom and fatigue for those who lie there.

At the time of the pharaohs, spring was celebrated with gifts of lotus flowers to wives or loved ones, and families enjoyed river outings on flower-decorated barges and *feluccas* (small sailing vessels).

CONTACT:
Egyptian Tourist Authority
645 N. Michigan Ave., Ste. 829
Chicago, IL 60611
312-280-4666; fax: 312-280-4788

SOURCES:
BkFestHolWrld-1970, p. 74
BkHolWrld-1986, Apr 28
Chases-1996, p. 183
FolkWrldHol-1992, p. 184

♦ 1781 ♦ **Shampoo Day**
Fifteenth day of sixth lunar month

In Korea, **Cold Water Shampoo Day** or **Yoodoonal** is a day spent near a stream or waterfall, where people bathe and wash their hair to ward off fever and other heat-related ills during the coming year. Macaroni, flour cakes, melons, and other fruits are offered at family shrines. For scholars, Shampoo Day is an opportunity to go on picnics, drink wine, and compose poems.

SOURCES:
FolkWrldHol-1992, p. 352

♦ 1782 ♦ **Shankaracharya Jayanti**
April–May; fifth or 10th day of waxing half of Hindu month of Vaisakha

Although he is believed to have lived between 788 and 820, Hindu tradition says that Adi Shankaracharya, one of India's greatest saint-philosophers, flourished in 200 B.C. He revived Brahmanism and raised Vedanta philosophy to new heights, producing a number of original philosophical works and commentaries on the Upanishads, Vedanta Sutras, and the *Bhagavad Gita*. Shankaracharya also composed many popular hymns, worked numerous miracles, and urged Hindus to devote themselves to God in all of his many forms and incarnations.

Shankaracharya's birthday, known as Shankaracharya Jayanti, is celebrated on the fifth day of Vaisakha in southern India and on the 10th day in northern India. It is usually spent fasting, meditating, and studying Shankaracharya's works.

SOURCES:
RelHolCal-1993, p. 114

♦ 1783 ♦ **Sharad Purnima**
September–October; full moon day of Hindu month of Asvina

Hindus devote this day to the moon god, Hari. In the belief that *amrit* (elixir) is showered on the earth by moonbeams, they prepare *khir* (milk thickened with rice and mixed with sugar) on this day and offer it to Hari amid the ringing of bells and chanting of hymns. The mixture is left out in the moonshine all night so that it may absorb the amrit falling from the moon. The resulting khir is believe to possess special qualities. In the evening, the moon god is worshipped and offered food. The next morning, the specially prepared khir is given to the devotees.

SOURCES:
RelHolCal-1993, p. 114

♦ 1784 ♦ **Shark Angling Competition, International**
April–May

Held annually in late April or early May, when sharks are more likely to swim close to shore, Gibraltar's International Shark Angling Competition dates back to 1964, when it was introduced on a much smaller scale. Today the competition attracts up to 1,000 competitors, with prizes for the heaviest shark and the largest total weight of all sharks caught. The boats leave Gibraltar's City Wharf, which is decorated with the flags of the competing countries, at 9:00 A.M. and return at 6:00 P.M. for the weighing. Both men and women participate in the competition. The local record for the largest shark is 203 pounds.

CONTACT:
British Tourist Authority
551 Fifth Ave., Ste. 702
New York, NY 10176
800-462-2748 or 212-986-2200
fax: 212-986-1188

SOURCES:
GdWrldFest-1985, p. 88

♦ 1785 ♦ **Shavuot (Shabuoth)**
Between May 16 and June 13; Sivan 6

Shavuot ('weeks') is the second of the three PILGRIM FESTIVALS (*see also* PASSOVER and SUKKOT). It follows Passover by 50 days and is also known in English as *Pentecost* from the Greek word meaning "fiftieth" (like the Christian PENTECOST, which comes 50 days after EASTER). It is also called the **Feast of Weeks** or **Feast of the Harvest**, because it originally marked the end of the seven weeks of the Passover barley harvest and the beginning of the wheat harvest. At one time, all adult male Jews were expected to bring their first *omer*, or 'sheaf', of barley to the Temple in Jerusalem as a thanksgiving offering. Today dairy dishes are associated with Shavuot, particularly cheese blintzes.

After the period of Jewish slavery in Egypt, Shavuot took on a new meaning: it celebrated Moses' return from the top of Mt. Sinai with the two stone tablets containing the Ten Commandments, the most fundamental laws of the Jewish faith, and is therefore also known as the **Festival of the Giving of the Law**. Orthodox and Conservative Jews in the Diaspora celebrate two days of Shavuot as full holidays, while Reform Jews and those living in Israel observe only the first day.

See also LAG BA-OMER

SOURCES:
AmerBkDays-1978, pp. 462,
544
BkFest-1937, p. 208
BkFestHolWrld-1970, p. 70
BkHolWrld-1986, May 25
DaysCustFaith-1957, pp. 137,
159, 161
DictWrldRel-1989, pp. 155,
390, 564, 678
FestSaintDays-1915, p. 119
FolkAmerHol-1991, p. 224
FolkWrldHol-1992, p. 321
RelHolCal-1993, pp. 102, 114

♦ 1786 ♦ Sheboygan Bratwurst Days
First weekend in August

A celebration in Sheboygan, Wis., that is scented with the smoke from 3,000 to 4,000 bratwursts being grilled. Sheboygan, billing itself the "Bratwurst Capital of the World," or alternatively, the "Wurst City of the World," is the home of several large sausage factories that ship bratwurst around the country and of numerous smaller markets that make tons of brat. (*Brat*, incidentally, rhymes with *cot*, not *cat*.)

The celebration's main event is a parade led by a 13-foot-tall balloon Bavarian figure in lederhosen who is known as the *Bratmeister*, or 'sausage master.' In 1991, a highlight of the parade was a float carrying giant twin brats—two 130-pound brats on a hard roll made from 40 pounds of dough.

The point of the festival is to eat brats, and the smell of them cooking on outdoor grills permeates the city. There are a brat-and-pancake breakfast and a brat-eating contest. (The record-holder is Roger Theobald who ate nine double-brats in 15 minutes in 1953). Other events include band concerts, a magic show, wrestling matches, competitions for children, and a stumpf-fiddle contest. The stumpf fiddle is an instrument combining bells, springs, BB-filled pie plates, wood blocks, and taxi horns on a wooden pole with a rubber ball at the bottom.

Germans settled in Sheboygan in the 1830s and 1840s and immediately began making sausage. In 1953, to celebrate the city's 100th birthday, a Bratwurst Day was held in August. The mayor's proclamation noted that the city "has achieved national fame and recognition for the exclusive manufacture of a special kind of roasting sausage . . ."

The celebration was canceled in 1966 because it had become too rowdy. In 1978 Bratwurst Days came back for the city's 125th anniversary. Today the festival attracts about 50,000 people.

CONTACT:
Wisconsin Division of Tourism
123 W. Washington Ave., 6th
Floor
Madison, WI 53703
800-432-8747 or 608-266-7621
fax: 608-266-3403

SOURCES:
Chases-1996, p. 319

♦ 1787 ♦ Sheelah's Day
March 18

Even the Irish aren't exactly sure who Sheelah was. Some say she was St. Patrick's wife; some say his mother. But one thing that they all seem to agree on is how this day should be celebrated: by drinking whiskey. The shamrock worn on St.

Patrick's Day is supposed to be worn on the following day as well, until it is "drowned" in the last glass of the evening. If someone should drop his shamrock into his glass and drink it before the "drowning ceremony" takes place, he has no choice but to get a fresh shamrock and another glass.

SOURCES:
AnnivHol-1983, p. 39
DaysCustFaith-1957, p. 81
DictDays-1988, p. 110
RelHolCal-1993, p. 114

♦ 1788 ♦ Shellfish Gathering (Shiohi-gari)
April 4

April 4 is approximately the date on which the tide is usually at its lowest in Japan. Families dress in brightly colored clothing and gather in coastal areas where the shellfish are known to be plentiful. They go out in boats decorated with red and white bunting and wait until the tide goes out and strands them on the bottom. Then they dig for clams, which they often cook and eat on the spot for lunch. Fishermen living nearby are more than willing to supplement their efforts, selling clams from their own stock to those whose digging has been unsuccessful. Most people buy a bag of shellfish to take home as well. The maritime police are usually kept busy rescuing those who go out too far and are caught by the incoming tide.

SOURCES:
BkFestHolWrld-1970, p. 76

♦ 1789 ♦ Shemini Atzeret
Between September 27 and October 25; Tishri 22

Shemini Atzeret, or 'eighth day of solemn assembly', is actually the eighth day of the festival of Sukkot, but it is celebrated as a separate holiday dedicated to the love of God. The second day of Shemini Atzeret is known as Simhat Torah and is also celebrated separately by Orthodox and Conservative Jews. Most Reform Jews celebrate Shemini Atzeret concurrently with Simhat Torah.

In ancient times, prayers for rain were recited on this day—a practice that is still part of Orthodox services. It is also one of four Jewish holidays on which the *Yizkor*, or memorial rite for the dead, is observed. The other three are Yom Kippur, the second day of Shavuot, and the last day of Passover.

SOURCES:
AmerBkDays-1978, p. 928
AnnivHol-1983, p. 172
Chases-1996, p. 407

♦ 1790 ♦ Shenandoah Apple Blossom Festival
Early May

A four-day celebration of the apple orchards of Virginia's Shenandoah Valley, held in Winchester, the state's apple center. The festival was inaugurated in 1924 to publicize the area's historic, scenic, and industrial assets. Its motto was "The bounties of nature are the gift of God." Winchester was settled in 1732, and George Washington, an early landlord in the area, required each tenant to plant four acres of apples.

The festival comes when the orchards are in bloom. About 250,000 people visit to enjoy the pink and white blossoms and the special events, including the coronation of Queen Shenandoah, a title once held by Luci Baines Johnson, former

President Lyndon B. Johnson's youngest daughter. Other attractions are a parade, concerts, an apple-pie baking contest, fireworks, and square- and folk-dancing.

CONTACT:
Virginia Dept. of Economic
    Development
Division of Tourism
901 E. Byrd St.
Richmond, VA 23219
804-786-4484; fax: 804-786-1919

SOURCES:
AmerBkDays-1978, p. 403
Chases-1996, p. 197
GdUSFest-1984, p. 202

♦ 1791 ♦ **Shepherd's Fair**
*Two weeks beginning the third or fourth Sunday
in August*

Also known as the **Schueberfo'er** or **Schuebermess**, the Shepherd's Fair held in Luxembourg City at the end of August every year dates back to 1340, when it was founded by John the Blind, Count of Luxembourg and King of Bohemia. Originally a market for the wool and sheep merchants of medieval Europe, the Shepherd's Fair has shifted its focus over the years. Today it is geared toward entertainment rather than commerce, with carousels, food stands, and candy booths everywhere. Practically the only remnant of the original fair is the *Marche des Moutons*, or 'March of the Sheep,' a parade of sheep decorated with ribbons and led by shepherds in folkloric costumes, accompanied by a band playing an ancient tune known as the *Hammelsmarsch*, or 'Sheeps' March.'

CONTACT:
Luxembourg National Tourist
    Office
17 Beekman Pl.
New York, NY 10022
212-935-8888; fax: 212-935-5896

SOURCES:
Chases-1996, p. 342
FestEur-1992, p. 81
GdWrldFest-1985, p. 129

♦ 1792 ♦ **Shichi-Go-San (Seven-Five-Three
Festival)**
November 15

An ancient Japanese celebration that marks the special ages of seven, five, and three. It has long been traditional for families to take girls aged seven, boys of five, and all three-year-olds, dressed in their finest, to the neighborhood Shinto shrine where their birth is recorded. There they are purified, and the priest prays to the tutelary deity for their healthy growth. At the end the priest gives each child two little packages: one containing cakes in the form of Shinto emblems (mirror, sword, and jewel), and the other holding sacred rice to be mixed with the evening meal. Afterwards, there are often parties for the children, and customarily they are given a special pink hard candy, called "thousand-year candy," to symbolize hopes for a long life. Because Nov. 15 is not a legal holiday, families now observe the ceremony on the Sunday nearest that date.

Legend says that the custom started because parents believed their children's mischievousness was caused by little worms that somehow entered their bodies. The visits to the shrines were to pray that the mischief-making worms would depart. A more likely story is that the festival began in the days when children often died young, and parents gave thanks for those who survived.

SOURCES:
AnnivHol-1983, p. 148

BkHolWrld-1986, Nov 15
Chases-1996, p. 450
FolkWrldHol-1992, p. 560

♦ 1793 ♦ **Shick-Shack Day (Shik-Shak Day,
Shicsack Day, Shitsack Day, Shig-Shag
Day)**
May 29

The *Oxford English Dictionary* suggests that this day takes its name from a corruption of *shitsack*, a derogatory term for the Nonconformists, Protestants who did not follow the doctrines and practices of the established Church of England. It was later applied to those who did not wear the traditional sprig of oak on May 29, or **Royal Oak Day**—the birthday of Charles II and the day in 1660 on which he made his triumphal entry into London as king after a 12-year interregnum.

The association of Charles II (1630–1685) and the oak tree dates back to 1651 when, after being defeated by Oliver Cromwell in battle (*see* CROMWELL'S DAY), legend has it he took refuge from his pursuers in an oak tree behind a house known as Boscobel. *Shick-shack* has since become synonymous with the oak-apple or sprig of oak itself, and May 29 is celebrated—particularly in rural areas of England—in memory of the restoration of King Charles and his preservation in the Royal Oak. Also called **Oak Apple Day, Oak Ball Day, Bobby Ack Day, Yack Bob Day, Restoration Day**, or **Nettle Day**.

CONTACT:
British Tourist Authority
551 Fifth Ave., Ste. 702
New York, NY 10176
800-462-2748 or 212-986-2200
fax: 212-986-1188

SOURCES:
AnnivHol-1983, p. 72
BkDays-1864, vol. I, p. 696
Chases-1996, p. 233
DictDays-1988, pp. 14, 81, 83,
    96, 98, 110, 134
FolkWrldHol-1992, p. 305

♦ 1794 ♦ **Shilla (Silla) Cultural Festival**
October in even-numbered years

An exuberant three-day festival, one of Korea's biggest and most impressive, to celebrate the country's ancient Shilla Kingdom. The celebrations are held in Kyongju, the capital of the Shilla Kingdom, and throughout the Kyongju Valley, where there is a great treasure of historic buildings: the Sokkuram Grotto, one of Asia's finest Buddhist shrines with a granite dome; Ch'omsongdae, a seventh-century bottle-shaped stone structure that is the world's earliest known extant observatory; royal tombs; palaces; and pleasure pavilions. The Shilla Kingdom in the southeastern portion of what is now Korea flourished from 57 B.C. to 935 A.D., and defeated two rival kingdoms, unifying all three in 676. The Unified Shilla Period is considered a golden age of Buddhist arts and especially of granite Buddhist sculpture.

The festival features concerts, wrestling matches, Buddhist pagoda dancing, games and contests, and lavish processions with elaborate floats.

CONTACT:
Korea National Tourism Corp.
205 N. Michigan Ave., Ste. 2212
Chicago, IL 60601
312-819-2560; fax: 312-819-2563

♦ 1795 ♦ **Shiprock Navajo Nation Fair**
Usually first weekend of October

Also known as the **Northern Navajo Fair**, this fair began in 1924 and is considered the oldest and most traditional of Navajo fairs. It is a harvest fair held in Shiprock, New Mexico, the largest populated community of the Navajo Nation.

The fair coincides with the conclusion of an ancient Navajo healing ceremony, the Night Chant. This is a nine-day chant known as the *Yei Bei Chei*, and is a complex ritual usually conducted after the first frost. Parts of the ceremony may be witnessed by the public. Among the more colorful public rituals are *Two Yei's Come*, a Saturday-afternoon dance, and the grand finale in which sacred masked dancers begin a dance late Saturday night and continue into the pre-dawn.

After watching the healing ceremony, spectators go on to other events of the fair such as an all-Indian rodeo, an inter-tribal powwow, a livestock show, a carnival, the Miss Northern Navajo Pageant, Indian arts and crafts exhibits, and a Saturday morning parade.

See also Navajo Nation Fair at Window Rock

CONTACT:
Navajo Tribal Council
P.O. Box 308
Window Rock, AZ 86515
602-871-4941

SOURCES:
IndianAmer-1989, p. 269
RelHolCal-1993, p. 115

♦ 1796 ♦ **Shitala Ashtami**
March–April; on or near eighth day of waxing half of Hindu month of Caitra

This Hindu festival honors Shitala, the goddess of smallpox, whose blessings are invoked for protection against the disease. Usually identified with either the devil or Durga, Shitala is depicted as roaming the countryside riding an ass.

Colorful fairs are held on this day in India at several locations where there is a shrine to Shitala. These fairs are characterized by singing, dancing, feasting, and merrymaking. Women usually visit the shrine in the morning, bringing offerings of rice, homemade sweets, cooked food, and holy water mixed with milk.

CONTACT:
India Tourist Office
30 Rockefeller Ave.
15 N. Mezzanine
New York, NY 10112
212-586-4901; fax: 212-582-3274

SOURCES:
RelHolCal-1993, p. 114

Shivah Asar be-Tammuz
See **Tammuz, Fast of the 17th of**

♦ 1797 ♦ **Shivaratri**
February–March; 13th day of waning half of Hindu month of Phalguna

A Hindu holiday observed throughout India and Nepal. Legend says that on this night Lord Shiva, the great god of destruction (who is also the restorer), danced the Tandav, his celestial dance of Creation, Preservation, and Destruction. Hindu devotees of Shiva eat only once on the day before this "Night of Shiva," and then fast and tell stories about him. In India, pilgrims throng the Shiva shrines in Chidambaram

(Tamil Nadu), Kalahasti (Andhra Pradesh), and Varanasi (Uttar Pradesh), where special celebrations are held. Mandi in Himachal Pradesh becomes one big party. Devotees carry deities on temple chariots, and there are folk dances and folk music. Hundreds of thousands make the pilgrimage to Pashupatinath Temple in Katmandu, Nepal, for worship, feasting, and ritual bathing in the holy Bagmati River. In Port Louis, Mauritius, wooden arches covered with flowers are carried to Grand Bassin, to get water from the holy lake to wash the symbols of Shiva.

CONTACT:
India Tourist Office
30 Rockefeller Ave.
15 N. Mezzanine
New York, NY 10112
212-586-4901; fax: 212-582-3274

Nepal Embassy
2131 Leroy Pl., N.W.
Washington, D.C. 20008
202-667-4550; fax: 202-667-5534

SOURCES:
AnnivHol-1983, p. 179
BkHolWrld-1986, Mar 10
FolkWrldHol-1992, p. 148
RelHolCal-1993, p. 92

♦ 1798 ♦ **Shrimp Festival, National**
Early October

A waterside festival held for four days in Gulf Shores, Ala., drawing crowds estimated at 200,000. This festival began in this shrimping and resort area in 1971 as a one-day event to liven things up after Labor Day. The big event was a shrimp-cooking contest, and shrimp dishes have been in the forefront since. About 30 percent of the food vendors' fare includes shrimp. This means lots of jambalaya and kabobs. Also on the menu are such dishes as shark and Greek foods including seafood gyros (pronounced YEER-ohs). Events of the festival include a parade, a sailboat regatta, musical entertainment, sky-diving exhibitions, a Miss Sunny beauty contest, and arts and crafts displays.

CONTACT:
Alabama Bureau of Tourism and
  Travel
P.O. Box 4927
Montgomery, AL 36103
800-252-2263 or 334-242-4169
fax: 334-242-4554

SOURCES:
Chases-1996, p. 411

♦ 1799 ♦ **Shrove Monday**
Between February 2 and March 8; Monday before Ash Wednesday

Many countries celebrate Shrove Monday as well as Shrove Tuesday, both days marking a time of preparation for Lent. It is often a day for eating pastry, as the butter and eggs in the house must all be used up before Lent. In Greece it is known as **Clean Monday** and is observed by holding picnics at which Lenten foods are served. In Iceland, the Monday before Lent is known as **Bun Day**. The significance of the name is twofold: It is a day for striking people on the buttocks with a stick before they get out of bed as well as a day for eating sweet buns with whipped cream. The latter custom is believed to have been introduced by Danish and Norwegian bakers who emigrated to Iceland during the late 19th century.

SOURCES:
Chases-1996, pp. 104, 105

411

♦ 1800 ♦ **Shrovetide in Norway (Fastelavn)**
*Between February 3 and March 9; Sunday before
Ash Wednesday*

Formerly observed on the Monday before Ash Wednesday, Fastelavn, or **Shrove Sunday**, is a holiday that Norwegian children anticipate eagerly. They rise at dawn and, armed with *fastelavnsris* (decorated birch or evergreen branches), they go from room to room and strike with their branches anyone who is still in bed. The children receive a hot cross bun for every victim they spank.

The fastelavnsris can be quite elaborate, often decorated with tinsel and paper streamers or brightly colored paper roses. Sometimes a doll with stiff, full skirts is tied to the topmost branch. The curious custom of switching with branches can most likely be traced to an ancient pagan rite heralding the fruitfulness of spring.

SOURCES:
BkFest-1937, p. 249
FestWestEur-1958, p. 151

♦ 1801 ♦ **Shrove Tuesday**
*Between February 3 and March 9; day before Ash
Wednesday*

There are a number of names in the West for the last day before the long fast of Lent. The French call it Mardi Gras (meaning 'Fat Tuesday'), because it was traditionally a time to use up all the milk, butter, and eggs left in the kitchen. These ingredients often went into pancakes, which is why the English call it Pancake Day and still celebrate it with games and races that involve tossing pancakes in the air. Other names include **Shuttlecock (or Football) Day**, after sports associated with this day; **Doughnut Day**; **Bannock (or Bannocky) Day** (a bannock being the Scottish equivalent of a pancake), and **Fastingong** (meaning 'approaching a time of fast'). The name "Shrove Tuesday" is derived from the Christian custom of confessing sins and being "shriven" (i.e., absolved) just before Lent.

In northern Sweden, people eat a meat stew. In the south, they eat "Shrove Tuesday buns" called *semlor*, made with cardamom, filled with almond paste, and topped with whipped cream.

No matter what its name, the day before Ash Wednesday has long been a time for excessive eating and merrymaking. The Mardi Gras parade in New Orleans is typical of the masquerades and dancing in the streets that take place in many countries on this day as people prepare for the long Lenten fast.

See also Carnival, Cheese Sunday, Cheese Week, Fastens-een, and Fasching

SOURCES:
Chases-1996, p. 106

♦ 1802 ♦ **Shrove Tuesday among the
Pennsylvania Dutch**
*Between February 3 and March 9; day before Ash
Wednesday*

Among the Pennsylvania Dutch, work is taboo on Shrove Tuesday, just as it is on other religious holidays. There is an old superstition that if a woman sews on Shrove Tuesday, she will prevent her hens from laying their eggs. Some believe that sewing on this day means that the house will be visited by snakes during the spring and summer.

A special kind of cake or doughnut known as a *fasnacht* is eaten on this day. Rectangular with a slit down the middle, it is often soaked with molasses and then dunked in saffron tea. Sometimes the fasnachts were crumbled and fed to the chickens in the belief that it would prevent the hawks from snatching the chicks in the spring. Another old custom associated with Shrove Tuesday is "barring out," or locking the teacher out of the local school. In many areas, Christmas is barring-out day.

SOURCES:
FolkAmerHol-1991, p. 96

♦ 1803 ♦ **Shrove Tuesday in Bohemia**
*Between February 3 and March 9; day before Ash
Wednesday*

In Bohemia in eastern Czech Republic, a mummer known as the "Oats Goat" traditionally is led from house to house on Shrove Tuesday. He dances with the women of the house, and in return they feed him and give him money. Like the Fastnachtsbär (or Shrovetide Bear) in parts of Germany, the Oats Goat is dressed in straw and wears horns on his head. He is associated with fertility; at one time it was widely believed that dancing with the Fastnachtsbär ensured the growth of crops.

SOURCES:
DictFolkMyth-1984, pp. 370,
807

♦ 1804 ♦ **Shrove Tuesday in Estonia**
*Between February 3 and March 9; day before Ash
Wednesday*

Schools are closed in Estonia on the last day before Lent, known as **Vastla Päev**, and children often spend the entire day sledding. At night, their mothers serve a traditional Shrove Tuesday soup, which is made from pigs' feet boiled with dried peas or lima beans. After dinner, the children play with the *vuriluu kont*, or the bones left over from the pigs' feet soup. A hole is drilled in each bone and a doubled rope is inserted through the hole. When the contrivance is manipulated in a certain way it causes a terrific rattle, which delights the children and is a traditional way to end the day's celebration.

SOURCES:
BkFest-1937, p. 102

♦ 1805 ♦ **Shrove Tuesday in Finland**
*Between February 3 and March 9; day before Ash
Wednesday*

Children in Finland often spend Shrove Tuesday, a school holiday, sledding and enjoying other outdoor sports. According to an old folk saying, the better the coasting and the longer the hills one rides on **Laskiaispäivä**, the more bountiful the coming harvest will be. A typical Finnish meal on this day would include pea soup and *blini*, or rich pancakes, served with caviar and *smetana*, a kind of sour milk. A typical dessert consists of wheat buns filled with almond paste, placed in deep dishes, and eaten with hot milk.

There are many folk beliefs surrounding Shrove Tuesday. At

one time, women would not spin on this day, believing that if they did, no flax would grow the following summer. Men refrained from planing wood, the common wisdom being that if farm animals walked on the chips made by the planes, their feet would become swollen and sore.

SOURCES:
BkFest-1937, p. 111

♦ 1806 ♦ Shrove Tuesday in the Netherlands
Between February 3 and March 9; day before Ash Wednesday

The day preceding the Lenten fast is known as **Vastenavond** (Fast Eve) in the Netherlands, where it is a time for feasting and merrymaking. In the provinces of Limburg and Brabant, it is customary to eat pancakes and *oliebollen*, or rich fried cakes with currants, raisins, and apples added. Brabant specializes in *worstebrood*, a special kind of bread that appears ordinary on the outside but is filled with spiced sausage meat.

In the southern part of the country, the CARNIVAL season lasts for three days, beginning on the Sunday before ASH WEDNESDAY. In other areas, the celebration is confined to one day. The farmers of Schouwen-en-Duiveland, on the island of Zeeland, still observe the old Vastenavond custom of gathering at the village green with their horses in the afternoon. The animals are carefully groomed and decorated with paper roses. The men ride their horses down to the beach, making sure the animals get their feet wet. The leader of the procession toots on a horn. It is possible that this custom originated in an ancient spring purification rite, when blowing horns was believed to drive away evil spirits and getting wet was a symbolic act of cleansing.

SOURCES:
BkFest-1937, p. 241
FestWestEur-1958, p. 124
FolkAmerHol-1991, p. 98

♦ 1807 ♦ Sierra Leone Republic Day
April 19

This national holiday celebrates the day Sierra Leone became a republic on April 19, 1971. It had gained independence from Britain on April 27, 1961.

Republic Day festivities are especially elaborate in the capital city of Freetown.

CONTACT:
Sierra Leone Embassy
1701 19th St., N.W.
Washington, D.C. 20009
202-939-9261; fax: 202-483-1793

SOURCES:
AnnivHol-1983, p. 53
Chases-1996, pp. 177, 189
NatlHolWrld-1968, p. 50

♦ 1808 ♦ Silent Days
Beginning between March 19 and April 22; Thursday, Friday, and Saturday before Easter

The last three days of HOLY WEEK—MAUNDY THURSDAY, GOOD FRIDAY, and HOLY SATURDAY—were at one time referred to as the **Swidages**, from an Old English word meaning 'to be

silent.' From this came Silent Days or **Still Days**—three days during which the church bells in England remained silent. The bells were rung again at the EASTER Vigil Mass.

SOURCES:
DictDays-1988, p. 111

♦ 1809 ♦ "Silent Night, Holy Night" Celebration
December 24

The world's best known Christmas carol, "Silent Night, Holy Night," was written and composed by Franz Gruber and Father Josef Mohr. The carol was first performed on CHRISTMAS EVE, 1818, at St. Nickola Church in Oberndorf, Austria. This event is commemorated in Oberndorf, Hallein, Wagrain, Salzburg, and other Austrian towns by holding a candlelight procession on December 24. Everyone sings the carol as they march to the church and again when they are inside. It is usually sung in various languages to honor the many nations where the birth of the Christ child is celebrated.

CONTACT:
Austrian National Tourist Office
P.O. Box 1142, Times Square
New York, NY 10148
212-944-6880; fax: 212-730-4568

SOURCES:
Chases-1996, p. 487
GdWrldFest-1985, p. 12

Simbang Gabi
See **Misa de Gallo**

♦ 1810 ♦ Simhat Torah
Between September 28 and October 26; Tishri 22 or 23

This Jewish holiday, which follows SUKKOT, celebrates the annual completion of the public reading of the Torah, or the first five books of the Bible, and the beginning of a new reading cycle. The hand-lettered scrolls of the Torah are removed from the Ark (a box-like container) and paraded around the synagogue—and sometimes through the streets—amidst singing and dancing. Simhat Torah means "rejoicing in the law," which is as good a description as any of what takes place on this day. To be chosen as the Bridegroom of the Law—to read the final verses of the last book, Deuteronomy—or the Bridegroom of the Beginning—to read the opening verses of the first book, Genesis—is considered a great honor.

In Israel and among Reform Jews, this festival is observed on the 22nd day of Tishri, concurrently with SHEMINI ATZERET; all other Jews celebrate it separately on the 23rd day. Israelis also hold a second *hakkafot* ('procession around the synagogue') on the night after Simhat Torah, frequently accompanied by bands and choirs.

Simhat Torah customs have varied from country to country. In Afghanistan all the scrolls are taken out of their Arks and heaped in a pyramid almost to the synagogue's roof. In Cochin, China, a carpet was laid on the courtyard flagstones, coconut oil lamps were heaped in a pyramid in front of the synagogue entrance, and the Scrolls of the Law carried around the outside of the synagogue. One synagogue in Calcutta, India, has 50 Scrolls, and the women go from scroll to scroll, kissing them. At the end of the holiday a Simhat

Torah ball is held and a beauty queen chosen. Young Yemeni children are taken to the synagogue for the first time on this holiday.

In southern France, two mourners stand on either side of the reader, crying bitterly as the death of Moses is related. The Bridegrooms of the Law in Holland are escorted home in a torchlight parade accompanied by music. A crown from one of the Torah Scrolls was placed on the head of every reader in medieval Spain, and in some places in Eastern Europe, the reader wore a large paper hat decorated with bells and feathers.

> **SOURCES:**
> *AmerBkDays-1978*, pp. 928, 950
> *BkHolWrld-1986*, Oct 11
> *BkFest-1937*, p. 204
> *DictWrldRel-1989*, pp. 155, 693
> *FolkAmerHol-1991*, p. 354
> *FolkWrldHol-1992*, p. 508

Simnel Sunday
See **Mothering Sunday**

Sinai Day
See **Egypt National Day**

◆ 1811 ◆ Singapore National Day
August 9

A public holiday in Singapore to commemorate its independence. Singapore was the administrative seat for the Straits Settlements, a British crown colony, from 1867 until it was occupied by Japan in World War II. It was restored to Britain in 1945, became a part of Malaysia in 1963, and became independent in 1965. The holiday is celebrated with a spectacular parade, cultural dances, and fireworks.

CONTACT:
Singapore Tourist Promotion
  Board
590 Fifth Ave., 12th Floor
New York, NY 10036
212-302-4861; fax: 212-302-4801

SOURCES:
AnnivHol-1983, p. 104
Chases-1996, p. 330
GdWrldFest-1985, p. 159

◆ 1812 ◆ Sinhala Avurudu
April

The New Year celebrated in Sri Lanka (formerly Ceylon) as a non-religious festival by both Sinhalese and Tamils. The exact hour of the new year is determined by astrologers, and often the new year does not begin when the old year ends. The few hours between the new and old year are known as the *nona gathe* ('neutral period'), and all activities, including eating and drinking, must stop for that time.

In the villages the new year traditionally begins with lighting a fire in the kitchen and wearing new clothes. The color of these clothes is determined by an almanac. The ceremonies reach a climax with an anointing ceremony. Oil is mixed with an herbal paste and a family elder rubs this oil on the heads of all the family members as they sit with a white cloth under their feet. The holiday is also a day of public festivities, including sports, games, dancing, and special dinners.

CONTACT:
Sri Lankan Embassy
2148 Wyoming Ave., N.W.
Washington, D.C. 20008
202-483-4025; fax: 202-232-7181

SOURCES:
AnnivHol-1983, p. 181
GdWrldFest-1985, p. 165
IntlThFolk-1979, p. 345

◆ 1813 ◆ Sinjska Alka
First weekend in August

A day of jousting on horseback in the small town of Sinj, near Split in Croatia (in the former Yugoslavia). The festival commemorates a victory of a peasant army over the Turks in 1715, even though the 60,000 Turks outnumbered the Sinj warriors by three to one. The annual tournament was supposedly instituted soon after the 1715 victory.

On this day, young men who have trained throughout the year ride horses headlong down the steep 140-yard run and try to spear an iron ring, or *alka*, suspended from a rope about nine feet off the ground. The ring has a diameter of six inches and within it is another two-inch ring. The jouster who most successfully spears the rings in three tries is the winner and receives a sash and silver medal. The band plays a triumphal march and shots are fired for all top scorers.

Before the contest, there is a ceremonial procession through the streets. The contestants march through Sinj accompanied by their mace bearers and shield bearers wearing 18th-century costumes decorated with gold and silver.

CONTACT:
Croatia Embassy
2343 Massachusetts Ave., N.W.
Washington, D.C. 20008
202-588-5899; fax: 202-588-8936

Atlas Tourism and Travel
60 E. 42nd St., Ste. 2235
New York, NY 10165
800-528-5275 or 212-697-6767
fax: 212-697-7678

SOURCES:
IntlThFolk-1979, p. 403

Sinterklass
See **St. Nicholas's Day**

◆ 1814 ◆ Sinulog Festival
Third weekend in January

A festival on the island of Cebu in the Philippines, held at the same time as the frenzied ATI-ATIHAN FESTIVAL in Kalibo and the more sedate DINAGYANG in Iloilo City. The word *sinulog* is derived from the rootword *sulog*, meaning 'river current', and the dancing of the festival is thought to flow like a river.

The festival celebrates both early Cebuano culture and the history of the Christianization of Cebu, combining the pageantry of early years with today's Christian ritual. An image of Cebu's patron saint, the Santo Niño ('the Holy Child,' Jesus), is carried in a procession along the streets, while drums beat in the ritual for a bountiful harvest and revelers dance in the streets.

CONTACT:
Philippine Department of Tourism
556 Fifth Ave.
First Floor Mezzanine
New York, NY 10036
212-575-7915; fax: 212-302-6759

♦ 1815 ♦ **Sithinakha**
May–June; sixth day of waxing half of Hindu month of Jyestha

This is the birthday of the Hindu god Kumara, also known as Skanda, the god of war and first-born son of Shiva. Kumara has six heads because he was nursed by the Karttikas—six women who as stars comprise the Pleiades. For this reason he is also called *Karttikeya*, 'son of Karttikas.' The six heads also represent the six senses (including extrasensory perception). He also has a large following under the name *Subrahmanya*, meaning 'dear to the Brahmanas.'

Most Hindus observe this day with a ritual purification bath followed by processions to the temples to honor Kumara. It is also considered a good opportunity to clean out wells and tanks, because the snake gods are off worshipping on this day and it's safe to enter their habitats. In Nepal, eight different kinds of cakes, made from eight different grains, are offered to Kumara on his birthday, and for this reason Sithinakha is sometimes referred to as the **Cake Festival**. Lotus-shaped windmills are often set on rooftops at this time, to symbolize the end of bad times and the onset of holier days.

SOURCES:
FolkWrldHol-1992, p. 319

♦ 1816 ♦ **Sitka Summer Music Festival**
June

A series of concerts featuring internationally known musicians, held during three weeks in June in Sitka, Alaska. Chamber music concerts are held on Tuesdays and Fridays, and there are programs ranging from classical to pop. The concerts are given in the Centennial Building auditorium, which has a wall of glass behind the stage. Since the nights are light in June, the audience can look at mountains, eagles, water, and mist while listening to the music. Violin virtuoso Paul Rosenthal founded the festival in 1972, producing the first musical event with four other musicians, and going on to emphasize a repertoire of 18th- and 19th-century classics.

CONTACT:
Anchorage Convention and Visitors Bureau
1600 'A' Street, Ste. 200
Anchorage, AK 99501
800-446-5352 or 907-276-4118
fax: 907-278-5559

SOURCES:
Chases-1996, p. 246
MusFestAmer-1990, p. 22

♦ 1817 ♦ **Sjomannadagur (Seaman's Day)**
First Sunday in June

A day honoring the role that fishing and fishermen have played in Icelandic history, celebrated in the coastal towns and cities of Iceland. Sailors take the day off, and the Sea-

man's Union sponsors many events. These include competitions in rowing and swimming, tugs-of-war, and sea rescue competitions. On the more solemn side, medals are awarded for rescue operations of the past year. Most celebrations begin with a church service and a trip to the local cemetery to honor sailors lost at sea. Afterward there are children's parades, dances, outdoor cookouts, and bonfires in the evening. The proceeds from the day's events throughout the country go to the national fund that supports old seamen's homes.

CONTACT:
Scandinavian Tourism, Inc.
P.O. Box 4649
New York, NY 10163-4649
212-949-2333; fax: 212-983-5260

SOURCES:
AnnivHol-1983, p. 75

♦ 1818 ♦ **Smithsonian Kite Festival**
Late March–early April

The Kite Festival held on the Mall in Washington, D.C., every spring is co-sponsored by the Smithsonian Resident Associate Program and the National Air and Space Museum. First held in 1966, the festival was started by Dr. Paul Garber, a kite fancier and historian emeritus of the National Air and Space Museum. Until his death in 1992, Dr. Garber served as master of ceremonies for the festivities.

A major focus of the annual festival is the competition for hand-made kites, which must be capable of flying at a minimum altitude of 100 feet for at least one minute. Kites are judged on the basis of appearance (design, craftsmanship, beauty) as well as on performance (takeoff, climb, angle, recovery). Trophies are awarded in many categories—for example, airplane, bird figure, box-kite, spacecraft, and delta—and age groups. Participants come from all regions of the United States as well as several foreign countries. Immediately following the kite display program, a kite-building workshop is held for members of the Smithsonian Resident Associate Program.

CONTACT:
National Air and Space Museum
Smithsonian Institution
Independence Ave. & 6th St., S.W.
Washington, D.C. 20560
202-357-2700; fax: 202-357-2426

SOURCES:
Chases-1996, p. 150

♦ 1819 ♦ **Snake-Antelope Dance**
August

An ancient Hopi Indian prayer for rain, the Snake-Antelope Dance is held in alternate years during the last dry week in August. Before the ceremony, the medicine men gather snakes, which are believed to have the power to bring rain, and wash them in suds made from the yucca plant. The Snake and Antelope priests come out of the kiva, where secret rituals are held, and perform a dance around the enclosure where the snakes are confined. Then they divide into groups of three, each consisting of a carrier, a hugger, and a gatherer. The carrier takes a snake in his mouth, the hugger puts his left hand on the carrier's shoulder, and the gatherer does the same thing to the hugger. Together they circle the area four times. Then the carrier releases the snake and the gatherer retrieves it. Eventually the snakes are set free so that they can carry out their mission and summon the rain.

Snake dances are common among Indian tribes, and vestiges of this ceremony can still be seen at the Zuni, Acoma, and Cochiti pueblos.

CONTACT:
Hopi Tribal Council
P.O. Box 123
Kykotsmovi, AZ 86039
602-734-2445

SOURCES:
DictFolkMyth-1984, p. 1030
EncyRel-1987, vol. 10, p. 520

♦ 1820 ♦ Snan Yatra
May–June; full moon day of Hindu month of Jyestha

This Hindu bathing festival is held in Orissa, India. Images of the gods Jagannath, Balbhadra, Subhadra, and Sudarshan are brought in a grand procession to the bathing platform for their ceremonial baths. As mantras from the Vedas, or Hindu sacred writings, are recited, consecrated water is poured over the deities. Then they are dressed in ceremonial robes before going into seclusion for 15 days. For Hindus, this is an occasion for rejoicing and merrymaking.

CONTACT:
India Tourist Office
30 Rockefeller Ave.
15 N. Mezzanine
New York, NY 10112
212-586-4901; fax: 212-582-3274

SOURCES:
RelHolCal-1993, p. 115

♦ 1821 ♦ Snowgolf Championship
February

A tongue-in-cheek winter event established to rescue the residents of Prince George, British Columbia, from their winter doldrums, the Snowgolf Championship was started in 1973 by members of the Prince George Golf Club who wanted to try playing their sport in the snow. Competitors show up in unusual winter costumes and play golf using six-inch tees and billiard-size, bright purple golf balls. Several hundred snowgolfers use three nine-hole courses for the event, which goes on for three days in February and is often attended by sports and entertainment celebrities. Prizes and souvenirs worth more than $10,000 are awarded to the golfer with the best costume, the golfer with the most unusual footwear, the most promotion-conscious golfer, and the coldest celebrity foursome. There are dinner dances in the evening, and the proceeds of the event go to a local charity.

CONTACT:
Tourism British Columbia
Parliament Buildings
Victoria, B.C.
Canada V8V 1X4
800-663-6000 or 604-663-6000

SOURCES:
GdWrldFest-1985, p. 32

Snow Hut Festival
See **Kamakura Matsuri**

♦ 1822 ♦ Sol
January–February; first day of first lunar month; January 1–2

One of the biggest holidays of the year in Korea, the LUNAR NEW YEAR is celebrated largely by rural people and is a two-day national holiday. January 1 and 2, also national holidays, are celebrated more by residents of cities. On Sol, tradition calls for families to gather in their best clothes and for children to bow to parents and grandparents to reaffirm family ties. A soup made of rice dumplings called *duggook* is always served, and it is customary to play *yut*, a game played with wooden blocks and a game board. Young girls see-saw standing up. During early Confucianism, women were not allowed any outdoor exercises. See-sawing this way bounced them above their enclosing walls, and they could see their boyfriends. This made see-sawing a love sport and not exercise. It is still very popular.

SOURCES:
FolkWrldHol-1992, p. 52

♦ 1823 ♦ Solomon Islands Independence Day
July 7

The Solomon Islands in the Southwest Pacific gained independence from Britain on this day in 1978. They had been under British control since 1900. Independence Day is a national holiday throughout the islands.

CONTACT:
Solomon Islands Mission to the
U.N.
820 Second Ave., Ste. 800-A
New York, NY 10017
212-599-6192

SOURCES:
AnnivHol-1983, p. 90
Chases-1996, p. 288

♦ 1824 ♦ Somalia Independence Days
June 26; July 1

Somalia celebrates two independence days. Before becoming a united republic, Somalia was divided up between Britain and Italy. The northern part of the region was British Somaliland, and other areas belonged to Italy. June 26 is the anniversary of independence of British Somaliland from Britain in 1960, while July 1, 1960, is the day the former Italian Somaliland became independent from Italy. On July 1, 1960, both areas were united as the Republic of Somalia.

SOURCES:
AnnivHol-1983, pp. 84, 87
NatlHolWrld-1968, p. 103

♦ 1825 ♦ Songkran (Pi Mai)
April 12–14; sixth or seventh moon of Dai calendar

The traditional NEW YEAR in Thailand and a public holiday. The celebration actually lasts for three days, from April 12–14, and takes the form of religious ceremonies as well as public festivities. Merit-making ceremonies are held at Buddhist temples, water is sprinkled on Buddhist images, and captive birds and fish are freed. Water-splashing on the streets is also a part of the festivities, especially among young people. The young do not splash older people, but instead sprinkle water on their hands or feet to honor them.

The celebration is held with special élan in Chiang Mai with beauty contests, parades, dancing, and, of course, water splashing.

The Dai people of the southwestern Xinan region of China, celebrate the birthday of Buddha (*see* VESAK) and the new year with the **Water-Splashing Festival**. In tropical Xishuangbanna, a land of elephants and golden-haired monkeys, the celebration begins with dragon-boat races and fireworks displays. On the second day, people visit Buddhist temples. The third day, which is New Year's Day, is the high point. Dressed in colorful local costumes, people carry buckets and pans of water to the temple to bathe the Buddha, and they then splash water at each other. The water symbolizes happiness and good health. It washes away the demons of the past year and welcomes in a new year of good harvests, better livestock, and increased prosperity.

CONTACT:	SOURCES:
Tourism Authority of Thailand	*AnnivHol-1983,* p. 182
5 World Trade Center, Ste. 3443	*BkFestHolWrld-1970,* p. 11
New York, NY 10048	*BkHolWrld-1986,* Apr 13
212-432-0433; fax: 212-912-0920	*FolkWrldHol-1992,* pp. 6, 244
	GdWrldFest-1985, p. 174
China National Tourist Office	*RelHolCal-1993,* p. 116
350 Fifth Ave., Ste. 6413	
New York, NY 10165	
212-760-9700; fax: 212-760-8809	

◆ 1826 ◆ **Song of Hiawatha Pageant**
Last two weekends in July and first weekend in August

Pipestone, Minnesota, was named for the soft red stone used by the Native American Dakota tribe to make their ceremonial pipes. The Dakotas believe that their tribe originated here, and that the stone was colored by the blood of their ancestors. On weekends in late July and early August each year, the story of Hiawatha (Haionhwat'ha, fl. c.1570)—the chief of the Onondaga tribe immortalized in Henry Wadsworth Longfellow's poem, "Song of Hiawatha"—is told in symbolic pantomime with traditional Indian music and dances. The audience watches the performance from the opposite side of a quiet reflecting pool that lies at the bottom of the pipestone quarry where the pageant is held.

The Great Spirit appears at the top of the cliff, where he shows his children the pink stone and makes a calumet or peace pipe. With the last whiff on his pipe, the Great Spirit disappears in a cloud of smoke. The Three Maidens, who once guarded the place where the Great Spirit lived, can be seen in the form of three huge boulders. The pageant ends with the death of Hiawatha and his departure on a "long and distant journey."

CONTACT:	SOURCES:
Minnesota Office of Tourism	*AmerBkDays-1978,* p. 215
121 E. 7th Pl. Metro Sq., Ste. 100	*Chases-1996,* p. 303
St. Paul, MN 55101	
612-296-5029 or 800-657-3700	
fax: 612-296-7095	

◆ 1827 ◆ **South Africa Republic Day**
May 31

A referendum held in South Africa on October 6, 1960, narrowly approved the formation of the Republic of South Africa, although "colored" voters were excluded as part of the country's long-standing policy of racial segregation known as apartheid. The closeness of the vote—52.14 percent in favor, 47.42 percent opposed—reflected the mixed feelings of both the Afrikaners and the British settlers, although the former generally supported the idea. The Union of South Africa became the Republic of South Africa on May 31, 1961, thus severing its long-standing ties to the old British

Empire. Also on this date in 1902 the Boer War ended. The Treaty of Vereeniging was signed by representatives of the South African Republic and the Orange Free State who had been waging war with Great Britain since October 12, 1899. Eight years later the Union of South Africa was inaugurated, uniting the Cape of Good Hope, Natal, the Transvaal, and the Orange Free State.

CONTACT:	SOURCES:
South African Tourism Board	*AnnivHol-1983,* p. 73
500 Fifth Ave.	*DictDays-1988,* pp. 95, 124
New York, NY 10110	*NatlHolWrld-1968,* p. 72
800-822-5368 or 212-730-2929	
fax: 212-764-1980	

◆ 1828 ◆ **South Carolina Peach Festival**
Mid-July

A 10-day festival in Gaffney, S.C., to salute the state's peach industry. Events of the festival include a parade, truck and tractor pulls, country-music concerts, and peach desserts. Gaffney's year-round tribute to the peach is the eye-catching "peachoid," a one-million-gallon water tank in the shape and color of a peach with a great metal leaf hanging over it.

CONTACT:
South Carolina Division of
Tourism
1205 Pendleton St.
Columbia, SC 29201
803-734-0122; fax: 803-734-0133

◆ 1829 ◆ **Southern 500 (Heinz Southern 500)**
September, Labor Day weekend

The oldest southern stock-car race, held in Darlington, S.C., since 1950. The race, which draws about 80,000 spectators, is one of the four so-called crown jewels in the NASCAR (National Association for Stock Car Auto Racing) Winston Cup circuit and is considered the forerunner of those races. The others are the DAYTONA 500 (in Florida), the WINSTON 500 (Talladega, Ala.), and the COCA-COLA 600 (Charlotte, N.C.).

The first of the southern super speedways, the Darlington track was promoted and built by Harold Brasington, a sometime racing driver, and a group of Darlington citizens. The track was built on land owned by Sherman J. Ramsey, a farmer, and he insisted that his minnow pond not be disturbed. So the track had to skirt around it. Sports writers dubbed the oddly configured raceway the "Lady in Black" supposedly because it was fickle with drivers, like a mysterious woman. The winner of the first race in 1950 was Johnny Mantz. The all-time winner of the most Southern 500s is Cale Yarborough, who zipped past everybody else in 1968, 1973, 1974, 1978, and 1982.

CONTACT:	SOURCES:
National Association for Stock Car	*FolkAmerHol-1991,* p. 330
Auto Racing	
P.O. Box 2875	
Daytona Beach, FL 32115	
904-253-0611; fax: 904-258-7646	

South Carolina Division of
Tourism
1205 Pendleton St.
Columbia, SC 29201
803-734-0122; fax: 803-734-0133

♦ 1830 ♦ **Southern Ute Tribal Sun Dance**
First weekend after July 4

A ritual ceremony of ancient origin held by the Southern Ute Indians in Ignacio, Colo., usually on the Sunday and Monday after July Fourth. The dancers who perform the ceremony are chosen from those who dream dreams and see visions, and they fast for four days before the dancing. While the public is allowed to attend, dress must be circumspect, and women are not allowed who are "on their moon," that is, having their menstrual period.

One aspect of the ceremony involves chopping down a tree, stripping its bark and then dancing around it. The SUN DANCE was at one time performed by most Plains tribes, and usually involved self-torture. The Utes, however, did not practice this.

CONTACT:
Southern Ute Tribal Council
P.O. Box 737
Ignacio, CO 81137
303-563-4525

SOURCES:
EncyRel-1987, vol. 14, p. 143
IndianAmer-1989, pp. 121, 360

♦ 1831 ♦ **Southwestern Exposition & Livestock Show & Rodeo**
Last two weeks of January

The oldest continuously running livestock show in the United States, held since 1896 in Fort Worth, Tex. The exposition calls to mind Fort Worth's past when it was considered the capital of the southwestern cattle empire, and stockyards ringed the city. The world's first indoor rodeo was featured here in 1918.

Events of the exposition include a parade, horse shows, a midway, big-name entertainers, and $600,000 in show premiums and rodeo purses. The more than 17,000 head of livestock include beef and dairy cattle, sheep, swine, goats, horses, donkeys, mules, pigeons, poultry, sheepdogs, and llamas. The latter have been found to be more effective against coyotes than guns, dogs, electric fences, or chemical repellants. About 500 of them are now guarding sheep in the Rocky Mountain region.

CONTACT:
Fort Worth Convention and Visitors Bureau
415 Throckmorton St.
Fort Worth, TX 76102
800-433-5747 or 817-336-8791
fax: 817-336-3282

SOURCES:
Chases-1996, p. 69

Spearing the Dragon
See **Drachenstich**

♦ 1832 ♦ **Spoleto Festival USA**
May–June

Pulitzer Prize-winning composer Gian Carlo Menotti founded the **Festival of Two Worlds** in Spoleto, Italy, in 1958, and brought it to Charleston, South Carolina, in 1977 under the name of **Spoleto USA**. The annual 17-day international arts festival focuses on new works and productions, and routinely offers more than 100 events in opera, chamber music, symphonic concerts, theater, dance, and art.

There has been some controversy recently over whether or not the Spoleto Festival should feature more contemporary

art forms, such as jazz. Menotti, who turned 80 in 1991, prefers to keep the festival more traditional and convinced the Board of Directors to keep it so. The festival and the composer have been associated for so long that "Menotti" and "Spoleto" have become nearly synonymous.

CONTACT:
Charleston Area Convention and Visitors Bureau
P.O. Box 975
Charleston, SC 29402
800-868-8118 or 803-853-8000

SOURCES:
GdUSFest-1984, p. 169
GdWrldFest-1985, p. 120
IntlThFolk-1979, p. 248
MusFestAmer-1990, p. 136

♦ 1833 ♦ **Spring Break**
February–April

An annual celebration of spring—and of school vacations—by an estimated two million college students who whoop it up, sunbathe, party, drink, dance, and listen to loud music. From the early 1950s until 1985, Fort Lauderdale, Fla., was a prime destination. In 1960 the movie, *Where the Boys Are* (based on the Glendon Swarthout novel of the same name), featuring Connie Francis, George Hamilton, and Yvette Mimieux, was all about spring break. It gave Fort Lauderdale great national exposure. But the hordes of students got to be too much; by 1985, 350,000 people took over the city for six weeks and tied up not just traffic but the legal system. Fort Lauderdale started clamping down, and now only about 20,000 students visit. The popular destinations today are Panama City Beach, Fla., which drew about 500,000 young revelers in 1992, Daytona Beach, Fla., South Padre Island, Tex., Palm Springs, Calif., the Bahamas, Jamaica, and Mexico. To lure the spring breakers, the various towns and resorts spend millions of dollars and offer an abundance of free activities, including beach sports, concerts, movie premieres, and contests.

See also BERMUDA COLLEGE WEEKS

CONTACT:
Florida Division of Tourism
126 W. Van Buren
Tallahassee, FL 32399
904-487-1462; fax: 904-921-9158

Spring Festival
See **Lunar New Year**

♦ 1834 ♦ **Springtime Festival**
Beginning between March 11 and April 15; four successive Thursdays before Orthodox Easter

Celebrated by peasants of all religious faiths, the Springtime Festival is a regional celebration throughout the Bekáa Valley, a region occupying parts of Syria, Lebanon, and the former Palestine. It takes place during LENT, on four successive Thursdays preceding the Eastern Orthodox EASTER.

The first Thursday, known as Thursday-of-the-Animals, is a day of rest for domestic working animals, whose heads are decorated with a spot of henna, which is symbolic of blood and life. On the following Thursday, known as Thursday-of-the-Plants, young children and unmarried girls wash themselves in water scented with crushed flowers. Next is Thursday-of-the-Dead, a day for visiting the graves of family and friends. Last is Thursday-of-the-Jumping, or Day of the Jumping, when people living in the mountains come down by the thousands to the plains to join in the festival activities. They visit the tomb of Noah and then the shrine of the Wali Zaur, a locally popular Muslim saint. There they receive blessings for good health. Eventually everyone returns to the village, where there is dancing in the streets and even on the mosque grounds.

SOURCES:
FolkWrldHol-1992, p. 123

♦ 1835 ♦ Spy Wednesday
Between March 19 and April 22; Wednesday before Easter

The Wednesday before EASTER Sunday is the day on which the disciple Judas Iscariot made the deal to betray Jesus. In order to arrest Jesus without exciting the populace, Judas led the Jewish priests to the Garden of Gethsemane, near Jerusalem, where Jesus had gone at night to pray with the other 11 disciples after the Last Supper (*see* MAUNDY THURSDAY). Judas identified Jesus by kissing him and addressing him as "Master." For this he was paid 30 pieces of silver, the price of a slave in the Old Testament.

The name "Spy Wednesday" is said to be of Irish origin, although the Bible never refers to Judas as a spy. His surname, Iscariot, is believed to be a corruption of the Latin *sicarius*, meaning 'murderer' or 'assassin.'

SOURCES:
DaysCustFaith-1957, p. 106
DictDays-1988, p. 113

♦ 1836 ♦ Sri Lanka Independence Day
February 4

The former British colony of Ceylon changed its name in 1972 to Sri Lanka, which means "Blessed Isle." Sri Lankans commemorate the granting of their independence from Great Britain on February 4, 1948, with public gatherings throughout the island and special services in the temples, churches, and mosques. There are also parades, folk dances, processions, and national games.

CONTACT:
Sri Lankan Embassy
2148 Wyoming Ave., N.W.
Washington, D.C. 20008
202-483-4025; fax: 202-232-7181

SOURCES:
AnnivHol-1983, p. 19
Chases-1996, p. 87
IntlThFolk-1979, p. 345
NatlHolWrld-1968, p. 22

Stamp Act Repealed
See Repudiation Day

♦ 1837 ♦ Stanton Day, Elizabeth Cady
November 12

Elizabeth Cady Stanton (1815–1902) was a pioneer in the struggle for women's rights. After graduating from the Troy Female Academy (now known as the Emma Willard School), one of the first schools devoted to providing better education for women, she married journalist and abolitionist Henry Brewster Stanton—although she carefully omitted the word "obey" from their wedding ceremony. With a group of other women, she helped organize the first women's rights convention, held at Seneca Falls, New York, in 1848. This is where Stanton drew up her famous bill of rights for women, which included the first formal demand for women's suf-

frage in the United States. But it was her partnership with Susan B. Anthony, beginning in 1851, that galvanized the women's rights movement. Together they organized the National Woman Suffrage Association, planned suffrage campaigns, spoke out in favor of liberal divorce laws, and fought for political, legal, and industrial equality for women. Stanton died, however, 18 years before the 19th Amendment to the Constitution, granting women the right to vote, became law in 1920.

Governor Herbert Lehman of New York declared November 12 Elizabeth Cady Stanton Day in 1941. But Stanton's birthday has long been observed by women's rights groups throughout the United States, particularly the National Organization for Women (NOW).

See also ANTHONY DAY, SUSAN B.

CONTACT:
National Organization for Women
1000 16th St., N.W., Ste. 700
Washington, D.C. 20036
202-331-0066; fax: 202-785-8576
E-mail: now@now.org
WWW: http://now.org/now/
home.html

SOURCES:
AmerBkDays-1978, p. 1016
AnnivHol-1983, p. 146
Chases-1996, p. 448

♦ 1838 ♦ Star Festival
January–February; 18th day of Chinese lunar year

To the Chinese, the stars and planets are the homes of sainted heroes who have the power to influence the course of human destiny. When LUNAR NEW YEAR is over, therefore, a day is set aside for men to worship the Star Gods. Women are traditionally forbidden to participate in the ceremony, which consists of setting up a small table or altar in the courtyard of the house with a very simple food offering—usually rice balls cooked in sugar and flour. Two pictures are placed on the altar, one of the Star Gods and another of the cyclical signs associated with them. In a sealed envelope is a chart of lucky and unlucky stars. The master of the house makes a special prayer to the star that presided over his birth and lights the special lamps, made of red and yellow paper and filled with perfumed oil, that have been arranged around the altar. They burn out quickly, after which each son of the house comes forward to honor his own star by relighting three of the lamps. If their flames burn brightly, it means he will have good luck in the coming year.

SOURCES:
BkFestHolWrld-1970, p. 25

Star Festival in Japan
See Tanabata

♦ 1839 ♦ State Fair of Texas
Late September through the beginning of October

Not surprisingly, one of the nation's biggest state fairs, claiming more than three million visitors to the 200-acre Fair Park in Dallas. The fair began in 1887, and in 1952 Big Tex, its symbol of bigness, arrived. Big Tex is a 52-foot-tall cowboy with a 30-foot chest and 7'8" biceps, wearing a five-foot-high, 75-gallon cowboy hat. The cowboy stands in the middle of the fairgrounds booming out welcomes and announcements. The skeleton of the cowboy was built in 1949 to be the world's tallest Santa Claus for a Christmas celebration in Kerens, Tex. It was sold to the State Fair, and Dallas artist Jack Bridges used baling wire and papier-mâché to create the cowboy that debuted in 1952. The following year, a motor was installed to move the cowboy's jaw in sync with a voice mechanism, and Big Tex has been booming ever since. Among fair events are a rodeo, college football game, and parades.

CONTACT:
Texas Department of Commerce
Tourism Division
1700 N. Congress Ave., Ste. 200
Austin, TX 78711
800-888-8839 or 512-462-9192
fax: 512-936-0089

SOURCES:
Chases-1996, p. 393
GdUSFest-1984, p. 181

♦ 1840 ♦ **State Opening of Parliament**
Early November

This colorful British ritual is observed at the beginning of November when the members of Parliament return after the long summer recess. Crowds assemble in the streets of Westminster, an inner borough of Greater London, in hopes of catching a glimpse of the Queen as she arrives in her horse-drawn coach, dressed in royal robes of state and escorted by the Household Cavalry. The Queen is not allowed to enter the House of Commons because she is not a commoner, so after being met by the Lord Chancellor she is led straight to the House of Lords. Seated on a magnificent throne and surrounded by various church and state officials in their robes, she reads aloud the speech that has been written for her by members of the government outlining their plans for the coming session.

An interesting tradition that accompanies the opening of Parliament is the searching of the cellars of both Houses. This goes back to 1605, when Guy Fawkes (*see* Guy Fawkes Day) and his accomplices tried to blow them up.

CONTACT:
British Tourist Authority
551 Fifth Ave., Ste. 702
New York, NY 10176
800-462-2748 or 212-986-2200
fax: 212-986-1188

SOURCES:
AnnivHol-1983, p. 180

♦ 1841 ♦ **Stewardship Sunday**
Second Sunday in November

This is the day on which many churches in the United States and Canada begin their campaign for financial support in the coming year. The term "stewardship" refers to Christian and Jewish teaching that all creation belongs to God and that each man and woman is an agent or steward to whom God's property is entrusted for a while. On this Sunday each year, churches appeal to their members' sense of responsibility as stewards of the money God has entrusted to them.

In the United States, Stewardship Sunday is sponsored by the National Council of Churches' Joint Department of Stewardship and Benevolence.

SOURCES:
DaysCustFaith-1957, p. 300

♦ 1842 ♦ **Stickdance**
Spring

A week of ceremonies to grieve for the dead, held by the Athapaskan Indians of Alaska. The ancient ceremony, usually held long after the deaths of those memorialized, is now observed only in two villages on the Yukon River—Kaltag and Nulato.

Each evening of the ceremony, people go to the community hall with traditional foods—moose, salmon, beaver, rabbit, ptarmigan (a kind of grouse)—for a meal called a *potlatch.* After the meal, the women stand in a circle, swaying and chanting traditional songs for the dead. The hall becomes more crowded each night. On Friday night, as the women dance in a circle, the men carry in a tall spruce tree stripped of branches and wrapped in ribbons. The tree is erected in the center of the room and wolf and fox furs are draped on it. The people then dance around it and chant continuously through the night. In the morning, the men tear the furs and ribbons from the stick and carry it away to the Yukon River, where they break it into pieces and throw the pieces on the river's ice.

On Saturday night, people representing the dead are ritually dressed in special clothes. Somberly, they leave the hall and go to the river where they shake the spirits from their clothing. On their return to the hall, the mood becomes festive; gifts are exchanged and a night of celebration begins. The following morning the people who have represented the dead walk through the village shaking hands with people, sharing food and drink, and saying farewell.

Stickdance is held at irregular intervals, since it takes months or longer to prepare for it. People must choose those who will represent the dead being honored and make their clothes, and they must also save up to buy gifts.

The Athapaskans, who may have descended from bands who crossed from Asia, have lived in Alaska longer than the Eskimos, and speak a language that is in the same family as that spoken by Navajos and Apaches.

CONTACT:
Alaska Division of Tourism
P.O. Box 110801
Juneau, AK 99811
907-465-2012; fax: 907-465-2287

♦ 1843 ♦ **Stiftungsfest**
Last weekend in August

Appropriately enough, Minnesota's oldest continuous festival is held in the town of Young America. Loosely translated as 'founders' day,' Stiftungsfest was created in 1861 by the Young America Maennerchor (men's choir) as a way of bringing the music of old Germany to the new world. Well-known bands and singing groups from Germany as well as local groups perform during the three-day event, which includes a traditional German beer garden, a flower show, and a Grand Parade, which is held every fifth year.

CONTACT:
Minnesota Office of Tourism
121 E. 7th Pl. Metro Sq., Ste. 100
St. Paul, MN 55101
612-296-5029 or 800-657-3700
fax: 612-296-7095

SOURCES:
Chases-1996, p. 347

♦ 1844 ♦ **Stir-Up Sunday**
November–December; Sunday before Advent

The collect for the Sunday preceding Advent in the Church of

England begins, "Stir up, we beseech Thee, O Lord, the wills of thy faithful people." But the real "stirring up" that takes place on this day is more literal: the stirring of the batter for the traditional CHRISTMAS pudding, which must be prepared weeks in advance. It is customary for each member of the family to take turns stirring the pudding with a wooden spoon (symbolic of Jesus' crib), which is thought to bring good luck. The stirring is done clockwise, with eyes closed, and the stirrer makes a wish.

SOURCES:
BkHolWrld-1986, Nov 22
DictDays-1988, p. 114
FolkWrldHol-1992, p. 572

◆ 1845 ◆ **Stockton Asparagus Festival**
Last weekend in April

A two-day celebration in Stockton, Calif., the heart of the region that claims to be the "Asparagus Capital of the Nation." In fact, California accounts for about 90 percent of the fresh-market asparagus production in the country, and most of that asparagus comes from Stockton's San Joaquin Delta region.

The festival began in 1986 to promote the asparagus and it now draws 85,000 spectators to the varied events. These include more than 50 food booths in Asparagus Alley, a wine-tasting booth, a fun run (some runners wear asparagus spears in their headbands), a car show of some 200 antique and classic cars, arts and crafts, live entertainment (bands, jugglers, mimes, magicians, etc.), and children's activities. There's also a recipe contest; among the past winning entries are enchiladas and lasagna made, of course, with asparagus. Other popular asparagus dishes served include asparaberry shortcake (it is said the asparagus gives a nutmeg flavor to the strawberries), asparagus-and-beef sandwiches, and asparagus bisque. The festival is also a time to promulgate information about the asparagus, and fair-goers learn that asparagus is a source of vitamins A and C; the first trainload of asparagus was sent east from California in 1900; the Greeks and Romans used asparagus as a medicine for bee stings, dropsy, and toothache, and also as an aphrodisiac.

CONTACT:
California Division of Tourism
801 K Street, Ste. 1600
Sacramento, CA 95814
800-862-2543 or 916-322-2881
fax: 916-322-3402

Store Bededag
See **Common Prayer Day**

◆ 1846 ◆ **Storytelling Festival, National**
First weekend in October

A three-day festival in Jonesborough, Tenn., that was started in 1973 to revive the ancient folk art of storytelling. The popularity of storytelling seemed to be dying, replaced by radio, television, and movies. The first festival was the idea of Jimmy Neil Smith, a Jonesborough schoolteacher who became executive director of the festival's sponsor, the National Association for the Preservation and Perpetuation of Storytelling (now known as the National Storytelling Association), which was formed in 1975 and is headquartered in Jonesborough. That first event drew about 60 people. At first,

people sat on bales of hay, then the festival moved to kitchens and parlors and porches, and finally into the large tents now used. The festival has inspired scores of similar events around the country as well as college courses in storytelling.

About 6,000 people now attend to listen to storytellers relating ghost stories, sacred stories, ballads, tall tales, myths, legends, and fairy tales. Restaurants set up food booths, and a resource tent provides tapes and other material. The 20th-anniversary celebration in 1992 brought together more than 80 storytellers who had all appeared at previous festivals. A highlight was a special ghost-story concert by tellers of supernatural tales.

See also TELLEBRATION

CONTACT:
National Storytelling Association
P. O. Box 309
Jonesborough, TN 37659
800-525-4514 or 423-753-2171
fax: 423-753-9331

SOURCES:
Chases-1996, p. 403
GdUSFest-1984, p. 174

◆ 1847 ◆ **Stratford Festival**
June–October

What started in Stratford, Ontario, in 1953 as a six-week Shakespearean drama festival under the artistic leadership of Alec Guinness and Irene Worth has since expanded into a 23-week event drawing an audience of half a million people. All of Shakespeare's plays have been performed here over the years, as well as works by Sophocles, Ibsen, Molière, Chekhov, Sheridan, Beckett, and a number of Canadian playwrights. The festival's repertory company, known as the Stratford Company, goes on tour during the months when the festival is not in session.

See also SHAKESPEARE FESTIVAL

CONTACT:
Ontario Travel
Queen's Park
Toronto, Ontario
Canada M7A 2R9
800-ONTARIO or 416-314-0944

SOURCES:
GdWrldFest-1985, p. 52
IntlThFolk-1979, p. 73
MusFestAmer-1990, p. 161

◆ 1848 ◆ **Strawberry Festival**
Strawberry time–usually June

One of several annual festivals held by Iroquois Indians. At Tonawanda, N.Y., the people congregate in their longhouse to hear a lengthy recitation of the words of Handsome Lake (Ganio 'Daí Io'; 1735–1815). In 1799 this Seneca prophet delivered a message calling for cooperative farming, abstention from hard drink, abandonment of witchcraft and magic, the prohibition of abortion, and other instructions. This is the basis of today's Longhouse religion.

Following the recitations and speeches are ceremonial dances accompanied by chants and the pounding of turtle-shell rattles. Lunch follows, with a strawberry drink and winding up with strawberry shortcake. The Iroquois say "you will eat strawberries when you die," because strawberries line the road to heaven.

Other traditional Iroquois celebrations are a New Year festival, a Maple Dance held at the time of making maple syrup and sugar, a Planting Festival, and the Green Corn Dance, at which the principal dish is succotash, made not just with corn and lima beans but also with squash and venison or beef.

CONTACT:
Tonawanda Band of Seneca
7027 Meadville Rd.
Basom, NY 14013
716-542-4600

SOURCES:
DictWorldRel-1989, p. 533
EncyRel-1987, vol. 6, p. 191

♦ 1849 ♦ **Styrian Autumn (Steirischer Herbst)**
October–November

Dedicated to the avant-garde in music, drama, literature, and the fine arts, this eight-week festival in Austria celebrates spontaneity and experimentation. Founded in 1968, its goal is to remove the barrier between the producers and consumers of culture by presenting world premieres of plays, operas, and musical works by contemporary artists, workshops and symposia on 20th-century composers, exhibitions of contemporary art, and a variety of fringe events that include circus acts and multimedia shows. Ticket prices are purposely kept low, and many festival events are offered free of charge.

"Musikprotokoll," a biennial radio program of contemporary musical compositions, is broadcast internationally from the festival. There is also the Styrian Academy, a scientific symposium on a special theme. The festival takes its name from the province of Styria, whose capital city, Graz, is where the work of Austria's modernists is performed and displayed.

CONTACT:
Austrian National Tourist Office
P.O. Box 1142, Times Square
New York, NY 10148
212-944-6880; fax: 212-730-4568

SOURCES:
GdWrldFest-1985, p. 12
IntlThFolk-1979, p. 33
MusFestEurBrit-1980, p. 28

♦ 1850 ♦ **Sudan Independence Day**
January 1

Sudan became an independent republic on New Year's Day in 1956, after having been a joint British-Egyptian territory since 1899.

Independence Day is celebrated as a national holiday with elaborate festivities in the capital city of Khartoum.

CONTACT:
Sudan Embassy
2210 Massachusetts Ave., N.W.
Washington, D.C. 20008
202-338-8565; fax: 202-667-2406

SOURCES:
AnnivHol-1983, p. 2
Chases-1996, p. 52
NatlHolWrld-1968, p. 10

♦ 1851 ♦ **Sugar Ball Show**
Sixteenth day of first lunar month

This temple festival is held at the Haiyun Buddhist Convent in Qingdao, Shandong Province, China. Set for the day of the first spring tide, this festival has been held since the convent was built in the 17th century near the end of the Ming Dynasty. Originally fishermen observed this time to pray for safety and a good harvest. Now sugar balls—yams, oranges, and dates dipped in hot syrup and then cooled until crisp—colorfully displayed on long skewers, are specialties of the fair. About 200,000 people attend the show.

CONTACT:
China National Tourist Office
350 Fifth Ave., Ste. 6413
New York, NY 10165
212-760-9700; fax: 212-760-8809

♦ 1852 ♦ **Sugar Bowl Classic**
January 1

New Orleans, Louisiana, has been host to football and lots of hoopla since the Sugar Bowl originated there in 1935. The Southeastern Conference champion is always awarded a berth in this yearly event. Alabama has won the most games. Nineteen ninety-three was their eighth victory when they rolled over Miami of Florida 34–13. That game ended Miami's 29-game winning streak and gave the Alabama Crimson Tide its first national collegiate football championship since 1979. The game is the grand finale in Sugar Bowl Week, a round of events that begins with a sailing regatta on Lake Pontchartrain and includes contests in basketball, tennis, and track.

CONTACT:
Sugar Bowl
1500 Sugar Bowl Dr.
New Orleans, LA 70012
504-525-8603

SOURCES:
BkFestHolWrld-1970, p. 3
GdUSFest-1984, p. 73

♦ 1853 ♦ **Sukkot (Sukkoth, Succoth)**
Begins between September 20 and October 18;
Tishri 15–21

After their escape from slavery in Egypt, the Jews wandered in the desert for 40 years under the leadership of Moses. For much of the time they lived in huts, or *sukkot*, made of wooden frames covered with branches or hay. The festival of Sukkot, also known as the **Feast of Tabernacles** or the **Feast of Booths**, commemorates this period in Jewish history. It is also one of the Pilgrim Festivals (*see also* Passover and Shavuot).

The traditional way of observing Sukkot was to build a small booth or tabernacle and live in it during the seven-day festival. Nowadays Orthodox congregations build a *sukkah* in the synagogue, while Reform Jews make miniature models of the ancient huts and use them as centerpieces on the family table. Although linked to the Exodus from Egypt, Sukkot also celebrates the fall harvest and is sometimes referred to as the **Feast of the Ingathering**.

A major part of the festival is the four species: a palm branch, citron, three myrtle twigs, and two willow branches. These are tied together and waved at different points in the service, to "rejoice before the Lord."

Like other Jewish holidays, Sukkot begins at sundown on the preceding evening, in this case the 14th day of Tishri. The seventh day of Sukkot is known as Hoshana Rabbah and is the last possible day on which one can seek and obtain forgiveness for the sins of the previous year—an extension of the Yom Kippur or the Day of Atonement. The eighth day of Sukkot is known as Shemini Atzeret, and the day after that is called Simhat Torah, which is now celebrated as a separate holiday by Orthodox and Conservative Jews.

SOURCES:
AmerBkDays-1978, pp. 928, 1053
BkFest-1937, p. 204

BkFestHolWrld-1970, pp. 118, 123
BkHolWrld-1986, Oct 1
DaysCustFaith-1957, p. 270
DictWrldRel-1989, pp. 155, 390, 723
FolkAmerHol-1991, p. 353
FolkWrldHol-1992, p. 488
RelHolCal-1993, pp. 102, 116

♦ 1854 ♦ Sumamao, Fiesta de
December 26

The Argentine ritual drama known as *sumamao*, which means 'beautiful river,' is named after the location in which it is traditionally performed—near the Rio Dulce. It used to take place in a deserted chapel near the river, but nowadays it is sponsored by a ranch owner, who sets up a small altar on his property. On San Esteban's (St. Stephen's) Day, December 26, an avenue of *arcos*, or arches—made from trees that have been stripped of their branches except for a tuft on top and tied together by cords hung with *ichas* (cakes in the form of puppets)—leads up to the altar. The drama begins at dawn with trumpets and fireworks, followed by a slow procession of men on horseback through the arches. The rest of the drama unfolds throughout the day, culminating in the demolition of the arcos and the eating of the ichas. A fiesta concludes the celebration.

The sumamao is primarily an agricultural ritual aimed at winning the favor of the gods by offering sacrifices and exorcizing evil spirits. Social dances—including the *zamba*, the *gato*, and the *chacarera*—have replaced the orgiastic behavior that followed the ritual in ancient times.

CONTACT:
Argentina National Tourist Office
12 W. 56th St.
New York, NY 10019
212-603-0443; fax: 212-315-5545

SOURCES:
DictFolkMyth-1984, p. 1086

♦ 1855 ♦ Summer Festival
July 4

Something for everybody on the FOURTH OF JULY in Owensboro, Ky. A highlight is the "Anything That Goes and Floats Race," in which contestants must have a vehicle that gets them to the Ohio River and then floats them for a decent distance on the river. Vehicles that have made it into the water include bicycles attached to a canoe, a skateboard tied to a plastic raft, and large pontoons powered by bicycles on land and paddlewheels in the water.

Other events of the day include a pops concert, a gospel music show, a lighted boat parade, and, of course, fireworks.

CONTACT:
Kentucky Dept. of Travel
  Development
500 Mero St., 22nd Floor
Frankfort, KY 40601
800-225-8747 or 502-564-4930
fax: 502-564-5695

♦ 1856 ♦ Summer Festival of the Arts
July 1–31

Canadian playwright Michael Cook and John C. Perlin, cultural affairs director for the province of Newfoundland, helped establish this festival of drama, music, and the arts in an attempt to provide a cultural program for the local residents of St. John's. Since the first festival was held in 1967, it has grown from three weeks to a month-long event featuring stage productions, classic films, pop and country and western music, craft displays, and a children's theater. Most of the events are held in the Arts and Culture Centre, an elaborate arts complex that was built as a joint project of the federal and provincial governments.

CONTACT:
Newfoundland and Labrador
  Dept. of Tourism and Culture
P.O. Box 8730
St. John's, Newfoundland
Canada A1B 4K2
800-563-NFLD or 709-729-2830

SOURCES:
GdWrldFest-1985, p. 41
IntlThFolk-1979, p. 65

♦ 1857 ♦ Summer Solstice
June 21–22 (Northern Hemisphere); December 21–22 (Southern Hemisphere)

There are times during the year, respectively in each hemisphere, when the sun is at its furthest point from the equator. It reaches its northernmost point around June 21, which is the longest day of the year for those living north of the equator, and its southernmost point around December 22, which is the longest day for those living in the Southern Hemisphere. The summer solstice marks the first day of the summer season—the word *solstice* is from the Latin word, *solstitium*, meaning 'sun-stopping,' since the point at which the sun appears to rise and set stops and reverses direction after this day.

Although it was very common to celebrate the Summer Solstice in ancient times, modern American observations are comparatively rare. The solstice celebration sponsored by the Institute of Advanced Thinking in Belfast, Maine, attempts to recreate the ancient rituals. People from five countries and up to 20 different states arrive in Belfast the night before the solstice equipped with tents and sleeping bags. They get up at dawn to greet and worship the sun with prayers and ritual chants. The celebration continues for three hours. There are also a number of solstice observances held by New Age and Neopagan groups throughout the United States.

See also MIDSUMMER DAY; WINTER SOLSTICE

CONTACT:
Institute of Advanced Thinking
50 Salmond St.
Belfast, ME 04915

SOURCES:
BkFest-1937, p. 136
Chases-1996, p. 264
DictDays-1988, pp. 69, 114
DictFolkMyth-1984, p. 1032
FestSaintDays-1915, p. 4
FestWestEur-1958, p. 68

♦ 1858 ♦ Sun Dance
Late June

Although many North American Indian tribes hold ritual dances in honor of the sun and its life-giving powers, the Sioux were known to hold one of the most spectacular. Usually performed during the SUMMER SOLSTICE, preparations for the dance included the cutting and raising of a tree that would be considered a visible connection between the heavens and earth, and the setting up of teepees in a circle to represent the cosmos. Participants abstained from food and drink during the dance itself, which lasted from one to four days, and decorated their bodies in the symbolic colors of red (sunset), blue (sky), yellow (lightning), white (light), and black (night). They wore deerskin loincloths, wristlets and anklets made out of rabbit fur, and carried an eagle-wing bone whistle in their mouths. The dance often involved self-laceration or hanging themselves from the tree-pole with their feet barely touching the ground. Sometimes the dancers fell unconscious or tore themselves loose, which was considered evidence that they'd had a visionary experience. After the dance, they were allowed to have a steam bath, food, and water.

SOURCES:
DictFolkMyth-1984, p. 1088
EncyRel-1987, vol. 14, p. 143

♦ 1859 ♦ **Sunday School Day**
First Sunday in May

In the Polynesian kingdom of Tonga, a group of islands whose inhabitants are primarily Methodist, the first Sunday in May is known as **Faka Me**, or Sunday School Day. The children rise early and bathe in the sea, after which they put on the new clothes that their mothers have made: *valas*, or kilts, for the boys and new dresses for the girls. Then they all go to church, where the youngest children sing a hymn or recite a verse of scripture in front of the congregation and the older children present biblical dramas. At the feast that always follows a church service, the children sit on mats spread on the ground. A variety of Polynesian specialties—including roast pig, lobster, chicken and fish steamed in coconut milk, and potato-like vegetables called *ufi*—are served to the children by the adults on long trays made of woven coconut fronds known as *volas*. The parents stand behind their children and fan them to keep them cool as they eat.

Sunday School Day is observed in various ways by Protestant children in other countries as well.

See also WHITE SUNDAY

SOURCES:
FolkWrldHol-1992, p. 259

♦ 1860 ♦ **Sun Fun Festival**
First week in June

A beach festival at Myrtle Beach, S.C., to celebrate the state's Grand Strand, a 60-mile stretch of white-sand ocean beach. Myrtle Beach is the central city on the strand and so the fitting place for this five-day celebration that includes fireworks, beauty pageants, beach games, music and dance performances, and a sandcastle-building contest. The record for the world's longest sandcastle was set here in 1990—the castle measured 10½ miles long. As many as 200,000 attend.

CONTACT:
South Carolina Division of
  Tourism
1205 Pendleton St.
Columbia, SC 29201
803-734-0122; fax: 803-734-0133

SOURCES:
Chases-1996, p. 247
GdUSFest-1984, p. 171

♦ 1861 ♦ **Sun Pageant Day**
January–March

It is not uncommon for towns in the northern part of Norway to observe **Solday**, or **Sun Day**, when the sun reappears at the end of January or in early February. In Narvik, for example, Sun Pageant Day is celebrated on February 8.

The sun's reappearance is particularly welcome for the people of Rjukan, which is nestled so deeply in a narrow valley that the sun doesn't shine there from early October to mid-March.

Although the date of the Sun Pageant in Rjukan varies from year to year, it always entails weeks of preparation. The town square is decorated with tall ice columns topped by flaming torches. At one end there is a throne on a raised wooden platform for the "Prince of the Sun," who leads a procession of costumed figures into the square and officially begins the celebration. The eating, singing, folk dancing, and fireworks continue for most of the day and night.

CONTACT:
Norwegian Tourist Board
655 Third Ave., 18th Floor
New York, NY 10017
212-949-2333; fax: 212-983-5260

SOURCES:
AnnivHol-1983, p. 21
BkHolWrld-1986, Jan 31

♦ 1862 ♦ **Sun Yat-sen, Birthday of**
November 12

Sun Yat-sen (1866–1925) was the leader of the Chinese Nationalist Party (Kuomintang). He served as the first provisional president of the Republic of China (1911–12) and later as its de facto ruler (1923–25). Because he possessed an exceptionally broad knowledge of the West and developed a grand plan for China's industrialization, he is known as "the father of modern China."

Sun Yat-sen's birthday is a holiday in Taiwan. The anniversary of his death, March 12, is observed as Arbor Day in Taiwan.

See also DOUBLE TENTH DAY

CONTACT:
Taiwan Visitors Association
1 World Trade Center, Ste. 7953
New York, NY 10048
212-466-0691; fax: 212-432-6436

SOURCES:
AnnivHol-1983, p. 146
Chases-1996, pp. 130, 448

♦ 1863 ♦ **Super Bowl Sunday**
Usually last Sunday in January

The day of the championship game of the National Football League, which marks the culmination of the American professional football season. The game is played at a preselected site, always either a warm-weather city or one with a covered stadium. The contestants are the winners from each of the league's two divisions, the American Football Conference and the National Football Conference.

The first game was played on Jan. 15, 1967, in the Los Angeles Coliseum; the Green Bay Packers beat the Kansas City Chiefs by a score of 35–10. Since then, the games have been identified by Roman numerals (e.g., Super Bowl II in 1968), and, in keeping with this pretension, are surrounded by hoopla reminiscent of Roman imperial excess. Fans vie for Super Bowl tickets, and corporations woo clients with lavish Super Bowl trips. Nationwide, the day is celebrated with at-home parties to watch the game on television, and many, many people watch: an estimated 130 million viewers in the U.S. tune to the Super Bowl—that's 45 percent of all U.S. households owning television sets. Millions more watch the game in other countries. At sports bars, fans gather to watch wall-sized television screens, drink beer, and cheer.

CONTACT:
National Football League
410 Park Ave.
New York, NY 10022
212-758-1500; fax: 212-758-1742
WWW: http://nflhome.com

SOURCES:
Chases-1996, p. 78

◆ 1864 ◆ Suriname Independence Day
November 25

Suriname had been under Dutch control for more than 200 years when it gained independence on this day in 1975, which is observed as a national holiday.

CONTACT:
Suriname Embassy
4301 Connecticut Ave., N.W., Ste. 108
Washington, D.C. 20008
202-244-7488; fax: 202-244-5878

SOURCES:
AnnivHol-1983, p. 151
Chases-1996, p. 460

◆ 1865 ◆ Svenskarnas Dag
Fourth Sunday in June

One of the largest festivals in the United States celebrating the traditions of a specific ethnic group, Svenskarnas Dag honors the Swedish heritage of the people of Minneapolis, Minnesota, and the longest day of the year. When the festival first started in 1934 it was observed in August, but in 1941 the day was changed to the fourth Sunday in June so that it would coincide with midsummer observances in Sweden (*see* MIDSUMMER DAY).

Held in Minnehaha Park in Minneapolis, the festival includes a band concert, Swedish folk dancing, choral group performances, and the crowning of a Midsummer Queen. A national celebrity of Swedish descent is often asked to officiate at this one-day event, which attracts more than 100,000 visitors each year.

CONTACT:
Greater Minneapolis Convention and Visitors Association
33 S. 6th St., Multifoods Tower, Ste. 4000
Minneapolis, MN 55402
800-445-7412 or 612-661-4700
fax: 612-348-8359

SOURCES:
AmerBkDays-1978, p. 586
GdUSFest-1984, p. 97

◆ 1866 ◆ Swallows of San Juan Capistrano
October 23

San Juan Capistrano was the name of a mission built on the Pacific Coast by Father Junipero Serra in 1777. Even after the buildings collapsed in an earthquake 35 years later, thousands of swallows continued to nest in the ruins of the church. Local people noticed that the swallows tended to fly south on October 23, the death anniversary of St. John of Capistrano, and returned on March 19, ST. JOSEPH'S DAY.

Beginning in 1940, the sentimental love song "When the Swallows Come Back to Capistrano" (words and music by Leon René) was recorded by a variety of artists. This brought attention to the event and media attention further made it known. A Swallow Festival is held each year at the mission in San Juan Capistrano near Los Angeles, California, around the time of the birds' return. Also known as the **Fiesta de las**

Golondrinas, it features the largest non-automotive parade in the country. In addition to the Swallow Festival, the Mission hosts various cultural and historic events throughout the year.

CONTACT:
Mission San Juan Capistrano
Visitors Center
P.O. Box 697
San Juan Capistrano, CA 92693
714-248-2049

SOURCES:
AnnivHol-1983, pp. 39, 136
BkHolWrld-1986, Oct 23
Chases-1996, pp. 138, 419, 427, 428
DictDays-1988, p. 116
FolkAmerHol-1991, p. 133

◆ 1867 ◆ Swan-Upping
Monday–Thursday of the third full week in July

The tradition of marking newborn swans goes back six centuries, to a time when most of the swans on England's public waters were owned by the queen. Later the members of two livery companies (trade guilds), the Company of Dyers and the Company of Vintners, were given the right to keep swans on the Thames River between London and Henley. Every year since 1363, the Queen's swan master and the swan wardens of the two livery companies row up the Thames, starting at Blackfriars in the center of London and continuing 40 miles west to Henley-on-Thames, and "up" all the swan families into the boats, where they pinion their wings so they can't fly away. Then they cut marks on the beaks of the cygnets—one nick for the Dyers, two for the Vintners, and none at all to indicate that they are owned by the Crown. There are very specific rules governing how ownership is decided, and the six boats, each flying a large silk flag as they row up the river, form a procession that has changed little over the centuries.

CONTACT:
British Tourist Authority
551 Fifth Ave., Ste. 702
New York, NY 10176
800-462-2748 or 212-986-2200
fax: 212-986-1188

SOURCES:
BkHolWrld-1986, Jul 21
GdWrldFest-1985, p. 95

◆ 1868 ◆ Swaziland Independence Day
September 6

Independence Day is a national holiday in Swaziland. On this day in 1968, Swaziland became self-governing after having been ruled by Britain since 1903. This national holiday was also known as **Sobhuza Day**, named after Sobhuza II (1899–1982), king of Swaziland from 1921 until his death. In 1973, he disregarded the constitution passed upon independence and assumed supreme power.

CONTACT:
Swaziland Embassy
3400 International Dr., N.W., Ste. 3M
Washington, D.C. 20008
202-362-6683; fax: 202-244-8059

SOURCES:
AnnivHol-1983, p. 115
Chases-1996, p. 366

◆ 1869 ◆ Swedish Flag Day
June 6

Constitution and Flag Day commemorates the adoption of the Swedish constitution on June 6, 1809, and the ascension of Gustavus I to the throne on June 6, 1523. It is observed throughout Sweden with patriotic meetings, parades, and the raising of flags. In Stockholm the main celebration takes place at the Stadium, where the Swedish national anthem is sung by a chorus of several thousand voices, and King Gustaf V awards flags to various schools, sports clubs, and other organizations. In the evening the celebration continues at Skansen, the oldest open-air museum in Europe.

CONTACT:
Swedish National Tourist Office
655 Third Ave., 18th Floor
New York, NY 10017
212-949-2333; fax: 212-983-5260

SOURCES:
AnnivHol-1983, p. 76
Chases-1996, p. 245

◆ 1870 ◆ Swedish Homage Festival
Second week in October in odd-numbered years

Svensk Hyllningsfest, or the Swedish Homage Festival, is a biennial event held for three days during the second week in October in Lindsborg, Kansas. It honors the Swedish pioneers who first settled the area and celebrates the heritage of Lindsborg's Swedish-American population. More than 50,000 people attend the festival, which started in 1941 and is now held only in odd-numbered years.

Events include Swedish folk dancing, singing, and band music; Swedish arts and crafts displays; and a huge *smörgasbord*, or hot and cold buffet, at Bethany College. Other highlights include an American-Swedish parade and the crowning of the Hyllningsfest Queen, who is traditionally a senior citizen of Swedish descent.

CONTACT:
Kansas Division of Travel and Tourism
700 S.W. Harrison St., Ste. 1300
Topeka, KS 66603
800-252-6727 or 913-296-2009
fax: 913-296-6988

SOURCES:
GdUSFest-1984, p. 61

◆ 1871 ◆ Sweetest Day
Third Saturday in October

More than 40 years ago, a man from Cleveland came up with the idea of showing the city's orphans and shut-ins that they hadn't been forgotten by distributing small gifts to them on a Saturday in October. Over the years, other Clevelanders took up the idea of spreading cheer not only to the underprivileged but to everyone. The celebration of what came to be called Sweetest Day soon spread to Detroit and other American cities.

This holiday is unusual in that it is not based on any one group's religious beliefs or on a family relationship. Because it falls mid-way between FATHER'S DAY and CHRISTMAS, however, it has come to be regarded as a merchandising opportunity. Although it is still supposed to be an occasion to remember others with a kind act, a word of encouragement, or a long-overdue letter, local merchants in cities where Sweetest Day is observed usually get together and promote the day as a time to purchase gifts.

SOURCES:
AnnivHol-1983, p. 134
Chases-1996, p. 424

◆ 1872 ◆ Sweetwater Rattlesnake Roundup
Second weekend in March

Billed "The World's Largest Rattlesnake Roundup," this is one of several rattlesnake roundups in Texas. It was started in 1958 by ranchers in Sweetwater to thin out the snakes plaguing them and their livestock, and now the average annual catch is 12,000 pounds of Western Diamondback Rattlesnake. Some 30,000 spectators watch the goings-on.

The roundup is sponsored by the Sweetwater Jaycees, who stress the focus on safety (hunters are governed by state hunting laws) and the benefits of the roundup. The venom milked from the snakes is used in medical research and as an antidote for bite victims, and the skins are used for such items as belts and boots. The roundup supports various Jaycee charitable causes.

The weekend events include snake-handling demonstrations, snake milking (to extract the venom), and the awarding of prizes for the most pounds and the biggest snake. (The record for the Sweetwater Roundup is 74", while the longest on record anywhere is 84".) There are also a Miss Snake Charmer Queen Contest, a parade, rattlesnake dances with country bands, and a rattlesnake meat-eating contest. A cook shack fries and serves more than 4,000 pounds of rattlesnake meat each year.

Other Texas rattlesnake roundups are held from February through April in Cleburne, Breckenridge, Brownwood, Big Spring, San Angelo, Jacksboro, Gainesville, and Freer. A number of other southern states also have rattlesnake roundups.

CONTACT:
Texas Department of Commerce
Tourism Division
1700 N. Congress Ave., Ste. 200
Austin, TX 78711
800-888-8839 or 512-462-9192
fax: 512-936-0089

SOURCES:
Chases-1996, p. 126
FolkAmerHol-1991, p. 112

Swing Day
See **Tano Festival**

◆ 1873 ◆ Swiss National Day
August 1

A nationwide celebration of the Swiss Confederation, observed with torchlight processions, fireworks, shooting contests, and folkloric events. The day commemorates the occasion in 1291 when representatives of the three original cantons of Schwyz, Uri, and Unterwalden met on the Rutli meadow and swore an oath of alliance and mutual defense to lay the foundations of the Confederation.

In 1991, year-long 700th-anniversary festivities set different themes for the different language areas. A celebration of the Federal Pact of 1291 was the theme for the German-speaking region; a Four Cultures Festival, demonstrating cultural diversity, for the French-speaking region; and a Festival of Solidarity, illustrating Switzerland's role in the international community, in the Romansh- and Italian-speaking areas.

CONTACT:
Swiss National Tourist Office
608 Fifth Ave.
New York, NY 10020
212-757-5944; fax: 212-262-6116

SOURCES:
AnnivHol-1983, p. 101
Chases-1996, p. 319
FestWestEur-1958, p. 224
NatlHolWrld-1968, p. 132

◆ 1874 ◆ **Syria National Day**
April 17

This national holiday commemorates the withdrawal of French troops on this day in 1946, when Syria proclaimed its independence after more than 20 years of French occupation. It is also known as **Independence Day** and **Evacuation Day**.

CONTACT:
Syrian Embassy
2215 Wyoming Ave., N.W.
Washington, D.C. 20008
202-232-6313; fax: 202-234-9548

SOURCES:
AnnivHol-1983, p. 52
Chases-1996, p. 174
NatlHolWrld-1968, p. 48

◆ 1875 ◆ **Syttende Mai Fest**
May 17

Norwegian Constitution Day (*see* NORWAY CONSTITUTION DAY) is celebrated each year by the descendants of the Norwegian immigrants who first settled in Spring Grove, Minnesota. The town, incorporated in 1889, was the first Norse settlement in Minnesota, and the Norwegian language can still be heard in the town's streets and cafes. The Syttende Mai Fest offers ethnic foods, folk music and costumes, a show of traditional Norwegian arts and crafts, and a grand parade led by the "King of Trolls." Young children dressed as *Nisse* roam the streets during the festival, wearing green caps and playing tricks on people. Unlike the trolls, who thrive on darkness and are known for making things go wrong, the Nisse bring luck and help out with household tasks. During the festival, the store windows often feature displays with trolls or Nisse peeking out.

Syttende Mai is celebrated by Norwegian communities in other states as well. The celebration in Stoughton, Wisconsin, takes place on the weekend nearest May 17 and features folk dancing, a Norwegian smorgasbord, and demonstrations of *rosemaling* (painted or carved floral designs) and *hardanger* (a form of pulled thread embroidery).

CONTACT:
Minnesota Office of Tourism
121 E. 7th Pl. Metro Sq., Ste. 100
St. Paul, MN 55101
612-296-5029 or 800-657-3700
fax: 612-296-7095

◆ 1876 ◆ **Szüret**
Late October

Since wine is the national drink of the Hungarian people, the Szüret, or **Grape Gathering**, is a time for great celebration. In fact, many peasant marriages take place after this yearly festival. As they have done since ancient times, the grape gatherers make an enormous "bouquet" out of grapes and two men carry it on a pole in procession to the vineyard owner's home, accompanied by musicians, clowns, and young girls dressed in white wearing flower wreaths on their heads. When they reach their destination, they hang the cluster of grapes from the ceiling and accept the vineyard owner's invitation to join in the feasting and dancing.

A traditional game known as robber is often played during the festival, either as the grapes are being gathered or during the dancing that takes place later. While several men guard the bouquet of grapes, the others try to steal the fruit off the vines. Anyone who gets caught is dragged before a mock judge and forced to pay a penalty—usually by performing a song, a solo dance, or a pantomime while his companions make fun of him.

CONTACT:
Hungarian Embassy
3910 Shoemaker St., N.W.
Washington, D.C. 20008
202-362-6730; fax: 202-966-8135

SOURCES:
BkFest-1937, p. 173
FolkWrldHol-1992, p. 451

T

◆ 1877 ◆ **Ta'anit Esther (Fast of Esther)**
Between February 13 and March 13; Adar 13

The **Fast of Esther** commemorates the three days that Queen Esther fasted before petitioning her husband, King Ahasuerus (Xerxes I) of Persia, to spare the Jews of her country from destruction by Haman, the Persian prime minister, in the sixth century B.C. (*See* PURIM.)

Ordinarily observed on the 13th day of the Jewish month of Adar, Ta'anit Esther is observed on the preceding Thursday (Adar 11) when Adar 13 falls on the Sabbath.

This date was originally a minor festival commemorating Judah Maccabee's defeat of the Syrian general Nicanor, known as the "Day of Nicanor." In time it gave way to the present Fast of Esther.

SOURCES:
AnnivHol-1983, p. 172
Chases-1996, p. 123

Tabernacles, Feast of
See **Sukkot**

◆ 1878 ◆ **Tabuleiros Festival (Festa dos Tabuleiros)**
Four days in mid-July every third year

The town of Tomar in Portugal has been celebrating the Tabuleiros ("headdresses") Festival for 600 years as a way of expressing gratitude for the harvest and charity for the poor. The highlight of the festival is the procession through town of 600 girls in traditional headdresses selected from Tomar and the surrounding communities.

The foundation of the headdress, which weighs about 33 pounds and must be at least as tall as the girl who carries it, is a round basket covered with a linen cloth. An elaborate framework of bamboo sticks and wires holds up 30 small loaves of bread arranged in five rows. Flowers made of colored paper disguise the wires and the entire structure is topped with a white dove or Maltese cross. The priest blesses the bread, and the girls keep their *tabuleiros* for the entire year to ward off sickness. This is also a time for making donations to the poor and the afflicted.

CONTACT:
Portuguese National Tourist
  Office
590 Fifth Ave., 4th Floor
New York, NY 10036
212-354-4403; fax: 212-764-6137

SOURCES:
AnnivHol-1983, p. 182
BkHolWrld-1986, Jul 8
FestWestEur-1958, p. 171
IntlThFolk-1979, p. 313

◆ 1879 ◆ **Tagore, Birthday of Rabindranath**
May 7

A commemoration of the works of Rabindranath Tagore (1861–1941), the great poet, philosopher, social reformer, dramatist, and musician of Calcutta, India. Born into a family of painters, writers, and musicians, Tagore possessed all these talents. In 1913, he was the first non-European to win the Nobel Prize for Literature. The Tagore family has been important in India's cultural history from the 19th century and is especially revered in Calcutta. Rabindranath Tagore's birthday is celebrated with a festival of his poetry, plays, music, and dance dramas. There are discussions at schools of his ideas on education and philosophy, and screenings of films based on Tagore's short stories and novels made by filmmaker and Calcutta native, Satyajit Ray.

CONTACT:
India Tourist Office
30 Rockefeller Ave.
15 N. Mezzanine
New York, NY 10112
212-586-4901; fax: 212-582-3274

SOURCES:
AnnivHol-1983, p. 63
Chases-1996, p. 203

◆ 1880 ◆ **Taiiku-no-Hi**
October 10

Taiiku-no-Hi, or **Health-Sports Day**, is a national legal holiday in Japan set aside to promote good physical and emotional health through athletic activity. Since 1966 it has been observed on the anniversary of the first day of the OLYMPIC GAMES held in Tokyo in 1964.

SOURCES:
AnnivHol-1983, p. 130
Chases-1996, p. 411

♦ 1881 ♦ Tako-Age (Kite Flying)
April, May, June

Kite-flying battles are a favorite sport in Japan, and numerous kite festivals take place in the spring. In the battles, the object is to cut down other kites by means of skillful maneuvering; broken glass embedded in the kite lines also helps.

The kite festivals of Nagasaki are held on April 29 and May 3, with teams of as many as 20 people controlling colossal kites up to 25' x 30' in size.

In Hamamatsu in Shizuoka Prefecture, a kite festival is held on the beach on May 3–5. It is thought to have originated in the mid-16th century when the lord of one of the fiefdoms celebrated the birth of a son by flying a giant kite. It is the biggest event now in the western region of the prefecture, with more than 1,000 kites sparring in the sky. Other festival events include parades of 50 floats in the evenings.

In Shirone in Niigata Prefecture, two teams on opposite banks of the Nakanokuchi River wage kite battles on June 5–12. This festival supposedly dates back some 300 years when the people of one village accidentally crashed a huge kite onto a neighboring village.

CONTACT:
Japan National Tourist
 Organization
630 Fifth Ave., Ste. 2101
New York, NY 10111
212-757-5640; fax: 212-307-6754

SOURCES:
AnnivHol-1983, p. 179
GdWrldFest-1985, p. 122

♦ 1882 ♦ Tam Kung Festival
May; eighth day of fourth lunar month

A celebration of the birthday of the god Tam Kung, held at the Tam Kung Temple in Shau Kei Wan on Hong Kong Island. Like TIN HAU, Tam Kung is a popular deity among fisherfolk. He is a Taoist child-god, whose powers were apparent when he was only 12 years old. His greatest gift was controlling the weather, but he could also heal the sick and predict the future. Residents of the Shau Kei Wan area believe he saved many lives during an outbreak of cholera in 1967. His birthday is marked with a grand procession, Cantonese opera, and lion and dragon dances.

CONTACT:
Hong Kong Tourist Association
590 Fifth Ave.
New York, NY 10036
212-869-5008; fax: 212-730-2605

♦ 1883 ♦ Tammuz, Fast of the 17th of (Shivah Asar be-Tammuz)
Between June 17 and July 24; Tammuz 17

The **Fast of Tammuz** commemorates the breaching of the walls of Jerusalem in 586 B.C., when the Babylonians conquered Judah, destroyed the Temple, and carried most of the Jewish population off into slavery. But this destruction had a happy ending: after 70 years the people returned and rebuilt the Temple. Then the Roman army breached the walls of Jerusalem in the year 70 A.D., dooming both the city and its Temple for the second time. This time the destruction and the scattering of the people—known as the Diaspora—had a far more tragic finality. Jews remain scattered over the face of the earth to this day. Other sad events associated with this day are the shattering of the first Tablets of the Law by

Moses, and the collapse of the sacrificial system caused by the Roman invasion in 70 A.D.

The Fast of Tammuz begins THREE WEEKS of mourning lasting until TISHA BE-AV.

See also ASARAH BE-TEVET

SOURCES:
Chases-1996, p. 282
DaysCustFaith-1957, p. 159
DictWrldRel-1989, p. 155

♦ 1884 ♦ Ta Mo's Day
Fifth day of 10th lunar month

Ta Mo was a sixth-century Indian monk who founded the Ch'an school of Buddhism in China, known in Japan as Zen Buddhism. He believed that the Law of Buddha could only be understood through contemplation, without the aid of books or rituals. According to legend, he spent nine years meditating in front of a cave wall, during which time his legs fell off. The Japanese, to whom he is known as Daruma, have a legless doll, constructed in such a way that no matter how it is placed on the ground, it always returns to a sitting position.

There is another legend that Ta Mo cut off his eyelids in a fit of anger after falling asleep during meditation. When they fell to the ground, his eyelids took root and grew up as the first tea plant. This legend is the basis for the practice among Zen monks of drinking tea to stay awake during meditation. Members of the Ch'an (or Zen) sect of Buddhism observe the fifth day of the 10th month as Ta Mo's Day.

SOURCES:
DictFolkMyth-1984, p. 1102

♦ 1885 ♦ Tanabata (Star Festival)
July 7, August 6–8

A Japanese festival based on a Chinese legend of parted lovers who are identified with two of the brightest stars in the night sky. In the legend, Vega, representing a weaver-princess, is permitted by the king to marry the simple cowherd, Altair. But after they marry, the princess neglects her weaving and the herdsman forgets his cows, so the king separates them, making them live on opposite sides of the River of Heaven, as the Milky Way is known in Japan. On the seventh day of the seventh month, the lovers are able to meet when a flock of magpies makes a bridge across the river. If it's rainy, the lovers have to wait another year.

The festival is observed throughout Japan, with people hanging colorful strips of paper on bamboo branches outside their homes. It is an especially colorful occasion in Sendai (Miyagi Prefecture), where it occurs a month later, on Aug. 6–8. The whole city is decked out with paper streamers and works of origami, the Japanese art of paper folding.

See also SEVEN SISTERS FESTIVAL

CONTACT:
Japan National Tourist
 Organization
630 Fifth Ave., Ste. 2101
New York, NY 10111
212-757-5640; fax: 212-307-6754

SOURCES:
AnnivHol-1983, p. 90
BkFest-1937, p. 199
BkHolWrld-1986, Jul 7
Chases-1996, p. 288
DictFolkMyth-1984, p. 540
FolkWrldHol-1992, p. 387

◆ 1886 ◆ **Tano Festival (Dano-nal; Swing Day)**
May–June; fifth day of fifth lunar month

An ancient spring agricultural festival in Korea that started as a planting ritual and a time to pray for a good harvest. It falls in the farming season between the planting of rice seedlings and their transplanting to the paddy fields. With the lunar SOL or New Year's Day and MID-AUTUMN FESTIVAL, it is one of the country's three great festivals on the lunar calendar. Festivities in the countryside include swinging contests for girls: swings are suspended from tall poles or bridges, and the girls, sometimes in pairs, try to ring a bell with their feet as they swing. Boys and men sometimes compete in this, but usually they take part in *ssirum*, native Korean wrestling, a sport that can be dated to 400 A.D. Today ssirum matches are nationally televised.

In the usually sleepy east coast town of Kangnung, the festival goes on for a week, from the third through the eighth days of the month. Activities include a mask dance-drama of ancient tradition and shaman *kut*, ritualistic ceremonies combining theatrics with music and dance.

The ceremonies are performed by a shaman, or *mudang*, a priestess who is able to appease spirits to prevent natural disasters. The mudang is also a talented performer with supernatural powers when in a trance. A long-lived indigenous shamanistic faith of uncertain origin involves the worship of spirits and demons who reside in natural objects—rocks, mountains, trees, and so on. Shamanists also believe the dead have souls, and that the mudangs can mediate between the living and the departed.

Korea is nominally more than 70 percent Buddhist and more than 15 percent Christian, but it actively remains about 90 percent shamanist.

CONTACT:
Korea National Tourism Corp.
205 N. Michigan Ave., Ste. 2212
Chicago, IL 60601
312-819-2560; fax: 312-819-2563

SOURCES:
BkHolWrld-1986, Jun 16
Chases-1996, p. 263
FolkWrldHol-1992, p. 315

◆ 1887 ◆ **Tanzania Independence Day**
December 9

A celebration of the independence from the British in 1961 of Tanganyika, which merged with Zanzibar in 1964 to become Tanzania. The day is a national holiday celebrated with parades, youth leagues marching before the president at the stadium in Dar-es-Salaam, school games, cultural dances, and aerobatics by the air force.

CONTACT:
Tanzanian Embassy
2139 "R" St., N.W.
Washington, D.C. 20008
202-939-6125; fax: 202-797-7408

SOURCES:
AnnivHol-1983, p. 158
Chases-1996, p. 477
NatlHolWrld-1968, p. 222

◆ 1888 ◆ **Tater Days**
First weekend and Monday in April

Considered the oldest trade day in the U.S., and now a celebration of the sweet potato in Benton, Ky. The event started in 1843 when sweet potatoes were a staple crop of the area. Today the "tater" is honored with a parade, flea market, quilt show, road races, rodeo, gospel music, arts and crafts exhibits, a gun, coin and knife show, horse and mule

pulls, and a Miss Tater Day contest. Most of the food served is some kind of sweet potato concoction.

CONTACT:
Kentucky Dept. of Travel
  Development
500 Mero St., 22nd Floor
Frankfort, KY 40601
800-225-8747 or 502-564-4930
fax: 502-564-5695

SOURCES:
Chases-1996, p. 150

◆ 1889 ◆ **Ta'u Fo'ou**
January 1

New Year's Day in Tonga, a Polynesian island kingdom in the South Pacific, is reminiscent of CHRISTMAS EVE celebrations in the United States and Western Europe, when carolers go from house to house singing Christmas songs. But because the new year arrives in the middle of the Southern Hemisphere's summer, when schoolchildren are on holiday and the weather is warm, the caroling custom has a cultural twist. Boys and girls go from house to house singing hymns, rounds, and other songs that they have created specifically for the occasion. Instead of offering them hot chocolate or coffee, their friends and neighbors show their appreciation by offering fruit or cool drinks. Sometimes the children will be given a piece of *tapa*, Polynesian bark cloth.

SOURCES:
FolkWrldHol-1992, p. 7

◆ 1890 ◆ **Tazaungdaing**
*October–November; full moon day of Burmese
month of Tazaungmone*

The Tazaungdaing festival was observed in Burma (now officially called Myanmar) even before the spread of Buddhism. It was held in honor of the God of Lights, and it marked the awakening of the Hindu god Vishnu from his long sleep. Burmese Buddhists later attached their own religious significance to the festival, saying that this was the night that Siddhartha's mother, sensing that her son was about to discard the royal robes of his birth and put on the robes of the monkhood, spent the entire night weaving the traditional yellow robes for him. To commemorate her achievement, a weaving contest is held at the Shwe Dagon Pagoda in Rangoon. Another festival activity is the offering of *Kathin* robes to the Buddhist monks to replace the soiled robes they have worn throughout the rainy season. This offering ceremony begins on the first waning day of THADINGYUT and continues until the full moon night of Tazaungmone.

The Tazaungdaing festival is celebrated by sending up fire balloons and lighting multi-colored lanterns, especially at the Sulamani Pagoda in Tavatimsa. Sometimes called the **Tawadeintha Festival**, this day commemorates the return of Gautama Buddha from his visit to heavenly Tawadeintha to visit his mother's reincarnated spirit. Holy men with lit candles illuminated his path back to earth.

CONTACT:
Myanmar Embassy
2300 'S' St., N.W.
Washington, D.C. 20008
202-332-9044; fax: 202-332-9046

SOURCES:
BkHolWrld-1986, Nov 19
FolkWrldHol-1992, p. 570

Teacher's Day in China and Taiwan
See **Confucius's Birthday**

♦ 1891 ♦ **Teachers' Day in the Czech Republic**
March 28

March 28 is the birthday of Jan Amos Komensky (1592–1670), a noted educational reformer and theologian in the former Czechoslovakia. Komensky was the first person to write an illustrated textbook for children. Published in 1658, it was pocket-sized and used for teaching Latin words. Komensky was also a proponent of compulsory education who pointed out the state's obligation to provide kindergarten training and schooling. Today children honor him on Teachers' Day, or **Komensky Day**, by bringing flowers and gifts to their teachers. The day is also observed with lectures, music, and educational activities.

SOURCES:
BkFest-1937, p. 85
BkHolWrld-1986, Mar 28
Chases-1996, p. 146

♦ 1892 ♦ **Teej (Tij; Green Teej)**
*July–August; third day of waxing half of Hindu
month of Sravana*

A welcome to the monsoon, the season when the wind from the Indian Ocean brings heavy rainfall. It is celebrated especially in the dry, desert-like state of Rajasthan in northwestern India. Because the monsoon augurs good crops and fertility, this is also a celebration for women and is dedicated to the Hindu goddess, Parvati, consort of Lord Shiva and patron goddess of women. On this day, she is supposed to have left the home of her father to go to Shiva.

On Teej women traditionally paint delicate designs on their hands and feet with henna. Specially decorated swings are hung from trees in every village, and women swing on them and sing songs in praise of Parvati. Married women go to their parents' home and receive gifts of clothes and jewelry. There are also local fairs and processions carrying the image of the goddess.

On this day in Katmandu, Nepal, Hindu women visit Pashupatinath Temple to worship Shiva and Parvati. Ritual bathing in the sacred Bagmati River is supposed to wash away the sins of the past year.

In Bundi and Jaipur, the capital of Rajasthan, the day is called **Gangaur**. Women dressed in their finest go out to the main temple with flowers and brass vessels filled with water to worship the goddess, Gauri (another name for Parvati), and sing her praise. On the final day, a palanquin carrying an image of Parvati is carried through the streets in a procession of decorated elephants, camels, horses, chariots, dancers, and musicians.

CONTACT:
India Tourist Office
30 Rockefeller Ave.
15 N. Mezzanine
New York, NY 10112
212-586-4901; fax: 212-582-3274

Nepal Embassy
2131 Leroy Pl., N.W.
Washington, D.C. 20008
202-667-4550; fax: 202-667-5534

SOURCES:
AnnivHol-1983, p. 182
BkHolWrld-1986, Aug 6
FolkWrldHol-1992, p. 405
RelHolCal-1993, pp. 83, 117

♦ 1893 ♦ **Tellabration**
November, Friday before Thanksgiving

A nationwide night of storytelling, started in 1988 by storyteller J. G. ("Paw-Paw") Pinkerton. The event began with storytelling going on in six communities in Connecticut. The next year, Texas and Missouri also had Tellebrations, and by 1991, storytelling on this night was happening in 72 communities in 27 states, as well as in locations in Bermuda and Canada. Proceeds of the event go toward developing the archives of the National Storytelling Association (formerly the National Association for the Preservation and Perpetuation of Storytelling) in Jonesborough, Tenn.

Pinkerton originated the event as a way to encourage storytelling for adults, feeling that storytelling keeps culture alive. He grew up in a small Texas town listening to family stories—especially those told by his grandfather who had herded cattle in the early days of Texas. Pinkerton became a mining executive and, after retiring in 1988, devoted his time to promoting storytelling from his Connecticut home.

See also STORYTELLING FESTIVAL, NATIONAL

CONTACT:
National Storytelling Association
P. O. Box 309
Jonesborough, TN 37659
800-525-4514 or 423-753-2171
fax: 423-753-9331

SOURCES:
Chases-1996, p. 458

♦ 1894 ♦ **Tell Play at Altdorf**
*Weekends in August–September during odd-
numbered years*

The Swiss legendary hero William Tell symbolized the struggle for individual and political freedom. When he defied the Austrian authorities, he was forced to shoot an apple off his son's head in order to gain his freedom. He was later arrested for threatening the governor's life, saved the same governor's life en route to prison, escaped, and ultimately killed the governor in an ambush. These events supposedly inspired the Swiss people to rebel against Austrian rule.

Although there is no hard evidence to support William Tell's existence, the story of his test as a marksman has passed into folklore. J. C. Friedrich von Schiller, the German dramatist, wrote a play about Tell in 1804. Set in the environs of Altdorf, the legendary site of the apple-shooting incident, Schiller's play has been performed by the local citizens there on a regular basis since 1899. The theater originally designed for the production has been rebuilt and renovated a number of times, but it still retains many features of the original structure. *Wilhelm Tell* is currently presented on weekends during August and September on a biennial basis during odd-numbered years.

See also WILLIAM TELL PAGEANT

CONTACT:
Swiss National Tourist Office
608 Fifth Ave.
New York, NY 10020
212-757-5944; fax: 212-262-6116

SOURCES:
IntlThFolk-1979, p. 348

♦ 1895 ♦ **Telluride Film Festival**
September, Labor Day weekend

A three-day celebration of the silver screen in Telluride, Colo., featuring free outdoor showings in Elks Park with the audience bundled in blankets and sleeping bags. The festival attracts celebrity film makers, actors, and film scholars from all over the globe for national and international premieres and viewings of experimental filmmaking, retrospectives, and tributes.

CONTACT:
Colorado Office of Tourism and
  Travel
1625 Broadway, Ste. 1700
Denver, CO 80202
800-592-1939; fax: 303-592-5510

SOURCES:
Chases-1996, p. 354
GdUSFest-1984, p. 28

◆ 1896 ◆ Telluride Hang Gliding Festival
Second week in September

The largest hang gliding event in the country, held in Telluride, Colo., the small mountain resort that began life as a mining town and is known today as the "festival capital of the Rockies." Top hang gliders from throughout the world come here to soar and spin above Town Park. On the last day of the six-day event, in the competition for the world acrobatic championship, fliers skid, loop, somersault, and pirouette from the heights of the ski mountain, trailing colored smoke from their wingtips.

CONTACT:
Colorado Office of Tourism and
  Travel
1625 Broadway, Ste. 1700
Denver, CO 80202
800-592-1939; fax: 303-592-5510

◆ 1897 ◆ Telluride Jazz Festival
Mid-August

Three days of jazz in Telluride, Colo. Top artists produce jazz of all schools—traditional, Chicago, blues, big band, and Latin. On Fridays, the music happens at the historic Sherman Opera House and at various pubs, and on Saturdays and Sundays, the concerts are open-air in the Town Park. The festival began in 1977.

Telluride also boasts a three-day Bluegrass and Country Music Festival in late June, and a Chamber Music Festival held during two weekends in August. A special feature of that festival is the gourmet dessert concert, when fancy treats are served with the music, and the concert closes with a classical jam session.

CONTACT:
Colorado Office of Tourism and
  Travel
1625 Broadway, Ste. 1700
Denver, CO 80202
800-592-1939; fax: 303-592-5510

SOURCES:
Chases-1996, p. 320
MusFestAmer-1990, p. 190

◆ 1898 ◆ Tennessee Walking Horse National Celebration
August–September, 10 days preceding the Saturday before Labor Day

Ten days and nights of pageantry and competition for about 2,100 Tennessee Walking Horses in Shelbyville, Tenn., the "Walking Horse Capital of the World." The horses compete for more than $600,000 in prizes and the title of World Grand Champion, awarded on the final night of the show. The celebration is the nation's largest horse show in terms of spectators (close to 250,000 fans come to this town of 13,000) and the second largest in numbers of entered horses.

The blood lines of the Tennessee Walking Horse are traced back to the Thoroughbred, the Standardbred, the Morgan, and the American Saddle Horse. It was bred pure in the early days of Tennessee for the three-fold purpose of riding, driving, and general farm work. Today, it's a pleasure mount and a show horse with distinctive high-stepping gaits.

The three natural gaits of the Tennessee Walker are the flat-foot walk, the running walk, and the canter. The flat-foot walk, the slowest, is a diagonally-opposed movement of the feet. The running walk starts like the flat-foot walk and, as speed increases, the hind foot overstrides the front track. It is the only gait of a horse where the forefoot strikes the ground a mere instant before the hindfoot. The canter is a rhythmic motion known as the "rocking-chair" movement.

The Shelbyville celebration began in 1939, at the initiative of horse owner Henry Davis of Wartrace, Tenn., who thought his county should celebrate its most important asset. The celebration has been held ever since without interruption. From 1939 through 1991, forty-eight horses have been crowned World Grand Champion, some winning more than once.

Besides the horse shows, the celebration features an equestrian trade fair, horse sales, an arts-and-crafts festival, and America's largest barn decoration competition. The barns and stalls are elegantly decorated with brass lanterns, chandeliers, fine art, rugs, and expensive furnishings.

CONTACT:
Tennessee Dept. of Tourism
  Development
P.O. Box 23170
Nashville, TN 37202
615-741-2158; fax: 615-741-7225

SOURCES:
Chases-1996, p. 346
GdUSFest-1984, p. 179

Tenth of Tevet
See **Asarah be-Tevet**

◆ 1899 ◆ Terlingua Chili Cookoff
First full weekend in November

A contest of chili chefs held in Terlingua, Tex., an abandoned mining town near the Big Bend desert area in the southwestern part of the state. More than 200 cooks from as many as 30 states and occasionally from foreign countries show up to prepare the official state dish, and thousands of spectators drive or fly in. Humorists Wick Fowler and H. Allen Smith staged the first cookoff in 1967, deciding to locate it in the hot desert because it was a contest for a hot dish. It has become such an institution that the number of entrants has to be kept down by earning points at preliminary cookoffs, especially the CHILYMPIAD, held in September in San Marcos, and the State Ladies Chili Cookoff, held in early October in Luckenbach.

CONTACT:
Texas Department of Commerce
Tourism Division
1700 N. Congress, Ste. 200
Austin, TX 78711
800-888-8839 or 512-462-9191
fax: 512-936-0089

♦ 1900 ♦ Terminalia
February 23

In ancient Rome, February 23 marked the end of the year and was therefore an appropriate time to honor Terminus, the god of boundaries and landmarks. The terminus, or boundary stone marking the outer limits of Rome, stood between the fifth and sixth milestones on the road to Laurentum. During the observance of the Terminalia, property owners would gather there—or at the boundary stones that marked their private lands—to place garlands around the stone and offer sacrifices. Afterward there would be singing and socializing among family members and servants.

Ceremonies that involve marking boundaries are common in England and Scotland as well (*see* Ascension Day and Common Ridings Day).

> SOURCES:
> *DictFolkMyth-1984*, pp. 129, 493, 1106

♦ 1901 ♦ Tet
January–February; first to seventh days of first lunar month

The Vietnamese New Year, an abbreviation for **Tet Nguyen Dan**, meaning 'first day.' This is the most important festival of the year, signifying both the beginning of the year and of spring. It's also seen as a precursor of everything that will happen in the coming year, and for that reason, efforts are made to start the year properly with family reunions, paying homage to ancestors, and wiping out debts. At the start of the festival, the Spirit of the Hearth goes to the abode of the Emperor of Jade to report on family members. The spirit should be in a good frame of mind, so a tree is built of bamboo and red paper to ward off evil spirits. At midnight the New Year and the return of the Spirit of the Hearth are welcomed with firecrackers, gongs, and drums. The festival then continues for a week, with special events on each day. A favorite food of the festival is *banh chung*, which is made of sticky rice, yellow beans, pig fat, and spices wrapped in leaves and boiled for half a day.

Tet became known worldwide in 1968 for the Tet Offensive of the Vietnam War. The lunar New Year truce was shattered on Jan. 31 with attacks by North Vietnam and the National Liberation Front against more than 100 South Vietnamese cities. The United States embassy in Saigon was attacked and parts of it held by the Viet Cong for six hours; the headquarters of U.S. Gen. William Westmoreland at Tan Son Nhut Airport outside Saigon was also attacked. The city of Hue was captured. The attacks were repulsed, and the U.S. and South Vietnam claimed victory. But television viewers had seen the ferocity of the attack and the flight of Saigon residents, and the offensive led to increased movements in the United States to end the war.

CONTACT:
Vietnamese Embassy
1233 20th St., N.W., Rm. 501
Washington, D.C. 20036
202-861-0737

SOURCES:
AnnivHol-1983, p. 182
FolkAmerHol-1991, p. 62
FolkWrldHol-1992, p. 59
RelHolCal-1993, p. 117

♦ 1902 ♦ Texas Citrus Fiesta
Last week in January

An annual festival held in Mission, Tex., to salute the Texas citrus industry and, especially, the Texas Ruby Red Grapefruit. Mission, in the Rio Grande Valley, was founded by the Catholic Missionary Society of the Oblate Fathers, who built a mission here in 1824. They also are credited with being the first to plant citrus fruit in the region, which is now famous for the Ruby Red Grapefruit.

Among the events of the fiesta are a style show featuring garments made of Rio Grande Valley agricultural products: dried orange peel, seeds, and onion skins are used in creating costumes that range from ballgowns to bikinis. Other events: parades, the coronation of a Citrus Queen, Mexican folklorico dance performances, and a Texas armadillo race.

CONTACT:
Texas Department of Commerce
Tourism Division
1700 N. Congress, Ste. 200
Austin, TX 78711
800-888-8839 or 512-462-9191
fax: 512-936-0089

♦ 1903 ♦ Texas Folklife Festival
First week in August

Often described as "the largest block party in Texas," the Texas Folklife Festival was founded in 1972 by O.T. Baker, exhibits manager at the Institute of Texan Cultures, as a celebration of the state's ethnic cultures and pioneer heritage. There are demonstrations of the crafts, work skills, costumes, foods, and customs of the more than 36 different ethnic groups living in Texas today. Visitors can learn how to make a cowhide chair, for example, or the proper way to pickle olives. There are lessons in Swiss yodeling, splitting shingles, and blacksmithing, as well as musical performances by German oompah bands, Czech accordionists, and Dutch singers. Attendees are encouraged to jump up on stage and learn the various dances or sing along with their favorite musicians. The four-day festival is sponsored by the University of Texas and is held at HemisFair Park in downtown San Antonio.

CONTACT:
Institute of Texan Cultures
81 S. Bowie St.
Box 1226
San Antonio, TX 78205
210-558-2300

SOURCES:
Chases-1996, p. 319
GdUSFest-1984, p. 187
MusFestAmer-1990, p. 229

♦ 1904 ♦ Texas Independence Day
March 2

A legal holiday in Texas, March 2 commemorates both the convention at Washington-on-the-Brazos held on this day in 1836, when delegates prepared for the separation of Texas from Mexico, and the birthday of Sam Houston (1793–1863), who led the Texans to victory over the Mexicans in the battle of San Jacinto. The convention formed an interim government, drew up a constitution, and made Sam Houston commander-in-chief of the Texan military forces. But their work was interrupted by the invading Mexican army. It wasn't until the following month that the Republic of Texas forced the issue of independence at the battle of San Jacinto (*see* San Jacinto Day). Texas is the only state to celebrate independence from a country other than England.

March 2 is also known as **Sam Houston Day** and **Texas Flag Day**, although these are "special observance days" rather than legal holidays. This period in Texas history, beginning with the Washington-on-the-Brazos convention and ending with Sam Houston's decisive victory at San Jacinto, is celebrated each year during "Texas Week."

CONTACT:
Texas Department of Commerce
Tourism Division
1700 N. Congress, Ste. 200
Austin, TX 78711
800-888-8839 or 512-462-9191
fax: 512-936-0089

SOURCES:
AmerBkDays-1978, p. 227
AnnivHol-1983, p. 32
Chases-1996, p. 120
DictDays-1988, p. 118

♦ 1905 ♦ Texas Rose Festival
October

An annual tribute to roses in Tyler, Tex., center of the region that produces more than a third of the field-grown roses in the United States. Tyler's Municipal Rose Garden, one of the largest rose gardens in the country, covers 22 acres and has some 38,000 rose bushes, representing 500 varieties. They blossom among pines, fountains, gazebos, and archways, peaking in May but continuing through October. The five-day festival features the coronation of a Rose Queen, a rose show, a parade of floats decorated with roses, and tours of the rose gardens. There are also arts and crafts shows, a square-dance festival, and a symphony concert.

CONTACT:
Texas Department of Commerce
Tourism Division
1700 N. Congress, Ste. 200
Austin, TX 78711
800-888-8839 or 512-462-9191
fax: 512-936-0089

♦ 1906 ♦ Thadingyut
September–October; full moon of Thadingyut

The period that begins with the full moon day of the 11th lunar month and continues until the full moon day of the 12th lunar month marks the end of the Buddhist Lent and the beginning of the *Kathin*, or pilgrimage season. Also known as **Robe Offering Month**, this is a time when Buddhists make pilgrimages to various temples, bringing food and gifts—particularly new robes—to the monks. In Burma, Thadingyut is the day on which the Buddha completed his preaching of the *Abhidhamma*, or 'philosophy', and it is sometimes referred to as **Abhidhamma Day**. In Laos, it is called **Boun Ok Vatsa**, or the **Festival of the Waters**, as it is a popular time for pirogue (canoe) races. In Thailand, it is called **Tod Kathin**—the *kathin* being a wooden frame on which scraps of cloth were stretched before being sewn together to make into robes.

See also TAZAUNGDAING; WASO

SOURCES:
AnnivHol-1983, pp. 180, 182, 183
BkHolWrld-1986, Jul 23, Sep 22, Oct 20, Oct 27, Oct 29
FolkWrldHol-1992, pp. 348, 525

♦ 1907 ♦ Thaipusam (Thai Poosam)
Three to 12 days in January–February

A dramatic Hindu festival celebrated in India, Malaysia, Sri Lanka, Singapore, South Africa, Mauritius, and elsewhere. The day marks the birthday and victory of the Hindu god Subramaniam, also known as Lord Murugar, over the demons, and is a time of penance and consecration to the god, usually involving self-mortification in a test of mind over pain.

In Malaysia, the festival is a public holiday in the states of Perak, Penang, and Selangor. In Georgetown, Penang, a statue of Subramaniam—covered with gold, silver, diamonds, and emeralds—is taken from the Sri Mariamman temple along with his consorts, Valli and Theivanai, and placed in a silver chariot. Then begins a grand procession to his tomb in the Batu Caves, near the capital city of Kuala Lumpur, where the statue is carried up 272 steep steps, and placed beside the permanent statue kept there. The next day about 200,000 people begin to pay homage, while movies, carousels, and other entertainments are provided for their amusement.

The most intense form of penance and devotion is the carrying of *kavadee*—a wooden arch on a wooden platform—which the Tamil people of Mauritius practice in a unique way—much more elaborately and solemnly than in other countries. Devotees, both male and female, abstain from meat and sex during the sacred 10 days before the festival. Each day they go to the temple (*kovil*) to make offerings, and in Port Louis, at Arulmigu Sockalingam Meenaatchee Amman Kovil, Murugar and his two consorts are decorated differently each day to depict episodes in the deity's life.

On the eve of the celebration, devotees prepare their kavadees and decorate them with flowers, paper, and peacock feathers. They may be built in other shapes, such as a peacock or temple, but the arch is most common. The next morning, priests pour cow milk into two brass pots and tie them to the sides of each kavadee. Fruits, or *jagger* (a coarse, brown sugar made from the East Indian palm tree), may also be placed on the platform. Then religious ceremonies are performed at the shrines to put the bearers in a trance. When ready, penitents have their upper bodies pierced symmetrically with *vels*, the sacred lance given to Lord Subramaniam by his mother, Parvati; some also have skewers driven through their cheeks, foreheads, or tongues.

The procession then begins, with the devotees carrying the kavadees on their shoulders. Some penitents draw a small chariot by means of chains fixed to hooks dug into their sides; some walk to the temple on sandals studded with nails. Groups of young men and women follow, singing rhythmic songs. Each region may have 40 to 100 kavadees, but in places like Port Louis there may be 600 to 800. At the temple, the kavadee is dismounted, the needles and skewers removed by the priest, and the milk in the pots—which has stayed pure—is poured over the deity from head to foot. The penitents then go out and join the crowds.

Some believe carrying the kavadee washes away sins through self-inflicted suffering; others say the kavadee symbolizes the triumph of good over evil.

In Durban, South Africa, these rites last 12 days and are also performed during Chitray Massum in April–May.

CONTACT:
Malaysian Tourism Promotion
    Board
818 W. Seventh St., Ste. 804
Los Angeles, CA 90017
213-689-9702; fax: 213-689-1530

Mauritius Government Tourist In-
    formation Service
8 Haven Ave., Ste. 227
Port Washington, NY 11050
516-944-3763; fax: 516-944-8458

♦ 1908 ♦ Thanh-Minh
Fifth day of third lunar month

Thanh-Minh (which means 'pure and bright') in Vietnam is a day to commemorate the dead. Families brings flowers, food, incense, and other offerings to the graves of deceased relatives. Sometimes they visit the graves a few days in advance to prepare for Thanh-Minh by raking or sweeping the surrounding area and painting the tombs.

See also QING MING

SOURCES:
FolkWrldHol-1992, p. 211

♦ 1909 ♦ Thanksgiving
Fourth Thursday in November (U.S.); second Monday in October (Canada)

The Pilgrim settlers of New England were not the first to set aside a day for expressing their gratitude to God for the harvest. The Greeks and the Romans paid tribute to their agricultural goddesses, the Anglo-Saxons celebrated LAMMAS and HARVEST HOME FESTIVAL, and the Jews have their eight-day SUKKOT, or Feast of Tabernacles. The first American Thanksgiving was entirely religious, and took place on December 4, 1619, when a group of 38 English settlers arrived at Berkeley Plantation on the James River. Their charter decreed that their day of arrival be celebrated yearly as a day of thanksgiving to God.

But most Americans think of the first "official" Thanksgiving as being the one that took place at Plymouth Colony in October 1621, a year after the Pilgrims first landed on the New England coast. They were joined in their three-day feast by Massasoit, the chief of the Wampanoag Indians, and about 90 of his fellow tribesmen. The Episcopal Church and many states declared Thanksgiving holidays, but it wasn't until 1863 that President Abraham LINCOLN proclaimed the last Thursday in November as a national day to give thanks. Each year thereafter, for 75 years, the president proclaimed the same day to be celebrated. In 1939, however, President Franklin D. ROOSEVELT moved it one week earlier to allow more time for Christmas shopping. Finally, Congress ruled that the fourth Thursday of November would be the legal federal holiday of Thanksgiving after 1941. Canadians celebrate their Thanksgiving on the second Monday in October.

Today Thanksgiving is a time for family reunions and traditions, most of which center around the preparation of an elaborate meal featuring turkey and a dozen or so accompanying dishes. Although some people go to special church services on Thanksgiving day, far more line the streets of Philadelphia, Detroit and New York City, where huge parades are held. In many places Santa Claus arrives in town on this day, and the widespread sales that begin in department stores the next day mark the start of the CHRISTMAS shopping season.

See also PILGRIM THANKSGIVING DAY; SCHWENKFELDER THANKS-GIVING

SOURCES:
AmerBkDays-1978, p. 1053
BkDays-1864, vol. II, p. 614
BkFest-1937, pp. 13, 19
BkFestHolWrld-1970, pp. 118, 124
BkHolWrld-1986, Nov 27
Chases-1996, pp. 462, 463
DaysCustFaith-1957, p. 300
FolkAmerHol-1991, p. 396
GdUSFest-1984, p. 89
RelHolCal-1993, p. 117

♦ 1910 ♦ Thargelia
May–June

This ancient Greek festival was celebrated in Athens on the sixth and seventh days of the ancient Greek month of Thargelion (which fell sometime during May and June) to honor Apollo. In addition to offerings of first fruits, or the first bread from the new wheat, it was customary to select two condemned criminals (either two men or a man and a woman) to act as scapegoats for community guilt. First they were led through the city and then driven out and banished. If circumstances warranted a greater sacrifice, they were killed—either thrown into the sea or burned on a pyre. On the second day of the festival there was an offering of thanksgiving, a procession, and the official registration ceremony for individuals who had been adopted.

SOURCES:
DictFolkMyth-1984, p. 67
DictMyth-1962, vol. II, p. 1552

♦ 1911 ♦ Thesmophoria
September or October; three days during ancient Greek month of Pynepsion

An ancient Greek festival held in honor of Demeter Thesmophoros, the goddess of fertility and the protectress of marriage; it is unclear whether this festival was named after the goddess or vice versa. It was celebrated by women, perhaps only married women, and lasted three days, between the 11th and the 13th (some say between the 14th and the 16th) of the month of Pynepsion (which fell between September and October), at the time of the autumn sowing of the new crops.

The festival was held in honor of the corn and harvest goddess Demeter, who was sometimes referred to as Thesmophorus. According to Greek mythology, Demeter's daughter, Kore, was gathering flowers near Eleusis one day when she was abducted by Pluto, god of the underworld, and taken away to his subterranean kingdom. By lowering pigs into chasms in the earth, the women commemorated the abduction of Kore. Some of the women had to enter the underground chambers themselves and bring up the putrefied remains of the pigs that had been cast there the year before. The rotten flesh was placed on altars and mixed with seed corn, which was then sown in the fields as a kind of magical fertilizer to ensure a good crop. The women fasted on the second day, and on the third they celebrated the magic of fertility in the animal as well as the plant kingdom.

In Athens and other Greek cities, the women who celebrated the Thesmophoria dressed in white robes and observed a period of strict chastity for several days before and during the ceremony. They would strew their beds with herbs that were supposed to ward off venereal diseases and sit on the ground to promote the fertility of the corn that had just been sown. Although the festival itself was taken very seriously, it was not uncommon for the women to joke among themselves, as if in doing so they could cheer the goddess Demeter, who suffered greatly over the loss of her daughter.

The Romans had a similar festival in honor of Ceres, called the CEREALIA.

SOURCES:
ClassDict-1984, p. 625
DictFolkMyth-1984, pp. 867, 870, 1108
SeasFeast-1961, p. 135

♦ 1912 ♦ Thingyan
Mid-April; during Burmese month of Tagu

The three-day feast of the New Year in Burma (now officially called Myanmar) is also known as the **Water Festival** because of the custom of throwing or squirting water on others. The festival has been traditional for centuries; King Narathihapate (1254–1287) built enclosed corridors running from his palace to the banks of the Irrawaddy River; inside them he and his courtiers reveled in water throwing.

During the celebration, pots of clear cold water are offered to monks at monasteries to wash or sprinkle images of Buddha. Everyone else gets drenched; young men and women roam the streets dousing everybody with buckets of water or turning hoses on them. On the final day, the traditional Burmese New Year, birds and fish are set free, and young people wash the hair of their elders. The water-splashing custom originated with the idea that by this the bad luck and sins of the old year were washed away. Now splashing people is more a frolicsome thing to do and also a way of cooling off. This is the hottest time of year in Burma, and temperatures can sizzle above 100 degrees.

See also LUNAR NEW YEAR and SONGKRAN

CONTACT:
Myanmar Embassy
2300 'S' St., N.W.
Washington, D.C. 20008
202-332-9044; fax: 202-332-9046

SOURCES:
AnnivHol-1983, p. 182
BkHolWrld-1986, Apr 13
DictFolkMyth-1984, pp. 913, 1108
DictMyth-1962, vol. II, p. 1556
FolkWrldHol-1992, pp. 41, 239
RelHolCal-1993, p. 117

♦ 1913 ♦ Third Prince, Birthday of the
April–May; eighth and ninth days of fourth lunar month

A Chinese Taoist festival to honor the Third Prince, a miracle-working child-god who rides on the wheels of wind and fire. In Singapore, Chinese mediums in trances dance, slash themselves with spiked maces and swords, and write charms on yellow paper with blood from their tongues. There is also a street procession of stilt-walkers, dragon dancers, and Chinese musicians.

CONTACT:
Singapore Tourist Promotion
  Board
590 Fifth Ave., 12th Floor
New York, NY 10036
212-302-4861; fax: 212-302-4801

♦ 1914 ♦ Three Choirs Festival
August

One of Europe's oldest continuing music festivals, the Three Choirs Festival alternates among the three English cathedral cities of Gloucester, Worcester, and Hereford. The festival opens with a performance by a choir of 300 voices, accompanied by a symphony orchestra, at the host cathedral. Concerts during the rest of the week-long event take place either in the cathedral or in local theaters and historic homes.

Records show that the festival was founded before 1719, and that it was held, as it is now, in succession at the three cathedrals. In the early days of the festival, it was customary for two or more wealthy patrons—called stewards—to underwrite the cost of the event. Today, subscribers to the festivals are still referred to as stewards, and money collected at the doors of the cathedral following a performance still benefits the Charity for the Relief of Widows and Orphans of Clergy, which has been affiliated with the festival since 1724.

CONTACT:
British Tourist Authority
551 Fifth Ave., Ste. 702
New York, NY 10176
800-462-2748 or 212-986-2200
fax: 212-986-1188

SOURCES:
GdWrldFest-1985, p. 91
MusFestEurBrit-1980, p. 61
MusFestWrld-1963, p. 27

Three Kings' Day
See **Día de los Tres Reyes; Epiphany**

♦ 1915 ♦ Three Kings Day in Indian Pueblos
January 6

A day for the installation of new officers and governors at most of the 19 Indian pueblos in New Mexico. The inaugural day begins with a church ceremony during which four walking canes, the symbols of authority, are passed on to the new governor. The governor is honored with a dance, which starts in mid-morning and is usually some form of an animal dance—often the EAGLE, Elk, Buffalo, and Deer dances. Spirited and animated, they are considered a form of prayer. Each dance is very different from the others, and the same dance differs from pueblo to pueblo, although certain aspects are similar. In the Deer Dance, for example, dancers "walk" holding two sticks that represent their forelegs. They wear elaborate costumes and antler headdresses.

New Mexico's 19 pueblos are: Acoma, Cochiti, Isleta, Jemez, Laguna, Nambe, Picuris, Pojoaque, Sandia, San Felipe, San Ildefonso, San Juan, Santa Ana, Santa Clara, Santo Domingo, Taos, Tesuque, Zia, and Zuni. Each of them celebrates its saint's feast day as well as other occasions with dances and ceremonies that are an expression of thanksgiving, prayer, renewal, and harmony with nature. Many dances tell stories, legends, or history. Besides the feast days and Three Kings Day (EPIPHANY), most pueblos observe these other major holidays: NEW YEAR'S DAY, EASTER, and CHRISTMAS, which is often celebrated for two to five days.

SOURCES:
AmerBkDays-1978, p. 38
DictFolkMyth-1984, pp. 346, 571
DictMyth-1962, vol. I, p. 516
FolkAmerHol-1991, p. 31
IndianAmer-1989, pp. 285, 306

Three Shrines Festival
See **Sanja Matsuri**

♦ 1916 ♦ Three Weeks
Begins between June 17 and July 24 and ends between July 17 and August 14; from Tammuz 17 until Av 9

The 17th of Tammuz, also known as **Shivah Asar be-Tammuz**, marks the day on which the walls of Jerusalem were breached by the Babylonians under Nebuchadnezzar (*see also* ASARAH BE-TEVET). The three-week period between this day and the ninth of Av (*see* TISHA BE-AV) is known in Hebrew as the period **Bén ha-Metsarim**, in reference to Lamentations 1:3, which describes the city of Jerusalem as having been overtaken by her persecutors 'between the straits.'

Because this period is associated with the destruction of the Temple, it is a time of mourning for the Jewish people. As the days draw closer to the ninth of Av, the signs of mourning increase in severity. Although there are differences between Ashkenazi and Sephardic customs, the restrictions include not shaving or cutting one's hair, not wearing new clothes, nor eating fruit for the first time in season. Beginning with the first day of Av, the Ashkenazi custom is not to eat any meat nor drink any wine until after Tisha be-Av, while Sephardim refrain from meat and wine beginning with the Sunday preceding the ninth of Av. On Tisha be-Av itself, it is not permitted to eat or drink, to wear leather shoes, to anoint with oil, to wash (except where required), or to engage in sexual relations. On each of the three Sabbaths during the Three Weeks, a special prophetic passage of the Old Testament, known as a *haftarah*, is read.

SOURCES:
Chases-1996, p. 282
DaysCustFaith-1957, p. 159
DictWrldRel-1989, p. 155

Throne Day
See **Morocco Independence Day**

♦ 1917 ♦ Tichborne Dole
March 25

The custom of handing out a dole or allotment of flour to the village poor in Tichborne, England, dates back to 1150. Lady Mabella Tichborne, who was on her deathbed at the time, begged her husband to grant her enough land to provide an annual bounty of bread to the poor, who were suffering from a recent failure of the wheat crop. Her husband, in a less charitable frame of mind, snatched a blazing log from the fire and said that his wife could have as much land as she was able to crawl across before the flames died out. Although she

had been bedridden for years, Lady Mabella had her servants carry her to the fields bordering the Tichborne estate and miraculously managed to crawl across 23 acres. With her dying breath, she proclaimed that if her heirs should ever fail to honor the bequest, the family name would die out.

On March 25, or LADY DAY, each year, villagers in need of assistance gather at the porch of Tichborne House to claim their portion of the gift: a gallon of flour for adults, half as much for children. The fields across which Lady Mabella dragged herself are still known as ''The Crawls.''

SOURCES:
AnnivHol-1983, p. 43
FolkCal-1930, p. 28
YrbookEngFest-1954, p. 41

♦ 1918 ♦ Tihar
October–November; waning half of Hindu month of Kartika

A five-day Hindu festival in Nepal which honors different animals on successive days. The third day of the festival, Lakshmi Puja, dedicated to the goddess of wealth, is known throughout India as DEWALI.

On the first day of the festival, offerings of rice are made to crows, thought to be sent by Yama, the god of death, as his ''messengers of death.'' The second day honors dogs, since in the afterworld dogs will guide departed souls across the river of the dead. Dogs are fed special food and adorned with flowers. Cows are honored on the morning of the third day; they, too, receive garlands and often their horns are painted gold and silver.

The third day is the most important day of the festival, when Lakshmi will come to visit every home that is suitably lit for her. Consequently, as evening falls, tiny candles and butter lamps flicker in homes throughout the country.

The fourth day is a day for honoring oxen and bullocks, and it also marks the start of the new year for the Newari people of the Katmandu Valley. On the fifth day, known as Bhai Tika, brothers and sisters meet and place *tikas* (dots of red sandalwood paste, considered emblems of good luck) on each other's foreheads. The brothers give their sisters gifts, and the sisters give sweets and delicacies to their brothers and pray to Yama for their brothers' long life. This custom celebrates the legendary occasion when a girl pleaded so eloquently with Yama to spare her young brother from an early death that he relented and the boy lived.

CONTACT:
Nepal Embassy
2131 Leroy Pl., N.W.
Washington, D.C. 20008
202-667-4550; fax: 202-667-5534

SOURCES:
FolkWrldHol-1992, p. 532

Tij
See **Teej**

♦ 1919 ♦ Time Observance Day
June 10

Emperor Tenchi of Japan (663–671) is credited with making the first water clock, a device that measured time by the amount of water leaking out of a vessel. Because keeping track of time was not standard practice in the seventh century, the Japanese honor their 38th emperor on June 10, the day on which he first ordered the hour to be announced by sounding temple bells and drums.

The Federation for the Improvement of Living Conditions, under whose auspices Time Observance Day, or **Punctuality Day**, is celebrated, carries out an annual campaign to get people to recognize the importance of keeping the correct time. On June 10 the Federation holds lectures and hands out honors to those whose actions have furthered its cause. In Tokyo, the organization used to have watchmakers stand at prominent locations throughout the city, offering free advice to pedestrians on how to adjust the controls on their clocks and watches.

While placing so much emphasis on keeping track of the time may sound odd to Americans, it is important to remember that the Japanese were traditionally lax in such matters, often failing to announce the time when a meeting or function would begin because it depended on the readiness of the person in charge.

SOURCES:
BkFestHolWrld-1970, p. 97

◆ 1920 ◆ Timqat (Timkat)
January 19–20

Because the Ethiopian CHRISTMAS, called GANNA, falls on January 7, EPIPHANY (Timqat) is celebrated on January 19. Timqat celebrates the baptism of Jesus in the Jordan River. It begins at sunset on Epiphany Eve, when people dress in white and go to their local church. From the church they form a procession with the *tabot*, or holy ark, in which the ancient Israelites put the Tablets of the Law, or Torah, the first five books of the Old Testament. Ethiopians do not believe it was lost, but that it is now preserved in the Cathedral of Axum in Ethiopia. Each Ethiopian Orthodox church has a blessed replica of it. They accompany it to a lake, stream, or pond. It is placed in a tent, where it is guarded all night while the clergy and villagers sing, dance, and eat until the baptismal service the following morning. At dawn the clergy bless the water and sprinkle it on the heads of those who wish to renew their Christian vows. Then the procession, again bearing the tabot, returns to the church. The festivities continue until the following day, January 20 or the feast of St. Michael.

Ethiopian religious processions are characterized by the priests' richly colored ceremonial robes, fringed, embroidered umbrellas, and elaborately decorated crosses. The national sport of *guks* is often played at Timqat. Warriors with shields of hippopotamus hide, wearing lion-mane capes and headdresses ride on caparisoned horses and try to strike each other with thrown bamboo lances.

CONTACT:
Ethiopian Embassy
2134 Kalorama Rd., N.W.
Washington, D.C. 20008
202-234-2281; fax: 202-328-7950

SOURCES:
BkFestHolWrld-1970, p. 23
FolkWrldHol-1992, p. 32

◆ 1921 ◆ Tin Hau Festival
Twenty-third day of third lunar month

A birthday celebration in Hong Kong for Tin Hau, Queen of Heaven and Goddess of the Sea. Also known as Tien-hou or Matsu, she is one of the most popular deities in Hong Kong; there are about 24 Tin Hau temples throughout the territory,

and fishermen often have shrines to her on their boats. Her story dates back many centuries when, it is said, a young girl, born with mystical powers in a fishing village in Fukien Province, saved her two brothers from drowning during a storm. Today she is revered for her ability to calm the waves and to guarantee bountiful catches, and for her protection from shipwrecks and sickness.

The festivities include parades, performances of Chinese opera, and the sailing of hundreds of junks and sampans, decked out with colorful streamers, through Hong Kong's waterways to the temples. The temple in Joss House Bay is especially known for its festival, with thousands of fisherfolk arriving. The original temple was built southwest of the present temple in 1012 by two brothers who said their lives were saved by the statue of Tin Hau that they clutched when they were shipwrecked. A typhoon destroyed that temple, and descendants of the brothers built another one on the present site in 1266.

See also MATSU, BIRTHDAY OF

CONTACT:
Hong Kong Tourist Association
590 Fifth Ave.
New York, NY 10036
212-869-5008; fax: 212-730-2605

SOURCES:
Chases-1996, p. 207

◆ 1922 ◆ Tirgul de fete de pe muntele Gaina (Maidens' Fair on Mount Gaina)
Third Sunday in July

A major folk festival held at Mount Gaina in Transylvania, Romania. It was originally a marriage fair, where young men came to choose their future wives, but is now an opportunity for people to display their talents in handicrafts, costume making, singing, and dancing. Thousands of people gather for the events of the fair, which include dance competitions and concerts by folk bands and singers. Other aspects of the festival are feasts and bonfires, and the chanting of satirical verses during certain folk dances.

CONTACT:
Romanian National Tourist Office
342 Madison Ave., Ste. 210
New York, NY 10173
212-697-6971; fax: 212-697-6972

◆ 1923 ◆ Tisha be-Av
Between July 17 and August 14; Av 9

The Jewish **Fast of Av** is a period of fasting, lamentation, and prayer in memory of the destruction of both the First and Second Temples in Jerusalem. When the Babylonians under Nebuchadnezzar destroyed the First Temple in 586 B.C., the Jews rebuilt it, but continued the fast day. Then the Second Temple was destroyed by the Romans under Titus, who burned it down in 70 A.D., and a long period of exile began for the Jews.

The Fast of Av begins at sunset the previous day and lasts for more than 24 hours. The nine days from the beginning of the month of Av through Tisha be-Av mark a period of intense mourning for the various disasters and tragedies that have befallen the Jewish people throughout history.

See also ASARAH BE-TEVET and THREE WEEKS

SOURCES:
AnnivHol-1983, p. 172
BkFest-1937, p. 209
BkHolWrld-1986, Aug 4
DaysCustFaith-1957, p. 197
FolkWrldHol-1992, p. 378

◆ 1924 ◆ Togo Independence Day
April 27

Togo became independent on this day in 1960, after being under French control from the end of World War I. Independence Day is a national holiday in Togo.

CONTACT:
Togolese Tourist Information
112 E. 40th St.
New York, NY 10016
212-490-3455; fax: 212-983-6684

SOURCES:
AnnivHol-1983, p. 57
Chases-1996, p. 189
NatlHolWrld-1968, p. 51

◆ 1925 ◆ Tok Race of Champions Dog Sled Race
Late March

The last race of the Alaska dog-mushing season, held since 1954 in Tok, which claims to be the Dog Capital of Alaska. Mushers from Alaska, Canada, and the lower 48 states participate in six-dog, eight-dog and open-class events for cash prizes.

Tok, a trade center for nearby Athapaskan Indian villages, is also a center for dog breeding, training, and mushing. It's not quite certain where the name of the town came from; some say it derives from a native word meaning 'peace crossing,' and others believe the village was originally called Tokyo and shortened to Tok during World War II.

CONTACT:
Alaska Division of Tourism
P.O. Box 110801
Juneau, AK 99811
907-465-2012; fax: 907-465-2287

◆ 1926 ◆ Tolling the Devil's Knell
December 24

To celebrate the birth of Christ and the death of the Devil, the Church of All Saints in Dewsbury, Yorkshire, rings its bell the same number of times as the number of the year (for example, 1,997 times in 1997) on CHRISTMAS EVE. The tolling starts at 11:00 P.M., stops during the church service from midnight to 12:45, and is then resumed until the years have been tolled away. The custom has been going on for almost 700 years, although there was an interruption in the early 19th century and again during World War II, when all bell-ringing was banned except to signal enemy invasion.

Although no one seems to remember exactly how the custom got started, there is a legend that says Sir Thomas Soothill donated the tenor bell to the Dunster parish church as a penance for murdering a young boy servant and then trying to conceal his body. The bell has been called "Black Tom of Soothill" since the 13th century, and **Tolling Black Tom** is supposed to keep the parish safe from the Devil for another 12 months.

CONTACT:
British Tourist Authority
551 Fifth Ave., Ste. 702
New York, NY 10176
800-462-2748 or 212-986-2200
fax: 212-986-1188

◆ 1927 ◆ Tom Sawyer Days, National
Week of July 4

Sponsored by the Hannibal, Missouri, Jaycees, the National Tom Sawyer Days celebration began in 1956 with a Tom Sawyer Fence Painting Contest and a Tom and Becky competition. Three years later, all of the events relating to the fictional character originally created by Mark Twain in his 1876 novel were combined with the traditional FOURTH OF JULY celebration in Hannibal, and Independence Day was officially proclaimed "Tom Sawyer Day." In 1961 it became a national event, and today the festival spans five days and includes a number of unique competitions.

Contestants for the fence-painting competition, who must be 10 to 13 years old, come primarily from the 10 states bordering the Mississippi River. They are judged on the authenticity of their costumes (which must be based on details from Mark Twain's book), the speed with which they can whitewash a four-by-five-foot section of fence, and the quality of their work.

The Frog Jump Competition is another of the festival's highlights, drawing up to 350 children and their pet frogs, each of whom is allowed three jumps. Competitors for the Tom and Becky competition must be seventh graders living in Hannibal, and the winners serve as goodwill ambassadors for the year.

See also CALAVERAS COUNTY FAIR AND FROG JUMPING JUBILEE

CONTACT:
Missouri Division of Tourism
P.O. Box 1055
Jefferson City, MO 65102
800-877-1234 or 314-751-4133
fax: 314-751-5160

SOURCES:
AmerBkDays-1978, pp. 624, 1065, 1067
Chases-1996, p. 281

◆ 1928 ◆ Tonga Emancipation Day
June 4

June 4 is a national holiday in the Kingdom of Tonga, celebrating its full independence from Britain in 1970. It had been a protectorate since 1900.

CONTACT:
Kingdom of Tonga Consulate
  General
360 Post St., Unit 604
San Francisco, CA 94108
415-781-0365

SOURCES:
AnnivHol-1983, p. 75
Chases-1996, p. 243

◆ 1929 ◆ Torch Festival
Twenty-fourth through twenty-sixth days of sixth lunar month

A traditional holiday of many of the minority national people in Yunnan and Sichuan provinces in China. Revelers dress in fine clothes, and the girls are especially colorful in embroidered gowns and headdresses of all colors. Celebrations begin with the sound of firecrackers, followed by folk dancing, athletic contests in such sports as pole-climbing and wrestling, and a bullfight. At night, huge bonfires are lit, dancers whirl around them, and a parade of people carrying torches brightens the night.

CONTACT:
China National Tourist Office
350 Fifth Ave., Ste. 6413
New York, NY 10165
212-760-9700; fax: 212-760-8809

♦ 1930 ♦ Tori-no-ichi
November

The **Bird Fair**, or **Eagle Market**, in Japan takes its name not only from the sacred crow that guided the first Mikado out of the wilderness by the light from its shining wings, but also from a play on the Japanese words signifying financial gain. This may be because many members of the Shinto sect who observe this festival are wealthy merchants and speculators, and the bamboo rakes that can be seen everywhere at this time are supposed to resemble the *kumade*, or bear-paw, which is the symbol of the Eagle market. People carry these rakes, usually decorated with good-luck emblems and the smiling face of the laughing goddess Okame, because they represent the power to pull toward them anything they desire. Some of the rakes are small enough to be worn in a woman's hair, while others are so large and heavily decorated that it takes several men to carry them through the streets. Sometimes, signs advertising restaurants or shops are hung from them and used throughout the year.

CONTACT:
Japan National Tourist
 Organization
630 Fifth Ave., Ste. 2101
New York, NY 10111
212-757-5640; fax: 212-307-6754

SOURCES:
FolkWrldHol-1992, p. 539

Toro Nagashi
See **Floating Lantern Ceremony**

♦ 1931 ♦ Torta dei Fieschi
August 14

When Count Fieschi of Lavagna in Genoa, Italy, was married in 1240, he invited his guests—and everyone else in town—to share a cake that was more than 30 feet high. The citizens of Lavagna haven't forgotten his generosity, and each year they celebrate the event on August 14. Dressed in costumes, they parade to the town square, where they pin to their clothes a piece of paper (blue for men, white for women) on which a word is written. When they find someone wearing the same word, the couple is given a piece of "Fieschi's cake."

CONTACT:
Italian Government Travel Office
630 Fifth Ave.
New York, NY 10111
212-245-4822

SOURCES:
BkHolWrld-1986, Aug 14

♦ 1932 ♦ Toshogu Haru-No-Taisai (Great Spring Festival of the Toshogu Shrine)
May 17–18

A festival—also known as the **Sennin Gyoretsu**, or **Proces-**

sion of 1,000 People**—that provides the most spectacular display of ancient samurai costumes and weaponry in Japan. The Toshogu Shrine, in Nikko, Tochigi Prefecture, was built in 1617 to house the mausoleum of Tokugawa Ieyasu (1543–1616), the first of the Tokugawa shoguns. The festival originated in honor of the reburial of Ieyasu in the new mausoleum.

On the first day of the festival, dignitaries and members of the Tokugawa family make offerings to the deities of the shrine. Also on this day, warriors on horseback shoot at targets with bows and arrows. On the morning of May 18 more than 1,000 people take part in the procession from Toshogu to Futaarasan Shrine, including hundreds of samurai warriors with armor, helmets and weaponry. Also marching are priests with flags; men with stuffed hawks representing huntsmen; men in fox masks to honor the fox spirits that protect the shrine; and musicians with drums and bells.

CONTACT:
Japan National Tourist
 Organization
630 Fifth Ave., Ste. 2101
New York, NY 10111
212-757-5640; fax: 212-307-6754

SOURCES:
GdWrldFest-1985, p. 123
JapanFest-1965, p. 33

♦ 1933 ♦ Tour de France
July

The world's greatest bicycle race and also the annual sports event with the most viewers—an estimated one billion who watch television coverage beamed around the world and 14.6 million who stand by the roadside. The tour, started in 1903, takes place mostly in France and Belgium, but also visits Spain, Italy, Germany, and Switzerland. It is divided into 21 timed stages, or legs, over three weeks, and has become a French national obsession. The newspaper sports columnist Red Smith once wrote that "an army from Mars could invade France, the government could fall, and even the recipe for sauce Béarnaise be lost, but if it happened during the Tour de France nobody would notice."

The route and distance of the tour is different each year, averaging 3,500 kilometers (about 2,100 miles, or the distance from Chicago to Los Angeles). It always includes strenuous mountain passes and a finale in Paris. The number of riders is limited to 200, and the rider with the lowest cumulative time for all stages is the winner. There have been three five-time winners: Jacques Anquetil (1957, 1961–1964), Eddy Merckx (1969–1972, 1974), and Bernard Hinault (1978, 1979, 1981, 1982, 1985). Merckx, a Belgian who seemed almost immune to pain, is considered the all-time greatest cycler. He competed in 1,800 races and won 525 of them. In 1986, Greg LeMond was the first American to win the tour. He was nearly killed in a 1987 hunting accident, and endured accidents and operations during the next two years, but came back to win the tour in 1989 and again in 1990.

The first tour in 1903 was organized as a publicity stunt by Henri Desgranges, bicyclist and publisher of the cycling magazine *L'Auto*. On July 1, 1903, 60 bikers started from the Alarm Clock Café on the outskirts of Paris, and three weeks later Maurice Garin was the winner, and the tour was born. In 1984, the Tour Feminin, a special women's race, was added to the tour, and is now a stage race of about 1,000 kilometers, run concurrently with the final two weeks of the men's tour. The first winner was an American, Marianne Martin.

CONTACT:
French Government Tourist Office
9454 Wilshire Blvd., Ste. 715
Beverly Hills, CA 90212
310-271-6665; fax: 310-276-2835

SOURCES:
BkHolWrld-1986, Jul 5

♦ 1934 ♦ **Tournament of Roses (Rose Parade)**
January 1

One of the world's most elaborate and most photographed parades, held every NEW YEAR'S DAY in Pasadena, Calif. The parade is made up of about 60 floats elaborately decorated—and completely covered—with roses, orchids, chrysanthemums, and other blossoms that portray the year's theme. Additionally there are more than 20 bands, 200 horses and costumed riders, a grand marshal, a Rose queen, and the queen's princesses. The parade is five and one-half miles long, attracts about 1.5 million spectators along the route, and is televised nationally.

The first festival, called the Battle of Flowers, was held on Jan. 1, 1890, under the auspices of the Valley Hunt Club. The man responsible was Charles Frederick Holder, a naturalist and teacher of zoology. He had seen the BATTLES OF THE FLOWERS on the French Riviera, and figured California could do something similar; his suggestion resulted in a parade of decorated carriages and buggies followed by amateur athletic events. The parade evolved gradually. Floral floats were introduced, and in 1902 the morning parade was capped by a football game, which was replaced in following years by chariot races. In 1916, football came back, and the ROSE BOWL GAME is now traditionally associated with the parade.

In 1992, the theme of the tournament was "Voyages of Discovery," and it kicked off the Columbus Quincentennial. Co-grand marshals were Cristobal Colon, a descendant of Christopher COLUMBUS, and Colorado Rep. Ben Nighthorse Campbell, a Cheyenne chief.

CONTACT:
Pasadena Tournament of Roses
391 S. Orange Grove Blvd.
Pasadena, CA 91184
818-449-4100; fax: 818-449-9066

SOURCES:
AmerBkDays-1978, p. 17
AnnivHol-1983, p. 3
Chases-1996, p. 53
FolkAmerHol-1991, p. 9

♦ 1935 ♦ **Town Meeting Day**
First Tuesday of March

An official state holiday in Vermont, this is the day on which nearly every town elects its officers, approves budgets, and deals with other civic issues in a day-long public meeting of the voters. It more or less coincides with the anniversary of Vermont's admission to the Union on March 4, 1791 (*see* Appendix A). Vermonters pride themselves on their active participation in these meetings, which often include heated debates on issues of local importance.

SOURCES:
AnnivHol-1983, p. 32
Chases-1996, p. 124
DictDays-1988, p. 121

♦ 1936 ♦ **Trafalgar Day**
October 21

This is the anniversary of the famous naval battle fought by the British off Cape Trafalgar, Spain, in 1805. The British navy, under the command of Viscount Horatio Nelson (1758–

1805), defeated the combined French and Spanish fleets, thus eliminating the threat of Napoleon's invasion of England. The victory that cost Lord Nelson his life was commemorated by the column erected in his honor in London's Trafalgar Square. Ceremonies on Trafalgar Day, or **Nelson Day**, include a naval parade from London's Mall to Trafalgar Square, where a brief service is held and wreaths are placed at the foot of Nelson's Column.

CONTACT:
British Tourist Authority
551 Fifth Ave., Ste. 702
New York, NY 10176
800-462-2748 or 212-986-2200
fax: 212-986-1188

SOURCES:
AnnivHol-1983, p. 135
Chases-1996, p. 426
DictDays-1988, p. 121

♦ 1937 ♦ **Transfer Day**
Last Monday in March

On March 31, 1917, the U.S. government formally purchased the Virgin Islands from Denmark for the sum of $25 million—about $295 an acre. Located about 34 miles east of Puerto Rico, the U.S. Virgin Islands consist of about 50 small islets and cays in addition to the three large islands of St. Thomas, St. John, and St. Croix. The United States purchased them primarily for their strategic importance, and they are still considered a vital key to the defense of the Panama Canal Zone and the Caribbean.

Transfer Day is usually observed with a parade and other public festivities. There was a major celebration in 1967, fifty years after the transfer took place, with events that underscored Danish-American friendship and a reenactment of the original transfer ceremony of 1917. The climax of the year-long semi-centennial celebration came when the governors of all 50 states as well as Guam, Puerto Rico, and American Samoa landed in St. Thomas for the 59th National Governors' Conference. Danish-American Week was observed at the same time.

CONTACT:
U.S. Virgin Islands Dept. of
  Tourism
P.O. Box 4538
Christiansted, St. Croix, VI 00822
809-773-0495

SOURCES:
AmerBkDays-1978, p. 310
AnnivHol-1983, p. 44
Chases-1996, p. 151

♦ 1938 ♦ **Transfiguration, Feast of the**
August 6

As described in the first three Gospels, when Jesus' ministry was coming to an end, he took his three closest disciples—Peter, James, and John—to a mountaintop to pray. While he was praying, his face shone like the sun and his garments became glistening white. Moses (symbolizing the Law) and Elijah (symbolizing the prophets) appeared and began talking with him, testifying to his Messiahship. Then a bright cloud came over them, and a voice from within the cloud said, "This is my beloved Son, with whom I am well pleased; listen to him." The disciples were awestruck and fell to the ground. When they raised their heads, they saw only Jesus (Matthew 17).

Observance of this feast began in the Eastern church as early as the fourth century, but it was not introduced in the Western church until 1457. It is observed by Roman Catholics, Orthodox Christians, Lutherans, and Anglicans; most Protestants stopped observing it at the time of the REFORMA-

TION. The mountaintop on which the Transfiguration took place is traditionally believed to be Mount Tabor, a few miles east of Nazareth in Galilee. However, many scholars believe it was Mount Hermon, or even the Mount of Olives.

SOURCES:
AmerBkDays-1978, p. 726
DaysCustFaith-1957, p. 201
FolkWrldHol-1992, p. 415
RelHolCal-1993, p. 118
SaintFestCh-1904, p. 358

◆ 1939 ◆ Transpac Race
Begins July 4 in odd-numbered years

It was in 1906, the year of the great San Francisco earthquake, that the first yacht race across the Pacific was held. Because of the earthquake, only three yachts participated, ranging in length from 48 feet to 115 feet overall. The course was from Los Angeles to Honolulu.

The Transpac Race was originally held in even-numbered years, with a long break between 1912 and 1923, and another interruption, after the Japanese attack on Pearl Harbor, between 1941 and 1947. It is currently held in odd-numbered years, beginning on the FOURTH OF JULY, and is sponsored by the Transpacific Yacht Racing Association.

The finish can be close: in the 1965 race, with 55 yachts participating, there were fewer than 100 yards between the first two finishers as they struggled up the Molokai Channel. One had lost her main boom and the other's boom was badly damaged.

CONTACT:
Hawaii Visitors Bureau
2270 Kalakaua Ave., Ste. 801
Honolulu, HI 96815
808-923-1811; fax: 808-922-8991

Los Angeles Convention and Visitors Bureau
633 W. Fifth St., Ste. 6000
Los Angeles, CA 90071
800-228-2452 or 213-624-7300
fax: 213-624-9746

Treaty of Paris Day
See Ratification Day

◆ 1940 ◆ Trial of Louis Riel
June–August

Louis Riel (1844–1885) was the leader of the métis, Canadians of mixed French and Indian ancestry. He became their champion in the struggle for Canadian unification during the late 19th century and was twice elected to the House of Commons but never seated. He became a U.S. citizen in 1883, but returned to Canada two years later to lead the North West Rebellion. Defeated, he was eventually tried for treason, convicted, and hanged at Regina, Saskatchewan, on November 16, 1885.

The transcripts of Riel's five-day trial are the basis for a full-length courtroom drama that is performed on Tuesdays, Wednesdays, and Fridays throughout the summer in Regina's Saskatchewan House, the site of the original trial. Riel's life and death are seen today as symbolic of the problems between French and English Canadians.

CONTACT:
Tourism Saskatchewan
1900 Albert St., Ste. 500
Regina, Saskatchewan
Canada S4P 4L9
800-667-7191 or 306-787-2300

SOURCES:
Chases-1996, pp. 315, 451
IntlThFolk-1979, p. 77

◆ 1941 ◆ Trinidad and Tobago Carnival
Between February 2 and March 8; Monday and Tuesday before Ash Wednesday

One of the most spectacular and frenzied CARNIVAL celebrations before LENT, the Trinidad and Tobago Carnival is a nonstop 48-hour festival in which almost everyone on the island participates. It started out in the late 19th century as a high-spirited but relatively sedate celebration involving a torch-light procession in blackface called *canboulay*—from *cannes brulées*, or 'burned cane'—patterned after the procession of slaves on their way to fight fires in the cane fields. There was also music in the streets and masked dancing, although slaves were not permitted to wear masks. With the emancipation of the slaves, Carnival became a free-for-all with raucous music and displays of near-nudity. The government tried to crack down on the celebrations, but in 1881 there were canboulay riots in which 38 policemen were injured. After that, a law was passed that forbade parading before six o'clock in the morning on Carnival Monday. That moment is still known as *jouvé* (possibly from *jour ouvert*, or 'daybreak').

Today the main events are the two carnival day parades, which involve 25 to 30 costumed bands, each with about 2,500 marchers and its own king and queen. There is a calypso competition in which steel bands and calypso composers vie for the title of "Calypso Monarch." Few get any sleep during the two-day celebration, and the event ends with the "*las lap*," which is a wild, uninhibited dance in the streets.

CONTACT:
Trinidad and Tobago Tourism Development Authority
25 W. 43rd St., Ste. 1508
New York, NY 10036
800-232-0082 or 212-719-0540
fax: 212-719-0988

SOURCES:
Chases-1996, p. 105
FolkWrldHol-1992, p. 117
GdWrldFest-1985, p. 175

◆ 1942 ◆ Trinidad and Tobago Emancipation Day
August 1

Since 1985, August 1 has been celebrated in Trinidad and Tobago as Emancipation Day, rather than COLUMBUS Discovery Day as in former years. Slavery was abolished in 1833 throughout the British Empire, and eventually slaves in the colony of Trinidad and Tobago were freed. The day begins with an all-night vigil and includes religious services, cultural events, processions past historic landmarks, addresses by dignitaries, and an evening of shows with a torchlight procession to the National Stadium.

CONTACT:
Trinidad and Tobago Tourism Development Authority
25 W. 43rd St., Ste. 1508
New York, NY 10036
800-232-0082 or 212-719-0540
fax: 212-719-0988

SOURCES:
AnnivHol-1983, p. 102
Chases-1996, p. 319

♦ 1943 ♦ Trinidad and Tobago Independence Day
August 31

After being subjected to British rule since 1802, Trinidad and Tobago became an independent commonwealth state on this day in 1962.

This national holiday is celebrated amid a Carnival atmosphere, with an elaborate military parade accompanied by calypsos at the Queen's Park Savannah. Religious services are varied to accommodate the Yoruba Orisha, Hindu, Muslim, Baptist, and other faiths represented in the citizenry. In the evening, awards are presented at the National Awards Ceremony to those who have notably served their country.

CONTACT:
Trinidad and Tobago Tourism Development Authority
25 W. 43rd St., Ste. 1508
New York, NY 10036
800-232-0082 or 212-719-0540
fax: 212-719-0988

SOURCES:
AnnivHol-1983, p. 112
Chases-1996, p. 357
NatlHolWrld-1968, p. 152

♦ 1944 ♦ Trinidad and Tobago Republic Day
September 24

On this day in 1976, Trinidad and Tobago became a republic. The constitution provided for a president, who replaced the British monarch as supreme ruler of the nation.

The month of September is crowded with festivals leading up to a historical parade with colorful floats held on the Sunday nearest September 24. During the first week in September, music and dancing permeates the Folk Fair, which includes more than 100 booths where traditional arts and crafts items, food, and beverages can be purchased. Around September 15, the Family Fair begins. During this 10-day festival, there are art exhibits, lectures, food, and shows every night.

CONTACT:
Trinidad and Tobago Tourism Development Authority
25 W. 43rd St., Ste. 1508
New York, NY 10036
800-232-0082 or 212-719-0540
fax: 212-719-0988

SOURCES:
Chases-1996, p. 390

♦ 1945 ♦ Trinity Sunday
Between May 17 and June 20; first Sunday after
Pentecost in the West and Monday after Pentecost
in the East

Trinity Sunday differs from other days in the Christian calendar in that it is not associated with a particular saint or historic event. Instead, it is a day that celebrates the central dogma of Christian theology: that the One God exists as three persons with one substance—as the Father, the Son, and the Holy Spirit. The idea of a festival in honor of the Trinity was first introduced by Stephen, Bishop of Liège, Belgium, in the 10th century. But it took several more centuries for a feast in honor of so abstract a concept to find its way into the church calendar. It became popular in England perhaps because of the consecration of Thomas à Becket on that day in 1162, but it wasn't until 1334 that it became a universal observance decreed by Pope John XXII. The day after Trinity is sometimes referred to as Trinity Monday.

Tradition has it that ST. PATRICK of Ireland used a shamrock as a symbol of the "three-in-one," triune God.

SOURCES:
DaysCustFaith-1957, p. 164
DictWrldRel-1989, p. 768
FestSaintDays-1915, p. 128
FolkWrldHol-1992, p. 286
RelHolCal-1993, p. 118
SaintFestCh-1904, p. 256

♦ 1946 ♦ Triple Crown Pack Burro Races
July–August

Three races of pack burros and human runners in the Colorado Rocky Mountains. The first leg of the triple crown starts in Fairplay and is held the last weekend in July. The second leg, the first weekend in August, starts in Leadville. The final race is two weeks later in Buena Vista. The first organized pack burro races were held in 1949 along a route over Mosquito Pass between Leadville and Fairplay; in 1979, the Buena Vista race became the final leg of the triple crown. The races cover from 15 to 30 miles over 13,500-foot mountain passes, sometimes in snow, and generally take the 20 to 25 entrants three to four hours. Women run a different shorter course than men. Contestants can't ride their burros, but must run alongside them. (They can and frequently do push the animals.) Winners of individual races get cash prizes; the total purse at Buena Vista is $5,020. The men's winner at Leadville gets $1,200.

The word *burro* is Spanish and means 'donkey'. The history of these animals in the West goes back to the Gold Rush days of the 1800s when pack burros carried great loads of machinery and supplies to mining camps. Pack burro racing is thought to have started in those times.

The race days are surrounded by a variety of activities and are now major events in the small Colorado towns. In Buena Vista, for example, there are bed races, toilet-seat races, simulated hangings, a horseshoe tournament, and a chili cookoff. Leadville holds contests in mine drilling events. There's also a triple crown outhouse race; each town in the burro triple crown also stages an outhouse race, with definite rules (e.g., one member of the outhouse team must sit in the outhouse during the race wearing colored underwear and/or a bathrobe).

CONTACT:
Colorado Office of Tourism and
Travel
1625 Broadway, Ste. 1700
Denver, CO 80202
800-592-1939; fax: 303-592-5510

♦ 1947 ♦ Trois Glorieuses
Third Saturday–Monday in November

The **Three Glorious Days** to which the name of this French wine festival refers occur in mid-November on the Côte d'Or in eastern France, and are observed in three different wine-producing centers. On the first day, at Nuits-Saint-Georges, the Confrerie des Chevaliers du Tastevin put on their red robes and square toques (a type of soft hat popular in the 16th century) to receive their new members—the *tastevin* is a small silver cup used to taste wines. This event is followed by a pig dinner during which a thousand bottles of wine are uncorked. The second day of the festival takes place at

Beaune, where a wine auction is held at the Hospice de Beaune, whose cellars are open to the public. On the third and final day in Meursault, everyone who has taken part in the work of the wine harvest is invited to a huge banquet. There is folk dancing and merrymaking as the festival draws to a close.

The Confrerie des Chevaliers du Tastevin was formed in 1934 to put the French wine industry back on its feet after a number of disastrous vintage failures. They hold a series of winetasters' banquets throughout Burgundy, but the most elaborate ones are part of this three-day festival.

CONTACT:
French Government Tourist Office
9454 Wilshire Blvd., Ste. 715
Beverly Hills, CA 90212
310-271-6665; fax: 310-276-2835

SOURCES:
AnnivHol-1983, p. 182
GdWrldFest-1985, p. 80

Trout Festival, National
See **Michigan Brown Trout Festival**

Tsom Gedalyah
See **Gedaliah, Fast of**

♦ 1948 ♦ **Tuan Wu (Double Fifth)**
May–June; fifth day of fifth lunar month

The fifth day of the fifth lunar month, or **Double Fifth**, is considered an auspicious day in the Chinese calendar. One reason why dragon boat races are often held on this day is that the dragon boats are believed to offer protection against disease, particularly for the paddlers. Another reason is that Ch'ü Yüan (c. 343–c. 289 B.C.), a renowned minister of the Ch'u kingdom and a famous poet, threw himself into the Mi Lo River on the fifth day of the fifth month. When the people heard about his suicide, they all jumped into their boats and paddled out to save him, but it was too late. So they wrapped rice in bamboo leaves or stuffed it into sections of bamboo tube and floated it on the river to provide sustenance for his spirit.

It is traditional to prepare and eat sticky rice dumplings known as *zong ze* on this day in honor of the drowned poet Ch'ü Yüan. Charms made from chunks of incense are used to ward off the so-called "five poisonous things"—which vary in different parts of China depending upon the climate and the local animal life. In Taiwan, for example, the five poisonous things are wall-lizards, toads, centipedes, spiders, and snakes. The charms are made in the shape of these harmful creatures, and sometimes small cakes resembling the creatures are eaten on this day.

Another custom associated with the Double Fifth is the placing of mugwort plants in the doorposts of each house. These branches are supposed to frighten evil spirits away and preserve those living in the house from summer diseases. Those who take a bath at noon on the fifth day of the fifth month are believed to be immune from illness for one year.

See also Dragon Boat Festival

SOURCES:
AnnivHol-1983, p. 176

FolkWrldHol-1992, p. 313

Tuan Yang Chieh
See **Dragon Boat Festival**

♦ 1949 ♦ **Tu Bishvat (Bi-Shevat; B'Shevat; Hamishah Asar Bishevat)**
Between January 16 and February 13; Shevat 15

Tu Bishvat, also known as **New Year for Trees**, is a minor Jewish festival similar to Arbor Day. It is first referred to in the late Second Temple period (515 B.C.–20 A.D.), when it was the cut-off date for levying the tithe on the produce of fruit trees. When Jewish colonists returned to Palestine during the 1930s, they reclaimed the barren land by planting trees wherever they could. It became customary to plant a tree for every newborn child: a cedar for a boy and a cypress or pine for a girl.

Today the children of Israel celebrate Tu Bishvat with tree planting and outdoor games. In other countries, Jews observe the festival by eating fruit that grows in the Jewish homeland—such as oranges, figs, dates, raisins, pomegranates, and especially, almonds, the first tree to bloom in Israel's spring.

SOURCES:
BkFest-1937, p. 206
BkFestHolWrld-1970, p. 18
BkHolWrld-1986, Jan 29
DaysCustFaith-1957, p. 40
FolkWrldHol-1992, p. 40
RelHolCal-1993, p. 63

♦ 1950 ♦ **Tucson Meet Yourself Festival**
Second weekend in October

The annual folk and ethnic festival known as Tucson Meet Yourself has been held in Tucson, Arizona, since 1974. Designed to promote southern Arizona's wide mix of cultures—which includes Mexican-, Czechoslovakian-, Italian-, German-, and Indian-American groups—the festival features formal presentations of traditional music and dance, demonstrations by folk artists and craftspeople, and workshops in which various experts on ethnic customs and traditions hold informal discussions, give lessons, and organize games.

Food, however, is the festival's primary attraction. Dozens of food booths, each operated by a non-profit organization identified with a specific cultural heritage and elaborately decorated to represent elements of "the old country," are set up throughout the park in which the event is held. Although American Indian and Mexican-American specialties predominate, the booths have featured Irish, Finnish, Hungarian, Ukrainian, Greek, Armenian, Vietnamese, Japanese, Sri Lankan, and many other ethnic dishes, giving the festival the well-earned nickname of "Tucson Eat Yourself."

CONTACT:
Tucson Convention and Visitors
  Bureau
130 S. Scott Ave.
Tucson, AZ 85701
800-638-8350 or 520-624-1817
fax: 520-884-7804

♦ 1951 ♦ **Tulip Time**
Second weekend in May

When a group of high school students in Pella, Iowa, staged an operetta called *Tulip Time in Pella* in 1935, the only tulips growing in the town were in wooden pots. But the musical performance gave the local chamber of commerce an idea for promoting the town's Dutch heritage. They hired tulip specialists from the Netherlands to teach them how to plant and care for tulips. Then they planted thousands of bulbs and got the local historical society started preserving the town's Dutch buildings and heirlooms. Today Pella (named 'city of refuge' by the first Dutch immigrants, who were fleeing religious intolerance in their homeland) has been renovated to resemble a typical village in the Netherlands. During the festival, townspeople dress in Dutch provincial costumes and engage in such activities as street-scrubbing, authentic Dutch dancing and folk music, and tours of the formal tulip gardens. One of these gardens features a Dutch windmill and a pond shaped like a wooden shoe.

Unlike most local festivals, Tulip Time is not a commercial event. There are no souvenir stands or food booths, although the local shops, museums, and restaurants offer a wide variety of Dutch specialties. Many of the events take place at the Tulip Torne, a tower with twin pylons more than 65 feet high that was built as a memorial to the early Dutch settlers.

CONTACT:
Iowa Tourism Office
200 E. Grand Ave.
Des Moines, IA 50309
800-345-4692 or 515-242-4705
fax: 515-242-4749

SOURCES:
Chases-1996, p. 206
GdWrldFest-1985, p. 59

♦ 1952 ♦ **Tunisia Constitution and National Day**
June 1

Tunisia Constitution and National Day is a public holiday. On this day in 1959, a constitution for the two-year-old Republic of Tunisia (*see* TUNISIA REPUBLIC DAY) was decreed.

CONTACT:
Tunisian Embassy
1515 Massachusetts Ave., N.W.
Washington, D.C. 20005
202-862-1850; fax: 202-862-1858

SOURCES:
AnnivHol-1983, p. 74
NatlHolWrld-1968, p. 76

♦ 1953 ♦ **Tunisia Independence Day**
March 20

Independence Day is a public holiday commemorating a treaty signed on this day in 1956 that formally recognized Tunisia's independence from France. It had been a French colony since the 1880s.

CONTACT:
Tunisian Embassy
1515 Massachusetts Ave., N.W.
Washington, D.C. 20005
202-862-1850; fax: 202-862-1858

SOURCES:
AnnivHol-1983, p. 40
Chases-1996, p. 139

♦ 1954 ♦ **Tunisia Republic Day**
July 25

This public holiday in Tunisia is held on the anniversary of the vote to abolish monarchical rule and found the republic on July 25, 1957.

CONTACT:
Tunisian Embassy
1515 Massachusetts Ave., N.W.
Washington, D.C. 20005
202-862-1850; fax: 202-862-1858

SOURCES:
AnnivHol-1983, p. 97

♦ 1955 ♦ **Tura Michele Fair**
September 29

On ST. MICHAEL'S DAY in Augsburg, Bavaria, there is an annual autumn fair that attracts visitors from all over Germany. One of the fair's chief attractions is the hourly appearance of figures representing the Archangel Michael and the Devil that are built into the foundation of Perlach Turm, or Tower, called *Tura* in local dialect. The slender structure, 225 feet high, standing next to Peter's Kirche (church) was originally a watch tower, but it was heightened in 1615 and converted into a belfry. Whenever the tower bell strikes on St. Michael's Day, the armor-clad figure of the Archangel appears and stabs with his pointed spear at the devil writhing at his feet.

Although the figures were destroyed during World War II, they were later replaced. For over four centuries spectators have gathered around the Tura to watch the symbolic drama reenacted on St. Michael's Day.

CONTACT:
German National Tourist Office
122 E. 42nd St., 52nd Floor
New York, NY 10168
212-661-7200; fax: 212-661-7174

SOURCES:
FestWestEur-1958, p. 71

♦ 1956 ♦ **Turkey Republic Day**
October 29

The Turkish Republic was founded by Mustafa Kemal Atatürk in 1923 after the fall of the Ottoman Empire. Kemal was named the first president on October 29, a full republican constitution was adopted the following April, and all members of the Ottoman dynasty were expelled from the country. Although Islam remained the state religion for several years, this clause was eventually removed from the constitution and in April 1928, Turkey became a purely secular state.

The public celebration, which lasts for two days, includes parades, music, torchlight processions, and other festivities in honor of the founding of the republic. The largest parades are held in Ankara and Istanbul.

CONTACT:
Republic of Turkey Embassy
1714 Massachusetts Ave., N.W.
Washington, D.C. 20036
202-659-8200; fax: 202-659-0744

SOURCES:
AnnivHol-1983, p. 138
Chases-1996, p. 433
IntlThFolk-1979, p. 373
NatlHolWrld-1968, p. 194

♦ 1957 ♦ **Turkmenistan Independence Day**
October 27

This national holiday commemorates Turkmenistan's independence from the U.S.S.R. on this day in 1991. Turkmenistan and other republics were gradually able to establish their own autonomous states due to the relaxation of Soviet rule influenced by the policy of perestroika. When the Soviet Union ceased to exist in December 1991, their independence was assured.

CONTACT:
Turkmenistan Embassy
1511 K St., N.W.
Washington, D.C. 20005
202-737-4800; fax: 202-737-1152

SOURCES:
Chases-1996, p. 432

♦ 1958 ♦ Turon
December; the week after Christmas

A Polish peasant festival observed in the week following CHRISTMAS, Turon is a remnant of an ancient festival in honor of the winter god Radegast. The *turon* is a legendary beast with a huge wooden head and jaws that open and close. This is one of several animal disguises that people wear as they go from house to house singing carols and receiving food and drink from their neighbors in return. Other traditional costumes worn in the celebration represent a wolf, a bear, and a goat. The original turon symbolized frost, consuming vegetation with its huge mouth.

SOURCES:
DictFolkMyth-1984, p. 1132
DictMyth-1962, vol. II, p. 1609

Tutti Day
See **Hocktide**

♦ 1959 ♦ Twelfth Night
January 5–6

The evening before EPIPHANY is called **Epiphany Eve**, or Twelfth Night, and it traditionally marks the end of the Christmas season, also called **Twelfthtide** in England. Since **Twelfth Day** is January 6, there is some confusion over exactly when Twelfth Night occurs, and it is often observed on the night of Epiphany rather than the night before.

Twelfth Night is an occasion for merrymaking, as reflected in Shakespeare's comedy, *Twelfth Night*. Celebrations reflect ancient WINTER SOLSTICE rites encouraging the rebirth of the New Year and also the Magis' visit to the Christ child. Pageants held on this night typically include fantastic masked figures, costumed musicians, and traditional dances, such as the Abbots Bromley Antler Dance, or HORN DANCE, in England. Customarily, the Twelfth Night cake is sliced and served and the man who gets the hidden bean and the woman the pea are the king ("King of the Bean" or "Lord of Misrule") and queen for the festivities.

SOURCES:
AmerBkDays-1978, pp. 29, 34, 43
BkDays-1864, vol. I, pp. 55, 58
BkFest-1937, pp. 51, 119
DictDays-1988, p. 123
DictFolkMyth-1984, pp. 114, 137, 689, 856
FestSaintDays-1915, p. 14
FestWestEur-1958, p. 123
FolkAmerHol-1991, p. 27
FolkWrldHol-1992, pp. 13, 18

U

◆ 1960 ◆ **Uganda Independence Day**
October 9

This national holiday commemorates Uganda's independence from Britain on this day in 1962, after 70 years of British rule. Uganda became a republic in 1963 on its one-year independence anniversary.

CONTACT:
Uganda Embassy
5909 16th St., N.W.
Washington, D.C. 20011
202-726-7100; fax: 202-726-1727

SOURCES:
AnnivHol-1983, p. 130
Chases-1996, p. 410
NatlHolWrld-1968, p. 187

◆ 1961 ◆ **Uganda Liberation Day**
April 11

On April 11, 1979, Tanzanian fighters joined forces with Ugandans in successfully ousting Idi Amin who, during his dictatorship, had assassinated a reported 300,000 political opponents. He had overthrown the government of Prime Minister Milton Obote in 1971, and by 1976, named himself president for life. This anniversary of this event is a national holiday celebrated in Uganda.

CONTACT:
Uganda Embassy
5909 16th St., N.W.
Washington, D.C. 20011
202-726-7100; fax: 202-726-1727

SOURCES:
Chases-1996, p. 166

◆ 1962 ◆ **Uhola Festival**
Various

Observed by the Dakkarkari people in Nigeria, the Uhola Festival is preceded by a housecleaning period during which the villages, the shrines, and the surrounding hills are cleaned up and put in order. This time is dominated by the drinking of local beer, called *m'kya*. The *Yadato*—boys and girls from wealthy families—go into seclusion for a four-week period prior to the Uhola, where they are properly fed and fattened, and encouraged to rest up for the celebration.

On the first day of the festival, the Yadato must dance in front of the chiefs' palace and present the chiefs with Uhola gifts. The celebration then moves to the village square, where they continue to dance and sing songs satirizing prostitutes, unmarried pregnant girls, irresponsible men—even political figures. The highlight of the second day of the festival is the wrestling contest, which also takes place in the village square. Sometimes the Dakkarkari wrestle against other tribes, and the victor in each match receives a prize from the chief. The wrestling, prize-giving, and speeches continue for about four more days, until the priest declares that the festival is over.

Only girls who are engaged to be married are allowed to participate in the Uhola. Their future husbands must have completed their *golmo*—a period of farm labor in lieu of paying for their brides. After the Uhola, the girls move into their prospective husbands' homes, while new boys go into golmo.

CONTACT:
Nigerian Embassy
1333 16th St., N.W.
Washington, D.C. 20036
202-986-8400; fax: 202-775-1385

SOURCES:
FolkWrldHol-1992, p. 455

◆ 1963 ◆ **Ukraine Independence Day**
August 24

On this day in 1991, just after a failed coup in Moscow, Ukraine declared its independence from the U.S.S.R. On December 1, 1991, ninety percent of the people voted for independence.

CONTACT:
Ukraine Embassy
3350 M St., N.W.
Washington, D.C. 20007
202-333-0606; fax: 202-333-0817

SOURCES:
Chases-1996, p. 348

◆ 1964 ◆ **Ullr Fest**
Third week in January

A winter festival in Breckenridge, Colo., to recognize Ullr, the Norse god of winter and a stepson of Thor. Highlights are a broomball tournament, town skiing championship races, skiing along lantern-lit trails, ice sculpture, fireworks, wine tasting, Norwegian dancing, and a Grand Ullr Ball.

CONTACT:
Colorado Office of Tourism and
  Travel
1625 Broadway, Ste. 1700
Denver, CO 80202
800-592-1939; fax: 303-592-5510

SOURCES:
Chases-1996, p. 61
DictFolkMyth-1984, p. 1148

♦ 1965 ♦ United Arab Emirates National Day
December 2

This national holiday commemorates the December 2, 1971, expiration of a British treaty that inhibited self-rule for the shaikhdoms on the Persian Gulf in the eastern Arabian peninsula, and the union of seven of the shaikhdoms in the former Trucial States to become the United Arab Emirates.

CONTACT:
United Arab Emirates Embassy
3000 K. St., N.W., Ste. 600
Washington, D.C. 20007
202-338-6500; fax: 202-337-7029

SOURCES:
AnnivHol-1983, p. 155
Chases-1996, p. 469

♦ 1966 ♦ United Nations Day
October 24

The international peace-keeping organization known as the United Nations was formally established on October 24, 1945, in the wake of World War II. Representatives from the United States, Great Britain, the Soviet Union, and Nationalist China first met in August and September of 1944 at the Dumbarton Oaks estate in Washington, D.C., to discuss the problems involved in creating such an agency, and the results of their talks became the basis for the United Nations Charter that was ratified the following year. Although it has not always been successful in maintaining world peace, the U.N. has served as an important international forum for the handling of conflicts in the Middle East, Korea, Somalia, the former Yugoslavia, and other troubled areas.

Each member nation observes October 24, and in some places the entire week is known as **United Nations Week**. In the United States, events taking place on this day include parades, international fairs, and dinners featuring foods from different countries. It is also common to hold debates and discussions designed to acquaint the public with the U.N.'s functions. Schools frequently observe United Nations Day by holding folk festivals that teach students the music, songs, and dances of different countries, or by organizing special programs focusing on their geography, products, government, and culture.

CONTACT:
United Nations
Dept. of Public Information
New York, NY 10017
212-963-1234; fax: 212-963-4879
WWW: http://www.undp.org

SOURCES:
AmerBkDays-1978, p. 953
AnnivHol-1983, p. 135
BkHolWrld-1986, Oct 24
Chases-1996, p. 428
DictDays-1988, p. 124

♦ 1967 ♦ United States Air and Trade Show
Third weekend in July; trade show biennially

Dayton, Ohio, has been a center for aeronautical research and development ever since two of its local residents, Orville and Wilbur Wright, created the first successful flying machine in their bicycle shop and tested their invention just a few miles outside of town (*see* WRIGHT BROTHERS' DAY). Dayton began celebrating its heritage as "the birthplace of aviation" by staging informal air shows shortly after the turn of the

century, and by the early 1970s, the **Dayton Air Fair** was a regular annual event consisting of flying demonstrations and aircraft displays. By 1988 it was called the **Dayton Air and Trade Show**, reflecting a growing emphasis on the commercial aspects of the aviation and aerospace industry. It was renamed the United States Air and Trade Show in 1990, when it became an international exposition, and since that time the trade show has been held biennially for six days in June. Every year, the third weekend in July is devoted to the air show, which features bi-planes, gliders, helicopters, and jets flown by some of the most famous names in the field of aviation.

Held at the Dayton International Airport, the show hosts over 250 exhibitors from the United States and other countries. Conferences and seminars, flight demonstrations, and tours of the latest makes and models of aircraft draw an international and largely professional crowd. Visitors and participants can also visit the United States Air Force Museum, the National Aviation Hall of Fame, the restored Wright Brothers Cycle Shop, and Wright-Patterson Air Force Base, which continues to play a major role in the development of aerospace technology.

CONTACT:
United States Air and Trade Show
Dayton International Airport
Dayton, OH 45377
513-898-5901

United States Independence Day
See **Fourth of July**

♦ 1968 ♦ United States Open Championship in Golf
Four days ending the third Sunday in June

The **U.S. Open**, conducted by the United States Golf Association, is the oldest golf tournament in North America, and was first held in 1895. More than 6,000 professional and amateur golfers vie for only 156 available places. Unlike the MASTERS, which is an invitational tournament, the U.S. Open is for anyone good enough to survive the qualifying rounds. Rather than being played on the same course each year, its location changes. It is traditionally played on the nation's best courses, such as Merion in Philadelphia, Oakland Hills in Birmingham, Mich., Baltusrol in Union County, New Jersey, Winged Foot in Mamaroneck, New York, and Pebble Beach on the Monterey Peninsula of California. Since the 1930s, it has been the U.S.G.A.'s practice every 10 to 15 years to take the Open back to certain courses that have demonstrated they can provide a rigorous test for the world's top golfers. The tournament itself takes four days. There is a qualifying round followed by three days of 18 holes each, for a total of 72 holes.

The U.S. Open is one of the most difficult golf championships to win. Its list of champions includes Bobby Jones, Walter Hagen, Gene Sarazen, Ben Hogan, Arnold Palmer, Jack Nicklaus, Lee Trevino, and Tom Watson. The 1913 tournament, which was won by an unknown 20-year-old store clerk named Francis Ouimet, is considered to have marked the transformation of golf in America from an elite game to a public pastime.

CONTACT:
U.S. Golf Association
Liberty Corner Rd.
Far Hills, NJ 07931
800-336-4446 or 908-234-2300
fax: 908-234-9687

SOURCES:
Chases-1996, p. 254

♦ 1969 ♦ **United States Open Tennis**
September

The final tournament in the four events that make up the Grand Slam of tennis. (The others are the AUSTRALIAN OPEN, the FRENCH OPEN and WIMBLEDON.) Also known as the **U.S. Championships**, the games are played on hard courts at Flushing Meadows Park in Queens, N.Y. They had been played from 1915 to 1978 in Forest Hills, also in Queens. Separate amateur and professional open championships were held in 1968 and 1969, and the tournament became exclusively an open in 1970.

The U.S. National Lawn Tennis Association was established in 1881, and the first official U.S. National Championship was played under its auspices that year in Newport, R.I. The first women's championship was played in 1887. The golden age at Forest Hills is considered to have been the 1920s when William T. "Big Bill" Tilden II dominated the game. He was U.S. Open champion seven times, from 1920–25 and in 1929. Other seven-time winners were Richard Sears (1881–87) and William Larned (1901, 1902, 1907–11). Jimmy Connors took the title five times (1974, 1976, 1978, 1982, 1983). In the women's championships, Molla Bjurstedt Mallory is the all-time champ; she won eight times (1915–18, 1920–22, 1926). Helen Wills Moody won seven times (1923–25, 1927–29, 1931). "Little Poker Face," as she was called, also won eight Wimbledons and four French Opens.

Ranking near the top of the excitement scale were the wins in the U.S. Championships that sewed up the Grand Slam championship. In 1938, Don Budge was the first to win all four Grand Slam titles. The feat wasn't equaled until 1962 when Rod Laver won all four. Then he did it again in 1969. In 1953, Californian Maureen Connolly became the first woman to sweep the Grand Slam titles. Known as "Little Mo," she had won her first U.S. Championship at the age of 16 in 1951. A horse-riding accident in 1954 cut her career short, and she died in 1969. Women who have won all Grand Slam titles since then are Margaret Smith Court in 1970 and Steffi Graf in 1988.

CONTACT:
United States Tennis Association
70 W. Red Oak Ln.
White Plains, NY 80604
914-696-7000; fax: 914-696-7167
WWW: http://www.usta.com

♦ 1970 ♦ **Universal Prayer Day (Dzam Ling Chi Sang)**
Usually June or July; 14th to 16th days of fifth Tibetan lunar month

A Tibetan Buddhist festival and a time for spiritual cleansing. At this time, people hang prayer flags on tree tops, burn juniper twigs, and build bonfires to worship the Buddha and local gods. Fire in the Tibetan culture is symbolic of cleansing. Family picnics are also common during the festival.

This is also the time of the once-a-year display of the famous giant *thangkas*, or 'scroll paintings', at Tashilhunpo (which means "heap of glory") Monastery in Shigatse, Tibet. Tashilhunpo, the seat of the Panchen Lamas, once had more than 4,000 monks, but the monastery was disbanded by the Chinese in 1960, and only about 600 monks remain.

At this time, three huge thangkas with images of the Buddha are displayed for three days on a nine-story wall on the monastery grounds. Thangkas, which are made in all sizes, were first known in Tibet in the 10th century, and were used in monastery schools as teaching devices. Before being hung, they were always consecrated.

Panchen Lamas came into being in the 17th century when the fifth Dalai Lama gave the title *panchen*, meaning 'great scholar,' to his beloved tutor. The tutor was then found to be the reincarnation of Amitabha, the Buddha of infinite light, and subsequent Panchen Lamas are new incarnations. As with Dalai Lamas, when a Panchen Lama dies, a search is made for an infant boy who is the new incarnation.

See also DALAI LAMA, BIRTHDAY OF THE

CONTACT:
India Tourist Office
30 Rockefeller Ave.
15 N. Mezzanine
New York, NY 10112
212-586-4901; fax: 212-582-3274

♦ 1971 ♦ **University of Pennsylvania Relay Carnival**
Seven days, beginning on the Sunday before the last weekend in April

The **Penn Relays** is the oldest and largest track and field event in the United States. The first relay meet held on the campus of the University of Pennsylvania in Philadelphia was on April 21, 1895—but even back then the tents and the festival atmosphere contributed to its reputation as a "carnival" rather than just a series of races. Since that time, the Penn Relays have served as a springboard for athletes who later went on to win OLYMPIC medals—such as Carl Lewis, Joan Benoit, Edwin Moses, and Frank Shorter. It is also a breeding ground for rising track and field stars, with more than 700 high school teams and 180 college teams participating.

The event begins on the Sunday before the last weekend in April (unless that day is EASTER, in which case the Relays would begin a week earlier) with a 20-kilometer road race. There is a heptathlon and a decathlon on Tuesday and Wednesday, and the rest of the week is filled with walk, sprint, distance, and field events for athletes of all ages and abilities—including Special Olympians. More than 70,000 spectators are drawn to the event, which receives wide press coverage.

CONTACT:
Philadelphia Convention and Visitors Bureau
1515 Market St., Ste. 2020
Philadelphia, PA 19102
800-537-7676 or 215-636-3300
fax: 215-636-3327

♦ 1972 ♦ **Up-Helly-Aa**
Last Tuesday in January

This ancient fire festival is observed by people of Lerwick in the Shetland Islands. In pre-Christian times their Norse ancestors welcomed the return of the sun god with YULE, a 24-day period of feasting, storytelling, and bonfires. The last night of the festival was called Up-Helly-Aa, or 'End of the Holy Days.'

Today a group known as the Guizers builds a 31-foot model of a Viking longship, complete with a dragon's head and many oars, in honor of those Viking invaders who decided to remain in Scotland. On the night of Up-Helly-Aa, the Guizers dress in Norse costumes and helmets and carry the boat to a large open field. There they throw lit torches into the ship and burn it.

Uphaliday originally referred to EPIPHANY, or January 6—the day when the Yuletide holidays came to an end. The shifting of the date to the end of January probably reflects the change from the Julian to the Gregorian calendar in 1752. This day is also referred to as **Uphelya, Up-Helly-Day, Uphalie Day**, or **Uphalimass**.

CONTACT:
British Tourist Authority
551 Fifth Ave., Ste. 702
New York, NY 10176
800-462-2748 or 212-986-2200
fax: 212-986-1188

SOURCES:
AnnivHol-1983, p. 16
BkHolWrld-1986, Jan 28
Chases-1996, p. 79
DictDays-1988, p. 124
FolkWrldHol-1992, p. 39
RelHolCal-1993, p. 119

♦ 1973 ♦ Urini Nal (Children's Day)
May 5

A national holiday in South Korea since 1975. Schools are closed and parks are packed with children. Events of the day may include wrestling and martial arts exhibitions, dancing, and the presentation of puppet shows and plays. Cake shops give away rice cake favors. The holiday is intended to forge the bonds of family life.

SOURCES:
AnnivHol-1983, p. 61
Chases-1996, p. 201

♦ 1974 ♦ Uruguay Independence Day
August 25

This national holiday commemorates the declaration of independence from Portuguese rule on this day in 1825. By 1828, Uruguay was officially autonomous.

Patriotic ceremonies are held in the capital city of Montevideo, with speeches and the singing of the national anthem.

CONTACT:
Uruguayan Tourist Bureau
747 Third Ave.
Doral Inn Hotel, 21st Floor
New York, NY 10017
212-753-8581; fax: 212-753-1603

SOURCES:
AnnivHol-1983, p. 110
Chases-1996, p. 349
NatlHolWrld-1968, p. 150

♦ 1975 ♦ Utah Arts Festival
Late June

The only state-sponsored arts festival in the country, bringing together more than 100 performing groups. The festival was founded in 1977 in Salt Lake City and is now a five-day event held on stages and in the streets, plazas, and galleries. Hundreds of booths are set up for native foods and for exhibits of sculpture, painting, pottery, folk arts, and photography. In a Children's Art Yard, stories are told of Utah mining days and natural history. Live performances of contemporary, jazz, bluegrass, folk, and salsa music are presented from two outdoor stages, and in the evening, there are dance, theater, symphony, and opera performances in the Utah Symphony Hall and restored 19th-century Capitol Theatre.

CONTACT:
Utah Tourism and Travel
Council House
Capitol Hill
Salt Lake City, UT 84114
800-200-1160; fax: 801-538-1000

SOURCES:
GdUSFest-1984, p. 191
MusFestAmer-1990, p. 141

♦ 1976 ♦ Ute Bear Dance
May, Memorial Day weekend

An ancient ceremony of the Southern Ute Indians held now on the Sunday and Monday of Memorial Day weekend in Ignacio, Colo. Originally the ritual was held in late February or early March, at the time of the bears awakening from their hibernation. It stemmed from the belief that the Utes were descended from bears, and the dance was given both to help the bears coming out of hibernation and to gain power from them, since bears were believed to cure sickness and to communicate with people in the Spirit World.

Today the dance is largely a social occasion, and is what is called a women's dance, since the women ask the men to dance. This practice is rooted in the habits of bears: supposedly the female bear wakes first and then chases the male bear. In earlier days, two bears—a man and woman wearing bearskins, with red paint around their mouths to suggest the bloody ferocity of the bears—romped around a corral, the female chasing the male, and both responding ferociously toward anyone who might laugh. In the present-day dance, lines of women and men advance toward each other, gradually dancing in pairs. The dancing goes on until sunset, when there is a feast.

CONTACT:
Southern Ute Tribal Council
P.O. Box 737
Ignacio, CO 81137
303-563-4525

SOURCES:
IndianAmer-1989, p. 121

V

◆ 1977 ◆ Vaisakh
April–May; first day of Hindu month of Vaisakha

The Hindu New Year and a harvest festival, celebrated primarily in northern India and Bangladesh with temple worship, ritual bathing in rivers, and a New Year's fair. For Sikhs, it is their most important holy day.

In Malaysia and India, especially in the Indian state of Punjab, where the gospel of the Sikhs began, **Baisakh** is particularly significant because on this day in 1689 Guru Gobind Singh chose the five leaders (called the *Panch Pyare*, or 'Beloved Five') who formed the Khalsa, the militant fraternity of the Sikhs. There the holiday is celebrated in the temples, with a 48-hour reading of the Granth Sahib (the Sikh holy book), prayers, hymns, and sermons. Castelessness, an important Sikh principle, is emphasized by everyone eating and sitting together. Afterwards, there is feasting and dancing of the *bhangra*, a popular and athletic folk dance for men, depicting the entire farming year.

In the Indian state of Kerala, the festival is known as **Vishu**. Activities include fireworks and what is called Vishu Kani, a display of grain, fruits, flowers, gold, new cloth, and money, which is supposed to ensure a prosperous year.

The festival is called **Bohag Bihu** in Assam, and there it is celebrated for a week with music, folk dances, and community feasting. Traditions include decorating cattle, smearing them with turmeric, and giving them brown sugar and eggplant to eat. Also during this time, there is a day on which young people look for marriage partners. The girls wear beautiful scarves, and the boys look for the most lovely orchids; they present these to each other and then dance.

CONTACT:
India Tourist Office
30 Rockefeller Ave.
15 N. Mezzanine
New York, NY 10112
212-586-4901; fax: 212-582-3274

Bangladesh Embassy
2201 Wisconsin Ave., N.W., Ste. 300
Washington, D.C. 20007
202-342-8372; fax: 202-333-4971

SOURCES:
AnnivHol-1983, pp. 173, 178
BkFest-1937, p. 157
DictFolkMyth-1984, p. 790
FolkWrldHol-1992, pp. 254, 255
RelHolCal-1993, pp. 60, 80, 87

◆ 1978 ◆ Valentine's Day
February 14

St. Valentine is believed to have been a Roman priest who was martyred on this day around 270. How he became the patron saint of lovers remains a mystery, but one theory is that the Church used the day of St. Valentine's martyrdom in an attempt to Christianize the old Roman LUPERCALIA, a pagan festival held around the middle of February. Part of the ancient ceremony entailed putting girls' names in a box and letting the boys draw them out. Couples would thus be paired off until the following year. The Church substituted saints' names for girls' names, in the hope that the participant would model his life after the saint whose name he drew. But by the 16th century, it was once again girls' names that ended up in the box. Eventually the custom of sending anonymous cards or messages to those one admired became the accepted way of celebrating **St. Valentine's Day**.

SOURCES:
AmerBkDays-1978, p. 177
BkDays-1864, vol. I, p. 255
BkFest-1937, p. 15
DaysCustFaith-1957, p. 54
DictFolkMyth-1984, p. 866
FestSaintDays-1915, p. 34
FolkAmerHol-1991, p. 74
FolkWrldHol-1992, p. 133
RelHolCal-1993, p. 112
SaintFestCh-1904, p. 103

◆ 1979 ◆ Valley of the Moon Vintage Festival
Last full weekend in September

California's oldest wine festival, held since the late 1890s in Sonoma, the cradle of the state's wine industry. Located in Sonoma Valley, which Jack London made famous as the "Valley of the Moon," the city was founded in 1835 by Gen. Mariano Guadalupe Vallejo. In 1846, the Northwest became part of the United States, and, on June 14 of that year, American settlers invaded Sonoma, captured Vallejo and his Mexican garrison, and raised an improvised Bear Flag to proclaim California a republic. On July 9, the flag was replaced by the Stars and Stripes. In the 1850s, Hungarian nobleman Count Agoston Haraszthy planted thousands of cuttings from European grape vines to establish the Buena

Vista Winery, now the state's oldest premium winery, becoming the father of California's wine industry. In 1863, a double wedding united the two prominent wine-making families—the Vallejos and the Haraszthys.

The two-day festival focuses on this history, presenting reenactments of the 1846 Bear Flag Revolt and of the double wedding. There are also wine tastings, parades, live music, cooking-with-wine demonstrations, a firemen's water fight, and grape stomps.

CONTACT:
California Division of Tourism
801 K Street, Ste. 1600
Sacramento, CA 95814
800-862-2543 or 916-322-2881
fax: 916-322-3402

◆ 1980 ◆ Vandalia Gathering
May, Memorial Day weekend

A folk festival held on the state capitol grounds in Charleston, W. Va., to exhibit the best of the state's traditional arts, music, dance, crafts, and food. Events include music by fiddlers, banjo players, and lap-dulcimer players, clogging, craft demonstrations, liars' contests, storytelling, and an exhibition of quilts made by West Virginia's top quilters. Held since 1976, the festival attracts about 35,000 people.

See also WEST VIRGINIA DAY

CONTACT:
Charleston Convention and Visitors Bureau
200 Civic Center Dr.
Charleston, WV 25301
800-733-5469 or 304-344-5075

◆ 1981 ◆ Vappu
May 1

A national holiday and celebration of the coming of spring in Finland. The holiday, once a pagan festival to rejoice at the end of the long northern winter, is also LABOR DAY, and factories that are said to "never close" do close on May 1 and CHRISTMAS Day.

For students (and even gray-bearded former students), the "anything goes" celebration begins at midnight on the eve of MAY DAY, called Vapunaatto, when they wear white student caps and indulge in anything not indecent or criminal. It's traditional in Helsinki for students to wade across the moat that surrounds the statue of Havis Amanda, a mermaid, and place their caps on her head. There are balloons, streamers, horns, and masks everywhere, and few get much sleep. On May Day itself, the students lead processions through the streets of Helsinki, and then enjoy carnivals and concerts. Workers in most provincial towns generally gather in more solemn fashion to celebrate with speeches and parades.

See also PREMIER MAY

CONTACT: SOURCES:
Finnish Tourist Board   *BkFest-1937*, p. 113
655 Third Ave., 18th Floor
New York, NY 10017
212-949-2333; fax: 212-983-5260

◆ 1982 ◆ Vaqueros, Fiesta de los
Four days beginning the last Thursday in February

A four-day event in Tucson, Ariz., featuring the world's longest non-motorized parade and the largest outdoor midwinter rodeo in the United States. The fiesta starts with the parade—a two-mile-long procession of some 300 entries, including such old horse-drawn vehicles as buckboards, surreys (with or without the fringe on top), western stagecoaches, and Conestoga wagons. The first parade was in 1925; now about 200,000 people line the parade route.

The three days of rodeo include the standard events as well as daily Mutton Bustin' contests. In these, four- to six-year-olds test their riding skills on sheep. There are also demonstrations by Appaloosa trick stallions and by the Quadrille de Mujeres, a women's precision-riding team.

CONTACT: SOURCES:
Tucson Convention and Visitors   *Chases-1996*, p. 107
  Bureau
130 S. Scott Ave.
Tucson, AZ 85701
800-638-8350 or 520-624-1817
fax: 520-884-7804

◆ 1983 ◆ Vasalopp
First Sunday in March

The biggest cross-country ski race in the world takes place in Sweden on the first Sunday in March each year. The course begins on the border between Norway and Sweden, in a huge frozen field outside the village of Sälen, and ends 54 miles away in the Swedish town of Mora. The race was named for a young Swedish nobleman, Gustav Vasa, who persuaded the people of Mora to help him drive out the Danes in 1520. He later ruled the country for almost 40 years as King Gustavus I.

More than 8,000 men compete in the annual race, which for even the strongest skier takes over five hours to complete. Because they consider this to be a test of their manhood, many Swedish men celebrate their 50th birthdays by entering the race. More than 70,000 have officially completed the Vasalopp since the race became a national ski festival in 1922.

CONTACT: SOURCES:
Swedish National Tourist Office *BkHolWrld-1986*, Mar 7
655 Third Ave., 18th Floor
New York, NY 10017
212-949-2333; fax: 212-983-5260

◆ 1984 ◆ Vasant Panchami (Basant Panchami)
January–February; fifth day of waxing half of Hindu month of Magha

A Hindu festival of spring, celebrated throughout India at the end of January or in early February. People wear bright yellow clothes, the color of the mustard flower that heralds the onset of spring, and mark the day with music, dancing, and kite-flying. In Shantiniketan, West Bengal, the festival is celebrated with special lavishness in honor of Sarasvati, the goddess of learning and the arts. Her images are taken in procession to rivers to be bathed, and books and pens are placed at her shrine.

CONTACT:
India Tourist Office
30 Rockefeller Ave.
15 N. Mezzanine
New York, NY 10112
212-586-4901; fax: 212-582-3274

SOURCES:
AnnivHol-1983, p. 173
BkHolWrld-1986, Feb 16
RelHolCal-1993, p. 120

◆ 1985 ◆ Vata Savitri
May–June; Hindu month of Jyestha

During this festival Hindu women bathe early in the morning, dress in their best clothes, then go out in groups to worship the banyan tree (*vata*). A type of fig tree which sends roots directly from the branches down to the ground, the banyan has special significance for Hindu women because Savitri, a deified woman in Hindu scriptures, was able to rescue her husband from Yama, the god of death, after she had worshipped the *Vata* tree.

During the worship ceremony, the tree is sprinkled with vermilion and its trunk is wrapped in raw cotton threads. The women walk around the tree seven times and place various articles of worship near it. Those who are unable to find a banyan tree on this day pay their respects to a twig of it in their homes and fast during worship.

See also KARWACHOTH

SOURCES:
BkFest-1937, p. 158
FolkWrldHol-1992, p. 320
RelHolCal-1993, p. 120

◆ 1986 ◆ Vegetarian Festival
September–October; first nine days of ninth lunar month

An annual nine-day affair observed on the island of Phuket off southwestern Thailand by residents of Chinese ancestry. During the nine days, observers eat only vegetarian foods. The festival begins with a parade in which devotees wear white, and continues with ceremonies at temples, performances of special feats by ascetics, and acts of self-mortification—walking on hot coals, piercing the skin, and so on. The festival celebrates the beginning of the month called "Taoist Lent," when devout Chinese abstain from meat. It is thought, however, that the self-mortification acts are derived from the Hindu festival of THAIPUSAM.

CONTACT:
Tourism Authority of Thailand
5 World Trade Center, Ste. 3443
New York, NY 10048
212-432-0433; fax: 212-912-0920

◆ 1987 ◆ Vendimia, Fiesta de la
Second week in September

Spain is famous for its sherry, and some of the best sherry comes from the southwestern part of the country, in a district known as Jerez de la Frontera. This is said to be one of the few remaining places where the juice of the grapes is extracted by trampling them in huge wooden vats, or *lagares*. Although most people think this is done with bare feet, the participants actually wear specially designed hobnail boots.

In mid-September Jerez de la Frontera holds its **Grape Harvest Festival**, or Fiesta de la Vendimia, which includes flamenco dancing, *cante jondo* singing (a distinctive and deeply moving variety of Spanish gypsy song), and bullfighting. There is also an official "blessing of the grapes" and the season's first wine before the statue of San Ginés de la Jara, the patron saint of the region's wine growers. The blessing is part of a colorful pageant held at the Collegiate Church of Santa Maria. All of the events that take place during the festival pay tribute in one way or another to wine sherry, the area's most famous product.

CONTACT:
Tourist Office of Spain
665 Fifth Ave.
New York, NY 10022
212-759-8822; fax: 212-980-1053

SOURCES:
AnnivHol-1983, p. 183
DictFolkMyth-1984, p. 483
FestWestEur-1958, p. 204
GdWrldFest-1985, p. 161

◆ 1988 ◆ Venezuela Independence Day
July 5; April 19

Revolutionary struggle against Spanish rule began in Venezuela in 1810. On July 5, 1811, a group of citizens in Caracas became the first in South America to proclaim a formal declaration of independence from Spain. Forces led by Simon Bolivar assured independence in 1821.

April 19 is another national holiday, known as both Declaration of Independence Day and Day of the Indian.

CONTACT:
Venezuelan Tourism Association
7 E. 51st St., 4th Floor
New York, NY 10022
212-826-1678; fax: 212-826-4175

SOURCES:
AnnivHol-1983, pp. 53, 89
Chases-1996, p. 285
NatlHolWrld-1968, p. 109

◆ 1989 ◆ Vermont Maple Festival
Last weekend in April

Vermont is the official maple capital of the world, and the maple festival held there each spring is really a statewide celebration. Maple sugaring—the process of tapping maple trees, gathering the sap, and boiling it in the sugarhouse to produce syrup—was a main source of income for the early settlers in Vermont as well as their main source of sweets. The sugaring industry flourished until World War II, when the number of producers dropped sharply. In the 1940s, 1950s and 1960s, the growing emphasis on dairy farming resulted in the suspension of many sugaring operations. Although there has been a resurgence of interest in recent years, mild winters have taken their toll on the maple sugar crop because cold nights are needed to make the sap flow.

Since 1968 the three-day festival in St. Albans has promoted Vermont maple products through educational exhibits, sugaring equipment displays, essay contests, syrup competitions, and maple cooking contests. In addition to maple syrup, the festival gives visitors an opportunity to sample maple cream, maple candy, and maple sugar on snow.

CONTACT:
Vermont Dept. of Travel and Tourism
134 State St.
Montpelier, VT 05602
800-837-6668 or 802-828-3236
fax: 802-828-3233

SOURCES:
Chases-1996, p. 177
GdUSFest-1984, p. 195

◆ 1990 ◆ Vernal Equinox
March 21 or 22

The vernal equinox, Latin for 'of spring' and 'equal night,' is one of the two occasions during the year when the sun crosses the equator, and the days and nights everywhere are nearly of equal length. It marks the beginning of spring in the Northern Hemisphere and the beginning of autumn in the Southern Hemisphere.

In Japan, the **Festival of the Vernal Equinox**, or **Shumbun-no-Hi**, is a day on which schools and places of business are closed and people are encouraged to love and appreciate nature and all living creatures.

See also AUTUMNAL EQUINOX

SOURCES:
AmerBkDays-1978, p. 276
BkDays-1864, vol. II, p. 364
Chases-1996, p. 139
DictDays-1988, p. 37
DictFolkMyth-1984, p. 1105
FolkWrldHol-1992, p. 183

◆ 1991 ◆ **Verrazano Day**
April 17

Observed in New York state, Verrazano Day commemorates the discovery of New York Harbor by the Italian navigator Giovanni da Verrazano on April 17, 1524. With the backing of King Francis I of France, Verrazano sailed his ship *La Dauphine* to the New World, reaching the Carolina coast in March 1524 and then sailing northward, exploring the eastern coast of North America. In addition to discovering the present-day site of New York City's harbor, he also discovered Block Island and Narragansett Bay in what is now Rhode Island, plus 32 islands off the coast of Maine, including Monhegan. Verrazano was the first European explorer to name newly discovered sites in North America after persons and places in the Old World.

In naming the Verrazano-Narrows Bridge, New York gave Verrazano official recognition. Spanning New York Harbor from Brooklyn to Staten Island, the 4,260-foot suspension bridge, built between 1959 and 1964, succeeded the Golden Gate Bridge in San Francisco as the world's longest suspension bridge until the Humber Bridge was completed in 1981 in Kingston upon Hull, England.

SOURCES:
AnnivHol-1983, p. 52
Chases-1996, p. 174

◆ 1992 ◆ **Vesak (Wesak; Buddha's Birthday)**
April–May; full moon of Hindu month of Vaisakha; April 8

This is the holiest of Buddhist holy days, celebrating the Buddha's birth, enlightenment, and death, or attaining of Nirvana. While these anniversaries are observed in all Buddhist countries, they are not always celebrated on the same day. In Theravada Buddhist countries, all three anniversaries are marked on the full moon of Vaisakha. In Japan and other Mahayana Buddhist countries, the three anniversaries are usually observed on separate days—the birth on April 8, the enlightenment on December 8, and the death on February 15.

Vesak is a public holiday in many countries, including Thailand, Indonesia, Korea, and Singapore.

This celebration differs from country to country, but generally activities are centered on the Buddhist temples, where people gather to listen to sermons by monks. In the evening, there are candle-lit processions around the temples. Homes are also decorated with paper lanterns and oil lamps. Because it's considered important to practice the virtues of kindness to all living things, it's traditional in some countries to free caged birds on this day. In some areas, booths are set up along streets to dispense food. In Burma, people water the Bodhi tree with blessed water and chant prayers around it.

The Buddha was born as a prince, Siddhartha Gautama, at Lumbini, Nepal, an isolated spot near the border with India, and Lumbini is one of the most sacred pilgrimage destinations for Buddhists, especially on Vesak. A stone pillar erected in 250 B.C. by the Indian emperor Ashoka designates the birthplace, and a brick temple contains carvings depicting the birth. Another center of celebrations in Nepal is the Swayambhunath temple, built about 2,000 years ago. On this day it is constantly circled by a procession of pilgrims. The lamas in colorful silk robes dance around the *stupa* (temple) while musicians play. On this day each year, the stupa's collection of rare *thangkas* (embroidered religious scrolls) and mandalas (geometrical and astrological representations of the world) is shown on the southern wall of the stupa courtyard.

Sarnath, India, is the place where the Buddha preached his first sermon, and a big fair and a procession of relics of the Buddha highlight the day there. Bodh Gaya (or Buddh Gaya) in the state of Bihar is also the site of special celebrations. It was here that Siddhartha Gautama sat under the Bodhi tree, attained enlightenment, and became known as the Buddha, meaning the 'Enlightened One.'

Gautama was born about 563 B.C. into a regal family and was brought up in great luxury. At the age of 29, distressed by the misery of mankind, he renounced his princely life and his wife and infant son to become a wandering ascetic and to search for a path that would give relief from suffering. For six years he practiced severe austerities, eating little. But he realized that self-mortification wasn't leading him to what he sought. One morning, sitting in deep meditation, under a ficus tree now called the Bodhi tree, he achieved enlightenment, or awakening. This was at Bodh Gaya in about 528 B.C., when Gautama was 35 years old. In the years that followed, he laid down rules of ethics (*see* MAGHA PUJA) and condemned the caste system. He taught that the aim of religion is to free oneself of worldly fetters in order to attain enlightenment, or Nirvana, a condition of freedom from sorrow and selfish desire. The Buddha trained large numbers of disciples to continue his work. He died in about 483 B.C.

From its start in northern India, Buddhism spread throughout Asia. The religion grew especially after Asoka, the first great emperor of India, adopted it as his religion in the third century B.C. and traveled about preaching and building hospitals and monasteries. He also sent his son, Mahinda, to preach the tenets of Buddhism in Sri Lanka (*see* PONSON). The Buddhism practiced in Southeast Asia is the oldest form of the religion, known as Theravada Buddhism, or 'The Way of the Elders.' As Buddhism went north, into Nepal, Bhutan, Tibet, China, Korea, and then Japan, it took a different form called Mahayana Buddhism, or 'The Great Vehicle.'

Vesak, or **Wesak**, is also known as **Waicak**, **Vesakha Puja** (Thailand), **Buddha Jayanti** (Nepal and India), **Phat Dan Day** (Vietnam), **Buddha Purnima** (India), **Full Moon of**

Waso or **Kason** (Burma), **Vixakha Bouxa** (Laos) and sometimes the **Feast of the Lanterns**.

See also BUN BANG FAI, HANA MATSURI, and SONGKRAN

SOURCES:
BkFestHolWrld-1970, pp. 76, 78
BkHolWrld-1986, May 26
DictWrldRel-1989, pp. 121, 135
FolkAmerHol-1991, p. 180
FolkWrldHol-1992, pp. 141, 253, 257, 308
IntlThFolk-1979, p. 345
RelHolCal-1993, pp. 64, 121

♦ 1993 ♦ Veterans Day
November 11; second Sunday in November in Great Britain

On November 11, 1918, the armistice between the Allied and Central Powers that halted the fighting in World War I was signed in Marshal Ferdinand Foch's railroad car in the Forest of Compiègne, France. In the United States, the name **Armistice Day** was changed to Veterans Day in 1954 to honor those who have served their country in other wars as well. In Great Britain, Canada, and France, it is dedicated primarily to those who died in both world wars. The British and Canadians call it **Remembrance Day**. In England it is also known as **Poppy Day** for the red paper flowers sold by the British Legion to benefit veterans. The association of poppies with World War I was popularized by the poet John McCrae, who wrote the lines "In Flanders fields the poppies blow/ Between the crosses, row on row." Flanders was the site of heavy fighting during the war, and for many who wrote about it later, the poppy came to symbolize both the beauty of the landscape and the blood that was shed there. Poppies are also sold by veterans' organizations in most countries. An attempt in 1971 to make Veterans Day conform to the "Monday Holiday Law" by observing it on the fourth Monday in October triggered widespread resistance, and seven years later it was moved back to the traditional November 11 date. In many places the 11th day of the 11th month is celebrated by observing a two-minute silence at 11:00 in the morning, the hour at which the hostilities ceased.

SOURCES:
AmerBkDays-1978, p. 1011
BkFest-1937, p. 19
BkHolWrld-1986, Nov 11
DaysCustFaith-1957, p. 287
DictDays-1988, pp. 5, 125
DictFolkMyth-1984, p. 976

Victoria Day
See **Commonwealth Day**

♦ 1994 ♦ Victory Day (Our Lady of Victories Day)
September 8

A national holiday in Malta in celebration of the lifting of two sieges:

In 1565, the Hospitallers, or the Knights of the Order of St. John of Jerusalem, with 6,000–9,000 men, held Malta against a four-month siege by some 29,000 Ottoman Turks. The onslaught left half the knights dead, but the Turks didn't fare well either—the knights used the heads of Turkish captives as cannonballs, and the defeat of the Turks humbled the Ottoman Empire. (Malta was under the control of the knights, a religious and military order of the Roman Catholic Church dedicated to tending the sick and poor and warring against Muslims, from 1530 until June 1798, when Napoleon took possession of the island.)

During World War II, the island fought off Axis powers (Germany and Italy) despite three years of severe air bombardment. In April 1942, air-raid alerts averaged about 10 a day; the ruins included the Royal Opera House in Valletta, destroyed by a German bomb. British Prime Minister Winston Churchill called Malta "our only unsinkable aircraft carrier." On April 15, 1942, England's King George VI awarded the island of Malta the George Cross, Britain's highest decoration for civilian gallantry, to "honour her brave people . . . to bear witness to a heroism and devotion which will long be famous in history." This was the first time a medal was conferred on any part of the commonwealth. At this time, Britain also declared that self-government would be restored at the end of hostilities.

The holiday is celebrated with parades, fireworks, and a colorful regatta and boat races in the Grand Harbour at Valletta. A highlight of the boat races is that of the *dgnajsas*, oared taxi boats with painted designs. They are thought to date back to Phoenician times (800 B.C.).

See also MALTA INDEPENDENCE DAY

CONTACT:
Malta National Tourist Office
350 Fifth Ave.
Empire State Bldg., Ste. 4412
New York, NY 10118
212-695-9520; fax: 212-695-8229

SOURCES:
Chases-1996, p. 369

Victory over Japan Day
See **V-J Day**

♦ 1995 ♦ Vidalia Onion Festival
Third weekend in May

No tears here: a tribute to Georgia's state vegetable, the sweet Vidalia onion, said to be burp-free, good for digestion, *and* tearless. The festival is held in Vidalia (nearby Glenville has a rival onion festival, usually a week earlier) at the height of the harvest season, which extends from mid-April to early June.

This onion is an interesting vegetable, officially the F-1 hybrid yellow granex, a round white onion with a yellow skin. Local folks hail it as the "world's sweetest onion," and, in fact, it has a sugar content of 12.5 percent, making it as sweet as a Valencia orange. If the seed is planted anywhere but Georgia, however, it becomes a normal sharp-tasting onion, probably due to the soil. Therefore, the name Vidalia may be given only to onions grown in 13 Georgia counties and parts of seven more (by act of the state legislature and federal directive).

According to a local story, Vidalia onions have been known since 1931, when a farmer discovered the onions didn't make him cry and so got a premium price for them even during the Depression. But they didn't become widely known until

Delbert Bland of Bland Farms, a big onion producer, started a marketing campaign and mail-order onion business in 1984. In 1990, the sweet-onion business in Georgia amounted to about $35 million.

The celebration of the onion includes standard festival fare—music, a street dance, a rodeo, and sports tournaments. It also has a Vidalia Onion Masquerade Contest and a competition for Miss Vidalia Onion (a beautiful high school or college woman). In 1991, other beauty pageant winners were Miss Vidalia Onion Seed (age 4), Miss Vidalia Onion Sprout (age 9), and Junior Miss Vidalia Onion (age 12). Finally, there are onion-eating contests, and a Vidalia Onion Cook-Off, which produces cakes, breads, and muffins made with onions.

CONTACT:
Georgia Dept. of Industry
Trade and Tourism
285 Peachtree Center Ave., N.E.
Marquis Tower II, Ste. 1000
Atlanta, GA 30303
800-847-4842 or 404-656-3592
fax: 404-651-9063

♦ 1996 ♦ Vienna Festival
May–June

This six-week festival, founded in 1951, regularly attracts more than a million people to the city of Vienna, Austria. There are more than 1,000 performances of music, opera, ballet, and drama by some of the best-known Austrian and foreign companies in the world—including the Royal Shakespeare Company, the Merce Cunningham Dance Company, the Martha Graham Dance Company, the Noh Theater of Japan, and the Malegot Ballet of St. Petersburg.

Like the EDINBURGH FESTIVAL, the Vienna Festival also includes many "fringe" events offered by independent theater, dance, and musical groups.

CONTACT:
Austrian National Tourist Office
P.O. Box 1142, Times Square
New York, NY 10148
212-944-6880; fax: 212-730-4568

SOURCES:
GdWrldFest-1985, p. 14
IntlThFolk-1979, p. 42
MusFestEurBrit-1980, p. 29
MusFestWrld-1963, p. 87

♦ 1997 ♦ Vietnam Independence Day
September 2

The Socialist Republic of Vietnam observes its declaration of independence from France as a national holiday. On this day in 1945 Ho Chi Minh (1890–1969) proclaimed the establishment of the Democratic Republic of Vietnam.

CONTACT:
Vietnamese Embassy
1233 20th St., N.W., Rm. 501
Washington, D.C. 20036
202-861-0737

SOURCES:
AnnivHol-1983, p. 113
Chases-1996, p. 362
NatlHolWrld-1968, p. 156

♦ 1998 ♦ Vinalia
April 23, August 19

There were two ancient Roman festivals that were sacred to Venus and known as the Vinalia. The first, observed on April 23, was called the **Vinalia Priora**; the second, on August 19, was the **Vinalia Rustica**. Both festivals, it seems, were originally sacred to Jupiter. But after the worship of Venus was introduced into Rome in the second century B.C., its popularity spread so quickly that the older association with Jupiter gradually faded.

April 23 was probably the day on which the wine-skins were first opened, the new wine having been brought into Rome just a few days earlier. Libations from the newly opened skins were made to Jupiter (later Venus, who was a deity of gardens and therefore of vineyards as well). After the libation, the wine was tasted. Wine-growers were warned not to bring the new wine into the city until the Vinalia had been proclaimed on the *nones*, or the ninth day before the IDES of the month.

There is some confusion about what went on at the August festival. Some believe that this—not April 23—was the day on which the new wine was brought into Rome. Others say that the Vinalia Rustica was a rite designed to protect the vintage that would follow from disease, storms, and other harmful influences.

SOURCES:
FestRom-1981, pp. 106, 177
RomFest-1925, p. 85

♦ 1999 ♦ Vinegrower's Day
January–February

This pre-harvest vineyard festival in Bulgaria involves pruning the vines and sprinkling them with wine. Ritual songs and dances are performed in hopes of a plentiful grape harvest. In some areas, a "Vine King" is crowned with a wreath of twigs from the vineyards. Everyone treats him with great respect, for it is believed that fertility depends on the King's happiness.

Participation in the **Trifon Zarezan** festivities is something that both locals and foreign tourists look forward to. Visits to well-known Bulgarian vineyards are organized, the vines are pruned, and guests are given an opportunity to sample the local wine and foods.

CONTACT:
Bulgarian Embassy
1621 22nd St., N.W.
Washington, D.C. 20008
202-387-7969; fax: 202-234-7973

SOURCES:
AnnivHol-1983, p. 24
Chases-1996, pp. 64, 96

♦ 2000 ♦ Virginia Scottish Games
Fourth weekend in July

Alexandria, Virginia, was founded by Scotsmen in 1749 and named for Scottish merchant John Alexander. The city celebrates its Scottish heritage with a two-day Celtic country fair featuring bagpipe bands, world-class athletes, Celtic dancers, a national fiddling championship, and an international harp competition.

One of the most colorful attractions is the Highland dancing, which involves hundreds of competitors ranging in age from pre-schoolers to adults. The highlight of the athletic contests is the caber toss, which is part of a seven-event competition known as the Highland Heptathlon. These contests trace their origins to the ancient Highland games of northern

Scotland, where military chiefs demonstrated their strength at annual clan gatherings.

See also ALMA HIGHLAND FESTIVAL AND GAMES, GRANDFATHER MOUNTAIN HIGHLAND GAMES AND GATHERING OF SCOTTISH CLANS, and HIGHLAND GAMES

CONTACT:
Virginia Dept. of Economic
  Development
Division of Tourism
901 E. Byrd St.
Richmond, VA 23219
804-786-4484; fax: 804-786-1919

SOURCES:
Chases-1996, p. 313

♦ 2001 ♦ Virgin of the Pillar, Feast of the
October 12

According to an ancient legend, the Virgin Mary appeared to Santiago, or St. James the Apostle, when he was in Saragossa, Spain. She spoke to him from the top of a pillar, which he interpreted as a sign that he should build a chapel where the column stood. *Nuestra Señora del Pilar* has since become a major pilgrimage center.

The 10-day Feast of the Virgin of the Pillar is observed with special Masses and processions in honor of *La Virgen*. The *Gigantes*—giant cardboard and canvas figures concealing the men who dance behind them—are brought out especially for the occasion. Often representing Spanish kings and queens or famous literary and historical figures, they can be 20- to 30-feet tall. The *cabezudos*, or 'big heads', on the other hand, are grotesque puppets with huge heads which are meant to poke fun at certain professions or personalities. Also characteristic of the festival are *jota* contests in which Aragon's regional folk dance is performed to the accompaniment of guitars, mandolins, and lutes.

See also ST. JAMES'S DAY

CONTACT:
Tourist Office of Spain
665 Fifth Ave.
New York, NY 10022
212-759-8822; fax: 212-980-1053

SOURCES:
AnnivHol-1983, p. 183
DictWrldRel-1989, p. 569
FestWestEur-1958, p. 205
IntlThFolk-1979, p. 344

♦ 2002 ♦ Visitation, Feast of the
May 31, Roman Catholic and Protestant; July 2,
Church of England

On this day churches in the West commemorate the Virgin Mary's visit to her cousin Elizabeth. After learning that she was to be the mother of Jesus, Mary went into the mountains of Judea to see her cousin, the barren wife of Zechariah, who had conceived a son who would come to be known as John the Baptist. According to the Gospel of Luke, Elizabeth's baby "leaped in her womb" (1:41) at the sound of Mary's voice. It was at this moment, according to the pious belief of some Roman Catholics, that John the Baptist was cleansed from original sin and filled with heavenly grace. Mary stayed with Elizabeth for three months and returned home just before John was born.

See also ST. ELIZABETH, FEAST OF; ST. JOHN'S DAY

SOURCES:
AnnivHol-1983, p. 73

BkDays-1864, vol. II, p. 11
BkFest-1937, p. 187
DaysCustFaith-1957, p. 168
RelHolCal-1993, p. 121
SaintFestCh-1904, p. 315

♦ 2003 ♦ Visvakarma Puja
August–September; end of Hindu month of
Bhadrapada

Dedicated to Visvakarma, the patron god of all Hindu artisans, the **Festival of Tools** is a workers' holiday dedicated to each individual's most important tool or instrument. A pitcher representing the god is set in a place of honor in every home and shop, and before it the people lay their most important tool. Students might place one of their schoolbooks there, musicians would place the instrument they play, artists would put their favorite brushes before the pitcher, tailors their scissors, gardeners their rakes, fishermen their nets, etc. A candle is lit in front of the pitcher, and sometimes incense is burned or scented water is sprinkled over the tool. Workers give thanks for their tools and implore Visvakarma's help in plying their trade.

After this ceremony is over, people gather in parks or public places and spend the rest of the day in games and feasting.

CONTACT:
India Tourist Office
30 Rockefeller Ave.
15 N. Mezzanine
New York, NY 10112
212-586-4901; fax: 212-582-3274

♦ 2004 ♦ V-J Day (Victory over Japan Day)
August 14

The anniversary of Japan's surrender to the Allies in 1945, ending World War II. The atomic bombs dropped on Hiroshima on Aug. 6 and Nagasaki on Aug. 9, and the Soviet Union's invasion of Manchuria in the previous week made the surrender inevitable. The announcement of the surrender by President Harry S. Truman set off street celebrations from coast to coast in the United States. In New York City, Times Square was jammed with people embracing and dancing. In Naples, Italy, the Andrews Sisters had just finished singing "Don't Sit Under the Apple Tree" to U.S. troops when Maxine Andrews was given a slip of paper and read the news; joyous bedlam ensued. The official end of the war didn't come until Sept. 2, when Gen. Douglas MACARTHUR accepted the Japanese surrender from Gen. Yoshijiro Umezu aboard the USS *Missouri* in Tokyo Bay. He said, "Today the guns are silent. A great tragedy has ended.... The holy mission has been completed." President Truman declared Sept. 2 as official V-J Day.

V-J Day is a legal holiday only in the state of Rhode Island, where it is called Victory Day. In Connecticut, the tiny village of Moosup (a section of the town of Plainfield) claims to have the only V-J Day parade in the country. Sponsored by the local American Legion post, it began small in 1961 and now features more than 200 units—marching bands, floats, civic groups, color guards, and Gold Star Mothers (women who lost a son or daughter in war)—and attracts some 10,000 spectators.

CONTACT:
Connecticut Tourism Division
865 Brook St.
Rocky Hill, CT 06067
800-282-6863 or 860-258-4355
fax: 860-258-4275

SOURCES:
AmerBkDays-1978, pp. 754, 794, 796
AnnivHol-1983, p. 107
Chases-1996, p. 336
DictDays-1988, p. 126

♦ 2005 ♦ **Vlöggelen**
Between March 22 and April 25; Easter Sunday and Monday

As practiced in the eastern Netherlands village of Ootmarsum, the Vlöggelen, or **Winging Ceremony**, is believed to be the remnant of an ancient spring fertility rite. It is a ritualistic dance through the narrow cobbled streets performed by villagers, linked to form a human chain that advances slowly, "like birds on the wing." The dancers enter the front doors of shops, inns, farmhouses, and barns, emerging through the back doors to the melody of an old EASTER hymn with so many verses that the dancers must read the words pinned to the back of the person in front of them.

See also EASTER MONDAY IN THE NETHERLANDS

CONTACT:
Netherlands Board of Tourism
355 Lexington Ave., 21st Floor
New York, NY 10017
212-370-7360; fax: 212-370-9507

SOURCES:
FestWestEur-1958, p. 130

♦ 2006 ♦ **Von Steuben Day**
September 17; fourth Sunday in September

Baron Friedrich Wilhelm Ludolf Gerhard Augustus von Steuben (1730–1794) was an experienced Prussian soldier who came to America in 1777 and volunteered to serve in the Continental army without rank or pay. He was sent to join General George WASHINGTON at Valley Forge, where he trained Washington's men in the intricacies of military drill, earning himself the sobriquet "Drill Master of the American Revolution." Von Steuben led one of Washington's divisions at the Battle of Yorktown (*see* YORKTOWN DAY), and his experience in siege warfare helped the American troops achieve the victory that soon brought the Revolutionary War to an end. In gratitude for his contributions, he was granted American citizenship and given a large piece of land in the Mohawk Valley and a yearly pension.

Von Steuben's birthday, September 17, was first celebrated by members of the Steuben Society of America, an organization founded in 1919 by U.S. citizens of German descent. The Society now has branches in many states, which observe the anniversary with patriotic exercises. At Valley Forge State Park in Pennsylvania, there is a von Steuben birthday celebration featuring German music and speeches at the monument to him erected in 1915. There is also a Steuben Day parade in New York City on the Saturday following September 17; in Philadelphia on the fourth Sunday in September; and in Chicago on or near the Prussian hero's birthday. These parades are usually large and colorful, with boys in *lederhosen* (leather shorts with suspenders) and girls in *dirndls* (skirts gathered at the waistband, with a bib top) marching to the sounds of polka-playing bands and martial music.

SOURCES:
AmerBkDays-1978, p. 851

Vossa
See **Waso**

♦ 2007 ♦ **Vulcanalia (Volcanalia)**
August 23

Vulcan was the ancient Roman god of volcanic or destructive fire—not to be confused with the Greek god Hephaestus, who was the god of the blacksmith's forge and therefore a kindly fire god. In offering sacrifices to Vulcan, it was customary to burn the whole victim—usually a calf or a boar—rather than reserving a part of the animal, as was common when worshipping other gods.

The Vulcanalia, or festival in honor of Vulcan, was held on August 23, right at the time of year when forest fires might be expected and when the stored grain was in danger of burning. For this reason Vulcan's cult was very prominent at Ostia, where Rome's grain was stored. At the Vulcanalia, which was observed in Egypt, in Athens, and in Rome, the priest or flamen Volcanis performed a sacrifice, and the heads of families burned small fish they had caught in the Tiber River.

It was the Emperor Augustus who divided the city of Rome into small districts to facilitate fire fighting, and who was honored as Volcanus Quietus Augustus.

SOURCES:
AmerBkDays-1978, p. 713
ClassDict-1984, p. 665
DictFolkMyth-1984, p. 1163

W

♦ 2008 ♦ **Waitangi Day**
February 6

A national public holiday in New Zealand, February 6 commemorates the signing of the 1840 Treaty of Waitangi, in which the Maori natives agreed to co-exist peacefully with the European settlers. Although it was first declared a national day of commemoration in 1960, Waitangi Day was not observed as a public holiday outside the North Island until it became **New Zealand Day** in 1973. It was observed as such until 1976, when it again became known as Waitangi Day.

The town of Waitangi is located on the Bay of Islands at the northern end of the North Island, and the day on which the treaty was signed is observed there by the Royal New Zealand Navy and the Maoris each year.

CONTACT:
New Zealand Tourism Board
501 Santa Monica Blvd., Ste. 300
Santa Monica, CA 90401
800-388-5494 or 310-395-7480
fax: 310-395-5453

SOURCES:
AnnivHol-1983, p. 20
Chases-1996, p. 89
DictDays-1988, p. 127
NatlHolWrld-1968, p. 24

♦ 2009 ♦ **Walpurgis Night (Walpurgisnacht)**
April 30

People who lived in the Harz Mountains of Germany believed for many centuries that witches rode across the sky on the eve of St. Walpurga's Day to hold a coven on Brocken Mountain. To frighten them off, they rang church bells, banged pots and pans, and lit torches topped with hemlock, rosemary, and juniper. The legend of Walpurgis Night is still celebrated in Germany, Austria, and Scandinavia with bonfires and other festivities designed to welcome spring by warding off demons, disaster, and darkness.

St. Walpurga (or Walburga) was an eighth-century English nun who later became a German abbess. She is the patron saint against dog bites and rabies. On the eve of May 1 her remains were moved from Heidenheim to Eichstätt, Germany, where her shrine became a popular place of pilgrimage. Legend has it that the rocks at Eichstätt give off a miraculous oil possessing curative powers. She is the saint who is also associated with protection against magic.

SOURCES:
AmerBkDays-1978, p. 404
BkFest-1937, p. 310
DaysCustFaith-1957, p. 102
DictDays-1988, p. 128
DictFolkMyth-1984, pp. 114,
    425, 961, 1165
FestWestEur-1958, pp. 25, 214
FolkAmerHol-1991, p. 187
FolkWrldHol-1992, p. 251
RelHolCal-1993, p. 64

♦ 2010 ♦ **Wangala (Hundred Drums Festival)**
Late fall, after harvest

A festival that lasts several days and celebrates the harvest, held in the Garo Hills of the state of Meghalaya in northeastern India. It involves a ceremony led by the village priest, climaxing in a dance to the sound of 100 drums and the music of gongs, flutes, and trumpets.

CONTACT:
India Tourist Office
30 Rockefeller Ave.
15 N. Mezzanine
New York, NY 10112
212-586-4901; fax: 212-582-3274

♦ 2011 ♦ **Waratambar**
August 24

Waratambar is observed by members of the Christian population of Papua New Guinea, who comprise about half of the country's two million people. It is a day for giving thanks to the Lord for what Christianity has done for people throughout the world. Farmers and their families take time off work to participate in the celebration, which focuses on singing and dancing. The songs express an appreciation of and closeness to nature and all creatures; the dances dramatize tribal wars. Costumes worn by the dancers are usually handmade—of ferns, moss, leaves, flowers, and other natural materials.

Waratambar is observed on different days in August in different provinces. In New Ireland, the date is August 24.

CONTACT:
Papua New Guinea Embassy
1615 New Hampshire Ave., N.W.,
   3rd Floor
Washington, D.C. 20009
202-745-3680; fax: 202-745-3679

SOURCES:
FolkWrldHol-1992, p. 424

♦ 2012 ♦ Warsaw Autumn Festival
Mid-September

Although it is officially called the **International Festival of Contemporary Music**, the Warsaw Autumn Festival's offerings are more conservative than the name would seem to indicate. Some experimental music is performed, and world premieres are not unheard of, but the Festival's offerings might be more accurately called "modern." Established in 1956 by a group of Polish composers who wanted to bring other East European as well as West European countries together, the Festival has presented the work of Luciano Berio, Michael Tippett, Krzysztof Penderlicki, Witold Lutoslawski, and other 20th-century composers. The concerts, which continue for nine days in mid-September, are held primarily in the concert hall of the Philharmonic Building, the Warsaw Opera House, and the concert hall of the National Conservatory. Orchestras that have performed in these locations include the Scottish National Orchestra of Glasgow, the Tokyo Metropolitan Symphony Orchestra, the Polish Chamber Orchestra, and the National Philharmonic Orchestra and Choir of Warsaw.

CONTACT:
Polish National Tourist Office
275 Madison Ave., Ste. 1711
New York, NY 10016
212-338-9412; fax: 212-338-9283

SOURCES:
GdWrldFest-1985, p. 154
IntlThFolk-1979, p. 298
MusFestEurBrit-1980, p. 130
MusFestWrld-1963, p. 254

♦ 2013 ♦ Washington's Birthday
February 22; observed third Monday in February

George Washington's birthday was not always celebrated in the United States as widely as it is today. The date itself was in question for a while, since the Gregorian calendar was adopted in England during Washington's lifetime and this shifted his birthday from February 11 to February 22 (*see* OLD CHRISTMAS DAY). Then there was a period when Washington's association with the Federalist party made the Antifederalists (or Jeffersonian Republicans) uncomfortable, and they put a damper on any official celebrations. It wasn't until Washington's death in 1799 that such feelings disappeared and he was regarded as a national hero.

As commander-in-chief of the Continental Army during the American Revolution and as the first president of the United States, George Washington looms large in American literature and legend. By the centennial of his birth in 1832, celebrations were firmly established, and his name had been given not only to the nation's capital, but to a state and more than 20 cities and towns. While the third Monday in February is observed as Washington's Birthday by the federal government and in most states, some combine it with the February birthday of another famous American president, Abraham LINCOLN, and call it **Washington-Lincoln Day** or PRESIDENTS' DAY.

At his death in 1799 Washington was a lieutenant general, then the highest military rank in the United States. That same year Congress had established the nation's highest military title, General of the Armies of the United States, intending it for him, but he didn't live to receive it. Subsequently, he was outranked by many U.S. Army officers, so in 1976 Congress finally granted it to him. He is now the senior general officer on Army rolls; General John J. Pershing is the only other officer to have been so honored—he received it in September 1919 for his work during World War I.

See also WASHINGTON'S BIRTHDAY CELEBRATION IN ALEXANDRIA, VIRGINIA and WASHINGTON'S BIRTHDAY CELEBRATION IN LOS DOS LAREDOS

SOURCES:
AmerBkDays-1978, p. 197
BkDays-1864, vol. I, p. 284
BkHolWrld-1986, Feb 22
Chases-1996, pp. 105, 108
GdUSFest-1984, p. 198

♦ 2014 ♦ Washington's Birthday Celebration in Alexandria, Virginia
Third Monday in February and preceding weekend

An array of activities in Alexandria, Va., including the nation's largest parade honoring the Father of His Country. Alexandria calls itself Washington's hometown; he kept a townhouse there, was one of the city's original surveyors, organized the Friendship Fire Company, and was a vestryman of Christ Church Parish and Charter Master of Masonic Lodge No. 22. A reminder of the president's association with the Masons is the George Washington Masonic National Memorial, a 333-foot-tall replica of the ancient lighthouse in Alexandria, Egypt.

Celebrations of Washington's birthday have been held in Alexandria since the president's lifetime. The first parade to honor him was in 1798, when he came from his Mt. Vernon home to review the troops in front of Gadsby's Tavern.

The present-day festivities get off to an elegant start on Saturday night with a banquet followed by the George Washington Birthnight Ball in Gadsby's Tavern, a duplication of the birthday-eve parties held in Washington's lifetime. People wear 18th-century dress, and the banquet toasts to Washington are usually delivered by people who are prominent in current events and who reflect Washington's military background. In 1991, Gen. Colin Powell, chairman of the U.S. Joint Chiefs of Staff proposed the toast. His name and face became widely known during the Persian Gulf War of 1991.

Sunday brings a Revolutionary War reenactment and the running of a 10-K road race. On Monday is the big parade. It lasts two hours and usually draws about 75,000 spectators. George and Martha Washington are depicted, along with other colonial personages. The paraders include a number of Scottish bagpipe groups (the city was founded by Scots), Masonic units, equestrian groups, color guards, fife and drum corps, and horse-drawn carriages.

See also WASHINGTON'S BIRTHDAY

CONTACT:
Virginia Dept. of Economic
   Development
Division of Tourism
901 E. Byrd St.
Richmond, VA 23219
804-786-4484; fax: 804-786-1919

SOURCES:
AmerBkDays-1978, p. 200
Chases-1996, p. 102
GdUSFest-1984, p. 198

◆ 2015 ◆ Washington's Birthday Celebration in Los Dos Laredos
Mid-February

A 10-day celebration in honor of George Washington, held since 1898 by Laredo, Tex., and its sister city on the other side of the Mexican border, Nuevo Laredo. The two Laredos (*los dos Laredos* in Spanish) are linked by history and by three bridges across the Rio Grande. Founded by the Spanish in 1755, Laredo has been under seven different national flags. Both cities also celebrate Mexican Independence Day during Expomex in September.

Washington's birthday events include dances, fireworks, mariachi music, an international bike race, a five-kilometer race, a waiters' race, a jalapeno-eating contest, and parades with lavishly decorated floats.

CONTACT:
Texas Department of Commerce
Tourism Division
1700 N. Congress, Ste. 200
Austin, TX 78711
800-888-8839 or 512-462-9191
fax: 512-936-0089

SOURCES:
AmerBkDays-1978, p. 200
Chases-1996, p. 99

◆ 2016 ◆ Washington State Apple Blossom Festival
May

The oldest blossom festival in the United States, this event has been held annually in Wenatchee, Washington, since 1920 (with the exception of the World War II years). It began with a suggestion from Mrs. E. Wagner, a Wenatchee resident who wanted to see something similar to the celebration held in her native New Zealand when the apple orchards were in bloom. Originally called **Blossom Days**, the event grew in size and popularity until it reached its current status as an 11-day festival drawing up to 100,000 spectators.

In 1947 the name of the festival was officially changed from the **Wenatchee Apple Blossom Festival** to its present name, although it continues to be held in Wenatchee, the "Apple Capital of the World." In addition to seeing the Wenatchee Valley orchards in full bloom, the events include apple relay races, a horse show, a foodfest, and a marching band competition. In 1967 the Aomori Apple Blossom Festival in Japan became Wenatchee's "sister festival," and the two towns have exchanged visitors a number of times.

CONTACT:
Washington State Tourism Development Division
P.O. Box 42500
Olympia, WA 98504
800-544-1800 or 360-753-5601
fax: 360-753-4470

SOURCES:
AnnivHol-1983, p. 173
BkFestHolWrld-1970, p. 89
Chases-1996, p. 184

◆ 2017 ◆ Waso (Buddhist Rains Retreat)
June–July to September–October; full moon of Buddhist month of Waso to full moon of Buddhist month of Thadingyut

A three-month period when monks remain in monasteries to study and meditate. At other times of the year, monks wander the countryside, but this is the time of monsoons in Southeast Asia, and the Buddha chose this period for retreat and prayer so they wouldn't walk across fields and damage young rice plants. However, even in China, Japan, and Korea—countries that don't have monsoons—the Waso is observed. It is also known as the **Buddhist Lent**. In Cambodia and India it is called **Vassa** or **Vossa**. In Burma and Thailand it is called **Phansa**, **Waso**, **Wasa**, or **Wazo Full Moon Day**; and in Laos, **Vatsa**.

The months are considered a time of restraint and abstinence. Weddings are not celebrated, and people try to avoid moving to new homes. Many young men enter the priesthood just for the retreat period, and therefore many ordinations take place. The new young monks have their heads shaved and washed with saffron, and they are given yellow robes. Many lay people attend the monasteries for instruction.

The day just prior to the retreat commemorates the Buddha's first sermon to his five disciples, 49 days after his enlightenment.

In Thailand, the start of the retreat, called Khao Phansa, is observed in the northeastern city of Ubon Ratchathani with the Candle Festival, in which beeswax candles carved in the shapes of birds and other figures, several yards high, are paraded and then presented to the temples. In many places, a beeswax candle is lit at the beginning of Waso and kept burning throughout the period. In Saraburi, people offer flowers and incense to monks who walk to the hilltop Shrine of the Holy Footprint where they present the offerings as tribute. It is traditional everywhere for people to bring food and other necessities to the monasteries.

The end of this period called **Ok-Barnsa,** or **Full Moon Day of Thadingyut,** is a time of thanksgiving to the monks, and also, according to legend, the time when the Buddha returned to earth after visiting his mother in heaven and preaching to her for three months. During the month of celebration (known as **Kathin**), lay people present monks with new robes and other items for the coming year.

Boat races are held on the rivers in Laos at Vientiane, Luang Phabang and Savannakhet, and in Thailand at numerous places. A special ceremony takes place in Bangkok when elaborate golden royal barges, rowed by oarsmen in scarlet, proceed to Wat Arun (the Temple of Dawn), where the king presents robes to the monks.

At Sakon Nakhon in northeastern Thailand, people build temples and shrines from beeswax and parade them through the streets to present them at temples. After the presentations, there are regattas and general festivities.

In Burma (now officially Myanmar), a Festival of Lights called the **Tassaung Daing** or TAZAUNGDAING Festival is held at this time, when the moon is full. Homes are lit with paper lanterns, and all-night performances are staged by dancers, comedians, and musicians. A major event of the festival is an all-night weaving contest at the Shwe Dagon pagoda in Rangoon (officially called Yangon); young unmarried women spend the night weaving robes, and at dawn they are offered to images of the Buddha at the pagoda. Similar weaving competitions are held throughout the country.

See also THADINGYUT

SOURCES:
AnnivHol-1983, pp. 180, 182, 183
BkHolWrld-1986, Jul 23, Sep 22, Oct 20, Oct 29
FolkWrldHol-1992, pp. 348, 525

♦ 2018 ♦ **Watch Night Service**
December 31

The custom of holding a "Watch Night" service on New Year's Eve was started in America by St. George's Methodist Church in Philadelphia in 1770. The custom has since been adopted by a number of denominations throughout the country. Methodists, Presbyterians, and others gather in their churches on the night of December 31. A five-minute period of silence is observed right before midnight, when a hymn of praise is sung.

Sometimes New Year's Eve is referred to as **Watch Night**, a time for people to gather and celebrate as they see the old year out and the new year in.

SOURCES:
AnnivHol-1983, p. 167
DaysCustFaith-1957, p. 325
DictDays-1988, p. 129

♦ 2019 ♦ **Water-Drawing Festival**
Beginning between September 20 and October 18; night following the first day of Sukkot and each night of the festival thereafter

The name of this ancient Jewish festival comes from Isaiah 12:3, which says, "Therefore with joy shall ye draw water out of the wells of salvation." The water-drawing ceremony, also known as **Simhat bet ha-Sho'evah**, was a matter of dispute between Pharisees, who regarded it as an oral tradition handed down from Sinai, and the Sadducees, who saw no basis for it and often showed outright contempt for the entire ritual. The more the Sadducees opposed it, the more emphasis the Pharisees placed on the water libation, which was considered a particularly joyful occasion and was performed in the temple on the night following the first day of Sukkot and then on each remaining night of the festival. Huge bonfires were lit throughout Jerusalem and the people stayed up dancing and singing for most of the night, often dozing off on each other's shoulders.

There have been attempts to revive the water-drawing festival in a more modern form, primarily among Israel's contemporary *kibbutzim*, or agricultural communities.

CONTACT:
Israel Ministry of Tourism
6380 Wilshire Blvd., Ste. 1700
Los Angeles, CA 90048
213-658-7462; fax: 213-658-6543

♦ 2020 ♦ **Watermelon-Eating and Seed-Spitting Contest**
Second Sunday in September

The only event of its kind sanctioned by the United States Department of Agriculture, the Watermelon-Eating and Seed-Spitting Contest held since 1965 in Pardeeville, Wisconsin, is attended by up to 9,000 people—eaters, spitters, and spectators. It takes eight people an entire day to cut up the 4,500–5,000 watermelons used in the contest. This festival also includes a watermelon volleyball competition, watermelon carving and growing contests, a parade, and a T-shirt design contest. But it is the eating and spitting contests that most people come to see. To date, the watermelon-eating record is 3.6 seconds for a two-pound slice. The spitting record is 48 feet.

Tongue-in-cheek rules for the spitting contest are strictly enforced: professional tobacco spitters are not eligible; denture wearers must abide by the judge's decision if their teeth go further than the seed; and no one is allowed to propel their seeds through a pipe, tube, or other hollow object. There is a team spitting competition, a couples' spitting competition, and separate competitions for men and women.

CONTACT:
Wisconsin Division of Tourism
123 W. Washington Ave., 6th Fl.
Madison, WI 53703
800-432-8747 or 608-266-7621
fax: 608-266-3403

♦ 2021 ♦ **Watermelon Thump**
Last weekend in June

A celebration of the watermelon harvest in Luling, Tex. The chief watermelon-related events are watermelon judging, a watermelon auction, watermelon-eating competitions, and watermelon seed-spitting contests leading to a Championship Seed Spit-Off. Among other activities are a parade, the coronation of the Watermelon Thump Queen, a fiddlers' contest, a carnival, and golf, baseball, and bowling tournaments.

CONTACT:
Texas Department of Commerce
Tourism Division
1700 N. Congress, Ste. 200
Austin, TX 78711
800-888-8839 or 512-462-9191
fax: 512-936-0089

SOURCES:
Chases-1996, p. 273

♦ 2022 ♦ **Wayne Chicken Show**
Second Saturday in July

This lighthearted one-day event takes place in Wayne, Nebraska, a town that is known primarily as a pork capital. But, as one of the festival's organizers admits, "We didn't want to make fun of pigs," and since there were some egg-processing plants and chicken farms in the area who were willing to contribute to the cause, the Wayne Chicken Show was "hatched" in 1981. Billed as an "eggszotic eggstravaganza," up to 10,000 people witness competitions in rooster crowing, chicken flying, egg dropping and catching, and a national cluck-off whose winner has appeared on the Tonight Show with Johnny Carson. There are prizes for the oddest egg, the most beautiful beak, and the best chicken legs on a human. The eggs and chefs for the free "omelette feed" are donated by egg producers in the area.

CONTACT:
Nebraska Travel and Tourism
  Division
700 S. 16th St.
Lincoln, NE 68508
800-228-4307 or 402-471-3794
fax: 402-471-3026

SOURCES:
Chases-1996, p. 296

♦ 2023 ♦ **Wedding Festivities in Galicnik, Macedonia**
July 12

It was common practice at one time in the former Yugoslavia for men to leave their villages or even to emigrate in search of higher paying work. On a specific day they would all return to their villages and mass wedding celebrations would be held. Galicnik is one of the last strongholds of this ancient custom, and on St. Peter's Day each year a multiple wedding feast is held. It begins on St. Peter's Eve with a torchlight procession of brides to three fountains where water is drawn for a purification ceremony. The most interesting feature of the wedding ceremony itself is that brides, bridegrooms, and guests knock their heads together. The first night of the marriage is spent in a complicated hide-and-seek game and the newlyweds do not sleep together. There is a great feast on the second day and that night the marriages are consummated.

Because the village of Galicnik is cut off from the rest of the world by snow for much of the winter, it is transformed during the summer, when many former residents and tourists come for the July 12 wedding festivities. Similar village wedding ceremonies are held in the Slovenian towns of Ljubljana at the end of July and in Bled in mid-August.

CONTACT:
Macedonia Consulate
866 UN Plaza, Ste. 4018
New York, NY 10017
212-317-1727; fax: 212-317-1484

SOURCES:
IntlThFolk-1979, p. 388

Weeks, Feast of
See **Shavuot**

Wesak
See **Vesak**

♦ 2024 ♦ **Western Samoa Independence Day**
June 1–3

Western Samoa gained independence from New Zealand on January 1, 1962. Because the rainy season in Western Samoa comes in January, however, celebrations are held in June during the first three days of the month.

CONTACT:
Western Samoa Embassy
820 Second Ave., Ste. 800
New York, NY 10017
212-599-6196; fax: 212-599-0797

SOURCES:
AnnivHol-1983, pp. 2, 74
NatlHolWrld-1968, p. 9

♦ 2025 ♦ **Western Stock Show, National**
Mid-January

The world's largest livestock exhibition and the show of shows in Denver, Colo. This is a 12-day trade show for the ranching industry, drawing visitors from throughout the U.S. as well as Mexico and Canada. On view at the stock show are more than 20,000 Hereford, Angus, Simmental, Shorthorn and Longhorn cattle. Plus Arabian, Morgan, draft, miniature and quarter horses, and ewes and lambs. Transactions in the millions of dollars are daily events; the livestock auctions as a matter of course can bring six figures for a single bull.

There are also daily rodeos, with more than 1,000 professional cowboys and cowgirls taking part in calf roping, bull and bronco riding, steer wrestling, and barrel racing. Sheep-shearing contests, displays for children, exhibits and sales of livestock supplies, and exhibitions of Western paintings are other features.

More than half a million people attend, among them ranch-

ers wearing belt buckles with diamonds and boots with the value of diamonds.

CONTACT:
Denver Convention and Visitors
  Bureau
1555 California St., Ste. 300
Denver, CO 80202
303-892-1112; fax: 303-892-1636

SOURCES:
Chases-1996, p. 59
GdUSFest-1984, p. 26

♦ 2026 ♦ **West Virginia Day**
June 20

A state holiday in West Virginia to celebrate its joining the Union in 1863 as the 35th state. The creation of the state was a result of the Civil War. The settlers of western Virginia defied the state's vote to secede from the Union, and President Lincoln justified the "secession" of West Virginia from Virginia as a war act. He proclaimed its statehood in April of 1863 and on June 20 West Virginia formally entered the Union as an anti-slave state. The western Virginians' movement for independence from Virginia had actually started long before the Civil War; as early as 1776, western Virginians had the idea of establishing a separate colony called Vandalia, named for Queen Charlotte, wife of British King George III, who believed herself to be a descendant of the Vandals of early Europe (*see also* Vandalia Festival).

The day is marked with ceremonies at the state capitol in Charleston and at the West Virginia Independence Hall in Wheeling. It was there that the conventions were held to declare West Virginia's independence from Virginia.

CONTACT:
Charleston Convention and Visitors Bureau
200 Civic Center Dr.
Charleston, WV 25301
800-733-5469 or 304-344-5075

SOURCES:
AmerBkDays-1978, p. 570
AnnivHol-1983, p. 82
Chases-1996, p. 264
DictDays-1988, p. 130

♦ 2027 ♦ **West Virginia Italian Heritage Festival**
September, Labor Day weekend

A three-day street festival in Clarksburg, W. Va., celebrating Italian culture. The festival began in 1979 and attracts from 175,000 to 200,000 visitors for tastes of food, music, dance, crafts, and sports. A queen, known as Regina Maria, reigns over the festivities. Distinctively Italian events are a bocci tournament, a homemade wine contest, a pasta cookoff (prizes for the best red sauce and best white sauce) for both professional and amateur cooks, and Italian religious observances. There are also strolling musicians, organ grinders, and puppeteers.

About 40 percent of Clarksburg's population is of Italian descent. Italians came here around the turn of the century for plentiful coal-mining jobs and it is said the mountains are reminiscent of those in northern Italy.

CONTACT:
West Virginia Tourism and Parks
  Division
2101 Washington St. E.
Charleston, WV 25305
800-225-5982 or 304-558-2200
fax: 304-558-0108

SOURCES:
Chases-1996, p. 354

♦ 2028 ♦ West Virginia Strawberry Festival
Usually late May or early June

A long-standing, good-tasting tradition in Buckhannon, W. Va., the center of a strawberry-growing region. The festival began in 1936, was suspended during World War II, and celebrated its 50th anniversary in 1991 with a block-long strawberry shortcake. Visitors, who numbered about 100,000, got free samples.

The festival focuses on what can be done culinarily to the strawberry: there are pancake breakfasts with strawberry jam, strawberry syrup, and fresh strawberries. There's a strawberry recipe contest, with recipes for such delights as strawberry cakes, pies, and cookies, kiwi-and-strawberry pizza, chicken glazed with strawberries, and strawberry stirring sticks (take drinking straws and fill with strawberries). The festival begins with a blessing of the berries, and moves on to the coronation of a king and queen, a Strawberry Party Gras (a street festival of music and dancing), strawberry auctions, the sweetest strawberry tasting contest, an antique-car show, and contests and parades.

CONTACT:
West Virginia Tourism and Parks
 Division
2101 Washington St. E.
Charleston, WV 25305
800-225-5982 or 304-558-2200
fax: 304-558-0108

SOURCES:
Chases-1996, p. 223

♦ 2029 ♦ Wexford Festival Opera
Late October

The Wexford Festival Opera is best known for its staging of obscure or seldom-heard operas from the 17th to the 20th centuries. Held in a small seaport community in the southeastern corner of Ireland since 1951, the festival has based its success on its choice of rare operas and relatively unknown singers, many of whom have later become quite famous. Three operas are staged during the two-week festival in Wexford's Georgian-style Theatre Royal, built in 1832. Some of the unusual operas presented there include Bedrich Smetana's *The Two Widows*, Joseph Haydn's *Il Monde della Luna*, and Francesco Cavalli's *Eritrea*, which had not been performed since 1652.

The festival also features celebrity recitals, choral concerts, band concerts, and traditional song and dance performances. There are also a number of "fringe" activities, including fishing competitions, hurling (an Irish game resembling field hockey), baby contests, and sculpture exhibitions.

CONTACT:
Irish Tourist Board
345 Park Ave., 17th Floor
New York, NY 10154
800-223-6470 or 212-418-0800
fax: 212-371-9052

SOURCES:
GdWrldFest-1985, p. 115
MusFestEurBrit-1980, p. 111

♦ 2030 ♦ Whale Festival
March

In Mendocino, Fort Bragg, and Gualala, on the northern coast of California, festivals to watch migrating whales are held on varying weekends.

At Mendocino, local vintners host a wine tasting, and there are also marine art exhibits, music, and lighthouse tours.

Fort Bragg offers tasting of beers from statewide microbreweries. Local restaurants compete in a chowder contest, and there is live music. Fort Bragg is also the home of what it calls the WORLD'S LARGEST SALMON BARBECUE.

Gualala has wine tastings, food buffets, an art show, photo contest, children's activities, and music.

CONTACT:
California Division of Tourism
801 K Street, Ste. 1600
Sacramento, CA 95814
800-862-2543 or 916-322-2881
fax: 916-322-3402

♦ 2031 ♦ Wheat Harvest
Late summer

In Transylvania, a region of Romania that was at one time part of Hungary, the gathering of the wheat harvest in late summer reflects traditional customs that have been largely supplanted by modern agricultural methods elsewhere. Here the owner of a farm must still rely on his friends and neighbors to gather his crops. When the last sheaf is harvested, a wreath made of wheat and wild flowers is taken to the farmer's house by young girls in traditional dress. The other farm laborers lie in wait for the procession, and ambush them by drenching everyone in water. When the landowner first appears in the harvest field, the harvesters tie him up and demand a ransom for his release.

When the procession arrives at the landowner's house, poems in his honor are recited. The wreath is hung in a special place where it will remain until the next harvest. There is a feast for everyone, followed by dancing to the music of a gypsy band. A special delicacy associated with the harvest feast is gingerbread cookies. In fact, elaborately shaped and decorated gingerbread cookies are considered a part of the region's folk art tradition.

SOURCES:
FolkWrldHol-1992, p. 452

♦ 2032 ♦ Wheat Harvest Festival in Provins, France
Last weekend of August

Like most harvest festivals, which date back to ancient Roman times, the Wheat Harvest Festival in Provins, a small village in central France honors Ceres, the ancient goddess of wheat and mother of the earth (*see* CEREALIA). On the last Saturday and Sunday of August, villagers celebrate a plentiful harvest by decorating their homes and shops with wheat and wildflowers. There are also exhibits of antique farming tools and parades featuring harvest floats pulled by tractors. The villagers reenact ancient rituals involving wheat and perform demonstrations of how the grain is separated, ground, and baked to make bread.

CONTACT:
French Government Tourist Office
9454 Wilshire Blvd., Ste. 715
Beverly Hills, CA 90212
310-271-6665; fax: 310-276-2835

♦ 2033 ♦ Whe'wahchee (Dance of Thanksgiving)
First full moon of August

The annual dance and celebration of the Omaha Indian tribe

of Nebraska, held on the Omaha Reservation in northeastern Nebraska. The 188th dance was held in 1991, making this the oldest powwow in the United States. Lewis and Clark encountered the Omahas in 1803 and mentioned the **Omaha Dance of Thanksgiving** in their journal. The time of the festival is set for the first full moon in August, because a full moon traditionally guarantees no rain.

CONTACT:
Omaha Tribal Council
P.O. Box 368
Macy, NE 68039
402-837-5391

♦ 2034 ♦ Whistlers Convention, National
Second or third weekend in April

A convocation of whistlers in Louisburg, N.C., highlighted by whistlers' contests for children, teenagers, and adults. Held since 1974, it grew out of a folk festival.

The convention features a school for whistlers, a concert in which the performer is usually someone who can both sing and whistle, and a processional march—a very short affair led by a man dressed as Benjamin Franklin (because the county is named for him). The town serves an annual salt herring breakfast on the day of the contest; the menu is salt herring, hush puppies, and sweet potatoes, all cooked in boiling pork fat. On the Sunday after the contest, whistlers whistle at church services and on Monday give demonstrations in schools.

The grand champion in 1992 was Sean Lomax of Murrieta, Calif., who whistled the First Movement of Beethoven's Fifth Symphony and a selection from Bizet's *Carmen*. This is serious whistling.

This convention isn't a big event, but it is the only one in the United States, and in 1992 it attracted people from 10 states and three Canadian provinces. In addition, Masaaki Moku, a whistler from Osaka, Japan, was there; he whistled the Japanese national anthem for the contest audience.

CONTACT:
North Carolina Travel and Tourism Division
430 N. Salisbury St.
Raleigh, NC 27603
800-847-4862 or 919-733-4171
fax: 919-733-8582

SOURCES:
Chases-1996, p. 174

♦ 2035 ♦ White Nights
June 21–29

The time of year in St. Petersburg (formerly Leningrad), Russia, when the nights are so short that the sky appears white, or light grey, and twilight lasts only 30 or 40 minutes. The city, with its many buildings painted in pastel shades of lavender, green, pink and yellow, has a particularly beautiful charm during the white nights. The time is celebrated with a fine-arts festival that focuses on ballet and folk dancing but also includes opera and musical theater. The Kirov Opera and Ballet Theatre presents its best productions of classical and Soviet ballets, and traditionally there are also performances by students of St. Petersburg's famous Vaganova School of Choreography. Concerts are given by the Symphony Orchestra of the Leningrad Philharmonic. About 250,000 attend each year.

CONTACT:
Russian Travel Information Office
Rockefeller Center
610 Fifth Ave., Ste. 603
New York, NY 10020
212-757-3884; fax: 212-459-0031

SOURCES:
GdWrldFest-1985, p. 182
IntlThFolk-1979, p. 373

♦ 2036 ♦ White Sunday
Second Sunday in October

This is a special day celebrated in the Christian churches of both American and Western Samoa to honor children. Each child dresses in white and wears a crown of white frangipani blossoms. The children line up and walk to church, carrying banners and singing hymns, while their parents wait for them inside. Instead of the usual sermon, the children present short dramatizations of Bible stories such as "the good Samaritan," "Noah's ark," and "the prodigal son." After the performance is over, the children return to their homes, where their parents serve them a feast that includes roast pig, bananas, taro, coconuts, and cakes. They are allowed to eat all they want, and in a reversal of the usual custom, **Lotu-A-Tamaiti** is the one day of the year when the adults don't sit down to eat first.

See also SUNDAY SCHOOL DAY

SOURCES:
AnnivHol-1983, p. 130
BkHolWrld-1986, Oct 14
Chases-1996, pp. 416, 417
FolkWrldHol-1992, p. 506

♦ 2037 ♦ Whitewater Wednesday
Third Wednesday in June

A day of whitewater rafting on the New River Gorge National River in West Virginia, as well as food and musical entertainment in Oak Hill. The New River is said to rival the Colorado when it comes to whitewater thrills. On Whitewater Wednesday, thousands of people raft down the river through the breathtaking New River Gorge and under the engineering marvel, the New River Gorge Bridge.

See also BRIDGE DAY

CONTACT:
West Virginia Tourism and Parks
  Division
2101 Washington St. E.
Charleston, WV 25305
800-225-5982 or 304-558-2200
fax: 304-558-0108

♦ 2038 ♦ Whit-Monday (Whitmonday)
*Between May 11 and June 14; Monday after
Pentecost*

The day after Whitsunday (PENTECOST) is known as Whit-Monday, and in Great Britain it is also known as the **Late May Bank Holiday** (*see* BANK HOLIDAY). The week that includes these two holidays, beginning on Whitsunday and ending the following Saturday, is called Whitsuntide.

Until fairly recently, Whit-Monday was one of the major holidays of the year in Pennsylvania Dutch country. In the period from 1835 to just after the Civil War, Whit-Monday was referred to as the "**Dutch Fourth of July**" in Lancaster, Pennsylvania, where rural people came to eat, drink, and be entertained. In Lenhartsville, another Pennsylvania Dutch town, Whit-Monday was known as **Battalion Day**, and it was characterized by music, dancing, and military musters. So much carousing went on that one Pennsylvania newspaper suggested that the name "Whitsuntide" be changed to "Whiskeytide."

SOURCES:
AmerBkDays-1978, p. 463
BkDays-1864, vol. I, p. 643
BkFest-1937, p. 98
BkFestHolWrld-1970, p. 65
DictDays-1988, p. 131
FestWestEur-1958, pp. 12, 26
FolkWrldHol-1992, p. 283

Whitsunday

See **Pentecost**

♦ 2039 ♦ Whole Enchilada Fiesta
First full weekend in October

Lots of red chili, lots of corn meal, lots of cheese, and lots of people. This festival in Las Cruces, New Mexico, draws about 100,000 people who scramble to get a taste of the world's biggest enchilada. It's 10 feet long and is made of 185 pounds of corn dough, 60 gallons of red chili sauce, and 175 pounds of cheese. The enchilada is prepared as the climactic Sunday afternoon event: while thousands watch and cheer, giant tortillas are lifted from 75 gallons of bubbling vegetable oil and smothered with the chili sauce and cheese and served. Before this grand moment, there will have been a parade, street dances, arts and crafts exhibits, and a horseshoe-pitching contest. Las Cruces is the largest business center in southern New Mexico, but its economic foundation is agriculture, and chilis are a big crop.

See also HATCH CHILE FESTIVAL

CONTACT:
New Mexico Tourism and Travel
  Division
491 Old Santa Fe Trail
Santa Fe, NM 87503
800-545-2040 or 505-827-7400
fax: 505-827-7402

♦ 2040 ♦ Wianki Festival of Wreaths
June 23

On St. John's Eve in Poland, young girls traditionally perform a ritual that can be traced back to pagan times. They weave garlands out of wild flowers, put a lit candle in the center, and set them afloat in the nearest stream. If the wreath drifts to shore, it means that the girl will never marry, but if it floats downstream, she will find a husband. If the wreath should sink, it means that the girl will die before the year is out. Since the boy who finds a wreath, according to the superstition, is destined to marry the girl who made it, boys hide in boats along the river banks and try to catch their girlfriends' wreaths as they float by.

A variation on this custom, known as the Wianki Festival of Wreaths (*wianki* means 'wreath' in Polish), is observed by Polish-Americans in Washington, D.C., on this same day every year. The wreaths are made out of fresh greens, the candles are lit at twilight, and they're set afloat in the reflecting pool in front of the Lincoln Memorial. Because there is no current, the wreaths don't drift much at all. But

young men gather around the pool anyway, in the hope that the wind will blow their girlfriends' wreaths toward them.

See also MIDSUMMER DAY and SEMIK

CONTACT:
Washington D.C. Convention and
  Visitors Association
1212 New York Ave., N.W., Ste.
  600
Washington, D.C. 20005
800-635-6338 or 202-789-7000
fax: 202-789-7037

SOURCES:
BkFest-1937, p. 263

♦ 2041 ♦ Wigilia
December 24

Christians in Poland, like Christians around the world, regard the entire period from CHRISTMAS EVE (December 24) to EPIPHANY (January 6) as part of the CHRISTMAS season. Although their customs and the timing of their specific Christmas celebrations may differ from village to village, it all occurs during these two weeks. The Wigilia—from the Latin *vigilare*, meaning 'to watch' or 'keep vigil', takes place on Christmas Eve and commemorates the vigil that the shepherds kept on the night of Christ's birth. But it's very possible that the celebration goes back to pre-Christian times. Showing forgiveness and sharing food were part of the Poles' ancient WINTER SOLSTICE observance, a tradition that can still be seen in what is known as the *Gody*—the days of harmony and good will that start with the Wigilia and last until Epiphany, or Three Kings Day.

Because some people still cling to the ancient belief that wandering spirits roam the land during the darkest days of the year, it is not uncommon for Poles to make an extra effort to be hospitable at Christmas time, leaving out a pan of warm water and a bowl of nuts and fruits for any unexpected visitors.

SOURCES:
BkFest-1937, p. 256
BkFestHolWrld-1970, p. 142
FolkWrldHol-1992, p. 627

♦ 2042 ♦ Williams Day, Roger
February 5 and Sunday nearest May 4

Roger Williams was the founder of the American Baptist Church. Born in Wales, he arrived in the Massachusetts colony on this day in 1631 and soon found himself in profound disagreement with the local Puritans. The latter admitted no distinction between crime and sin, while Williams contended that the civil authorities only had a right to punish those who had committed a civil offense. The argument led to a court trial in 1635, and soon afterward Williams was banished from the colony. He fled south to what is now called Providence and founded the Rhode Island colony. Under his leadership, the people of Rhode Island were the first to establish a Baptist congregation on American soil (in 1638) and the first to build a community based on this principle of religious liberty.

Baptists in the United States still celebrate the day of his arrival in America. On the Sunday nearest RHODE ISLAND INDEPENDENCE DAY, May 4, the First Baptist Meeting House in

Providence holds its annual Forefathers Service, honoring Williams as its founder and often using the 18th-century order of worship.

SOURCES:
AmerBkDays-1978, p. 143
AnnivHol-1983, p. 20
DaysCustFaith-1957, p. 47
RelHolCal-1993, p. 58

♦ 2043 ♦ **William Tell Pageant**
September, Labor Day weekend

New Glarus, Wisconsin, was settled by a group of Swiss immigrants in 1845 and is still referred to as "Little Switzerland." It is the location of several annual events designed to draw attention to the area's Swiss heritage. These include the Heidi Festival in June and the Volksfest in August. But one of the most popular is the William Tell Pageant that has been performed each year on Labor Day weekend since 1938.

The highlight of the William Tell story, of course, is the famous "apple scene" where the imprisoned patriot is given a chance at freedom if he can shoot an apple off his son's head. The play includes performances by the famous New Glarus yodelers and the costumed usherettes, who perform Swiss folk dances. The play is given in Swiss-German on Sunday afternoon and in English on Monday. The pageant weekend includes dancing on the green, Swiss singing, and other traditional Swiss forms of entertainment.

See also Tell Play at Altdorf

CONTACT:
Wisconsin Division of Tourism
123 W. Washington Ave., 6th Fl.
Madison, WI 53703
800-432-8747 or 608-266-7621
fax: 608-266-3403

♦ 2044 ♦ **Wimbledon**
Late June–early July; six weeks before first
Monday in August

The oldest and most prestigious tennis tournament in the world, the **Lawn Tennis Championships** at Wimbledon are held for 13 days each summer, beginning six weeks before the first Monday in August, on the manicured courts of the All England Lawn Tennis and Croquet Club. The first competition in 1877 was supposedly an attempt to raise money to purchase a new roller for the croquet lawns, and it featured only the men's singles event. Today the world's best tennis players compete for both singles and doubles titles that are the most coveted in tennis. The event is watched on television by tennis fans all over the world, many of whom get up at dawn or conduct all-night vigils around their television sets so as not to miss a single match. Members of the English royal family often watch the finals from the Royal Box.

The Centre Court at Wimbledon, where the championships are held, is off-limits to members and everyone except the grounds staff. On the Saturday before the competition begins, four women members of the club play two or three sets to "bruise" the grass and make sure the courts are in good shape.

CONTACT:
British Tourist Authority
551 Fifth Ave., Ste. 702
New York, NY 10176
800-462-2748 or 212-986-2200
fax: 212-986-1188

♦ 2045 ♦ **Wind Festival**
First day of second lunar month

In the rural districts of Korea's Kyongsang-namdo and Kyongsang-pukto provinces, a grandmother known as *Yungdeung Mama* comes down from heaven every year on the first day of the second lunar month and returns on the 20th day. If she brings her daughter with her, there is no trouble; but if she brings her daughter-in-law, who is an epileptic, it means that a stormy wind known as *Yungdeung Baram* will wreck ships and ruin the crops. To prevent such devastation, farmers, fishermen, and sailors offer special prayers and sacrifices to Yungdeung Mama and her daughter-in-law. Tempting foods and boiled rice are set out in the kitchen or garden, and little pieces of white paper containing the birthdates of family members are burned for good luck: the higher the ashes fly, the better the luck. Sometimes altars are made out of bamboo branches with pieces of cloth or paper tied to them. Sacrifices are laid under the altars, which remain standing until the 20th day of the month.

SOURCES:
FolkWrldHol-1992, p. 143

♦ 2046 ♦ **Windjammer Days**
Last Wednesday–Friday in June

The annual Windjammer Days Festival in Boothbay Harbor, Maine, celebrates the U.S. Coast Guard's 200 years of service to coastal Maine. The three-day festival is also a salute to the large sailing merchant ships that once carried trade along the New England coast. The locals claim that this festival, which has been going on since 1963, was the original gathering of "tall ships," although they are for the most part sailing schooners rather than the full-rigged clipper ships and barks that have gathered in New York, Boston, and other port cities for more recent celebrations.

The festival begins with a boat parade in which the owners compete for prizes in various classes. That afternoon the coastal schooners sail into Boothbay Harbor and are met by a flotilla of local vessels with flags flying. There is a competition for Miss Windjammer and Captain Windjammer, and band concerts, lobster suppers, and street dances add to the merrymaking. The ships leave Boothbay the last morning of the festival—again watched by thousands on the water and from the shore.

In the 19th century the Boothbay region played an active role in the shipping trade, carrying lumber to South America and the West Indies. There was a time when more than a hundred of these coastal vessels might have been seen in Boothbay Harbor, waiting out a spell of bad weather.

CONTACT:
Maine Office of Tourism
33 Stone St.
Augusta, ME 04333
800-533-9595 or 207-287-5711
fax: 207-287-5701

SOURCES:
Chases-1996, p. 271
GdUSFest-1984, p. 76

♦ 2047 ♦ **Wings 'n Water Festival**
Third weekend in September

This two-day event celebrates the coastal environment of southern New Jersey. It is sponsored by the Wetlands Institute, an organization dedicated to conserving coastal salt marshes and educating the public about marshland ecology. Since 1983 the Institute has held the Wings 'n Water Festival in September every year to raise funds for its various educational and research projects as well as to raise public awareness of the salt marsh by offering activities that relate to its unique environment. Salt marsh safaris and boat cruises, a decoy and decorative bird-carving show, exhibits of naturalist and maritime art, and a wildlife craft market are among the events. There is also a Black Lab retriever demonstration, musical entertainment featuring traditional American instruments, and various booths serving oysters, clams on the half shell, "shrimpwiches," chowders, Maryland hard-shelled crabs, and Maine lobster. Festival events are held along a 15-mile stretch of the South Jersey coast that includes Avalon, Stone Harbor, and Cape May Court House.

CONTACT:
Wetlands Institute
1075 Stone Harbor Blvd.
Stone Harbor, NJ 08247
609-368-1211; fax: 609-368-3871

SOURCES:
Chases-1996, p. 386

♦ 2048 ♦ **Winnipeg Folk Festival**
Second weekend in July

The largest event of its kind in North America, the Winnipeg Folk Festival is essentially a music festival featuring bluegrass, gospel, jazz, Cajun, swing, Celtic, and other performers from Canada and around the world. Held at Birds Hill Park, about 19 miles northeast of Winnipeg, the festival has seen performances by such world-renowned artists as Odetta, Bonnie Raitt, Bruce Cockburn, Pete Seeger, Eric Bogle, Ladysmith Black Mambazo, and Billy Bragg. There are concerts, jam sessions, a juried handcrafts village, children's performances, and folk dancing. The festival was started in 1974 by Mitch Podolak, a veteran in the folk music field, and although it only lasts for three days, it also operates on a year-round basis as a folklore and music center.

CONTACT:
Travel Manitoba
155 Carlton St., 7th Floor
Winnipeg, Manitoba
Canada R3C 3H8
800-665-0040 or 204-945-3777

SOURCES:
GdWrldFest-1985, p. 36
MusFestAmer-1990, p. 234

♦ 2049 ♦ **Winston 500**
First Sunday in May

This 500-mile stock-car race is Alabama's biggest sporting event. It's held at the Talladega Superspeedway, known as the "World's Fastest Speedway." The Winston 500 is one of the Big Four NASCAR (National Association for Stock Car Auto Racing) Winston Cup events, the others being the DAYTONA 500, the COCA-COLA 600, and the SOUTHERN 500. The Winston is considered the fastest of the four. The winner in Talladega in 1991 was 51-year-old Harry Gant, who had never won two races in a row in his 11 years on the circuit and was the surprise of the season. He won four straight in 1991,

beginning with the Southern 500 at Darlington International Raceway in South Carolina. "Age don't have nothing to do with it," Gant said about the streak. His day's work at Talladega driving an average speed of 165.62 miles an hour entitled him to $81,950.

Talladega, which opened in 1969, has 83,200 permanent grandstand seats and each year attracts more than 350,000 spectators.

CONTACT:
National Association for Stock Car
   Auto Racing
P.O. Box 2875
Daytona Beach, FL 32115
904-253-0611; fax: 904-258-7646

Alabama Bureau of Tourism and
   Travel
P.O. Box 4927
Montgomery, AL 36103
800-252-2263 or 334-242-4169
fax: 334-242-4554

♦ 2050 ♦ **Winter Festival of Lights**
Early November through late January

A premier light show in Wheeling, W. Va., started in 1985 and now considered a rival of the light show at Niagara Falls (*see* LIGHTS, FESTIVAL OF). More than a million people visit each year to see half a million lights on the downtown Victorian buildings, dozens of giant displays, 200 lighted trees, and about 10 miles of drive-by light displays with architectural and landscape lighting designed by world-famous lighting designers. Some 300 acres of the city's Oglebay Park (a former private estate that was left to the city) are covered with animated light displays that depict symbols of HANUKKAH and CHRISTMAS and general winter scenes. There are also nighttime parades and storefront animations.

CONTACT:
Wheeling Convention and Visitors
   Bureau
1310 Market St.
Wheeling, WV 26003
800-828-3097 or 304-233-7709

SOURCES:
Chases-1996, p. 436

♦ 2051 ♦ **Winterlude**
Ten days in February

A midwinter civic festival held in Ottawa, Canada, Winterlude is primarily a celebration of winter sports. The Rideau Canal, which has been referred to as "the world's longest skating rink," is eight kilometers long and provides an excellent outdoor skating facility. There is also snowshoeing, skiing, curling (a game in which thick heavy stone and iron disks are slid across the ice toward a target), speedskating, dogsled racing, barrel jumping, and tobogganing. For those who prefer not to participate in the many sporting events, there is an elaborate snow sculpture exhibit known as Ice Dream. Nearly half a million people attend the 10-day festival each year.

CONTACT:
Ontario Travel
Queen's Park
Toronto, Ontario
Canada M7A 2R9
800-ONTARIO or 416-314-0944

SOURCES:
Chases-1996, p. 83
FolkWrldHol-1992, p. 88

♦ 2052 ♦ **Winter Solstice**
*June 21–22 (Southern Hemisphere); December
21–22 (Northern Hemisphere)*

This is the shortest day of the year, respectively in each
hemisphere, when the sun has reached its furthest point from
the equator. It also marks the first day of winter.

The winter solstice has played an important role in art,
literature, mythology, and religion. There were many pre-
Christian seasonal traditions marking the winter solstice,
and huge bonfires were an integral part of these ancient solar
rites. Although winter was regarded as the season of dor-
mancy, darkness, and cold, the gradual lengthening of the
days after the winter solstice brought on a more festive
mood. To many peoples this return of the light was cause for
celebration that the cycle of nature was continuing.

See also Midsummer Day and Summer Solstice

> SOURCES:
> *AmerBkDays-1978*, p. 1127
> *BkFest-1937*, p. 82
> *DictDays-1988*, pp. 110, 131
> *FestSaintDays-1915*, p. 4
> *FolkWrldHol-1992*, p. 599
> *RelHolCal-1993*, p. 105
> *SaintFestCh-1904*, p. 32

♦ 2053 ♦ **Wizard of Oz Festival**
Weekend in September

Since 1982 the classic 1939 film has come to life again every
September in the town of Chesterton, Ind., as townspeople
dress up and portray Dorothy, the Scarecrow, the Tin Man,
the Cowardly Lion, Glinda the Good Witch, and other characters. A huge sculpture of the Tin Man overlooks the
proceedings from the top of a downtown building. The
festival also serves as a reunion site for actors who played the
Munchkins in the film—many come every year to meet fans
and participate in the annual hour-long Oz Fantasy Parade,
Munchkin autograph parties, a Munchkin celebrity dinner
and dance, and a Munchkin breakfast.

As if all this were not enough, the festival also has a town
crier competition, Auntie Em's pie contest, a juried arts and
crafts display, Oz memorabilia collectors' gatherings, and a
teddy bear parade and tea party.

CONTACT:
Duneland Chamber of Commerce
303 Broadway
Chesterton, IN 46394
219-926-5513

♦ 2054 ♦ **Wolfe Festival, Thomas**
October 3

A celebration of writer Thomas Wolfe's birthday in 1900 in
Asheville, N.C. The celebrations usually extend several days
beyond the actual birthday and include dramatizations of
Wolfe's works, the performance of musical compositions
based on his writings, workshops conducted by Wolfe scholars, and a walking tour of "Wolfe's Asheville." This includes
a visit to Riverside Cemetery, where Wolfe and members of
his family, as well as some of the people he fictionalized in his
novels, are buried.

The center of the celebration is the Thomas Wolfe Memorial
State Historic Site, the boarding house run by his mother,
where Thomas Wolfe grew up. It still has the sign of his
mother's time hanging over the porch, "Old Kentucky Home."
In his famous first novel, *Look Homeward, Angel*, published in
1929, Wolfe fictionalized Asheville as Altamont and called
the boarding house "Dixieland."

Other works by Wolfe include *Of Time and the River*, published in 1935, and *The Web and the Rock* and *You Can't Go
Home Again*, both published after his death in 1938.

CONTACT:
North Carolina Travel and Tourism Division
430 N. Salisbury St.
Raleigh, NC 27603
800-847-4862 or 919-733-4171
fax: 919-733-8582

♦ 2055 ♦ **Wolf Trap Summer Festival Season**
May–September

Located just 30 minutes from downtown Washington, D.C.,
in Vienna, Virginia, Wolf Trap Farm Park for the Performing
Arts hosts musical performances on a year-round basis. But
Wolf Trap is best known for the Summer Festival Season.
Recent seasons have featured productions by the New York
City Opera, the National Symphony Orchestra, the Kirov
Ballet from Leningrad (now St. Petersburg), the Bolshoi
Ballet, and the Joffrey Ballet as well as performances by Ray
Charles, Johnny Cash, John Denver, Willie Nelson, Emmylou
Harris, and jazz trumpeter Wynton Marsalis.

Concerts are held in the 6,900-seat Filene Center II, about
half of which is exposed to the open sky. Many concertgoers
bring a picnic supper and dine on the grass. Smaller concerts
are held during the off-season in the pre-Revolutionary, 350-
seat German Barn.

CONTACT:
Wolf Trap Farm Park for the
Performing Arts
1551 Trap Rd.
Vienna, VA 22182
703-255-1800; fax: 703-255-1918

SOURCES:
MusFestAmer-1990, p. 149

♦ 2056 ♦ **Women's Day, International**
March 8

Not only is this day commemorating working women one of
the most widely observed holidays of recent origin, but it is
unusual in that it began in the United States and was adopted
by many other countries, including the former U.S.S.R. and
the People's Republic of China. This holiday has its roots in
the March 8, 1857, revolt of American women in New York
City, protesting conditions in the textile and garment industries, although it wasn't proclaimed as a holiday until 1910.

In Great Britain and the United States, International Wom-
en's Day is marked by special exhibitions, films, etc., in praise
of the working woman. In the former U.S.S.R., women
received honors for distinguished service in industry, aviation, agriculture, military service, and other fields of endeavor.

> SOURCES:
> *AnnivHol-1983*, p. 34

BkFest-1937, p. 284
BkFestHolWrld-1970, p. 73
Chases-1996, p. 126
FolkWrldHol-1992, p. 160

♦ 2057 ♦ Wood Art Festival, Grant
Second Sunday in June

American artist Grant Wood (1892–1942) is best known for his painting, *American Gothic,* of a dour-looking farmer holding a pitchfork as he stands with his daughter in front of their 19th-century Gothic revival farmhouse. The annual Grant Wood Art Festival in Stone City-Anamosa, Iowa, celebrates the area's heritage as "Grant Wood Country" with juried art exhibits, children's and adults' "Art Happenings," dramatic and musical presentations, and guided bus tours of Stone City.

Born in Anamosa, Wood traveled to Europe several times, where he was exposed to Flemish and German primitive art. But he eventually returned to Iowa to paint the scenes he knew best in the clean-cut, realistic style for which he became famous. He established an art colony in the Stone City valley in 1932–33, and replicas of the colorful ice wagons used as housing by the students and instructors serve as a backdrop for the exhibits of contemporary artists during the festival.

The original *American Gothic*—one of the most widely parodied paintings in the world—is on display at the Chicago Art Institute.

CONTACT:
Iowa Tourism Office
200 E. Grand Ave.
Des Moines, IA 50309
800-345-4692 or 515-242-4705
fax: 515-242-4749

♦ 2058 ♦ Wood Promenade Concerts, Henry
Mid-July to mid-September

Popularly known as **The Proms,** the nine-week concert series that has been held in London since 1895 presents solo recitals, operas, symphonies, chamber music, and popular music to enormous audiences. Tens of thousands of listeners tune in to the concerts on their radios or televisions, and 7,000–8,000 crowd into the Royal Albert Hall. The series is named after Henry Wood, a pianist and singing teacher who served as conductor at the Proms for 46 years and who is credited with establishing its first permanent orchestra, introducing young and aspiring musicians to the public, and attracting the primarily youthful crowd that attends the Proms every year. The idea for the series came from France, where "promenade concerts"—in other words, concerts where strolling around and socializing took precedence over listening to the music—were popular.

A highlight of the Proms is "Last Night," which occurs on a Saturday in mid-September. *Fantasia of Sea Songs,* composed by Henry Wood, is a traditional part of the Last Night program, as is a setting of Blake's "Jerusalem" and Elgar's "Pomp and Circumstance." Many festival patrons wear party hats, throw streamers, and chant rhymes similar to those heard at football games as the festival draws to a close.

CONTACT:
British Tourist Authority
551 Fifth Ave., Ste. 702
New York, NY 10176
800-462-2748 or 212-986-2200
fax: 212-986-1188

SOURCES:
DictDays-1988, p. 66
MusFestEurBrit-1980, p. 58

♦ 2059 ♦ World Championship Crab Races
Sunday before third Monday of February

A sporting event in Crescent City, Calif., featuring races of the nine- to 11-inch Dungeness crabs that are caught off this northern California coastal city. The crabs are urged down a four-foot raceway, prizes are awarded, and the winning crab gets a trip back to the harbor for a ceremonious liberation. This is also an eating event: throughout the day about 3,000 pounds of fresh cracked crab are served.

The event began in 1976, but its origins are older. Traditionally, local fisherman returned to port after a day of crabbing and celebrated the catch by racing their liveliest crabs in a chalked circle.

CONTACT:
California Division of Tourism
801 K Street, Ste. 1600
Sacramento, CA 95814
800-862-2543 or 916-322-2881
fax: 916-322-3402

♦ 2060 ♦ World Cup
June–July, every four years

The world series of soccer. Since 1930 (except during World War II), the international championship games have been played every four years, sandwiched between the Olympic Games. The series was started under the auspices of the Fédération Internationale de Football Association (FIFA) and is now the best attended sporting event in the world. It's claimed that, including television viewers, more than 500 million people watch it.

Soccer is also called football or association football; the word soccer comes from assoc., an abbreviation for "*association.*" It originated in England in the public schools (which are actually more like American private schools), and spread to universities and then into local clubs, attracting more and more working-class players. British sailors took the game to Brazil in the 1870s, and businessmen carried it to Prague and Vienna in the 1880s and 1890s. Belgium and France began an annual series of games in 1903. In 1904, international competition was such that FIFA was formed, and by 1982, it claimed 146 member nations. In 1946, the trophy was named the Jules Rimet Cup for the president of FIFA from 1921 to 1954.

The World Cup is played on a rotating basis in six different regions—Africa, North and Central America and the Caribbean, South America, Europe, Asia, and Oceana.

In 1991, the first women's World Cup Tournament was held and was won by the U.S. It was the first cup ever taken by the United States.

The first World Cup was played in Montevideo, Uruguay, and Uruguay won. Three countries have been three-time winners: Italy, Brazil, and West Germany. Brazil's wins came in 1958, 1962, and 1970 under the leadership of Edson Arantes do Nascimento, better known as Pelé and sometimes as the *Pérola Negra*, or 'Black Pearl.' A Brazilian national hero and at the time one of the best-known athletes in the world, the 5'8" Pelé combined kicking strength and accuracy with the knack of anticipating other players' moves. He announced his retirement in 1974 but in 1975 signed a three-year $7 million contract with the New York Cosmos; after leading them to the North American Soccer League championship in 1977, he retired for good.

CONTACT:
International Federation of Asso-
  ciation Football
Hitzigweg 11
Postfach 85
CH-8030 Zurich, Switzerland
011-41-1-555400

SOURCES:
BkHolWrld-1986, Jul 30
Chases-1996, p. 260

♦ 2061 ♦ World Environment Day
June 5

The United Nations General Assembly designated June 5 World Environment Day in 1972. The date was chosen because it marked the opening day of the United Nations Conference on the Human Environment in Stockholm, which led to the establishment of the United Nations Environment Programme, based in Nairobi. The conference was convened again 20 years later, in the hope that nations would recapture the enthusiasm of the 1972 conference and take up the challenge of preserving and enhancing the environment.

The General Assembly urges countries and organizations to mark this day with activities that educate people about threats to the environment and encourage them to strike a balance between development and concern for the earth's future.

CONTACT:
United Nations
Dept. of Public Information
New York, NY 10017
212-963-1234; fax: 212-963-4879
WWW: http://www.undp.org

SOURCES:
Chases-1996, p. 243

♦ 2062 ♦ World Eskimo-Indian Olympics
Mid-July

A gathering in Fairbanks, Alaska, of native people from throughout the state and Canada to participate in games of strength and endurance. Events include the popular blanket toss, which originated in whaling communities as a method of tossing a hunter high enough to sight far-off whales. The tossees are sometimes bounced as high as 28 feet in the air. Also on the program are a sewing competition, a seal-skinning contest, native dancing, and such events as the knuckle-hop contest, in which contestants get on all fours and hop on their knuckles. The winner is the one who goes the farthest.

CONTACT:
Fairbanks Convention and Visitors
  Bureau
550 First Ave.
Fairbanks, AK 99701
800-327-5774 or 907-456-5774
fax: 907-452-2867

SOURCES:
GdUSFest-1984, p. 9

♦ 2063 ♦ World Food Day
October 16

Proclaimed in 1979 by the conference of the Food and Agri-

culture Organization (FAO) of the United Nations, World Food Day is designed to heighten public awareness of the world food problem and to promote cooperation in the struggle against hunger, malnutrition, and poverty. October 16 is the anniversary of the founding of the FAO in Quebec, Canada, in 1945.

CONTACT:
United Nations
Dept. of Public Information
New York, NY 10017
212-963-1234; fax: 212-963-4879
WWW: http://www.undp.org

SOURCES:
Chases-1996, p. 419

♦ 2064 ♦ World Population Day
July 11

World Population Day was established by the Governing Council of the United Nations Development Programme to focus public attention on the issue of population growth. Schools, businesses, and organizations around the world are urged to observe July 11 with speeches, programs, and activities that address population issues and encourage people to think of solutions to the health, social, and economic problems associated with population growth. World Population Day is an outgrowth of the Day of Five Billion, which was observed on July 11, 1987, to mark the approximate date when the world's population reached five billion.

Currently growing at an annual rate of 1.7 percent, the world's population is expected to reach 6.2 billion at the end of this century, and could surpass eight billion by the year 2019, according to U.N. estimates.

CONTACT:
United Nations
Dept. of Public Information
New York, NY 10017
212-963-1234; fax: 212-963-4879
WWW: http://www.undp.org

SOURCES:
Chases-1996, p. 292

♦ 2065 ♦ World Religion Day
Third Sunday in January

A day initiated in 1950 by the National Spiritual Assembly of the Baha'i faith in the United States. The purpose was to call attention to the harmony of the world's religions and empha-size that the aims of religion are to create unity among people, to ease suffering, and to bring about peace. The day is observed with gatherings in homes, public meetings and panel discussions, and proclamations by government officials.

CONTACT:
Baha'is of the U.S.
Office of Public Information
866 United Nations Plaza, Ste. 120
New York, NY 10017-1822
212-803-2500; fax: 212-803-2573

SOURCES:
AnnivHol-1983, p. 10
Chases-1996, p. 72
RelHolCal-1993, p. 122

♦ 2066 ♦ World's Biggest Fish Fry
Last full week in April

A four-day spring festival in Paris, Tenn., that makes use of the catfish in nearby Kentucky Lake. The fish fry began in 1954, and by the next year more than 1,600 pounds of catfish

471

were served. Now, some 13,000 pounds of catfish are cooked from Wednesday through Saturday, and about 100,000 people show up in this town of 10,000 to eat, fish, and look around. Events include a car show, arts and crafts exhibits, a two-hour parade and a smaller Small Fry Parade, and the coronation of a Queen of the Tennessee Valley and a Junior King and Queen. In the Fishing Rodeo, prizes are awarded for the biggest bass and biggest crappie, which must be caught in Kentucky Lake using legal sport equipment. Besides fried fish to eat, there are hush puppies, small deep-fat fried corn meal balls; some say these were originally made and tossed to puppies to keep them from begging while meals were being prepared.

CONTACT:
Tennessee Dept. of Tourism
  Development
P.O. Box 23170
Nashville, TN 37202
615-741-2158; fax: 615-741-7225

SOURCES:
GdUSFest-1984, p. 178

♦ 2067 ♦ World's Championship Duck Calling Contest and Wings Over the Prairie Festival
November, Tuesday through Saturday of Thanksgiving week

An annual sporting event in Stuttgart, Ark., the "Rice and Duck Capital of the World." The first duck-calling contest was held in 1937 and attracted 17 contestants. The winner that year was Thomas E. Walsh of Mississippi who was awarded a hunting coat valued at $6.60. Today, there are hundreds of participants in the various calling events (including the women's, intermediate, and junior world's championships). The main World's Championship contest is limited to between 50 and 80 callers who have qualified in sanctioned state and regional calling events. These elite duck callers vie for a top cash prize of $5,000. This celebration of the waterfowl hunting season is held when the rice fields around Stuttgart have been harvested and the ducks have ample opportunity for feeding. The duck hunting here is billed as the finest in the world.

Ducks are called by blowing a "duck call," a device about the size of a cigar. Originally the callers had to demonstrate four calls—the open-water call, the woods call, the mating call, and the scare call. Now contestants are judged on the hail, or long-distance, call; the mating, or lonesome-duck, call; the feed, or chatter, call; and the comeback call. Judges sit behind a screen so they can't see the contestants. And since 1955, a "Champion of Champions" contest for former World Champions has been staged every five years.

The related events that have sprung up around the contest have been formalized as the Wings Over the Prairie Festival. Included are fun shoots, an arts and crafts fair, a sportsmen's dinner and dance, a retriever demonstration, children's duck-call clinics, and a duck-gumbo cookoff. In 1957 the Grand Prairie Beauty Pageant debuted in which a Queen Mallard is crowned.

CONTACT:
Arkansas Dept. of Parks and
  Tourism
1 Capitol Mall
Little Rock, AR 72201
800-628-8725 or 501-682-7777
fax: 501-682-1364

SOURCES:
Chases-1996, p. 465

♦ 2068 ♦ World Series
October

Also known as the **Fall Classic**, this best-of-seven-games play-off is between the championship baseball teams of the American and National Leagues. Games are played in the home parks of the participating teams, but the Series is truly a national event. For many it marks the spiritual end of summer and is a uniquely American occasion—like the FOURTH OF JULY. At workplaces, Series betting pools are common; in the days before night telecasts, radios droned the play-by-play broadcasts.

The first World Series was played in 1903 between the Boston Red Sox and the Pittsburgh Pirates. There was a lapse in 1904, but the Series resumed in 1905 and has been played annually ever since. The seven-game format was adopted in 1922.

Highlights of the Series mirror the symbolism of life that some see in the game itself; they include moments of athletic perfection and of human error, of drama and of scandal.

The scandal came when eight team members of the Chicago White Sox (ever afterwards to be known as the Black Sox) were accused of conspiring with gamblers to lose the 1919 World Series. Star left fielder "Shoeless" Joe Jackson admitted his part in the scandal, and on leaving court one day, heard the plea of a tearful young fan, "Say it ain't so, Joe."

Brooklyn Dodgers catcher Mickey Owen brought groans from fans with an error that has resounded in Series history. He let a ball get away from him—in 1941, in the ninth inning, on the third strike, with the Dodgers ahead of the New York Yankees by one run. The Yankee team revived and went on to win. Fifteen years later, in 1956, Yankee pitcher Don Larsen gave fans a rare thrill when he pitched a perfect game (no hits, no walks, no runners allowed on base) against the Dodgers, beating them 2-0. It remains the only perfect game pitched in a Series. Both these World Series were called Subway Series, because New York City fans could commute by subway from the Dodgers' Ebbets Field in Brooklyn to Yankee Stadium in the Bronx.

Another dramatic moment came in the 1989 Series. On Oct. 17, at 5:04 P.M., while 60,000 fans were waiting for the introduction of the players at San Francisco's Candlestick Park, an earthquake struck and the ballpark swayed. Players and fans were safely evacuated (although 67 people in other parts of the city died in the quake), and 10 days later the Series resumed in the same park. The Oakland Athletics mowed down the San Francisco Giants in four straight games.

CONTACT:
Office of the Baseball
  Commissioner
350 Park Ave., 17th Floor
New York, NY 10022
212-339-7800; fax: 212-355-0007
WWW: http://
  www.majorleaguebaseball.com

SOURCES:
BkHolWrld-1986, Oct 17

♦ 2069 ♦ World's Largest Salmon Barbecue
Late June or early July

Some 5,000 pounds of salmon are barbecued for close to 5,000 visitors in the city of Fort Bragg on the northern coast of California. Besides salmon freshly caught in local waters and freshly barbecued, the menu offers corn on the cob, salad, hot bread and ice cream. The feasting is followed by fireworks and dancing. The event is sponsored by the Salmon Restoration Association of California, and proceeds from it help restore the once abundant salmon runs on the rivers of the area. Fort Bragg also hosts a WHALE FESTIVAL in March.

CONTACT:
California Division of Tourism
801 K Street, Ste. 1600
Sacramento, CA 95814
800-862-2543 or 916-322-2881
fax: 916-322-3402

♦ 2070 ♦ World Wristwrestling Championships
Second Saturday of October

The original world championship matches in wrist-wrestling, which is similar to but slightly different from armwrestling. The one-day competitions, held in Petaluma, Calif., since 1962, originated in Mike Gilardi's Saloon in 1957. A bank building has now replaced Gilardi's. The excitement generated by the first backroom bar contests led Bill Soberanes, a columnist for the *Petaluma Argus-Courier*, to transform the bar sport into an international championship.

Fifty men entered the first world championship in 1962. The final pairings that year pitted David-and-Goliath contestants Earl Hagerman, at 5'8", and Duane Benedix, 6'4". In four seconds, Hagerman won. There was only one division at that time; now there are five men's divisions and three women's. Contestants number from 250 to 300 with wrestlers coming from as far away as Australia, Germany, and Russia. The event has been viewed by a TV audience of 200 million. Sometimes there are cash prizes, sometimes not. In the past a purse of $7,500 has been split among the winning contestants. But there are always medals and trophies awarded.

CONTACT: SOURCES:
California Division of Tourism   *Chases-1996*, p. 416
801 K Street, Ste. 1600
Sacramento, CA 95814
800-862-2543 or 916-322-2881
fax: 916-322-3402

♦ 2071 ♦ Wright Brothers Day
December 17

It was on the morning of December 17, 1903, that Wilbur and Orville Wright became the first men to fly and control a powered heavier-than-air machine. Orville Wright took his turn at piloting on this particular day and his historic 12-second flight (120 feet) near Kitty Hawk, North Carolina, was witnessed by only a handful of observers. It wasn't until the brothers went on to set additional flight records that they received widespread acclaim for their achievements. Their original plane (patented in 1906) can be seen today at the National Air and Space Museum in Washington, D.C.

Although Wright Brothers Day has been observed in one way or another and under various names throughout the United States almost since the flight took place, the more notable observations include the annual Wright Brothers Dinner held in Washington, D.C., by the National Aeronautic Association, and the awarding of the Kitty Hawk Trophy at an annual dinner on this day in Los Angeles. Celebrations are also held in North Carolina at Kitty Hawk and in Dayton, Ohio, where the brothers were born and where they opened their first bicycle shop in 1892. Events on December 17

traditionally include a "flyover" by military aircraft and a special ceremony held at the Wright Brothers National Memorial, a 425-acre area that features a 60-foot granite pylon on top of Kill Devil Hill, where the Wright Brothers' camp was located. The flyover takes place at precisely 10:35 A.M., the time of the original flight in 1903.

See also UNITED STATES AIR AND TRADE SHOW

CONTACT: SOURCES:
North Carolina Travel and Tour- *AmerBkDays-1978*, p. 1111
  ism Division   *AnnivHol-1983*, p. 162
430 N. Salisbury St.   *Chases-1996*, p. 483
Raleigh, NC 27603
800-847-4862 or 919-733-4171
fax: 919-733-8582

♦ 2072 ♦ Wurstfest (Sausage Festival)
End of October through first week in November

A festival billed as "The Best of the Wurst," held in the town of New Braunfels, Tex., to celebrate the sausage-making season and recall the town's German heritage. New Braunfels was settled in 1845 by German immigrants led by Prince Carl of Solms-Braunfels, a cousin of Queen Victoria. The prince chose lands along the Comal and Guadalupe rivers, envisioning a castle on the riverbanks. But the rigors of the wilderness proved too much, and he abandoned his castle plans and went home, while those who had followed him were left behind. They were decimated by starvation and disease, but the survivors eventually prospered, finding abundant water and rich soil.

The eight-day festival features polka music, German singing and dancing, arts and crafts, sporting events, a biergarten, and German food—especially sausage.

CONTACT: SOURCES:
Texas Department of Commerce   *Chases-1996*, p. 438
Tourism Division
1700 N. Congress, Ste. 200
Austin, TX 78711
800-888-8839 or 512-462-9191
fax: 512-936-0089

♦ 2073 ♦ Wuwuchim
Eve of the new moon in November

The new year for the Hopi Indians, observed in northeastern Arizona. This is thought to be the time when *Katchina* spirits emerge from *Shipap*, the underworld, to stay a short time on earth. It is the most important of Hopi rituals because it establishes the rhythms for the year to come. For four days, prayers, songs, and dances for a prosperous and safe new year are led by the priests in the *kivas*, or ceremonial chambers. The men of the tribe dance, wearing embroidered kilts, and priests from the Bear Clan chant about the time of creation. It may also serve as an initiation rite for boys.

CONTACT: SOURCES:
Hopi Tribal Council   *DictFolkMyth-1984*, p. 1185
P.O. Box 123   *DictMyth-1962*, vol. II, p.
Kykotsmovi, AZ 86039   1694
602-734-2445   *IndianAmer-1989*, p. 265
                                 RelHolCal-1993, p. 122

Y

◆ 2074 ◆ Yale-Harvard Regatta
Usually during first weekend in June

This famous college crew race has been held since 1865 between arch-rivals Yale and Harvard on the Thames River (pronounced THAYMZ) in New London, Connecticut. The event, which claims to be the oldest crew competition in the country, is timed to coincide with the turning of the tide, either upriver or downriver. It begins with a two-mile freshman race, followed by a two-mile combination race featuring the best rowers from all classes. Then there is a three-mile junior varsity race. But the highlight is the four-mile varsity race.

Prior to World War II, crowds of up to 60,000 used to line the banks of the Thames to watch the race, but nowadays only a third as many come to watch—many of them by boat.

CONTACT:
Yale University
Sports Information Office
P.O. Box 208216
New Haven CT, 06520
203-432-1456

SOURCES:
GdUSFest-1984, p. 30

Harvard University
Sports Information Office
60 John F. Kennedy St.
Cambridge, MA 02138
617-495-2206; fax: 617-495-2130

◆ 2075 ◆ Yellow Daisy Festival
Second weekend in September

A tribute to a rare flower, the Yellow Daisy, or *Viguiera porteri*, that blooms on Stone Mountain near Atlanta, Ga. The flowers, two and one-half feet tall, grow in granite crevices, sprouting in April and not blooming until September, when they give the mountain a golden blanket. They wilt if they are picked and seem to thrive only in the crevices. They were first discovered in 1846 by Pennsylvania missionary Thomas Porter, who sent a specimen to noted botanist Asa Gray for identification. Gray decided it was the *Viguiera* genus, comprising about 60 other species that grow largely in Central America and Mexico. The only other place in the United States the "yellow daisy" has been identified is California, but there the plant is larger and woodier.

The festival, held since 1969 at Georgia's Stone Mountain Park, offers tours to view the daisy and much more: one of the South's largest arts and crafts shows, bluegrass music, and puppet shows. A Yellow Daisy Princess reigns over it all.

CONTACT:
Georgia Dept. of Industry
Trade and Tourism
285 Peachtree Center Ave., N.E.
Marquis Tower II, Ste. 1000
Atlanta, GA 30303
800-847-4842 or 404-656-3592
fax: 404-651-9063

SOURCES:
Chases-1996, p. 366
GdUSFest-1984, p. 40

◆ 2076 ◆ Yemen Independence and National Days
May 22; November 30

Independence Day in Yemen is November 30, a national holiday to commemorate Yemen's independence from the British. It was won on that day in 1967, when evacuation of British soldiers was complete and the leading political group, the National Liberation Front, declared the formation of the independent state of the People's Republic of South Yemen. The British had occupied key portions of the country since the 1830s.

National Day observes the official proclamation of the unification of the Yemen Arab Republic (North Yemen) and the People's Democratic Republic of Yemen (South Yemen) on May 22, 1990. An agreement to a common constitution, government, and economy between both had been signed the day before.

CONTACT:
Yemen Embassy
2600 Virginia Ave., N.W., Ste. 705
Washington, D.C. 20037
202-965-4760

SOURCES:
AnnivHol-1983, p. 153
Chases-1996, p. 223

◆ 2077 ◆ Yemen Revolution Days
September 26; October 14

Yemen observes two Revolution Days: one commemorates the revolutionary movement that overthrew the monarchy of Imam Muhammad al-Badr on September 26, 1962, and helped pave the way for the creation of the Yemen Arab

Republic. Before that could occur, however, British occupation of the area remained another force impeding independence. Revolts against the British then ensued in 1962–63, and by 1967, the British granted Yemen its sovereignty (*see* YEMEN INDEPENDENCE AND NATIONAL DAYS). These revolts are commemorated on October 14.

CONTACT:
Yemen Embassy
2600 Virginia Ave., N.W., Ste. 705
Washington, D.C. 20037
202-965-4760

SOURCES:
AnnivHol-1983, pp. 123, 132
Chases-1996, p. 391
NatlHolWrld-1968, p. 178

Yodeling Festivals
See **Jodlerfests**

Yom ha-Shoah
See **Holocaust Day**

♦ 2078 ♦ **Yom ha-Zikkaron**
Between April 15 and May 13; Iyyar 4

In Israel, the **Day of Remembrance** honors those who died fighting for the establishment of the Israeli state. It is observed on the day preceding Yom ha-Atzma'ut, or ISRAELI INDEPENDENCE DAY. During Shahavit (the morning service), a candle is lit in memory of fallen soldiers, the ark is opened, and Psalm 9, "Over the death of the son," is recited. This is followed by a prayer for the war dead and other prayers for lost relatives. The service concludes with a reading of Psalm 114.

At the end of the day, sirens are sounded and a few minutes of silence are observed throughout Israel. At sundown, Yom ha-Atzma'ut begins and the mood shifts to one of celebration.

CONTACT:
Israel Ministry of Tourism
6380 Wilshire Blvd., Ste. 1700
Los Angeles, CA 90048
213-658-7462; fax: 213-658-6543

♦ 2079 ♦ **Yom Kippur**
Between September 15 and October 13; Tishri 10

Also known as the **Day of Atonement** or **Yom ha-Din**, the **Day of Judgment**, Yom Kippur is the holiest and most solemn day in the Jewish calendar, and the last of the 10 High Holy Days, or Days of Penitence, that begin with ROSH HASHANAH, the Jewish New Year. It is on this day that Jews acknowledge transgressions, repent through confession, then make atonement to God to obtain his forgiveness, with the hope of being inscribed in the Book of Life. It is not uncommon for Jews to spend the entire 24 hours at the synagogue, where five services are held.

Yom Kippur is a strict day of fast; not even water may be taken from sundown to sundown. It is also a day of reconciliation for those who have done each other harm during the past year and a day of charity toward the less fortunate. It is the only fast day that is not postponed if it falls on the Sabbath.

SOURCES:
AmerBkDays-1978, p. 910
BkFest-1937, p. 203
BkFestHolWrld-1970, p. 6
BkHolWrld-1986, Sep 28

DaysCustFaith-1957, p. 246
DictFolkMyth-1984, p. 1009
DictWrldRel-1989, pp. 65,
  155, 390, 817
FolkAmerHol-1991, p. 352
FolkWrldHol-1992, p. 481
RelHolCal-1993, p. 123

♦ 2080 ♦ **Yom Yerushalayim**
Between May 9 and June 6; Iyyar 28

Jerusalem Day commemorates the capture and reunification of Jerusalem during the Six-Day War (on 28 Iyyar 5727 on the Jewish calendar—June 7, 1967), after which Israel gained possession of the Old City of Jerusalem, which had been under Jordanian rule, and other Arab lands. It is the most recent addition to the Jewish calendar and is observed primarily in Israel.

Although there are no specific rituals connected with this relatively new holiday, it is common to recite the Hallel (Psalms 115–118), Psalm 107, and the Aleinu, or concluding prayer. Because this day falls during the LAG BA-OMER period—which begins on the second night of PASSOVER and continues through SHAVUOT—the mourning customs traditionally observed during this time are suspended for the day.

CONTACT:
Israel Ministry of Tourism
6380 Wilshire Blvd., Ste. 1700
Los Angeles, CA 90048
213-658-7462; fax: 213-658-6543

♦ 2081 ♦ **York Festival and Mystery Plays**
June–July, every three years

From 1350 until 1570, a series of "mystery plays"—dramas recounting the story of mankind from the Creation to the Last Judgment—were produced in the city of York, England, on CORPUS CHRISTI by the medieval craft guilds. The event was revived in 1951 and has been held on a triennial basis since then, beginning in mid-June and extending through early July. Modern adaptations of the original plays are performed in the garden of the Abbey of St. Mary—with the exception of one that is given in medieval style on a wagon in the street.

In addition to the mystery plays, there is a festival of music and the arts, with piano and violin recitals, orchestral performances, opera, and art exhibitions.

CONTACT:
British Tourist Authority
551 Fifth Ave., Ste. 702
New York, NY 10176
800-462-2748 or 212-986-2200
fax: 212-986-1188

SOURCES:
GdWrldFest-1985, p. 97
IntlThFolk-1979, p. 181
MusFestEurBrit-1980, p. 64

♦ 2082 ♦ **Yorktown Day**
October 19

On October 19, 1781, Lord Cornwallis surrendered his British and German troops to General George Washington's Allied American and French troops at Yorktown, Virginia. Although the peace treaty recognizing American independence was not ratified until January 14, 1784, the fighting was only sporadic in the intervening two years, and the Battle of Yorktown is widely considered to mark the end of the Revolutionary War.

There has been some sort of patriotic observance of this day since its first anniversary in 1782. But since 1949, Yorktown Day activities have been planned and sponsored by the Yorktown Day Association, composed of representatives from 13 different patriotic and government organizations. Events held at the Colonial National Historical Park in Yorktown include a commemorative ceremony at the French Cemetery and the placing of a wreath at both the French Monument and the Monument to Alliance and Victory. There are other patriotic exercises, 18th-century tactical demonstrations, a parade of military and civilian units, and musical presentations by fife and drum units from all over the eastern United States. The events are often attended by visiting French dignitaries.

CONTACT:
Yorktown Day Association
P.O. Box 210
Yorktown, VA 23690
804-898-3400; fax: 804-898-3400

SOURCES:
AmerBkDays-1978, p. 943
AnnivHol-1983, p. 134
Chases-1996, p. 424

♦ 2083 ♦ Young Woman of the Year Finals
Late June

The final competitions and awards for the title of Young Woman of the Year has been held since 1958 in Mobile, Ala. The winner, a high school senior chosen on the basis of scholarship, fitness, creativity, and human relations, receives a $30,000 college scholarship. More than 26,000 participants in 50 states take part in local programs that lead to the Mobile finals.

The program traces its start to the late 1920s when the Mobile Junior Chamber of Commerce organized an annual azalea program. After World War II, to make this program more attractive, the Jaycees invited high school senior girls from the area to compete for modest awards, and a court of Azalea Trail Maids was selected. By 1957, girls from Florida and Mississippi were joining the Alabama girls, and the Jaycees decided to set up a national program. It got under way in 1958 as the **Junior Miss Pageant** with 18 states represented; the winner that year was Phyllis Whitnack of West Virginia. The name of the pageant was changed to its present one in 1989. Probably the best-known one-time Junior Miss is Diane Sawyer of Kentucky, who took the title in 1963 and went on to become a star television journalist for ABC.

CONTACT:
Mobile Convention and Visitors
  Corp.
1 S. Water St.
Mobile, AL 36602
800-666-6282 or 334-415-2000
fax: 334-415-2060

♦ 2084 ♦ Ysyakh
On or near December 21

This is a celebration of the midnight sun, observed in the Jatutsk region in the northeastern part of Russia. The festivities include foot races, horse races, and often sled dog and reindeer races. Folk dancing and feasting—primarily on boiled beef and *kumiss*, or fermented mare's milk—complete the celebration, which often goes on all night.

CONTACT:
Russian Travel Information Office
Rockefeller Center
610 Fifth Ave., Ste. 603
New York, NY 10020
212-757-3884; fax: 212-459-0031

SOURCES:
FolkWrldHol-1992, p. 596

Yuan Hsiao Chieh
See **Lantern Festival**

Yuki Matsuri
See **Sapporo Snow Festival**

Yukon Discovery Day
See **Klondike Gold Discovery Day**

♦ 2085 ♦ Yule
December 22; December 25

Also known as **Alban Arthan**, Yule is one of the 'Lesser Sabbats' of the Wiccan year, a time when ancient believers celebrated the re-birth of the Sun God and the lengthening of the days. This took place annually around the time of the WINTER SOLSTICE and lasted for 12 days.

The Sabbats are the eight holy days generally observed in modern witchcraft (Wicca) and Neopaganism. They revolve around the changing of the seasons and agricultural events, and were generally celebrated outdoors with feasting, dancing, and performances of poetry, drama, and music. There are four 'Greater Sabbats,' falling on February 2 (*see* IMBOLC), April 30, July 31, and October 31 (*see* SAMHAIN). The Lesser Sabbats fall on the solstices and equinoxes.

Yule, or **Yule Day**, is also an old Scottish expression for CHRISTMAS day, 'Yule' deriving from the old Norse word *jól*, referring to the pre-Christian winter solstice festival. CHRISTMAS EVE is sometimes referred to as 'Yule-Even.'

See also JUUL, FEAST OF

SOURCES:
BkDays-1864, vol. II, pp. 735, 745
DaysCustFaith-1957, p. 352
FestSaintDays-1915, pp. 9, 232
FolkAmerHol-1991, p. 468
FolkWrldHol-1992, pp. 625, 626, 632
RelHolCal-1993, p. 123
SaintFestCh-1904, p. 40

Z

♦ 2086 ♦ **Zaire Independence Day**
June 30

Zaire gained independence from Belgium on this day in 1960. It had been a Belgian colony since 1907, and powerful movements had struggled for self-rule since the 1950s. The people celebrated the first independence day with fireworks and bonfires in the capital city of Léopoldville. In 1966, the capital moved to Kinshasa.

CONTACT:
Zaire Embassy
1800 New Hampshire Ave., N.W.
Washington, D.C. 20009
202-234-7690

SOURCES:
AnnivHol-1983, p. 86
Chases-1996, p. 276
NatlHolWrld-1968, p. 92

♦ 2087 ♦ **Zambia Independence Day**
October 24

On this day in 1964, the British colony of Northern Rhodesia became the independent Republic of Zambia, after decades of nationalist struggle.

For two days, including October 24, celebrations and parades are held all over Zambia, but the most elaborate are in the capital city of Lusaka. Labor and youth organizations march along with the armed forces with dancing and music. Various tribal dances from all over the country are performed in Independence Stadium, and there are gymnastics performances by children. October 24 is also the occasion for the final game of the annual Independence Soccer Trophy.

CONTACT:
Zambia National Tourist Board
237 E. 52nd St.
New York, NY 10022
212-308-2155; fax: 212-758-1319

SOURCES:
AnnivHol-1983, p. 136
Chases-1996, p. 428
GdWrldFest-1985, p. 188
NatlHolWrld-1968, p. 190

♦ 2088 ♦ **Zarthastno Diso**
April 30; May 29; June 1

This is the day on which the followers of Zoroaster (or Zarathustra), the sixth-century Persian prophet and religious reformer, commemorate their founder's death in 551 B.C. Zoroaster was a legendary figure associated with occult knowledge and the practice of magic on the one hand, and on the other, with the monotheistic concept of God familiar in modern-day Christianity and Judaism. The largest group of his followers are the Parsis of India, although they can also be found in isolated areas of Iran.

Zoroaster's death is observed on April 30 by the Fasli sect of the Parsis, on May 29 by the Kadmi sect, and on June 1 by the Shahenshai sect.

CONTACT:
India Tourist Office
30 Rockefeller Ave.
15 N. Mezzanine
New York, NY 10112
212-586-4901; fax: 212-582-3274

Iran Mission to the U.N.
622 Third Ave., 34th Floor
New York, NY 10017
212-687-2020

♦ 2089 ♦ **Zibelemarit (Onion Market)**
Fourth Monday in November

A great celebration of onions and the principal festival of Bern, the capital of Switzerland, known for its bear pit and mechanical clock that displays a parade of wonderful mechanical figures every hour. The onion market is said to date back to the great fire of 1405, after which farmers of the lake region of Canton Fribourg were given the right to sell their products in Bern because they helped rebuild the city. This story is probably a made-up one, since the first documented mention of onions came in the middle of the 19th century.

Farmers at hundreds of stalls offer for sale more than 100 tons of strings of onions, as well as other winter vegetables and nuts. There is a carnival spirit, with confetti battles, people dressed in disguises, and jesters doing satires of the year's events.

CONTACT:
Swiss National Tourist Office
608 Fifth Ave.
New York, NY 10020
212-757-5944; fax: 212-262-6116

SOURCES:
AnnivHol-1983, p. 151
Chases-1996, p. 460
FestWestEur-1958, p. 238

♦ 2090 ♦ **Zimbabwe Independence Day**
April 18

The major holiday in Zimbabwe, which means 'stone dwelling' in Bantu. An independent constitution was written for Zimbabwe in London in 1979. The country was then known as Southern Rhodesia. Independence followed on April 18, 1980, with the first national budget adopted in July 1980. Robert Mugabe was the first prime minister.

Cecil Rhodes formed the British South Africa Company in 1889 to colonize the region, and European settlers began arriving in the 1890s. Rhodes's company governed the country until 1922 when the 34,000 European settlers chose to become a self-governing British colony. In 1923, Southern Rhodesia was annexed by the British Crown. In the fight for independence in the 1970s, black guerrilla organizations launched sporadic attacks, and thousands died in the warfare. The white minority finally consented to multiracial elections in 1980, which Mugabe won in a landslide.

Independence Day is celebrated in every city and district of the nation with political rallies, parades, traditional dances, singing, and fireworks.

CONTACT:
Zimbabwe Tourist Office
1270 Avenue of the Americas
Rockefeller Center, Ste. 412
New York, NY 10020
212-332-1090; fax: 212-332-1093

SOURCES:
AnnivHol-1983, p. 52
Chases-1996, p. 176

♦ 2091 ♦ **Zulu Festival**
First day in July to the last Sunday

The Zulu Festival, also known as the **Shembe Festival**, for Isaiah Shembe (c. 1870–1935), the sect's founder, is one of three annual festivals observed by the Nazareth Baptist Church (Church of the Ama Nazaretha). It takes place at the Ematabetulu village near Inanda, South Africa. The other two are the October festival, observed at Judia near Ginginglovu, and the January festival observed on Inhlangakazi Mountain. All aspects of worship, ritual, dress, and festivals were established by Shembe in 1911. The church's beliefs are a mixture of pagan, Old Testament, and Christian ideas.

The **July Festival** is the most popular of the three, and church members come from all over South Africa to attend it. Some live in temporary encampments for the three- to four-week festival, which begins on the first day of July and ends on the last Sunday. Throughout this period there are alternate days of dancing and rest. The sacred dancing that takes place on the final Sunday usually draws large numbers of spectators. Other activities during the festival include sermons by a variety of preachers, testimonies by church members, and prayer for the sick.

The men and women dance separately, and their costumes vary considerably. The two male groups of dancers, for example, are the Njobo and the Iscotch. The Njobo, who are mostly older men, wear traditional Zulu dress, as do the female groups. But the younger male dancers of the Iscotch group wear a long white smock with a tasseled hem over a black pleated kilt, a white pith helmet, black army boots with black-and-white football socks, and a light green tie bearing icons of the prophet Shembe and other church leaders.

The dances, which can last an entire day, involve rows of 50 or more dancers, each of which takes its turn at the front and then gradually works its way to the back, allowing those who tire to leave the group without being noticed.

CONTACT:
South African Tourism Board
500 Fifth Ave.
New York, NY 10110
800-822-5368 or 212-730-2929
fax: 212-764-1980

SOURCES:
FolkWrldHol-1992, p. 357
GdWrldFest-1985, p. 159

Appendices

1. Admission Days and Facts about the States and Territories

This section lists for each of the fifty states of the United States: the date of admission; information about observances, if applicable; state nicknames, mottoes, animals, birds, flowers, and other symbols; sources noting admission days; and selected state offices. For territories, listed are year of association with the U.S.; nicknames; mottoes, animals, flowers, birds, and other symbols; and government offices.

2. United States Presidents

Lists all U.S. presidents in the order in which they held office, their birth dates and places, spouses, death dates and places, burial sites, political parties, nicknames, career highlights, and notable landmarks.

3. Domestic Tourism Information Sources

Lists, in alphabetical order by state, contact information for travel and tourism offices and selected convention and visitors bureaus and chambers of commerce in all 50 states and the District of Columbia.

4. International Tourism Information Sources

Lists, in alphabetical order by country, contact information for tourism offices for more than 80 countries and embassies or consulate offices for more than 150 countries around the world.

5. Bibliography

Includes sources cited or consulted in the *HFCWD*, as well as other sources for further reading.

6. Web Sites on Holidays

This listing of holiday-related web sites includes descriptions of sites, major subject categories, and e-mail and web site addresses as well as mailing addresses, phone and fax numbers (when available).

APPENDIX 1

Admission Days and Facts about the States and Territories

This section lists for each of the fifty states: the date and order of admission to the Union; information about current or past admission day observances, if applicable; state nicknames, mottoes, animals, flowers, and other symbols; reference sources noting the admission day; and offices to contact for further information. This last item includes governors' offices, secretaries of state, state libraries, and state tourism and travel offices. For territories, listed are year of association with the U.S.; nicknames, mottoes, flowers, and other symbols; and offices to contact.

Alabama

Twenty-second state; admitted on December 14, 1819 (seceded from the Union on January 11, 1861, and was readmitted on June 25, 1868)

Alabama does not observe the anniversary of its admission day, but did hold festivities in 1969 in honor of the 150th, or sesquicentennial, anniversary of statehood. There were historical pageants, a boat parade, formal balls, music, fireworks, and the issuance of a commemorative stamp.

Nicknames: The Heart of Dixie; The Yellowhammer State; The Camellia State
State motto: *Audemus jura nostra defendere* (Latin 'We dare defend our rights')
State barbecue championship: Demopolis Christmas on the River Barbecue Cook-Off
State bird: Yellowhammer (*Colaptes auratus*)
State butterfly and mascot: Easter tiger swallowtail
State championship horse show: Alabama State Championship Horse Show
State dance: Square dance
State fish: saltwater: Tarpon (*Megalops atlantica*); **freshwater:** Largemouth bass (*Micropterus punctulatus*)
State flower: Camellia (*Camellia japonica*)
State fossil: Basilosaurus cetoides
State gemstone: Star blue quartz
State horse: Rocking horse
State insect: Monarch butterfly (*Danaus plexippus*)
State mineral: Hematite
State nut: Pecan
State reptile: Red-bellied turtle (*Pseudemys rubriventris*)
State rock: Marble
State shell: *Scaphella junonia johnstoneae*
State song: "Alabama"
State stone: Marble
State tree: Southern (longleaf) pine (*Pinus palustris*)

SOURCES:
AmerBkDays-1978, p. 1102

AnnivHol-1983, p. 160
Chases-1996, p. 480

STATE OFFICES:
Office of the Governor
600 Dexter Ave.
Montgomery, 36130
334-242-7100
Fax: 334-242-4541

Secretary of State
P.O. Box 5616
Montgomery, 36103
334-242-7200
Fax: 334-242-4993

State Library
6030 Monticello Dr.
Montgomery, 36117
334-213-3900
Fax: 334-213-3993

Tourism and Travel
P.O. Box 4927
Montgomery, 36103
800-ALABAMA
Fax: 334-242-4554

Alaska

Forty-ninth state; admitted on January 3, 1959

See ALASKA DAY

Nicknames: Last Frontier; Land of the Midnight Sun
State motto: North to the Future
State bird: Willow ptarmigan (*Lagopus lagopus*)
State fish: Chinook (king) salmon (*Oncorhynchus tshawytscha*)
State flower: Forget-me-not (*Myosotis sylvatica* or *M. scorpioides*)
State fossil: Woolly mammoth (*Mammuthus primigenius*)
State gem: Jade

State marine mammal: Bowhead whale (*Balaena mysticetus*)
State mineral: Gold
State song: "Alaska's Flag"
State sport: Dogteam racing (mushing)
State tree: Sitka spruce (*Picea sitchensis*)

SOURCES:
AmerBkDays-1978, p. 22
AnnivHol-1983, p. 3
Chases-1996, pp. 55, 421

STATE OFFICES:
Office of the Governor
P.O. Box 110001
Juneau, 99811
907-465-3500
Fax: 907-465-3532

Lieutenant Governor
P.O. Box 110015
Juneau, 99811
907-465-3520
Fax: 907-465-5400

State Library
P.O. Box 110571
Juneau, 99811
907-465-2910
Fax: 907-465-2151

Tourism and Travel
P.O. Box 110801
Juneau, 99811
907-465-2012
Fax: 907-465-2287

Arizona

Forty-eighth state; admitted on February 14, 1912

Admission Day is a legal holiday in Arizona. State offices close and schools may hold observances, but there are no official celebrations.

Nickname: Grand Canyon State
State motto: *Ditat Deus* (Latin 'God Enriches')
State bird: Cactus wren (*Campylorhynchus brunneicapillus*)
State fish: Arizona trout (*Salmo apache*)
State flower: Blossom of the saguaro cactus (*Carnegiea gigantea*)
State fossil: Petrified wood
State gemstone: Turquoise
State neckwear: Bola tie
State reptile: Arizona ridgenose rattlesnake (*Crotalus willardi*)
State songs: "Arizona March Song" and "Arizona"
State tree: Paloverde (*Cercidium floridum*)

SOURCES:
AmerBkDays-1978, p. 180
AnnivHol-1983, p. 24
Chases-1996, p. 96

STATE OFFICES:
Office of the Governor
1700 W. Washington
Phoenix, 85007
602-542-4331
Fax: 602-542-7601

Secretary of State

1700 W. Washington
West Wing, 7th Floor
Phoenix, 85007
602-542-4285
Fax: 602-542-1575

State Library
1700 W. Washington, Rm. 200
Phoenix, 85007
602-542-4035
Fax: 602-542-4972

Tourism and Travel
1100 W. Washington
Phoenix, 85007
800-842-8257
Fax: 602-542-4068

Arkansas

Twenty-fifth state; admitted on June 15, 1836 (seceded from the Union on May 6, 1861, and was readmitted in June 1868)

Nickname: The Land of Opportunity; Bowie State; Toothpick State; Hot Water State
State motto: *Regnat populus* (Latin 'The people rule')
State beverage: Milk
State bird: Mockingbird (*Mimus polyglottos*)
State flower: Apple blossom (*Malus sylvestris*)
State folk dance: Square dance
State fruit and vegetable: South Arkansas vine-ripe pink tomato
State gem: Diamond
State insect: Honeybee (*Apis mellifera*)
State language: English
State mineral: Quartz crystal
State musical instrument: Fiddle
State rock: Bauxite
State songs: "Arkansas," "Arkansas (You Run Deep in Me)," "Oh Arkansas," and "The Arkansas Traveler"
State tree: Pine (*Pinus palustris*)

SOURCES:
AmerBkDays-1978, p. 558
AnnivHol-1983, p. 80
Chases-1996, p. 257

STATE OFFICES:
Office of the Governor
State Capitol, Rm. 250
Little Rock, 72201
501-682-2345
Fax: 501-682-1382

Secretary of State
State Capitol, Rm. 256
Little Rock, 72201
501-682-1010
Fax: 501-682-3510

State Library
1 Capitol Mall, 5th Floor
Little Rock, 72201
501-682-1527
Fax: 501-682-1529

Tourism and Travel
1 Capitol Mall
Little Rock, 72201
800-NATURAL
Fax: 501-682-1364

California

Thirty-first state; admitted on September 9, 1850

City and state offices, banks, and public schools close in California to mark this legal holiday. Two organizations—the Native Sons of the Golden West and the Native Daughters of the Golden West—have sponsored annual programs in different locations throughout the state each year. In addition, many communities hold festivities of their own, including parades, music, food, and dancing.

Nickname: The Golden State
State motto: *Eureka* (Greek 'I Have Found It')
State animal: California grizzly bear (*Ursus (arctos) horribilis*)
State bird: California valley quail (*Callipepla californica*)
State dance: West Coast swing dance
State fish: South Fork golden trout (*Salmo aguabonita*)
State folk dance: Square dance
State fossil: California saber-toothed cat (*Smilodon californicus*)
State flower: Golden poppy (*Eschscholtzia californica*)
State gemstone: Benitoite
State insect: California dog-face butterfly (flying pansy)
State marine mammal: California gray whale (*Eschrichtius robustus*)
State mineral: Native gold
State prehistoric artifact: Chipped stone bear
State reptile: California desert tortoise (*Gopherus agassizii*)
State rock: Serpentine
State song: "I Love You, California"
State trees: Two species of California redwoods (*Sequoia sempervirens* and *Sequoia gigantea*)

SOURCES:
AmerBkDays-1978, p. 827
AnnivHol-1983, p. 116
Chases-1996, p. 371

CONTACT:
Native Sons of the Golden West
414 Mason, Rm. 300
San Francisco, CA 94102
415-392-1223; fax: 415-392-1224

STATE OFFICES:
Office of the Governor
State Capitol, 1st Floor
Sacramento, 95814
916-445-2841
Fax: 916-445-4633

Secretary of State
1230 "J" St.
Sacramento, 95814
916-445-6371
Fax: 916-324-4573

State Library
P.O. Box 942837
Sacramento, 94237
916-654-0261
Fax: 916-654-0064

Tourism and Travel
801 "K" St., Ste. 1600
Sacramento, 95814
800-862-2543
Fax: 916-322-3402

Colorado

Thirty-eighth state; admitted on August 1, 1876

Colorado Day is observed on the first Monday in August with the closing of state, county and city offices throughout the state, but Central City hosts the best-known festivities. The Central City Opera House sponsors different events each year, but there is usually a banquet in a former miners' hotel, the Teller House, including a speech on Colorado's history. In past years, there have been pageants, receptions, cultural events, and tours of historic homes.

Nickname: Centennial State; Switzerland of America; Highest State
State motto: *Nil sine Numine* (Latin 'Nothing without Providence')
State animal: Bighorn sheep (*Ovis canadensis*)
State bird: Lark bunting (*Calamospiza melanocorys*)
State flower: Columbine (*Aguilegia caerula*)
State gem: Aquamarine
State song: "Where the Columbines Grow"
State tree: Blue spruce (*Picea pungens*)

SOURCES:
AmerBkDays-1978, p. 714
AnnivHol-1983, p. 101
Chases-1996, p. 325
DictDays-1988, p. 22

CONTACT:
Central City Opera House
621 17th St.
Denver, CO 80293
303-582-5202; fax: 303-292-4958

STATE OFFICES:
Office of the Governor
State Capitol Bldg., Rm. 136
Denver, 80203
303-866-2471
Fax: 303-866-2003

Secretary of State
1560 Broadway, Ste. 200
Denver, 80202
303-894-2200
Fax: 303-894-7734

State Library
201 E. Colfax
Denver, 80203
303-866-6725
Fax: 303-866-6940

Tourism and Travel
1625 Broadway, Ste. 1700
Denver, 80202
800-592-1939
Fax: 303-592-5510

Connecticut

Fifth state; adopted the U.S. Constitution on January 9, 1788

Nicknames: The Constitution State; The Nutmeg State; Land of Steady Habits; Blue Law State
State motto: *Qui Transtulit Sustinet* (Latin 'He Who Transplanted Still Sustains')
State animal: Sperm whale (*Physeter catodon*)
State bird: American robin (*Turdus migratorius*)
State composer: Charles Edward Ives (1874-1954)

State flower: Mountain laurel (*Kalmia latifolia*)
State fossil: *Eubrontes giganteus*
State hero: Nathan Hale (1755-1776)
State insect: Praying mantis (*Mantis religiosa*)
State mineral: Garnet
State shellfish: Eastern oyster (*Crassostrea virginica*)
State ship: USS *Nautilus* (first nuclear submarine)
State song: "Yankee Doodle"
State tree: White oak (*Quercus alba*)

SOURCES:
AmerBkDays-1978, p. 54
AnnivHol-1983, p. 6
Chases-1996, p. 61

STATE OFFICES:
Office of the Governor
Executive Chambers
210 Capitol Ave.
Hartford, 06106
203-566-4840
Fax: 203-566-4677

Secretary of State
State Capitol, Rm. 101
Hartford, 06106
203-566-2739
Fax: 203-566-6318

State Library
231 Capitol Ave.
Hartford, 06106
203-566-4777
Fax: 203-566-2133

Tourism and Travel
865 Brook St.
Rocky Hill, 06067
800-CT-BOUND
Fax: 860-258-4275

Delaware

First state; adopted the U.S. Constitution on December 7, 1787

December 7 is Delaware Day, commemorating the day it became the first state to ratify the Constitution. In 1939 the state legislature decreed that a commission be set up to organize the annual celebration. Since then, the observance has consisted mainly of the singing of patriotic songs, recitations of the Pledge of Allegiance and "Our Heritage," a poem by Herman Hanson, and speeches and readings on the state's history.

Nicknames: The First State; The Diamond State; The Blue Hen State
State motto: Liberty and Independence
State beverage: Milk
State bird: Blue Hen chicken
State fish: Weakfish (*Cynoscion regalis*)
State flower: Peach blossom (*Prunus persica*)
State insect: Ladybug (*Hippodamia convergens*)
State rock: Sillimanite
State song: "Our Delaware"
State tree: American holly (*Ilex opaca*)

SOURCES:
AmerBkDays-1978, p. 1080
AnnivHol-1983, p. 157
Chases-1996, p. 474

STATE OFFICES:
Office of the Governor
Carvel State Bldg.
820 N. French
Wilmington, 19801
302-739-4101
Fax: 302-739-2775

Secretary of State
Townsend Bldg.
P.O. Box 898
Dover, 19903
302-739-4111
Fax: 302-739-3811

State Library
43 S. DuPont Hwy.
Dover, 19901
302-739-4748
Fax: 302-739-6787

Tourism and Travel
99 Kings Hwy.
P.O. Box 1401
Dover, 19903
800-441-8846
Fax: 302-739-5749

Florida

Twenty-seventh state; admitted on March 3, 1845 (seceded from the Union on January 10, 1861, and was readmitted on June 25, 1868)

Florida does not hold regular admission day celebrations, but a centennial observance did occur in 1945. A three-cent stamp was issued, schools gave presentations, and there were local exhibits and commemorations. The Library of Congress hosted an exhibit on Florida from March 3 through May 31.

Nicknames: The Sunshine State; Alligator State; Everglades State; Southernmost State; Orange State
State motto: In God We Trust
State animal: Florida panther (*Felis concolor*)
State band: St. Johns River City Band
State beverage: Orange juice
State bird: Mockingbird (*Mimus polyglottos*)
State fiddle contest: Sponsored by Florida State Fiddlers' Association, held at Stephen Foster State Folk Culture Center
State fish: freshwater: Largemouth bass (*Micropterus salmoides*); **saltwater:** Atlantic sailfish (*Istiophorus platypterus*)
State flower: Orange blossom; **wildflower:** Coreopsis
State gem: Moonstone
State litter control symbol: "Glenn Glitter," trademark of Florida Federation of Garden Clubs, Inc.
State marine mammals: Manatee (*Trichechus manatus*) and dolphin (*Tursiops truncatus*)
State moving image center and archive: Louis Wolfson II Media History Center, Inc., Miami
State opera program: Greater Miami Opera Association, Orlando Opera Company, Florida State University School of Music
State railroad museums: Orange Blossom Special Museum; Gold Coast Railroad Museum, Inc., and Gold Coast Railroad, Inc.; Florida Gulf Coast Railroad Museum
State shell: Horse conch (*Pleuroploca gigantea*)

State soil: Myakka fine sand
State song: "Old Folks at Home" (also known as "Swanee River")
State stone: Agatized coral
State transportation museum: Florida Museum of Transportation and History in Fernandina Beach
State tree: Sabal palmetto palm (*Sabal palmetto*)

SOURCES:

AmerBkDays-1978, p. 231
AnnivHol-1983, p. 32
Chases-1996, p. 121

STATE OFFICES:

Office of the Governor
The Capitol
Tallahassee, 32399
904-488-4441
Fax: 904-487-0801

Secretary of State
The Capitol
Plaza Level, Rm. 2
Tallahassee, 32399
904-488-3680
Fax: 904-487-2214

State Library
R. A. Gray Bldg.
Tallahassee, 32399
904-487-2651
Fax: 904-488-2746

Tourism and Travel
126 W. Van Buren
Tallahassee, 32399
904-487-1462
Fax: 904-921-9158

Georgia

Fourth state; adopted the U.S. Constitution on January 2, 1788 (seceded from the Union on January 19, 1861, and was readmitted on July 15, 1870)

Nicknames: The Empire State of the South; The Peach State; The Goober State; The Peachtree State
State mottoes: Wisdom, Justice, Moderation; Agriculture and Commerce, 1776
State atlas: *The Atlas of Georgia*
State bird: Brown thrasher (*Toxostoma rufum*)
State fish: Largemouth bass (*Micropterus salmoides*)
State flower: Cherokee rose (*Rosa laevigata*); **wildflower:** Azalea
State fossil: Shark tooth
State gem: Quartz
State historic drama: *The Reach of Song*
State insect: Honeybee (*Apis mellifera*)
State marine mammal: Right whale (*Baleana glacialin*)
State mineral: Staurolite
State reptile: Gopher tortoise
State seashell: Knobbed whelk (*Busycon carica*)
State song: "Georgia on My Mind"
State tree: Live oak (*Quercus virginiana*)
State vegetable: Vidalia sweet onion
State waltz: "Our Georgia"
State wildflower: Azalea (*Rhododendron*)

SOURCES:

AmerBkDays-1978, p. 20

AnnivHol-1983, p. 3
Chases-1996, p. 54

STATE OFFICES:

Office of the Governor
203 State Capitol
Atlanta, 30334
404-656-1776
Fax: 404-657-7332

Secretary of State
State Capitol, Rm. 214
Atlanta, 30334
404-656-2881
Fax: 404-656-0513

State Library
156 Trinity Ave., S.W., 1st Floor
Atlanta, 30303
404-657-6220
Fax: 404-651-9447

Tourism and Travel
P.O. Box 1776
Atlanta, 30301
800-847-4842
Fax: 404-651-9063

Hawaii

Fiftieth state; admitted on August 21, 1959

Hawaii's admission day anniversary is observed as a state holiday on the third Friday in August every year.

Nicknames: Aloha State; Paradise of the Pacific; Pineapple State
State motto: *Ua mau ke ea o ka aina i ka pono* (Hawaiian 'The Life of the Land Is Perpetuated in Righteousness')
State bird: Nene or Hawaiian goose (*Nesochen sandvicensis*)
State fish: Humuhumunukunukuapuaa (*Rhinecantus aculeatus*)
State flower: *Pua aloalo* (Hibiscus; *rosa-sinensis*)
State gem: Black coral
State song: "Hawaii Ponoi"
State team sport: Outrigger canoe paddling
State tree: *Kukui* (candlenut; *Aleurites moluccana*)

SOURCES:

AmerBkDays-1978, p. 768
AnnivHol-1983, p. 109
Chases-1996, pp. 339, 344

STATE OFFICES:

Office of the Governor
State Capitol
Executive Chamber, 15th Floor
Honolulu, 96813
808-586-0034
Fax: 808-586-0006

Lieutenant Governor
P.O. Box 3226
Honolulu, 96801
808-586-0255
Fax: 808-586-0231

State Library
478 S. King
Honolulu, 96813
808-586-3500

Tourism and Travel

P.O. Box 2359
Honolulu, 96804
808-586-2550

Idaho

Forty-third state; admitted on July 3, 1890

In 1963, Idaho held a centennial celebration marking the anniversary of its becoming a territory of the United States. From June 27 to July 6, numerous activities were sponsored by more than 165 organizations in the Boise area, including "Old Fashioned Bargain Days," balls, parades, singing, street dancing, fireworks, a rifle shoot, sports events, an art exhibit, rodeo, picnics, a poetry reading, an air show, and a historical pageant presenting memorable episodes from the state's history.

Nicknames: Gem State; Gem of the Mountains
State motto: *Esto perpetua* (Latin 'May it endure forever')
State bird: Mountain bluebird (*Sialia currucoides*)
State fish: Cutthroat trout (*Salmo clarki*)
State flower: Syringa (*Philadelphus lewisii*)
State folkdance: Square dance
State fossil: Hagerman horse (*Equus simplicidens*)
State gem: Star garnet
State horse: Appaloosa
State song: "Here We Have Idaho"
State tree: Western white pine (*Pinus strobus*)

SOURCES:
AmerBkDays-1978, p. 616
AnnivHol-1983, p. 88
Chases-1996, p. 281

STATE OFFICES:
Office of the Governor
P.O. Box 83720
Boise, 83720
208-334-2100
Fax: 208-334-2175

Secretary of State
P.O. Box 83720
Boise, 83720
208-334-2300
Fax: 208-334-2282

State Library
325 W. State
Boise, 83702
208-334-2150
Fax: 208-334-4016

Tourism and Travel
P.O. Box 83720
Boise, 83720
800-635-7820
Fax: 208-334-2631

Illinois

Twenty-first state; admitted on December 3, 1818

The 150th, or sesquicentennial, anniversary of Illinois' statehood was celebrated throughout the state during 1968. In December 1967, a year-long exhibit on Illinois history opened at Chicago's Field Museum of Natural History. Miniature replicas of historic rooms—Carl Sandburg's birthplace, Jane Addams's Hull House office, and the Palmer House Hotel's Silver Dollar Barber Shop of 1875—were on display in Carson Pirie Scott department stores. Lincoln's birthday on February 12 was observed with programs commemorating his career in Illinois. On July 4, there was a parade, drama, musical events, fireworks, and speeches at Steeleville. As part of the year-long celebration, the Old State House in Springfield was restored.

Nicknames: Prairie State; Land of Lincoln; Corn State
State motto: State Sovereignty, National Unity
State animal: White-tailed deer (*Odocoileus virginianus*)
State bird: Cardinal (*Cardinalis cardinalis*)
State dance: Square dance
State fish: Bluegill (*Lepomis macrochirus*)
State flower: Violet (*Viola*)
State folk dance: Square dance
State fossil: Tully Monster (*Tullimonstrum gregarium*)
State insect: Monarch butterfly (*Danaus plexippus*)
State language: English
State mineral: Fluorite
State prairie grass: Big bluestem (*Andropogon furcatus*)
State song: "Illinois"
State tree: White oak (*Quercus alba*)

SOURCES:
AmerBkDays-1978, p. 1072
AnnivHol-1983, p. 155
Chases-1996, p. 469

STATE OFFICES:
Office of the Governor
Capitol Bldg., Rm. 207
Springfield, 62706
217-782-6830
Fax: 217-782-3560

Secretary of State
Capitol Bldg., Rm. 213
Springfield, 62756
217-782-2201
Fax: 217-785-0358

State Library
300 S. Second
Springfield, 62701
217-782-2994
Fax: 217-785-4326

Tourism and Travel
100 W. Randolph, Ste. 3-400
Chicago, 60601
800-2-CONNECT
Fax: 312-814-1800

Indiana

Nineteenth state; admitted on December 11, 1816

Indiana Day, December 11, is not a legal holiday, but has been observed sporadically since Indiana's General Assembly proclaimed the holiday in February 1925. Schools often hold commemorative programs. The sesquicentennial anniversary in 1966, however, was marked throughout that year with historical pageants and recreations of such notable events as the signing of the state's constitution.

Nickname: Hoosier State
State motto: The Crossroads of America
State bird: Cardinal (*Cardinalis cardinalis*)
State flower: Peony (*Paeonia*)
State language: English

State poem: "Indiana"
State song: "On the Banks of the Wabash, Far Away"
State stone: Indiana limestone
State tree: Tulip tree (yellow poplar; *Liriodendron tulipfera*)

SOURCES:
AmerBkDays-1978, p. 1094
AnnivHol-1983, p. 158
Chases-1996, p. 478
DictDays-1988, p. 59

STATE OFFICES:
Office of the Governor
State Capitol, Rm. 206
Indianapolis, 46204
317-232-1048
Fax: 317-232-3443

Secretary of State
State House, Rm. 201
Indianapolis, 46204
317-232-6531
Fax: 317-233-3283

State Library
140 N. Senate Ave.
Indianapolis, 46204
317-232-3675
Fax: 317-232-3728

Tourism and Travel
1 N. Capitol, Ste. 700
Indianapolis, 46204
800-289-6646
Fax: 317-233-6887

Iowa

Twenty-ninth state; admitted on December 28, 1846

Nicknames: The Hawkeye State; The Corn State
State motto: Our Liberties We Prize, and Our Rights We
   Will Maintain
State bird: Eastern goldfinch (*Carduelis tristis*)
State flower: Wild rose (*Rosa pratincola*)
State song: "The Song of Iowa"
State stone: Geode
State tree: Oak (*Quercus*)

SOURCES:
AmerBkDays-1978, p. 1157
AnnivHol-1983, p. 165
Chases-1996, p. 491

STATE OFFICES:
Office of the Governor
State Capitol Bldg.
Des Moines, 50319
515-281-5211
Fax: 515-281-6611

Secretary of State
State House
Des Moines, 50319
515-281-5204
Fax: 515-242-5952

State Library
E. 12th and Grand
Des Moines, 50319
515-281-4105
Fax: 515-281-6191

Tourism and Travel

200 E. Grand
Des Moines, 50309
800-345-4692
Fax: 515-242-4749

Kansas

Thirty-fourth state; admitted on January 29, 1861

Kansas Day has been observed since 1877, most often in school programs about the state.

Nicknames: Sunflower State; Wheat State; Breadbasket of
   America; Jayhawk State
State motto: *Ad Astra per Aspera* (Latin 'To the Stars
   Through Difficulties')
State animal: American buffalo or bison (*Bison bison*)
State bird: Western meadowlark (*Sturnella neglecta*)
State flower: Sunflower (*Helianthus annuus*)
State insect: Honeybee (*Apis mellifera*)
State march: "The Kansas March"
State reptile: Ornate box turtle
State song: "Home on the Range"
State tree: Cottonwood (*Populus deltoides*)

SOURCES:
AmerBkDays-1978, p. 117
AnnivHol-1983, p. 15
Chases-1996, p. 79

STATE OFFICES:
Office of the Governor
State Capitol, 2nd Floor
Topeka, 66612
913-296-3232
Fax: 913-296-7973

Secretary of State
State House, 2nd Floor
Topeka, 66612
913-296-2236
Fax: 913-296-4570

State Library
State House
300 S.W. 10th Ave., 3rd Floor
Topeka, 66612
913-296-3296
Fax: 913-296-6650

Tourism and Travel
700 S.W. Harrison, Ste. 1300
Topeka, 66603
800-2-KANSAS
Fax: 913-296-6988

Kentucky

Fifteenth state; admitted on June 1, 1792

Admission Day is not regularly observed in Kentucky, although festivities were held on the 100th, 150th, and 175th anniversaries of statehood.

Nicknames: The Bluegrass State; The Hemp State; The
   Tobacco State; The Dark and Bloody Ground
State motto: United We Stand, Divided We Fall
State bird: Cardinal (*Cardinalis cardinalis*)
State flower: Goldenrod (*Solidago nemoralis*)
State language: English
State song: "My Old Kentucky Home"

State tree: Kentucky coffee tree (*Gymnocladus dioicus*)
State tug-of-war championship: Nelson County Fair Tug-of-War Championship Contest
State wild animal: Gray squirrel (*Sciurus carolinensis*)

SOURCES:
AmerBkDays-1978, p. 510
AnnivHol-1983, p. 74
Chases-1996, p. 238
DictDays-1988, p. 113

STATE OFFICES:
Office of the Governor
The Capitol
700 Capitol Ave.
Frankfort, 40601
502-564-2611
Fax: 502-564-2517

Secretary of State
150 Capitol Bldg.
700 Capital Ave.
Frankfort, 40601
502-564-3490
Fax: 502-564-5687

State Library
300 Coffee Tree Rd.
P.O. Box 537
Frankfort, 40602
502-875-7000
Fax: 502-564-5773

Tourism and Travel
Capital Plaza Tower, 24th Floor
500 Mero St.
Frankfort, 40601
800-225-8747
Fax: 502-564-5695

Louisiana

Eighteenth state; admitted on April 30, 1812 (seceded in 1861 and was readmitted on June 25, 1868)

Nicknames: The Pelican State; The Bayou State; Fisherman's Paradise; Child of the Mississippi; Sugar State
State motto: Union, Justice, and Confidence
State bird: Eastern brown pelican (*Pelecanus erythrorhynchos*)
State crustacean: Crawfish
State dog: Louisiana Catahoula leopard dog
State doughnut: Beignet
State drink: Milk
State environmental song: "The Gifts of Earth"
State flower: Magnolia; **wildflower:** Louisiana iris (*Giganticaerulea*)
State fossil: Petrified palm wood
State gem: Agate
State insect: Honeybee (*Apis mellifera*)
State musical instrument: Diatonic ("Cajun") accordion
State songs: "Give Me Louisiana"; "You Are My Sunshine"
State tree: Bald cypress (*Taxodium distichum*)

SOURCES:
AmerBkDays-1978, p. 401
AnnivHol-1983, p. 58
Chases-1996, p. 192

STATE OFFICES:
Office of the Governor
P.O. Box 94004
Baton Rouge, 70804
504-342-7015
Fax: 504-342-7099

Secretary of State
P.O. Box 94125
Baton Rouge, 70804
504-342-4857
Fax: 504-342-5577

State Library
P.O. Box 131
Baton Rouge, 70821
504-342-4913
Fax: 504-342-3547

Tourism and Travel
P.O. Box 94291
Baton Rouge, 70804
800-334-8626
Fax: 504-342-8390

Maine

Twenty-third state; admitted on March 15, 1820

Nicknames: The Pine Tree State; The Lumber State; The Border State; The Old Dirigo State
State motto: *Dirigo* (Latin 'I direct')
State animal: Moose (*Alces alces*)
State berry: Wild blueberry
State bird: Chickadee (*Parus atricapillus*)
State cat: Maine coon cat
State fish: Landlocked salmon (*Salmo salar*)
State flower: White pine cone and tassel (*Pinus strobus*)
State fossil: *Pertica quadrifaria*
State insect: Honeybee (*Apis mellifera*)
State language of the deaf community: American Sign Language
State mineral: Tourmaline
State song: "State of Maine Song"
State tree: Eastern white pine (*Pinus strobus*)
State vessel: Schooner *Bowdoin*

SOURCES:
AmerBkDays-1978, p. 257
AnnivHol-1983, p. 37
Chases-1996, p. 133

STATE OFFICES:
Office of the Governor
State House Station 1
Augusta, 04333
207-287-3531
Fax: 207-287-1039

Secretary of State
State House Station 148
Augusta, 04333
207-626-8400
Fax: 207-287-8598

State Library
State House Station 64
Augusta, 04333
207-287-5600
Fax: 207-622-0933

Tourism and Travel
33 Stone St.

Augusta, 04333
800-533-9595
Fax: 207-287-5701

Maryland

Seventh state; adopted the U.S. Constitution on April 28, 1788

Nicknames: The Old Line State; Free State
State mottoes: *Fatti maschii, parole femine* (Latin 'Manly deeds, womanly words'); *Scuto Bonae Voluntatis Tuae Coronasti Nos* (Latin 'With favor wilt Thou compass us as with a shield')
State bird: Baltimore oriole (*Icterus galbula*)
State boat: Skipjack
State crustacean: Maryland blue crab (*Callinectes sapidus*)
State dog: Chesapeake Bay retriever
State fish: Rockfish or striped bass (*Roccus saxatilis*)
State flower: Black-eyed Susan (*Rudbeckie hirta*)
State fossil shell: *Ecphora quadricostata*
State insect: Baltimore checkerspot butterfly (*Euphydryas phaeton*)
State song: "Maryland, My Maryland"
State sport: Jousting
State summer theater: Olney Theatre (Montgomery County)
State theater: Center State (Baltimore)
State tree: White oak (*Quercus alba*)

SOURCES:
AmerBkDays-1978, p. 393
AnnivHol-1983, p. 58
Chases-1996, p. 190

STATE OFFICES:
Office of the Governor
State House
Annapolis, 21401
410-974-3901
Fax: 410-974-3275

Secretary of State
State House
Annapolis, 21401
410-974-5521
Fax: 410-974-5190

State Library
400 Cathedral St.
Baltimore, 21201
410-396-5430

Tourism and Travel
217 E. Redwood, 9th Floor
Baltimore, 21202
800-543-1036
Fax: 410-333-6643

Massachusetts

Sixth state; adopted the U.S. Constitution on February 6, 1788

Nicknames: The (Old) Bay State; The Old Colony State; The Puritan State; The Baked Bean State; The Pilgrim State
State motto: *Ense petit placidam sub libertate quietem* (Latin 'By the sword we seek peace, but peace only under liberty')
State bean: Baked navy bean
State beverage: Cranberry juice
State bird: Chickadee (*Parus atricapillus*)
State building and monument stone: Granite
State cat: Tabby cat
State ceremonial march: "The Road to Boston"
State designation of citizens: Bay Staters
State dog: Boston terrier
State explorer rock: Dighton Rock
State fish: Cod (*Gadus morhua*)
State flower: Mayflower (also called ground laurel or trailing arbutus; *Epigaea repens*)
State folk dance: Square dance
State folk song: "Massachusetts"
State fossil: Theropod dinosaur tracks
State gem: Rhodonite
State heroine: Deborah Sampson (1760-1827; while disguised as a man under the name of Robert Shirtliff, she fought with the Continental Army against the British)
State historical rock: Plymouth Rock
State horse: Morgan horse
State insect: Ladybug (*Hippodamia convergens*)
State marine mammal: Right whale
State memorial to honor Vietnam War veterans: Memorial in Worcester
State mineral: Babingtonite
State muffin: Corn muffin
State patriotic song: "Massachusetts (Because of You Our Land is Free)"
State poem: "Blue Hills of Massachusetts"
State rock: Roxbury pudding stone (Roxbury conglomerate)
State shell: New England neptune (*Neptuna decemcostata*)
State soil: Paxton soil series
State song: "All Hail to Massachusetts"
State tree: American elm (*Ulmus americana*)

SOURCES:
AmerBkDays-1978, p. 150
AnnivHol-1983, p. 20
Chases-1996, p. 88

STATE OFFICES:
Office of the Governor
Executive Office
State House
Boston, 02133
617-727-3600
Fax: 617-727-9725

Secretary of State
State House, Rm. 337
Boston, 02133
617-727-9180
Fax: 617-742-4722

State Library
State House, Rm. 341
Boston, 02133
617-727-2590
Fax: 617-727-5819

Tourism and Travel
100 Cambridge St., 13th Floor
Boston, 02202
800-447-6277
Fax: 617-727-6525

Michigan

Twenty-sixth state; admitted on January 26, 1837

The anniversary of Michigan's statehood was previously observed as Michigan Day, but is no longer a holiday.

Nicknames: The Wolverine State; The Water Wonderland; the Upper Peninsula is often referred to as the Land of Hiawatha
State motto: *Si quaeris peninsulam amoenam, circumspice* (Latin 'If you seek a pleasant peninsula, look about you')
State bird: Robin (*Turdus migratorius*)
State fish: Brook trout (*Salvelinus fontinalis*)
State flower: Apple blossom (*Malus sylvestris*)
State gem: Chlorastrolite
State soil: Kalkaska Soil Series
State song: "Michigan, My Michigan"
State stone: Petosky stone
State tree: White pine (*Pinus strobus*)

SOURCES:
AmerBkDays-1978, p. 113
AnnivHol-1983, p. 14
Chases-1996, p. 76

STATE OFFICES:
Office of the Governor
P.O. Box 30013
Lansing, 48909
517-373-3400
Fax: 517-335-6826

Secretary of State
Treasury Bldg.
430 W. Allegan, 1st Floor
Lansing, 48918
517-373-2510
Fax: 517-373-0727

State Library
717 W. Allegan
P.O. Box 30007
Lansing, 48909
517-373-1580
Fax: 517-373-5700

Tourism and Travel
333 S. Capitol, Ste. F
Lansing, 48909
800-543-2937
Fax: 517-373-0059

Minnesota

Thirty-second state; admitted on May 11, 1858

Nicknames: North Star State; Gopher State; Bread and Butter State; The Land of 10,000 Lakes
State motto: *L'Etoile du Nord* (French 'The North Star')
State bird: Common loon (*Gavia immer*)
State drink: Milk
State fish: Walleye (*Stizostedion vitreum*)
State flower: Pink and white lady's slipper (*Cypripedium reginae*)
State gem: Lake Superior agate
State grain: Wild rice or manomin (*Zizania aquatica*)
State muffin: Blueberry muffin
State mushroom: Morel or sponge mushroom (*Morchella esculenta*)

State song: "Hail! Minnesota"
State tree: Norway (red) pine (*Pinus resinosa*)

SOURCES:
AmerBkDays-1978, p. 442
AnnivHol-1983, p. 64
Chases-1996, p. 208

STATE OFFICES:
Office of the Governor
State Capitol, Rm. 130
St. Paul, 55155
612-296-3391
Fax: 612-296-2089

Secretary of State
100 Constitution Ave., Rm. 180
St. Paul, 55155
612-296-2079
Fax: 612-296-9073

State Library
345 Kellogg Blvd. W.
St. Paul, 55102
612-296-2143
Fax: 612-297-7436

Tourism and Travel
100 Metro Sq., Ste. 100
121 E. Seventh Pl.
St. Paul, 55101
800-657-3700
Fax: 612-296-7095

Mississippi

Twentieth state; admitted on December 10, 1817 (seceded on January 9, 1861, and was readmitted on February 23, 1870)

No admission day celebrations occur, but in 1917, the state held centennial ceremonies including speeches and music. On the sesquicentennial, or 150th, anniversary in 1967, there were exhibits at the Old Capitol Building museum, and efforts got underway to preserve state historical documents (including appropriating $1,120,000 for building a new archives center).

Nickname: The Magnolia State; Eagle State; Border-Eagle State; Bayou State; Mud-cat State
State motto: *Virtute et armis* (Latin 'By valor and arms')
State beverage: Milk
State bird: Mockingbird (*Mimus polyglottos*)
State butterfly: Spicebush swallowtail (*Papilio troilus*)
State fish: Largemouth or black bass (*Micropterus salmoides*)
State flower: Magnolia blossom (*Magnolia grandiflora*)
State fossil: Prehistoric whale
State insect: Honeybee (*Apis mellifera*)
State language: English
State mammal: land: White-tailed deer (*Odocoileus virginianus*); **water:** Bottle-nosed dolphin (*Tursiops truncatus*)
State shell: Oyster shell
State song: "Go, Mississippi"
State stone: Petrified wood
State tree: Magnolia (*Magnolia grandiflora*)
State waterfowl: Wood duck (*Aix sponsa*)

SOURCES:
AmerBkDays-1978, p. 1091

Chases-1996, p. 477

STATE OFFICES:
Office of the Governor
P.O. Box 139
Jackson, 39215
601-359-3100
Fax: 601-359-3741

Secretary of State
P.O. Box 136
Jackson, 39205
601-359-1350
Fax: 601-354-6243

State Library
P.O. Box 1040
Jackson, 39215
601-359-3672

Tourism and Travel
P.O. Box 849
Jackson, 39205
800-927-6378
Fax: 601-359-5757

Missouri

Twenty-fourth state; admitted on August 10, 1821

Nicknames: Show Me State; Mother of the West; Bullion State; Cave State; Lead State; Ozark State
State motto: *Salus populi suprema lex esto* (Latin 'The welfare of the people shall be the supreme law')
State bird: Bluebird (*Sialia sialis*)
State flower: Hawthorn blossom (*Crataegus*)
State fossil: Crinoid
State insect: Honeybee (*Apis mellifera*)
State mineral: Galena
State musical instrument: Fiddle
State rock: Mozarkite (chert or flint rock)
State song: "Missouri Waltz"
State tree: Flowering dogwood (*Cornus florida*)
State tree nut: Eastern black walnut (*Juglans nigra*)

SOURCES:
AmerBkDays-1978, p. 744
AnnivHol-1983, p. 105
Chases-1996, p. 332

STATE OFFICES:
Office of the Governor
P.O. Box 720
Jefferson City, 65102
314-751-3222
Fax: 314-751-1491

Secretary of State
P.O. Box 778
Jefferson City, 65102
314-751-2379
Fax: 314-751-2490

State Library
600 W. Main
P.O. Box 387
Jefferson City, 65102
314-751-2862
Fax: 314-751-3612

Tourism and Travel
P.O. Box 1055
Jefferson City, 65102
800-877-1234

Fax: 314-751-5160

Montana

Forty-first state; admitted on November 8, 1889

Nicknames: Treasure State; Big Sky Country; Bonanza State; Stub Toe State
State motto: *Oro y Plata* (Spanish 'Gold and Silver')
State animal: Grizzly bear (*Ursus (arctos) horribilis*)
State arboretum: University of Montana, Missoula campus
State ballad: "Montana Melody"
State bird: Western meadowlark (*Sturnella neglecta*)
State fish: Black-spotted (cutthroat) trout (*Salmo clarki*)
State flower: Bitterroot (*Lewisia rediviva*)
State fossil: Duck-billed dinosaur (*Maiasaura peeblesorum*)
State gems: Yogo sapphire; Montana agate
State grass: Bluebunch wheatgrass (*Agropyron spicatum*)
State song: "Montana"
State tree: Ponderosa pine (*Pinus ponderosa*)
State Vietnam veterans' memorial: Memorial in Rose Park, Missoula

SOURCES:
AmerBkDays-1978, p. 1002
AnnivHol-1983, p. 143
Chases-1996, p. 444

STATE OFFICES:
Office of the Governor
Capitol Station
Helena, 59620
406-444-3111
Fax: 406-444-4151

Secretary of State
State Capitol, Rm. 225
Helena, 59620
406-444-2034
Fax: 406-444-3976

State Library
1515 E. Sixth Ave.
Helena, 59620
406-444-3004
Fax: 406-444-5612

Tourism and Travel
1424 Ninth Ave.
Helena, 59620
800-VISIT-MT
Fax: 406-444-1800

Nebraska

Thirty-seventh state; admitted on March 1, 1867

Nebraska's admission day anniversary is marked as State Day. On March 1 every year, state law requires the governor to issue a proclamation about the anniversary and call on citizens to celebrate. Schools may mark the occasion with programs about the state's history. The centennial celebration was held during much of 1967 with festivals, rodeos, pageants, and exhibits.

Nicknames: Cornhusker State; Tree Planters' State; Antelope State; Bug-eating State
State motto: Equality Before the Law
State bird: Western meadowlark (*Sturnella neglecta*)

491

State flower: Goldenrod (*Solidago gigantea*)
State fossil: Mammoth
State gem: Blue agate (blue chalcedony)
State grass: Little bluestem (*Schizachyrium scoparium*), also called "bunch grass" or "beard grass"
State insect: Honeybee (*Apis mellifera*)
State mammal: Whitetail deer (*Odocoileus virginianus*)
State rock: Prairie agate
State soil: Holdrege series
State song: "Beautiful Nebraska"
State tree: Cottonwood (*Populus deltoides*)

SOURCES:
AmerBkDays-1978, p. 224
AnnivHol-1983, p. 31
Chases-1996, p. 118

STATE OFFICES:
Office of the Governor
State Capitol Bldg., 2nd Floor
Lincoln, 68509
402-471-2244
Fax: 402-471-6031

Secretary of State
State Capitol Bldg., Rm. 2300
Lincoln, 68509
402-471-2554
Fax: 402-471-3666

State Library
1200 "N" St., Ste. 120
Lincoln, 68508
402-471-2045
Fax: 402-471-2083

Tourism and Travel
700 S. 16th St.
P.O. Box 94666
Lincoln, 68509
800-228-4307
Fax: 402-471-3026

Nevada

Thirty-sixth state; admitted on October 31, 1864

Nevada Day is a legal holiday throughout the state, but the most festive celebrations take place in Carson City, where the Admission Day parade has been held since 1938. There are historical Indian pageants, a costume ball, a Miss Nevada crowning, and dancing, picnicking, games, and other events. Students have entered a historical essay contest since 1959, and the winners are awarded during the festivities.

Nicknames: Silver State; Sagebrush State; Mining State
State motto: All for Our Country
State animal: Desert bighorn sheep (*Ovis canadensis*)
State bird: Mountain bluebird (*Sialia currucoides*)
State colors: Silver and blue
State fish: Lahontan cutthroat trout (*Salmo clarki henshawi*)
State flower: Sagebrush (*Artemisia tridentata*)
State fossil: Ichthyosaur (*Stenopterygius quadriscissus*)
State grass: Indian ricegrass (*Oryzopsis hymenoides*)
State metal: Silver
State precious gemstone: Virgin Valley Black Fire opal
State reptile: Desert tortoise (*Gopherus agassizii*)
State rock: Sandstone
State semi-precious gemstone: Turquoise
State song: "Home Means Nevada"

State trees: Single-leaf piñon (*Pinus monophylla*), and Bristlecone pine (*Pinus aristata*)

SOURCES:
AmerBkDays-1978, p. 972
AnnivHol-1983, p. 138
Chases-1996, p. 435
DictDays-1988, p. 81

STATE OFFICES:
Office of the Governor
Capitol Complex
Carson City, 89710
702-687-5670
Fax: 702-687-4486

Secretary of State
Capitol Complex
Carson City, 89710
702-687-5203
Fax: 702-687-3471

State Library
Capitol Complex
Carson City, 89710
702-687-5160
Fax: 702-687-8311

Tourism and Travel
Capitol Complex
Carson City, 89710
800-638-2328
Fax: 702-687-6779

New Hampshire

Ninth state; adopted the U.S. Constitution on June 21, 1788

Nickname: The Granite State; The Mother of Rivers; Switzerland of America
State motto: Live Free or Die
State amphibian: Spotted newt (*Notophthalmus viridescens*)
State animal: White-tailed deer (*Odocoileus virginianus*)
State bird: Purple finch (*Carpodacus purpureus*)
State flower: Purple lilac (*Syringa vulgaris*); **wildflower:** Pink lady's slipper (*Cypripedium acaule*)
State gem: Smoky quartz
State insect: Ladybug (*Hippodamia convergens*)
State mineral: Beryl
State rock: Granite
State song: "Old New Hampshire"; "New Hampshire, My New Hampshire"
State tree: White birch (*Betula pendula*)

SOURCES:
AmerBkDays-1978, p. 578
AnnivHol-1983, p. 82
Chases-1996, p. 265

STATE OFFICES:
Office of the Governor
107 N. Main, Rm. 208
Concord, 03301
603-271-2121
Fax: 603-271-2130

Secretary of State
State House, Rm. 204
Concord, 03301
603-271-3242

State Library
20 Park St.

Concord, 03301
603-271-2392
Fax: 603-271-2205

Tourism and Travel
P.O. Box 1856
Concord, 03302
800-386-4664
Fax: 603-271-2629

New Jersey

Third state; adopted the U.S. Constitution on December 18, 1787

Nickname: The Garden State; Clam State
State motto: Liberty and Prosperity
State animal: Horse
State bird: Eastern goldfinch (*Carduelis tristis*)
State dinosaur: Hadrosaurus foulki
State fish: Brook trout (*Salvelinus fontinalis*)
State flower: Purple violet (*Viola sororia*)
State insect: Honeybee (*Apis mellifera*)
State memorial tree: Dogwood (*Cornus florida*)
State tree: Red oak (*Quercus rubra*)

SOURCES:
AmerBkDays-1978, p. 1116
AnnivHol-1983, p. 162
Chases-1996, p. 484

STATE OFFICES:
Office of the Governor
State House
CN 001
Trenton, 08625
609-292-6000
Fax: 609-292-3454

Secretary of State
State Capitol Bldg.
CN 300
Trenton, 08625
609-984-1900
Fax: 609-292-7665

State Library
185 W. State
CN 520
Trenton, 08625
609-292-6200
Fax: 609-777-4099

Tourism and Travel
20 W. State
Trenton, 08625
800-JERSEY-7
Fax: 609-633-7418

New Mexico

Forty-seventh state; admitted on January 6, 1912

New Mexico does not regularly observe the anniversary of its statehood, but in 1972, the 60th anniversary of its admission to the U.S., a commemoration was held in Santa Fe. There was a reception at the Palace of Governors, where members of the Sociedad Folklórica dressed in costumes of the 1910s.

Nickname: Land of Enchantment; Cactus State; Spanish State
State motto: *Crescit Eundo* (Latin 'It Grows as It Goes')

State animal: Black bear (*Ursus americanus*)
State ballad: "Land of Enchantment—New Mexico"
State bird: Chaparral bird or roadrunner (*Geococcyx californianus*)
State cookie: Biscochito
State fish: Cutthroat trout (*Salmo clerki*)
State flower: Yucca flower
State fossil: Coelophysis dinosaur
State gem: Turquoise
State grass: Blue grama (*Bouteloua gracilis*)
State insect: Tarantula hawk wasp (*Pepsis formosa*)
State poem: "A Nuevo Mexico"
State song: "O, Fair New Mexico"
State tree: Piñon or nut pine (*Pinus edulis*)
State vegetables: Chile (*Capsicum annum*) and *frijol* or pinto bean (*Phaseolus vulgaris*)

SOURCES:
AmerBkDays-1978, p. 40
AnnivHol-1983, p. 5
Chases-1996, p. 59

STATE OFFICES:
Office of the Governor
State Capitol
Santa Fe, 87503
505-827-3000
Fax: 505-827-3026

Secretary of State
State Capitol, Rm. 420
Santa Fe, 87503
505-827-3601
Fax: 505-827-3634

State Library
325 Don Gaspar Ave.
Santa Fe, 87503
505-827-3800
Fax: 505-827-3888

Tourism and Travel
491 Old Santa Fe Trail
Santa Fe, 87503
800-545-2040
Fax: 505-827-7402

New York

Eleventh state; adopted the U.S. Constitution on July 26, 1788

Nicknames: The Empire State; Excelsior State; Knickerbocker State
State motto: *Excelsior* (Latin 'Ever upward')
State animal: Beaver (*Castor canadensis*)
State beverage: Milk
State bird: Bluebird (*Sialia sialis*)
State fish: Brook or speckled trout (*Salvelinus fontinalis*)
State flower: Rose
State fossil: Prehistoric crab (*Eurypterus remipes*)
State fruit: Apple (*Malus sylvestris*)
State gem: Garnet
State insect: Ladybug (*Hippodamia convergens*)
State muffin: Apple muffin
State shell: Bay scallops (*Agropecten irradians*)
State tree: Sugar maple (*Acer saccharum*)

SOURCES:
AmerBkDays-1978, p. 696
AnnivHol-1983, p. 97

493

Chases-1996, p. 311

STATE OFFICES:
Office of the Governor
State Capitol
Executive Chambers
Albany, 12224
518-474-8390

Secretary of State
162 Washington Ave.
Albany, 12231
518-474-0050
Fax: 518-474-4765

State Library
Cultural Education Center, 7th Floor
Albany, 12230
518-474-5355
Fax: 518-474-2718

Tourism and Travel
1 Commerce Plaza
Albany, 12245
800-CALL-NYS
Fax: 518-486-6416

North Carolina

Twelfth state; adopted the U.S. Constitution on November 21, 1789 (joined the Confederacy on May 20, 1861, and was readmitted to the Union on June 25, 1868)

Nickname: The Tarheel State; Old North State; Turpentine State
State motto: *Esse quam videri* (Latin 'To be rather than to seem')
State bird: Cardinal (*Cardinalis cardinalis*)
State colors: Red and blue
State fish: Channel bass (*Sciaenops ocellatus*)
State flower: Dogwood blossom (*Cornus florida*)
State insect: Honeybee (*Apis mellifera*)
State mammal: Gray squirrel (*Sciurus carolinensis*)
State mineral: Emerald
State reptile: Eastern box turtle
State rock: Granite
State shell: Scotch bonnet
State song: "The Old North State"
State stone: Emerald
State tartan: Carolina tartan
State toast: "A Toast" (to North Carolina)
State tree: Pine (*Pinus palustris*)

SOURCES:
AmerBkDays-1978, p. 1038
AnnivHol-1983, p. 149

STATE OFFICES:
Office of the Governor
116 W. Jones St.
Raleigh, 27603
919-733-5811
Fax: 919-733-2120

Secretary of State
300 N. Salisbury St.
Raleigh, 27603
919-733-4161
Fax: 919-733-5172

State Library
109 E. Jones St.

Raleigh, 27601
919-733-2570
Fax: 919-733-8748

Tourism and Travel
430 N. Salisbury St.
Raleigh, 27603
800-847-4862
Fax: 919-733-8582

North Dakota

Thirty-ninth state; admitted on November 2, 1889

Nicknames: Flickertail State; Sioux State; Land of the Dakotas; Peace Garden State
State motto: Liberty and Union, Now and Forever, One and Inseparable
State art gallery: University of North Dakota Art Gallery on the Grand Forks campus
State beverage: Milk
State bird: Western meadowlark (*Sturnella neglecta*)
State fish: Northern pike (*Esox lucius*)
State flower: Wild prairie rose (*Rosa blanda* or *R. arkansana*)
State fossil: Teredo petrified wood
State grass: Western wheatgrass (*Agropyron smithii*)
State language: English
State march: "Spirit of the Land"
State railroad museum: Mandan Railroad Museum
State song: "North Dakota Hymn"
State tree: American elm (*Ulmus americana*)

SOURCES:
AmerBkDays-1978, p. 984
AnnivHol-1983, p. 141
Chases-1996, p. 439

STATE OFFICES:
Office of the Governor
600 E. Boulevard
Bismarck, 58505
701-328-2200
Fax: 701-328-2205

Secretary of State
600 E. Boulevard
Bismarck, 58505
701-328-2900
Fax: 701-328-2992

State Library
604 E. Boulevard
Bismarck, 58505
800-472-2104
Fax: 701-328-2040

Tourism and Travel
604 E. Blvd. Ave.
Bismarck, 58505
800-HELLO-ND
Fax: 701-328-4878

Ohio

Seventeenth state; admitted on March 1, 1803

Nicknames: Buckeye State; Mother of Presidents; Gateway State
State motto: With God All Things Are Possible
State animal: White-tailed deer (*Odocoileus virginianus*)

State beverage: Tomato juice
State bird: Cardinal (*Cardinalis cardinalis*)
State flower: Scarlet carnation (*Dianthus caryophyllus*);
  wildflower: Large white trillium (*Trillium grandiflorum*)
State fossil: Trilobite
State gemstone: Ohio flint
State insect: Ladybird beetle (ladybug; *Hippodamia convergens*)
State invertebrate fossil: Isotelus
State song: "Beautiful Ohio"
State rock song: "Hang on Sloopy"
State tree: Buckeye (*Aesculus glabra*)

SOURCES:
AmerBkDays-1978, pp. 194, 225
AnnivHol-1983, p. 31
Chases-1996, p. 118

STATE OFFICES:
Office of the Governor
77 S. High St., 30th Floor
Columbus, 43215
614-644-0813
Fax: 614-644-9354

Secretary of State
30 E. Broad St., 14th Floor
Columbus, 43266
614-466-4980
Fax: 614-466-2892

State Library
65 S. Front St.
Columbus, 43215
614-644-7061
Fax: 614-466-3584
WWW: http://winslo.ohio.gov

Tourism and Travel
77 S. High St., 29th Floor
P.O. Box 1001
Columbus, 43266
800-282-5393
Fax: 614-466-6744

Oklahoma

Forty-sixth state; admitted on November 16, 1907

Since 1921, November 16 has been designated Oklahoma Statehood Day. It has also been Oklahoma State Flag Day since 1968. In 1957, in honor of the 50th anniversary of statehood, the state legislature decreed the week of November 11–16 to be Oklahoma Week. And, in 1965, the lawmakers mandated public schools to conduct programs on the state's history and achievements on November 16.

Annual observance of the day began in 1921 under the sponsorship of the Oklahoma Memorial Association, which continues to hold a dinner at the state capital at which notable Oklahomans are inducted into the Oklahoma Hall of Fame. Oklahoma Statehood Day is also observed annually with a ceremony at the Washington Cathedral in the nation's capital.

See also OKLAHOMA DAY

Nicknames: The Sooner State; The Boomer State
State motto: *Labor omnia vincit* (Latin 'Labor conquers all things')
State animal: American buffalo (*Bison bison*)

State bird: Scissor-tailed flycatcher (*Muscivora forficatus*)
State colors: Green and white
State fish: White (sand) bass (*Morone chrysops*)
State floral emblem: Mistletoe (*Phoradendron serotinum*)
State grass: Indian grass (*Sorghastrum nutans*)
State poem: "Howdy Folks"
State reptile: Collared lizard (mountain boomer; *Crotaphytus collaris*)
State song: "Oklahoma!"
State stone: Barite rose (rose rock)
State tree: Redbud (*Cercis canadensis*)

SOURCES:
AmerBkDays-1978, p. 1025
AnnivHol-1983, p. 148
Chases-1996, p. 451

CONTACT:
Oklahoma Heritage Association
201 N.W. 14th St.
Oklahoma City, OK 73103
405-235-2714; fax: 405-235-4458

STATE OFFICES:
Office of the Governor
State Capitol, Rm. 212
Oklahoma City, 73105
405-521-2342
Fax: 405-521-3353

Secretary of State
101 State Capitol
Oklahoma City, 73105
405-521-3911
Fax: 405-521-3771

State Library
200 N.E. 18th St.
Oklahoma City, 73105
405-521-2502
Fax: 405-525-7804

Tourism and Travel
Will Rogers Bldg.
2401 N. Lincoln Blvd., Ste. 500
Oklahoma City, 73105
800-652-6552
Fax: 405-521-4883

Oregon

Thirty-third state; admitted on February 14, 1859

While Admission Day is often commemorated by programs in schools, it is not a legal holiday in Oregon.

Nicknames: Beaver State; Pacific Wonderland; Webfoot State
State motto: *Alis volat propriis* (Latin 'She flies with her own wings'; motto since 1987); The Union (motto from 1859 to 1987)
State animal: Beaver (*Castor canadensis*)
State bird: Western meadowlark (*Sturnella neglecta*)
State colors: Navy blue and gold
State dance: Square dance
State fish: Chinook salmon (*Oncorhynchus tshawytscha*)
State flower: Oregon grape (*Berberis aquifolium*)
State gemstone: Oregon sunstone
State insect: Swallowtail butterfly (*Papilio oregonius*)
State nut: Hazelnut (*Corylus avellana*)
State rock: Thunderegg (geode)

State song: "Oregon, My Oregon"
State tree: Douglas fir (*Pseudotsuga menziesii*)

SOURCES:
AmerBkDays-1978, p. 182
AnnivHol-1983, p. 24
Chases-1996, p. 97

STATE OFFICES:
Office of the Governor
State Capitol, Rm. 254
Salem, 97310
503-378-3111
Fax: 503-378-4863

Secretary of State
State Capitol, Rm. 136
Salem, 97310
503-986-1500
Fax: 503-373-7414

State Library
250 Winter St., N.E.
State Library Bldg.
Salem, 97310
503-378-4243
Fax: 503-588-7119

Tourism and Travel
775 Summer St. N.E.
Salem, 97310
800-547-7842
Fax: 503-986-0001

Pennsylvania

Second state; adopted the U.S. Constitution on December 12, 1787

Nicknames: Keystone State; Quaker State
State motto: Virtue, Liberty, and Independence
State animal: White-tailed deer (*Odocoileus virginianus*)
State beverage: Milk
State bird: Ruffed grouse (*Bonasa umbellus*)
State dog: Great Dane
State fish: Brook trout (*Salvelinus fontinalis*)
State flagship: U.S. Brig *Niagara*
State flower: Mountain laurel (*Kalmia latifolia*)
State fossil: Phacops rana
State insect: Firefly (*Photuris pennsylvanica*)
State plant: Penngift crownvetch (*Coronilla varia*)
State song: "Pennsylvania"
State tree: Eastern hemlock (*Tsuga canadensis*)

SOURCES:
AmerBkDays-1978, p. 1098
AnnivHol-1983, p. 159
Chases-1996, p. 479

STATE OFFICES:
Office of the Governor
Main Capitol Bldg., Rm. 225
Harrisburg, 17120
717-787-2500
Fax: 717-783-1396

Secretary of Commonwealth
North Office Bldg., Rm. 302
Harrisburg, 17120
717-787-7630
Fax: 717-787-1734

State Library
Walnut and Commonwealth Ave.

P.O. Box 1601
Harrisburg, 17105
717-787-2646
Fax: 717-783-2070

Tourism and Travel
453 Forum Bldg.
Harrisburg, 17120
800-VISIT-PA
Fax: 717-234-4560

Rhode Island

Thirteenth state; adopted the U.S. Constitution on May 29, 1790

Nicknames: The Ocean State; Little Rhody; Plantation State
State motto: Hope
State American folk art symbol: Charles I. D. Looff Carousel
State bird: Rhode Island red chicken
State flower: Violet (*Viola palmata*)
State fruit: Rhode Island greening apple
State mineral: Bowenite
State rock: Cumberlandite
State shell: Quahaug (*Mercenaria mercenaria*)
State song: "Rhode Island"
State tree: Red maple (*Acer rubrum*)

SOURCES:
AmerBkDays-1978, p. 498
AnnivHol-1983, p. 72
Chases-1996, p. 234

STATE OFFICES:
Office of the Governor
State House
Providence, 02903
401-277-2080
Fax: 401-272-5729

Secretary of State
State House, Rm. 218
Providence, 02903
401-277-2357
Fax: 401-277-1356

State Library
300 Richmond St.
Providence, 02903
401-277-2726
Fax: 401-831-1131

Tourism and Travel
7 Jackson Walkway
Providence, 02903
800-556-2484
Fax: 401-277-2102

South Carolina

Eighth state; adopted the U.S. Constitution on May 23, 1788 (seceded from the Union in December 1860, and was readmitted on June 25, 1868)

Nickname: The Palmetto State; The Rice State; The Swamp State; The Iodine State
State motto: *Animis opibusque parati* (Latin 'Prepared in mind and resources'); *Dum spiro spero* (Latin 'While I breathe, I hope')
State animal: White-tailed deer (*Odocoileus virginianus*)

State beverage: Milk
State bird: Carolina wren (*Thryothorus ludovicianus*)
State dance: The shag
State dog: Boykin spaniel
State fish: Striped bass (*Morone saxatilis*)
State flower: Yellow jessamine (*Gelsemium sempervirens*)
State fruit: Peach
State gem: Amethyst
State insect: Carolina mantid, or praying mantis (*Mantis religiosa*)
State language: English
State reptile: Loggerhead turtle (*Caretta caretta*)
State shell: Lettered olive (*Oliva sayana*)
State song: "Carolina"; "South Carolina on My Mind"
State stone: Blue granite
State tree: Palmetto
State wild game bird: Wild turkey (*Meleagris gallopavo*)

SOURCES:
AmerBkDays-1978, p. 478
AnnivHol-1983, p. 70
Chases-1996, p. 224

STATE OFFICES:
Office of the Governor
P.O. Box 11369
Columbia, 29211
803-734-9818
Fax: 803-734-1598

Secretary of State
P.O. Box 11350
Columbia, 29211
803-734-2155
Fax: 803-734-2164

State Library
P.O. Box 11469
Columbia, 29211
803-734-8666
Fax: 803-734-8676

Tourism and Travel
1205 Pendleton, Ste. 106
Columbia, 29201
803-734-0122
Fax: 803-734-0133

South Dakota

Fortieth state; admitted on November 2, 1889

Nicknames: Coyote State; Sunshine State; Blizzard State; Artesian State
State motto: Under God the People Rule
State animal: Coyote (*Canis latrans*)
State bird: Ring-necked pheasant (*Phasianus colchicus*)
State drink: Milk
State fish: Walleye (*Stizostedion vitreum*)
State flower: American pasque (*Pulsatilla hisutissima*)
State fossil: Triceratops
State gem: Fairburn agate
State grass: Western wheatgrass (*Agropyron smithii*)
State insect: Honeybee (*Apis mellifera*)
State jewelry: Black Hills gold
State mineral: Rose quartz
State musical instrument: Fiddle
State soil: Houdek soil
State song: "Hail, South Dakota"

State tree: Black Hills spruce (*Picea glauca densata*)

SOURCES:
AmerBkDays-1978, p. 989
AnnivHol-1983, p. 141
Chases-1996, p. 439

STATE OFFICES:
Office of the Governor
500 E. Capitol Ave.
Pierre, 57501
605-773-3212
Fax: 605-773-4711

Secretary of State
500 E. Capitol, Ste. 204
Pierre, 57501
605-773-3537
Fax: 605-773-6580

State Library
800 Governors Dr.
Pierre, 57501
605-773-3131
Fax: 605-773-4950

Tourism and Travel
711 E. Wells Ave.
Pierre, 57501
800-952-3625
Fax: 605-773-3256

Tennessee

Sixteenth state; admitted on June 1, 1796 (seceded on June 8, 1861, and was readmitted on July 24, 1866)

In 1929, the state legislature designated June 1 as Statehood Day in Tennessee.

Nicknames: The Volunteer State; The Big Bend State; The Mother of Southwestern Statesmen
State motto: Agriculture and Commerce
State agricultural insect: Honeybee (*Apis mellifera*)
State animal: Raccoon (*Procyon lotor*)
State bird: Mockingbird (*Mimus polyglottos*)
State commercial fish: Channel catfish
State fine art: Porcelain painting
State flower: cultivated: Iris; **wild:** Passion flower (*Passiflora incarnata*)
State folk dance: Square dance
State game bird: Bobwhite quail (*Colinus virginianus*)
State gem: Tennessee pearl
State insects: Ladybug (*Hippodamia convergens*); firefly (*Photuris pennsylvanica*)
State language: English
State poem: "Oh Tennessee, My Tennessee"
State public school song: "My Tennessee"
State railroad museum: Tennessee Valley Railroad Museum in Hamilton County
State rocks: Limestone; agate
State slogan: Tennessee—America at Its Best
State songs: "When It's Iris Time in Tennessee"; "The Tennessee Waltz"; "My Homeland, Tennessee"; "My Tennessee"; "Rocky Top"
State sport fish: Largemouth bass (*Micropterus salmoides*)
State tree: Tulip poplar (*Liriodendron tulipfera*)

SOURCES:
AmerBkDays-1978, p. 516

AnnivHol-1983, p. 74
Chases-1996, p. 240
DictDays-1988, p. 113

STATE OFFICES:
Office of the Governor
State Capitol
Nashville, 37243
615-741-2001
Fax: 615-741-1416

Secretary of State
State Capitol, 1st Floor
Nashville, 37243
615-741-2817
Fax: 615-741-5962

State Library
403 Seventh Ave. N.
Nashville, 37243
615-741-2754
Fax: 615-741-6471

Tourism and Travel
P.O. Box 23170
Nashville, 37202
615-741-2158
Fax: 615-741-7225

Texas

Twenty-eighth state; admitted on December 29, 1845 (seceded from the Union on February 1, 1861, and was readmitted on March 30, 1870)

Nickname: The Lone Star State; The Beef State; The Banner State
State motto: Friendship
State bird: Mockingbird (*Mimus polyglottos*)
State flower: Bluebonnet (*Lupinus subcarnosus*)
State flower song: "Bluebonnets"
State gem: Topaz
State plays: *The Lone Star; Texas; Beyond the Sundown; Fandangle*
State songs: "Texas, Our Texas"; "The Eyes of Texas"
State stone: Palmwood
State tree: Pecan (*Carya illinoensis*)

SOURCES:
AmerBkDays-1978, p. 1163
AnnivHol-1983, p. 165
Chases-1996, p. 492

STATE OFFICES:
Office of the Governor
State Capitol
P.O. Box 12428
Austin, 78711
512-463-2000
Fax: 512-463-1849

Secretary of State
P.O. Box 12697
Austin, 78711
512-463-5770
Fax: 512-475-2761

State Library
P.O. Box 12927
Austin, 78711
512-463-5460
Fax: 512-463-5436

Tourism and Travel

1700 N. Congress Ave., Ste. 200
Austin, 78711
800-888-8839
Fax: 512-936-0089

Utah

Forty-fifth state; admitted on January 4, 1896

Nickname: Beehive State; Salt Lake State
State motto: Industry
State animal: Elk (*Cervus canadensis*)
State bird: California gull (*Larus californius*)
State emblem: Beehive
State fish: Rainbow trout (*Salmo gairdnerii*)
State flower: Sego lily (*Calochortus nuttallii*)
State fossil: Allosaurus
State gem: Topaz
State grass: Indian ricegrass (*Oryzopsis hymenoides*)
State insect: Honeybee (*Apis mellifera*)
State railroad museum: Ogden Union Station
State rock: Coal
State song: "Utah, We Love Thee"
State tree: Blue spruce (*Picea pungens*)

SOURCES:
AmerBkDays-1978, p. 27
AnnivHol-1983, p. 4
Chases-1996, p. 57

STATE OFFICES:
Office of the Governor
210 State Capitol
Salt Lake City, 84114
801-538-1000
Fax: 801-538-1528

Lieutenant Governor
210 State Capitol
Salt Lake City, 84114
801-538-1040
Fax: 801-538-1557

State Library
2150 S. 300 W., Ste. 16
Salt Lake City, 84115
801-466-5888
Fax: 801-533-4657

Tourism and Travel
Council House
Capitol Hill
Salt Lake City, 84114
800-200-1160
Fax: 801-538-1000

Vermont

Fourteenth state; admitted on March 4, 1791

Town meetings held all over the state on the first Tuesday in March serve in part to commemorate Vermont's Admission Day (*see* Town Meeting Day).

Nickname: The Green Mountain State
State motto: Freedom and Unity
State animal: Morgan horse
State beverage: Milk
State bird: Hermit thrush (*Hylocichla guttata*)
State butterfly: Monarch butterfly (*Danaus plexippus*)

State fish: cold water: Brook trout (*Salvelinus fontinalis*);
warm water: Walleye pike (*Stizostedion vitreum vitreum*)
State flower: Red clover (*Trifolium pratense*)
State gem: Grossular garnet
State insect: Honeybee (*Apis mellifera*)
State mineral: Talc
State rocks: Marble, granite, and slate
State soil: Tunbridge soil series
State song: "Hail, Vermont!"
State tree: Sugar maple (*Acer saccharum*)

SOURCES:
AmerBkDays-1978, p. 233
AnnivHol-1983, p. 33
Chases-1996, p. 123

STATE OFFICES:
Office of the Governor
109 State St.
Montpelier, 05609
802-828-3333
Fax: 802-828-3339

Secretary of State
109 State St.
Montpelier, 05609
802-828-2363
Fax: 802-828-2496

State Library
109 State St.
Montpelier, 05609
802-828-3265
Fax: 802-828-2199

Tourism and Travel
134 State St.
Montpelier, 05609
800-VERMONT
Fax: 802-828-3233

Virginia

Tenth state; adopted the U.S. Constitution on June 25, 1788 (seceded from the Union in April 1861, and was readmitted on January 26, 1870)

Nicknames: Old Dominion; Mother of Presidents; Mother of Statesmen
State motto: *Sic semper tyrannis* (Latin 'Thus ever to tyrants')
State beverage: Milk
State bird: Cardinal (*Cardinalis cardinalis*)
State boat: *Chespeake Bay Deadrise*
State dog: American foxhound
State flower: American dogwood (*Cornus florida*)
State folk dance: Square dance
State folklore center: Blue Ridge Institute in Ferrum
State insect: Tiger swallowtail butterfly (*Papilio glaucus Linne*)
State shell: Oyster shell (*Crassostraea virginica*)
State song: "Carry Me Back to Old Virginia"
State tree: American dogwood (*Cornus florida*)

SOURCES:
AmerBkDays-1978, p. 595
AnnivHol-1983, p. 84
Chases-1996, p. 270

STATE OFFICES:
Office of the Governor
Capitol Bldg., 3rd Floor
Richmond, 23219
804-786-2211
Fax: 804-371-6351

Secretary of Commonwealth
Old Finance Bldg.
Capitol Square
Richmond, 23219
804-786-2441
Fax: 804-371-0017

State Library
11th St. and Capitol Square
Richmond, 23219
804-786-2332
Fax: 804-786-5855

Tourism and Travel
901 E. Byrd St.
Richmond, 23219
804-786-4484
Fax: 804-786-1919

Washington

Forty-second state; admitted on November 11, 1889

Admission Day is observed in Washington by closing public schools (however, schools are expected to hold special patriotic and historic programs on the preceding Friday). Former significant anniversaries of statehood—the 25th, 50th, and 75th—were commemorated with speeches (by President Franklin D. Roosevelt in 1939) and ceremonies.

Nickname: Evergreen State; Chinook State
State motto: *Alki* (unspecified American Indian language 'By and By')
State bird: Willow goldfinch (*Spinus tristis salicamans*)
State colors: Green and gold
State dance: Square dance
State fish: Steelhead trout (*Salmo gairdnerii*)
State flower: Coast or pink rhododendron (*Rhododendron macrophyllum*)
State folk song: "Roll on, Columbia, Roll on"
State fruit: Apple (*Malus sylvestris*)
State gem: Petrified wood
State grass: Bluebunch wheatgrass (*Agropyron spicatum*)
State ship: Container ship *President Washington*
State song: "Washington, My Home"
State tartan: A set made up of a green background with blue, white, yellow, red, and black stripes
State tree: Western hemlock (*Tsuga heterophylla*)

SOURCES:
AmerBkDays-1978, p. 1015
AnnivHol-1983, p. 145
Chases-1996, p. 448

STATE OFFICES:
Office of the Governor
Legislative Bldg.
Olympia, 98504
360-753-6780
Fax: 360-753-4110

Secretary of State
P.O. Box 40220
Olympia, 98504

360-753-7121
Fax: 360-586-5629

State Library
P.O. Box 42464
Olympia, 98504
360-753-2915
Fax: 360-586-7575

Tourism and Travel
P.O. Box 42500
Olympia, 98504
800-544-1800
Fax: 360-753-4470

West Virginia

Thirty-fifth state; admitted on June 20, 1863

The centennial celebration took place throughout the state during the year of 1963 with parades, pageants, sporting events, historical exhibits and reenactments, various arts contests, musical events, fireworks, and, on June 20 at the capitol in Charleston, a speech by President John F. Kennedy.

See also WEST VIRGINIA DAY

Nicknames: The Mountain State; The Panhandle State
State motto: *Montani Semper Liberi* (Latin 'Mountaineers are always free')
State animal: Black bear (*Ursus (Euarctos) americanus*)
State bird: Cardinal (*Cardinalis cardinalis*)
State fish: Brook trout (*Salvelinus fontinalis*)
State flower: Big laurel (*Rhododendron maximum*)
State fruit: Apple (*Malus sylvestris*)
State songs: "The West Virginia Hills"; "West Virginia, My Home Sweet Home"; "This Is My West Virginia"
State tree: Sugar maple (*Acer saccharum*)

SOURCES:
AmerBkDays-1978, p. 570
AnnivHol-1983, p. 82
Chases-1996, p. 264
DictDays-1988, p. 130

STATE OFFICES:
Office of the Governor
State Capitol
1900 Kanawha Blvd. E.
Charleston, 25305
304-558-2000
Fax: 304-342-7025

Secretary of State
State Capitol
1900 Kanawha Blvd. E.
Bldg. 1, Ste. 157-K
Charleston, 25305
304-558-6000
Fax: 304-558-0900

State Library
Cultural Center
1900 Kanawha Blvd. E.
Charleston, 25305
304-558-2041
Fax: 304-558-2044

Tourism and Travel
2101 Washington St. E.
Charleston, 25305
800-CALL-WVA
Fax: 304-558-0108

Wisconsin

Thirtieth state; admitted on May 29, 1848

Nicknames: Badger State; America's Dairyland; Copper State
State motto: Forward
State animal: Badger (*Taxidea taxus*); **wildlife animal:** White-tailed deer (*Odocoileus virginianus*); **domestic animal:** Dairy cow (*Bos taurus*)
State beverage: Milk
State bird: Robin (*Turdus migratorius*)
State dog: American water spaniel
State fish: Muskellunge (muskie; *Esox masquinongy*)
State flower: Wood violet (*Viola papilionacea*)
State fossil: Trilobite
State grain: Corn (*Zea mays*)
State insect: Honeybee (*Apis mellifera*)
State mineral: Galena
State rock: Red granite
State soil: Antigo silt loam
State song: "On, Wisconsin!"
State symbol of peace: Mourning dove (*Zenaidura macroura*)
State tree: Sugar maple (*Acer saccharum*)

SOURCES:
AmerBkDays-1978, p. 500
AnnivHol-1983, p. 72
Chases-1996, p. 234

STATE OFFICES:
Office of the Governor
P.O. Box 7863
Madison, 53707
608-266-1212
Fax: 608-267-8983

Secretary of State
P.O. Box 7848
Madison, 53707
608-266-8888
Fax: 608-267-6813

State Library
P.O. Box 7841
Madison, 53707
608-266-2205
Fax: 608-267-1052

Tourism and Travel
123 W. Washington Ave., 6th Floor
P.O. Box 7970
Madison, 53707
800-432-8747
Fax: 608-266-3403

Wyoming

Forty-fourth state; admitted on July 10, 1890

Nicknames: Equality State; Cowboy State; Big Wyoming
State motto: Equal Rights
State bird: Meadowlark (*Sturnella neglecta*)
State fish: Cutthroat trout (*Salmo clerki*)
State flower: Indian paintbrush (*Castilleja linariaefolia*)
State fossil: Knightia
State gemstone: Jade (nephrite)
State mammal: Bison (*Bison bison*)
State song: "Wyoming"

State tree: Plains cottonwood (*Populus sargentii*)

SOURCES:
AmerBkDays-1978, p. 650
AnnivHol-1983, p. 91
Chases-1996, p. 291

STATE OFFICES:
Office of the Governor
State Capitol
Cheyenne, 82002
307-777-7434
Fax: 307-632-3909

Secretary of State
State Capitol
Cheyenne, 82002
307-777-7378
Fax: 307-777-6217

State Library
2301 Capitol Ave.
Cheyenne, 82002
307-777-7281
Fax: 307-777-6289

Tourism and Travel
I-25 and College Dr.
Cheyenne, 82002
800-225-5996
Fax: 307-777-6940

American Samoa

American Samoa has been a U.S. territory since 1899; its inhabitants are considered U.S. nationals.

Motto: *Samoa—Muamua le Atua* (Samoan 'Samoa—Let God Be First')
Flower: Paogo (Ula-fala)
Plant: Kava
Song: "Amerika Samoa"
Tree: Paogo or pandanus

GOVERNMENT OFFICES:
Office of the Governor
Pago Pago, 96799
011-684-633-4116

Samoan Affairs Department
Pago Pago, 96799
011-684-633-5201

Office of Library Services
P.O. Box 1329
Pago Pago, 96799
011-684-633-1181

Tourism and Travel
P.O. Box 1147
Pago Pago, 96799
011-684-633-1091

Guam

Guam has been a territory of the U.S. since 1898, but has been allowed autonomy in local affairs since 1950; native inhabitants are citizens of the U.S. but cannot vote in U.S. elections.

Nicknames: Where America's Day Begins; America's Paradise in the Pacific
Bird: Totot (also known as the Mariana fruit dove or love bird; *Ptilinopus roseicapilla*)

Flower: Puti tai nobio (bougainvillea)
Hymn: "Guam Hymn"
Languages: Chamorro; English
March: "Guam March"
Tree: Ifit (*Intsia bijuga*)

GOVERNMENT OFFICES:
Office of the Governor
Executive Chamber
P.O. Box 2950
Agana, 96910
011-671-472-8931

Lieutenant Governor
P.O. Box 2950
Agana, 96910
011-671-472-8931

Memorial Library
254 Martyr St.
Agana, 96910
011-671-477-6913

Tourism and Travel
P.O. Box 3520
Tamuning, 96911
011-671-646-5279

Puerto Rico

Puerto Rico became a territory of the U.S. in 1917, and, on July 25, 1952, a commonwealth with autonomous local governmental units.

See PUERTO RICO CONSTITUTION DAY

Nickname: Island of Enchantment
Motto: *Joannes est nomen ejus* ('John Is His Name')
Animal: Coqui (*Francolinus coqui*)
Bird: Reinita
Languages: English; Spanish
Mother's Day flower: Honeysuckle
Song: "La Borinquena"
Tree: Ceiba (*Ceiba pentandra*)

GOVERNMENT OFFICES:
Office of the Governor
La Fortaleza
P.O. Box 82
San Juan, 00901
809-725-1666

State Department
P.O. Box 3271
San Juan, 00902
809-723-4343

University of Puerto Rico Library System
Rio Piedras Campus
P.O. Box 23302
San Juan, 00931
809-764-0000

Puerto Rico Tourism Company
575 Fifth Ave.
New York, NY 10017
212-599-6262

U.S. Virgin Islands

The U.S. Virgin Islands were purchased by the U.S. on March 31, 1917; in 1927 native inhabitants were made U.S. citizens.

Nickname: The American Paradise
Motto: United in Pride and Hope
Bird: Yellow breast (bananaquit; *Coereba flaveola*)
Flower: Yellow elder or yellow cedar (*Tecoma stans*)
Song: "Virgin Islands March"

GOVERNMENT OFFICES:

Office of the Governor
Kogens Glade
St. Thomas, 00802
809-774-0001

Lieutenant Governor

Kogens Glade
St. Thomas, 00802
809-774-2991

Division of Libraries, Archives and Museums
23 Dronningens Gade
St. Thomas, 00802
809-774-3407

Commission of Tourism Office
P.O. Box 6400
Charlotte-Amalie, St. Thomas, 00801
800-USVINFO

APPENDIX 2

United States Presidents

This section lists all U.S. presidents in the order in which they held office, their birth dates and places, spouses, death dates and places, burial sites, political parties, nicknames, career highlights, and notable landmarks commemorating them. It should be noted that some of these landmarks are private residences, and do not permit visitors. The diamond symbol (♦) indicates that an entry on a festival celebrating the president appears in the main text.

♦ George Washington

First president (1789-97)
Born Feb 22, 1732, Pope's Creek (now Wakefield), Westmoreland County, Va.
Married Martha Dandridge Custis, 1759
Died Dec 14, 1799, Mt. Vernon, Va.
Buried in family vault, Mt. Vernon, Va. 22121, 703-780-2000

Federalist. "Father of His Country." Fought in French and Indian War. Served in Continental Congress. Commander-in-Chief during Revolutionary War. Bill of Rights passed. Laid cornerstone of Capitol in Washington, D.C.

LANDMARKS:

Birth site: George Washington Birthplace National Monument, R.R. 1, Box 717, Pope's Creek (now Wakefield), VA 22443, 804-224-1732

Anderson House Museum, 2118 Massachusetts Ave., N.W., Washington, DC 20008, 202-785-2040

Brandywine Battlefield Park, Box 202, Chadds Ford, PA 19317, 610-459-3342

Deshler-Morris House, 5442 Germantown Ave., Philadelphia, PA 19144, 215-596-1748

Dey Mansion, 199 Totowa Rd., Wayne, NJ 07470, 201-696-1776

1815 Masonic Lodge, Princess Anne and Hanover Sts., Fredericksburg, VA 22404, 540-373-5885

Federal Hall National Memorial, 26 Wall St., New York, NY 10005, 212-825-6888

Gadsby's Tavern Museum, 134 N. Royal St., Alexandria, VA 22314, 703-838-4242

George Washington Masonic National Memorial, 101 Callahan Dr., Alexandria, VA 22301, 703-683-2007

Grist Mill Historical State Park, 5514 Mount Vernon Memorial Hwy., Alexandria, VA 22309, 703-780-3383

Mary Washington House, 1200 Charles St., Fredericksburg, VA 22401, 540-373-1569

Military Headquarters Museum, 140 Virginia Rd., North White Plains, NY 10601, 914-949-1236

Military Headquarters State Historic Site, 84 Liberty St., Newburgh, NY 12550, 914-562-1195

Military Office Museum, Braddock and Cork Sts., Winchester, VA 22601, 540-662-4412

Morristown National Historic Park, Washington Place, Morristown, NJ 07960, 201-539-2085

Mount Vernon, Mount Vernon, VA 22121, 703-780-2000

Museum of the Valley Forge Historical Society, Valley Forge National Historical Park, Box 122, Valley Forge, PA 19481, 610-783-0535

Rockingham State Historic Site, Route 518, Rocky Hill, NJ, 609-921-8835

Valley Forge National Historical Park, Box 953, Valley Forge, PA 19481, 610-783-1000

Wallace House, 38 Washington Place, Somerville, NJ 08878, 908-725-1015

Washington Monument, National Mall between 15th and 17th Sts., Washington, DC 20242, 202-485-9880

John Adams

Second president (1797-1801)
Born Oct 30, 1735, Braintree (now Quincy), Mass.
Married Abigail Smith, 1764
Died Jul 4, 1826, Quincy, Mass.
Buried at United First Parish Church (Church of the Presidents), 1306 Hancock St., Quincy, Mass. 02169, 617-773-1290 or 617-773-0062

Federalist. "Father of American Independence." Served in Continental Congress. Helped draft and signed Declaration of Independence. Secretary of War. Minister to Great Britain, Netherlands. Vice President. First occupant of

♦ Indicates that an entry on a festival celebrating the president appears in the main text

White House. Son was sixth president (*see* **John Quincy Adams**).

LANDMARKS:

Birth site: Adams National Historic Site, 135 Franklin St., Quincy, MA 02269, 617-773-1177

Peacefield-Adams Mansion, 135 Adams St., Quincy, MA 02269, 617-773-1177

♦ Thomas Jefferson

Third president (1801-09)
Born Apr 13, 1743, Shadwell, Charlottesville, Goochland County (now Albemarle County), Va.
Married Martha Wayles Skelton, 1772
Died Jul 4, 1826, Charlottesville, Va.
Buried at Monticello, Charlottesville, Va. 22902, 804-984-9800

Democratic-Republican. "Father of the Declaration of Independence." Served in Continental Congress. Drafted Declaration of Independence. Governor of Virginia. Minister to France. Secretary of State. Vice President. Louisiana Purchase completed.

LANDMARKS:

Birth site: Shadwell, Charlottesville, VA 22902

Jefferson Memorial, Washington, DC 20242, 202-619-7222 or 202-426-6841

Jefferson National Expansion Memorial (Gateway Arch), St. Louis, MO 63102, 314-425-4465

Monticello, Box 316, Charlottesville, VA 22902, 804-984-9800

Poplar Forest, Box 419, Forest, VA 24551, 804-525-1806

Tuckahoe Plantation, 12601 River Rd., Richmond, VA 23233, 804-784-5736

James Madison

Fourth president (1809-17)
Born Mar 16, 1751, Port Conway, Va.
Married Dolley Dandridge Payne Todd, 1794
Died Jun 28, 1836, Orange County, Va.
Buried at Montpelier, Orange County, Va. 22957, 703-672-2728

Democratic-Republican. "Father of the Constitution." Served in Continental Congress. Signed Constitution. U.S. Representative. Secretary of State. Participated in War of 1812. Forced to flee White House when British invaded Washington, D.C.

LANDMARKS:

Birth site (marker): Belle Grove, Port Conway, VA

James Madison Museum, 129 Caroline St., Orange, VA 22960, 703-672-1776

Montpelier, Box 67, Montpelier Station, VA 22957, 703-672-2728

The Octagon, 1799 New York Ave., N.W., Washington, DC 20006, 202-638-3105

James Monroe

Fifth president (1817-25)
Born Apr 28, 1758, Westmoreland County, Va.
Married Elizabeth Kortright, 1786
Died Jul 4, 1831, New York, N.Y.
Buried at Marble Cemetery, New York, N.Y.; removed 1858 to Hollywood Cemetery, Cherry and Albemarle Sts., Richmond, Va. 23224, 804-648-8501

Democratic-Republican. "Era of Good Feeling President." Fought in Revolutionary War. Served in Continental Congress. Governor of Virginia. U.S. Senator. Secretary of State. Secretary of War. First inauguration held outdoors. Author of the Monroe Doctrine.

LANDMARKS:

Birth site (marker): Monrovia, State Hwy. V.A. 205 between Oak Grove and Colonial Beach, VA

Ash Lawn-Highland residence, Route 6, Box 37, Charlottesville, VA 22902, 804-293-9539

James Monroe Museum and Memorial Library, 908 Charles St., Fredericksburg, VA 22401, 540-654-1043

Oak Hill residence, Aldie, Loudoun County, VA 22001 (private residence)

John Quincy Adams

Sixth president (1825-29)
Born Jul 11, 1767, Braintree (now Quincy), Mass.
Married Louisa Catherine Johnson, 1797
Died Feb 23, 1848, Washington, D.C.
Buried at United First Parish Church, 1306 Hancock St., Quincy, Mass. 02269, 617-773-0062

Democratic-Republican. "Old Man Eloquent." Minister to Great Britain, Netherlands, Russia. U.S. Senator. Secretary of State. U.S. Representative. Father was second president (*see* **John Adams**).

LANDMARKS:

Birth site: 141 Franklin St., Quincy, MA 02269, 617-773-1177

Peacefield-Adams Mansion, 135 Adams St., Quincy, MA 02269, 617-773-1177

♦ Andrew Jackson

Seventh president (1829-37)
Born Mar 15, 1767, Waxhaw, S.C.
Married Rachael Donelson Robards, 1791
Died Jun 8, 1845, Nashville, Tenn.
Buried at the Hermitage estate, 4580 Rachael's Lane, Hermitage, TN 37076, 615-889-2941

Democrat (Democratic-Republican). "Old Hickory." Governor of Florida. U.S. Representative and Senator. Fought against Indians and in War of 1812. First president born in a log cabin.

LANDMARKS:

Birth site (disputed): Andrew Jackson State Park and

♦ Indicates that an entry on a festival celebrating the president appears in the main text

Museum, 196 Andrew Jackson Park Rd., Lancaster, SC 29720, 803-285-3344

Birth site (disputed): Andrew Jackson Birthplace Marker, NC 25 (S. Main) at Rehobeth Rd., Waxhaw, NC 28173

McCamie Cabin site marker, Mecklenburg County, NC

Springfield Plantation, Route 1, Box 201, Fayette, MS 39069, 601-786-3802

Martin Van Buren

Eighth president (1837-41)
Born Dec 5, 1782, Kinderhook, N.Y.
Married Hannah Hoes, 1807
Died Jul 24, 1862, Kinderhook, N.Y.
Buried at Kinderhook Cemetery, Albany Ave., Kinderhook, N.Y.

Democrat (Democratic-Republican). "Sage of Kinderhook." U.S. Senator. Governor of New York. Secretary of State. Vice President. First president born a U.S. citizen.

LANDMARKS:

Birth site (marker): 46 Hudson St., Kinderhook, NY 12106

Lindenwald residence, 1013 Old Post Rd., P.O. Box 545, Kinderhook, NY 12106, 518-758-9689

William Henry Harrison

Ninth president (1841)
Born Feb 9, 1773, Berkeley, Charles City County, Va.
Married Anna Tuthill Symmes, 1795
Died Apr 4, 1841, Washington, D.C.
Buried at Harrison Tomb State Memorial, Loop Ave., North Bend, Ohio

Whig. "Old Tippecanoe." Fought against Indians and in War of 1812. U.S. Representative. U.S. Senator. Died in office, serving shortest term of a president. Grandson was twenty-third president (*see* **Benjamin Harrison**).

LANDMARKS:

Birth site: Berkeley Plantation, 12602 Harrison Landing Rd., Charles City, VA 23030, 804-829-6018

Grouseland, 3 West Scott St., Vincennes, IN 47591, 812-882-2096

John Tyler

Tenth president (1841-45)
Born Mar 29, 1790, Greenway, Charles City County, Va.
Married Letitia Christian, 1813; Julia Gardiner, 1844
Died Jan 18, 1862, Richmond, Va.
Buried at Hollywood Cemetery, 4125 Cherry, Richmond, Va. 23220, 804-648-8501

Whig. "Accidental president." U.S. Representative. Governor of Virginia. U.S. Senator. Succeeded presidency upon death of William Henry Harrison. Elected representative to Confederate Congress.

LANDMARKS:

Birth site: Greenway, Charles City County, VA (private residence)

Sherwood Forest Plantation, Box 8, Charles City, VA 23030, 804-829-5377

James Knox Polk

Eleventh president (1845-49)
Born Nov 2, 1795, near Pineville, Mecklenburg County, N.C.
Married Sarah Childress, 1824
Died Jun 15, 1849, Nashville, Tenn.
Buried at Polk Place, Nashville, Tenn.; removed 1893 to State Capitol Grounds, Nashville, Tenn. 37243, 615-741-1621

Democrat. "Napoleon of the Stump." U.S. Representative. Speaker of the House. Governor of Tennessee. First inauguration ceremony relayed by telegraph. Acquired much of western and southwestern U.S.

LANDMARKS:

Birth site: U.S. 521, Box 475, Pineville, NC 28134, 704-889-7145

Polk home, 301 W. Seventh St., Columbia, TN 38402, 615-388-2354

Zachary Taylor

Twelfth president (1849-50)
Born Nov 24, 1784, Montebello, Gordonsville, Va.
Married Margaret Mackall Smith, 1810
Died Jul 9, 1850, Washington, D.C.
Buried at Zachary Taylor National Cemetery, 4701 Brownsboro Rd., Louisville, Ky. 40207, 502-893-3852

Whig. "Old Rough and Ready." Fought against Indians and in War of 1812 and Mexican War. Son-in-law was Jefferson Davis. Died in office.

LANDMARKS:

Birth site (marker): Montebello, Gordonsville, VA

Springfield, 5608 Apache Rd., Louisville, KY 40207, 502-897-9990

Millard Fillmore

Thirteenth president (1850-53)
Born Jan 7, 1800, Summerhill, Cayuga County, N.Y.
Married Abigail Powers, 1826; Caroline Carmichael McIntosh, 1858
Died Mar 8, 1874, Buffalo, N.Y.
Buried at Forrest Lawn Cemetery, 1411 Delaware Ave., Buffalo, N.Y. 14209, 716-885-1600

Whig. "His Accidency." U.S. Representative. Succeeded presidency upon death of Zachary Taylor.

LANDMARKS:

Birth site (marker): Fillmore Rd., Summerhill, NY

♦ Indicates that an entry on a festival celebrating the president appears in the main text

Birth site (replica): Fillmore Glen State Park, Rd. 3, Box 26, Moravia, NY 13118, 315-497-0130

Childhood home (marker): Carver Rd., New Hope, NY

Millard Fillmore House Museum, 24 Shearer Ave., East Aurora, NY 14052, 716-652-8875

Franklin Pierce

Fourteenth president (1853-57)
Born Nov 23, 1804, Hillsborough (now Hillsboro), N.H.
Married Jane Means Appleton, 1834
Died Oct 8, 1869, Concord, N.H.
Buried at Old North Cemetery, North State St., Concord, N.H. 03301, 603-225-3911

Democrat. "Young Hickory of the Granite Hills." U.S. Representative. U.S. Senator. Fought in Mexican War.

LANDMARKS:

Birth site: Hillsboro, NH

Pierce Homestead, State Hwy. 31, Box 896, Hillsboro, NH 03244, 603-478-3165

Pierce House (marker), 52 South Main St., Concord, NH

Pierce Manse, 14 Penacook St., Box 425, Concord, NH 00302, 603-224-7668

James Buchanan

Fifteenth president (1857-61)
Born Apr 23, 1791, Cove Gap, PA
Died Jun 1, 1868, Lancaster, PA
Buried at Woodward Hill Cemetery, 538 East Strawberry St., Lancaster, PA

Democrat. "Bachelor president." Fought in War of 1812. U.S. Representative. Minister to Russia. U.S. Senator. Secretary of State. Minister to Great Britain.

LANDMARKS:

Birth site (marker): Buchanan's Birthplace Historical State Park, c/o Cowans Gap State Park, HC 17266, Fort Loudon, PA 17224, 717-485-3948

Birth site (cabin): Mercersburg Academy, Mercersburg, PA 17236, 717-328-2151

James Buchanan Hotel (marker), 17 North Main St., Mercersburg, PA 17236, 717-328-3008

Wheatland, 1120 Marietta Ave., Lancaster, PA 17603, 717-392-8721

Abraham Lincoln

Sixteenth president (1861-65)
Born Feb 12, 1809, Hodgenville, Hardin County (now Larue County), Ky.
Married Mary Todd, 1842
Died Apr 15, 1865, Washington, D.C.
Buried at Oak Ridge Cemetery, 1441 Monument Ave., Springfield, Ill. 62702, 217-782-2717

Republican. "Honest Abe." Fought in Blackhawk War.

U.S. Representative. U.S. divided by Civil War while president. Issued Emancipation Proclamation. Author of Gettysburg Address. First president assassinated.

LANDMARKS:

Birth site: Lincoln Birthplace National Historic Park, 2995 Lincoln Farm Rd., Hodgenville, KY 42748, 502-358-3874

Childhood home: Knob Creek Farm, 7120 Bardstown Rd., Hodgenville, KY 42748, 502-549-3741

Abraham Lincoln Museum, Lincoln Memorial University, Cumberland Gap Pkwy., Harrogate, TN 37752, 615-869-6235

Chicago Historical Society Museum, Clark St. at North Ave., Chicago, IL 60614, 312-642-4600

Civil War Library and Museum, 1805 Pine St., Philadelphia, PA 19103, 215-735-8196

Ford's Theatre National Historic Site, Petersen House, 516 Tenth St., N.W., Washington, DC 20004, 202-426-6924

Lincoln Boyhood National Memorial, IN 162, Box 1816, Lincoln City, IN 47552, 812-937-4541

Lincoln College Museum, Lincoln College, 300 Keokuk, Lincoln, IL 62656, 217-732-3155

Lincoln Depot, Monroe St. between Ninth and Tenth Sts., Springfield, IL 62704, 217-544-8695

Lincoln-Herndon Law Offices State Historic Site, 2 S. Old Capitol Plaza, Springfield, IL 62703, 217-785-7289

Lincoln Home National Historic Site, 413 S. Eighth St., Springfield, IL 62701, 217-492-4241

Lincoln Homestead State Park, 5079 Lincoln Park Rd., Springfield, KY 40069, 606-336-7461

Lincoln Log Cabin Courthouse, 5580 N. Fork, Decatur, IL 62521, 217-422-4919

Lincoln Memorial, 23rd St., N.W., Washington, DC 20242, 202-619-7222/426-6841

Lincoln Memorial Shrine, 125 West Vine St., Redlands, CA 92373, 909-798-7636

Lincoln Monument, Sherman Hill, Laramie, WY

Lincoln Monument, Lafayette and Oakland Ave., Council Bluffs, IA

Lincoln Museum, 66 Lincoln Square, Hodgenville, KY 42748, 502-358-3163

Lincoln Museum, 200 E. Berry, Fort Wayne, IN 46802, 219-455-3864

Lincoln Room Museum, 12 Lincoln Square, Gettysburg, PA 17325, 717-334-8188

Mount Pulaski Courthouse State Historic Site, Washington St., Mount Pulaski, IL 62548, 217-792-3919

New Salem State Historic Site, State Rte. 97, Box 244-A, Petersburg, IL 62675, 217-632-4000

Old State Capitol State Historic Site, 1 Old State Capitol Plaza, Springfield, IL 62701, 217-785-8363

Postville Courthouse (replica) State Historic Site, 914 Fifth St., Lincoln, IL 62656, 217-732-8930

Postville Courthouse, Greenfield Village, 20900 Oakwood Blvd, Dearborn, MI 48121, 313-271-1620

♦ Indicates that an entry on a festival celebrating the president appears in the main text

Union Pacific Historical Museum, 1416 Dodge St., Omaha, NE 68179, 402-271-3530

Andrew Johnson

Seventeenth president (1865-69)
Born Dec 29, 1808, Raleigh, N.C.
Married Eliza McArdle, 1826
Died Jul 31, 1875, Carter's Station, Tenn.
Buried at Andrew Johnson National Cemetery, P.O. Box 1088, Greeneville, Tenn. 37744, 615-638-3551

Democrat. "Tennessee Tailor." U.S. Representative. Governor of Tennessee. U.S. Senator. Succeeded presidency upon assassination of Abraham Lincoln. Only president to be impeached (acquitted).

LANDMARKS:

Birth site: Mordecai Historic Park, 1 Mimosa St., Raleigh, NC 27604, 919-834-4844

Andrew Johnson National Cemetery, P.O. Box 1088, Greeneville, TN 37744, 615-638-3551

Andrew Johnson National Historic Site, P.O. Box 1088, Greeneville, TN 37744, 615-638-3551

Ulysses Simpson Grant

Eighteenth president (1869-77)
Born Apr 27, 1822, Point Pleasant, Ohio
Married Julia Boggs Dent, 1848
Died Jul 23, 1885, Mt. McGregor, N.Y.
Buried at General Grant National Memorial, Riverside Dr. and W. 122nd St., New York, N.Y. 10016

Republican. "United States Grant." Fought in Mexican War. General in Civil War. Fifteenth Amendment (right of suffrage) ratified.

LANDMARKS:

Birth site: Grant Birthplace Historic Site, 1591 State Rt. 232, Point Pleasant, OH 45153, 513-553-4911

Childhood home: 219 E. Grant Ave., Georgetown, OH 45121 (private residence)

City Point Unit residence, Petersburg National Battlefield, Box 549, Petersburg, VA 23804, 804-732-3531

Grant Cottage State Historic Site, Mount McGregor, P.O. Box 990, Saratoga Springs, NY 12866, 518-587-8277

Grant's "Hardscrabble" Farm, 10501 Gravois Rd., St. Louis, MO 63123, 314-843-1700

Grant's Home at White Haven, 7400 Grant Rd., St. Louis, MO 63123, 314-842-1867

U.S. Grant Home, 511 Bouthillier St., Box 333, Galena, IL 61036, 815-777-0248

U.S. Grant House, Michigan State Fair Grounds, 1120 W. State Fair, Detroit, MI 48203, 313-369-8250

Rutherford Birchard Hayes

Nineteenth president (1877-81)

Born Oct 4, 1822, Delaware, Ohio
Married Lucy Ware Webb, 1852
Died Jan 17, 1893, Fremont, Ohio
Buried at Spiegel Grove National Historic Landmark, Rutherford B. Hayes Presidential Center, 1337 Hayes Ave., Fremont, Ohio 43420, 419-332-2081

Republican. "Dark Horse President." Fought in Civil War. U.S. Representative. Governor of Ohio. Some electoral votes in dispute; election decided by special electoral commission.

LANDMARKS:

Birth site (marker): East William and Winter St., Delaware, OH

Spiegel Grove National Historic Landmark, Rutherford B. Hayes Presidential Center, 1337 Hayes Ave., Fremont, OH 43420, 419-332-2081

James Abram Garfield

Twentieth president (1881)
Born Nov 19, 1831, Orange (now Moreland Hills), Ohio
Married Lucretia Rudolph, 1858
Died Sep 19, 1881, Elberon, N.J.
Buried at Lake View Cemetery, 12316 Euclid Ave., Cleveland, Ohio 44106, 216-421-2665

Republican. "Martyr President." Fought in Civil War. U.S. Representative. Died of wounds 2½ months after being shot by assassin.

LANDMARKS:

Birth site (marker): Abram Garfield Farm Site Park, S.O.M. Center and Jackson Rd., Moreland Hills, OH

Garfield House, 6825 Hinsdale St., Hiram, OH (private residence; closed to the public)

Lawnfield, President Garfield National Historic Site, 8095 Mentor Ave., Mentor, OH 44060, 216-255-8722

Chester Alan Arthur

Twenty-first president (1881-85)
Born Oct 5, 1829, Fairfield, Vt.
Married Ellen Lewis Herndon, 1859
Died Nov 18, 1886, New York, N.Y.
Buried at Albany Rural Cemetery, Cemetery Ave., Menands, N.Y.

Republican. "Elegant Arthur." Succeeded presidency upon death of James Garfield.

LANDMARKS:

Childhood home (replica): North Fairfield, VT 05450, 802-933-8362

Arthur House, 123 Lexington Ave., New York, NY (private residence; closed to the public)

◆ Indicates that an entry on a festival celebrating the president appears in the main text

Grover Cleveland

Twenty-second and twenty-fourth president (1885-89; 1893-97)
Born Mar 18, 1837, Caldwell, N.J.
Married Francis Folsom, 1886
Died Jun 24, 1908, Princeton, N.J.
Buried at Princeton Cemetery, 29 Greenview Ave., Princeton, N.J. 08542, 609-924-1369

Democrat. "Sage of Princeton." Governor of New York. Only president to serve two non-consecutive terms. Only president married in White House.

LANDMARKS:

Birth site: 207 Bloomfield Ave., Caldwell, NJ 07006, 201-226-1810

Childhood home: 109 Academy St., Fayetteville, NY (private residence)

Cleveland House, Cleveland Hill Rd., Tamworth, NH (private residence)

Cleveland Park, Washington, DC

Grover Cleveland Cottage, Deer Park Hotel Rd., Deer Park, MD (private residence)

Oak View, 3536 Newark St., N.W., Washington, DC

Westland, 15 Hodge Rd., Princeton, NJ (private residence; closed to the public)

Benjamin Harrison

Twenty-third president (1889-93)
Born Aug 20, 1833, North Bend, Ohio
Married Caroline Lavinia Scott, 1853; Mary Scott Lord Dimmick, 1896
Died Mar 13, 1901, Indianapolis, Ind.
Buried at Crown Hill Cemetery, 700 W. 38th St., Indianapolis, Ind. 46208, 317-925-8231

Republican. "Centennial President." Served in Civil War. U.S. Senator. Grandfather was ninth president (*see* **William Henry Harrison**).

LANDMARKS:

Birth site (location): grounds of Harrison Tomb State Memorial, Loop Ave., North Bend, OH

Benjamin Harrison Home, 1230 N. Delaware St., Indianapolis, IN 46202, 317-631-1898

William McKinley

Twenty-fifth president (1897-1901)
Born Jan 29, 1843, Niles, Ohio
Married Ida Saxton, 1871
Died Sep 14, 1901, Buffalo, N.Y.
Buried at McKinley National Memorial, 800 McKinley Monument Dr., N.W., Canton, Ohio 44708, 216-455-7043

Republican. "Idol of Ohio." Served in Civil War. U.S. Representative. Governor of Ohio. Died of wounds almost two weeks after being shot by assassin.

LANDMARKS:

Birth site (marker): 36 S. Main St., Niles, OH (replica of McKinley birthplace to be built on site)

The McKinley, 800 McKinley Monument Dr., N.W., Canton, OH 44708, 216-455-7043

National McKinley Birthplace Memorial and Library, 40 N. Main St., Niles, OH 44446, 216-652-1704

Saxton-Barber House, 331 Market Ave. S., Canton, OH 44702, 216-454-3426

♦ Theodore Roosevelt

Twenty-sixth president (1901-09)
Born Oct 27, 1858, New York, N.Y.
Married Alice Hathaway Lee, 1880; Edith Kermit Carow, 1886
Died Jan 6, 1919, Oyster Bay, N.Y.
Buried at Young's Memorial Cemetery, Cove Neck Rd. and East Main St., Oyster Bay, N.Y.

Republican. "Hero of San Juan Hill." Fought in Spanish-American War. Governor of New York. Succeeded presidency upon assassination of William McKinley. Youngest man to become president. Awarded Nobel Peace Prize.

LANDMARKS:

Birth site: 28 E. 20th St., New York, NY 10003, 212-260-1616

Sagamore Hill National Historic Site, 20 Sagamore Hill Rd., Oyster Bay, NY 11771, 516-922-4447/4788

Theodore Roosevelt Inaugural National Historic Site, 641 Delaware Ave., Buffalo, NY 14202, 716-884-0095

Theodore Roosevelt Island, Potomac River, Washington, DC 22101, 202-426-6922; 703-285-2598

Theodore Roosevelt National Park, Maltese Cross Cabin, Box 7, Medora, ND 58645, 701-623-4466

William Howard Taft

Twenty-seventh president (1909-13)
Born Sep 15, 1857, Cincinnati, Ohio
Married Helen Herron, 1886
Died Mar 8, 1930, Washington, D.C.
Buried at Arlington National Cemetery, Arlington, Va. 22211, 703-697-2131

Republican. Solicitor General. Governor-General of Philippines. Secretary of War. First president to throw out baseball on opening day. Sixteenth amendment enacted. Chief Justice of the Supreme Court.

LANDMARKS:

Birth site: 2038 Auburn Ave., Cincinnati, OH 45219, 513-684-3262

The Quarry, 1763 E. McMillan St., Cincinnati, OH (private residence)

2215 Wyoming Ave., N.W., Washington, DC 20008 (Syrian Embassy)

♦ Indicates that an entry on a festival celebrating the president appears in the main text

Woodrow Wilson

Twenty-eighth president (1913-21)
Born Dec 29, 1856, Staunton, Va.
Married Ellen Louise Axson, 1885; Edith Bolling Galt, 1915
Died Feb 3, 1924, Washington, D.C.
Buried at National Cathedral, Massachusetts and Wisconsin Ave., N.W., Washington, D.C. 20016, 202-537-6200

Democrat. "Professor." Governor of New Jersey. Held first presidential press conference. Author of Fourteen Points plan. Eighteenth and Nineteenth Amendments enacted. Awarded Nobel Peace Prize.

LANDMARKS:

Birth site: Woodrow Wilson Birthplace and Museum, 18 N. Coalter St., Box 24, Staunton, VA 24402, 703-885-0897

Early childhood home: 419 Seventh St., Augusta, GA 30901, 706-724-0436

Childhood home: 1705 Hampton St., Columbia, SC 29201, 803-252-1770

Woodrow Wilson House Museum, 2340 "S" St., N.W., Washington, DC 20008, 202-387-4062

Warren Gamaliel Harding

Twenty-ninth president (1921-23)
Born Nov 2, 1865, Blooming Grove (now Corsica), Ohio
Married Florence Kling De Wolfe, 1891
Died Aug 2, 1923, San Francisco, Calif.
Buried at Harding Memorial, Vernon Heights Blvd., Marion, Ohio

Republican. U.S. Senator. First presidential election returns broadcast on radio. Teapot Dome Scandal. Died in office.

LANDMARKS:

Birth site (marker): State Hwy. 97, east of County Rd. 20, Corsica, OH

Harding Home and Museum, 380 Mt. Vernon Ave., Marion, OH 43302, 614-387-9630

♦ Calvin Coolidge

Thirtieth president (1923-29)
Born Jul 4, 1872, Plymouth Notch, Vt.
Married Grace Anna Goodhue, 1905
Died Jan 5, 1933, Northampton, Mass.
Buried at Plymouth Notch Cemetery, Plymouth Notch, Vt.

Republican. "Silent Cal." Governor of Massachusetts. Succeeded presidency upon death of Warren Harding. First inaugural speech broadcast on radio.

LANDMARKS:

Birth site: P.O. Box 247, Plymouth Notch, VT 05056, 802-672-3773

The Beeches, 16 Hampton Terrace, Northampton, MA (private residence; closed to the public)

Calvin Coolidge Memorial Room, Forbes Library, 20 West St., Northampton, MA 01060, 413-584-6037

Coolidge Homestead, P.O. Box 247, Plymouth Notch, VT 05056, 802-672-3773

Northampton Home, 21 Massasoit St., Northampton, MA (private residence; closed to the public)

Herbert Clark Hoover

Thirty-first president (1929-33)
Born Aug 10, 1874, West Branch, Iowa
Married Lou Henry, 1899
Died Oct 20, 1964, New York, N.Y.
Buried at Herbert Hoover National Historic Site, Parkside Dr. and Main St., P.O. Box 607, West Branch, Iowa, 52358, 319-643-2541

Republican. "Grand Old Man." Involved in Boxer Rebellion in China. Chairman of Commission for Relief in Belgium. Secretary of Commerce. Wall Street crash (Black Tuesday), 1929.

LANDMARKS:

Birth site: Herbert Hoover National Historic Site, Downey and Penn St., P.O. Box 607, West Branch, IA 52358, 319-643-2541

Herbert Hoover Academic Bldg., George Fox College, Newberg, OR 97132, 503-538-8383

Herbert Hoover Presidential Library and Museum, 210 Parkside Dr., Box 488, West Branch, IA 52358, 319-643-5301

Hoover Institution on War, Revolution and Peace, Stanford University, Palo Alto, CA 94305, 415-723-1754

Hoover-Minthorn House Museum, 115 South River St., Newberg, OR 97132, 503-538-6629

Lou Henry Hoover House, Stanford University, 623 Miranda Ave., Palo Alto, CA 94305 (official residence of university president; closed to the public)

Shenandoah Camp Hoover, Shenandoah National Park, Rapidan River, VA (Park: Rte. 4, Box 348, Luray, VA 22835, 703-999-2243)

♦ Franklin Delano Roosevelt

Thirty-second president (1933-45)
Born Jan 30, 1882, Hyde Park, N.Y.
Married Eleanor Roosevelt, 1905
Died Apr 12, 1945, Warm Springs, Ga.
Buried at Franklin D. Roosevelt National Historic Site, 519 Albany Post Rd., Hyde Park, N.Y. 12538, 914-229-9115

Democrat. "F.D.R." Governor of New York. Author of the "New Deal." Only four-term president. Died in office.

LANDMARKS:

Birth site: Franklin D. Roosevelt National Historic Site, 519 Albany Post Rd., Hyde Park, NY 12538, 914-229-9115

Franklin D. Roosevelt Library and Museum, 511 Albany Post Rd., Hyde Park, NY 12538, 914-229-8114

♦ Indicates that an entry on a festival celebrating the president appears in the main text

Little White House State Historic Site, State Rte. 1, Box 10, Warm Springs, GA 31830, 706-655-5870

Roosevelt Campobello International Park, Campobello Island, New Brunswick, Canada E0G 3H0, 506-752-2922

♦ Harry S. Truman

Thirty-third president (1945-53)
Born May 10, 1884, Lamar, Mo.
Married Elizabeth "Bess" Virginia Wallace, 1919
Died Dec 26, 1972, Kansas City, Mo.
Buried at Harry S. Truman Library and Museum, U.S. Highway 24 and Delaware St., Independence, Mo. 64050, 816-833-1225

Democrat. "Give 'Em Hell Harry." Fought in World War I. U.S. Senator. Succeeded presidency upon death of Franklin D. Roosevelt. Authorized use of atomic bomb against Japan. Implemented the "Fair Deal."

LANDMARKS:

Birth site: Harry S. Truman Birthplace State Historic Site, 1009 Truman Ave., Lamar, MO 64759, 417-682-2279

Childhood home: 909 West Waldo St., Independence, MO (private residence; closed to the public)

Harry S. Truman Courtroom and Office, Independence Square Courthouse, 111 E. Maple, Independence, MO 64051, 816-881-4467

Harry S. Truman Key West Little White House Museum, 111 Front St., Key West, FL 33040, 305-294-9911

Harry S. Truman Library and Museum, U.S. Highway 24 and Delaware St., Independence, MO 64050, 816-833-1400

Harry S. Truman National Historic Site, 219 N. Delaware St., Independence, MO 64050, 816-254-7199

Truman Farm Home, 12301 Blue Ridge Blvd., Grandview, MO 64030, 816-254-2720

Dwight David Eisenhower

Thirty-fourth president (1953-61)
Born Oct 14, 1890, Denison, Tex.
Married Marie "Mamie" Geneva Doud, 1916
Died Mar 28, 1969, Washington, D.C.
Buried at Eisenhower Center, 200 Southeast 4th St., Abilene, Kan. 67410, 913-263-4751

Republican. "Ike." General in World War II. Commander of NATO. First televised press conference.

LANDMARKS:

Eisenhower Birthplace State Historical Park, 208 E. Day St., Denison, TX 75020, 903-465-8908

Eisenhower Center, Dwight D. Eisenhower Library, Eisenhower Museum, family home, 200 SE 4th St., Abilene, KS 67410, 913-263-4751

Eisenhower National Historic Site, 97 Taneytown, Gettysburg, PA 17325, 717-334-1124

Fort Sam Houston Museum, 1207 Stanley, Fort Sam Houston, San Antonio, TX 78234, 210-221-0019

♦ John Fitzgerald Kennedy

Thirty-fifth president (1961-63)
Born May 29, 1917, Brookline, Mass.
Married Jacqueline Lee Bouvier, 1953
Died Nov 22, 1963, Dallas, Tex.
Buried at Arlington National Cemetery, Arlington, Va. 22211, 703-697-2131

Democrat. "J.F.K." Served in World War II. U.S. Representative. U.S. Senator. First president born in twentieth century. Youngest elected president. Fourth president assassinated.

LANDMARKS:

Birth site: 83 Beals St., Brookline, MA 02146, 617-566-7937

Dallas County Administration Bldg. (formerly the Texas School Book Depository), 411 Elm, Ste. 120, Dallas, TX 75202, 214-653-6666

Hammersmith Farm, Ocean Dr., Newport, RI 02840, 401-846-0420

John F. Kennedy Library and Museum, Columbia Point, Boston, MA 02125, 617-929-4523

John F. Kennedy Memorial Plaza, Elm and Houston St., Dallas, TX

Kennedy Compound, Irving and Merchant Ave., Hyannis Port, MA (private residence; closed to the public)

♦ Lyndon Baines Johnson

Thirty-sixth president (1963-69)
Born Aug 27, 1908, near Stonewall, Tex.
Married Claudia Alta "Lady Bird" Taylor, 1934
Died Jan 22, 1973, San Antonio, Tex.
Buried at Johnson Family Cemetery, LBJ Ranch Unit, Box 329, Lyndon B. Johnson National Historic Park, Stonewall, Tex. 78636, 210-868-7128

Democrat. "L.B.J." U.S. Representative. Served in World War II. U.S. Senator. Succeeded presidency upon assassination of John F. Kennedy. Author of the "Great Society."

LANDMARKS:

Birth site: Junction School, LBJ Ranch, LBJ Ranch Unit, Lyndon B. Johnson National Historical Park, Stonewall, TX, 210-868-7128

Childhood home: 9th St. between "F" and "G" Sts., Johnson City, TX 78636

Alumni House, Southwest Texas State University, 400 North LBJ Dr., San Marcos, TX 78666, 512-245-2371

Johnson Settlement, Johnson City Unit, Lyndon B. Johnson Historical Park, Johnson City, TX 78636, 210-868-7128

Lyndon Baines Johnson Library and Museum, University of Texas at Austin, 2313 Red River St., Austin, Tex. 78705, 512-482-5137

Lyndon Baines Johnson Memorial Grove on the Potomac, Lady Bird Johnson Park, George Washington Memorial Pkwy., Arlington, VA

Lyndon Baines Johnson National Historical Park Visitor

Center, 9th and "G" Sts., Johnson City, TX 78636, 210-868-7128

Lyndon B. Johnson State Historical Park, U.S. 290, Stonewall, TX 78691, 210-644-2252

Richard Milhous Nixon

Thirty-seventh president (1969-74)
Born Jan 9, 1913, Yorba Linda, Calif.
Married Patricia Ryan, 1940
Died Apr 22, 1994, New York, N.Y.
Buried at Richard Nixon birthplace, 18001 Yorba Linda Blvd., Yorba Linda, Calif. 92686, 714-993-3393

Republican. Served in World War II. U.S. Representative. U.S. Senator. Vice President. First president to visit communist China. First and only president to resign (Watergate scandal).

LANDMARKS:

Birth site: 18001 Yorba Linda Blvd., Yorba Linda, CA 92686, 714-993-3393

California White House, Del Presidente Ave., San Clemente, CA (private residence; closed to the public)

Florida White House, 500 & 516 Bay Lane, Key Biscayne, FL (private residence; closed to the public)

Nixon Presidential Materials, Staff National Archives at College Park, 8601 Adelphi Rd., College Park, MD 20740, 301-713-6950

Richard Nixon Library, 18001 Yorba Linda Blvd., Yorba Linda, CA 92686, 714-993-3393 (privately held)

Gerald Rudolph Ford

Thirty-eighth president (1974-77)
Born Jul 14, 1913, Omaha, Neb.
Married Betty Bloomer Warren, 1948

Republican. Served in World War II. U.S. Representative. First vice president to take office under Twenty-fifth Amendment. Succeeded presidency upon resignation of Richard Nixon. Only president to serve in office without being elected.

LANDMARKS:

Birth site park: 3212 Woolworth Ave., Omaha, NE 68105, 402-444-5900

Childhood home: 649 Union Ave, S.E., Grand Rapids, MI (private residence; closed to the public)

Family home: 514 Crown View Dr., Alexandria, VA (private residence; closed to the public)

Gerald R. Ford Library, University of Michigan at Ann Arbor, 1000 Beal Ave., Ann Arbor, MI 48109, 313-741-2218

Gerald R. Ford Museum, 303 Pearl St., N.W., Grand Rapids, MI 49504, 616-451-9290

Retirement home, Thunderbird Country Club, 40-471 Sand Dune Rd., Rancho Mirage, CA 92270 (private residence; closed to the public)

James Earl Carter

Thirty-ninth president (1977-81)
Born Oct 1, 1924, Plains, Ga.
Married Rosalynn Smith, 1946

Democrat. "Jimmy." Governor of Georgia. First president to walk from Capitol to White House after inauguration. Camp David accords signed between Israel and Egypt. U.S. embassy staff held hostage in Tehran, Iran.

LANDMARKS:

Birth site: Plains Nursing Center, 225 Hospital St., Plains, GA

Childhood home: Preston Rd., Archery, GA (private residence)

Carter Center and Jimmy Carter Library, One Copenhill Ave., Atlanta, GA 30307, 404-331-0296

Jimmy Carter National Historic Site, P.O. Box 392, Plains, GA 31780, 912-824-3413

Retirement home, Woodland Dr., Plains, GA (private residence)

Ronald Wilson Reagan

Fortieth president (1981-89)
Born Feb 6, 1911, Tampico, Ill.
Married Jane Wyman, 1940, divorced 1949; Nancy Davis, 1952

Republican. "Great Communicator." Movie actor. Non-combat duty in World War II. Governor of California. Oldest president. Only president to be wounded in assassination attempt and survive. Iran-contra affair.

LANDMARKS:

Birth site: 111 Main St., Tampico, IL 61283, 815-438-2815

Childhood home: 816 S. Hennepin Ave., Dixon, IL 61021, 815-288-3404

California White House, Rancho del Cielo, 3333 Refugio Canyon, Santa Barbara, CA (private residence; closed to the public)

Retirement home, 668 St. Cloud Rd., Bel Air, CA 90077 (private residence; closed to the public)

Ronald Reagan Presidential Library, 40 Presidential Dr., Simi Valley, CA 93065, 805-522-8444

George Herbert Walker Bush

Forty-first president (1989-93)
Born Jun 12, 1924, Milton, Mass.
Married Barbara Pierce, 1945

Republican. Served in World War II. U.S. Representative. U.N. Ambassador. C.I.A. Director. Vice President. First acting president under Twenty-fifth amendment. Fall of Berlin Wall. Dissolution of Soviet Union. Persian Gulf War.

♦ Indicates that an entry on a festival celebrating the president appears in the main text

LANDMARKS:

Birth site: 173 Adams St., Milton, MA 02187 (private residence; closed to the public)

Childhood home: Grove Lane, Greenwich, CT (private residence; closed to the public)

Family summer home: Walker's Point, Kennebunkport, ME (private residence; closed to the public)

George Bush Library, Texas A&M University, College Station, TX 77843

Bill Clinton

Forty-second president (1993-)
Born Aug 19, 1946, Hope, Ark.

Married Hillary Rodham, 1975

Democrat. Rhodes Scholar. Governor of Arkansas. Proposed national health care plan. North American Free Trade Agreement. Middle East peace accord. Dayton Agreement for peace in Bosnia and Herzegovina.

LANDMARKS:

Childhood home: 117 S. Hervey St., Hope, AR (private residence)

Childhood home: 321 E. 13th St., Hope, AR (private residence)

Childhood home (marker): 1011 Park Ave., Hot Springs, AR (private residence)

♦ Indicates that an entry on a festival celebrating the president appears in the main text

APPENDIX 3

Domestic Tourism Information Sources

The following list includes, in alphabetical order by state, contact information for travel and tourism offices and selected convention and visitors bureaus and chambers of commerce in all 50 states and the District of Columbia.

State travel and tourism offices publish visitors guides that include information on lodging, dining, festivals and other recreational opportunities, and other travel resources. Many also publish calendars of events, state maps, and trip planning tips. Some state travel and tourism offices in the United States maintain World Wide Web (WWW) pages on the Internet to provide up-to-date information on a variety of travel-related topics.

City convention and visitors bureaus and tourism offices provide a wealth of travel-related material, including information on lodging and dining, local attractions and festivals, transportation, and calendars of events. Visitors guides for each city are usually available free of charge for the asking. There is also a great deal of information on cities available over the Internet. Some useful sites include:

CityNet - **http://www.city.net**
Cool City Hyperlinks - **http://www.iflyswa.com/info/coolcity.html**
USA CityLink - **http://www.usacitylink.com/citylink**

Local chambers of commerce can provide information on businesses, including restaurants, accommodations, and attractions.

Alabama

Bureau of Tourism and Travel
P.O. Box 4927
Montgomery, AL 36103
800-252-2262 or 334-242-4169
fax: 334-242-4554
WWW: http://alaweb.asc.edu/ala_tours/tours.html

[Birmingham] Greater Birmingham Convention and Visitors
  Bureau
2200 Ninth Ave., N.
Birmingham, AL 35203
800-458-8085 or 205-458-8000
fax: 205-458-8086

Birmingham Area Chamber of Commerce
2027 First Ave., N.
Birmingham, AL 35202
205-323-5461; fax: 205-250-7669

Huntsville/Madison County Convention and Visitors Bureau
700 Monroe St.
Huntsville, AL 35801
800-772-2348 or 205-551-2230
fax: 205-551-2324

Huntsville Chamber of Commerce
225 Church St.
Huntsville, AL 35801
205-535-2000; fax: 205-535-2015

Mobile Convention and Visitors Corp.
1 S. Water St.
Mobile, AL 36602
800-566-2453 or 334-415-2000
fax: 334-415-2060

Mobile Chamber of Commerce
P.O. Box 2187
Mobile, AL 36652
334-433-6951; fax: 334-432-1143

Montgomery Area Chamber of Commerce
P.O. Box 79
Montgomery, AL 36101
334-240-9455

Tuscaloosa Convention and Visitors Bureau
P.O. Box 032167
Tuscaloosa, AL 35403
800-538-8696 or 205-391-9200
fax: 205-391-2125

Alaska

Division of Tourism
P.O. Box 110801
Juneau, AK 99811
907-465-2012; fax: 907-465-2287

Anchorage Convention and Visitors Bureau
524 W. Fourth Ave.
Anchorage, AK 99501
800-446-5352 or 907-276-4118
fax: 907-278-5559

Anchorage Chamber of Commerce
441 W. Fifth Ave., Ste. 300
Anchorage, AK 99501
907-272-7588; fax: 907-272-4117

Fairbanks Convention and Visitors Bureau
550 First Ave.
Fairbanks, AK 99701
800-327-5774 or 907-456-5774
fax: 907-452-2867

Fairbanks Chamber of Commerce
546 Ninth Ave., Ste. 100
Fairbanks, AK 99701
907-452-1105; fax: 907-456-6968

Juneau Convention and Visitors Bureau
369 S. Franklin St., Ste. 201
Juneau, AK 99801
907-586-1737; fax: 907-586-1449

Juneau Chamber of Commerce
124 W. Fifth St.
Juneau, AK 99801
907-586-6420; fax: 907-463-5670

Arizona

Office of Tourism
2702 N. Third St., Ste. 4015
Phoenix, AZ 85004
800-842-8257 or 602-230-7733
fax: 602-240-5475
WWW: http://www.arizonaguide.com

Flagstaff Convention and Visitors Bureau
211 W. Aspen Ave.
Flagstaff, AZ 86001
800-217-2367 or 520-779-7611
fax: 520-556-1305

Flagstaff Chamber of Commerce
101 W. Rt. 66
Flagstaff, AZ 86001
520-774-4505; fax: 520-779-1209

Mesa Chamber of Commerce
120 N. Center St.
Mesa, AZ 85201-6627
602-969-1307; fax: 602-827-0727

Phoenix Valley of the Sun Convention and Visitors Bureau
400 E. Van Buren, 1 Arizona Center, Ste. 600
Phoenix, AZ 85004
602-254-6500; fax: 602-253-4415

Phoenix Chamber of Commerce
201 N. Central Ave., Ste. 2700
Phoenix, AZ 85073
602-254-5521; fax: 602-495-8913

Tucson Convention and Visitors Bureau
130 S. Scott Ave.
Tucson, AZ 85701
800-638-8350 or 520-624-1817
fax: 520-884-7804

Tucson Metropolitan Chamber of Commerce
465 W. St. & Mary's Rd.
Tucson, AZ 85701
520-792-1212; fax: 520-882-5704

Arkansas

Department of Parks and Tourism
1 Capitol Mall
Little Rock, AR 72201
800-628-8725 or 501-682-7777
fax: 501-682-1364
WWW: http://www.state.ar.us/html/ark_parks.html

Fort Smith Convention and Visitors Bureau
2 North B St.
Fort Smith, AR 72901
800-637-1477 or 501-783-8888
fax: 501-784-2421

Fort Smith Chamber of Commerce
P.O. Box 1668
Fort Smith, AR 72902
501-783-6118; fax: 501-783-6110

Hot Springs Convention and Visitors Bureau
P.O. Box K
Hot Springs, AR 71902
800-772-2489 or 501-321-2277
fax: 501-321-2136

[Hot Springs] Greater Hot Springs Chamber of Commerce
659 Ouichita Ave.
Hot Springs, AR 79101
501-321-1700; fax: 501-624-2064

Little Rock Convention and Visitors Bureau
P.O. Box 3232
Little Rock, AR 72203
800-844-4781 or 501-376-4781
fax: 501-374-2255

[Little Rock] Greater Little Rock Chamber of Commerce
101 S. Spring St.
Little Rock, AR 72201
501-374-4871; fax: 501-374-6018

California

Division of Tourism
801 K St., Ste. 1600
Sacramento, CA 95814
800-862-2543 or 916-322-2881
fax: 916-322-3402
WWW: http://gocalif.ca.gov:8000

Fresno Convention and Visitors Bureau
808 M St.
Fresno, CA 93721
800-788-0836 or 209-233-0836
fax: 209-445-0122

Fresno Chamber of Commerce
2331 Fresno St.
Fresno, CA 93721
209-495-4800; fax: 209-495-4811

Lake Tahoe Visitors Authority
1156 Ski Run Blvd.
South Lake Tahoe, CA 96150
800-288-2463 or 916-544-5050
fax: 916-544-2386

Long Beach Convention and Visitors Council
1 World Trade Center, Ste. 300
Long Beach, CA 90831
800-452-7829 or 310-436-3645
fax: 310-435-5653

Long Beach Area Chamber of Commerce
1 World Trade Center, Ste. 350
Long Beach, CA 90831
310-436-1251; fax: 310-436-7099

Los Angeles Convention and Visitors Bureau
633 W. Fifth St., Ste. 6000
Los Angeles, CA 90071
800-228-2452 or 213-624-7300
fax: 213-624-9746

Los Angeles Area Chamber of Commerce
350 S. Bixel St.
Los Angeles, CA 90017
213-580-7500; fax: 213-580-7511

Oakland Convention and Visitors Bureau
550 10th St., Ste. 214
Oakland, CA 94607
800-262-5526 or 510-839-9000
fax: 510-839-5924

Oakland Chamber of Commerce
475 14th St.
Oakland, CA 94612
510-874-4800; fax: 510-839-8817

Sacramento Convention and Visitors Bureau
1421 K St.
Sacramento, CA 95814
916-264-7777; fax: 916-264-7788

Sacramento Metropolitan Chamber of Commerce
917 Seventh St.
Sacramento, CA 95814-2561
916-552-6800; fax: 916-443-2672

San Diego Convention and Visitors Bureau
401 B St., Ste. 1400
San Diego, CA 92101
619-232-3101; fax: 619-696-9371

[San Diego] Greater San Diego Chamber of Commerce
402 W. Broadway, Ste. 1000
San Diego, CA 92101
619-232-0124; fax: 619-234-0571

San Francisco Convention and Visitors Bureau
201 Third St., Ste. 900
San Francisco, CA 94103
415-974-6900; fax: 415-227-2602

San Francisco Chamber of Commerce
465 California St.
San Francisco, CA 94104
415-392-4520; fax: 415-392-0485

San Jose Convention and Visitors Bureau
333 W. San Carlos St., Ste. 1000
San Jose, CA 95110
800-726-5673 or 408-295-9600
fax: 408-295-3937

San Jose Metropolitan Chamber of Commerce
180 S. Market St.
San Jose, CA 95113
408-291-5250; fax: 408-286-5019

Colorado

Boulder Convention and Visitors Bureau
2440 Pearl St.
Boulder, CO 80302
800-444-0447 or 303-442-2911
fax: 303-938-8837

Boulder Chamber of Commerce
P.O. Box 73
Boulder, CO 80306
303-442-1044; fax: 303-938-8837

Colorado Springs Convention and Visitors Bureau
104 S. Cascade, Ste. 104
Colorado Springs, CO 80903
800-368-4748 or 719-635-7506
fax: 719-635-4968

Colorado Springs Chamber of Commerce
P.O. Box B
Colorado Springs, CO 80903
719-635-1551; fax: 719-635-1571

Denver Convention and Visitors Bureau
1555 California St., Ste. 300
Denver, CO 80202
303-892-1112; fax: 303-892-1636

[Denver] Greater Denver Chamber of Commerce
1445 Market St.
Denver, CO 80202
303-534-8500; fax: 303-534-3200

Connecticut

Tourism Division
865 Brook St.
Rocky Hill, CT 06067
800-282-6863 or 860-258-4355
fax: 860-258-4275

[Bridgeport] New Bridgeport Chamber of Commerce
360 Granville Ave.
Bridgeport, CT 06610
203-332-1995; fax: 203-334-6702

[Hartford] Greater Hartford Convention and Visitors Bureau
1 Civic Center Plaza
Hartford, CT 06103
800-446-7811 or 860-728-6789
fax: 860-293-2365

[Hartford] Greater Hartford Chamber of Commerce
250 Constitution Plaza
Hartford, CT 06103-1882
860-525-4451; fax: 860-293-2592

[New Haven] Greater New Haven Convention and Visitors
  Bureau
1 Long Wharf Dr.
New Haven, CT 06511
800-332-7829 or 203-777-8550
fax: 203-495-6949

[New Haven] Greater New Haven Chamber of Commerce
195 Church St.
New Haven, CT 06510
203-787-6735; fax: 203-782-4329

[Stamford] Coastal Fairfield County Convention and Visitors
  Bureau
655 Washington Blvd., Ste. 502
Stamford, CT 06901
800-473-4868 or 203-327-1622
fax: 203-327-1828

Domestic Tourism

Stamford Chamber of Commerce
1 Landmark Sq.
Stamford, CT 06901
203-359-4761; fax: 203-363-5069

Delaware

Tourism Office
99 Kings Hwy.
Dover, DE 19901
800-441-8846 or 302-739-4271
fax: 302-739-5749
WWW: http://www.state.de.us/tourism/intro.htm

[Dover] Kent County/Dover Convention and Visitors Bureau
9 E. Loockerman St.
Dover, DE 19901
800-233-5368 or 302-734-1736
fax: 302-678-0189

[Dover] Central Delaware Chamber of Commerce
Treadway Towers, Ste. 2-B
Dover, DE 19903
302-678-3028; fax: 302-678-0189

[Wilmington] Greater Wilmington Convention and Visitor's
  Bureau
1300 N. Market St., Ste. 504
Wilmington, DE 19801
302-652-4088; fax: 302-652-4726

District of Columbia

Washington DC Convention and Visitors Association
1212 New York Ave., N.W., Ste. 600
Washington, DC 20005
202-789-7000; fax: 202-789-7037

Washington DC Chamber of Commerce
1301 Pennsylvania Ave., Ste. 309
Washington, DC 20004
202-347-7201; fax: 202-347-3538

Florida

Division of Tourism
126 W. Van Buren
Tallahassee, FL 32399
904-487-1462; fax: 904-921-9158

Fort Lauderdale Convention and Visitors Bureau
1850 Eller Dr., Ste. 303
Fort Lauderdale, FL 33316
800-356-1662 or 954-765-4466
fax: 954-765-4467

[Fort Lauderdale] Greater Fort Lauderdale Chamber of
  Commerce
512 N.E. Third Ave.
Fort Lauderdale, FL 33301
954-462-6000; fax: 954-527-8766

Jacksonville Convention and Visitors Bureau
3 Independent Dr., 1st Fl.
Jacksonville, FL 32202
800-733-2668 or 904-353-9736
fax: 904-798-9103

Jacksonville Chamber of Commerce
3 Independent Dr.
Jacksonville, FL 32202
904-366-6600; fax: 904-632-0617

[Miami] Greater Miami Convention and Visitors Bureau
701 Brickell Ave., Ste. 2700
Miami, FL 33131
800-933-8448 or 305-539-3000
fax: 305-539-3113

[Miami] Greater Miami Chamber of Commerce
1601 Biscayne Blvd., Ballroom Level
Miami, FL 33132
305-350-7700; fax: 305-374-6902

Orlando/Orange County Convention and Visitors Bureau
6700 Forum Dr., Ste. 100
Orlando, FL 32821
407-363-5800; fax: 407-363-5899

[Orlando] Greater Orlando Chamber of Commerce
P.O. Box 1234
Orlando, FL 32802
407-425-1234; fax: 407-839-5020

Saint Petersburg-Clearwater Area Convention and Visitors
  Bureau
1 Stadium Dr., Florida Thunder Dome, Ste. A
Saint Petersburg, FL 33705
813-582-7892; fax: 813-582-7949

Saint Petersburg Area Chamber of Commerce
100 Second Ave. N.
Saint Petersburg, FL 33701
813-821-4069; fax: 813-895-6326

Tallahassee Area Convention and Visitors Bureau
P.O. Box 1369
Tallahassee, FL 32302
800-628-2866 or 904-413-9200
fax: 904-487-4621

Tampa/Hillsborough Convention and Visitors Association
111 E. Madison St., Ste. 1010
Tampa, FL 33602
800-448-2672 or 813-223-1111
fax: 813-229-6616

[Tampa] Greater Tampa Chamber of Commerce
P.O. Box 420
Tampa, FL 33601-0420
813-228-7777; fax: 813-223-7899

Georgia

Department of Industry, Trade, and Tourism
285 Peachtree Center Ave., N.E., Marquis Tower II, Ste. 1000
Atlanta, GA 30303
800-847-4842 or 404-656-3590
fax: 404-651-9063
WWW: http://www.georgia-on-my-mind.org/code/
  welcome.html

Atlanta Convention and Visitors Bureau
233 Peachtree St., N.E., Ste. 2000
Atlanta, GA 30303
800-285-2682 or 404-521-6600
fax: 404-584-6331

Atlanta Chamber of Commerce
P.O. Box 1740
Atlanta, GA 30301
404-880-9000; fax: 404-586-8464

Augusta-Richmond County Convention and Visitors Bureau
32 Eighth St.
Augusta, GA 30901
800-726-0243 or 706-823-6600
fax: 706-826-6609

[Augusta] Metro Augusta Chamber of Commerce
600 Broad Street Plaza
Augusta, GA 30913
706-821-1300; fax: 706-821-1330

Savannah Area Convention and Visitors Bureau
P.O. Box 1628
Savannah, GA 31402
800-444-2427 or 912-944-0456
fax: 912-944-0468

Savannah Area Chamber of Commerce
222 W. Oglethorpe Ave., Ste. 100
Savannah, GA 31402
800-444-2427 or 912-944-0444
fax: 912-944-0468

Hawaii

Visitors Bureau
2270 Kalakaua Ave., Ste. 801
Honolulu, HI 96815
808-923-1811; fax: 808-922-8991
WWW: http://www.visit.hawaii.org

Idaho

Tourism Division
700 W. State St.
Boise, ID 83720
800-635-7820 or 208-334-2017
fax: 208-334-2631
WWW: http://www.idoc.state.id.us/irti/Main.html

Boise Convention and Visitors Bureau
168 N. Ninth St., Ste. 200
Boise, ID 83702
800-635-5240 or 208-344-7777
fax: 208-344-6236

Boise Area Chamber of Commerce
300 N. Sixth St.
Boise, ID 83702
208-344-5515; fax: 208-344-5849

[Pocatello] Greater Pocatello Chamber of Commerce
P.O. Box 626
Pocatello, ID 83204
208-233-1525; fax: 208-233-1527

Illinois

Bureau of Tourism
100 W. Randolph St., Ste. 300
Chicago, IL 60601
800-226-6632 or 312-814-4732
fax: 312-814-6581

Chicago Convention and Tourism Bureau
2301 S. Lake Shore Dr.
Chicago, IL 60616-1490
312-567-8500; fax: 312-567-8533

Chicago Office of Tourism
78 E. Washington St.
Chicago, IL 60602
312-744-2400; fax: 312-744-2359

Chicago Chamber of Commerce
330 N. Wabash
Chicago, IL 60611
312-494-6700; fax: 312-494-0196

Rockford Area Convention and Visitors Bureau
211 N. Main St.
Rockford, IL 61101
800-521-0849 or 815-963-8111
fax: 815-963-4298

Rockford Area Chamber of Commerce
P.O. Box 1747
Rockford, IL 61110
815-987-8100; fax: 815-987-8100

[Springfield] Central Illinois Tourism Council
629 E. Washington
Springfield, IL 62701
800-262-2482 or 217-525-7980
fax: 217-525-8004

Springfield Convention and Visitors Bureau
109 N. Seventh St.
Springfield, IL 62701
800-545-7300 or 217-789-2360
fax: 217-544-8711

Springfield Chamber of Commerce
S. Old State Capitol Plaza, Ste. 3
Springfield, IL 62701
217-525-1173; fax: 217-525-8768

Indiana

Tourism Division
1 N. Capitol Ave., Ste. 700
Indianapolis, IN 46204
800-289-6646 or 317-232-8860
fax: 317-233-6887
WWW: http://www.state.in.us/acin/tourism/index.html

Evansville Convention and Visitors Bureau
623 Walnut St.
Evansville, IN 47708
800-433-3025 or 812-425-5402
fax: 812-421-2207

Evansville Chamber of Commerce
100 N.W. Second St., Ste. 202
Evansville, IN 47708
812-425-8147; fax: 812-421-5883

Fort Wayne/Allen County Convention and Visitors Bureau
1021 S. Calhoun St.
Fort Wayne, IN 46802
800-767-7752 or 219-424-3700
fax: 219-424-3914

Fort Wayne Chamber of Commerce
826 Ewing St.
Fort Wayne, IN 46802
219-424-1435; fax: 219-426-7232

Indianapolis Convention and Visitors Association
200 S. Capitol Ave., 1 RCA Dome, Ste. 100
Indianapolis, IN 46225
800-323-4639 or 317-639-4282
fax: 317-639-5273

Indianapolis Chamber of Commerce
320 N. Meridian St., Ste. 928
Indianapolis, IN 46204
317-464-2200; fax: 317-464-2217

South Bend/Mishawaka Convention and Visitors Bureau
P.O. Box 1677
South Bend, IN 46634
800-828-7881 or 219-234-0051
fax: 219-289-0358

[South Bend] Chamber of Commerce of Saint Joseph County
401 E. Colfax Ave., Ste. 310
South Bend, IN 46634
219-234-0051; fax: 219-289-0358

Iowa

Tourism Office
200 E. Grand Ave.
Des Moines, IA 50309
800-345-4692 or 515-242-4705
fax: 515-242-4749

Cedar Rapids Area Convention and Visitors Bureau
P.O. Box 5339
Cedar Rapids, IA 52406
800-735-5557 or 319-398-5009
fax: 319-398-5089

Cedar Rapids Area Chamber of Commerce
P.O. Box 74860
Cedar Rapids, IA 52407
319-398-5317; fax: 319-398-5228

[Des Moines] Greater Des Moines Convention and Visitors
   Bureau
601 Locust St., Ste. 222
Des Moines, IA 50309
800-451-2625 or 515-286-4960
fax: 515-244-9757

[Des Moines] Greater Des Moines Chamber of Commerce
601 Locust St., Ste. 100
Des Moines, IA 50309
515-286-4950; fax: 515-286-4974

Kansas

Division of Travel and Tourism
700 S.W. Harrison St., Ste. 1300
Topeka, KS 66603
800-252-6727 or 913-296-2009
fax: 913-296-6988

Topeka Convention and Visitors Bureau
1275 S.W. Topeka Blvd.
Topeka, KS 66612
800-235-1030 or 913-234-1030
fax: 913-234-8282

Topeka Chamber of Commerce
120 S.E. Sixth, Ste. 110
Topeka, KS 66603
913-234-2644; fax: 913-234-8656

Wichita Convention and Visitors Bureau
100 S. Main St., Ste. 100
Wichita, KS 67202
800-288-9424 or 316-265-2800
fax: 316-265-0162

Wichita Area Chamber of Commerce
350 W. Douglas
Wichita, KS 67202
316-265-7771; fax: 316-265-7502

Kentucky

Department of Travel Development
500 Mero St., 22nd Fl.
Frankfort, KY 40601
800-225-8747 or 502-564-4930
fax: 502-564-5695
WWW: http://www.state.ky.us/tour/tour.htm

Frankfort/Franklin County Tourist and Convention Commission
100 Capitol Ave.
Frankfort, KY 40601
800-960-7200 or 502-875-8687
fax: 502-227-2604

Frankfort Chamber of Commerce
100 Capitol Ave.
Frankfort, KY 40601
502-223-8261; fax: 502-227-2604

[Lexington] Greater Lexington Convention and Visitors Bureau
301 E. Vine St.
Lexington, KY 40507
800-845-3959 or 606-233-7299
fax: 606-254-4555

Lexington Chamber of Commerce
330 E. Main St.
Lexington, KY 40507
606-254-4447; fax: 606-233-3304

Louisville Convention and Visitors Bureau
400 S. First St.
Louisville, KY 40202
800-626-5646 or 502-582-3732
fax: 502-584-6697

Louisville Area Chamber of Commerce
600 W. Main St.
Louisville, KY 40202
502-625-0000; 502-625-0010

Louisiana

Office of Tourism
P.O. Box 94291
Baton Rouge, LA 70804
800-334-8626 or 504-342-8119
fax: 504-342-8390
WWW: http://hob.com/louisiana

Baton Rouge Area Convention and Visitors Bureau
730 North Blvd.
Baton Rouge, LA 70802
800-527-6843 or 504-383-1825
fax: 504-346-1253

[Baton Rouge] Greater Baton Rouge Chamber of Commerce
564 Laurel St.
Baton Rouge, LA 70801
504-381-7125; fax: 504-336-4306

Bossier Chamber of Commerce
710 Benton Rd.
Bossier City, LA 71111
318-746-0252; fax: 318-746-0357

New Orleans Metropolitan Convention and Visitors Bureau
1520 Sugar Bowl Dr.
New Orleans, LA 70112
800-672-6124 or 504-566-5011
fax: 504-566-5046

New Orleans and River Region Chamber of Commerce
601 Poydras St., Ste. 1700
New Orleans, LA 70130
504-527-6900; fax: 504-527-6950

Shreveport-Bossier Convention and Tourist Bureau
P.O. Box 1761
Shreveport, LA 71166
800-551-8682 or 318-222-9391
fax: 318-222-0056

Shreveport Chamber of Commerce
P.O. Box 20074
Shreveport, LA 71120
318-677-2500; fax: 318-677-2541

Maine

Office of Tourism
33 Stone St.
Augusta, ME 04333
800-533-9595 or 207-287-5711
fax: 207-287-5701

[Augusta] Kennebec Valley Chamber of Commerce
P.O. Box E
Augusta, ME 04332
207-623-4559; fax: 207-626-9342

Bangor Convention and Visitors Bureau
519 Main St.
Bangor, ME 04401
207-947-5205; fax: 207-990-1427

[Bangor] Greater Bangor Chamber of Commerce
P.O. Box 1443
Bangor, ME 04402
207-947-0307; fax: 207-990-1427

[Portland] Convention and Visitors Bureau of Greater Portland
305 Commercial St.
Portland, ME 04101
207-772-5800; fax: 207-874-9043

[Portland] Greater Portland Chamber of Commerce
145 Middle St.
Portland, ME 04101
207-772-2811; fax: 207-772-1179

Maryland

Office of Tourism Development
217 E. Redwood St., 9th Fl.
Baltimore, MD 21202
800-543-1036 or 410-767-3400
fax: 410-333-6643
WWW: http://www.mdisfun.org/mdisfun

Annapolis and Anne Arundel Conference and Visitors Bureau
26 West St.
Annapolis, MD 21401
410-268-8687; fax: 410-263-9591

Annapolis Chamber of Commerce
1 Annapolis St.
Annapolis, MD 21401
410-268-7676; fax: 410-268-2317

Baltimore Area Convention and Visitors Association
100 Light St., 12th Fl.
Baltimore, MD 21202
800-343-3468 or 410-659-7300
fax: 410-727-2308

Baltimore Chamber of Commerce
204 E. Lombard St., Herget Harbor Bldg., 3rd Fl.
Baltimore, MD 21202
410-837-7102; fax: 410-837-7104

Massachusetts

Office of Travel and Tourism
100 Cambridge St., 13th Fl.
Boston, MA 02202
800-447-6277 or 617-727-3201
fax: 617-727-6525
WWW: http://www.magnet.state.ma.us/travel/travel.html

[Boston] Greater Boston Convention and Visitors Bureau
P.O. Box 990468
Boston, MA 02199-0468
800-374-7400 or 617-536-4100
fax: 617-424-7664

[Boston] Greater Boston Chamber of Commerce
1 Beacon St., 4th Fl.
Boston, MA 02108
617-227-4500; fax: 617-227-7505

[Springfield] Greater Springfield Convention and Visitors Bureau
1500 Main St.
Springfield, MA 01115-5589
800-723-1548 or 413-787-1548
fax: 413-781-4607

[Springfield] Greater Springfield Chamber of Commerce
1277 Main St., 3rd Fl.
Springfield, MA 01103
413-787-1555; fax: 413-787-6645

Worcester County Convention and Visitors Bureau
33 Waldo St.
Worcester, MA 01608
508-753-2920; fax: 508-754-8560

Worcester Area Chamber of Commerce
33 Waldo St.
Worcester, MA 01608
508-753-2924; fax: 508-754-8560

Michigan

Travel Bureau
105 W. Allegan St.
Lansing, MI 48933
800-543-2937 or 517-373-0670
fax: 517-373-0059
WWW: http://www.travel-michigan.state.mi.us

Ann Arbor Area Convention and Visitors Bureau
120 W. Huron
Ann Arbor, MI 48104
313-995-7281; fax: 313-995-7283

Ann Arbor Area Chamber of Commerce
425 S. Main
Ann Arbor, MI 48104
313-665-4433; fax: 313-665-4191

Detroit Visitor Information Center
100 Renaissance Center, Ste. 1900
Detroit, MI 48243
800-338-7648 or 313-259-4333

[Detroit] Metropolitan Detroit Convention and Visitors Bureau
100 Renaissance Center, Ste. 1900
Detroit, MI 48243
800-225-5389 or 313-259-4333
fax: 313-259-7583

[Detroit] Greater Detroit Chamber of Commerce
600 W. Lafayette Blvd.
Detroit, MI 48232
313-964-4000; fax: 313-964-0531

Grand Rapids/Kent County Convention and Visitors Bureau
140 Monroe Center, Ste. 300
Grand Rapids, MI 49503-2832
800-678-9859 or 616-459-8287
fax: 616-459-7291

Grand Rapids Area Chamber of Commerce
111 Pearl St. N.W.
Grand Rapids, MI 49503
616-771-0300; fax: 616-771-0318

[Lansing] Greater Lansing Convention and Visitors Bureau
P.O. Box 15066
Lansing, MI 48901
800-648-6630 or 517-487-6800
fax: 517-487-5151

Lansing Regional Chamber of Commerce
P.O. Box 14030
Lansing, MI 48901
517-487-6340; fax: 517-486-6910

Minnesota

Office of Tourism
121 E. Seventh Pl., Metro Sq., Ste. 100
Saint Paul, MN 55101
800-657-3700 or 612-296-5029
fax: 612-296-2800
WWW: http://www.tccn.com/mn.tourism/mnhome.html

Duluth Convention and Visitors Bureau
1000 Lake Place Dr.
Duluth, MN 55802
800-438-5884 or 218-722-4011
fax: 218-722-1322

[Minneapolis] Greater Minneapolis Convention and Visitors
    Association
33 S. Sixth St., Multifoods Tower, Ste. 4000
Minneapolis, MN 55402
800-445-7412 or 612-661-4700
fax: 612-348-8359

[Minneapolis] Greater Minneapolis Chamber of Commerce
81 S. Ninth St., Ste. 200
Minneapolis, MN 55402
612-370-9132; fax: 612-370-9195

Rochester Convention and Visitors Bureau
150 S. Broadway, Ste. A
Rochester, MN 55904
800-634-8277 or 507-288-4331
fax: 507-288-9144

Rochester Chamber of Commerce
220 S. Broadway, Ste. 100
Rochester, MN 55904
507-288-1122; fax: 507-282-8960

Saint Paul Convention and Visitors Bureau
55 E. Fifth St., Norwest Center, Ste. 102
Saint Paul, MN 55101
800-627-6101 or 612-297-6985
fax: 612-297-6879

Saint Paul Area Chamber of Commerce
332 Minnesota St., Ste. N-205
Saint Paul, MN 55101
612-223-5000; fax: 612-223-5119

Mississippi

Division of Tourism Development
P.O. Box 849
Jackson, MS 39205
800-927-6378 or 601-359-3297
fax: 601-359-5757

Biloxi Visitors Center
710 Beach Blvd.
Biloxi, MS 39530
800-245-6943 or 601-374-3105
fax: 601-435-6248

Biloxi Chamber of Commerce
P.O. Box 1928
Biloxi, MS 39533
601-374-2717; fax: 601-374-2764

[Gulfport] Mississippi Beach Convention and Visitors Bureau
P.O. Box 6128
Gulfport, MS 39506
800-237-9493 or 601-896-6699
fax: 601-896-6796

Gulfport Chamber of Commerce
P.O. Box FF
Gulfport, MS 39502
601-863-2933; fax: 601-863-3080

[Jackson] Metro Jackson Convention and Visitors Bureau
921 N. President St.
Jackson, MS 39202
800-354-7695 or 601-960-1891
fax: 601-960-1827

Jackson Chamber of Commerce
201 S. President St.
Jackson, MS 39225
601-948-7575; fax: 601-352-5539

Missouri

Division of Tourism
P.O. Box 1055
Jefferson City, MO 65102
800-877-1234 or 573-751-4133
fax: 573-751-5160
WWW: http://www.ecodev.state.mo.us/tou/home.htm

Jefferson City Convention and Visitors Bureau
213 Adams St.
Jefferson City, MO 65101
800-769-4183 or 573-634-3616
fax: 573-634-3805

Jefferson City Chamber of Commerce
213 Adams St.
Jefferson City, MO 65101
573-634-3616; fax: 573-634-3805

[Kansas City] Convention and Visitors Bureau of Greater Kansas
    City
1100 Main St., Ste. 2550
Kansas City, MO 64105
800-767-7700 or 816-221-5242
fax: 816-691-3855

[Kansas City] Greater Kansas City Chamber of Commerce
911 Main St.
Kansas City, MO 64105
816-221-2424; fax: 816-221-7440

Saint Louis Convention and Visitors Commission
10 S. Broadway, Ste. 1000
Saint Louis, MO 63102
800-325-7962 or 314-421-1023
fax: 314-421-0039

[Saint Louis] Regional Commerce & Growth Association
100 S. Fourth St., Ste. 500
Saint Louis, MO 63102
314-231-5555; fax: 314-444-1122

Springfield Convention and Visitors Bureau
3315 E. Battlefield Rd.
Springfield, MO 65804
800-678-8766 or 417-881-5300
fax: 417-881-2231

Springfield Chamber of Commerce
320 N. Jefferson
Springfield, MO 65806
417-862-5567; fax: 417-862-1611

Montana

Travel Promotion Division
1424 Ninth Ave.
Helena, MT 59620
800-847-4868 or 406-444-2654
fax: 406-444-1800
WWW: http://travel.mt.gov

Billings Convention and Visitors Bureau
P.O. Box 31177
Billings, MT 59107
406-245-4111; fax: 406-245-7333

Billings Area Chamber of Commerce
815 S. 27th St.
Billings, MT 59107
406-245-4111; fax: 406-245-7333

Great Falls Area Chamber of Commerce
P.O. Box 2127
Great Falls, MT 59403
406-761-4434; fax: 406-454-2995

Helena Area Chamber of Commerce
201 E. Lyndale
Helena, MT 59601
800-743-5362 or 406-442-4120
fax: 406-449-5631

Nebraska

Travel and Tourism Division
700 S. 16th St.
Lincoln, NE 68508
800-228-4307 or 402-471-3794
fax: 402-471-3026
WWW: http://www.ded.state.ne.us/tourism.html

Lincoln Convention and Visitors Bureau
P.O. Box 83737
Lincoln, NE 68501
800-423-8212 or 402-476-7511
fax: 402-476-7552

Lincoln Chamber of Commerce
1221 'N' St., Ste. 320
Lincoln, NE 68508
402-476-7511; fax: 402-476-7552

[Omaha] Greater Omaha Convention and Visitors Bureau
6800 Mercy Rd., Ste. 202
Omaha, NE 68106-2627
800-332-1819 or 402-444-4660
fax: 402-444-4511

[Omaha] Greater Omaha Chamber of Commerce
1301 Harney St.
Omaha, NE 68102
402-346-5000; fax: 402-346-7050

Nevada

Commission on Tourism
5151 S. Carson St., Capitol Complex
Carson City, NV 89710
800-638-2328 or 702-687-4322
fax: 702-687-6779

Carson City Convention and Visitors Bureau
1900 S. Carson St., Ste. 200
Carson City, NV 89701
800-638-2321 or 702-687-7410
fax: 702-687-7416

Carson City Chamber of Commerce
1900 S. Carson St., Ste. 100
Carson City, NV 89701
702-882-1565; fax: 702-882-4179

Las Vegas Convention and Visitors Authority
3150 Paradise Rd.
Las Vegas, NV 89109
800-332-5333 or 702-892-0711
fax: 702-892-2824

Las Vegas Chamber of Commerce
711 E. Desert Inn Rd.
Las Vegas, NV 89109
702-735-1616; fax: 702-735-2011

[Reno] Greater Reno-Sparks Chamber of Commerce
405 Marsh Ave.
Reno, NV 89509
702-686-3030; fax: 702-686-3038

New Hampshire

Office of Travel and Tourism Development
P.O. Box 1856
Concord, NH 03302
800-386-4664 or 603-271-2343
fax: 603-271-6784
WWW: http://www.visitnh.gov

Concord Convention and Visitors Bureau
P.O. Box 1856
Concord, NH 03302-1856
603-271-2343; fax: 603-271-6784

Concord Chamber of Commerce
244 N. Main St.
Concord, NH 03301
603-224-2508; fax: 603-224-8128

Manchester Convention and Visitors Bureau
55 John E. Devine. Dr.
Manchester, NH 03103
800-932-4282 or 603-635-9000

[Manchester] Greater Manchester Chamber of Commerce
889 Elm St.
Manchester, NH 03101
603-666-6600; fax: 603-626-0910

New Jersey

Division of Travel and Tourism
20 W. State St.
Trenton, NJ 08625
800-537-7397 or 609-292-2470
fax: 609-633-7418

Atlantic City Convention and Visitors Authority
2314 Pacific Ave.
Atlantic City, NJ 08401
609-348-7100; fax: 609-347-9186

Domestic Tourism

[Atlantic City] Greater Atlantic City Region Tourism Council
P.O. Box 7457
Atlantic City, NJ 08404
609-345-0300

[Atlantic City] Greater Atlantic City Chamber of Commerce
1125 Atlantic Ave.
Atlantic City, NJ 08401
609-345-5600; fax: 609-345-4524

[Newark] Metro Newark Chamber of Commerce Regional
    Business Partnership
1 Newark Center
Newark, NJ 07102
201-242-6237; fax: 201-824-6587

Trenton Convention and Visitors Bureau
Lafayette and Barrack
Trenton, NJ 08608
609-777-1770; fax: 609-292-3771

[Trenton] Mercer County Chamber of Commerce
214 W. State St.
Trenton, NJ 08608
609-393-4143; fax: 609-393-1032

New Mexico

Tourism and Travel Division
491 Old Santa Fe Trail
Santa Fe, NM 87503
800-545-2040 or 505-827-7400
fax: 505-827-7402

Albuquerque Convention and Visitors Bureau
20 First Plaza, Ste. 601
Albuquerque, NM 87102
800-284-2282 or 505-842-9918
fax: 505-247-9101

[Albuquerque] Greater Albuquerque Chamber of Commerce
401 Second St. N.W.
Albuquerque, NM 87102
505-764-3700; fax: 505-764-3714

Santa Fe Convention and Visitors Bureau
P.O. Box 909
Santa Fe, NM 87504
800-777-2489 or 505-984-6760
fax: 505-984-6679

Santa Fe County Chamber of Commerce
P.O. Box 1928
Santa Fe, NM 87504
505-983-7317; fax: 505-984-2205

New York

Division of Tourism
1 Commerce Plaza
Albany, NY 12245
800-225-5697 or 518-474-4116
fax: 518-486-6416
WWW: http://iloveny.state.ny.us

Albany County Convention and Visitors Bureau
52 S. Pearl St.
Albany, NY 12207
800-258-3582 or 518-434-1217
fax: 518-434-0887

Albany-Colonie Chamber of Commerce
540 Broadway
Albany, NY 12207
518-434-1214; fax: 518-434-1339

[Buffalo] Greater Buffalo Convention and Visitors Bureau
107 Delaware Ave.
Buffalo, NY 14202
800-283-3256 or 716-852-0511
fax: 716-852-0131

[Buffalo] Greater Buffalo Partnerships
300 Main Place Tower
Buffalo, NY 14202
716-852-7100; fax: 716-852-2761

New York Convention and Visitors Bureau
2 Columbus Cir.
New York, NY 10019
800-692-8474 or 212-484-1200
fax: 212-247-6193

New York Chamber of Commerce & Industry
1 Battery Park Plaza
New York, NY 10004
212-493-7400; fax: 212-334-3344

Niagara Falls Convention and Visitors Bureau
310 Fourth St.
Niagara Falls, NY 14303
800-421-5223 or 716-285-2400
fax: 716-285-0809

[Rochester] Greater Rochester Visitors Association
126 Andrews St.
Rochester, NY 14604
800-677-7282 or 716-546-3070
fax: 716-232-4822

North Carolina

Travel and Tourism Division
430 N. Salisbury St.
Raleigh, NC 27603
800-847-4862 or 919-733-4171
fax: 919-733-8582

Asheville Area Convention and Visitors Bureau
151 Haywood St.
Asheville, NC 28801
800-257-1300 or 704-258-6111
fax: 704-254-6054

Asheville Area Chamber of Commerce
151 Haywood St.
Asheville, NC 28802
704-258-6101; fax: 704-251-0926

Charlotte Convention and Visitors Bureau
122 E. Stonewall St.
Charlotte, NC 28202
800-231-4636 or 704-334-2282
fax: 704-342-3972

Charlotte Chamber of Commerce
330 S. Tryon St.
Charlotte, NC 28202
704-378-1300; fax: 704-374-1903

Durham Convention and Visitors Bureau
101 E. Morgan St.
Durham, NC 27701
800-446-8604 or 919-687-0288
fax: 919-683-9555

[Durham] Greater Durham Chamber of Commerce
300 W. Morgan St., Ste. 1400
Durham, NC 27702
919-682-2133; fax: 919-688-8351

Greensboro Area Convention and Visitors Bureau
317 S. Greene St.
Greensboro, NC 27401
800-344-2282 or 910-274-2282
fax: 910-230-1183

Greensboro Area Chamber of Commerce
125 S. Elm St.
Greensboro, NC 27401
910-275-8675; fax: 910-230-1867

[Raleigh] Greater Raleigh Convention and Visitors Bureau
225 Hillsborough St., Ste. 400
Raleigh, NC 27603
800-849-8499 or 919-834-5900
fax: 919-831-2887

[Raleigh] Greater Raleigh Chamber of Commerce
800 S. Salisbury St.
Raleigh, NC 27602
919-664-7000; fax: 919-664-7099

Winston-Salem Convention and Visitors Bureau
P.O. Box 1408
Winston-Salem, NC 27102
910-777-3787; fax: 910-773-1404

[Winston-Salem] Greater Winston-Salem Chamber of Commerce
P.O. Box 1408
Winston-Salem, NC 27102
910-725-2361; 910-721-2209

North Dakota

Tourism Office
604 E. Boulevard Ave.
Liberty Memorial Bldg.
Bismarck, ND 58505
800-435-5663 or 701-328-2525
fax: 701-328-4878

Bismarck Mandan Convention and Visitors Bureau
P.O. Box 2274
Bismarck, ND 58502
800-767-3555 or 701-222-4308
fax: 701-222-0647

Bismarck Chamber of Commerce
P.O. Box 1675
Bismarck, ND 58502
701-223-5660; fax: 701-255-6125

Fargo-Moorhead Convention and Visitors Bureau
P.O. Box 2164
Fargo, ND 58103
800-235-7654 or 701-282-3653
fax: 701-282-4366

Fargo Chamber of Commerce
P.O. Box 2443
Fargo, ND 58108
701-237-5678; fax: 701-233-3233

[Grand Forks] Greater Grand Forks Convention and Visitors
 Bureau
4251 Gateway Dr.
Grand Forks, ND 58203
800-866-4566 or 701-746-0444
fax: 701-746-0775

Grand Forks Chamber of Commerce
202 N. Third St.
Grand Forks, ND 58203
701-772-7271; 701-772-9238

Ohio

Division of Travel and Tourism
P.O. Box 1001
Columbus, OH 43216
800-282-5393 or 614-466-8844
fax: 614-466-6744
WWW: http://www.travel.state.oh.us

Akron/Summit County Convention and Visitors Bureau
77 E. Mill St.
Akron, OH 44308
800-245-4254 or 330-374-7560
fax: 330-374-7626

[Akron] Regional Development Board
Cascade Plaza, Ste. 800
Akron, OH 44308
330-376-5550; fax: 330-379-3164

[Cincinnati] Greater Cincinnati Convention and Visitors Bureau
300 W. Sixth St.
Cincinnati, OH 45202
800-621-2142 or 513-621-2142
fax: 513-621-5020

[Cincinnati] Greater Cincinnati Chamber of Commerce
441 Vine St., Carew Tower, Ste. 300
Cincinnati, OH 45202
513-579-3100; fax: 513-579-3102

[Cleveland] Convention and Visitors Bureau of Greater Cleveland
50 Public Sq., Tower City Center, Ste. 3100
Cleveland, OH 44113
800-321-1001 or 216-621-4110
fax: 216-621-5967

[Cleveland] Greater Cleveland Growth Associates
200 Tower City Center
Cleveland, OH 44113
216-621-3300

[Columbus] Greater Columbus Convention and Visitors Bureau
10 W. Broad St., Ste. 1300
Columbus, OH 43215
800-354-2657 or 614-221-6623
fax: 614-221-5618

Columbus Area Chamber of Commerce
37 N. High St.
Columbus, OH 43215
614-221-1321; fax: 614-221-1408

Dayton/Montgomery County Convention and Visitors Bureau
5th & Main Sts., 1 Chamber Plaza, Ste. A
Dayton, OH 45402
800-221-8235 or 513-226-8248
fax: 513-226-8294

Dayton Area Chamber of Commerce
Chamber Plaza
Dayton, OH 45402
513-226-1444; fax: 513-226-8254

[Toledo] Greater Toledo Convention and Visitors Bureau
401 Jefferson Ave.
Toledo, OH 43604
800-243-4667 or 419-321-6404
fax: 419-255-7731

Toledo Area Chamber of Commerce
300 Madison Ave., Ste. 200
Toledo, OH 43604
419-243-8191; fax: 419-241-8302

Domestic Tourism

Oklahoma

Tourism and Recreation Department
2401 N. Lincoln Blvd.
Will Rodgers Bldg., Ste. 500
Oklahoma City, OK 73105
800-652-6552 or 405-521-2413
fax: 405-521-4883

Oklahoma City Convention and Visitors Bureau
123 Park Ave.
Oklahoma City, OK 73102
800-225-5652 or 405-297-8910
fax: 405-297-8916

Oklahoma City Chamber of Commerce
123 Park Ave.
Oklahoma City, OK 73102
405-297-8900; fax: 405-297-8916

Tulsa Convention and Visitors Bureau/
Chamber of Commerce
616 S. Boston Ave., Ste. 100
Tulsa, OK 74119
800-558-3311 or 918-585-1201
fax: 918-592-6244

Oregon

Tourism Commission
775 Summer St., N.E.
Salem, OR 97310
800-547-7842 or 503-986-0000
fax: 503-986-0001

Eugene/Springfield Convention and Visitors Bureau
P.O. Box 10286
Eugene, OR 97440
800-547-5445 or 541-484-5307
fax: 541-343-6335

Eugene Chamber of Commerce
P.O. Box 1107
Eugene, OR 97440
541-484-1314; fax: 541-484-4942

Portland Visitors Association
26 S.W. Salmon St.
Portland, OR 97204
800-962-3700 or 503-275-9750
fax: 503-275-9774

Portland Metropolitan Chamber of Commerce
221 N.W. Second Ave.
Portland, OR 97209
503-228-9411; fax: 503-228-5126

Salem Convention and Visitors Association
1313 Mill St. S.E.
Salem, OR 97301
800-874-7012 or 503-581-4325
fax: 503-581-4540

Salem Chamber of Commerce
1110 Commercial St. N.E.
Salem, OR 97301
503-581-1466; fax: 503-581-0972

Springfield Chamber of Commerce
P.O. Box 155
Springfield, OR 97477
541-746-1651; fax: 541-726-4727

Pennsylvania

Office of Travel and Tourism
453 Forum Bldg.
Harrisburg, PA 17120
800-237-4363 or 717-787-5453
fax: 717-234-4560
WWW: http://www.state.pa.us/Visit/index.html

Erie Area Tourist and Convention Bureau
1006 State St.
Erie, PA 16501
814-454-7191; fax: 814-459-0241

Erie Area Chamber of Commerce
1006 State St.
Erie, PA 16501
814-454-7191; fax: 814-459-0241

Harrisburg-Hershey-Carlisle Tourism and Convention Bureau
114 Walnut St.
Harrisburg, PA 17101
800-995-0969 or 717-232-1377
fax: 717-232-4364

[Harrisburg] Capital Region Chamber of Commerce
114 Walnut St.
Harrisburg, PA 17108
717-232-4121; fax: 717-232-4364

Philadelphia Convention and Visitors Bureau
1515 Market St., Ste. 2020
Philadelphia, PA 19102
800-537-7676 or 215-636-3300
fax: 215-636-3327

[Philadelphia] Greater Philadelphia Chamber of Commerce
1234 Market St., Ste. 1800
Philadelphia, PA 19107
215-545-1234; fax: 215-972-3900

Pittsburgh Convention and Visitors Bureau
4 Gateway Center, 18th Fl.
Pittsburgh, PA 15222
800-366-0093 or 412-281-7711
fax: 412-644-5512

[Pittsburgh] Greater Pittsburgh Chamber of Commerce
3 Gateway Center
Pittsburgh, PA 15222
412-392-4500; fax: 412-392-4520

[Scranton] Greater Scranton Chamber of Commerce
P.O. Box 431
Scranton, PA 18501
800-722-5289 or 717-342-7711
fax: 717-347-6262

Rhode Island

Tourism Division
One W. Exchange St.
Providence, RI 02903
800-556-2484 or 401-277-2601
fax: 401-277-2102

Newport County Convention and Visitors Bureau
23 America's Cup Ave.
Newport, RI 02840
800-326-6030 or 401-849-8048
fax: 401-849-0291

Newport County Chamber of Commerce
45 Valley Rd.
Middletown, RI 02842-6377
401-847-1600; fax: 401-849-5848

[Providence] Greater Providence Convention and Visitors Bureau
30 Exchange Terr.
Providence, RI 02903
800-233-1636 or 401-274-1636
fax: 401-351-2090

[Providence] Greater Providence Chamber of Commerce
30 Exchange Terr.
Providence, RI 02903
401-521-5000; fax: 401-751-2434

South Carolina

Division of Tourism
1205 Pendleton St.
Columbia, SC 29201
803-734-0122; fax: 803-734-0133
WWW: http://www.sccsi.com/sc/home.html

Charleston Area Convention and Visitors Bureau
P.O. Box 975
Charleston, SC 29402
800-868-8118 or 803-853-8000
fax: 803-853-0444

Charleston Metro Chamber of Commerce
P.O. Box 975
Charleston, SC 29402
803-723-1773; fax: 803-723-4853

Columbia Metropolitan Convention and Visitors Bureau
P.O. Box 15
Columbia, SC 29202
800-264-4884 or 803-254-0479
fax: 803-799-6529

[Columbia] Greater Columbia Chamber of Commerce
950 Richland St.
Columbia, SC 29202
803-733-1110; fax: 803-733-1149

Greenville Convention and Visitors Bureau
P.O. Box 10527
Greenville, SC 29603
800-351-7180 or 864-421-0000
fax: 864-421-0005

[Greenville] Greater Greenville Chamber of Commerce
P.O. Box 10048
Greenville, SC 29603
864-242-1050; fax: 864-282-8549

South Dakota

Department of Tourism
711 E. Wells Ave.
Pierre, SD 57501
800-732-5682 or 605-773-3301
fax: 605-773-3256
WWW: http://www.state.sd.us/state/executive/tourism/
  tourism.html

Pierre Convention and Visitors Bureau
800 W. Dakota
Pierre, SD 57501
800-962-2034 or 605-224-7361
fax: 605-224-6485

Pierre Area Chamber of Commerce
P.O. Box 548
Pierre, SD 57501
800-962-2034 or 605-224-7361

Rapid City Convention and Visitors Bureau
P.O. Box 747
Rapid City, SD 57709
800-487-3223 or 605-343-1744
fax: 605-348-9217

Rapid City Area Chamber of Commerce
P.O. Box 747
Rapid City, SD 57709
605-343-1744; fax: 605-343-1916

Sioux Falls Convention and Visitors Bureau
200 N. Phillips Ave., Ste. 102
Sioux Falls, SD 57102
800-333-2072 or 605-336-1620
fax: 605-336-6499

Sioux Falls Area Chamber of Commerce
200 N. Phillips Ave., Ste. 102
Sioux Falls, SD 57102
605-336-1620; fax: 605-336-6499

Tennessee

Department of Tourist Development
P.O. Box 23170
Nashville, TN 37202
615-741-2158; fax: 615-741-7225
WWW: http://www.state.tn.us

Chattanooga Convention and Visitors Bureau
1001 Market St.
Chattanooga, TN 37402
800-231-4636 or 423-756-8687
fax: 423-265-1630

Chattanooga Area Chamber of Commerce
1001 Market St.
Chattanooga, TN 37402
423-756-2121; fax: 423-267-7242

Knoxville Convention and Visitors Bureau
810 Clinch Ave.
Knoxville, TN 37902
800-727-8045 or 423-523-7263
fax: 423-673-4400

Knoxville Chamber of Commerce
301 E. Church Ave.
Knoxville, TN 37915
423-637-4550; fax: 423-523-2071

Memphis Convention and Visitors Bureau
47 Union Ave.
Memphis, TN 38103
800-873-6282 or 901-543-5300
fax: 901-574-5350

Memphis Area Chamber of Commerce
22 N. Front St., Ste. 200
Memphis, TN 38103
901-575-3500; fax: 901-575-3510

Nashville Convention and Visitors Bureau
161 Fourth Ave. N.
Nashville, TN 37219
615-259-4730; fax: 615-244-6278

Nashville Chamber of Commerce
161 Fourth Ave. N.
Nashville, TN 37219
615-259-4755; fax: 615-256-3074

Texas

Department of Commerce, Tourism Division
1700 N. Congress Ave., Ste. 200
Austin, TX 78711
800-452-9292 or 512-462-9191
fax: 512-936-0089
WWW: http://travel.state.tx.us

Amarillo Convention and Visitor Council
P.O. Box 9480
Amarillo, TX 79105
806-374-1497; fax: 806-373-3909

Austin Convention and Visitors Bureau
201 E. Second St.
Austin, TX 78701
800-926-2282 or 512-474-5171
fax: 512-474-5183

[Austin] Greater Austin Chamber of Commerce
111 Congress Ave.
Austin, TX 78701
512-478-9383; fax: 512-478-9615

Corpus Christi Convention and Visitors Bureau
1201 N. Shoreline Blvd.
Corpus Christi, TX 78401
800-678-6232 or 512-881-1888
fax: 512-887-9023

Corpus Christi Business Alliance
1201 N. Shoreline Blvd.
Corpus Christi, TX 78401
512-881-1888; fax: 512-888-5627

Dallas Convention and Visitors Bureau
1201 Elm St., Ste. 2000
Dallas, TX 75270
214-746-6677; fax: 214-746-6688

[Dallas] Greater Dallas Chamber of Commerce
1201 Elm St., Ste. 2000
Dallas, TX 75270
214-746-6600; fax: 214-746-6799

El Paso Civic Convention and Tourist Center
1 Civic Center Plaza
El Paso, TX 79901
800-351-6024 or 915-534-0600
fax: 915-534-0686

[El Paso] Greater El Paso Chamber of Commerce
10 Civic Center Plaza
El Paso, TX 79901
915-534-0500; fax: 915-534-0513

Fort Worth Convention and Visitors Bureau
415 Throckmorton St.
Fort Worth, TX 76102
800-433-5747 or 817-336-8791
fax: 817-336-3282

Fort Worth Chamber of Commerce
777 Taylor St., Ste. 900
Fort Worth, TX 76102
817-336-2491; fax: 817-877-4034

[Houston] Greater Houston Convention and Visitors Bureau
801 Congress St.
Houston, TX 77002
800-365-7575 or 713-227-3100
fax: 713-227-6336

[Houston] Greater Houston Partnership
1200 Smith, Ste. 700
Houston, TX 77002
713-651-2100; fax: 713-221-2299

Lubbock Convention and Visitor's Bureau
P.O. Box 561
Lubbock, TX 97408
800-747-1419 or 806-747-5232
fax: 806-763-2311

Lubbock Chamber of Commerce
1120 14th St.
Lubbock, TX 79401
806-763-4666; fax: 806-763-2311

San Antonio Convention and Visitors Bureau
P.O. Box 2277
San Antonio, TX 78205
800-447-3372 or 210-270-8700
fax: 210-270-8782

[San Antonio] Greater San Antonio Chamber of Commerce
P.O. Box 1628
San Antonio, TX 78205
210-229-2100; fax: 210-229-1600

Utah

Travel Council
Council Hall, Capitol Hill, 300 N State St.
Salt Lake City, UT 84114
801-538-1030; fax: 801-538-1399
WWW: http://www.utah.com

Ogden-Weber County Convention and Visitors Bureau
2501 Wall Ave., Union Stn.
Ogden, UT 84401
800-255-8824 or 801-627-8288
fax: 801-399-0783

Ogden-Weber County Chamber of Commerce
2404 Washington Blvd., Ste. 1100
Ogden, UT 84401
801-621-8300; fax: 801-392-7609

[Provo] Mountainland Travel Region Office
2545 N. Canyon Rd.
Provo, UT 84604
801-377-2262; fax: 801-377-2317

Provo Chamber of Commerce
51 S. University Ave., Ste. 215
Provo, UT 84601
801-379-2555; fax: 801-379-2557

Salt Lake City Convention and Visitors Bureau
180 S. West Temple
Salt Lake City, UT 84101
800-541-4955 or 801-521-2822
fax: 801-355-9323

Salt Lake City Area Chamber of Commerce
175 E. 400 South, Ste. 600
Salt Lake City, UT 84111
801-364-3631

Vermont

Department of Travel and Tourism
134 State St.
Montpelier, VT 05602
800-837-6668 or 802-828-3236
fax: 802-828-3233
WWW: http://www.genghis.com/tourism/vermont.htm

[Barre] Central Vermont Chamber of Commerce
P.O. Box 336
Barre, VT 05641
802-229-5711; fax: 802-229-5713

Burlington Convention and Visitors Bureau
60 Main St., Ste. 100
Burlington, VT 05401
802-863-3489; fax: 802-863-1538

[Burlington] Lake Champlain Regional Chamber of Commerce
60 Main St., Ste. 100
Burlington, VT 05401
802-863-3489; fax: 802-863-1538

Virginia

Department of Economic Development, Division of Tourism
901 E. Byrd St.
Richmond, VA 23219
804-786-4484; fax: 804-786-1919
WWW: http://www.state.va.us/home/visitor.html

Norfolk Division, Hampton Roads Chamber of Commerce
420 Bank St.
Norfolk, VA 23510-2421
757-622-2312; fax: 757-622-5563

[Richmond] Metropolitan Richmond Convention and Visitors
  Bureau
550 E. Marshall St.
Richmond, VA 23219
800-370-9004 or 804-782-2777
fax: 804-780-2577

[Richmond] Central Virginia Chamber of Commerce
2318 Goodes Bridge Rd.
Richmond, VA 23224
804-745-6000; fax: 804-745-6695

Roanoke Valley Convention and Visitors Bureau
114 Market St.
Roanoke, VA 24011
800-635-5535 or 540-342-6025
fax: 540-342-7119

[Roanoke] Salem/Roanoke Valley Chamber of Commerce
P.O. Box 832
Salem, VA 24153
540-387-0267; fax: 540-837-4110

Virginia Beach Department of Convention and Visitor
  Development
2101 Parks Ave., Ste. 500
Virginia Beach, VA 23451
757-437-4700; fax: 757-437-4747

Virginia Beach Division, Hampton Roads Chamber of Commerce
4512 Virginia Beach Blvd.
Virginia Beach, VA 23462
757-490-1221; fax: 757-473-8208

Williamsburg Area Convention and Visitors Bureau
P.O. Box 3585
Williamsburg, VA 23187
800-368-6511 or 757-253-0192
fax: 757-229-2047

Washington

State Tourism Development Division
P.O. Box 42500
Olympia, WA 98504
800-544-1800 or 360-753-5601
fax: 360-753-4470

Olympia/Thurston County Chamber of Commerce
P.O. Box 1427
Olympia, WA 98501
800-753-8474 or 360-357-3362
fax: 360-357-3376

Seattle-King County Convention and Visitors Bureau
520 Pike St., Ste. 1300
Seattle, WA 98101
360-461-5840; fax: 360-461-5855

[Seattle] Greater Seattle Chamber of Commerce
1301 Fifth Ave., Ste. 2400
Seattle, WA 98101
206-389-7200; fax: 206-389-7288

Spokane Convention and Visitors Bureau
926 W. Sprague, Ste. 180
Spokane, WA 99204
509-624-1341; fax: 509-623-1297

Spokane Area Chamber of Commerce
W. 1020 Riverside Ave.
Spokane, WA 99204
509-624-1393; fax: 509-747-3230

Tacoma-Pierce County Visitor and Convention Bureau
906 Broadway
Tacoma, WA 98402
800-272-2662 or 206-627-2836
fax: 206-627-8783

Tacoma-Pierce County Chamber of Commerce
950 Pacific Ave.
Tacoma, WA 98401
206-627-2175; fax: 206-597-7305

West Virginia

Tourism and Parks Division
2101 Washington St. E.
Charleston, WV 25305
800-225-5982 or 304-558-2200
fax: 304-558-0108

Charleston Convention and Visitors Bureau
200 Civic Center Dr.
Charleston, WV 25301
800-733-5469 or 304-344-5075
fax: 304-344-1241

Charleston Chamber of Commerce
106 Capitol St., Ste. 100
Charleston, WV 25301
304-345-0770; fax: 304-345-0776

[Morgantown] Greater Morgantown Convention and Visitors
  Bureau
709 Beechurst Ave.
Morgantown, WV 26505
800-458-7373 or 304-292-5081
fax: 304-291-1354

Morgantown Area Chamber of Commerce
1009 University Ave.
Morgantown, WV 26505
304-292-3311; fax: 304-296-6619

Wheeling Convention and Visitors Bureau
1310 Market St.
Wheeling, WV 26003
800-828-3097 or 304-233-7709
fax: 304-233-1320

Wheeling Area Chamber of Commerce
1310 Market St.
Wheeling, WV 26003
304-233-2575; fax: 304-233-1320

Wisconsin

Division of Tourism
123 W. Washington Ave., 6th Fl.
Madison, WI 53703
800-432-8747 or 608-266-7621
fax: 608-266-3403
WWW: http://badger.state.wi.us/agencies/tourism/
    index.html

Green Bay Area Visitor and Convention Bureau
P.O. Box 10596
Green Bay, WI 54307
800-236-3976 or 414-494-9507
fax: 414-494-9229

Green Bay Area Chamber of Commerce
400 S. Washington St.
Green Bay, WI 54301
414-437-8704; fax: 414-437-1024

[Madison] Greater Madison Convention and Visitors Bureau
615 E. Washington Ave.
Madison, WI 53703
800-373-6376 or 608-255-2537
fax: 608-258-4950

[Madison] Greater Madison Chamber of Commerce
615 E. Washington Ave.
Madison, WI 53703
608-256-8348; fax: 608-256-0333

[Milwaukee] Greater Milwaukee Convention and Visitors Bureau
510 W. Kilbourn Ave.
Milwaukee, WI 53203
800-231-0903 or 414-273-3950
fax: 414-273-5596

[Milwaukee] Metropolitan Milwaukee Association of Commerce
756 N. Milwaukee St.
Milwaukee, WI 53202
414-287-4100; fax: 414-271-7753

Wyoming

Division of Tourism
I-25 and College Dr.
Cheyenne, WY 82002
800-225-5996 or 307-777-7777
fax: 307-777-6904
WWW: http://www.state.wy.us/state/tourism/tourism.html

Casper Area Convention and Visitors Bureau
P.O. Box 399
Casper, WY 82602
800-852-1889 or 307-234-5311
fax: 307-265-2643

Casper Area Chamber of Commerce
P.O. Box 399
Casper, WY 82602
307-234-5311; fax: 307-265-2643

Cheyenne Area Convention and Visitors Bureau
P.O. Box 765
Cheyenne, WY 82003
800-426-5009 or 307-778-3133
fax: 307-778-3190

[Cheyenne] Greater Cheyenne Chamber of Commerce
301 W. 16th St.
Cheyenne, WY 82001
307-638-3388; fax: 307-778-1450

APPENDIX 4

International Tourism Information Sources

The following list contains, in alphabetical order by country, contact information for tourism offices for more than 80 countries and embassies or consulate offices for more than 150 countries around the world.

Many foreign countries maintain tourism offices in the United States that can provide information on a wide range of travel-related subjects, including the country's history and culture, geography and climate, local customs, holidays and festivals, lodging and dining, places of interest, and transportation. Multiple listings are provided for some countries.

Foreign embassies located in Washington, D.C., are not only responsible for maintaining diplomatic relations with the United States, but can provide information on passport and visa requirements as well as general tourism information about their countries. Those with access to the Internet may obtain information from a number of foreign embassies located in the U.S. online at The Embassy Page, **http://www.embpage.org/usemb.html**. Many of the individual embassies' sites include links that contain tips for travelers and other information of interest to tourists.

Afghanistan

Republic of Afghanistan Embassy
2341 Wyoming Ave., N.W.
Washington, DC 20008
202-234-3770; fax: 202-328-3516

Albania

Republic of Albania Embassy
1511 K St., N.W., Ste. 1000
Washington, DC 20005
202-223-4942; fax: 202-628-7342

Algeria

Democratic and Popular Republic of Algeria Embassy
2118 Kalorama Rd., N.W.
Washington, DC 20008
202-265-2800; fax: 202-667-2174

Andorra

Andorra Bureau for Tourism and Information
6800 N. Knox Ave.
Lincolnwood, IL 60646
708-674-3091; fax: 708-329-9470

Angola

Republic of Angola Embassy
1819 L St., N.W., Ste. 400
Washington, DC 20036
202-785-1156; fax: 202-785-1258

Anguilla

Anguilla Tourist Board
P.O. Box 1388, Sactory Plaza
The Valley, Anguilla
British West Indies
800-553-4939 or 809-497-2759
fax: 809-497-2710

Antigua and Barbuda

Department of Tourism
610 Fifth Ave., Ste. 311
New York, NY 10020
212-541-4117; fax: 212-757-1607

Antigua and Barbuda Embassy
3216 New Mexico Ave., N.W.
Washington, DC 20016
202-362-5122; fax: 202-362-5225

Argentina

National Tourist Office
2655 Le Jeune Rd., Penthouse 1, Ste. F
Coral Gables, FL 33134
305-442-1366; fax: 305-441-7029

National Tourist Office
12 W. 56th St.
New York, NY 10019
212-603-0443; fax: 212-315-5545

Argentine Republic Embassy
1600 New Hampshire Ave., N.W.
Washington, DC 20009
202-939-6400; fax: 202-332-3171

Armenia

Republic of Armenia Embassy
1660 L St., N.W., 11th Fl.
Washington, DC 20036
202-628-5766; fax: 202-628-5769

Aruba

Aruba Tourism Authority
1000 Harbor Blvd.
Weehawken, NJ 07087
800-862-7822 or 201-330-0800
fax: 201-330-8757

Australia

Australian Tourist Commission
2049 Century Pk. E.
Los Angeles, CA 90067
800-753-0998 or 310-229-4870
fax: 310-552-1215

Australian Tourist Commission
100 Park Ave., 25th Fl.
New York, NY 10017
212-687-6300; fax: 212-661-3340

Commonwealth of Australia Embassy
1601 Massachusetts Ave., N.W.
Washington, DC 20036
202-797-3000; fax: 202-797-3168

Austria

National Tourist Office
11601 Wilshire Blvd., Ste. 2480
Los Angeles, CA 90025
310-477-2038; fax: 310-477-5141

National Tourist Office
500 N. Michigan Ave., Ste. 1950
Chicago, IL 60611
312-644-8029; fax: 312-644-6526

National Tourist Office
P.O. Box 1142, Times Sq.
New York, NY 10148
212-944-6880; fax: 212-730-4568

Republic of Austria Embassy
3524 International Ct., N.W.
Washington, DC 20008
202-895-6700; fax: 202-895-6750

Azerbaijan

Republic of Azerbaijan Embassy
927 15th St., N.W., Ste. 700
Washington, DC 20005
202-842-0001; fax: 202-842-0004

Bahamas

Bahamas Tourism Center
3450 Wilshire Blvd., Ste. 208
Los Angeles, CA 90010
800-422-4262 or 213-385-0033
fax: 213-383-3966

Bahamas Tourist Office
150 E. 52nd St., 28th Fl. N.
New York, NY 10022
800-422-4262 or 212-758-2777
fax: 212-753-6531

Commonwealth of the Bahamas Embassy
2220 Massachusetts Ave., N.W.
Washington, DC 20008
202-319-2660; fax: 202-319-2668

Bahrain

State of Bahrain Embassy
3502 International Dr., N.W.
Washington, DC 20008
202-342-0741; fax: 202-362-2192

Bangladesh

People's Republic of Bangladesh Embassy
2201 Wisconsin Ave., N.W., Ste. 300
Washington, DC 20007
202-342-8372; fax: 202-333-4971

Barbados

Barbados Tourism Authority
3440 Wilshire Blvd.
Los Angeles, CA 90010
800-221-9831 or 213-380-2198
fax: 213-384-2763

Barbados Tourism Authority
800 Second Ave.
New York, NY 10017
212-986-6516; fax: 212-573-9850

Barbados Embassy
2144 Wyoming Ave., N.W.
Washington, DC 20008
202-939-9200; fax: 202-332-7467

Belarus

Republic of Belarus Embassy
1619 New Hampshire Ave., N.W.
Washington, DC 20009
202-986-1604; fax: 202-986-1805

Belgium

Belgian Tourist Office
780 Third Ave.
New York, NY 10017
212-758-8130; fax: 212-355-7675

Kingdom of Belgium Embassy
3330 Garfield St., N.W.
Washington, DC 20008
202-333-6900; fax: 202-333-3079

Belize

Belize Tourist Board
421 Seventh Ave., Ste. 1110
New York, NY 10001
800-624-0686 or 212-563-6011
fax: 212-563-6033

Belize Embassy
2535 Massachusetts Ave., N.W.
Washington, DC 20008
202-332-9636; fax: 202-332-6888

Benin

Republic of Benin Embassy
2737 Cathedral Ave., N.W.
Washington, DC 20008
202-232-6656; fax: 202-265-1996

Bermuda

Department of Tourism
245 Peachtree Center Ave., N.E., Ste. 803
Atlanta, GA 30303
800-223-6106 or 404-524-1541
fax: 404-586-9933

Department of Tourism
310 Madison Ave., Ste. 201
New York, NY 10017
800-223-6106 or 212-818-9800
fax: 212-983-5289

Bhutan

Kingdom of Bhutan Consulate General
2 U.N. Plaza, 27th Floor
New York, NY 10017
212-826-1919; fax: 212-826-2998

Bolivia

Republic of Bolivia Embassy
3014 Massachusetts Ave., N.W.
Washington, DC 20008
202-483-4410; fax: 202-328-3712

Bonaire

Government Tourist Office
10 Rockefeller Plaza, Ste. 900
New York, NY 10020
800-826-6247 or 212-956-5911
fax: 212-956-5913

Bosnia and Herzegovina

Bosnia and Herzegovina Embassy
1707 L St., N.W., Ste. 760
Washington, DC 20036
202-833-3612; fax: 202-833-2061

Botswana

Republic of Botswana Embassy
3400 International Dr., N.W.
Intelfat Bldg., Ste. 7M
Washington, DC 20008
202-244-4990; fax: 202-244-4164

Brazil

Federative Republic of Brazil Embassy
3006 Massachusetts Ave., N.W.
Washington, DC 20008
202-745-2700; fax: 202-745-2827

Britain. *See* United Kingdom

British Virgin Islands

Tourist Board
1804 Union St.
San Francisco, CA 94123
800-835-8530 or 415-775-0344
fax: 415-775-2554

Tourist Board
370 Lexington Ave.
New York, NY 10017
800-835-8530 or 212-696-0400
fax: 212-949-8254

Brunei

State of Brunei Darussalam Embassy
2600 Virginia Ave., N.W., Ste. 300
Washington, DC 20037
202-342-0159; fax: 202-342-0158

Bulgaria

Bulgaria-Balkan Holidays-U.S.A.
317 Madison Ave., Ste. 508
New York, NY 10017
800-852-0944 or 212-573-5530
fax: 212-573-5538

Republic of Bulgaria Embassy
1621 22nd St., N.W.
Washington, DC 20008
202-387-7969; fax: 202-234-7973

Burkina Faso

Burkina Faso Embassy
2340 Massachusetts Ave., N.W.
Washington, DC 20008
202-332-5577

Burma. *See* Myanmar

Burundi

Republic of Burundi Embassy
2233 Wisconsin Ave., N.W., Ste. 212
Washington, DC 20007
202-342-2574; fax: 202-342-2578

Cameroon

Republic of Cameroon Embassy
2349 Massachusetts Ave., N.W.
Washington, DC 20008
202-265-8790; fax: 202-387-3826

Canada

Canadian Tourism Commission
4th Floor, East Tower
235 Queen St.
Ottawa, Ontario K1A 0H6
Canada
800-577-2266

Canadian Embassy
501 Pennsylvania Ave., N.W.
Washington, DC 20001
202-682-1740; fax: 202-682-7726

Cape Verde

Republic of Cape Verde Embassy
3415 Massachusetts Ave., N.W.
Washington, DC 20007
202-965-6820; fax: 202-965-1207

Cayman Islands

Cayman Islands Department of Tourism
3440 Wilshire Blvd., Ste. 1202
Los Angeles, CA 90010
213-738-1968; fax: 213-738-1829

Cayman Islands Department of Tourism
420 Lexington Ave., Ste. 2733
New York, NY 10170
800-346-3313 or 212-682-5582
fax: 212-986-5123

Central African Republic

Central African Republic Embassy
1618 22nd St., N.W.
Washington, DC 20008
202-483-7800; fax: 202-332-9893

Chad

Republic of Chad Embassy
2002 R St., N.W.
Washington, DC 20009
202-462-4009; fax: 202-265-1937

Chile

Republic of Chile Embassy
1732 Massachusetts Ave., N.W.
Washington, DC 20036
202-785-1746; fax: 202-887-5579

China

China National Tourist Office
333 W. Broadway, Ste. 201
Glendale, CA 91204
818-545-7505; fax: 818-545-7506

China National Tourist Office
350 Fifth Ave., Ste. 6413
New York, NY 10108
212-760-9700; fax: 212-760-8809

People's Republic of China Embassy
2300 Connecticut Ave., N.W.
Washington, DC 20008
202-328-2500; fax: 202-234-4055

Colombia

Republic of Colombia Embassy
2118 Leroy Pl., N.W.
Washington, DC 20008
202-387-8338; fax: 202-232-8643

Comoros

Federal Islamic Republic of Comoros Embassy
336 E. 45th St., 2nd Fl.
New York, NY 10017
212-972-8010; fax: 212-983-4712

Congo

Republic of Congo Embassy
4891 Colorado Ave., N.W.
Washington, DC 20011
202-726-0825; fax: 202-726-1860

Costa Rica

Republic of Costa Rica Embassy
2114 'S' St., N.W.
Washington, DC 20008
202-234-2945; fax: 202-265-4795

Cote D'Ivoire (Ivory Coast)

Republic of Cote D'Ivoire Embassy
2424 Massachusetts Ave., N.W.
Washington, DC 20008
202-797-0300; fax: 202-483-8482

Croatia

Atlas Tourism and Travel
60 E. 42nd St., Ste. 2235
New York, NY 10165
800-528-5275 or 212-697-6767
fax: 212-697-7678

Republic of Croatia Embassy
2343 Massachusetts Ave., N.W.
Washington, DC 20008
202-588-5899; fax: 202-588-8936

Curacao

Curacao Tourist Board
330 Biscayne Blvd., Ste. 808
Miami, FL 33132
800-445-8266 or 305-374-5811
fax: 305-374-6741

Curacao Tourist Board
475 Park Ave. S., Ste. 2000
New York, NY 10016
800-270-3350 or 212-683-7660
fax: 212-683-9337

Cyprus

Cyprus Tourism Organization
13 E. 40th St.
New York, NY 10016
212-683-5280; fax: 212-683-5282

Republic of Cyprus Embassy
2211 R St., N.W.
Washington, DC 20008
202-462-5772; fax: 202-483-6710

Czech Republic

Viktor Corp. [Tourism]
10 E. 40th St.
New York, NY 10016
212-689-9720; fax: 212-481-0597

Czech Republic Embassy
3900 Spring of Freedom St., N.W.
Washington, DC 20008
202-363-6315; fax: 202-966-8540

Denmark

Danish Tourist Board
655 Third Ave., 18th Fl.
New York, NY 10017
212-949-2333; fax: 212-983-5260

Kingdom of Denmark Embassy
3200 Whitehaven St., N.W.
Washington, DC 20008
202-234-4300; fax: 202-328-1470

Djibouti

Republic of Djibouti Embassy
1156 15th St., N.W., Ste. 515
Washington, DC 20005
202-331-0270; fax: 202-331-0302

Dominica

Commonwealth of Dominica Consulate General
820 Second Ave., 9th Floor
New York, NY 10017
212-949-0853; fax: 212-808-4975

Dominican Republic

Dominican Republic Tourist Board
1501 Broadway, Ste. 410
New York, NY 10036
212-575-4966; fax: 212-575-5448

Dominican Republic Embassy
1715 22nd St., N.W.
Washington, DC 20008
202-332-6280; fax: 202-265-8057

Ecuador

Ecuador Trade Center
2600 Douglas Rd., Ste. 401
Coral Gables, FL 33134
305-461-2363; fax: 305-446-7755

Republic of Ecuador Embassy
2535 15th St., N.W.
Washington, DC 20009
202-234-7200

Egypt

Egyptian Tourist Authority
8383 Wilshire Blvd., Ste. 215
Beverly Hills, CA 90211
213-653-8815; fax: 213-653-8961

Egyptian Tourist Authority
645 N. Michigan Ave., Ste. 829
Chicago, IL 60611
312-280-4666; fax: 312-280-4788

Egyptian Tourist Authority
630 Fifth Ave., Ste. 1706
New York, NY 10111
212-332-2570; fax: 212-956-6439

Arab Republic of Egypt
3521 International Ct., N.W.
Washington, DC 20008
202-895-5400; fax: 202-244-4319

El Salvador

Republic of El Salvador Embassy
2308 California St., N.W.
Washington, DC 20008
202-265-9671

Equatorial Guinea

Republic of Equatorial Guinea Embassy
57 Magnolia Ave.
Mount Vernon, NY 10553
914-667-6913; fax: 914-667-6838

Eritrea

State of Eritrea Embassy
1708 New Hampshire Ave., N.W.
Washington, DC 20009
202-319-1991; fax: 202-319-1304

Estonia

Republic of Estonia Embassy
2131 Massachusetts Ave., N.W.
Washington, DC 20008
202-588-0101; fax: 202-588-0108

Ethiopia

Ethiopia Embassy
2134 Kalorama Rd., N.W.
Washington, DC 20008
202-234-2281; fax: 202-328-7950

European Commission

European Commission
2300 M St., N.W., 3rd Fl.
Washington, DC 20037
202-862-9500; fax: 202-429-1766

Fiji

Fiji Visitors Bureau
5777 W. Century Blvd., Ste. 220
Los Angeles, CA 90045
800-932-3454 or 310-568-1616
fax: 310-670-2318

Republic of Fiji Embassy
2233 Wisconsin Ave., N.W., Ste. 240
Washington, DC 20007
202-337-8320; fax: 202-337-1996

Finland

Finnish Tourist Board
655 Third Ave., 18th Fl.
New York, NY 10017
212-949-2333; fax: 212-983-5260

Republic of Finland Embassy
3301 Massachusetts Ave., N.W.
Washington, DC 20008
202-298-5800; fax: 202-298-6030

France

French Government Tourist Office
9454 Wilshire Blvd., Ste. 715
Beverly Hills, CA 90212
310-271-6665; fax: 310-276-2835

French Government Tourist Office
676 N. Michigan Ave., Ste. 3360
Chicago, IL 60611
312-751-7800; fax: 312-337-6339

French Government Tourist Office
444 Madison Ave.
New York, NY 10022
212-838-7800; fax: 212-838-7855

French Republic Embassy
4101 Reservoir Rd., N.W.
Washington, DC 20007
202-944-6000; fax: 202-944-6116

French West Indies

French West Indies Tourist Board
610 Fifth Ave.
New York, NY 10020
212-757-1125; fax: 212-247-6468

French West Indies Tourist Office
9454 Wilshire Blvd., Ste. 715
Beverly Hills, CA 90212
310-271-6665; fax: 310-276-2835

Gabon

Gabon Tourist Information Office
347 Fifth Ave., Ste. 810
New York, NY 10016
212-447-6701; fax: 212-447-1532

Gabonese Republic Embassy
2034 20th St., N.W.
Washington, DC 20009
202-797-1000; fax: 202-332-0668

Gambia

Republic of Gambia Embassy
1155 15th St., N.W., Ste. 1000
Washington, DC 20005
202-785-1399; fax: 202-785-1430

Georgia

Republic of Georgia Embassy
1511 K St., N.W., Ste. 424
Washington, DC 20005
202-393-6060; fax: 202-393-4537

Germany

German National Tourist Office
11766 Wilshire Blvd., Ste. 750
Los Angeles, CA 90025
310-575-9799; fax: 310-575-1565

German National Tourist Office
122 E. 42nd St., 52nd Fl.
New York, NY 10168
212-661-7200; fax: 212-661-7174

Federal Republic of Germany Embassy
4645 Reservoir Rd., N.W.
Washington, DC 20007
202-298-4000; fax: 202-298-4249

Ghana

Republic of Ghana Embassy
3512 International Dr., N.W.
Washington, DC 20008
202-686-4520; fax: 202-686-4527

Greece

Greek National Tourist Organization
611 W. Sixth St., Ste. 2198
Los Angeles, CA 90017
213-626-6696; fax: 213-489-9744

Greek National Tourist Organization
645 Fifth Ave.
New York, NY 10022
212-421-5777; fax: 212-826-6940

[Greece] Hellenic Republic Embassy
2221 Massachusetts Ave., N.W.
Washington, DC 20008
202-939-5800; fax: 202-939-5824

Grenada

Grenada Office of Tourism
820 Second Ave., Ste. 900D
New York, NY 10017
800-927-9554 or 212-687-9554
fax: 212-573-9731

Grenada Embassy
1701 New Hampshire Ave., N.W.
Washington, DC 20009
202-265-2561; fax: 202-265-2468

Guatemala

Republic of Guatemala Embassy
2220 R St., N.W.
Washington, DC 20008
202-745-4952; fax: 202-745-1908

Guinea

Republic of Guinea Embassy
2112 Leroy Pl., N.W.
Washington, DC 20008
202-483-9420; fax: 202-483-8688

Guinea-Bissau

Republic of Guinea-Bissau Embassy
918 16th St., Mezzanine Ste.
Washington, DC 20006
202-872-4222; fax: 202-872-4226

Guyana

Cooperative Republic of Guyana Embassy
2490 Tracy Pl., N.W.
Washington, DC 20008
202-265-6900; fax: 202-232-1297

Haiti

Republic of Haiti Embassy
2311 Massachusetts Ave., N.W.
Washington, DC 20008
202-332-4090; fax: 202-745-7215

Honduras

Republic of Honduras Embassy
3007 Tilden St., N.W.
Washington, DC 20008
202-966-7702; fax: 202-966-9751

Hong Kong

Hong Kong Tourist Association
10940 Wilshire Blvd., Ste. 1220
Los Angeles, CA 90024
800-282-4582 or 310-208-4582
fax: 310-208-1869

Hong Kong Tourist Association
610 Enterprise Dr., Ste. 200
Oak Brook, IL 60521
708-575-2828; fax: 708-575-2829

Hong Kong Tourist Association
590 Fifth Ave.
New York, NY 10036
212-869-5008; fax: 212-730-2605

Hungary

Hungarian National Tourist Office
150 E. 58th St., 33rd Fl.
New York, NY 10155
212-355-0240; fax: 212-207-4130

Republic of Hungary Embassy
3910 Shoemaker St., N.W.
Washington, DC 20008
202-362-6730; fax: 202-966-8135

Iceland

Icelandic Tourist Board
655 Third Ave., 18th Fl.
New York, NY 10017
212-949-2333; fax: 212-983-5260

Republic of Iceland Embassy
1156 15th St., N.W.
Washington, DC 20005
202-265-6653; fax: 202-265-6656

India

India Tourist Office
3550 Wilshire Blvd., Ste. 204
Los Angeles, CA 90010
800-422-4634 or 213-380-8855
fax: 213-380-6111

India Tourist Office
30 Rockefeller Plaza, 15 N. Mezzanine
New York, NY 10112
800-953-9399 or 212-586-4901
fax: 212-582-3274

Republic of India Embassy
2107 Massachusetts Ave., N.W.
Washington, DC 20008
202-939-7000; fax: 202-939-7027

Indonesia

Indonesian Tourist Promotion Office
3457 Wilshire Blvd., Ste. 104
Los Angeles, CA 90010
213-387-2078; fax: 213-380-4876

Republic of Indonesia Embassy
2020 Massachusetts Ave., N.W.
Washington, DC 20036
202-775-5200; fax: 202-775-5365

Iraq

Republic of Iraq Embassy
1801 P St., N.W.
Washington, DC 20036
202-483-7500; fax: 202-462-5066

Ireland

Irish Tourist Board
345 Park Ave., 17th Fl.
New York, NY 10154
800-223-6470 or 212-418-0800
fax: 212-371-9052

Republic of Ireland Embassy
2234 Massachusetts Ave., N.W.
Washington, DC 20008
202-462-3939; fax: 202-232-5993

Israel

Israel Economic Commission and Tourist Office
800 Second Ave.
New York, NY 10017
212-499-5600; fax: 212-499-5715

Israel Ministry of Tourism
6380 Wilshire Blvd., Ste. 1700
Los Angeles, CA 90048
213-658-7462; fax: 213-658-6543

State of Israel Embassy
3514 International Dr., N.W.
Washington, DC 20008
202-364-5500; fax: 202-364-5610

Italy

Italian Government Travel Office
12400 Wilshire Blvd., Ste. 550
Los Angeles, CA 90025
310-820-0098; fax: 310-820-6357

Italian Government Travel Office
630 Fifth Ave., Ste. 1565
New York, NY 10111
212-245-4822; fax: 212-586-9249

Italian Republic Embassy
1601 Fuller St., N.W.
Washington, DC 20009
202-328-5500; fax: 202-328-5542

Ivory Coast. *See* Cote D'Ivoire, Republic of

Jamaica

Jamaica Tourist Board
3440 Wilshire Blvd., Ste. 1207
Los Angeles, CA 90010
213-384-1123; fax: 213-384-1780

Jamaica Tourist Board
1320 S. Dixie Hwy., Ste. 1100
Coral Gables, FL 33146
305-665-0557; fax: 305-666-7239

Jamaica Tourist Board
801 Second Ave., 20th Fl.
New York, NY 10017
212-856-9727; fax: 212-856-9730

Jamaica Embassy
1520 New Hampshire Ave., N.W.
Washington, DC 20036
202-452-0660; fax: 202-452-0081

Japan

Japan National Tourist Organization
624 S. Grand Ave., Ste. 1611
Los Angeles, CA 90017
213-623-1952; fax: 213-623-6301

Japan National Tourist Organization
401 N. Michigan Ave., Ste. 770
Chicago, IL 60611
312-222-0874; fax: 312-222-0876

Japan National Tourist Organization
1 Rockefeller Plaza, Ste. 1250
New York, NY 10020
212-757-5640; fax: 212-307-6754

Japan Embassy
2520 Massachusetts Ave., N.W.
Washington, DC 20008
202-939-6700; fax: 202-328-2187

Jordan

Jordan Information Bureau
2319 Wyoming Ave., N.W.
Washington, DC 20008
202-265-1606; fax: 202-667-0777

Hashemite Kingdom of Jordan Embassy
3504 International Dr., N.W.
Washington, DC 20008
202-966-2664; fax: 202-966-3110

Kazakhstan

Republic of Kazakhstan Embassy
3421 Massachusetts Ave., N.W.
Washington, DC 20007
202-333-4504; fax: 202-333-4509

Kenya

Kenya Tourist Office
9150 Wilshire Blvd., Ste. 160
Beverly Hills, CA 90212
310-274-6635; fax: 310-859-7010

Kenya Tourist Office
424 Madison Ave.
New York, NY 10017
212-486-1300; fax: 212-688-0911

Republic of Kenya Embassy
2249 R St., N.W.
Washington, DC 20008
202-387-6101; fax: 202-462-3829

Kiribati

Republic of Kiribati Honorary Consulate
850 Richards St., Ste. 503
Honolulu, HI 96813
808-521-7703

Korea

Korea National Tourism Organization
3435 Wilshire Blvd., Ste. 1110
Los Angeles, CA 90010
213-382-3435; fax: 213-480-0483

Korea National Tourism Organization
205 N. Michigan Ave., Ste. 2212
Chicago, IL 60601
312-819-2560; fax: 312-819-2563

Republic of Korea Embassy
2450 Massachusetts Ave., N.W.
Washington, DC 20008
202-939-5600; fax: 202-797-0595

Kuwait

State of Kuwait Embassy
2940 Tilden St., N.W.
Washington, DC 20008
202-966-0702; fax: 202-966-0517

Kyrgyzstan

Republic of Kyrgyzstan Embassy
1511 K St. N.W., Ste. 705
Washington, DC 20005
202-347-3732; fax: 202-347-3718

Laos

Lao People's Democratic Republic Embassy
222 'S' St., N.W.
Washington, DC 20008
202-332-6416; fax: 202-332-4923

Latvia

Republic of Latvia Embassy
4325 17th St., N.W.
Washington, DC 20011
202-726-8213; fax: 202-726-6785

Lebanon

Republic of Lebanon Embassy
2560 28th St., N.W.
Washington, DC 20008
202-939-6300; fax: 202-939-6324

Lesotho

Kingdom of Lesotho Embassy
2511 Massachusetts Ave., N.W.
Washington, DC 20008
202-797-5533; fax: 202-234-6815

Liberia

Liberia Tourist Information
5303 Colorado Ave., N.W.
Washington, DC 20011
202-723-0437; fax: 202-723-0436

Republic of Liberia Embassy
5303 Colorado, N.W.
Washington, DC 20011
202-723-0437; fax: 202-723-0436

Lithuania

Republic of Lithuania Embassy
2622 16th St., N.W.
Washington, DC 20009
202-234-5860; fax: 202-328-0466

Luxembourg

Luxembourg National Tourist Office
17 Beekman Pl.
New York, NY 10022
212-935-8888; fax: 212-935-5896

Grand Duchy of Luxembourg Embassy
2200 Massachusetts Ave., N.W.
Washington, DC 20008
202-265-4171; fax: 202-328-8270

Macau

Macau Tourist Information Bureau
70A Greenwich Ave., Ste. 316
New York, NY 10011
212-206-6828; fax: 212-727-3222

Madagascar

Democratic Republic of Madagascar Embassy
2374 Massachusetts Ave., N.W.
Washington, DC 20008
202-265-5525; fax: 202-265-3034

Malawi

Republic of Malawi Embassy
2408 Massachusetts Ave., N.W.
Washington, DC 20008
202-797-1007; fax: 202-265-0976

Malaysia

Malaysian Tourism Promotion Board
818 W. Seventh St.
Los Angeles, CA 90017
800-336-6842 or 213-689-9702
fax: 213-689-1530

Malaysia Embassy
2401 Massachusetts Ave., N.W.
Washington, DC 20008
202-328-2700; fax: 202-483-7661

Mali

Republic of Mali Embassy
2130 R St., N.W.
Washington, DC 20008
202-332-2249; fax: 202-332-6603

Malta

Malta National Tourist Office
350 Fifth Ave., Empire State Bldg., Ste. 4412
New York, NY 10118
212-695-9520; fax: 212-695-8229

Malta Embassy
2017 Connecticut Ave., N.W.
Washington, DC 20008
202-462-3611; fax: 202-387-5470

Marshall Islands

Republic of the Marshall Islands Embassy
2433 Massachusetts Ave., N.W.
Washington, DC 20008
202-234-5414; fax: 202-232-3236

Martinique. *See* **French West Indies**

Mauritania

Islamic Republic of Mauritania Embassy
2129 Leroy Pl., N.W.
Washington, DC 20008
202-232-5700; fax: 202-319-2623

Mauritius

Mauritius Government Tourist Information Service
8 Haven Ave., Ste. 227
Port Washington, NY 11050
516-944-3763; fax: 516-944-8458

Mauritius Embassy
4301 Connecticut Ave., N.W., Ste. 441
Washington, DC 20008
202-244-1491; fax: 202-966-0983

Mexico

Mexican Government Tourism Office
10100 Santa Monica Blvd., Ste. 224
Los Angeles, CA 90067
310-203-8191; fax: 310-203-8316

Mexican Government Tourism Office
2333 Ponce de Leon Blvd., Ste. 17
Coral Gables, FL 33134
800-446-3942 or 305-443-9160
fax: 305-443-1186

Mexican Government Tourism Office
405 Park Ave., Ste. 1401
New York, NY 10022
800-446-3942 or 212-755-7261
fax: 212-753-2874

United Mexican States Embassy
1911 Pennsylvania Ave., N.W.
Washington, DC 20006
202-728-1600; fax: 202-728-1698

Micronesia

Federated States of Micronesia Embassy
1725 'N' St., N.W.
Washington, DC 20036
202-223-4383; fax: 202-223-4391

Moldova

Republic of Moldova Embassy
1511 K St., N.W., Ste. 329
Washington, DC 20005
202-783-3012; fax: 202-783-3342

Monaco

Monaco Government Tourist and Convention Office
845 Third Ave., 19th Fl.
New York, NY 10022
800-753-9696 or 212-759-5227
fax: 212-754-9320

Principality of Monaco Honorary Consulate
888 16th St., N.W., Ste. 300
Washington, D.C. 20006
202-887-1400

Mongolia

Mongolia Embassy
2833 M St., N.W.
Washington, DC 20007
202-333-7117; fax: 202-298-9227

International Tourism

Morocco

Moroccan National Tourist Office
20 E. 46th St., Ste. 1201
New York, NY 10017
212-557-2520; fax: 212-949-8148

Kingdom of Morocco Embassy
1601 21st St., N.W.
Washington, DC 20009
202-462-7979; fax: 202-265-0161

Mozambique

Republic of Mozambique Embassy
1990 M St., N.W., Ste. 570
Washington, DC 20036
202-293-7146; fax: 202-835-0245

Myanmar (Burma)

Union of Myanmar Embassy
2300 'S' St., N.W.
Washington, DC 20008
202-332-9044; fax: 202-332-9046

Namibia

Republic of Namibia Embassy
1605 New Hampshire Ave., N.W.
Washington, DC 20009
202-986-0540; fax: 202-986-0443

Nauru

Republic of Nauru Honorary Consulate
841 Bishop St., Ste. 506
Honolulu, HI 96813
808-523-7821

Nepal

Kingdom of Nepal Embassy
2131 Leroy Pl., N.W.
Washington, DC 20008
202-667-4550; fax: 202-667-5534

Netherlands

Netherlands Board of Tourism
225 N. Michigan Ave., Ste. 326
Chicago, IL 60601
800-953-8824 or 312-819-0300
fax: 312-819-1740

Netherlands Board of Tourism
355 Lexington Ave., 21st Fl.
New York, NY 10017
212-370-7360; fax: 212-370-9507

Kingdom of the Netherlands Embassy
4200 Wisconsin Ave.
Washington, DC 20016
202-244-5300; fax: 202-362-3430

New Zealand

New Zealand Tourism Board
501 Santa Monica Blvd., Ste. 300
Santa Monica, CA 90401
800-338-5494 or 310-395-7480
fax: 310-395-5453

New Zealand Embassy
37 Observatory Cir., N.W.
Washington, DC 20008
202-328-4800; fax: 202-667-5227

Nicaragua

Republic of Nicaragua Embassy
1627 New Hampshire Ave., N.W.
Washington, DC 20009
202-939-6570; fax: 202-939-6542

Niger

Republic of Niger Embassy
2204 R St., N.W.
Washington, DC 20008
202-483-4224; fax: 202-483-3169

Nigeria

Federal Republic of Nigeria Embassy
1333 16th St., N.W.
Washington, DC 20036
202-986-8400; fax: 202-775-1385

Northern Ireland

Northern Ireland Tourist Board
551 Fifth Ave., Ste. 701
New York, NY 10176
800-326-0036 or 212-922-0101
fax: 212-922-0099

Norway

Norwegian Tourist Board
655 Third Ave., 18th Fl.
New York, NY 10017
212-949-2333; fax: 212-983-5260

Kingdom of Norway Embassy
2720 34th St., N.W.
Washington, DC 20008
202-333-6000; fax: 202-337-0870

Oman

Sultanate of Oman Embassy
2535 Belmont Rd., N.W.
Washington, DC 20008
202-387-1980; fax: 202-745-4933

Pakistan

Islamic Republic of Pakistan Embassy
2315 Massachusetts Ave., N.W.
Washington, DC 20008
202-939-6200; fax: 202-387-0484

Panama

Republic of Panama Embassy
2862 McGill Terr., N.W.
Washington, DC 20008
202-483-1407; fax: 202-483-8413

Papua New Guinea

Papua New Guinea Embassy
1615 New Hampshire Ave., N.W., Ste. 300
Washington, DC 20009
202-745-3680; fax: 202-745-3679

Paraguay

Republic of Paraguay Embassy
2400 Massachusetts Ave., N.W.
Washington, DC 20008
202-483-6960; fax: 202-234-4508

Peru

Republic of Peru Embassy
1700 Massachusetts Ave., N.W.
Washington, DC 20036
202-833-9860; fax: 202-659-8124

Philippines

Philippine Department of Tourism
556 Fifth Ave., 1st Fl. Mezzanine
New York, NY 10036
212-575-7915; fax: 212-302-6759

Republic of the Philippines Embassy
1600 Massachusetts Ave., N.W.
Washington, DC 20036
202-467-9300; fax: 202-328-7614

Poland

Polish National Tourist Office
275 Madison Ave., Ste. 1711
New York, NY 10016
212-338-9412; fax: 212-338-9283

Republic of Poland Embassy
2640 16th St., N.W.
Washington, DC 20009
202-234-3800; fax: 202-328-6271

Portugal

Portuguese National Tourist Office
590 Fifth Ave., 4th Fl.
New York, NY 10036
800-767-8842 or 212-354-4403
fax: 212-764-6137

Republic of Portugal Embassy
2125 Kalorama Rd., N.W.
Washington, DC 20008
202-328-8610; fax: 202-462-3726

Qatar

State of Qatar Embassy
4200 Wisconsin Ave., Ste. 200
Washington, DC 20016
202-274-1600; fax: 202-237-0061

Romania

Romanian National Tourist Office
342 Madison Ave., Ste. 210
New York, NY 10173
212-697-6971; fax: 212-697-6972

Romania Embassy
1607 23rd St., N.W.
Washington, DC 20008
202-232-4747; fax: 202-232-4748

Russia

Russian Travel Information Office (Intourist U.S.A.)
610 Fifth Ave., Rockefeller Center, Ste. 603
New York, NY 10020
212-757-3884; fax: 212-459-0031

Russian Federation Embassy
2650 Wisconsin Ave., N.W.
Washington, DC 20007
202-298-5700; fax: 202-298-5735

Rwanda

Republic of Rwanda Embassy
1714 New Hampshire Ave., N.W.
Washington, DC 20009
202-232-2882; fax: 202-232-4544

Saint Kitts and Nevis

Saint Kitts and Nevis Department of Tourism
414 E. 75th St.
New York, NY 10021
800-582-6208 or 212-535-1234
fax: 212-734-6511

State of Saint Kitts and Nevis Embassy
3216 New Mexico Ave., N.W.
Washington, DC 20016
202-686-2636; fax: 202-686-5740

Saint Lucia

Saint Lucia Tourist Board
820 Second Ave., Ste. 900E
New York, NY 10017
800-456-3984 or 212-867-2950
fax: 212-867-2795

Saint Lucia Embassy
3216 New Mexico Ave., N.W.
Washington, DC 20016
202-364-6792; fax: 202-364-6723

Saint Vincent and the Grenadines

Saint Vincent and the Grenadines Tourist Information Office
801 Second Ave., 21st Fl.
New York, NY 10017
800-729-1726 or 212-687-4981
fax: 212-949-5946

Saint Vincent and the Grenadines Embassy
3216 New Mexico Ave., N.W.
Washington, DC 20036
202-364-6730; fax: 202-364-6736

San Marino

Republic of San Marino Honorary Consulate General
1899 L St., N.W., Ste. 500
Washington, D.C. 20036
202-223-3517

Sao Tome and Principe

Democratic Republic of Sao Tome and Principe Embassy
122 E. 42nd St., Rm. 1604
New York, NY 10168
212-697-4211; fax: 212-687-8389

Saudi Arabia

Kingdom of Saudi Arabia Embassy
601 New Hampshire Ave., N.W.
Washington, DC 20037
202-342-3800; fax: 202-337-3233

Scandinavia

Scandinavian Tourist Board
655 Third Ave., 18th Fl.
New York, NY 10017
212-949-2333; fax: 212-983-5260

Senegal

Senegal Tourist Office
310 Madison Ave., Ste. 724
New York, NY 10017
800-443-2527 or 212-286-0977
fax: 212-286-0172

Republic of Senegal Embassy
2112 Wyoming Ave., N.W.
Washington, DC 20008
202-234-0540; fax: 202-332-6315

Seychelles

Seychelles Tourist Office
820 Second Ave., Ste. 900-F
New York, NY 10017
212-687-9766; fax: 212-922-9177

Republic of Seychelles Embassy
820 Second Ave., Ste. 900-F
New York, NY 10017
212-687-9766; fax: 212-922-9177

Sierra Leone

Republic of Sierra Leone Embassy
1701 19th St., N.W.
Washington, DC 20009
202-939-9261; fax: 202-483-1793

Singapore

Singapore Tourist Promotion Board
8484 Wilshire Blvd., Ste. 510
Beverly Hills, CA 90211
213-852-1901; fax: 213-852-0129

Singapore Tourist Promotion Board
590 Fifth Ave., 12th Fl.
New York, NY 10036
212-302-4861; fax: 212-302-4801

Republic of Singapore Embassy
3501 International Pl., N.W.
Washington, DC 20008
202-537-3100; fax: 202-537-0876

Slovakia

Viktor Corp. [Tourism]
10 E. 40th St.
New York, NY 10016
212-689-9720; fax: 212-481-0597

Slovakia Embassy
2201 Wisconsin Ave., N.W., Ste. 350
Washington, DC 20007
202-965-5161; fax: 202-965-5166

Slovenia

Republic of Slovenia Embassy
1525 New Hampshire Ave., N.W.
Washington, DC 20036
202-667-5363; fax: 202-667-4563

South Africa

South African Tourism Board
9841 Airport Blvd.
Los Angeles, CA 90045
800-782-9772 or 310-641-8444
fax: 310-641-5812

South African Tourism Board
500 Fifth Ave., Ste. 2040
New York, NY 10110
800-822-5368 or 212-730-2929
fax: 212-764-1980

Republic of South Africa Embassy
3051 Massachusetts Ave., N.W.
Washington, DC 20008
202-232-4400; fax: 202-265-1607

Spain

Tourist Office of Spain
8383 Wilshire Blvd., Ste. 960
Beverly Hills, CA 90211
213-658-7188; fax: 213-658-1061

Tourist Office of Spain
1221 Brickell Ave., Ste. 1850
Miami, FL 33131
305-358-1992; fax: 305-358-8223

Tourist Office of Spain
665 Fifth Ave., 35th Fl.
New York, NY 10022
212-265-8822; fax: 212-265-8864

Spain Embassy
2375 Pennsylvania Ave., N.W.
Washington, DC 20037
202-452-0100; fax: 202-833-5670

Sri Lanka

Democratic Socialist Republic of Sri Lanka Embassy
2148 Wyoming Ave., N.W.
Washington, DC 20008
202-483-4025; fax: 202-232-7181

Sudan

Republic of the Sudan Embassy
2210 Massachusetts Ave., N.W.
Washington, DC 20008
202-338-8565; fax: 202-667-2406

Suriname

Republic of Suriname Embassy
4301 Connecticut Ave., N.W., Ste. 108
Washington, DC 20008
202-244-7488; fax: 202-244-5878

Swaziland

Kingdom of Swaziland Embassy
3400 International Dr., N.W., Ste. 3M
Washington, DC 20008
202-362-6683; fax: 202-244-8059

Sweden

Swedish National Tourist Office
655 Third Ave., 18th Fl.
New York, NY 10017
212-949-2333; fax: 212-983-5260

Kingdom of Sweden Embassy
1501 M St., N.W.
Washington, DC 20005
202-467-2600; fax: 202-467-2699

Switzerland

Swiss National Tourist Office
222 N. Sepulveda Blvd., Ste. 1570
El Segundo, CA 90245
310-335-5980; fax: 310-335-5982

Swiss National Tourist Office
608 Fifth Ave.
New York, NY 10020
212-757-5944; fax: 212-262-6116

Swiss Confederation Embassy
2900 Cathedral Ave., N.W.
Washington, DC 20008
202-745-7900; fax: 202-387-2564

Syria

Syrian Arab Republic Embassy
2215 Wyoming Ave., N.W.
Washington, DC 20008
202-232-6313; fax: 202-234-9548

Tahiti

Tahiti Tourism Board
300 Continental Blvd., Ste. 180
El Segundo, CA 90245
310-414-8484; fax: 310-414-8490

Taiwan

Taiwan Visitors Association
166 Geary St., Ste. 1605
San Francisco, CA 94108
415-989-8677; fax: 415-989-7242

Taiwan Visitors Association
1 World Trade Center, Ste. 7953
New York, NY 10048
212-466-0691; fax: 212-432-6436

Tanzania

United Republic of Tanzania Embassy
2139 R St., N.W.
Washington, DC 20008
202-939-6125; fax: 202-797-7408

Thailand

Tourism Authority of Thailand
3440 Wilshire Blvd., Ste. 1101
Los Angeles, CA 90010
800-842-4526 or 213-382-2353
fax: 213-389-7544

Tourism Authority of Thailand
5 World Trade Center, Ste. 3443
New York, NY 10048
212-432-0433; fax: 212-912-0920

Kingdom of Thailand Embassy
1024 Wisconsin Ave., N.W.
Washington, DC 20007
202-944-3600; fax: 202-944-3611

Togo

Togolese Tourist Information
112 E. 40th St.
New York, NY 10016
212-490-3455; fax: 212-983-6684

Republic of Togo Embassy
2208 Massachusetts Ave., N.W.
Washington, DC 20008
202-234-4212; fax: 202-232-3190

Tonga

Kingdom of Tonga Consulate General
360 Post St., Unit 604
San Francisco, CA 94108
415-781-0365

Trinidad and Tobago

Trinidad and Tobago Tourism Development Authority
7000 Blvd. E.
Guttenberg, NJ 07093
800-748-4224 or 201-662-3403
fax: 201-869-7628

Republic of Trinidad and Tobago Embassy
1708 Massachusetts Ave., N.W.
Washington, DC 20036
202-467-6490; fax: 202-785-3130

Tunisia

Republic of Tunisia Embassy
1515 Massachusetts Ave., N.W.
Washington, DC 20005
202-862-1850; fax: 202-862-1858

Turkey

Republic of Turkey Embassy
1714 Massachusetts Ave., N.W.
Washington, DC 20036
202-659-8200; fax: 202-659-0744

Turkmenistan

Republic of Turkmenistan Embassy
2207 Massachusetts Ave., N.W.
Washington, DC 20008
202-588-1500; fax: 202-588-0697

Turks and Caicos Islands

Turks and Caicos Islands Tourist Board
P.O. Box 128, Pond St.
Grand Turk, Turks and Caicos Islands
800-241-0824 or 809-946-2321
fax: 809-946-2733

Uganda

Republic of Uganda Embassy
5911 16th St., N.W.
Washington, DC 20011
202-726-7100; fax: 202-726-1727

International Tourism

Ukraine

Ukraine Embassy
3350 M St., N.W.
Washington, DC 20007
202-333-0606; fax: 202-333-0817

United Arab Emirates

United Arab Emirates Embassy
3000 K St., N.W., Ste. 600
Washington, DC 20007
202-338-6500; fax: 202-337-7029

United Kingdom

British Tourist Authority
551 Fifth Ave., Ste. 701
New York, NY 10176
800-462-2748 or 212-986-2200
fax: 212-986-1188

United Kingdom of Great Britain and Northern Ireland Embassy
3100 Massachusetts Ave., N.W.
Washington, DC 20008
202-462-1340; fax: 202-898-4255

Uruguay

Uruguayan Tourist Bureau
747 Third Ave., 21st Fl.
New York, NY 10017
212-753-8581; fax: 212-753-1603

Republic of Uruguay Embassy
1918 F St., N.W.
Washington, DC 20006
202-331-1313; fax: 202-331-8142

Uzbekistan

Republic of Uzbekistan Embassy
1511 K St., N.W., Ste. 619
Washington, DC 20005
202-638-4266; fax: 202-638-4268

Vatican City

The Holy See Embassy
3339 Massachusetts Ave., N.W.
Washington, DC 20008
202-333-7121; fax: 202-337-4036

Venezuela

Venezuelan Tourism Association
P.O. Box 3010
Sausalito, CA 94966
800-331-0100 or 415-331-0100

Venezuelan Tourism Association
7 E. 51st St., 4th Fl.
New York, NY 10022
212-826-1678; fax: 212-644-7471

Republic of Venezuela Embassy
1099 30th St., N.W.
Washington, DC 20007
202-342-2214; fax: 202-342-6820

Virgin Islands, U.S.

U.S. Virgin Islands Department of Tourism
900 17th St., N.W., Ste. 500
Washington, DC 20006
202-293-3707; fax: 212-785-2542

Western Samoa

Independent State of Western Samoa Embassy
820 Second Ave., Ste. 800
New York, NY 10017
212-599-6196; fax: 212-599-0797

Yemen

Republic of Yemen Embassy
2600 Virginia Ave., N.W., Ste. 705
Washington, DC 20037
202-965-4760; fax: 202-337-2017

Yugoslavia

Federal Republic of Yugoslavia Embassy
2410 California St., N.W.
Washington, DC 20008
202-462-6566; fax: 202-797-9663

Zaire

Republic of Zaire Embassy
1800 New Hampshire Ave., N.W.
Washington, DC 20009
202-234-7690

Zambia

Zambia National Tourist Board
237 E. 52nd St.
New York, NY 10022
212-758-1110 - Phone and Fax

Republic of Zambia Embassy
2419 Massachusetts Ave., N.W.
Washington, DC 20008
202-265-9717; fax: 202-332-0826

Zimbabwe

Zimbabwe Tourist Office
1270 Ave. of the Americas
Rockefeller Center, Ste. 2315
New York, NY 10020
800-621-2381 or 212-332-1090
fax: 212-332-1093

Republic of Zimbabwe Embassy
1608 New Hampshire Ave., N.W.
Washington, DC 20009
202-332-7100; fax: 202-483-9326

APPENDIX 5

Bibliography

The annotated bibliography includes sources cited or consulted in *HFCWD*, as well as other sources for further reading. Sources are listed under the following categories: Reference and Other Background Works on Holidays (including Calendars and Time-Reckoning Systems; Festival Organization; Philosophy, Theory and Analysis of Festivity; and Teaching Aids); Holidays of Religious Traditions; Holidays of Ethnic Groups and Geographic Regions; Individual Holidays; and Journals. Sources marked with the diamond symbol (♦) are cited in the entries in the main text.

Reference and Other Background Works on Holidays

General Works

Augur, Helen. *The Book of Fairs.* Introduction by Hendrik Willem Van Loon. Illustrated by James MacDonald. 1939. Reprinted by Omnigraphics, Inc., 1992. 308 pp. Index.

Traces the development of trade, customs, and social life in connection with fairs in history up to the 1939 World's Fair. Includes discussion of fairs and festivals in ancient Tyre, Athens and Rome, the Kinsai Fairs in 13th-century Cathay, festivals in 13th-century France, 15th-century Belgium and Germany, medieval England, Ireland and Scotland, Russia, and the modern expositions.

♦ Chambers, Robert, ed. *The Book of Days: A Miscellany of Popular Antiquities in connection with the Calendar, including Anecdote, Biography, & History, Curiosities of Literature, and Oddities of Human Life and Character.* New introduction by Tristram Potter Coffin. 1862–64. Reprinted by Omnigraphics, Inc., 1990. Vol. I, 832 pp.; Vol. II, 840 pp. Illustrated. Index (Vol. II).

British tome organized chronologically and covering popular Christian festivals and saints' days; seasonal phenomena; folklore of the British Isles, especially that connected with the passing of time and seasons of the year; "Notable Events, Biographies, and Anecdotes connected with the Days of the Year"; "Articles of Popular Archaeology, of an entertaining character, tending to illustrate the progress of Civilization, Manners, Literature, and Ideas in these kingdoms"; and other miscellaneous items. [Cited in the text as *BkDays-1864*]

♦ *Chase's Annual Events: The Day-by-Day Directory.* Chicago: Contemporary Books, Inc. Annual. Illustrated. Index.

This chronological guide provides more than 10,000 brief entries on annual events, holidays, festivals, religious days, anniversa-ries, and state and national days around the world. Special features include introductory section describing "banner" events, including important anniversaries; presidential proclamations issued each year for the year; a listing of national days throughout the world; various civil and religious calendars for the year; and other miscellaneous information, including facts about the states and presidents, astronomical events predicted for the year, and major entertainment awards given throughout the year. Approximately 70 percent of entries describe U.S. events or anniversaries. [Cited in the text as *Chases-1996*]

Deems, Edward M., comp. *Holy-Days and Holidays.* 1902. Reprinted by Omnigraphics, Inc., 1968. 768 pp. Bibliography. Index.

Divided into two major sections—religious and secular holidays—both arranged chronologically. Covers events observed in the United States, Canada, and United Kingdom. For each holiday, the compiler presents an introductory essay, a selection of prose essays, sermons and speeches, an alphabetical list of "suggestive thoughts," and poetry pertaining to the occasion.

♦ Dobler, Lavinia. *National Holidays around the World.* Illustrated and designed by Vivian Browne. New York: Fleet Press Corporation, 1968. 233 pp. Bibliography. Index.

Covers national and independence days from more than 130 countries. Written for a young audience. Entries are chronologically arranged and provide brief recounting of historical and political circumstances leading up to the observance of the day and a description of the nation's flag. [Cited in the text as *NatlHolWrld-1968*]

Dossey, Donald E. *Holiday Folklore, Phobias and Fun: Mythical Origins, Scientific Treatments and Superstitious "Cures."* Los Angeles: Outcomes Unlimited Press, Inc., 1992. 231 pp. Appendices. Bibliography. Index.

An expert on phobias and anxiety and stress disorders conducts informal survey of origins of various holiday customs—New Year's, St. Valentine's Day, St. Patrick's Day, Friday the 13th,

♦ Indicates a book cited in the main text

Easter, April Fools' Day, Halloween, Thanksgiving, Christmas—while offering advice on dealing with holiday stress and anxiety. Appendices include some folklore recipes, tips for cognitive refocusing and keying, and list of phobias and symptoms.

♦ Dunkling, Leslie. *Dictionary of Days.* New York: Facts on File, 1988. 156 pp.

Alphabetical listing of more than 700 named days: local days, fictional days (such as *The Day of the Jackal* and Lewis Carroll's "unbirthday"), expressions (such as "hey-day" and "turkey day"), generic (e.g., Friday) and technical terms (e.g., sidereal day) as well as names of holidays and other observed events. Much cross-referencing. Emphasis is on providing general-interest etymological information on the name itself in addition to giving basic definition of the day's significance. Often gives Scottish and northern English dialectical forms. Many entries include relevant literary quotations. A special feature is a calendar that chronologically maps the days discussed. [Cited in the text as *DictDays-1988*]

Eddy, Lloyd Champlin, *Holidays.* Boston, MA: The Christopher Publishing House, 1928. 304 pp. Index.

Day-by-day listing of holidays and birthdays worldwide, followed by chapters on various religious and secular events observed by a broad range of ethnic groups and religions.

Eichler, Lillian. *The Customs of Mankind With Notes on Modern Etiquette and Entertainment.* Pen and ink drawings by Phillipps Ward. Garden City, NY: Garden City Publishing Company, Inc., 1924. 753 pp. Illustrated. Bibliography. Index.

One chapter covers origins of holidays and customs accompanying them.

Frazer, James George. *The Golden Bough: A Study in Magic and Religion.* One volume, abridged edition. New York: Collier Books, 1950. 864 pp. Index.

Numerous festivals are discussed in this classic work on legends, mythology, and religions throughout the world, abridged in one volume.

Gaer, Joseph. *Holidays around the World.* Drawings by Anne Marie Jauss. Boston, MA: Little, Brown and Company, 1953. 212 pp. Index.

Covers more than 30 Chinese, Hindu, Jewish, Christian, and Muslim holidays, as well as United Nations Day. List of principal holidays in the United States.

♦ Gregory, Ruth W. *Anniversaries and Holidays.* Fourth edition. American Library Association, 1983. 262 pp. Bibliography. Index.

Organized chronologically, this book offers more than 2,600 short entries on religious and civic holidays and anniversaries marking notable people and events. The first and longest part of the book covers fixed days according to the Gregorian calendar. Months begin with an introductory note covering how the month was named, notable historical events or festivals occurring in the month, and flowers and birthstones associated with it. Entries are grouped together under each date by "Holy Days and Feast Days," "Holidays and Civic Days," and "Anniversaries and Special Events Days." Movable days are listed in the second part of the book and are organized by the Christian, Islamic, and Jewish calendars, followed by movable events observed according to the lunar calendar or other chronological criteria. The annotated bibliography describes 875 books related to holidays and anniversaries and is broken down by subject. [Cited in the text as *AnnivHol-1983*]

Hammerton, J. A., ed. *Manners and Customs of Mankind: An Entirely New Pictorial Work of Great Educational Value Describing the Most Fascinating Side of Human Life.* 4 vols. London: The Amalgamated Press, Ltd.; New York: Wm. H. Wise & Co., 193?. 1356 pp. Illustrated. Indexes.

Essays cover such topics as Animal Dances of the East, Midsummer Beliefs and Practices, and Food Taboos and Their Meaning, and are presented in no evident order. Subject headings under which essays are grouped are: Agricultural Customs; Children and the Young; Costume, Special Customs; The Dance; Death and the Disposal of the Dead; Education, Customs in; Etiquette and Conventions; The Family; Fetish and Fetish Worship; Folk Lore; Food and Food Gathering; Games and Amusement; Habitations; Law and Justice; Local Customs; Magic, Primitive; Marriage; Medicine and Treatment of the Sick; Miscellaneous; Music; Nature Lore and Superstitions; Naval and Sea Customs; Personal Adornment; Racial Manners; Religion and Religious Customs; Seasonal Customs; Sex Customs; Sport; Springtide; Summer; Taboo; War and Military Customs; and Witch Doctors and Witchcraft. Classified Index to Chapter Titles. General Index (including illustrations).

Heinberg, Richard. *Celebrate the Solstice: Honoring the Earth's Seasonal Rhythms Through Festival and Ceremony.* Foreword by Dolores LaChapelle. Wheaton, IL: Quest Books, The Theosophical Publishing House, 1993. 199 pp. Illustrated. Notes. Bibliography. Index.

Discusses the celebration of winter and summer solstices and world renewal rites and myths throughout history around the world. Suggests activities for contemporary observance.

Helfman, Elizabeth S. *Celebrating Nature: Rites and Ceremonies Around the World.* Illustrated by Carolyn Cather. New York: The Seabury Press, 1969. 165 pp. Index.

Describes for young readers celebrations associated with the seasons from ancient times among Egyptians, Hebrews, Babylonians, Greeks, Romans, Ashanti, Yoruba, Ga and Kikuyu peoples in Africa, New Guinea peoples, Thai people, Chinese, Japanese, Hindus, Saora people, Muslims, Incans, Mapuche Indians, Aztecs, and North American Indians, as well as observance of Christian holidays throughout the world. Pronunciation guide. Further reading list.

Hone, William. *The Every-Day Book; or, Everlasting Calendar of Popular Amusements, Sports, Pastimes, Ceremonies, Manners, Customs, and Events, Incident to Each of the Three Hundred amd Sixty-Five Days, in Past and Present Times; Forming a Complete History of the Year, Months, & Seasons, and a Perpetual Key to the Almanack; Including Accounts of the Weather, Rules for Health and Conduct, Remarkable and Important Anecdotes, Facts, and Notices, in Chronology, Antiquities, Topography, Biography, Natural History, Art, Science, and General Literature; Derived from the Most Authentic Sources, and Valuable Original Communications, with Poetical Elucidations, for Daily Use and Diversion.* Introduction by Leslie Shepard. 2 vols. 1827. Reprinted by Omnigraphics, 1967. Vol. 1, 1720 pp.; vol. 2, 1711 pp. Illustrated. Indexes.

Each volume presents a different collection of miscellany on holy days, festivals, and anniversaries from January 1 through December 31. Indexes of general subjects, Romish saints, poetry, flowers

♦ Indicates a book cited in the main text

and plants, and engravings are found in both volumes. Bibliography of works by William Hone.

♦ Humphrey, Grace. *Stories of the World's Holidays.* 1924. Reprinted by Omnigraphics, Inc., 1990. 335 pp. Index.

Twenty stories for young readers describing the origins of commemorated historical events in the United States, England, France, Italy, China, Japan, Poland, Ireland, Czechoslovakia, and South America, arranged in chronological order. Suggested reading list. [Cited in the text as *StoryWrldHol-1924*]

♦ Ickis, Marguerite. *The Book of Festivals and Holidays the World Over.* Drawings by Richard E. Howard. New York: Dodd, Mead & Co., 1970. 164 pp. Index.

A selection of "holidays and festivals that are current and give promise of continuing indefinately," twelve chapters in chronological order cover customs and legends associated with New Year's, Epiphany, Lent, Holy Week, Easter, Advent, and Christmas, as well as more than 80 winter, spring, summer, and fall festivals in nearly 50 countries. [Cited in the text as *BkFestHolWrld-1970*]

♦ James, E. O. *Seasonal Feasts and Festivals.* 1961. Reprinted by Omnigraphics, Inc., 1993. 336 pp. Bibliography. Index.

Covers more than 100 season-based rituals, dances, plays, and festivals of the Palaeolithic era, vegetation cults, Egypt, Mesopotamia, Palestine, Hebrew, Asia Minor and Greece, Rome, Christianity, and medieval to eighteenth-century Europe. Examines Egyptian, Babylonian, Greek, Roman, Julian, and Christian calendars. [Cited in the text as *SeasFeast-1961*]

♦ Jobes, Gertrude. *Dictionary of Mythology, Folklore and Symbols.* 3 vols. New York: Scarecrow Press, 1962. 1759 pp., plus 482 pp. Index (vol. 3). Bibliography.

Several thousand entries cover mythology, folklore, and symbols from around the world and from all religions, past and present. Includes names and their meanings, deities with their genealogy, function, attributes, emblems, behavior, depictions in art, and parallel deities; characters from novels and plays; animals, vegetables, and minerals with their symbolism, significance in dreams; Freemasonry, heraldry, the occult, religion, and mythology; constellations; significance of the parts of the body and body postures; festivals, holidays, and dances. Cross-referencing. The third volume, the Index, contains symbols and abbreviations used, a table of Deities, Heroes, and Personalities, and a table of Mythological Affiliations (supernatural forms, realms, things). [Cited in the text as *DictMyth-1962*]

♦ Leach, Maria, ed. *Funk & Wagnalls Standard Dictionary of Folklore, Mythology & Legend.* New York: Harper & Row, 1984. 1236 pp. Index.

This first one-volume edition contains "a representative sampling," contributions from 34 anthropologists and folklorists of more than 4,500 entries on animals, minerals, vegetables and objects, rituals, festivals and practices, songs, legends and games, and gods, monsters and other entities associated with the folklore and mythology of over 2,000 cultures, peoples, and countries and other geographical regions in the world. More than 50 longer essays surveying the folklore of various cultures and folkloric methodologies, themes and elements conclude with bibliographies. In addition, sources are occasionally inserted throughout in individual entries. [Cited in the text as *DictFolkMyth-1984*]

Long, Kim. *The Almanac of Anniversaries.* Santa Barbara, CA: ABC-CLIO, 1992. 270 pp. Bibliography. Index.

Timeline-like structure provides 25th, 50th, . . . 500th anniversaries relating to notable events and people that will take place between 1993 and 2001. Within each year, anniversaries are given chronologically. Calendar Locator chart provides cross-reference of years and milestones.

♦ MacDonald, Margaret R., ed. *The Folklore of World Holidays.* Detroit, MI: Gale Research Inc., 1992. 739 pp. Index.

Chronologically arranged collection of customs, legends, songs, food, superstitions, games, pageants, etc., associated with more than 340 festivals and holidays in over 150 countries. The United States and, for the most part, Canada, are not included. The editor provides a brief explanation of the holiday, followed by excerpts from written material describing actual observances of the event. Bibliographic information for each source follow the excerpts. [Cited in the text as *FolkWrldHol-1992*]

♦ Merin, Jennifer, with Elizabeth B. Burdick. *International Directory of Theatre, Dance, and Folklore Festivals.* Westport, CT: Greenwood Press, 1979. 480 pp. Bibliography. Appendix.

More than 850 festivals involving theater, dance or folklore in over 50 countries are covered. The United States is not included. Entries are organized by country and often contain mailing addresses, phone numbers, contact names, and dates of occurrence. Length of festival description varies from a few lines to a few paragraphs. Festival entries are followed by a country-by-country chronological listing of festivals, bibliography, an appendix listing the number of festivals in each country, and index of festivals by festival name. [Cited in the text as *IntlThFolk-1979*]

Mossman, Jennifer, ed. *Holidays and Anniversaries of the World.* Second edition. Detroit, MI: Gale Research Inc., 1990. 1,080 pp. Glossary. Index.

Lists 23,000 brief entries on secular, religious, and historic holidays and special observances, and anniversaries of notable people and occurrences in chronological order. Perpetual calendar covers the years 1753–2100.

Nickerson, Betty. *Celebrate the Sun: A Heritage of Festivals Interpreted through the Art of Children from Many Lands.* New York: J. B. Lippincott Company, 1969. 128 pp. Illustrated. Bibliography. Index.

Covers more than 30 holidays worldwide, as well as provides descriptions of such events as spring festivals, weddings, parades, processions, fairs, circuses, and side shows—all accompanied by over 40 paintings by children around the world.

Patten, Helen Philbrook. *The Year's Festivals.* Boston, MA: Dana Estes & Company, 1903. 270 pp. Illustrated.

One chapter each covers New Year's Day, Twelfth Night, St. Valentine's Day, All Fool's Day, Easter, May Day, Halloween, Thanksgiving, and Christmas. Discussion includes the general historical nature of observance, including customs, poems, songs, legends, often as represented in works of literature.

♦ Shemanski, Frances. *A Guide to World Fairs and Festivals.* Westport, CT: Greenwood Press, 1985. 309 pp. Appendix. Index.

Following the format of *A Guide to Fairs and Festivals in the United States* by the same author, this volume includes entries on more than 280 fairs and festivals held in 75 countries. A country-by-

Bibliography

country chronological listing of festivals follows the main text. Appendix lists festivals by type. [Cited in the text as *GdWrldFest-1985*]

♦ Spicer, Dorothy Gladys. *Book of Festivals.* Foreword by John H. Finley. 1937. Reprinted by Omnigraphics, Inc., 1990. 429 pp. Appendix. Bibliography. Index of festivals.

The main part of the book is broken down into 35 chapters, each covering an ethnic or major religious (Hindu, Jew, and Muslim or Mohammedan) group or nationality. Groups were chosen on the basis of their representation in the United States. Geographic areas covered include Asia, Eastern and Western Europe, India, the Middle East, and the United States. Within each chapter, holidays and festivals are listed and described in chronological order. Part II of the book is devoted to discussions of the Armenian, Chinese, Gregorian, Hindu, Jewish, Julian, and Mohammedan calendars. Topics include rate of variation between the Julian and Gregorian calendars, dates of Easter computed between 1938 and 1950, and dates of major Jewish holidays computed between 1936 and 1951. The appendix is a glossary of religious and festival terms. The bibliography, with notes, organizes sources by ethnic group or nationality. [Cited in the text as *BkFest-1937*]

Spielgelman, Judith. *UNICEF's Festival Book.* Illustrated by Audrey Preissler. New York: U.S. Committee for UNICEF, 1966. 26 pp.

For young readers. Presents New Year (Enkutatash) in Ethiopia, Divali in India, Now-ruz (Nawruz) in Iran, Hanukkah in Israel, Doll Festival (Hina Matsuri) in Japan, Posadas in Mexico, Sinterklaas (St. Nicholas's Day) in the Netherlands, end of Ramadan ('Id al-Fitr) in Pakistan, Easter in Poland, Lucia Day (St. Lucy's Day) in Sweden, Songkran in Thailand, and Halloween in Canada and the United States.

♦ Stoll, Dennis Gray. *Music Festivals of the World: A Guide to Leading Festivals of Music, Opera and Ballet.* London: Pergamon Press, Ltd., 1963. 310 pp. Illustrated.

Describes more than 50 music festivals in over 20 countries that run for at least eight days, feature performers known around the world, and show signs of continuing indefinitely. Book is organized into thematic chapters containing essays discussing each event's special features and background and addresses for obtaining tickets. Index of festivals. [Cited in the text as *MusFestWrld-1963*]

♦ Van Straalen, Alice. *Book of Holidays around the World.* New York: E. P. Dutton, 1986. Illustrated. Appendices. Index.

Brief datebook-style entries provide at least one observance or anniversary for each day of the year. Photographs and reproductions of literary illustrations and artwork punctuate nearly every page. Appendices offer brief descriptions of Buddhist, Chinese, Christian, Hindu, Islamic, and Jewish calendars, followed by alphabetical listing of movable festivals and holidays. [Cited in the text as *BkHolWrld-1986*]

Walsh, William S. *Curiosities of Popular Customs and of Rites, Ceremonies, Observances, and Miscellaneous Antiquities.* 1914. Reprinted by Omnigraphics, Inc., 1966. 1018 pp. Illustrated.

Dictionary-style coverage of Christian, Jewish, Islamic, Buddhist, Japanese, Chinese, Hindu, ancient, and secular holidays and feasts including entries on people, places, customs, and relics associated with them. Also contains entries on birthdays, the months, and various calendars.

Wasserman, Paul, ed. *Festivals Sourcebook: A Reference Guide*

to *Fairs, Festivals and Celebrations in Agriculture, Antiques, The Arts, Theater and Drama, Arts and Crafts, Community, Dance, Ethnic Events, Film, Folk, Food and Drink, History, Indians, Marine, Music, Seasons, and Wildlife.* Detroit, MI: Gale Research Company, 1977. 656 pp. Indexes.

More than 3,800 entries cover festive events in the United States and Canada. Organized by 18 subject areas, then alphabetically by state, entries list location, dates, contact name and address, description of the event, and date event first occurred. Does not include widely celebrated holidays, such as the Fourth of July, or sports events, religious holidays, rodeos, county fairs, and beauty pageants. Chronological, Event Name, Geographic, and Subject Indexes.

Webster, Hutton. *Rest Days; The Christian Sunday, the Jewish Sabbath, and Their Historical and Anthropological Prototypes.* 1916. Reprinted by Omnigraphics, Inc., 1992. 325 pp. Index.

The standard work on the origin of holy days and their religious and sociological development. Among topics covered are the tabooed days at critical epochs, the holy days, lunar superstitions and festivals, lunar calendars and the week, market days, unlucky days, the Babylonian "evil days," and the Shabattum.

Calendars and Time-Reckoning Systems

Achelis, Elisabeth. *The Calendar for Everybody.* 1943. Reprinted by Omnigraphics, Inc., 1990. 141 pp. Index.

Traces the calendar from its beginning, relating little-known facts about our present calendar and proposes a new calendar system and presents advantages to be gained by using it. Discusses the earth's time, the Egyptian, Julian, Gregorian, and world calendars.

Asimov, Isaac. *The Clock We Live On.* Revised edition. Illustrated by John Bradford. New York: Abelard-Schuman, 1965. 172 pp. Diagrams. Index.

The scientist-science fiction writer explains the solar and lunar systems by which humans have learned to tell time. Surveys devices for keeping time, from ancient to modern clocks and calendars. Discussion of solar, lunar, Egyptian, Hebrew, Christian, Julian, Gregorian, and French Revolutionary calendars, and chronological eras.

Aveni, Anthony F. *Empires of Time: Calendars, Clocks, and Cultures.* New York: Kodansha International, 1995. 371 pp. Illustrated. Index.

A far-reaching examination of concepts of time and calendar systems across cultures and throughout history. Discusses historical development and workings of various calendar and time-reckoning schemes, pointing out their contribution to cultural systems as well as illustrating the connection between political power and control over the calendar. Explores the evidence for the earliest known calendar systems, including Neolithic time-reckoning systems, calendar systems of the ancient Greeks, and the Stonehenge controversy. Detailed coverage of the Western (Gregorian), Mayan, Aztec, Incan, and Chinese calendars, as well as discussion of the calendar systems of two tribal groups, the Nuer of East Africa, and the Trobriand Islanders of the Pacific.

Coleman, Lesley. *A Book of Time.* Camden, NJ: Thomas Nelson, Inc., 1971. 144 pp. Illustrated. Bibliography. Index.

Survey of Sumerian, Babylonian, Muslim, Christian, Jewish, Egyptian, Roman, Julian, Gregorian, and French Revolutionary calendars and the proposed World Calendar. Includes discussion of

♦ Indicates a book cited in the main text

546

timepieces, clockmakers, navigation, and some theories and literature dealing with time.

Couzens, Reginald C. *The Stories of the Months and Days.* 1923. Reprinted by Omnigraphics, Inc., 1990. 160 pp. Illustrated.

Explains how the months and days were named, telling stories about the Greek, Roman, Anglo and Saxon gods, goddesses, and emperors with whom they are associated.

Irwin, Keith Gordon. *The 365 Days.* Illustrated by Guy Fleming. New York: Thomas Y. Crowell Company, 1963. 182 pp. Maps. Index.

Discusses solar, lunar, and astronomical cycles, ancient calendars of Egypt, Babylon, Chaldea, Rome, and the Mayas. Traces origins and development from the Julian to the Gregorian calendars. Note on various calendars proposed in recent history. Section on dating the observance of Easter and Christmas. Discussion of carbon-dating and tree rings.

Krythe, Maymie R. *All About the Months,* New York: Harper & Row, Publishers, 1966. 222 pp. Bibliography. Index.

Discussion, in chronological order, of how each month was named, anniversaries occurring within each month, lore and literature associated with the month, mention of ancient holidays and festivals, and each month's gem and flower.

O'Neil, W. M. *Time and the Calendars.* Sydney, Australia: Sydney University Press, 1975. 138 pp. Appendix. Bibliography. Index.

Examines Egyptian, Roman, Babylonian, Indian, Chinese, Meso-American, and Gregorian calendars, and the day, week, month, and year. Appendix gives names of the days in various languages.

Parise, Frank, ed. *The Book of Calendars.* New York: Facts on File, Inc., 1982. 387 pp. Index.

Summarizes the history and organization of the Babylonian, Macedonian, Hebrew, Seleucid, Olympiad, Roman, Armenian, Islamic, Fasli, Zoroastrian, Yezdezred, Jelali, Egyptian, Coptic, Ethiopian, Iranian, Afghanistan, Akbar, Fasli Deccan, Parasuram, Burmese and Arakanse, Chinese, Tibetan, Mayan, Julian, Gregorian, and Christian eras and calendars. Tables throughout convert the various ancient and other calendars to Julian or Gregorian dates or years. Dates of Easter provided from the year 1 through 1999. Calendar of Christian saints. Explanations of the French Revolutionary calendar and the Soviet calendar. Table depicts dates various regions in Europe celebrated New Year's Day.

Tannenbaum, Beulah, and Myra Stillman. *Understanding Time: The Science of Clocks and Calendars.* Illustrated by William D. Hayes. New York: Whittlesey House, 1958. 143 pp. Index.

Explanation for young readers of time and clocks, calendars, and other measuring systems used throughout history. Each chapter includes suggested experiments.

Festival Organization

Goldblatt, Joe Jeff. *Special Events: The Art and Science of Celebration.* Foreword by Linda Faulkner, Social Secretary to the White House during the Reagan Administration. New York: Van Nostrand Reinhold, 1990. 386 pp. Illustrated. Appendices. References. Glossary. Index.

Guide to the special events industry, including social, retail, corporate and government events, meetings, and conventions. Provides techniques for budgeting, planning, and creating events such as theme parties, awards ceremonies, holidays, fairs, festivals, sporting events, and more. Appendices list related books and organizations and provide the text of the Flag Code.

Wilson, Joe, and Lee Udall. *Folk Festivals: A Handbook for Organization and Management.* Knoxville, TN: The University of Tennessee Press, 1982. 278 pp. Illustrations. Tables. Bibliography. Index.

Guide for folklore festival organizers covering such topics as administration, progamming concepts, planning, publicity, and production. Part Two describes three folk festivals produced in the United States (Tucson, Meet Yourself Festival, Mississippi Valley Folk Festival, and Open Fiddlers' Contest), including an interview with a festival performer and samples of media releases and public service announcements.

Philosophy, Theory and Analysis of Festivity

Browne, Ray B., and Michael T. Marsden, eds. *The Cultures of Celebrations.* Bowling Green, OH: Bowling Green State University Popular Press, 1994. 244 pp.

Collection of 15 case studies from scholars working in areas relating to popular culture studies. Essays analyze various celebrations and forms of entertainment, including Shi'ite rituals, folk festivals in Australia, Lord Mayor's Procession, Columbus celebrations from the 18th to the 20th centuries, and seasonal festivals in Manitoba.

Cantwell, Robert. *Ethnomimesis: Folklife and the Representation of Culture.* Chapel Hill, NC: The University of North Carolina Press, 1993. 323 pp. Notes. Bibliography. Index.

Describes the Festival of American Folklife, held annually on the Mall in Washington, D.C., and discusses it as a cultural artifact that can yield insights on "festivity, identity, and memory."

Cox, Harvey. *The Feast of Fools: A Theological Essay on Festivity and Fantasy.* Cambridge, MA: Harvard University Press, 1969. 204 pp. Appendix. Notes. Index.

Adapted from the William Belden Noble Lectures given by the author in 1968 at Harvard University. Theological examination of spiritual aspects of festivity and fantasy as practiced in Western cultures. Uses the medieval Feast of Fools and its eventual disappearance as a symbol for thesis that Western civilization needs a rebirth of "the spirit represented by the Feast of Fools."

Falassi, Alessandro, ed. *Time Out of Time: Essays on the Festival.* Albuquerque, NM: University of New Mexico Press, 1987. 311 pp.

Collection of essays by Goethe, Hemingway and Aldous Huxley, and Victor Turner, Vladimir Propp, and other folklorists describing and analyzing festivals celebrated in Europe, North and South America, Africa, Asia, and Oceania such as the Palio at Siena, the Roman Carnival, bullfighting, Olojo Festival, Carnival at Rio de Janeiro, the Holy Ghost Festival in the Azores, and more.

Handelman, Don. *Models and Mirrors: Towards an Anthropology of Public Events.* Cambridge, England: Cambridge University Press, 1990. Figures. Notes. Bibliography. Index.

Analyses of such festivals as the Palio of Siena, Christmas mumming in Newfoundland, observance of Jewish and state holidays in

Bibliography

Israel and in Israeli kindergartens, and katchina dancers as well as other forms of public ritual play.

MacAloon, John J., ed. *Rite, Drama, Festival, Spectacle: Rehearsals Toward a Theory of Cultural Performance.* Philadelphia, PA: Institute for the Study of Human Issues, Inc., 1984. 280 pp. Notes.

Papers from 10 scholars in the humanities delivered at the 76th Burg Wartenstein Symposium, sponsored by the Wenner-Gren Foundation for Anthropological Research. Academic essays concerned with various cultural and performative implications of festival and ritual in literature and in actuality: "Liminiality and the Performative Genres," Victor Turner; "Charivari, Honor, and the Community in Seventeenth-Century Lyon and Geneva," Natalie Zemon Davis; "'Rough Music' in The Duchess of Malfi: Webster's Dance of Madmen and Charivari Tradition," Frank W. Wadsworth; "Borges's 'Immortal': Metaritual, Metaliturature, Metaperformance," Sophia S. Morgan; "Arrange Me into Disorder: Fragments and Reflections on Ritual Clowning," Barbara A. Babcock; "The Diviner and the Detective," Hilda Kuper; "A Death in Due Time: Construction of Self and Culture in Ritual Drama," Barbara G. Myerhoff; "The Ritual Process and the Problem of Reflexivity in Sinhalese Demon Exorcisms," Bruce Kapferer; "Carnival in Multiple Planes," Roberto Da Matta; and "Olympic Games and the Theory of Spectacle in Modern Societies," John J. MacAloon.

Pieper, Josef. *In Tune with the World: A Theory of Festivity.* Translated by Richard and Clara Winston. New York: Harcourt, Brace & World, Inc., 1965. 81 pp.

Philosophical essay discusses what festivity means from a predominantly Western and Christian orientation. Includes consideration of festivity in relation to art, labor, and modern commercialization of history.

Thompson, E. P. *Customs in Common: Studies in Traditional Popular Culture.* New York: The New Press, 1993. 547 pp. Illustrated. Index.

Scholarly study of English working-class culture in the 18th and early 19th centuries. Includes examination of the historical contexts of such events as beating the bounds, the Horn Fair, and others.

Turner, Victor, ed. *Celebration: Studies in Festivity and Ritual.* Washington, DC: Smithsonian Institution Press, 1982. 318 pp. Illustrated.

This companion volume to the Smithsonian Institution's exhibition of celebratory objects is a collection of essays exploring such topics as objects used in festivals, celebrations as rites of passage, and political, economic and religious festivals. Events included within the discussions are Juneteenth, Penitentes, Trinidad Carnival, Incwala, Juggernaut (Rath Yatra), Dragon Boat Festival in China, Rama festivals in India, German-American Passion Plays in the United States, and more.

Teaching Aids

Bauer, Caroline Feller. *Celebrations: Read-Aloud Holiday and Theme Book Programs.* Drawings by Lynn Gates Bredeson. New York: H. W. Wilson Company, 1985. 301 pp. Index.

Education specialist offers 16 theme book programs dealing with holidays and such invented celebrations as National Nothing Day and Pigmania for teachers and other professionals working with primarily middle-grade children. Each program includes some prose and poetry selections, ideas for bulletin boards, recipes,

activities and jokes, and lists of related books marked for various age groups.

Dupuy, Trevor Nevitt, ed. *Holidays; Days of Significance for All Americans.* New York: Franklin Watts, Inc., 1965. 162 pp. Index.

Intended for elementary-school teachers. Brief essays from contributors to, and members of, the Historical Evaluation and Research Organization cover 27 patriotic holidays and commemorative days observed in the United States. Further reading list.

Green, Victor J. *Festivals and Saints Days: A Calendar of Festivals for School and Home.* Poole, Dorset, England: Blandford Press Ltd., 1978. 161 pp. Index.

Beginning with New Year's Day and following the calendar, the book covers more than 30 secular, Christian, Jewish, Hindu and Muslim holidays observed in Britain. Also includes Independence Day and Thanksgiving in the United States. Further reading list.

Hopkins, Lee Bennett, and Misha Arenstein. *Do You Know What Day Tomorrow Is? A Teacher's Almanac.* New York: Citation Press, 1975. Appendices.

Guide intended to integrate chronologically presented information about people, places, and events with elementary-school curriculum. Provided for each month are a brief explanation of its name, flower and birthstone, representative poem, and descriptive listings in chronological order of events in history, anniversaries associated with notable people, holidays, admission days, and other events that occur on each day of the year. Appendices include a reference bibliography for teachers and list of sources cited.

Purdy, Susan. *Festivals for You to Celebrate.* New York: Lippincott Company, 1969. 192 pp. Illustrated. Bibliography. Index.

Holiday-related craft projects for group or individual celebrations. Thirty festivals of various religions and locales are discussed; emphasis is on holidays observed in the United States, and their origins and counterparts elsewhere. Activities subject index.

Holidays of Religious Traditions
General Works

♦ Crim, Keith, ed. *Perennial Dictionary of World Religions* (originally published as *Abingdon Dictionary of Living Religions*). San Francisco, CA: Harper & Row, 1989. 830 pp. Illustrations. Maps. Charts.

One hundred sixty-one scholars contributed more than 1,600 entries on the world's major living systems of faith: deities, saints and other holy figures, religious sites, art and architecture, movements, sects and societies, authors and texts, creeds, prayers, mantras, and spiritual practices. Some bibliograpy provided throughout in individual entries. Long survey article on each major religion. Good cross-referencing. Guide to abbreviations and pronunciation table. Listing of key entries pertaining to major religions. [Cited in the text as *DictWrldRel-1989*]

♦ Eliade, Mircea, ed. *The Encyclopedia of Religion.* New York: Macmillan, 1987. 16 vols. About 8,000 pp. Index in Volume 16.

♦ Indicates a book cited in the main text

548

A comprehensive collection of articles by leading scholars and religious figures touching on all aspects of religion. Reflects the significant increase in knowledge and changing interpretive frameworks which have marked the study of religion in the last 60 years. Treats religious ideologies and practices, as well as sociological aspects of religions from Paleolithic times to the present. Generates broad view of topics through composite entries joining several articles under a common heading. Articles list works cited and give suggestions for further reading. Ample coverage of non-Western religions. Extensively cross-referenced. [Cited in the text as *EncyRel-1987*]

♦ Gross, Ernie. *This Day in Religion.* New York: Neal-Schuman Publishers, Inc., 1990. 294 pp. Bibliography. Glossary. Index.

Offers a day-by-day listing of significant events in the world of religion from biblical times to the present. Focuses on Christianity, but some coverage of Judaism and Eastern religions. Includes saints' days, the birth or death of religious leaders or notable figures in the world of religion, appointments, canonizations, feast days, founding dates of organizations and associations, and other important events. [Cited in the text as *DayRel-1990*]

♦ Harper, Howard V. *Days and Customs of All Faiths.* 1957. Reprinted by Omnigraphics, Inc., 1990. 399 pp. Index.

Part One contains more than 300 entries in chronological order that cover Roman, Jewish, and Christian religious festivals, saints' days and major secular holidays observed, especially in the United States. Part Two consists of chapters covering Jewish customs, major Christian holiday customs, including New Year's, words and expressions associated with various lore, and wedding customs. [Cited in the text as *DaysCustFaith-1957*]

Hinnells, John R., ed. *The Penguin Dictionary of Religions.* Harmondsworth, Middlesex, England: Penguin Books, 1984. 550 pp. Maps. Bibliography. Indexes.

More than 1,000 entries contributed by 29 scholars cover deities, beliefs, people, places, texts, institutions, practices, rituals, and festivals associated with the world's religions, past and present. List of contents by subject area and contributor. Maps of Europe, ancient Near East and west Asia, Africa, the Indian Sub-Continent, Southeast Asia, Japan, China, Southwest Pacific and Australasia, North America, Mesoamerica, and Latin America. Substantial bibliography by subject area, cross-referenced with the entries. Synoptic index. General index.

Ickis, Marguerite. *The Book of Religious Holidays and Celebrations.* With drawings by Richard E. Howard. New York: Dodd, Mead & Company, 1966. 161 pp.

Covers Jewish holidays, Christian holidays, the New Year in the United States, Europe, Japan, China, India, Africa, and the Middle East. Includes legends, food, music, songs, prayers, symbols and emblems, and examples of programs and pageants. Discussion of plant lore. Further reading list.

♦ Kelly, Aidan, Peter Dresser, and Linda M. Ross. *Religious Holidays and Calendars: An Encyclopaedic Handbook.* Detroit, MI: Omnigraphics, Inc., 1993. 163 pp. Bibliography. Indexes.

Part One consists of chapters explaining the history and organization of calendars of the world: Babylonian, Hebrew, Greek, Christian, Islamic, Indian, Buddhist, Chinese, Egyptian, Roman, Julian, Gregorian. Part Two provides alphabetical listing by name of religious holiday, dates celebrated, and brief description of its history and current practice, if applicable. Monthly Index of

Holidays. Religions Index. Master Index. [Cited in the text as *RelHolCal-1993*]

A second edition, edited by Karen Bellenir, is forthcoming by Omnigraphics, Inc. The second edition contains more than 100 new entries and is organized into two sections. Part One features coverage of calendars. Part Two consists of chapters on 14 major religious groups. Each chapter provides background of the religion, overview of the religion's calendar, and descriptions of the religion's holidays. Listing of Internet resources. Bibliography arranged by topic. General Index, Calendars Index, and indexes of holidays alphabetically and chronologically.

Magida, Arthur J., ed. *How to Be a Perfect Stranger: A Guide to Etiquette in Other People's Religious Ceremonies.* Woodstock, VT: Jewish Lights Publishing, 1996. 417 pp. Glossary.

Provides an overview of the content of and the expected dress and behavior at the services of 20 religious and denominational groups. Covers the Assemblies of God, Baptist, Buddhist, Christian Scientist, Disciples of Christ, Episcopalian, Greek Orthodox, Hindu, Islamic, Jehovah's Witnesses, Jewish, Lutheran, Methodist, Mormon, Presbyterian, Quaker, Catholic, Seventh-day Adventist, and United Church of Christ ceremonies. Lists each group's major religious holidays and their significance. Reviews the calendar systems of the major religions, and furnishes a calendar listing of their holidays for the years 1996 to 1998.

Parrinder, Geoffrey. *A Dictionary of Non-Christian Religions.* Philadelphia, PA: The Westminster Press, 1971. 320 pp. Illustrated.

More than 2,400 entries provide A to Z coverage of people, deities, rites, locations, festivals, texts, philosophies, etc., associated with ancient and living non-Christian religions, including various African religions, Aztec, Baha'i, Buddhism, Confucianism, Hinduism, Islam, Jainism, Judaism, Maori religion, Native American religions, Shinto, Sikhism, Taoism, Theosophy, Yoruba, Zoroastrianism, religions of ancient Rome, Greece, Babylon, and of the Celts, Egyptians, Incans, Mayans, Scandinavians, and others. Cross-referencing. Lists of Egyptian, Chinese, and Islamic dates and dynasties. Further reading list.

♦ Pike, Royston. *Round the Year with the World's Religions.* 1950. Reprinted by Omnigraphics, Inc., 1993. 208 pp. Illustrated. Index.

Chronologically arranged chapters covering customs, legends, and stories behind religious observances in ancient Rome and Greece, Europe, India, Tibet, China, Japan, and Ceylon (Sri Lanka), and among ancient Romans, Greeks and Egyptians, Jews, Christians, Hindus, Jains, Muslims, Buddhists, Incans, and Aztecs. [Cited in the text as *RoundYr-1950*]

African

King, Noel Q. *Religions of Africa: A Pilgrimage into Traditional Religions.* New York: Harper & Row, Publishers, 1970. 116 pp. Glossary. Index.

Discusses Ashanti, Yoruba, and others' religious festivals, ceremonies, and customs, such as the Egungun Festival and ceremonies for Yoruba deities, as well as birth, initiation, marriage, and death customs among various African ethnic groups. Notes on pronunciation. Good further reading list, including many works in English.

Lawson, E. Thomas. *Religions of Africa: Traditions in Transformation.* Religious Traditions of the World Series. San Fran-

♦ Indicates a book cited in the main text

cisco, CA: Harper & Row, 1984. 106 pp. Illustrated. Glossary. Notes.

Surveys history and religious traditions of the Zulu and Yoruba peoples. Covers customs, legends, and ceremonies associated with birth, puberty, marriage, and death. Festivals described include Zulu (or Shembe) Festival, New Year's, and the New Yam Festival. Further reading list.

Murphy, Joseph M. *Working the Spirit: Ceremonies of the African Diaspora.* Boston, MA: Beacon Press, 1994. 263 pp. Notes. Glossary. Bibliography. Index.

Describes history, significance, and performance of religious ceremonies, practices, music, and dances observed through voodoo in Haiti, candomblé in Brazil, santería in Cuba and among Cuban-Americans, Revival Zion in Jamaica, and "the Black Church" in the United States, in attempt to show how all are connected to a common spiritual foundation.

Baha'i

Gaver, Jessyca Russell. *The Baha'i Faith: Dawn of a New Day.* New York: Hawthorn Books, Inc., 1967. 223 pp. Index.

Surveys the development of the Baha'i faith and its major prophets, beliefs, and laws and obligations. Discussion of observance of the Nineteen-Day Feast, New Year (Nawruz), and the Ridvan Festival.

Buddhism

Snelling, John. *Buddhist Festivals.* Holidays and Festivals Series. Vero Beach, FL: Rourke Enterprises, Inc., 1987. 48 pp. Illustrated. Maps. Glossary. Index.

For young readers. Provides historical background on Buddha and discusses Buddhist festivals in Thailand, Sri Lanka, Tibet, and Japan, as well as brief notes on Buddhist observances in Asia, the United States, and Britain. Further reading list.

Christianity

Attwater, Donald. *The Penguin Dictionary of Saints.* Second edition revised and updated by Catherine Rachel John. London: Penguin Books, 1983. 352 pp. Bibliography. Glossary.

Covers, in alphabetical order, more than 750 saints. Scope is international. Includes obscure and early, as well as more popular and recent saints. List of emblems associated with saints. Chronological list of feast days.

Bentley, James. *A Calendar of Saints: The Lives of the Principal Saints of the Christian Year.* New York: Facts on File Publications, 1986. 256 pp. Illustrated. Index.

Brief biographies of more than 300 saints are provided. Inspirational quotes from saints preface each month and also appear throughout. Richly illustrated, over 300 paintings are reproduced.

♦ Brewster, H. Pomeroy. *Saints and Festivals of the Christian Church.* 1904. Reprinted by Omnigraphics, Inc., 1990. 558 pp. Index.

Much of the book originally appeared as a series of articles published in the *Union and Advertiser* in Rochester, New York, which the author subsequently revised, adding more material to be published in the form reprinted in 1990. A yearbook of sorts of

the Christian calendar, entries are arranged in chronological order, beginning with Advent. At least one saint or church feast is discussed for nearly every day of the year. Chronological list of the bishops and popes of the Christian church since St. Peter. Alphabetical list of canonized saints and others. General Index. [Cited in the text as *SaintFestCh-1904*]

Cowie, L. W., and John Selwyn Gummer. *The Christian Calendar: A Complete Guide to the Seasons of the Christian Year Telling the Story of Christ and the Saints from Advent to Pentecost.* Springfield, MA: G & C Merriam Company, Publishers, 1974. 256 pp. Illustrated. Index.

Introduction gives historical background on the development of the Christian calendar. Part one discusses each Christian holiday and Sunday of the liturgical year, from Advent to the 24th Sunday after Pentecost, discussing the scripture and/or festival associated with each day covered. Part two provides entries, in chronological order, on saints' days and feasts for every day of the Gregorian year. List of patron saints, in alphabetical order by saint. Glossarial index.

Denis-Boulet, Noële M. *The Christian Calendar.* Vol. 113 of the *Twentieth Century Encyclopedia of Catholicism.* Translated by P. Hepburne-Scott. New York: Hawthorn Books, 1960. 126 pp. Bibliography.

Provides historical background on how the Christian calendar evolved from earlier calendars. Discussion of the observance of Sunday, Easter, and other feasts. History of martyrologies. Calendar reforms through history and contemporary reform proposal of a world calendar.

Farmer, David Hugh. *The Oxford Dictionary of Saints.* Second edition. Oxford, England: Oxford University Press, 1987. 478 pp. Appendices.

Covers, in alphabetical order, more than 1,000 saints venerated in the Christian church—mainly in Great Britian, but this edition also includes some Greek and Russian saints from Eastern Orthodoxy. Bibliographical sources conclude the entries. Appendices include a list of English people who have been candidates for canonization and are associated with a popular cult; a list of patronages of saints; iconographical emblems of saints; places in Great Britain and Ireland associated with saints; and a calendar of feast days for saints.

Gwynne, Rev. Walker. *The Christian Year: Its Purpose and Its History.* 1917. Reprinted by Omnigraphics, Inc., 1990. 143 pp. Appendix. Index.

Beginning chapters address the purpose and development of the Christian liturgical year. Discussion of Jewish holidays, as well as early Christians' observance of Jewish feasts and and transformation of these into Christian feasts. Church calendar is explained, along with technical terms associated with it. History and description of observances of holidays and saints' days. Appendix includes liturgical colors and questions for review or examination.

Hamilton, Mary. *Greek Saints and Their Festivals.* London: William Blackwood and Sons, 1910. 211 pp. Index.

Describes the observance of saints' days and other religious, as well as a few secular, holidays as celebrated in Greece, by the Greek Orthodox Church, and in Italy, Sicily, and Sardinia.

Holweck, Frederick George. *A Biographical Dictionary of the Saints, with a General Introduction on Hagiology.* 1924. Reprinted by Omnigraphics, Inc., 1990. 1053 pp.

Covers thousands of saints—all those venerated in any Christian

♦ Indicates a book cited in the main text

church, including those not officially canonized but with popular cult following. Brief bibliographical notices.

Monks, James L. *Great Catholic Festivals.* Great Religious Festivals Series. New York: Henry Schuman, 1951. 110 pp. Illustrated. Index.

Discusses origins and Catholic observance of Christmas, Epiphany, Easter, Pentecost, Corpus Christi, and Assumption.

Rodgers, Edith Cooperrider. *Discussion of Holidays in the Later Middle Ages.* New York: Columbia University Press, 1940. Reprinted by AMS Press, 1967. 147 pp. Bibliography. Index.

Examines holy days observed (or not observed), the Church's position on feasts, rules of observance, and nature of actual observance of religious holidays between 1200 and the Reformation.

Secretariat, Bishops' Committee on the Liturgy, National Conference of Catholic Bishops [Gurrieri, John A.]. *Holy Days in the United States.* Washington, DC: United States Catholic Conference, 1984. 100 pp. Notes.

Description of history, meaning, and liturgical and popular observance of the six holy days of obligation, as well as saints' days, with discussion of American saints, and other special days for Roman Catholics in the United States. Questions for discussion and suggested reading list conclude each chapter.

♦ Urlin, Ethel L. *Festivals, Holy Days, and Saints' Days: A Study in Origins and Survivals in Church Ceremonies & Secular Customs.* 1915. Reprinted by Omnigraphics, Inc., 1992. 272 pp. Illustrated. Bibliography. Index.

Entries cover, in chronological order, major Christian festivals and saints' days in England and Europe. Some mention of ancient Roman and Greek festivals where they figure in the origins of current Christian feasts. Listing of liturgical colors and the festivals during which they are worn by clergy. English calendar of Christian festivals and saints' days. [Cited in the text as *FestSaintDays-1915*]

Walsh, Michael, ed. *Butler's Lives of the Saints.* Concise edition. Foreword by Cardinal Basil Hume. San Francisco, CA: Harper & Row, Publishers, 1985. Index.

Abridgement of the four-volume *Lives of the Saints, or The Lives of the Fathers, Martyrs and other Principal Saints: Compiled from Original Monuments and other authentick records: Illustrated with the Remarks of judicious modern criticks and historians*, by Alban Butler, originally published in London between 1756 and 1759. The original contained nearly 1,500 entries. Later editions expanded to include 2,500. This edition provides biographical sketches and legends associated with one saint for each day of the year, in chronological order. List of patron saints.

Weiser, Francis X. *Handbook of Christian Feasts and Customs: The Year of the Lord in Liturgy and Folklore.* New York: Harcourt, Brace & World, Inc., 1958. 366 pp. Glossary. Index.

Part I discusses Christian significance of Sunday and other days of the week, ember days, and rogation days. Part II is organized according to the Christian calendar and presents description of major Christian feasts. Part III deals with the veneration of saints and Mary and provides some background on a few of the most popular saints.

Hinduism

Gupte, Rai Bahadur B. A. *Hindu Holidays and Ceremonials with Dissertations on Origin, Folklore and Symbols.* Calcutta and Simla, India: Thacker, Spink & Co., 1919. 285 pp. Illustrated.

The main text contains dictionary-style entries on Hindu festivals, days and places of worship and ceremony, and mythological and historical persons along with constellations associated with them. Brief glossary precedes main text with entries on animals and plants with folkloric significance.

Mitter, Swasti. *Hindu Festivals.* Holidays and Festivals Series. Vero Beach, FL: Rourke Enterprises, Inc., 1989. 48 pp. Illustrated. Glossary. Index.

Background for young readers on Hindu beliefs, history, and festivals inside and outside India. Note on the Hindu calendar and chronological table of Hindu holidays by month.

Sivananda, Sri Swami. *Hindu Fasts and Festivals.* India: The Yoga-Vedanta Forest Academy Press, 1983. 176 pp. Illustrated.

Explains religious significance and customs and observances of 27 popular Hindu festivals. Also discusses folklore surrounding eclipses and special days. Includes some Hindu prayers. Concludes with an essay on the "Philosophy of Idol Worship."

Thomas, P. *Hindu Religion, Customs and Manners, Describing the Customs and Manners, Religious, Social and Domestic Life, Arts and Sciences of the Hindus.* Second revised Indian edition. Bombay, India: D. B. Taraporevala Sons & Co., Ltd., 1948? 161 pp. Illustrated. Glossary and Index.

Covers Hindu history and creation theories, the caste system, religious sects, beliefs and practices, philosophy, social and domestic life, superstitions, etiquette, dress and ornamentation, literature and languages, ceremonies, music, dance, the calendar and holidays, architecture, the fine arts, and courtship and love.

Islam

Ahsan, M. M. *Muslim Festivals.* Holidays and Festivals Series. Vero Beach, FL: Rourke Enterprises, Inc., 1987. 48 pp. Illustrated. Glossary. Index.

Presents Islamic beliefs, holidays, and rites for young readers. Note on Islamic calendar. Chronological table of Muslim holidays by Islamic month. Further reading list.

Glassé, Cyril. *The Concise Encyclopedia of Islam.* Introduction by Huston Smith. San Francisco, CA: Harper & Row, 1989. 472 pp. Illustrated. Maps. Appendices. Bibliography.

More than 1,100 entries cover people, places, texts, beliefs, rituals, festivals, and practices associated with the Islamic faith and its branches. Appendices include historical synopsis of the Islamic world, maps of Mecca and description of the Hajj, schematic representation of branches of Islam, genealogical tables, and chronology.

Sanders, Paula. *Ritual, Politics, and the City in Fatimid Cairo.* Albany, NY: State University of New York Press, 1994. 231 pp. Maps. Notes. Bibliography. Index.

Examines court ritual practices, ceremonial processions, and such festivals as Nawruz, Ramadan, and the Festival of Breaking the Fast ('Id al-Fitr) in fourth- and fifth-century Cairo in terms of social and political culture.

Bibliography

♦ Indicates a book cited in the main text

Trimingham, J. Spencer. *Islam in West Africa*. London: Oxford University Press, 1959. 262 pp. Map. Appendices. Glossary. Indexes.

Describes history, beliefs, practices, and observances of Muslim West Africans. Explanation of Islamic calendar, saints, social customs. Glossary-Index of Arabic and African terms. General index.

♦ Von Grunebaum, Gustave E. *Muhammadan Festivals*. Introduction by C. E. Bosworth. New York: Olive Branch Press, 1988. 107 pp. Illustrated. Bibliographical notes and references. Index.

Provides historical background on Islam, as well as discussion of beliefs, prayers, saints, and worship services. Festivals covered are the pilgrimage to Mecca, Ramadan, Nawruz, Muhammad's birthday (Mawlid al-Nabi), feasts of saints, and the death anniversary of Husain (Ashura). [Cited in the text as *MuhFest-1988*]

Judaism

Cashman, Greer Fay. *Jewish Days and Holidays*. Illustrated by Alona Frankel. New York: SBS Publishing, Inc., 1979. 64 pp.

Describes for young readers the history of, and traditions and customs associated with, major Jewish holidays, including the Sabbath. Sidebars depict foods and other items used during celebrations. Concludes with quiz on matching sidebar items with appropriate holiday.

Edidin, Ben M. *Jewish Customs and Ceremonies*. Illustrated by H. Norman Tress. New York: Hebrew Publishing Company, 1941. 178 pp. Bibliography. Index and Glossary.

A companion to *Jewish Holidays and Festivals* (see below), intended as an educational supplemental text, describes everyday customs as well as those associated with holidays and other important events, such as birth, bar and bat mitzvah, marriage, burial, and worship.

Edidin, Ben M. *Jewish Holidays and Festivals*. Illustrated by Kyra Markham. 1940. Reprinted by Omnigraphics, Inc., 1993. 66 pp. Bibliography. Index and Glossary.

Discusses history, significance and customs associated with Jewish holidays and anniversaries.

Eisenberg, Azriel. *The Story of the Jewish Calendar*. Wood engravings by Elisabeth Friedlander. New York: Abelard-Schuman, 1958. 62 pp.

A short story of two teenaged boys watching for the new moon prefaces a brief history of the Jewish calendar. Explanation of Jewish holidays and names of months and Sabbaths and their significance. Glossary of Hebrew terms and place-names.

Gaster, Theodor H. *Festivals of the Jewish Year*. New York: William Sloane Associates Publishers, 1953. 308 pp. Bibliography.

Presents origins of Jewish festivals and holy days, draws comparisons to other religious and ethnic holidays, and describes evolving nature of their observance throughout history.

Goldin, Hyman E. *A Treasury of Jewish Holidays: History, Legends, Traditions*. New York: Twayne Publishers, 1952. 308 pp. Illustrated. Index.

Examines Jewish festivals, explaining their meanings, describing

customs and traditional beliefs associated with them, and telling the stories of their historical origins. Calendar of Jewish festivals from 1951 to 1971.

Hacohen, Devorah, and Menahem Hacohen. *One People; The Story of the Eastern Jews: Twenty Centuries of Jewish Life in North Africa, Asia and Southeastern Europe*. Introduction by Yigal Allon. Translated by Israel I. Taslitt. New York: Sabra Books, 1969. 195 pp. Illustrated. Glossary. Bibliography.

Discusses history, folklore, beliefs and customs, ceremonies, and observance of holidays among Jews in Iraq and Kurdistan, Persia, the Caucasus, Bukhara, Morocco, Algeria, Tunisia and Jreba, Libya, Cyrenaica, Egypt, Syria, Yemen, Hadramaut, Aden, Turkey, Salonika, Bulgaria, and India.

Rockland, Mae Shafter. *The Jewish Party Book: A Contemporary Guide to Customs, Crafts, and Foods*. New York: Schocken Books, 1978. 264 pp. Illustrated. Appendix. Index.

Traditional customs, foods, and activities associated with birth, bar and bat mitzvah, marriage, reunions, housewarmings, and holidays. Appendix provides explanation of Jewish calendar and table of holiday dates from 1978 to 2000.

Rosenau, William. *Jewish Ceremonial Institutions*. Third and revised edition. 1925. Reprinted by Omnigraphics, Inc., 1992. 190 pp. Illustrated. Index.

Adapted from a series of lectures given by the author at the Oriental Seminary of the Johns Hopkins University in 1901. Origin and purpose of the synagogue and explanatory commentary on its worship services and customs. Discussion of the Jewish calendar and observance of holidays and festivals at home and at the synagogue. Practices associated with birth, marriage, bar and bat mitzvah, divorce, mourning, and related laws and practices.

Strassfeld, Michael. *The Jewish Holidays: A Guide and Commentary*. Illustrated by Betsy Platkin Teutsch. New York: Harper & Row, 1985. 248 pp. Appendices. Index.

Each of 11 chapters deals with a holiday and its specific practices in depth. Appendices on the Jewish calendar, laws pertaining to holidays, Torah reading list for the holidays, glossary of Hebrew blessings, glossary of Hebrew terms, and dates of holidays to the years 1999–2000.

Trepp, Leo. *The Complete Book of Jewish Observance: A Practical Manuel for the Modern Jew*. New York: Behrman House, Inc./Simon & Schuster, 1980. 370 pp. Illustrated. Index.

Covers Jewish prayers, practices, customs, and laws in addition to festivals and fasts.

Turck, Mary. *Jewish Holidays*. New York: Crestwood House, 1990. 48 pp. Illustrated. Index.

Explanations for young readers of reasons for celebrating the holidays, ways in which they are observed, and food, blessings, and prayers associated with them. Brief further reading list.

Turner, Reuben. *Jewish Festivals*. Holidays and Festivals Series. Vero Beach, FL: Rourke Enterprises, Inc., 1987. 48 pp. Illustrated. Map. Glossary. Index.

Presents scriptural background for young readers on the Jewish feasts, along with customs and traditions, recipes and food, and activities associated with them. Sections explaining the Jewish calendar, including a calendar of festivals, and the Hebrew alphabet. Further reading list.

♦ Indicates a book cited in the main text

Wigoder, Geoffrey, ed. *The Encyclopedia of Judaism.* New York: Macmillan, 1989. 768 pp. Illustrated. Glossary. Index.

Several hundred entries cover religious life and development, from the major and minor prophets to dietary laws, from festivals and ceremonies to definitions of concepts and terms. Cross-referencing.

Sikhism

Cole, William Owen, and Piara Singh Sambhi. *The Sikhs: Their Religious Beliefs and Practices.* Boston, MA: Routledge & Kegan Paul, 1978. 210 pp. Illustrated. Maps. Glossary. Bibliography. Appendices. Index.

Covers historical background, beliefs and practices of the Sikh faith, including discussion of founder Guru Nanak and others, scripture, places and style of worship, ethics, ceremonies, birth, marriage and death rites, and calendar of festivals. Appendices cover the Rehat Maryada, or guide to the Sikh way of life; prayers and meditations; population statistics; and explanation of the structure of the Guru Granth Sahib—the scriptural hymns.

Kapoor, Sukhbir Singh. *Sikh Festivals.* Holidays and Festivals Series. Vero Beach, FL: Rourke Enterprises, Inc., 1989. 48 pp. Illustrated. Glossary. Index.

Background for young readers on Sikh religious beliefs, history, and ceremonies and festivals. Chronological table of holidays by Hindu month. List of Sikh gurus. Further reading list.

Holidays of Ethnic Groups and Geographic Regions

Africa

Beier, Ulli. *Yoruba Myths.* Cambridge, England: Cambridge University Press, 1980. 82 pp. Illustrated.

The author and contributors present 41 myths from Nigeria about Yoruba deities, including Ogun and Oranmiyan.

Levine, Donald N. *Wax & Gold: Tradition and Innovation in Ethiopian Culture.* Chicago: The University of Chicago Press, 1965. 315 pp. Illustrations. Maps. Glossary. Index.

Social scientist examines history, traditions, lifestyles, literature, art, and religion of Amhara people in Ethiopia. Festivals discussed include Maskal (Exaltation of the Cross), St. Michael's Day and other saints' days, Christmas (Ganna), and Timqat (Epiphany).

Westermarck, Edward. *Ritual and Belief in Morocco.* 2 vols. London: Macmillan and Co., Ltd., 1926. Vol. 1, 608 pp.; vol. 2, 629 pp. Map. Illustrations. Index (vol. 2).

Author presents results of on-site research, discussing peoples living in Morocco and their religions, beliefs and practices, saints, charms and superstitions. Calendar and agricultural rites and festivals are covered in vol. 2. List of tribes and locales.

Ancient World (Western)

♦ Avery, Catherine B., ed. *The New Century Classical Handbook.* New York: Appleton-Century-Crofts, Inc., 1962. 1162 pp. Illustrated.

This book has more than 6,000 dictionary-style entries, with pronunciations, covering mythological and historical figures, texts, places, festivals, legends, and artifacts in ancient Greece and Rome. Some cross-referencing. [Cited in the text as *NewCentClassHand-1962*]

♦ Brumfield, Allaire Chandor. *The Attic Festivals of Demeter and Their Relation to the Agricultural Year.* Salem, NH: Ayer Company, 1981. 257 pp. Appendix. Bibliography. Glossary. Indexes.

Scholarly investigation of the various Attic (ancient Greek) festivals of Demeter. Covers Proerosia, Thesmophoria, Haloa, Cloaia, the Lesser Mysteries, various harvest festivals, Skira, and the Eleusinian Mysteries. Argues that these festivals attempted to ritually ensure a good harvest and to consolidate community attention on important moments of the agricultural cycle. List of Athenian months. Appendix provides a glossary of Greek agricultural words. General index and index of Greek words. [Cited in the text as *AtticFest-1981*]

♦ Fowler, W. Warde. *The Roman Festivals of the Period of the Republic: An Introduction to the Study of the Religion of the Romans.* London, England: Macmillan and Co., Ltd., 1899. Reprinted in 1925. 373 pp. Indexes.

Describes the Roman calendar and Roman festivals of the Republican era in chronological order, from *Mensis Martius*, or March, to *Mensis Februarius*, or February. Chronological table of calendar festivals, according to the Republican calendar. Indexes of subjects, Latin words, Latin authors quoted, and Greek authors quoted. [Cited in the text as *RomFest-1925*]

♦ Grant, Michael. *A Guide to the Ancient World: A Dictionary of Classical Place Names.* New York: H. W. Wilson Company, 1986. 728 pp. Bibliography. Maps.

Covers place names throughout the Mediterranean world and Europe. Gives location, history of settlement, major historical events, incorporation into states or empires, and current remains. Furnishes 15 maps of various European and Mediterranean regions, with ancient place names marked. Provides a bibliography of sources in the following ancient and modern languages: Greek, Latin, Aramaic, Armenian, Coptic, German, Hebrew, Syriac, and English. Also lists relevant journals and archeological reports. [Cited in the text as *GdAnctWrld-1986*]

♦ Hammond, N.G.L., and H. H. Scullard. *The Oxford Classical Dictionary.* Second edition. Oxford, England: Clarendon Press, 1970. 1176 pp. Bibliography. Index.

Covers the ancient Greek and Roman worlds. Treats place names, mythological figures, legends, notable individuals, institutions, customs, natural features, political and administrative units, festivals, cults, and more. Entries are substantial; most list sources. Offers bibliography of books in many languages. Index includes people, places, and things mentioned throughout, but not titles of entries. [Cited in the text as *OxClassDict-1970*]

♦ *Lemprière's Classical Dictionary of Proper Names mentioned in Ancient Authors Writ Large.* Third edition. Introduction by R. Willets. London, England: Routledge & Kegan Paul, 1984. 675 pp. Table.

More than 10,000 dictionary-style entries cover historical and mythological figures, places, festivals, and other terms relevant to the classical world from the 12th century B.C. to the 15th century A.D. Chronological table of events, from the Trojan War to the fall of Trebizond in 1461, precedes the text of the *Dictionary.* Original-

♦ Indicates a book cited in the main text

Bibliography

ly published in 1788, this source had particular influence on 19th-century English literature. [Cited in the text as *ClassDict-1984*]

♦ Parke, H. W. *Festivals of the Athenians*. Ithaca, NY: Cornell University Press, 1977. 208 pp. Illustrated. Notes. Bibliography. Index.

Describes festivals celebrated in ancient Athens. Part one presents, in chronological order, the festivals associated with a specific calendar date. Part two covers local and movable festivals. Gives background information on Athenian religion and daily life. Includes a calendar of Athenian festivals and a map of Athens showing principal sanctuaries. [Cited in the text as *FestAth-1977*]

♦ Scullard, H. H. *Festivals and Ceremonies of the Roman Republic*. Ithaca, NY: Cornell University Press, 1981. 288 pp. Illustrated.

Describes numerous holidays and ceremonies of the Republic. Part one provides introduction to Roman religion. Part two gives historical background of festivals and identifies (when possible) deity or event celebrated, manner of observance, legends and temple sites associated with the celebration, and references made to the festival in ancient texts. Part three covers other ceremonies, such as those connected with triumphs, ovations, and meetings of the Senate. Provides a map of Rome identifying sites of temples and buildings, a further reading list, a list of Roman calendars and festivals, a complete Roman calendar, and a list of temples and their dates of consecration. [Cited in the text as *FestRom-1981*]

Asia and the Middle East

GENERAL WORKS

Festivals in Asia. Asian Copublication Programme Series Two. Sponsored by the Asian Cultural Centre for Unesco. Tokyo, Japan: Kodansha International Ltd., 1975. 66 pp. Illustrated.

For young readers. Describes, in chronological order, the New Year in Singapore, Festival of Fire (New Year) in Iran, Dolls' Day and Boys' Day in Japan, Bengali New Year in Bangladesh, the Water Festival in Burma, New Year in Cambodia, New Year in Laos, Sinhala and Tamil New Year in Sri Lanka, and Maytime in the Philippines, often through storytelling.

Jettmar, Karl, ed. *Cultures of the Hindukush: Selected Papers from the Hindu-Kush Cultural Conference Held at Moesgård 1970*. Wiesbaden, Germany: Franz Steiner Verlag, 1974. Illustrated. Maps. Bibliography. Index.

These papers and notes by more than a dozen scholars were compiled from the conference in 1970 on cultures of peoples in the valley regions of the Hindukush mountain range in Central Asia, including the Kafirs, Kalasha, and Kom. Topics covered include languages, history, festivals, religion, cosmology, mythology, customs, and political organization.

More Festivals in Asia. Asian Copublication Programme Series Two. Sponsored by the Asian Cultural Centre for Unesco. Tokyo, Japan: Kodansha International Ltd., 1975. 66 pp. Illustrated.

For young readers. Describes, in chronological order, Tano Day in Korea, Eid-ul-Fitr in Pakistan, Lebaran in Indonesia, Hari Raya Puasa in Malaysia, Mid-Autumn Festival in Vietnam, Dasain in Nepal, Diwali Festival of Lights in India, Loy Krathong in Thailand, and the Buzkashi Game in Afghanistan, often through storytelling.

CHINA

Bredon, Juliet, and Igor Mitrophanow. *The Moon Year: A Record of Chinese Customs and Festivals*. Shanghai, China: Kelly & Walsh, Ltd., 1927. 522 pp. Illustrated. Bibliography. Index.

Chapters on the Chinese calendar, imperial ceremonies, and the many Chinese gods and cults associated with them, including a discussion of the rise of Confucianism, Taoism and Buddhism. A chapter is then devoted to each month of the Chinese year, describing the observance of festivals within each month.

Burkhardt, V. R. *Chinese Creeds & Customs*. 2 vols. Hong Kong: The South China Morning Post, Ltd., 1953–55. Vol. 1, 181 pp. + index, i-v; vol. 2, 201 pp. + index, i-ix Illustrated. Appendices. Bibliography.

Author describes customs and observance of more than 20 festivals and ceremonies in China, as well as legends, foods, objects, symbols, and fine arts, and discussion of the calendar. Appendices include list of the 24 segments of the Chinese year, the 10 celestial stems and 12 earthly branches, and a table of Chinese temples that lists each temple's locale, god(s) worshipped, and date founded.

Eberhard, Wolfram. *Chinese Festivals*. Great Religious Festivals Series. New York: Henry Schuman, 1952. 152 pp. Illustrated. Index.

Essays on observance and folklore associated with the New Year, Dragon Boat Festival, Mid-Autumn Festival, Spring Festival, Feast of the Souls, Sending the Winter Dress Festival, and the Weaving Maid and the Cowherd Festival.

Hodous, Lewis. *Folkways in China*. London: Arthur Probsthain, 1929. 248 pp. Illustrated. Bibliography. Index.

Author relates his travels to more than 20 festivals in China, covering history, lore, superstitions, customs, and foods. List of Chinese names.

Latsch, Marie-Luise. *Chinese Traditional Festivals*. Beijing, China: New World Press, 1984. 107 pp.

Discusses seven major Chinese festivals and their changing significance through history. Festivals covered are New Year Lantern Festival, Pure Brightness Festival (Qing Ming), Dragon Boat Festival, Mid-Autumn Festival, Honoring the Kitchen God, and the Lunar New Year's Eve.

Qi Xing, comp. *Folk Customs at Traditional Chinese Festivals*. Translated by Ren Jiazhen. Illustrated by Yang Guanghua. Beijing, China: Foreign Languages Press, 1988. 125 pp. Appendices.

Describes customary festivities for 13 traditional Chinese festivals, including the Spring Festival, the Lantern Festival, Spring Dragon Day, Clear and Bright Festival, Dragon Boat Festival, Heaven's Gift Day, Double Seventh Night, Middle of the Year Festival, Mid-Autumn Festival, Double Ninth Day, Eighth Day of the Twelfth Month, Kitchen God's Day, and New Year's Eve. Also gives brief descriptions of 10 minor festivals. Covers major festivals of 15 ethnic minority groups, for example Tibetans and Mongolians, as well as 20 minor ethnic festivals. Appendices explain various elements of the traditional Chinese calendar systems, including the 24 solar terms, the 10 heavenly stems and 12 earthly branches, list modern China's commemorative days, and provide a brief chronology of periods in Chinese history.

Stepanchuk, Carol, and Charles Wong. *Mooncakes and Hun-*

♦ Indicates a book cited in the main text

gry Ghosts: Festivals of China.* San Francisco, CA: China Books & Periodicals, 1991. 145 pp. Illustrated. Maps. Appendices. Glossary. Notes. Bibliography.

Covers legends, history, foods, superstitions, poems, objects, and customs associated with such major Chinese holidays as New Year, Dragon Boat Festival, Mid-Autumn Festival, Clear Brightness Festival, Feast of the Hungry Ghosts, Festival of the Cowherd and the Weaving Maiden, Tian Hou, Protectress of Seafarers, and Double Yang Day, as well as 12 holidays observed by national minorities in China. Appendices include explanation of the Chinese calendar, listing of major festivals by the calendar, table of related symbols, notes on arranging food, pictorial glossary of symbols, Chinese character glossary, and chronology of dynasties.

Tun Li-Ch'en. *Annual Customs and Festivals in Peking.* Translated by Derk Bodde. Second edition (revised). Hong Kong: Hong Kong University Press, 1965 (first edition, 1936). 147 pp. Illustrated. Bibliography. Appendices. Index.

Originally written in 1900, this book describes more than 100 annual events in Peking, arranged chronologically by Chinese month. Appendices discuss the Chinese calendar and list units of measure, English equivalents of Chinese names, dynasties and emperors, and concordance of Chinese and Gregorian calendars from 1957–1984.

HONG KONG

Ward, Barbara E., and Joan Law. *Chinese Festivals in Hong Kong.* The Guidebook Company, Ltd., 1993. 95 pp. Illustrated. Map. Glossary. Index.

Presents 30 Chinese festivals and ceremonies as they are observed in contemporary Hong Kong. Explanation of solar calendar and chart. Map of festival locations. Festival calendar, including table converting solar dates from 1992 to 2004.

INDIA AND SRI LANKA

Welbon, Guy R., and Glenn E. Yocum, eds. *Religious Festivals in South India and Sri Lanka.* New Delhi, India: Manohar, 1982. 341 pp. Index.

Scholars in anthropology, religious studies, and history of Indian art contribute twelve essays that derive from a workshop at the Conference on Religion in South India, held in 1971 at Haverford College. Essays are entitled: "The Hindu Festival Calendar," Karen L. Merrey; "Festivals in Pancaratra Literature," H. Daniel Smith; "The Cycle of Festivals at Parthasarathi Temple," James L. Martin; "The Candala's Song," Guy R. Welbon; "Two Citra Festivals in Madurai," D. Dennis Hudson; "Chronometry, Cosmology, and the Festival Calendar in the Murukan Cult," Fred W. Clothey; "Mahasivaratri: The Saiva Festival of Repentance," J. Bruce Long; "The Festival Interlude: Some Anthropological Observations," Suzanne Hanchett; "The End is the Beginning: A Festival Chain in Andhra Pradesh," Jane M. Christian; "Kalam Eluttu: Art and Ritual in Kerala," Clifford R. Jones; "The Kataragama and Kandy Asala Peraharas: Juxtaposing Religious Elements in Sri Lanka," Donald K. Swearer; and "An-keliya: A Literary-Historical Approach," Glenn E. Yocum. [Cited in the text as *RelFestSriLank-1982*]

JAPAN

♦ Bauer, Helen, and Sherwin Carlquist. *Japanese Festivals.* Garden City, NY: Doubleday & Company, Inc., 1965. 224 pp. Illustrated. Index.

Essays on 11 major festivals. Chapters on food and flower festi-

vals. Second half of book is a chronological arrangement of Japanese festivals. Back matter includes a pronunciation guide and summary of Japan's history. [Cited in the text as *JapanFest-1965*]

Casal, U. A. *The Five Sacred Festivals of Ancient Japan: Their Symbolism & Historical Development.* Tokyo, Japan: Charles E. Tuttle Company, Inc., and Sophia University, 1967. 114 pp. Illustrated. Index.

Covers historical background, traditions, legends and myths, food, customs, and current observance of the New Year Festival, the Girls' Festival, the Boys' Festival, the Star Festival, and the Chrysanthemum Festival in Japan.

KOREA

Chun Shin-yong, ed. *Customs and Manners in Korea.* Part of the 10-volume Korean Culture Series. Seoul, Korea: International Cultural Foundation and Si-sa-yong-o-sa, Inc., 1982. 132 pp. Illustrated.

Scholars from various academic specialties contribute 10 essays on Korean traditions and values, rituals and rites, mental health, literature and mythology. The essay, "Annual Ceremonies and Rituals," by Choi Gil-sung, discusses the timing, significance, and observance of various festivals throughout Korea. Kim Yol-kyu's "Several Forms of Korean Folk Rituals, Including Shaman Rituals" examines folk dance and festivals.

NEPAL

Anderson, Mary M. *The Festivals of Nepal.* London: George Allen & Unwin Ltd., 1971. 288 pp. Illustrated. Bibliography. Index.

Author describes, in chronological order of occurrence, more than 30 Hindu, Buddhist, and Nepalese festivals attended in Nepal, as well as legends and customs associated with them.

VIETNAM

Crawford, Ann Caddell. *Customs and Culture of Vietnam.* Foreword by Henry Cabot Lodge. Illustrations by Hau Dinh Cam. Rutland, VT: Charles E. Tuttle Co., Publishers, 1966. 259 pp. Map. Bibliography.

In addition to providing a calendar and description of festivals and holidays, this book is a survey of mainly South Vietnamese geography, history, culture, religion, education, media, arts, medicine, agriculture, and industry against the backdrop of the Vietnam War. Customs, ceremonies, legends, and points of interest are also included.

Caribbean and Latin America

Bettelheim, Judith, ed. *Cuban Festivals: An Illustrated Anthology.* New York: Garland Publishing, Inc., 1993. 261 pp. Illustrated. Index.

Scholars from various academic disciplines present essays on Cuban festivals: "The Afro-Cuban Festival 'Day of the Kings'," Fernando Ortiz; "Annotated Glossary for Fernando Ortiz's The Afro-Cuban Festival 'Day of the Kings'," David H. Brown; "Glossary of Popular Festivals," Rafael Brea and José Millet; "Carnival in Santiago de Cuba" and "Appendix: The Tumba Francesa and Tajona of Santiago de Cuba," Judith Bettelheim; and "Flashback on Carnival, a Personal Memoir," Pedro Pérez Sarduy.

Dunham, Katherine. *Dance of Haiti.* Foreword by Claude

♦ Indicates a book cited in the main text

Lévi-Strauss. Photographs by Patricia Cummings. Los Angeles: University of California, 1983. 78 pp. Glossary.

In a revised version of her thesis, the dancer-anthropologist surveys religious, social, and festive uses of dance in Haiti, including some commentary on dance and Lent, Mardi Gras, Holy Week, and Easter.

Hill, Errol. *The Trinidad Carnival: Mandate for a National Theatre.* Austin, TX: University of Texas Press, 1972. 139 pp. Illustrations. Appendices. Bibliography. Index.

Historical survey of Trinidad and the Carnival, calypso, and masquerades, including descriptions of observance from the 19th century. Argues that elements of the Carnival and its related traditions should be harnessed toward producing a national theater. Appendices provide an example of calypso drama as well as a list of 50 renowned calypsos.

Milne, Jean. *Fiesta Time in Latin America.* Los Angeles: The Ward Ritchie Press, 1965. 236 pp.

Organized chronologically, this book discusses more than 80 festivals celebrated in Mexico and Central and South America. Concludes with list of festivals by country.

MEXICO

Beezley, William H., Cheryl English Martin, and William E. French, eds. *Rituals of Rule, Rituals of Resistance: Public Celebrations and Popular Culture in Mexico.* Wilmington, DE: Scholarly Resources, Inc., 1994. 374 pp.

Fifteen papers presented by scholars at the Eighth Conference of Mexican and North American Historians in San Diego, 1990. Essays analyze popular culture, rituals, customs, and festivals in Mexico in the context of political power and colonial domination.

Burland, C. A. *The Gods of Mexico.* New York: G. P. Putnam's Sons, 1967. 219 pp. Illustrated. Maps. Appendices. Bibliography. Index.

Alphabetical listing of Aztec gods. Guide to pronunciation. Covers Aztec, Mayan, Toltec, and Olmec cultures, cities, calendar systems, deities, and religions. Aztec ceremonies and festivals described. Appendices discuss Mayan, Aztec, and other Mexican codices and tlachtli, a ball game.

Fergusson, Erna. *Fiesta in Mexico.* Illustrated by Valentín Vidaurreta. New York: Alfred A. Knopf, 1934. 267 pp. + i-iv, index.

Account of travel to festivals throughout Mexico, including Pilgrimage to Chalma, Moors and Christians in Tuxpan, La Fiesta de Nuestra Señora de la Soledad in Oaxaca, Passion Play in Tzintzuntzan, Los Voladores in Coxquihui, a Yaqui Indian *Pascola*, Deer Dance, Coyote Dance, Los Matachines, Holy Week, Good Friday and Holy Saturday in Tlaxcala, Day of the Dead, All Saints' Day and All Souls' Day, Lent, Fiesta of Nuestra Señora de la Santa Vera Cruz, *El Viernes de Dolores* (fifth Friday in Lent) in Santa Anita, Christmas and Posadas. Also includes historical discussion of ancient Aztec, Christian, and secular celebrations.

Marcus, Rebecca B., and Judith Marcus. *Fiesta Time in Mexico.* Champaign, IL: Garrard Publishing Company, 1974. 95 pp. Index.

Intended for young readers, this book describes the following holidays and festivals observed in Mexico: Day of the Dead, Our Lady of Guadalupe, Christmas, New Year's, Day of the Three Kings, St. Anthony the Abbot's Day, Holy Week and Easter, St.

John's Day, Mexican Independence Day, Fifth of May, and the Twentieth of November. Pronunciation guide.

Toor, Frances. *A Treasury of Mexican Folkways: The Customs, Myths, Folklore, Traditions, Beliefs, Fiestas, Dances, and Songs of the Mexican People.* New York: Bonanza Books, 1985. 566 pp. Illustrated. Map. Notes. Bibliography. Glossary. Index.

Covers agricultural, religious, and folk festivals and ceremonies celebrated by the various peoples in Mexico, including dances, songs, folk arts, legends, riddles, and idiomatic expressions.

SOUTH AMERICA

Buechler, Hans C. *The Masked Media: Aymara Fiestas and Social Interaction in the Bolivian Highlands.* The Hague, Netherlands: Mouton Publishers, 1980. 399 pp. Illustrated. Appendices. Glossary. References. Indexes.

Anthropologist presents results of fieldwork on festivals, saints' fiestas, and other rituals among the Aymara people in Bolivia. Appendices offer notes on musical instruments employed during different festivals throughout the year; a description of the Fiesta of the Skulls at the main cemetery in La Paz; comparative table of food and drink expenditures for sponsors of rural and urban festivals during the 1960s and 1970s; a fiesta sponsor's list of participants' contributions to and involvement with a fiesta held in Lamacachi; and a note on recent use of brass bands in Compi fiestas. Index of authors referenced. Index of subjects.

Europe

GENERAL WORKS

Cooper, Gordon. *Festivals of Europe.* 1961. Reprinted by Omnigraphics, Inc., 1994. 172 pp. Illustrated. Appendix. Index.

Traveller-oriented guide provides brief mentions or descriptions of more than 1,000 festivals in 25 Western and Eastern European countries. Arranged alphabetically by country, festivals are discussed by type of event: agricultural, carnival, cultural, national, religious, sporting, trade, wine and food. Chapter offering travel hints. Directory of tourist offices for 24 countries.

Cosman, Madeleine Pelner. *Medieval Holidays and Festivals: A Calendar of Celebrations.* New York: Charles Scribner's Sons, 1981. 136 pp. Illustrated. Index.

Describes customs, activities, food and recipes, music, costume and decoration associated with 12 holidays from the 12th through the 16th centuries, mainly in England, France, Italy, and Germany: Twelfth Night, Valentine's Day, Easter, All Fool's Day, May Day, Midsummer Eve, St. Swithin's Day, Lammas, Michaelmas, Halloween, St. Catherine's Day, and Christmas. Further reading list.

Hanawalt, Barbara A., and Kathryn L. Reyerson, eds. *City and Spectacle in Medieval Europe.* Minneapolis, MN: University of Minnesota Press, 1994. 331 pp. Index.

Twelve papers from a conference at the University of Minnesota in 1991 explore various kinds of ritual and ceremony observed in medieval Europe, including liturgical rites in France, Holy Thursday in Spain, Midsummer in London, accounts of several festivals in medieval Castile, and more.

♦ Johnson, Margaret M. *Festival Europe! Fairs & Celebrations throughout Europe.* Memphis, TN: Mustang Publishing Co., 1992. 236 pp. Maps.

♦ Indicates a book cited in the main text

Tourist-oriented guide organized by region. Entries on more than 700 festivals in 21 countries are in chronological order, from May to October. Includes descriptions of types of events held in each country. Addresses of tourist boards are provided. [Cited in the text as *FestEur-1992*]

Madden, Daniel M. *A Religious Guide to Europe*. New York: Macmillan Publishing Co., Inc., 1975. 529 pp. Index.

Describes making pilgrimages to hundreds of shrines, sanctuaries, and other holy places in more than 15 European countries, from Ireland to Turkey. Travel and accommodation information, as well as descriptions of secular points of interest are provided.

Perl, Lila. *Foods and Festivals of the Danube Lands: Germany, Austria, Czechoslovakia, Hungary, Yugoslavia, Bulgaria, Romania, Russia*. Illustrated by Leo Glueckselig. Cleveland, OH: The World Publishing Company, 1969. 287 pp. Index.

Discusses foods, festivals, and traditions in countries bordering the Danube River. Provides historical overview on the region and on each country's people and lifestyles, often stretching back to prehistoric times. Heavy coverage of foods prepared and consumed in each country, including recipes.

♦ Rabin, Carol Price. *Music Festivals in Europe and Britain*. Stockbridge, MA: Berkshire Traveller Press, 1980. 163 pp. Index.

More than 90 music festivals in 21 European countries are described, arranged by country. Entries provide historical background, type of music offered, notable features and performers from past festivals, contact names, addresses and phone numbers for obtaining tickets and accommodation, and recommended attire. Listing of addresses and phone numbers of government tourist offices. Suggested reading list. [Cited in the text as *MusFestEurBrit-1980*]

♦ Spicer, Dorothy Gladys. *Festivals of Western Europe*. 1958. Reprinted by Omnigraphics, Inc., 1994. 275 pp. Index.

Major festivals in 12 western European countries described in more than 250 entries. Some material duplicates or is revised from that found in the author's *Book of Festivals*. Table of dates for Easter and other Christian movable days from 1958 to 1988. Glossary of festival terms. Suggested reading list. Indexes of festivals by country and by names of festivals. [Cited in the text as *FestWestEur-1958*]

EASTERN EUROPE AND FORMER SOVIET UNION

Dömötör, Tekla. *Hungarian Folk Customs*. Translated by Judith Elliott. Corvina, Budapest, Hungary: Corvina Press, 1972. 86 pp. + plates. Illustrated. Map. Bibliography.

Brief survey of folk customs and beliefs, and their study in Hungary. Discussion of history and observance of seasonal, religious, and secular festivals, as well as birth, marriage, and burial practices.

Martin, Pat, comp. *Czechoslovak Culture: Recipes, History and Folk Arts*. Iowa City, IA: Penfield Press, 1989. 176 pp. Illustrated.

Focus is on Czech-American culture, including traditions and stories carried over from Czechoslovakia. Essays on pioneer experiences, observance of holidays, including lengthy treatment of decorating Easter eggs, folk art, foods and recipes. Profiles of famous Czechs and Czech Americans. A partial list of Czech festivals throughout the United States and tips on planning Czech festivals.

Watson, Jane Werner. *A Parade of Soviet Holidays*. Illustrated by Ben Stahl. Champaign, IL: Garrard Publishing Company, 1974. 96 pp. Pronunciation guide. Index.

Aimed at a young audience, discussion of significance and celebration of more than 20 holidays and festivals observed throughout the former Soviet Union.

FRANCE

Janvier, Thomas A. *The Christmas Kalends of Provence*. 1902. Reprinted by Omnigraphics, Inc., 1990. 262 pp. Illustrated.

Relates tales about rites and celebrations of ancient feasts and festivals practiced in France.

Ozouf, Mona. *Festivals and the French Revolution*. Translated by Alan Sheridan. Cambridge, MA: Harvard University Press, 1988. 378 pp. Notes. Bibliography. Index.

Historian examines the Revolutionary festivals observed between 1789 and 1799, and their role in the French Revolution. Discussion of Revolutionary calendar. Brief chronology of the Revolution.

GERMANY

Russ, Jennifer M. *German Festivals & Customs*. London: Oswald Wolff, 1982. 166 pp. Illustrated. Appendices. Bibliography. Indexes.

Origins and observance of more than 50 religious, historical, and food festivals, pageants, and social customs and ceremonies. Includes rhymes, food, legends, and songs associated with events. Appendices include list of legal holidays in the Federal Republic of Germany. Subject index. Index of names and places.

GREECE

Megas, George A. *Greek Calendar Customs*. Athens, Greece: Press and Information Department, 1958. 159 pp. Illustrated.

Covers customs, beliefs, legends, food, and songs associated with more than 60 saints' days, holidays, festivals, and agricultural activities in Greece (especially rural traditions), according to the seasons of the year.

ITALY

Ashby, Thomas. *Some Italian Scenes and Festivals*. New York: E. P. Dutton and Company, Inc., c1928. 179 pp. Illustrated. Index.

Describes several religious and folk festivals observed in Italy, while providing impressions of the landscape and peoples, as well as some historical background.

Toor, Frances. *Festivals and Folkways of Italy*. New York: Crown Publishers, Inc., 1953. 312 pp. Illustrated. Appendix. Bibliography. Index.

Describes the author's observations of holidays, festivals and folk customs in Sicily, southern Italy and Sardinia, and Rome and its outskirts. Appendix includes notes on Italian festas, beliefs, folk arts, and folklore bibliography.

SCANDINAVIA

Wyndham, Lee. *Holidays in Scandinavia*. Illustrated by Gordon Laite. Champaign, IL: Garrard Publishing Company, 1975. 95 pp. Index.

Discusses 10 holidays and festivals in Sweden, Norway, and Denmark for young readers. Pronunciation guide.

SPAIN

Epton, Nina. *Spanish Fiestas (Including Romerías, Excluding Bull-Fights).* New York: A. S. Barnes and Company, 1968. 250 pp. Illustrated. Map. Index.

Descriptions of Easter, Corpus Christi, midsummer, Christmas, New Year's, and Carnival celebrations throughout Spain, as well as Moors and Christians fiestas, and more than 30 other festivals, holy days, and romarías (pilgrimages) observed in Spain.

UNITED KINGDOM

Brand, John. *Observations on Popular Antiquities, Chiefly Illustrating the Origin of Our Vulgar Customs, Ceremonies, and Superstitions; with the Additions of Sir Henry Ellis.* London: Chatto and Windus, 1877. 807 pp. Illustrated.

Chronologically arranged discussion, with historical background, of more than 60 holidays and festivals as observed in western Europe, especially England. Collection of lore on hundreds of items falling under such headings as sports and games, charms and omens, witchcraft and mythology, marriage, child-bearing, death, and drinking customs.

Drake-Carnell, F. J. *Old English Customs and Ceremonies.* New York: Charles Scribner's Sons; London: B. T. Batsford Ltd., 1938. 120 pp. Illustrated. Index.

Survey of religious, municipal (London), legal, commercial, military, school, marine, and royal ceremonies, customs and protocol relating to the House of Parliament, and rural festivals and traditions—such as the Furry Dance, Beating the Bounds, and Plough Monday—observed in England.

♦ Hole, Christina. *English Custom & Usage.* 1941–42. Reprinted by Omnigraphics, Inc., 1990. 152 pp. Illustrated. Index.

Discusses the celebration of various holidays in England and examines the transformation of pre-Christian observances and rituals into Christian holy days. [Cited in the text as *EngCustUse-1941*]

♦ Howard, Alexander. *Endless Cavalcade: A Diary of British Festivals and Customs.* London: Arthur Barker Limited, 1964. 300 pp. Illustrations. Bibliography. Index.

Arranged in chronological order, over 360 entries describe at least one holiday, festival, civic event or custom for every day of the year, as observed in Britain. [Cited in the text as *EndlessCaval-1964*]

Jones, T. Gwynn. *Welsh Folklore and Folk-Custom.* 1930. Reprint. Suffolk, England: D. S. Brewer, 1979. 255 pp. Bibliography. Glossary. Index.

Collection of Welsh folklore regarding gods, ghosts, fairies, monsters, caves, lakes, magic, marriage, birth, and death. Recounting of some folk tales. Chapters 9–10 deal with customs concerning such holidays as May Day, Midsummer, Christmas, New Year's, Easter, Mari Lwyd, and others.

Kightly, Charles. *The Customs and Ceremonies of Britain: An*

Encyclopaedia of Living Traditions. London: Thames & Hudson Ltd., 1986. 248 pp. Illustrated. Bibliography.

Book opens with a Calendar of Customs, listing events and holidays in chronological order. Next, in alphabetical order, more than 200 entries describe the observance and historical background of religious holidays, secular festivals, and other elements of social life. Practices associated with other types of events are discussed under such general headings as "Bells and Bellringing Customs," "Birth," "Civic Customs," "Coronations," "Fairs," and "Harvest Customs." Regional listing of events.

♦ Long, George. *The Folklore Calendar.* 1930. Reprinted by Omnigraphics, Inc., 1990. 240 pp. Illustrations. Index.

Arranged in chronological order, entries provide historical background for, and cover observance of, more than 40 holidays, festivals, ceremonies, and other events in Great Britain. [Cited in the text as *FolkCal-1930*]

Owen, Trefor M. *A Pocket Guide: The Customs and Traditions of Wales.* Cardiff, Wales: University of Wales Press, 1991. 136 pp. Illustrated. Notes. Index.

Discusses agricultural traditions, customs associated with the home and domestic life, Mari Lwyd, St. Thomas's Day, Twelfth Night, Candlemas, St. David's Day, religious and communal observances and events, and eisteddfod from the 19th century to the present day. Historical survey of the study of folk customs in Wales. Selected reading list by chapter.

♦ Spicer, Dorothy Gladys. *Yearbook of English Festivals.* 1954. Reprinted by Omnigraphics, Inc., 1993. 298 pp. Glossary. Map. Indexes.

Chronologically arranged descriptions of more than 200 English holidays, ceremonies, anniversaries, and local festivals and traditions. Map of England depicting regions and counties. Explanation of Julian and Gregorian calendars and their coexistence in parts of the country. List of movable Christian feasts dependent upon the date of Easter. List of liturgical colors, what they symbolize and when they are used. Table of dates of Easter for 1954 to 1984. Suggested reading list. Indexes by name of event, county, and region. [Cited in the text as *YrbookEngFest-1954*]

Wright, A. R. *British Calendar Customs.* 3 vols. Preface by S. H. Hooke. London: William Glaisher Ltd., 1936. Vol. I, 212 pp.; vol. II, 272 pp.; vol. III, 333 pp. Illustrated. Index in Volumes I and III.

Volumes I through III cover popular customs, lore, superstitions, weather omens, and songs associated with holidays and festivals observed in England. Volume I deals with Christian movable holidays from Shrovetide to Corpus Christi, as well as other movable festivals and harvest customs. Volumes II and III survey nearly 100 secular and religious festivals occurring on fixed dates, presented in chronological order.

North America

CANADA

Parry, Caroline. *Let's Celebrate! Canada's Special Days.* Toronto, Ontario, Canada: Kids Can Press Ltd., 1987. 256 pp. Illustrated. Index.

For young readers. Entries cover more than 250 secular and religious holidays and festivals celebrated in Canada, including Muslim, Hindu, Chinese, Jewish, Baha'i, Sikh, Jaina, Buddhist, and Christian holy days. Entries are organized by season of the

♦ Indicates a book cited in the main text

year and, in addition to discussion of the holiday's background, include riddles, games, poems, crafts, and other activities. Explanation of the calendar, as well as sidebars providing brief background notes on various religious and ethnic groups.

NATIVE NORTH AMERICA

Campbell, Liz, comp. *1993 Powwow Calendar: Guide to North American Powwows and Gatherings U.S.A. and Canada.* Summertown, TN: The Book Publishing Company, 1992. 96 pp. Illustrated.

Lists, in chronological order, more than 400 powwows and other events observed by Native Americans in the United States and Canada. Entries include contact addresses and phone numbers.

♦ Eagle/Walking Turtle. *Indian America: A Traveller's Companion.* Santa Fe, NM: John Muir Publications, 1989. 413 pp. Illustrated. Glossary. Bibliography. Appendix. Index.

More than 300 Indian tribes in the United States are listed and arranged by geographical region. Entries provide mailing address and location, phone numbers, public ceremony or powwow dates, visitor information, and historical background. The appendix offers chronological listing of Indian Moons according to tribe; powwow calendar for North America; Indian arts and crafts shows; Navajo rug auctions; museums with major American Indian collections; Indian-owned and -operated museums and cultural centers, stores, rodeos, and community colleges; populations by state as of April 1980; reservations, rancherias and pueblos with population figures; and urban Indian centers in major metropolitan areas. [Cited in the text as *IndianAmer-1989*]

Faris, James C. *The Nightway: A History and a History of Documentation of a Navajo Ceremonial.* Albuquerque, NM: University of New Mexico Press, 1990. 288 pp. Charts and figures. Notes. Bibliography. Index.

Anthropologist presents a study of recordings of the Navajo Nightway Ceremony and its stories, songs, beliefs, prayers and practices, including sandpainting. Charts and figures detail genealogies of medicine men who have led the Nightway, as well as specific elements of Nightways observed over the last 100 years.

Fergusson, Erna. *Dancing Gods: Indian Ceremonials of New Mexico and Arizona.* Foreword by Tony Hillerman. Albuquerque, NM: University of New Mexico Press, 1931. Sixth paperback printing, 1991. 286 pp. Illustrated. Index.

Describes history, meaning, and performance of religious and social dances and ceremonies observed among the Pueblo, Hopi, Navajo, and Apache peoples, including prayers, customs, and some historical background on each.

Fewkes, Jesse Walter. *Hopi Snake Ceremonies; An Eyewitness Account.* Selections from Bureau of American Ethnology, Annual Reports Nos. 16 and 19 for the years 1894–95 and 1897–98. Albuquerque, NM: Avanyu Publishing, Inc., 1986. Illustrated.

Reprint of two papers published in annual reports. Author describes ceremonies performed by the Hopi Snake Society during the 1890s.

Fewkes, Jesse Walter. *Tusayan Katcinas and Hopi Altars.* Introduction by Barton Wright. Albuquerque, NM: Avanyu Publishing, Inc., 1990. Illustrated.

Reprint of two texts by Fewkes, one an article, "The Katcina Altars in Hopi Worship," that appeared in the Annual Report of the Board of Regents of The Smithsonian Institution for 1926. Both represent author's late 19th-century endeavor to describe and analyze katchina ceremonials among the Hopis, including the Powamû ceremony.

Tiller, Veronica E., ed. *Discover Indian Reservations USA: A Visitors' Welcome Guide.* Foreword by Ben Nighthorse Campbell. Denver, CO: Council Publications, 1992. 402 pp. Illustrated. Maps. Appendices. Index.

Travel-oriented information provided on more than 350 federal and state Indian reservations in 33 states, listed in alphabetical order by state. Entries include a brief profile on the reservation's land, population, and structure, its location and address, cultural institutes, special events (festivals, powwows, rodeos, etc.), businesses and organizations, accommodations, and special restrictions. Appendix I lists tribes alphabetically and gives their location. Appendix II is a powwow directory by state, then month.

UNITED STATES—General Works and Background on Holidays

Anyike, James C. *African American Holidays: A Historical Research and Resource Guide to Cultural Celebrations.* Chicago: Popular Truth, Inc., 1991. 102 pp. Appendices. Bibliography.

Covers holidays celebrated by slaves between the 17th and 19th centuries as well as Martin Luther King, Jr. birthday observances, Black History Month, African Liberation Day, Juneteenth, Umoja Karamu (Unity Feast), and Kwanzaa. Appendices include timeline of important dates in history and brief historical background on major holidays observed in the United States. List of related sources and organizations.

Bailey, Carolyn Sherwin. *Stories for Every Holiday.* 1919. Reprinted by Omnigraphics, Inc., 1990. 277 pp.

Twenty-seven stories for young readers about 19 Christian and secular holidays observed in the United States. Arranged in chronological order, beginning with Labor Day.

Coffin, Tristram P., and Hennig Cohen, eds. *Folklore in America: Tales, Songs, Superstitions, Proverbs, Riddles, Games, Folk Drama, and Folk Festivals with 17 Folk Melodies.* 1966. Reprinted by University Press of America, Inc., 1986. 256 pp. Source notes.

Presents numerous examples of folk tradition among more than 30 ethnic groups in the United States. Index of ethnic groups and geographic locations. Index of titles and first lines of songs. List of tale types and motifs.

Cohen, Hennig, and Tristram Potter Coffin. *America Celebrates! A Patchwork of Weird & Wonderful Holiday Lore.* Detroit, MI: Visible Ink Press, 1991. 355 pp. Illustrated.

Drawing from oral history and newspaper and journal accounts, this book collects more than 200 traditions, legends, beliefs, superstitions, recipes, food, games, dances, poems, riddles, and music associated with over 60 religious, patriotic, commemorative, agricultural, ethnic, and folk holidays and festivals observed among various ethnic, regional, and occupational groups in North America.

♦ Cohen, Hennig, and Tristram Potter Coffin, eds. *The Folklore of American Holidays: A Compilation of More Than 500 Beliefs, Legends, Superstitions, Proverbs, Riddles, Poems, Songs, Dances, Games, Plays, Pageants, Fairs, Foods, and Processions Associ-*

ated with Over 120 American Calendar Customs and Festivals. Detroit, MI: Gale Research Company, 1991. 509 pp. Indexes.

Chronologically arranged collection of lore associated with more than 120 holidays and festivals in the United States. Various ethnic, occupational and religious groups living in the United States are represented. The editors provide brief background information on the event's history, followed by excerpts from written material describing actual observances of the event, as well as accompanying customs, legends, games, recipes, music, etc. Bibliographic information for each source follows the excerpts. Subject Index; Ethnic and Geographic Index; Collectors, Informants, and Translators Index; Song Titles and First Significant Lines Index; and Motif and Tale Types Index. [Cited in the text as *FolkAmerHol-1991*]

Craig, Darrin, and Julie Craig. *The Festival Hopper's Guide to California & Nevada.* Third edition. San Jose, CA: Creative Chaos, 1991. 519 pp. Maps. Indexes.

Information on more than 450 festivals, fairs, rodeos, and arts and music events held in California and Nevada. Entries are organized by northern, central, and southern California, and Nevada, then chronologically within each region or state. Information provided within each entry includes a map, population of the town and festival attendance, average outdoor temperature during the time of the event, festival location, where to call for more information, and checklist of the event's features and existence of regulations, accommodations, and fees. Town index and festival index. List of festival coordinators and vendors with addresses and phone numbers.

Craig, Darrin, and Julie Craig. *The Festival Hopper's Guide to the Rocky West.* San Jose, CA: Creative Chaos, 1991. 209 pp. Maps. Indexes.

Covers more than 150 festivals, fairs, rodeos, and arts and music events held in Arizona, Colorado, New Mexico, Utah, and Wyoming. Entries are organized alphabetically by state, then chronologically within each state. Information provided within each entry is the same as in the authors' *The Festival Hopper's Guide to California & Nevada.* Town index and festival index. List of festival coordinators and vendors with addresses and phone numbers.

Curtis, Mary I. *Why We Celebrate Our Holidays.* Illustrated by Jewel Morrison. New York and Chicago: Lyons and Carnahan, 1924. 148 pp.

Intended for a young audience, the author describes reasons for major observances of the year in the United States.

Dillon, Philip Robert. *American Anniversaries; Every Day of the Year; Presenting Seven Hundred and Fifty Events in United States History, from the Discovery of America to the Present Day.* c1918. Reprinted by Omnigraphics, Inc., 1991. 349 pp. + index, pp. i-xv.

Opens with a chronology of principal events during World War I and summary of armistice. Book is organized chronologically. At least one anniversary is given for each day of the year. Entries cover anniversaries of historical events and people in politics and legislation, commerce and invention, arts and letters.

Greif, Martin. *The Holiday Book: America's Festivals and Celebrations.* New York: The Main Street Press, 1978. 255 pp. Illustrated. Bibliography.

Lengthy entries cover, in chronological order, traditions, customs, and poetry associated with 20 major patriotic, religious, and commemorative holidays observed in the United States. Shorter

entries discuss background and observance of 20 more special days.

Gutiérrez, Ramón, and Geneviève Fabre, eds. *Feasts and Celebrations in North American Ethnic Communities.* Albuquerque, NM: University of New Mexico Press, 1995. 200 pp.

Twelve essays analyze celebrations and practices surrounding such events as funerals, holidays such as Halloween and Easter, folk festivals, and harvest rites among African Americans, Hispanics, Filipinos, West Indians, urban and rural Americans and gays throughout North and South America.

♦ Hatch, Jane M. *The American Book of Days.* Third ed., New York: H. W. Wilson, 1978. 1214 pp. Appendix. Index.

Contains more than 700 entries pertaining to American holidays, festivals, and anniversaries organized by month. Selections reflect events in American history, including entries on each U.S. president and chief justice. There is at least one entry for every day of the year. Entries tend to be lengthy, averaging about 1,300 words. Each month begins with an essay recounting the origin of the month, ancient festivals observed, and the month's birthstone. Four essays comprise the appendix and cover "The Calendar," "The Era," "The Days of the Week," and "Signs of the Zodiac." [Cited in the text as *AmerBkDays-1978*]

Hill, Kathleen Thompson. *Festivals U.S.A.* Foreword by Willard Scott. New York: John Wiley & Sons, Inc., 1988. 242 pp. Glossary. Index.

More than 1,000 art, drama, ethnic, music, food, and promotional festivals held in the United States are organized by geographic region, then state. Estimated annual attendance provided for some entries. Information on event's date and location, foods served, admission price, accommodations, restaurants, and contact information provided within the entries, when known.

Hobbie, Margaret, comp. *Italian American Material Culture: A Directory of Collections, Sites, and Festivals in the United States and Canada.* Westport, CT: Greenwood Press, 1992. 173 pp. Bibliography. Indexes.

Lists nearly 100 museum collections related to Italian-American culture, more than 40 sites around the U.S. significant in Italian American history, and more than 100 religious, folk, agricultural, art, music, food, and commemorative festivals associated with Italian-American material culture. Festival entries provide information on event's location, sponsor address and phone number, dates observed, estimated annual attendance and date first observed, and brief description of festival activities. Sponsor name index. Subject index.

Kincade, Kathy, and Carl Landau. *Festivals of New England: Your Guided Tour to the Festivals of Connecticut, Maine, Massachusetts, New Hampshire, Rhode Island, and Vermont.* San Francisco, CA: Landau Communications, 1990. 218 pp. Illustrated.

Covers more than 200 agricultural, ethnic, food and wine, marine, music, historical, art, and community festivals in New England in chronological order. List of festivals by state and by type of festival.

Krythe, Maymie R. *All About American Holidays.* New York: Harper & Row, 1962. 275 pp. Bibliography. Index.

Surveys historical background and contemporary observance of

♦ Indicates a book cited in the main text

51 religious days (Christian and Jewish), secular holidays, and patriotic anniversaries celebrated in the United States.

Landau, Carl, and Katie Landau, with Kathy Kincade. *California Festivals* (paper). Third edition. San Francisco, CA: Landau Communications, 1992. 270 pp. Illustrated.

A guide to more than 300 California festivals, arranged by month. Provides date, brief description of activities and attractions, fees, attendance, years in existence, location, and phone number. Lists of festivals by theme and by general location follow the main listings.

Murphy, Joseph M. *Santería: African Spirits in America.* Boston, MA: Beacon Press, 1988. 189 pp. Notes. Glossary. References. Index.

Traces origins and presents beliefs, rituals, ceremonies, songs, gestures, foods, and herbs associated with the practice of the Santería ("the way of the saints") religion, an Afro-Cuban outgrowth of the Yoruba religion in Nigeria, as observed by African Americans in New York.

Myers, Robert J., with the editors of Hallmark Cards. *Celebrations: The Complete Book of American Holidays.* Illustrations by Bill Greer. Garden City, NY: Doubleday & Company, Inc., 1972. 386 pp. Selected bibliography. Index.

Covers origins and observance of 45 religious, ethnic, and patriotic holidays in the United States, including dates of first observance, and summarizes another 14.

Olcott, Frances Jenkins. *Good Stories for Anniversaries.* Illustrated by Hattie Longstreet Price. 1937. Reprinted by Omnigraphics, Inc., 1990. 237 pp. Index.

More than 120 stories for children relating to holidays and events in the history of the United States, such as Inauguration Day, Bunker Hill Day, and pioneer days. Arranged chronologically by the school year.

♦ Rabin, Carol Price. *The Complete Guide to Music Festivals in America: Classical, Opera, Jazz, Pops, Country, Folk, Bluegrass, Old-Time Fiddlers, Cajun.* Fourth edition. Illustrated by Celia Elke. Great Barrington, MA: Berkshire Traveller Press, 1990. 271 pp. Index.

Covers more than 150 music festivals in 40 of the United States and territories, as well as Canada, arranged by type of music. Within each section, festivals are listed by the state in which they take place. Entries include a description of the event and addresses and phone numbers to obtain information on purchasing tickets and finding accommodations. Listing of music festivals by location, with maps. Suggested reading list. Index by name of festival. [Cited in the text as *MusFestAmer-1990*]

Sandak, Cass R. *Patriotic Holidays.* New York: Crestwood House, 1990. 48 pp. Index.

Covers 16 patriotic holidays in the United States, and a handful of others elsewhere, for young readers. Further reading list.

Santino, Jack. *All Around the Year: Holidays and Celebrations in American Life.* Urbana and Chicago: University of Illinois Press, 1994. 227 pp. Notes. Bibliography. Index.

Discusses origins and meanings of holidays observed in the United States, and customs, ephemera, and symbols associated with them.

Schaun, George and Virginia Schaun. *American Holidays and Special Days.* Illustrations by David Wisniewski. Lanham, MD: Maryland Historical Press, 1986. 194 pp. Bibliography. Index.

Alphabetical and chronological listings of holidays. List of dates on which states were admitted to the United States. Part I discusses the various calendars, names of the months and days of the week, movable days, and reasons for observance of special days. Part II consists of more than 60 entries on holidays, festivals, and commemorative days observed in the United States in chronological order.

Schibsby, Marian, and Hanny Cohrsen. *Foreign Festival Customs.* Revised edition. New York: American Council for Nationalities Service, 1974. 74 pp.

Describes Christmas, New Year's, and Easter customs, traditions, and recipes from more than 30 immigrant groups to the United States. Discusses Thanksgiving and harvest traditions from Europe.

♦ Shapiro, Larry. *A Book of Days in American History.* New York: Charles Scribner's Sons, 1987. [150 pp.] Illustrated. Index.

Brief entries are arranged in calendar order and cover at least one event in U.S. history. Focus is on European settlement and history from pre-Revolutionary days through the 1970s. [Cited in the text as *BkDaysAmerHist-1987*]

♦ Shemanski, Frances. *A Guide to Fairs and Festivals in the United States.* Westport, CT: Greenwood Press, 1984. 339 pp. Appendix. Index.

Following the format of *A Guide to World Fairs and Festivals* by the same author, this volume covers more than 260 fairs and festivals in the United States, American Samoa, Puerto Rico, and the U.S. Virgin Islands. Entries are arranged alphabetically by state and city, then by territory. Each entry provides a description of the festival's history, purpose, and idiosyncracies of observance. A state-by-state chronological listing of festivals follows the main text. Appendix lists festivals by type. [Cited in the text as *GdUSFest-1984*]

Spicer, Dorothy Gladys. *Folk Festivals and the Foreign Community.* 1923. Reprinted by Omnigraphics, Inc., Detroit, 1990. 152 pp. Bibliography.

Offers advice on administration and production gleaned from folk festivals organized during the 1920s that were attempts to bond recent immigrants with those born in the United States by fostering understanding and appreciation of cultural diversity.

Spivack, Carol, and Richard A. Weinstock. *Best Festivals of North America: A Performing Arts Guide.* Third edition. Ventura, CA: Printwheel Press, 1989. Indexes.

Entries on more than 150 classical music, chamber music, opera, dance, theater, film, jazz, folk music, bluegrass, ethnic, and children's festivals held in the United States, ordered by type of event, then state. Entries include information on points of interest, ticket prices, accommodations, and contact addresses and phone numbers. Index of festivals by name and state. Index of other attractions near festivals. Chronological Index by month.

Thornton, Willis. *Almanac for Americans.* 1941. Reprinted by Omnigraphics, Inc., 1973. 418 pp. Illustrated. Index.

A "Book of Days of the Republic," arranged chronologically, focuses on patriotic holidays and historical events in the United States.

♦ Indicates a book cited in the main text

Tuleja, Tad. *Curious Customs: The Stories Behind 296 Popular American Rituals.* New York: Harmony Books, 1987. 210 pp. Bibliography.

Provides historical information and occasionally tongue-in-cheek observations on major American holidays as well as customs and superstitions surrounding various social activities including gestures, apparel, etiquette, eating, and courtship.

Young, Judith. *Celebrations: America's Best Festivals, Jamborees, Carnivals & Parades.* Foreword by Ray Bradbury. Santa Barbara, CA: Capra Press, 1986. Series title: American Holidays: Volume One. 183 pp. Photos.

Arranged by region of the United States, then by season. Describes more than 200 festivals in the United States and a few in Canada. Includes state maps, admission fee information, contact addresses, index of ethnic festivals by region, and index of Native American festivals by region.

UNITED STATES—Works on the Presidents

Benbow, Nancy D. Myers, and Christopher H. Benbow. *Cabins, Cottages and Mansions: Homes of the Presidents of the United States.* Gettysburg, PA: Thomas Publications, 1993. 234 pp. Illustrated. Bibliography.

A foreword by Pres. James A. Garfield's great-grandson leads off detailed entries on each president as well as the featured sites. Black-and-white photos and addresses, telephone numbers and traveling directions are included, as is an entry describing the White House.

Haas, Irvin. *Historic Homes of the American Presidents.* New York: Dover Publications, Inc., 1991. 184 pp. Illustrated. Index.

Entries on the homes or birthplaces of thirty-five U.S. presidents include excellent black-and-white photos (some exterior, some interior) and many detailed descriptions of the residences, though length of the entries varies. Addresses, telephone numbers, and traveling directions are included. The White House is also listed.

Kane, Joseph Nathan. *Facts About the Presidents.* New York: H. W. Wilson Company, 1993. 433 pp. Illustrated. Index.

This is a detailed and exhaustive source for "facts about the presidents." Biographical information on immediate family is included, with selected events of the president's life and administration highlighted. Comparative data (religion, military service and so on) is included along with election information and a section on the vice presidents.

Kern, Ellyn R. *Where the American Presidents Lived, including a Guide to the Homes that are Open.* Indianapolis, IN: Cottontail Publications, 1982. 120 pp. Illustrated. Bibliography.

Presidential lives broken down by years, with black-and-white photos and line drawings, followed by brief descriptions and history of sites with addresses, telephone numbers, and locations on line maps organized geographically.

Kochmann, Rachel M. *Presidents: A Pictorial Guide to the Presidents' Birthplaces, Homes and Burial Sites.* Osage, MN: Osage Publications, 1994. 158 pp. Illustrated.

Black-and-white photographs accompany the brief text which includes basic facts, dates and a quote from each president. Addresses and traveling directions are listed along with locations on line maps.

Kruh, David, and Louis Kruh. *Presidential Landmarks.* New York: Hippocrene Books, 1992. 480 pp. Illustrated. Indexes.

Each entry opens with a two- to three-page overview of each president and his administration, followed by descriptions of sites and addresses, telephone numbers and traveling directions. An entry on "multi-presidential" sites is also included. Photos are black-and-white.

UNITED STATES—Works on the States

Abate, Frank, ed. *American Places Dictionary: A Guide to 45,000 Populated Places, Natural Features, and Other Places in the United States.* 4 volumes. Detroit, MI: Omnigraphics, Inc., 1994. Maps. Bibliography. Appendix. Indexes.

Organized first by state, then by county, this reference work provides coverage of the following places throughout the U.S.: states, counties and county equivalents, incorporated places (cities, towns, etc.), unincorporated places (certain townships, villages, Census Designated Places, etc.), American Indian reservations, major military installations, and geographic features. Place entries for each state are preceded by various geographic and demographic data on the state, including symbols and name origin information, a description of the local government, and an essay on the state's history and boundaries. Place entries provide legal place name and status, latitude and longitude, population, land and water areas, notable background information and name origin. Miscellany on American Places and American Names—Curiosities and Peculiarities. State indexes. Complete index in volume 4.

Kane, Joseph Nathan, Janet Podell, and Steven Anzovin. *Facts about the States.* 2nd edition. New York: H. W. Wilson Company, 1993. 624 pp. Tables.

This reference book presents the following information about each state, organized alphabetically by state: admission date and rank; explanations of state name, nicknames, seal and flag; motto, song, and symbols; geographic and climatic data; national sites; chronology of significant dates in the state's history; demographic data; local government, political history, finances, economy, environment, ethnic groups, educational and cultural facilities; miscellaneous state facts; and bibliography containing fiction and nonfiction works about the state. The District of Columbia and Puerto Rico are also covered. Comparative tables on land areas and shorelines, population, settlement by non-native Americans, geography, finances, transportation, military installations, and educational facilities.

Worldmark Encyclopedia of the States. Detroit, MI: Gale Research Inc., 1995. 758 pp. Glossary. Tables. Maps.

Arranged alphabetically by state, this reference work provides information on each state including its location, size, topography, climate, flora, fauna and environmental condition, population, languages and ethnic groups, religions, transportation, history, government, political parties and voting history, economy, income, industries, education, housing, famous people, and more. A bibliography is included for each state. Includes sections on U.S. dependencies and territories.

Individual Holidays
Christmas

Auld, William Muir. *Christmas Tidings.* 1933. Reprinted by Omnigraphics, Inc., 1990. 156 pp. Illustrated.

♦ Indicates a book cited in the main text

Describes legends, verse, and such historic liturgies as the Roman Breviary and the Missal.

Auld, William Muir. *Christmas Traditions.* 1931. Reprinted by Omnigraphics, Inc., 1992. 179 pp. Index.

This history of Christmas surveys origins, antecedents, changes, and developments of the traditions through the ages. Covers ancient English carols, the yule log, the tree, bells, and more. Excerpts from literature, legends, and historical accounts.

Ballam, Harry, and Phyllis Digby Morton, eds. *The Christmas Book.* 1947. Reprinted by Omnigraphics, Inc., 1990. 260 pp. Illustrated. Appendices.

Collection of articles and stories by such writers as Charles Dickens, Aldous Huxley, Washington Irving, Bram Stoker, and others on the subject of Christmas. Several holiday quizzes are included, for which the Appendices provide the answers.

Bauer, John E. *Christmas on the American Frontier, 1800–1900.* 1961. Reprinted by Omnigraphics, Inc., 1993. 320 pp. Illustrated.

Seventeen chapters cover such topics as "A California Festival of Good Will," "Down a Prairie Chimney," "Giving Christmas to the Indians," and more. Contains eyewitness accounts of frontier holidays.

Buday, George. *The History of the Christmas Card.* 1954. Reprinted by Omnigraphics, Inc., 1992. 304 pp. Illustrated. Bibliography. Appendices. Index.

Traces the rise of the Christmas card and discusses its forerunners, old Christmas card creators, children's cards, religious cards, and wartime Christmas cards. Appendices list artists and designers, old Christmas card sentiment writers, and Christmas card publishers.

Crippen, Thomas G. *Christmas and Christmas Lore.* 1923. Reprinted by Omnigraphics, Inc., 1990. 223 pp. Illustrated. Index.

Collection of customs, traditions, and legends relating to Christmas, drawn from chapbooks and pamphlets of the 17th and 18th centuries and from various books dealing with antiquities and legends.

Dawson, W. F. *Christmas: Its Origins and Associations.* 1902. Reprinted by Omnigraphics, Inc., 1990. 366 pp. Illustrated. Index.

Arranged chronologically, this book covers the holiday's origin, its historical events, and festive celebrations during the course of 19 centuries. Considers the evolving tradition in Britain and includes information on the celebration of Christmas in various lands.

Duncan, Edmondstoune. *The Story of the Carol.* 1911. Reprinted by Omnigraphics, Inc., 1992. 253 pp. Illustrated. Appendices. Bibliography. Index.

Surveys development of the forms and purposes of carols, as well as the days, feasts, pageants, and religious rites associated with them. Includes words and music to traditional carols. Appendices include brief biographical notes on relevant individuals, glossary, chronological table of development of carols, and list of manuscript carols held in the British Museum.

Foley, Daniel J. *Christmas the World Over: How the Season of Joy and Good Will Is Observed and Enjoyed by Peoples Here and Everywhere.* Illustrated by Charlotte Edwards Bowden. Philadelphia and New York: Chilton Books, 1963. 128 pp. Index.

Customs and traditions associated with Christmas in more than 30 countries around the world. Heavy coverage of Europe and Latin America.

Foley, Daniel J., ed. *Christmas in the Good Old Days: A Victorian Album of Stories, Poems, and Pictures of the Personalities Who Rediscovered Christmas.* 1961. Reprinted by Omnigraphics, Inc., 1994. 224 pp. Illustrated. Bibliography. Index.

Anthology of stories and poems written during the Victorian era by such authors as Louisa May Alcott, Washington Irving, Bret Harte, O. Henry, Charles Dickens, Hans Christian Andersen, Herman Melville, and others. Includes brief sketches on the authors.

Hole, Christina. *Christmas and Its Customs: A Brief Study.* Illustrated by T. Every-Clayton. New York: M. Barrows and Company, Inc., 1957. 95 pp. Bibliography. Index.

Discusses origins of the holiday, as well as garlands, gift-giving, carols, food, and legends and superstitions. Also covers Twelfth Night and the New Year.

Hottes, Alfred Carl. *1001 Christmas Facts and Fancies.* 1946. Reprinted by Omnigraphics, Inc., 1990. 308 pp. Illustrated.

Facts and fancies, stories and legends gathered from author's personal experiences and obscure literature.

Miles, Clement A. *Christmas in Ritual and Tradition; Christian and Pagan.* 1912. Reprinted by Omnigraphics, Inc., 1968. Illustrated. Notes. Bibliography. Index.

Part I deals with the Christian observance, examining Latin and European hymns and poetry, liturgy, popular customs, and dramas, pageants, and plays. Part II covers pre-Christian winter festivals and their surviving customs. Includes discussion of the Christmas tree, gifts, cards, and mumming, as well as more than 20 saints' days and other holidays and festivals observed throughout the year in Europe.

Miller, Daniel, ed. *Unwrapping Christmas.* Oxford, England: Clarendon Press, 1993. 239 pp. Index.

Ten anthropological essays by scholars in various academic fields on contemporary, and international, observance and meaning of Christmas: "A Theory of Christmas" and "Christmas against Materialism in Thailand," Daniel Miller; "Father Christmas Executed," Claude Lévi-Strauss; "The Rituals of Christmas Giving," James Carrier; "Materialism and the Making of the Modern American Christmas," Russell Belk; "Cinderella Christmas: Kitsch, Consumerism, and Youth in Japan," Brian Moeran and Lise Skov; "The English Christmas and the Family: Time out and Alternative Realities," Adam Kuper; "Christmas Cards and the Construction of Social Relations in Britain Today," Mary Searle-Chatterjee; "Christmas Present: Christmas Public," Barbara Bodenhorn; and "The Great Christmas Quarrel and Other Swedish Traditions," Orvar Löfgren.

Schauffler, Robert, ed. *Christmas: Its Origin, Celebration and Significance as Related in Prose and Verse.* New foreword by Tristram Potter Coffin. 1907. Reprinted by Omnigraphics, Inc., 1990. 354 pp. Index.

Collection of prose and poetry, hymns and carols divided into sections on origins, celebration, and the significance and spirit of Christmas.

♦ Indicates a book cited in the main text

Bibliography

Sechrist, Elizabeth Hough. *Christmas Everywhere: A Book of Christmas Customs of Many Lands.* New revised and enlarged edition. Philadelphia, PA: Macrae Smith Company, 1962. 186 pp. Illustrated.

For young readers. Stories and customs associated with Christmas in 20 locales around the world.

Walsh, William S. *The Story of Santa Klaus: Told for Children of All Ages from Six to Sixty.* 1909. Reprinted by Omnigraphics, Inc., 1991. 231 pp. Illustrated.

Discusses the origin and development of the Klaus legend, mythological concepts absorbed by Christianity, the Three Kings, Twelfth Night customs, Father Christmas, and Christmas traditions and observances in various countries. Illustrations by artists of all times from Fra Angelico to Henry Hutt.

Weiser, Francis X. *The Christmas Book.* Illustrated by Robert Frankenberg. 1952. Reprinted by Omnigraphics, Inc., 1990. 188 pp. Reference notes. Index.

Relates the story of the celebration of Christmas, from the beginning with its gospel and history, through the festivities of the Middle Ages, to the decline and eventual revival of Christmas customs in Europe and the United States. Ancient and familiar hymns are included, as well as a section on holiday breads and pastries.

Wernecke, Herbert H. *Christmas Customs Around the World.* Philadelphia, PA: The Westminster Press, c1959. 188 pp. Bibliography. Indexes.

Covers historical background, customs and legends, holiday recipes, and pageants and programs. Describes observance of the holiday in more than 60 countries on all continents.

Easter

The Book of Easter. Introduction by William C. Doane. 1910. Reprinted by Omnigraphics, Inc., 1990. 246 pp. Illustrated.

Collection of Easter poems, stories, hymns, and essays from various sources including the Bible, and by such writers as Elizabeth Barret Browning, Walter Pater, Robert Browning, Alfred Tennyson, George Herbert, Thomas Hardy, and others. Reproductions of famous paintings relating to Easter by such artists as Rembrandt, Rubens, and Fra Angelico. Provides historic accounts and descriptions of customs and legends associated with Good Friday, Easter, and the Ascension.

Hazeltine, Alice Isabel, and Elva Sophronia Smith, eds. *The Easter Book of Legends and Stories.* Illustrated by Pamela Bianco. 1947. Reprinted by Omnigraphics, Inc., 1992. 392 pp. Notes. Indexes.

Compilation of literature relating to Easter including biblical narrative, poems, plays, legends, and stories by such authors as Robert Frost, Emily Dickinson, A. E. Houseman, and others. Indexes of authors and titles.

Lord, Priscilla Sawyer, and Daniel J. Foley. *Easter the World Over.* Philadelphia, PA: Chilton Book Company, 1971. 289 pp. Illustrated. Bibliography. Index.

Discusses origins of, and traditions, practices, rhymes, songs and music, fine arts, and food associated with, Easter, Holy Week, and Carnival or Mardi Gras in the Middle East, United States, Europe, Bermuda, the Caribbean, and South and Central America. Also

covers the spring festivals of Ching-ming (Qing Ming) in China and Setsubun in Japan.

Mardi Gras

Mitchell, Reid. *All on a Mardi Gras Day: Episodes in the History of New Orleans Carnival.* Cambridge, MA: Harvard University Press, 1995. 243 pp. Illustrated. Index.

Retells the story of a number of incidents occuring on or around Mardi Gras, from the early 1800s to the 1990s. Provides a unique window on the history of Mardi Gras, its meaning to various ethnic and social groups across time, and the history and culture of New Orleans. Gives suggested reading list.

Memorial Day

Schauffler, Robert, ed. *Memorial Day; Its Celebration, Spirit, and Significance as Related in Prose and Verse, with a Non-sectional Anthology of the Civil War.* 1940. Reprinted by Omnigraphics, Inc., 1990. 339 pp. Index.

Compilation of 140 stories and poems relating the significance of Memorial Day in the United States.

Mother's Day

Schauffler, Robert, ed. *Mother's Day; Its History, Origin, Celebration, Spirit, and Significance as Related in Prose and Verse.* 1927. Reprinted by Omnigraphics, Inc., 1990. 380 pp. Index.

Collection of poetry and stories about mother-worship in pagan times, mother-love antedating Christianity, and some of the ancient customs and rites honoring mothers throughout the centuries. Suggestions for Mother's Day programs for school exercises also included.

New Year

Blackwood, Alan. *New Year.* Holidays and Festivals Series. Vero Beach, FL: Rourke Enterprises, Inc., 1987. 48 pp. Illustrated. Glossary. Index.

For young readers. Discusses ancient celebrations of the New Year in Egypt, Babylonia, and Rome, and among Celts. Explanation of the Jewish and Chinese calendars, the Muslim and Hindu New Year, the New Year throughout Asia, the New Year in the United States and Britain, and some mentions of customs in various European countries. Entries on St. Sebastian and St. Basil. Further reading list.

Journals

African Arts. UCLA James S. Coleman African Studies Center, 1967-

African Studies. Witwatersrand University Press, 1921-

American Anthropologist. American Anthropological Association, 1899-

Anthropology and Archeology of Eurasia; a journal of translations from Soviet sources. M. E. Sharpe, Inc., 1962-

Asian Folklore Studies. Nanzan University, Nanzan Anthropological Institute, 1942-

British Federation of Festivals Yearbook. British Federation of Festivals, 1921-

Canadian Geographic. Royal Canadian Geographic Society, 1930-

Cavalcade of Arts & Attractions. BPI Communications, 1894-

Comparative Studies in Society and History. Cambridge University Press, 1959-

Dance Magazine. Dance Magazine, Inc., 1926-

Directory of North American Fairs, Festivals and Expositions (Amusement Business's Directory North American Fairs; until 1972, known as Cavalcade and Directory of Fairs). BPI Communications, 1888-

The Drama Review. MIT Press, 1955-

Ethnos. Folkens Museum, National Museum of Ethnography, Stockholm, Sweden, 1936-

Folklore. Folklore Society, 1878-

Folklore Forum. Folklore Institute, Bloomington, IN, 1968-

International Migration Review (International Migration Digest). Center for Migration Studies of New York, Inc., 1964-

Jewish Folklore & Ethnology Review. YIVO Institute for Jewish Research, 1978-

Journal of American Culture. Bowling Green Popular Press, 1967-

Journal of American Folklore. American Folklore Society, 1888-

Journal of Ethnic Studies. Western Washington University, 1973-

Journal of Folklore Research. Indiana University, Folklore Institute, 1964-

Journal of Latin American Lore. UCLA Latin American Center, 1974-

The Journal of Polynesian Society. Polynesian Society, Inc., 1892-

Journal of Popular Culture. Bowling Green State University, 1967-

Lore and Language. Centre for English Cultural Tradition and Language, 1969-

National Geographic. National Geographic Society, 1888-

Native American Directory. National Native American Co-Op, 1969-

Nigeria Magazine. Ministry of Culture and Social Welfare, Lagos, Nigeria, 1927-1988.

Western Folklore. California Folklore Society, 1942-

World's Fair. World's Fair, Inc., 1981-

♦ Indicates a book cited in the main text

APPENDIX 6

Holiday Web Sites

This listing of holiday-related web sites includes descriptions of sites and web site addresses (URL), as well as mailing addresses, phone and fax numbers, and e-mail addresses, when available. Sites chosen represent a broad sampling of holiday, festival, and celebration material available on the World Wide Web, and the sites are thought to be relatively stable as gauged by communication with the sites' sponsors or the well-known status of the sponsoring organization (e.g. B'nai B'rith). The names of web sites appear in boldface.

Blake & Associates: First Tier Sites

URL: http://banzai.neosoft.com/citylink/blake/ftier.html
Sponsor: Blake & Associates
Phone: 504-898-2158
Fax: 504-892-8535
E-mail: citylink@neosoft.com

This site will link visitors to sites about Halloween, Christmas, Valentine's Day, Mardi Gras, the Fourth of July, and St. Patrick's Day. Each of these sites is hosted by Blake & Associates, a group of Internet marketing consultants headed by Carol Blake, who is responsible for founding the massive **USA CityLink** site, which may be found at http://usacitylink.com/. These holiday sites all tie back to **USA CityLink**, but each offers some combination of commercial products and services, traditional recipes, crafts, music, history, celebration ideas, and links to related sites. According to Carol Blake, "all of our seasonal sites are into their third year and we have no plans of taking them down."

Chinese New Year

URL: http://www.chinascape.org/chinascape/ChineseNewYear/
Sponsor: Chinascape
E-mail: china@chinascape.org

This site, one page from Chinascape's home page (found at http://www.chinascape.org), is a growing list of links to information on the Chinese New Year. Besides links to essays on the history and celebration of the Chinese New Year, visitors will find links to Chinese calendars, songs, astrology, and information on specific celebrations planned around the world. This site also contains a Holidays section with links to information on official, traditional, and minority nationality holidays celebrated by the Chinese. Finally, there is a growing list of links—in the What's New section—to such far flung topics of Chinese interest as hotels in China, the folk art of the Taiwan Traditional Puppet Show (Bo-De-Hi), and Chinese newsgroups and mailing lists.

Festival Finder: Music Festivals of North America

URL: http://www.festivalfinder.com/fest.home.html
Sponsor: The Clyness Group
5616 N. Broadway
Chicago, IL 60640
Phone: 312-878-2523
E-mail: rudy@festivalfinder.com

Festival Finder is a massive, well-indexed page listing hundreds of music festivals in the United States and Canada. Visitors can locate information by linking to Alternative, Bluegrass, Blues, Cajun Zydeco, Classical, Country, Eclectic, Folk, Jazz, Reggae and World Music, Rock, and Miscellaneous subject categories. The site is organized as a database where visitors can search by festival name, performer, genre, date, state/province, or region. Each of the twelve subject categories has a search option, a list of the current month's offerings, an index of all the festivals in the particular category, and a newsgroup-style discussion area. Links to individual festivals yield dates, artists scheduled to appear, location, directions, contact information for tickets and tourists, and detailed descriptions of the history and happenings of each festival.

Good Stories for Great Holidays: Arranged for Story-Telling and Reading Aloud and for the Children's Own Reading by Frances Jenkins Olcott

URL: http://ftp.sunet.se/ftp/pub/etext/gutenberg/etext95/sthol10.txt
Sponsor: Project Gutenberg
P. O. Box 2782
Champaign, IL 61825
E-mail: dircompg@ux1.cso.uiuc.edu

Visitors to this site will find the entire ASCII text of *Good Stories for Great Holidays* (originally published in 1914), by Frances Jenkins Olcott. In this book, the author "endeavored to bring together myths, legends, tales, and historical stories suitable to holiday occasions." The text contains over 100 traditional stories to be read or told for New Year's Day, Abraham Lincoln's Birthday, St. Valentine's Day, George Washington's Birthday, Easter, May Day, Mother's Day, Memorial Day, Independence Day, Labor Day, Columbus Day, Halloween, Thanksgiving, Christmas, and Arbor Day. This title is one of hundreds of complete "Etexts" (electronic texts) made available by Project Gutenberg, found at http://gutenberg.etext.org/. Project Gutenberg is a non-profit organization whose goal is to make 10,000 public domain titles available in electronic format by the end of the year 2001.

Holidays on the Net

URL: http://www.holidays.net/
Sponsor: Studio Melizo
53 Meadow Lane
Levittown
New York, NY 11756
Phone: 516-520-0366
Fax: 516-520-0379
E-mail: infojp@melizo.com

Studio Melizo's *Holidays on the Net* site is rich in the current multimedia technologies available to Web authors today, including 3-D animation, sound, and video. This site offers links to Studio Melizo's own sites on Christmas, Hanukkah, Thanksgiving, Halloween, Rosh Hashanah and Yom Kippur, Independence Day, Father's Day, Shavuot, Mother's Day, Easter, Passover, Purim, and St. Valentine's Day. Each site provides a history of the particular holiday and its traditional elements, and many include information on legends and customs, ideas for celebrations, and traditional recipes and songs. Studio Melizo also announces *Holidays on the Net on CD* and *Jewish Holidays on the Net on CD* to be released in 1997.

The Jewish Holidays

URL: http://bnaibrith.org/caln.html
Sponsor: B'nai B'rith, Washington, D.C.
E-mail: internet@bnaibrith.org

This site is a calendar listing the specific days on which major Jewish holidays will fall from 1996–2006 (or the traditional Jewish years of 5757–5766). A brief description follows each of the nine holidays listed. This site is a single page, originating from **B'nai B'rith Interactive**, found at http://bnaibrith.org/index.html. B'nai B'rith is an international organization of volunteers supporting the Jewish community around the world. See **B'nai B'rith Interactive** for contact information in each of the United States and 54 other countries around the world.

Merry Christmas

URL: http://www.algonet.se/~bernadot/christmas/
calendar.html
E-mail: bernadot@algonet.se
Sponsor: Beradottesdolen
E2 (Christmas Calendar)
Bernadotte School
Hellerupvej 11
2900 Hellerup
Denmark

This site is a project hosted by children and teachers at Bernadotteskolen: The International School in Denmark. Visitors will find an advent calendar of links—23 of which appear in the shape of presents under the 24th link, the Christmas tree. The hosts invite visitors to "open a new page every day to find out how Christmas and other winter holidays are celebrated in different countries and cultures." The links contain submissions from students at Bernadotteskolen, as well as those solicited from children around the world. Within these links are recipes, songs (some with audio files), and children's

drawings, pictures, and descriptions of holiday traditions and legends from around the world.

The National Arbor Day Foundation

URL: http://www.arborday.org/
Sponsor: The National Arbor Day Foundation
100 Arbor Ave.
Nebraska City, NE 68410
Phone: 402-474-5655

Visitors to this site will find information on the history of Arbor Day, suggestions for celebrations, and—since Arbor Day is celebrated on different dates in different states according to the best tree-planting times in various regions—the specific dates on which Arbor Day is celebrated in each of the fifty states, the Virgin Islands, and Guam. Main sections at this site include Planting & Caring for Trees, Teaching Youth About Trees, and Conferences & Workshops. This site also contains membership information and descriptions of major Foundation programs and awards.

The Sikhism Home Page

URL: http://www.sikhs.org/topics.htm
Sponsor: Sandeep Singh Brar
E-mail: sandeep@sikhs.org

This page is a storehouse of information on the Sikh religion, including in its many sections: Philosophy, The Sikh Gurus, Translations of Selected Scriptures, Audio Prayers, Sikh Ceremonies and Festivals, and Dates in Sikh History. The Ceremonies section contains descriptions of ceremonies and festivals for the naming of children, baptism, marriage, funerals, anniversaries associated with the lives of gurus, and the traditional celebrations of Baisakhi, Diwali, Maghi, Hola Mohalla, and Sangrand. The Dates section lists the calendar dates on which major Sikh holidays and festivals will fall through the year 2000, a descriptive overview of the Sikh calendar, and actual historical dates associated with the lives of Sikh gurus. This page is well organized into major sections and includes an extensive bibliography as well as a section containing additional resources such as Sikh organizations, student groups, and other Sikh-related sites.

Web Home for UU/Pagans

URL: http://world.std.com/~notelrac/cuups.dir/
index.html
Sponsor: Notelrac Starshine
E-mail: notelrac@starshine.ziplink.net

This page contains "information of interest to Unitarian Universalists, Pagans, Wiccans, and followers of various other alternative religious paths." Main sections in this site include: What is Unitarian Universalism, What is Paganism, and an expansive Essay section with links to essays on subjects such as Unitarian Universalism, Paganism, Wicca, and Rituals. The Rituals section contains a calendar of Pagan holidays and festivals, and links to over 50 essays on subjects such as the Winter Solstice, February Eve, the Vernal Equinox, May Eve, the Summer Solstice, August Eve, the Autumnal Equinox, Samhain, and various rituals.

The World Wide Holiday and Festival Page

URL: http://smiley.logos.cy.net/bdecie/
Sponsor: Brian Prescott-Decie
P. O. Box 5704
1311 Nicosia, Cyprus
E-mail: bdecie@logos.cy.net

One of the most thorough and well-indexed holiday sites on the

Web, **The World Wide Holiday and Festival Page** contains over 300 links divided among movable holidays, national holidays, and links. Movable holidays contains links to the Chinese New Year calculated through the year 2000, Christian fixed and movable feasts for both the Western and Orthodox calendars, Hindu festivals for the coming year, Sikh holidays and festivals through the year 2000 (four of which have links to more detailed information), and links to other organizations' pages providing similar information for Islam, Jainism, and Judaism. The national holidays section provides separate links for more than 200 countries, each listing national holidays, and, where a particular religion dominates, movable holidays for that particular religion. Finally, the manageable links section points visitors to related pages for more information.

Year 2000 and Millennium Threshold Observances Around the World

URL: http://www.igc.org/millennium/events/ index.html

Sponsor: The Millennium Institute
1117 N. 19th St., Ste. 900
Arlington, VA 22209-1708
Phone: 703-841-0048
Fax: 703-841-0050
E-mail: millennium@igc.apc.org

Toward its goal of helping to "create the conditions for the peoples of the world to achieve a sustainable future for Earth and to use the energy of the year 2000 to begin building a diverse alliance committed to this task," The Millennium Institute, whose home page is found at http://www.igc.org/millennium, has published this page of events for the coming millennium. This site lists contact information for millennium events by region, country, and major city. Other sections include: International and/or Synchronized Millennium Activities, listing organizations planning events leading up to and during the year 2000; Special Events, highlighting individual events; and Mega Events, in which the Institute expects more than one million people to participate (for instance, Earth Day 2000 and the Olympics). Finally, visitors will find links to further information about the Millennium Institute, as well as more than 50 links to millennium-related sites on the Web.

Indexes

Eight indexes provide reference to entries (as appropriate) for each of the following categories:

INDEX 1

Ethnic and Geographic Index

Indexed below are ethnic groups and peoples observing events, and geographic locales (regions, cities, states, provinces, countries) in which holidays and festivals occur.

576

582

E

F

K

N

O

S

618

U

V

W

X

Y

Z

Religious Groups Index

Indexed below are events with a significant religious element by the religious group observing it. In some cases, the line between culture and religion is not distinct enough to comfortably place an observance in either camp. Therefore, entries that describe events observed by a particular ethnic group that contain sacred components (not affiliated with any major religion) are listed in this index under the ethnic group as well as in the Ethnic and Geographic Index.

Religious Groups Index

INDEX 3

Chronological Index

The Chronological Index lists entries by Fixed Days and Events—for holidays that are celebrated on a specific date—and by Movable Days—for events whose date of celebration is not fixed, particularly those that are observed according to non-Gregorian calendars and those that depend on the date of Easter.

Fixed Days and Events Index

Entries are indexed below according to the month or specific date(s) on which they are observed. For each month, those holidays within the month are given first, followed by holidays celebrated on specific date(s), then those observed at the same time every year, although not on a fixed date (e.g., the first Monday, the last week, etc.).

Movable Days Index

The index below lists entries that are observed according to the dates of non-Gregorian calendars, including the Jewish calendar, Hindu calendar, and movable Christian holidays that depend on the date of Easter. (Hindu dates are approximate, since some Hindu sects begin reckoning new months at the new moon, while others begin reckoning from the full moon.)

The listings for each month are followed by listings of other calendar dates, including those of the lunar Chinese and Buddhist calendars and dates according to the Islamic calendar.

INDEX 4

Special Subject Index

Entries are indexed into one of the six categories below, as appropriate. Some events may be categorized in more than one of the categories. For instance, the **Burning of Judas** in Venezuela is listed under the Religious Groups Index (for its Christian significance), Ancient/Pagan (for its almost certain growth out of similar pagan customs), and Folkloric (for its folkloric aspects).

Ancient/Pagan Index

Indexed below are holidays rooted in ancient Greece, ancient Rome, or in Europe before the spread of Christianity.

Ancient/Pagan Index

Calendar Index

Indexed below are festivals that deal specifically with the calendar or that are held in celebration of the time of the year (solstices and equinoxes), the beginning and end of seasons, etc.

Folkloric Index

Indexed below are festivals deeply rooted in folklore and tradition, as well as those celebrating specific folk tales.

Historic Index

Indexed below are festivals commemorating specific events from history, such as battles, the birth dates of famous people, national independence, etc.

685

Promotional Index

Indexed below are festivals that promote everything from city, state, and national pride to agricultural products; from activities (film, quilting, rodeo) to social values (conservation, harmony among peoples).

Sporting Index

Indexed below are events that are based on or revolve around sporting events. This index does not include the many fairs and festivals in which games and contests form only a part, although these games, etc., can be found in the Subject Index.

Legal Holidays by State Index

The "standard six" holidays observed throughout the United States are:

Jan 1	New Year's Day	1294
May, last Mon	Memorial Day	1178
	(not celebrated in Alabama)	
Jul 4	Fourth of July (Independence Day)	0667
Sep, first Mon	Labor Day	1025
Nov, fourth Thurs	Thanksgiving	1909
Dec 25	Christmas	0385

Indexed below are legal holidays observed by the various states, Washington, D.C., American Samoa, Guam, Puerto Rico, and the U.S. Virgin Islands. Under each state or territory, holidays are listed in Gregorian calendar order, followed by entry number(s). For Jewish holidays and those holidays based on the Christian calendar (Good Friday, Corpus Christi, etc.), we have given the range of months during which the day may fall. The more precise dates may be found at the main entry.

Alabama

Jan, third Mon	Martin Luther King, Jr.'s	
	Birthday	0993
	Robert E. Lee's Birthday	1046
Feb, third Mon	Washington's Birthday	2013
Apr, fourth Mon	Confederate Memorial Day	0432
Jun, first Mon	Jefferson Davis's Birthday	0491
Oct, second Mon	Columbus Day	0424
	Fraternal Day	0674

Alaska

Jan 19	Martin Luther King, Jr. Day	0993
Feb, third Mon	Presidents' Day	1480
Mar, last Mon	Seward's Day	1770
Oct 18	Alaska Day	0025

Arizona

Jan, third Mon	Martin Luther King, Jr. Day and Civil	
	Rights Day	0993
Feb, second Mon	Lincoln's Birthday	1065
Feb, third Mon	Washington's Birthday	2013
May, second Sun	Mother's Day	1236
Jun, third Sun	Father's Day	0628
Sep 17	Constitution Day (Citizenship	
	Day)	0417
Oct, second Mon	Columbus Day	0424

Arkansas

Jan, third Mon	Martin Luther King, Jr.'s	
	Birthday	0993
	Robert E. Lee's Birthday	1046
Feb, third Mon	Washington's Birthday	2013
Dec 24	Christmas Eve	0386

California

Jan, third Mon	Martin Luther King, Jr. Day	0993
Feb 12	Lincoln's Birthday	1065
Feb, third Mon	Washington's Birthday	2013
Mar–Apr: Fri		
before Easter	Good Friday	0733
Sep 9	Admission Day	0010, Appendix 1
Oct, second Mon	Columbus Day	0424

Colorado

Jan, third Mon	Martin Luther King Jr.'s	
	Birthday	0993
Feb, third Mon	Washington-Lincoln Day	1065, 2013
Oct, second Mon	Columbus Day	0424

Connecticut

Jan, first Mon on		
or after Jan 15	Martin Luther King, Jr. Day	0993
Feb 12	Lincoln's Birthday	1065
Feb, third Mon	Washington's Birthday	2013

Oct, second Mon	Columbus Day	0424

Delaware

Jan, third Mon	Martin Luther King, Jr. Day	0993
Feb, third Mon	Presidents' Day	1480
Oct, second Mon	Columbus Day	0424

District of Columbia

Jan, third Mon	Martin Luther King, Jr. Day	0993
Feb, third Mon	Washington's Birthday	2013
Oct, second Mon	Columbus Day	0424

Florida

Jan 15	Martin Luther King, Jr.'s Birthday	0993
Jan 19	Robert E. Lee's Birthday	1046
Feb 12	Lincoln's Birthday	1065
Feb 15	Susan B. Anthony's Birthday	0070
Feb, third Mon	Washington's Birthday	2013
Mar–Apr: Fri before Easter	Good Friday	0733
Apr 2	Pascua Florida Day	1417
Apr 26	Confederate Memorial Day	0432
Jun 3	Jefferson Davis's Birthday	0491
Jun 14	Flag Day	0650
Oct, second Mon	Columbus Day	0424

Georgia

Jan 19	Robert E. Lee's Birthday	1046
Jan, third Mon	Martin Luther King, Jr.'s Birthday	0993
Feb, third Mon	Washington's Birthday	2013
Apr 26	Confederate Memorial Day	0432
Jun 3	Jefferson Davis's Birthday	0491
Oct, second Mon	Columbus Day	0424

Hawaii

Jan, third Mon	Martin Luther King, Jr.'s Birthday	0993
Feb, third Mon	Presidents' Day	1480
Mar 26	Jonah Kuhio Kalanianole Day	1483
Mar–Apr: Fri before Easter	Good Friday	0733
Jun 11	King Kamehameha I Day	0996
Aug, third Fri	Admission Day	0010, Appendix 1

Idaho

Jan, third Mon	Martin Luther King, Jr.'s Birthday	0993
Feb, third Mon	Washington's Birthday	2013
Oct, second Mon	Columbus Day	0424

Illinois

Jan, third Mon	Martin Luther King, Jr.'s Birthday	0993
Feb 12	Lincoln's Birthday	1065
Feb, third Mon	Washington's Birthday	2013
Mar, first Mon	Casimir Pulaski's Birthday	1492

Mar–Apr: Fri before Easter	Good Friday	0733
Oct, second Mon	Columbus Day	0424

Indiana

Jan, third Mon	Martin Luther King, Jr.'s Birthday	0993
Feb 12	Lincoln's Birthday	1065
Feb, third Mon	Washington's Birthday	2013
Mar–Apr: Fri before Easter	Good Friday	0733
Oct, second Mon	Columbus Day	0424

Iowa

Jan, third Mon	Martin Luther King, Jr.'s Birthday	0993
Feb, third Mon	Washington's Birthday	2013

Kansas

set by governor	Martin Luther King Day	0993
Feb 12	Lincoln's Birthday	1065
Feb, third Mon	Washington's Birthday	2013
Oct, second Mon	Columbus Day	0424

Kentucky

Jan 19	Robert E. Lee's Birthday	1046
Jan, third Mon	Martin Luther King, Jr. Day	0993
Jan 30	Franklin D. Roosevelt Day	1564
Feb 12	Lincoln's Birthday	1065
Feb, third Mon	Washington's Birthday	2013
Jun 3	Confederate Memorial Day	0432
	Jefferson Davis Day	0491
Oct, second Mon	Columbus Day	0424

Louisiana

Jan 8	Battle of New Orleans Day	0159
Jan 19	Robert E. Lee's Birthday	1046
Jan, third Mon	Martin Luther King, Jr.'s Birthday	0993
Feb, third Mon	Washington's Birthday	2013
Mar–Apr: Fri before Easter	Good Friday	0733
Jun 3	Confederate Memorial Day	0432
Aug 30	Huey P. Long Day	1076
Oct, second Mon	Columbus Day	0424
Nov 1	All Saints' Day (New Orleans)	0038

Maine

Jan, third Mon	Martin Luther King, Jr. Day	0993
Feb, third Mon	Washington's Birthday	2013
Apr, third Mon	Patriot's Day	1420
Oct, second Mon	Columbus Day	0424

Maryland

Jan 15	Martin Luther King, Jr.'s Birthday	0993
Feb 12	Lincoln's Birthday	1065
Feb, third Mon	Washington's Birthday	2013

Mar 25	Maryland Day 1139	
Mar–Apr: Fri before Easter	Good Friday 0733	
Sep 12	Defenders' Day 0503	
Oct 12	Columbus Day 0424	

Massachusetts

Jan 15	Martin Luther King, Jr.'s Birthday 0993
Feb, third Mon	Washington's Birthday 2013
Apr, third Mon	Patriot's Day 1420
Oct, second Mon	Columbus Day 0424

Michigan

Jan, third Mon	Martin Luther King, Jr. Day 0993
Feb 12	Lincoln's Birthday 1065
Feb, third Mon	Washington's Birthday 2013
Oct, second Mon	Columbus Day 0424

Minnesota

Jan, third Mon	Martin Luther King, Jr.'s Birthday 0993
Feb, third Mon	Washington-Lincoln Day .. 1065, 2013
Oct, second Mon	Columbus Day 0424

Mississippi

Jan, third Mon	Robert E. Lee's Birthday 1046
	Martin Luther King, Jr.'s Birthday 0993
Feb, third Mon	Washington's Birthday 2013
Apr, last Mon	Confederate Memorial Day 0432
May, last Mon	National Memorial Day and Jefferson Davis's Birthday 0491

Missouri

Jan, third Mon	Martin Luther King, Jr. Day 0993
Feb 12	Lincoln's Birthday 1065
Feb, third Mon	Washington's Birthday 2013
Oct, second Mon	Columbus Day 0424

Montana

Jan, third Mon	Martin Luther King, Jr. Day 0993
Feb, third Mon	Washington's Birthday 2013
	Lincoln's Birthday 1065
Oct, second Mon	Columbus Day 0424

Nebraska

Jan, third Mon	Martin Luther King, Jr. Day 0993
Feb, third Mon	Presidents' Day 1480
Apr, last Fri	Arbor Day 0080
Oct, second Mon	Columbus Day 0424

Nevada

Jan, third Mon	Martin Luther King, Jr.'s Birthday 0993
Feb, third Mon	Washington's Birthday 2013
Oct 12	Columbus Day 0424
Oct 31	Nevada Day .... Appendix 1

New Hampshire

Jan, third Mon	Civil Rights Day (Martin Luther King, Jr.'s Birthday) 0993
Feb, third Mon	Washington's Birthday 2013
Apr, fourth Mon	Fast Day 0625
Oct, second Mon	Columbus Day 0424

New Jersey

Jan, third Mon	Martin Luther King, Jr.'s Birthday 0993
Feb 12	Lincoln's Birthday 1065
Feb, third Mon	Washington's Birthday 2013
Mar–Apr: Fri before Easter	Good Friday 0733
Oct, second Mon	Columbus Day 0424

New Mexico

Jan, third Mon	Martin Luther King, Jr.'s Birthday 0993
Oct, second Mon	Columbus Day 0424

New York

Jan, third Mon	Martin Luther King, Jr. Day 0993
Feb 12	Lincoln's Birthday 1065
Feb, third Mon	Washington's Birthday 2013
Jun, second Sun	Flag Day 0650
Oct, second Mon	Columbus Day 0424

North Carolina

Jan 19	Robert E. Lee's Birthday 1046
Jan, third Mon	Martin Luther King, Jr.'s Birthday 0993
Feb, third Mon	Washington's Birthday 2013
Mar 25	Greece Independence Day 0760
Mar–Apr: Fri before Easter	Good Friday 0733
Apr 12	Halifax Day 0794
May 10	Confederate Memorial Day 0432
May 20	Mecklenburg Independence Day 1170
Sep–Oct	Yom Kippur 2079
Oct, second Mon	Columbus Day 0424

North Dakota

Jan, third Mon	Martin Luther King, Jr.'s Birthday 0993
Feb, third Mon	Washington's Birthday 2013
Mar–Apr: Fri before Easter	Good Friday 0733

Ohio

Jan, third Mon	Martin Luther King, Jr.'s Birthday 0993
Feb, third Mon	Washington-Lincoln Day .. 1065, 2013
Oct, second Mon	Columbus Day 0424

Oklahoma

Jan, third Mon	Martin Luther King, Jr.'s Birthday	0993
Feb, third Mon	Washington's Birthday	2013
Apr 22	Oklahoma Day	1344
May, second Sun	Mothers' Day	1236
Sep 16	Cherokee Strip Day	0360
Sep, first Sat after full moon	Indian Day	0052
Oct 10	Oklahoma Historical Day	1345
Nov 4	Will Rogers's Day	1560

Oregon

Jan, third Mon	Martin Luther King, Jr.'s Birthday	0993
Feb, third Mon	Presidents' Day	1480

Pennsylvania

Jan, third Mon	Martin Luther King, Jr. Day	0993
Feb, third Mon	Presidents' Day	1480
Mar–Apr: Fri before Easter	Good Friday	0733
Jun 14	Flag Day	0650
Oct, second Mon	Columbus Day	0424

Rhode Island

Jan, third Mon	Martin Luther King, Jr.'s Birthday	0993
Feb, third Mon	Washington's Birthday	2013
May 4	Rhode Island Independence Day	1549
Aug, second Mon	V-J Day (Victory Day)	2004
Oct, second Mon	Columbus Day	0424

South Carolina

Jan 15	Martin Luther King, Jr.'s Birthday	0993
Jan 19	Robert E. Lee's Birthday	1046
Feb, third Mon	Washington's Birthday	2013
May 10	Confederate Memorial Day	0432
Jun 3	Jefferson Davis's Birthday	0491

South Dakota

Jan, third Mon	Martin Luther King, Jr.'s Birthday	0993
Oct, second Mon	Native Americans' Day	0052

Tennessee

Jan, third Mon	Martin Luther King, Jr. Day	0993
Feb, third Mon	Washington's Birthday	2013
Mar–Apr: Fri before Easter	Good Friday	0733
Oct, second Mon	Columbus Day	0424

Texas

Jan 19	Confederate Heroes Day	0432
Jan, third Mon	Martin Luther King, Jr. Day	0993
Feb, third Mon	Washington's Birthday	2013
Mar 2	Texas Independence Day	1904
Apr 21	San Jacinto Day	1718, 1729
Jun 19	Emancipation Day	0594, 0953
Aug 27	Lyndon B. Johnson's Birthday	Appendix 2

Utah

Jan, third Mon	Martin Luther King, Jr.'s Birthday and Human Rights Day	0993
Feb, third Mon	Presidents' Day	1480
Jul 24	Mormon Pioneer Day	1228
Oct, second Mon	Columbus Day	0424

Vermont

Jan, third Mon	Martin Luther King, Jr.'s Birthday	0993
Feb 12	Lincoln's Birthday	1065
Feb, third Mon	Washington's Birthday	2013
Mar, first Tues	Town Meeting Day	1935
Aug 16	Bennington Battle Day	0176
Oct, second Mon	Columbus Day	0424

Virginia

Jan, third Mon	Lee-Jackson-King Day	0924, 0993, 1046
Feb, third Mon	Washington's Birthday	2013
Oct, second Mon	Columbus Day	0424
	Yorktown Day	2082

Washington

Jan, third Mon	Martin Luther King, Jr.'s Birthday	0993
Feb, third Mon	Presidents' Day	1480
Oct 12	Columbus Day	0424

West Virginia

Jan, third Mon	Martin Luther King, Jr.'s Birthday	0993
Feb 12	Lincoln's Birthday	1065
Feb, third Mon	Washington's Birthday	2013
Jun 20	West Virginia Day	2026
Oct, second Mon	Columbus Day	0424

Wisconsin

Jan, third Mon	Martin Luther King, Jr. Day	0993
Feb, third Mon	Washington-Lincoln Day	1065, 2013
Oct, second Mon	Columbus Day	0424

Wyoming

Jan, third Mon	Martin Luther King, Jr.'s Birthday and Wyoming Equality Day	0993
Feb, third Mon	Washington-Lincoln Day	1065, 2013

American Samoa

Jan, third Mon	Martin Luther King, Jr. Day	0993
Oct, second Mon	Columbus Day	0424

Guam

Jan, third Mon	Martin Luther King, Jr.'s Day	 0993
Feb, third Mon	Presidents' Day	 1480
Mar 6	Magellan Day	 1101
Mar–Apr: Fri before Easter	Good Friday	 0733
Oct, second Mon	Columbus Day	 0424
Nov 2	All Souls' Day	 0041
Dec 8	Our Lady of Camarin	 0893

Puerto Rico

Jan 11	Hostos Day	 0867
Mar–Apr: Fri before Easter	Good Friday	 0733
Jul 17	Muñoz-Rivera Day	 1251

Jul 25	Constitution Day	 1491
Sep, first Mon	Labor Day	 1025
Nov 19	Discovery Day	.... 0521, 0935

Virgin Islands

Jan 6	Three Kings Day	 0599
Jan, third Mon	Martin Luther King, Jr.'s Day	 0993
Feb, third Mon	Presidents' Day	 1480
Mar, last Mon	Transfer Day	 1937
Mar–Apr: Thurs before Easter	Holy Thursday	 1151
Fri before Easter	Good Friday	 0733
Mon after Easter	Easter Monday	 0569
Jul, fourth Mon	Hurricane Supplication Day	 0878
Oct, third Mon	Hurricane Thanksgiving Day	 0878

Legal Holidays by Country Index

This index of legal holidays celebrated by the various countries of the world is arranged by Gregorian calendar order, followed by entry number(s). The holidays for the republics of the former U.S.S.R. and Yugoslavia are included when information was available; former legal holidays are also included because many of them are still observed by people, and because they are often referred to in literature.

For Jewish holidays and those holidays based on the Christian calendar (Easter, Pentecost, etc.), we have given the range of months during which the day may fall. The more precise dates and the dates on the Jewish calendar may be found at the main entry. Some Christians still use the Julian calendar to determine all holy days, and therefore their dates for major feasts will be different.

The Islamic calendar dates are given for both Muslim holy days and holidays in Islamic countries since the Gregorian date varies according to the lunar Islamic calendar.

Asian festival dates fluctuate from country to country and may even be different in various parts of the same country because of the variety of traditions observed and calendars used. (See the section on **Calendar Systems around the World** for a detailed explanation of calendar systems.)

Afghanistan

Aug, late	Jeshn (Independence Day)	0938

Albania

Jan 11	Republic Day (Anniversary Day)	0028
Nov 28	Independence Day	0027

Algeria

Jan 1	New Year	1294
May 1	Labor Day	1025
Jul 3	Independence Day	0033
Nov 1	National Day (Revolution Day)	0034

Andorra

Sep 8	National Day	0060

Angola

Nov 11	Independence Day	0062
Dec 25	Family Day	0621

Antigua and Barbuda

Jan 1	New Year	1294
Mar–Apr: Fri before Easter	Good Friday	0733
Mar–Apr: Mon after Easter	Easter Monday	0569
May 6	Labor Day	1025
May–Jun: Mon after Pentecost	Whit Monday	2038
Jun 8	Queen's Birthday	1508
Aug 5–6	Carnival	0071
Nov 1	Independence Day	0071
Dec 25–26	Christmas	0385

Argentina

Jan 1	New Year	1294
Mar–Apr: Thurs before Easter	Maundy Thursday	1151
Mar–Apr: Fri before Easter	Good Friday	0733
May 1	Labor Day	1157
May 25	Independence Day	0081
Jun 20	Flag Day	0081
Jul 9	National Day	0081
Aug 17	San Martín Day	1733
Oct 12	Columbus Day	0424
Dec 8	Immaculate Conception	0893
Dec 25	Christmas	0385

Armenia

Sep 23	Independence Day	0085

Australia

Jan 1	New Year	1294
Jan 26 or following Mon	Australia Day	0102
Mar–Apr: Fri before Easter	Good Friday	0733
Mar–Apr: Mon after Easter	Easter Monday	0569
Apr 25	Anzac Day	0074
Jun 15	Queen Elizabeth II Birthday	1508
Dec 25	Christmas	0385

Austria

Jan 1	New Year	1294
Jan 6	Epiphany	0600, 1431
Mar–Apr: Mon after Easter	Easter Monday	0569
Apr–Jun	Ascension Day	0089
May 1	Labor Day	1157
May–Jun	Corpus Christi	0443
May–Jun: Mon after Pentecost	Whit Monday	2038
Aug 15	Assumption Day	0095
Oct 26	National Day	0104
Nov 1	All Saints' Day	0038
Dec 8	Immaculate Conception	0893
Dec 25–26	Christmas	0385

Azerbaijan

Mar 21	Nawruz	1275
May 28	Independence Days	0112
Oct 18	Independence Days	0112

Bahamas

Jan 1	New Year	1294
Mar–Apr: Fri before Easter	Good Friday	0733
Mar–Apr: Mon after Easter	Easter Monday	0569
May–Jun: Mon after Pentecost	Whit Monday	2038
Jun 7	Labor Day	1025
Jul 10	Independence Day	0123
Aug, first Mon	Emancipation Day	0122, 0670
Oct 12	Discovery Day	0424
Dec 25–26	Christmas	0385

Bahrain

Jan 1	New Year	1294
Dec 16	National Day	0127

Bangladesh

Feb 21	Shaheed Day	1775
Mar 26	Independence Day	0133
Apr–May	Vaisakh (New Year)	1977
May 1	May Day	1157
Dec 16	Victory Day	0134
Dec 25	Christmas	0385

Barbados

Jan 1	New Year	1294
Jan 21	Errol Barrow Day	0144
Mar–Apr: Fri before Easter	Good Friday	0733
Mar–Apr: Mon after Easter	Easter Monday	0569
May 1	Labor Day	1157
May–Jun: Mon after Pentecost	Whit Monday	2038
Aug 5	Kadooment Day	0467
Oct 1	United Nations Day	1966
Nov 30	Independence Day	0139
Dec 25–26	Christmas	0385

Belarus

Jan 1	New Year	1294
Jan 6	Christmas (Orthodox)	1349, 1584
Mar 8	Women's Day	2056
May 1	Labor Day	1157
Jul 27	Independence Days	0167
Aug 25	Independence Days	0167
Nov 7	Bolshevik Revolution Day	0218
Dec 25	Christmas	0385

Belgium

Jan 1	New Year	1294
Mar–Apr: Mon after Easter	Easter Monday	0553, 0569
Apr–Jun	Ascension Day	0089
May 1	May Day	1157
May–Jun: Mon after Pentecost	Whit Monday	2038
Jul 21	Independence Day	0169
Aug 15	Assumption Day	0095, 0096
Nov 1	All Saints' Day	0038
Nov 11	Armistice Day	1993
Nov 15	King's Birthday	0997
Dec 25–26	Christmas	0385

Belize

Jan 1	New Year	1294
Mar 9	Baron Bliss Day	0143
Mar–Apr: Fri before Easter	Good Friday	0733
Mar–Apr: Sat before Easter	Holy Saturday	0848
Mar–Apr: Mon after Easter	Easter Monday	0569
May 1	Labor Day	1157
May 25	Commonwealth Day	0427
Sep 10	National Day (St. George's Caye Day)	0171
Sep 21	Independence Day	0170
Oct 12	Columbus Day	0424
Dec 25–26	Christmas	0385

Benin

Aug 1	Independence Day	0175

Bermuda

Jan 1	New Year	1294
Mar–Apr: Fri before Easter	Good Friday	0735
May 24	Bermuda Day	0182
Jun 17	Queen's Birthday	1508
Sep 2	Labour Day	1025
Nov 11	Remembrance Day (Veterans Day)	1993
Dec 25–26	Christmas	0385

Bolivia

Jan 1	New Year	1294
Mar–Apr: Fri before Easter	Good Friday	0733
May 1	Labor Day	1157
May–Jun	Corpus Christi	0443
Aug 6	Independence Day	0216
Nov 1	All Saints' Day	0038
Dec 25	Christmas	0385

Botswana

Jan 1–2	New Year	1294
Mar–Apr: Fri before Easter	Good Friday	0733
Mar–Apr: Sat before Easter	Holy Saturday	0848
Mar–Apr: Mon after Easter	Easter Monday	0569
Apr–Jun	Ascension Day	0089
Jul 15	President's Day	0230
Sep 30–Oct 1	Independence Day	0230
Dec 25–26	Christmas	0385

Brazil

Jan 1	New Year	1294, 1304
Mar–Apr: Fri before Easter	Good Friday	0733
Mar–Apr: Mon after Easter	Easter Monday	0569
Apr 21	Tiradentes Day	0897
May 1	Labor Day	1157
May–Jun	Corpus Christi	0443
Sep 7	Independence Day	0241
Oct 12	Our Lady Aparacida Day	1373
Nov 1	All Saints' Day	0038
Nov 15	Proclamation of the Republic	0242
Dec 25–26	Christmas	0385

Brunei

Feb 23	National Day	0249

Bulgaria

Jan 1	New Year	1294
Mar 3	Liberation Day	0258
May 1	Labor Day	1157
May 24	Bulgaria Culture Day	0257
Sep 9–10	National Day	0259
Nov 7	Bolshevik Revolution Day	0218

Burkina Faso

Aug 4–5	Independence Day	0268
Dec 11	Republic Day	0269

Burma

Jan 4	Independence Day	0270
Apr, mid	Thingyan (New Year)	1912
Dec 25	Christmas	0385

Burundi

Jul 1	Independence Day	0275

Cambodia

Nov 9	Independence Day	0290

Cameroon

Jan 1	New Year	1294
Mar–Apr: Fri before Easter	Good Friday	0733
Mar–Apr: Mon after Easter	Easter Monday	0569
Apr–Jun	Ascension Day	0089
May 1	Labor Day	1157
May 20	National Day	0293
Aug 15	Assumption Day	0095
Dec 25	Christmas	0385
Dhu al-Hijjah 10–12	'Id al-Adha	0885

Canada

Jan 1	New Year	1294
Mar–Apr: Fri before Easter	Good Friday	0733
Mar–Apr: Mon after Easter	Easter Monday	0569
May 24 or Mon before	Commonwealth Day	0427
Jul 1	Canada Day	0295
Sep, first Mon	Labour Day	1025
Oct, second Mon	Thanksgiving Day	1909
Nov 11	Remembrance Day	1993
Dec 25–26	Christmas	0235, 0385

Cape Verde

Jul 5	Independence Day	0301

Central African Republic

Aug 13	Independence Days	0341
Dec 1	Independence Days	0341

Chad

Aug 11	Independence Day	0346
Nov 28	Republic Day	0347
Dhu al-Hijjah 10–12	'Id al-Adha	0885

Chile

Jan 1	New Year	1294
Mar–Apr: Fri before Easter	Good Friday	0733
Mar–Apr: Sat before Easter	Easter Saturday	0848
May 1	Labor Day	1157
May–Jun	Corpus Christi	0443
Jun 29	Sts. Peter and Paul Day	1699
Aug 15	Assumption Day	0095
Sep 18	Independence Day	0376
Oct 12	Columbus Day	0424
Nov 1	All Saints' Day	0038
Dec 8	Immaculate Conception	0893
Dec 25	Christmas	0385

China

Jan 1	New Year	1294
Jan–Feb	Lunar New Year	1090
Mar 8	Women's Day	2056
May 1	Labor Day	1157
Sep, mid	Mid-Autumn Festival	1192
Oct 1–2	National Days	0378

Colombia

Jan 1	New Year	1294
Jan 6	Epiphany	0599
Mar 19	St. Joseph's Day	1659
Mar–Apr: Thurs before Easter	Holy Thursday	1151
Mar–Apr: Fri before Easter	Good Friday	0733
Apr–Jun	Ascension Day	0089
May 1	Labor Day	1157
Jul 1	Sts. Peter and Paul Day	1699
Jul 20	Independence Day	0423
Aug 15	Assumption Day	0095
Oct 12	Columbus Day	0424
Nov 1	All Saints' Day	0038
Dec 8	Immaculate Conception	0893
Dec 25	Christmas	0385

Comoros

Jul 6	Independence Day	0428

Congo

Jan 1	New Year	1294
Mar 8	Women's Day	2056
May 1	Labor Day	1157
Aug 13–15	Independence Day celebration	0434
Dec 25	Children's Day	0374
Dec 31	Republic Day	0435

Costa Rica

Jan 1	Liberation Day and New Year	0449
May 1	Labor Day	1157
Jul 26	National Day	0449
Sep 15	Independence Day	0449

Côte d'Ivoire. *See* Ivory Coast

Cuba

Jan 1	Liberation Day	0472
May 1	Labor Day	1157
May 20	Independence Day	0471
Jul 26	National Day	0472

Cyprus

Jan 1	New Year	1294, 1605
Jan 6	Epiphany	1370
Mar 25	Greece Independence Day	0760
Mar–Apr: Fri before Easter	Good Friday	0733
Mar–Apr: Mon after Easter	Easter Monday	0553, 0569
May 1	May Day	1157
Aug 15	Assumption	0095
Oct 1	Independence Day	0478
Dec 25–26	Christmas	0385

Czech Republic

Jan 1	New Year	1294
Mar–Apr: Mon after Easter	Easter Monday	0569
May 1	May Day	1161, 1164
May 9	Liberation Day	0480
Oct 28	Independence Day	0480
Dec 25–26	Christmas	0385

Denmark

Jan 1	New Year	1295
Mar–Apr: Thurs before Easter	Maundy Thursday	1151
Mar–Apr: Fri before Easter	Good Friday	0733
Mar–Apr: Mon after Easter	Easter Monday	0569
Apr–May: fourth Fri after Easter	Common Prayer Day	0425
Apr–Jun	Ascension Day	0089
May–Jun: Mon after Pentecost	Whit Monday	2038
Jun 5	Constitution Day	0504
Jun 15	Flag Day	0505
Dec 25–26	Christmas	0385, 0390

Djibouti

Jun 27	Independence Day	0525

Dominica

Nov 3	Independence Day	0536

Dominican Republic

Jan 26	Duarte Day	0537
Feb 27	Independence Day	0537

Ecuador

Jan 1	New Year	1294, 1305
Mar–Apr: Fri before Easter	Good Friday	0733
May 1	Labor Day	1157
May 24	Battle of Pichincha Day	0572
Aug 10	Independence Day	0572
Oct 12	Columbus Day	0424
Dec 25	Christmas	0385

Egypt

Apr 25	Sinai Day	0579
Apr–May	Sham el-Nesim	1780
May 1	Labor Day	1157
Jul 23	National Day	0579
Oct 6	Armed Forces Day	0083
Muharram 1	Ashura	0092
Rabi al-Awwal 12	Mawlid al-Nabi	1156
Shawwal 1–3	'Id al-Fitr (Ramadan Bairam)	0886
Dhu al-Hijjah 10–12	'Id al Adha (Grand Bairam)	0885

El Salvador

Sep 15	Independence Day	0592

England

Jan 1	New Year	1294
Mar–Apr: Fri before Easter	Good Friday	0736
Mar–Apr: Mon after Easter	Easter Monday	0569
May 1	May Day	1157
May–Jun: Mon after Pentecost	Whit Monday Bank Holiday	2038
Jun 15	Queen Elizabeth II Birthday	1508
Dec 25–26	Christmas	0235, 0385

Equatorial Guinea

Oct 12	Independence Day	0608

Estonia

Jan 1	New Year	1294
Feb 24	Independence Day	0612
Mar–Apr: Fri before Easter	Good Friday	0733
May 1	Spring Day (May Day)	1157
Jun 23	Victory Day	1197
Jun 24	St. John's Day	1197
Dec 25–26	Christmas	0395

Ethiopia

Jan 7	Ganna (Orthodox Christmas)	0695
Jan 19	Timqat (Orthodox Epiphany)	1920
Mar–Apr: Fri before Easter	Good Friday	0733
May 1	Labor Day	1157
Sep 12	National Day	0613, 0787

Finland

Jan 1	New Year	1294
Jan 19	Epiphany	0599
Mar–Apr: Fri before Easter	Good Friday	0733
Mar–Apr: Mon after Easter	Easter Monday	0569
Apr–Jun	Ascension Day	0089
May 1	Vappu (May Day)	1981
Jun 24, Sat nearest	Juhannus (Midsummer)	0951
Nov 1	All Saints' Day	0038
Dec 6	Independence Day	0641
Dec 24–26	Christmas	0385, 0391

France

Jan 1	New Year	1296
Mar–Apr: Mon after Easter	Easter Monday	0569
Apr–Jun	Ascension Day	0089
May 1	Labor Day (Premier Mai)	1478
May–Jun: Mon after Pentecost	Whit Monday	2038
Jul 14	Bastille Day	0149
Aug 15	Assumption Day	0095
Nov 1	All Saints' Day	0039
Nov 11	Armistice Day	1993
Dec 25	Christmas	0385, 0392

French Polynesia

Jan 1	New Year	1294
Mar–Apr: Fri before Easter	Good Friday	0733
Mar–Apr: Mon after Easter	Easter Monday	0569
Apr–Jun	Ascension Day	0089
May 1	Labor Day	1478
May–Jun: Mon after Pentecost	Whit Monday	2038
Jul 14	Bastille Day	0149
Aug 15	Assumption Day	0095
Nov 1	All Saints' Day	0038
Nov 11	Armistice Day	1993
Dec 25	Christmas	0385

Gabon

Jan 1	New Year	1294
Mar–Apr: Mon after Easter	Easter Monday	0569
Apr–Jun	Ascension Day	0089
May 1	Labor Day	1157
May–Jun: Mon after Pentecost	Whit Monday	2038
Aug 15	Assumption Day	0095
Aug 16–18	Independence Day celebration	0685
Nov 1	All Saints' Day	0038

Gambia

Jan 1	New Year	1294
Feb 18	Independence Day	0691

Mar–Apr: Fri before Easter	Good Friday	0733
May 1	Labor Day	1157
Aug 15	Assumption Day	0095
Dec 25–26	Christmas	0385

Germany

Jan 1	New Year	1297, 1306
Jan 6	Epiphany	0602
Mar–Apr: Fri before Easter	Good Friday	0733
Mar–Apr: Mon after Easter	Easter Monday	0559, 0569
Apr–Jun	Ascension Day	0089
May 1	Labor Day	1157
May–Jun	Corpus Christi	0445
May–Jun: Mon after Pentecost	Whit Monday	1175, 2038
Aug 15	Assumption Day	0095
Nov 1	All Saints' Day	0038
Dec 25–26	Christmas	0385, 0406

Ghana

Jan 1	New Year	1294
Mar 6	Independence Day	0711
Mar–Apr: Fri before Easter	Good Friday	0733
Mar–Apr: Mon after Easter	Easter Monday	0569
May 1	May Day	1157
Jul 1	Republic Day	0711
Dec 25–26	Christmas	0385

Gibraltar

Jan 1	New Year	1294
Mar 12	Commonwealth Day	0427
Mar–Apr: Fri before Easter	Good Friday	0733
Mar–Apr: Mon after Easter	Easter Monday	0569
May 1	May Day	1157
May 28	Bank Holiday	0135
Jun 17	Queen's Birthday	1508
Aug 27	Bank Holiday	0135
Dec 25–26	Christmas	0385

Greece

Jan 1	New Year	1294, 1605
Jan 6	Epiphany	1370
Feb–Mar	Shrove Monday	1799
Mar 25	Independence Day	0760
Mar–Apr: Fri before Easter	Good Friday	0733
Mar–Apr: Mon after Easter	Easter Monday	0569
May 1	Labor Day	1157
Aug 15	Assumption Day	0095
Oct 28	Oxi Day	1382
Dec 25–26	Christmas	0385, 0396

Grenada

Feb 7	Independence Day	0765
Mar 13	National Day	0766

Guatemala

Sep 15	Independence Day	0773

Guinea

Oct 2	Independence Day	0777

Guinea-Bissau

Sep 24	Independence Day	0776

Guyana

Feb 23	Republic Day	0783
May 26	Independence Day	0783

Haiti

Jan 1	Independence Day and New Year	0789
Dec 5	Discovery Day	0521

Honduras

Sep 15	Independence Day	0855

Hong Kong

Jan 1	New Year	1294
Jan–Feb	Lunar New Year	1090
Mar–Apr: Fri before Easter	Good Friday	0733
Mar–Apr: Mon after Easter	Easter Monday	0569
Jun 15–17	Queen's Birthday	1508
Aug, last Mon	Liberation Day	0857
Sep–Oct	Chung Yeung	0411
Dec 25–26	Christmas	0385

Hungary

Jan 1	New Year	1295
Mar 15	Anniversary of Revolution	0874
Mar–Apr: Mon after Easter	Easter Monday	0569
May 1	Labor Day	1157
Aug 20	Constitution Day (St. Stephen of Hungary Day)	0874
Oct 23	Revolution Day	0874
Dec 24–26	Christmas	0385

Iceland

Jan 1	New Year	1294
Mar–Apr: Thurs before Easter	Maundy Thursday	1151
Mar–Apr: Fri before Easter	Good Friday	0733
Mar–Apr: Mon after Easter	Easter Monday	0569

Apr 19–25, Thurs between	First Day of Summer	0645
Apr–Jun	Ascension Day	0089
May 1	Labor Day	1157
May–Jun: Mon after Pentecost	Whit Monday	2038
Jun 17	Independence Day	0881
Dec 25–26	Christmas	0385

India

Jan 1	New Year	1294
Jan 26	Republic Day	0901
Mar–Apr: Fri before Easter	Good Friday	0733
May 1	Labor Day	1157
Aug 15	Independence Day	0901
Oct 2	Gandhi Jayanti	0692
Dec 25	Christmas	0385

Indonesia

Jan 1	New Year	1294
Mar 21, near	Nyepi (New Year)	1331
Mar–Apr: Fri before Easter	Good Friday	0733
Apr–May	Vesak (Buddha's Birthday)	1992
Apr–Jun	Ascension Day	0089
Aug 17	Independence Day	0902
Dec 25	Christmas	0385
Rabi al-Awwal 12	Mawlid al-Nabi (Muhammad's Birthday)	1156

Iran

Mar 21	Nawruz (New Year)	1275

Iraq

Jan 1	New Year	1294
May 1	Labor Day	1157

Ireland

Jan 1	New Year	1294
Mar 17	St. Patrick's Day	1683
Mar–Apr: Fri before Easter	Good Friday	0733
Mar–Apr: Mon after Easter	Easter Monday	0569
Dec 25	Christmas	0385

Israel

Feb–Mar	Purim	1494
Mar–Apr	Passover	1419
Apr–May	Independence Day	0914
May–Jun	Shavuot	1785
Sep–Oct	Rosh Hashanah	1571
	Yom Kippur	2079
	Sukkot	1853
	Simhat Torah	1810
Nov–Dec	Hanukkah	0807

Italy

Jan 1	New Year	1294
Jan 6	Epiphany	0164
Mar–Apr: Mon after Easter	Easter Monday	0569
Apr 25	Liberation Day	0918
May 1	Labor Day	1157, 1159
Jun 2	Republic Day	0919
Aug 15	Assumption Day	0097
Nov 1	All Saints' Day	0038
Dec 8	Immaculate Conception	0893
Dec 25–26	Christmas	0385, 0393

Ivory Coast (Côte d'Ivoire)

Jan 1	New Year	1294
Mar–Apr: Fri before Easter	Good Friday	0733
Mar–Apr: Mon after Easter	Easter Monday	0569
Apr–Jun	Ascension Day	0089
May 1	Labor Day	1157
May–Jun: Mon after Pentecost	Whit Monday	2038
Aug 15	Assumption Day	0095
Nov 1	All Saints' Day	0038
Dec 7	Independence Day	0921
Dec 25	Christmas	0385

Jamaica

Jan 1	New Year	1294
Feb–Mar	Ash Wednesday	0093
Mar–Apr: Fri before Easter	Good Friday	0733
Mar–Apr: Mon after Easter	Easter Monday	0569
May 23	Labor Day	1025
Aug, first Mon	Independence Day	0926, 0927
Dec 25–26	Christmas	0385

Japan

Jan 1–3	Oshogatsu (New Year)	1361, 1372
Jan 15	Seijin-no-Hi (Coming of Age)	1761
Feb 11	National Foundation Day	0934
Mar 21 or 22	Vernal Equinox Day	0823, 1990
Apr 29	Greenery Day	0761
May 3	Constitution Memorial Day	0790, 0934
May 5	Kodomo-no-Hi (Children's Day)	0790, 1010
Sep 15	Keiro-no-Hi (Respect for the Aged)	0978
Sep 23 or 24	Autumnal Equinox Day	0106, 0823
Oct 10	Taiiku-no-Hi (Health-Sports Day)	1880
Nov 3	Bunka-no-Hi (Culture Day)	0263
Nov 23	Labor Thanksgiving Day	1025
Dec 23	Emperor's Birthday	0933

Jordan

Jan 1	New Year	1294

May 1	Labor Day	1157
May 25	Independence Day	0946
Dec 25	Christmas	0385, 0389

Kenya

Jan 1	New Year	1294
Mar–Apr: Fri before Easter	Good Friday	0733
Mar–Apr: Mon after Easter	Easter Monday	0569
May 1	Labor Day	1157
Dec 12	Jamhuri (Independence Day)	0929
Dec 25–26	Christmas	0385

Kiribati

Jul 12	Independence Day	1001

Korea, North

Aug 15	Liberation Day	1014

Korea, South

Jan 1–2	New Year	1090, 1822
Mar 1	Samil-jol (Independence Movement Day)	1717
Apr–May	Vesak (Buddha's Birthday)	1992
May 5	Urini Nal (Children's Day)	1973
Aug 15	Liberation Day	1014
Oct 3	National Foundation Day	1015
Oct 9	Han'gul Day	0806
Dec 25	Christmas	0385

Kuwait

Jan 1	New Year	1294
Feb 25	National Day	1023
Jun 19	Independence Day	1022

Lebanon

Jan 1	New Year	1294
Mar–Apr: Fri before Easter	Good Friday	0733
May 1	Labor Day	1157
Aug 15	Assumption Day	0095
Nov 1	All Saints' Day	0038
Nov 22	National Day	1044
Dec 25	Christmas	0385

Lesotho

Jan 1	New Year	1294
Mar 12	Moshoeshoe's Day	1232
Mar–Apr: Fri before Easter	Good Friday	0733
Mar–Apr: Mon after Easter	Easter Monday	0569
Apr–Jun	Ascension Day	0089
Oct 4	Independence Day	1053
Dec 25–26	Christmas	0385

Liberia

Jan 1	New Year	1294
Jul 26	Independence Day	1056
Dec 25	Christmas	0385

Libya

Jan 1	New Year	1294
Sep 1	National Day	1058
Dec 24	Independence Day	1057
Rabi al-Awwal 12	Mawlid al-Nabi	1156

Liechtenstein

Aug 15	Prince's Birthday	1484

Lithuania

Jan 1	New Year	1294
Feb 16	Independence Day	1067
Mar–Apr: Mon after Easter	Easter Monday	0569
Nov 1	All Saints' Day	0038
Dec 24–26	Christmas	0385, 0395

Luxembourg

Jan 1	New Year	1294
Mar–Apr: Mon after Easter	Easter Monday	0569
Apr–Jun	Ascension Day	0089
May 1	Labor Day	1157
May–Jun: Mon after Pentecost	Whit Monday	2038
Jun 23	National Day	1093
Aug 15	Assumption Day	0095
Nov 1	All Saints' Day	0038
Nov 2	All Souls' Day	0041
Dec 25–26	Christmas	0385

Macau

Sep–Oct	Chung Yeung	0411

Madagascar

Jun 26	Independence Day	1098
Dec 30	Republic Day	1098

Malawi

Jan 1	New Year	1294
Mar–Apr: Fri before Easter	Good Friday	0733
Mar–Apr: Mon after Easter	Easter Monday	0569
Jul 6	Republic Day	1112
Dec 25–26	Christmas	0385

Malaysia

Jan–Feb	Lunar New Year	1090
May 1	Labor Day	1157
Aug 31	Merdeka (Independence Day)	1182

Dec 25	Christmas	0385

Maldives

Jul 26	Independence Day	1114
Nov 11	Republic Day	1114

Mali

Sep 22	Independence Day	1115

Malta

Jan 1	New Year	1294
Feb 10	St. Paul's Shipwreck	1685
Mar–Apr: Fri before Easter	Good Friday	0733
May 1	St. Joseph the Worker Day	1660
Jun 29	Mnarja (Sts. Peter and Paul Feast)	1212
Aug 15	Assumption Day	0095
Sep 8	Victory Day (Our Lady of Victories)	1994
Sep 21	Independence Day	1117
Dec 8	Immaculate Conception	0893
Dec 13	Republic Day	1117
Dec 25	Christmas	0385

Mauritania

Nov 28	Independence Day	1153

Mauritius

Jan 1–2	New Year	1294
Jan–Feb	Lunar New Year	1090
Mar 12	Independence Day	1154
May 1	Labor Day	1157
Nov 1	All Saints' Day	0038
Dec 25	Christmas	0385

Mexico

Jan 1	New Year	1294
Jan 6	Día de los Tres Reyes (Epiphany)	0513
Mar–Apr: Thurs before Easter	Maundy Thursday	1151
Mar–Apr: Fri before Easter	Good Friday	0738
May 1	Labor Day	1157
May 5	Cinco de Mayo	0413
Sep 15–16	Independence Day Festival	1186
Oct 12	Columbus Day	0424
Dec 25	Christmas	0385, 0405, 1473

Mongolia

Jul 11	Nadam (Revolution Day)	1257

Morocco

Jan 1	New Year	1294
Jan 11	Independence Manifesto	1229
Mar 3	Throne Day	1229
May 1	May Day	1157
May 23	National Day	1229
Aug 14	Allegiance of Wadi-Eddahab	1229
Aug 20	Anniversary of the King's and People's Revolution	1229
Nov 6	Green March Anniversary	1229
Nov 18	Independence Day	1229
Muharram 1	Ashura	0092
Rabi al-Awwal 12	Mawlid al-Nabi (Muhammad's Birthday)	1156
Shawwal 1	'Id al-Fitr	0886
Dhu al-Hijjah 10–12	'Id al-Adha	0885

Mozambique

Jan 1	New Year	1294
May 1	Labor Day	1157
Jun 25	Independence Day	1245

Myanmar. *See* Burma

Namibia

Jan 1	New Year	1294
Mar–Apr: Fri before Easter	Good Friday	0733
Apr–Jun	Ascension Day	0089
Dec 25–26	Christmas	0385

Nauru

Jan 31	Independence Day	1273

Nepal

Jan 11	Unity Day	1281
Feb 18	National Day	1281
Nov 8	Constitution Day	1281
Dec 28	King's Birthday	0995

Netherlands

Jan 1	New Year	1302
Mar–Apr: Fri before Easter	Good Friday	0733
Mar–Apr: Mon after Easter	Easter Monday	0567, 0570, 2005
Apr 30	Queen Juliana's Birthday	1509
Apr–Jun	Ascension Day	0089, 0510
May 5	Dutch Liberation Day	0550
May–Jun: Mon after Pentecost	Whit Monday	2038
Dec 25–26	Christmas	0385

New Zealand

Jan 1	New Year	1294
Feb 6	Waitangi Day	2008
Mar–Apr: Fri before Easter	Good Friday	0773
Mar–Apr: Mon after Easter	Easter Monday	0569
Apr 25	Anzac Day	0074

Jun 3	Queen's Birthday	1508
Oct, last Mon	Eight Hour Day	0580
Dec 25–26	Christmas	0385

Nicaragua

Sep 15	Independence Day	1310

Niger

Aug 3	Independence Day	1313
Dec 18	Republic Day	1313

Nigeria

Jan 1	New Year	1294
Mar–Apr: Fri before Easter	Good Friday	0733
Mar–Apr: Mon after Easter	Easter Monday	0569
May 1	Labor Day	1157
Oct 1	National Day	1312
Dec 25–26	Christmas	0385

Northern Ireland

Jan 1	New Year	1294
Mar 17	St. Patrick's Day	1681, 1683
Mar–Apr: Fri before Easter	Good Friday	0733
Mar–Apr: Mon after Easter	Easter Monday	0569
May 1	May Day	1157
May–Jun: Mon after Pentecost	Whit Monday Bank Holiday	2038
Jun 15	Queen Elizabeth II Birthday	1508
Dec 25–26	Christmas	0385

Norway

Jan 1	New Year	1294
Mar–Apr: Thurs before Easter	Maundy Thursday	1151
Mar–Apr: Fri before Easter	Good Friday	0733
Mar–Apr: Mon after Easter	Easter Monday	0562, 0567
Apr–Jun	Ascension Day	0089
May 1	Labor Day	1157, 1162
May 17	Constitution Day	1328, 1875
May–Jun: Mon after Pentecost	Whit Monday	2038
Dec 25–26	Christmas	0397

Oman

Dhu al-Hijjah 10	'Id al-Adha	0885
Shawwal 1	'Id al-Fitr	0886

Pakistan

Mar 23	Pakistan Day	1387
May 1	Labor Day	1157
Aug 14	Independence Day	1388

Panama

Jan 1	New Year	1294
Mar–Apr: Fri before Easter	Good Friday	0733
Nov 3	Independence Day	1398
Nov 28	Independence Day	1398
Dec 25	Christmas	0385

Papua New Guinea

Sep 16	Independence Day	1404

Paraguay

Jan 1	New Year	1294
Mar–Apr: Thurs before Easter	Maundy Thursday	1151
Mar–Apr: Fri before Easter	Good Friday	0733
May 1	Labor Day	1157
May 14–15	Independence and Flag Day	1405
Dec 8	Immaculate Conception	0893
Dec 25	Christmas	0385

Peru

Jan 1	New Year	1294
Mar–Apr: Fri before Easter	Good Friday	0733
May 1	Labor Day	1157
Jun 28–29	Independence Day	1432
Jun 29	Sts. Peter and Paul Day	1699
Aug 23	St. Rose of Lima Day	1693
Nov 1	All Saints' Day	0038
Dec 8	Immaculate Conception	0893
Dec 25	Christmas	0385

Philippines

Jan 1	New Year	1294
Feb 25	Fiesta sa EDSA (People Power Day)	0638
Mar–Apr: Thurs before Easter	Holy Thursday	1151
Mar–Apr: Fri before Easter	Good Friday	0733
May 1	Labor Day	1157
May 6	Bataan Day (Heroes Day)	0151
Jun 12	Independence Day	1436
Nov 1	All Saints' Day	0038
Dec 25	Christmas	0385, 0714, 1206
Dec 30	Rizal Day	1555

Poland

Jan 1	New Year	1294
Mar–Apr: Mon after Easter	Easter Monday	0563, 0569
May 1	Labor Day	1157
May 3	Constitution Day	1459
May–Jun	Corpus Christi	0443
Jul 22	Liberation Day	1461
Aug 15	Assumption Day	0095, 0540
Nov 1	All Saints' Day	0038

Nov 11	Independence Day	1460
Dec 25–26	Christmas	0385, 2041

Portugal

Jan 1	New Year	1298
Mar–Apr: Fri before Easter	Good Friday	0733
Apr 25	Liberation Day	1469
May 1	Labor Day	1157
May–Jun	Corpus Christi	0443
Jun 10	National Day	1470
Aug 15	Assumption Day	0095
Oct 5	Republic Day	1471
Nov 1	All Saints' Day	0038
Dec 1	Restoration of Independence Day	1472
Dec 8	Immaculate Conception	0893
Dec 24	Christmas Eve	0386
Dec 25	Christmas	0385

Qatar

Sep 3	Independence Day	1500

Romania

Jan 1–2	New Year	1299, 1303
May 1–2	Workers Holiday	1157
Dec 1	National Day	1562

Russia

Jan 1–2	New Year	1301
Jan 7	Christmas (Orthodox)	1584, 1585
Mar 8	Women's Day	2056
May 1–2	Labor Day (May Day)	1157
Nov 7	Bolshevik Revolution Day	0218

Rwanda

Jul 1	Independence Day	1586

St. Lucia

Feb 22	Independence Day	1665

St. Maarten

Nov 11	Concordia Day	0430

St. Vincent

Oct 27	Independence and Thanksgiving Day	1710

San Marino

Sep 3	St. Marinus Day	1667

Sao Tome and Principe

Jul 12	National Independence Day	1741

Saudi Arabia

Shawwal 1	'Id al-Fitr	0886
Dhu al-Hijjah 10	'Id al-Adha	0885

Scotland

Jan 1	New Year	1294
Jan 2	Bank Holiday	0135
Mar–Apr: Fri before Easter	Good Friday	0733
Mar–Apr: Mon after Easter	Easter Monday	0569
May 1	May Day	1157
May–Jun: Mon after Pentecost	Whit Monday Bank Holiday	2038
Jun 15	Queen Elizabeth II Birthday	1508
Aug 5	Bank Holiday	0135
Dec 25–26	Christmas	0235, 0385

Senegal

Jan 1	New Year	1294
Mar–Apr: Fri before Easter	Good Friday	0733
Mar–Apr: Mon after Easter	Easter Monday	0569
Apr 4	Independence Day	1765
Apr–Jun	Ascension Day	0089
May 1	Labor Day	1157
Aug 15	Assumption Day	0095
Nov 1	All Saints' Day	0038
Dec 25	Christmas	0385

Seychelles

Jan 1–2	New Year	1294
Mar–Apr: Fri before Easter	Good Friday	0733
May 1	Labor Day	1157
May–Jun	Corpus Christi	0443
Jun 5	Liberation Day	1772
Jun 29	Independence Day	1771
Aug 15	Assumption Day	0095
Nov 1	All Saints' Day	0038
Dec 8	Immaculate Conception	0893
Dec 25	Christmas	0385

Sierra Leone

Apr 19	Republic Day	1807

Singapore

Jan 1	New Year	1294
Jan–Feb	Lunar New Year	1090
Mar–Apr: Fri before Easter	Good Friday	0733
Apr–May	Vesak (Buddha's Birthday)	1992
May 1	Labor Day	1157
Aug 9	National Day	1811
Dec 25	Christmas	0385

Solomon Islands

Jul 7	Independence Day	1823

Somalia

Jun 26	Independence Days	1824
Jul 1	Independence Days	1824

South Africa

Jan 1	New Year	1294
Mar–Apr: Fri before Easter	Good Friday	0733
Mar–Apr: Mon after Easter	Family Day (Easter Monday)	0621
Apr–Jun	Ascension Day	0089
May 31	Republic Day	1827
Dec 16	Day of the Covenant	0494
Dec 25	Christmas	0400
Dec 26	Day of Good Will	0235

Spain

Jan 1	New Year	1294, 1307
Jan 6	Epiphany	0605
Mar 19	St. Joseph's Day	1659
Mar–Apr: Fri before Easter	Good Friday	0740
Mar–Apr: Mon after Easter	Easter Monday (Barcelona and Mallorca only)	0565, 0569
May 1	Labor Day	1157
May–Jun	Corpus Christi	0443
Jul 25	St. James's Day	1645
Aug 15	Assumption Day	0095
Nov 1	All Saints' Day	0038
Dec 8	Immaculate Conception	0893
Dec 25	Christmas	0401

Sri Lanka

Dec–Jan	Pongal	1464
Feb 4	Independence Day	1836
Mar–Apr: Fri before Easter	Good Friday	0733
May 1	May Day	1157
Dec 25	Christmas	0385

Sudan

Jan 1	Independence Day and New Year	1850
Dec 25	Christmas	0385

Suriname

Nov 25	Independence Day	1864

Swaziland

Jan 1	New Year	1294
Mar–Apr: Fri before Easter	Good Friday	0733
Mar–Apr: Mon after Easter	Easter Monday	0569

Apr–Jun	Ascension Day	0089
Sep 6	Independence Day	1868
Dec 25–26	Christmas	0385

Sweden

Jan 1	New Year	1294
Jan 6	Epiphany	0606
Mar–Apr: Fri before Easter	Good Friday	0733
Mar–Apr: Mon after Easter	Easter Monday	0566, 0569
Apr–Jun	Ascension Day	0089
May 1	Labor Day	1157, 1162
May–Jun: Mon after Pentecost	Whit Monday	2038
Jun 6	Flag and Constitution Day	1869
Jun 24	Midsummer Day	1197
Nov 1	All Saints' Day	0038
Dec 25	Christmas	0402
Dec 31	New Year's Eve	1303

Switzerland

Jan 1	New Year	1300
Jan 2	Berchtold's Day	0177
Mar–Apr: Fri before Easter	Good Friday	0733, 1455
Mar–Apr: Mon after Easter	Easter Monday	0569
Apr–Jun	Ascension Day	0089, 0136
May–Jun: Mon after Pentecost	Whit Monday	2038
Aug 1	Swiss National Day	1873
Dec 25	Christmas	0385, 0394

Syria

Jan 1	New Year	1294
Apr 17	National Day	1874
May 1	Labor Day	1157
Dec 25	Christmas	0403

Taiwan

Jan–Feb	Lunar New Year	1090
Mar–Apr	Qing Ming (Tomb-Sweeping Day)	1501
May–Jun	Dragon Boat Festival	0542
Sep 28	Confucius's Birthday	0433
Oct 10	Double Tenth Day (National Day)	0539
Nov 12	Sun Yat-sen's Birthday	1862

Tanzania

Jan 1	New Year	1294
Mar–Apr: Fri before Easter	Good Friday	0733
Mar–Apr: Mon after Easter	Easter Monday	0569
May 1	International Workers Day	1157
Jul 7	Saba Saba Day (Farmers' Day)	1587
Dec 9	Independence Day	1887
Dec 25	Christmas	0385

Thailand

Jan 1	New Year	1294
Mar–Apr	Magha Puja	1102
Apr 6	Chakri Day	0348
Apr 12–14	Songkran	1825
Apr–May	Vesakha Puja	0262, 1992
Aug 12	Queen's Birthday	1511
Oct 23	Chulalongkorn Day	0410
Dec 5	King's Birthday	0999
Dec 31	New Year's Eve	1303

Togo

Apr 27	Independence Day	1924

Tonga

Jan 1	Ta'u Fo'ou (New Year)	1889
Jun 4	Emancipation Day	1928

Trinidad and Tobago

Jan 1	New Year	1294
Mar–Apr: Fri before Easter	Good Friday	0733
Mar–Apr: Mon after Easter	Easter Monday	0569
May–Jun: Mon after Pentecost	Whit Monday	2038
May–Jun	Corpus Christi	0443
Jun 19	Labor Day	1025
Aug 1	Emancipation Day	1942
Aug 31	Independence Day	1943
Sep 24	Republic Day	1944
Dec 25–26	Christmas	0385

Tunisia

Jan 1	New Year	1294
Mar 20	Independence Day	1953
May 1	Labor Day	1157
Jun 1	Constitution and National Day	1952
Jul 25	Republic Day	1954

Turkey

Jan 1	New Year	1294
Apr 23	Children's Day	0374
Oct 29	Republic Day	1956

Turkmenistan

Jan 1	New Year	1294
Mar 8	Women's Day	2056
Mar 21	Novrus Bairam	1275
Oct 27	Independence Day	1957

Uganda

Jan 1	New Year	1294
Mar–Apr: Fri before Easter	Good Friday	0733
Mar–Apr: Mon after Easter	Easter Monday	0569
Apr 11	Liberation Day	1961

May 1	Labor Day	1157
Oct 9	Independence Day	1960
Dec 25–26	Christmas	0385

Ukraine

Jan 1	New Year	1301
Jan 7	Christmas (Orthodox)	1584
Mar 8	Women's Day	2056
May 1–2	Labor Day	1157
Aug 24	Independence Day	1963

Union of Soviet Socialist Republics (U.S.S.R., former)

Jan 1	New Year	1301
Mar 8	Women's Day, International	2056
May 1	Labor Day	1157
Nov 7	Bolshevik Revolution Day	0218

United Arab Emirates

Jan 1	New Year	1294
Dec 2	National Day	1965
Dec 25	Christmas	0385

United Kingdom. *See* England, Northern Ireland, Scotland, and Wales

Uruguay

Jan 1	New Year	1294
Jan 6	Epiphany	0599
Mar–Apr: Thurs before Easter	Holy Thursday	1151
Mar–Apr: Fri before Easter	Good Friday	0733
Mar–Apr: Sat before Easter	Holy Saturday	0848
Mar–Apr: Mon after Easter	Easter Monday	0569
May 1	Labor Day	1157
Aug 25	Independence Day	1974
Oct 12	Columbus Day	0424
Nov 2	All Souls' Day	0041
Dec 25	Christmas	0385

Venezuela

Jan 1	New Year	1294
Jan 6	Epiphany	0513, 0599
Mar–Apr: Thurs before Easter	Holy Thursday	1151
Mar–Apr: Fri before Easter	Good Friday	0733
Apr 19	Declaration of Independence Day	1988
Apr–Jun	Ascension Day	0089
May 1	Labor Day	1157
May–Jun	Corpus Christi	0443
Jun 29	Sts. Peter and Paul Day	1699
Jul 5	Independence Day	1988

Aug 15	Assumption Day	0095
Oct 12	Columbus Day	0424
Nov 1	All Saints' Day	0038
Dec 8	Immaculate Conception	0893
Dec 25	Christmas	0385, 0386

Vietnam

Jan–Feb	Tet (New Year)	1901
Sep 2	Independence Day	1997

Wales

Jan 1	New Year	1294
Mar–Apr: Fri before Easter	Good Friday	0733
Mar–Apr: Mon after Easter	Easter Monday	0569
May 1	May Day	1157
May–Jun: Mon after Pentecost	Whit Monday Bank Holiday	2038
Jun 15	Queen Elizabeth II Birthday	1508
Dec 25–26	Christmas	0385

Western Samoa

Jun 1–3	Independence Day celebration	2024

Yemen

Jan 1	New Year	1294
May 1	Labor Day	1157
May 22	National Day	2076
Sep 26	Revolution Days	2077
Oct 14	Revolution Days	2077
Nov 30	Independence Day	2076

Yugoslavia (former)

Jan 1–2	New Year	1294
May 1–2	Labor Day	1157

Zaire

Jan 1	New Year	1294
May 1	Labor Day	1157
Jun 30	Independence Day	2086
Dec 25	Christmas	0385

Zambia

Jan 1	New Year	1294
Mar–Apr: Fri before Easter	Good Friday	0733
Mar–Apr: Sat before Easter	Holy Saturday	0848
May 1	Labor Day	1157
Oct 24	Independence Day	2087
Dec 25	Christmas	0385

Zimbabwe

Jan 1	New Year	1294
Mar–Apr: Fri before Easter	Good Friday	0733
Mar–Apr: Sat before Easter	Easter Saturday	0848
Mar–Apr: Mon after Easter	Easter Monday	0569
Apr 18	Independence Day	2090
May 1	Workers' Day	1157
Dec 24–25	Christmas	0385

General Index, Alphabetical by Name, and Key-Word

Indexed below are names of main entries in *HFCWD* (in boldface type), alternate and foreign names of events, and English translations (when available) of foreign names, by key-word. For instance, the **National Old-Time Fiddlers' Contest** is listed under its main entry name (**Old-Time Fiddlers' Contest, National**), as well as under "Fiddlers," "Contest," and "National." And the entry **Janmashtami,** for example, is also listed under its alternate rendering, "Krishnastami," as well as by key-word in its English translation, "Krishna's Birthday" and "Birthday of Krishna."

General Index

General Index

General Index

G

General Index

H

I

General Index

735

L

General Index

General Index

N

O

General Index

Q

R

General Index

S

General Index

T

General Index

U

V

General Index

Subject Index

The Subject Index lists people, places, institutions, and other items of significance appearing within the text of the entries. For example, foods, animals, music, customs, and activities closely associated with an event are indexed—both those that are the subject of an observance and those that play significant roles in observances. We have identified celebratory elements common to various cultures, such as burning (effigies, mock, rituals), courtship (ceremonies and festivals, customs and lore), and planting and weather lore, and these elements are indexed accordingly. In addition, some religious groups and geographic locations are listed in this index when entries provide substantial information about a religion's background or a location's history. Such headings in the Subject Index *do not* list every holiday and festival celebrated by those religious groups or in those locations—however, cross references at those headings point to such listings that are provided in, respectively, the Religious Groups Index and the Ethnic and Geographic Index. A diamond (♦) next to a listing indicates cross references to other indexes. Listings in the Subject Index provide the entry number or numbers.

A

♦ Indicates cross references to other indexes

Subject Index

♦ Indicates cross references to other indexes

Subject Index

♦ Indicates cross references to other indexes

♦ Indicates cross references to other indexes

Subject Index

♦ Indicates cross references to other indexes

♦ Indicates cross references to other indexes

♦ Indicates cross references to other indexes

♦ Indicates cross references to other indexes

♦ Indicates cross references to other indexes

Subject Index

1579, 1590, 1595, 1598, 1600, 1652, 1655, 1656, 1663, 1669, 1676, 1695, 1723, 1763, 1768, 1822, 1977, 1978
cowboy festivals
   See also rodeos
   Brazil 0336
   Colombia 1503
   Hungary 0863
   Portugal 1538
   U.S. 0194, 0455, 0484, 1266, 1423, 1426
cows. *See* animals
crabs. *See* animals; food: festivals: seafood; races
Crandall, Prudence 0459
Crandall Museum, Prudence (Canterbury, Conn.) ... 0459
creation stories
   Incan 0514
   Korean 1015
   Mescalero Apache 0076
crèche. *See* Christmas
crickets. *See* animals
The Crisis (Thomas Paine) 1386
Croagh Patrick (Ireland) 1087, 1540
Crockett, Davy 0024
Cromm Dub 0463
Cromwell, Oliver 0464, 1793
Cromwell Association (England) 0464
Cronus (Greek god) 0465
croquet. *See* games
cross (Christian) 0093, 0404, 0512, 0566, 1146, 1163, 1370, 1486, 1487, 1597, 1608, 1657
   Feast of the 0595, 0617
   Finding of the 0617
   Stations of the 0733, 0734
cross-dressing 0630, 0861, 1456, 1644, 1745
   and Carnival 0315, 0320, 0321, 0967
   in dance 0321, 0604, 1774
crossroads 0096, 0429, 0712, 0733, 1079, 1203, 1528
Crow, Joe Medicine 1068
Crow Agency (Mont.) 1068
crows. *See* animals
crucifix. *See* cross (Christian)
Cruft, Charles 0470
Cruising Club of America 1292
Crusades 0501, 0842
   and children 1439
   and plenary indulgence 0661
Cuauhtemoc (Aztec emperor) 0853
♦ Cuba
   See also Index 1
   and Fidel Castro 0472
   independence from Spain 0471
   Spanish-American War 1110
Cucklet Dell (Eyam, Derbyshire, England) 1454
cuckoos. *See* animals
Custer, George Armstrong 0728, 1068
Custer's Last Stand 1068
Cuvilliés-Theater (Munich, Germany) 1250
Cybele (Phrygian goddess) 1086, 1173, 1366
Cynonfardd Literary Society (Pa.) 0477
♦ Cyprus
   See also Index 1
   independence from England 0478

Cyrus (king of Persia) 1588
♦ Czechoslovakia (Czech Republic)
   See also Index 1
   independence from Austria 0480
   World War II 0480

D

Daciens 1241
Dagini (mother of Indra) 0903
Daikakuji Temple (Kyoto, Japan) 1192
daisies. *See* flowers
Dalada Maligava (Temple of the Tooth, Kandy, Sri Lanka) 0609
Dalai lamas. *See* lamas
Dam Square (Amsterdam, Netherlands) 0550
dance dramas. *See* theatrical performances
dances 0063, 0153, 0168, 0183, 0283, 0292, 0502, 0574, 0718, 0752, 0856, 0882, 0915, 1074, 1093, 1253, 1266, 1371, 1450, 1680, 1735, 1760, 1832, 1860, 1872, 2014, 2015
   See also processions
   Afghanistan 0938
   Argentine 1854
   Athapaskan Indian 1842
   Ati (Philippines) 0100
   Austrian folk 1431
   Bahamian 0670
   ballet 0009, 0099, 0132, 0154, 0178, 0243, 0281, 0335, 0635, 0651, 0656, 0818, 0838, 0913, 0925, 0952, 1094, 1166, 1167, 1250, 1526, 1744, 1996, 2035, 2055
   balls 0058, 0153, 0250, 0451, 0575, 0657, 0699, 0743, 0877, 0967, 0982, 1032, 1056, 1075, 1097, 1140, 1187, 1436, 1505, 1584, 1719, 1735, 1737, 1810, 1964, 2014
   balls (Carnival) 0128, 0313, 0315, 0316, 0320, 0321, 0324, 0329, 0967, 1122, 1569
   balls (inauguration) 0896
   Baltic folk 0130
   Barbados 0467
   Basque 0147
   Blackfeet Indian 1583
   block 1718
   Bolivia 1734
   Brazil 0889
   buck 1357
   Buddhist 0820, 1035, 1138, 1362, 1413
   Bulgarian 0558, 1026
   Bundi 1440
   Cajun 1122
   Calinda 0289
   calypso 0989
   Cherokee Indian 0359
   Chhau 0369
   Chilean 0376
   Chinese 0433, 0546, 0720, 1929
     dragon 0367, 0720, 1090, 1192, 1193, 1882, 1913
     lion 0215, 0367, 0720, 1090, 1193, 1882
   Choctaw Indian 0382
   classical 1739
   clog 0091, 0148, 0366, 1350, 1357, 1358, 1383, 1980

♦ Indicates cross references to other indexes

♦ Indicates cross references to other indexes

♦ Indicates cross references to other indexes

E

Subject Index

♦ Indicates cross references to other indexes

G

♦ Indicates cross references to other indexes

♦ Indicates cross references to other indexes

Subject Index

H

♦ Indicates cross references to other indexes

Subject Index

♦ Indicates cross references to other indexes

788

Subject Index

Subject Index

♦ Indicates cross references to other indexes

M

Subject Index

Subject Index

Subject Index

♦ Indicates cross references to other indexes

◆ Indicates cross references to other indexes

Subject Index

P

♦ Indicates cross references to other indexes

♦ Indicates cross references to other indexes

♦ Indicates cross references to other indexes

♦ Indicates cross references to other indexes

R

♦ Indicates cross references to other indexes

♦ Indicates cross references to other indexes

807

S

♦ Indicates cross references to other indexes

♦ Indicates cross references to other indexes

811

♦ Indicates cross references to other indexes

Subject Index

♦ Indicates cross references to other indexes

T

♦ Indicates cross references to other indexes

◆ Indicates cross references to other indexes

♦ Indicates cross references to other indexes

V

♦ Indicates cross references to other indexes

X

Y

Z

♦ Indicates cross references to other indexes